*Images of the Mind*

# IMAGES OF

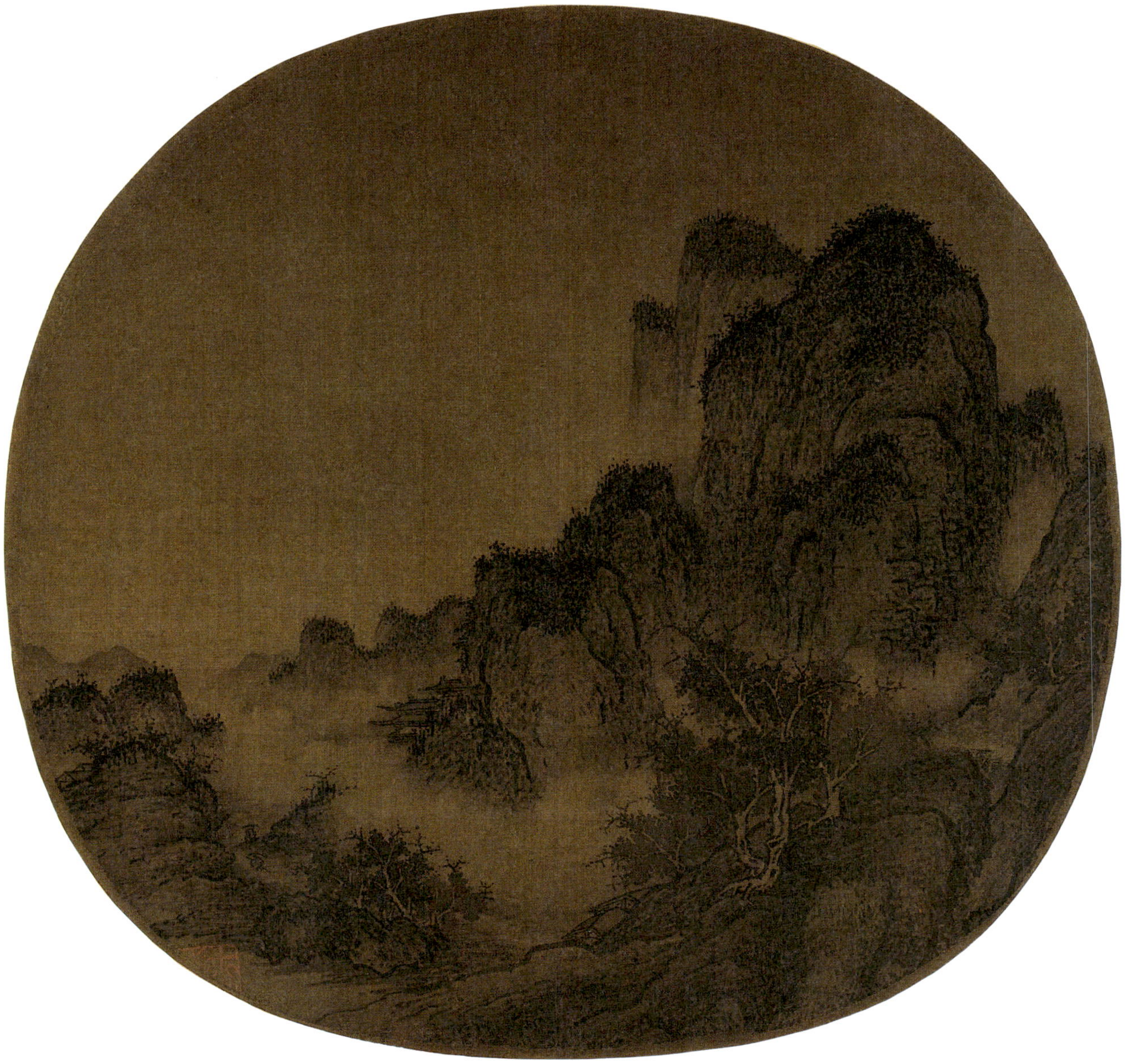

# THE MIND

*Selections from the Edward L. Elliott Family and John B. Elliott Collections of Chinese Calligraphy and Painting at The Art Museum, Princeton University*

WEN C. FONG
*And Alfreda Murck, Shou-chien Shih, Pao-chen Ch'en, and Jan Stuart*

THE ART MUSEUM, PRINCETON UNIVERSITY

Dates of the exhibition: April 15–June 17, 1984

Designed by Bruce Campbell
Set in type by The Stinehour Press
Printed by The Meriden Gravure Company

Cover: Chao Meng-fu, *The Mind Landscape of Hsieh Yu-yü* (no. 6)
Frontispiece: Anonymous, *Landscape in the Style of Fan K'uan* (no. 3)

Copyright © 1984 by the Trustees of Princeton University.
All rights reserved. No part of this book may be reproduced in any form or by any electronic or mechanical means including information storage and retrieval systems without permission in writing from The Art Museum, Princeton University, except by a reviewer, who may quote brief passages in a review.

Library of Congress Catalogue Card Number 83–43056
ISBN 0–943012–04–X

Published by The Art Museum, Princeton University,
Princeton, New Jersey 08544

This catalogue has been fully supported by the
Edward Elliott Foundation.

*To the memory of*
Edward Elliott

# Contents

# *Foreword*

THERE ARE MANY NAMES that quickly come to mind to account for the great fortune and reputation The Art Museum enjoys in its collection of Chinese art: DuBois S. Morris, Lionberger Davis, Dr. Arthur M. Sackler, Mr. and Mrs. Earl Morse, Jeannette Shambaugh Elliott, and, as this exhibition and catalogue so impressively demonstrate, the Edward Elliott family—Ellen, John B., and David Elliott.

John B. Elliott and Wen C. Fong, both members of the Class of 1951 majoring in history at Princeton, shared several favorite courses, including a particularly memorable one, Art 304, a popular undergraduate survey of Chinese art taught by the late Professor George Rowley. In the late 1960s the two friends met again; by then John was a collector, and Wen, as Professor Rowley's successor in the Department of Art and Archaeology, was cofounder, with Professor Frederick W. Mote of the Department of East Asian Studies, of the Ph.D. Program in Chinese Art and Archaeology at Princeton. Agreeing to serve on the councils of Professors Fong's and Mote's respective departments, John Elliott proposed to build a collection of Chinese calligraphy and painting to be used for teaching and research purposes at Princeton.

As John's collecting gained pace, he was joined in his enthusiasm and activities by other members of his family, especially his mother, Ellen. One of the Museum's most valued volunteer docents, Ellen Elliott not only aided and participated in John's collecting, but also informed herself on Chinese art and culture as only the most committed collectors do. Over the years Ellen, John, and David have made many important gifts of major works in their collections to the Museum. In 1980 John communicated to the University his mother's wish to donate the remainder of the Edward L. Elliott Family Collection of Chinese paintings to The Art Museum, Princeton University, over a ten-year period.

The achievement of the Elliott family in the formation of the collection is remarkable, and their generosity to Princeton overwhelming. This achievement is shared by Wen Fong. Both John and Ellen Elliott value their friendship and close working relationship with Professor Fong, and the stature of the Far Eastern program has benefited immeasurably from the opportunity to teach with works of such quality and historical importance as those in the Elliott collection. It was with a deep sense of responsibility that Professor Fong undertook the organization of the exhibition and his contribution to this publication. His introductory essay, "Images of the Mind," is an important work and will stand as a fundamental text on the history of Chinese art. It is a splendid measure of his affection and respect for the Elliott family, a rich return in the partnership of scholar and collector and the fulfillment of John Elliott's desire that a collection be formed to "serve as a resource for the field."

The other contributors to the catalogue are also Princetonians and students of Professor Fong's. Alfreda Murck is now Assistant Curator and Administrator, Department of Far Eastern Art, The Metropolitan Museum of Art, and her essay on one of the masterpieces of the Elliott Collection, *The Eight Views of the Hsiao and Hsiang Rivers* by Wang Hung, is the subject of her Ph.D. dissertation. It is a special pleasure and satisfaction to count her among the authors of this important publication. Shou-chien Shih, a graduate student in the Department of Art and Archaeology at Princeton, is to be congratulated for his essay on the great revivalist painting *The Mind Landscape of Hsieh Yu-yü* by Chao Meng-fu. Pao-chen Ch'en and Jan Stuart, also graduate students at Princeton, wrote the catalogue entries and accompanying essays, and their research and insights will serve students and scholars in their appreciation of the Elliott Collection for many years to come.

Few people could have edited this catalogue with the authority, professionalism, and good nature of Lauren Shakely. We are grateful to her for undertaking this enormous task, which she has brought to such an impressive completion. Jill Guthrie, editor of publications at the Museum, worked closely with all involved and bore the considerable burden of the production of the catalogue, and the result is another example of why she is so greatly valued and appreciated by the Museum.

Lucy L. Lo's importance to the Museum cannot be measured, and, as in all matters pertaining to Far Eastern art at Princeton, she has been indispensable to the enterprise. We are as always most grateful to her and hold her dearly as a colleague and friend.

Our exhibitions of Far Eastern art and our publications in this field, as scholarly contributions and as handsome publications, are of special pride to the Museum. The superb visual and technical quality of this publication is due to the intelligence and taste of Bruce Campbell, the designer, and to the Stinehour Press and the Meriden Gravure Company, with special thanks to Meriden's president John Peckham, Princeton Class of 1940.

The Edward L. Elliott Family Collection is a major collection, and the discernment and sense of purpose with which the collection was formed has set a standard for us. We hope that John, Ellen, David, and other members of the Elliott family will accept this exhibition and catalogue as a measure of our respect for their achievement and our gratitude for their extraordinary generosity and support of the program in Far Eastern studies at Princeton University.

Allen Rosenbaum
*Director*

# *Preface*

My introduction to Chinese art was almost absurd. In the winter of 1944–45 *Life* magazine featured an eight-page spread of Chinese paintings, primarily from the Museum of Fine Arts, Boston, all in dreadful color. I was amazed and entranced at their simplicity of line, their spare elegance. The earth seemed so grand and large. Men were not masters in these landscapes but diminutive in them. Those pages from *Life* were on my walls for the balance of the school year.

At Princeton I took Professor George Rowley's one-semester course in Chinese painting. I remember very little of what I studied. What I do remember most clearly is a small album by Chu Ta of grasshoppers and bamboo. Perhaps the most lasting benefit of that exposure to Chinese art was my meeting, at Rowley's suggestion, Mathias Komor. Mr. Komor had lived many years in China and enjoyed reminiscing. He also dealt in Chinese art. Many Saturday afternoons I would stop by his gallery and, if he was free, he would produce a few objects from his closet and have me look at them, hard, while he talked and taught. Mr. Komor gave his time and attention to the early training of my eye. For this I remain grateful.

I did not begin seriously to collect until 1967. I had read somewhere that the Chinese have always considered calligraphy, after poetry, their noblest art. I asked Wen Fong—whom I had known as a student and with whom I had remained in contact—if anyone in the United States was collecting Chinese calligraphy and learned that only John Crawford had a truly splendid collection. I decided that here was an opportunity and asked Wen to attempt to locate some outstanding scrolls. He tested my commitment by introducing me to Huang T'ing-chien's *Scroll for Chang Ta-t'ung* (no. 1) and Hsien-yü Shu's *Admonitions to the Imperial Censors*. It was a promising start.

In 1968–71 I plunged. When the effort got beyond my carrying capacity, I enlisted the help of my mother and my brother David. The results of the plunge continue to give us pride—pride in possessing so much that is genuinely beautiful—and at the same time to humble us in the knowledge that we are only custodians, the most recent keepers of these objects that others will guard and prize after us. But the pleasures of collecting extend far beyond the collection itself. The eye is enriched—how often I have seen three receding ranges of hills or mountains in California or Massachusetts that I first saw in Southern Sung landscapes. From art grew an interest in the land, and the land has confirmed my readings of paintings. On a recent trip to Mount O-mei in Szechuan province I discerned nine receding ranges with empty, misty distances separating them. Passing through the Yangtze gorges I saw Hsia Kuei's cliffs. On the hills around Hang-chou four- and-five-stroke pines still march along the ridges.

Beyond the eye there are the people, among them many friends, to whom this art has brought me. They are too numerous to name, but I shall mention a few—first Wen Fong and his wife, Connie; Mike Hearn; Christian and Alfreda Murck; Lucy and James Lo; Professor and Mrs. Shūjirō Shimada; Michael Nylan; Marilyn Wong Fu; Shen Fu; and Yoshiaki Shimizu. With a few of these we have been able to share individual works from the collections—works that became the subjects of dissertations. This sharing for scholarship has been a continuing joy.

The art has inevitably expanded our activities. My mother has for years been a docent at Princeton's Art Museum. It is a commitment: she is in the Museum three or four times a week filling regular shifts and instructing visiting groups—high school students, alumni—in the Museum's exhibitions of Chinese art; and for the last ten or eleven years she has audited undergraduate courses in Chinese art and history. She always keeps a few objects from her collection in her home for the pleasure and sense of space they give.

My involvement has also progressed. From art my interests grew to Chinese culture and history. I met and was befriended by Professor Frederick Mote and his wife, Hsiao-lan. Fritz Mote has introduced me to

Princeton's Department of East Asian Studies, perhaps the finest such department for the study of imperial China existing in the world. I am a member of the Advisory Council to the Department.

Foremost for my mother and myself is the sharing—with friends, with new scholars, with a wider public through exhibitions. It amazed and heartened me that the exhibition of Chinese calligraphy, organized for the Philadelphia Museum of Art by Tseng Yu-ho Ecke in 1971 and later exhibited in New York, drew so many people. Some of my calligraphies were among those on view. Most Americans are innocent of calligraphy, yet the audience I wandered among was intent, serious, reaching. Remarks were few but warming: "Beautiful," "the strength of the line." I could not have said much more myself.

I have not learned a great deal, but I do know what it can mean to have a form of writing in which many characters still reveal their pictorial origins. The hand can produce its own poetry within canons of form that reach back three millennia. In contemplating calligraphy, as in painting, I am aware of the immediate present, the act of creation sparking from the vast and looming tradition, the act personalizing and renewing that which is already ancient.

Part of our collection is now housed in The Metropolitan Museum of Art, thanks to the generosity of Douglas Dillon. My mother's collection of paintings is promised to The Art Museum, Princeton. She is happy with this decision, for Princeton is her home and has given her much. I am happy too, for the University is one of my primary affections. I hope these collections involve more parts of the institution than I can now envision—more than the Department of Art and Archaeology and the Program in East Asian Studies. We cannot understand the pulse and rhythms of a culture without some sensibility to its art.

Lastly I wish to recognize Wen Fong. Throughout our collecting he has guided and shaped. The collections may bear our names, but they are his creations. It is appropriate here to acknowledge with gratitude and deep friendship the two paintings (nos. 10, 13) that Connie and he have presented to The Art Museum at Princeton in commemoration of our enterprise together.

John B. Elliott

# *Acknowledgments*

LIKE THE Edward L. Elliott Family Collection published in this volume, this catalogue is a Princeton Family venture. Colleagues and friends in and out of Princeton have aided the project in countless ways. As I wrote my essay for the catalogue, I was reminded of how much of my understanding of Chinese painting and calligraphy is owed to seminar teaching and discussion with colleagues and students. Topic after topic in my essay recalled names and faces from over the years—questions posed, insights gained, and problems solved or left unsolved by generations of fresh, inquiring minds. My wish for all participants of the Princeton seminars, past and present, is that they continue to find these topics and problems as continually rich and rewarding as I do. Since the text and notes of my essay can refer only to published individual contributions, I wish to note here a number of outstanding unpublished seminar papers that helped to sharpen my own thoughts: Roberta Bickford on Wang Fu; Robert Harrist on Tao-chi; Julia K. Murray on Kao-tsung's calligraphy; Matthew Kercher on Chü-jan; Shou-chien Shih on Tung Ch'i-ch'ang; and Jan Stuart on Fan K'uan.

I must also thank my close colleagues and associates in the Departments of Art and Archaeology and East Asian Studies who help me guide graduate students in our Ph.D. Program in Chinese Art and Archaeology: especially Professors Frederick W. Mote (cultural history), James T. C. Liu (institutional history), Ta-tuan Chen (language), Yu-kung Kao (poetry), and Robert L. Thorp (archaeology). Professors Mote and John Shearman, Chairman of the Department of Art and Archaeology, took time to read the manuscript of my essay and made valuable suggestions.

The principal reason for recent interests and activities in Chinese art at Princeton has been the vigorous growth of library and museum resources in this area. Building on the strengths of the Frederick Peterson and the DuBois Schanck Morris, Class of 1893, collections of Chinese paintings, acquired under the guidance of the late Professor George Rowley, The Art Museum at Princeton University has been enriched in the past decades by many wonderful gifts of Chinese works from such noted collectors as Irene and Earl Morse, Dr. Arthur M. Sackler, and Jeannette Shambaugh Elliott. For more than a dozen years John Elliott and his mother, Ellen, have extended themselves beyond the gifts and loans of the works of art in their collections; they worked closely with individual students and their projects by offering the use of major works in their collections as dissertation topics and providing—with characteristic modesty—anonymous funds for fellowships, books, photographs, and travel. As much as the quality and importance of the collections they have assembled, John's and Ellen's exceptional generosity and sensitivity have motivated the enthusiasm and dedication of everyone involved in the writing and production of this catalogue.

Lucy L. Lo, curator of the Far Eastern Art Seminar, acting as majordomo, bore the burden of the many crises endemic to such a complex project with infinite grace and efficiency. Her good nature and devotion, well known to generations of students she has helped, made the experience of creating this book a smooth and nearly painless one.

Lauren Shakely, who must be the brightest and the most effective editor I know, coordinated and gave unity to this book, which has so many parts written by authors of different experiences and backgrounds. I feel especially fortunate to have enjoyed Lauren's help. Her acute criticisms and suggestions throughout the endeavor were invaluable. I am also full of affection and admiration for Bruce Campbell, whose sensitive design makes the book a pleasure to behold. And I thank Pao-chen Ch'en and Jan Stuart, who not only wrote the catalogue entries and essays, but also devoted much time to the project's many details.

In addition, I am very grateful to Allen Rosenbaum, director of The Art Museum, and his efficient staff for their warm and active support. Allen took the initiative that led to the Museum's acquisition, in 1980, of two of the most important Elliott paintings (nos. 4, 6), and he kept a lively interest in the catalogue project, giving active help and, on occasions, a much appreciated boost to the working team's morale. Robert Lafond, the Museum's registrar, and Jill Guthrie, the Museum's coordinating editor, have worked so hard and so closely with us that they are all but chartered alumni of the Far Eastern Art Seminar.

We are grateful to Mary Schmidt, curator of the Marquand Library, and Diane Perushek, curator of the Gest Oriental Library, for their help and cooperation in making Princeton's rich library resources constantly ready and available to us.

Colleagues and friends outside Princeton, indeed all over the world, have been kind and generous in supplying photographs and permissions to publish materials from their institutions. We thank especially: Deputy Director Yang Poda, Palace Museum, Peking; Director Yang Renkai, Liaoning Provincial Museum; Ma Chengyuan, Curator, Shanghai Museum; Deputy Director Chiang Chao-shen and Hu Sai-lan, National Palace Museum, Taipei; Shen C. Y. Fu, Freer Gallery of Art, Washington, D.C.; Maxwell Hearn and Alfreda Murck, The Metropolitan Museum of Art, New York; Wai-kam Ho, Cleveland Museum of Art; Nakagawa Keniji, Osaka Municipal Museum of Fine Art; Director Marc Wilson, Nelson Gallery-Atkins Museum, Kansas City; and T'ung Wu of the Museum of Fine Arts, Boston. The keen interest and warm support shown us by our outside colleagues are received with deep appreciation and heartfelt thanks.

Wen C. Fong

# Chronology

| | | | |
|---|---|---|---|
| Hsia dynasty | 21st–16th century B.C. | | |
| Shang dynasty | 16th–11th century B.C. | | |
| Chou dynasty | 11th century–256 B.C. | | |
| *Spring and Autumn period* | 770–476 B.C. | | |
| *Warring States period* | 475–221 B.C. | | |
| Ch'in dynasty | 221–206 B.C. | | |
| Han dynasty | 206 B.C.–A.D. 220 | | |
| Three Kingdoms | 220–265 | | |
| Western Tsin dynasty | 265–317 | | |
| Southern dynasties | 317–589 | Northern dynasties | 386–581 |
| *Eastern Tsin* | 317–420 | *Northern Wei* | 386–534 |
| *Liu Sung* | 420–479 | *Eastern Wei* | 534–549 |
| *Southern Ch'i* | 479–502 | *Western Wei* | 535–556 |
| *Liang* | 502–557 | *Northern Ch'i* | 550–577 |
| *Ch'en* | 557–589 | *Northern Chou* | 557–581 |
| Sui dynasty | 581–618 | | |
| T'ang dynasty | 618–906 | | |
| Five Dynasties | 907–960 | Northern China and Manchuria | |
| *Later Liang* | 907–923 | *Liao dynasty* | 907–1125 |
| *Later T'ang* | 923–937 | | |
| *Later Tsin* | 937–946 | | |
| *Later Han* | 947–950 | | |
| *Later Chou* | 951–960 | | |
| Sung dynasty | 960–1279 | Chin dynasty | 1115–1234 |
| *Northern Sung* | 960–1127 | | |
| *Southern Sung* | 1127–1279 | | |
| Yüan dynasty | 1279–1368 | | |

Ming dynasty

| YEAR OF ACCESSION | EMPEROR'S TEMPLE OR MEMORIAL TITLE | REIGN TITLE | YEAR OF ADOPTION OF REIGN TITLE |
|---|---|---|---|
| 1368 | T'ai-tsu | Hung-wu | 1368 |
| 1398 | Hui-ti | Chien-wen | 1399 |
| 1402 | Ch'eng-tsu | Yung-lo | 1403 |
| 1424 | Jen-tsung | Hung-hsi | 1425 |
| 1425 | Hsüan-tsung | Hsüan-te | 1426 |
| 1435 | Ying-tsung | Cheng-t'ung | 1436 |
| 1449 | Ching Ti | Ching-t'ai | 1450 |
| 1457 | Ying-tsung* | T'ien-shun | 1457 |
| 1464 | Hsien-tsung | Ch'eng-hua | 1465 |
| 1487 | Hsiao-tsung | Hung-chih | 1488 |
| 1505 | Wu-tsung | Cheng-te | 1506 |
| 1521 | Shih-tsung | Chia-ching | 1522 |
| 1567 | Mu-tsung | Lung-ch'ing | 1567 |

*restored to throne

| | YEAR OF ACCESSION | EMPEROR'S TEMPLE OR MEMORIAL TITLE | REIGN TITLE | YEAR OF ADOPTION OF REIGN TITLE |
|---|---|---|---|---|
| Ming dynasty | 1572 | Shen-tsung | Wan-li | 1573 |
| | 1620 | Kuang-tsung | T'ai-ch'ang | 1620 |
| | 1620 | Hsi-tsung | T'ien-ch'i | 1621 |
| | 1627 | Ssu-tsung | Ch'ung-chen | 1628 |
| | 1644 | Fu Wang | Hung-kuang | 1645 |
| | 1645 | T'ang Wang | Lung-wu | 1645 |
| | 1646 | T'ang Wang | Shao-wu | 1646 |
| | 1646 | Yung-ming Wang | Yung-li | 1647 |
| Ch'ing dynasty | 1643 | Shih-tsu | Shun-chih | 1644 |
| | 1661 | Sheng-tsu | K'ang-hsi | 1662 |
| | 1722 | Shih-tsung | Yung-cheng | 1723 |
| | 1735 | Kao-tsung | Ch'ien-lung | 1736 |
| | 1796 | Jen-tsung | Chia-ch'ing | 1796 |
| | 1820 | Hsüan-tsung | Tao-kuang | 1821 |
| | 1850 | Wen-tsung | Hsien-feng | 1851 |
| | 1861 | Mu-tsung | T'ung-chih | 1862 |
| | 1875 | Te-tsung | Kuang-hsü | 1875 |
| | 1908 | Hsüan-t'ung-ti | Hsüan-t'ung | 1909 |

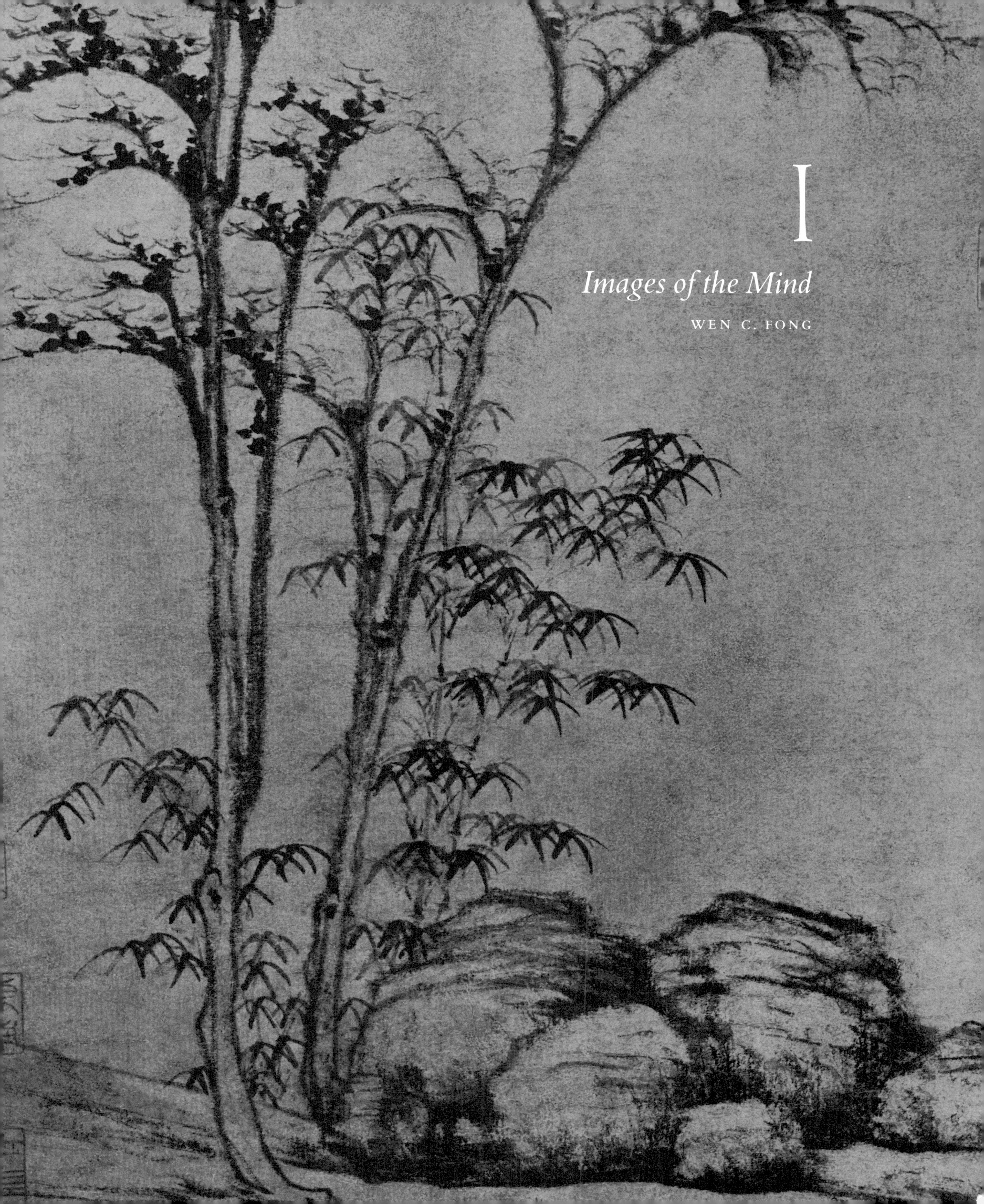

# I

# *Images of the Mind*

WEN C. FONG

# *Introduction: The Great Tradition*

It is impossible to consider the great paintings of the Sung, Yüan, Ming, and Ch'ing dynasties without first examining the traditions behind them. Mindful of the diversity of human activity and suspicious of established orthodoxy, modern critics fairly blanch at the mention of a moral and intellectual tradition, or a unitary view of art. Yet Chinese literature, calligraphy, and painting—the last being by far the youngest of the three—not only had a single, uninterrupted history, but also developed with a tradition of a strong moral ethos, a sense of spiritual purpose and commitment that still allowed for freedom and diversity. Chinese artists stressed the "correctness" of a Great Tradition, not to emphasize man-made, doctrinal truths, but to reaffirm an order larger than the ways of man. Without an acknowledgment of the Great Way (Tao) of their cultural tradition, Chinese scholars believed, any individualistic or eccentric thought, however dazzling, could only be a work of revision, not one that would chart a new course for history. The story of Chinese painting tells of imaginative uses of the past—major episodes of stylistic change and continuity that testify to the leading Chinese painters' infinite resourcefulness, courage, and creativity, and their abiding faith in their tradition and in themselves.

Confucius (551–479 B.C.) expressed an early rationale for literature and by extension for the arts in general: "When there is intent [*chih*; "wish" or "purpose"], it is speech [*yen*] that fulfills the intent, and literature [*wen*] that carries out speech. Without speech, how shall the intent be known? If speech is not literary, speech shall not travel far."[1] Art is necessary, the scholar believed, because expression without art neither lasts long nor "travels far."

All forms of artistic expression, according to early Chinese thinkers, must embody or convey the Great Way, the same Great Way that must be manifested in all human endeavors and institutions. In the beginning, literature served a useful moral or didactic purpose. In the *Analects* Confucius admonished, "When substance [*chih*] exceeds ornament [*wen*], we have rusticity; when ornament exceeds substance, we have the writing of history. When ornament and substance are in harmony, we shall then have [the way] of a gentleman."[2] The aesthetic aspect of literature was first recognized and analyzed around the end of the Han period, in the early third century A.D. During the Six Dynasties period (A.D. 316–618), when literary forms became increasingly elaborate and ornamental, the first critical awareness of a historical development began to appear: "the ancient was simple, and the modern is beautiful" (*ku-p'u chin-li*).[3]

Early Chinese written script, like literature, evolved slowly through more than two millennia, from the "simple" to the "beautiful": from the "oracle bone" (*chia-ku*) and the "seal" (*chuan*) script forms of the Shang, Chou, and Ch'in periods (ca. 1500–200 B.C.), through the "clerical" (*li*) of the Han (ca. 200 B.C.–A.D. 200) to the "cursive," or "grass" (*ts'ao*), the "regular" (*cheng* or *k'ai*), and the "running" (*hsing*) forms of the Wei, Tsin, and the Six Dynasties periods (ca. A.D. 200–600). Starting with the free curvilinear and picturelike forms of the "great seal," drawn in strokes of even thickness with a stylus or brush, the written character moved first toward a standardized, squared-off shape and uniform size in the small seal and the early clerical scripts, with vertical and horizontal strokes crossing each other at right angles; then, reflecting the flexible movements of the brush, which replaced the stylus as the writing instrument in the later clerical script, slanting as well as undulating brushstrokes of varying thickness developed, finally transforming the character into a subtle composition of intricately balanced brush forces (*pi-shih*) in the regular and running scripts.

Unlike the Greeks, who saw *mimesis*, or imitation of nature, as the principal objective in art, the Chinese tried to apprehend the principles of nature through graphic means: according to the fifth-century scholar Yen Yen-chih (384–456), painting (*hua*), defined as "representing nature's forms" (*t'u-hsing*), was but one of the three diagrammatic representations; the other two were the written language, defined as "representing concepts" (*t'u-shih*), and the magical Eight Trigrams of the *Book of Changes (I-ching)*, which "represent nature's principles" (*t'u-li*).[4] Just as words must carry meaning and symbols must be magically efficacious, successful painting must mirror and complete nature's creation. And, like the written word and the magical symbol, painting was based on graphic conventions.

Thus a unique characteristic of Chinese painting is its close relationship to writing. From the myth of Ts'ang-chieh inventing written characters by drawing forms of nature in the sand to the great late seventeenth-century monk-painter Tao-chi's (1642–1707) theory of *i-hua*, the "primordial line" or "painting of oneness," Chinese writers reaffirmed the belief that calligraphy and painting were one, and that the practice of these arts was the mark of the civilized man: not only do writing and painting express the same substantial truths about the universe, they also share the common technique of brushwork. In the course of time the simultaneous use of pictorial and verbal modes of expression became integral to individual works of art.

The common tool for both Chinese writing and painting is a brush tapering to a point, made of animal hair—in ascending order of stiffness, goat, horse, rabbit, or weasel hair, or mouse whiskers. Pliant yet resilient and capable of infinite shades of subtlety, the brush became a potent instrument in the hand of a master and was often compared to a powerful battlefield weapon—or the Hindu god Indra's invincible "diamond club"—that is at once a physical extension of the artist's arm and a magic wand that gives him access to the powers of creation. The very simplicity of the instrument, as well as the physical nature of its application, inevitably determined the characterization of its function in Chinese cosmogonic terms: the blank wall, silk, or paper came to represent an undifferentiated oneness; the first stroke establishes a primary yin and yang relationship; the second stroke combines with the first to create all kinds of new yin and yang situations, each successive combination begetting stroke after stroke, until the multitudinous are reconciled and reunited into a harmonious whole.

According to the essay *Nine Forces* (*Chiu-shih*), attributed to Ts'ai Yung (A.D. 132–192), but composed in the seventh or eighth century (T'ang dynasty), "calligraphy derives from nature. When nature was established, there appeared yin and yang. When yin and yang appeared, forms and forces emerged. By 'hiding the head' and 'protecting the tail' [of each stroke], the calligrapher stores power in each character. In the application of his brush, and the transmitting of power through it, he creates beautiful muscle and skin [in each stroke]."[5] The brush techniques are also characterized in yin and yang, contrasting and complementary terms: tilting the brush to one side, using the broad side and the sharp tip of the brush, the writer makes a square (*fang*) or angular or oblique (*ts'e*) brushstroke; holding the brush upright, always carefully keeping the brushtip hidden (*ts'ang*) within the stroke, he makes a round (*yüan*) or centered (*chung*) brushstroke; the sharp, oblique brushstrokes with angular turns are often made with a flicking motion of the fingers and the wrist, while the self-contained round ones are made by moving the whole arm, simultaneously pressing down and lifting up the brush, in order to generate and maintain a high level of energy throughout the brushstroke. With the tip of the brush the artist makes fine lines, and, saturating the brush with ink, he covers broad areas with ink wash; brush and ink, in their infinite line-and-surface, bone-and-flesh, thin-and-thick, hard-and-soft, and dry-and-wet relationships, can represent nearly everything in a monochrome universe.

A well-executed brushstroke, expressing beauty and joy through movement, involves not only the muscle actions of the artist's finger, wrist, and arm, but also his mental, emotional, and psychic states. Like signatures and autographs, calligraphy is said to reveal a person's innermost being. Thus the Chinese refer to both calligraphy and painting as the artist's *hsin-yin*, or "imprint of the mind."[6] As an imprint, or image, of the mind, a work of calligraphy or painting is said to reflect the artist—the man, his ideas, his thoughts, and his self-cultivation.

## *Formal Likeness and Beyond Likeness*

For the ancient Chinese, painting, like the diagrammatic emblems (*hsiang*) of the *Book of Changes*, was invested with the magic power of creation.[7] The painter's goal was to participate in the dynamic energies and transformations of creation, rather than to fashion a mere counterfeit of nature. Painting must invoke and capture reality.

The purpose of painting, according to the leading figural painter of the late fourth and early fifth centuries, Ku K'ai-chih (ca. 344–ca. 406), was "to portray the spirit through the form" (*i-hsing hsieh-shen*).[8] While descriptive likeness was a necessary means for "transmitting the spirit" (*ch'uan-shen*), the goal of the painter was to capture the spirit; form was the vehicle used to reach the goal. Toward the end of the fifth century, the critic Hsieh Ho (fl. ca. 479–502) set forth the so-called Six Principles (*liu-fa*) in painting, the first of which was "breath-resonance-life-motion" (*ch'i-yün-sheng-tung*).[9] According to Hsieh and other literary and art critics of the Wei, Tsin, and Six Dynasties period, the active operative force in a work of art, as well as in the whole universe, is *ch'i*—the all-pervasive ether, the dynamic energy, the "breath" of life that permeates, animates, and motivates all things. In a series of two-word descriptive compounds, Hsieh writes of two kinds of *ch'i*: the objective, descriptive qualities of the representation, such as the *shen-ch'i*, "breath of the spirit," or the *sheng-ch'i*, "breath of life," of the depiction; and the individual and personal qualities of the creator, such as the *chuang-ch'i*, "robust breath," the *ch'i-hou*, "breath cultivation," or the *ch'i-li*, "breath force," of a certain artist.[10] The word *yün* (resonance) refers to another critical concern of the Six Dynasties period, namely, the harmonious manner of execution in a work of art.[11] By *ch'i-yün-sheng-tung*, Hsieh Ho meant that a good painting should be vital in its "breath" (both personal and representational), harmonious, alive, and full of motion in its execution.

Commenting on Hsieh Ho's first principle, the T'ang dynasty art historian and critic Chang Yen-yüan (fl. ca. mid-9th century), in his *Record of Famous Paintings in Successive Dynasties* (*Li-tai ming-hua chi*), compiled in 847, contrasted "breath-resonance" (*ch'i-yün*) with "formal likeness" (*hsing-ssu*) in painting and complained that "in paintings today, even if by chance there is formal likeness, the breath-resonance is not lively." Chang advised painters to aim at "that which lies beyond formal likeness," insisting that "if a painter had only sought for breath-resonance in his painting, formal likeness would be present in his work."[12]

Finally, at the end of the T'ang dynasty, the leading landscape master Ching Hao (fl. ca. 870–930), in his treatise *Notes on Brush Method* (*Pi-fa chi*), addressed himself to the question "What is painting?" in an imaginary dialogue between himself and a wise old man of the mountains:

> I said, "Painting is ornamentation [*hua*, decorative beauty and splendor]. The important thing is formal likeness and attainment of the correct appearance. . . ." The old man replied: "Not so. Painting is imaging [*hua*; to measure, estimate, or divine]. Having examined the appearance of the thing, one seizes its true essence. . . .[13]

Ching Hao's idea that "having examined the appearance of the thing, one seizes its true essence" reflected the late T'ang Neo-Confucian theories about investigating the "principles" (*li*) and the "nature" (*hsing*) of things in the universe.

During the Five Dynasties and early Northern Sung periods (10th century), a monumental style of landscape painting developed. Its aim was to seize the universe and partake wholly of the secrets of its vast grandeur and multiplicity; its objective approach to the study of nature paralleled the teachings of the Neo-Confucian School of Principles (*li-hsüeh*), which emphasized "the investigation of things leading to the extension of knowledge" (*ko-wu chih-chih*). For Sung painters, formal likeness in representation was essential to seizing an object's inner reality, even though their critics, in order to stress inner reality, often derided them for capturing merely the appearance of an object. Making a careful distinction between "constant forms" (*ch'ang-hsing*) and "constant principles" (*ch'ang-li*), Su Shih (1036–1101), the leading scholar-artist of the late Northern Sung period, observed that "the artisans of this world may be able to capture the forms perfectly, but when it comes to the principles, only a superior man of outstanding talent can discern them."[14] Yet it was the Sung painter's inspired and enthusiastic pursuit of perfection in forms, as well as in principles, that led, step by step, to a successful conquest of illusion in landscape painting by the end of the Southern Sung dynasty, in the late thirteenth century .

By the eleventh century scholar-officials had replaced China's hereditary aristocracy as the dominant force in government and culture. Su Shih's views, representing the powerful, newly emerged scholar-artist's aesthetic, proved to be of enormous influence on painters of the later centuries. Preferring to see painting as self-expression rather than objective representation, Su made the following pronouncement: "To discuss paintings in terms of formal resemblance / Is a view comparable to a child's."[15] The scholar-critics emphasized Hsieh Ho's definition of *ch'i-yün* (breath-resonance) in painting as the personal, individual quality of the artist. While stating that "a painting must fully show breath-resonance before it can be hailed as a treasure of its age," Kuo Jo-hsü (fl. ca. 1075), in his *Experiences in Painting* (*T'u-hua chien-wen chih*; completed in 1074), argued that, "if a painter's personal qualities are lofty, his breath-resonance cannot but be lofty also."[16] In other words only a scholar of exceptional "breath-resonance" can be considered a true artist. To make this point clear, Shen Kua (1029–1093), a noted contemporary of Su Shih's, suggested that if a work possessed uncommon "breath-resonance," it might even forgo formal likeness or common-sense logic altogether; according to Shen Kua, for example, a banana tree in a snow scene done by a superior artist could be quite wonderful.[17]

By the fourteenth century, when illusion in painting had been fully mastered, leading Yüan dynasty painters sought increasingly for extrarepresentational qualities in painting. It was then that the idea of *pu-ssu* (beyond likeness) was seriously discussed. Ni Tsan (1301–1374) wrote, for example,

> I only use bamboo painting to write out the exceptional exhilaration in my breast, that is all. Why should I bother about whether it shows likeness or not, whether the leaves are too dense or too sparse, or whether the branches are slanted or upright?[18]

The term *pu-ssu*, literally "without likeness" or "lacking in likeness," took on positive connotations as "beyond likeness" or "more than likeness" when painters, developing new expressive possibilities through calligraphy, learned to "write ideas or feelings" (*hsieh-i*) in painting.

By spurning formal realism the scholar-artists of the Yüan and later periods sought not to lay bare the truth of the universe, but rather to confront the personal psychological realities of the moment. For the scholar-artist a painting was "written" rather than carefully drawn or dazzlingly painted: a scholar-artist's work prevails neither by vivid technique nor by dramatic invention, but by a profundity of thought and taste wholly expressive of the artist's inner self.

## *Eremitism, Individualism, and Eccentricity*

Because a scholar-painter was typically also a literary man, poet, calligrapher, and, in some notable instances, a prominent official and public figure, the histories of his day—or his own existing writings—offer much information, often quite detailed, about his life. When the anthologies of a scholar's literary works exist, much can be learned about his times and his friendships, and about how he thought and felt, and how he sought happiness and contentment, or coped with misfortunes. Ni Tsan's collected works, for example, include not only the artist's own poetry, prose, and letters, but also biographies of him, anecdotes, encomiums, poems written for him by his friends, comments on his works by later writers, and even a selection of recipes attributed to him.[19]

As intimate revelations of their private thoughts and feelings, the artists' poems—many of them inscribed on their paintings—deal largely with themes of loneliness, depression, or downright misery. To judge by their verses it would appear that most Chinese artists had lived in sad times or painted their best works in melancholy moods. Both perhaps were true, but the frequency of these topics also reflects the strong Chinese tradition of using art to "speak one's mind" (*yen-chih*; speak one's intent).[20] This tradition reflects the Confucian belief in the power of the word, as embodied in the argument contained in the classic *Spring and Autumn Annals* (*Ch'un-ch'iu*): a scholar may right a wrong and "execute" the wrongdoer with words. In their quest for self-expression, scholar-artists of the fourteenth century and later learned to blend pictorial, calligraphic, and poetic images in single works of art.

In the normal career pattern, a Chinese scholar first attained official degrees through three stages of competitive examinations—county, prefectural, and metropolitan. At the successful conclusion of his metropolitan examinations, he became a *chin-shih* (presented scholar). Then he received his first official assignment, a post either in court or in a provincial administrative center. Finally, with ability and luck, he advanced through the nine ranks of officialdom. This active life of service was neatly balanced—in practice and by long cultural tradition—by periods of withdrawal, during which the official turned, ideally, to moral and spiritual self-cultivation. In the illustration by Li Kung-lin (ca. 1049–1106) of *The Classic of Filial Piety* (*Hsiao-ching t'u*), on loan to The Art Museum, Princeton University, a scene showing how "the virtuous man serves his sovereign" illustrates this line: "When he advances [*chin*] he thinks of total loyalty and commitment to his duties; when in retreat [*t'ui*] he contemplates how to repair his moral failings."[21] The principle of retreat or reclusion corrected as well as restored the principle of advance or active engagement, while at all times the reflective self had to keep both body and mind keen and well-balanced.

It is not surprising that scholar-artists turned to artistic self-expression mostly during their times of reclusion. Though most men experienced retreat from time to time, some chose it, especially in times of trouble, as a permanent way of life. Thus recluses and their ideals of a moral, eremitic existence play a special role in the history of Chinese poetry and painting.

Chinese official histories and gazetteers often contain a special section devoted to "recluses" (*yin-i*), and another to persons of "singular conduct" (*tu-hsing*). The latter, referring to men of outstanding character and strength, often also include recluses—men withdrawn from society who showed commendable courage and devotion to moral principles.[22] As a cultural phenomenon, eremitism in Chinese history has been related to the spirit of resistance in an authoritarian society.[23] Frederick W. Mote, in his "Confucian Eremitism in the Yüan Period" (1960), described it as an "alternative life of particular importance in time of disorder and impending doom, when thoughtful pessimism seemed more attractive to educated men than the normal pattern of life."[24] In the Chinese scheme of things reclusion represented a morally positive rather than negative course of action: when the whole world seemed to have gone awry, only men of "singular conduct" had the courage and strength to withdraw and stand up singly for the righteous Great Way. Thus, after the Mongol conquest of the Southern Sung in 1279, Cheng Ssu-hsiao (fl. ca. 1240–1310), a leading Sung loyalist, wrote about the ancient recluses:

> We revere the likes of Hsü Yu [who washed his ears when Yao offered him the throne], and Po-i and Shu-ch'i [who starved themselves when the Chou vanquished the Shang]. . . . If such men had not existed, all later generations would have to walk in the shadows of tyrants, who, by killing men's spirit, would have made them all slaves. . . .[25]

For Cheng the noble recluse was a passive, nonviolent person, who in his "lofty embrace of unyielding virtue" gained a stature so heroic that even the mightiest rulers and conquerors must show him deference.

During the Ming period, scholars and artists often affected the style of reclusive "mountain men" (*shan-jen*), or "wild men" (*k'uang-shih*)—dressing strangely, flouting social conventions, imitating Taoist or Buddhist eccentrics, and abandoning themselves to wine, women, and song. As cultural antiheroes, many found inspiration and strength in the Ming Neo-Confucian School of the Mind (*hsin-hsüeh*). Instead of stressing objective principles, as the Neo-Confucian School of Principles did, the School of the Mind proposed that "the universe is the mind, and the mind the universe," and taught individualism—the fulfillment of what is within oneself. An extreme case of late Ming individualism was the iconoclast Li Chih (1527–1602), a Neo-Confucian scholar turned Buddhist, who was scathingly scornful of everything and everyone—"sages" as well as the so-called mountain men: "They call themselves mountain men, but their hearts are those of merchants. Their lips are full of the Tao and virtue, but their ambition is to become thieves of virtue."[26] Vilified by orthodox scholars as a pervert and a heretic, Li committed suicide in prison. Although his books were officially burned and banned, his irreverence, cynicism, and taste for the sensational had a profound appeal for late Ming intellectuals.

## *Orthodoxy and Change*

The early evolution of literature, calligraphy, and painting can be divided into distinct phases, each representing the accumulation of experience and the acquisition of new skills. Thus, as Chinese art history unfolded, critics and historians could begin to judge artists according to their success in reaching accepted standards of development. During the Six Dynasties period, when literary concepts and forms evolved rapidly, critics became interested in the problem of *hsin-pien*, or "new transformation." Hsiao Tzu-hsien (489–537), for instance, wrote that "without newness and transformation, one cannot become the [literary] figure of his generation."[27] To counter such argument, Liu Hsieh (ca. 465–522), author of *The Literary Mind and the Carving of Dragons* (*Wen-hsin tiao-lung*), wrote about *t'ung-pien*, or "understanding transformation":

> The color blue is prepared from indigo, and the color red comes from madder. Although blue and red seem to be brighter than their sources, they are incapable of further change. . . . If one wishes to refine upon the blue and to purify the red, one must return to the indigo and the madder and begin there; in the same way, to correct pretentiousness and cure superficiality, a writer must return to the classics and begin there. Only when a writer is able to strike a balance between substance [*chih*] and the ornament [*wen*], and to make the right choice between a graceful and vulgar expression, is he a man with whom we may discuss the problem of "understanding transformation."[28]

The direction was set for the argument on the question of old and new styles in Chinese critical literature. Since to "understand transformation" was to perceive the fundamental nature and substance (*chih*) of the arts, the real revolution in taste, it was argued, lay in the renewal or revival of ancient styles and principles, which had been based on such an understanding. By this reasoning the hapless searcher for "new" techniques inevitably fell into old beaten tracks, while the true vanguard opened up future aesthetic horizons by returning to ancient truths.

Judging calligraphy by two standards, *kung-fu* (skill) and *t'ien-jan* (naturalness)—thus echoing "ornament" versus "substance" in literary criticism—Yü Chien-wu, a critic of the Southern Liang dynasty (502–556), found Wang Hsi-chih (ca. 307–ca. 365) more "skilled" but less "natural" than Chung Yu (A.D. 151–230).[29] One possible inference was that as the art of calligraphy developed away from archaic simplicity, it became more beautiful but less natural, hence declined. The early T'ang calligrapher Sun Ch'ien-li (Sun Kuo-t'ing; 648?–703?), however, defended modernity:

> From substance to ornament [calligraphy] went through three stages of transformation. Sudden changes like wild ducks fleeing are the constant order of things. What is important is that the ancient must not become out of date, and the modern must not share in [today's] corruption. It is said an equal blend of the ornament and the substance marks the gentleman. Why should anyone exchange his sculpted palace for a cave dwelling or his jade chariot of state for a primitive wheel?[30]

The same concept of three stages of development was applied to the history of painting. In the ninth century Chang Yen-yüan gave his assessment of these three periods: "In paintings of Early Antiquity, the drawing is simple, the expression is plain and yet elegant and noble. . . . Paintings of Middle Antiquity are fine and detailed, exquisitely finished and exceedingly beautiful. . . . Paintings of more recent times are brilliantly executed, and they excel in [representational] completeness.[31]

Although Chang regarded the tendency toward beauty, brilliance, and representational completeness as something of a mixed blessing, he was unequivocal in his praise of modern accomplishments in the newly emerged art of landscape painting. Chang's pride in landscape painting was justified by the subsequent development of that art during the Northern Sung period, when Kuo Jo-hsü pronounced this verdict:

> If it is a question of Buddhist and Taoist icons, secular figure themes, gentlewomen, or cattle and horses, then the modern works do not measure up to the ancient. In the case of landscapes, trees and rocks, flowers and bamboo, or birds and fish, then the ancient works cannot equal the modern.[32]

Su Shih, at the end of the eleventh century, concluded that artistic development had come to an end in the eighth century:

> By the time poetry produced a Tu Fu [712–707], prose writing produced a Han Yü, calligraphy produced a Yen Chen-ch'ing [709–785], and painting produced a Wu Tao-tzu [fl. ca. 710–60], the ability to change in history had reached its limits in these various fields. . . . The [ancient] calligraphic styles of Chung [Yu] and Wang [Hsi-chih] are relaxed, easy, simple, and remote; they evince a wonderful taste beyond the brushwork. . . . As for Yen and Liu [Kung-ch'üan, 778–865], who have summarized all the brush methods of the ages, they have nearly exhausted all the potentials, reaching the limits of change in calligraphic art. Ever since, everyone under heaven chose to follow Yen and Liu as masters, and the brush methods of Chung and Wang have been in steady decline.[33]

Su Shih developed his notion of decline from the Buddhist theory of the four *kalpas* (world periods): birth, maturity, transformation, and destruction.[34] It seemed clear to the late Northern Sung artists and critics alike that, after the inevitable latter-day transformation and decline, renewal in art lay in the return to the archaic and simple. Even in later times, successive renewals had to depend on successive revivals of ancient styles.

The belief in the cycle of renewing traditional principles thus lies at the heart of the Chinese practice of imitating (*fang*) ancient models. In imitating an ancient model, the exceptional artist examined the model more intently, more purely, and more receptively than ordinary artists, yet he used his model only as a metaphor or as a point of departure. In order to express and realize himself in his work, he always had to "transform" (*pien*) his model by formulating his own special techniques and methods of articulation.

With the practice of imitating ancient models came the need for identifying the right models. It was Mencius (ca. 371–289 B.C.) who, tracing the lineage of ancient sages "from Yao and Shun through T'ang, from T'ang to King Wen, and from King Wen to Confucius," first espoused the notion of a *tao-t'ung* (orthodox tradition of the Tao).[35] In the T'ang period Han Yü, leader of the revivalist movement in literature, who believed art to be inseparable from the Tao, or the ancient sages' teachings, considered the Great Tradition in literature (*wen-t'ung*) as the same as the Tradition of the Tao. By early Sung period, the belief in a common heritage in art and the Tao became widespread; Liu K'ai (947–1001), for instance, wrote: "Our Tao is the Tao of Confucius, Mencius, Yang Hsiung [53 B.C.–A.D. 18], and Han Yü."[36]

While the revivalists stressed the importance of rules (*ko*) and methods (*fa*) in imitating ancient models, the antitraditionalists emphasized self-realization and the discovery of a personal style. During the late fifth century, when the calligraphic styles of the two Wangs, Wang Hsi-chih and Wang Hsien-chih (344–386), had become universally accepted models, the calligrapher Chang Yung (fl. 479–501) made a great impression by declaring: "Rather than regretting that I do not share the methods of the two Wangs, I deeply regret that the two Wangs had not shared my methods!"[37] Chang's boast became the war cry of defiance among antitraditionalists throughout the centuries. During the Ming period, when revivalism predominated, antirevivalist sentiments also rose to an unprecedented height. Li Chih, for example, insisted that the only "true mind" was the "childlike mind" (*t'ung-hsin*), uncontaminated by learning. Accordingly, if the childlike mind prevailed, true art naturally expressed the true self, obviating the need for imitation of ancient styles.[38]

There is, however, a subtle wrinkle in the apparent dichotomy of these two approaches: as suggested by Liu Hsieh's argument of *t'ung-pien*, or "understanding transformation," the correct method of imitation must lie in individual transformation, without which the new and unorthodox is but an orthodoxy of the unorthodox. This paradox explains why Mi Fu (1052–1107), the greatest "imitator" of ancient styles of the eleventh century, was also a preeminent individualist: even as Mi exemplified the encyclopedic approach to style, he broadly criticized every major ancient model he emulated, claiming that he had "washed off the ugly styles of the Two Wangs."[39] The radicals of the late Ming period, in attacking the "falsehood" of imitation, merely vaunted eccentric and fantastic styles, which were, in the eyes of the traditionalists, yet another form of falsehood. The heterodox art and criticism of the late Ming period was denounced by the mainstream artists as mad or deviant, or as the "fox spirit," Ch'an Buddhism.

## *A Structural Analysis*

The historical pattern seen by the Chinese artist is not one of progress, in which the new must replace the old, and any return to the old can play a secondary, critical role; rather it was seen as an enduring effort on the part of succeeding generations of artists to gain or restore life and truth to art. Ancient models took their places in a nonhistorical continuum, in which the chronologically later masters, in achieving self-realization through inner responses to ancient models, emerged as equals rather than followers.

However compelling as a theory of creativity, such a view tends to obscure, rather than foster, an understanding of history. The traditional four-stage periodization of birth-maturity-transformation-destruction, for instance, when translated in poetry criticism as Early T'ang–High T'ang–Middle T'ang–Late T'ang, deals only with the first evolutionary phase of a genre; it cannot be applied to the later periods of successive revival movements. When a Ming critic used such a scheme to describe prose writing or poetry, he saw it as a system for assigning value: for prose writing the proper model had to be the high prose style of Ch'in and Han, and for poetry, that of High T'ang. In searching for creative renewal, the Ming critic concerned himself only with the general and timeless problem of quality and change. Modern historical inquiry seeks to establish the precise historical context of this change.

The same problem is faced by the historians of Chinese thought, as Fung Yu-lan explained in his *History of Chinese Philosophy* (1953):

> Former scholars of Chinese civilization have either not known how to separate genuine ancient writings from forgeries, or when they did, they have considered such forgeries to lack any value. . . . We historians of Chinese philosophy maintain that such a distinction between false and genuine writings must be made, because only after this has been done can the true aspect of the thought of each period be made evident.[40]

Recognizing the familiar pattern of an evolutionary development followed by successive renewals through revival (*fu-ku*) movements, Fung divided the history of Chinese thought into two principal parts: the Period of the Philosophers, which began with Confucius in the sixth century B.C. and ended about 100 B.C., followed by the Period of Classical Learning, which extended from about 100 B.C. until modern times. "The philosophy of medieval and modern times in China," Fung suggested, "must for the most part be found within the scholarly studies made upon the early Confucian classics and the Buddhist sutras." Yet, he cautioned, "such [later] men as Tung Chung-shu [ca. 179–93 B.C.] and Wang Yang-ming [1472–1529] are not merely commentators. Their philosophic works represent their own philosophy and not that preceding them."[41]

In the history of literature and literary criticism, too, the pattern of an evolutionary phase followed by successive revivals has been clearly recognized. In dividing early Chinese literature into two periods, the Period of Evolution of Literary Concepts (Chou through Six Dynasties) and the Period of Revival of Literary Concepts (Sui through Northern Sung), Kuo Shao-yü showed (1955) that, during the first period, literature developed from the point of view of form, while, in the second, revivalism was motivated by a desire to return to content. Kuo further separated his third period, Growth and Completion of Literary Criticism, dialectically into three subphases: the Establishment of Critical Systems (Southern Sung–Yüan), followed by the Polarization of Critical Theories (Ming), ending with the Resolution and Synthesis of Critical Theories (Ch'ing).[42]

For the history of Chinese painting, Max Loehr proposed that the 1,500 years between the Han dynasty and the end of the Southern Sung dynasty (ca. 200 B.C.–ca. A.D. 1300) be seen as the "phase of representational art in China, revealing a progress from images of isolated objects toward images of the visual phenomenon of pure space."[43] Before the Han period, according to Loehr, "there is no trace of a pictorial art but only some representational non-art [on the level of diagrams]."[44] Beginning with Yüan, "the content or intrinsic meaning of landscape painting changed abruptly. . . . Pictorial art from now on became an intellectualized, supra-representational art."[45] In the Han and Yüan periods, Loehr contended, "there occurred radical and profound shifts of motivation. They were marked by the phenomenon of a cessation of stylistic changes; instead of changes of style we observe critical ruptures." Ming and Ch'ing painting, for Loehr, was "painting about painting, allusive, commentatorial, and increasingly abstract because its content was thought."[46]

It was Loehr's belief that "an analysis of the [changing] content . . . should lead us to a meaningful periodization of painting history."[47] Pointing to the "changing nature of the [concept of] style" in history, Loehr classified the development of Chinese painting in four major phases:

1. Ornamental art (Neolithic through Chou), when style was "the formal substance (as in proto-representational images)."
2. Representational art (Han through Southern Sung), when style served as "a tool like an instrument to recover or capture reality."
3. Suprarepresentational art (Yüan), when "the objective representation of Sung was discarded for subjective expression. . . . Style now became the central problem of each individual."
4. Historically oriented art (Ming and Ch'ing), when "styles of the past began to function as subject-matter and to be explored as if they were the primary reality."

Loehr pointed out, however, that in defining "[each] phase [as] determined by its content," he gave "no historical [and] stylistic descriptions."[48]

Loehr's system is an adequate beginning, but in order to argue convincingly that a profound shift of motivation occurred in Yüan painting, the shift would have to be described and the impact of this change of motivation accounted for in formal, technical, and compositional terms. Most important, a way to analyze stylistic changes between successive revival movements, and waves of imitation of older styles, has to be found, so that—in Fung Yu-lan's words—the "distinction between false and genuine [works can] be made." If Ming and Ch'ing painting is "painting about painting" and "its content was thought," the challenge for the art historian is to devise a way to describe its self-reflexive nature in stylistic terms.

A useful modern contribution to the study of Chinese painting has been the development of stylistic analysis. This method classifies rather than narrates; it concentrates upon periods rather than individuals. In order to classify a style, modern historians deal not only with formal elements, motifs, and techniques, which are earmarks of individual styles, but also with formal relationships and visual structures (the way forms are perceived and organized in painting), which are group characteristics. The formal peculiarities of an individual work are interpreted as specific solutions to generic problems of delineation, modeling, and composition. While individual motifs and techniques do not give sufficient evidence for a fixed visual position in time, morphological analysis of successive visual structures in history provides useful clues for dating a painting. When external (historical or archaeological) documentation is lacking, style can be used, in most cases, to establish the approximate date or the origin of an anonymous work.[49]

As an abstract concept defining general structural problems rather than specific motifs and qualities of a work of art, "period styles" can be articulated only when they are seen within a larger developmental framework. Once a large stylistic goal or motivation has been identified, structural analysis may be used to reconstruct the formal problem to which stylistic changes provided the solution.[50] From the fourth century to the ninth century A.D. for figure painting and from the fourth century to the fourteenth century A.D. for landscape painting, pictorial representation of nature's forms in space became a clearly discernible stylistic motivation. As successive generations of artists moved steadily toward the conquest of illusion of depth and natural movement in painting through mastery of representational skills, structural changes in the conventions of representation also progressed through clearly defined stages.

In the history of the arts of the world, Chinese pictorial art appears to be the only living pictorial tradition that can trace its origins directly and continuously to the Neolithic past. Myths about the origins of the Chinese written language and art were an integral part of the early history of man, and the mastery of crucial skills in the arts in China seems to have occurred totally within the Chinese cultural context, independent of—and only occasionally touched by—outside influences.

The first chapter in this evolution is early Chinese figural representation, which echoes the so-called Greek miracle or revolution of the figure "awakening" from frozen archaic stiffness and becoming an organically articulated form moving freely in space.[51] Next was landscape painting, the story of the development from ideographic mountain and tree motifs in the two-dimensional picture plane to the creation of illusionistic space with a three-dimensional, receding ground plane. After representation ceased to be a challenge, the Chinese painter began to reinvestigate the two-dimensional picture plane. He first explored the unlimited possibilities of design through surface abstraction, then using simplified brush formulas, ultimately learned to "write" landscapes as kinetic, calligraphic designs. Since Chinese painters produced neither scientific theories of vision nor the modern Western "desperate revolt against illusion,"[52] Chinese paintings remained "images of the mind."

A good illustration of how structural analysis works is provided by its application to Chang Yen-yüan's three stages of the early history of Chinese painting. His Early Antiquity–Middle Antiquity–Recent Antiquity progression, from "simple" to "detailed" to "complete," actually covers a long, slow evolution spanning well over a millennium, from the late Eastern Chou period (4th century B.C.) through the T'ang dynasty (9th century), during which the Chinese artist gradually mastered the representational skills necessary to render human and animal figures as three-dimensional, organically integrated forms in space. From the late Eastern Chou to the early Six Dynasties period (early 6th century A.D.), Chinese figural representation remained in the archaic mode of linear, two-dimensional, and largely frontal forms. This archaic mode of representation seems to have been shared by many of the "original" cultures of the world—besides China, the ancient Near East, Egypt, and Greece, as well as the indigenous cultures of Africa, Oceania, and America—whose artists literally had to "learn" to draw and sculpt for the first time. Offering psychological explanation of the so-called Law of Frontality, Emanuel Loewy theorized, in his *Rendering of Nature in Early Greek Art* (1907), that archaic artists created according to "memory images," presenting the form as it could best be distinguished from other forms.[53] Archaic representations share certain features: the figures are shown to the spectator with each of their parts in its more characteristic aspect, either the profile or the frontal view; figures break up into fractional parts—the face, the shoulders, the body and limbs—each seen as a schematic motif, and together organized on an additive basis, there being neither concern for the organic whole nor interest in organic connectives, such as necks, wrists, or ankles; foreshortening is avoided, and thus diagonal recession is distorted to keep motifs in the lateral picture plane; and power to move does not lie in the figure, which is two-dimensional and nonorganic, but in the rhythm of the silhouette. Loewy's observations agree well with Chang Yen-yüan's description of the "simple" style of Early Antiquity of Han, Wei, Tsin, and early Six Dynasties: "The human figures are larger than the mountains, . . . [which] look like silver hairpins, or the teeth of a comb. . . . They are arranged like outstretched arms or spread fingers."[54]

In a late Eastern Chou drawing, *Lady with a Phoenix and a Dragon*, dated to the fifth or fourth century B.C. (fig. 1), the female figure consists of three additive parts: a profile head, an outstretched arm in a draping sleeve, and the lower body in a gown spread out over the ground like the base of a vase. On a painted basket from Lo-lang, Korea, dated around A.D. 100 (fig. 2), the figures are done in two kinds of brushstrokes: the face and the hands in fine lines that animate the figures with expressive movements of the eyes, the mouth, and hand gestures; and the drapery folds in broad sweeping strokes that suggest bulk and surface movement. The broad crescent-shaped brushstrokes seem to echo the wavelike ending strokes of the clerical script calligraphy of the later Han period. Smooth and swelling, the brushstrokes follow the movement of the artist's hand, first pressing down, then lifting up, and give the billowing surfaces a life of their own. In *Admonitions to the Court Ladies* (*Nü-shih chen*; now in The British Museum, London; fig. 3), the well-known handscroll attributed to Ku K'ai-chih—who was, according to Chang Yen-yüan, one of the two leading painters of Early Antiquity—complex allegorical themes are expressed in simple but effective linear characterization, with great elegance and nobility of bearing. The flat figures—their torsos, hips, and raised hands all turned into the lateral picture plane—stand against a blank background with little overlapping between them. The swirling gossamer brushlines animate the drawing but disregard the body beneath the garment. This additive method of visualizing forms was also used to depict the landscape setting behind figures. At Tun-huang, Kansu province, in northwestern China, where the best visual record of early Chinese Buddhist art is preserved, Cave 285, dated 538–39 (fig. 4), shows "space cells" created by series of triangular mountain motifs, running both horizontally and diagonally, around a given scene; "the human

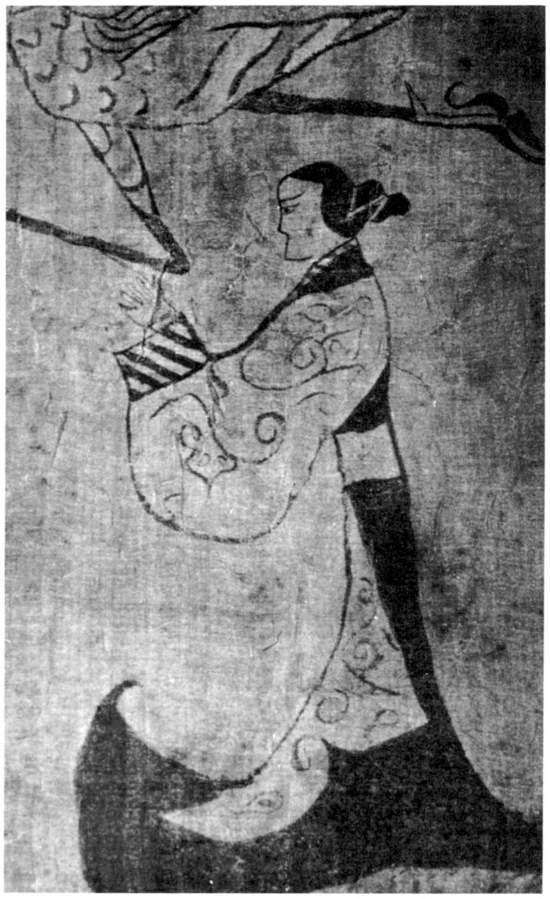

Fig. 1. Anonymous, *Lady with a Phoenix and a Dragon*. Undated, 5th–4th century B.C. Drawing, ink on coarse silk, from a tomb at Ch'ang-sha, Hunan. Historical Museum, Peking

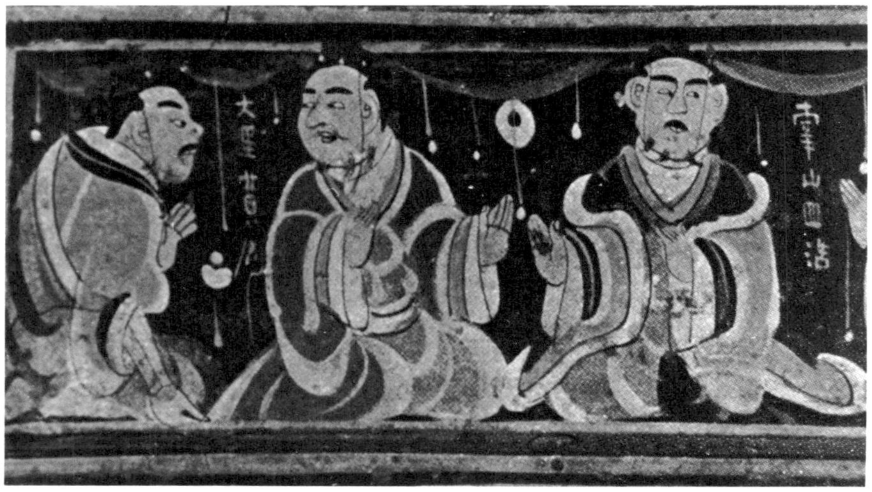

Fig. 2. Anonymous, painted basket from a tomb at Lo-lang, Korea. Undated, ca. A.D. 100. Ink and color on lacquer

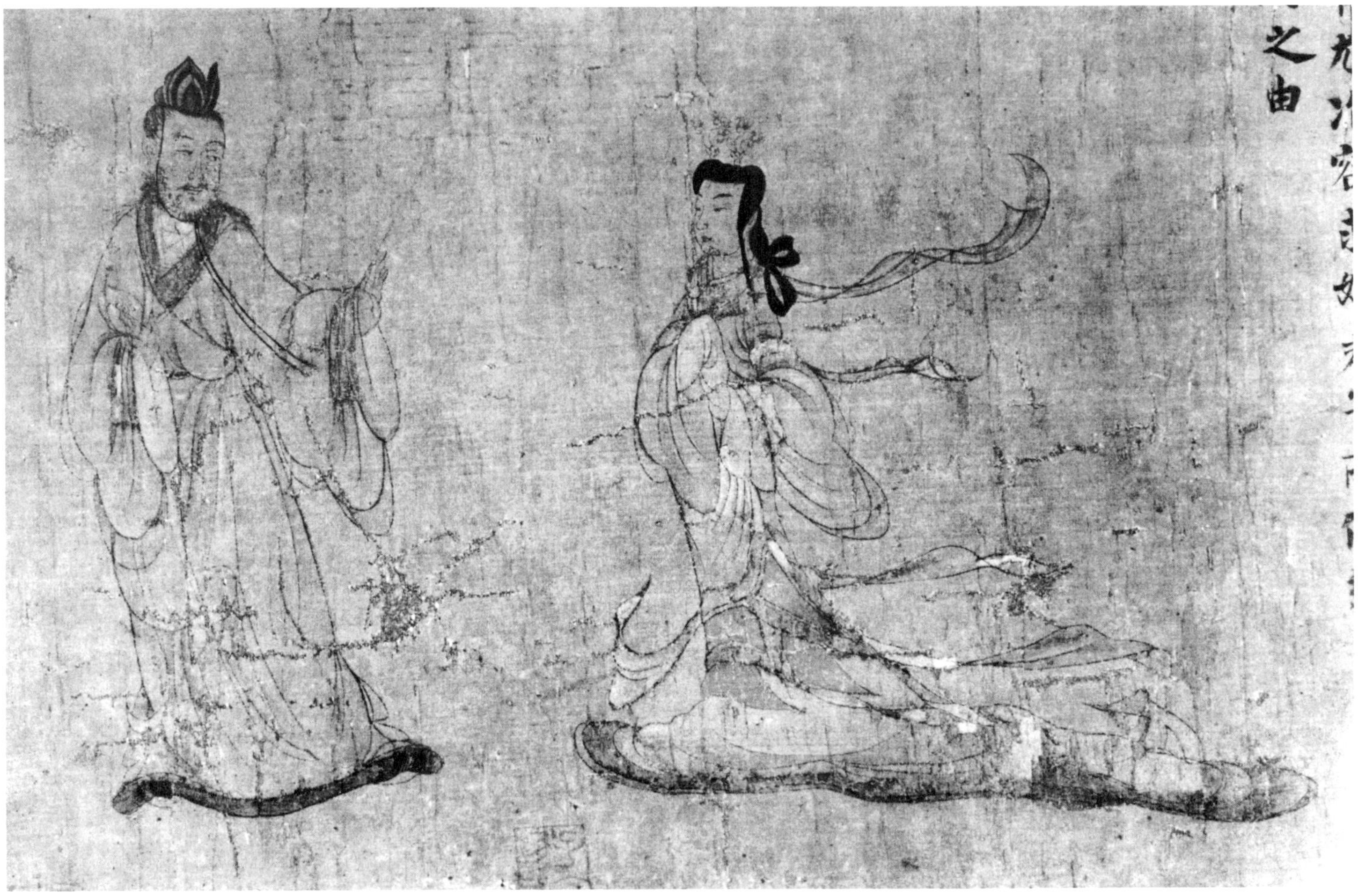


Fig. 3. Attributed to Ku K'ai-chih, detail, *Admonitions to the Court Ladies* (*Nü-shih chen*). Undated, early T'ang tracing copy (?). Handscroll, ink and color on silk. The British Museum, London

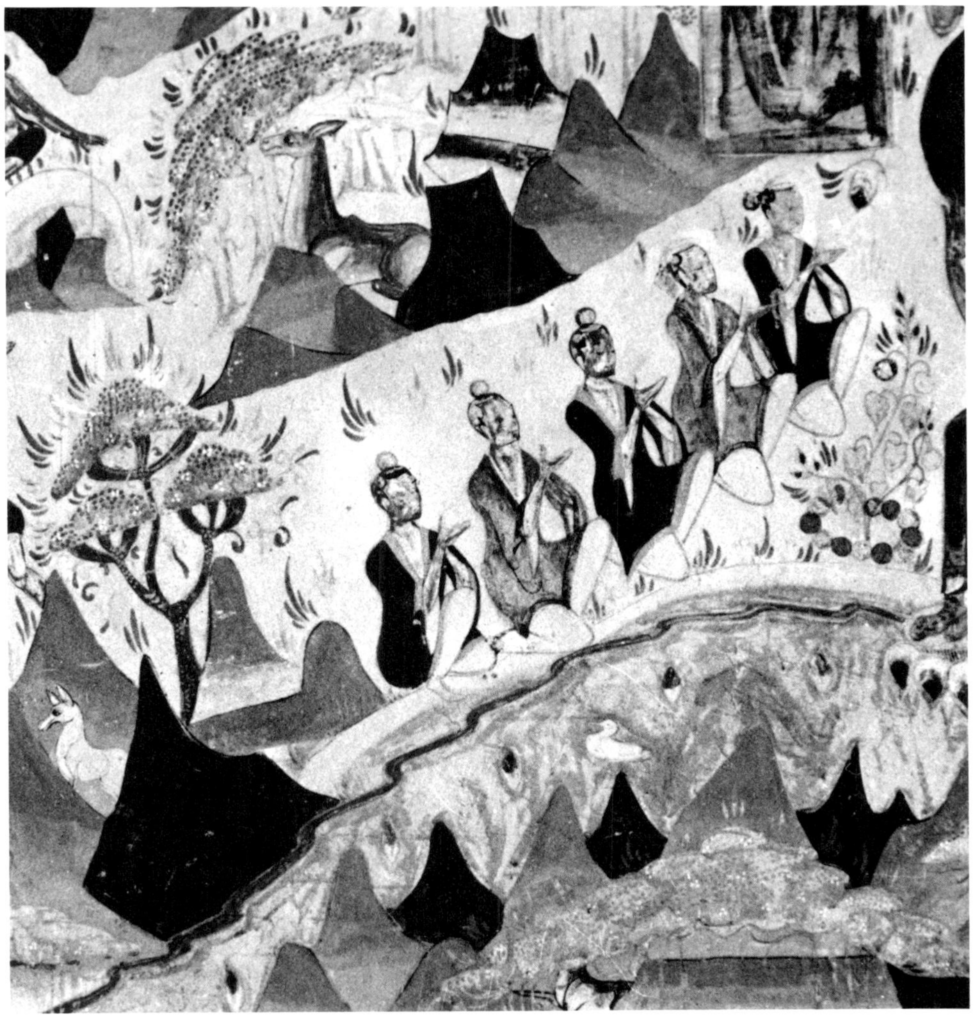

Fig. 4. Anonymous, detail, wall painting. Dated 538–39. Cave 285, Tun-huang, Kansu province

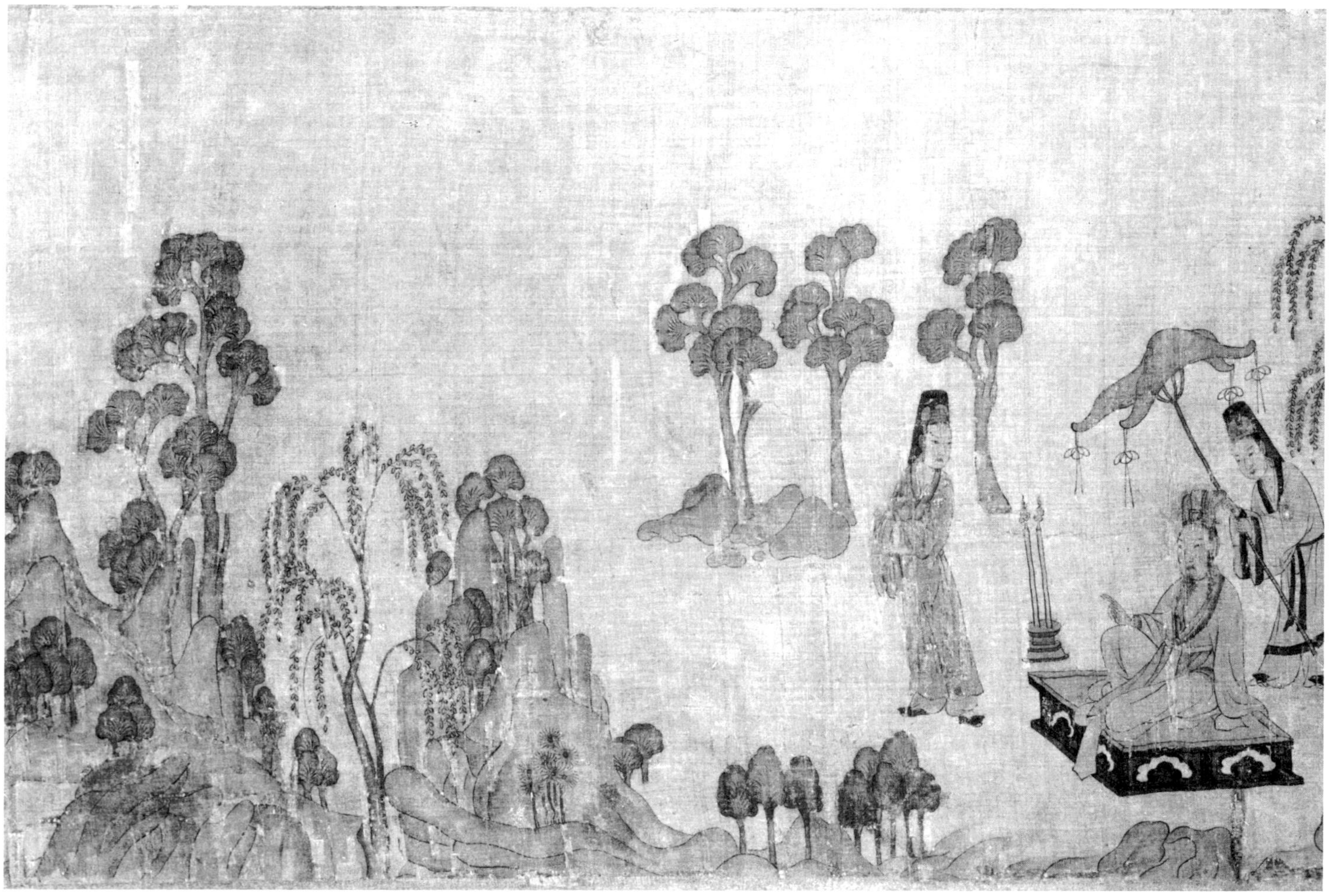

Fig. 5. Attributed to Ku K'ai-chih, detail, *Nymph of the Lo River* (*Lo-shen t'u*). Undated, Sung dynasty copy. Handscroll, ink and color on silk. 24.0 x 310.0 cm (9½ in. x 10 ft. 2 in.). Freer Gallery of Art, Washington, D.C.

figures are larger than the mountains, . . . [which] look like . . . the teeth of a comb," and the disjointed series of mountain motifs indicate a spatial setting without describing a receding, physically articulated space. The same method of landscape setting is seen in the handscroll *Nymph of the Lo River* (*Lo-shen t'u*) attributed to Ku K'ai-chih, a copy of which is in the Freer Gallery of Art, Washington, D.C. (fig. 5).

With the introduction of Buddhism into China in the first century A.D., the chiaroscuro modeling method of India and Central Asia, with its concomitant concern for mass, volume, and a well-articulated human figure, had a powerful impact on Chinese painting. As the Buddhist cave paintings at Tun-huang show, the imported shading style, known in Chinese as *ao-t'u hua*, or "receding-and-protruding painting," dominates the earliest extant caves, dated to the fifth century.[55] But the Western modeling technique, which emphasized color and shading, was essentially foreign to the Chinese, and they at first produced merely flat schematic patterns with bands and circles of color. Gradually the Chinese artists devised their own method of rendering receding and protruding forms; rejecting colored shading, they indicated three dimensions with a modulated, thickening-and-thinning brushline.

In Chang Yen-yüan's *Record of Famous Paintings*, the next painting phase is represented by the Southern Liang dynasty painter Chang Seng-yu (fl. ca. 500–550), known for his Indian-influenced receding-and-protruding style: "Chang Seng-yu made his dots, drag strokes, hacking and sweeping strokes in accordance with Lady Wei's [early 4th century] [treatise on calligraphy] *Battle Array of the Brush* (*Pi-ch'eng-t'u*)."[56] These "dots, drag strokes, hacking and sweeping strokes" reflect the increasingly complex brush techniques developing in the regular and running scripts of the time. Although Chang Seng-yu's paintings have not survived, the Tun-huang cave paintings of the second half of the sixth century show the success of these new techniques: in Cave 428, the receding-and-protruding flower paintings in its ceiling (fig. 6), when

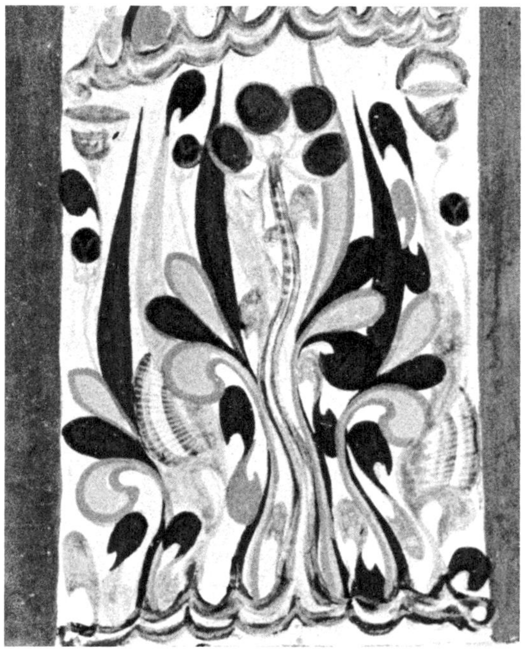

Fig. 6. Anonymous, detail, *Flower*. Undated, mid-6th century. Wall painting, Cave 428, Tun-huang, Kansu province

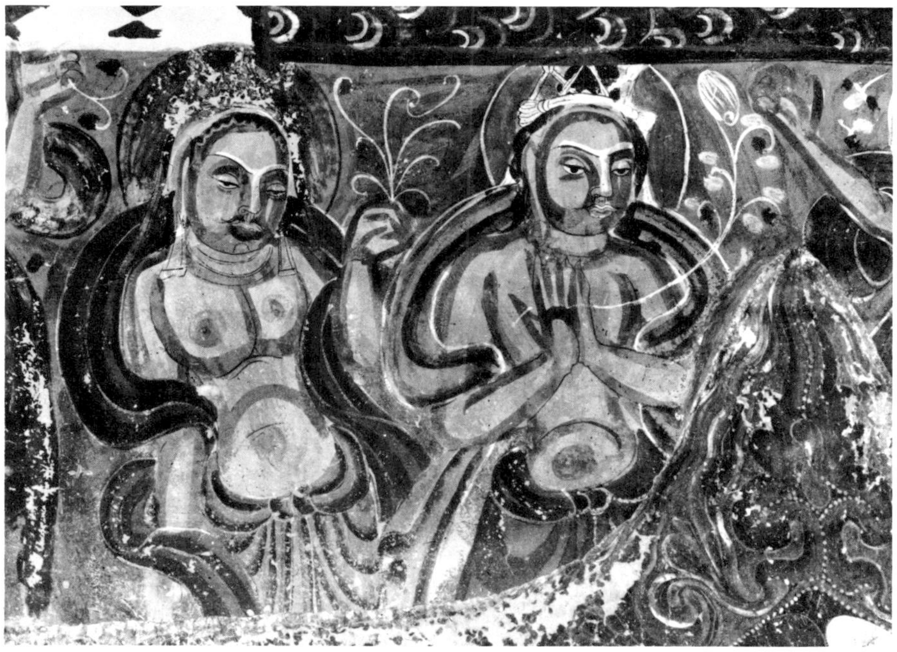

Fig. 7. Anonymous, detail, *Bodhisattvas*. Undated, mid-sixth century. Wall painting, Cave 428, Tun-huang, Kansu province

compared with earlier examples (such as the ones in Cave 288), appear to recede and protrude more successfully by virtue of their twisting and turning leaves, which reveal a good knowledge of foreshortening and perspective. In the fully modeled figures of Cave 428 (fig. 7), the forms were built first with the usual band of color shading, then with white highlighting, and finally with modulated brushstrokes in ink outlining the principal features of the face and the body. The drawing shows a sophisticated sense of bone structure: the lines of the eyelids and eye sockets, for instance, wrap around the eyes, the curved nostrils and the upturned corners of the lips describe the curvature of the cheeks, and together the firmly articulated facial features rest in the T-frame formed by the arching eyebrows and the bridge of the nose. The

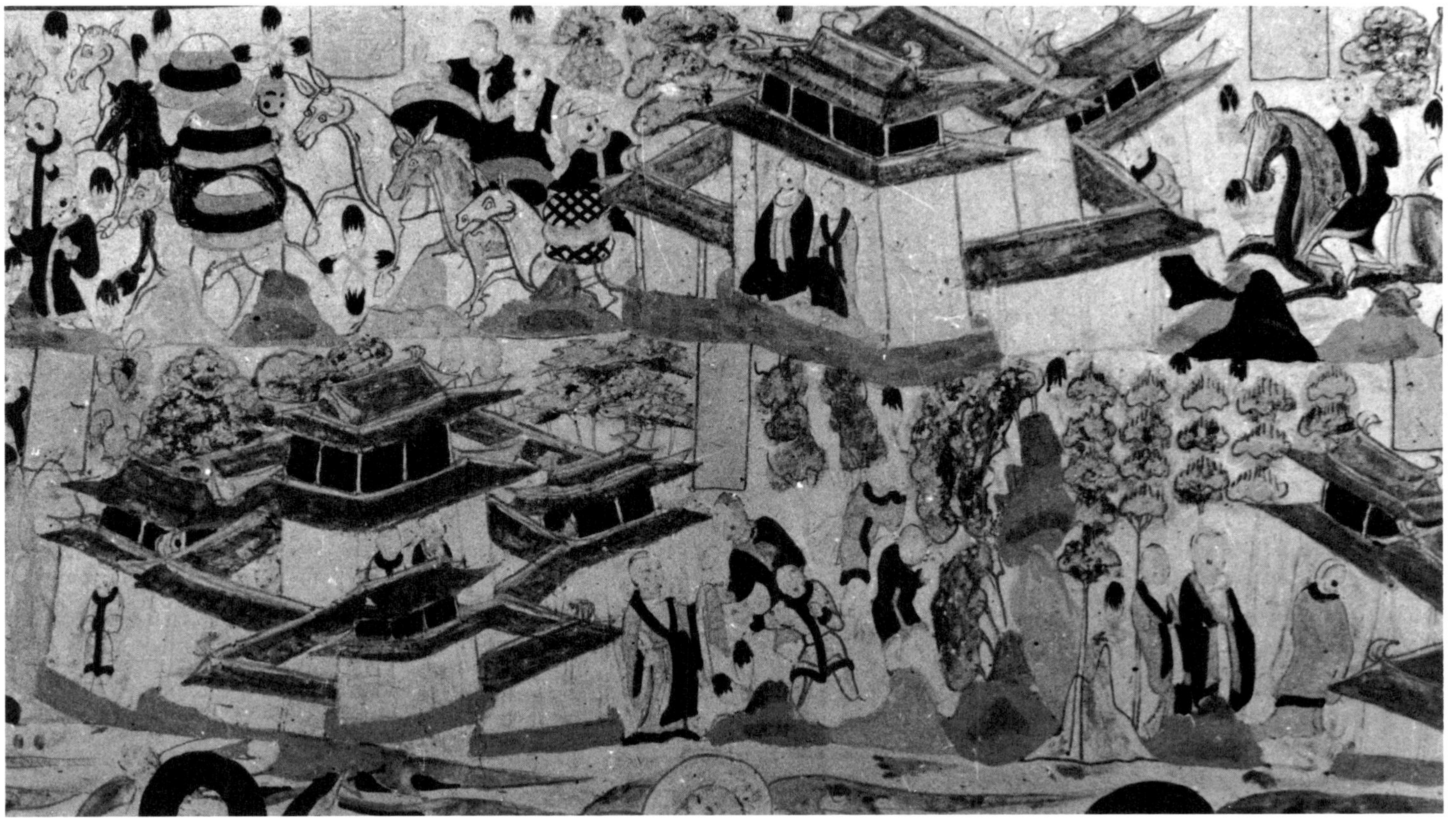

Fig. 8. Anonymous, detail, wall painting. Undated, late 6th century. Cave 296, Tun-huang, Kansu province

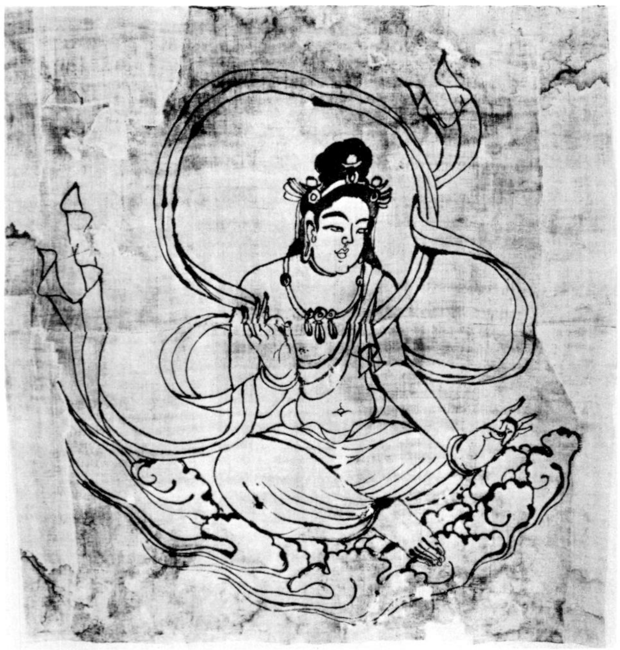

Fig. 9. Anonymous, *Bodhisattva*. Undated, mid-8th century. Drawing, ink on burlap. Shōsōin Treasury, Nara

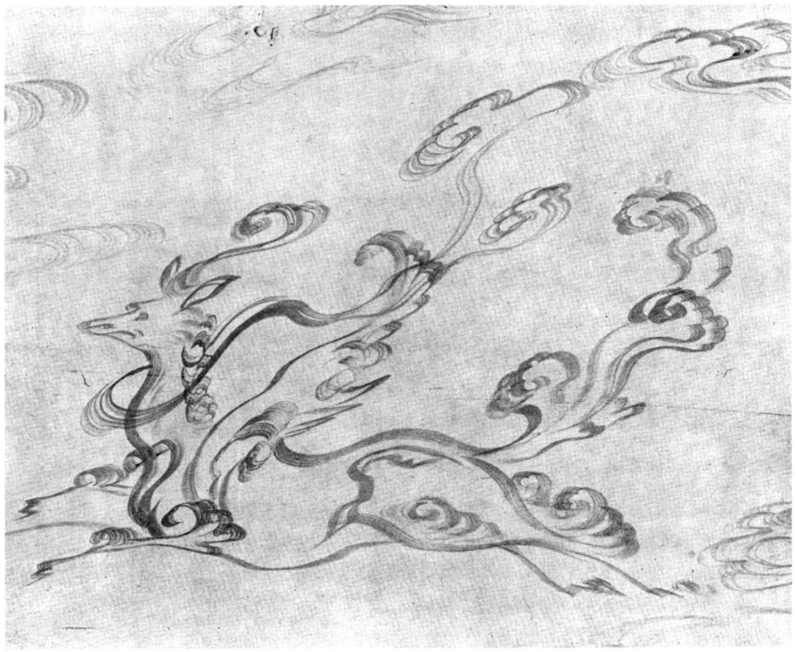

Fig. 10. Anonymous, *Flying Deer*. Undated, 8th century. Drawing, light color on decorated paper. Shōsōin Treasury, Nara

sculptured images in these late sixth-century caves also indicate a new interest in the columnar form of the body, and in organic relationships between parts of the figure. In the narrative illustrations of the late sixth century, such as those in Cave 296 (fig. 8), figures, horses, and buildings—all conceived as forms receding and protruding in space—seem to push out of the narrow confines of the horizontal register. To emphasize recession the artist played with the zigzag lines of a city wall; each building is turned at an angle, with one corner lying in the picture plane and the two sides moving into the distance. Chronologically these paintings belong to the period Chang Yen-yüan called Middle Antiquity, and they justify his descriptions of works of the period as "fine and detailed, exquisitely finished and exceedingly beautiful."[57]

By the eighth century, the "painting sage" of Chang's Recent Antiquity period, Wu Tao-tzu, was able to render a fully articulated three-dimensional figure with such forceful thickening-and-thinning brushstrokes that they needed neither shading nor colors. "When we gaze at the works of Wu Tao-tzu," Chang wrote, "we may say that all Six Principles are complete, and the myriad phenomena have been wholly expressed. Some god must be painting through his hand, so completely does his work fathom the power of Creation itself."[58] Wu's three-dimensional drawing style, of which no original is extant, is best reflected at Tun-huang in the figure of Vimalakirti in the mid-eighth-century Cave 103. An ink sketch on burlap representing the figure of a Bodhisattva, at the Shōsōin Treasury in Nara, Japan, dated in the mid-eighth century (fig. 9), is an excellent example of Wu's *pai-hua* ("white painting" or "pure-line drawing") style. The powerful thickening-and-thinning brushstrokes describe a fully plastic sculptural image. With a keen eye for bulk and foreshortening, the artist mastered three-dimensionality with lines alone. On a decorated paper specimen at the Shōsōin (fig. 10), a flying deer with cloud scrolls is executed in the split-hair, flying-white (*fei-pai*) brush technique; the same technique is used in calligraphy, as seen in the inscription on the late eighth-century portraits of the Chen-yen (Shingon) patriarchs by Li Chen (fl. ca. 780–804) in the Tō-ji, Kyoto.

Despite the playful decorative effect of streaks of flying white showing through the flat folding and turning brushstrokes, the animal form is beautifully conceived in the round as a fully integrated organic unity. Such effective drawing, a special achievement of T'ang painting, can only be produced when the artist is able to visualize and depict forms in organic three-dimensional terms. As the representation of human figures became more and more convincing in three-dimensionality and freedom of movement, the landscape elements around the figures also became more natural in scale and appearance. In the illustrations of the life of Buddha on silk banners from Tun-huang, dated in the ninth century and now in The British Museum, London (fig. 11), the landscape elements provide a convincing stagelike setting for human activity; the developed triangular mountain form shows parallel folds on two sides and a receding ridge, or spine, in the middle of the mountain mass; the mountain folds are modeled by softly rubbed, parallel *ts'un* (texture strokes), and the colors are modulated—greens for the exposed grass-covered surfaces and browns and blacks for the shaded earth-covered areas. In terms of representational achievement, Chinese painting by the mid- and late T'ang period had reached a peak.

After this height of naturalism in the ninth century, both figure and landscape paintings of the tenth century became flat and schematic (fig. 12). The "decline" may be attributed, in part, to the terrible turmoil and sufferings that occurred during the collapse of the T'ang dynasty at the end of the ninth century. The schematic idiom may also have signified a return to archaic simplicity and the discovery of an expressionistic style of nostalgia and pathos. As a full stylistic cycle of developing naturalism came to an end, it prompted a logical desire to turn to surface abstraction. Such a return to archaistic styles occurred periodically in Chinese art history, primarily during times of dynastic change: at the end of the Five Dynasties period, after the tenth century; toward the end of the northern Sung in about 1120; at the end of the Southern Sung, toward 1300; and at the end of the Ming period, about 1600.[59] At the end of the T'ang period, even as figure painting began to wane, another genre emerged: after the tenth century the history of painting in China was to turn decisively toward landscape.

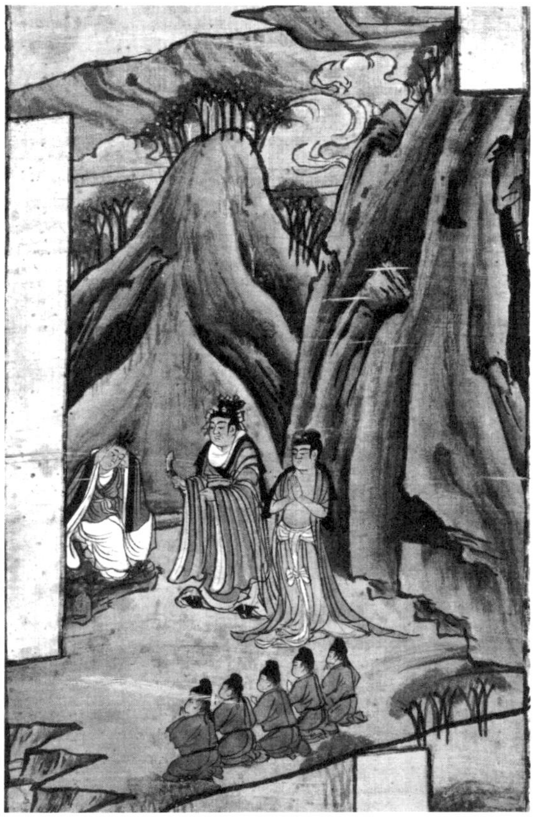

Fig. 11. Anonymous, detail, *Life of Buddha*. Undated, 9th century. Banner, ink and color on silk, from Tun-huang, Kansu province. The British Museum, London

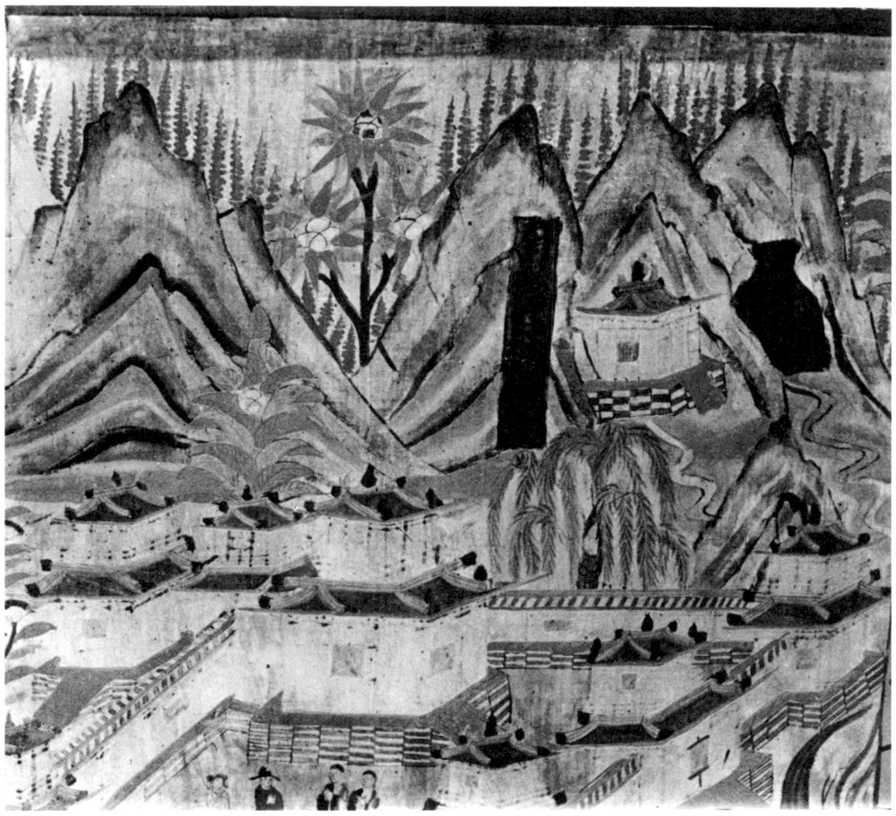

Fig. 12. Anonymous, detail, *Mount Wu-t'ai* (*Wu-t'ai-shan*). Undated, 10th century. Wall painting, Cave 61, Tun-huang, Kansu province

## NOTES

1. James Legge, trans., "Duke Seang, Twenty-fifth Year," in *Spring and Autumn Annals with Tso-chuan Commentary (Ch'un-ch'iu yü Tso-chuan), The Chinese Classics*, vol. 5 (1872; repr. ed., 1939), pt. 2, p. 515.
2. James Legge, trans., *Confucian Analects (Lun-yü), The Chinese Classics*, vol. 1, (1895; repr. ed., 1935), p. 39.
3. For the emergence of a historical criticism in literature, see Kuo Shao-yü, *Chung-kuo wen-hsüeh p'i-p'ing shih* (History of Chinese literary criticism) (Shanghai: Chung-hua shu-chü, 1961), pp. 84 ff.
4. Chang Yen-yüan, *Li-tai ming-hua chi* (Record of famous painters of successive dynasties), in Yü An-lan, ed., *Hua-shih ts'ung-shu* (Compendium of painting histories) (Shanghai: Shanghai jen-min mei-shu ch'u-pan-she, 1963), vol. 1, *chüan* 6, p. 80; see William R. B. Acker, *Some T'ang and Pre-T'ang Texts on Chinese Painting* (Leiden: E.J. Brill, 1954), pp. 65–66.
5. See Wang Yüan-ch'i et al., comps., *P'ei-wen-chai shu-hua-p'u* (Manual on calligraphy and painting of the P'ei-wen Studio) (1708; repr. ed., Taipei, 1969), *chüan* 3, p. 1a.
6. See Kuo Jo-hsü, *T'u-hua chien-wen chih* (Experiences in painting), in Yü An-lan, ed., *Hua-shih ts'ung-shu*, vol. 1, *chüan* 1, p. 9; Alexander C. Soper, *Kuo Jo-hsü's Experiences in Painting* (Washington, D.C.: American Council of Learned Societies, 1951), p. 15.
7. Wang Wei (fifth century A.D.), as quoted in Chang Yen-yüan, *Li-tai ming-hua chi*, *chüan* 6, p. 80.
8. For a biography of Ku K'ai-chih, see Chang Yen-yüan, *Li-tai ming-hua chi*, *chüan* 5, pp. 70–71.
9. See Wen C. Fong, "Ch'i-yün-sheng-tung: Vitality, Harmonious Manner and Aliveness," *Oriental Art* 8, no. 3 (Autumn 1966): 159–64.
10. Ibid.: 160.
11. Ibid.: 160–62.
12. Chang Yen-yüan, *Li-tai ming-hua chi*, *chüan* 1, p. 15; William R. B. Acker, *Some T'ang and Pre-T'ang Texts on Chinese Painting*, p. 149.
13. Ching Hao, *Pi-fa chi* (Notes on brush method), in Yü Chien-hua, ed., *Chung-kuo hua-lun lei-pien* (Classified compilation of writings on Chinese painting) (Hong Kong: Chung-hua shu-chü, 1973), vol. 1, p. 605; see Munakata Kiyohiko, *Ching Hao's "Pi-fa chi": A Note on the Art of Brush, Artibus Asiae* Supplementum 31 (1974): 11–12.
14. Su Shih, *Ching-chin Tung-p'o wen-chi shih-lüeh* (Collected prose of Su Shih), Ssu-pu ts'ung-k'an, vol. 10 (Taipei: Shang-wu yin-shu-kuan, 1967), *chüan* 54, pp. 9a–b.
15. Su Shih, *Chi-chu fen-lai Tung-p'o hsien-sheng shih* (Annotated poetry of Master Tung-p'o), Ssu-pu ts'ung-k'an, vol. 5 (Taipei: Shang-wu yin-shu-kuan, 1967), *chüan* 11, p. 29a.
16. Kuo Jo-hsü, *T'u-hua chien-wen chih*, *chüan* 1, p. 9.
17. Shen Kua, *Meng-ch'i pi-t'an chiao-cheng* (Notes written in Meng-ch'i), in *Ts'ung-shu chi-ch'eng* (Shanghai: Shang-wu yin-shu-kuan, 1935–37), *chüan* 17, p. 107.
18. Ts'ao P'ei-lien, ed., *Ch'ing-pi-ko ch'üan-chi* (Collected works of the Pure and Secluded Pavilion [of Ni Tsan]), Yüan-tai chen-pen wen-chi hui-kan, vol. 10 (1713; repr. ed, Taipei: Kuo-li chung-yang t'u-shu-kuan, 1970), *chüan* 9, p. 428.
19. The National Central Library (Kuo-li chung-yang t'u-shu-kuan) reprint of Ni Tsan's *Ch'ing-pi-ko ch'üan-chi* (Taipei, 1970) consists of a total of twelve *chüan*: eight *chüan* of ancient and regulated poems, two *chüan* of *yüeh-fu* poems and miscellaneous writings, and two *chüan* known as *wai-chi* (addenda), which include anecdotes, epitaphs, critiques, and colophons.
20. For a lucid introduction to this topic, see James J. Y. Liu, *The Art of Chinese Poetry* (Chicago: The University of Chicago Press, 1962), pp. 70–76.
21. For an alternative translation, see Richard Barnhart, "Li Kung-lin's *Hsiao Ch'ing t'u*, Illustrations of *The Classic of Filial Piety*" (Ph.D. diss., Princeton University, 1967), p. 127.
22. Ni Tsan, for instance, is found under "recluses" (*yin-i*) in Ch'in Hsiang-yeh et al., comps., *Wu-hsi Chin-kuei hsien-chih* (Gazetteer of Wu-hsi [Kiangsu province]) (1881; repr. ed., Taipei: Wu-hsi t'ung hsiang-hui, 1968), p. 451.
23. See Nemoto Makoto, *Sensei-shakai ni okeru teiku-seishin Chūgoku-teki initsu no kenkyu* (The spirit of resistance in authoritarian society: a study of Chinese eremitism) (Tokyo: Sōgen-sha, 1952).
24. Frederick W. Mote, "Confucian Eremitism in the Yüan Period," in Arthur F. Wright, ed., *The Confucian Persuasion* (Stanford, California: Stanford University Press, 1960), p. 205.
25. Cheng Ssu-hsiao, *Wo-chia Ch'ing-feng-lou chi* (A record of my own "Pavilion of Pure Breeze"), in *Cheng So-nan hsien-sheng wen-chi* (Collected prose writings of Cheng Ssu-hsiao), Chih-pu-tsu-chai ts'ung-shu, vol. 9 (1776; repr. ed., Taipei: Hsing-chung shu-chü, 1964), pp. 1–2.
26. See William Theodore de Bary, "Individualism and Humanitarianism in Late Ming Thought," in William Theodore de Bary, ed., *Self and Society in Ming Thought* (New York: Columbia University Press, 1970), p. 205.
27. Quoted in Kuo Shao-yü, *Chung-kuo wen-hsüeh p'i-p'ing-shih*, p. 84.
28. For a translation, see Vincent Yu-chung Shih, trans., *The Literary Mind and the Carving of Dragons by Liu Hsieh* (New York: Columbia University Press, 1959), p. 167.
29. See Chang Yen-yüan, comp., *Fa-shu yao-lu* (Selections of writings on calligraphy), I-shu ts'ung-pien, vol. 1 (Taipei: Shih-chieh shu-chü, 1967), *chüan* 2, p. 28.
30. Sun Ch'ien-li [Sun Kuo-t'ing], *Shu-p'u* (Treatise on calligraphy), I-shu ts'ung-pien, vol. 1 (Taipei: Shih-chieh shu-chü, 1962), p. 1; see Roger Goepper, "Shu-p'u, Der Traktat zur Schriftkunst des Sun Kuo-t'ing," in *Studien zur Ostasiatischen Schriftkunst*, vol. 2 (Weisbaden: Franz Steiner, 1974); for facsimile of *Shu-p'u*, see also table, pp. 8–66.
31. Chang Yen-yüan, *Li-tai ming-hua-chi*, *chüan* 2, p. 15. For a translation, see William R. B. Acker, *Some T'ang and Pre-T'ang Texts on Chinese Painting*, p. 149.
32. Kuo Jo-hsü, *T'u-hua chien-wen chih*, *chüan* 2, p. 14. For another translation, see Alexander C. Soper, *Kuo Jo-hsü's Experiences in Painting*, pp. 21–22.
33. Su Shih, "Shu Wu Tao-tzu hua-hou" (Writings on a painting by Wu Tao-tzu), in *Tung-p'o t'i-pa* (Colophons by Su Shih), I-shu ts'ung-pien, vol. 22 (Taipei: Shih-chieh shu-chü, 1962), *chüan* 5, p. 95.
34. For the Buddhist *kalpas*, see Fung (Feng) Yu-lan, *A History of Chinese Philosophy*, trans. Derk Bodde (Princeton: Princeton University Press, 1953), vol. 2, pp. 474, 519. Liang Ch'i-ch'ao (1873–1929), in his *Ch'ing-tai hsüeh-shu k'ai-lun* (A survey of Ch'ing dynasty scholarship) (1921; repr. ed., Taipei: Shang-wu yin-shu-kuan, 1972), p. 2, describing the four Buddhist *kalpas*, states that "the development of every intellectual trend of any country, at any given time, seems to follow this pattern."
35. James Legge, trans., *The Works of Mencius (Meng-tzu), The Chinese Classics*, vol. 2 (1895; repr. ed., 1939), p. 522.
36. See Kuo Shao-yü, *Chung-kuo wen-hsüeh p'i-p'ing-shih*, pp. 140–41.
37. See Wang Yüan-ch'i et al., comps., *P'ei-wen-chai shu-hua-p'u*, *chüan* 24, p. 6a.
38. See Kuo Shao-yü, *Chung-kuo wen-hsüeh p'i-p'ing-shih*, pp. 349–51.
39. T'ang Hou, *Ku-chin hua-chien* (Mirror of past and present painting), I-shu ts'ung-pien, vol. 11 (Taipei: Shih-chieh shu-chü, 1962), p. 38.
40. Fung (Feng) Yu-lan, *History of Chinese Philosophy*, vol. 1, p. 5.
41. Ibid.
42. Kuo Shao-yu, *Chung-kuo wen-hsüeh p'i-p'ing-shih*, pp. 2–7.
43. Max Loehr, "Some Fundamental Issues in the History of Chinese Painting," *The Journal of Asian Studies* 23, no. 2 (February 1964): 186.
44. Max Loehr, "The Fate of Ornament in Chinese Art," *Archives of Asian Art* 21 (1967/68): 8–19.
45. Max Loehr, "Phases and Content in Chinese Painting," in National Palace Museum, ed., *Proceedings of the International Symposium on Chinese Painting* (Taipei: National Palace Museum, 1970), p. 286.
46. Max Loehr, "Some Fundamental Issues": 186–92.
47. Max Loehr, "Phases and Content," p. 286.
48. Ibid., pp. 286, 304. By insisting that historical and stylistic descriptions are "on a level below" his own analysis, Loehr arrives at a periodization of painting history not dependent upon description. While he has made a useful contribution to Chinese art history by pointing out the changing content of the works of the Sung, Yüan, and Ming-Ch'ing periods, his emphasis on "critical ruptures" and a "cessation of stylistic changes"

between the periods can lead to oversimplified views of Yüan and Ming–Ch'ing paintings. To characterize Ni Tsan's painting, which is typically Yüan, as suprarepresentational, disregards that Ni, as well as other Yüan painters, had continued to work in the illusionistic visual structure inherited from his Southern Sung predecessors.

49. See Wen C. Fong, "Toward a Structural Analysis of Chinese Landscape Painting," *Art Journal* 28, no. 4 (Summer 1969): 388–97; Wen C. Fong, "How to Understand Chinese Painting," *Proceedings of the American Philosophical Society* 115, no. 4 (August 1971): 282–92.
50. See George Kubler, *The Shape of Time* (New Haven: Yale University Press, 1962), pp. 33 ff.
51. For "Reflections on the Greek Revolution," see E. H. Gombrich, *Art and Illusion: A Study in the Psychology of Pictorial Representation*, Bollingen Series, vol. 35.5 (New York: Pantheon Books, 1960), pp. 116 ff.
52. Ibid., p. 281.
53. Emanuel Loewy, *The Rendering of Nature in Early Greek Art*, trans. John Fothergill (London, 1907), p. 12.
54. Chang Yen-yüan, *Li-tai ming-hua chi, chüan* 1, p. 16.
55. See Wen C. Fong, "*Ao-t'u-hua* or 'Receding-and-Protruding Painting' at Tun-huang," in *Kuo-chi Han-hsüeh hui-i lun-wen chi* (Proceedings of the International Sinological Conference) (Taipei: Chung-yang yen-chiu so, 1981), pp. 73–94.
56. Chang Yen-yüan, *Li-tai ming-hua chi, chüan* 2, p. 22. In *chüan* 1, Chang cites two late sixth-century painters, Chan Tzu-chien and Cheng Fa-shih, in Middle Antiquity.
57. Chang Yen-yüan, *Li-tai ming-hua chi, chüan* 1, p. 15.
58. Ibid.
59. See Wen C. Fong, "Archaism as a Primitive Style," in Christian F. Murck, ed., *Artists and Traditions: Uses of the Past in Chinese Culture* (Princeton: The Art Museum, 1976), pp. 89–109.

# 1 *Pictorial Representation in Chinese Landscape Painting*

THE EARLY FOUNDERS of the monumental style of landscape painting—Ching Hao (fl. ca. 870–930), Kuan T'ung (fl. ca. 907–23), Tung Yüan (fl. 937–76), Chü-jan (fl. 960–80), and Li Ch'eng (919–967)—who lived and worked in the Five Dynasties period and early Northern Sung period, are known to us only through attributed paintings, copies of their works, and copies of copies. To assess whether a particular work represents an "early" or "late" imitation of a painter's style along a linear sequence from representation to surface abstraction ignores the complexities of stylistic permutations, mixed influences, and inventions, much of which easily eludes attention unless a particular work is considered in the context of the whole development. The process of dating an early Chinese painting leads in a circular direction: individual works are dated according to our conception of a period style, which in turn must be defined, expanded, and refined on the basis of specific paintings. As more studies are carried out, and key "monuments" fall one by one into their proper stylistic context, individual works as monuments become evidence for documenting other attributed works.

Chinese landscape painters conquered illusion in three stages. In the first phase, beginning about A.D. 700 and continuing to about A.D. 1050 (see diagrams, figs. 13a, b; cf. fig. 18), the composition proceeded from the front to the back in three separate stages. Individual mountain and tree forms, each fully outlined and modeled, are viewed frontally and organized additively part by part, motif by motif. Even juxtaposed elements do not physically connect or relate to one another. Although overlapping triangular mountain motifs suggest diagonal recession, each sequence of mountains is limited to three or four steps; then the chain breaks off, jumps to a higher level in the picture plane, and starts again. The treatment of space is thus compartmentalized: foreground, middle ground, and far distance occupy three separate levels in the picture plane, each with its own angle of recession. These levels exist in three parallel planes, each with its own suggested ground plane tilting at a different angle away from the viewer.

During the second phase, from about 1050 to 1250 (see diagrams, figs. 14a, b; cf. fig. 53), both the modeling and composition techniques change to accommodate and match more closely the natural vision that collects landscape forms in a unified spatial continuum: the modeling of the forms, relying heavily on the use of ink wash, softens to a generalized surface to suggest atmosphere; and overlapping forms are ranged from the front to the back in a continuous sequence. The advanced spatial relationship still describes no real ground plane. Mountain forms are still seen frontally and individually; they fan out into the distance like a deck of playing cards, in parallel vertical planes. Disconnected silhouettes dissolve artfully into surrounding mists at their bases, which gives the impression of a unified vision.

Finally, during the third phase, from about 1250 to about 1400 (see diagrams, figs. 15a, b; cf. fig. 66), the landscape was depicted as a spatially integrated, physical environment. Foreshortening was discovered: the elements are no longer superimposed along the vertical picture plane; those far away are seen behind and through those in front. Brushwork and ink wash, in mixed values and tones, fuse and blur to create an atmospheric surface. The ground plane recedes continuously, physically linking the landscape elements.

Because the Chinese emphasized brush methods and ancient styles, the phenomenon that Heinrich Wölfflin calls "the effect of picture on picture"[1] was at least as great as the effect of the observation of nature on pictorial representation. Throughout the history of Chinese painting, the persistence of old styles, as well as periodic revivals of them, seemed to lead inevitably toward stylization and surface abstraction. In order to date paintings correctly, the archaistic or revivalist styles of different periods must be distinguished not only from their ancient models, but also from each other.

Assuming that early painters followed both early art and nature as models, their reduction of earlier techniques to brush methods always proceeded hand in hand with the creation of new representational

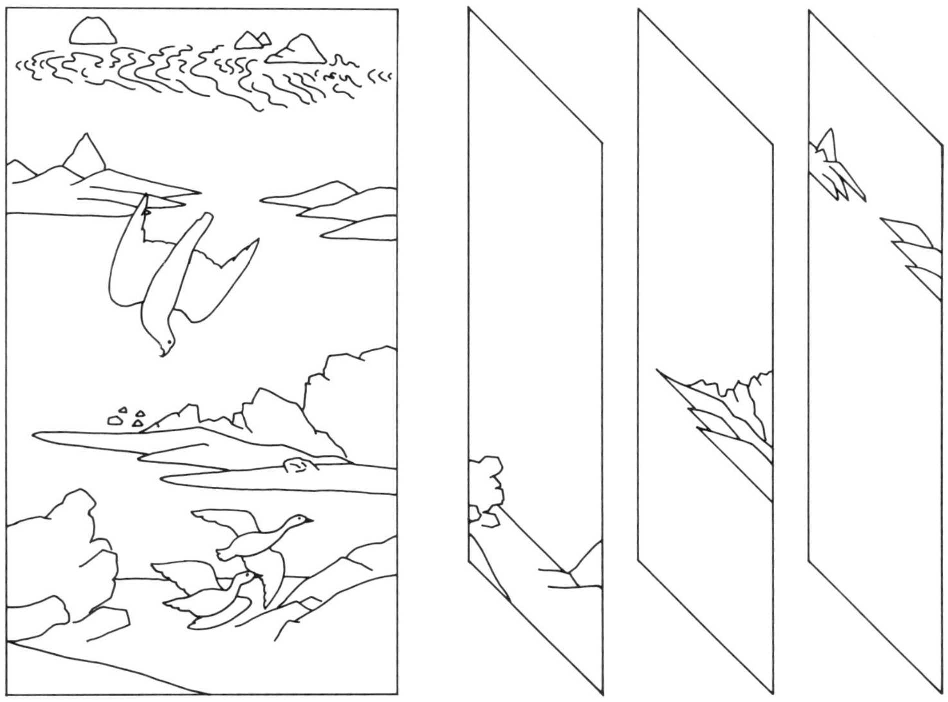

Figs. 13a, b. Diagrams of *Hawk and Ducks*, fig. 18, showing additive mountain motifs receding in three separate stages

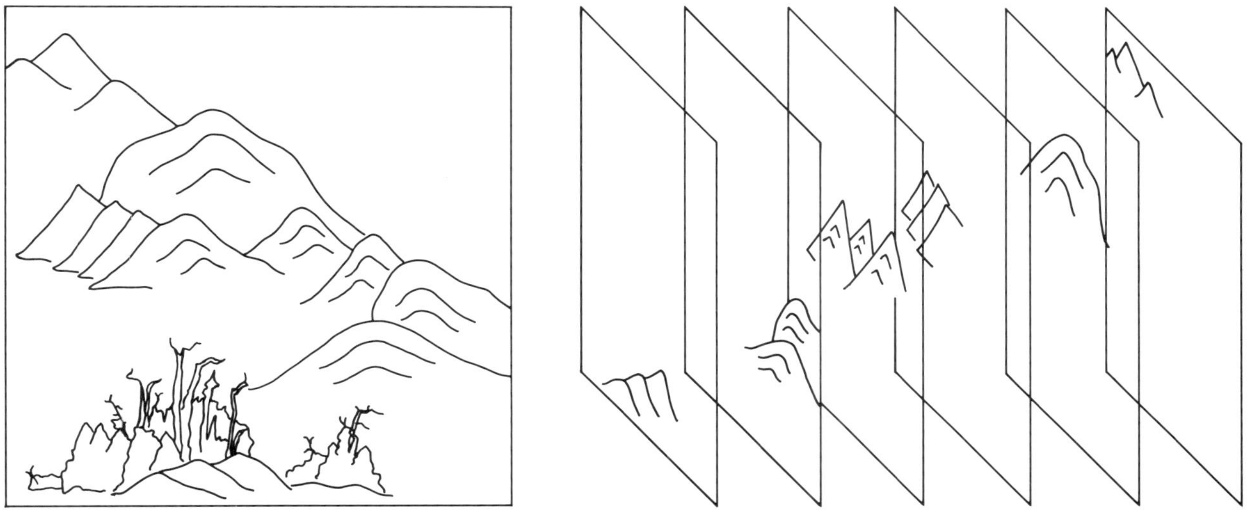

Figs. 14a, b. Diagrams of Li-sheng, *Dream Journey through the Hsiao and Hsiang Rivers*, fig. 53, showing overlapping mountain motifs receding in a continuous sequence

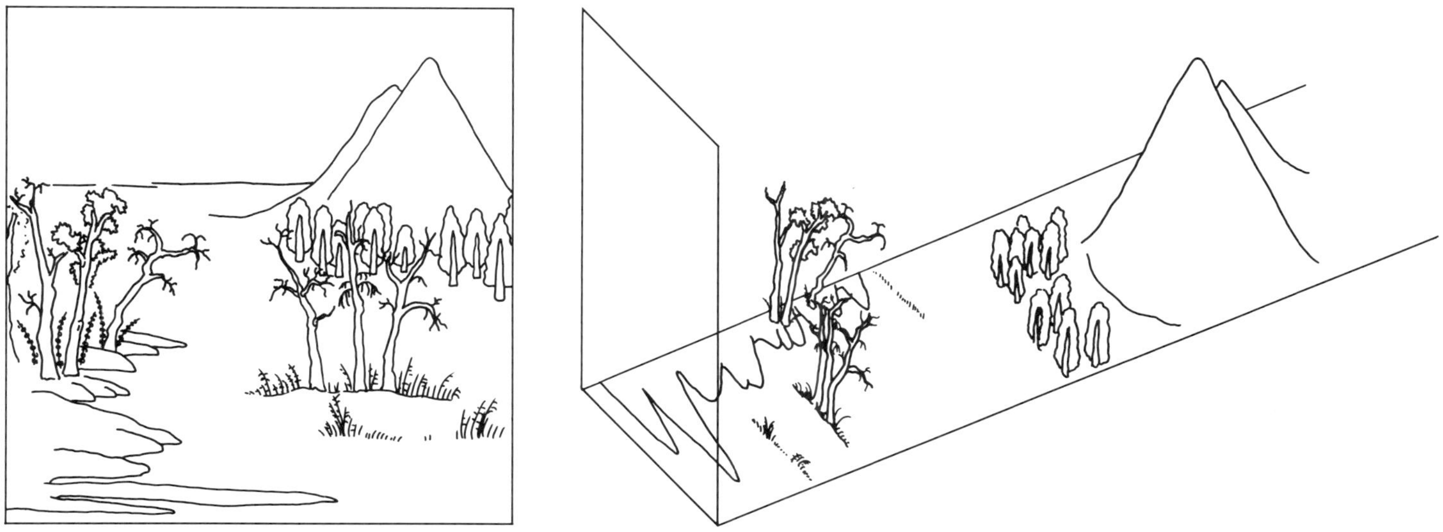

Figs. 15a, b. Diagrams of Chao Meng-fu, *Autumn Colors on the Ch'iao and Hua Mountains*, fig. 66, showing landscape elements arranged along a continuously receding ground plane

styles. Later copyists and imitators, in consciously trying to reproduce archaism, clung to superficial elements, brush techniques, and compositional motifs. In expanding the original solution and giving it fresh understanding, however, the later artists inevitably deviated from the original and made subtle structural changes. In short, later painters did not reproduce archaic styles, but transmitted and interpeted them through the visual structures and articulations of their own times. While formal elements, techniques, and individual motifs may be copied, the subtler formal relationships, both the macrostructure of visual organization and the microstructure of the artist's hand movements, cannot be exactly duplicated.

## *Building the Vocabulary*

Landscape elements first appeared in Chinese art as a background to figure painting. In the Han and Six Dynasties periods, from the third century B.C. to the seventh century A.D., representations of mountains and trees resemble their ideographic counterparts: *shan* 山 comprising three peaks, a "host" mountain flanked by two "guests," and *mu* 木 describing forking branches above and anchoring roots below. The earliest representations of foliage patterns, found, for example, in the fifth-century B.C. silk manuscript from Ch'ang-sha, now in the Arthur M. Sackler collection (figs. 16a, b), illustrate seasonal changes: leaves of deciduous trees, indicated by circular outlines, stand for spring and summer, and evergreen branches, with needle patterns, for fall and winter.

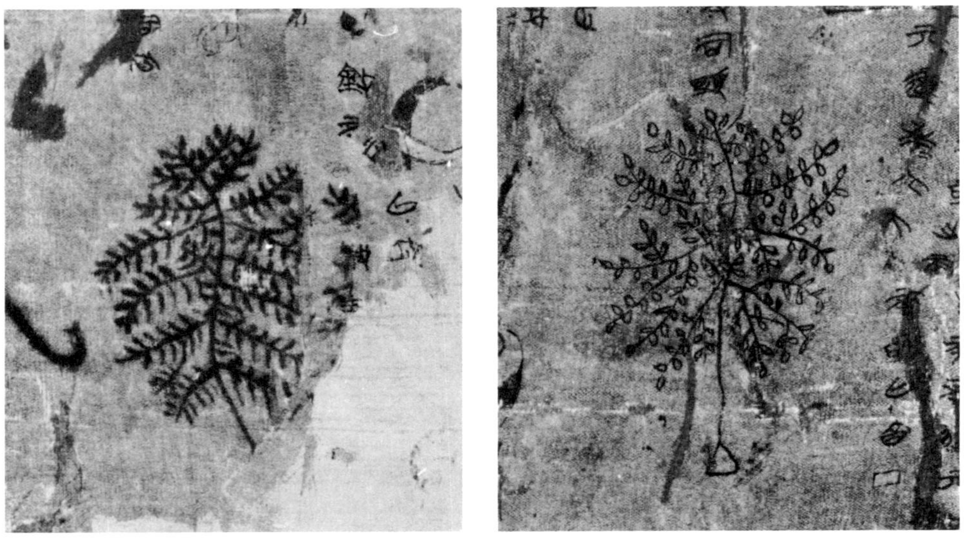

Figs. 16a, b. Anonymous, details, *Ritual Drawings and Text*. Undated, 5th century B.C. Silk manuscript, from a tomb at Ch'ang-sha, Hunan province. Arthur M. Sackler collection

Landscape painting appeared in the fourth century as part of man's new mystic desire, under the influence of Taoism, to project himself into the domain of spirits. A late fourth-century Taoist painter, Tsung Ping (375–443) explained that

> mountains and water have material existence that reaches out into the spiritual domain. . . . While the spirits may be untraceable, they nonetheless reside in physical forms, stirring responses in man, and there are principles in their manifestations. If a painter can describe these cleverly, he will be doing all there is to be done. . . . The joy of the spirit is my goal. When the spirit is joyful, what more is there?

To describe the vastness of landscape Tsung Ping suggested the use of graphic symbols of mountains and trees, in shorthand fashion, both to compress and to enlarge the feeling of distance:

> Mount K'un-lun is large but the pupil of the eye is small. If we try to measure the mountain close up, we will not be able to see its true appearance. . . . When we stretch out a piece of plain silk to capture the distant scenery, the appearance of K'un-lun may be encompassed within a square inch. A vertical stroke of three inches may equal a height of several thousand feet; a horizontal stroke of ink of a few feet may represent a distance of a hundred *li*.[2]

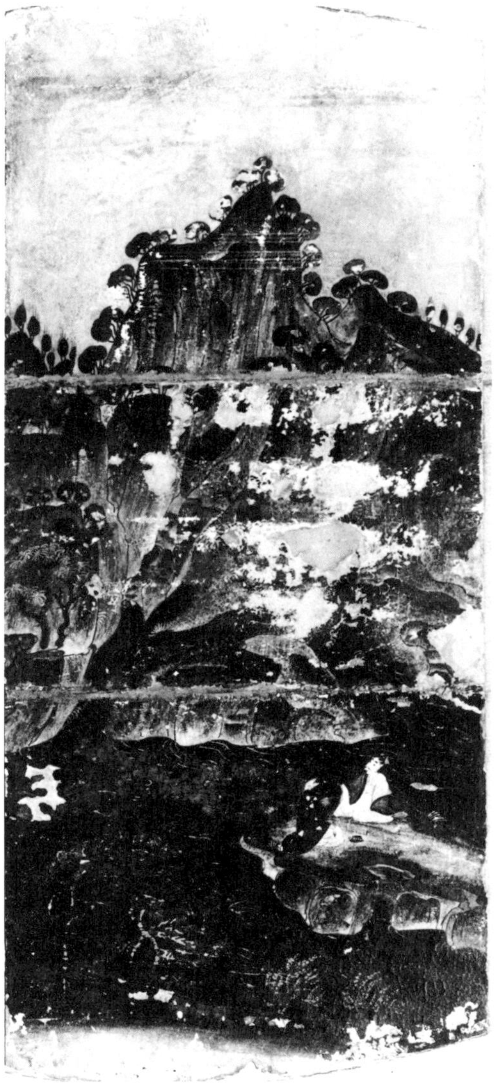

Fig. 17. Anonymous, *Sitting under a Mountain*. Undated, 8th century. Painting on a plectrum guard of a biwa. Shōsōin Treasury, Nara

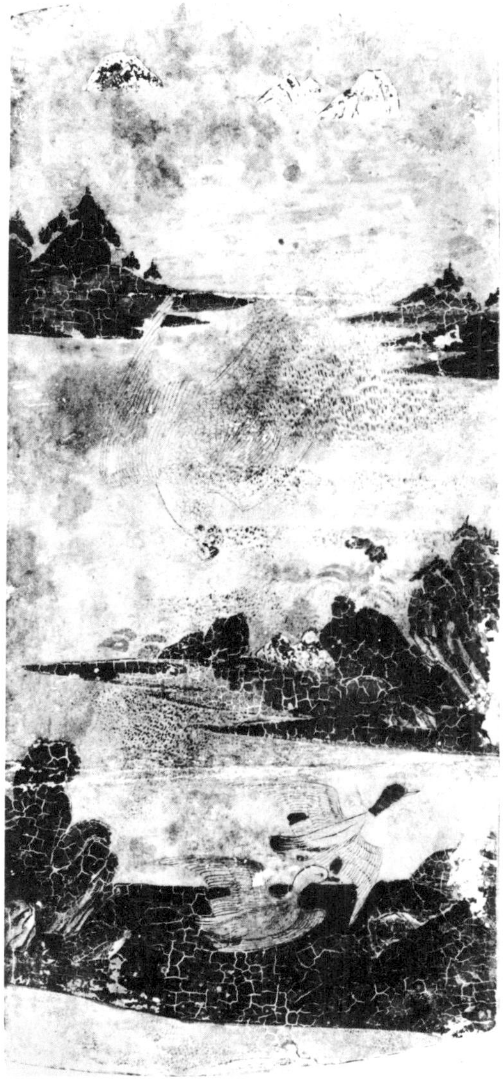

Fig. 18. Anonymous, *Hawk and Ducks*. Undated, 8th century. Painting on a plectrum guard of a biwa. Shōsōin Treasury, Nara

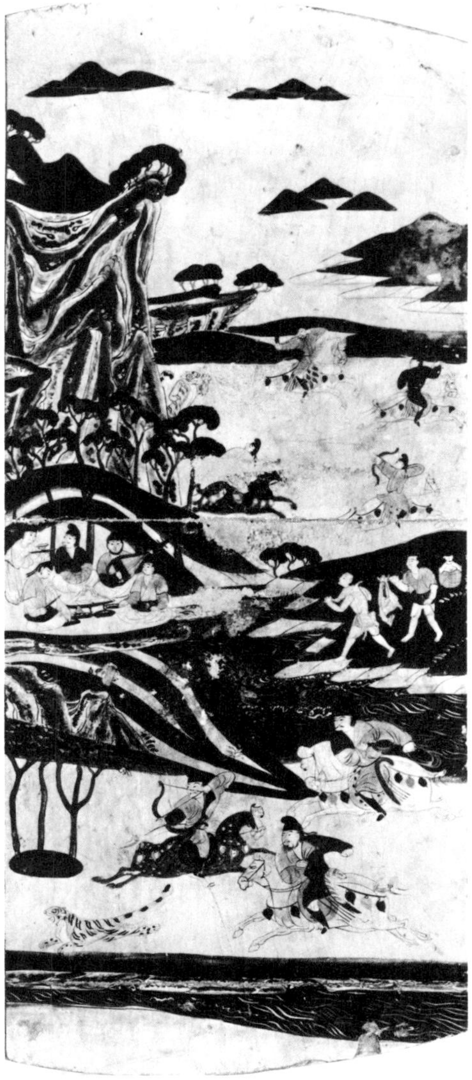

Fig. 19. Anonymous, *Tiger Hunt*. Undated, 8th century. Painting on a plectrum guard of a biwa. Shōsōin Treasury, Nara

The first important compositional discovery was that overlapping triangles— 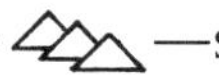 —suggest recession. During the T'ang period, in the late seventh and early eighth centuries, three basic compositional schemes began to emerge. The first is exemplified in *Sitting under a Mountain*, an eighth-century painting on a biwa (lute) now in the Shōsōin Treasury, Nara, Japan (fig. 17). Here a towering central mountain is flanked by two smaller ones. The composition progresses in three stages: water and reeds in the foreground, two seated figures in the middle distance directing their gaze upward, and soaring peaks in the background. *Hawk and Ducks*, a painting on another eighth-century biwa at the Shōsōin (fig. 18) shows the second scheme, an open panoramic view progressing from front to back in three stages of horizontal elements. *Tiger Hunt*, on a third biwa at the Shōsōin (fig. 19), combines vertical elements at the left and horizontal ones at the right to form a valley scene.

Beginning in the eighth century these three schemes were standardized as the three ways of viewing mountain scenery. In his treatise on landscape, *Lofty Aims in Forests and Streams* (*Lin-ch'üan kao-chih chi*), the leading landscape master of the second half of the eleventh century, Kuo Hsi (ca. 1010–ca. 1090), discussed mountains as having "three distances" (*san-yüan*):

> The bottom of the mountain looking up toward the top, this is called the "high distance" [*kao-yüan*]. From the front of the mountain peering toward the back of the mountain, this is called the "deep distance" [*shen-yüan*]. From a nearby mountain looking past distant mountains, this is called the "flat distance" [*p'ing-yüan*].[3]

Although all of the compositions found on the Shōsōin biwas are vertical, they were adapted for a horizontal format to fit handscrolls.[4]

Quite as important to the artist as his types of composition were his methods of modeling forms. The beginnings of *ts'un*, texture patterns for describing rocks, can be seen in another eighth-century biwa painting at the Shōsōin, *Musicians Riding on an Elephant* (fig. 20). The artist has combined graded shading technique with thickening-and-thinning contour lines. Tentative texture strokes, as well as softly rubbed parallel brushstrokes, appear in the shaded crevices, following the parallel swelling contours of the mountain. A very different kind of rock modeling is seen in *Lady Standing under a Tree*, an eighth-century screen painting also at the Shōsōin (fig. 21). The rock, an ornamental garden specimen from Lake T'ai, south of the Yangtze River, has been contoured in jagged and stippled texture strokes.

In early Sung literature, a description of the stippled technique is found in Huang Hsiu-fu's *Record of Famous Paintings in I-chou [Szechuan province] (I-chou ming-hua lu)*, completed before 1006. According to Huang, a Szechuan painter named Huang Chü-pao rendered garden rocks in about 990 by

> using the tip of his brush in stippling and rubbing motions, making his rock rich in both ornament [*wen*] and principles [*li*]. The rocks, with sand and pebbles in their surfaces, have sharp and angular contours. They look like reptiles and tigers waiting to strike: their shapes and attitudes are not limited to any single kind.[5]

But it was again Kuo Hsi who, forever formulating principles, identified two contrasting landscape modes, the "earthen" and the "rocky": "Some mountains are covered with earth; others are covered with rocks. On earthen mountains that are covered with rocks, the forests and trees are lean and tall; on rocky mountains that are covered with earth, the forests and trees are fat and luxuriant."[6] The smooth and jagged texture patterns, corresponding to earthen and rocky mountain forms, became in time two opposed landscape idioms.

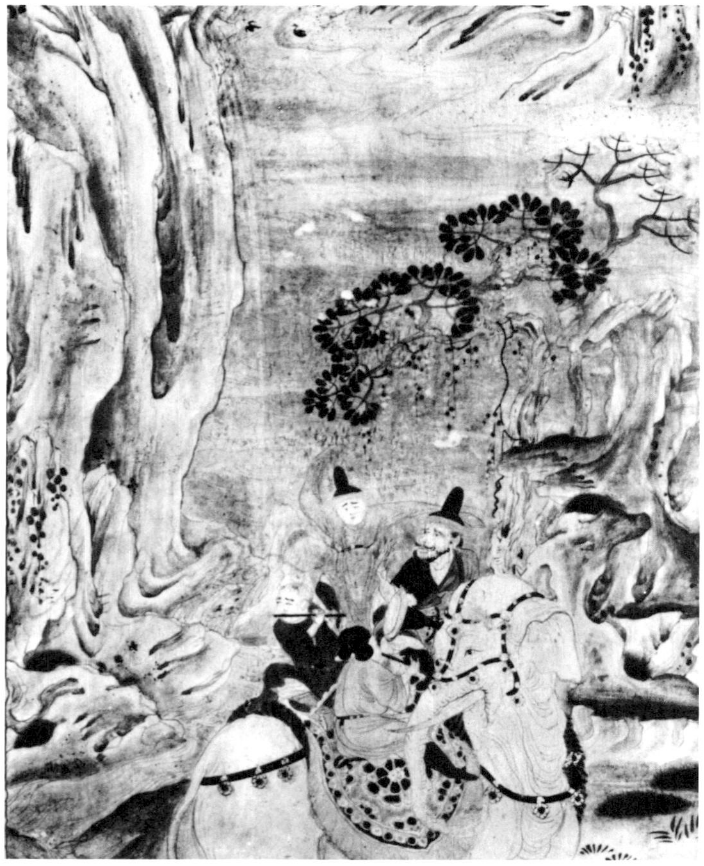

Fig. 20. Anonymous, detail, *Musicians Riding on an Elephant*. Undated, 8th century. Painting on a plectrum guard of a biwa. Shōsōin Treasury, Nara

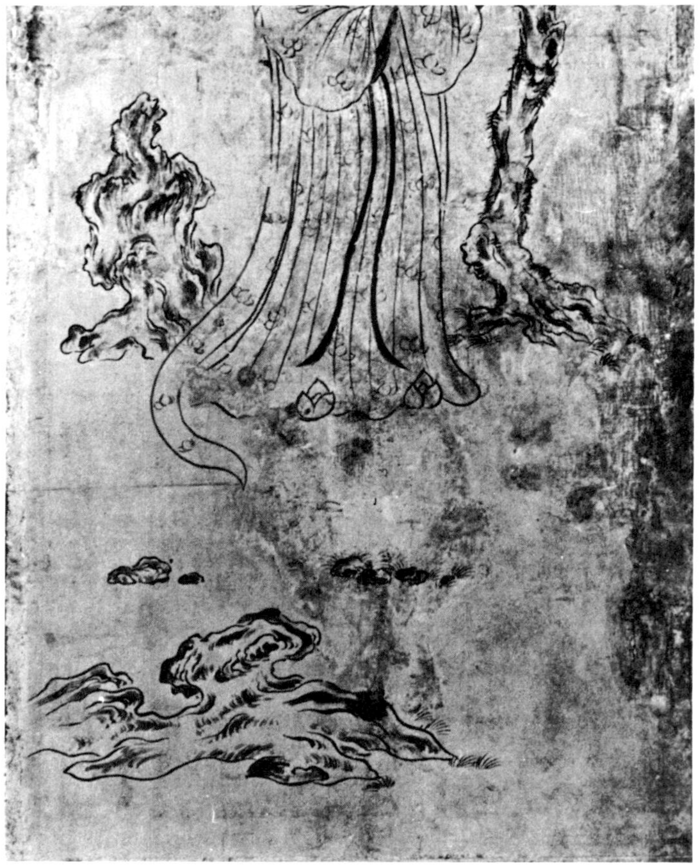

Fig. 21. Anonymous, detail, *Lady Standing under a Tree*. Undated, 8th century. Painting on a screen. Shōsōin Treasury, Nara

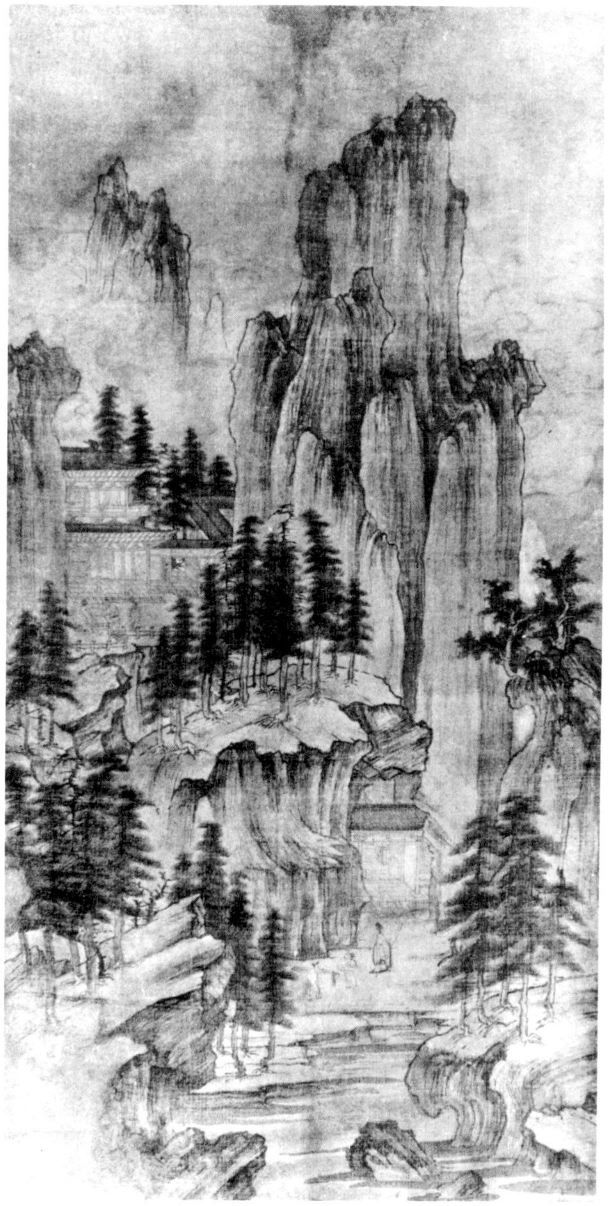

Fig. 22. Anonymous, *Landscape* (*Shan-shui*). Undated, ca. 959–86. Hanging scroll, ink and color on silk, from a tomb at Fa-k'u, Yeh-mao-t'ai, Liaoning. Liaoning Provincial Museum

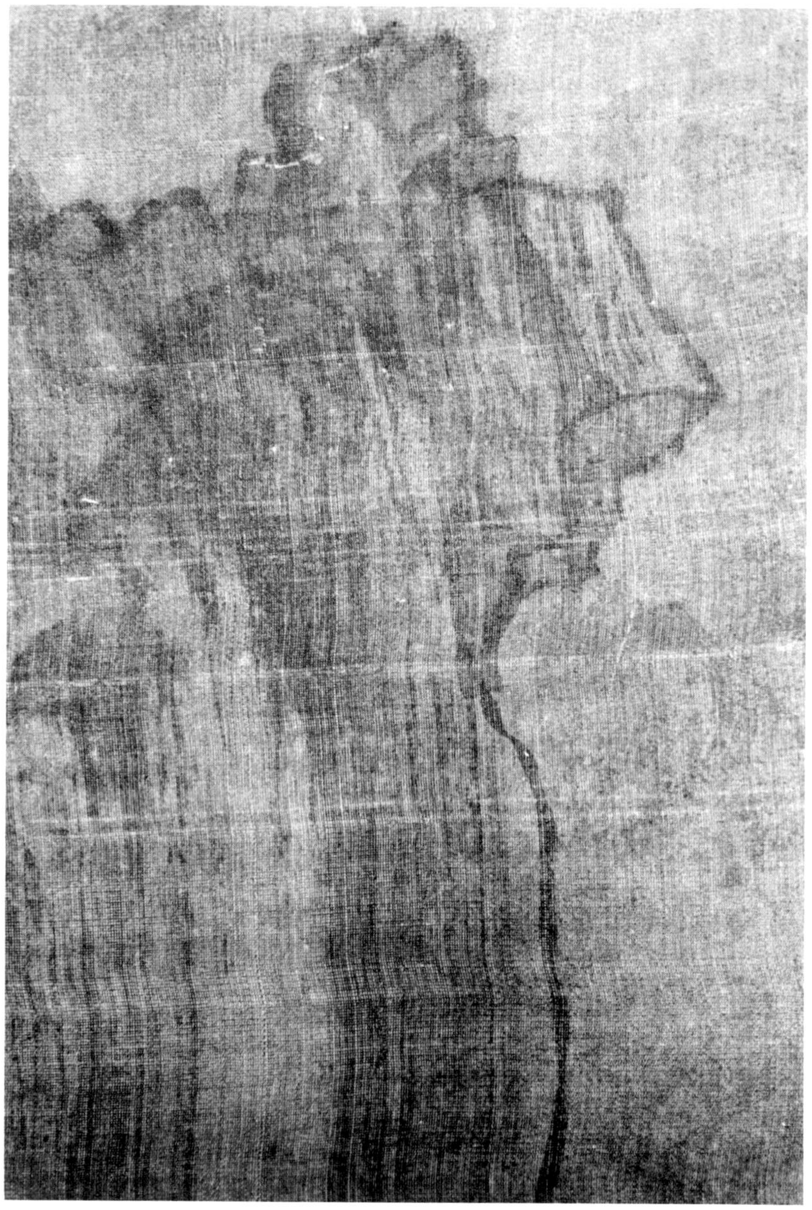

Fig. 22a. Detail, fig. 22

A recently archaeologically discovered painting from a Liao dynasty burial dated about 959–86 (fig. 22), now in the Liaoning Provincial Museum, is the earliest indubitable tenth-century silk hanging scroll with a landscape subject.[7] In subject matter as well as in composition, the scroll may be compared with *Sitting under a Mountain* (cf. fig. 17); both pictures show the theme of "lofty scholars" (*kao-shih*) in a high-distance mountain scheme. Whereas the two men seated on a promontory in the eighth-century composition reside in a relatively simple landscape of spectacular peaks soaring overhead, the recluse scholars in the tenth-century painting find themselves in an isolated mountain valley with splendid palatial buildings, which can only represent an abode of the immortals. The mountain forms in the tenth-century scroll, organized additively, are columnar and sculptural: the central peak resembles the lid of a Han dynasty incense burner representing the mountain isle of the immortals (fig. 23). In the incense burner multiple secondary mountains cluster like colonnettes around a central massif. The columnar forms are modeled by shading as well as softly rubbed, parallel, vertical texture strokes, done in the flying-white (*fei-pai*) brush technique (fig. 22a). The massed trees, mostly conical evergreens, diminish in size from front to back. The hanging scroll achieves an added sense of depth and seclusion by combining the high-distance view with a deep-distance valley scene in the foreground. Overlapping plateau motifs, ranging diagonally from the foreground in several sequences, and stopping at the middle distance, represent a bluff overlook-

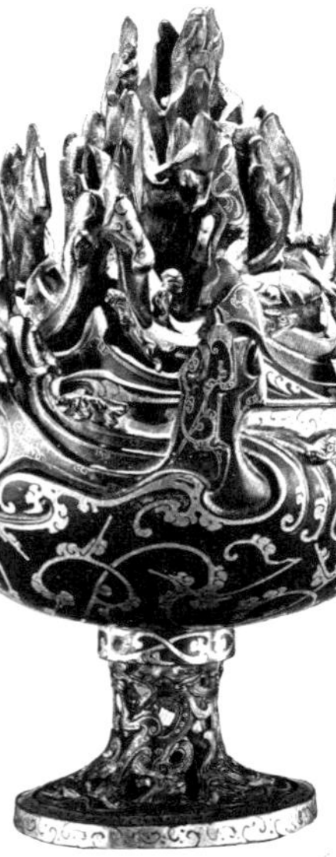

Fig. 23. Anonymous, incense burner. 2nd half 2nd century B.C. Bronze, from tomb of Prince Liu Sheng, Man-ch'eng. Hopei Provincial Museum

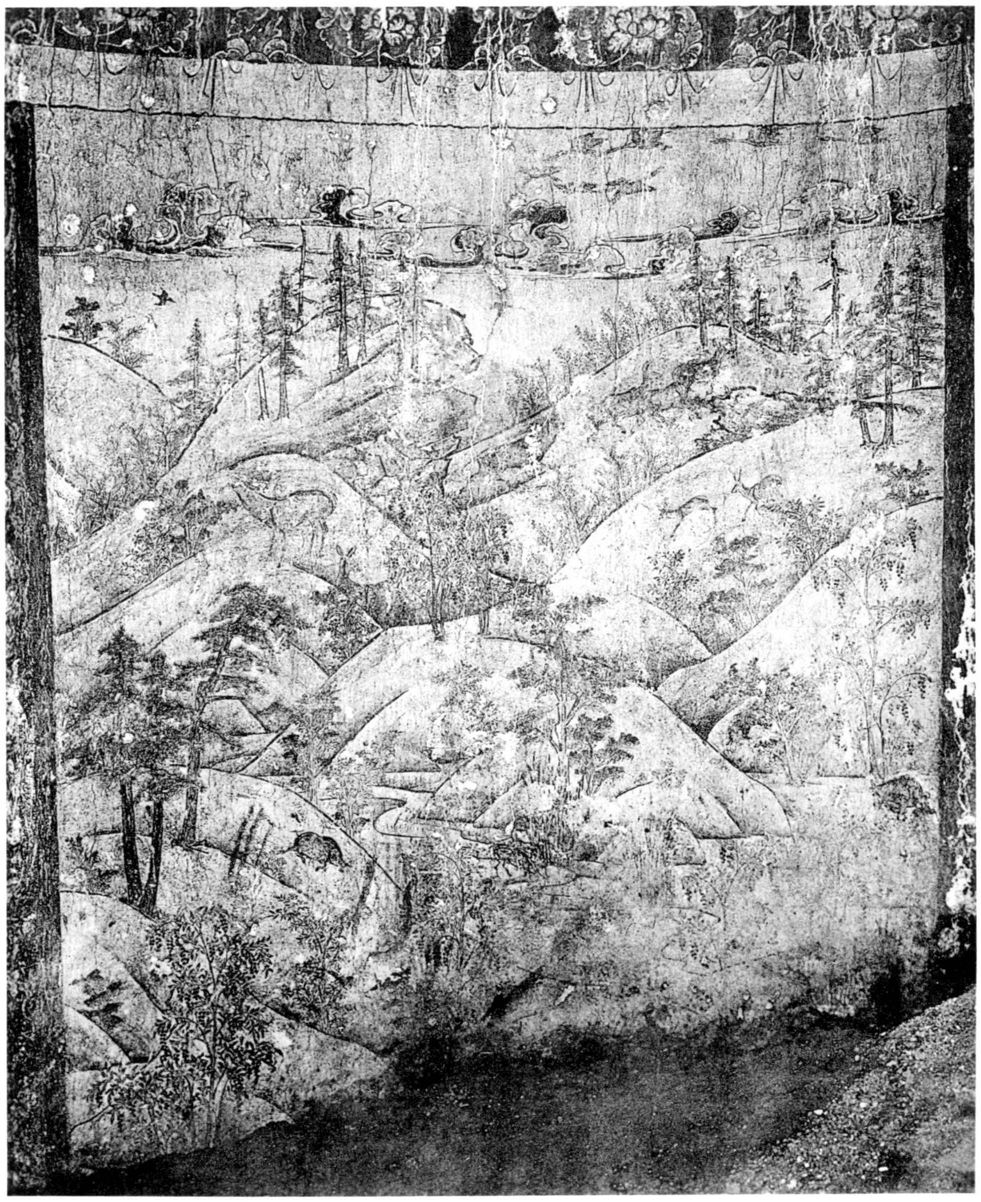

Fig. 24. Anonymous, *Autumn*, from *The Four Seasons* (*Ssu-ching shan-sui*). Ca. 1030. Wall painting, Ch'ing-ling, eastern Mongolia

ing a winding chasm; above and behind the treetops tall peaks rise to fill the vertical picture plane, the most distant pinnacle in the upper left corner suggesting the beginnings of the treatment of mist that characterizes landscapes of two centuries later.

Further archaeological evidence of early landscape painting is provided by a series of wall paintings called *The Four Seasons* (*Ssu-ching shan-sui*), at Ch'ing-ling, in eastern Mongolia, dated around 1030.[8] The four wall paintings are placed at the cardinal directions of a circular chamber, representing spring at the east, summer at the south, autumn at the west (fig. 24), and winter at the north; the cyclical change of the seasons is indicated by two lines of geese, flying counterclockwise, returning north in the spring and departing for the south in the autumn. All four landscapes show panoramic flat-distance views: triangular mountain motifs are piled up additively; in the middle of the picture, a stream zigzagging into the distance is described by an interlocking pattern of overlapping triangular spits of land, which range back diagonally to the left and to the right, each time in short sequences of three or four steps. The four seasons are represented by vegetation and activities appropriate to their times of the year: spring shows budding flowers and trees, tall reeds, and ducks and geese paddling in a full stream; summer displays large blossoming tree peonies, with boars and herds of deer grazing lazily in the valley; autumn exhibits a great variety of evergreen trees and bushes, and its animals, some baying and running, are nervously alert; winter is appropriately solemn and desolate, with a dry and frozen stream, and animals roaming in packs, scavenging for food. The rock forms were first drawn in bold outlines, then filled in with a few texture strokes and color washes. Although the simple mountain motifs recall T'ang models, the trees are carefully scaled and differentiated to suggest recession in space. In *Autumn* the large pine trees in the foreground are individually portrayed, but the distant fir forest is indicated by simplified patterns of vertical brushstrokes and by layers of foliage in green color washes.

## *Monumental Landscape Painting*

Beginning in the late T'ang period, Neo-Confucian scholars borrowed a phrase from the Confucian classic *The Great Learning* (*Ta-hsüeh*) to describe their approach to learning and self-cultivation: *ko-wu chih-chih*, or "the investigation of things leading to the extension of knowledge." The late T'ang scholar Li Ao (d. ca. 844) offered an explication of the phrase: "*Wu* [things] means 'all things.' *Ko* [investigation] means 'arriving' or 'coming.' When things come [before me], the mind should clearly understand and distinguish among them, yet at the same time should not be moved by them. Such is *chih-chih* [the extension of knowledge]. It is the bringing of knowledge to completion."[9] The essential point about knowledge, according to Li Ao, is that "the mind . . . should not be moved by things [through emotions]."

For Neo-Confucian thinkers, the highest reality was the *li*, the metaphysical principles that underlie and transcend the physical universe. In answer to the question "What constitutes knowledge?" the Neo-Confucian quoted from a passage in the *Book of Changes* (*I-ching*): "[The sage] plumbs the principles [*li*] [of the things] to their depths, completely penetrates the nature [*hsing*] [of the things], and thereby arrives at an understanding of the destiny [*ming*] [of the things]."[10] A corollary of principles was therefore the nature of things, which in its absolute, objective "truthfulness" was carefully differentiated from *ch'ing*, or man's subjective emotions or feelings.

Central to the Neo-Confucian "system"—which, as it became fully developed by the Northern Sung period, included the study of emblems, numerology, cosmic diagrams, cosmological chronology, cosmogony, theories of heavenly principles and the natures of man and things, and political philosophy—was the notion of the sage (*sheng*): the perfect being who is able to articulate and follow the principles of heaven, earth, and man. In Li Ao's words, "that which enables man to become a sage is his nature; that which betrays the nature of man is his feelings or emotions. When the emotions cause obscurement, man's nature is thereby drowned. That is not the fault of man's nature, but of the ceaseless intermingling of the seven [emotions], which does not permit this nature to fulfill itself."[11]

Shao Yung (1011–1077), a leading thinker of the mid-eleventh century, put it a slightly different way:

> To observe things in terms of things is to follow the nature [of things]; to observe things in terms of one's self is to follow one's emotions. Nature is impartial and enlightened, but emotions are partial and blind. . . . To give free play to one's self leads to emotions, emotions lead to obscuring, and obscuring leads to benightedness. But to follow things [objectively] leads to their nature; this nature leads to spirituality, and spirituality leads to enlightenment.[12]

Shao Yung proposed seeing things "with the mind" and "in the light of their own principles," rather than the eye, since only the mind could perceive the underlying principles of an object.

Escaping the turmoil and destruction that took place at the end of the T'ang dynasty, the reclusive artists of the ensuing Five Dynasties (907–60) and the early Northern Sung period (960–1127) sought to capture the truth of the universe by investigating the principles and the nature of the things in landscape painting. In his treatise *Notes on Brush Method* (*Pi-fa chi*) Ching Hao (fl. ca. 870–930) distinguished likeness from truth in painting: "A picture of likeness reproduces the outward form [*hsing*], but neglects the breath [*ch'i*] [of the things], while a picture of truth shows the breath and physical substance [*chih*] in equal perfection." Insisting that "calligraphy and painting can be learned only by the wise," Ching Hao advised, "If you love to paint clouds and forests, mountains and streams, you must learn to understand the origins of the outer appearances of the things. When a tree grows, it follows its own nature received from heaven. . . .

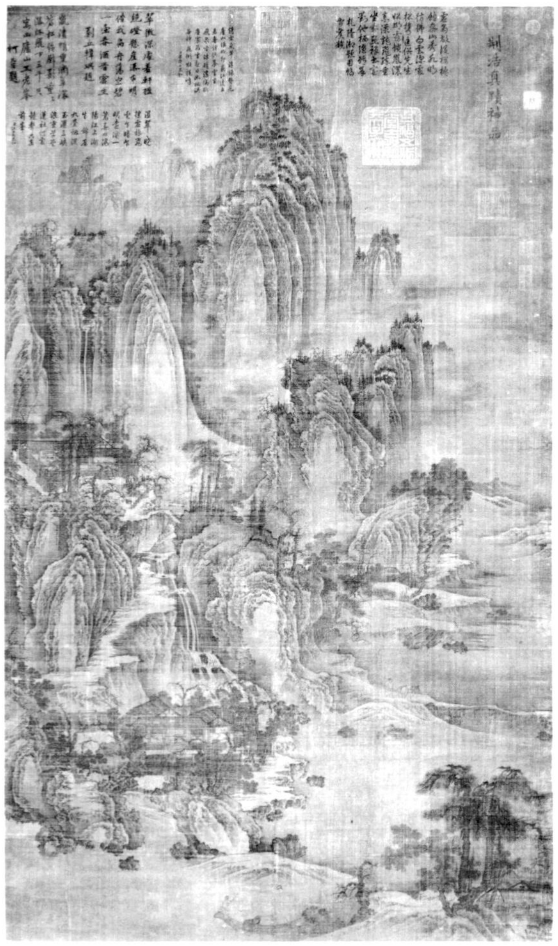

Fig. 25. Anonymous, after Ching Hao, *Mount K'uang-lu* (*K'uang-lu t'u*). Undated, late 12th–early 13th century (?). Hanging scroll, ink on silk. 185.8 x 106.8 cm (6 ft. 1 1/8 in. x 3 ft. 6 in.). National Palace Museum, Taipei

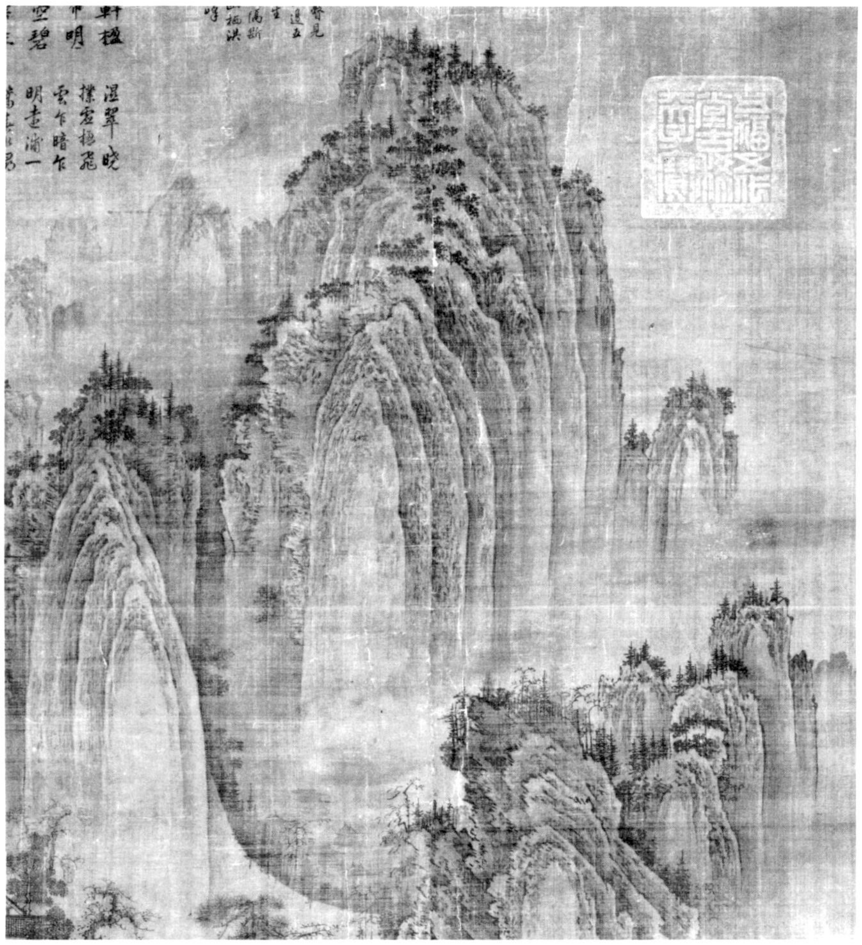

Fig. 25a. Detail, fig. 25

Even as a sapling, [a pine tree] stands upright, its budding heart already harbors noble ambitions. Once it grows up . . . it seems to possess the virtuous air of a gentleman."[13] Landscape painting, for Ching Hao, was the noble undertaking of a superior man, a scholar and philosopher—in short, a sage who painted.

The six essentials for landscape painting, according to Ching Hao, were

*Ch'i* (life breath): As the heart responds and the brush moves forward, forms are seized without hesitation.

*Yün* (resonance and elegance): Where forms are omitted or elaborated upon, the choice is not vulgar.

*Ssu* (thought): By sorting out the essentials, the painter conceives forms with great concentration.

*Ching* (scenery): By observing the laws of nature and the seasons, he searches out the wonderful and creates a true landscape.

*Pi* (brushwork): Though following certain basic methods, it must move freely and know how to improvise. It must not be too solid or assume too definite a form; it must look as if in flight and constant motion.

*Mo* (ink wash): High and low peaks are described by a light ink wash, which also makes objects stand out in either shallow or deep relief. The drawing and ink wash are so natural that they do not seem to be made by a brush.[14]

Ching Hao, "father" of the Northern Sung monumental style of landscape painting, was born in Ch'in-shui in northern Honan province. A learned Confucian scholar, he fled to Mount T'ai-hang in northern Honan after the fall of the T'ang dynasty in A.D. 907; there he lived as a recluse-painter and left behind *Notes on Brush Method*, which offered the first coherent theory of Chinese landscape painting. An important work attributed to Ching Hao is a hanging scroll entitled *Mount K'uang-lu* (*K'uang-lu t'u*), now in the National Palace Museum, Taipei (fig. 25). An imposing composition just over 6 feet tall, the painting shows a range of towering peaks with deeply fissured surfaces in the "rocky" mountain mode of the Northern Sung landscape tradition (fig. 25a). Max Loehr, in *The Great Painters of China* (1980), accepts the painting as a work of the tenth century; James Cahill, in *An Index of Early Chinese Painters* (1980), calls it "probably a late Sung (Chin?) work, perhaps after an old composition"; and Sofukawa Hiroshi, in "A Study of Landscape Painting of the Five Dynasties and Early Northern Sung Period" (1977), suggests a Yüan (fourteeth-century) date for the work.[15] The painting shows two Yüan dynasty inscriptions by Han Yü and K'o Chiu-ssu (1290–1343), and a line of six characters, "Ching Hao chen-chi shen-p'in" (An authentic work by Ching Hao, divine class), which some authorities attribute to the Southern Sung emperor Kao-tsung (r. 1127–62).[16] Shen Fu, in "Two Anonymous Sung Dynasty Paintings and the Lu Shan Landscape" (1968), provisionally accepts the attribution of the six-character inscription to Kao-tsung and dates the painting to "the middle or late Northern Sung," or the eleventh century.[17]

The best way to understand Ching Hao's landscape style is to analyze works securely dated to Ching Hao's time. In comparison with paintings of the eighth and ninth centuries, figure as well as landscape representations of the tenth century found on the Tun-huang wall and silk paintings (cf. fig. 12) show a marked taste for schematized archaistic forms, with simplified, triangular mountain motifs, stylized outlines, and flat bands of color.[18] Among extant arcaheological monuments elsewhere in China, this stylized treatment is seen also in the tenth-century sculptured reliefs at the Ch'i-hsia-ssu near Nanking (fig. 26) and the carvings at the mausoleum of the Northern Sung emperor Jen-tsung (r. 1023–63) in Honan.[19]

The best-known example of the early tenth-century schematic style, however, is the set of paintings of the sixteen lohans (*arhat* in Sanskrit, *rakan* in Japanese) by Kuan-hsiu (832–912), the best version of which is preserved in the Imperial Household Museum in Tokyo (fig. 27).[20] Here the facial features, the body, and

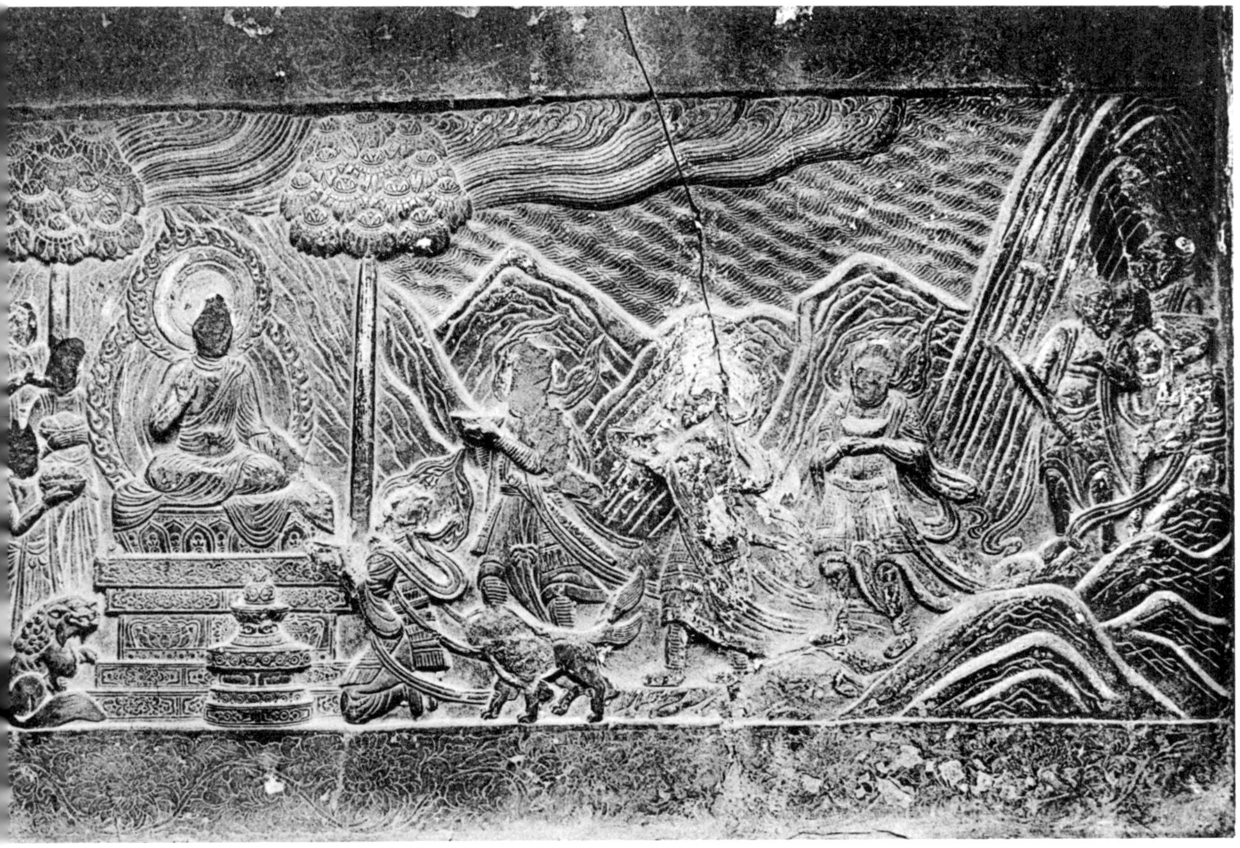

Fig. 26. Anonymous, stone relief. Undated, 10th century. Ch'i-hsia-ssu, near Nanking

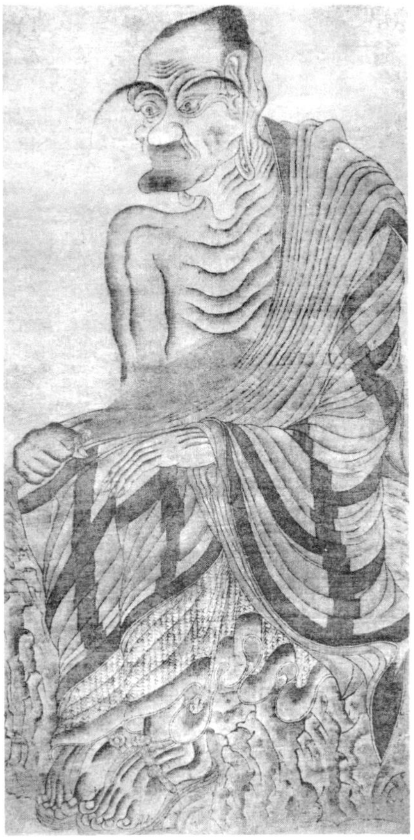

Fig. 27. Anonymous, after Kuan-hsiu, one of the set *Sixteen Lohans*. Undated, 10th century (?). Hanging scroll, ink and color on silk. Imperial Household Museum, Tokyo

the drapery of the figure, as well as the rock and tree forms of the background setting, are expressed in swirling parallel patterns of tense, unmodulated lines, shaded with ink wash. Born in Teng-kao (Lan-ch'i), Chekiang province, and ordained a Buddhist priest in 851, Kuan-hsiu had known the same kind of turmoil and horror experienced by Ching Hao at the end of the Tang dynasty; in these images, as Loehr has noted, "there is a richness of experience, imagination, and vision . . . that is not sufficiently acknowledged by an insistence on the ugly, grotesque or repellent appearance of these types."[21] The late Northern Sung imperial *Painting Catalogue of the Hsüan-ho Era [1119–25] (Hsüan-ho hua-p'u)*, of 1120, describes Kuan-hsiu's art as *ku-yeh* (archaic and rustic).[22] In renouncing the highly naturalistic style of the early ninth century and reducing forms to flat, intensely stylized abstract patterns, the early tenth-century archaism, as exemplified by Kuan-hsiu, represents a powerful, innovative expressionist style.

Loehr suggested that "T'ang classic and anticlassic currents were fused and transformed in [Ching Hao's] work, which became a foundation for the grand conceptions of the tenth-century masters, Kuan T'ung [fl. ca. 907–23] and Fan K'uan [ca. 960–1030]."[23] The problem is that the hanging scroll *Mount K'uang-lu*, though it may in some way reflect an original work by Ching, seems to date stylistically no earlier than the late twelfth century. Compared to the late tenth-century Liao hanging scroll (cf. fig. 22), *Mount K'uang-lu* shows a highly stylized *ts'un* texture pattern, and its continuous overlapping mountain

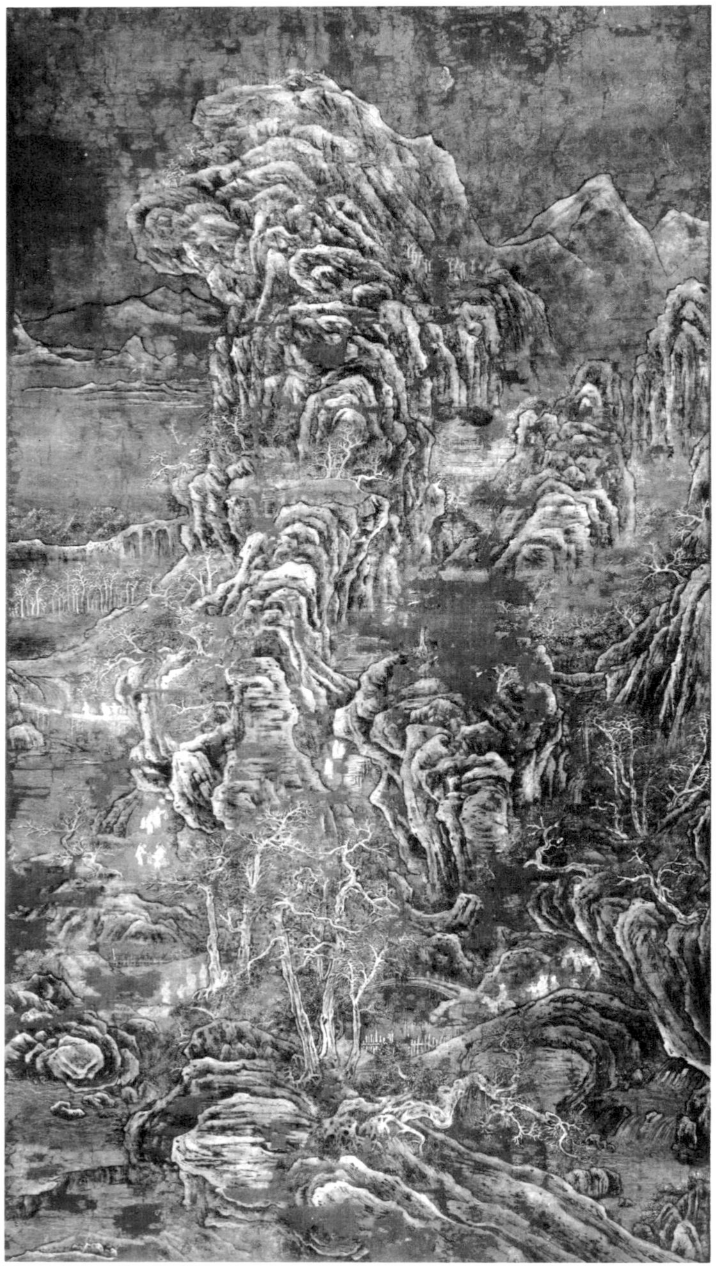

Fig. 28. Anonymous (signature of Ching Hao), *Travelers in Snow-covered Mountains (Hsüeh-shan hsing-lü)*. Undated, 16th century(?). Hanging scroll, ink, white pigment, and light color on silk. 136.0 x 75.0 cm (4 ft. 5 1/2 in. x 29 1/2 in.). Nelson Gallery–Atkins Museum, Kansas City

Fig. 28a. Detail, fig. 28

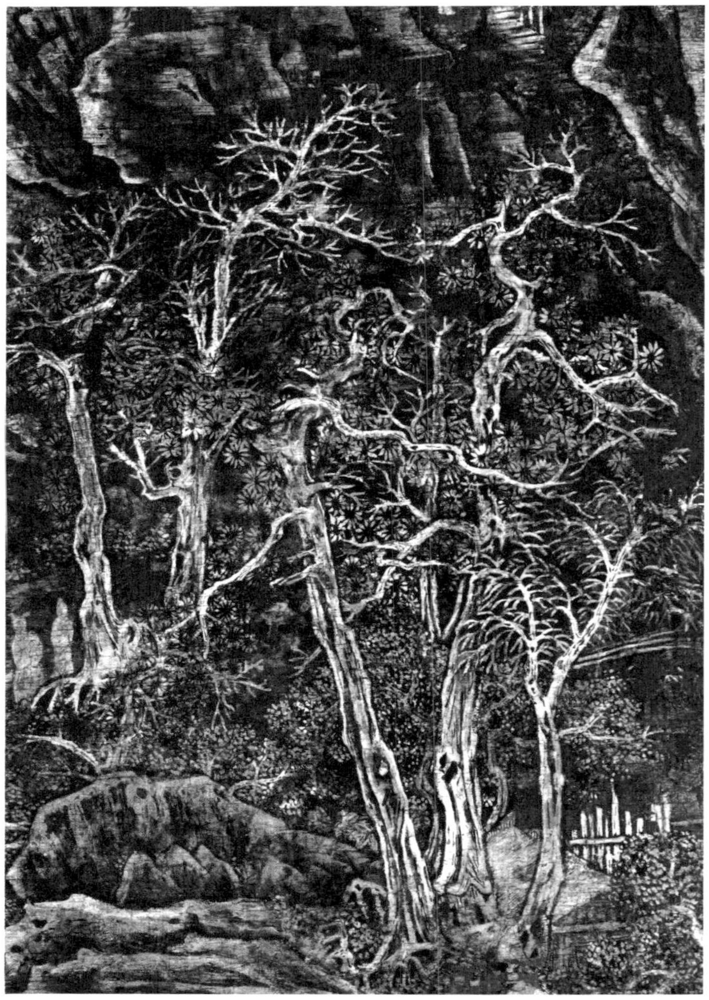

forms, gives the illusion of a unified, continuous space (cf. figs. 14a, b). Moreover, the tree forms in *Mount K'uang-lu*, as Shen Fu points out, relate to the late eleventh-century Kuo Hsi tradition. As a late twelfth-century or early thirteenth-century archaistic re-creation of Ching Hao's style, *Mount K'uang-lu* tells us more about the late Southern Sung than about the original Ching Hao.

Another hanging scroll, *Travelers in Snow-covered Mountains*, in the Nelson Gallery–Atkins Museum, Kansas City (fig. 28), said to have been recovered from a tomb, has been discussed recently as a possible work by Ching Hao.[24] Loehr, however, dates the painting to before Ching Hao's time,[25] and Cahill, believing that "the signature, reading Hung-ku-tzu, is of later date," calls it "probably after an early design." Cahill points out that "the upper part of the [Kansas City] composition is based on the same design as one of the pair of 'Anonymous Sung' paintings," which Shen Fu dates as early twelfth-century works in the Kuo Hsi tradition.[26]

Compared to *Mount K'uang-lu*, which shows overlapping triangular mountain motifs placed frontally in and parallel to the picture plane, the mountain forms of *Travelers in Snow-covered Mountains* are complex and irregularly shaped: they show three-dimensional foreshortening, with rock facets growing and expanding as a single organic mass into a dynamically twisting and turning central massif. The rock and tree outlines, instead of describing forms, have an independent calligraphic rhythm; and the rock texture pattern, a mixture of broad and thin stippling and hatching strokes, is equally abstract, rather than descriptive of the rock surface. The drawing of the bare tree branches, while superficially resembling the ornamental lacelike patterns of T'ang archaic trees, in fact shows knowledge of foreshortening and movement in depth; and the calligraphic outlines of the distant mountains, in the upper reaches of the composition, betray a naturalistic tendency to treat landscape forms as organically interrelated masses receding diagonally in space. In composition the complex, organically intertwined mountain forms, rather than moving back in a natural, open space, are strongly surface-and-frame-conscious. The landscape elements are cut and framed by the borders of the painting: brought forward to the bottom edge the tall trees stemming from the foreground boulders function as a foreground repoussoir, and along the two sides elements are superimposed to intersect carefully with the frame. While damage and repainting have made certain passages difficult to read, the overall impression of naturalism combined with surface abstraction in this unusual work points to a conscious archaistic imitation dating to the later Ming period (2nd half 16th century).

The second of the early founders of the Northern Sung style was a leading follower of Ching Hao, Kuan T'ung. Kuan was a native of Ch'ang-an, Shensi province, who worked with the master in K'ai-feng, Honan, possibly between 895 and 907.[27] Of the three major works attributed to Kuan T'ung (all in the National Palace Museum, Taipei) Sofukawa Hiroshi (1977) considers *Autumn Mountains at Dusk* (*Ch'iu-shan wan-ts'ui*; fig. 29) as best reflecting Kuan's original style.[28] In this painting the circular ring of mountains forms a "space cell" reminiscent of that in the eighth-century composition *The Wang-ch'üan Villa* (*Wang-ch'üan t'u*) by Wang Wei (699–759); the stacked mountain forms are carefully balanced, with the central host peaks supported on two sides by guest peaks, and the columnar mountain forms, modeled by parallel vertical texture strokes, recall those found in the Liao hanging scroll (cf. fig. 22). The rock and tree forms of this painting seem to echo a description of Kuan T'ung's style by Kuo Jo-hsü (fl. ca. 1075): "His rock formations are hard and solid; the [clumps of] mixed trees are luxuriant and dense. . . ."[29] Though not yet as stylized as *Mount K'uang-lu* attributed to Ching Hao, the layers of triangular mountain forms placed in parallel picture planes, as well as the mountain folds modeled by parallel texture strokes in this painting, seem to suggest the beginning of a schematic-archaistic formula. The painting may be dated to the first half of the twelfth century.

A second work attributed to Kuan T'ung, *Travelers at a Mountain Pass* (*Kuan-shan hsing-lü*), in the National Palace Museum, Taipei (fig. 30), bears a seal of the late Southern Sung minister Chia Ssu-tao (1213–1275), as well as the Yüan palace seal "T'ien-li-chih-pao" (Treasure of the T'ien-li reign), used about 1330.[30] The massive peak, silhouetted against the blank silk, shows a deeply pitted bulbous form in the

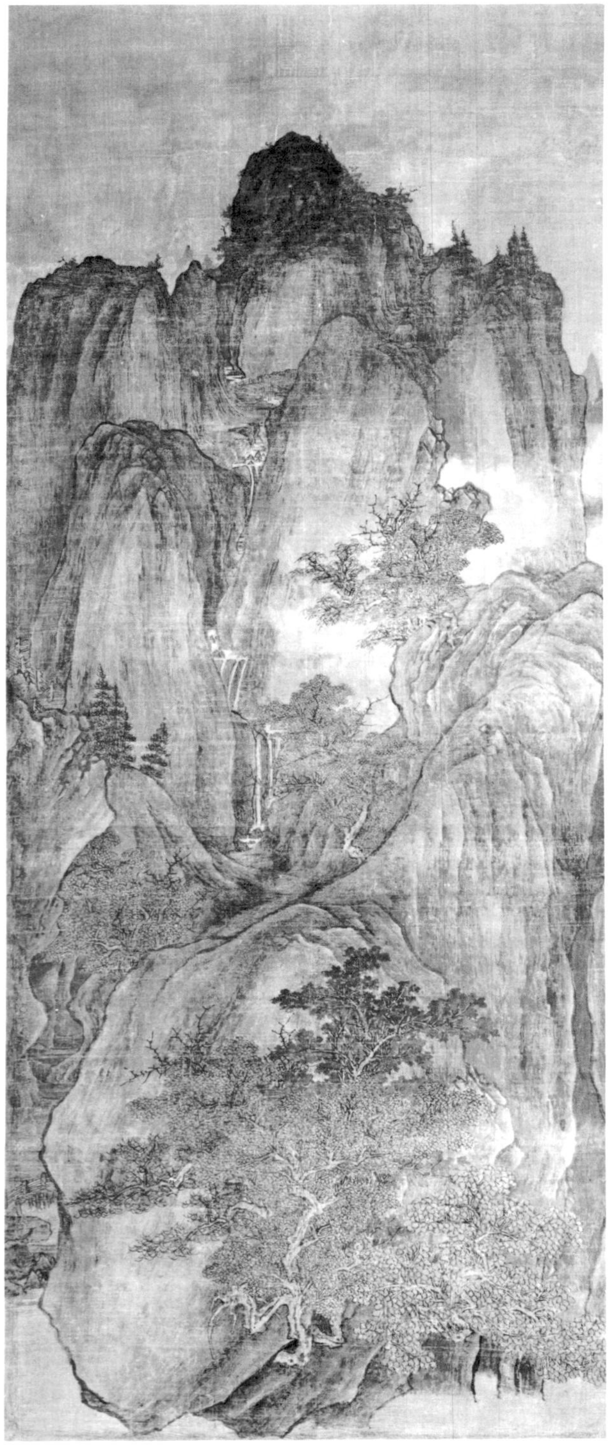

Fig. 29. Anonymous, after Kuan T'ung, *Autumn Mountains at Dusk* (*Ch'iu-shan wan-ts'ui*). Undated, 1st half 12th century(?). Hanging scroll, ink on silk. 140.5 x 57.3 cm (4 ft. 7¼ in. x 22½ in.). National Palace Museum, Taipei

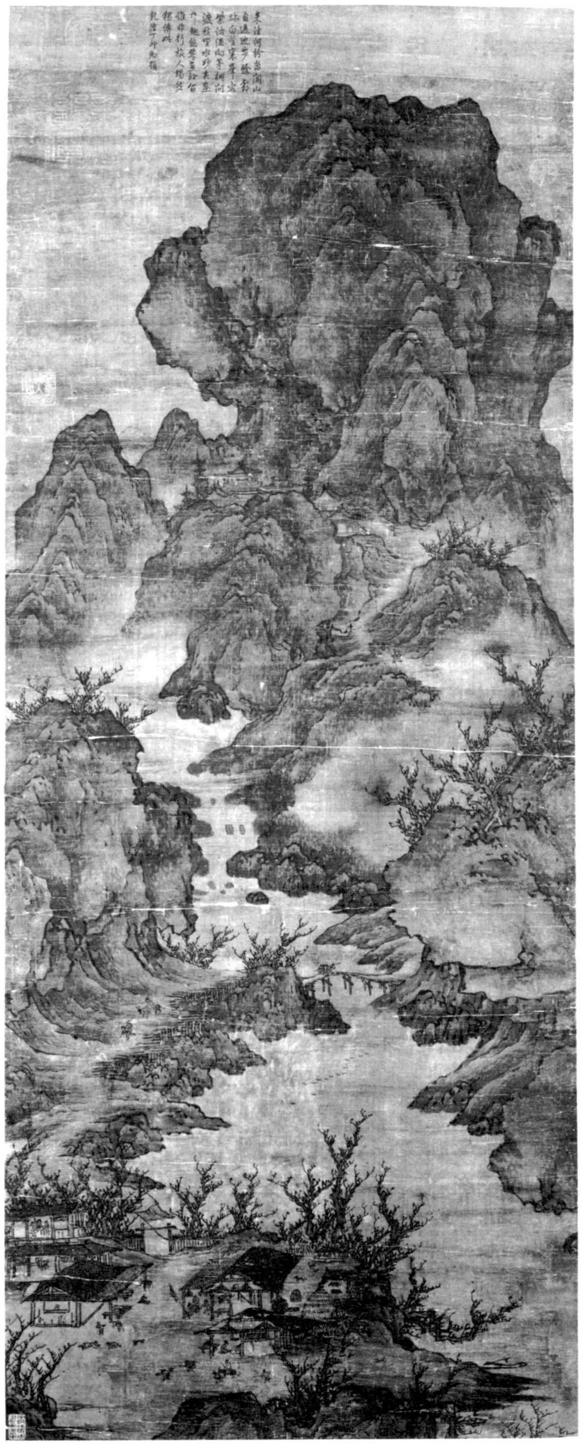

Fig. 30. Anonymous, formerly attributed to Kuan T'ung, in the Li Ch'eng–Yen Wen-kuei tradition, *Travelers at a Mountain Pass* (*Kuan-shan hsing-lü*). Undated, mid-12th century(?). Hanging scroll, ink and light color on silk. 144.4 x 56.8 cm (4 ft. 8⅞ in. x 22⅜ in.). National Palace Museum, Taipei

manner of two later Sung painters, Li Ch'eng and Yen Wen-kuei. The outlines of the rock forms are lively and varied: while they represent an exaggerated mannerism of the jerky, thickening-and-thinning contour lines of the Yen Wen-kuei tradition, they nevertheless work in concert with modeling texture strokes and ink washes to give plasticity to the rock masses. The mountain forms are piled up continuously without a receding ground plane; and triangular mountain slopes are stacked in parallel vertical picture planes, becoming, without transition, the towering vertical massif in the top part of the scroll. The painting is a powerful evocation of the Northern Sung grand manner in the Li Ch'eng and Yen Wen-kuei tradition, done not by Kuan T'ung but by an artist working around the middle of the twelfth century.

Finally a third work attributed to Kuan T'ung, *Waiting to Cross a Mountain Stream* (*Shan-ch'i tai-tu*), in the National Palace Museum, Taipei (fig. 31), which bears a Jurchen Chin imperial seal of the Ming-ch'ang

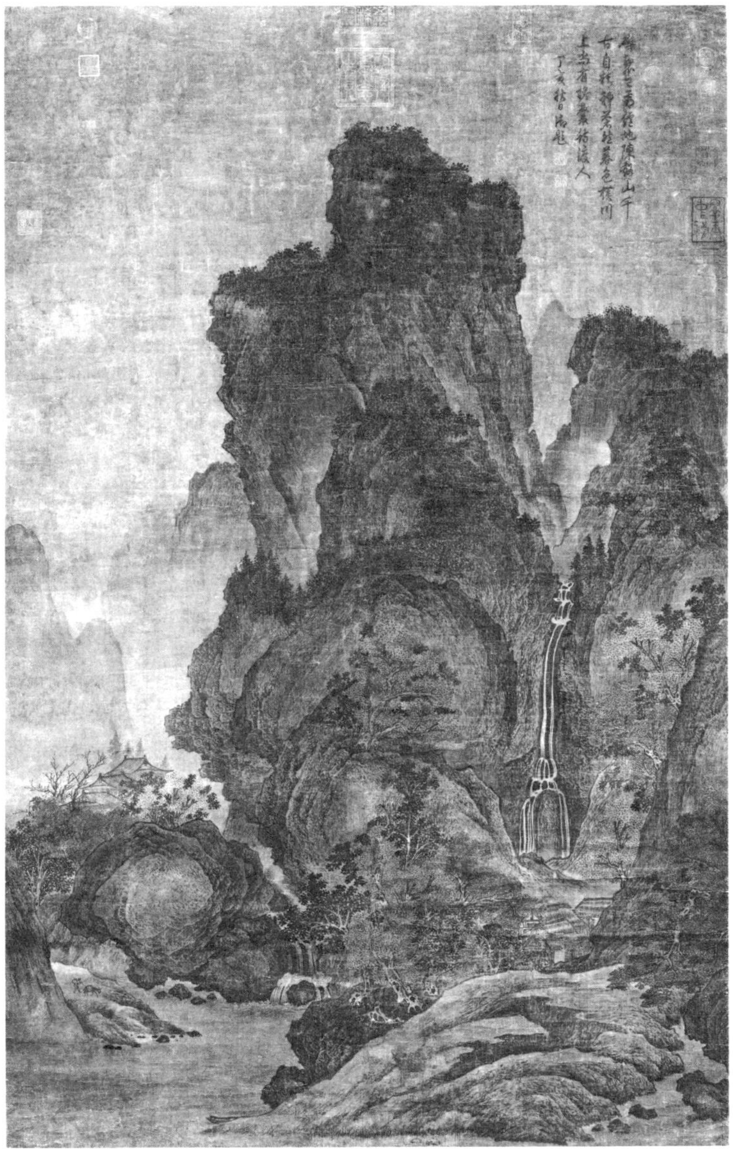

Fig. 31. Anonymous, formerly attributed to Kuan T'ung, in the style of Fan K'uan, *Waiting to Cross a Mountain Stream* (*Shan-ch'i tai-tu*). Undated, mid-12th century(?). Hanging scroll, ink and light color on silk. 156.6 x 99.6 cm (5 ft. 1 5/8 in. x 3 ft. 3 1/4 in.). National Palace Museum, Taipei

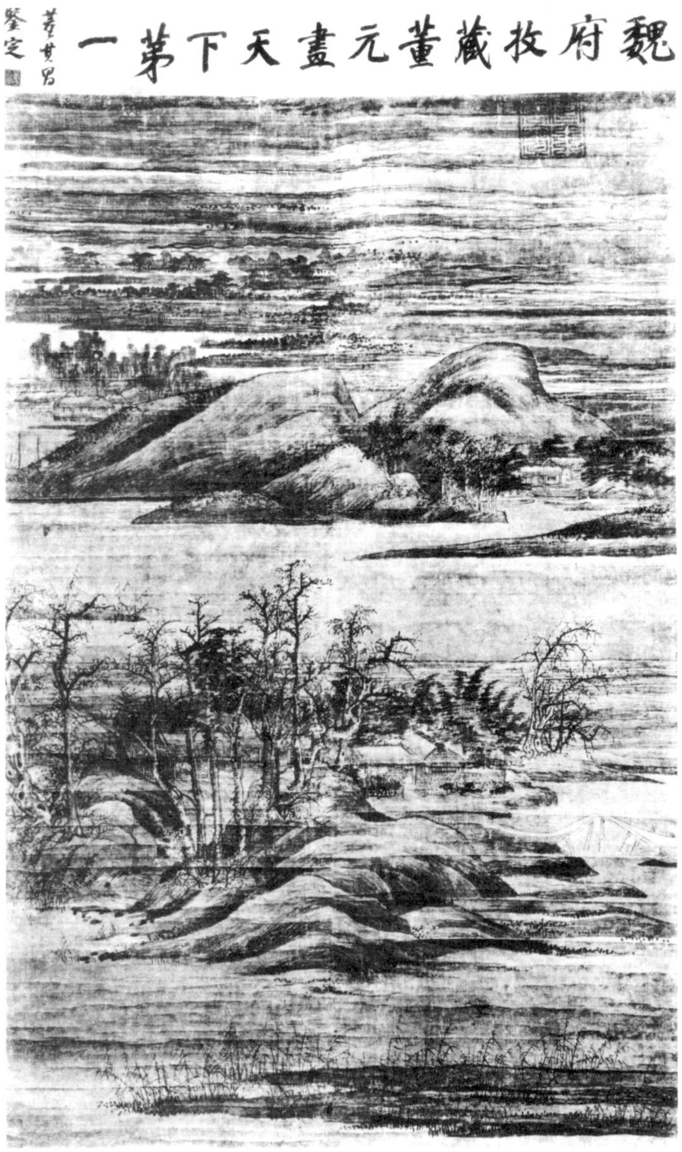


Fig. 32. Anonymous, after Tung Yüan, *Wintry Groves and Layered Banks* (*Han-lin ch'ung-t'ing*). Undated, 10th century(?). Hanging scroll, ink and light color on silk. 181.5 x 116.5 cm. (5 ft. 11 1/2 in. x 3 ft. 9 7/8 in.). Kurokawa Institute, Ashiya, Japan

era (1190–95), shows the pointillistic "raindrop" idiom developed by Fan K'uan, working fifty years after Kuan T'ung's death. In this painting, a texture pattern, originally a representational technique, has been codified into a system of standardized brushstrokes for landscape painting. This is a work in the style of Fan K'uan, done probably also around the middle of the twelfth century.

An assistant keeper of the North Park in Nanking, Kiangsu province, in the Southern T'ang principality, toward the end of the Five Dynasties period, Tung Yüan (fl. 937–76), from Chung-ling (Nanking), was said to have painted a wide range of subject matter, in the older colored style as well as the new monochrome ink wash (*shui-mo*) style.[31] According to Shen Kua (1029–1093), in his *Notes Written in Meng-ch'i* (*Meng-ch'i pi-t'an*), he painted "far vistas in autumnal vapors portraying the hills of Chiang-nan [south of the Yangtze River] without any strange cliffs. . . . If viewed closely, they seem without merit; but when seen at a distance . . . they are evening scenes, with the summits of faraway mountains rendered as if they were reflecting the light [of the setting sun]."[32] Mi Fu (1052–1107), in his *Painting History* (*Hua-shih*), wrote that "Tung Yüan's paintings excel in a plain, light, and natural quality; such a style did not exist in the T'ang period. . . . His peaks emerging or disappearing, his clouds and mist clearing or thickening, they are without any artificial, clever pretensions, but possess a natural truthfulness."[33]

In *Wintry Groves and Layered Banks* (*Han-lin ch'ung-t'ing*), attributed to Tung Yüan, now at the Kurokawa Institute, Ashiya, Japan (fig. 32), the gently rolling grassy knolls and the marshy plains are typical of the rich and moist landscape of the lower Yangtze delta region in south China. The painting bears two imperial seals, "Ch'i-hsi-tien pao" (treasure of the Ch'i-hsi palace; in use ca. 1233) and "Hsüan-wen-ko pao" (treasure of the Hsüan-wen imperial pavilion; in use 1341–67).[34] Mounted on top of the painting, in a horizontal line of boldly written characters, is an inscription by the late Ming connoisseur and painter Tung Ch'i-ch'ang (1555–1636), which reads: "Painting by Tung Yüan, from the collection of the duke of Wei [General Hsü Ta, 1332–1385], the best under heaven."

*Wintry Groves* shows a flat-distance compositional scheme similar to that of *Hawk and Ducks* (cf. fig. 18), but the softer, more natural mountain forms, with parallel folds and softly rubbed parallel texture strokes, show Tung Yüan's innovations: in the far distance, near the top of the painting, the broad brushstrokes, combined with ink wash illustrate perfectly Shen Kua's description of "faraway mountains . . . reflecting the light [of the setting sun]."[35] The landscape forms in this work compare closely with those of the handscroll *Travelers in Early Snow along the River* (*Chiang-hsing ch'u-hsüeh*) by Chao Kan (fl. ca. 961–75), now in the National Palace Museum, Taipei. Chao, "a student of the Painting Academy" in the Southern T'ang palace in Nanking, had apparently been influenced by Tung Yüan's style.

The art historical importance of the *Wintry Groves* composition to Yüan dynasty painters is well documented. In Chao Meng-fu's (1254–1322) short handscroll *Autumn Colors on the Ch'iao and Hua Mountains* (*Ch'iao-Hua ch'iu-se*) of 1296 (cf. fig. 66), the group of trees and layered banks in the center of the composition seems consciously modeled after those of *Wintry Groves*. The collected works of Wu Chen (1280–1354), *Ink Legacy of Wu Chen* (*Mei-tao-jen i-mo*), contains an inscription that states that Wu had studied and copied Tung's *Wintry Groves*.[36] A recently discovered work by Wu Chen in the Palace Museum, Peking, entitled *Winter Geese among Reedy Banks* (*Lu-hua han-yen*), [37] shows a striking composition of four horizontal bands of reed-covered banks that can only be derived from Tung's *Wintry Groves*.

While the reliability of *Wintry Groves* as a representative of Tung Yüan's style is not in doubt, the style of the work has been called "a frozen Tung Yüan style" because, according to Loehr, "the dots [in this painting] do not build up the forms but are non-essential additions."[38] A large hanging scroll, measuring almost exactly 6 feet in height, the work is extraordinarily bold and powerful in both conception and execution. The simple additive triangular mountain motifs, with continuous contour lines and softly rubbed parallel texture strokes modeling and shading the forms, recall the columnar sculptural treatment of the mountain forms in the tenth-century Liao hanging scroll (cf. fig. 22). The well-shaded, columnar tree trunks, as well as the simple but powerfully articulated wintry branches, compare closely with not only the trees in Chao Kan's *Travelers*, but also those in the Ch'ing-ling wall paintings. In composition the forms are built up in three horizontal sections across the picture plane, each tilted at a different angle away from the viewer. If it is a copy, *Wintry Groves* has admirably preserved both the form and the structure of a tenth-century original masterpiece by Tung Yüan.

Closely related in manner to *Wintry Groves* are three handscrolls attributed to Tung Yüan: *Hsiao and Hsiang Rivers* (*Hsiao-Hsiang t'u*) in the Palace Museum, Peking (fig. 33); *Summer Mountains* (*Hsia-shan t'u*) in the Shanghai Museum (fig. 34); and *Awaiting the Ferry at the Mouth of Summer Mountains* (*Hsia-k'ou tai-tu t'u*) in the Liaoning Provincial Museum. Richard Barnhart, in *Marriage of the Lord of the River* (1970), demonstrated that the Peking and Liaoning scrolls represent parts of a lost single handscroll composition and are from versions of different dates.[39] Loehr (1980) believes that *Hsiao and Hsiang Rivers* "may be an original work" and considers *Summer Mountains* in Shanghai as one that "exemplifies to perfection the early writers' descriptions of Tung Yüan's [depiction of ] . . . impressionistic effects."[40]

Most other scholars, however, place *Hsiao and Hsiang Rivers* in the late Northern Sung period, in about 1100.[41] Compared to *Wintry Groves* and Chao Kan's *Travelers*—in which the mountain form is clearly outlined and modeled, and the scattered dots represent foliage patterns on the mountain surface—dots and ink wash in *Hsiao and Hsiang Rivers*, replacing linear characterization, combine to create a vibrant, visually unified atmospheric surface typical of the late eleventh century; and in *Hsiao and Hsiang Rivers*, overlapping

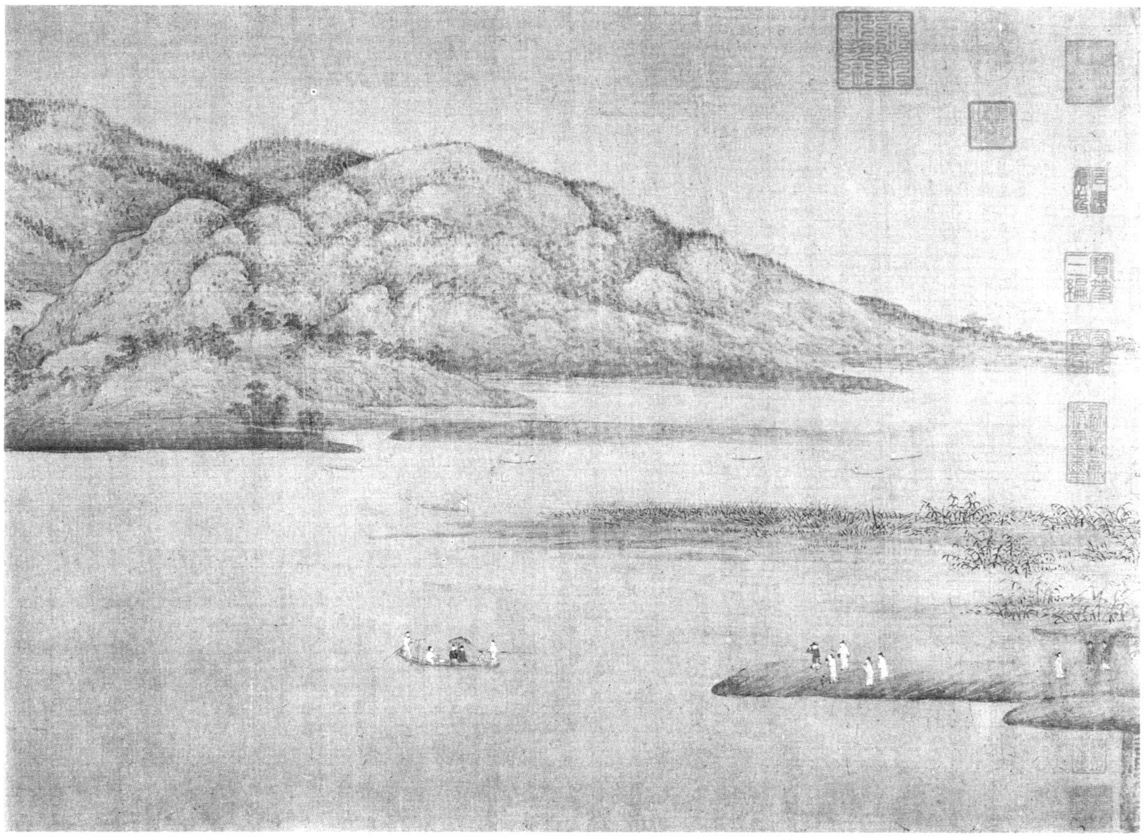

Fig. 33. Anonymous, after Tung Yüan, detail, *Hsiao and Hsiang Rivers* (*Hsiao-Hsiang t'u*). Undated, ca. 1100(?). Handscroll, ink and light color on silk. 50.2 x 140.0 cm (19¾ in. x 4 ft. 7⅛ in.). Palace Museum, Peking

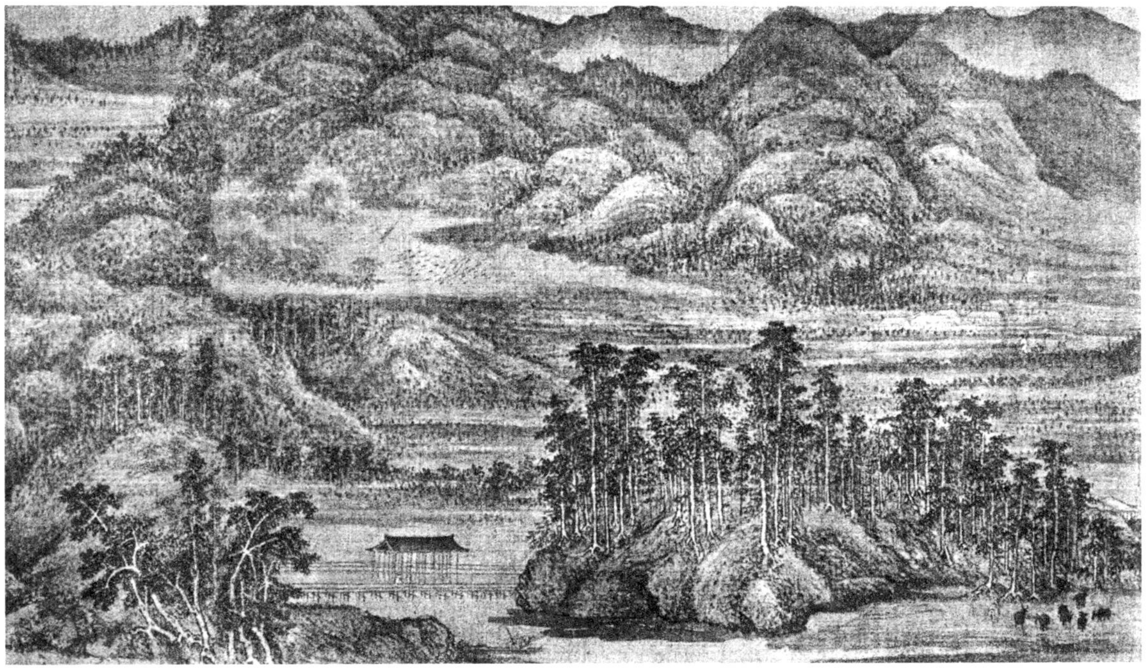

Fig. 34. Anonymous, after Tung Yüan, detail, *Summer Mountains* (*Hsia-shan t'u*). Undated, 1st half 13th century(?). Handscroll, ink and light color on silk. 49.4 x 313.2 cm (19½ in. x 10 ft. 3¼ in.). Shanghai Museum

triangular mountain motifs, ranging diagonally from front to back in a continuous sequence, strongly enhance the impression of spatial continuity. This emphasis on blurred form and spatial illusion is further developed in *Summer Mountains*, where dots and ink wash totally deny formal clarity and definition, in favor of visual fusion and surface pattern. *Summer Mountains*, which bears the seals of Chia Ssu-tao, is the work of a Southern Sung Tung Yüan follower who worked in the first half of the thirteenth century.

Chü-jan, a Buddhist priest from Nanking, is known as the principal follower of Tung Yüan. About 975 he accompanied the vanquished Southern T'ang prince Li Hou-chu to the Sung capital at K'ai-feng, Honan province, where he presented himself at the Sung court and began to earn a reputation as a painter.

Despite the immense popularity of his works during the Ming and Ch'ing periods, when the clearly formulated brush idiom attributed to him became the representative technique of the so-called Tung

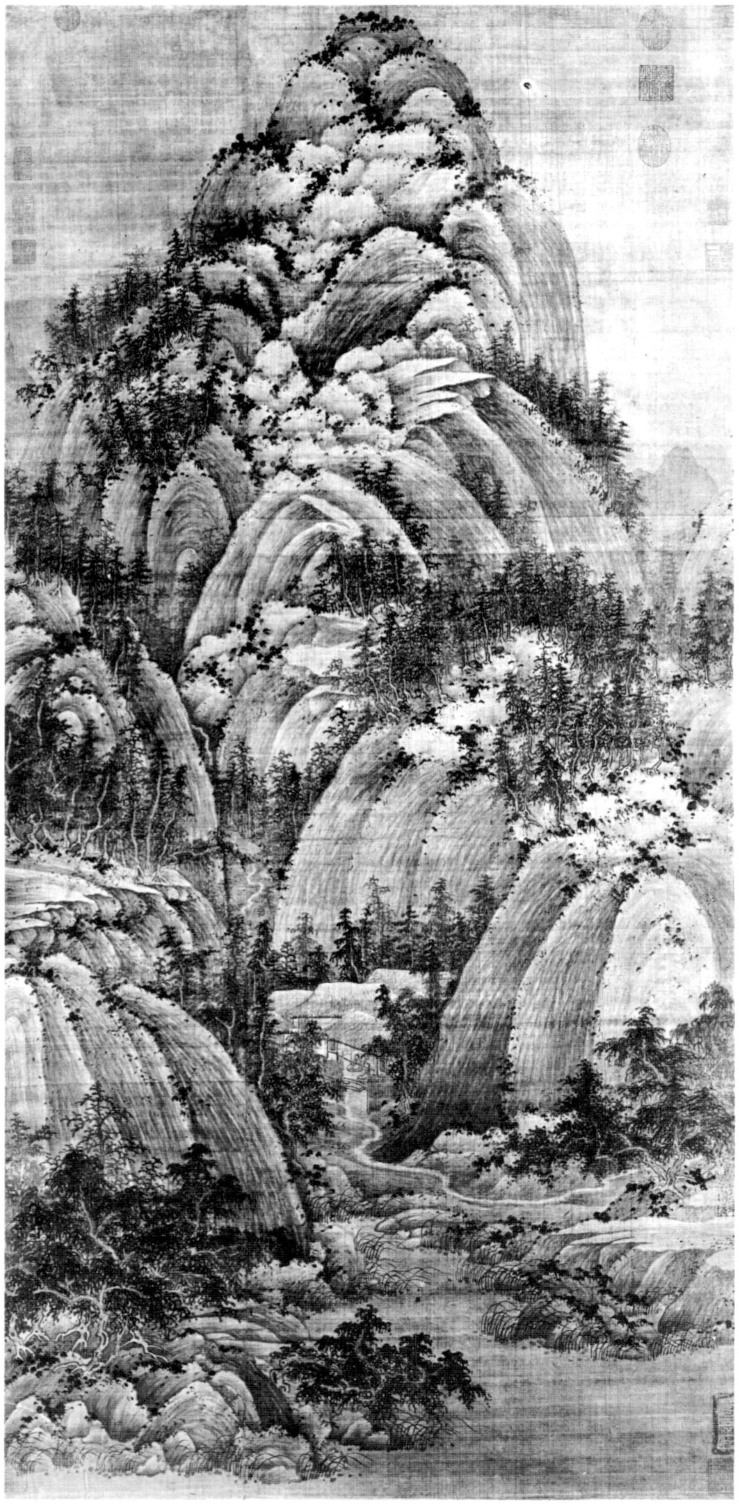

Fig. 35. Anonymous, formerly attributed to Chü-jan, *Seeking the Tao in Autumn Mountains* (*Ch'iu-shan wen-tao*). Undated, 14th century or later(?). Hanging scroll, ink on silk. 156.2 x 77.2 cm (5 ft. 1 1/2 in. x 30 3/8 in.). National Palace Museum, Taipei

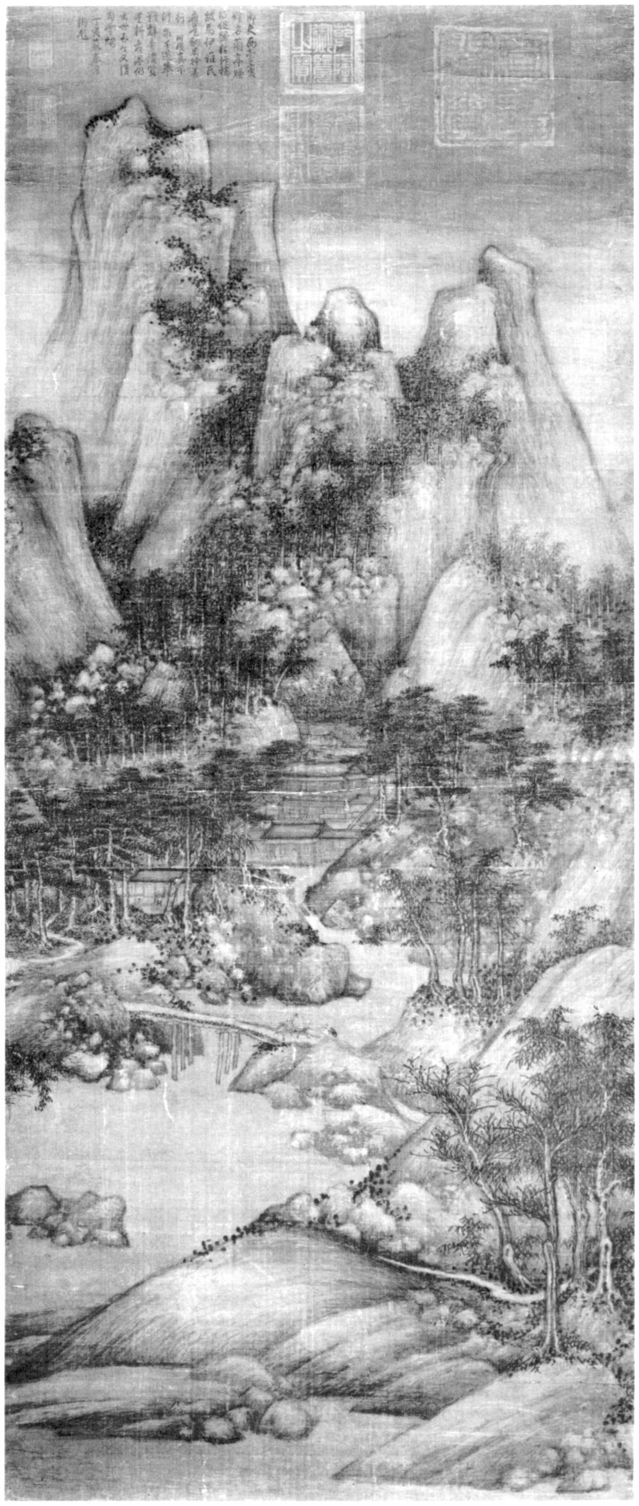

Fig. 36. Anonymous, after Chü-jan, *Hsiao I Seizing the Lan-t'ing [Manuscript] by Trickery* (*Hsiao I chuan Lan-t'ing*). Undated, late 11th century(?). Hanging scroll, ink and color on silk. 144.1 x 59.6 cm (4 ft. 8 3/4 in. x 23 1/2 in.). National Palace Museum, Taipei

(Yüan)–Chü(-jan) tradition, early Northern Sung writers had little to say about Chü's style. Kuo Jo-hsü remarked only that Chü "excelled in the depiction of mist and atmosphere, and the high and wide aspects of mountain and river scenery, but he was not at his best in drawing trees and forests."[42]

The painting that best exemplifies what was widely understood as the typical Chü-jan brush idiom during the late Ming and Ch'ing periods is *Seeking the Tao in Autumn Mountains* (*Ch'iu-shan wen-tao*), now in the National Palace Museum, Taipei (fig. 35). It shows a massive mountain piled up from rounded, "earthen" hills in repeated and uniform shapes—with rounded rock formations, known as "alum heads" (*fan-t'ou*), on hilltops; round, calligraphic, parallel "hemp-fiber" (*p'i-ma*) texture strokes and scattered large round "moss dots" (*t'ai-tien*) covering the mountain surface; and massed uniformly shaped trees with crooked trunks covered with round foliage dots. The painting bears a seal purporting to be that of the late Northern Sung minister Ts'ai Ching (1047–1126), but has no earlier documentation before it was recorded in the third series of the Ch'ing imperial catalogue, *Treasured Boxes of the Stony Moat* (*Shih-ch'ü pao-chi san-pien*) of 1793–1817.[43]

In "A Comparative Study of the Extant Works of Chü-jan" (1967), Shen Fu, provisionally accepting the evidence of Ts'ai Ching's seal on the painting, called *Seeking the Tao* "the finest representative of the Chü-jan style extant today."[44] Li Lin-ts'an, however, in "A Study of *Ts'un*-texture Methods in Chinese Landscape Painting" (1973) and "A Study of Moss Dots in Chinese Landscape Painting" (1975), pointed out that the formularized hemp-fiber texture strokes and large, round moss dots, both prominent features of *Seeking the Tao*, were developments of the fourteenth century, practiced by such notable Yüan painters as Huang Kung-wang (1269–1354) and Wu Chen.[45] Accordingly, a number of important works attributed to Chü-jan and other tenth-century masters that are closely related in style to *Seeking the Tao* must be dated to Yüan or later periods.

Another hanging scroll in the National Palace Museum, Taipei, *Hsiao I Seizing the Lan-t'ing [Manuscript] by Trickery* (*Hsiao I chuan Lan-t'ing*; fig. 36), illustrating a well-known story about Wang Hsi-chih's *Lan-t'ing* manuscript, represents a better reflection of Chü-jan's original style. The painting bears two barely legible seals purporting to be those of the first Southern Sung emperor Kao-tsung, and a clear seal of the last Yüan emperor Shun-ti, "Treasure of the Hsüan-wen Pavilion" (in use 1341–67).[46] The alum-head texture strokes and the moss dots, while related to their formularized statements as seen in *Seeking the Tao*, are less schematic and more descriptive of the natural mountain form. The triangular slopes in the foreground, with their continuous outlines and softly rubbed parallel texture strokes, closely resemble those in

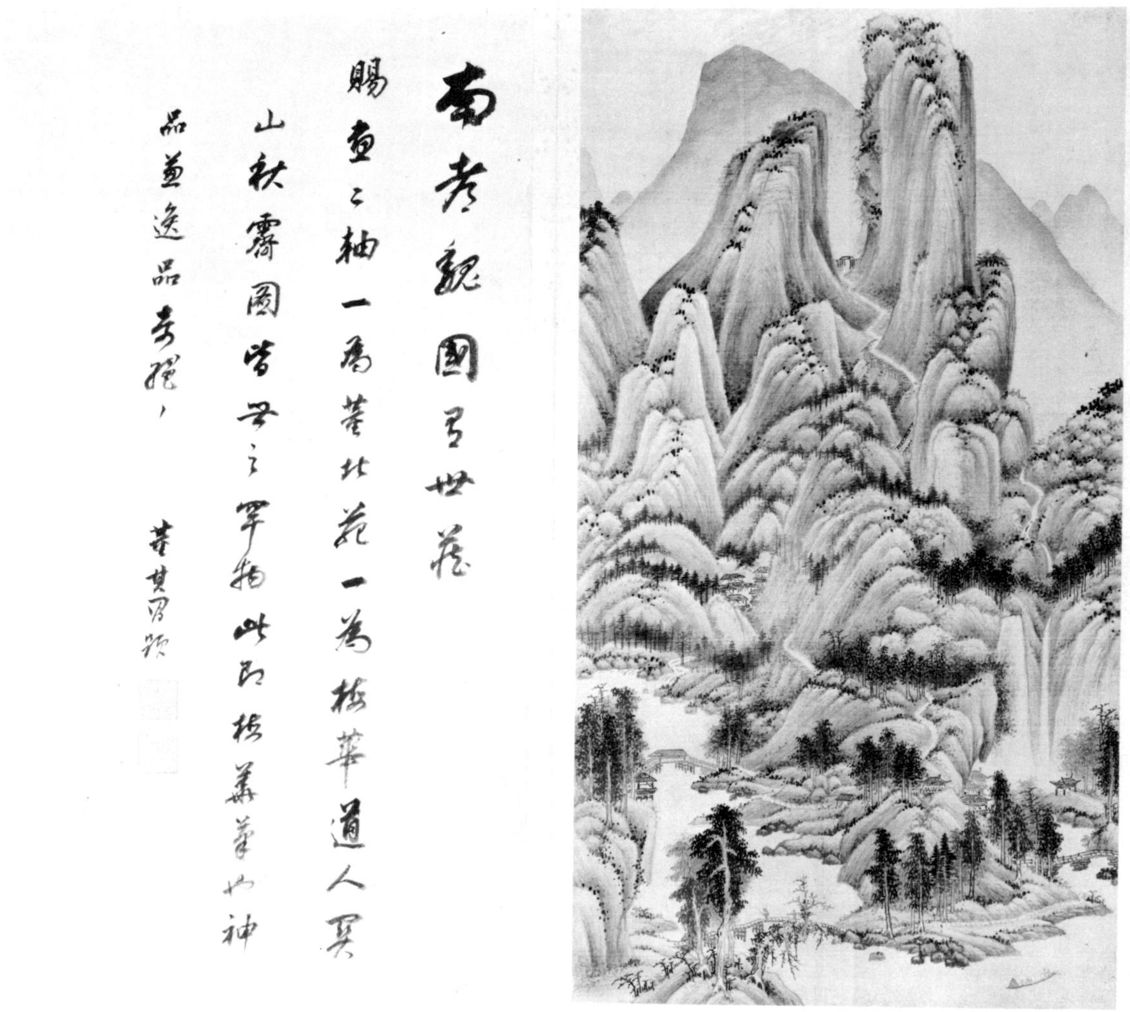

Fig. 37. Wang Shih-min, "After Wu Chen." Undated, late 1620s. Album leaf 15 of *Within Small See Large* (*Hsiao-chung hsien-ta*), ink on silk. 70.2 x 40.2 cm ($27\,^{5}/_{8}$ x $15\,^{7}/_{8}$ in.). National Palace Museum, Taipei

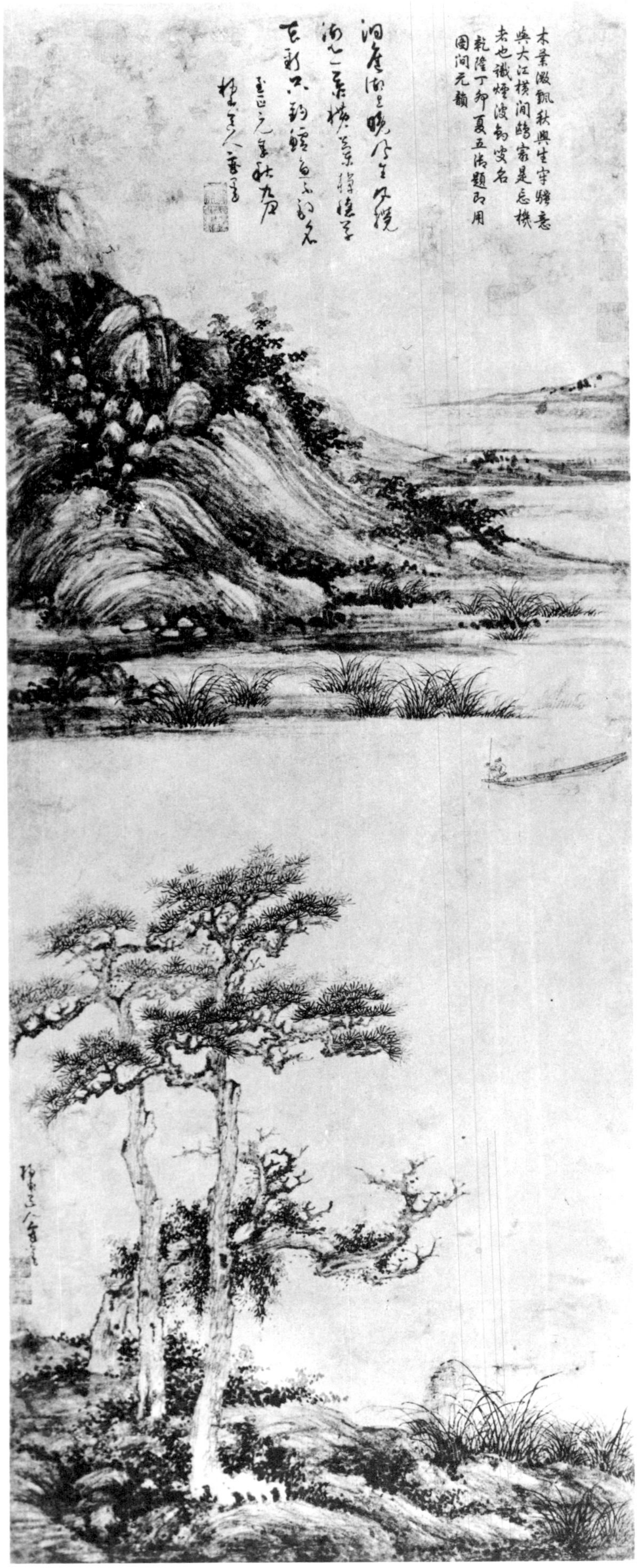

Fig. 38. Wu Chen, *Hermit Fisherman at Tung-t'ing* (*Tung-t'ing yü-yin*). Dated 1341. Hanging scroll, ink on paper. 146.4 x 58.6 cm (4 ft. 9⅝ in. x 23⅛ in.). National Palace Museum, Taipei

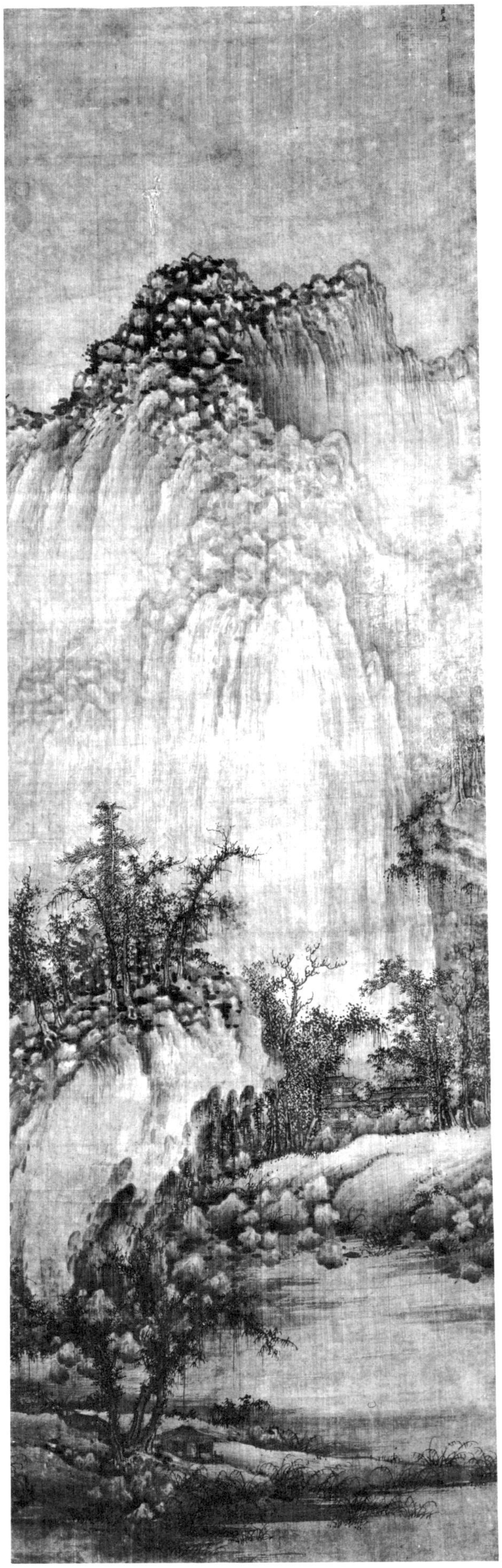

Fig. 39. Anonymous, after Chü-jan, *Buddhist Monastery by Streams and Mountains* (*Ch'i-shan lan-jo*). Undated, ca. 1100. Hanging scroll, ink on silk. 185.4 x 57.5 cm. (6 ft. ⅛ in. x 22⅝ in.). Cleveland Museum of Art

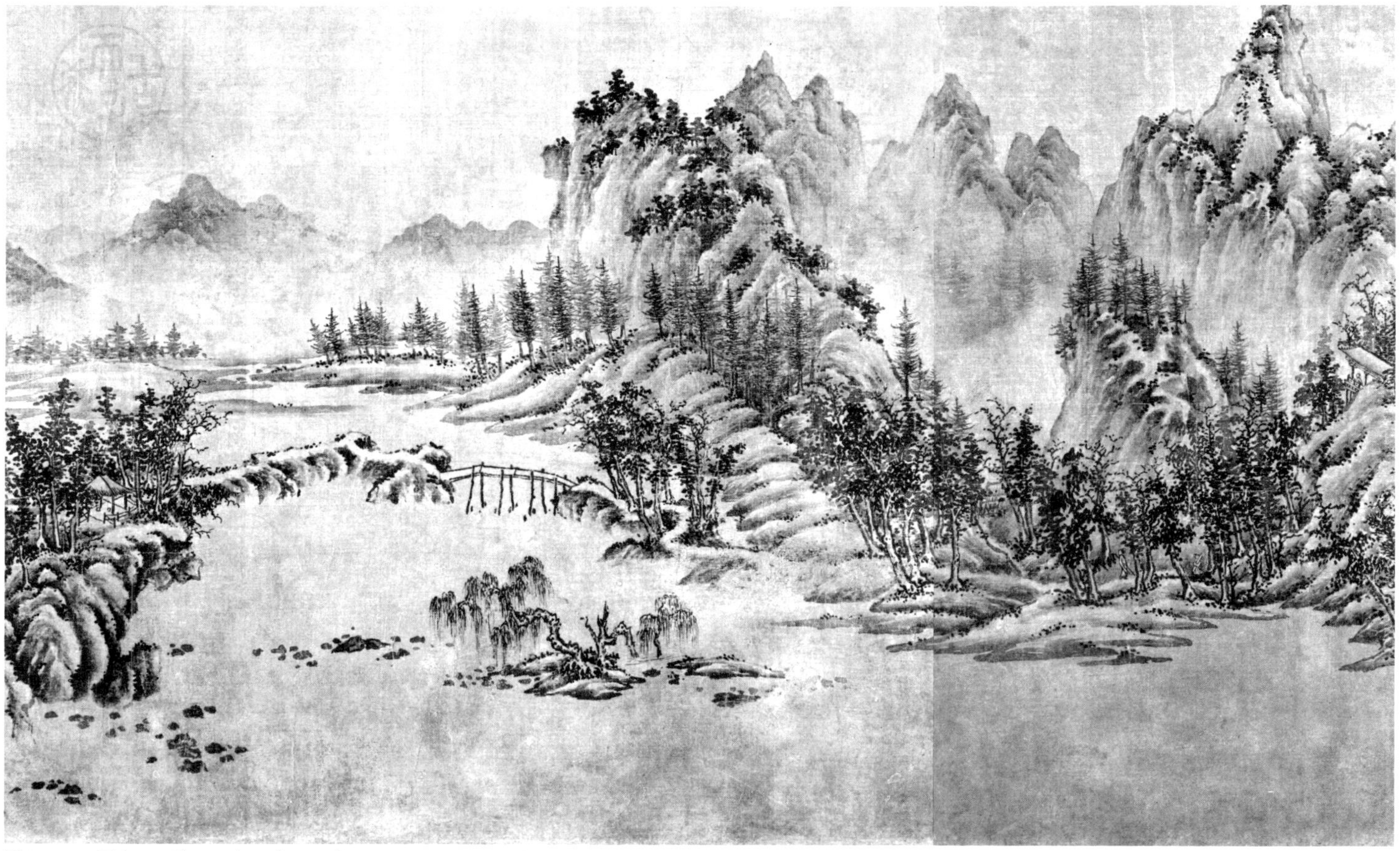

Fig. 40. Chiang Shen, detail, *Verdant Mountains* (*Lin-luan chi-ts'ui*). Undated, early 12th century. Handscroll, ink and light color on silk. 30.6 x 296.0 cm (12 in. x 9 ft. 8½ in.). Nelson Gallery–Atkins Museum, Kansas City

*Wintry Groves and Layered Banks* attributed to Tung Yüan (cf. fig. 32), while the vertical peaks in the background, again individually outlined and shaded, recall the columnar mountain forms seen in the archaeologically recovered tenth-century Liao hanging scroll (cf. fig. 22).

An early seventeenth-century album of paintings after Sung and Yüan compositions, commonly known as *Within Small See Large* (*Hsiao-chung hsien-ta*), in the National Palace Museum, Taipei, has copies of two large, presumably early, compositions by Wu Chen (fig. 37; cf. fig. 147c). According to Tung Ch'i-ch'ang's colophons on these paintings, Wu Chen had followed Chü-jan in these compositions;[47] indeed, the mountain forms in these seventeenth-century copies reflect fairly accurately the columnar, naturally shaded peaks in *Hsiao I Seizing the Lan-t'ing*, which could conceivably have been one of Wu Chen's models for the Chü-jan style. In Wu's *Hermit Fisherman at Tung-t'ing* (*Tung-t'ing yü-yin*) of 1341 (fig. 38), the Yüan master, combining the transmitted images of Tung Yüan (cf. fig. 32) and Chü-jan (cf. fig. 36), formulated a new calligraphic brush idiom, with clustered alum heads, parallel hemp-fiber texture strokes, and round moss dots.

*Buddhist Monastery by Streams and Mountains* (*Ch'i-shan lan-jo*), in the Cleveland Museum of Art (fig. 39), is a third kind of Chü-jan painting. The painting bears a Sung official seal, "Shang-shu-sheng-yin" (seal of the Council of State), which Wai-kam Ho (1980) dates to about 1083–1126.[48] Shen Fu, comparing this work with paintings of Chiang Shen (ca. 1090–1138), dates it to the end of the Northern Sung and beginning of the Southern Sung, in the early twelfth century.[49] Chiang's landscapes represent an atmospheric treatment of the Chü-jan style in the early 1100s; like *Hsiao and Hsiang Rivers* attributed to Tung Yüan, dated about 1100 (cf. fig. 33), Chiang's *Verdant Mountains* (*Lin-luan chi-ts'ui*), in the Nelson Gallery–Atkins Museum, Kansas City (fig. 40), combines dots and ink wash in a fused visual surface, with overlapping mountain forms ranging continuously in a unified space. Although in Ming and Ch'ing writings Chiang Shen was regarded solely as a Chü-jan follower, in Chiang's own time his painting style was said to derive from Li Ch'eng (919–967) and Kuo Hsi, as well as Tung Yüan.[50] In the Cleveland painting, the leafless tree forms show the influence of the Li Ch'eng–Kuo Hsi tradition most popular around 1100. In composition and treatment of scale, the Cleveland hanging scroll compares closely to *Winter Landscape* by Li Kung-nien (fl. ca. 1120), in The Art Museum, Princeton University (cf. fig. 51), which shows superimposed elements ranging continuously through space, without a receding ground plane.

Two other Chü-jan attributions in the National Palace Museum, Taipei—*Layered Mountains and Dense Trees* (*Ts'eng-yen ts'ung-shu*) and *Mountain Stream between Wooded Shores* (*Ch'i-shan lin-shu*)—show this atmospheric treatment of the Chü-jan idiom, with superimposed elements. Both works may be dated to the early twelfth century.

Li Ch'eng, the first of the early Northern Sung masters, was also the most influential. Although no original work by Li has survived, he was clearly the primary source for Northern Sung landscape styles, and his influence is equally strong in the works of Fan K'uan and Yen Wen-kuei (fl. ca. 970–ca. 1030), leading masters at the turn of the eleventh century, as it is in those of Kuo Hsi and Hsü Tao-ning (fl. ca. 1030–67) in the third quarter of the eleventh century, more than a century after Li's death.

Born in Ch'ing-chou, Shantung province, to a family of scholars descended from the T'ang imperial clan, Li Ch'eng probably lived and worked in the Northern Sung capital at K'ai-feng between 957 and 964.[51] It is said that because of his aristocratic background, Li was ashamed of his career as a painter, and that in the Ching-yü era (1034–37), one of his grandsons, then governor of K'ai-feng, bought up all of his paintings, presumably in deference to the painter's wish not to leave them in unworthy hands. Although the late Northern Sung emperor Hui-tsung's *Painting Catalogue of the Hsüan-ho Era [1119–25]* (*Hsüan-ho hua-p'u*) lists 159 works attributed to Li Ch'eng, the author of the catalogue readily admitted that Li had many imitators.[52] At the beginning of the twelfth century, Mi Fu had indeed theorized that by his time no original work by Li had survived.[53]

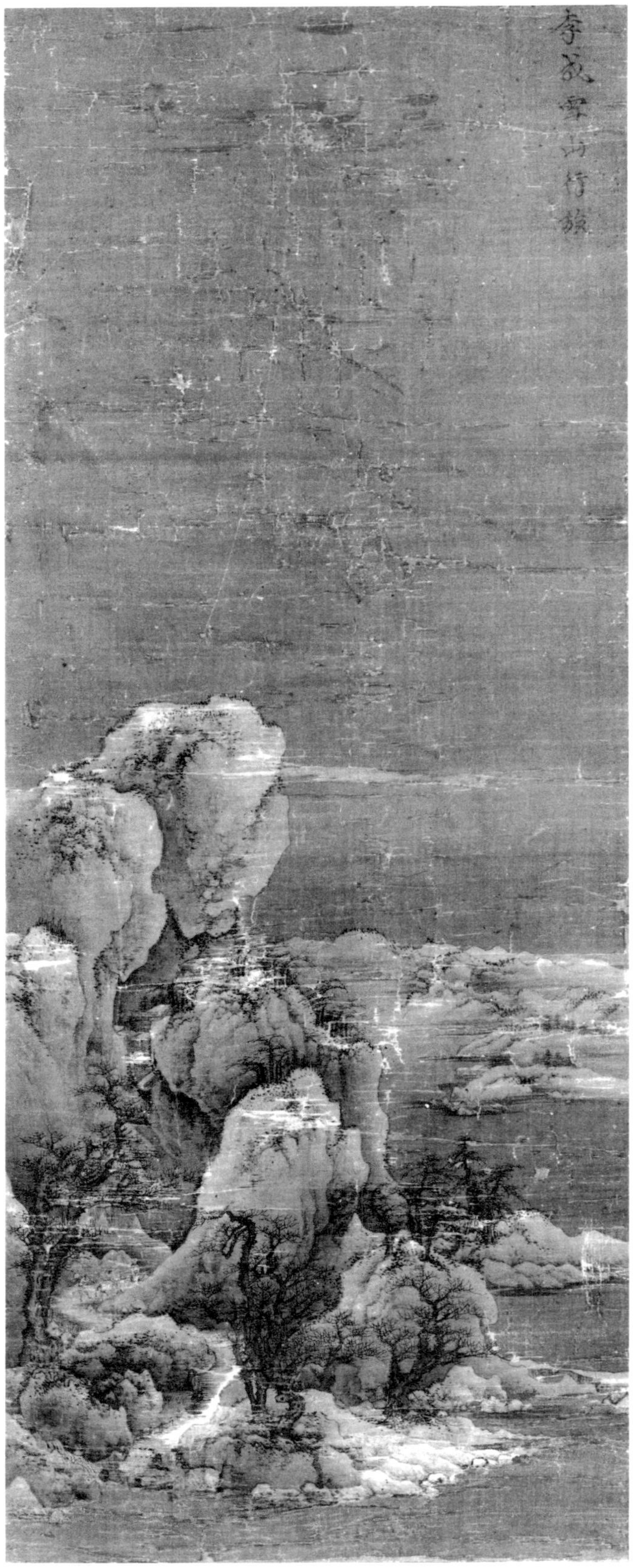

Fig. 41. Anonymous, after Li Ch'eng, *Travelers among Snowy Peaks* (*Hsüeh-shan hsing-lü*). Undated, ca. 1100(?). Hanging scroll, ink and light color on silk. 99.3 x 37.0 cm (3 ft. 3 1/8 in. x 14 5/8 in.). Museum of Fine Arts, Boston

*Travelers among Snowy Peaks* (*Hsüeh-shan hsing-lü*), a hanging scroll in the Museum of Fine Arts, Boston (fig. 41), offers insight into the style of the lost works of Li Ch'eng. The mountain forms in this painting are rounded, with deeply pitted crevices shaded by ink wash and accented and enlivened by darker moss dots. The composition, with an overhanging precipice on one side combined with a rolling pan-

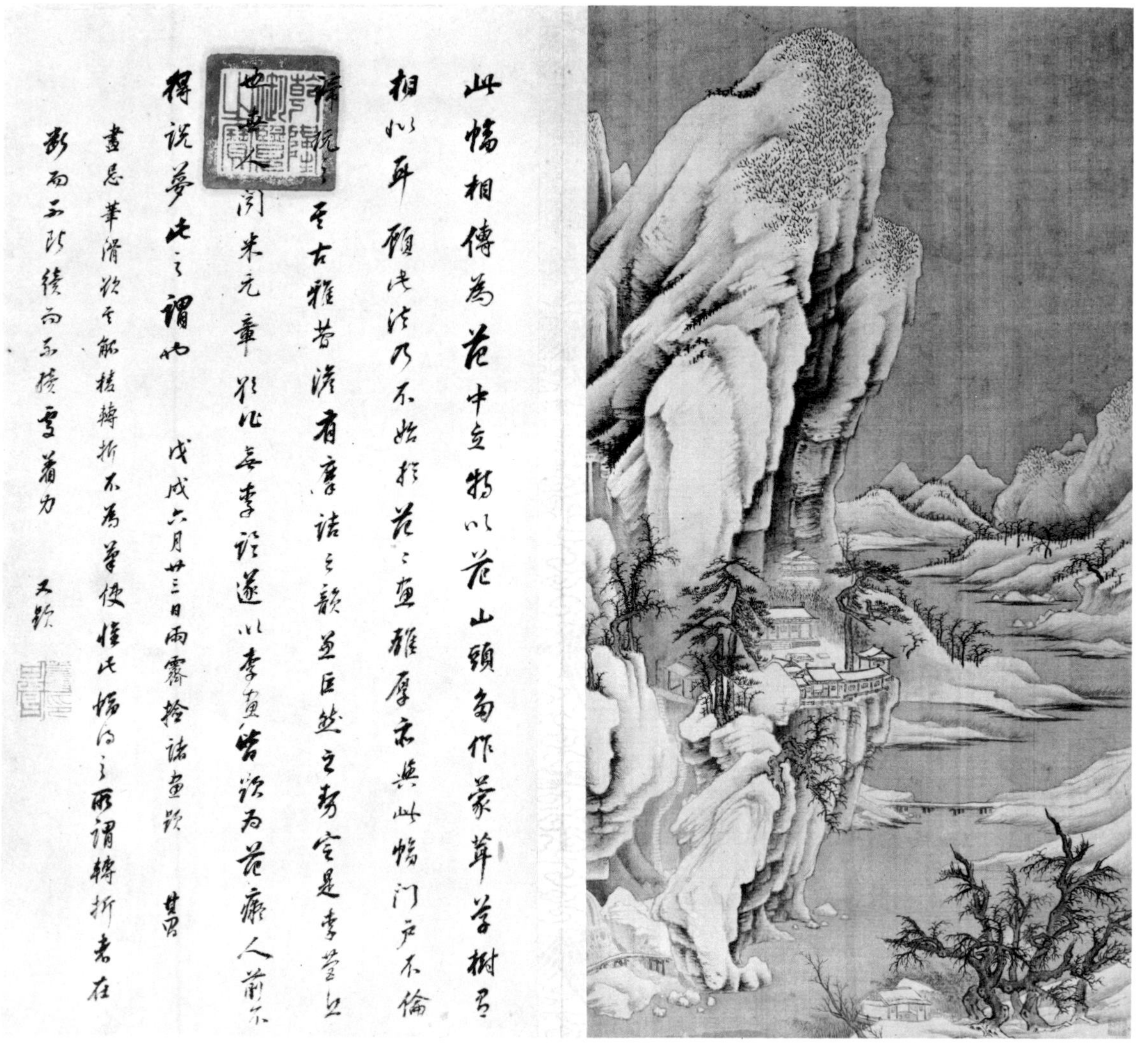

Fig. 42. Wang Shih-min, "After Li Ch'eng," and inscription by Tung Ch'i-ch'ang. Undated, late 1620s. Album leaf 1 of *Within Small See Large* (*Hsiao-chung hsien-ta*), ink on paper. 70.2 x 40.2 cm (27 5/8 x 15 7/8 in.). National Palace Museum, Taipei

oramic view on the other—the third of the T'ang compositional schemes—is echoed by *Snow Scene* attributed to Li Ch'eng by Tung Ch'i-ch'ang (1555–1636), as seen in the early seventeenth-century album of copies of early compositions, *Within Small See Large* (fig. 42).[54] The work agrees well with Sung descriptions of Li Ch'eng's style. Kuo Jo-hsü described "[Li's] atmosphere" as "desolate and thin; his misty forests are pure and wild. His brush point is as fine as a needle, his ink infinitely precise but light."[55] According to Mi Fu, "Li Ch'eng's use of light ink makes [his forms] appear as if in dreamlike mist; his rocks are like drifting clouds."[56] This image of "rocks like drifting clouds" became an important stylistic keynote for later artists working in the Li Ch'eng idiom. In an album entitled *In Pursuit of Antiquity* (*Ch'ü-ku*), dated 1673, in The Art Museum, Princeton University, for example, Wang Hui (1632–1717) created a lyrical snowy scene after Li Ch'eng, piling rocks to look like windblown clouds (fig. 43).

*Snowy Peaks* appears to be a work of the first half of the twelfth century: the brushwork and modeling of the rocks are concerned more with the pictorial surface than with the substance of the rock form; the forms are stacked vertically along the picture plane; the mountain peaks looming over distant shores are compressed together and pushed back so that they seem remote in the surrounding vast open space.[57] The generalized mountain forms have great lyric feeling: billowing, snow-clad silhouettes, insubstantial and "cloudlike," lie still and melancholy in a deep windswept valley.

The cloudlike rock recalls the Lake T'ai garden rock found in the eighth-century screen *Lady Standing under a Tree* (cf. fig. 21): the bulbous rock forms with deeply pitted crevices are portrayed by thin descriptive outlines and dry, softly rubbed texture strokes. The goal of early Northern Sung landscape painters was the representation of forms in nature: Tung Yüan's hemp-fiber (*p'i-ma*) strokes (cf. fig. 32)—before they became calligraphic and truly ropelike—were the perfect technique for describing the grassy "earthen" knolls of the south, and Fan K'uan's raindrop (*yü-tien*) dots—before they became uniform raindrops—were

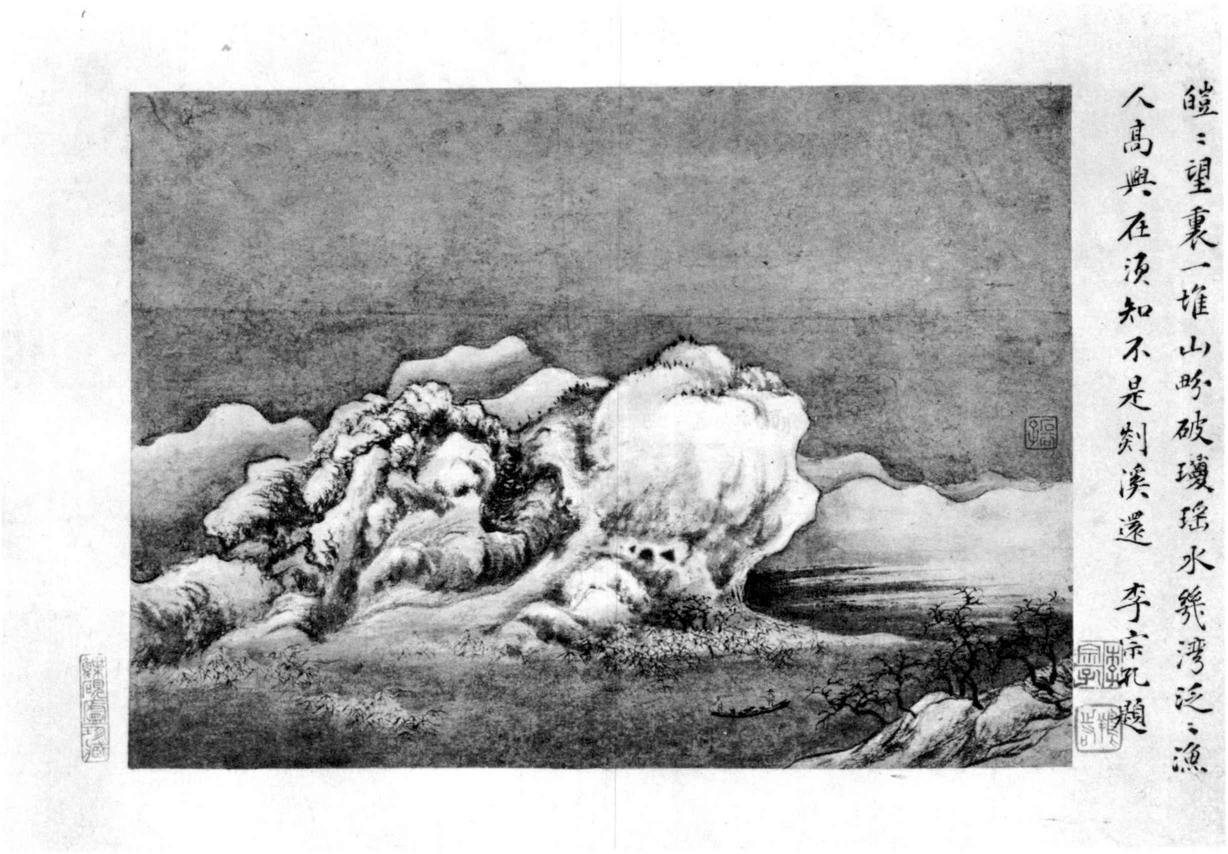


Fig. 43. Wang Hui, "After Li Ch'eng." Dated 1673. Album leaf 11 of *In Pursuit of Antiquity* (*Ch'ü-ku*), ink on paper. 22.3 x 31.1 cm (8¾ x 12¼ in.). The Art Museum, Princeton University

Fig. 44. Yen Wen-kuei, detail, *Pavilion by Rivers and Mountains* (*Chiang-shan lou-kuan*). Undated, ca. 1000. Handscroll, ink and light color on paper. 32.0 x 161.0 cm (12⅝ in. x 5 ft. 3⅜ in.). Osaka Municipal Museum of Fine Art

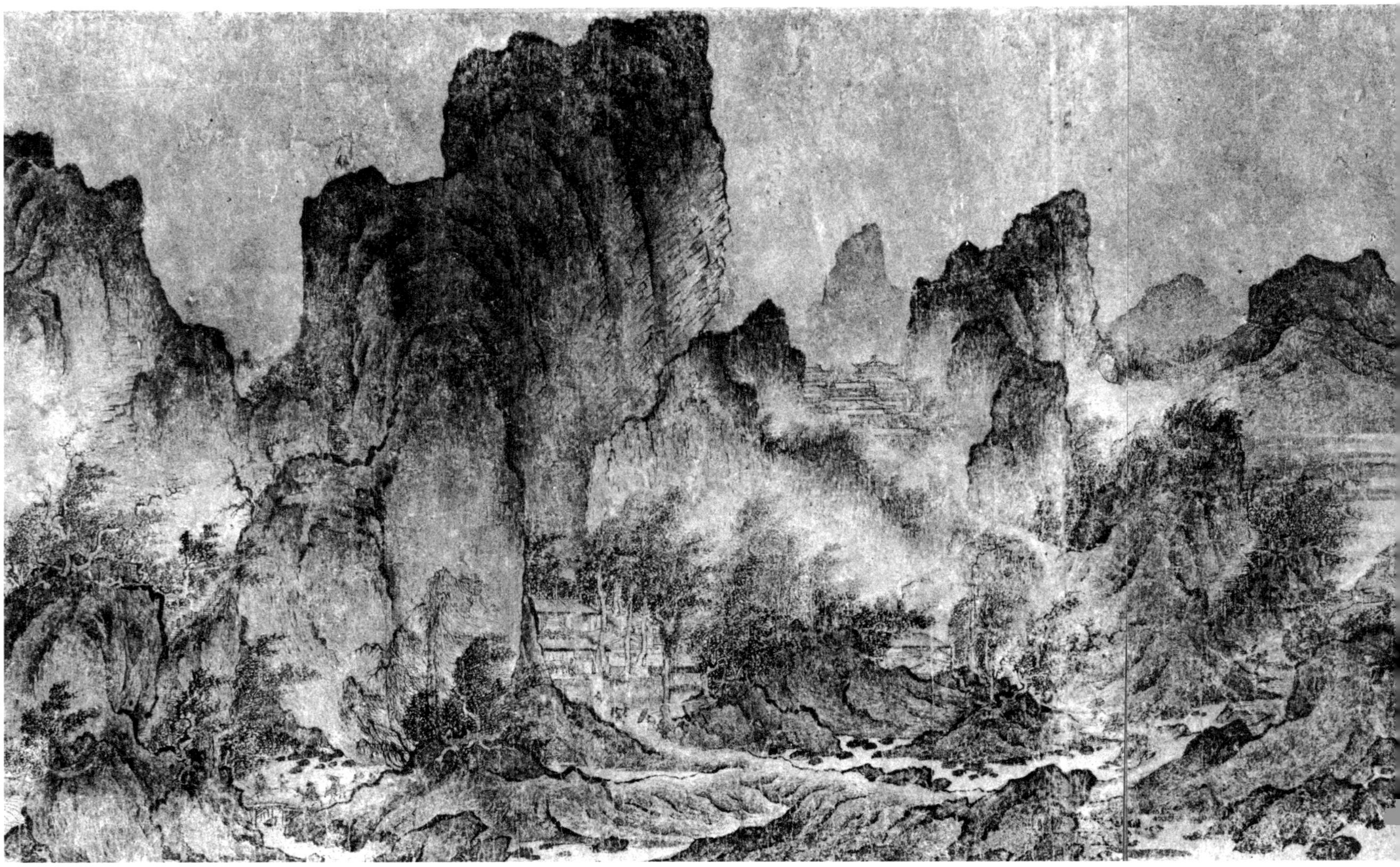

a natural interpretation of the gritty-surfaced bare rocky cliffs of the northwest. In the same way, Li Ch'eng's cloudlike pattern—before it became actual billowing clouds—was an effective technique for rendering the loess-covered, deeply pitted rounded boulders of the northeast. Li Ch'eng probably conceived his rock forms much as other tenth-century painters did—in a solid, tactile fashion with clearly defined outlines and texture strokes, mostly in dry brushwork.

In Yen Wen-kuei's *Pavilion by Rivers and Mountains* (*Chiang-shan lou-kuan*; fig. 44), about 1000, the influence of Li Ch'eng is seen in the tactually descriptive thickening-and-thinning rock contours and the varied texture strokes and ink shading for modeling the creviced rock forms. Viewed next to Fan K'uan's *Travelers among Streams and Mountains* (*Ch'i-shan hsing-lü*; cf. fig. 48), also about 1000, Yen's painting shows the legacy of Li Ch'eng in the ability of the early Northern Sung landscape masters to capture and represent the rocky essence of the mountain form, while choosing different texture patterns and brush motifs according to their personal preference and individual temperament.

*A Buddhist Temple amid Clearing Peaks* (*Ch'ing-luan hsiao-ssu*), a small hanging scroll attributed to Li Ch'eng, in the Nelson Gallery–Atkins Museum, Kansas City (fig. 45), bears a Northern Sung official seal, "Shang-shu-sheng-yin" (seal of the Council of State), of about 1083–1126.[58] The modeling method of *A Buddhist Temple* shows a mixture of influences of Li Ch'eng and Fan K'uan: while the front part of the central peak is cloudlike in the style of Li Ch'eng, most of the rock forms are filled with long raindrop texture dots like those of Fan K'uan; the brushwork of the painting is generally broader and looser than either Fan's or Yen Wen-kuei's. Instead of proceeding in distinct steps, first making contour lines, then

Fig. 45. Anonymous, after Li Ch'eng, *A Buddhist Temple amid Clearing Peaks* (*Ch'ing-luan hsiao-ssu*). Undated, ca. 1050(?). Hanging scroll, ink and light color on silk. 111.8 x 56.0 cm (3 ft. 8 in. x 22 in.). Nelson Gallery–Atkins Museum, Kansas City

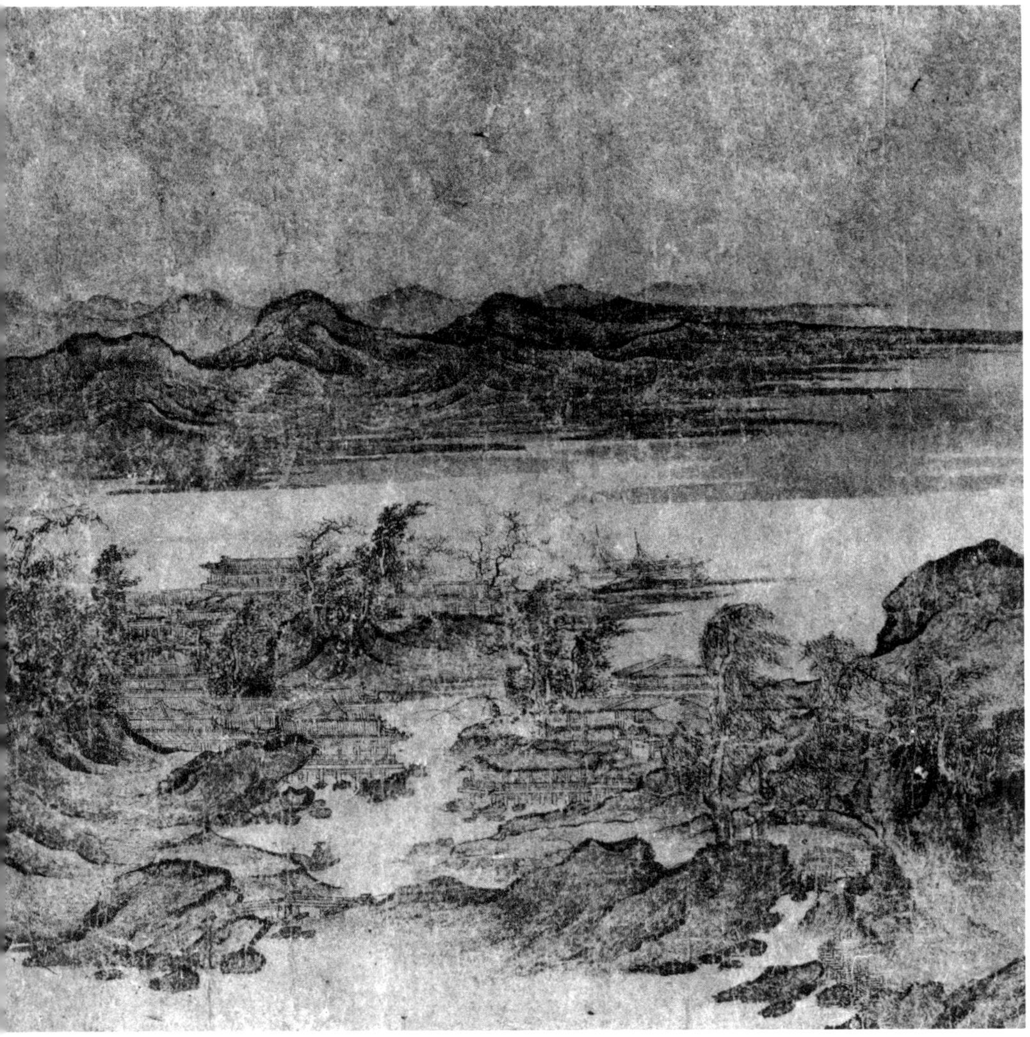

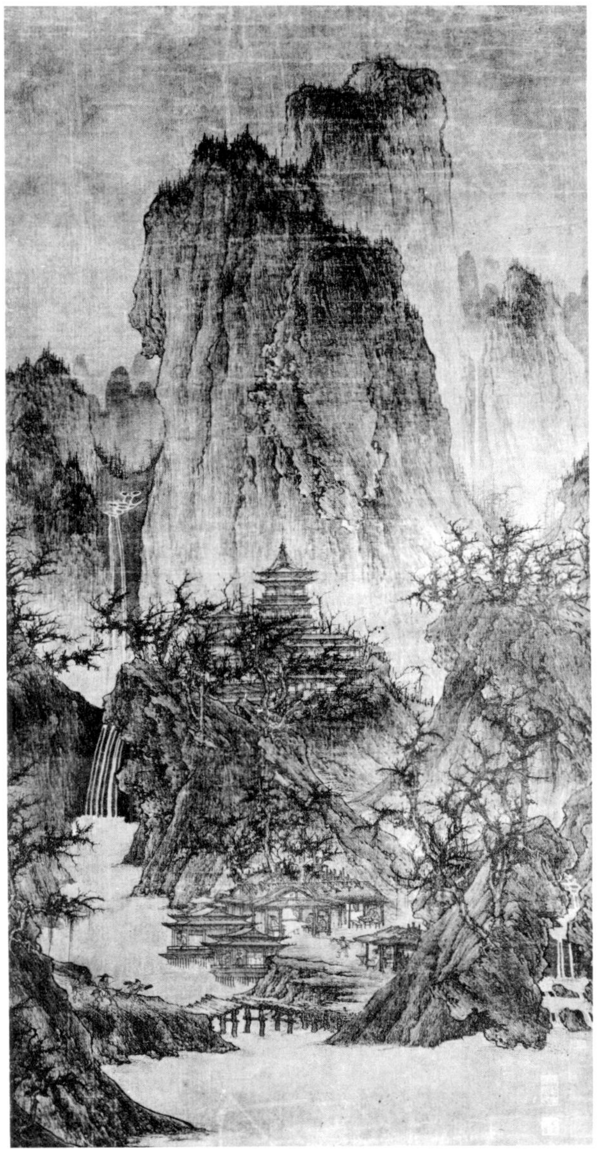

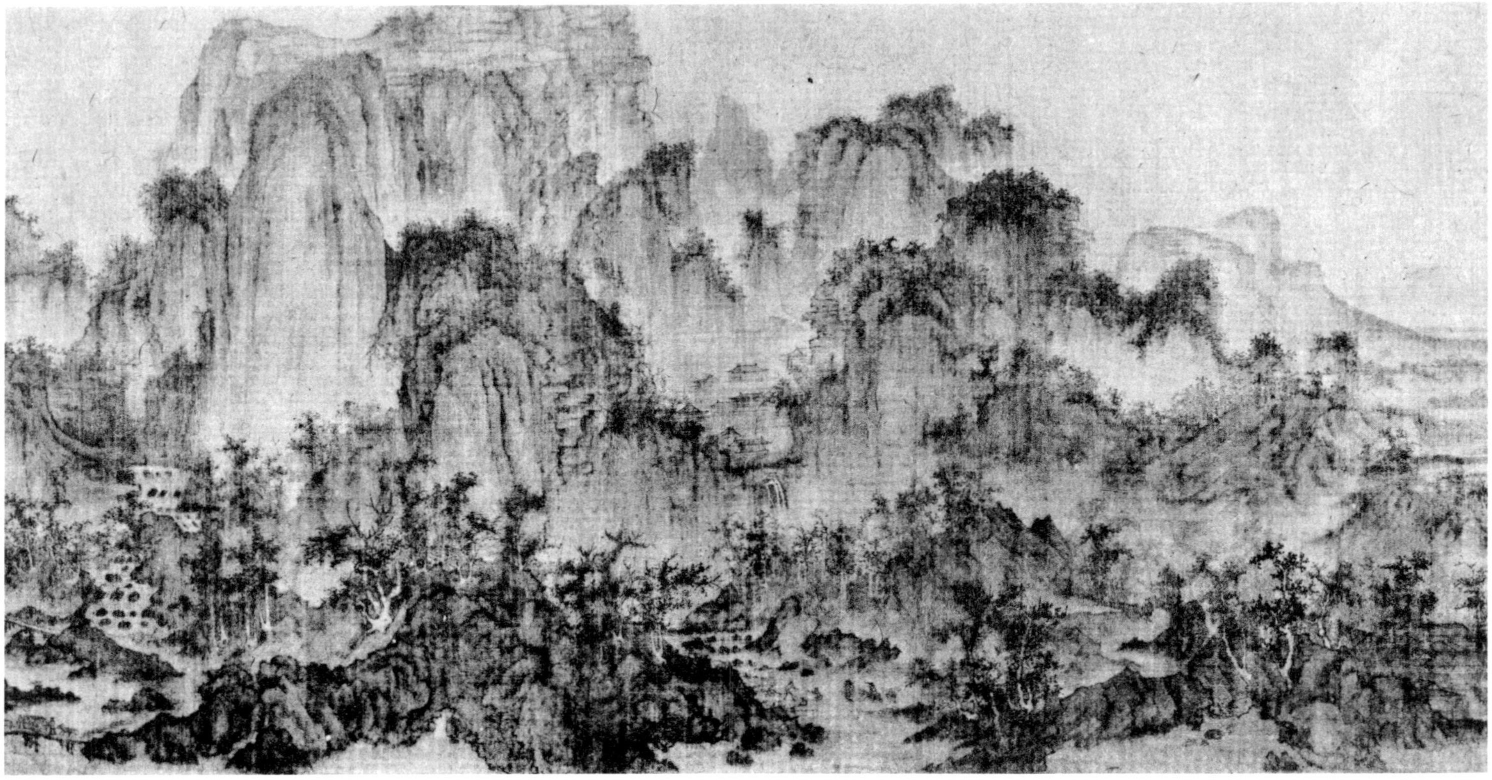

Fig. 46. Anonymous, formerly attributed to Li Ch'eng, in the Li Ch'eng–Yen Wen-kuei tradition, *Luxuriant Forest among Distant Peaks* (*Mao-lin yüan-hsiu*). Undated, ca. 1050(?). Handscroll, ink on silk. 45.4 x 141.8 cm (17 7/8 in. x 4 ft. 7 7/8 in.). Liaoning Provincial Museum

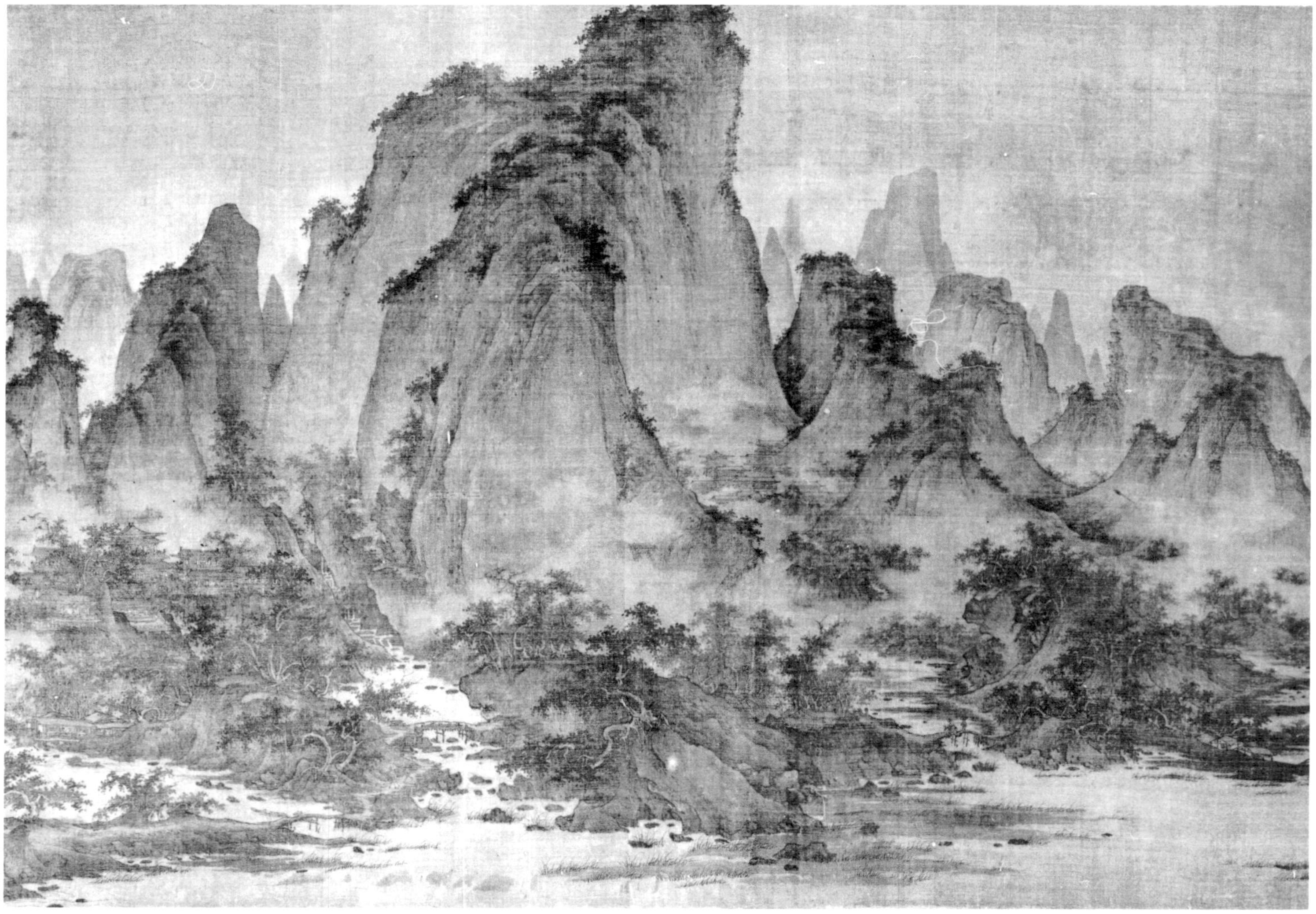

Fig. 47. Attributed to Ch'ü Ting, detail, *Summer Mountains* (*Hsia-shan t'u*). Undated, ca. 1050. Handscroll, ink and light color on silk. 45.2 x 114.9 cm (17 3/4 in. x 3 ft. 9 1/4 in.). The Metropolitan Museum of Art, New York

adding texture strokes, and finally shading with graduated ink wash—as painters worked in the early eleventh century—the artist of *A Buddhist Temple* blended the looser, broken contour lines and modeling strokes with ink washes to suggest a visually fused surface. The composition is made up of forms piled continuously in the vertical picture plane. The painting stands midway between Fan K'uan and Kuo Hsi in style, suggesting a date about 1050.[59]

A recently published handscroll in the Liaoning Provincial Museum, *Luxuriant Forest among Distant Peaks* (*Mao-lin yüan-hsiu*; fig. 46), has also been attributed to Li Ch'eng. According to a colophon dated 1219, the scroll, originally mounted as a small folding screen, was brought south by a family named Hsiang after the fall of K'ai-feng in 1126; a second colophon on the scroll, dated 1365, is by Ni Tsan (1301–1374), who, viewing the painting at the home of his friend Lu Heng (Lu Shan-fu), in Su-chou, praised it as a rare and wonderful original work by Li Ch'eng.[60] The horizontal landscape, bathed in an atmosphere of splendor, appears to be in Yen Wen-kuei's miniaturist style (cf. fig. 44). In form and composition, it is particularly close to the handscroll *Summer Mountains* (*Hsia-shan t'u*), in The Metropolitan Museum of Art, New York (fig. 47), which has been attributed to Ch'ü Ting (fl. ca. 1023–50), a follower of Yen.[61] The central peaks of *Luxuriant Forest* also compare closely in their organization with those of *Buddhist Temple amid Clearing Peaks* (cf. fig. 45): instead of painting a single row of a host peak flanked by guest peaks, as in Yen Wen-kuei's and Fan K'uan's compositions (cf. figs. 44, 48), the artist of this work has wrapped the overlapping folds of the mountains behind the near peaks, creating a compact layered mass. Similarly, at the foot of the mountains in Yen's and Fan's paintings, series of V-curves as valleys, echoing the overlapping peaks above, provide a ladder of spaces for nestling temple buildings or cascading waterfalls. The Liaoning handscroll, which shows a mixture of Li Ch'eng and Yen Wen-kuei influences, seems to date to about 1050.

Fan K'uan's incomparable *Travelers among Streams and Mountains*, about 1000, in the National Palace Museum, Taipei (figs. 48, 48a), epitomizes the early Northern Sung monumental style of landscape painting. Nearly seven feet in height, the hanging-scroll composition encompasses universal creation in its totality, and does so with the most economic of means. The awesome high-distance view is accomplished in three stages: two immense boulders occupy the foreground; above and behind them two men driving a band of laden mules proceed along a mountain road, behind which a large flat-topped mountain, covered with giant hardwood trees, firs, and temple roofs, stands high above a mountain cataract; beyond the bluff the great central massif, a solid screen of rock occupying nearly two-thirds of the picture, flanked by two smaller peaks, rises from a mist-filled ravine, its sheer height accentuated by a waterfall jetting from the summit and disappearing into the ravine below in two straight, lightninglike silvery streaks. The mountain form vividly captures the geological peculiarities of southern Shensi and northwestern Honan provinces, where thick vegetation grows only at the top of the bare steep-sided cliffs in thick layers of fine-grained soil deposited by the wind. The mountains, each a generalized triangle with parallel enveloping folds, are conceived frontally, and additively, yet the depiction, with its nervously charged contours, deep crevices, and pointillistic texture dots describing the gritty, soil-covered surfaces, conveys a powerful and immediate sense of tactile realism.

Fan modeled the mountain in three separate steps: incisive thickening-and-thinning contour strokes; subtly modulated texture dots, which develop the lines into surfaces; and finally a filling-in and rounding-out with a graduated blue-gray ink wash. Powerful brushstrokes define the twisted and gnarled ancient trunks of the large hardwood shade trees, and fine outlined foliage patterns fill the branches. The fir trees are silhouetted along the upper edge of the bluff; subdued touches of color enhance the tree foliage.

In contrast to the primitive tenth-century Liao painting (cf. fig. 22), Fan K'uan's masterpiece achieves its special sense of monumental grandeur with a lucidity of purpose that echoes the Neo-Confucian theory of "observing things in the light of their own principles." For the Northern Sung landscape painter, it seemed neither desirable nor indeed feasible to paint as the human eye sees. About 1071 Shen Kua, one of

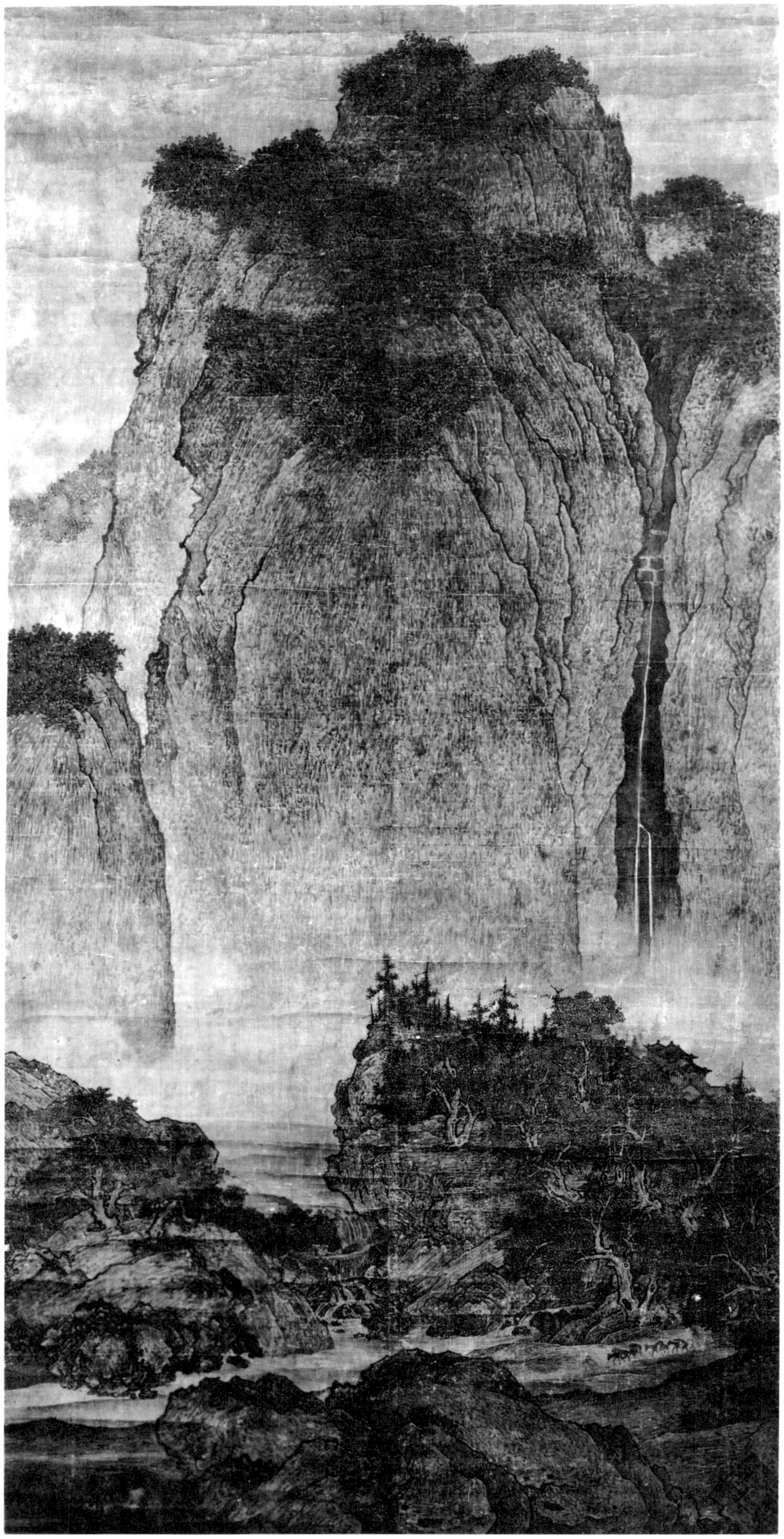

Fig. 48. Fan K'uan, *Travelers among Streams and Mountains* (*Ch'i-shan hsing-lü*). Undated, ca. 1000. Hanging scroll, ink and light color on silk. 206.3 x 103.3 cm (6 ft. 9¼ in. x 3 ft. 4⅝ in.). National Palace Museum, Taipei

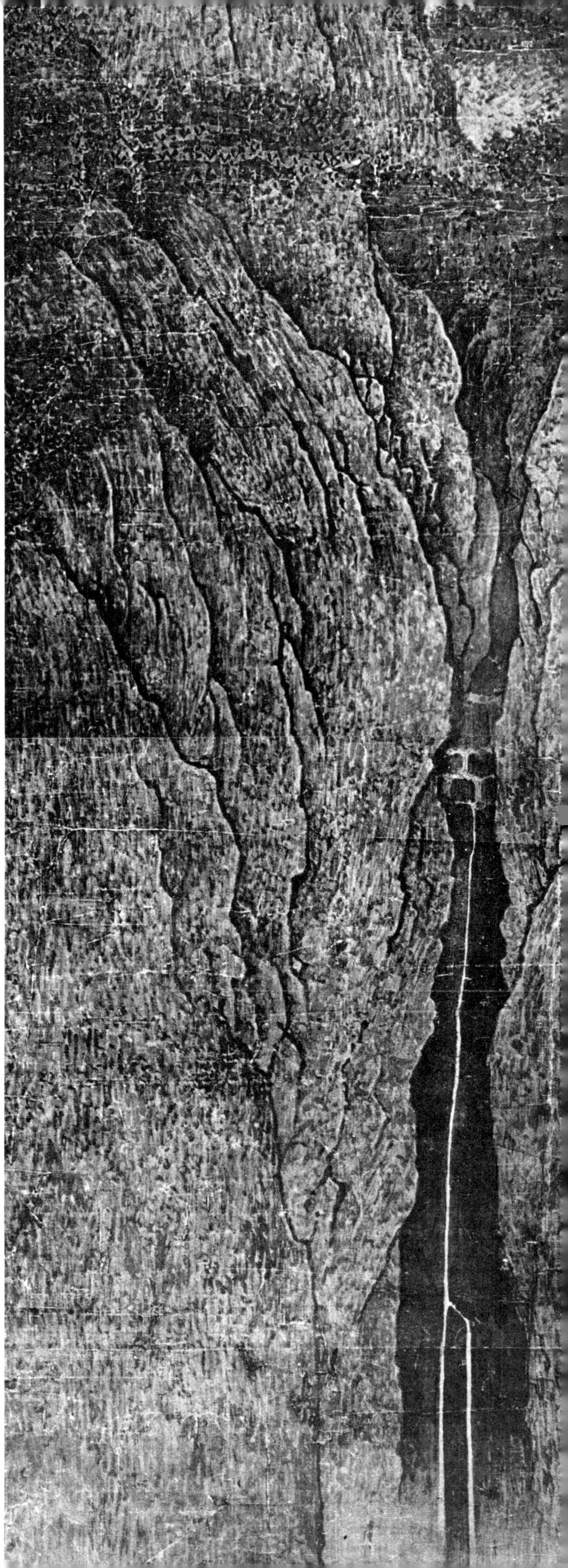

Fig. 48a. Detail, fig. 48

China's early "scientific" writers, observed that "if one paints as one sees, one will show only one peak; one will not see layer upon layer of mountaintops, nor will one see what goes on within the valleys."[62] By seeing things not through the human eye, but "in the light of their own principles," Fan was able to organize and present different aspects of a landscape within a single composition—on an additive basis and with a constantly shifting viewpoint.

To convey the sheer size of the landscape in *Travelers among Streams and Mountains*, he relied on suggestion—calling on memory and inviting anticipation—rather than description. The blank intervals of space between the three distances act as pauses between changing views. Because the additive images do not physically connect, they are comprehended separately. The viewer is invited to roam freely in imagination, leaping from one distance to the next, from one view to another, through immeasurable space.

As the macrocosmic image of a moral and orderly universe, Northern Sung landscape painting is said to embody contemporary theories of physiognomy as well as the Neo-Confucian philosophy of social order. Kuo Hsi described mountain scenery in anthropomorphic terms: "A mountain has watercourses as its arteries, grass and trees as its hairs, mist and clouds as its complexion. . . . Waters have the mountains as their face, pavilions and kiosks as their eyebrows and eyes, and fishing and angling to give them animation."[63] The great simplicity and directness of Fan's painting style was thought to be a reflection of his open character and generous disposition. Just as the subject of Fan's painting is humble and mundane, its spirit is grand and noble: the great host peak, in Kuo Hsi's words, sits "like a ruler among his subjects, a master among servants."[64]

The unsurpassed grandeur and monumentality of Fan's composition is expressed through the skillful use of scale. Kuo Hsi spoke of the "three degrees of magnitude" (*san-ta*), pointing out that mountains looked large painted next to small trees, which in turn dwarfed human figures.[65] Fan's landscape shows how the use of this leaping scale can dramatically heighten the sense of vastness and space. Lilliputian figures stand beside immense trees, and peaks of cosmic proportions tower over both. The relationship among the "three degrees of magnitude" is conceptual, aesthetic, and psychological rather than physical; it works almost musically, through rhythm, structure, and the harmony of the whole.

In the mid-eleventh century painters freely mixed influences of the early Northern Sung masters, but at the same time they continued to develop increasingly complex representational techniques. So far no visible effort had been made to codify or exactly reproduce earlier techniques; instead they employed them randomly to explore representational effects. In the third quarter of the eleventh century, Kuo Hsi developed Li Ch'eng's rock forms into an exuberantly mysterious mist-filled atmospheric style. Kuo's masterpiece, the large hanging scroll *Early Spring* (*Tsao-ch'un*), dated 1072, in the National Palace Museum, Taipei (fig. 49), represented the triumph of a temperament, as well as of a style. To have been Kuo Hsi, and to have painted what he saw, neither Fan K'uan's severely monumental nor Yen Wen-kuei's miniaturist but dramatic style would have sufficed.

A native of Wen-hsien in northern Honan, Kuo Hsi was made a member of the Imperial Painting Academy during the reign of Emperor Sung Jen-tsung (r. 1023–63) and rose to become the favorite painter of the emperor Sung Shen-tsung (r. 1067–85).[66] His paintings were usually large, intended to decorate screens and walls of the imperial palaces and of the Buddhist and Confucian temples. He was said to have worked with tremendous speed, "completing a composition with a single wave of the arm" (*i-hui erh-ch'eng*). His favorite topics were the infinite faces of the landscape under ever-changing atmospheric conditions, and he gave his paintings such evocative titles as *Morning Mist in Early Spring* (*Tsao-ch'un hsiao-yen*), *Water and Rocks in Wind and Rain* (*Feng-yü shui-shih*), *Mist Rising in Jagged Peaks* (*Yen-sheng luan-shan*), and *Morning Sun above the Treetops* (*Chao-yang shu-shao*).[67]

Fan K'uan's brush technique and use of ink had been severely exact, but Kuo Hsi's, as seen in *Early Spring*, were rich and extravagant. He cast aside clarity of definition in favor of a dramatic interpenetration of solids and voids: landscape elements simultaneously emerge from and recede behind dense, wafting mists. Kuo Hsi's outline, texture strokes, and modeling ink washes fuse into a single technique; thickening-and-thinning brushstrokes in tones ranging from transparent blue-gray to charcoal-black are overlaid so that they run into each other to create a wet, blurry surface. In drawing the bristling ancient trees, he alternated dark and light ink tones, effectively distinguishing the near from the far, cutting across the tops of trees with a veil of mist. Kuo gave detailed instructions for creating this effect. "After the outlines are made clear by dark ink strokes," he advised, "use ink washes mixed with blue to retrace these outlines repeatedly, so that even if the ink outlines are clear, they appear always as if they had just come out of the mist and dew."[68]

Extraordinary also in *Early Spring* is the treatment of light. Kuo observed that mountains changed in appearance depending on whether they stood in full sunlight or in shadow,[69] and he used his ink washes to render this distinction. As in all Chinese paintings, however, *Early Spring* does not indicate a specific light source that casts a shadow in any consistent manner. Through a subtle use of ink that yields a profoundly realistic effect of interpenetrating light and dark values, the mist-enveloped *Early Spring* seems drenched in early morning sunlight—warm, fresh, and radiantly alive.

A complex landscape, *Early Spring* suggests great depth in several parts of its composition, yet the painting remains a composite of compartmentalized pockets of space. The parallel folds of the mountain peaks zigzag to build a compact mass of layered peaks. From one part of the painting to another, the mountain forms, in Kuo Hsi's words, "viewed at a close range have one appearance, viewed from a distance of several miles still another. Every time one moves away, one gets a different view. This is why it is said that the mountain forms change with every step one takes."[70] At the same time Kuo attempted to create a unified composition by linking the different parts of the painting into a rhythmically flowing whole. The cloudlike mountains seem to float in the picture plane: as in Fan K'uan's *Travelers*, spatial recession, which is deep and immeasurable, is implied rather than physically depicted.

As objective description of nature, the winding central mountain mass in *Early Spring* has structural ambiguities that are concealed only by the artful use of mist. As a landscape of the imagination, however, the twisting and turning peaks are truly spellbinding. Ogawa Hiromitsu suggested that in painting mountains like clouds, Kuo painted by visual association and psychological projection.[71] An anecdote recorded by the twelfth-century author Teng Ch'un, in *A Continuation of Painting History* (*Hua-chi*, preface dated 1167):

> Kuo Hsi saw [the eighth-century sculptor Yang Hui-chih's sculpted wall landscapes] and derived new ideas from them. He told the plasterer not to use the trowel, but to throw the plaster on the wall, leaving undisturbed whatever concave or convex surfaces were thus created. After the plaster dried, he used ink to modify the forms [of the plaster], rendering mountain peaks, forests, and valleys, and adding towered buildings and human figures, making them look as if they were made by heaven.[72]

In addition to describing nature objectively or reflecting a state of mind, Kuo Hsi in *Early Spring* added a further dimension to Northern Sung landscape art through his occult Taoist's belief in magic and power. According to his son Kuo Ssu, Kuo Hsi "had in his youth devoted himself to the study of Taoism, learning 'the breathing out of the old and the swallowing of the new' and keeping company with religious Taoists and Buddhist monks."[73] Taoists practiced the so-called inner elixir in an attempt to exert control over nature; to quote from a thirteenth-century mystic, Yü Yen, "If a person seizes for himself the secret springs of heaven and earth in order thereby to compound for himself the great elixir of the golden fluid, he will then exist coeval with heaven and earth from beginning to end, and he will be called the true man."[74] In creating a macrocosmic vision of the universe, Kuo Hsi became, for the moment of his creative expression, coequal with Creation itself.

OPPOSITE PAGE: Fig. 49. Kuo Hsi, *Early Spring* (*Tsao-ch'un*). Dated 1072. Hanging scroll, ink and light color on silk. 158.3 x 108.1 cm (5 ft. 2 3/8 in. x 3 ft. 6 1/2 in.). National Palace Museum, Taipei

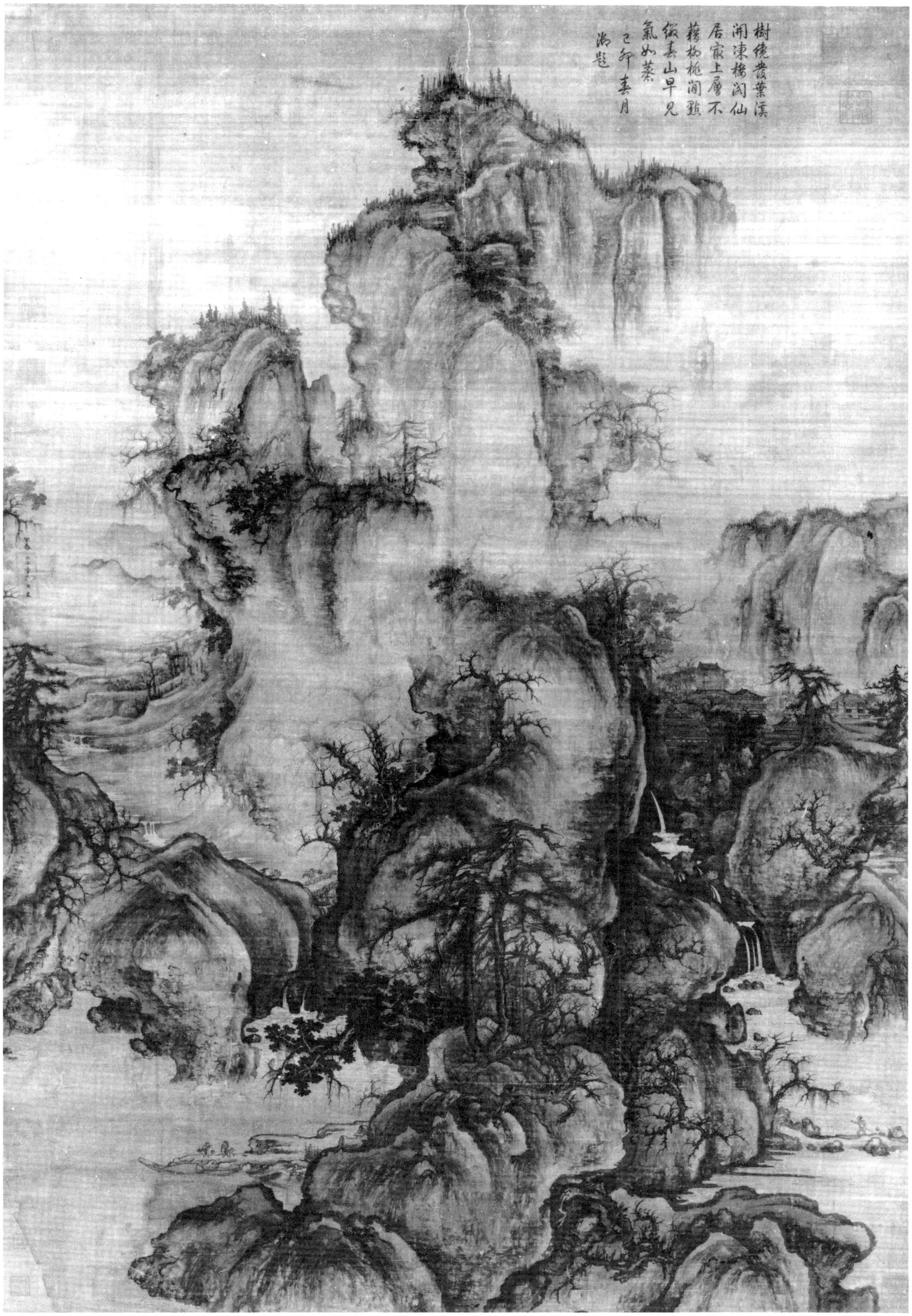

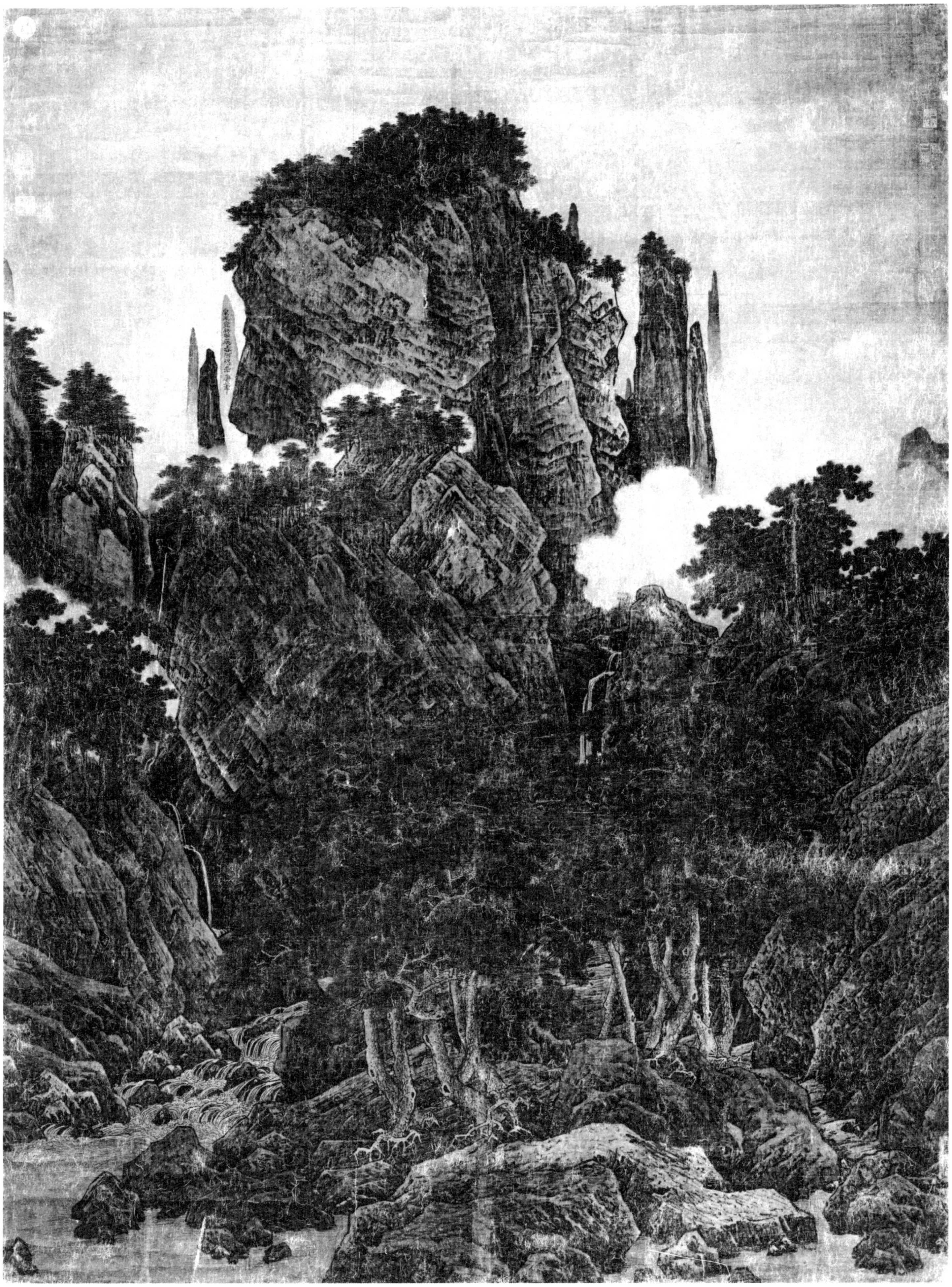

Fig. 50. Li T'ang, *A Myriad Ravines, Wind in the Pines* (*Wan-ho sung-feng-t'u*). Dated 1124. Hanging scroll, ink and light color on silk. 188.7 x 139.8 cm (6 ft. 2 1/4 in. x 4 ft. 7 in.). National Palace Museum, Taipei

## *The First Revival*

The most dynamic phase of Northern Sung landscape painting ended with Kuo Hsi's death in about 1090. Coinciding with the completion of a full stylistic cycle of developing naturalism in the second half of the eleventh century was the rise of the scholar-artist aesthetic. Greatly concerned with the distinction between the work of a scholar and that of an artisan, this aesthetic stressed self-expression over representational skills. Apart from rhetoric two important factors determined the method of a scholar-artist: as a literary artist he excelled in calligraphy, so he relied on calligraphy to express himself in painting; and as an antiquarian he learned as much from art as from nature, looking to the past for inspiration and renewal.

The nobleman-collector-painter Chao Ling-jang (fl. ca. 1070–1100), for instance, was said to have followed T'ang masters—Pi Hung (fl. ca. 742–56), Wei Yen (fl. late 7th–early 8th century), Li Ssu-hsün (651–716), and Wang Wei—as his models.[75] As a cousin of Emperor Sung Shen-tsung, Chao was obliged to live within the environs of K'ai-feng and therefore never had the opportunity to visit the great northern mountain ranges that had inspired the earlier Northern Sung landscape masters. By turning from monumental realism to intimate lyricism, painting the romantic dream world of a city-bound artist, Chao became a forerunner of the introspective landscape mode of the Southern Sung.

Among the leaders of scholar-artists of this period were Li Kung-lin (ca. 1049–1106) and Mi Fu. As the foremost figure painter of his time, Li studied and copied T'ang and pre-T'ang models, distilling and transforming them in a neoclassical *pai-miao* line (pure-line drawing) style. As the preeminent connoisseur and critic, Mi advocated simplicity and "naturalness" in landscape art; he rediscovered Tung Yüan's Southern style of landscape painting, thus anticipating Southern Sung developments, if not in technique, then in taste and psychological expression.

These developments resulted in great change and diversity in landscape painting in the early twelfth century, which began with the reign of the artist-emperor Sung Hui-tsung (r. 1101–25) and continued

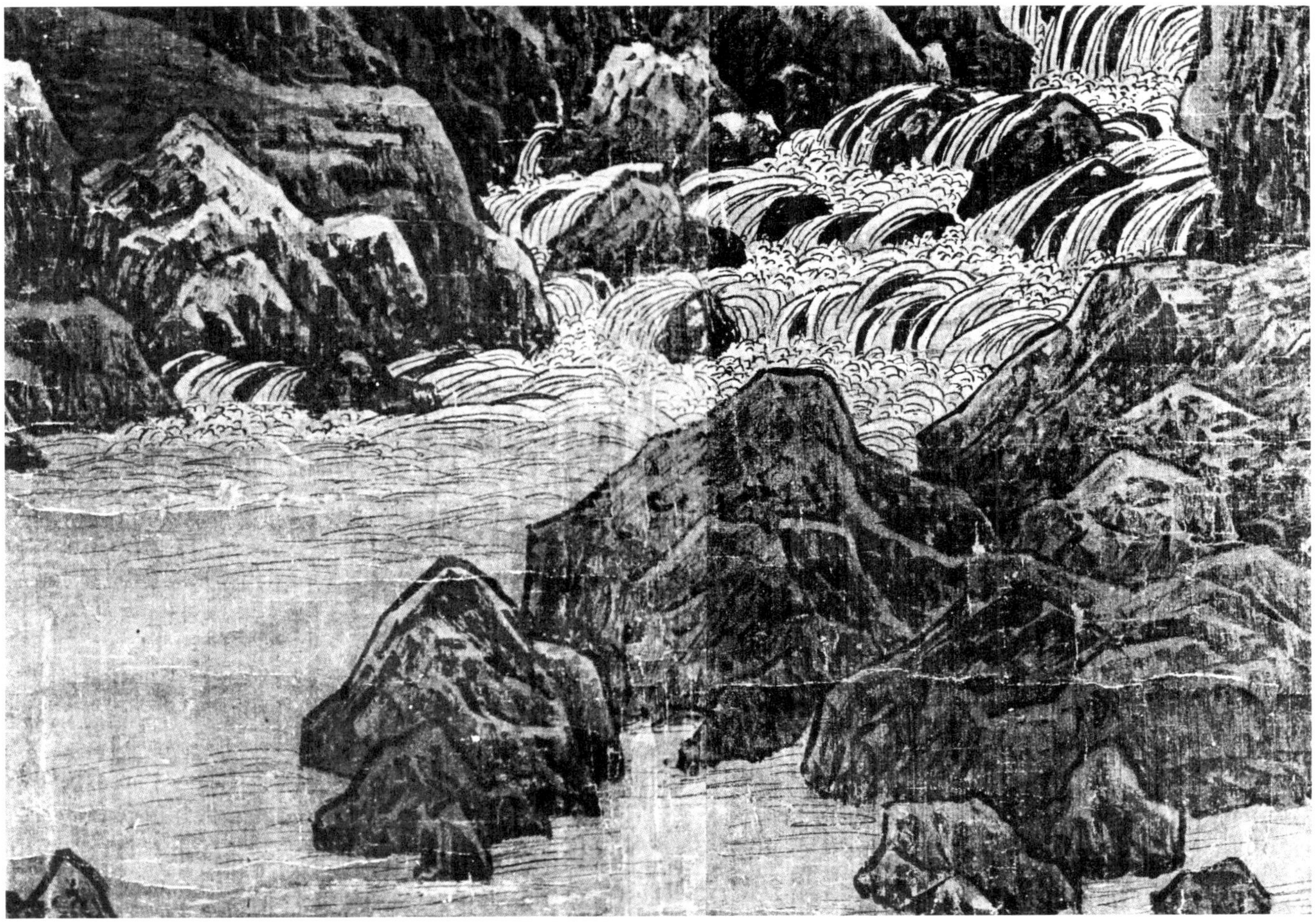

Fig. 50a. Detail, fig. 50

through the traumatic sack of K'ai-feng in 1126 by the Jurchen Chin, a Tungusic people who originated in eastern Manchuria and created the Chin dynasty in 1115. In a colophon to the writings of Han Cho (fl. early 12th century), a member of Sung Hui-tsung's Imperial Painting Academy, *Collection of Ch'un-ch'üan's Essays on Landscape Painting* (*Shan-shui Ch'un-ch'üan chi*; epilogue dated 1121), Chang Huai provided the first complete theoretical statement of the monumental landscape painting style:

> Painting distinguishes the "black" of heaven from the "yellow" of the earth, and discloses the secrets of the yin and yang of creation. . . . Whatever can be comprehended through the emblems and numbers of the *Book of Changes* [*I-ching*] may be represented in their physical forms. . . . Since man is the most sentient of all the myriad creatures, he alone is suited for painting. When a painter attains the principles, he is able to describe the wonders of the things; but when the principles are obscure, the truth of things will be lost. Why is this so? Because [painting] has to do with the heavenly nature [of things] and its secret springs. This nature receives its physical forms from heaven, and its secret springs may be operated by both men and gods. Once the spring sets in motion, a myriad transformations will take place. If a painter can grasp the principles and by following the nature of things discern their wonderful subtleties, his mind will come to meet and his spirit will become one [with the things]. Then, quietly meditating movement or stillness with his painting brush, casting it forward to depict the myriad emblematic forms, he will create both lively form and substance, as well as spirited breath [*ch'i*] and resonance [*yün*], in his painting. If the painter is ignorant of the principles, his mind will be driven by his emotions, and his own nature will be moved by things. Lost in the dust of the world, and distracted by motives of profit and expediency, he will be a mere slave to his brush and ink. How can he speak of capturing the truth [*chen*] of heaven and earth?[76]

That this admirable explanation of the monumental landscape painting style should appear at a time when the style was already in decline only proves the maxim that theories justify rather than inspire creativity. Han Cho's essays, to which Chang Huai's remarks were appended, represent a catalogue and description in overwhelming detail of the prevailing forms and techniques in early twelfth-century landscape painting. Han Cho enumerates, for instance, the various kinds of texture patterns for modeling rocks:

> There is the *p'i-ma* [draping hemp fibers] *ts'un*, the *tien-ts'o* [dotting and crossing] *ts'un*. . . , the *cho-t'a* [cutting] *ts'un*, the *heng* [horizontal] *ts'un*, and the *yün-erh-lien-shui* [uniform and connected, waterlike] *ts'un*. For every dot and every stroke there are ancient and modern schools, and special manners and rules exist.[77]

Han Cho's list marks an early effort to describe and catalogue representational techniques as graphic formulas. What scholars now recognize as Fan K'uan's pointillistic technique is here called a dotting (*t'ien*) pattern, while that of Li T'ang (ca. 1070s–ca. 1150s), which features a dot enlarged to a broad angular stroke, is a cutting (*cho-t'a*) method. *P'i-ma* is used to describe round, stringy, ropelike parallel brushstrokes; *yün-erh-lien-shui* refers to thinner parallel texture strokes.

Han Cho did not connect specific texture patterns with individual painters or even painting traditions. He merely listed the various techniques as part of the generic landscape painting vocabulary. Only the graphically vivid term *p'i-ma* remained a familiar designation in later painting literature; Han's other terms were either dropped or replaced by more colorful ones, such as *yü-tien* (raindrop) or *fu-p'i* (ax-cut).[78]

Li T'ang, from Ho-yang, northern Honan province, who had entered the Imperial Painting Academy under Emperor Sung Hui-tsung around 1120, later rejoined the Southern Sung court in Lin-an (Hang-chou) and was promoted to higher office under Emperor Sung Kao-tsung. In the large hanging scroll *A Myriad Ravines, Wind in the Pines* (*Wan-ho sung-feng t'u*), dated 1124, in the National Palace Museum, Taipei (figs. 50, 50a), the early Li T'ang rejected Kuo Hsi's extravagantly atmospheric style in favor of a more somber, tactile treatment of the great host mountain so prominent in the paintings of Fan K'uan. Developing Fan's stippled texture dots into broader cutting strokes, Li constructed his forms with layers of hatching strokes of varying sizes and ink values, creating a wet, shimmering rock surface. When compared with Fan K'uan's and Kuo Hsi's works, Li's composition represents a further step toward visual and spatial continuity in landscape. Li's mountain forms, for example, are broken up into many more facets than those of Fan K'uan, and they are more irregularly shaped. Frontally viewed mountains and trees move back sequentially and continuously through space in *Wind in the Pines*; the trees range diagonally across the picture plane, steadily diminishing in size, from the lower half of the picture to the top. Enhancing the feeling of depth, the great pine trees in the foreground occupy nearly half the height of the large composition; as a result, the mountain peaks seem much reduced, an illusion increasingly common in paintings of the twelfth and thirteenth centuries. In earlier Northern Sung vertical compositions, whenever the high-distance view was shown, foreground trees were usually kept small, emphasizing the height of the vertical mountain peaks; large foreground trees appeared only in panoramic, flat-distance views, where an impression of depth was the primary goal. The more naturalistic scale found in Li T'ang's painting is gained, however, only at the expense of the feeling of infinite space. In exchanging the immeasurable vastness of the earlier Northern Sung landscapes for a more limited, more realistic view, Li moved painting a step closer, in 1124, to the intimate landscapes of the Southern Sung period.

About the same time that Li T'ang painted *Wind in the Pines*, Li Kung-nien painted the somber and restrained *Winter Landscape* (*Tung-ching shan-shui*), now at The Art Museum, Princeton University (fig. 51). According to the *Painting Catalogue of the Hsüan-ho Era [1119–25]* (*Hsüan-ho hua-p'u*), of 1120, Li served as a prison official in Hang-chou, later capital of the Southern Sung; one of Li's paintings in Sung Hui-tsung's collection showed "a winter sun slowly emerging through the mist . . . with shapes appearing and disappearing in vast emptiness, hovering between existence and nothingness."[79] In the Princeton painting, which anticipates the Southern Sung Academy landscape style, the stippling strokes on its central peaks are a simplified version of Fan K'uan's texture dots, while the trees and the small overhanging cliff in the foreground follow the Li Ch'eng–Kuo Hsi tradition. In his rock forms, modeled with clearly defined outlines and texture strokes, and evenly graduated ink wash, Li Kung-nien seems to ignore the influence of Kuo Hsi. The landscape elements in the Princeton composition are greatly reduced in scope; mountain forms are linked and stacked in layers at the top, but fade and disappear into the mist at the base. The overlapping triangular motifs, each a frontal and discrete form, range through space continuously, without a receding ground plane. As a transitional work between the Northern and Southern Sung, Li Kung-nien's landscape strikes a curious halfway expression between the monumental and the intimate. Hauntingly beautiful, the work speaks eloquently for the anxieties of a troubled time. While the innovation of continuous spatial recession makes the landscape more naturalistic than its predecessors, the dwarfed human figures carried over from the Northern Sung idiom imbue the wintry scene with an unreal, eery, and bitterly desolate feeling.

As both the Sung empire and its official landscape style at its Imperial Painting Academy underwent dramatic transformation, Li T'ang's long career spanned and survived the change. According to Teng Ch'un, "Li T'ang, from Ho-yang, came to [the Southern Sung capital] Lin-an [Hang-chou] after the upheaval, when he was already about eighty years old. Kuang-yao [Emperor Sung Kao-tsung] was extremely fond of his landscapes."[80] Most later scholars, following Hsia Wen-yen in *Treasured Mirror of Painting* (*T'u-hui pao-chien*) of 1365, assumed that Li had rejoined the Painting Academy in Hang-chou in the Chien-yen era (1127–30), in the early years of Sung Kao-tsung's reign.[81] In a recent article, "A Tentative Theory Concerning Li T'ang's Moving to the South, and the Change in [Landscape] Style after the Reestablishment of the [Imperial Painting] Academy" (1981), however, Suzuki Kei raises the possibility that the Painting Academy was not reestablished in the south until the Shao-hsing era (1131–62), and that Li T'ang did not resettle in Hang-chou until the mid-1150s, when he was about eighty years old,[82] as reported by Teng Ch'un.

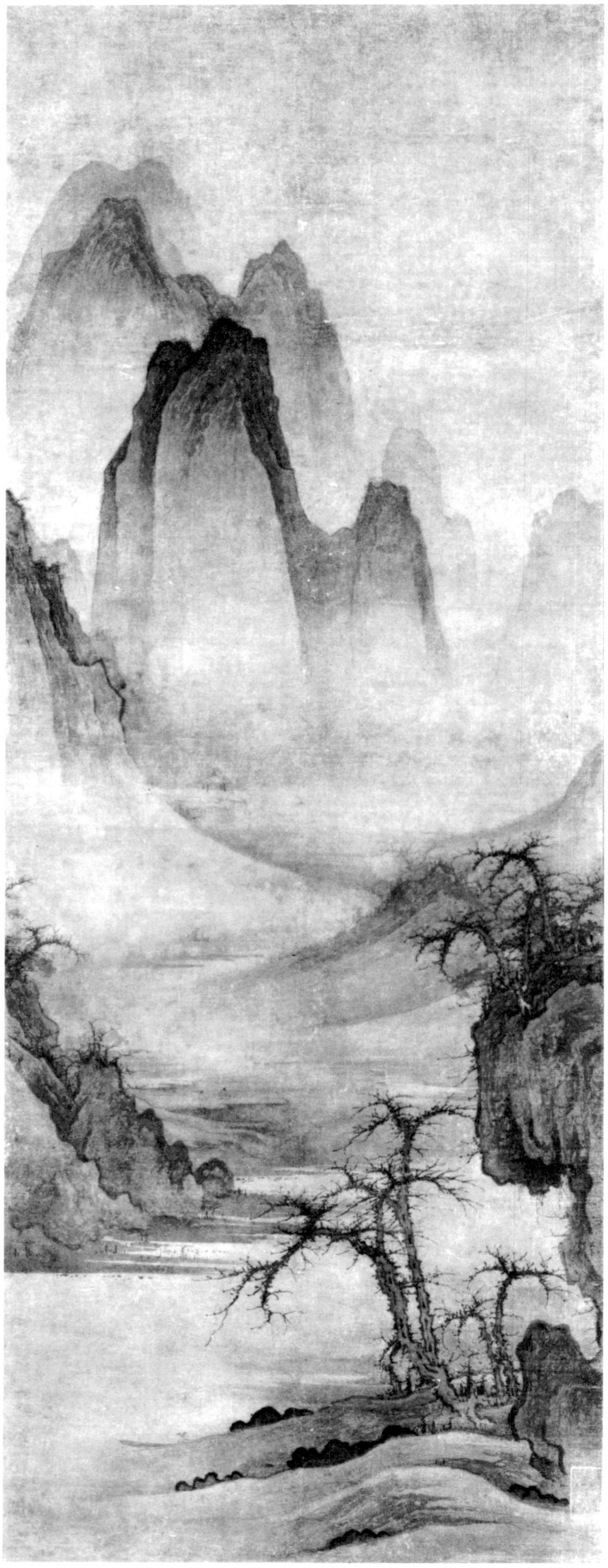

Fig. 51. Li Kung-nien, *Winter Landscape* (*Tung-ching shan-shui*). Undated, ca. 1120. Hanging scroll, ink and light color on silk. 129.5 x 48.2 cm (4 ft. 3 in. x 19 in.). The Art Museum, Princeton University

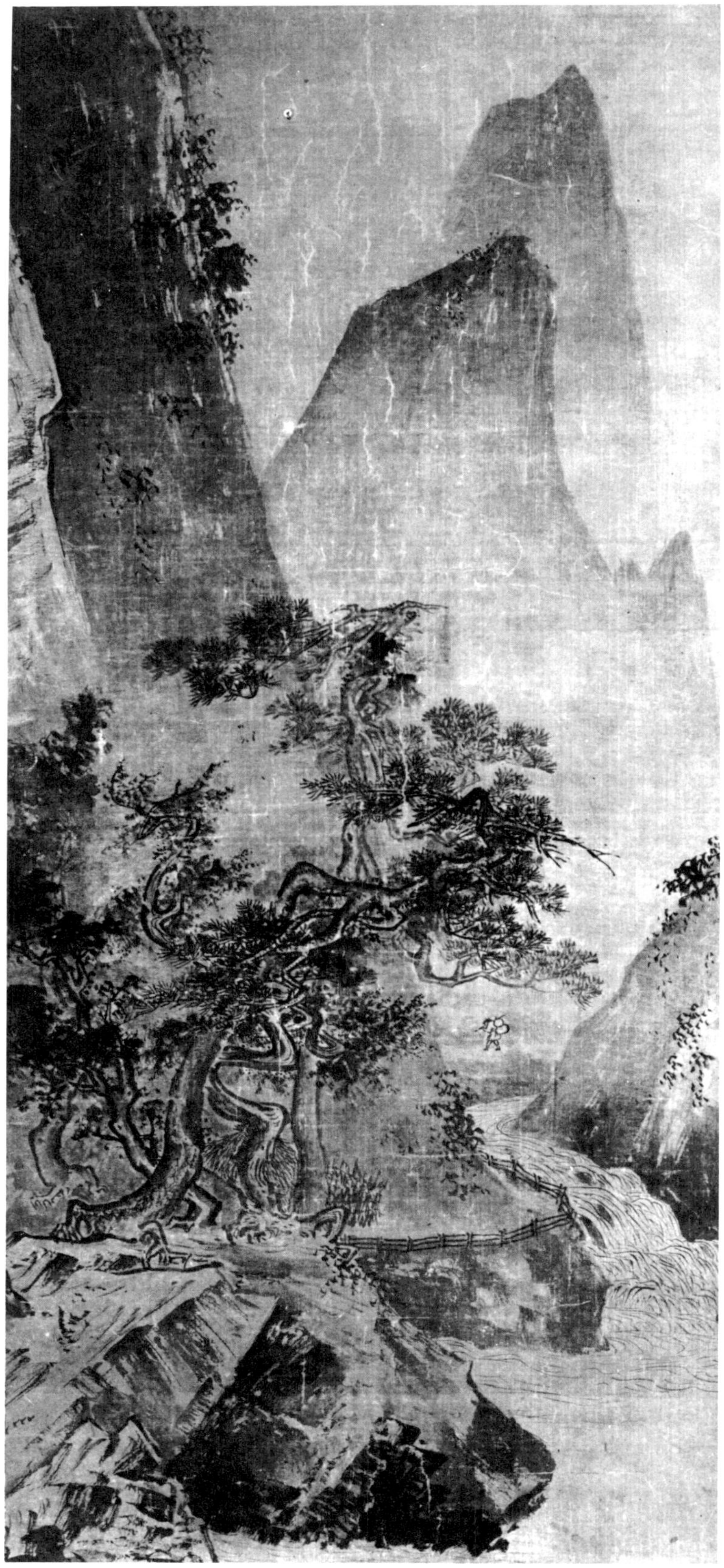

Fig. 52. Li T'ang, *Autumn*. Undated, ca. 1150s. Hanging scroll, ink on silk. 98.0 x 43.5 cm (3 ft. 2⅝ in. x 17⅛ in.). Kōtō-in, Daitoku-ji, Kyoto

A pair of landscape hanging scrolls, representing autumn and winter, in the Kōtō-in, Daitoku-ji, Kyoto (fig. 52), has been seen as examples of Li T'ang's late (Southern Sung) style, ever since Shimada Shujiro (in 1950) discovered a partially erased signature of Li T'ang on the *Autumn* scene.[83] The attribution has troubled some scholars, simply because of the apparent gap in style that exists between the large *Wind in the Pines* of 1124 in Taipei and the Kōtō-in paintings.[84] If the latter landscapes were to be dated in the 1150s, some thirty years later than the earlier work, as Suzuki suggests, however, they would serve well to explain how the protean genius Li T'ang had led Sung Kao-tsung's Painting Academy to formulate a typical Southern Sung landscape style.

Structurally the Kōtō-in Li T'ang compares closely with Li Kung-nien's *Winter Landscape*, which is dated about 1120 (cf. fig. 51): individual elements overlap, but there is no physical connection or receding ground plane between them. The powerful *cho-t'a* modeling, in describing the rugged, chipped-off facets of the rock surface, effectively combines texturing and shading in a single stroke. These brushstrokes vary in shape and size; they bring out the glistening hardness and individuality of the rocks; they are anything but a stylized, pattern-conscious *fu-p'i* (ax-cut) convention. In enlarged details they show the same tactile strength and display the same mental discipline and concentration as those of the earlier *Myriad Ravines* (cf. fig. 50a). The foreground trees in the Kōtō-in landscapes, now extending to two-thirds of the height of the painting, have replaced the earlier Northern Sung heroic mountain peaks as the focal point of the composition. The scale of the landscape is intimate, and the proportions of the elements within the painting are natural. The tensions caused by the conflicting modes of monumental and natural, as seen in Li Kung-nien's *Winter Landscape*, have disappeared.

Before the age of fifty Li T'ang had painted in a conservative mode, returning to an earlier model, Fan K'uan, in order to recapture the old monumental vision, but restating the earlier conventions in such a way as to incorporate new tastes and visual discoveries. In the Kōtō-in landscapes the grand old master Li now continued to paint the same shimmering rocks and great pine trees with a simpler style that expressed the new taste for natural space and a narrower, more concentrated vision. Once accomplished, Li T'ang's new style became the standard landscape idiom for Southern Sung Academy painters.

## *The Southern Sung Idiom*

By the mid-twelfth century the shift from monumental to intimate was complete, often expressed on personal objects of much diminished size from the grand six-foot scrolls of the Northern Sung. In an anonymous fan painting, *Landscape in the Style of Fan K'uan* (*Fang Fan K'uan shan-shui*), dated about 1150, in the Edward L. Elliott Family Collection at The Art Museum, Princeton University (no. 3), the elements of Fan K'uan's *Travelers* (cf. fig. 48) have been rearranged and adapted to the fan format in a visually unified, lyrical structure. The Fan K'uan idiom was divided here into three distinct types of brushstrokes: thickening-and-thinning contour strokes, stippled raindrop dots, and foliage dots mixed with branch patterns on the mountaintops. Though conventionalized, these brush patterns are representationally successful. In scale and spatial relationship the mountain and tree forms in the fan painting follow Li T'ang's *Myriad Ravines* (cf. fig. 50). Although Fan K'uan's compartmentalized treatment of space has been replaced by a unified composition, the landscape elements remain frontal and additive. The mountaintops recede in overlapping silhouettes, but no single ground plane links or contains the elements; they are held together only by the mist that curls through the valley. With the central mountain peaks placed to one side so that the scenery stretches out into a wide view, the Elliott fan represents a typical Southern Sung "one-corner" composition, which gradually replaced the Northern Sung style of landscape.

In 1121 Han Cho amended Kuo Hsi's principles of landscape composition—the flat-distance, middle-distance, high-distance system—by proposing an alternative set of three distances:

> From a nearby shore of a broad expanse of water, viewing far-reaching distant mountains is called the "wide distance" [*k'uo-yüan*]. When wilderness mists are vast and hazy, wild streams faintly cross and then disappear, it is called the "lost distance" [*mi-yüan*]. When the scenery and objects diminish to the extreme, becoming tiny and drifting away in vast space, it is called the "remote distance" [*yu-yüan*].[85]

Han Cho's scheme, a division based less on physical space than on atmosphere and its psychological dimensions, heralded the more personal visions of the Southern Sung painters, who emphasized the lyrical moment. The wide-distance scheme developed from the Northern Sung flat-distance, panoramic view. Having moved south of the Yangtze, where the great river and its many tributaries dominated the lives of the inhabitants, Southern Sung painters naturally tended to specialize in the river scene. In the preferred Southern Sung formats of fans, album leaves, and handscrolls, the wide-distance view stretched out diagonally to become a one-corner composition.

The early Southern Sung preoccupation with atmosphere and lyrical mood in landscape is clearly seen in the set of horizontal compositions *Eight Views of the Hsiao and Hsiang Rivers* (*Hsiao-Hsiang Pa-ching*) by Wang Hung (fl. ca. 1131–61), dated about 1150, in the Edward L. Elliott Family Collection at The Art Museum, Princeton University (no. 4). The region of the Hsiao and Hsiang rivers, which flow into Lake Tung-t'ing in Hunan province, is renowned for rain and misty scenery. According to literary records, the theme of the Eight Views of the Hsiao and Hsiang Rivers was first painted by Sung Ti, a contemporary of Kuo Hsi's, and like Kuo a follower of the Li Ch'eng tradition.[86] Shen Kua's *Notes Written in Meng-ch'i* (*Meng-ch'i pi-t'an*) gives the following poetic titles: "Wild Geese Descending to Sandbar" (*P'ing-sha yen-lo*); "Returning Sail off Distant Shore" (*Yüan-p'u fan-kuei*); "Mountain Market, Clear with Rising Mist" (*Shan-shih ch'ing-lan*); "River and Sky in Evening Snow" (*Chiang-shan mu-hsüeh*); "Autumn Moon over Lake Tung-t'ing" (*Tung-t'ing ch'iu-yüeh*); "Night Rain on Hsiao and Hsiang" (*Hsiao-Hsiang yeh-yü*); "Evening Bell from Mist-shrouded Temple" (*Yen-ssu wan-chung*); "Fishing Village in Evening Glow" (*Yü-ts'un lo-chao*).[87]

In Wang Hung's interpretations of the scenes, the artist's signature appears at the beginning (the right border) of "Night Rain." As arranged by the late Ming owners of the present double scrolls, the eight scenes appear as follows: "Night Rain," "Autumn Moon," "Geese Descending," "Returning Sail," "Evening Bell," "Evening Glow," "Mountain Market," and "Evening Snow."

Little is known about Wang Hung, except that he was active in the Shao-hsing era (1131–62) and that he painted in the Fan K'uan tradition.[88] In the eight horizontal landscapes, which probably were derived from Sung Ti's compositions, the artist borrowed liberally from Northern Sung landscape idioms to create a variety of special and frequently complex pictorial effects. In "Night Rain" the flat-distance view extending diagonally into a wide distance recalls the late eleventh-century horizontal composition of Chao Ling-jang; the boulders in the foreground are done in the Fan K'uan idiom. The dark forest violently whipped up by the storm and the steam rising densely from the ground seem to glisten and shimmer with a rain-drenched surface. In "Autumn Moon," where the open sky appears cool and clear, the rock's ax-cut texture strokes recall Li T'ang's crisp, crystalline forms. The bare-branched trees in "Geese Descending" derive from Li Ch'eng's; the piling-up of the sandy banks and low-lying hills vertically along the picture plane shows the apparent influence of an earlier flat-distance composition of the eleventh century. "Returning Sail," a diagonal composition showing the great distance the sailboat has traveled from the lower left corner of the painting to the upper right, is a good example of Han Cho's wide-distance view; the season depicted seems to be spring, and the painting seems to illustrate Han Cho's words "spring mountains are beautiful and seductive, as if smiling."[89] The tree and mountain forms recall those of Kuo Hsi's *Early Spring* (cf. fig. 49). In "Evening Bell" a scholar and his page stand by the shore under two tall pine trees, listening to the distant temple bell reverberating in the mountain peaks across the river; and in "Evening Glow" a fishing boat returns to a bay aglow under a russet sky. In both compositions the pointed craggy mountains set off against a broad river scene are reminiscent of Yen Wen-kuei's style (cf. fig. 44). "Mountain Market" shows bustling activities in a mountain village nestled in a valley under a sunny but hazy sky; its style again resembles Fan K'uan's. Finally, in "Evening Snow," the frozen mountains, the trees, and the river under the cover of snow are dark and peaceful; the trees and mountains derive from both Li Ch'eng and Fan K'uan.

Wang Hung's survey of Northern Sung landscape idioms parallels Han Cho's attempt, discussed previously, to catalogue representational techniques as graphic formulas. In Wang Hung's paintings the reduction of earlier techniques to "brush methods" serves new representational purposes. Wang did not consciously copy, or re-create, the styles of the earlier masters. The diagonal river scenes are distinctly new, pointing to the Southern Sung Academy compositions of Ma Yüan (fl. ca. 1190–1264) and Hsia Kuei (fl. 1st half 13th century; fig. 54). The sophisticated pictorial descriptions, with their complex seasonal, atmospheric, and coloristic effects, expand and develop the image of the poetic titles. Compared to Kuo Hsi's atmospheric *Early Spring*, Wang Hung's riverscapes are unified compositions viewed from a consistent vantage point. Although no ground plane actually connects the elements of each scene, the treatment of space is unified and continuous. Frontal silhouettes of mountains and trees, floating and fading into the mist, move sequentially and diagonally into the distance.

The handscroll *Dream Journey through the Hsiao and Hsiang Rivers* (*Hsiao-Hsiang wo-yu t'u*) by a certain Master Li (Li-sheng), dated about 1170, in the Tokyo National Museum (fig. 53), is another important representation of the Hsiao-Hsiang river scene. Suzuki Kei, in "Concerning the Handscroll *Dream Journey through the Hsiao and Hsiang Rivers*" (1973), suggests that this Li, a Southern Sung professional painter working in the landscape tradition of Tung Yüan, was possibly related to the great Northern Sung painter Li Kung-lin.[90] The scroll—according to one of its colophons, dated 1171—was painted for an old retired

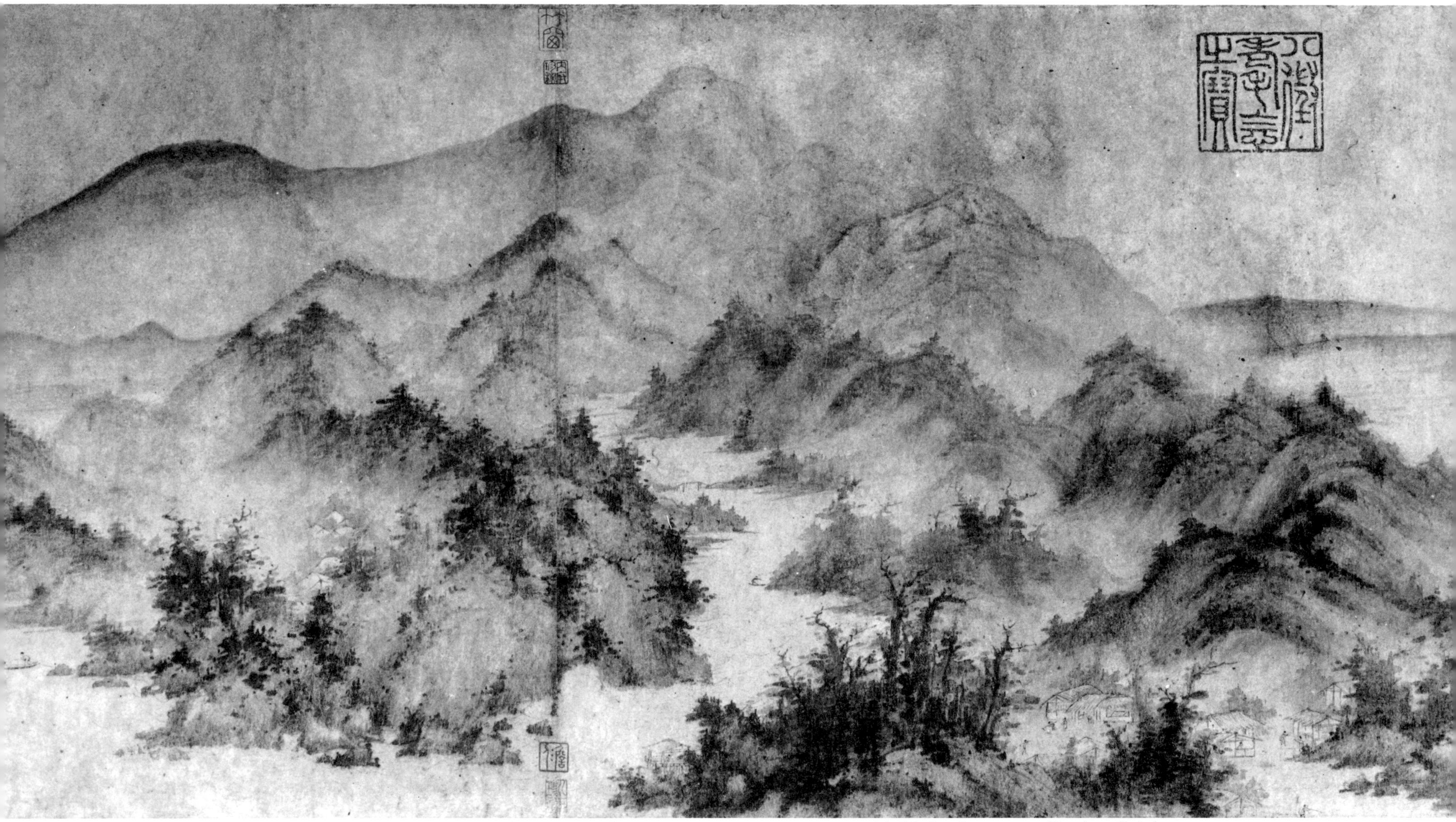

Fig. 53. Li-sheng, detail, *Dream Journey through the Hsiao and Hsiang Rivers* (*Hsiao-Hsiang wo-yu t'u*). Undated, ca. 1170. Handscroll, ink on paper. 30.3 x 403.6 cm (11⅞ in. x 13 ft. 2⅞ in.). Tokyo National Museum

Ch'an Buddhist priest, Yün-ku, in Wu-hsing, Chekiang province, who "for thirty years as a mendicant monk had visited almost all the famous mountains and rivers . . . but regretted that he never saw Hsiao and Hsiang [rivers]," so now, with this scroll, "without leaving home, the master could journey to Hsiao and Hsiang." Another writer (colophon dated 1170) spoke of the psychological dimension in viewing such an imaginary journey: "People of the past could see painting in a collapsed wall. It is not that a collapsed wall can paint; it is how the viewer's mind meets with it, and a painting emerges."[91] The painting, executed in faint ink and pale wash, shows a vast remote-distance view of tiny overlapping triangular mountain silhouettes drifting away in space. This dreamy, open landscape is a superbly rational image of the mind, with generalized mountain forms in a unified spatial continuum, overlapping triangular mountain motifs and jutting sandbanks neatly aligned on a diagonal across the picture plane, and individual linking and turning mountain forms as frontal silhouettes floating and dissolving in a mist, in parallel vertical planes.

A fan painting in the Museum of Fine Arts, Boston, *Sailboat in the Rain* (*Feng-yü kuei-chou*; fig. 54) by Hsia Kuei, who was from Ch'ien-t'ang, Chekiang province, and served as a leading court painter (*tai-chao*) in the early thirteenth century, sums up the taste and accomplishment of the Southern Sung Imperial Painting Academy in about 1200. Hsia Kuei inherited and formalized not only Li T'ang's ax-cut texture strokes, but also Li's favorite tree motifs, a powerful duet of opposing or intertwining pine trees and scrub oaks, as seen in the Kōtō-in *Autumn* landscape (cf. fig. 52). In the Boston fan the artist viewed nature through the microcosm of two or three trees and one or two rocks. The drawing is precise and economical; the visual experience is totally concentrated: windblown and rain-drenched trees occupy the foreground; a

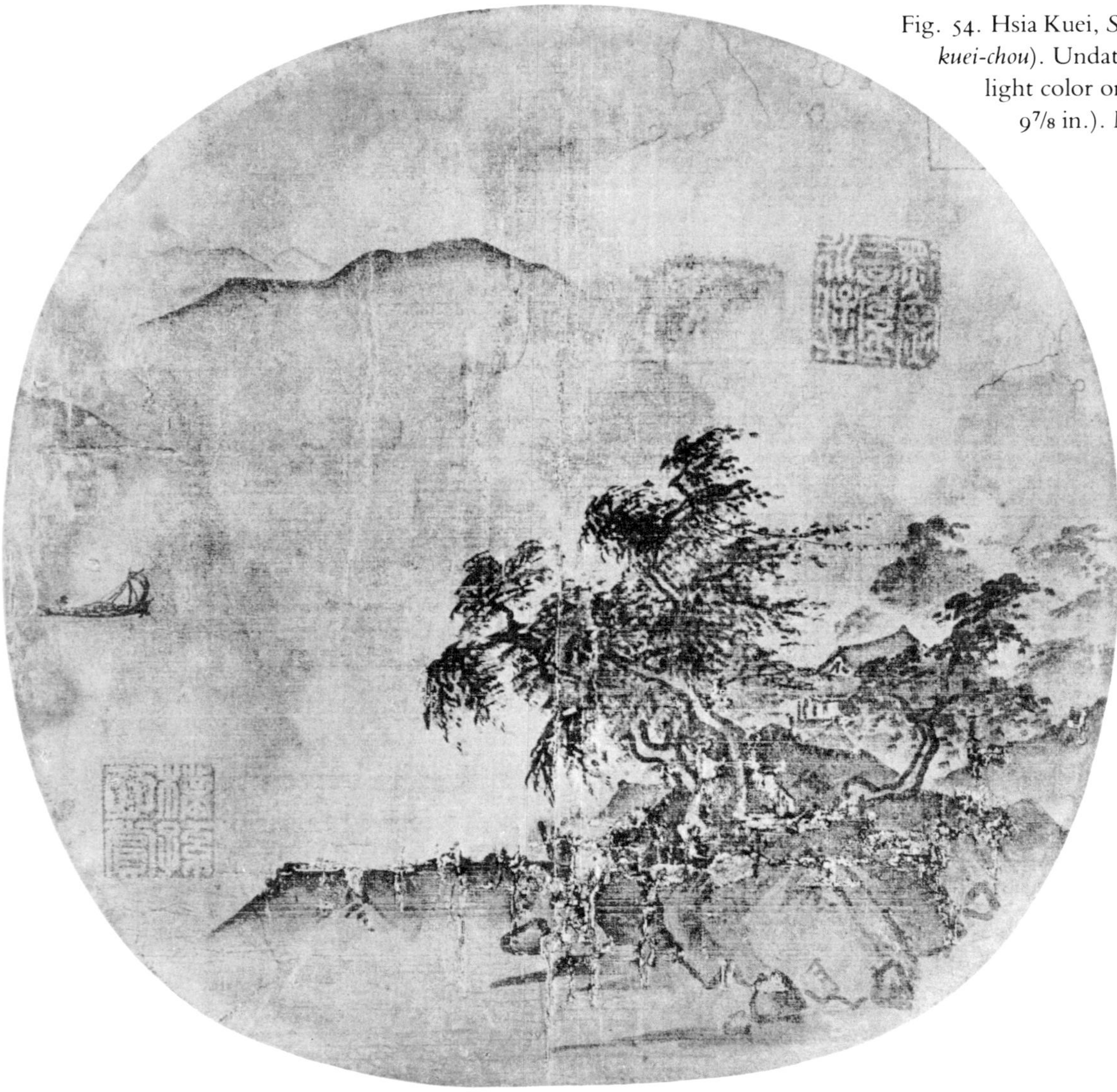

Fig. 54. Hsia Kuei, *Sailboat in the Rain* (*Feng-yü kuei-chou*). Undated, ca. 1200. Fan, ink and light color on silk. 23.9 x 25.1 cm ($9^3/_8$ x $9^7/_8$ in.). Museum of Fine Arts, Boston

tiny skiff sails swiftly in the wind in the middle distance; two faint distant mountain silhouettes, like thin eyebrows, mark the mist-covered distant shore. Despite the painter's total commitment to the exact rendering of nature, no superfluous description is allowed. No receding ground plane (or water surface) connects the shorelines; silhouettes of mountains and shores appear to float and fade into an infinite void.

This reductionist approach, favored by the Southern Sung academy painters, found a religious expression in the works of the thirteenth-century Ch'an Buddhist monk painters. Yü-chien's rendering of one of Eight Views of the Hsiao and Hsiang Rivers, *Mountain Market, Clear with Rising Mist* (*Shan-shih ch'ing-lan*), dated about 1250, in the Tokyo National Museum (see page 228), seems to emphasize not only spontaneity in execution, but also a religious belief in instantaneous communication that ultimately denies both form and technique. The broken and fused brushstrokes, mixing charcoal-black with pale and translucent ink tones, describe a vibrant mist-filled space. In visual structure Yü-chien's painting marks an important step beyond the works discussed so far. Yü-chien's abbreviated mountain forms are no longer silhouettes viewed in parallel vertical planes, as seen in Master Li's *Dream Journey through the Hsiao and Hsiang Rivers*. In spite of their blurred and indistinct outlines, Yü-chien's ink blotches clearly represent solid, three-dimensional landscape forms. Behind the veil of mist, these forms are foreshortened, fused together, and physically integrated and contained by a receding ground plane.

This decisive change in the visual structure of landscape painting in about 1250 can be confirmed by archaeologically recovered works dating roughly to the same period. The visual structure of landscape painting in the late twelfth and early thirteenth centuries is clearly shown by a number of landscape

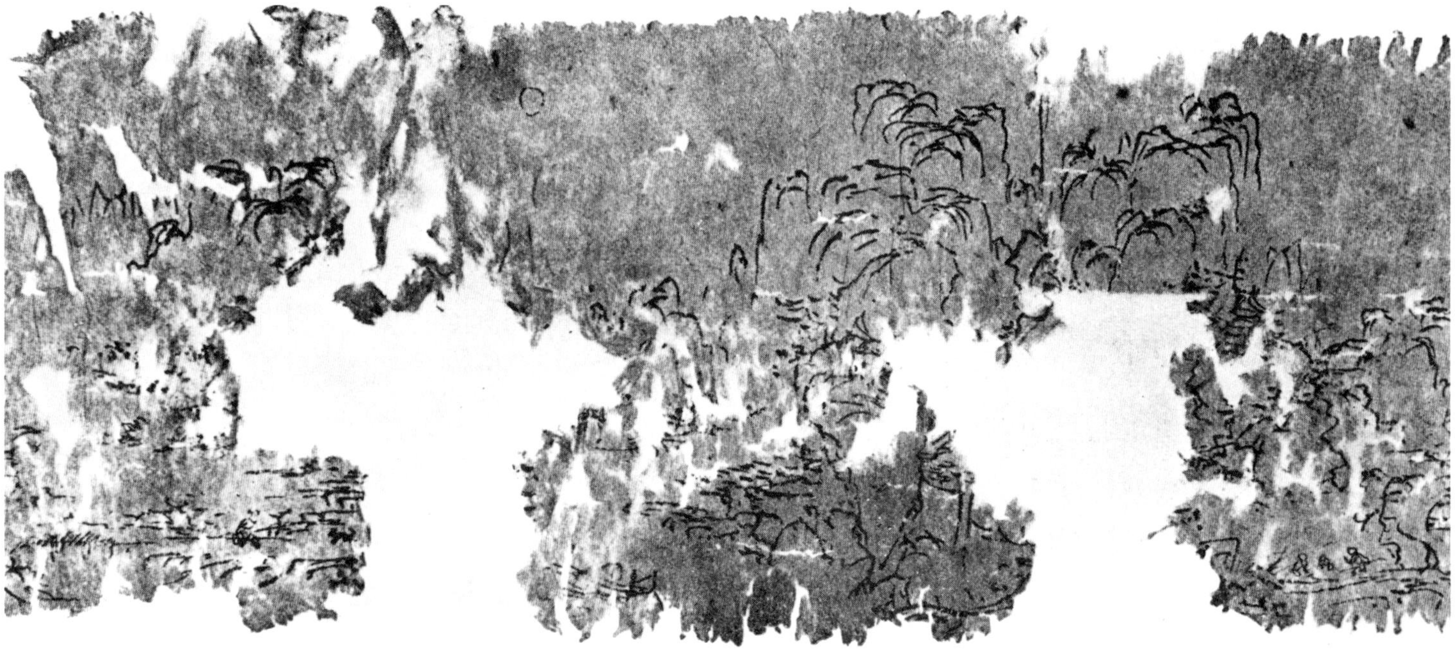

Fig. 55. Anonymous, *Landscape* (*Shan-shui*). Undated, late 12th–early 13th century. Silk fragment, from Kara-khoto

fragments discovered at the Central Asian site Kara-khoto, dated before 1226.[92] The largest of these (fig. 55) shows, in a horizontal format, a range of mountains rising in two crescendos. Traveling figures dot the foreground, mountain paths lead into the middle distance, and towering peaks fill two-thirds of the picture's height. The sketchy landscape is drawn with great sensitivity. The artist began at the mountaintop with contour strokes, building both to the left and to the right, until mountain spines emerged; the result suggests an organically complex and visually fused mountain mass. Interestingly this complex formation is limited to the upper half of the mountain; the artist simply let each mountain motif, viewed frontally, fade into mist and water, thus avoiding the problem of building a fully articulated mountain base. The composition is both harmonious and continuous: the rising and falling peaks range sequentially, and their silhou-

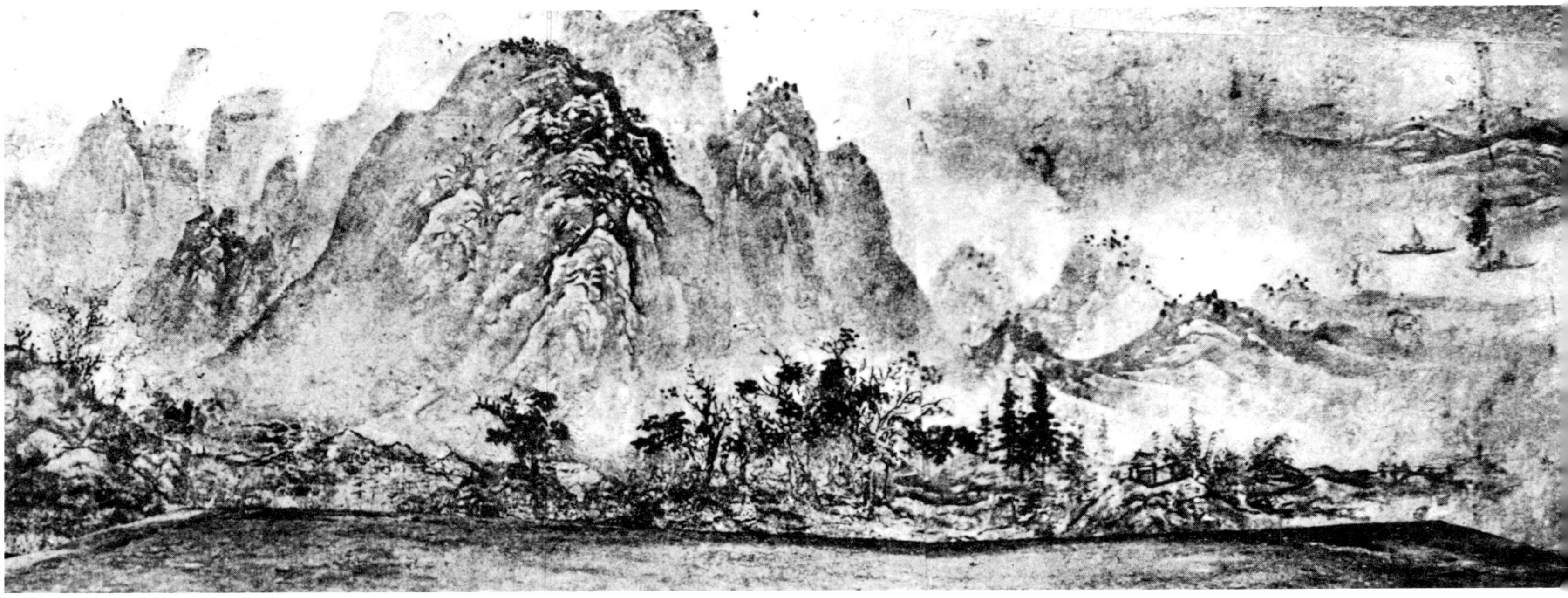

Fig. 56. Anonymous, *Landscape* (*Shan-shui*). Undated, ca. 1265. Wall painting, tomb of Feng Tao-chen, near Ta-t'ung, Shansi province

ettes, at once separated and bound by the mist, appear to float weightlessly in space. The mood of the landscape is dreamy and lyrical. Both in compositional structure and in expression, the Kara-khoto landscape fragment indeed closely resembles the *Dream Journey through the Hsiao and Hsiang Rivers* of about 1170 (cf. fig. 53).

In the wall painting at the tomb of Feng Tao-chen, dated about 1265, near Ta-t'ung, Shansi province, in north China (fig. 56),[93] the painter has established the physical integration of landscape elements through the use of a consistent receding ground plane. Here broad brushstrokes, applied with mixed ink tones, are fused and blurred to create variegated illusionistic surfaces in the foliage and mountains. The mountain forms, though descended from Fan K'uan's, are now set at an angle, with foreshortened shoulders and sides; the subsidiary peaks are clustered around and behind the central peak, and their common broad three-dimensional base sits firmly in the surrounding terrain. With the introduction of foreshortening in the tree trunks and branches, the painter has succeeded in suggesting three-dimensional relationships among objects along a receding ground plane: the forms of the vista to the right curve around in space and merge into forms behind them.

## *Survival of Northern Sung Idioms*

Modern scholars had once assumed that after the end of the Northern Sung in the early twelfth century, the Northern Sung styles of landscape persisted only in the north under the Chin. More recent evidence has shown, however, that outside the Imperial Painting Academy situated in the capital Lin-an (Hang-chou), where the simplified taste of the Ma Yüan–Hsia Kuei landscape idiom prevailed, the earlier grand manners of the Northern Sung, the Ching Hao–Kuan T'ung, Li Ch'eng–Kuo Hsi, and Fan K'uan–Yen Wen-kuei idioms, had also been carried on in the south under the Southern Sung.

The idea of a retrogressive style was first mentioned in Sherman Lee and Wen C. Fong's study (1956) of an anonymous handscroll *Streams and Mountains without End* (*Ch'i-shan wu-chin*), in the Cleveland Museum of Art, which dated the painting to the transitional period between the Northern and Southern Sung dynasties, in the early twelfth century.[94] In *Chinese Art Treasures* (1961), a catalogue of a selected group of objects from the National Palace Museum and the National Central Museum, Taipei, Aschwin Lippe and James Cahill assigned two works, a handscroll *The Red Cliff* (*Ch'ih-pi t'u*) formerly attributed to Chu Jui of the early twelfth century (now assigned to Wu Yüan-chih; fl. ca. 1190s) and an anonymous hanging scroll in the Kuo Hsi tradition, *Clearing after Snow on the Min Mountains* (*Min-shan hsüeh-chi*), to the Jurchen Chin dynasty. *Min Mountains*, according to the catalogue entry writer, "belongs to the northern tradition of Li Ch'eng and Kuo Hsi which in the Southern Sung period had declined to the status of a minor local tradition, carried on chiefly in the north under the Chin."[95] In an article entitled "*Clearing after Snow on the Min Mountains*, and Chin Landscape Painting" (1965), Susan Bush uses *Min Mountains* as a focal point for describing a group of possible Chin landscape paintings, presumably done in north China in the twelfth and thirteenth centuries.[96]

Since there is little or no external documentation for these paintings, they can only be dated through style. In twelfth- and thirteenth-century works in the grand manner of the Northern Sung, texture patterns gradually codified into systems of standard brush techniques, and specific texture patterns became hallmarks of individual painting traditions. As the later painters re-created earlier Northern Sung manners, they tended to reduce earlier representational techniques to surface patterns and graphic formulas.

One such stylistic sequence is shown by five large hanging scrolls in the style of Fan K'uan. One of these, *Sitting Alone by the Stream* (*Lin-liu tu-tso*), in the National Palace Museum, Taipei (figs. 57, 57a), has been dated to the late Sung dynasty, the thirteenth century.[97] An earlier date for this work is indicated, however, by its rock modeling, which shows not the simplified and standardized ax-cut texture stroke seen in Hsia Kuei's paintings, for example, but descriptive cutting strokes of varying sizes and ink values, as in the work of Li T'ang (cf. figs. 50a, 52). In characterizing the chipped, diagonal facets of the rocks, the

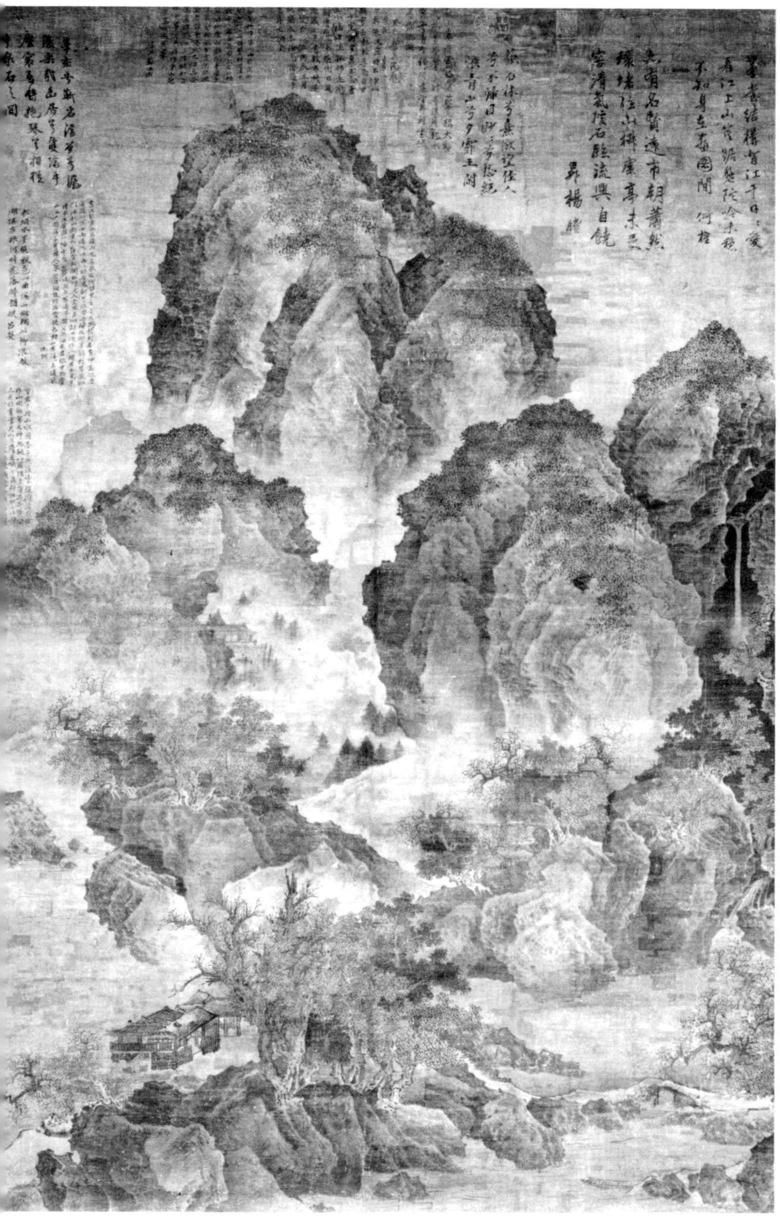

Fig. 57. Anonymous, in the style of Fan K'uan, *Sitting Alone by the Stream* (*Lin-liu tu-tso*). Undated, 1st half 12th century(?). Hanging scroll, ink and light color on silk. 156.1 x 106.3 cm (5 ft. 1 1/2 in. x 3 ft. 7/8 in.). National Palace Museum, Taipei

Fig. 57a. Detail, fig. 57

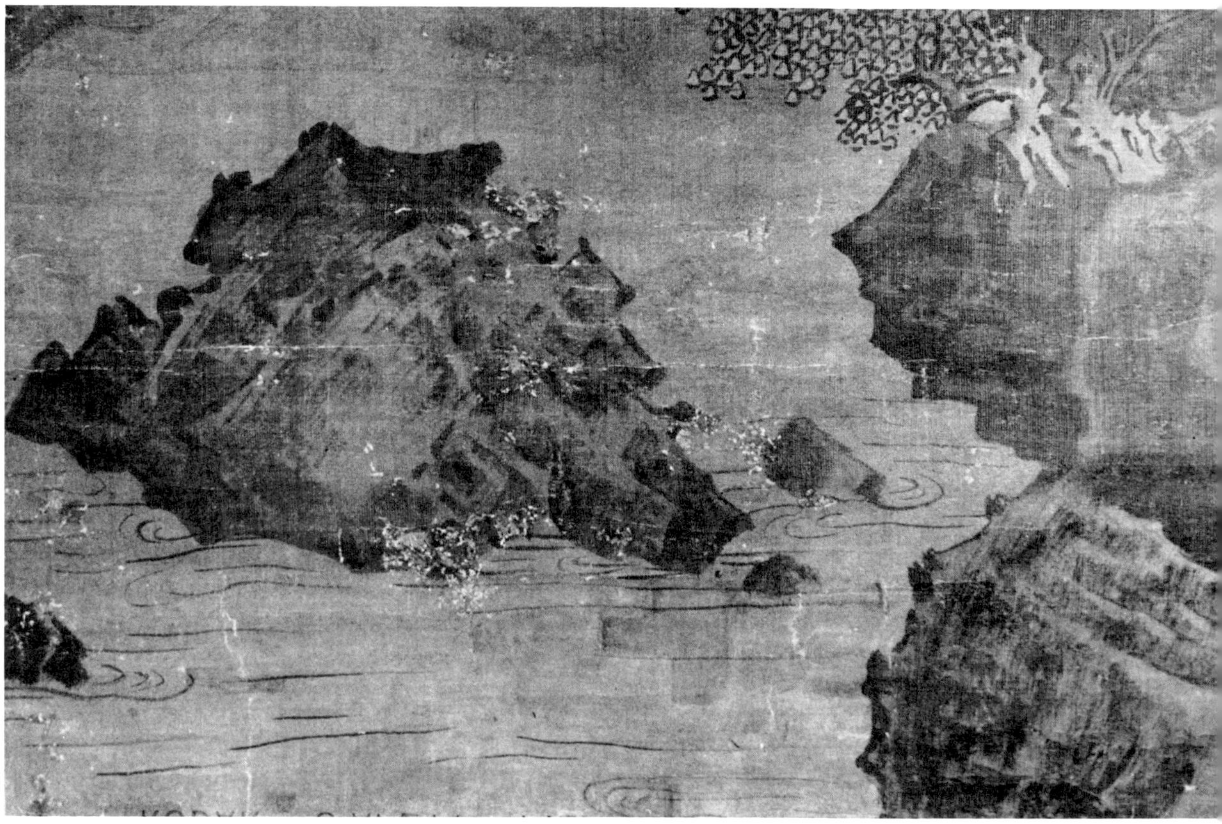

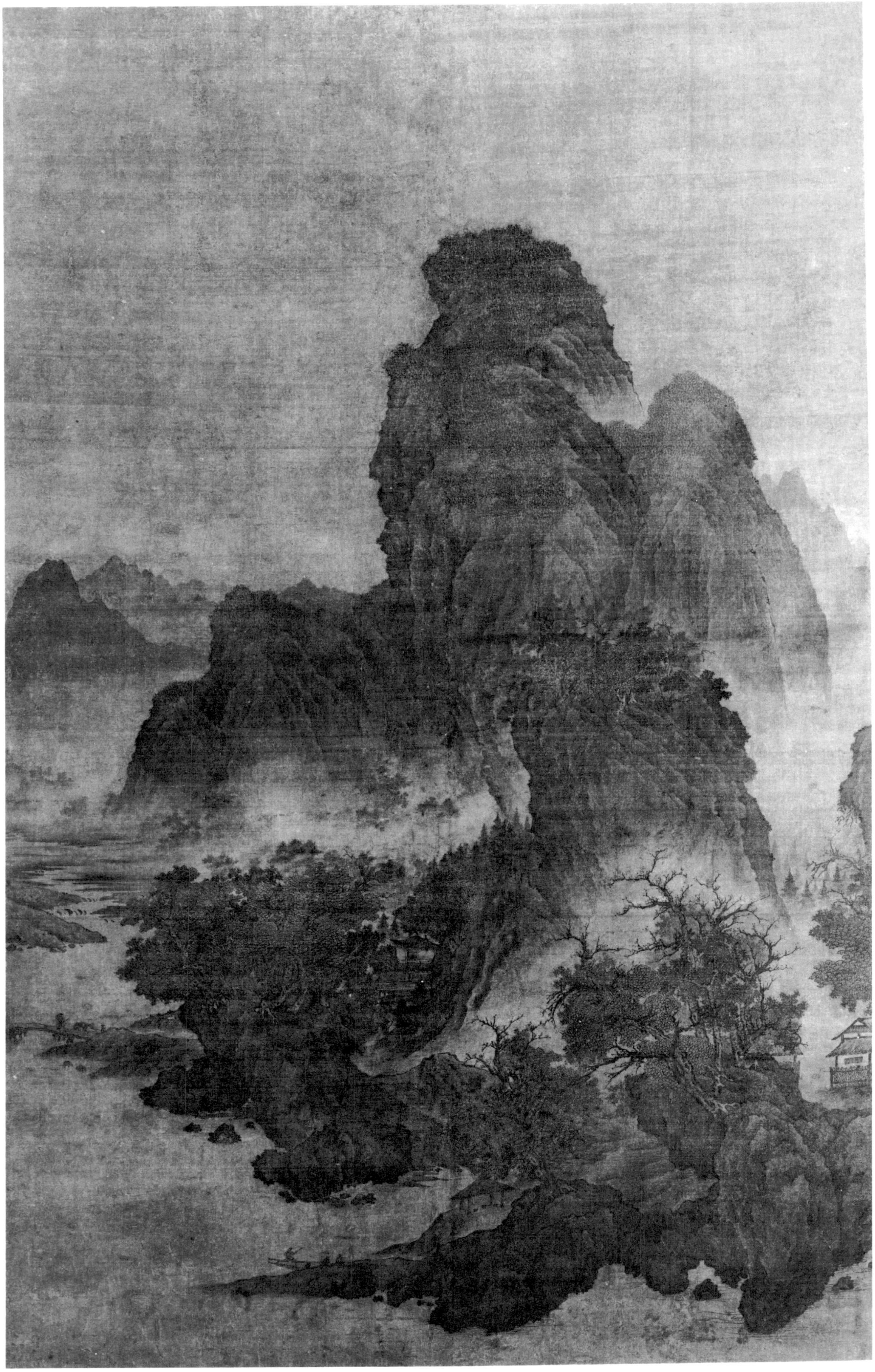

Fig. 58. Anonymous, *Landscape in the Style of Fan K'uan* (*Fang Fan K'uan shan-shui*). Undated, ca. 1150(?). Hanging scroll, ink and light color on silk. 164.78 x 103.8 cm (5 ft. 4⅞ in. x 3 ft. 4⅞ in.). The Metropolitan Museum of Art, New York

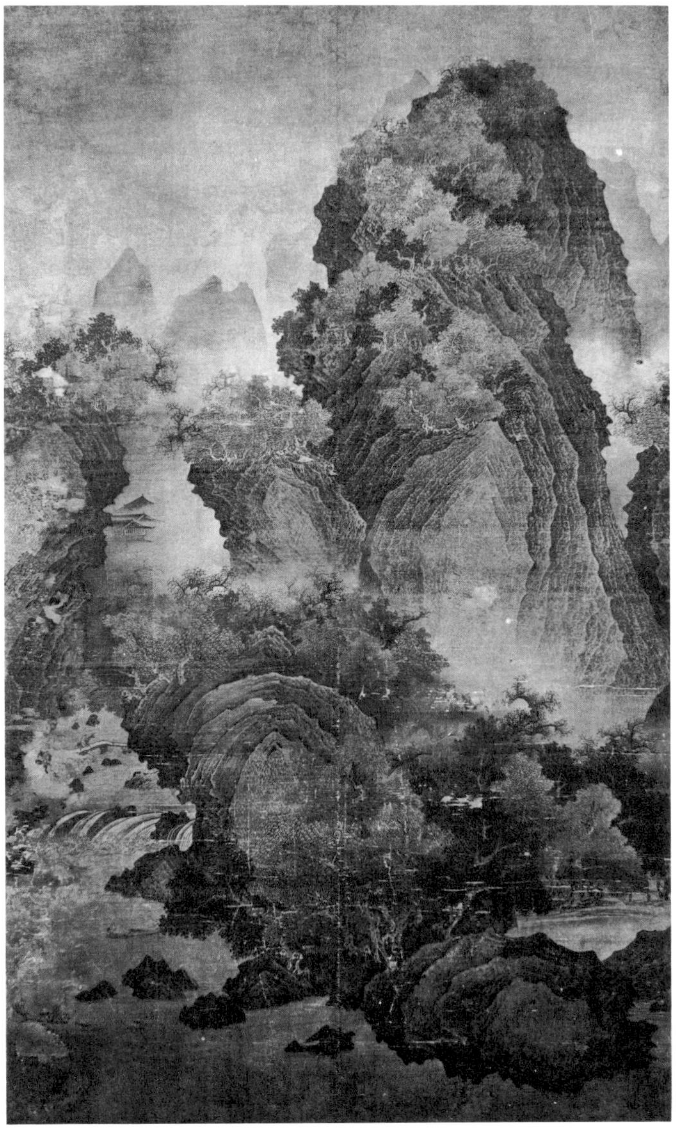

Fig. 59. Anonymous, *Landscape in the Style of Fan K'uan* (*Fang Fan K'uan shan-shui*). Undated, early 13th century(?). Hanging scroll, ink and light color on silk. 175.2 x 105.4 cm (5 ft. 9 in. x 3 ft. 5½ in.). The Art Museum, Princeton University

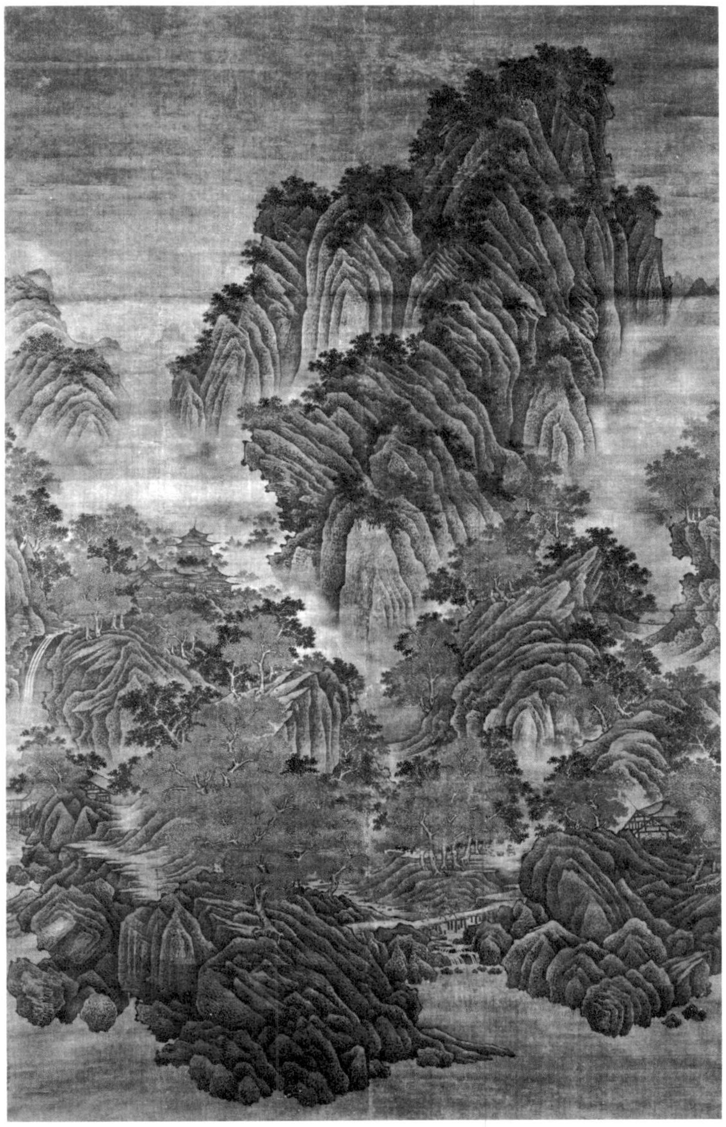

Fig. 60. Anonymous, *Landscape in the Style of Fan K'uan* (*Fang Fan K'uan shan-shui*). Undated, 1st half 13th century(?). Hanging scroll, ink on silk. Freer Gallery of Art, Washington, D.C.

Fig. 60a. Detail, fig. 60

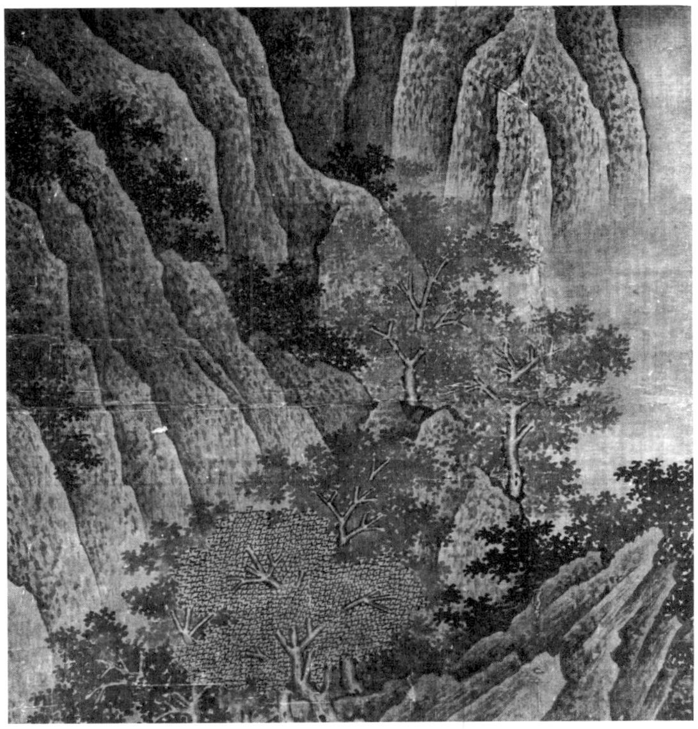

painter developed Fan K'uan's tactile stippling texture dots into broad diagonal hatching strokes, combining texturing and shading into single brushstrokes. Here, too, Fan K'uan's monolithic mountain masses have been fragmented into a more diffuse overall design, but have not been integrated into an organic structure with a receding ground plane. The painter of *Sitting Alone* seems to be of Li T'ang's generation, working between about 1120 and 1150.

In *Landscape in the Style of Fan K'uan* (*Fang Fan K'uan shan-shui*) in The Metropolitan Museum of Art, New York (fig. 58), a composition faintly resembling *Sitting Alone*, the landscape forms are pushed back into space. The rocks are described by angular, nervously charged contour strokes, and soft pointillistic dots cover the rock surfaces. Both in its systematic approach in texture modeling and in its psychological sense of remove from the viewer in composition, this *Landscape in the Style of Fan K'uan* compares closely to *Waiting to Cross a Mountain Stream*, attributed to Kuan T'ung (cf. fig. 31); in *Waiting to Cross a Mountain Stream* the principal stylistic clue is the swirling pattern of raindrop texture dots. The painters of both hanging scrolls probably belonged to Wang Hung's generation, active about 1150.

In *Landscape in the Style of Fan K'uan* in the DuBois Morris Schanck collection at The Art Museum, Princeton University (fig. 59), Fan K'uan's texture dotting technique has turned into a conscious mannerism of a uniform salt-and-pepper surface pattern. Finally, in *Landscape in the Style of Fan K'uan*, at the Freer Gallery of Art, Washington, D.C. (figs. 60, 60a), the Fan K'uan idiom is transformed into a schematic archaistic formula, with triangular mountain motifs divided into schematic parallel folds, and a flat, evenly modulated raindrop-patterned surface. The Freer work bears a colophon dated 1340, which sets a terminus date for the painting.

The appearance of a schematic patternistic formula in late Southern Sung painting may be documented by dated Southern Sung Buddhist paintings preserved in Japan. In the second half of the twelfth century, professional painters of Buddhist subjects in Ning-po, Chekiang province, possessed a fluent command of a range of texture patterns. In the set of *Five Hundred Lohans* (*Wu-pai lo-han*), dated 1178–81, most of which are now at the Zen monastery Daitoku-ji, in Kyoto, and two of which are at the Freer Gallery (fig. 61), the artists Chou Ch'i-ch'ang and Lin T'ing-kuei (late 12th century) easily switch from ax-cut strokes to the connected waterlike parallel texture pattern or to the "devil-face" (*kuei-mien*) pattern. The various texture patterns of the landscape painting vocabulary are used for different representational purposes; they are natural and descriptive of the landscape forms they depict. In the set of *Sixteen Lohans* (*Shih-liu lo-han*) by Lu Hsin-chung (early 13th century) at the Shōkoku-ji, Kyoto (fig. 62), however, the texture patterns are

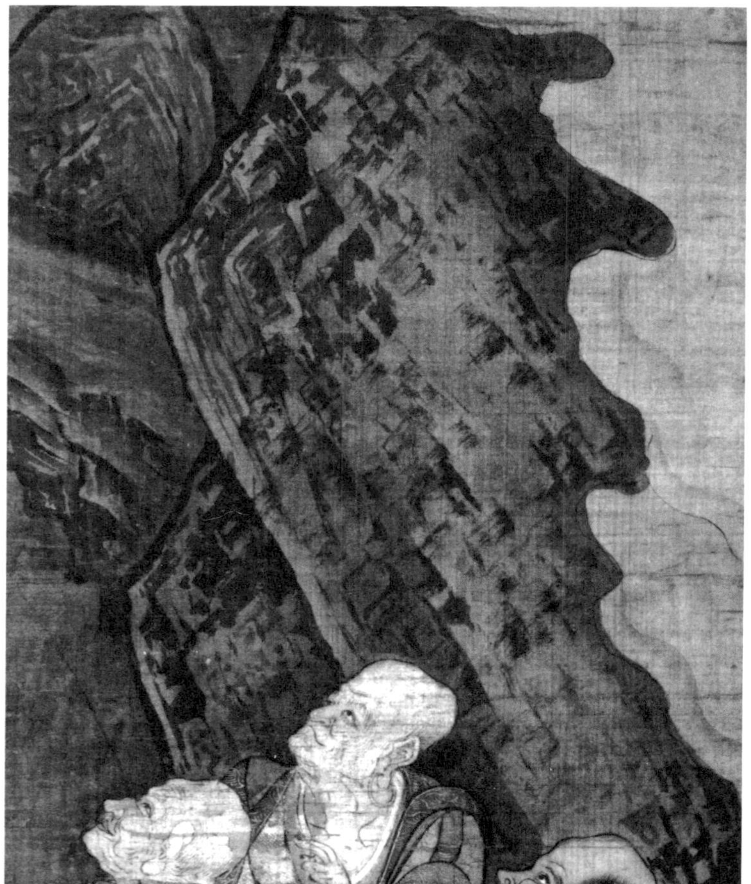

Fig. 61. Chou Chi-ch'ang, detail, one of *Five Hundred Lohans* (*Wu-pai lo-han t'u*). Dated 1178–81. Hanging scroll, ink and color on silk. 109.4 x 52.4 cm (3 ft. 7 1/8 in. x 20 5/8 in.). Freer Gallery of Art, Washington, D.C.

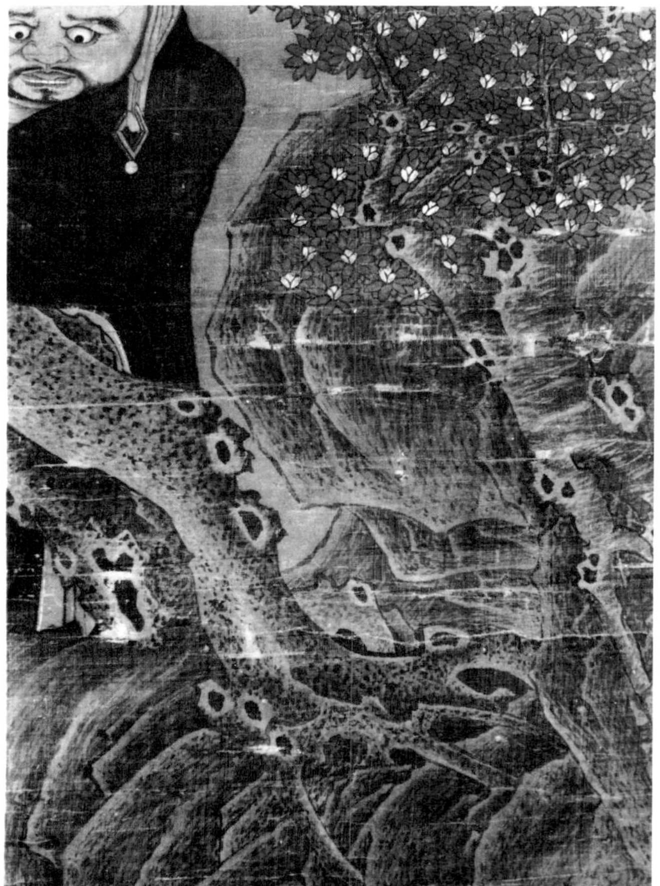

Fig. 62. Lu Hsin-chung, detail, *Sixteen Lohans* (*Shih-liu lo-han*). Undated, 1st half 13th century. Hanging scroll, ink and color on silk. Shōkoku-ji, Kyoto

schematic and patternistic. Lu included in his inscription the city name Ch'ing-yüan-fu. Since the city name of Ning-po was changed from Ming-chou to Ch'ing-yüan-fu in 1195 and to Ching-yüan-lu in 1277, Lu Hsin-chung's paintings, which show strong patternistic tendencies, must date from the first half of the thirteenth century.

The schematic archaistic formula, which shows triangular mountain motifs with parallel folds, and a flat, evenly textured surface, represents the generalized idea—the graphic symbol—of archaic style. A fan painting in the Liaoning Provincial Museum, *A Bridge over a Stream among Steep Mountains* (*Chün-ling ch'i-ch'iao*; fig. 63) expresses the essence of this formula: a bird's-eye view of a vast expanse of mountain peaks in archaistic triangular motifs without trees; only foliage dots along the mountain contours reinforce the design. The mountain motifs, piled up continuously in the vertical picture plane, and the curving, receding shoreline on the right side—a hint of a receding ground plane—suggest that the painting dates to the early thirteenth century.

The texture pattern of the Liaoning fan is a generalized dotting technique, which by this time referred not only to Fan K'uan, but also to Fan's antecedents, Ching Hao and Kuan T'ung. It is this same generic archaistic formula, with folds and dots, that distinguished *Mount K'uang-lu*, attributed to Ching Hao, in the National Palace Museum, Taipei (cf. fig. 25a), as well as the Freer Gallery *Landscape in the Style of Fan K'uan* (cf. fig. 60a). The receding shorelines in these hanging-scroll compositions, though mainly consisting of frontally viewed motifs, begin to merge visually into a continuous receding ground plane. Both paintings are Southern Sung archaistic re-creations of the early Northern Sung grand manner, done either at the very end of the twelfth century or in the first half of the thirteenth century.

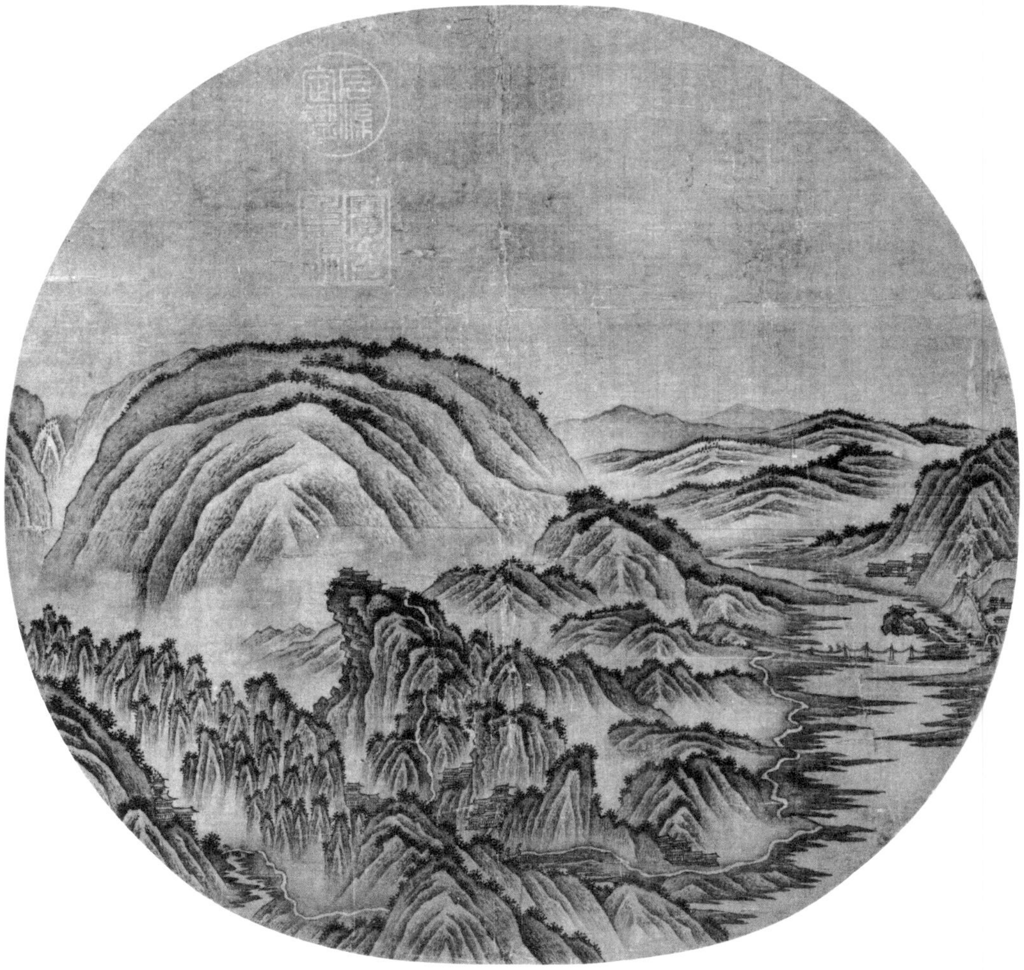

Fig. 63. Anonymous, *A Bridge over a Stream among Steep Mountains* (*Chün-ling ch'i-ch'iao*). Undated, early 13th century. Fan, ink and light color on silk. 25.0 x 27.0 cm ($9^7/_8$ x $10^5/_8$ in.). Liaoning Provincial Museum

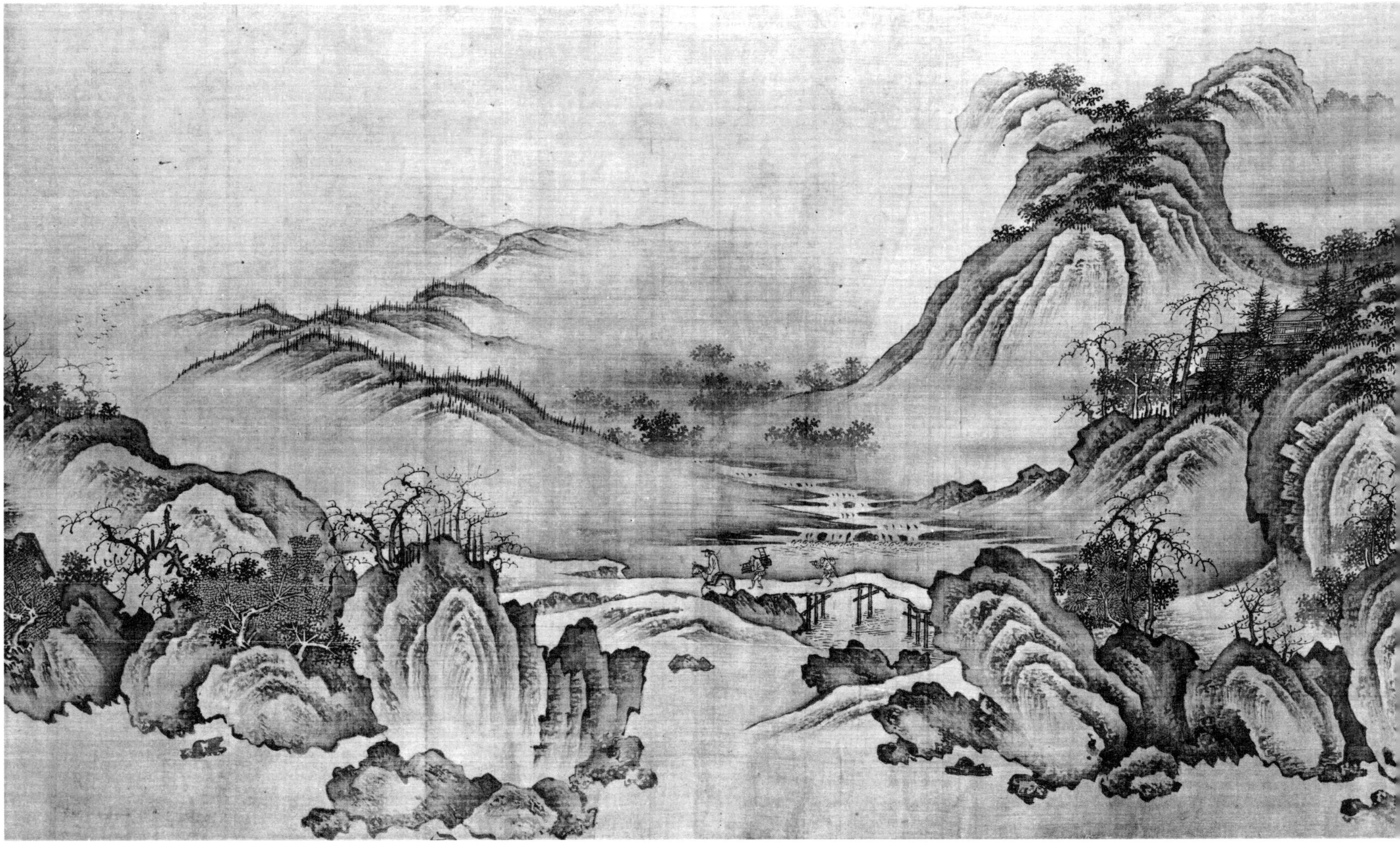

Fig. 64. Anonymous, in the style of Yen Wen-kuei, detail, *A Buddhist Monastery in Autumn Mountains* (*Ch'iu-shan hsiao-ssu*). Undated, ca. 1200. Handscroll, ink and light color on silk. 32.5 x 321.4 cm (12¾ in. x 10 ft. 6½ in.). The Metropolitan Museum of Art, New York

*A Buddhist Monastery in Autumn Mountains* (*Ch'iu-shan hsiao-ssu*), a handscroll attributed to Yen Wen-kuei, recently acquired by The Metropolitan Museum of Art, New York (figs. 64, 64a), is another splendid example of this Southern Sung retrogressive movement, in a survival, rather than a revival, of the Northern Sung monumental landscape style. Bearing a spurious signature of Yen Wen-kuei at the left end of the handscroll composition, the painting was done about 1200, probably in Wu-hsing, Chekiang province, the hometown of Yen Wen-kuei. During the mid-fourteenth century twelve colophons were added to the handscroll, including inscriptions by Ni Tsan and Lu Kuang (fl. mid-14th century). As a major Yen Wen-kuei attribution in the Chiang-nan area, the painting served as an important model of Northern Sung landscape style for the late Yüan and early Ming painters; its stylized twisting and turning peaks are reflected in many works dated to the late 1360s by such artists as Lu Kuang, Chao Yüan (fl. ca. 1360–75), Wang Meng (ca. 1308–1385; cf. fig. 119), and Hsü Pen (1335–1380; cf. fig. 121).[98]

*A Buddhist Monastery* shows stylized mountain folds in the archaistic mode, a mixed dotting and small ax-cut texture pattern, and intricately drawn spiky-branched trees in the Li Ch'eng–Kuo Hsi tradition. Painted during Hsia Kuei's time, when landscapes were generally simplified, the painting's monumental idiom in the Yen Wen-kuei tradition nevertheless reveals the Southern Sung taste for precisely drawn details, with a smoothly finished ink-wash surface. Turning necessity into a virtue, the painter transformed his multitudinous details into highly stylized silhouetted forms, and by perfectly orchestrating his smooth angular outlines with a neatly modulated texture pattern and ink wash, created a polished, hard-edged style on silk that exemplifies technical perfection in Southern Sung landscape painting (cf. fig. 54).

A very different style is seen in the mid- or late thirteenth-century handscroll on paper, *Travelers among Rivers and Mountains* (*Chiang-shan hsing-lü*), by a painter who called himself T'ai-ku i-min (A leftover citizen

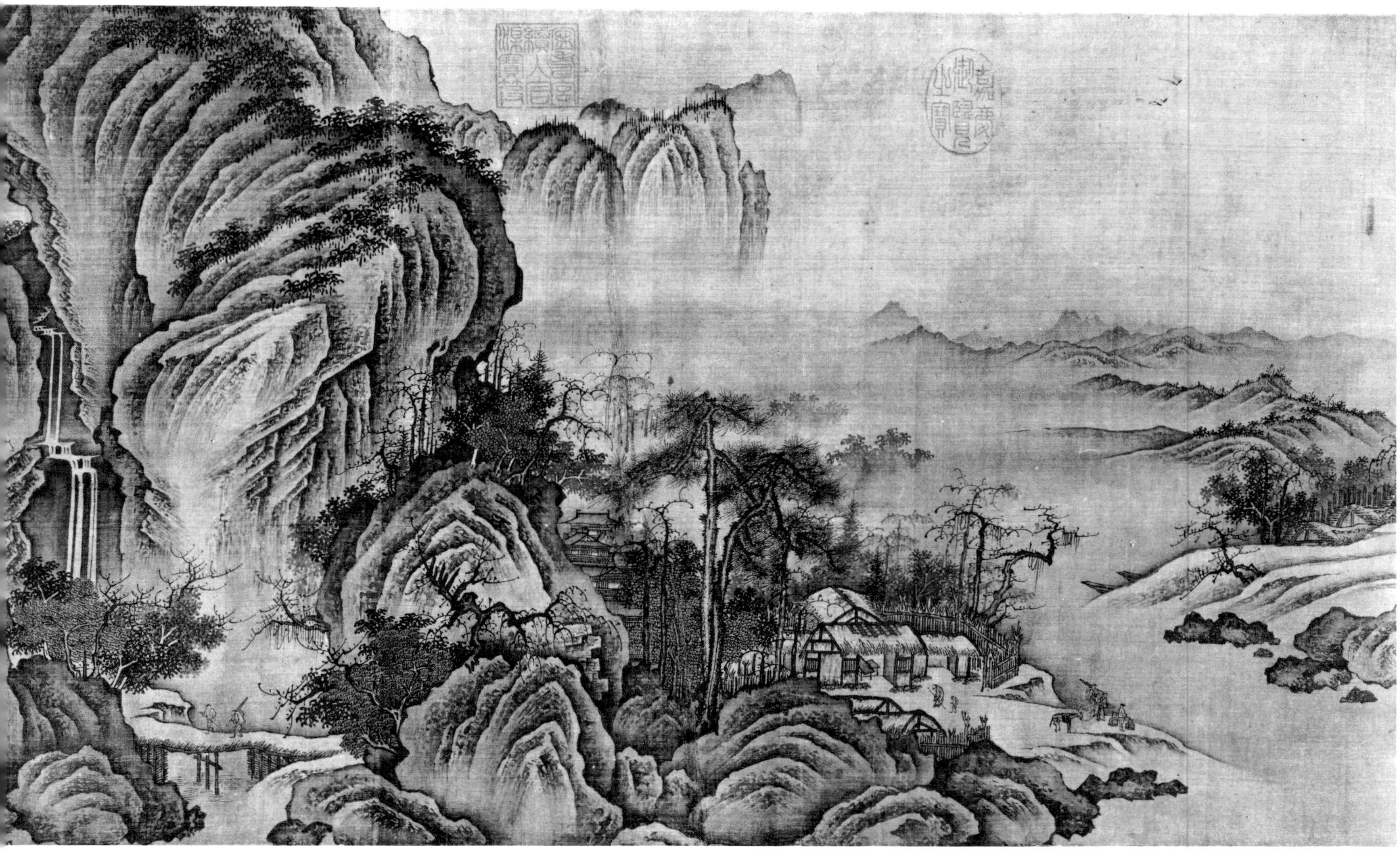

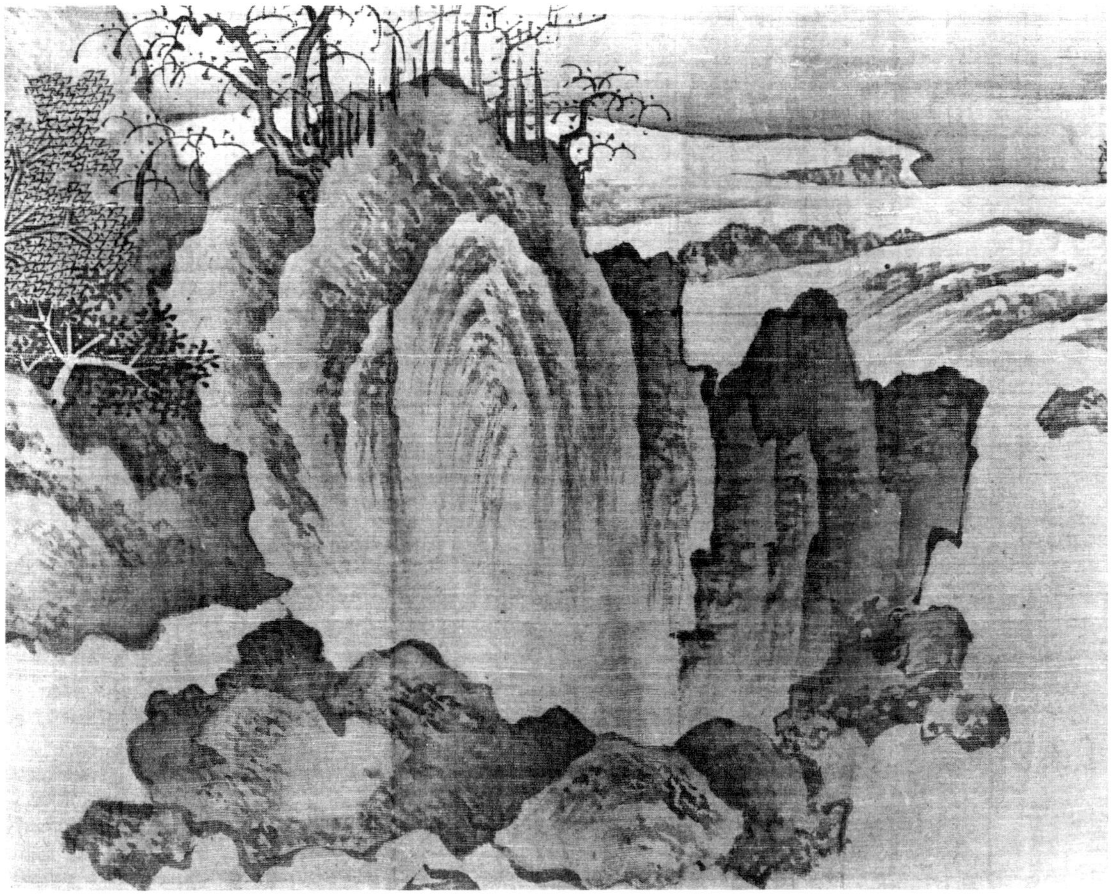

Fig. 64a. Detail, fig. 64

from remote antiquity), in the Nelson Gallery–Atkins Museum, Kansas City (figs. 65, 65a).[99] The scroll bears at its left end a collector's seal belonging to Ni Tsan, "Yün-lin Ni-shih chia-ts'ang" (Family collection of Yün-lin of surname Ni). In depicting his new vision of a spatially integrated landscape with a physically receding ground plane, the artist abandoned the smooth ink wash technique of the Southern Sung and adopted a free calligraphic brushwork style that anticipated the Yüan scholar-painter's calligraphic landscape style. The work is fresh and vital in its experimentation, offering new ways of portraying physical depth and structural complexities in landscape scenery and an anthology of recognized texture patterns: ax-cut (*fu p'i*), T-shape (*ting-hsiang*), and horse-teeth (*ma-chih*), deriving from the Northern landscape traditions of Ching Hao, Kuan T'ung, and others, as well as the draping hemp-fiber technique of the Southern masters Tung Yüan and Chü-jan. In translating the earlier smooth, hard-edged rock forms into freer and more independently assertive brushstrokes, however, T'ai-ku i-min abandoned the Southern Sung ink wash idiom without achieving a totally satisfactory new calligraphic style. The historical significance of T'ai-ku i-min's *Travelers* lies in its use of calligraphic brush formulas as a natural development in late thirteenth-century landscape painting. As calligraphic landscape style, however, T'ai-ku i-min's painting succeeded only in posing the question to which the leading Yüan dynasty masters were to supply the answer.

## *Illusionism Fully Mastered*

The short handscroll *Autumn Colors on the Ch'iao and Hua Mountains* (*Ch'iao-Hua ch'iu-se*), dated 1296, by Chao Meng-fu, in the National Palace Museum, Taipei (fig. 66), though the best example of the early Yüan scholar-painting aesthetic because of its skillful use of archaistic motifs and calligraphic brushwork, nevertheless features as its dominant compositional element a continuous receding ground plane.[100] Across the

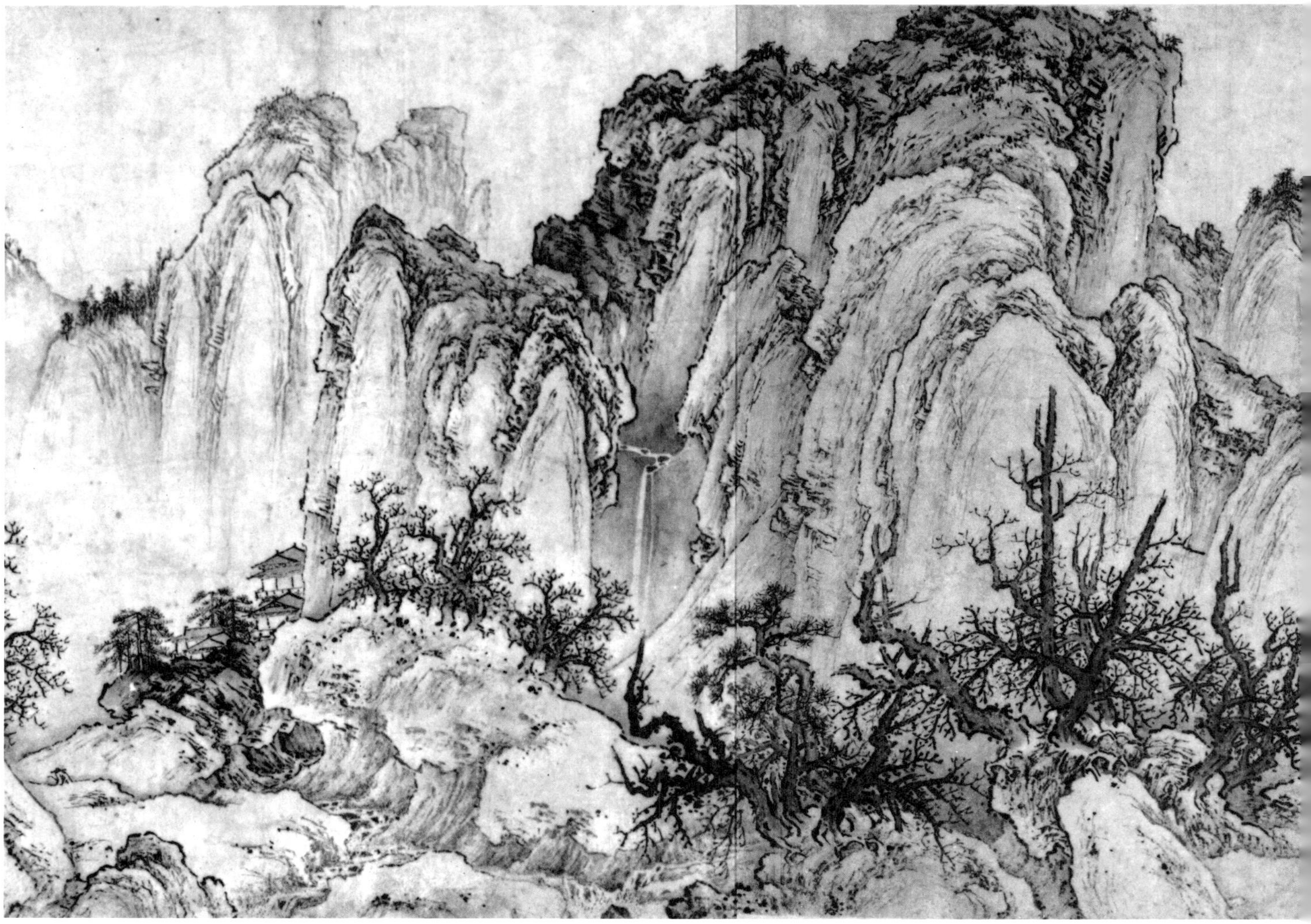

Fig. 65. T'ai-ku i-min, detail, *Travelers among Rivers and Mountains* (*Chiang-shan hsing-lü*). Undated, 2nd half 13th century. Handscroll, ink on paper. 38.4 x 418.0 cm (15 1/8 in. x 13 ft. 8 5/8 in.). Nelson Gallery–Atkins Museum, Kansas City

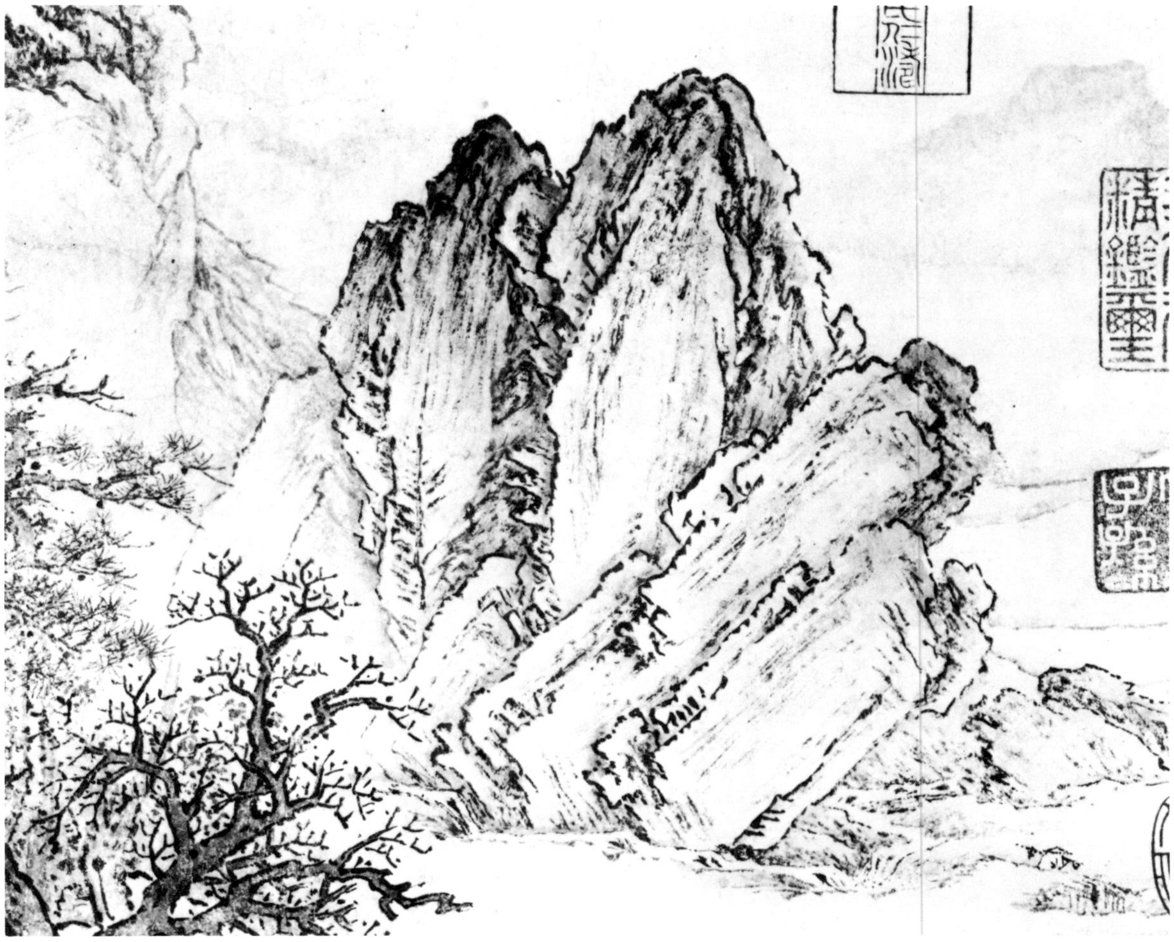

Fig. 65a. Detail, fig. 65

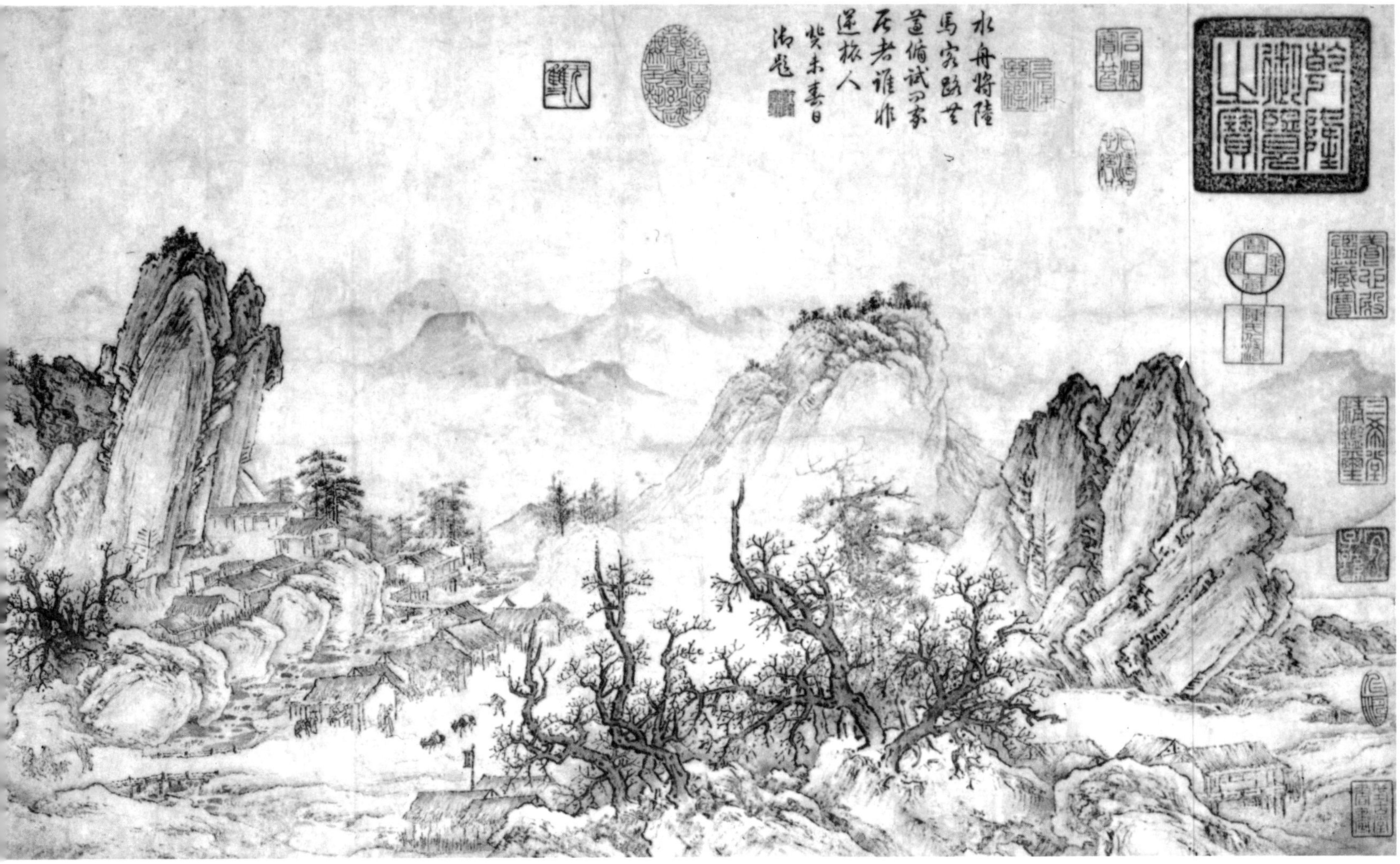

short handscroll two schematic mountain motifs, one triangular and the other semicircular, rendered in an archaistic blue and green color scheme, rise above the flat marshland. Below the twin peaks, trees and houses are arranged in circular patterns reminiscent of those of Wang Wei's *The Wang-ch'üan Villa* (*Wang-ch'üan t'u*). In modeling the mountains and sandy beaches, Chao Meng-fu uses a draping hemp-fiber texture pattern derived from Tung Yüan; the dry calligraphic brushstrokes are blurred and fused, creating an atmospheric effect around the trees and mountains. Every element in the composition relates closely to a consistently receding ground plane; the space appears to be physical and measurable. The central section of *Autumn Colors* seems consciously reminiscent of Tung Yüan's *Wintry Groves and Layered Banks* (cf. fig. 32). Chao's treatment of the thick clumps of trees in the middle distance, however, expertly transformed Tung's additive composition into a naturalistic vista, with a physically continuous and properly foreshortened ground plane.

In *Secrets of Landscape Painting* (*Hsieh shan-shui chüeh*), the leading mid-fourteenth-century master, Huang Kung-wang (1269–1354), noted that "painters of recent times follow mostly the two traditions of Tung Yüan and Li Ch'eng."[101] Huang Kung-wang, as well as other leading late Yüan dynasty masters, such as Wu Chen, Ni Tsan, and Wang Meng, relied heavily on Tung Yüan's texture method for modeling. Huang described how to modify Tung's hemp fibers into a calligraphic technique:

> At the foot of Tung Yüan's mountain slope there are many small rocks. This is the appearance of the Chien-k'ang mountain [near Nanking]. Tung's rock modeling is called the hemp-skin [*ma-p'i*] texture pattern. At the foot of the slope first use a slanted brush to draw an outline, then start making texture strokes. Later add lighter strokes to break into the deep recessed areas. . . . Tung Yüan's smaller rocks are called alum heads [*fan-t'ou*], and there is mist and vapor in the mountain. All this describes the Ching-ling [Nanking] mountain scenery. The modeling method should be moist and soft, with sandy ground below. Sweep [the ground] with light strokes, making curved lines, and repeatedly use lighter strokes to break [the individual lines].

This passage describes an illusionistic brush technique of creating forms with fused and mixed brush-strokes. To create his masterpiece *Dwelling in the Fu-ch'un Mountains* (*Fu-ch'un-shan chü*), dated 1350, in the National Palace Museum, Taipei (fig. 67), Huang first sketched broad outlines of the mountain with brushstrokes in medium shades of ink, then softened and blurred these outlines with lighter strokes. Finally he completed the form with dark accent strokes and moss dots (*t'ai-tien*). "In painting rocks," Huang advised, "start with light inkstrokes, so that alterations and revisions can be made, then gradually build with darker ink. . . . In landscape painting, individual brushstrokes should be linked like sinews and bones. There is a distinction between the uses of the brush and the ink. In modeling one blurs and blends the individual brushstrokes [*hu-t'u ch'i-pi*]. This is called the use of ink."[103]

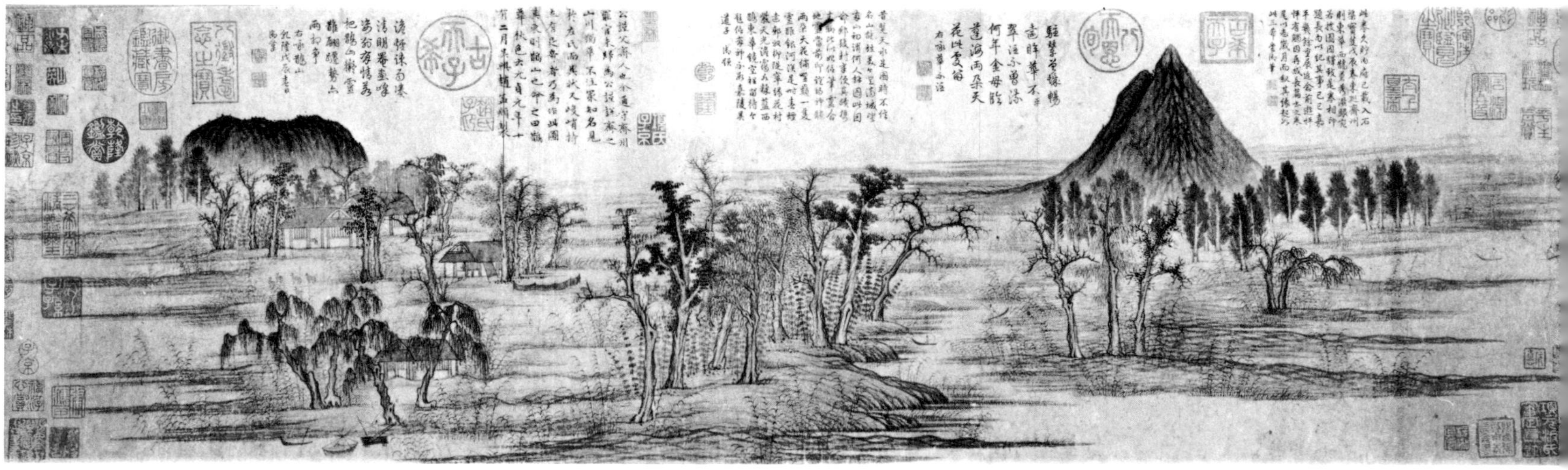

Fig. 66. Chao Meng-fu, *Autumn Colors on the Ch'iao and Hua Mountains* (*Ch'iao-Hua ch'iu-se*). Dated 1296. Handscroll, ink and color on paper. 28.4 x 93.2 cm (11 1/8 in. x 3 ft. 3 in.). National Palace Museum, Taipei

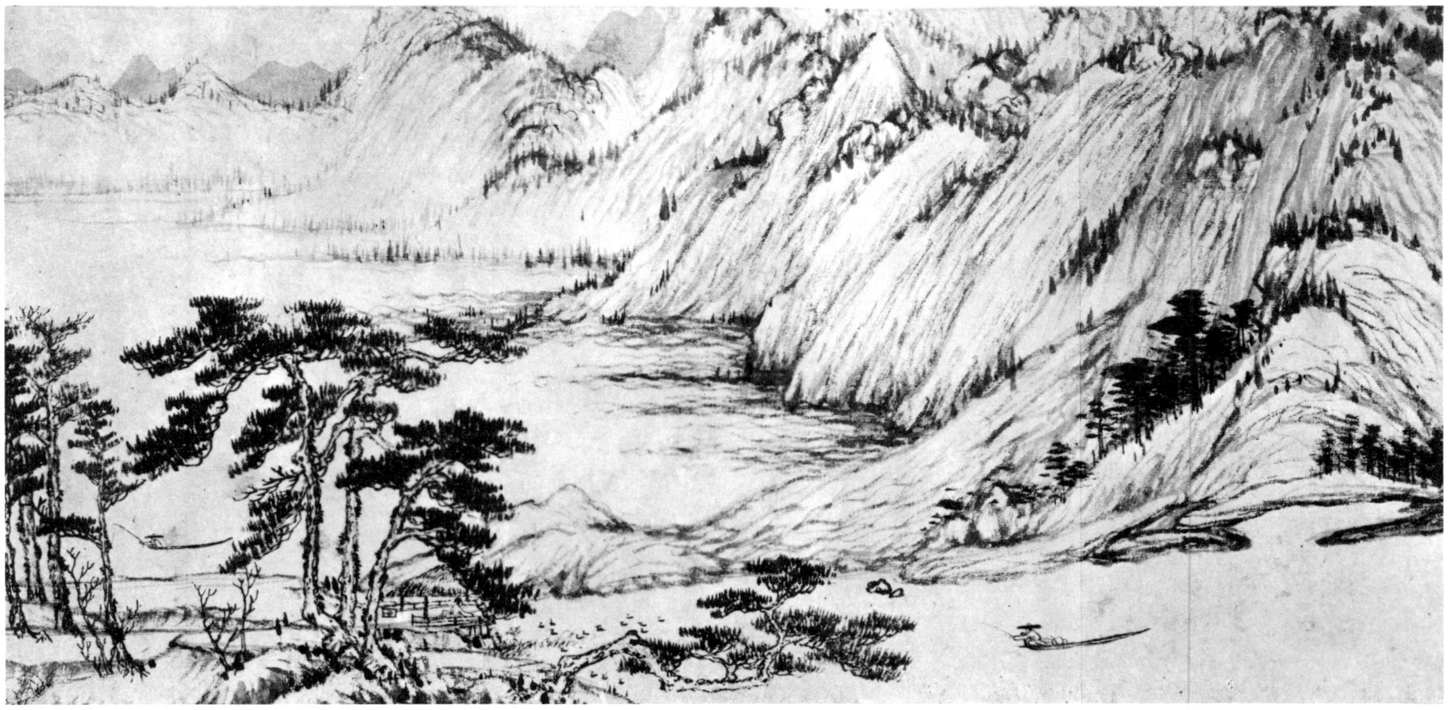

Fig. 67. Huang Kung-wang, detail, *Dwelling in the Fu-ch'un Mountains* (*Fu-ch'un shan-chü*). Dated 1350. Handscroll, ink on paper. 32.9 x 589.2 cm (13 in. x 19 ft. 4 in.). National Palace Museum, Taipei

Huang Kung-wang was a careful observer of forms in nature, recommending that "a painter should carry his brushes in a leather satchel, so that whenever he encounters good scenery or sees some extraordinarily shaped trees, he may draw and record them."[104] In the *Fu-ch'un* scroll he took advantage of his careful observations to portray rocks and trees from the top as well as from the sides; they are properly foreshortened and spatially integrated, with tree branches moving from the front to the back, in and out of the picture plane. For the painting of rocks Huang stressed "form-likeness. . . . A single side, whether it is the top or the left, can also be used."[105] "A tree," he wrote, "should have branches and twigs on all sides. . . . Trees should have good figures . . . should turn and overlap in a proper manner. . . . Those laden with leaves should show branches gently bent. Both in front and back there should be branches bending upward.[106]

Although the *Fu-ch'un* scroll follows, horizontally, the traditional convention of a tripartite design, the earlier additive spatial organization has been eclipsed by the overall flow of the composition:

> The mountain peaks should turn and link together, change direction and turn again, and yet the mountain veins always follow through smoothly. This method makes the landscape come alive. The multitude of peaks seem to bow and make way for each other, with ten thousand trees following along like a great army, grand and unopposed.[107]

All of the elements of the traditional three distances—the near, the middle, and the far—have become part of an integrated vision that extends from the front to the back along a continuous receding ground plane. The earlier distant-tree motifs, represented by simple vertical strokes crossed by horizontal dots, are now freely used as space fillers in the foreground. With landscape elements moving from right to left, the mountains and trees have approximately the same scale relationship; as a result the taller mountains are obliged to rise beyond the upper border of the scroll.

Thus, in Huang's painting, realism has taken its toll: physical description of nature is achieved only through the loss of the earlier ability to suggest infinite space. When compared with the monumental precipices of the Northern Sung landscape, the naturalistically proportioned peaks in Yüan painting appear to be mere hillocks.[108] But the Yüan scholar-painters, living under the Mongol rule, had a different goal than the perfection of pictorial representation. Turning away from the objective reality of Sung painting, they combined painting, poetry, and calligraphy in works that expressed their alienation and unhappiness.

## NOTES

1. Wölfflin points out that representational art is both imitation and decoration: "But even in the history of representative art, the effect of picture on picture as a factor in style is much more important than what comes directly from the imitation of nature. Pictorial imitation developed from decoration—the design as representation once arose from the ornament—and the after-effects of this relation have affected the whole of art history"; see Heinrich Wölfflin, *Principles of Art History: The Problem of the Development of Style in Later Art*, trans. M. D. Hottinger (New York: Dover, 1932), p. 230.
2. Tsung Ping, *Hua shan-shui hsü* (Introduction to landscape painting), in Yü Chien-hua, ed., *Chung-kuo hua-lun lei-pien* (Classified compilation of writings on Chinese painting) (Hong Kong: Chung-hua shu-chü, 1973), vol. 1, p. 583.
3. Kuo Hsi and Kuo Ssu, *Lin-ch'üan kao-chih chi* (Lofty aims in forests and streams), in Yü Chien-hua, ed., *Chung-kuo hua-lun lei-pien*, vol. 1, p. 639.
4. See Wen C. Fong, "*Rivers and Mountains after Snow* (*Chiang-shan hsüeh-chi*) attributed to Wang Wei (A.D. 699–759)," *Archives of Asian Art* 30 (1976–77): 19 ff.
5. Huang Hsiu-fu, *I-chou ming-hua lu* (Record of famous paintings in I-chou [Szechuan province]), in *Hua-shih ts'ung-shu* (Compendium of painting histories) (Taipei: Wen-shih-che ch'u-pan-she, 1974), vol. 3, *chüan* 2, p. 21.
6. Kuo Hsi and Kuo Ssu, *Lin-ch'üan kao-chih chi*, p. 642.
7. Yang Jen-k'ai, "Yeh-mao-t'ai Liao-mu ch'u-t'u ku-hua te shih-tai chi ch'i-t'a" (Ancient paintings excavated from the Liao dynasty tomb at Yeh-mao-t'ai, their dates and other problems), *Wen-wu* 1975, no. 12: 37–39.
8. Tamura Jitsuzō and Kōbayashi Yukio, *Keiryo* (Tombs and mural paintings of Ch'ing-ling) (Kyoto: Kyōtō diagaku bungakubu, 1952–53), vol. 1, pp. 70–82, figs. 86–89, 92–94; vol. 2, pls. 45–72.
9. Fung (Feng) Yu-lan, *A History of Chinese Philosophy*, trans. Derk Bodde (Princeton: Princeton University Press, 1953), vol. 2, p. 421.
10. James Legge, trans., *I-ching* (Book of changes), in Max Muller, ed., *Sacred Books of the East* (Oxford: Clarendon Press, 1899), appendix V, p. 422.
11. See Fung (Feng) Yu-lan, *History of Chinese Philosophy*, vol. 2, p. 414.
12. Ibid., pp. 466–68.
13. Ching Hao, *Pi-fa chi* (Notes on brush method), in Yü Chien-hua, ed., *Chung-kuo hua-lun lei-pien*, vol. 1, pp. 605, 607.
14. Ibid., p. 608; see notes and comments by Hsü Fu-kuan, *Chung-kuo i-shu ching-shen* (The spirit of Chinese fine arts) (Taipei: Hsüeh-sheng shu-chü, 1974), pp. 292–98.
15. Max Loehr, *The Great Painters of China* (New York: Harper and Row, 1980), p. 90; James Cahill [incorporating the work of Osvald Sirén and Ellen Johnston Laing], *An Index of Early Chinese Painters and Paintings: T'ang, Sung and Yüan* (Berkeley: University of California Press, 1980), pp. 26–27; Sofukawa Hiroshi, "Godai Hokusō shoki sansuiga no ichikōsatsu: Keikō, Kan Dō, Kaku Chūjo to En Bunki" (A study of landscape painting of the Five Dynasties and early Northern Sung period: Ch'ing Hao, Kuan T'ung, Kuo Chung-shu, Yen Wen-kuei), *Tōhō gakuhō* 49 (1977): 185–86.
16. Sun Tui-ku (1592–1676), *Keng-tzu hsiao-hsia chi* (Record of whiling away the summer in the *keng-tzu* year [1660]), Hsüeh-ku-chai chin-shih ts'ung-shu, vol. 3 (1904; repr. ed., Taipei: Hua-wen shu-chü, 1970), *chüan* 3, p. 9b; and National Palace Museum, Taipei, comp., *Ku-kung shu-hua lu* (A descriptive catalogue of the painting and calligraphy in the National Palace Museum) (Taipei: National Palace Museum, 1965), vol. 2, *chüan* 5, pp. 12–13.
17. Shen C. Y. Fu, "Two Anonymous Sung Dynasty Paintings and the Lu Shan Landscape: The Problem of Their Stylistic Origins," *National Palace Museum Bulletin* 2, no. 6 (January–February 1968): 1–16; 3, no. 3 (July–August 1968): 6–10.
18. See Wen C. Fong, "Archaism as a Primitive Style," in Christian F. Murck, ed., *Artists and Traditions: Uses of the Past in Chinese Culture* (Princeton: The Art Museum, 1976), pp. 93–112.
19. See Osvald Sirén, *Chinese Sculpture from the Fifth to the Fourteenth Century* (New York: Charles Scribner's Sons, 1925), pls. 558, 559.
20. See Wen C. Fong, "Archaism as a Primitive Style," pp. 94–98. For a detailed discussion of Kuan-hsiu's paintings of the sixteen lohans, see Wen C. Fong, "Five Hundred Lohans at the Daitoku-ji" (Ph.D. diss., Princeton University, 1956).
21. Max Loehr, *Great Painters of China*, p. 58.
22. *Hsüan-ho hua-p'u* (Painting catalogue of the Hsüan-ho era [1119–25]), I-shu ts'ung-pien, vol. 9 (Taipei: Shih-chieh shu-chü, 1962), *chüan* 3, p. 116.
23. Max Loehr, *Great Painters of China*, p. 90.
24. Wai-kam Ho et al., eds., *Eight Dynasties of Chinese Painting* (Cleveland: The Cleveland Museum of Art and Indiana University Press, 1980), pp. 12–13.
25. Max Loehr, *Great Painters of China*, pp. 85–86.
26. James Cahill, *Index of Early Chinese Painters and Paintings*, p. 27; and see Shen C. Y. Fu, "Two Anonymous Sung Dynasty Paintings," fig. 1.
27. See Kiyohiko Munakata, *Ching Hao's "Pi-fa chi": A Note on the Art of Brush, Artibus Asiae* Supplementum 31 (1974): 52–53.
28. Sofukawa Hiroshi, "Godai Hokusō shoki sansuiga no ichikōsatsu": 168–84.
29. Kuo Jo-hsü, *T'u-hua chien-wen chih* (Experiences in painting), in *Hua-shih ts'ung-shu* (Taipei: Wen-shih-che ch'u-pan-she, 1974), vol. 1, *chüan* 1/12, p. 158.
30. See Fu Shen, *Yüan-tai huang-shih shu-hua shou-ts'ang shih-lüeh* (A brief history of Yüan dynasty imperial collections of calligraphy and painting) (Taipei: National Palace Museum, 1981), p. 53.
31. See Kuo Jo-hsü, *T'u-hua chien-wen chih*, *chüan* 3/37, p. 183.
32. Shen Kua, *Meng-ch'i pi-t'an chiao-cheng* (Notes written in Meng-ch'i), ed. Hu Tao-ching, (Shanghai, 1956), vol. 1, *chüan* 17, p. 565; for a translation, see Max Loehr, *Great Painters of China*, pp. 111–12.
33. Mi Fu, *Lun shan-shui hua* [Excerpts from *Hua-shih*] (Discussion of landscape painting, from *Painting History*), in Yü Chien-hua, ed., *Chung-kuo hua-lun lei-pien*, vol. 2, p. 653.
34. See Fu Shen, *Yüan-tai huang-shih shu-hua shou-ts'ang shih-lüeh*, p. 72.
35. Shen Kua, *Meng-ch'i pi-t'an chiao-cheng*, pp. 111–12.
36. See Wu Chen, *Mei-tao-jen i-mo* (Ink legacy of Wu Chen), I-shu ts'ung-pien, vol. 11 (Taipei: Shih-chieh shu-chü, 1962), p. 54. *Wintry Groves and Layered Banks* also bears the Southern Sung emperor Li-tsung's (r. 1225–64) seal. The fact that Chao Meng-fu and Wu Chen had known the work suggests that the painting was in private hands in Chiang-nan before entering the late Yüan emperor Shun-ti's (r. 1333–67) collection.
37. See Wango H. C. Weng and Yang Boda, *The Palace Museum: Treasures of the Forbidden City* (New York: Harry N. Abrams, 1982), p. 195, pl. 97.
38. Max Loehr, *Great Painters of China*, p. 130.
39. See Richard Barnhart, *Marriage of the Lord of the River: A Lost Landscape by Tung Yüan, Artibus Asiae* Supplementum 27 (1970).
40. Max Loehr, *Great Painters of China*, p. 124.
41. For a review of scholarly opinions on *Hsiao and Hsiang Rivers*, see Barnhart, *Marriage of the Lord of the River*: 38.
42. Kuo Jo-hsü, *T'u-hua chien-wen chih*, *chüan* 4/55, p. 201.
43. See National Palace Museum, comp., *Ku-kung shu-hua lu*, vol. 2, *chüan* 20, pp. 21–22.
44. Fu Shen, "Chü-jan ts'un-shih hua-chi chih pi-chiao yen-chiu" (A comparative study of the extant works of Chü-jan), *National Palace Museum Quarterly* 2, no. 2 (October 1967): 51–79 (English summary, p. 22).
45. Li Lin-ts'an, "Chung-kuo shan-shui hua chung te 'ts'un-fa' yen-chiu" (A study of ts'un-texture methods in Chinese landscape painting), *National Palace Museum Quarterly* 8, no. 2 (Winter 1973): 1–26; and "Chung-kuo shan-shui hua shang t'ai-tien chih yen-chiu" (A study of moss dots in Chinese landscape painting), *National Palace Museum Quarterly* 9, no. 4 (Summer 1975): 25–46.
46. See Fu Shen, *Yüan-tai huang-shih shu-hua shou-ts'ang shih-lüeh*, pl. 56.
47. National Palace Museum, comp., *Ku-kung shu-hua lu*, vol. 4, *chüan* 6, p. 71–75; see inscription by Tung Ch'i-ch'ang on leaf 11 of the *Hsiao-chung hsien-ta* album.
48. Wai-kam Ho et al., eds., *Eight Dynasties of Chinese Painting*, p. 17.
49. Fu Shen, *Yüan-tai huang-shih shu-hua shou-ts'ang shih-lüeh*, pp. 73–74.
50. See Kwan S. Wong, "Chiang Shen te chia-shih sheng-p'ing shih-k'ao"

(A study of Chiang Shen's family background and life), *Su-chou University Journal of Chinese Art History* 11 (July 1981): 26–48, esp. p. 36.
51. For a study of Li Ch'eng's biography, see Wai-kam Ho, "Li Ch'eng and the Mainstream of Northern Sung Painting," in *Proceedings of the International Symposium on Chinese Painting* (Taipei: National Palace Museum, 1970), pp. 251–83.
52. *Hsüan-ho hua-p'u*, vol. 2, *chüan* 11, pp. 114–15.
53. Mi Fu, *Lun shan-shui hua*, vol. 2, p. 652.
54. National Palace Museum, comp., *Ku-kung shu-hua lu*, vol. 4, *chüan* 6, p. 72.
55. Kuo Jo-hsü, *T'u-hua chien-wen chih*, *chüan* 1, p. 12.
56. Mi Fu, *Hua-shih* (Painting history), I-shu ts'ung-pien, vol. 10 (Taipei: Shih-chieh shu-chü, 1975), p. 53.
57. For a discussion of compressed mountain forms receding in space in works of about 1100, see Wen C. Fong, *Summer Mountains: The Timeless Landscape* (New York: The Metropolitan Museum of Art, 1975), text accompanying pls. 31–33.
58. See Wai-kam Ho et al., eds., *Eight Dynasties of Chinese Painting*, p. 13.
59. See Wen C. Fong, *Summer Mountains*, pls. 16–21.
60. See Liaoning Provincial Museum, ed., *Liao-ning sheng po-wu-kuan ts'ang-hua chi* (Catalogue of the painting collection in the Liaoning Provincial Museum) (Peking: Wen-wu ch'u-pan-she, 1980), 2nd ser., vol. 1, pls. 4–8.
61. See Wen C. Fong, *Summer Mountains*, pls. 13–15.
62. Shen Kua, *Meng-ch'i pi-t'an chiao-cheng*, *chüan* 17, pp. 546–47.
63. Kuo Hsi and Kuo Ssu, *Lin-ch'üan kao-chih chi*, p. 639.
64. Ibid., p. 642.
65. Ibid., p. 639.
66. See Suzuki Kei, "*Rinsen kōchi shu* no gaki to kaku ki ni tsuite" (Kuo Hsi and "Record of Painting" in Kuo's *Lofty Aims in Forests and Streams*), *Bijutsushi* 109 (November 1980): 1–11; trans. (into Chinese) Wang Weiming, "*Lin-ch'üan kao-chih chi* hua-chi yü Kuo Hsi," *Mei-shu yen-chiu* 4 (1982): 70–76.
67. Kuo Hsi and Kuo Ssu, *Lin ch'üan kao-chih chi*, p. 646.
68. Ibid., p. 643.
69. Ibid., p. 637.
70. Ibid., p. 635.
71. See Ogawa Hiromitsu, "Tō Sō sansuiga shi ni okeru imajinēshan—hatsuboku kara *Sōshunzu*, *Shōsō gayū zukan* made" (Imagination in the history of T'ang and Sung landscape painting—from *p'o-mo* to *Early Spring* and *Dream Journey on the Hsiao and Hsiang Rivers*), *Kokka* 1034 (June 1980): 5–17; 1036 (July 1980): 25–36.
72. Teng Ch'un, *Hua-chi* (A continuation of painting history), in *Hua-shih ts'ung-shu*, vol. 1, *chüan* 9/72, p. 342.
73. Kuo Hsi and Kuo Ssu, *Lin-ch'üan kao-chih chi*, preface, p. 631.
74. Fung (Feng) Yu-lan, *History of Chinese Philosophy*, vol. 2, p. 432.
75. See Teng Ch'un, *Hua-chi*, *chüan* 2/5, p. 275.
76. See Chang Huai, "Hou-hsü" (Epilogue), in Han Cho, *Shan-shui Ch'un-ch'üan chi* (Collection of Ch'un-ch'üan's essays on landscape painting), in Yü Chien-hua, ed., *Chung-kuo hua-lun lei-pien*, vol. 2, p. 680.
77. Ibid., p. 667; Robert Maeda, *Two Twelfth-Century Texts on Chinese Painting*, Michigan Papers in Chinese Studies, no. 8 (Ann Arbor: Center for Chinese Studies, The University of Michigan, 1970), p. 25.
78. In the late Ming period, Wang K'o-yü (fl. ca. 1640) listed fourteen *ts'un* patterns: hemp-skin (*ma-p'i*), straightly rubbed (*chih-ch'a*), rain-drop (*yü-tien*), small ax-cut (*hsiao fu-p'i*), large ax-cut (*ta fu-p'i*), long ax-cut (*ch'ang fu-p'i*), short-stroked (*tuan-pi*), pulling nails out of mud (*ni-li pa-ting*), dragging in mud and water (*t'o-ni tai-shui*), confused cloud pattern (*luan-yün*), pellet-riddled (*tan-wo*), devil-faced (*kuei-mien*), skeleton (*k'u-lou*), and horse-teeth (*ma-ch'ih*); see Wang K'o-yü, *Shan-hu-wang hua-fa* (Painting methods of the Studio of Netted Corals), I-shu ts'ung-pien, vol. 13 (Taipei: Shih-chieh shu-chü, 1962), p. 243. See also Benjamin March, *Some Technical Terms of Chinese Painting* (Baltimore: Waverly Press, 1935), pp. 33–37. See also below, chap. 5, s.v. Tao-ch'i.
79. *Hsüan-ho hua-p'u*, vol. 2, *chüan* 12/132, p. 506.
80. Teng Ch'un, *Hua-chi*, *chüan* 6/50, p. 320.
81. See Hsia Wen-yen, *T'u-hui pao-chien* (Treasured mirror of painting), in *Hua-shih ts'ung-shu*, vol. 2, *chüan* 4/100, p. 772.
82. Suzuki Kei, "Ri Tō no nanto fukuin to sono Yōshi-ki hensen ni tsuite no ichi-shiren (A tentative theory concerning Li T'ang's moving to the south, and the change in [landscape] style after the reestablishment of the [Imperial Painting] Academy), *Kokka* 1047 (December 1981): 5–20; 1053 (July 1981): 13–23.
83. Shimada Shujiro, "Kōtō-in shozō no sansuiga ni tsuite" (On the landscape paintings in the Koto-in Temple, Kyoto), *Bijutsu kenkyū* 4, no. 165 (1950): 136–49.
84. See Richard Edwards, "The Landscape Art of Li T'ang," *Archives of the Chinese Art Society of America* 12 (1958): 48–60; Richard Barnhart, "Li T'ang (c. 1050–c. 1130) and the Kōtō-in Landscape," *The Burlington Magazine* 24, no. 830 (May 1972): 305–14; James Cahill, *Index of Early Chinese Painters and Paintings*, p. 124.
85. Han Cho, *Shan-shui Ch'un-ch'üan-chi*, vol. 2, p. 662.
86. See Shimada Shujiro, "Sō Teki to *Shōshō hakkei*" (Sung Ti and the *Eight Views of the Hsiao and Hsiang Rivers*), *Nanga Kansho* 104 (1941): 6–13; and below, "Eight Views of the Hsiao and Hsiang Rivers by Wang Hung" by Alfreda Murck.
87. Shen Kua, *Meng-ch'i pi-t'an chiao-cheng*, *chüan* 17, pp. 9–10.
88. Hsia Wen-yen, *T'u-hui pao-chien*, vol. 2, *chüan* 4/118, p. 790.
89. Han Cho, *Shan-shui Ch'un-ch'üan chi*, p. 662.
90. Suzuki Kei, "Shōsō gayū zukan ni tsuite" (Concerning the handscroll *Dream Journey through the Hsiao and Hsiang Rivers*), *Tōyō bunka kenkyūchiyō* 59 (March 1973): 1–61; 79 (March 1979): 1–84.
91. Ibid.: 28. This remark recalls Teng Ch'un's story about Kuo Hsi; see Teng Ch'un, *Hua-chi*, p. 342.
92. See M. A. Stein, *Innermost Asia* (Oxford: Clarendon Press, 1928), vol. 1, chap. 8, esp. pp. 435 ff., 450–51; vol. 2, pl. 61, Expedition No. Kara-khoto II, 0313.b.
93. *Wen-wu* 1962, no. 10: 45.
94. Sherman Lee and Wen C. Fong, *Streams and Mountains without End: A Northern Sung Handscroll and Its Significance in the History of Early Chinese Painting*, *Artibus Asiae* Supplementum 14 (1956): 25 ff.
95. *Chinese Art Treasures: A Selected Group of Objects from The Chinese National Palace Museum and The Chinese National Central Museum, Taichung, Taiwan* (Geneva: Skira, 1961), p. 111.
96. Susan Bush, "*Clearing after Snow in the Min Mountains* and Chin Landscape Painting," *Oriental Art* 11, no. 3 (Autumn 1965): 163–72.
97. James Cahill, *Index of Early Chinese Painters and Paintings*, p. 82.
98. See Richard Vinograd, "New Light on Tenth-century Sources of Landscape Painting Styles of the Late Yüan Period," in *Suzuki Kei sensei kanreki-kinen: Chūgoku ega-shi ron* (Celebrating Professor Suzuki Kei's sixtieth birthday: collected essays on Chinese painting history) (Tokyo: Yoshikawa, 1981), pp. 15 ff.
99. Wai-kam Ho et al., eds., *Eight Dynasties of Chinese Painting*, pp. 44–47.
100. Chu-tsing Li, "*The Autumn Colors on the Ch'iao and Hua Mountains*": *A Landscape by Chao Meng-fu*, *Artibus Asiae* Supplementum 21 (1965).
101. Huang Kung-wang, *Hsieh shan-shui chüeh* (Secrets of landscape painting), in Yü Chien-hua, ed., *Chung-kuo hua-lun lei-pien*, vol. 2, p. 696.
102. Ibid.
103. Ibid.
104. Ibid., p. 697.
105. Ibid., p. 696.
106. Ibid.
107. Ibid., p. 697.
108. See Wen C. Fong, "*Rivers and Mountains after Snow*," pp. 23–24.

# 2 Northern Sung Calligraphy: The Picture of the Mind

CALLIGRAPHY, RATHER THAN PAINTING, was the natural medium for the scholar-artist. Beginning in the late Han period, in the early third century A.D., the history of calligraphy as a fine art saw the completion of its full cycle of development long before landscape painting became a dominant art form. The rise of landscape art in later periods owed much to the artist's experience in, and knowledge of, calligraphy.

By the fourth century A.D., when the Chinese script had completed its evolution from the archaic seal (*chuan-shu*) and clerical (*li-shu*) to the modern regular (*k'ai-shu*) and running (*hsing-shu*) forms, there appeared the most famous of all calligraphers, the two Wangs of the Eastern Tsin period: Wang Hsi-chih (ca. 307–ca. 365) and his son Wang Hsien-chih (344–386). The two Wangs came to be considered archetypes; the renowned calligrapher and poet of the eleventh century, Huang T'ing-chien (1045–1105), comparing calligraphy with literature, equated the older Wang with the great ancient historian Tso-ch'iu Ming (fl. ca. 274 B.C.?), a model of judiciousness, keen perception, and profound learning, and the younger Wang with the Taoist mystic Chuang-tzu (399–295 B.C.), who epitomized brilliant insight and intuition.[1] Since every student of calligraphy began by imitating ancient models, particularly the two Wangs, each calligrapher had to create a distinctive personal style within the established tradition.

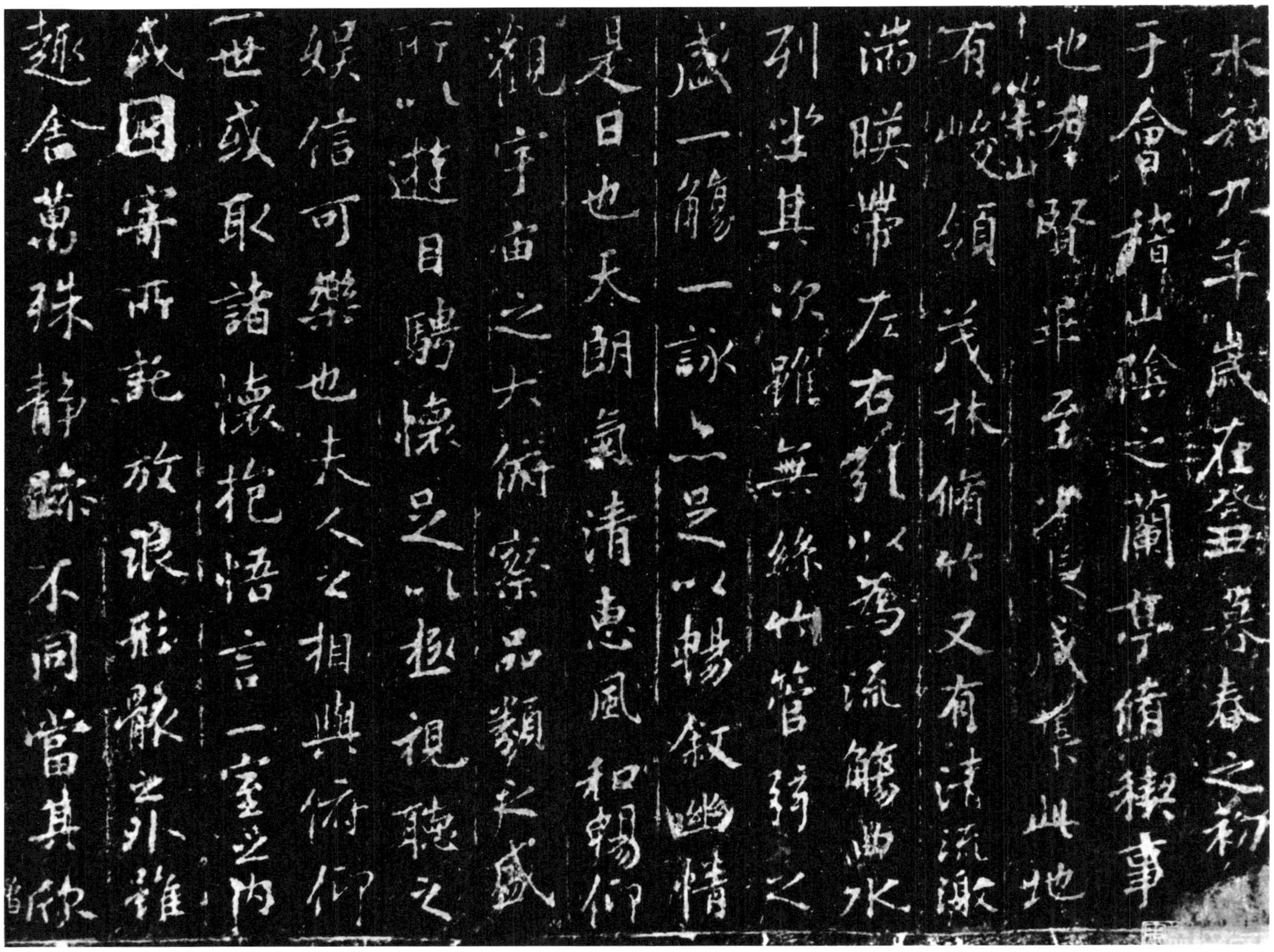

Fig. 68. Attributed to Wang Hsi-chih, *Preface to the Orchid Pavilion Gathering* (*Lan-t'ing chi hsü*). Dated 353. Ting-wu rubbing version, carved ca. 998–1061

The leading calligrapher-painter-theorist of the early seventeenth century, Tung Ch'i-ch'ang (1555–1636) still grappled with the problem:

> The calligraphic styles of Wang Hsi-chih and his son were exhausted by the Ch'i and Liang periods. In the early T'ang period, when Yü Shih-nan [558–638], Ch'u Sui-liang [596–658], and others transformed the two Wangs' methods, a new correspondence [*ho*] with the ancient methods was discovered through the change. Wang Hsi-chih and son were alive again.[2]

In other words, learning calligraphy has more to do with what one studies to be than with what one studies. To learn calligraphy from either a living or an ancient model is to perform a physical act generated from within: to do it well one must first know oneself. Therefore the wise student aims not for slavish imitation, but for spiritual responses (*shen-hui*) to his models, and for the growth and cultivation of the self through art.

Although excellent calligraphers abound in history, great stylistic innovators of lasting achievement are comparatively rare. In early Northern Sung calligraphy the principal models were Wang Hsi-chih (fig. 68) and Yen Chen-ch'ing (709–785; fig. 69), the leading mid-T'ang master of the regular script. In 992 the emperor Sung T'ai-tsung (r. 976–97) commissioned a selected anthology, *Calligraphic Works in the Ch'un-hua Palace* (*Ch'un-hua-ko t'ieh*), to be prepared from calligraphic specimens in the imperial collection and printed in ten *chüan*, or volumes, five of which were devoted to works attributed to the two Wangs. Compiled by the court calligrapher Wang Chu (fl. ca. 990), whose connoisseurship was less than perfect, the rubbings made from the numerous recuttings of the original carvings of 992 achieved a wide circulation, which resulted in a lowering of artistic standards. As the luster of the two Wangs became tarnished, the more immediate models of the T'ang dynasty, particularly Yen Chen-ch'ing, gained in influence over the regular script of the eleventh century. Leading literary figures and calligraphers of the time, such as Ou-yang Hsiu (1007–1072), Ts'ai Hsiang (1012–1067), and Su Shih (1036–1101), all followed Yen's square and robust regular script style.

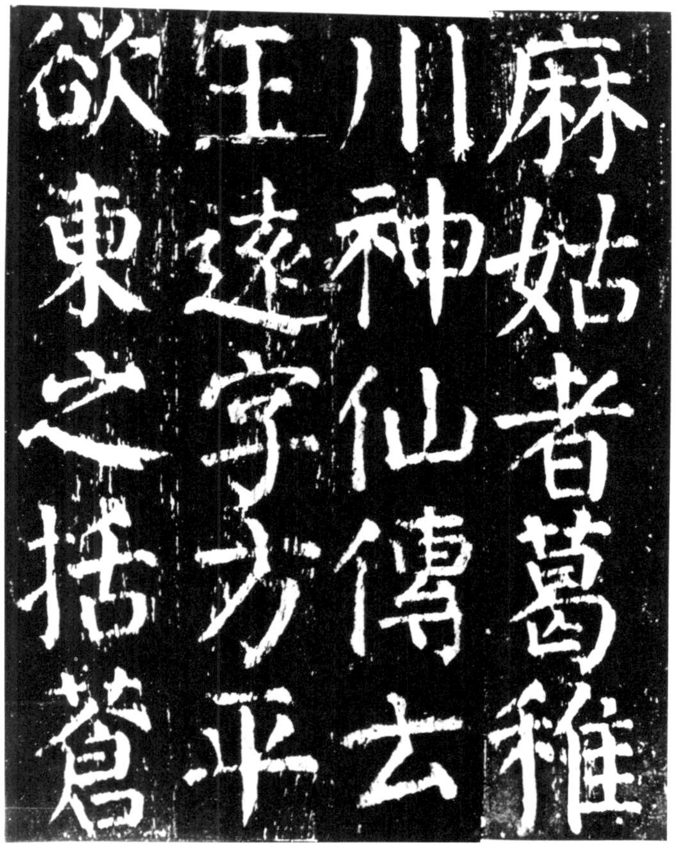


Fig. 69. Yen Chen-ch'ing, *Record of the Altar of the Goddess Ma-ku* (*Ma-ku hsien-t'an chi*). Dated 771. Rubbing of inscription

During the eleventh century scholar-artists heatedly debated the relationship between art and the Tao—the Great Way in general and the teachings of the sages in particular. The Neo-Confucian scholar Chou Tun-i (1017–1073) insisted that art must convey, or serve, the Tao (*wen-i tsai-tao*). Pure art—"the painting of small branches and leaves"—was "harmful to the Tao," it was held, while the only proper justification for art was the "illumination of the Tao" (*ming-tao*).[3]

For the brilliant scholar Su Hsün (1009–1066) and his even more talented son Su Shih, however, art was a means of achieving the power of the Tao (*wen-i kuan-tao*). Their interest in Taoist and Buddhist philosophy prompted them to appreciate "naturalness" and spontaneity in art. "Tao can be made to come," Su Shih wrote, "but cannot be sought."[4] In emphasizing spontaneity and naturalness, he compared art with such physical skills as swimming, which through total mastery become second nature[5]: "My essay writing swells up like ten thousand bushels full of water at the fountainhead, bursting out through the ground, spilling over a flat valley, and running for thousands of miles a day without difficulty. . . . My calligraphy follows my own hand, without bothering with details."[6]

Emphasizing a scholar-artist's personal qualities, the critic Kuo Jo-hsü (fl. ca. 1075) reiterated Yang Hsiung's (53 B.C.–A.D. 18) famous dictum: "Speech is the sound of the mind; calligraphy is the picture of the mind [*hsin-hua*]."[7] Two of Su Shih's younger contemporaries, Huang T'ing-chien and Mi Fu (1052–1107), took these sentiments to heart and, by reaching beyond Wang Hsi-chih and Yen Chen-ch'ing to even earlier sources, developed personal styles that were among the most individual and expressive in calligraphic history.

## *Huang T'ing-chien: Monumental Simplicity*

A native of Fen-ning, in modern Kiangsi province, Huang T'ing-chien (1045–1105) was the son of a poet, Huang Shu (1018–1058); nephew of a book collector, Li Ch'ang (1027–1090); and, through two successive marriages, son-in-law of two respected literary figures, Sun Chüeh (1028–1090) and Hsieh Ching-ch'u (1019–1084). From his uncle Li Ch'ang, young Huang T'ing-chien acquired a love of books. Achieving his *chin-shih* degree in 1067, he was made a professor in 1072 at the Imperial Academy in the northern capital Ta-ming-fu, in modern Hopei province. In 1080 he returned to Kiangsi as subprefect of T'ai-ho district in Chi-chou, and was transferred north again, in 1084, to Te-p'ing-chen in Te-chou, modern Shantung province. In 1085, at the age of forty, he was made a reader at the Imperial Library at the capital at K'ai-feng, and for the next nine years he assisted in the compilation of the *Veritable Records* (*Shih-lu*) of emperor Sung Shen-tsung's (r. 1067–85) reign. By this time he was well established as a poet. Through poetry and other artistic interests, he formed close friendships with such eminent scholar-officials as Ssu-ma Kuang (1019–1086), Wen Yen-po (1006–1097), and Su Shih, who, as advocates of the "conservative policy," had vigorously opposed the "new party" led by Wang An-shih (1021–1086). In 1094, upon the death of the dowager empress Kao, who supported the conservative policy, the new party regained power at the court. Although Huang T'ing-chien never held any office high enough to involve him directly in the political struggle, his association with the conservative leaders was reason enough to cause his exile. He was sent to Fu-chou, Szechuan province, in southwestern China, moving to Jung-chou, Szechuan, in 1098.

During his exile he turned for solace increasingly to the Taoist philosophy of Chuang-tzu and to Ch'an (Zen) Buddhism. In Jung-chou, referring to a passage by Chuang-tzu, he wrote, "My body is like dry wood and my mind is like dead ashes. I am nothing but a useless unshaven monk."[8] Nevertheless he learned to strengthen himself through the practice of calligraphy and poetry.

In 1100, when Emperor Sung Hui-tsung ascended the throne, first under the regency of the dowager empress Hsiang, a brief effort was made to reconcile the two rival parties, but the new party quickly regained power in the following year. Huang T'ing-chien was pardoned, started on his eastward journey down the Yangtze River in early 1101, returned home to Fen-ning a year later for a brief visit, and traveled on to a post in Anhui for only nine days before he was dismissed and sent to I-chou in Hupei province, where he remained for more than a year. At the end of 1103 he was sent on his second exile, this time to I-chou, Kuangsi. He died there in November 1105.[9]

As a calligrapher Huang T'ing-chien did not come into his full power until late in life. He wrote that his early models were Yang Ning-shih (873–957) and Chou Yüeh (fl. ca. 1020–50) for the grass, or cursive, script (*ts'ao-shu*), and Yen Chen-ch'ing for regular script.[10] During the Yüan-yu reign (1086–93), when he was in the Sung capital, he was strongly influenced by Su Shih, with whom he studied and frequently discussed calligraphy. "I am extremely fond of Yen Chen-ch'ing's calligraphy, and I often practice my interpretation of it," Huang wrote. "My brushwork seems to have gotten something of Yen's style, but [when it is] compared to Su Shih's, I am still far behind."[11] In a colophon Huang praised Yen Chen-ch'ing's writing as "exceptionally monumental, elegant, and extraordinary. It combines the superior style and

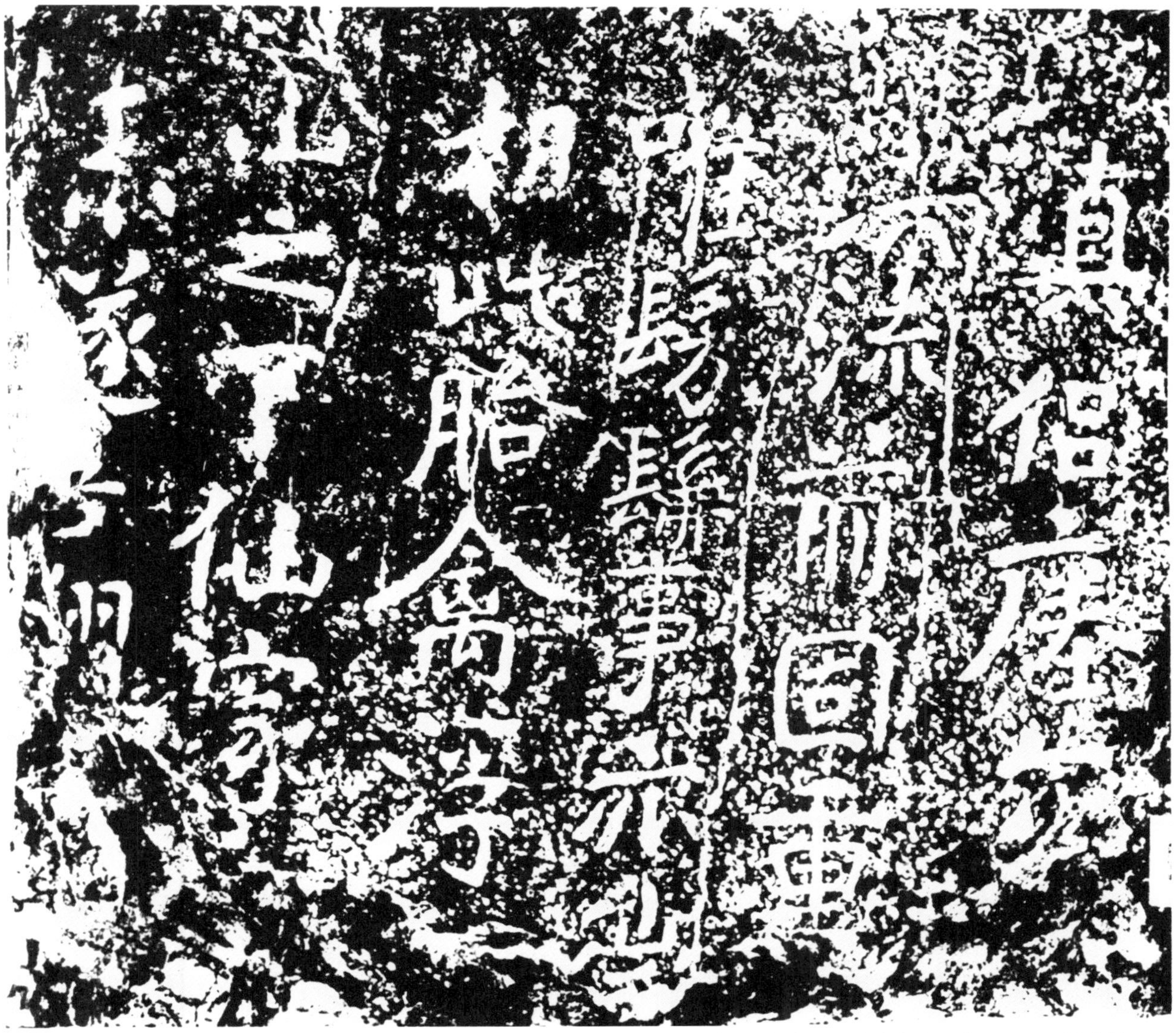

Fig. 70. Attributed to T'ao Hung-ching, detail, *Inscription for Burying a Crane* (*I-ho-ming*). Undated, 512–14. Rubbing of inscription. Chen-chiang, Kiangsu province

structure of the Wei, Tsin, Sui, and T'ang [masters]."[12] Except for Yen Chen-ch'ing, Huang T'ing-chien found most T'ang calligraphic models wanting: "I once spoke of an untrammeled spirit in the calligraphy of the two Wangs and felt that this quality was lacking in Ou-yang Hsün [557–641] Yü Shih-nan, Ch'u Sui-liang, and Hsüeh Chi [649–713]. Then, with Hsü Hao [703–782], and Shen Ch'uan-shih [769–827], it completely disappeared. Only Yen Chen-ch'ing and Yang Ning-shih [873–954] still had this quality."[13]

As a calligraphy theorist Huang T'ing-chien began with the observation made by Su Shih: "In writing large characters the difficulty lies in how to make them look balanced and compact, yet without a feeling of looseness. In writing small characters the difficulty lies in how to make them look spacious and monumental, with a roomy feeling."[14] As the exemplar for small-size writing, Huang cited *Preface to the Orchid Pavilion Gathering* (*Lan-t'ing-chi hsü*), dated 353 and attributed to Wang Hsi-chih (cf. fig. 68). And for large-size writing "that is compact, and without a feeling of looseness, *Inscription for Burying a Crane* [*I-ho-ming*; fig. 70] comes closest to the ideal."[15] He called *Burying a Crane* "the great ancestor of monumental writing."[16]

In the large-size running script Huang T'ing-chien introduced a style that was totally new and revolutionary, both in concept and in technique. Because of the popularity of the Ch'un-hua Palace anthology, which showed only small-size writings of letters and draft manuscripts, large-size monumental writing had been in decline; when practiced at all, it was merely a weak reflection of the Yen Chen-ch'ing style. Huang T'ing-chien's admiration for *Burying a Crane* stemmed from his dissatisfaction with the rigidity and oversophistication of the conventional regular-script writings based on the T'ang models; in *Burying a Crane* he found an antique style of monumental simplicity, with a free and "untrammeled" quality, the very antithesis of the restrictive, laborious forms that he detested.

On the island Chiao-shan, near Chen-chiang on the southern shore of the Yangtze River, the cliff bearing the sixth-century inscription *Burying a Crane* was struck by lightning sometime before the eleventh century, and, falling into the waters below, it broke into several pieces. Nothing was written about the inscription before the Northern Sung period, but, during the eleventh century, the broken stones, visible in fall and winter when the river receded from its banks, became an exciting topic among antiquarian scholars. Most observers of the time regarded the large, magnificent writing as the work of Wang Hsi-chih. Huang T'ing-chien, who "saw the large characters of *Burying a Crane* on the broken cliff at Ching-kou [Chen-chiang, Kiangsu]," considered the monumental script "surely Wang Hsi-chih's writing. Its greatness cannot be described. . . . If one considers this *Burying a Crane* stele as Wang's writing, surely no one can object."[17] But Ou-yang Hsiu (1007–1072), identifying the author of the text of *Burying a Crane* as a T'ang period Taoist priest named Ku K'uang, linked the writing style to Yen Chen-ch'ing: "The characters are unusual and special, but they do not resemble Wang Hsi-chih's brush style. . . . It seems closer to Yen Chen-ch'ing's writing."[18] It was not until the early twelfth century that Huang Po-ssu (1079–1118) and Tung Yü (fl. ca. 1120s) determined that the inscription was composed and executed by T'ao Hung-ching during the T'ien-chien reign of the southern Liang dynasty, between the years 512 and 514.[19]

The interest and controversy generated by *Burying a Crane* during the eleventh century reflected a general enthusiasm among the Northern Sung scholars for archaeology and epigraphical studies of *chin-shih-wen* (bronze and stone writings). Important archaeological publications of the time ranged from private compilations, such as *Catalogue of Collected Antiquities* (*Chi-ku lu*) by Ou-yang Hsiu, *Illustrated Catalogue of Archaeology* (*K'ao-ku t'u*) by Lü Ta-lin (1044–1093), and *Catalogue of Texts on Bronzes and Stones* (*Chin-shih lu*) by Chao Ming-ch'eng (1081–1129), to the catalogue of the imperial collection of the emperor Sung Hui-tsung *Illustrated Catalogue of Antiquities Known in the Hsüan-ho Era [1119–25]* (*Hsüan-ho po-ku-t'u*). The study of ancient scripts by scholars and calligraphers alike included not only stone carvings and inscriptions on ancient ritual bronze vessels, but also cast metal seals and brush or stylus writings on bamboo slips. Studying such inscriptions more for their calligraphy than their historical significance, Huang T'ing-chien and others saw important connections between the brush techniques and compositional principles of different script styles. In a colophon dated 1099 Huang made an insightful comment that would have a significant effect on the subsequent history of Chinese calligraphy: "The cursive writing shares the method and ideas of the tadpole, the seal, and the clerical scripts."[20]

Unlike regular script, where the uniform-size characters rigidly fill the square spaces of a grid pattern, the seal and cursive writings (figs. 71, 72) contract and expand freely, creating dynamic, fluid pictorial designs. Moreover the bold and simple individual brushstrokes of the seal and grass writings contrast strongly with the carefully modulated brushstrokes of the regular script, which change direction with sharp turns, often ending with a flick of the wrist to show the point of the brush. In both freedom of composition and simplicity of brushwork *Burying a Crane* seems to combine the best features of the seal and cursive writings. In contrast to the regular, upright forms made by T'ang calligraphers, the individual characters of *Burying a Crane*, with their range of heights, achieve compactness and balance in an irregular and asymmetrical fashion: individual parts of a character lean in different directions, but the character as a whole—and the relationship between characters—maintains a dynamic equilibrium. Such bold compositions must have required extraordinary psychic energy and confidence. Commenting on the mysteriously "round" (*yüan*) and powerful brushwork of *Burying a Crane*, Huang Po-ssu observed that "the cliff stone must have been difficult to carve. Moreover, the surface of the writing has been eroded by water, so that the writing shows no sign of a sharp brush point. It looks as if it were made by a worn-out, blunt-tipped brush."[21]

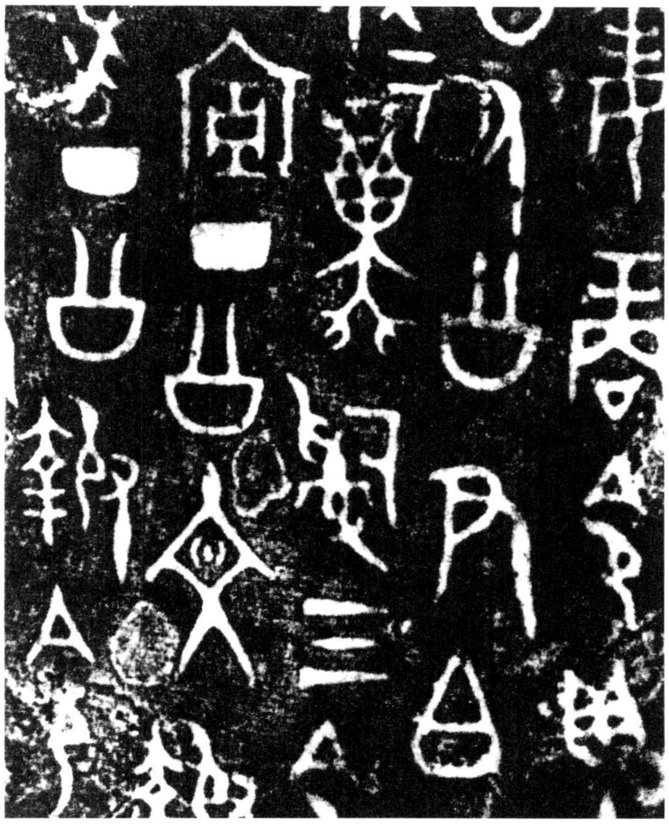

Fig. 71. Anonymous, detail, inscription on a ritual bronze vessel, the Ling *kuei*. Undated, early 11th century B.C. Rubbing of inscription. David Weill collection

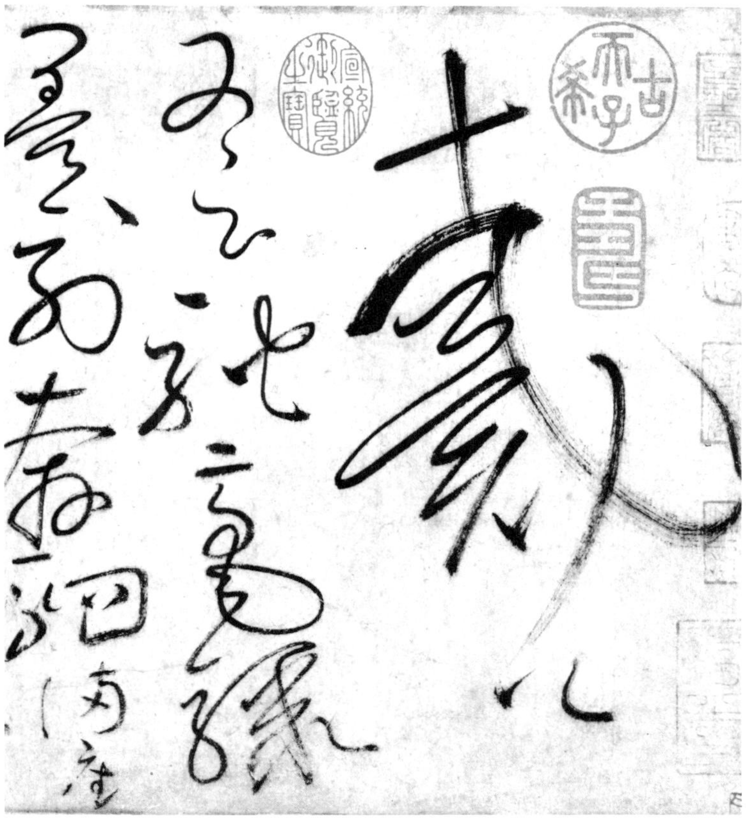

Fig. 72. Huai-su, detail, *Autobiography* (*Tzu-hsü t'ieh*). Dated 777. Handscroll, ink on paper. 28.3 x 755.0 cm (11 1/8 in. x 24 ft. 9 1/4 in.). National Palace Museum, Taipei

The notion of round brushwork— that is, brushstrokes with smooth, round silhouettes—played an important role in Chinese calligraphy and painting criticism: its significance is not only technical and visual, but also moral and philosophical. The ancient essay on calligraphy *Nine Forces* (*Chiu-shih*; attributed to Ts'ai Yung; A.D. 132–192) advises that in executing brushstrokes the writer must "hide the head" and "protect the tail" of each stroke: "Touching the paper with a rounded brush, keep the tip of the brush moving in the middle of the dot or stroke. . . . When the force of a stroke or dot is spent, use full power to halt and pull back."[22] A round brushstroke is strong, deep, and restrained; it is smooth, calm, and self-contained, and hides its own brilliance; "roundness" suggests a graceful appearance and spiritual harmony. Even as a cultivated scholar did not flaunt his mastery of technique, his brushwork ideally betrayed "no trace of the brush." Perhaps the idea of the brushless brushstroke derived from the antiquarian's study of ancient inscriptions cast in bronze or engraved in stone, made not by laying ink on paper with a brush, but by incising a clay matrix with a stylus. Indeed T'ang calligraphers had described good brushstrokes as "drawn in sand" (*ju-hua-sha*) or as resembling "bent hairpins" (*che-ch'ai-ku*). The Sage of Cursive Calligraphy, Huai-su (725–785; fig. 72) is said to have remarked to Yen Chen-ch'ing: "When I see extraordinary mountains in summer clouds, I try to imitate them. Good calligraphy resembles a flock of birds darting out of the trees, or startled snakes scurrying into the grass, or cracks bursting in a shattered wall." Whereupon Yen Chen-ch'ing replied, "What about stains from a leaky roof [*wu-lou-hen*]?"[23] In capturing nature's rhythms and movements, good calligraphy creates a reality all its own.

In studying *Burying a Crane*, Huang T'ing-chien did not copy it; he selected the salient features of his model and forged a strong new individual style that illuminates the calligraphy it draws upon even as it achieves its own imaginative purposes. Besides *Burying a Crane*, Huang's calligraphy seems to have been informed by other sixth-century monumental stone inscriptions, such as *Inscription on the Stone Gate* (*Shih-men-ming*), dated 509 (fig. 75), and *Stele for Cheng Hsi* by Cheng Tao-chao (d. 515), dated 511. In breaking away from the small-size writing tradition of the Northern Sung, Huang fully assimilated the

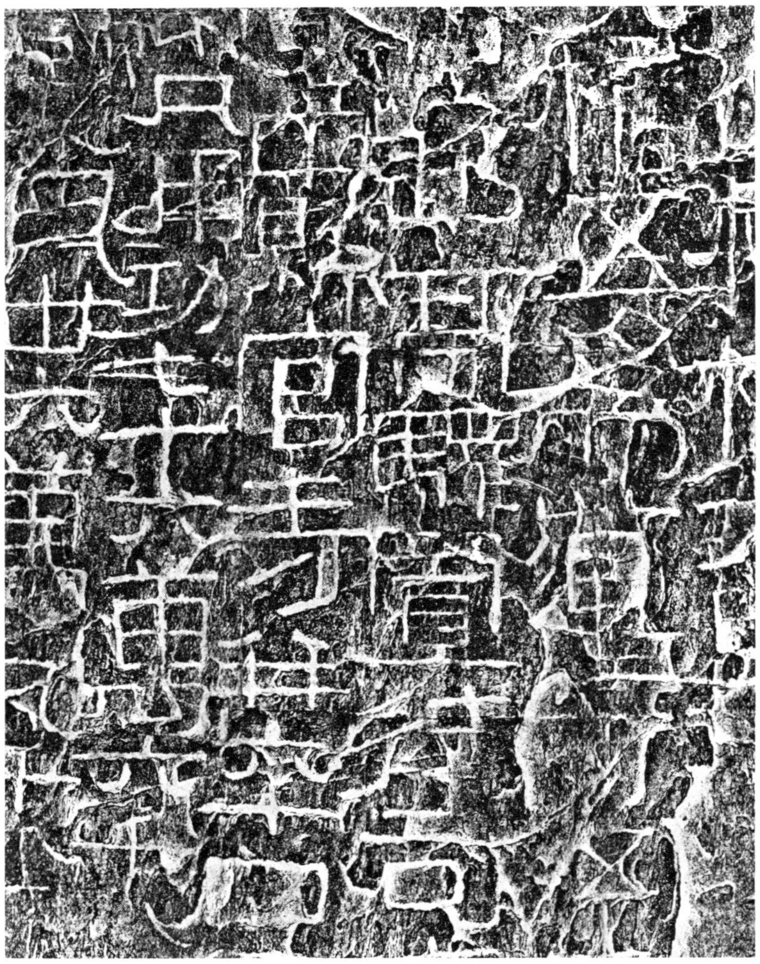

Fig. 73. Anonymous, *Opening the Pao-hsieh Mountain Pass* (*K'ai-t'ung Pao-hsieh-tao k'o-shih*) A.D. 66. Rubbing of inscription on mountain cliff, Pao Valley, Shensi province

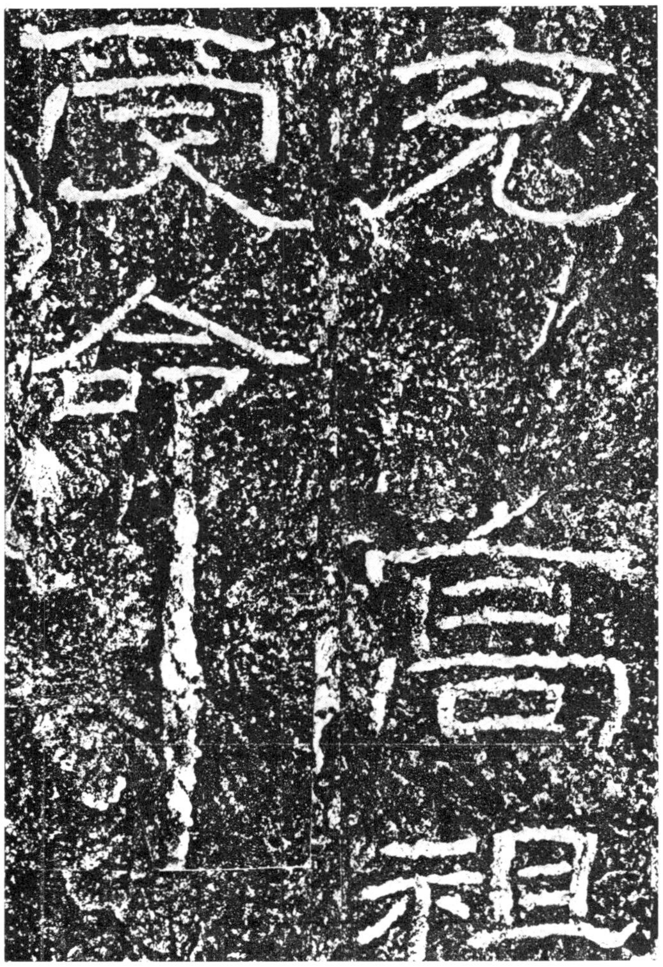

Fig. 74. Anonymous, *Eulogy on the Stone Gate* (*Shih-men-sung*). Dated A.D. 148. Rubbing of inscription, Pao-ch'eng-hsien, Shensi province

influence of a special genre of ancient calligraphy called *mo-yai*, or monumental inscriptions carved on "polished faces of mountainsides."[24]

Although the product of a southern dynasty, *Burying a Crane* belonged firmly to this northern monumental tradition. The earliest extant example of this genre is the inscription *Opening the Pao-hsieh Mountain Pass* (*K'ai-t'ung Pao-hsieh tao k'o-shih*) located at the southern end of the Pao Valley in Shensi in northwestern China and dated A.D. 66 (fig. 73), which commemorated the completion of a strategic mountain pass linking the then metropolitan China with Szechuan in the southwest. Important for military purposes, the pass was repeatedly blocked and destroyed in times of trouble, and its successive rebuildings were celebrated at Pao-ch'eng-hsien, Shensi province, by the *Eulogy on the Stone Gate* (*Shih-men-sung*), dated A.D. 148 (fig. 74), and the *Inscription on the Stone Gate* of 509. All three inscriptions are executed in a bold and free archaizing form, with plain round brushstrokes that look more like natural markings in the stone than the work of human hands. In their form and rhythm they blend into the ancient mountain face upon which they are engraved, becoming symbols of eternity. The earliest of the three inscriptions, written in an archaizing cursive clerical script (*ts'ao-li-shu*) form, shows characters in straight lines and varying sizes, like the markings on ancient ritual tortoise shells. Although the characters of the *Eulogy* of 148 generally fall into a grid pattern, long vertical strokes occupy one or two additional squares on the grid, recalling those of the free cursive clerical script found on bamboo slips dated to the early Han period. The *Inscription on the Stone Gate* of 509, in echoing the free and round brushwork of the earlier *Eulogy*, contrasts strongly with the neatly formed regular-script writing then fashionable at the Northern Wei court, for example the *Tomb Epitaph of Prince Yüan Hsiang* (*Yüan Hsiang mu-chih*) dated 507 (fig. 76), which betrays the influence of the more elegant southern tradition of Wang Hsi-chih.

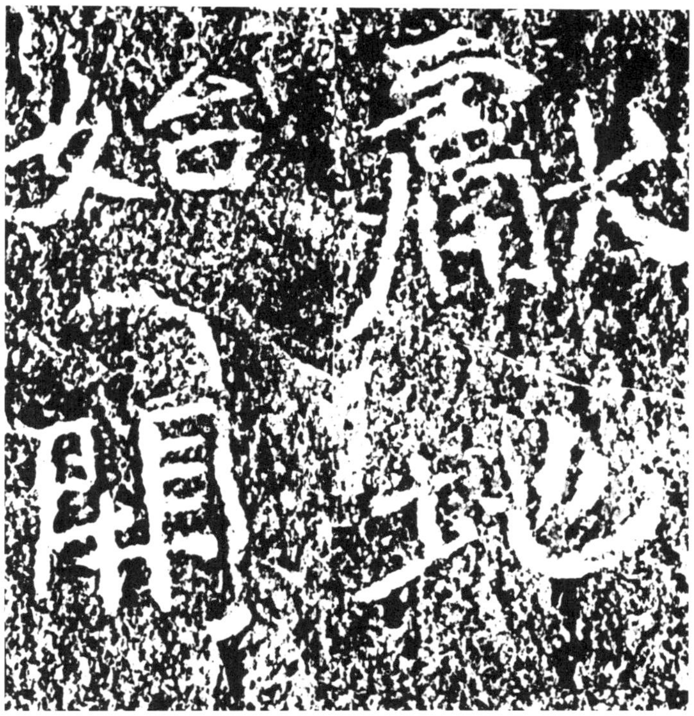

Fig. 75. Anonymous, *Inscription on the Stone Gate* (*Shih-men-ming*). Dated 509. Rubbing of inscription, Pao-ch'eng-hsien, Shensi province

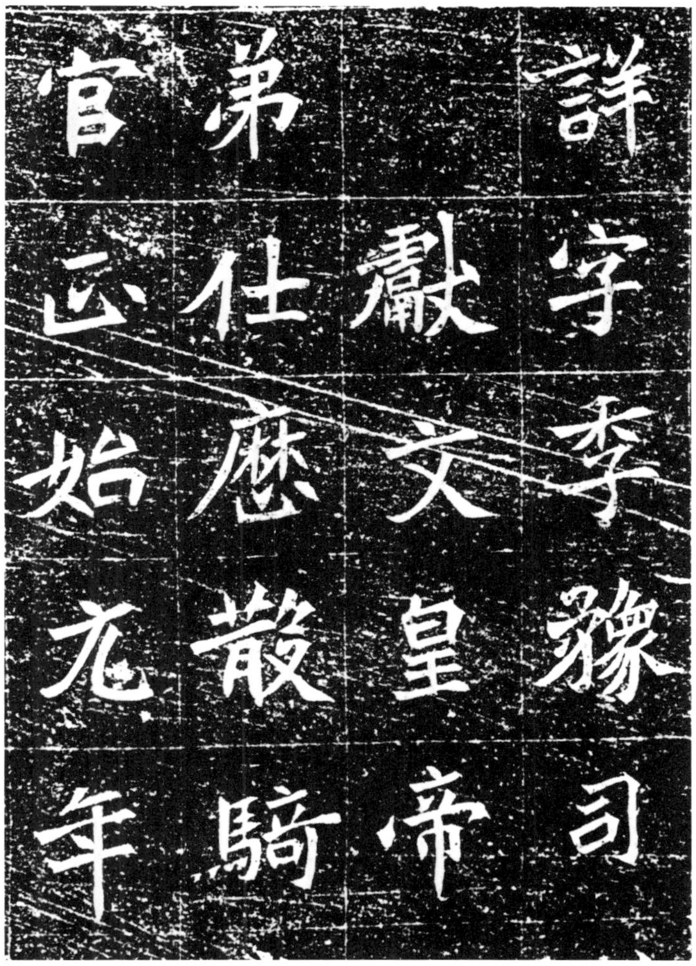

Fig. 76. Anonymous, *Tomb Epitaph of Prince Yüan Hsiang* (*Yüan Hsiang mu-chih*). Dated 507. Rubbing of inscription, Ch'ang-ling, Loyang

In 511 Cheng Tao-chao (d. 515), the powerful prefect of Kuangchou in Shantung and a great calligrapher, carved onto high mountains south of Yeh-hsien two stone steles extolling the virtue and career of his father, Cheng Hsi.[25] This grand act of filial piety, through which he also publicized and immortalized his own literary composition and calligraphic art, apparently so exhilarated him that he went on to write and carve dozens more of his poems at sites ranging from Yeh-hsien in the east, to P'ing-tu in the south, then to I-tu in the west, adding comments and signs on choice peaks. One splendid example is *Poem on Ascending Cloud-Peak Mountain and Discussing the Classics* (*Teng Yün-feng-shan lun-ching-shu shih*), dated 511 (fig. 77), which shows marked similarities in both brushwork and composition of individual characters to *Burying a Crane*, written about the same time. It has been argued by scholars who are accustomed to thinking of the south as more artistically "advanced" than the north that Cheng Tao-chao was influenced by some "new style of a southern dynasty," namely

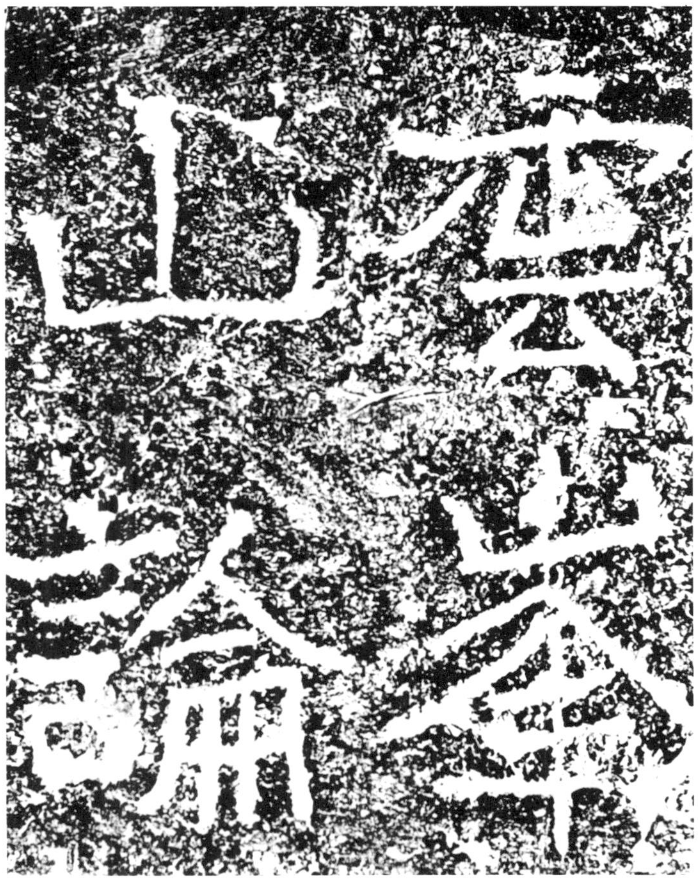

Fig. 77. Cheng Tao-chao, *Poem on Ascending Cloud-Peak Mountain and Discussing the Classics* (*Teng Yün-feng-shan lun-ching-shu shih*). Dated 511. Rubbing of inscription, Yeh-hsien, Shantung province

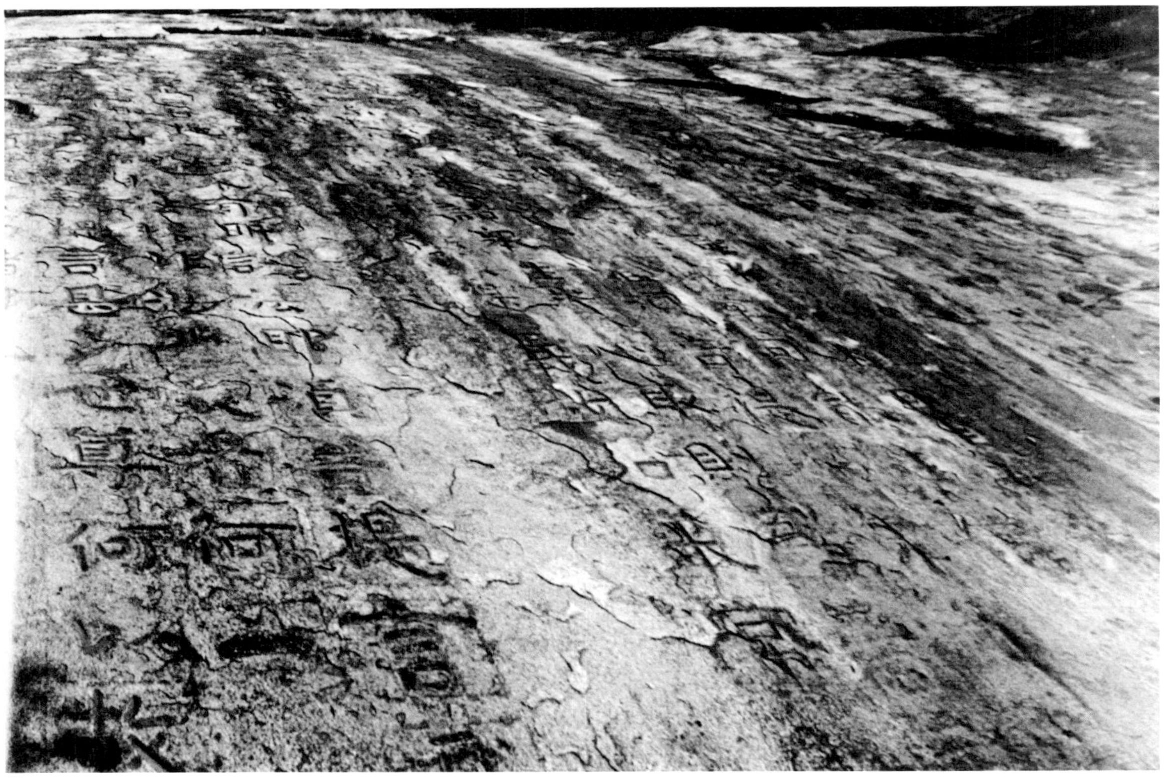

Fig. 78. Monumental carvings at Sutra Stone Valley. Undated, 560s–570s. T'ai-an-hsien, Shantung province

that of *Burying a Crane*.[26] But since both Cheng Tao-chao's work and *Burying a Crane* bear close resemblance to the *Inscription on the Stone Gate* of 509, it seems probable that all three had belonged to the northern monumental tradition, which continued to flourish through the second half of the sixth century. In the 560s and 570s, Cheng Tao-chao's son Cheng Shu-tsu, who followed his father as prefect, added more inscriptions on the same mountains.[27] During the same period there appeared among the splendid peaks of the sacred Mount T'ai range in Shantung, from T'ai-an in the north to Tsou-hsien in the south, about two dozen giant monumental carvings of Buddhist sacred texts. The largest of these, cut into a streambed named Sutra Stone Valley, once consisted of more than 2,000 characters (about 900 remain), each more than 1 foot wide (fig. 78). The large characters revert to the wide rectangle form of the archaic clerical script, with simple round brushstrokes. In physical grandeur matched only by the colossal rockcut images of Buddha at Yün-kang and Lung-men, these enormous writings bearing the words of Buddha, here permanently engraved on the bones of the earth under the vault of heaven, testify not only to man's spiritual devotion, but also to his unique creative power.

Unlike small-size writings, which are seen close up, large-size calligraphy must be viewed from a distance. To accommodate this shift, in the words of Huang T'ing-chien, "when the ancients studied calligraphy, they did not copy exactly. . . . They spread out an earlier master's work on the wall, and looked at it in complete concentration. Then, when they put their own brushes to paper, they naturally wrote in accordance with the earlier master's ideas."[28]

One of Huang T'ing-chien's masterpieces in the large running script (average character 3 inches in height), *Scroll for Chang Ta-t'ung* (*Tseng Chang Ta-t'ung ku-wen t'i-chi*), dated 1100, when the artist was living in exile in Jung-chou, is now in the John B. Elliott Collection, on loan to The Art Museum, Princeton University (no. 1).[29] The text reads, in part:

> I have made my home to the south of the city next to the butchers. Weeds grow in my house, and rats share my path. Still there are young people who constantly ask me to show them composition and calligraphy. Now I, Fu-weng, am fifty-six. I have foot trouble and cannot bend over. My stomach feels hard, as if carrying a tile or stone. I do not know if, on another day, I will be able to write characters like these again.

Despite Huang's fears about his failing powers, the scroll brims with energy and is in fact but one of many great works from his late years. It seems to bear out the popular Chinese notion that great art is often the product of a hard and bitter life. Just as earlier calligraphers had spread a work on the wall and examined it for its overall conception, so the individual characters in *Scroll for Chang Ta-t'ung* must be seen not as separate entities, but as critically linked elements of a total design: they move freely, almost three-dimensionally—contracting, expanding, and interlocking, thoroughly activating the composition.

Huang T'ing-chien treated his composition of large characters as pure energy and movement in abstract space. "Speaking of a calligrapher's brush force [*pi-shih*]," he once commented, "how Mi Fu has attained its limits."[30] In his own work Huang concentrated on the concept of *shih* (kinetic force or momentum). In the words of the *Nine Forces*, "When the *shih* rushes forward, it cannot be restrained; when the *shih* backs away, it cannot be stopped."[31] Huang wrote with his wrist and arm suspended above the table (*hsüan-wan*); he gripped the brush tightly, carefully hiding the brushtip in the center of the stroke, while pressing down and lifting up the brush vertically. This way he followed through each stroke with the power of his entire arm and body, rather than flicking the brush with his fingers and wrist: "Use two fingers [the fore and the middle], one on top of the other, and press hard against the fourth [which pushes forward]," he instructed. "Hold the palm round and hollow, while the fingers [grip the brush] firmly and solidly." In wielding the brush, he stressed the importance of "holding back as well as releasing energy" (*ch'in-tsung*) and "driving every stroke with full force" (*pi-chung yung-li*).[32] His grasp was so firm that occasionally he struggled with the brush, giving a halting or jerky motion to the stroke.

In discussing the imitation of ancient models, Huang T'ing-chien used the Taoist metaphors of "grabbing the fetus" (*to-t'ai*), meaning "capturing the essence of life," and "changing the bones" (*huan-ku*), or "reorganizing the structure" of the original. A master in the use of colloquial expressions in poetry, he had advocated the "turning of the common into the elegant, and the old into the new. . . . When we use in our compositions a familiar quotation from the ancient, it becomes an elixir that transforms iron into gold."[33] The secret in imitation, he believed, was to allow "the mind to respond to the subtle suggestions" (*hsin-hui chi miao-ch'u*) of the model. In his calligraphy he borrowed a single element from *Burying a Crane*—two long diagonal strokes, the roof radical, from the character *ch'in* (cf. fig. 80)—as the hallmark of his personal style (fig. 79), and that particular motif became the "elixir" that transmuted his "mortal bones."

Seeing his calligraphy as abstract movement, Huang described it with a musical concept, *yün* (resonance). *Yün* also means "rhyming" in poetry. Toward the end of the fifth century, along with the differentiation of the four tones (*ssu-sheng*) in the Chinese language, used for metrical purposes in poetry, a carefully regulated rhyme scheme was developed. According to Liu Hsieh (ca. 465–522), author of *The Literary Mind and the Carving of Dragons* (*Wen-hsin tiao-lung*), "by *ho* is meant the harmony of words of different sounds, and by *yün* is meant the consonant response of words of the same tone."[34] While early critics carefully laid down the "laws" and spelled out the "defects" in rhyming, they failed to define rules that would guarantee harmony (*ho*) in poetry. As Liu Hsieh pointed out, "rhyming has definite patterns; but the *ho* elements are sometimes low and sometimes high, so it is difficult to harmonize all the sounds."[35] In painting criticism the

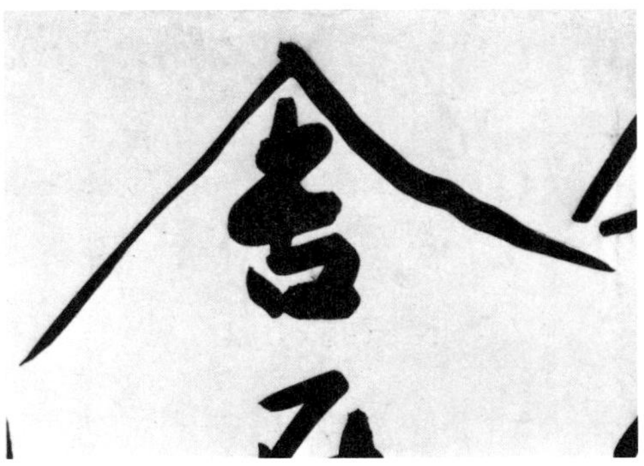

Fig. 79. The character *she*, detail, Huang T'ing-chien, *Scroll for Chang Ta-t'ung* (*Tseng Chang Ta-t'ung ku-wen t'i-chi*), no. 1

Fig. 80. The character *ch'in*, detail, attributed to T'ao Hung-ching, *Inscription for Burying a Crane* (*I-ho-ming*). Undated, 512–14. Rubbing of inscription, Chen-chiang, Kiangsu province

word *yün* came to refer to the tasteful and harmonious manner in composition, something equivalent to the concept of *ho* and equally difficult to define. Ching Hao (fl. ca. 870–930), in *Notes on Brush Method* (*Pi-fa chi*), for instance, tersely defined *yün* as *pu-su* (not vulgar),[36] but Huang T'ing-chien offered his own, more descriptive definition:

> In calligraphy and painting, one should look for *yün*. Li Kung-lin [ca. 1049–1106], in depicting [the captured Han] General Li Kuang [1077–1155] seizing a horse and fleeing southward, pictured the general pointing a fully drawn bow at the pursuing enemy. Where the arrows should strike, men and horses would fall at the sound of the bowstring. Li Kung-lin remarked with a smile: "Suppose a vulgar craftsman were to do this scene: he would have shown arrows striking the pursuing horsemen."[37]

Like Li Kung-lin, Huang T'ing-chien preferred taseful suggestion to dramatic exaggeration. Since calligraphy has no representational content, its beauty lies not so much in the artist's knowledge or ideas as in how he absorbs and responds to influences and how he graphically expresses the turn, the connection, and the gesture of thought. For Huang good brushwork had to have resonance—that is, good taste.

Using two popular models in poetry, Tu Fu (712–770) and T'ao Ch'ien (365–427), Huang T'ing-chien once explained that while artistry, as exemplified by Tu Fu, is founded on methods and rules, magic in art, as shown by T'ao Ch'ien, lies outside them and is indescribable: "For Tu Fu, there is the 'eye' of his phrase; / For T'ao Ch'ien, his is the music of a stringless zither."[38] As committed or "useful" art, poetry must say things—with an "eye" in every phrase; yet for pure imagination true music is found beyond the notes played on an instrument. Though a hardworking, highly disciplined Confucian scholar, Huang learned about inspiration and enlightenment from Chuang-tzu and Ch'an Buddhism. He was careful to point out that the way of art is born of a paradox: "The marvel is in harmonizing with all light and in uniting with all dust [i.e., uniting with the world] / But the description must be deep and penetrating." For "deep and penetrating" description (*kou-shen ju-shen*) he followed the earnest, striving humanist Tu Fu; but for "harmonizing with all light and in uniting with all dust" (*ho-kuang t'ung-ch'en*) he modeled himself after the incomparably natural and plain T'ao Ch'ien.[39]

In Huang's calligraphy, although the composition of individual characters seems difficult and eccentric, the brushwork is completely natural and straightforward. In *Scroll for Chang Ta-t'ung* the artist, ravaged but not humbled, marched forward clenching his brush in his fist, leaving behind an image of a strong, indomitable man. Huang's mentor and close friend Su Shih characterized Huang's calligraphy with a set of contrasting yet complementary qualities:

> He creates oblique and crooked characters with a view of equilibrium;
> He engages in playful methods with a straight and sincere countenance;
> He executes trivial matters with a large and open personality.[40]

## *Mi Fu: Eclecticism and Spontaneity*

Mi Fu (1052–1107) was an artistic personality very different from Huang T'ing-chien. Whereas Huang led a sad but conventional life of a scholar-official, and lived and died where his assignment and exiles took him, Mi Fu never earned a degree and served for most of his life in bureaucratic and secretarial positions, freely roaming the country as a scholar-artist and connoisseur. While Huang was a noted poet and counted calligraphy as but one of his accomplishments, Mi began to practice calligraphy earnestly at the age of six or seven and pursued it with a singular passion and as his principal occupation. The characters and styles of the two men's handwritings are also markedly different: with Huang the individual characters are tightly knit and asymmetrical, while the powerfully round brushwork, slow and measured, is plain and basically consistent; Mi Fu's character formation appears less adventurous, but his brushwork is brilliantly complex and lively, richly informed by his incomparable knowledge and experience as a collector and connoisseur.

Born in 1052 in Hsiang-yang, in Hupei province, Mi Fu had the good fortune to grow up in the Northern Sung capital at K'ai-feng, in the household of the heir apparent, the future Emperor Sung Ying-tsung (r. 1064–67), where his mother served as a lady-in-waiting to the future empress. His forebears had probably emigrated to the capital from the Central Asian region of Sogdia in the early seventh century.[41] Several of Mi Fu's immediate ancestors held military positions; Fu's father Mi Tso, a military official, was a lover of antiquities and calligraphy. This unusual family background undoubtedly affected Mi Fu's personality and career. His great pride in his native Hsiang-yang, which inspired him to imagine himself a descendant of the ancient kings of Ch'u (rulers of Hsiang-yang during the Warring States period), suggests that he may have been sensitive to his origins.[42]

Because of his mother's services to the imperial household, Mi Fu was made a reader at the Imperial Library in the capital in 1070, at about eighteen, and soon afterward was sent south to be a district official in Kuangtung province, then was transferred in 1073 to Kuei-lin in Kuangsi, where the ebullient young official left a self-portrait at a popular scenic spot, the stalactite wonder called the Cave of the Returned Pearl.[43] After less than five years in the south, Mi Fu, desiring to be near home, secured a clerical position in 1075 in Ch'ang-sha, where he stayed for about six years. In 1080 he gave up the position and started to tour the various provinces in Chiang-nan, south of the Yangtze River, assiduously collecting antique calligraphy and painting. For about ten years, except for two brief periods serving in minor official functions in Hang-chou (1084–85) and Yang-chou (1088–89), he traveled continually in Hunan, Hupei, Kiangsi, Kiangsu, Chekiang, Kuangtung, and Honan provinces. During this period he visited such eminent scholars and statesmen as Su Shih (1082) and Wang An-shih (1083), and attended with Su Shih the famous literary gathering held by Wang Shen (ca. 1036–ca. 1089) at the Western Garden in K'ai-feng in 1088. Among the places he preferred were Su-chou (1080 and 1087) and Jun-chou (Chen-chiang; 1091) in Kiangsu. Between 1086 and 1088, he also finished his first work on ancient calligraphy, *Catalogue of Precious Specimens of Calligraphy Visited* (*Pao-chang tai-fang lu*).

In 1092 he was appointed subprefect of Yung-ch'iu district in Honan, a post he held for two years, leaving after a dispute with an imperial inspector in 1094. Returning east, with a sinecure as superintendent of the Chung-yüeh Temple, he enjoyed two independent years living mostly at Jun-chou, Kiangsu. In 1097 he assumed the post of military commander of Lien-shui district in Kiangsu. Between 1099 and 1101 he was assigned to the Office of Regulator and Intendant of Exchange between the Yangtze and Huai rivers and the Hupei and Chekiang circuits. Traveling in the Lake T'ai region and along the Grand Canal to the north, he sailed with his collection of calligraphy and painting scrolls, in a houseboat bearing a sign that read "The Mi Family's Calligraphy and Painting Barge."[44]

By that time he had earned a wide reputation as a calligrapher, painter, and connoisseur. In 1103 he was called to the capital as a calligrapher and made a doctor of the Imperial Sacrifices, but his temperament and unconventional behavior were unsuited for life at the court, and he was banished to Anhui, as military commander of the Wu-wei district. In 1106 he was recalled and made the only doctor of calligraphy and painting at the emperor Sung Hui-tsung's newly founded Calligraphy and Painting Academy (Shu-hua-yüan)[45] and shortly afterward was briefly promoted to assistant division chief on the Board of Rites. Again an imperial censor had him demoted to head the military command of the Huai-yang district in Kiangsu. He died at that post in 1107.

Extraordinarily proud and independent, Mi Fu ranks with the great eccentric scholar-artists in Chinese history. He called himself "The Wild Scholar of Hsiang-yang" (Hsiang-yang man-shih) and was widely known as "Mi the Crazy" (Mi-tien). A man of obsessive passions, he pursued his love of fine painting and calligraphy, strangely shaped rocks, and old inkstones with a rare single-mindedness. Once, disappointed in his efforts to acquire a work attributed to the Eastern Tsin calligrapher Hsieh An (320–385), he vomited blood and fainted.[46] Because he never craved worldly success (he distributed most of his family wealth among poor relations), his admirers overlooked his strange conduct in collecting as a harmless personal foible. During a lifetime of travels he saw and described most of the best paintings and calligraphic works in private collections throughout China. Although he had encountered treasures in remote places, great concentrations of choice objects were located in the Chiang-nan area, particularly in Su-chou, in the capital city of K'ai-feng, and in the ancient eastern capital, Lo-yang, in Honan. As a minor official, Mi Fu had to rely on his knowledge and wit in order to curry favor with such high imperial clansmen and collectors as Wang Shen, Li Wei (second half of the eleventh century), and Chao Ling-jang (fl. ca 1070–1100). In his writings Mi decried these privileged but less than knowledgable collectors, boasting of his successes in tricking them with copies and forgeries. Yet he encountered nothing but generosity and high esteem among leading scholars and statesmen of the time. Wang An-shih praised him highly; Su Shih pronounced him "a first-class talent under heaven;"[47] and even Emperor Sung Hui-tsung was supposed to have remarked, "Such a brilliant man should not be judged by ordinary etiquette."[48] Sung Hui-tsung's prime minister, Ts'ai Ching (1047–1126), is said to have reported to his emperor, "Mi Fu is the kind of person of whom we must have one, but cannot afford two!"[49]

Of Mi Fu's unprecedented knowledge of ancient styles, the artist has given his own account in an essay collected in the *Calligraphic Works in the Ch'ün-yü-t'ang Studio* (*Ch'ün-yü-t'ang t'ieh*):

> In the beginning I studied Yen Chen-ch'ing; I was then seven or eight *sui* [six or seven years old]. I practiced characters in a large format, and I was not able to do letter-size writings. Then I was attracted to the tight composition of Liu Kung-ch'üan [778–865], so I started to study his *Diamond Sutra* [*Chin-kang Ching*]. After a while I realized that Liu had derived his style from Ou-yang Hsün, so I studied Ou-yang, but before long my writing looked like printed blocks or the sliding beads on an abacus. I then became enamored of the Ch'u Sui-liang style, which I studied the longest. I also admired the supple turns and folds of Tuan Chi [fl. ca. 806–20] and the multidimensional quality of his work, but, after a while, I discovered that Tuan had derived himself solely from [Wang Hsi-chih's] *Preface to the Orchid Pavilion Gathering*. So I went through all the anthologies of rubbings [of the two Wangs' calligraphy]. Gradually I moved back to the [Western] Tsin and Wei styles, cultivating more and more the plain and light [*p'ing-tan*] taste, eventually passing over the method of Chung Yu [A.D. 151–230] to study the *Stele of Liu K'uan* by Shih-i-kuan [ca. A.D. 168–88]. For seal script I loved *A Chant Cursing the Ch'u People* [*Tsu-Ch'u wen*; ca. 320 B.C.] and *The Stone Drum Inscription* [*Shih-ku wen*; ca. 420 B.C.]. I also gained insights into the writings on bamboo slips, done with a bamboo stylus dipped in lacquer, as well as the wonders of the archaic inscriptions on bronze vessels. . . .[50]

Keenly aware of the pitfalls of this encyclopedic approach to studying calligraphy, Mi Fu strove throughout his life to make his style distinctive: "In my maturing years, before I was able to establish my own style, people criticized my calligraphy as collector-antiquarian's writing. I used to select from the best styles and combine them in my own. It was not until after reaching old age that I found my own style. Now on seeing my calligraphy no one can tell who is my real model."[51]

Although Mi prided himself as a calligrapher in all five script types, he primarily used the running script. Following the example of the Eastern Tsin calligraphers, he devoted special attention to letter writing as a fine art, using it as a vehicle for personal expression; consequently his letters were especially treasured by collectors. Three superb letters by Mi Fu, datable to 1093–94, are in the John B. Elliott Collection, now on loan to The Art Museum, Princeton University (no. 2). Known by key phrases in the texts, they are: "Abundant Harvest" ("Sui-feng t'ieh"; Leaf A), "Escaping Summer Heat" ("T'ao-shu t'ieh"; Leaf B), and "Hasty Reply before Guests" ("Tui-k'o ts'ao-ts'ao t'ieh"; Leaf C). Closely resembling a poem written in Jun-chou after he had "passed forty" in 1091,[52] and a letter addressed to "Brother Lo" ("Lo-hsiung t'ieh"), dated 1095 and now in Tokyo (fig. 81),[53] the Elliott letters, together with the Tokyo letter, relate events that took place in 1092–94, when Mi Fu served as subprefect of Yung-ch'iu district in

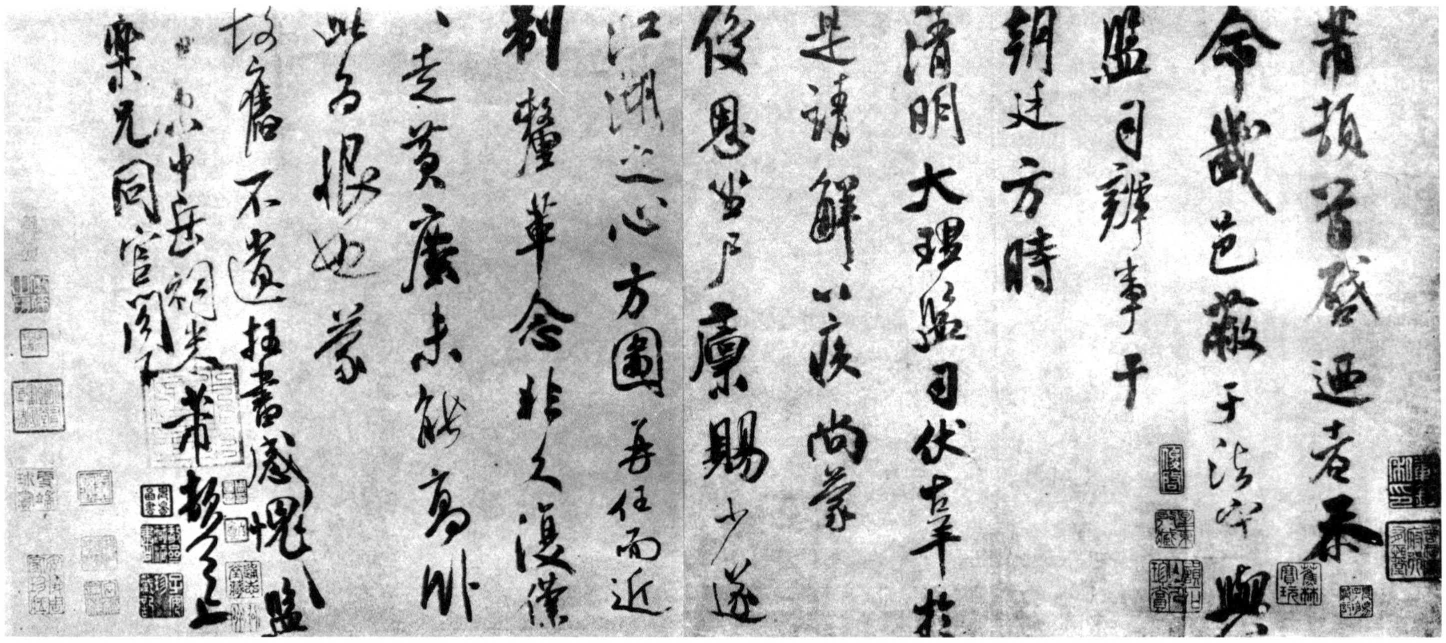

Fig. 81. Mi Fu, *Letter to Brother Lo* (*Lo-hsiung t'ieh*). Dated 1095. Album leaf, ink on paper. 29.0 x 66.0 cm (11 3/8 x 26 in.)

Honan.[54] Appointed a full-fledged civil magistrate, Mi Fu did well at his post until he entered into a dispute over grain-tax collection with a government inspector. In "Abundant Harvest," which was probably written early in 1093, the artist, evidently secure and pleased with himself, greeted a newly arrived fellow magistrate of a neighboring district with some kind words of advice:

> I, Fu, bow my head and ask to speak again. In my district we are blessed with an abundant harvest and no unusual happenings; thus I am allowed to continue cultivating my incompetence and earning a salary, since there is not so much to do. But Your Excellency, who has just arrived in your new position, must remember to help your people to live a good long life. A good magistrate must follow the wishes of the people while helping to spread a civilizing influence. I shall daily wipe my eyes clean and carefully listen [for good news from you]. . . .

Unfortunately, Mi Fu's naïve assumption that a good magistrate should always place the people's welfare before all else soon brought him into conflict with harsh reality.

Later that year the harvest was bad. The court dispatched an inspector to hasten the collection of grain taxes, and Mi Fu resisted the order. "Escaping Summer Heat," probably written in the summer of 1094, when the artist was escaping from a rise in political as well as seasonal temperatures, betrays a less happy state of mind:

> I, Fu, escaping summer heat, have come to the mountain and am comfortable here. We live a life of illusions. [One character missing] gives us fever, while heat causes us to be vexed. As the saying goes, rich [or poor] we all suffer from the heat. Ya-chih is located in the middle of the [undecipherable character], north of Southern Mountain. All summer [we sleep under] covers. When I am vexed by heat and able to escape here, am I not fortunate? By autumn I should be able to leave this place. . . .

"Hasty Reply before Guests," written for a waiting messenger while entertaining guests, probably dates to the summer of 1094:

> Earlier you came by and left a note, and I did not get to see you. I am still feeling disappointed. Now you inform me that my luggage has arrived. Because of the inspection visit of the official Lin, I have chosen to avoid him either by pleading to stay home or by running for the ferry landing before he arrives. . . . I reply to you hastily before guests. . . .

Finally, in the letter in Tokyo, signed with his new sinecure title, "Superintendent of Chung-yüeh Temple," Mi summarizes the whole affair:

> Some time ago I received orders to govern a territorial district. Because of my ignorance of government policy an inspector had my affairs brought to the court. In time the fair judge of the supreme Ta-li court declared me guilty as charged. So I asked to be released from official duties on account of poor health, and I was, by imperial grace, given an honorary position with salary and a chance to satisfy my "wish for living among rivers and lakes." . . . I am fortunate not to be forgotten by an old friend, so I write this to express my gratitude and shame—my gratitude and shame! Superintendent [characters missing] of Chung-yüeh Temple, Mi Fu, bowing his head, presenting this to His Excellency, Brother Lo.

In these letters, which represent Mi Fu's mature calligraphy, there is an easy mixture of stylistic sources. Rather than exhibiting the entire range of his knowledge, the artist adopted a style suited to the occasion, referring to earlier styles only as the spirit moved him. In their basic format these letters follow Wang Hsi-chih: the line of salutation, "I, Fu, bow my head, . . ." for example, clearly acknowledges Mi's indebtedness to the elder Wang, who opens his letters with the same characters (figs. 82a–d), while both single characters and the composition of the characters show an intimate familiarity with Wang's *Preface to the Orchid Pavilion Gathering* (cf. fig. 68) and the popular T'ang compendium of Wang's calligraphy in Priest Huai-jen's *Preface to the Sacred Teaching* (*Sheng-chiao hsü*) of 672. In "Abundant Harvest," which is a formal and polite missive complete with the artist-magistrate's seal, "Yü-hsiung hou-jen" (descendant of Yü-hsiung of the ancient Ch'u kingdom), affixed over the signature, "Fu," in the concluding line, Mi Fu employs the "beautiful" style of Ch'u Sui-liang, with finely modulated brushstrokes (fig. 83); and in "Escaping Summer Heat" the artist vents his anger and vexation through the angular and "severe" style of Ou-yang Hsün (fig. 84). Befitting the occasion and his state of mind, "Hasty Reply before Guests" reflects passion and abandon in a free running script.

The individualistic character of Mi Fu's writing style lies in his approach to brushwork, which seems to have been the opposite of Huang T'ing-chien's:

> People these days, when writing large characters, often grip the brush as hard as they can, and yet their calligraphy ends up looking deficient in sinews and bones, and lacks a spirited air. In writing in the round brushwork, they make the ends of their brushstrokes look like steamed breads. How laughable! [Large characters] should really look as if they were small ones, complete with all the sharp-edged movements, and preferably without a labored and artificial look.[55]

(a) (b) (c) (d)

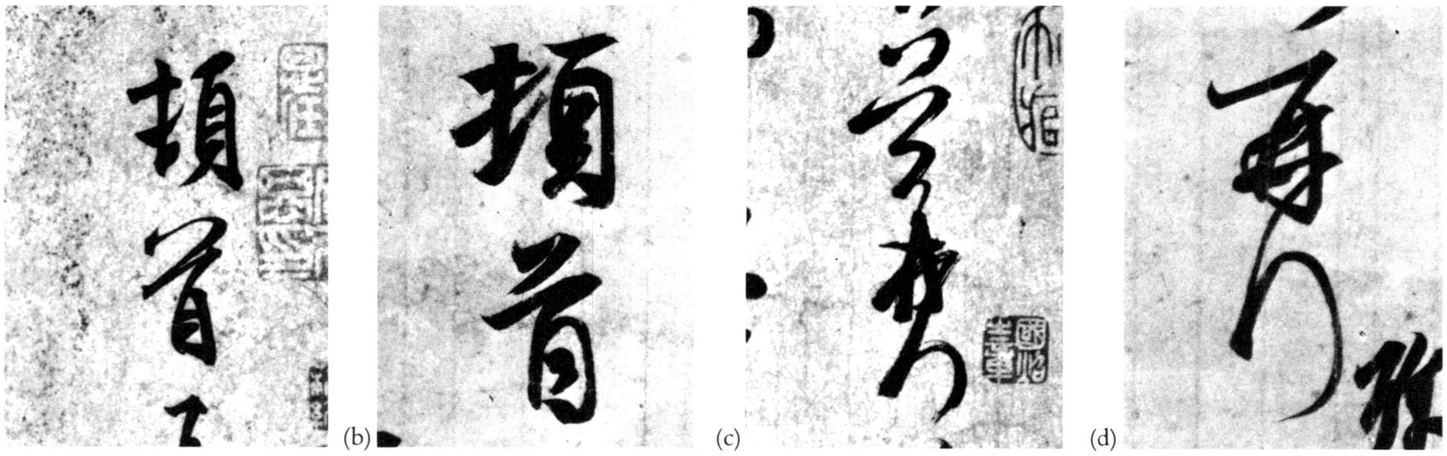

Figs. 82a–d. The characters *tun-shou* (bowing my head), details: Mi Fu, "Escaping Summer Heat" ("T'ao-shu t'ieh"), no. 2B(a) and Wang Hsi-chih *Disordered at the Time of Mourning* (*Sang-luan t'ieh*). Handscroll, ink on paper. 28.7 x 63.0 cm (11 1/4 x 24 3/4 in.). Imperial Household Museum, Tokyo (b); the characters *tsai-pai* (bow again), details: Mi Fu, "Hasty Reply before Guests" ("Tui k'o ts'ao-ts'ao t'ieh"), no. 2C (c) and Wang Hsi-chih, *Disordered at the Time of Mourning* (d)

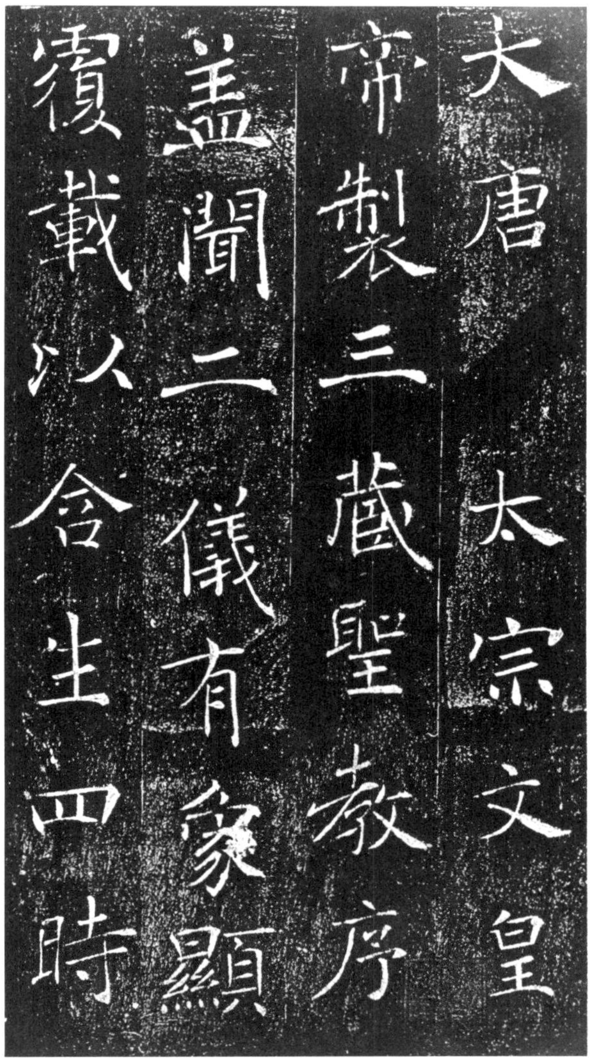


Fig. 83. Ch'u Sui-liang, *Preface to the Sacred Teaching Stele* (*Sheng-chiao-hsü pei*). Dated 654. 23.5 x 14.9 cm (9¼ x 5⅞ in.). Rubbing of inscription, Hsi-an (Sian), Shensi province

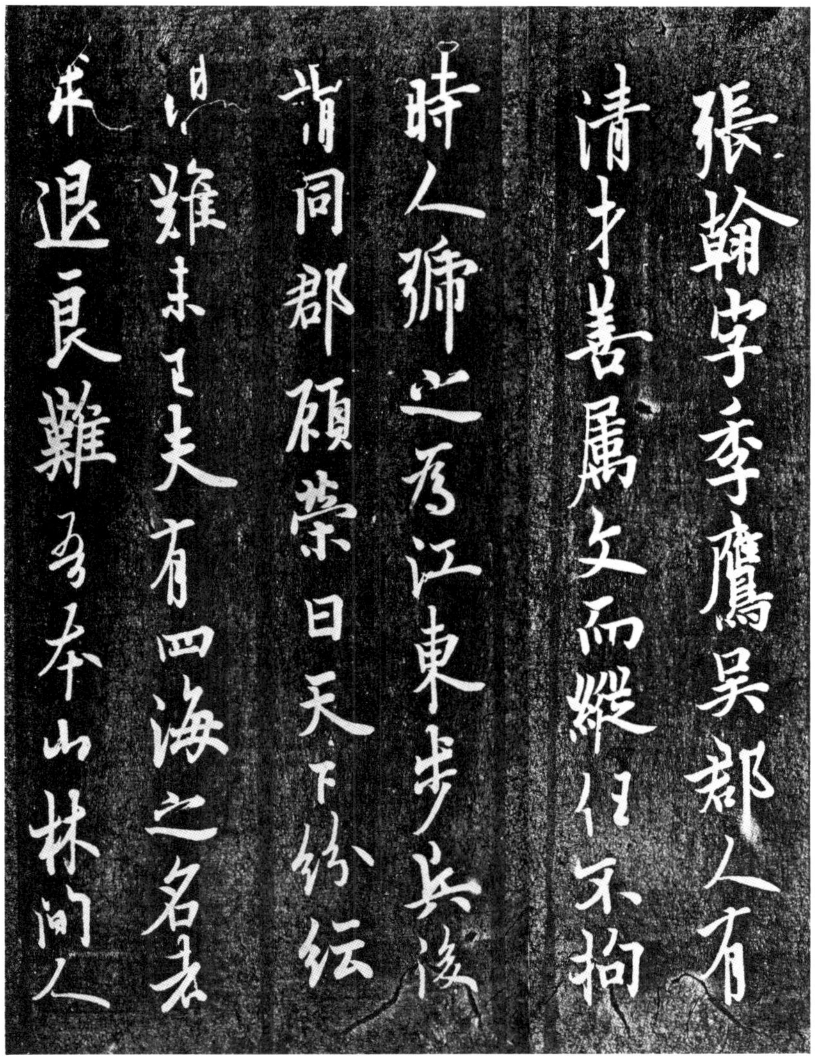


Fig. 84. Ou-yang Hsün, *The Story of Chang Han* (*Chang Han t'ieh*). 27.5 x 13.4 cm (10⅞ x 5¼ in.). Rubbing of inscription

In writing these letters Mi Fu makes each turning and shifting gesture fully realized and expressive, so that all characters have the same polish and completeness of detail as large, monumental designs. Instead of holding the brush tightly and "driving every brushstroke with full force," as Huang taught, Mi recommended that the calligrapher learn how to handle the brush lightly: "The palm should arch loosely and freely. The movements should be swift, natural, and true, and [they should] emerge unintentionally. . . . No stroke resembles another. In the character *san* [three] each of the three strokes is different. The pressure on the brush should not be the same, and the differences should appear natural and spontaneous."[56]

Yet the tense, round brushstroke technique, the hallmark of Huang T'ing-chien's style, also appears in Mi Fu's running script. By alternating his normally light, flicking movements with blunt-ended strokes, Mi achieved the variety, richness, and unpredictability that he valued.

Su Shih described Mi's writing style as "a sailboat in a gust of wind, or a warhorse charging into battle,"[57] and Huang T'ing-chien compared it to "a sharp sword cutting through a battle array or a strong arrow shooting across a thousand miles, piercing every obstacle on its way."[58] Because of the emphasis on speed and spontaneity, Mi Fu's calligraphy disregards fine technique and workmanship. As he explained, "When a craftsman makes a metal or jade vessel, if something goes wrong he can always redo his work. In what period of history was there ever a lack of fine craftsmanship? In calligraphy, even if the writer is still alive and is willing to repeat what he writes, the result will not always be satisfactory. This is why calligraphy must be natural, true, and spontaneous. The outcome is totally unpredictable."[59]

The three Elliott letters, couched in three different expressive modes, sum up both Mi Fu's varied experiences and his essential approach to calligraphy. He had a definite aesthetic goal, which he called a "natural taste," which he found lacking in the work of some of the most respected calligraphers: "Ever since Yen Chen-ch'ing derived his style from Ch'u Sui-liang, achieving fame for his flicking and kicking [*t'iao-t'i*] brushstrokes, his style became too affected. It lacks the plain, light, and naturally accomplished quality [*p'ing-tan t'ien-ch'eng*]."[60]

Probing for sources earlier than the T'ang masters, Mi developed a strong preference for the younger of the two Wangs, Wang Hsien-chih (fig. 85), whose work he described as "natural, true, transcendental, and untrammeled [*t'ien-chen ch'ao-i*]."[61] About one of Wang Hsien-chih's works he wrote, "The brushwork is like fire tongs drawing in ash; every line is interconnected, without beginning and without end. It looks so totally without premeditation, it has been called the calligraphy of one single continuous brushstroke [*i-pi-shu*]."[62] In Mi's "Hasty Reply" the linked characters done in one continuous brushstroke approximate Wang Hsien-chih's "natural" and "untrammeled" "single brushstroke calligraphy."

Reaching even further into antiquity, Mi Fu passed over Chung Yu, presumably Wang Hsi-chih's model, since he had "not seen a single inkwork from the Wei period."[63] For styles earlier than the third

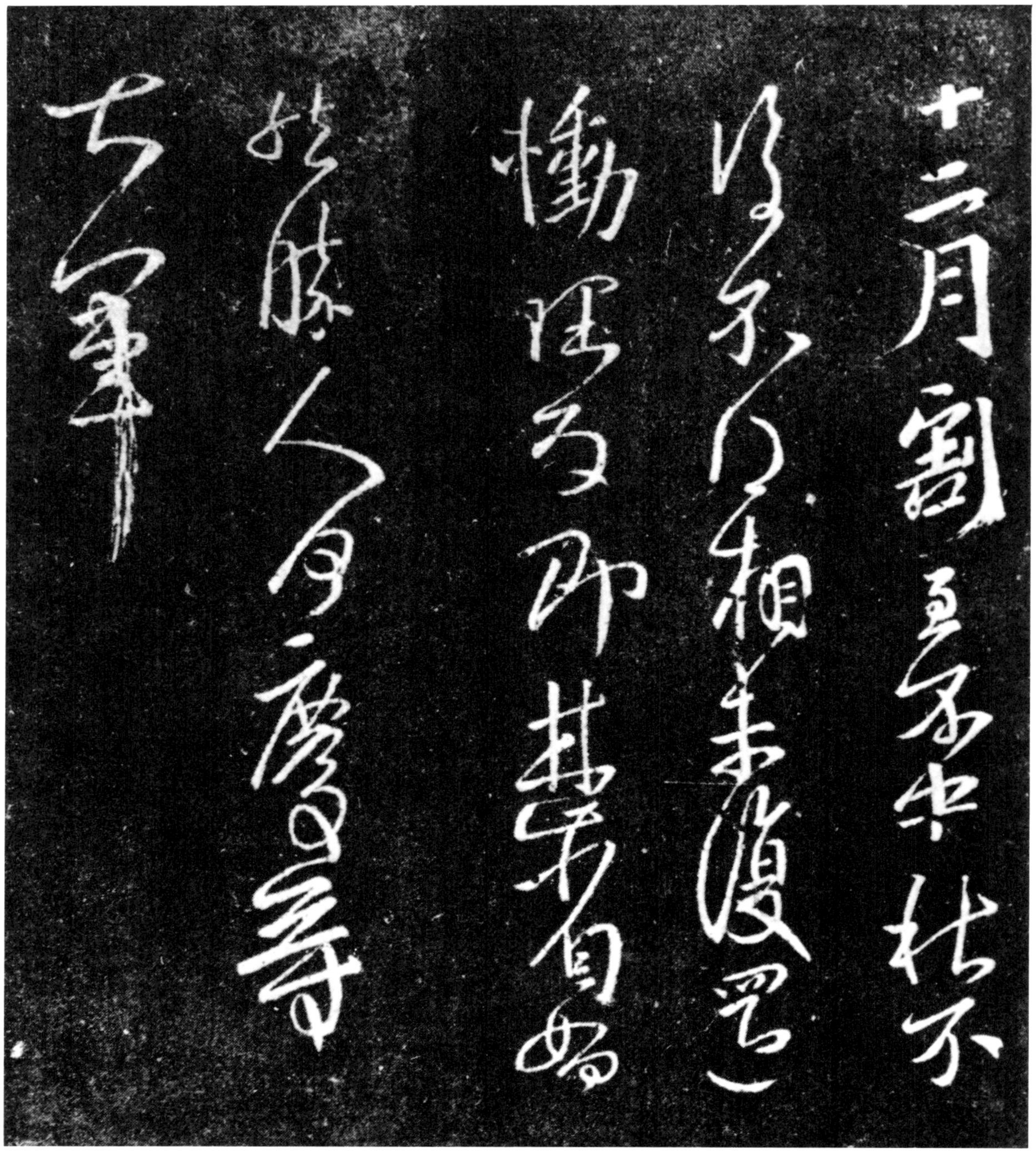

Fig. 85. Attributed to Wang Hsien-chih, *The Twelfth Month* (*Shih-erh-yüeh t'ieh*). Undated, late 4th century. H: 29.3 cm (11 1/2 in.). Rubbing version

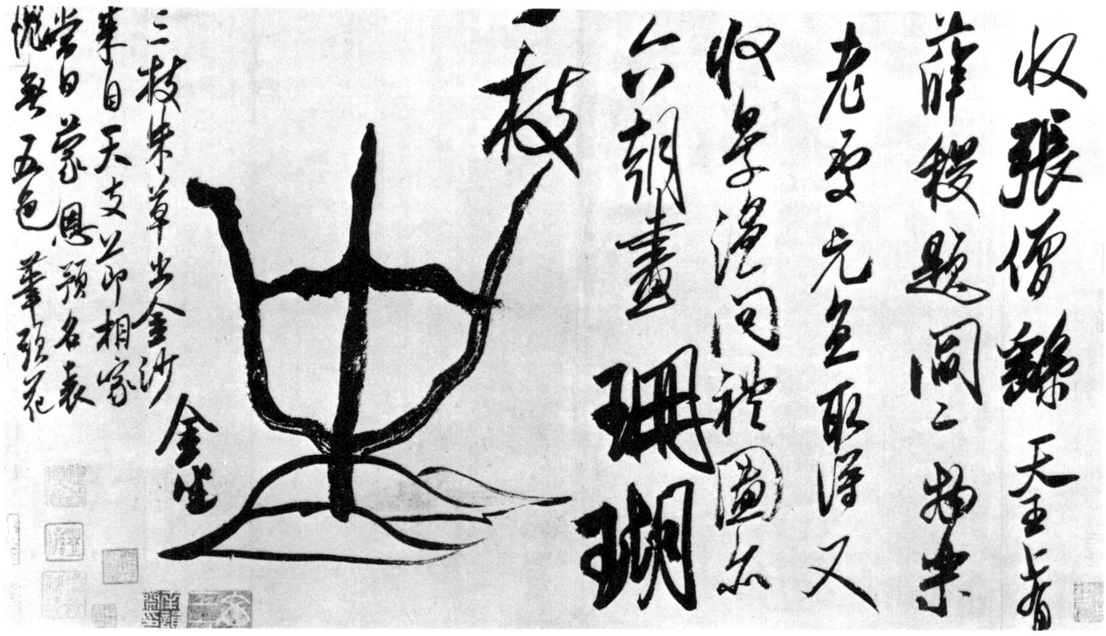

Fig. 86. Mi Fu, *Coral Tree* (*Shan-hu t'ieh*). Undated, ca. 1100. Handscroll(?), ink on paper. Palace Museum, Peking

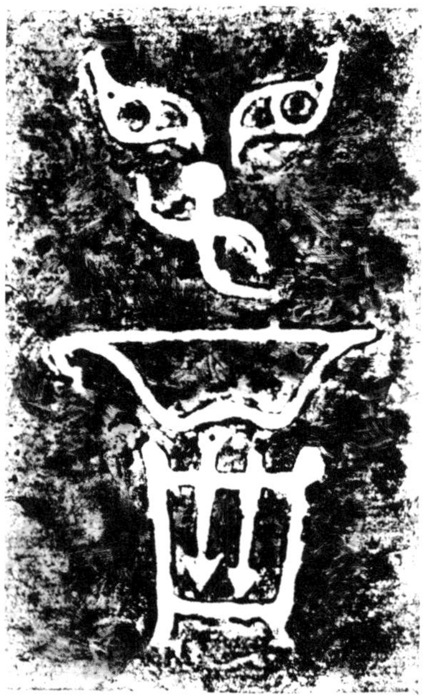

Fig. 87. Anonymous monogram, inscription on a ritual bronze vessel *yu*. Undated, ca. 1300 B.C. Rubbing of inscription. The Art Museum, Princeton University

century he turned instead to archaeological materials such as bamboo slips, stones, and bronze inscriptions. He was fascinated by the seal script, the earliest of all script types:

> By the time the clerical script emerged in calligraphy, the ancient method of the great seal was destroyed. In the seal script, individual characters are sometimes large and sometimes small; they symbolize the forms of hundreds of things [in nature]—alive and full of motion, round and complete, each is a self-contained image. With the clerical script there appeared the compositional force [*shih*] of spreading and contracting. The methods of the Three Dynasties [Hsia, Shang, and Chou, ca. 2000–220 B.C.] were finished.[64]

In one of the most dramatic examples of his later works, *A Coral Tree* (*Shan-hu t'ieh*), dated to the early 1100s (fig. 86), the artist listed an inventory of antique scrolls and curios he had just acquired, and, in mentioning a piece of coral, drew a magnificent three-branched coral mounted on a metal stand. At that instant Mi Fu seems to have experienced the very beginnings of the Chinese script: the pictograph, which resembles a splendid Shang dynasty monogram (fig. 87), is indeed "alive and full of motion, round and complete, . . . a self-contained image."

In executing the round brushstrokes of the coral-tree pictograph, Mi Fu employed a brush technique similar to Huang T'ing-chien's (cf. fig. 79): the brush is held tightly and upright, with the tip kept carefully hidden in the center of the stroke. In order to control the intense energy of the stroke he resisted the direction of the brush, producing a twisting, writhing movement.

Mi's pictograph confirms Huang's discovery that the cursive and the seal writings are closely related.[65] With the commanding pictograph at its center, the composition of the highly expressive cursive writing seems to correspond to Mi's description of seal-script characters as varying in size and symbolism. The convoluted brushstrokes give the individual characters a three-dimensional quality—what Mi Fu calls an "eight-sided" (*pa-mien*) appearance. The rounded archaic brushwork, free and natural, seems to speak with the primeval voice and authority of mountains and oceans. With Mi Fu cursive calligraphy became free-flowing abstract painting. It was only natural that in the following centuries scholar-painters should begin to tap the art of calligraphy for inspiration.

NOTES

1. Huang T'ing-chien, "Pi-fa t'ieh" (Colophons on exemplary calligraphic specimens), in *Shan-ku t'i-pa* (Colophons by Huang T'ing-chien), I-shu ts'ung-pien, vol. 22 (Taipei: Shih-chieh shu-chü, 1962), *chüan* 4, p. 34.
2. Mo Shih-lung or Tung Ch'i-ch'ang, *Hua-shuo* (Notes on painting), Mei-shu ts'ung-shu, 4th ser., vol. 1 (Taipei: Kuang-wen, 1963), p. 308.
3. See Kuo Shao-yü, *Chung-kuo wen-hsüeh p'i-p'ing shih* (History of Chinese literary criticism) (Shanghai: Chung-hua shu-chü, 1961), p. 156.
4. Ibid., pp. 165 ff.
5. See Susan Bush, *The Chinese Literati on Painting: Su Shih (1037–1101) to Tung Ch'i-ch'ang (1555–1636)*, Harvard-Yenching Institute Studies, no. 27 (Cambridge, Mass.: Harvard University Press, 1971), p. 40.
6. Su Shih, *Ching-chin Tung-p'o wen-chi shih-lüeh* (Collected prose of Su Shih), Ssu-pu ts'ung-k'an ch'u pien so pen, vol. 10 (Taipei: Shang-wu yin-shu-kuan, 1967), *chüan* 57, p. 16a; see also Su Shih, "P'ing ts'ao-shu" (Discussing grass writing), in *Tung-p'o t'i-pa* (Colophons by Su Shih), I-shu ts'ung-pien, vol. 22 (Taipei: Shih-chieh shu-chü, 1962), *chüan* 4, pp. 79–80.
7. Kuo Jo-hsü, *T'u-hua chien-wen chih* (Experiences in painting), in Yü An-lan, ed., *Hua-shih ts'ung-shu* (Compendium of painting histories), (Shanghai: Shanghai jen-min mei-shu ch'u-pan-she, 1963), vol. 1, *chüan* 1, p. 9.
8. See *Huang Shan-ku shih ch'üan-chi* (Complete compilation of poems by Huang T'ing-chien) (1899; repr. ed., Shanghai: Chu-i t'ang shu-chü, 1919), vol. 1, *chüan* 3, p. 2a. The references to "dried-up wood" and "dead ashes" are from Chuang-tzu.
9. The most complete source of information on Huang T'ing-chien's life and career is *Huang Shan-ku hsien-sheng nien-p'u* (Chronology of Master Huang T'ing-chien) (1914; repr. ed., Taipei: Hsüeh-hai ch'u-pan-she, 1979), compiled by a fourth-generation descendant of Huang's, Huang Hsüan (fl. 1147–1212). For Huang's chronology as a calligrapher, see Shen C. Y. Fu, "Huang T'ing-chien's Calligraphy and His Scroll for Chang Ta-t'ung: A Masterpiece Written in Exile" (Ph.D. diss., Princeton University, 1976).
10. See Ma Tsung-ho, comp., *Shu-lin tsao-chien* (Collected writings on calligraphy) (1936; repr. ed., Taipei: Shang-wu yin-shu-kuan, 1965), vol. 2, *chüan* 9, p. 219; and Huang T'ing-chien, "Pa Tung-p'o shu" (Colophons on Su Shih's calligraphy), in *Shan-ku t'i-pa*, *chüan* 5, p. 44.
11. Huang T'ing-chien, "Tsa-shu" (Miscellaneous comments), in *Shan-ku t'i-pa*, *chüan* 7, p. 64.
12. Huang T'ing-chien, "T'i Yen Lu-kung t'ieh" (Colophon on Yen Chen-ch'ing's calligraphy), in *Shan-ku t'i-pa*, *chüan* 4, p. 39.
13. Huang T'ing-chien, "Pa Tung-po t'ieh-hou" (Colophon on Su Shih's writing), in *Shan-ku t'i-pa*, *chüan* 5, p. 45.
14. For Su Shih's statement, see Su Shih, "Pa Wang Chin-ch'ing so-ts'ang Lien-hua-ching" (Colophon on the *Lotus Sutra* in Wang Shen's collection), in *Tung-p'o t'i-pa*, *chüan* 4, p. 86; Huang T'ing-chien quotes this statement in "Shu Wang Chou-yen Tung-p'o t'ieh" (Colophon on Su Shih's calligraphy in Wang Chou-yen's collection), dated 1101, in *Shan-ku t'i-pa*, *chüan* 9, p. 92.
15. Huang T'ing-chien, "Shu tseng Fu-chou Ch'en Chi-yüeh" (Written for Ch'en Chi-yüeh from Fu-chou), in *Shan-ku t'i-pa*, *chüan* 5, p. 49.
16. Huang T'ing-chien, *Shan-ku t'i-pa*, *chüan* 4, p. 40.
17. Huang T'ing-chien, "Shu *I-chiao-ching* hou" (Colophon at the end of *I-chiao-ching*), in *Shan-ku t'i-pa*, *chüan* 4, p. 36.
18. Ou-yang Hsiu, *Chi-ku lu pa-wei* (Colophon to catalogue of collected antiquities), Shih-k'o shih-liao hsin-pien, vol. 24 (1887; repr. ed., Taipei: Hsin Wen-feng ch'u-pan-kung-ssu, 1977), *chüan* 10, p. 3.
19. See Kanda Kiichiro et al., eds., *Shodō zenshū* (Reproductions of well-known works of calligraphy) (Tokyo: Heibon-sha, 1966–69), vol. 5, p. 21.
20. Huang T'ing-chien, "Pa Tz'u-chun-hsüan shih" (Colophon to poems written at Tz'u-chun-hsüan), dated 1099, in *Shan-ku t'i-pa*, *chüan* 8, p. 79.
21. Huang Po-ssu, *Tung-kuan yü-lun* (Addendum at Tung-kuan), Hsüeh-chin hao-yüan, t'ao-yüan, vol. 185, (Taipei, 1965), *chüan* 2, pp. 60–61.
22. Attributed to Ts'ai Yung, "Chiu-shih" (Nine forces), in Wang Yüan-ch'i et al., comps., *P'ei-wen-chai shu-hua p'u* (Manual on calligraphy and painting of the P'ei-wen Studio) (1708; repr. ed., Taipei, 1969), *chüan* 3, p. 1a.
23. Wang Yüan-ch'i et al., comps., *P'ei-wen-chai shu-hua p'u*, *chüan* 5, p. 9b.
24. Toyama Gunji, "Magai ni tsuite" (Concerning the *mo-yai* tradition), in Kanda Kiichiro et al., *Shodō zenshū*, vol. 6.
25. Ibid., pp. 166–67, notes at pls. 6–9.
26. Ibid., introduction by Kanda Kiichiro, p. 13.
27. For Cheng Shu-tsu's calligraphy, see ibid., pls. 90, 91; fig. 40.
28. Huang T'ing-chien, "Pa yü Chang Tsai-hsi shu chuan-wei" (Colophon to calligraphy written for Chang Tsai-hsi), in *Shan-ku t'i-pa*, *chüan* 5, p. 49.
29. The scroll is the subject of Shen C. Y. Fu, "Huang T'ing-chien's Calligraphy and His Scroll for Chang Ta-t'ung."
30. Huang T'ing-chien, "Pa Mi Yüan-chang shu" (Colophon on Mi Fu's calligraphy), in *Shan-ku t'i-pa*, *chüan* 5, p. 53.
31. Attributed to Ts'ai Yung, "Chiu-shih," *chüan* 3, p. 1a.
32. For Huang's ideas on brushwork, see "Pa yü Chang Tsai-hsi shu chuan-wei" and "Pa *Hsiang-t'ieh* ch'ün-kung shu" (Colophon to various masters' works in the anthology *Hsiang-t'ieh*), in *Shan-ku t'i-pa*, *chüan* 5, pp. 49–51; see discussion by Shen C. Y. Fu, "Huang T'ing-chien's Calligraphy and His Scroll for Chang Ta-t'ung."
33. Huang T'ing-chien, "Tsai tz'u-yün Yang Ming-shu ssu-shou" (Four poems following the rhymes of Yang Ming-shu), in Jen Yüan et al., *Shan-ku shih chi-chu* (Annotated collected poems by Huang T'ing-chien) (Taipei: I-wen yin-shu-kuan, 1969), *chüan* 12, p. 710; see Kuo Shao-yü, *Chung-kuo wen-hsüeh p'i-p'ing shih*, pp. 182–84.
34. Liu Hsieh, "Sheng-lu" (Musicalness), in *Wen-hsin tiao-lung* (The literary mind and the carving of dragons), Ssu-pu pei-yao, *chüan* 7, p. 6b; for another translation see Vincent Yu-chung Shih, trans. *The Literary Mind and the Carving of Dragons by Liu Hsieh* (New York: Columbia University Press, 1959), p. 184.
35. Ibid.
36. Ching Hao, *Pi-fa chi* (Notes on brush method), in Yü Chien-hua, ed., *Chung-kuo hua-lun lei-pien* (Classified compilation of writings on Chinese painting) (Hong Kong: Chung-hua shu-chü, 1973), vol. 1, p. 606.
37. See Wang Yüan-ch'i et al., comps., *P'ei-wen-chai shu-hua-p'u*, *chüan* 15, p. 4a.
38. Huang T'ing-chien, "Tseng Kao Tzu-mien [Kao Ho-tzu] ssu-shou" (Poems presented to Kao Tzu-mien), in Jen Yüan et al., *Shan-ku shih chi-chu*, *chüan* 16, p. 881.
39. Ibid.; see also Kuo Shao-yü, *Chung-kuo wen-hsüeh p'i-p'ing shih*, p. 184.
40. Su Shih, "Pa Lu-chih wei Wang Chin-ch'ing hsiao-shu *Erh-ya*" (Colophon on Huang T'ing-chien's transcription of the *Erh-ya* in small writing, done for Wang Shen), in Su Shih, *Tung-p'o t'i-pa*, *chüan* 4, p. 86.
41. See Edwin G. Pulleyblank, "A Sogdian Colony in Inner Mongolia," *T'oung-pao* 41, nos. 4–5 (1953): 320. For modern biographies of Mi Fu, see Nicole Vandier-Nicolas, *Art et sagesse en Chine, Mi Fou (1051–1107), peintre et connaisseur d'art dans la perspective de l'esthétique des lettrés*, Annales du Musée Guimet, vol. 70 (Paris: Presses Universitaires de France, 1963); Wai-kam Ho, "Mi Fei," in *Encyclopedia of World Art* (New York: McGraw-Hill, 1959–68), vol. 10, pp. 84–90; Cheng Chin-fa, "Mi Fu Shu-ssu t'ieh" (Mi Fu's writing on Shu silk) (Master's thesis, National Taiwan University, Taipei, 1974); Lothar Ledderhose, *Mi Fu and the Classical Tradition of Chinese Calligraphy* (Princeton: Princeton University Press, 1979).
42. Mi Fu's seal "Yü Hsiung hou-jen" (Descendant of Yü Hsiang [King of Ch'u]) is affixed on his signature "Fu" on "Abundant Harvest" (no. 2A).
43. See *Nagel's Encyclopedia-Guide: China* (Geneva: Nagel Publishers, 1975), p. 1219.
44. See Huang T'ing-chien, "Hsi-tseng Mi Yüan-chang erh-shou" (Two poems playfully presented to Mi Fu), in *Shan-ku ch'üan-chi* (Complete works of Huang T'ing-chien), Ssu-pu p'ei-yao (Taipei: Chung-hua shu-chü, 1965), *chüan* 15.
45. See Mi Fu's biography in *Hsüan-ho shu-p'u* (Catalogue of [Emperor Sung Hui-tsung's] calligraphy collection during the Hsüan-ho era [1119–25]), I-shu ts'ung-pien, vol. 1 (Taipei: Shih-chieh shu-chü, 1962), *chüan* 12, p. 283.
46. See Mi Fu, "T'ai-shih-heng chi Wang T'ai-shih Yen-chou" (Song of T'ai-shih presented to Wang Yen-chou), in *Pao-Tsin Ying-kuang chi* (Collections of Treasuring the Tsin and the Brilliant Lights [Mi Fu's

studios]), Ts'ung-shu chi-ch'eng chien-pien (Taipei: Shang-wu yin-shu-kuan, 1966), *chüan* 3, pp. 15–16.

47. See Mi Fu, "Su Tung-p'o wan-shih wu-shou" (Five poems mourning Su Shih), in *Pao-Tsin Ying-kuang chi*, *chüan* 4, pp. 24–25.
48. See Chang Ch'ou, *Ch'ing-ho shu-hua-fang* (Painting and calligraphy barge at Ch'ing-ho) (1616; repr. ed., Taipei: Hsüeh-hai shu-chü, 1975), *chüan* 9, as cited in Cheng Chin-fa, "Mi Fu Shu-ssu t'ieh."
49. See Ho Wei, *Ch'un-chu chi-wen* (Reports from a spring bank), Hsüeh-chin t'ao-yüan, vols. 209–11 (Taipei: 1965), *chüan* 7, as cited in Cheng Chin-fa, "Mi Fu Shu-ssu t'ieh," p. 20.
50. Mi Fu, *Pao-Tsin Ying-kuang chi*, *chüan* 8, p. 66; see also rubbing in Mi Fu, *Ch'ün-yü-t'ang t'ieh* (Calligraphic works in the Ch'ün-yü studio), in *Shoseki meihin sōkan* 43 (1960): 3–11, 16–59, 67.
51. Mi Fu, *Hai-yüeh ming-yen* (Famous sayings of Mi Fu), I-shu-ts'ung-pien, vol. 2 (Taipei, Shih-chieh shu-chü, 1972), p. 1.
52. For illustration of this poem, see *Su Tung-p'o mu-shih t'u t'i shih* (*Poem written on Su Shih's Tree and Rock*), in Kanda Kiichiro et al., *Shodō zenshū*, vol. 15, pl. 90, fig. 17.
53. See Kanda Kiichiro et al., *Shodō zenshū*, vol. 15, pls. 105, 106.
54. See Mi Fu, *Pao-Tsin Ying-kuang chi*: "Ts'ui-tsu" (Hastening tax collection), *chüan* 3, p. 21; "Ch'iu Chien-miao tso" (Written to request the post of superintendent of the temple), *chüan* 5, p. 33; "Pai Chung-yüeh ming-tso" (Written on being made superintendent of the Chung-yüeh Temple), addendum, p. 81.
55. Mi Fu, *Hai-yüeh ming-yen*, p. 2.
56. Mi Fu, *Pao-Tsin Ying-kuang chi*, *chüan* 8, p. 66.
57. Ma Tsung-ho, *Shu-lin tsao-chien*, vol. 2, *chüan* 9, p. 226b.
58. Huang T'ing-chien, "Pa Mi Yüan-chang shu," in *Shan-ku t'i-pa*, *chüan* 5, p. 53.
59. Mi Fu, *Shu-shih* (Calligraphy history), I-shu ts'ung-pien, vol. 2 (Taipei: Shih-chieh shu-chü, 1972), p. 53.
60. Mi Fu, *Hai yüeh t'i-pa* (Colophons by Mi Fu), I-shu ts'ung-pien, vol. 22 (Taipei: Shih-chieh shu-chü, 1962), pp. 16–17.
61. Mi Fu, *Shu-shih*, p. 11.
62. Ibid., p. 8.
63. Lothar Ledderhose, *Mi Fu and the Classical Tradition*, p. 3.
64. Mi Fu, *Hai-yüeh ming-yen*, p. 3.
65. See Huang T'ing-chien, "Pa Tz'u-chun-hsüan shih," *chüan* 8, p. 79.

# 3 *The Yüan Dynasty: The Rise of Self-Expression*

During the Sung dynasty period, the artist characteristically meditated on an object through a universalized self; Yüan painters more commonly concentrated on the personal inner self. As China underwent profound political and social change during the Yüan period, self-expression, or "speaking one's mind" (*yen-chih*), became firmly established as the chief purpose of poetry and painting. In Yüan landscape the artist's inner feelings were the primary subject; the actual scene set down by the artist was secondary.

The factor that most determined the lives of artists during this period was the Mongol conquest. Suspicious of the southern Chinese, the Mongols entrusted administration of their Yüan dynasty to western and central Asians, Tartars, and northern Chinese; Mongol or other alien supervisors (*darughachi*) were found at all levels of local government. The traditional literati elite of the Chiang-nan region, the delta south of the Yangtze River, became a disenfranchised class and turned to the arts both as a way to occupy their time and as a means of expressing themselves. As never before, works of art became autobiographical in content, and the personal histories of the painters provide the best key to understanding Yüan dynasty paintings.

From the point of view of style, the reductionism and retreat represented by Southern Sung landscape came to an end with the Mongol conquest. Just as Huang T'ing-chien (1045–1105) and Mi Fu (1052–1107), facing the end of a development in calligraphy in the late eleventh century, had renewed their art through a revival of earlier styles, Chao Meng-fu (1254–1322) now spearheaded in both calligraphy and painting a return to the ancient models. But the Yüan revival of Northern Sung idioms did not bring back the Northern Sung monumental style of landscape. Instead of objectified images of nature, the Yüan scholar-artists, applying calligraphic techniques to painting, created a new calligraphic landscape style expressive of the subjective state of mind of the artist.

## *Chao Meng-fu: Calligraphy as Landscape*

Born in 1254 in Wu-hsing, to the southwest of Lake T'ai, in modern Chekiang province, Chao Meng-fu was an eleventh-generation descendant of the founder of the Sung dynasty, Emperor T'ai-tsung; his great-great-grandfather Po-kuei was a brother of the second Southern Sung emperor, Hsiao-tsung (r. 1162–89). In 1267, two years after his father died, the young Meng-fu received a commission as a guard (*ts'an-chün*) in Chen-chou, Kiangsu. After the Southern Sung capital Lin-an (Hang-chou) fell to the Mongols in 1276, he remained in Wu-hsing in order to pursue his studies. Then, in 1286, the emperor Yüan Shih-tsu, better known as Khubilai Khan (r. 1260–94), in an effort to enlist the support of the literati class in the south, sent the imperial censor Ch'eng Chü-fu (1249–1318), a southerner, to recruit Chiang-nan scholars to serve at the court, and Chao Meng-fu, then thirty-two, agreed to present himself at the Yüan capital Ta-tu (Peking). A well-known scion of the Sung imperial family and a strikingly handsome man, Chao Meng-fu immediately caught Khubilai Khan's attention. At the court, first as a member of the war ministry supervising the postal service (1287), then as a member of the Academy of Worthies (1290), he effectively contributed to a more humane policy regarding criminal code and taxation in the south, argued against the "court beatings" of ministers, and even helped to oust the powerful and feared Muslim councillor Sengge in 1291. In 1292 he was posted to the Chi-nan circuit (modern Shantung province) as director-general. Summoned back to the capital in 1295 to participate in the compiling of the annals of the reign of the emperor, who had died in the preceding year, he was sent in 1297 as prefect of Feng-chou (in Shansi), then dispatched to Hang-chou in 1299 as director of Confucian studies in the Chiang-Che provincial government, a position he held until 1308. After briefly returning to Wu-hsing in 1309, he was made a reader at the Han-lin Academy in the capital in 1310. With the ascension of the emperor Yüan Jen-tsung in 1312, he became a lecturer of the Academy of Worthies in 1313, and the head of the Han-lin Academy in 1316. After his retirement in 1319, he returned to Wu-hsing and died there in 1322. He was posthumously honored with the title Duke of Wei (Wei-kuo kung).[1]

The emperor Yüan Jen-tsung (Ayurbarwada; r. 1312–20) is said to have enumerated seven outstanding qualities in Chao Meng-fu: he was descended from the Sung imperial family, endowed with an elegant appearance, widely learned, of pure character and righteous conduct, accomplished in literature, skilled in calligraphy and painting, and possessed of a profound knowledge of Buddhist and Taoist teachings.[2] The style of Chao Meng-fu's regular-script calligraphy reflects these qualities, not only providing an acute portrait of an individual, but also, by extension, summing up the outlook of a class and of a period. In serving the Mongols, Chao Meng-fu braved criticism from his Sung loyalist countrymen in the south. Yet the very presence and success of Chao and others like him at the Mongol court played an important role in insuring the continued vitality of Chinese culture and art during the Yüan period. After the last Southern Sung provincial examination in 1274, the Yüan government did not reinstate the examination system until 1315. Only through the presence at court of such eminent scholars and connoisseurs as Chao, Yü Chi (1272–1348), K'o Chiu-ssu (1290–1343), and K'ang-li Nao-nao (1295–1345) were the high cultural achievements of the Chinese introduced to the Mongol rulers. Members of the Yüan imperial family, such as the emperor Yüan Jen-tsung, his sister Princess Ta-chang (ca. 1282–1332), the emperor Yüan Wen-tsung (r. 1328–32), and the emperor Yüan Shun-ti (r. 1333–68), all took a lively interest in ancient Chinese calligraphy and painting, and gained at least a superficial understanding of its traditions.[3] Among these scholar-artists Chao was the undisputed leader, not only in preserving the ancient arts of painting and calligraphy, but also in advancing them.

For the most part Southern Sung calligraphers had followed the styles of the Northern Sung masters, especially those of Su Shih, Huang T'ing-chien, and Mi Fu. A distinctive personal style was achieved, however, by the emperor Sung Kao-tsung (r. 1127–62), who at first was an ardent follower of Huang T'ing-chien, but later developed a squat, archaizing regular-script style (fig. 88) by following pre-T'ang models, particularly an early seventh-century work, the *Thousand-character Essay in Regular and Cursive Scripts* (*Chen-ts'ao ch'ien-tzu wen*) by the priest Chih-yung (late 6th–early 7th century; fig. 89), who, in turn, had worked in the style of the first renowned master of the regular script, Chung Yu (A.D. 151–230) of the Wei period (cf. fig. 107). Sung Kao-tsung's style, widely imitated in the court circles, was popular and influential throughout the Southern Sung period, yet, as a primarily small-size-character style, it also epitomized certain inherent weaknesses in Southern Sung calligraphy. At the end of the period the painter and calligrapher Chao Meng-chien (1199–1267), a cousin of Chao Meng-fu's, whose writing style reflected the Sung Kao-tsung legacy, criticized the calligraphy of his day for stressing surface appearance to the detriment of overall structure:

> Following the T'ang is not as good as following the [Eastern] Tsin—this is what everyone says. Yet how can the Tsin be easily followed? To follow the T'ang is to learn basic methods and principles. To follow the Tsin without first mastering the T'ang is to misjudge one's own capabilities. If one merely makes one's characters slant, trying to make them attractive and not succeeding, it is like trying to draw a tiger and making a dog instead. Why so? In calligraphy every character must rest firmly on a frame of supports and walls; only then will it not look weak and crooked. In Ssu-ling's [Emperor Sung Kao-tsung's] calligraphy, which is certainly smooth and fluent, the writer has not paid enough attention to the building of supports and walls. This problem must be discussed among the connoisseurs.[4]

According to Chao Meng-fu the balance of a written character is a combined function of brushwork (*yung-pi*) and composition (*chieh-tzu*). The problem may be illustrated with examples of a simple character

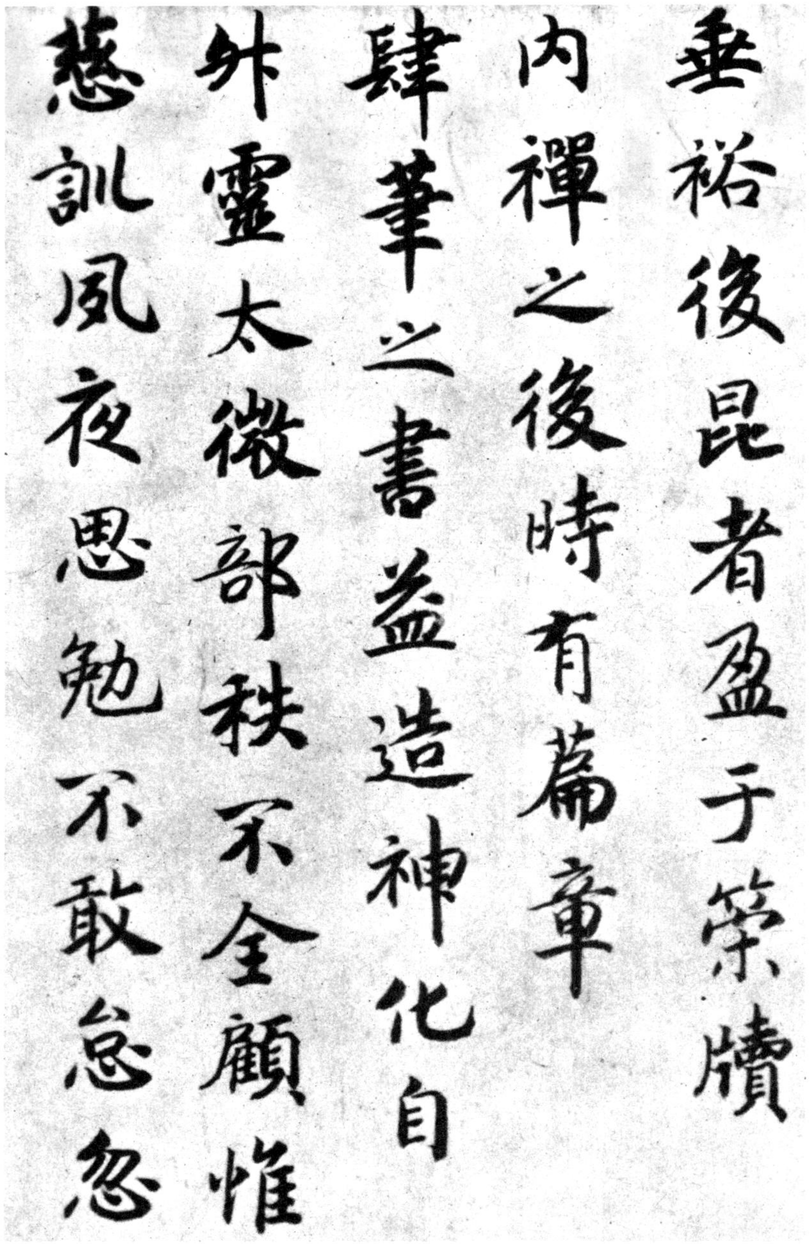

Fig. 88. Emperor Sung Kao-tsung, *Preface to the Anthology by Emperor Hui-tsung [r. 1101–25] (Hui-tsung wen-chi hsü)*. Dated 1154. Album leaf, ink on paper

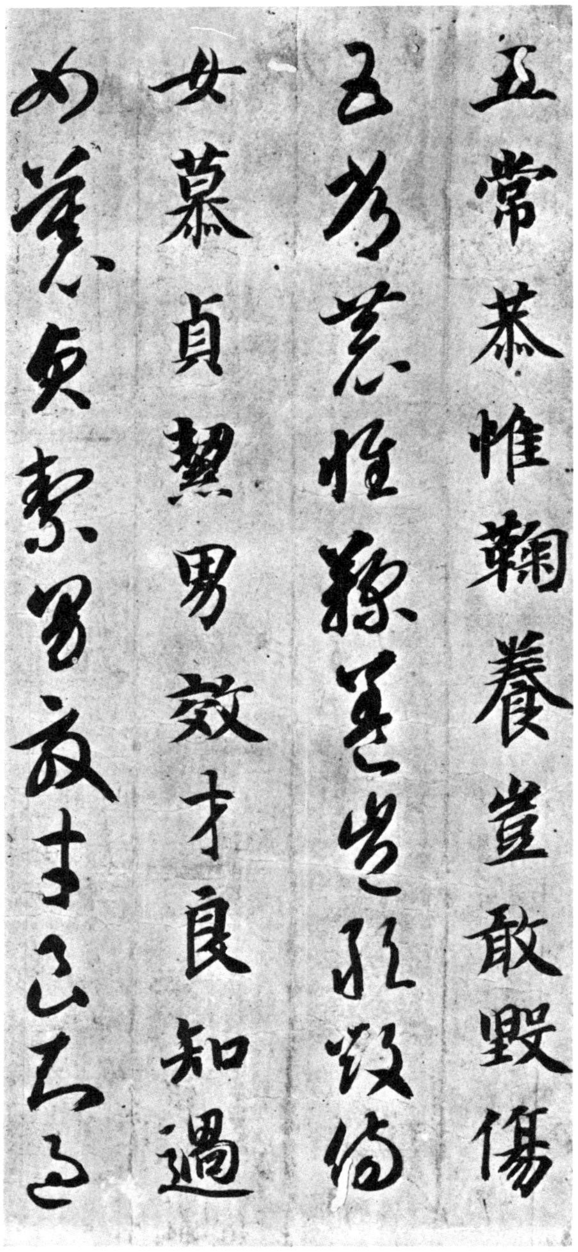

Fig. 89. Attributed to Chih-yung, detail, *Thousand-character Essay in Regular and Cursive Scripts (Chen-ts'ao ch'ien-tzu-wen)*. Undated, early 7th century. Handscroll, ink on paper. H. 24.7 cm (9¾ in.). Ogawa Family collection

*san* (three), showing three horizontal lines, written in the seal, clerical, and regular scripts. In the seal script, written with a stylus, the character *san* consists of three parallel strokes of uniform thickness and length (fig. 90a); the writer may place the three strokes either horizontally or slightly inclined. In a late Han clerical-script version of the character (fig. 90b), which is written with a brush, the upper two strokes remain parallel and of uniform thickness and length, but the bottom stroke, much longer than the two upper ones, has the pressed-down wavy (*p'o* or *che*) ending, a hallmark of the "spreading [like the character] eight" (*pa-fen*, late clerical) style. As the regular-script writing style evolved, the freedom and complexity of the brushwork and the composition of individual characters increased; brushstrokes in a variety of shapes and forms, turning and responding to one another, are held together in each character in a dynamic equilibrium. In the *san* of Ch'u Sui-liang (596–658; fig. 90c) the shorter upper strokes arch gently upward, while the longer bottom stroke bends subtly downward in response; in spite of the varied angles of the individual strokes, the finished character rests firmly in repose. Ch'u's brushwork likewise combines fluid movement with a stable balance. To insure that each stroke was perfectly executed he reversed direction at each end of the stroke, first pushing to the left before moving to the right, then descending toward the lower right,

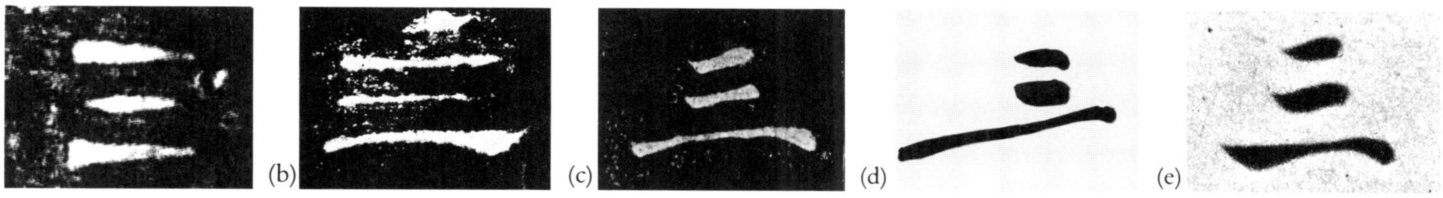

(a) (b) (c) (d) (e)

Figs. 90a–e. The character *san*: seal script, detail, inscription on a bronze ritual vessel, the Ling *kuei*. Undated, early 11th century B.C. Rubbing of inscription. David Weill collection (a); detail, *Ritual Implements in Confucius's Temple Stele* (*K'ung-miao li-ch'i pei*). A.D. 156. Ch'ü-fu, Shantung (b); Ch'u Sui-liang, *Preface to the Sacred Teaching Stele* (*Sheng-chiao-hsü pei*). Dated 654. Rubbing of inscription (c); Huang T'ing-chien, detail, *Scroll for Chang Ta-t'ung* (*Tseng Chang Ta-t'ung ku-wen t'i-chi*), no. 1 (d); and Sung Kao-tsung, detail, *Preface to the Anthology by Emperor Hui-tsung [r. 1101–25]* (*Hui-tsung wen-chi hsü*). Dated 1154. Album leaf, ink on paper (e)

moving the brushtip to the upper left again, before finally lifting the brush from the paper. Huang T'ing-chien's asymmetrical style, done in *chung-feng* (round or centered brushwork; fig. 90d), illustrates Mi Fu's statement, cited in chapter II, that "in the character *san* [three] each of the three horizontal strokes is different."[5] Finally, in the emperor Sung Kao-tsung's *san* (fig. 90e), which is in small writing done with the tip of the brush, the writer has touched down gently, leaving a point at the beginning of each stroke. Compared to Ch'u Sui-liang's example of T'ang dynasty *san* (cf. fig. 90c), the Southern Sung *san*, with brushstrokes manipulated by the writer's fingers rather than the whole arm, lacks a firm structure. This weakness Chao Meng-fu set out to correct.

Early calligraphy by Chao Meng-fu, however, reflects the influence of Sung Kao-tsung's style; in a colophon he wrote on the inkwork *The Great Tao* (*Ta-tao t'ieh*; fig. 91) attributed to Wang Hsi-chih (ca.

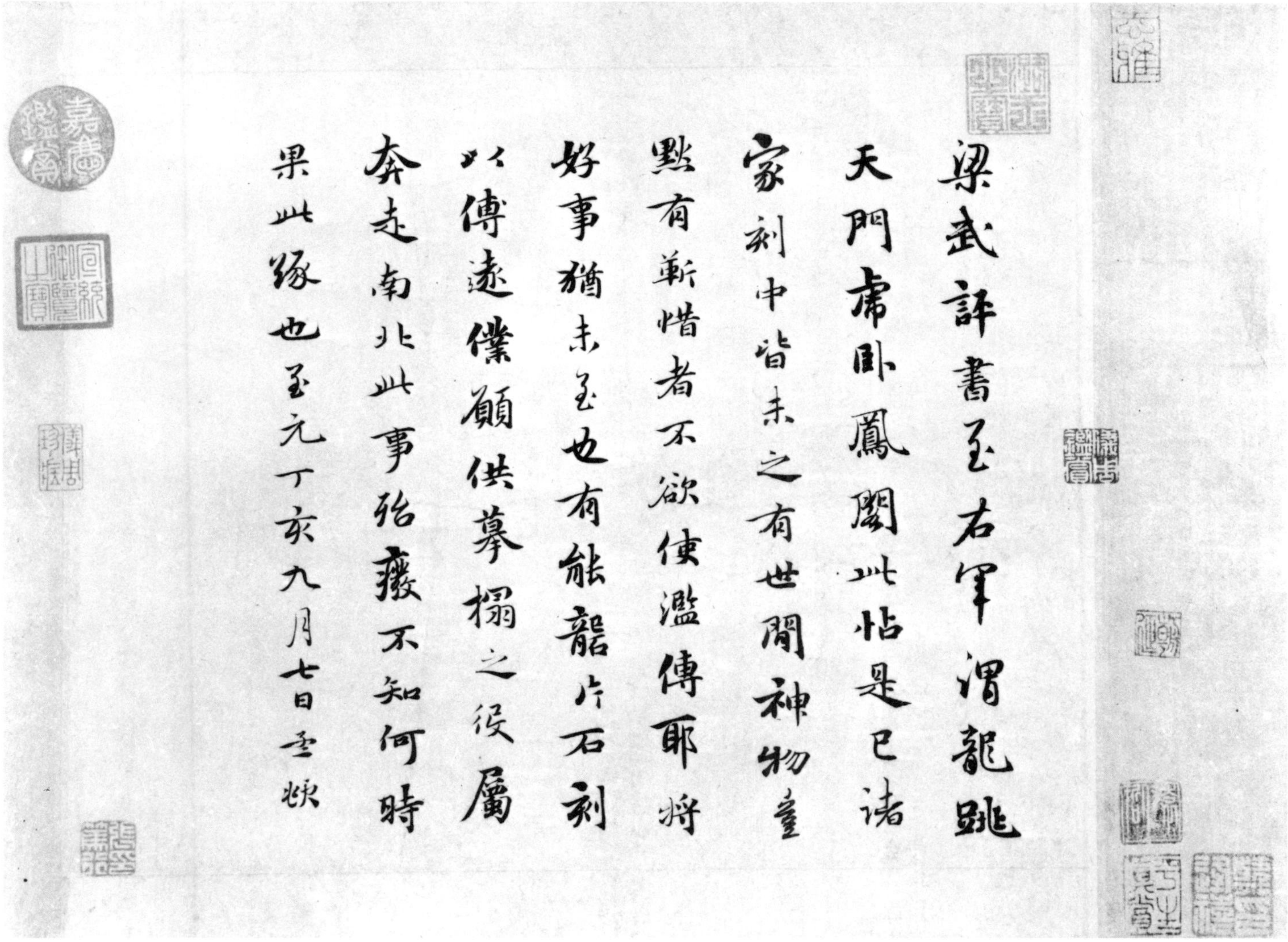

Fig. 91. Chao Meng-fu, colophon, dated 1287, to *The Great Tao* (*Ta-tao t'ieh*) attributed to Wang Hsi-chi. Handscroll, ink on paper. National Palace Museum, Taipei

307–ca. 365) and dated 1287, soon after Chao went to Peking, he used Sung Kao-tsung's squat style, with smooth modulated brushstrokes revealing the pointed brushtip. Throughout the 1290s, apparently agreeing with Chao Meng-chien's view that the T'ang style at least provided a background in basic methods, Chao carefully studied the T'ang masters Ou-yang Hsün (557–641), Yen Chen-ch'ing (709–785), Li Yung (678–747), and others. In a colophon dated 1291 on Ou-yang Hsün's *Confucius Making an Offering in a Dream* (*Chung-ni meng-tien t'ieh*; fig. 92), Chao wrote in the Yen Chen-ch'ing style, while in a poem written for his friend Chou Mi (1232–1298), dated the same year, he followed Li Yung's style (fig. 93).

During his years in Hang-chou, between 1299 and 1308, Chao concentrated on the earlier models of the Wei and Tsin periods, especially that of Wang Hsi-chih. Chao openly acknowledged his indebtedness to his predecessors, insisting that no calligrapher could ever ignore the ancient methods of composing characters. In his *Thirteen Colophons to the Preface to the Orchid Pavilion Gathering* (*Lan-t'ing shih-san pa*), dated 1310, Chao made important observations on brushwork and composition:

> In calligraphy brushwork comes first, yet one should also work on the composition of each character. While the composition of a character changes with time, brushwork remains the same throughout a thousand ages. In Yu-chün's [Wang Hsi-chih's] calligraphy the compositional forces of his characters represent a major transformation of the ancient methods; yet his powerful but elegant qualities are a natural gift. Thus from ancient times until now calligraphers have regarded his work as the exemplary model. As for the masters of the Ch'i and Liang periods, it is not that their compositions are not ancient, but that a certain elegance of the spirit is missing. This is a matter of personal style, but in any case one should never ignore the ancient [compositional] methods.[6]

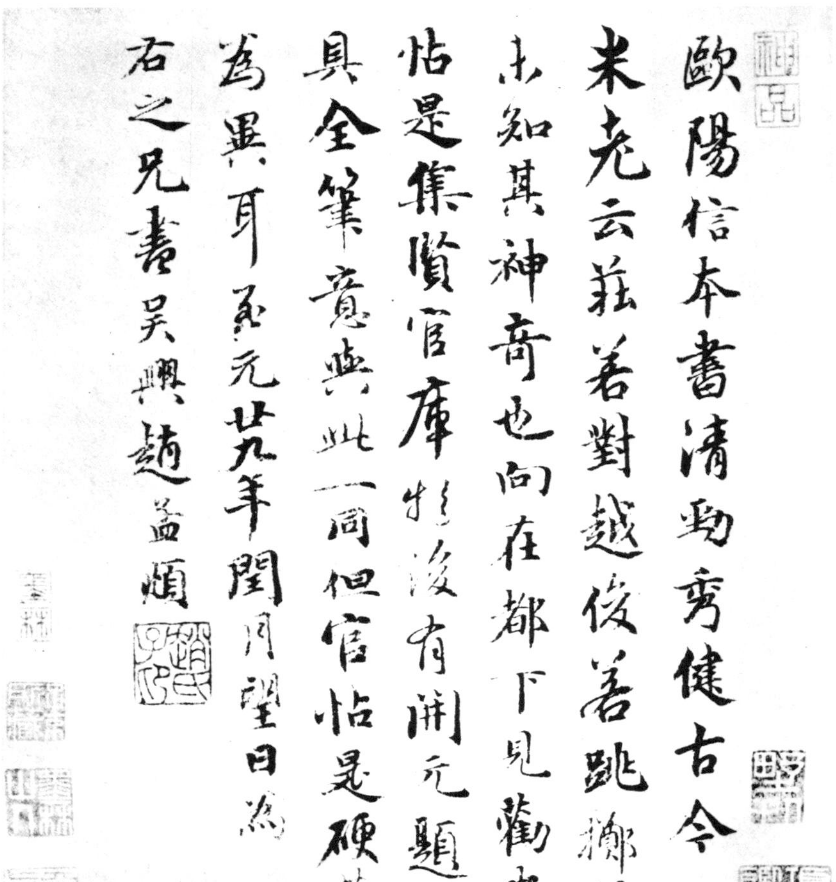

Fig. 92. Chao Meng-fu, colophon, dated 1291, to *Confucius Making an Offering in a Dream* (*Chung-ni meng-tien t'ieh*) by Ou-yang Hsün. Handscroll, ink on paper. Liaoning Provincial Museum

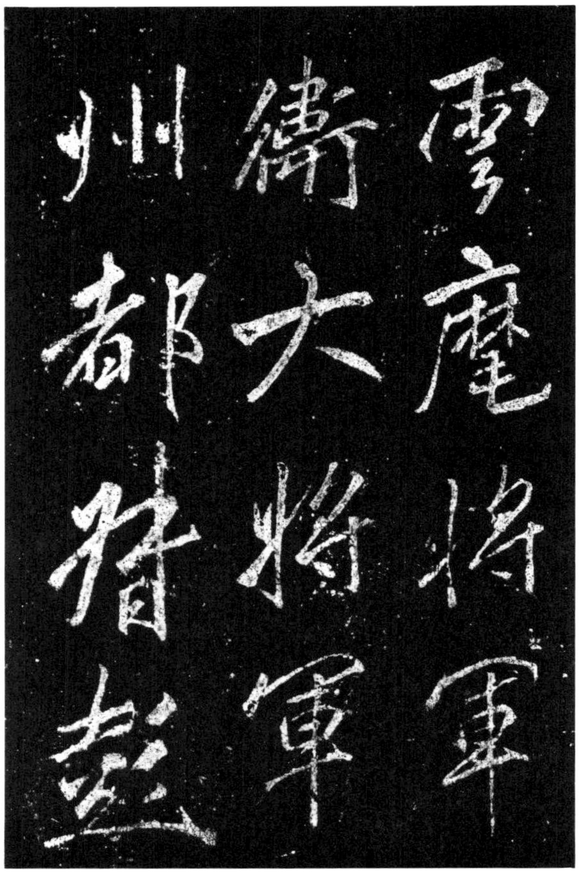

Fig. 93. Li Yung, *Epitaph of the Yün-hui General, Li Ssu-hsün pei* (*Yün-hui chiang-chün Li Ssu-hsün pei*). Undated, after 739. 23.6 x 11.2 cm (9¼ x 4⅜ in.). Rubbing of inscription. P'u-ch'eng, Shensi province

For Chao Meng-fu the necessary evolution of "the composition of a character" had to be inspired by a reexamination of the "ancient methods." As a master of the ancient scripts and creator of a new regular-script style, Chao sought the traditional Confucian goal of a Great Synthesis (Ta-ch'eng) of the past; by mastering the Great Tradition he emerged as rescuer and arbiter of history.

*Record of the Miao-yen Monastery* (*Hu-chou Miao-yen-ssu chi*), written in late 1309 or early 1310, now in the John B. Elliott Collection on loan to The Art Museum, Princeton University (no. 7), is a major work in Chao Meng-fu's mature large regular-script style. Located in the Wu-ch'eng district outside Wu-hsing, the monastery of the title was originally the Eastern Temple (Tung-chi-yüan) in the Southern Sung Chia-hsi era (1237–40) and was renamed Miao-yen (Wonderful Countenance) by the well-known Ch'an priest Yen-ch'i Kuang-wen (fl. 1257–81), who headed a popular sect of Buddhism called Pai-yün (White Cloud).[7] Toward the end of the Southern Sung period, the temple buildings were destroyed by fire. Rebuilt by the then abbot Tao-an (fl. 2nd half 13th century) who during the Chih-yüan era (1264–93) went twice to the Yüan capital to gain permission for the cutting and printing of a new set of the *Tripitaka*, the Buddhist scriptures, the temple was renamed a *ssu*, or a full-fledged monastery, in 1292. Upon the completion of an ambitious building program, Mou Hsien (1227–1311), a renowned Confucian scholar, was invited to compose a temple record, and Chao Meng-fu was asked to write the calligraphy for the inscription (the stone of which, however, was never cut).

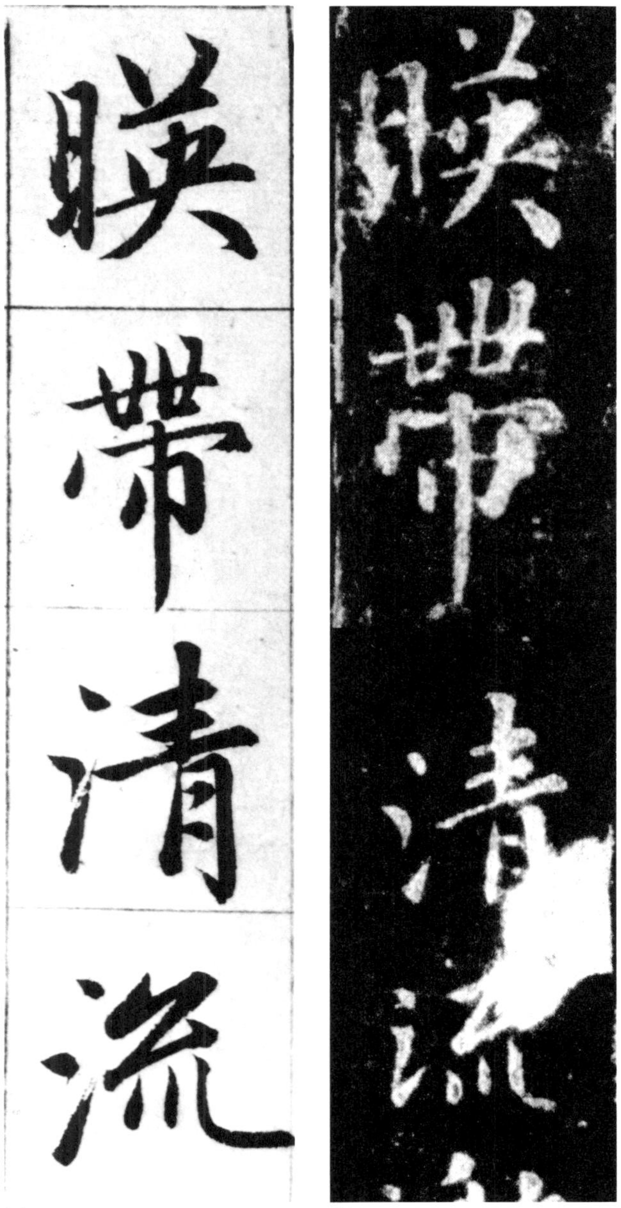

(a) (b)

Figs. 94a, b. The phrase *ying-tai ch'ing-liu*, details: Chao Meng-fu, *Record of the Miao-yen Monastery* (*Hu-chou Miao-yen-ssu chi*), no. 7 (a) and attributed to Wang Hsi-chih, *Preface to the Orchid Pavilion Gathering* (*Lan-t'ing chi hsü*). Dated 353 (b)

For the *Miao-yen Monastery* inscription Chao took as his primary models Wang Hsi-chih and Yen Chen-ch'ing, adding to them the influences of Ch'u Sui-liang, Li Yung, and Huang T'ing-chien (1045–1105), among others. The four characters *ying-tai ch'ing-liu* (fig. 94a) recall stroke for stroke those of the principal work attributed to Wang Hsi-chih, the *Preface to the Orchid Pavilion Gathering* (fig. 94b). Having copied the *Orchid Pavilion* innumerable times, Chao remembered every character and every movement of it by heart. The *Orchid Pavilion*, however, is in small writing. In enlarging the characters to almost 1 square inch, Chao had to invent a new repertory of brushstrokes.

Chao's mature brushwork derived mostly from Yen Chen-ch'ing, who was the accepted model for large-size regular script throughout the Sung period. In Chao's *wei*, *t'u*, *shih*, and *shih* (fig. 95a) the influence of Yen's square form and fully modulated brushwork (fig. 95b) remains strong. Chao preferred for the most part, however, a trimmer style, so he turned to Ch'u Sui-liang, who was Yen's model.

The characters *ting*, *ssu*, *hsia*, *wu*, *fang*, *yüeh*, *chiang*, and *wen* (fig. 96a) reveal the influence of the early T'ang master Ch'u Sui-liang. As can be seen in his *ting* and *hsia* (fig. 96b), Ch'u mixed broad horizontal

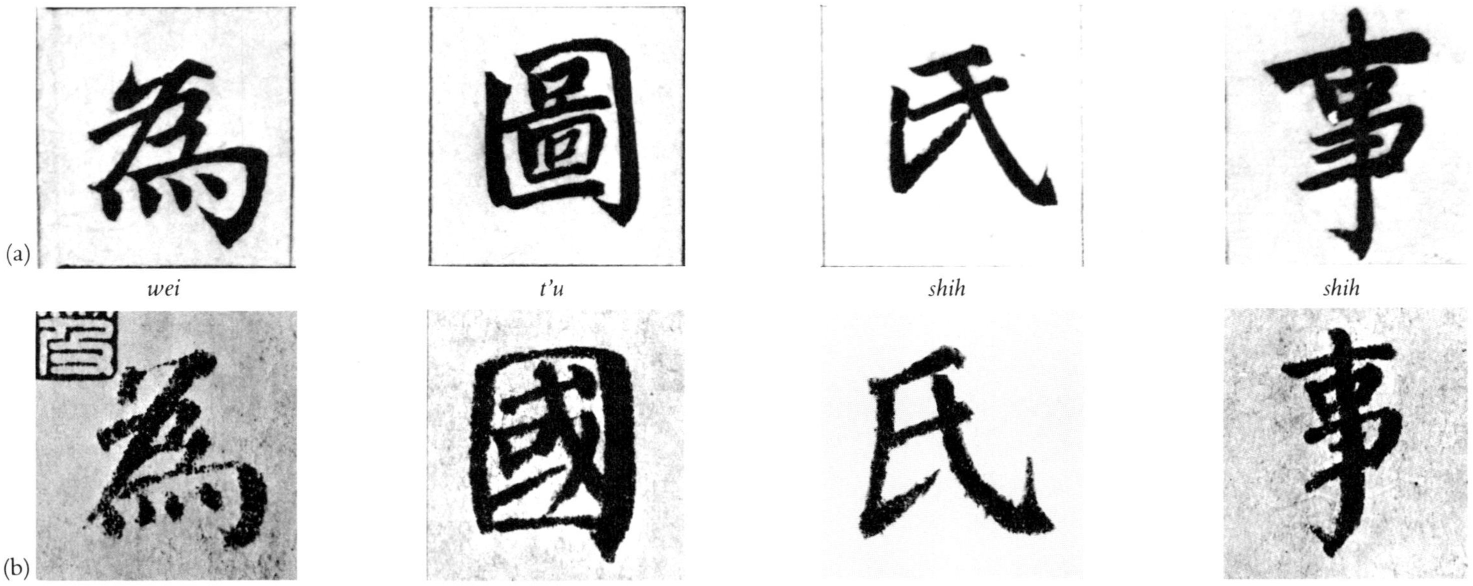


Figs. 95a, b. The characters *wei*, *t'u*, *shih*, and *shih*, details: Chao Meng-fu, *Record of the Miao-yen Monastery* (*Hu-chou Miao-yen-ssu chi*), no. 7 (a) and Yen Chen-ch'ing, *Certificate of Appointment* (*Kao-shen t'ieh*). Dated 780. Handscroll, ink on paper. 30.0 x 220.8 cm (11 7/8 in. x 7 ft. 2 7/8 in.). Museum of Calligraphy, Tokyo (b)

strokes in clerical technique with more elegantly modulated vertical elements; his characters are both lively and structurally stable. Chao's well-modulated individual brushstrokes derive equally from Yen Chen-ch'ing and Ch'u Sui-liang. In his characters with hooked strokes—*ssu*, *fang*, *yüeh*, *chiang*, and *wen*, for example—a moderate bulge on the outside of the stroke and a hook that springs directly from the end of the stroke to form an arrowhead shape recall the style of Ch'u Sui-liang; a fully developed bulge and a hook in which the brush retracts into the stroke before lifting up refers to the brush method of Yen Chen-ch'ing (cf. fig. 95b).

In his later years Chao was increasingly drawn to the style of Li Yung (fig. 97b), whose slanting brushstrokes and angular folds lend speed and momentum to the running script. In certain characters, such as *yeh*, *nai*, *chi*, *hsiu*, *chih*, Li Yung's influence became an integral part of Chao's regular-script style (fig. 97a).

Finally, Chao was not impervious to the powerful influence of the great late Northern Sung master Huang T'ing-chien. The *shu* and *yang* of Huang T'ing-chien (fig. 98b) have no level or upright strokes; all of the normally parallel strokes, both horizontal and vertical, here tilt at different angles and move at a varied speed and rhythm, so that the entire character is tangled and wound up, bursting with tension and liveliness. Huang's round brushwork uses the reversed-brushtip (*ni-feng*) or twisted-brushtip (*chiao-feng*) technique. Touching the brush to the paper in a reverse motion—hiding the tip—the writer pulls away powerfully with the brushtip folded inside the stroke, keeping his wrist locked and writing with his whole

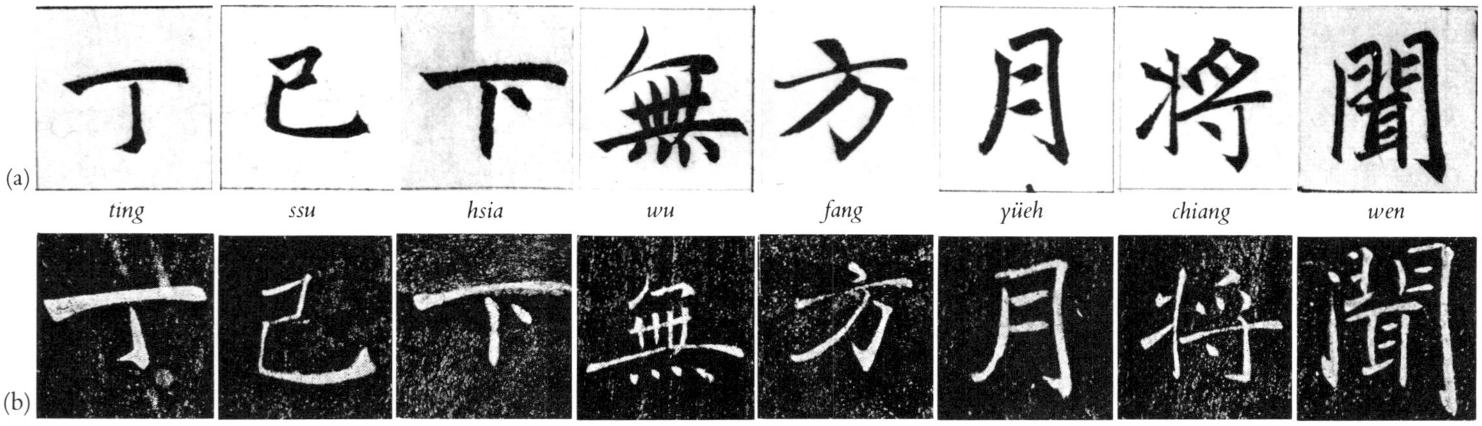


Figs. 96a, b. The characters *ting*, *ssu*, *hsia*, *wu*, *fang*, *yüeh*, *chiang*, and *wen*, details: Chao Meng-fu, *Record of the Miao-yen Monastery* (*Hu-chou Miao-yen-ssu chi*), no. 7 (a) and Ch'u Sui-liang, *Preface to the Sacred Teaching Stele* (*Sheng-chiao-hsü pei*). Dated 654. Rubbing of inscription (b)

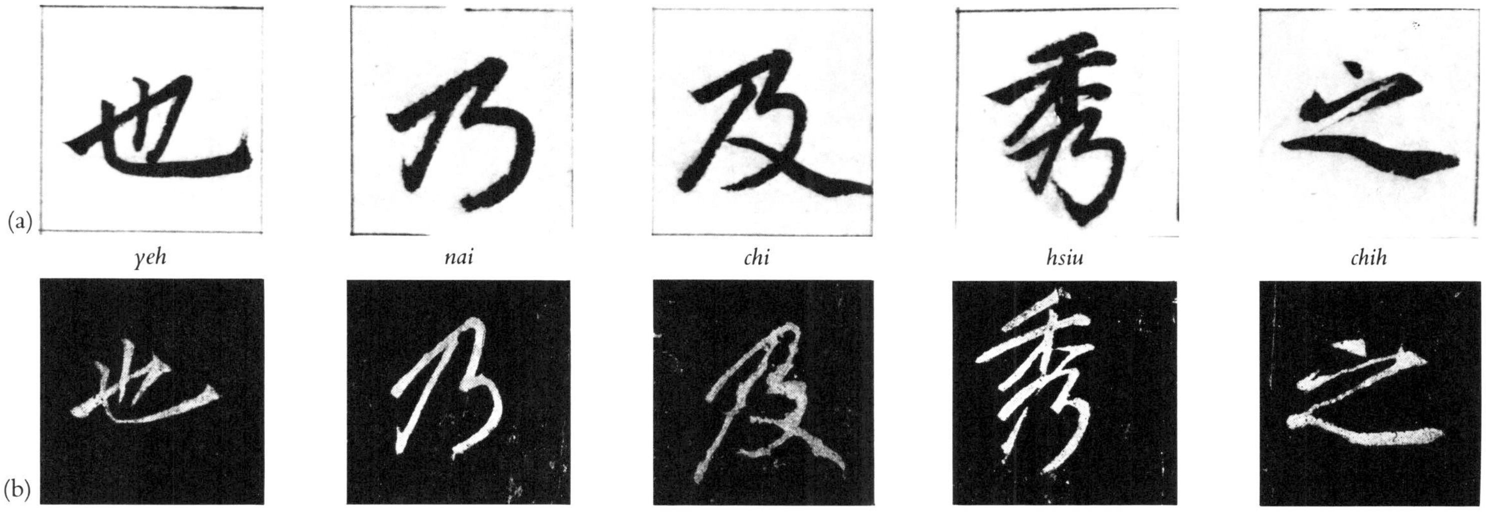


Figs. 97a, b. The characters *yeh*, *nai*, *chi*, *hsiu*, and *chih*, details: Chao Meng-fu, *Record of the Miao-yen Monastery* (*Hu-chou Miao-yen-ssu chi*), no. 7 (a) and Li Yung, *Epitaph of the Yün-hui General, Li Ssu-hsün* (*Yün-hui chiang-chün Li Ssu-hsün pei*). Undated, after 739. Rubbing of inscription

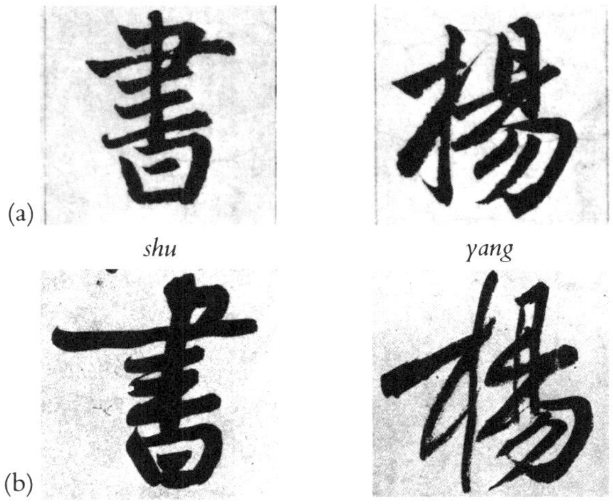


Figs. 98a, b. The characters *shu* and *yang*, details: Chao Meng-fu, *Record of the Miao-yen Monastery* (*Hu-chou Miao-yen-ssu chi*), no. 7 (a) and Huang T'ing-chien, detail, colophon, ca. 1100, to *Poem on the Cold-food Festival at Huang-chou* (*Huang-chou Han-shih shih*) by Su Shih. Handscroll, ink on paper. Private collection (b)

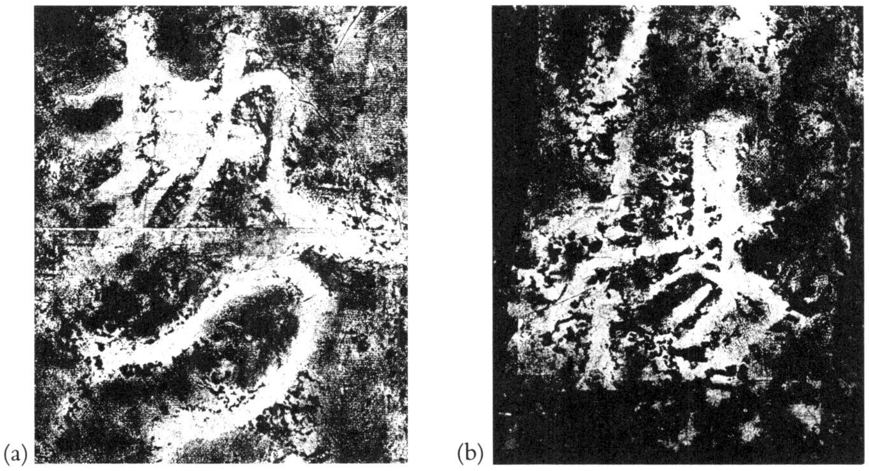


Figs. 99a, b. The characters *shih* and *yang*, details, T'ao Hung-ching, *Inscription for Burying a Crane* (*I-ho-ming*). Dated 514

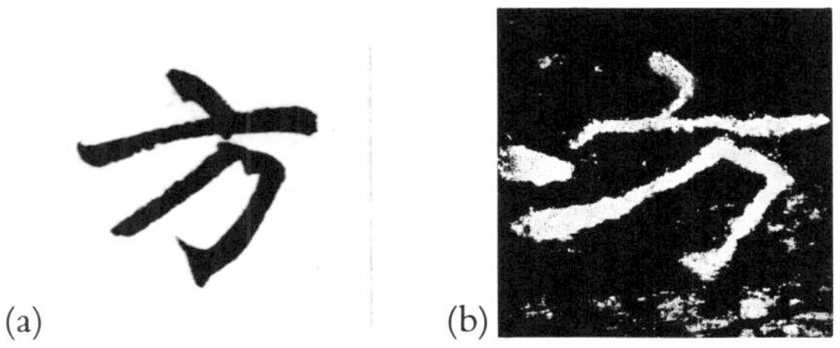


Figs. 100a, b. The character *fang*, details: Chao Meng-fu, detail, *Record of the Miao-yen Monastery* (*Hu-chou Miao-yen-ssu chi*), no. 7 (a) and *Ritual Implements in Confucius's Temple Stele* (*K'ung-miao li-ch'i pei*). Dated A.D. 156. Rubbing of inscription (b)

arm, as if applying the ink with his bare knuckles. In Chao's *shu* and *yang* (fig. 98a), the forms are relaxed and structurally stable, but their indebtedness to Huang T'ing-chien is apparent.

At the end of the eleventh century, as discussed in chapter II, Huang T'ing-chien had revived ancient sources in order to liberate calligraphy from the overly rigid influence of the Yen Chen-ch'ing style; at the beginning of the fourteenth century Chao Meng-fu turned to the same antique sources for a very different purpose: to provide the "supports and walls" late Southern Sung calligraphy lacked. The result can be seen, for instance, in the character *yang*. Both Huang's and Chao's renditions of the character derive from the early sixth-century stone inscription *Burying a Crane*, but Huang stressed the diagonal movement, while Chao emphasized overall stability and balance. The crucial form in this character is the diagonal element in the lower right corner. *Burying a Crane* shows two different treatments of this diagonal element: in the character *shih* (fig. 99a) the form is loose and powerful and the diagonal force is extreme, but in the *yang* (fig. 99b) the diagonal motif is a quadrangular form standing on one corner, a diamond framed by an imaginary square. The balanced geometrical treatment developed from the earlier Han clerical script, as seen in the simple character *fang* (fig. 100b) in the *Ritual Implements in Confucius's Temple Stele* (*K'ung-miao Li-ch'i pei*), dated A.D. 156. Previous masters of regular-script calligraphy, from Chung Yu and Wang Hsi-chih to Ch'u Sui-liang and Yen Chen-ch'ing, had arrived at no clearly defined method for forming this motif, but in his *Miao-yen Monastery* inscription Chao Meng-fu devised a geometric formula to give the character *fang* a look of consistency and solidity (fig. 100a). Indeed all diagonal strokes in Chao's regular-script writing are set at a 45-degree angle, thereby acting as structural braces for the "walls" of individual characters.

The early Ming scholar and patriot Fang Hsiao-ju (1357–1402) commented that Chao Meng-fu's "calligraphy resembles [the famous Han general] Ch'eng Pu-shih's way of commanding an army: the orders are always clear and strict, never allowing a single hair to stray from methods and principles."[8] Chao's regular script not only has beautifully modulated and well-balanced features, but also displays an easily recognized and repeatable array of brushstrokes. Chao's was the first new regular script since Yen Chen-ch'ing's that could be adapted successfully to both small and large writing, with characters measuring from the size of "the head of a fly" to the height of several inches. By the early decades of the fourteenth century the Chao style easily dominated the calligrapher's universe. Its all-pervasive influence is evident even in printed books, which after the 1330s showed a script type in the attractive, easily legible Chao style.

Yet, despite its fundamental stability, compared to the robust Yen Chen-ch'ing style Chao's seems soft, even effeminate. The early Ming scholar Sung Lien (1310–1381) remarked that "some people . . . denigrate it as resembling a pretty girl wearing flowers."[9] In the harsh judgment of the chauvinistic Ming period, historians never forgave Chao Meng-fu for agreeing to serve the Mongols and seized upon his sensuous calligraphic style as evidence of moral weakness.

A true reflection of Chao's state of mind during the early years of his service under the Mongols may be seen in his well-known landscape handscroll in the archaic blue and green idiom, *The Mind Landscape of Hsieh Yu-yü* (*Yu-yü ch'iu-ho*), now in the Edward L. Elliott Family Collection at The Art Museum, Princeton University (no. 6). While serving at court in the late 1280s and early 1290s, Chao Meng-fu painted this image of the Eastern Tsin courtier Hsieh K'un (280–322), who claimed to have preserved the purity of his mind in the mountains and valleys even while serving at court.[10] Through this theme of the recluse at court Chao communicated to his countrymen in the south his feelings of conflict between service and reclusion, engagement and withdrawal, the active and the contemplative life. Judging from the colophons attached to this painting, Chao's contemporaries had fully understood and appreciated the inner turmoil he suffered.

Rejecting realistic description, Chao returned to the archaic blue and green idiom. The archaizing calligraphic brush technique was consciously applied to landscape for expressive purposes: every element of the painting is depicted with the same calligraphic brushstroke. Although the composition shows an advanced understanding of spatial continuity, with foreground rocks and shorelines receding along a continuous ground plane, the drawing of trees and rocks follows the seal-cutting principles of positive and negative designs (figs. 101, 102): round, controlled iron-wire (*t'ieh-hsien*) lines are done in the seal-script style of calligraphy, and the outlines of tree and rock forms define the spaces between these forms as well as the spaces within them. Indeed individual tree and rock forms are now visualized as seal-script pictographs. For example, Chao's rendering of the ancient mythological *lien-li* (twin tree with joined roots and branches) may be compared with the designs of his own large seal-script characters at the beginning of the *Miao-yen Monastery* handscroll (fig. 103). Written over a network of squares marked on paper for design reference, the subtle curves and balances of round seal-script strokes that seem to embody in their slow, glacial movements nature's primordial forces. Applied to Chao's blue and green painting, the linear patterns of the mountains, surging like ocean waves, and those of the trees, echoing the sounds of celestial music (*t'ien-lai*),

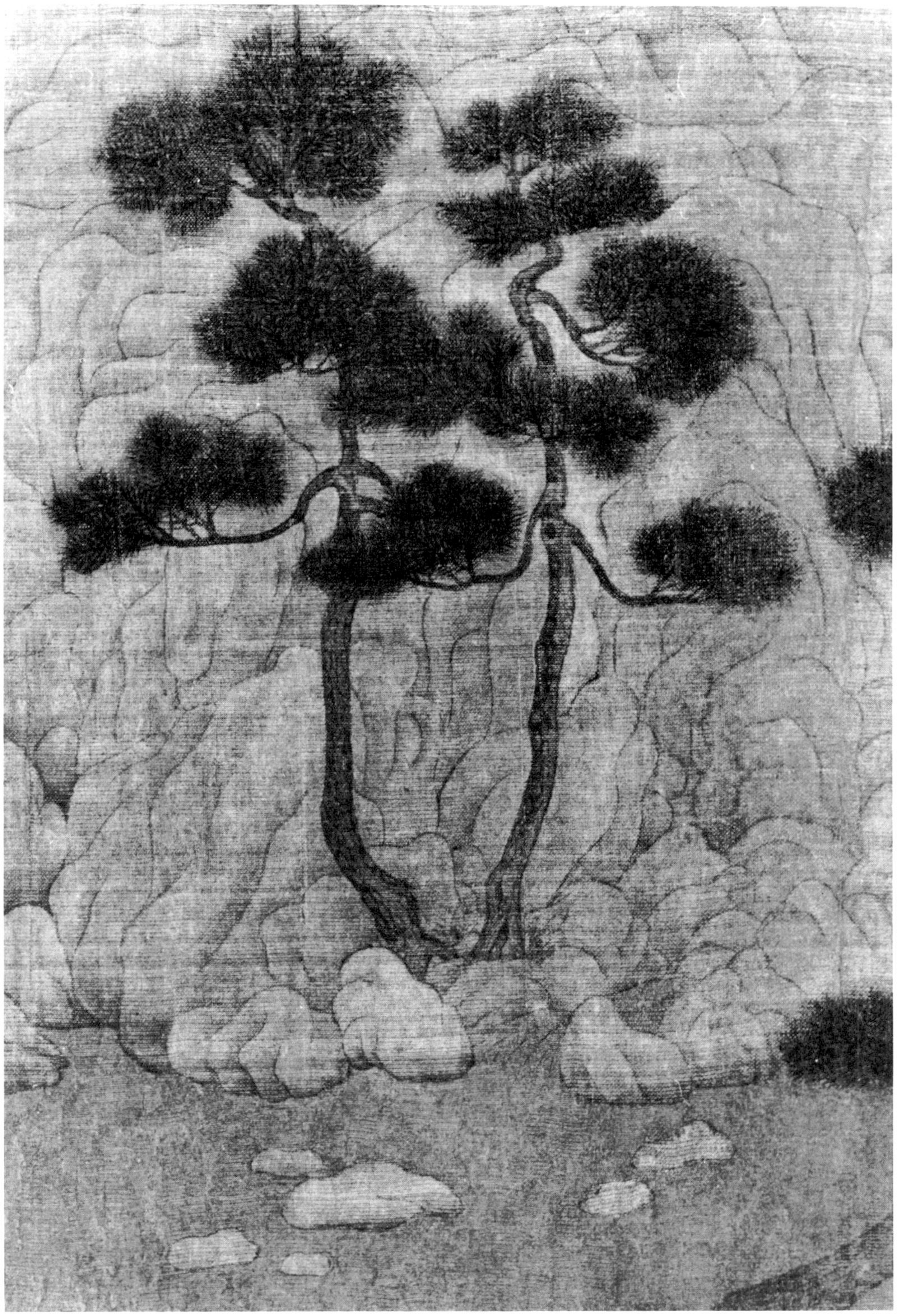

Fig. 101. Chao Meng-fu, detail, *The Mind Landscape of Hsieh Yu-yü* (*Yu-yü ch'iu-ho*), no. 6

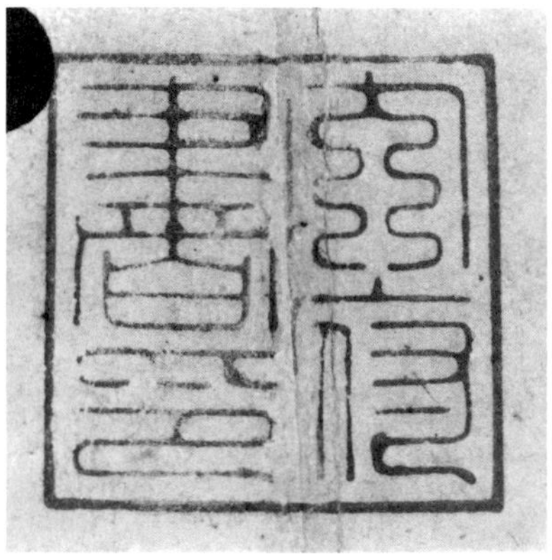

Fig. 102. Seal of Emperor Sung Kao-tsung on Huang T'ing-chien, *Scroll for Chang Ta-t'ung* (*Tseng Chang Ta-t'ung ku-wen t'i-chi*), no. 1

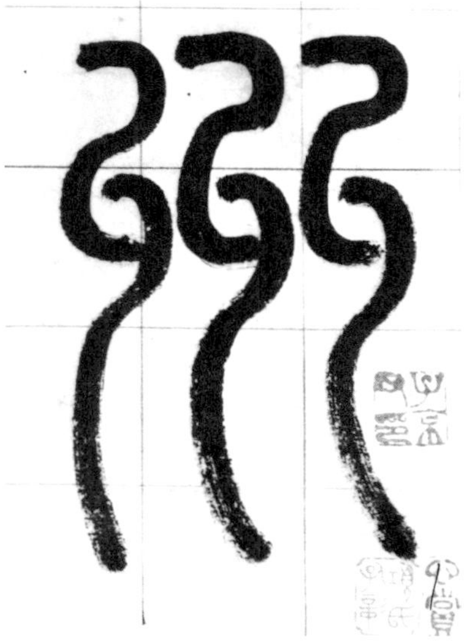

Fig. 103. Chao Meng-fu, detail of frontispiece, *Record of the Miao-yen Monastery* (*Hu-chou Miao-yen-ssu chi*), no. 7

the calligraphic brushstrokes seem to evoke rocks and trees in their quintessential forms, ageless and vibrantly alive.

In the 1290s and 1300s, when he was posted to Chi-nan in Shantung and Hang-chou in Chekiang, Chao Meng-fu practiced a variety of calligraphic brush idioms in several kinds of figure, animal, and landscape paintings. In *Man Riding Horse* (*Jen-ma t'u*), dated 1296, in the Palace Museum, Peking, he used the iron-wire seal-script technique. In *Autumn Colors on the Ch'iao and Hua Mountains*, dated in early 1296 (cf. fig. 66), he painted in the Tung Yüan (fl. 937–76) idiom using a fine regular-script brushwork style.[11] In *Twin Pines against a Flat Vista* (*Shuang-sung p'ing-yüan*), painted about 1310 (now in The Metropolitan Museum of Art, New York; fig. 104),[12] Chao boldly executed the Li Ch'eng–Kuo Hsi idiom of devil-face (*kuei-mien*) rocks and crab-claw (*hsieh-chao*) tree branches in the cursive and seal-script manners. In chapter 1

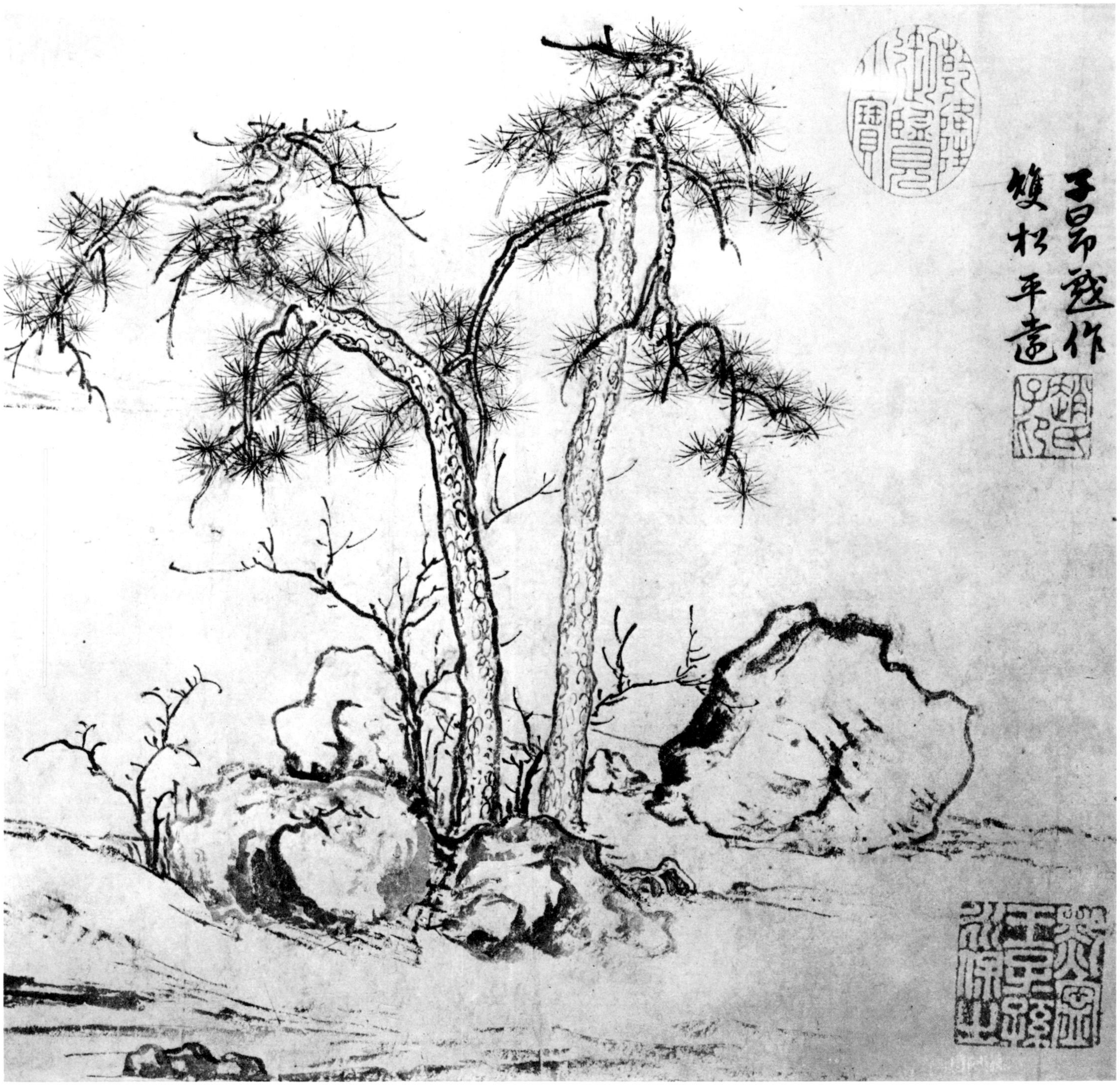

Fig. 104. Chao Meng-fu, detail, *Twin Pines against a Flat Vista* (*Shuang-sung p'ing-yüan*). Undated, ca. 1310. Handscroll, ink on paper. 26.7 x 107.3 cm (10½ in. x 3 ft. 6¼ in.). The Metropolitan Museum of Art, New York

we saw how illusionism was finally achieved in Chao's *Autumn Mountains*. But visual representation was no longer the Yüan painter's principal concern. Executed in calligraphic brushwork, Chao's landscape forms are calligraphically expressive. Like Mi Fu's coral tree (cf. fig. 86), Chao's rocks and trees in *Twin Pines* are "written" as pictographs: the twin trees show trunks and bark patterns drawn calligraphically in the round brushwork of cursive or seal script.

In a poetic colophon appended to a painting of *Elegant Rocks and Sparse Trees* (*Hsiu-shih shu-lin t'u*) in the Palace Museum, Peking (fig. 105), Chao summed up his calligraphic method of painting:

> Rocks as in flying white [*fei-pai*], trees as in seal [*chuan*] script;
> When painting bamboo, one should master the spreading-eight [*pa-fen*, late clerical script] method.
> Those who understand this principle thoroughly
> Will recognize that calligraphy and painting have always been one.[13]

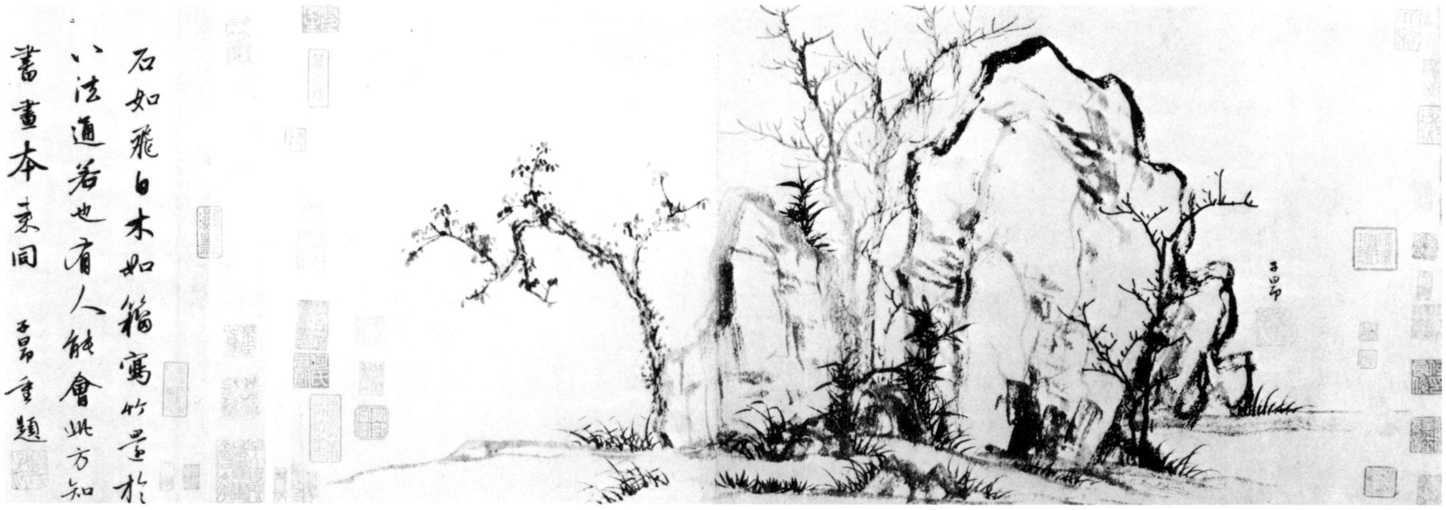

Fig. 105. Chao Meng-fu, *Elegant Rocks and Sparse Trees (Hsiu-shih shu-lin t'u)*. Undated, ca. 1310. Handscroll, ink on paper. 27.3 x 92.8 cm (10¾ in. x 3 ft. ½ in.). Palace Museum, Peking

In treating painting as calligraphy, the calligraphic painter, rather than investigating nature through painting, sought through calligraphic brushwork to merge self and object.

Unlike his calligraphy, however, Chao's calligraphic explorations of various landscape idioms did not yield a personal stylistic synthesis. While it is possible to recognize the master behind his many guises, Chao Meng-fu invented no single, distinctive style in landscape painting. It was not until the generation after Chao that landscape painting saw the development of unmistakably personal calligraphic styles.

## *Ni Tsan: The Noble Recluse*

What is known of Ni Tsan's life is found mostly in three tomb inscriptions composed soon after the artist's death in 1374: one by Wang Pin (ca. 1335–1405), another by Ni's close friend Chou Nan-lao (1308–1383), and a third by Chang Tuan (ca. 1320–1380).[14] According to Chou Nan-lao, in *Tomb Epitaph for the Yüan Dynasty Recluse, Master [Ni] Yün-lin (Yüan ch'u-shih Yün-lin hsien-sheng mu-chih-ming)*, Ni's family descended from Ni Kuan, an imperial censor of the Han period. Tsan's tenth-generation ancestor Shih went to live among the Hsi-hsia (Tangut) people. Then, sometime during the Ching-yu era (1034–37) of the emperor Sung Jen-tsung, Shih returned to Sung China as the Tangut ambassador. Thereafter the family lived in Tu-liang (modern Anhui province). During the early Chien-yen reign (1127–30) one of Tsan's fifth-generation ancestors, I, journeyed south with the Southern Sung and settled in Chih-t'o village in Wu-hsi.[15] There the Ni family prospered.

Ni Tsan and his elder brother Ying were the sons of their father's concubine Yen. Their father died when the brothers were young, and they were raised by their eldest half brother, Ni Chao-kuei (1279–1328), whose lavish contributions toward the building of temples garnered him important positions in the Taoist hierarchy, culminating in the title of *chen-jen*, or primate, conferred shortly before his death. Since Ying was a mental incompetent, after Chao-kuei's death Ni had to assume the responsibility of managing the large household. Although this role ill suited his personal inclinations, Ni Tsan led a seemingly idyllic, and by choice secluded, existence at his family estate for another twenty years. Through the mid-1340s he spent most of his time among precious books, antique paintings, calligraphy, and flowers, in his favorite studio, which he named the Pure and Secluded Pavilion (Ch'ing-pi-ko). According to Chou Nan-lao,

> where [Ni Tsan] lived there was a two-storied building called Ch'ing-pi, which was quiet, remote, and spotless. In it he kept thousands of volumes of books, which he had personally annotated and collated—classics, histories, anthologies, as well as Buddhist, Taoist, and medical texts, which he read all

> day long. There ancient ritual tripods and vessels and well-known zithers were displayed. And around the building grew pines and cassia trees, orchids, bamboo, and chrysanthemums; and beyond these were great hardwood trees and bamboo groves, which were luxuriantly thick and fine. This is why he called himself Yün-lin [Cloudy Forest]. . . . He had no other hobby outside of his love for collecting scrolls of ancient calligraphy and painting. Dealers came and sold them to him at the cost of hundreds of cash, but he never minded the prices.[16]

In addition to the Pure and Secluded Studio, Ni Tsan's elaborate garden villa included a Hall of the Cloudy Forest (Yün-lin-t'ang), a Pavilion of Leisurely Immortals (Hsiao-hsien-hsien-t'ing), a Guest House of the Vermilion Sun (Chu-yang-pin-kuan), a Cave of Snowy Cranes (Hsüeh-ho-tung), and a Pavilion of Mi Fu's Calligraphy and Painting (Hai-yüeh-weng-shu-hua-hsüan). According to Chang Tuan, in *Epitaph of Yün-lin, Master Ni* (*Yün-lin Ni hsien-sheng mu-piao*),

> The Pure and Secluded Studio was covered with blue carpets and was equipped with a hundred pairs of rope slippers, so that guests could change into them before entering. . . . The Cave of Snowy Cranes was covered with white carpets, and the tables inside were covered by a paper decorated with green cloud patterns. . . . In front of these buildings were planted flowers of many different colors, and the flowerbeds were lined with white glazed tiles. When the flowers were watered, the fallen petals were picked up with a long bamboo pole so that the beds would not be dirtied by footprints.[17]

An ardent admirer of the great Northern Sung eccentric artist and connoisseur Mi Fu, Ni shared two of Mi's passions: cleanliness and generosity to friends. Stories about Ni's passion for cleanliness reveal a streak of arrogance in his character. It is said that he would have the large hardwood trees surrounding his studio washed daily, and that, attending a party given by the wealthy well-known poet Yang Wei-chen (1296–1370), he had to leave in disgust because carousing party guests began to pass around a young woman's shoes filled with wine.[18] In Ni Tsan's epitaph Chang Tuan recounted that "if Ni met with some common person asking for a handout, he would lay down the money at some distance for this person to pick up so that he would not be physically touched by such a person."[19]

An anonymous portrait of Ni Tsan dated in the early 1340s (a copy of which is in the National Palace Museum, Taipei; fig. 106) shows the artist was something of a dandy, as well as a perfectionist: dressed in immaculate white linen, flanked by two well-groomed attendants—one holding a feather duster and the other carrying a towel and washing implements—he sits on a couch surrounded by a painted screen, scrolls, an inkstone, and antique bronze and ceramic implements. At the left of the painting Ni's close friend the Taoist scholar Chang Yü (1283–1350) wrote a eulogy:

> Born in Ching-man [Kiangsu Province],
> He lodges at the Cloudy Forest.
> His eyes are blue and white,[20]
> His voice is like metal and jade.
>
> For ten days he paints a stretch of water, for five more he draws a rock—this is how he pores over details;
> After three paces he turns his head, and after five more he sits down—this is how he spends his time.
> He turns his back on the dust of the "lacquer-tree nursery" and the "wild horses,"[21]
> And prefers the cool and snowy white complexion of the goddess Ku-she.
> Waving a jade-handled duster, he is immaculately neat and supremely elegant.
> If an uncouth person washes without using a towel, he is not allowed to speak of cleanliness.
>
> His thoughts follow Wang Wei's,
> His spirits befriend Mi Fu's.

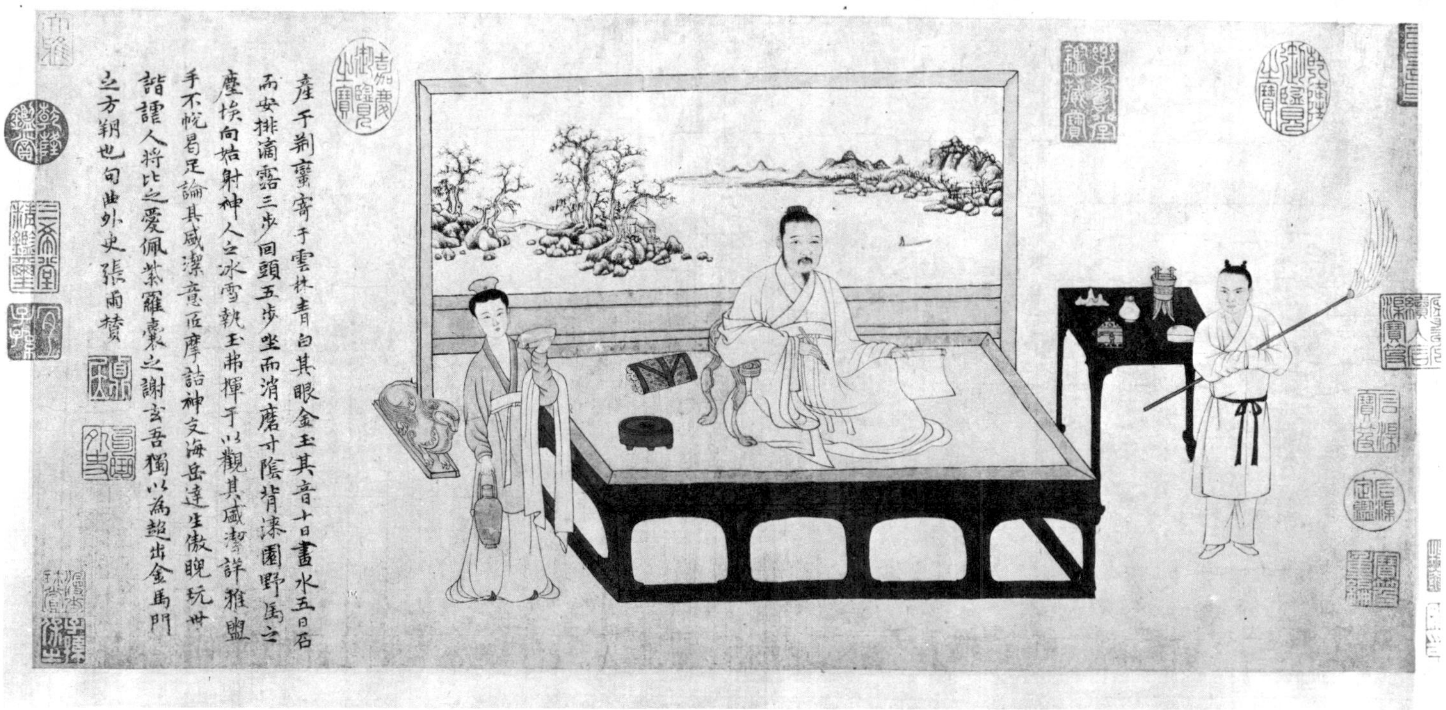

Fig. 106. Anonymous, *Portrait of Ni Tsan (Ni Tsan hsiang)*. Undated, early 1340s. Handscroll, ink and color on paper. 28.2 x 60.9 cm (11 1/8 x 24 in.). National Palace Museum, Taipei

> An enlightened person, yet he looks down upon the world;
> He looks upon life as play, full of humorous jokes.
> People see him as [an aristocratic] Hsieh Hsüan [fl. ca. 400] beautifully decked out with a purple silk sachet,
> I believe him to be even wiser than Tung-fang Shuo at the Chin-ma [palace] gate.[22]

Tung-fang Shuo (ca. 161–87 B.C.) was a Han dynasty court jester who could challenge the emperor without incurring punishment because he always did so wittily. Beneath Ni Tsan's cool and dandyish surface Chang Yü saw a similarly troubled but humane and wise person.

Ni's generosity to friends in need was legendary. Wang Pin recounted how Ni had arranged the funeral of his teacher Wang Jen-fu as if he was a member of his own family and made a generous grant of money to his aging friend Chang Yü.[23] According to Chou Nan-lao,

> If some out-of-town officials died in Ni's town and their coffins could not be returned to their distant homes, Ni would donate mountain property to bury them. . . . He was kind and generous to relatives and friends, and always gladly helped people in need. His demeanor was bright as the autumn moon and warm and kind as the spring sun.[24]

Yet his open and often impulsive behavior also brought him awkward moments. T'ao Tsung-i (ca. 1320–after 1402), author of *Notes Taken after Setting Aside the Plow* (*Cho-keng lu*), related how once Ni presented at a party a gift of 100 piculs of rice to a scholar named Ch'en Po, who, feeling publicly embarrassed, distributed the rice among the assembled courtesans and attendants, and broke off his friendship with Ni.[25]

By the mid-1340s Ni Tsan's halcyon days at the Pure and Secluded Pavilion were over. Beginning in the 1330s natural disasters—floods, droughts, and locusts—had struck China year after year, causing relentless famine and plague. From spring to fall in 1335 no rain had fallen in Chiang-nan, which produced the bulk of the country's grain. By 1337, according to one account, Chekiang and Kiangsu provinces alone had more than 400,000 starving families.[26] The Mongol government responded by heavily taxing wealthy families in the region, including Ni Tsan's. The government's system of forcing the wealthy to "contribute rice to earn official ranks" (*ju-su pu-kuan*) temporarily forestalled disaster, but soon the officials had to coerce the landowners, on threat of imprisonment and physical punishment, to accept titles and make payments.

Even under the best of circumstances, Ni Tsan would probably have found his life difficult, since his bookish predilections and religious friends encouraged him to disdain worldly affairs, including management of his property. As Wang Pin pointed out, "At the beginning of the Chih-cheng era [in the early 1340s], even before insurrections broke out, he started to sell off his family's farm properties. He never worked at what wealthy people usually do, but instead worked hard at being a poet. People would privately laugh at him and think him a fool."[27]

Reacting to the overly ornate poetic style of the early Yüan dynasty and reflecting the chaotic social conditions of the late Yüan time, mid-fourteenth-century Chinese writers emphasized feelings and self-expression in their works. Ni Tsan's poetry was a prominent example of this new realism. In Chou Nan-lao's opinion, Ni Tsan's poetry "does not try to be technically perfect, yet its thoughts are harmonious and light, quiet and relaxed [*ch'ung-tan hsiao-san*], and at the same time full of a sense of moral integrity [*ch'i-chieh*]."[28] Insisting that "poetry must say things," Ni Tsan preferred a realistic approach and stressed feelings over style in his poems. In the late 1360s he compared his time to happier eras:

> In the present [Yüan] dynasty earlier poets, such as Chao [Meng-fu] and Yü [Chi] had sung praises of a peaceful and prosperous era, but after nearly forty years of [rebel] warfare few poets these days can refrain from spinning words of pessimism, anxiety, and troubles. . . . There are those who moan and groan without illness, feign and pretend [suffering] with no sense of integrity [*chieh*]. This is the major sickness of some poets: they are worthless people.[29]

Upholding T'ao Ch'ien (364–427) and Tu Fu (712–770) as his two ideals, Ni Tsan found T'ao's work to exemplify a "harmonious, light, and peaceful" (*ch'ung-tan ho-p'ing*) style that "captures the moral aspect of man's nature and emotions" (*hsing-ch'ing chih-cheng*), and Tu's poems to be "inspired by world affairs" (*yin-shih hsing-huai*) and "patriotic, righteous, and passionate" (*chung-i chi-lieh*).[30] For Ni it was this moral aspect (*cheng*) in man's nature and emotions that, when released, restored to him his sense of joy and rapture in human existence. A good poet, according to Ni, "never wastes a single sentence without saying something real, never devotes himself to empty decoration alone"; good poetry "is like silk, hemp, and grain, which are immediately needed in the world, and is not like carved ice sculpture or fancily embossed paper, which are merely wasted effort. . . . One must guard against affectation and indolence," he cautioned. "One must never imitate or plagiarize; above all one must avoid using difficult language and superficial ideas."[31]

Throughout his difficult life Ni Tsan amused and sustained himself by writing verse. Composing in both the ancient (*ku*) and the regulated (*lü*) styles, he left behind several long autobiographical poems, but wrote mostly shorter ones, especially in the quatrain form, in either five-character or seven-character lines. Composed casually wherever he happened to be, whether at home or traveling, these poems usually record what he was doing, what he saw, or how he felt. Many of them were inscribed on his paintings, and they echo the same feelings and perceptions as his visual expressions. The poems now help us to reconstruct moments of his life in surprising detail.

In a preface to two poems dated 1347, Ni Tsan lamented, "Now that I am a farmer, I am tied to sowing and harvesting, and because of burdensome tax duties, I am constantly running between the prefecture and county government offices."[32] A sad and urgent note fills every poem, painting, and calligraphic work by Ni Tsan at this time. In his autobiographical poem "Speaking My Thoughts" ("Shu-huai"), composed in the late 1340s, the artist bemoaned his past and current circumstances:

Pity me that I lost my father in childhood.
I was raised by my eldest brother.
I was determined to pursue the life of a scholar,
To live by righteous deeds and to uphold pure principles. . . .

Noble positions and great wealth I disdained:
I wished only to leave behind a good name.
Suddenly my eldest brother died,
And our mother [his father's official wife] soon followed. . . .

I fished and farmed, and kept company with my own mother,
But public and private affairs daily troubled me.
I strove hard for twenty years—
Now the whole world is in great confusion.

I pay taxes until I am bled dry.
I handle government business while worrying about a sick child.
I am truly depressed by squalid, vulgar problems;
Unruly disputes upset and frighten me.
Giving everything away, I must bow to government clerks.
Under starlight I wait in the magistrate's courtroom.
In days past I have known the glories of springtime—
Now I struggle to survive in frozen snow.

He considered escaping, but felt trapped by family responsibilities:

How can I not think of running away from all this?
But the thought brings me deeper emotions:
I am afraid of causing my mother worry,
So how can I leave on a long trip?
Even if I gave away my family's inheritance,
I would have to swallow my sorrow and remain to till the land.
It is not that I want to live like an ant;
My real desire is to sail away into the vast sea. . . .

When Yeh-chang [Confucius's disciple] was in prison,
He was highly praised by Confucius;
But when Chi K'ang [223–263 B.C.] indulged in reckless behavior,
His only distinction was to get himself killed.
Even dressed in coarse clothes I can still hold a jade in my heart;
High rank in heaven needs no external trappings.
No physical abuse can blemish my character,
While protesting against violence may amount only to boastfulness.
If an orchid grows in the midst of brambles,
The brambles will not hide its delicate fragrance.[33]

Seeking spiritual consolation, Ni Tsan associated more and more frequently with Taoist and Buddhist priests, who counseled total detachment and retreat as a means of escape from physical harm. In a poem composed as a colophon to an early edition of Ni's poems, completed in the late 1340s, Chang Yü wrote:

You are drawn to mountains and valleys.
A powerless scholar, you find the times against you.
Like serpents, the strong and mighty will swallow you;
Like tigers, endlessly greedy, they will gnaw at you.
Why do you risk so much danger?
You are merely burdened by your land and property:
Like an old elephant stuck in the mire,
To extricate yourself you need courage and resolve.

Who but yourself can break the chain of causality?
Between morning and night there will be many vicissitudes of fortune.
Thus only the intelligent and the wise
Know how to place themselves outside these changes.
How worthy was Chü Po-yü [Confucius's disciple]
Who, discovering his errors, had no regrets about them.[34]

In 1351, after a disastrous flood inundated the Huai region in the north China plain, full-scale rebellions broke out all over China. Soon fires and fierce fighting between rebel forces had lain waste to much of Hang-chou, the city that had been the seat of the Southern Sung dynasty. Su-chou, the nearest city to Ni Tsan's home in Wu-hsi, was relatively safe because of its superior government defenses. The water country of Lake T'ai and the three rivers of Lou, Wu, and Sung—with their network of small streams, innumerable bays, inlets, and islands covered with mulberry trees and aquatic plants—afforded hiding places for many wealthy refugees. In early 1352 Ni Tsan loaded some of his worldly possessions onto a houseboat and set sail. For years he had to maintain this nomadic life, stopping at the homes of friends along the way and moving on at a moment's notice. Like Mi Fu's Calligraphy and Painting Barge, Ni's houseboat was filled with books and scrolls, tea implements, and trays of painting brushes.[35]

As a moral Neo-Confucian scholar, Ni was deeply offended by the very thought of rebellion, as he wrote in the poem "On Becoming Aware" ("Ching-shih"):

A lamb kneels while it suckles—in order to show deference;
When birds put food in the beaks of their young—the chicks never disobey.
These are small creatures that show heaven's principles.
Deeply I sigh, my tears running down my lapels.[36]

Instead, as he set down in "Wind and Rain" ("Feng-yü"), he reacted to his life of exile with feelings of defeat and melancholy:

In wind and rain, desolate and bleak, I chant a mournful tune.
Old memories rush back to me, but already they seem faint.
My mountain friend urges more wine on me, while the moon rises through the flowers;
A girl from Ch'in-huai plays on the zither "The Mulberry Trees in the Field."
The shadow cast by a lamp fills half the window pane, recalling a dream a thousand *li* away.
Another day spent on the muddy road churns up my stomach a full nine times.
In this life any hostel may serve as adequate shelter;
I deceive myself by imagining that every town is my own.[37]

After a year of wandering he stopped at the home of a relative, Lu Hsüan-su, at Fu-li, in early 1353.[38] There he sent for his wife and his mother. In "Composed on the Sixth Day [of the Lunar Month]" ("Liu-jih t'i"), Ni described his family members' flight from Wu-hsi:

Stopping over with the Ch'iu family they stole some rest,
The whole family fleeing, headed for the border pass at night.
The county officials were arresting everyone, emptying entire neighborhoods—
Bringing the family through was like escaping from the gates of hell.[39]

As Ni Tsan and his family were preparing to take leave from the Lu family at Fu-li (in about April 1353), Ni wrote this poem, "Farewell to a Daughter of the Lu Family" ("Pieh Lu shih nu"):

To leave or to stay—both are sad choices.
The Lord of Heaven must have plans for us.
There may be a safe haven ahead of our journey;
Do not believe everything will go wrong for me.[40]

He asked a friend named Han Po-ch'ing in a poem, "Chi Han Po-ch'ing," about a more permanent home:

Where may I rent a farm property?
I have no dream of a golden hall or a jade-filled room—
Just a place for raising vegetables and herbs, collecting firewood, and fishing,
Preferably close to some mountain or a green lake.[41]

And, struggling to maintain his mental equilibrium, he composed "Fair or Foul" ("Shun-ni"):

Fair or foul, I shall have neither love nor resentment,
Like white clouds above untouched by worldly dust.
If worldly affairs are like fire, my mind should be like water;
In my inner house I must remain my own master.[42]

After hiding his family in a safe place, he often returned to Wu-hsi, surreptitiously visiting his ancestral home. In one "miscellaneous poem" (*tsa-fu*) he wrote:

Once I built a fishing jetty over a river;
Now the vermilion gates and beautiful houses have all changed.
I am like the sparrow of the [once powerful] Wang and Hsieh families [of the Six Dynasties period];
Year after year it flies by the white-boarded windows.[43]

On one of these surreptitious visits, in 1355, he was seized by the local authorities, and jailed and beaten, as he recalled in "Chih-cheng Era, I-wei Year [1355], Poem on Man in White" ("Chih-cheng i-wei su-i shih"):

My white clothes stained,
A prisoner in the public courtrooms.
Covered with wounds and confined,
My heart is full of fear.
Cruel officials behave like tigers:
They have no pity.
They treat people like swine,
Killing them, heaping abuse on them.
Though I conduct myself with propriety,
I know I have myself to blame.
Even considering the family property,
And my mother in homeless exile,
To linger and not stay away
Is the cause of my sorrow.

> To have my body abused and parent endangered
> Is against filial piety and righteous behavior. . . .
>
> There are orchids in empty valleys,
> Where it is secluded and vast.
> There is a quiet little cottage
> With simple sustenance, harmony, and happiness.
> I can hunt, I can fish,
> My heart will not be confused;
> Peacefully I can cultivate myself;
> Awake or asleep I can forget my troubles.
> I shall realize my old resolve:
> In retirement I shall find simple enjoyment.[44]

So, returning to their refugee home on the river, Ni Tsan and his family settled down to a life of "simple sustenance, harmony, and happiness." For about ten years, between 1356 and 1366, they lived in the water country of Li-tse, at a place Ni nicknamed the "Snail Hut" (Kua-niu-lu). Compared to the Wu-hsi days, this was "another lifetime," though the family's circumstances seem to have been stable and even well-to-do. In 1357 Ni wrote to the scholar Ch'en Chih (1292–1362) to engage him as a tutor for his youngest son, Yang-cheng, who was seven years old: "To teach him where to go, and how always to aim for propriety and righteousness, we must not neglect the beginning."[45]

In March 1356 the rebel Chang Shih-ch'eng's forces crossed the Yangtze River and seized Su-chou and other areas east of Lake T'ai. Chang established ministries and bureaus in imitation of an imperial administration and invited talented scholars to join his government. Many well-known literary figures around the Su-chou and Sung-chiang areas joined the Chang regime immediately, and more followed in late 1357 and early 1358, when Chang legitimized himself by accepting a Mongol appointment as grand marshal (*t'ai-wei*) for the region he controlled. But Ni Tsan steadfastly declined Chang's repeated invitations. In 1363 Chang again declared himself independent, calling himself prince of Wu. By the summer of 1365 Chu Yüan-chang (1328–1398), the future founder of the Ming dynasty, who started his career as a Red Turban rebel occupying the area west of Lake T'ai with Nanking as his base, began his campaign against Chang Shih-ch'eng to the east. After a long and bitter struggle (from December 1366 to August 1367) Chang surrendered Su-chou to Chu's general, Hsü Ta.

Once again Ni Tsan had to abandon his home, this time to the marauding soldiers. He appears to have been completely alone by this time; his wife, Chiang Yüan-chao, had died in 1363,[46] and there is no further mention in the poems and other documents of his youngest child. Between December 21, 1366, and January 6, 1368—as he recalled in a preface to a poem—he spent his time sailing on the Mao River.[47] Soon after the establishment of the Ming dynasty on January 23, 1368, he sailed back briefly to Li-tse and Su-chou, then spent the next few years wandering throughout the Chiang-nan area, visiting old haunts he had not seen for twenty or thirty years. According to his epitaph writer,

> in his late years, he became quieter and more withdrawn than ever. Having lost or given away everything he ever owned, he did his best to forget his worries. Wearing a yellow [Taoist] cap and country clothes, he roamed the lakes and mountains, leading a recluse's life. His appearance became loftier than ever: he would not utter one word of flattery to please an official, nor set foot inside the doors of a grandee. . . . When the world began to settle down [i.e., after January 1368], he came back to the city. Mingling in the crowd of refugees, he carefully hid his light and avoided trouble.[48]

In the autumn of 1374 Ni Tsan finally returned to Wu-hsi from Su-chou. There he fell ill at the home of a relative, Tsou Wei-kao, where he died, according to Chou Nan-lao, on the eleventh day of the eleventh lunar month of the *chia-yin* year (December 13, 1374).

## *A Rustic Style*

As a calligrapher Ni Tsan, the recluse, presents an interesting contrast to Chao Meng-fu, who had practiced his art under the aegis of the Yüan court. In 1359 Chang Ching (Chang Te-chi), the newly appointed magistrate of Su-chou under the rebel government of Chang Shih-ch'eng, refurbished and expanded the buildings of the Su-chou county (*hsien*) school. After commissioning the well-known scholar Cheng Yüan-yu (1292–1369) to compose a eulogy for the dedicatory stele to be placed at the school gate,[49] the magistrate asked his father Chang Chien (1281–1370), a friend of Ni Tsan's, to inquire if Ni would be the calligrapher for the stone inscription. Ni firmly declined the invitation, replying to the elder Chang:

> The essay for the stone has a charming archaic and plain flavor; it is truly a masterpiece by the venerable Cheng. But my faulty calligraphy is not suited for such a formal place of learning; its dots and strokes are not strong and graceful, and its character formations are common and ugly. Furthermore I can write only small-size characters and am no good at all at large-size ones. If the magistrate wants the stele to be a lasting monument, he should ask someone with not only great calligraphic skill, but also an uncommonly superior moral character; then the calligraphy will match the literary composition. How can my faulty calligraphy equal such lofty demands?[50]

The unspoken reason for Ni's firm refusal was probably political. In asking Ni to be the calligrapher on that occasion, the magistrate Chang Ching may well have intended to entangle him officially with the rebel Chang Shih-ch'eng's government. In spite of his friendship with the magistrate's father, Ni may not have wished to appear to lend his personal endorsement to an official function. Yet the reasons that Ni gave for declining the invitation were genuine. As a calligrapher he was not, either by temperament or by training, suited to the writing of a monumental inscription for a commemorative stele. He was exclusively a writer of informal *hsiao-k'ai*, or "small-size script"; his individual characters seldom exceed three-quarters of an inch in height.

Growing up just across Lake T'ai from Wu-hsing, the home of Chao Meng-fu, Ni Tsan absorbed some of Chao's influences. Yet the calligraphic styles of the two men represent, in a psychological as well as a social sense, unalterably different ways of life. As a countrified recluse, Ni could no more be expected to write in Chao's elegant, tightly organized regular script than to assume Chao's official robes and courtly formality.

By following a primitive, rustic mode of writing, Ni Tsan created a distinctive style for the eccentric, reclusive scholar who lived "in the wilderness" (*tsai-yeh*). The calligrapher he chose as a model was Chung Yu, the Wei dynasty master who developed the archaic clerical form of the Han period into an early regular script. A well-known work attributed to Chung Yu, *Memorial to Recommend Chi-chih* (*Chien Chi-chih piao*; fig. 107) was found at that time in the collection of Lu Hsing-chih (1275–after 1349), a clansman of Ni Tsan's relative Lu Hsüan-su who lived at Lake Fen, not far from Fu-li. In a colophon dated 1349 Lu Hsing-chih, who classified Chung Yu as "of the Han period," wrote of the work as one of "lofty antiquity, pure and simple . . . without a trace of the Tsin–T'ang look of a pretty girl wearing flowers."[51] The phrase "pretty girl wearing flowers" was used by critics of that time to denigrate Chao Meng-fu's overelegant calligraphic style.[52] While Chao had based his regular script on Tsin and T'ang models, Ni Tsan used Chung Yu's style to re-create an earlier running-clerical style, with squat or square characters, mostly level strokes, generally simplified brushwork, and prominent wavelike ending strokes.

Since his intention was to use calligraphy to express himself, Ni Tsan's handwriting from the mid-1340s on, when he began to roam the lakes to dodge tax collectors, fully reflected his highly charged emotional state. In *The Six Gentlemen* (*Liu chün-tzu*), dated 1345 (fig. 108), a small hanging scroll in the Shanghai Museum, Ni Tsan's colophon to the left of the trees reads:

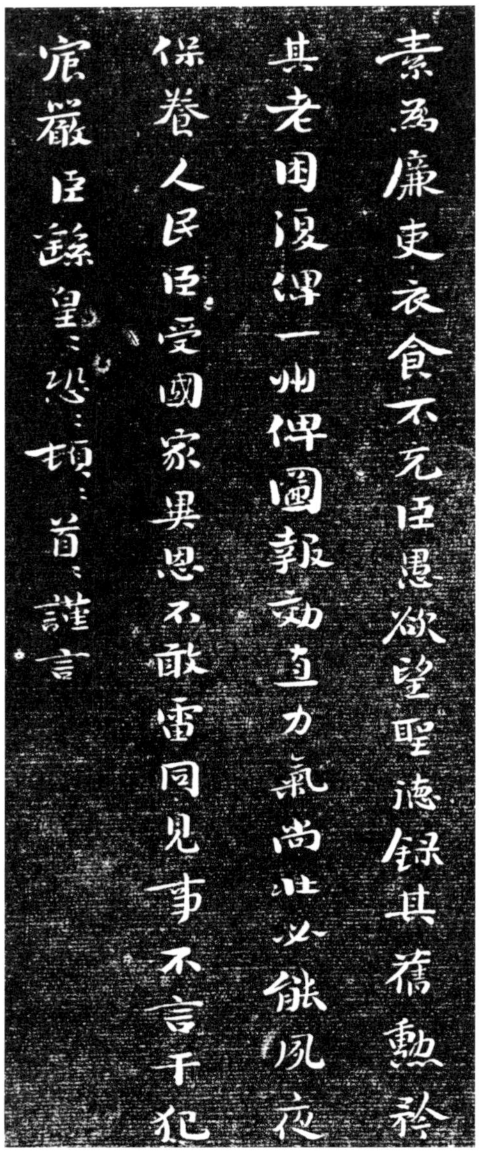

Fig. 107. Attributed to Chung Yu, *Memorial to Recommend Chi-chih* (*Chien Chi-chih piao*). Undated, A.D. 2nd–3rd century. 25.7 x 13.7 cm (10 1/8 x 5 3/8 in.). Rubbing of inscription

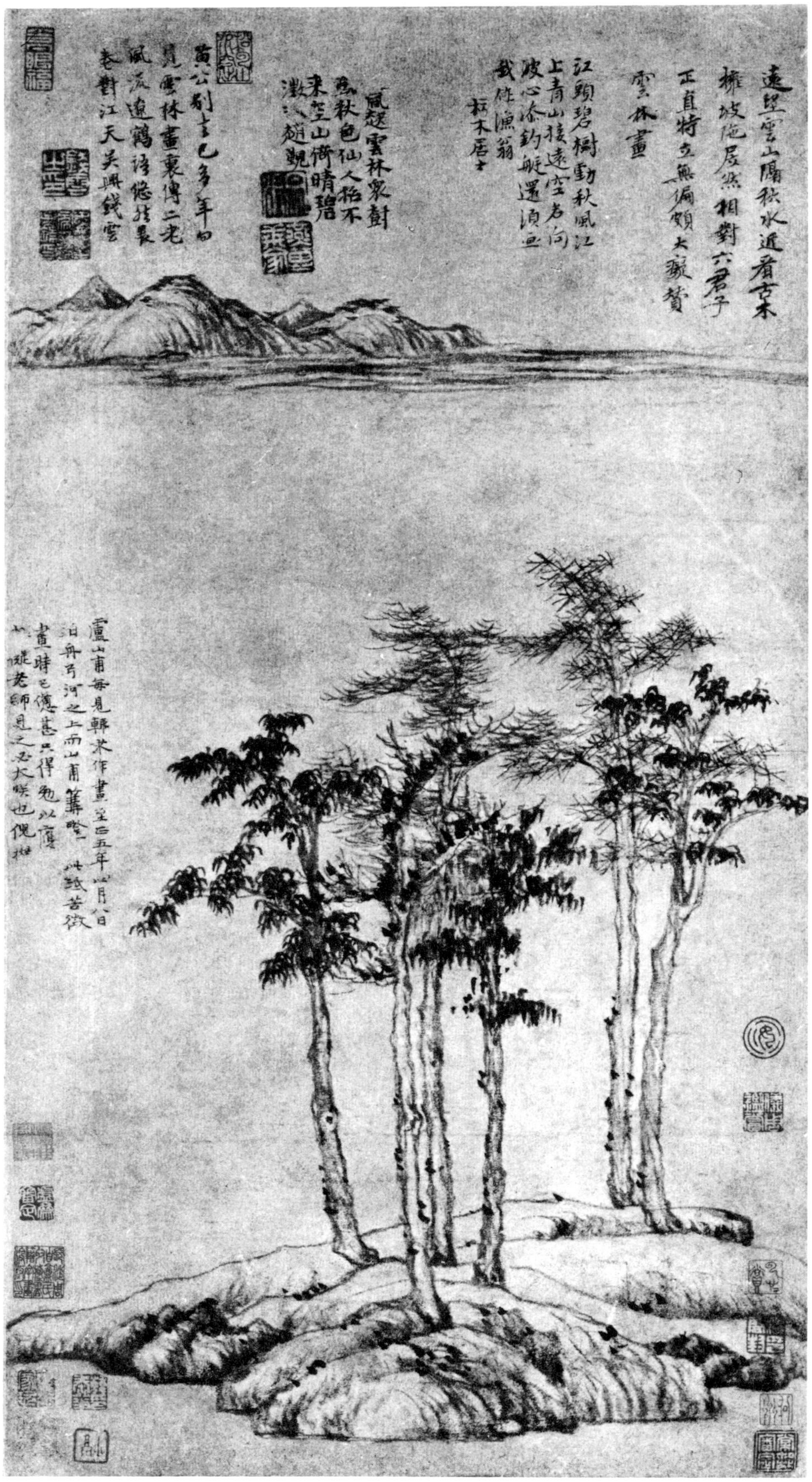

Fig. 108. Ni Tsan, *The Six Gentlemen* (*Liu chün-tzu*). Dated 1345. Hanging scroll, ink on paper. Shanghai Museum

Every time Lu Shan-fu [Lu Heng] sees me, he urges me to paint for him. On the eighth day of the fourth lunar month of the fifth year of the Chih-cheng era [May 10, 1345] I had just docked my boat on the Bow River when he greeted me with a lamp and a piece of paper, insisting strenuously that I paint for him. I was feeling extremely weary from the journey, but did my best to answer his request. When the old master Ta-ch'ih [Huang Kung-wang; 1269–1354] sees this, he will have a good laugh over it.

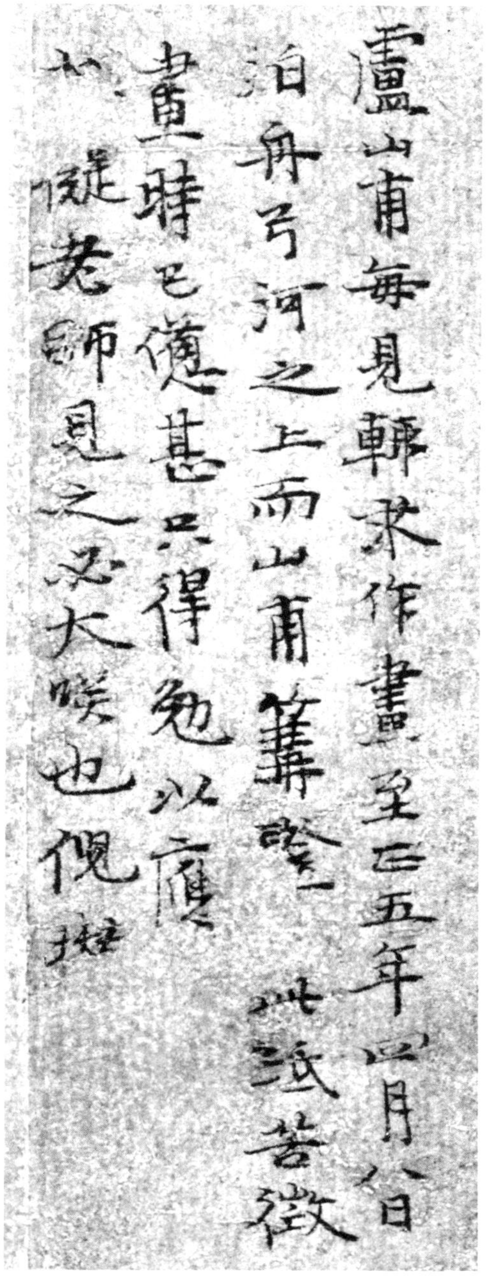

Fig. 108a. Detail of inscription by Ni Tsan, fig. 108

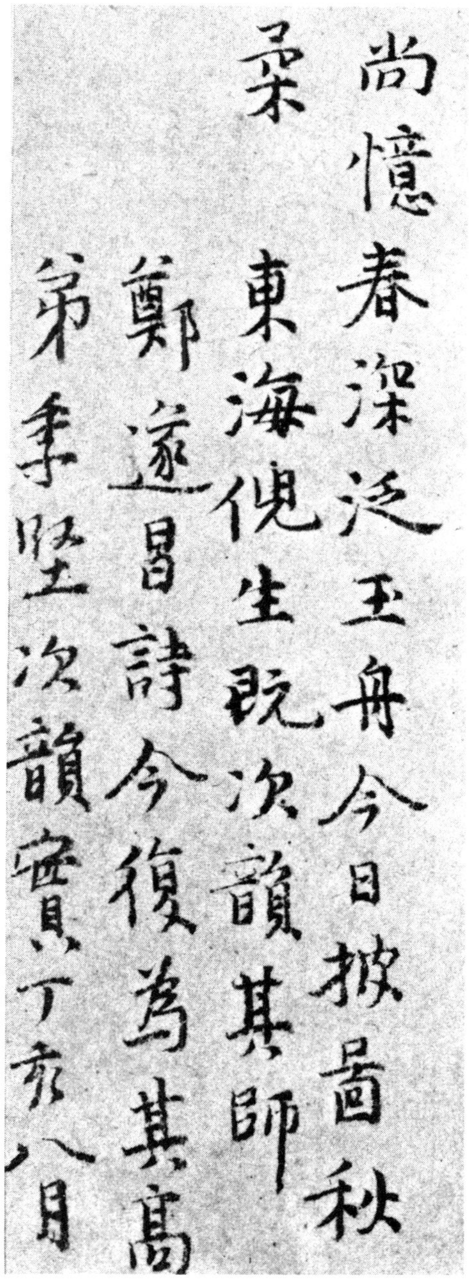

Fig. 109. Ni Tsan, inscription, dated 1347, on *Bright Peonies* (*Mu-tan*) by Ch'ien Hsüan. Handscroll, ink and color on paper. National Palace Museum, Taipei

The calligraphy (fig. 108a) shows a nervous energy and tensile strength: the brushwork is taut and bony, and certain elements in the writing are tightly wound up and lopsided. The writer deliberately exaggerated the contradictions between the regular- and the clerical-script types to create tension and interest: the naturally slanting regular-script elements are forced into the horizontal clerical compositional structure. In a poetic colophon of 1347 (fig. 109), written on a painting of brightly colored peonies by Ch'ien Hsüan (ca. 1235–1300), a Southern Sung loyalist who felt he had outlived his time, Ni Tsan wrote:

> Red and purple filling the table, like a piece of rich brocade from Shu [Szechuan province],
> It reminds me of some late spring days when I sailed in a jade-studded boat.
> Now I see this painting in autumn, in the eighth moon;
> How sad are the bare branches, which have lost their soft fragrant flowers.

The handwriting, that of a frightened fugitive, is spare and unadorned; the mood is somber and subdued.

The expression of emotion also influences the style and composition of Ni's paintings. *The Six*

*Gentlemen* shows six bleak looming spikes dominating the riverbank. A thin mist seems to drift across the river, giving a sense of utter isolation from everything except the river and the lonely trees. Lu Heng, Ni Tsan's host after his tiring journey and the recipient of this painting, was a noted scholar and connoisseur in Su-chou who often played host to well-known scholars and artists of the time.[53] It appears that when Ni arrived at Lu's home that night other distinguished guests were present—among them the old Taoist scholar and painter Huang Kung-wang. It was Huang who gave Ni's painting its title, by inscribing in the upper right corner of the painting a four-line poem:

> Distant cloudy mountains range across the autumn river;
> Nearby, ancient trees huddle by the sloping shore.
> Six gentlemen stand facing one another,
> Upright, straight, outstanding, and unbending.

Ni's work, painted in homage to Huang Kung-wang, resembles in its brushwork Huang's masterpiece *Dwelling in the Fu-ch'un Mountains*, dated 1350 (cf. fig. 67). The modeling of the rocks in both paintings follows Tung Yüan's hemp-skin (*ma-p'i*) idiom. The loosely directed texture strokes build, layer upon layer, until the forms emerge. The individual brushstrokes are—in Huang Kung-wang's words—"blurred and blended" (*hu-t'u ch'i-pi*)[54] to suggest atmospheric forms in space; and the tree branches and foliage dots project and recede three-dimensionally. The composition of the trees and slopes is a fully realized, realistic spatial structure: all the elements near and far extend in an integrated vision along a convincingly receding ground plane. Ni's round (*chung feng*) brushstrokes "write" the trees and rock forms as in seal and cursive calligraphy. Compared to Chao Meng-fu's *Twin Pines against a Flat Vista* (cf. fig. 104), Ni's round brushwork is "plain, light, and natural." Ni's slow and gentle cursive brushwork, though full of emotion and inner excitement, struggles to maintain an outward calm and balance, befitting a man who insisted, "In my inner house I must remain my own master."[55]

Traditionally, tall pine trees, in the words of the tenth-century master Ching Hao, "possess the virtuous air of a gentleman."[56] In early Yüan painting (fig. 110) a new emotionalism appeared in the rendering of the old theme of "wintry trees," contorted tree trunks with spiky branches, devil-face rocks peeking out from under the snow, an icy river, and restless, hungry crows tumbling and squawking against the dark sky. All of these elements convey a somber, gloomy mood that recalls the patriotic lament of Tu Fu: "The nation is broken, but the mountains and rivers remain."[57] In Ni Tsan's paintings ordinary trees, many of them gaunt and dry, stripped by age or harsh weather, seem larger than life. They emanate an impression of grandeur that seems to symbolize the artist's own noble and unbending spirit.

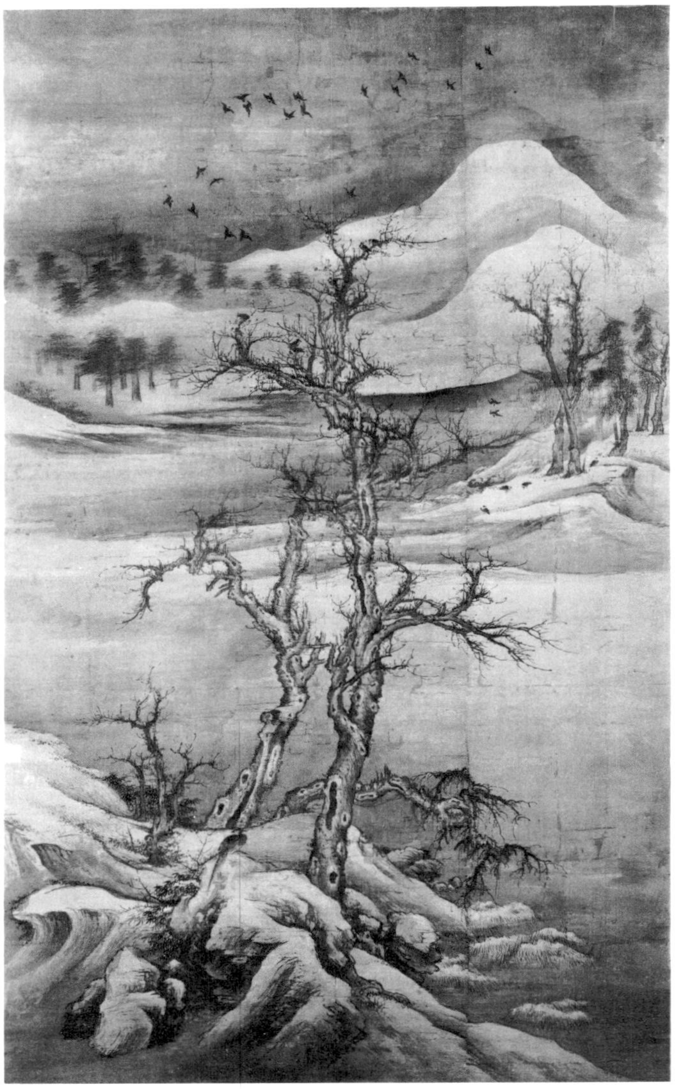

Fig. 110. Lo Chih-ch'uan, *Crows in Old Trees* (*Han-lin kuei-ya*). Undated, early 14th century. Hanging scroll, ink and light color on silk. 150.8 x 80.0 cm (4 ft. 11 3/8 in. x 31 1/2 in.). The Metropolitan Museum of Art, New York

The metaphor of clustered trees as lonely friends

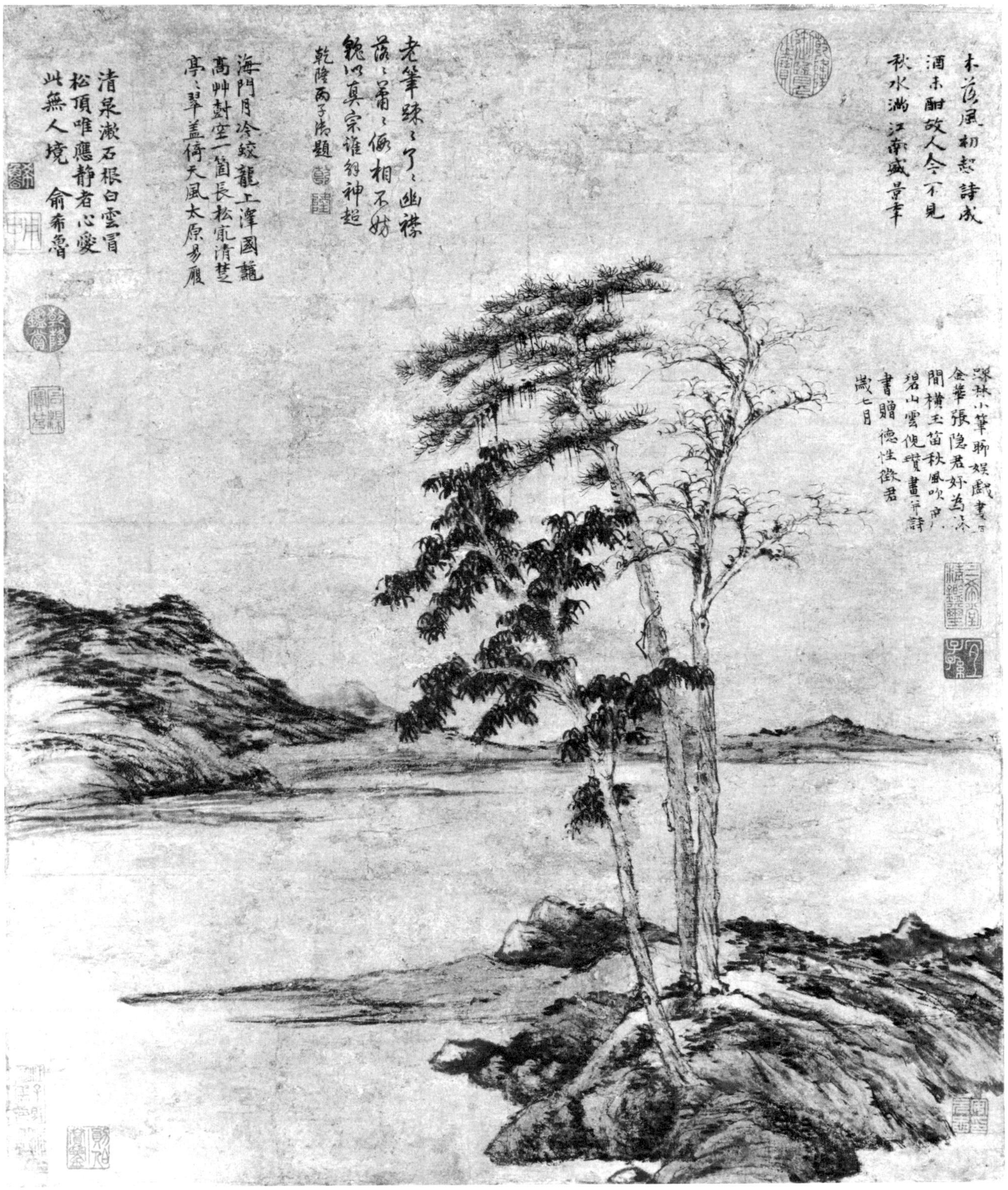

Fig. 111. Ni Tsan, *A Sparse Grove* (*Shu-lin hsiao-pi*). Undated, ca. 1345. Hanging scroll, ink on paper. Osaka Municipal Museum of Fine Art

is used in many of Ni Tsan's works during this period. In *A Sparse Grove* (*Shu-lin hsiao-pi*), painted about 1345 for Ni's friend Chang Te-hsing (another son of Chang Chien's) (Abe Collection, Osaka Municipal Museum of Fine Art; fig. 111), the artist shows three trees huddled together by a deserted riverbank. On the painting Ni inscribed this poem:

> A sparse grove done with a playful small brush;
> I painted this for the recluse Master Chang from Chin-hua [in Chekiang province].
> You enjoy playing a jade lute in the forest,
> When autumn wind blows the cloud away from the green hills.

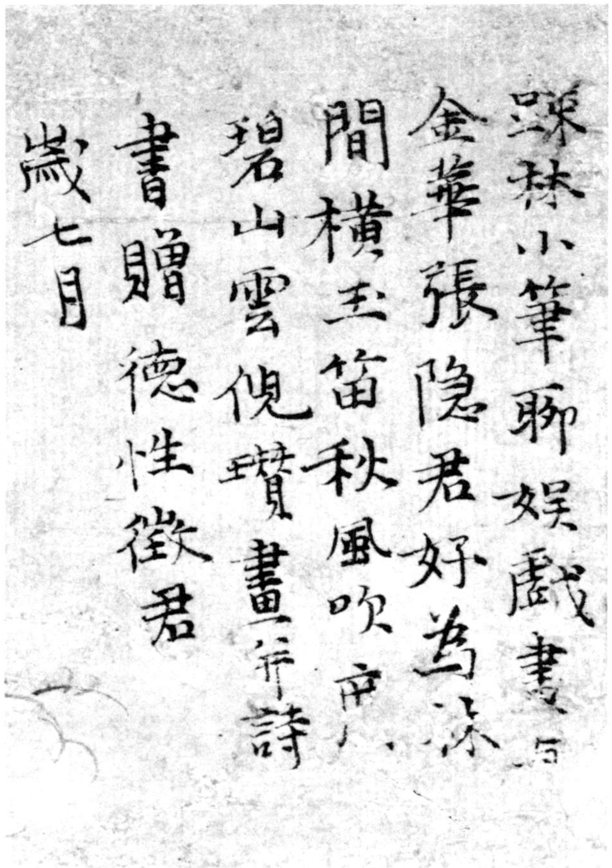

Fig. 111a. Detail of inscription by Ni Tsan, fig. 111

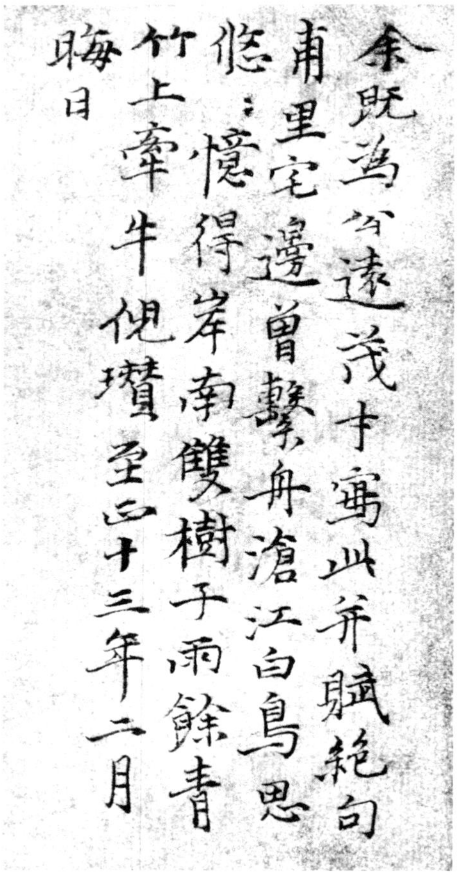

Fig. 112a. Ni Tsan, inscription on *Twin Trees by the South Bank* (*An-nan shuang-shu*), no. 10

Although the calligraphy of this inscription (fig. 111a) compares closely with that of *The Six Gentlemen* (cf. fig. 108a), the painting has a completely different overall appearance. The rock forms, covered with seemingly careless, almost messy strokes and horizontal dots, reflect an educated taste for childish daubing. For Ni Tsan brushwork, here delightfully playful (*hsi*), is painting—the blending of the various kinds of brushstrokes to reveal not only the true landscape, but also the anxious feelings of the artist. The painting records the moment when transient emotion becomes pure feeling (*ch'ing*), combining urgency with detachment, a characteristic that is uniquely Ni Tsan's.

Another of these symbolic friendship paintings, *Twin Trees by the South Bank* (*An-nan shuang-shu*), was executed at the end of his stay at Fu-li. A small hanging-scroll painting on paper dated "on the last day of the second lunar month of the thirteenth year of the Chih-cheng era," or April 4, 1353 (now in The Art Museum, Princeton University; no. 10), *Twin Trees* was a farewell present for a younger friend, perhaps one of Ni Tsan's hosts. In the upper right corner of the composition the artist inscribed a poem with a prefatory remark (fig. 112a):

> Having "written" this picture for the young scholar Kung-yüan, I further composed a quatrain:
>
> I once tied my boat near the cottage at Fu-li,
> Where the green river and white gulls stirred my melancholy thoughts.
> I shall remember the two trees on the south bank,
> How the blue-green bamboo clings, after rain, like morning glories.[58]

In *Twin Trees* the space evoked is open and natural. It shows two beautifully composed trees—one taller, bristling with dry twigs, standing upright, accompanied and balanced by a shorter tree with tender growths, leaning gracefully to one side (fig. 112b); these clearly represent Ni and the friend, Kung-yüan, to whom the painting is dedicated, as close companions who, during Ni's four months' stay at Fu-li, must

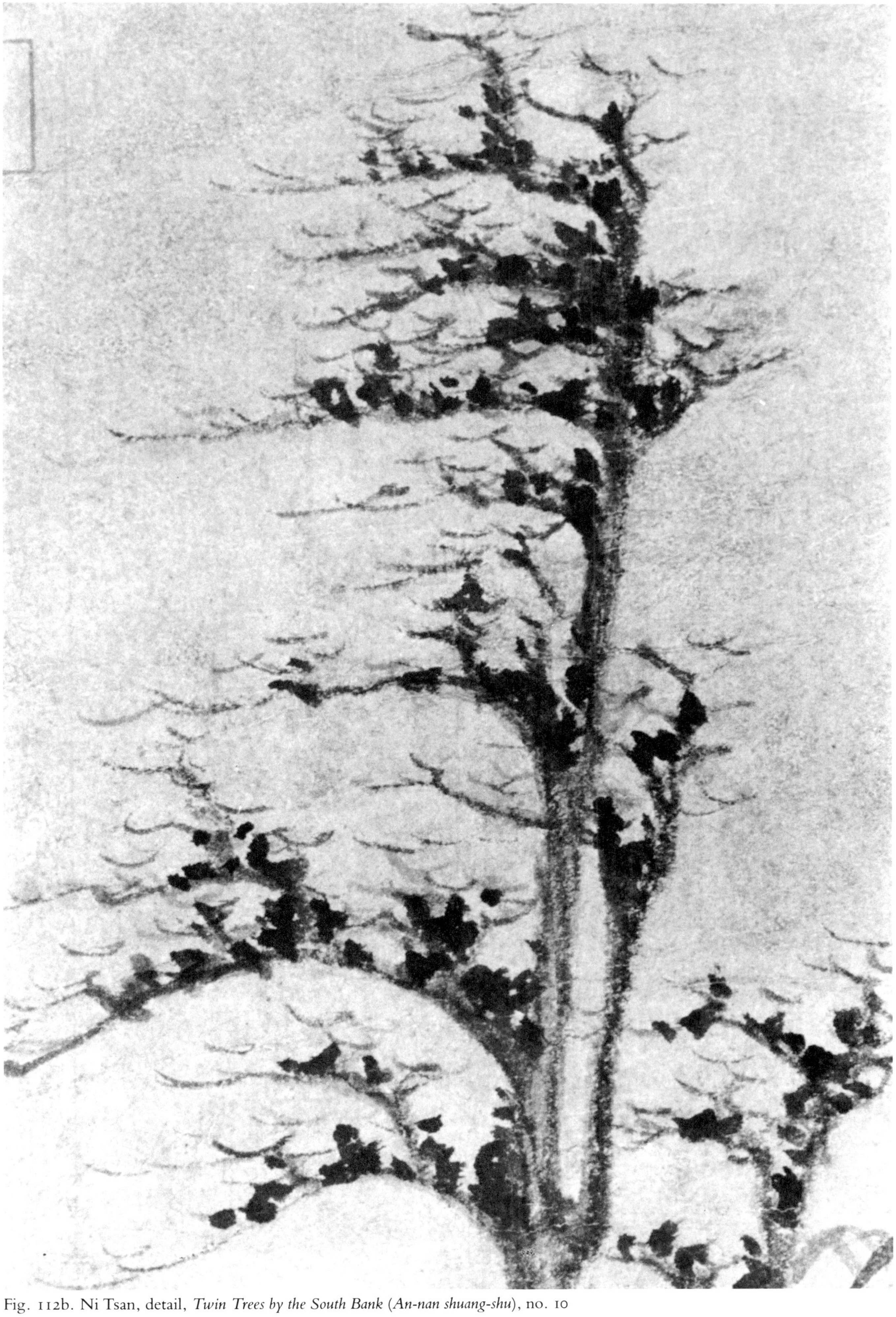

Fig. 112b. Ni Tsan, detail, *Twin Trees by the South Bank* (*An-nan shuang-shu*), no. 10

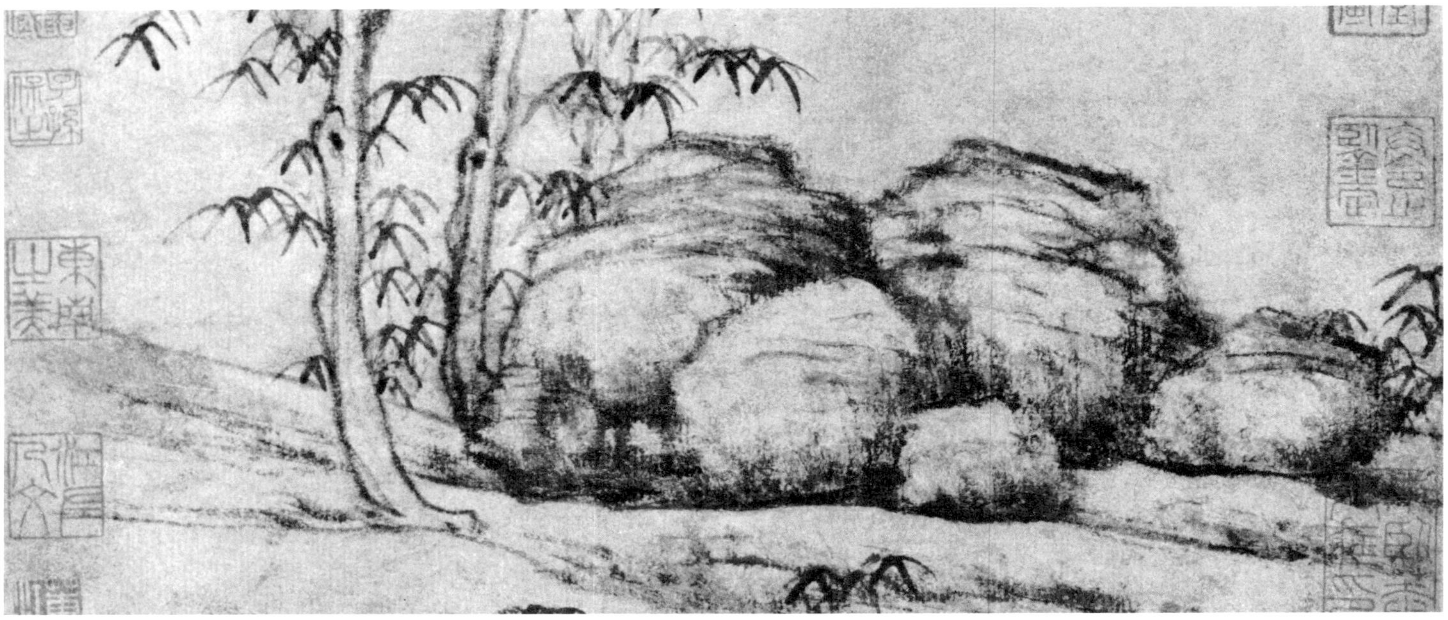

Fig. 112c. Ni Tsan, detail, *Twin Trees by the South Bank* (*An-nan shuang-shu*), no. 10

have spent long hours together on the south bank, exchanging ideas and thoughts while watching the green river, the white gulls, and the clinging blue-green bamboo mentioned in Ni's poem. These paintings and poems, which Ni Tsan created for friends as personal gifts and exchanges, capture isolated moments in what must have been a continual outpouring of feelings and thoughts between close friends. Though outwardly quiet, they are fiercely impassioned. The poem on each painting tempts us to eavesdrop on a private world of intimacies and lost conversations, but the sublime image admits no superfluous details, and presents instead a pure and privileged domain of trees and rocks. Ni Tsan repeated this composition of trees and rocks over and over, refining and distilling, until each work emerged as a pure image of the mind.

The manner of painting these two trees was something Ni Tsan had studied and considered carefully over a long time. Echoing Huang Kung-wang's advice that "a painter should carry his brushes in a leather satchel . . . to draw and record [from nature],"[59] Ni Tsan once wrote in a poem presented to Fang Yai, a Buddhist priest and painter in Su-chou:

> When I first learned to use a brush,
> Seeing an object I tried to capture its likeness.
> Whenever I traveled, in country or in town,
> I sketched object after object, keeping them in my painting basket.
> I ask my master Fang I,
> What is illusion, what is real?
> From the inkwell I take some inkdrops,
> To lodge in my painting a boundless feeling of spring.[60]

In the *Painting Manual* (*Hua-p'u*), in the National Palace Museum, Taipei—which is attributed to Ni Tsan and dated 1350, and seems to be an accurate, though not brilliant, copy of an original—the artist shows how two trees with a clump of bamboo between them may be composed (fig. 113); Ni's comments on the left of the illustration read:

> For the larger tree the brushwork should be soft, so that its branches look tender; for the smaller tree the brushwork should be ancient, so that it looks archaic. If the larger tree is seen from the front, the smaller tree should grow to one side. These are things a beginner must learn to master. In painting trees the space between them may be filled with bamboo, which need not be done with too much precision. But if the trees are seen on a sunny day, then they should be matched with sunny bamboo. This means the bamboo leaves should all point upward.[61]

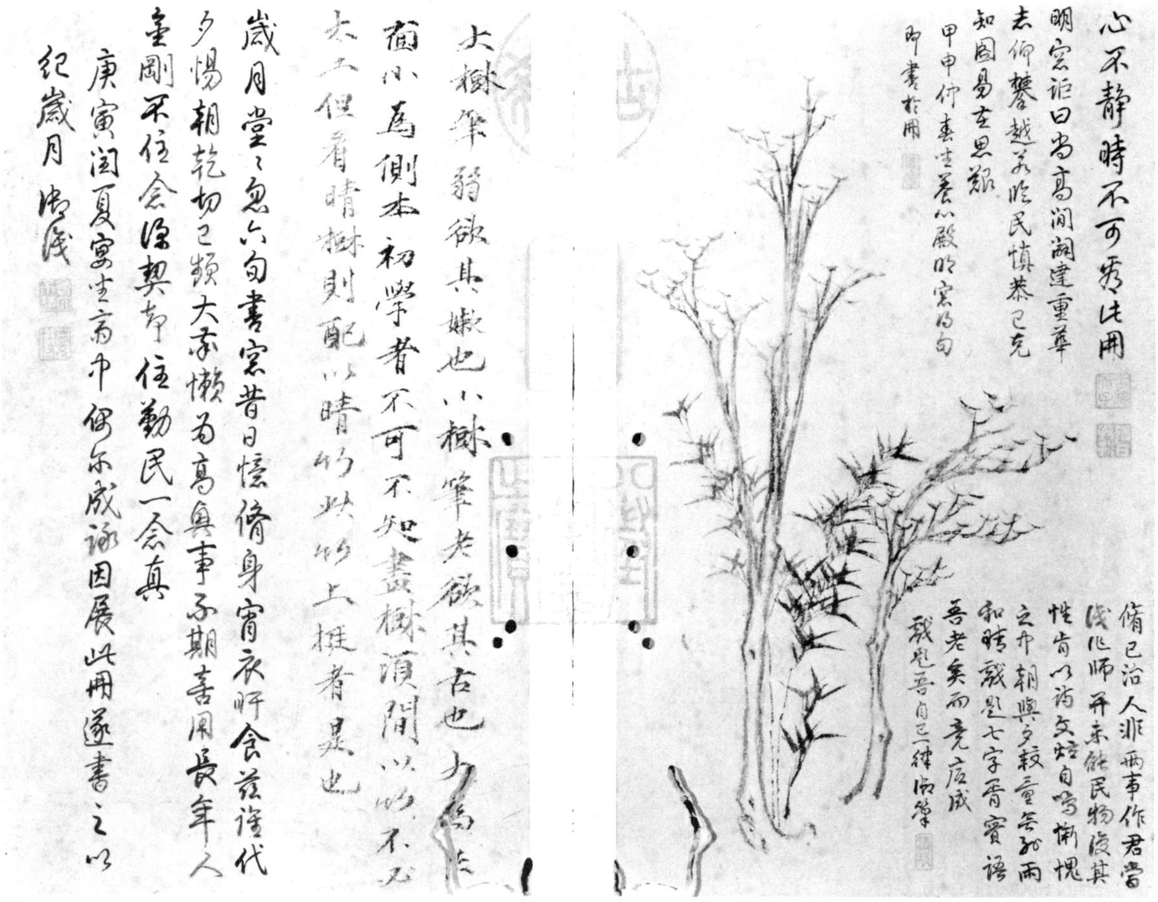

Fig. 113. Anonymous, after Ni Tsan, "Two Trees." Album leaf 2 of *Painting Manual* (*Hua-p'u*), ink on paper. Dated 1350. 23.6 x 14.2 cm (9¼ x 5⅝ in.). National Palace Museum, Taipei

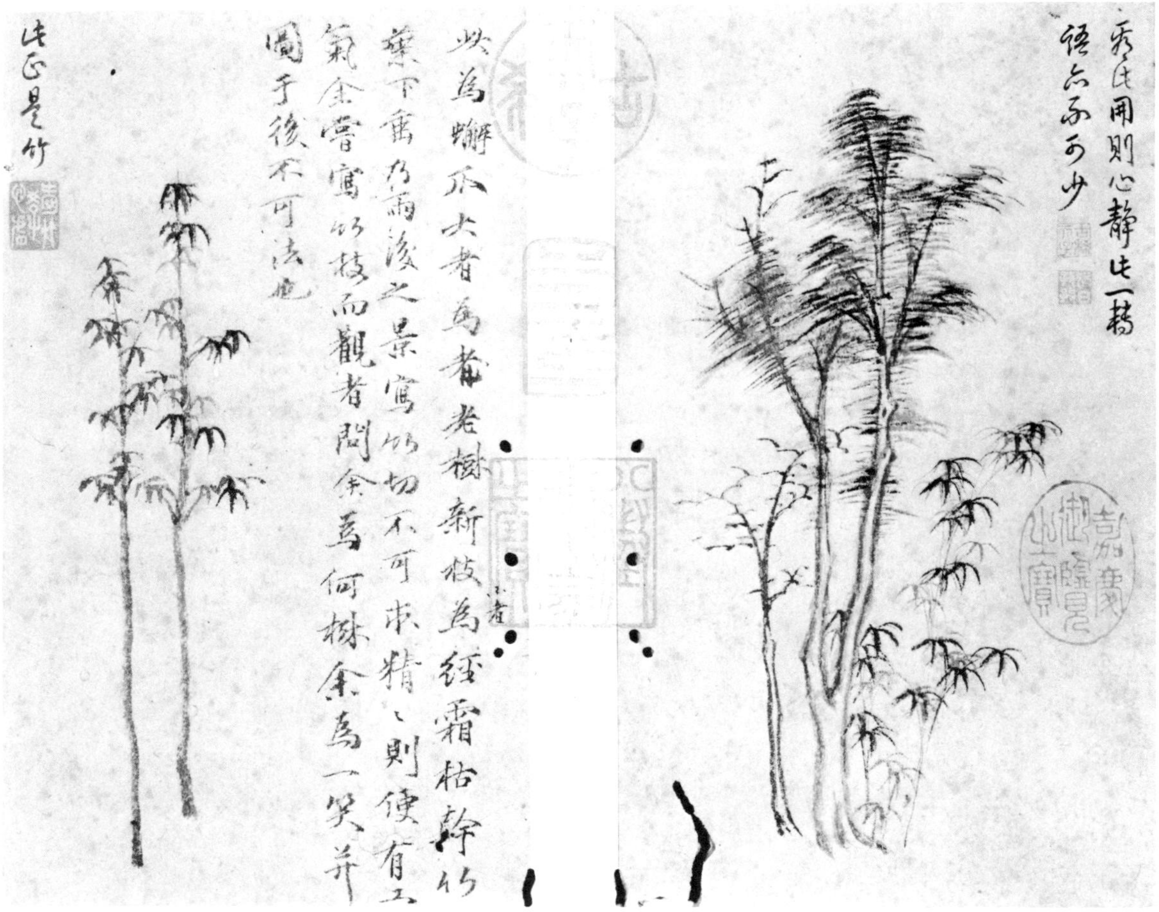

Fig. 114. Anonymous, after Ni Tsan, "Bamboo with Leaves Drooping." Album leaf 3 of *Painting Manual* (*Hua-p'u*), ink on paper. 23.6 x 14.2 cm (9¼ x 5⅝ in.). National Palace Museum, Taipei

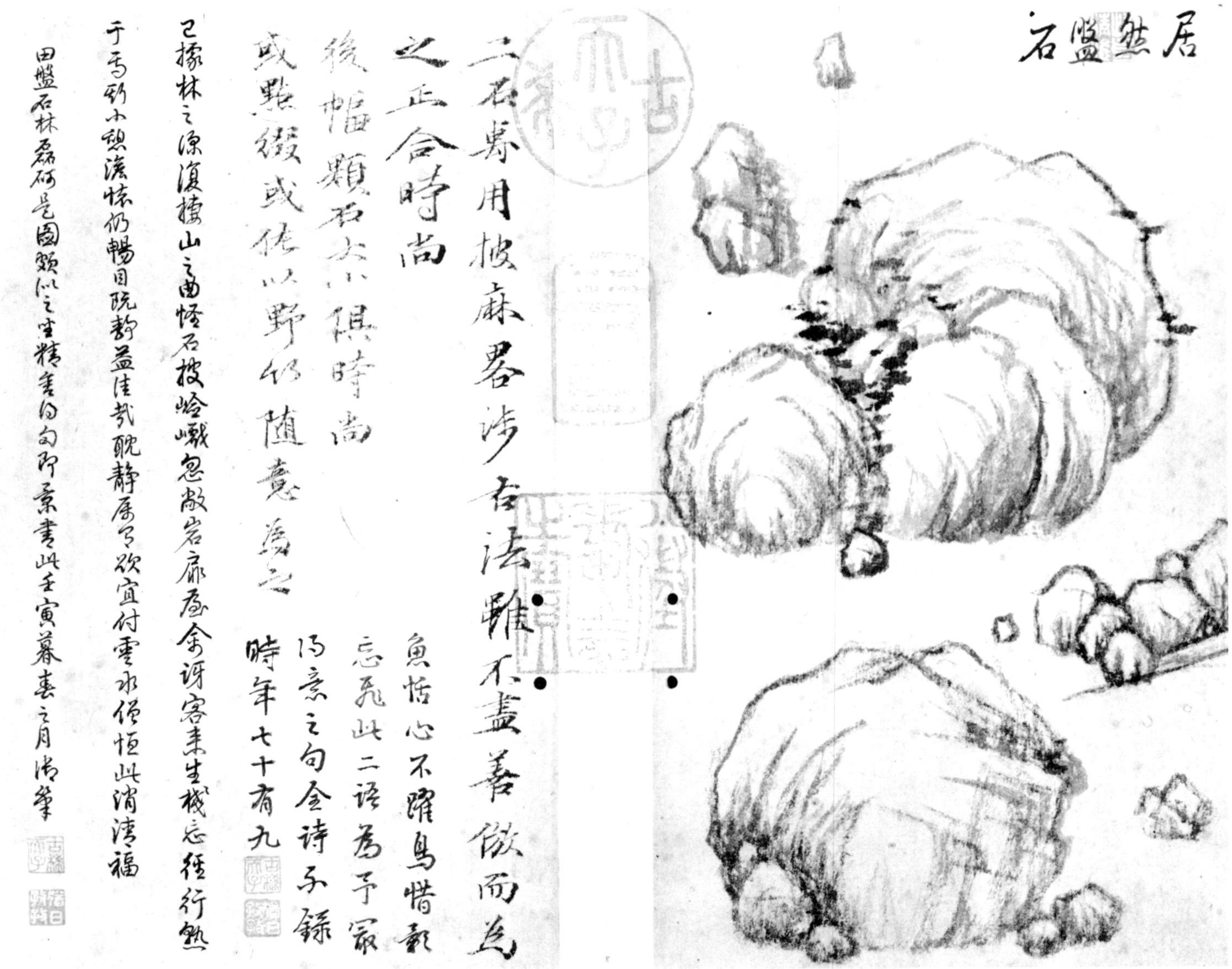

Fig. 115. Anonymous, after Ni Tsan, "Round Boulders." Album leaf 7 of *Painting Manual* (*Hua-p'u*), ink on paper. 23.6 x 14.2 cm (9¼ x 5⅝ in.). National Palace Museum, Taipei

In *Twin Trees*, which its poem says is "after rain," the tree branches droop toward the ground, and the bamboo leaves also point downward. The next illustration in the *Painting Manual* (fig. 114) is captioned: "Bamboo with leaves drooping downward describe a scene after rain."[62]

The rocks in *Twin Trees* are round boulders done with parallel draping hemp-fiber texture strokes (cf. fig. 112c). In another illustration in the *Painting Manual* (fig. 115), Ni Tsan pictures the round boulders, noting that "in these two groups of rocks I use especially the draping hemp-fiber [*p'i-ma*] technique, bringing it somewhat closer to the ancient method. Even if a student does not do this perfectly, by following it he will be in step with the taste of the time."[63]

By "taste of the time" Ni Tsan meant the brush idiom of Tung Yüan. By the mid-fourteenth century the southern landscape tradition of Tung Yüan—which Kuo Hsi had characterized as the "earthen" mode of landscape—had become the preferred idiom of the scholar-painters in Chiang-nan. By the very nature of its brush techniques, the Li Ch'eng idiom was more suited for descriptive realism, while the Tung Yüan hemp-fiber pattern encouraged free calligraphic expression. The contrast between styles of representational realism and self-expression can be seen in Ni Tsan's *Twin Trees* and Ts'ao Chih-po's (1272–1355) fan painting *Trees and Rocks* (*Shu shih t'u*) done about 1340 (The Art Museum, Princeton University; fig. 116).[64] Ts'ao, a wealthy gentleman-painter from the Hua-t'ing district (modern Sung-chiang), on the Wu-sung River, specialized in the Li Ch'eng and Kuo Hsi idioms; like his hanging scroll *Twin Pines*, dated 1329 (now in the National Palace Museum, Taipei), the Princeton fan follows the style of Li Ch'eng. In the Princeton painting, the tree and rock motifs complement and echo the curved edge of the silk fan, subtly creating a series of richly interacting large-and-small, high-and-low, front-and-back, dry-and-moist, spiky-and-smooth yin-yang relationships. Two large trees accompanied by two small rocks in the left foreground, for example, are balanced by a group of small trees and a large cluster of rocks in the right background; the leafless tall tree in the front, covered with a dessicated vine, raises its branches, while the shorter, luxuriant broad-leaved tree behind it bends and spreads its foliage. Ts'ao's brushwork is highly descriptive: the devil-face rocks and "crab-claw" (*hsieh-chao*) tree branches are first drawn with thickening-and-thinning brushstrokes, then modeled with softly rubbed texture strokes and a modulated ink wash, and finished with moss-dot accents; individual brushstrokes, in serving the representational purpose, do not stand out as independent kinesthetic brush movements. In composition the artist shows a keen awareness of foreshortening and three-dimensional spatial relationships in his treatment of the foreground rocks, the intertwining tree branches, and the physically described receding ground plane. The small fan painting offers no revelation of cosmic significance, but it is nevertheless an exquisite example of a fourteenth-century scholar-painter's thorough mastery of nature's "principles" in pictorial representation.

For Ni Tsan, as for Huang Kung-wang, however, painting had to be more than an accurate rendering of nature. According to Huang, "When every boulder or rock shows free and untrammeled ink [strokes], then the painting will have a scholar's air [*shih-ch'i*]. If it is too laborious, the painting will resemble the work of a craftsman."[65] In the *Painting Manual* Ni Tsan wrote: "You should try to do it in a sketchy manner. . . . Develop the form with a free hand . . . by following your ideas and feelings. . . . Too much precision will give a work the air of craftsmanship [*kung-ch'i*]."[66]

When Ni used the Tung Yüan idiom of hemp-fiber pattern, he reaffirmed his belief in the continuity of the ancient and the present. Although in Ni's paintings references to ancient masters were made not as

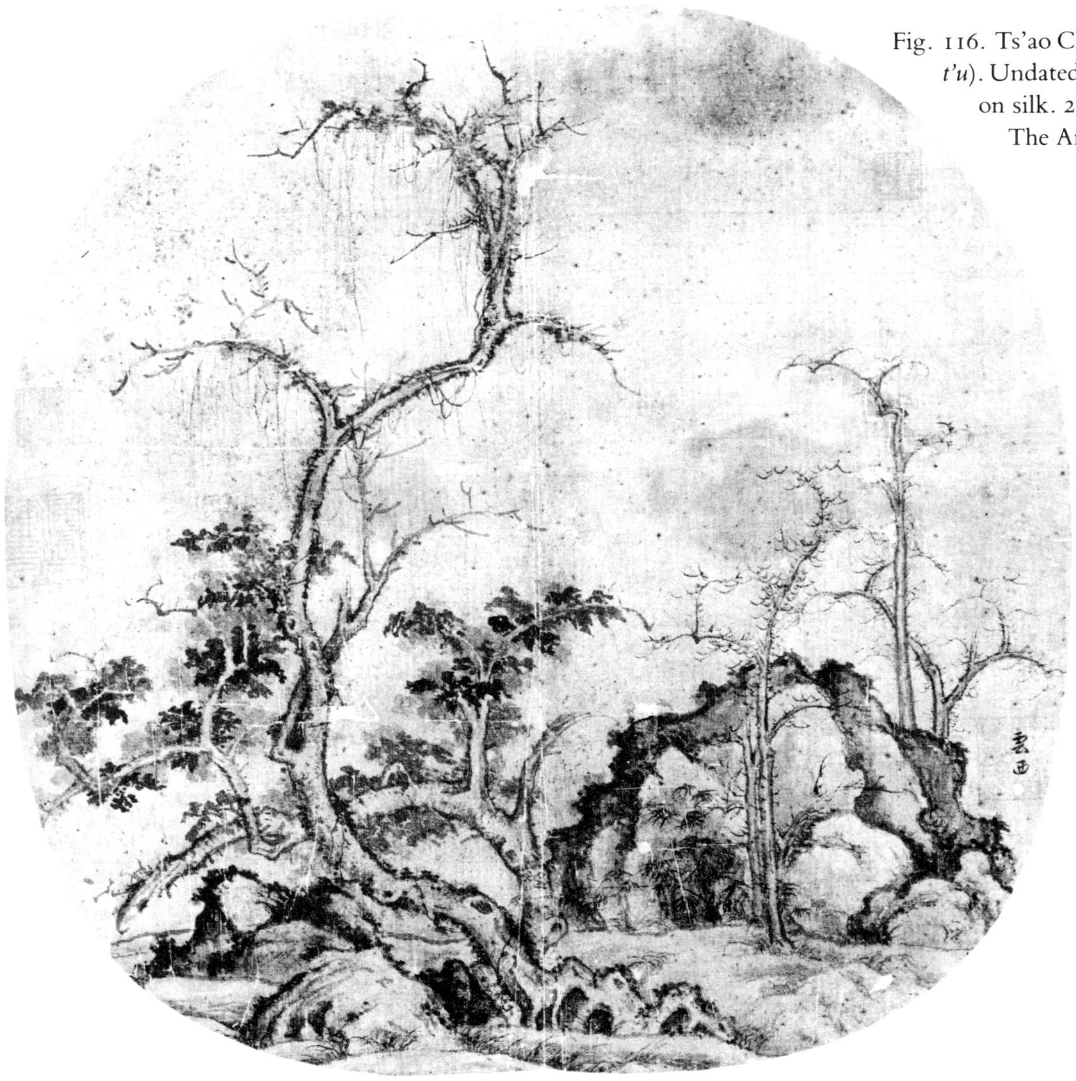

Fig. 116. Ts'ao Chih-po, *Trees and Rocks* (*Shu shih t'u*). Undated, ca. 1340. Fan, ink and light color on silk. 27.0 x 27.4 cm (10 5/8 x 10 3/4 in.). The Art Museum, Princeton University

imitations but as expressions of feelings and moods, Ni had also sought in his works to combine and sum up the best of the ancient styles. In the *Painting Manual* he wrote:

> In drawing rocks, one should not use the outlined [*kou*, "hooked"] method. Outlines make the rocks look stiff. One should develop the form with a free hand. . . . To make the rocks look ancient and simple, one should use texture strokes only sparingly; and to make them look elegant and beautiful, one should make use of a wash [*jan*] technique. . . . In placing two rocks [as illustrated], with an elegant one above and a simple one below, one should use whatever is best for the situation and avoid the unsuitable. Never limit oneself to using only one kind of texture method. The ancients had used the ax-cut [*fu-p'i*], the clove or T-shaped [*ting-hsiang*], the "horse-teeth" [*ma-ch'ih*], and other kinds of texture methods. But some modern painters, unable to master all the methods, claiming that some of them have a vulgar, craftsmanlike quality, follow only the [ax-cut of] Li T'ang and the [Tung Yüan] draping hemp-fiber methods. To try to follow the ancients and fail is to be twice a loser. In these two rocks I have used a mixture of several ancient and modern methods.[67]

In the accompanying illustration (fig. 117) are two rocks, the rounded one at the lower left done in hemp-fiber strokes, and the angular one above in a mixture of ax-cut, T-shaped, and horse-teeth patterns. Compared to the angular rock forms in *Travelers among Rivers and Mountains* by T'ai-ku i-min (cf. fig. 65a), a painting that Ni Tsan had ownd in the 1340s, Ni's rocks avoid a stiff, outlined approach, and develop their forms by building with dry, blurred brushstrokes—Ni called the technique *jan* (wash)—which create a visually fused pictorial surface.

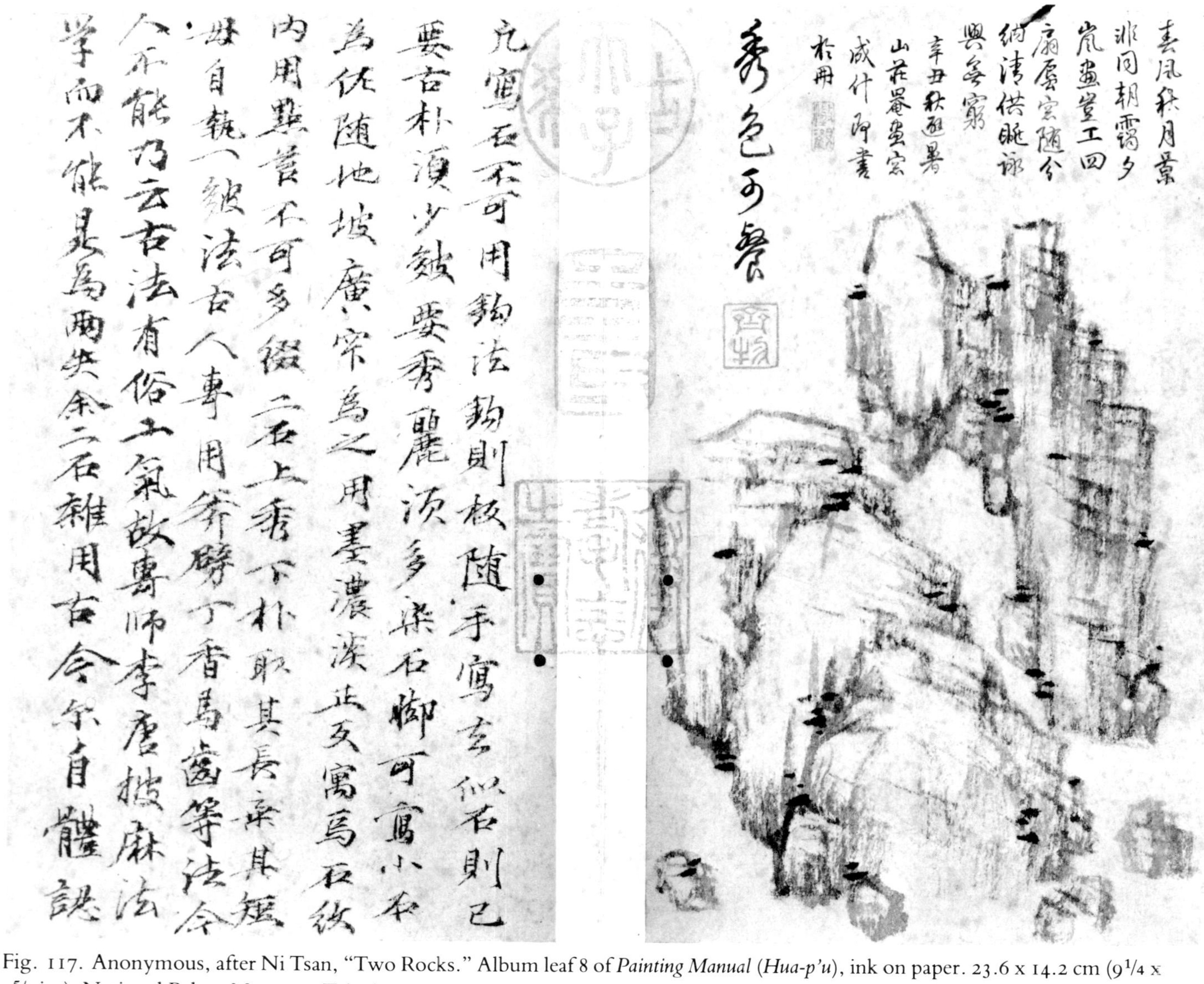

Fig. 117. Anonymous, after Ni Tsan, "Two Rocks." Album leaf 8 of *Painting Manual* (*Hua-p'u*), ink on paper. 23.6 x 14.2 cm (9 1/4 x 5 5/8 in.). National Palace Museum, Taipei

By mixing in his brushwork the hemp-fiber and ax-cut idioms, which were popular in the mid-fourteenth century, with T-shaped, horse-teeth, and other less familiar methods of the Northern Sung landscape styles, Ni Tsan thus forged a new creative synthesis in the great tradition of landscape painting. As a scholar-connoisseur, Ni Tsan saw every great work of art, ancient or modern, as a vital link in the great tradition. Admiring a brilliant composition by Hsia Kuei, *A Thousand Peaks Competing in Elegance (Ch'ien-yen ching-hsiu)*, Ni allowed in a colophon, dated 1344, that "it was because Li T'ang [ca. 1070s–ca. 1150s] had derived himself from Ching Hao [fl. ca. 870–930] and Fan K'uan [ca. 960–1030]: and Hsia Kuei [fl. 1st half 13th century], Ma Yüan [fl. ca. 1190–1264], and others had followed Li T'ang, that this painting [by Hsia Kuei] could have such impressive forms."[68]

In a well-known colophon written on the handscroll *Lion Grove Garden* (*Shih-tzu-lin t'u*), dated 1373, Ni Tsan wrote: "Master Chao Shan-ch'ang [Chao Yüan; fl. ca. 1360–75] and I, after some discussion, made this painting of the Lion Grove Garden. Truly it attains the ideas Ching [Hao] and Kuan [T'ung; fl. 907–23]. It is not something that Wang Meng [ca. 1308–1385] and others could have imagined in their dreams."[69] In *Woods and Valleys of Mount Yü* (*Yü-shan lin-ho*), dated 1372 (The Metropolitan Museum of Art, New York; fig. 118), the angular, crystalline rock forms—perhaps echoing the sharp-edged rocks in *A Buddhist Monastery in Autumn Mountains* attributed to Yen Wen-kuei (cf. fig. 64a), which Ni saw and inscribed in 1369—are done with a dry wash (*jan*) technique of softly rubbed, richly fused brushstrokes, "a mixture of several ancient and modern methods." Developing his forms with a free hand, Ni combined the different ax-cut, T-shaped, and horse-teeth patterns in his protean brushwork, creating a new calligraphic, illusionistic style that, in perpetuating the essence of the ancient, rocky landscape mode, "attains the ideas inherited from Ching [Hao] and Kuan [T'ung]."

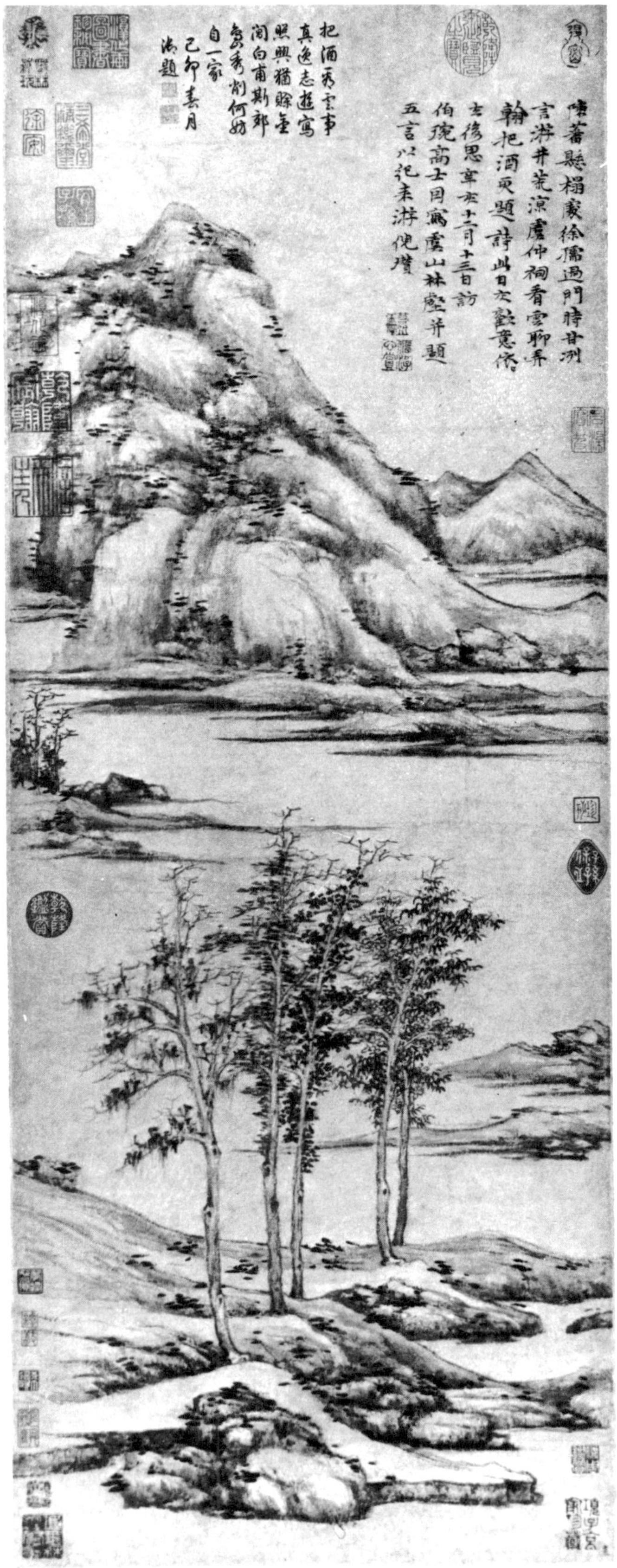

Fig. 118. Ni Tsan, *Woods and Valleys of Mount Yü* (*Yü-shan lin-ho*). Dated 1372. Hanging scroll, ink on paper. 95.2 x 33.2 cm (3 ft. 1 1/2 in. x 13 1/8 in.). The Metropolitan Museum of Art, New York

The secret of Ni's painting lies in the wide range of effects he achieved with his brushwork. In *The Six Gentlemen* of 1345 (cf. fig. 108) he acknowledged Huang Kung-wang's achievements while convincingly standing on his own stylistic ground, and in *A Sparse Grove* of about the same time (cf. fig. 111) he gave his rock modeling a purposely casual and "clumsy" (*cho*) quality. In *Twin Trees* of 1353, the painting does not imitate the calligraphy, but the same rhythmic cadence and "brush ideas" pervade both (cf. figs. 112a, b, c).

The movement of the brush, gentle yet incisive, speaks in a voice that is both plaintive and lyrical. Dry and moist brushstrokes combine to form flowing patterns and tonal passages, achieving an effect that is pure mood and poetry. Finally, in Ni's late masterpiece *Woods and Valleys of Mount Yü* of 1372 (cf. fig. 118), the artist invests so much personal vitality in the dry-brush wash strokes that the sparse landscape appears monumental.

Thus Ni Tsan's style, though deceptively simple and unassuming, proved to be inimitable. Shen Chou (1427–1509) nurtured a lifelong ambition to imitate Ni Tsan, yet, according to one story, every time he applied his brush to paper his teacher would shout: "No, no, you have overdone it again."[70] Ni Tsan succeeded in maintaining an exquisite balance and tension in every stroke, conveying his inner sentiments of protest and urgent communication without resorting to overstatement. As products of a brutal, disorderly time, Ni Tsan's simple rocks and trees represent—if we could only decode them—poignant and vivid testimony to his extraordinary emotional and artistic energy, his indomitable personality, and his longing for peace and beauty.

## *The Legend of Ni Tsan*

The irony was that just as Ni Tsan, the meek and eccentric recluse, was lionized in spite of his distaste for celebrity, his paintings, however private and undecorative, attracted a large public audience. He was harassed by demands for his paintings, as his dilemma was clearly expressed in a letter he wrote to someone named Chang Tsao-chung:

> I, Tsan, having received your command to illustrate the story of Ch'en Tzu-ching's Hsien-yüan, do not wish to disobey you. Lately I have spent much time in town and have not had any time for quiet thought. Only today, after coming to a place outside the city, have I finally read the story of the Hsien-yüan. Unfortunately, to portray all the elaborate scenery, vividly describing every detail, is beyond my ability. Yet, to do the job sketchily, without the necessary colors and descriptions, would only fail your purpose in having such a painting. What I call painting is merely sketching with a few untrammeled brushstrokes. I never seek for formal likeness, because I paint only for my own amusement. Lately when I come to town people asking me to paint often insist that I paint in a certain way and finish at a certain time. They even resort to insults, angry words, or worse. This is not fair. Would anyone blame a eunuch for not growing a beard? What have I done to deserve such trouble?[71]

In the course of time Ni Tsan, the "noble recluse," became something of a legend, and his life story was frequently retold. He was admired first of all for his genuine and total detachment; in the face of brute force Ni responded like a truly civilized person, retreating into an egocentric, self-imposed isolation. As Ch'ien P'u, a prominent Ming scholar-official from Wu-hsi, wrote in 1460 in a preface to a collection of Ni Tsan's poems, the political turmoil of Ni Tsan's time bred fierce opportunism, with only those who truly believed in themselves managing to remain principled and aloof:

> Those who achieved success and fame at that time all vanished like wind or flashes of lightning, leaving not a trace behind. Yet Master Ni's poems and paintings have survived in this world; every scrap of paper bearing his work is regarded as a prized treasure. And as we peruse them, we feel ourselves refreshed and exhilarated as if by a pure breeze. How could this have happened if the man did not have supreme faith in himself?[72]

In a popular story about Ni Tsan's courageous refusal to join Chang Shih-ch'eng's rebel government, Chang's younger brother Shih-hsin was said to have sent Ni Tsan a large present of money and bolts of silk, only to have Ni tear up the silk and return the money. One day sometime after this incident, as the younger Chang was entertaining on a boat on the lake, he and his guests detected the aroma of an exotic incense issuing from the water reeds, and concluded that Ni Tsan must be nearby. Chang's bodyguards had him brought to Chang and beat him nearly to death. Throughout the ordeal Ni never uttered a word. Asked about it later, he replied, "To open my mouth would be vulgar!"[73]

In *Biographies of Worthies of Chin-ling* (*Chin-ling ch'ung-ssu hsien-hsien chuan*), a work compiled in the 1550s, the editors summed up Ni Tsan's outstanding qualities:

> The recluse, in abandoning his fortune, showed heroism [*hsia*]; in tearing up a gift of silks, he showed integrity [*chieh*]; in safely preserving himself, he showed wisdom [*chih*]; and in refusing to serve in either war or peace, he showed singularity of conduct [*tu-hsing*]. The important thing is that he did all this because he was by nature independent and forthright, and not because he wanted to show his heroism, integrity, wisdom, or exceptional conduct.[74]

In the late Ming period, with ominous signs of "barbarian" (Manchu) trouble reappearing on China's northeastern border, and a growing sense of moral and political decline at home, Ni Tsan became a symbol of patriotism and moral regeneration. In the expanded edition of Ni's poems and prose writings, called *Manuscripts from the Pure and Secluded Studio* (*Ch'ing-pi-ko i-kao*; 1591–1600), a nascent nationalism appeared. A colophon dated 1600 by a descendant named Ni Ching begins with the words "My ancestor Yün-lin lived in the days when the barbarian Yüan dynasty contaminated the world."[75] And, in a preface to the same compilation, dated 1599, the essayist T'u Lung (1542–1605) tried to portray Ni Tsan as a resistance hero under the Mongols: "In the spirit of resistance he refused to serve the Yüan. [In his works] he wrote only cyclical dates and never the reigning titles of the Yüan emperors."[76] The truth was quite the reverse. Ni Tsan, for all his personal misfortunes, always considered himself a loyal subject of the Yüan. In his works he consistently used Chih-cheng, the reign designation for the last emperor of the Yüan dynasty, and it was only after the establishment of the Ming in 1368 that he used cyclical dates alone, steadfastly avoiding use of the reigning title of the first Ming emperor, Hung-wu.[77] For the late Ming writers, however, it was important that Ni Tsan, the noble recluse, be exalted as a cultural hero through whom the human mind might gain a new strength in adverse times. In times of trouble, when human institutions apparently failed, the one person who stood "unmatched in shining glory" was the noble recluse, whose quiet but constant effort to keep faith with himself represented man's ultimate stand for sanity.

Moreover, in the Confucian scheme of things, if the emperor was supposed to govern with the mandate of heaven, it was the recluse, the antiruler, who was thought to embody all the moral principles that underlay this mandate. Thus toward the end of the Ming period an elaborate argument upheld Ni Tsan as a moral ally of the first Ming emperor. In 1600 Ku Hsien-ch'eng (1550–1612), founder of the Tung-lin Academy in Wu-hsi, a martinet who fancied himself both an adviser to the throne and a noble scholar, invented a Ni Tsan who was an imaginary precursor for himself:

> When the world is in great turmoil, and evil forces have finally run their course, there usually appear a sage ruler to sweep things clean from the top and some extraordinary scholar to cause radical changes from below. Their respective functions reinforce each other, and they are incomplete without one another. . . . It is said that when our First Emperor eagerly recruited scholars [to serve], signal bows and banners were sent around the empire, yet Master Ni Tsan could not be recruited. . . . In those days, for planning and devising stratagems there were men like Liu Chi, Li Shan-ch'ang, and others; for winning battles and taking cities there were generals like Hsü Ta, Ch'ang Yü-ch'un, and others; and for establishing rituals and music there were learned scholars like Sung Lien, T'ao An, and others. . . . While all those great officials accomplished their work in state and territorial affairs, it was Master Ni who upheld moral standards in people's hearts, social mores, and customs. . . . Thus our first emperor used Master Ni, and Master Ni allowed himself to be used by our emperor, and both did so by silent mutual consent.[78]

If Ni Tsan were to read this, his only response might be: "To open my mouth would be vulgar!"

## NOTES

1. For Chao Meng-fu's biography, see *Yüan-shih* (History of the Yüan dynasty), Pai-na-pen erh-shih-ssu shih, vol. 36 (1369; repr. ed., Taipei: Shang-wu yin-shu-kuan, 1967), *chüan* 172, pp. 28,607–10. See also Chu-tsing Li, *The Autumn Colors on the Ch'iao and Hua Mountains: A Landscape by Chao Meng-fu*, *Artibus Asiae* Supplementum 21 (1964); Chu-tsing Li, "Chao Meng-fu chih yen-chiu" (Studies on Chao Meng-fu), pts. I, II, *National Palace Museum Quarterly* 16, no. 2 (Winter 1981): 33–40; no. 3 (Spring 1982): 1–13.
2. See Yang Tsai, "Chao Meng-fu hsing-chuang" (Biography of Chao Meng-fu), in *Sung-hsüeh-chai ch'üan-chi* (Collected works of the Sung-hsüeh Studio [of Chao Meng-fu]), Li-tai hua-chia shih-wen chi, vol. 3 (Taipei: Hsüeh-sheng shu-chü, 1970), addenda, pp. 487–510.
3. See Fu Shen, *Yüan-tai huang-shih shu-hua shou-ts'ang shih-lüeh* (A brief history of Yüan dynasty imperial collections of calligraphy and painting) (Taipei: National Palace Museum, 1981); see also Chiang I-han, *Yüan-tai K'uei-chang-ko chi K'uei-chang-ko jen-wu* (The K'uei-chang palace during the Yüan period and some personalities at the K'uei-chang palace) (Taipei: Lien-ching shu-chü, 1981).
4. Chao Meng-chien, "Chao Tzu-ku shu-fa lun" (Chao Meng-chien's discussion of calligraphy), in Pien Yung-yü, ed., *Shih-ku-t'ang shu-hua hui-kao* (Classified record of calligraphy and painting of Shih-ku Hall) (1682; repr. ed., Taipei: Cheng-chung shu-chü, 1956), vol. 1, *chüan* 3, p. 506.
5. Mi Fu, *Pao-Tsin Ying-kuang chi* (Collections of Treasuring the Tsin and the Brilliant Lights [Mi Fu's studios]), Ts'ung-shu chi-ch'eng chien-pien (Taipei: Shang-wu yin-shu-kuan, 1966), *chüan* 8, p. 66.
6. An Ch'i, *Mo-yüan hui-kuan lu* (A comprehensive record of ink acquaintances: a catalogue of An Ch'i's collection of calligraphy and painting), Kuo-hsüeh ch'i-pen ts'ung-shu, vol. 155 (1742; repr. ed., Taipei: Shang-wu yin-shu-kuan, 1968), *chüan* 2, pp. 111–13. A complete rubbing version of Chao Meng-fu's thirteen colophons is found in Feng Ch'üan, ed., *K'uai-hsüeh-t'ang fa-shu* (Anthology of calligraphy in the K'uai-hsüeh Hall collection) (preface 1779), *chüan* 5, pp. 32b–42b; fragments of the original, which has been damaged by fire, are reproduced in Kanda Kiichiro et al., eds., *Shodō zenshū* (Reproductions of well-known works of calligraphy) (Tokyo: Heibon-sha, 1966–69), vol. 17, pls. 6–9. See Nakata Yūjirō, "Rantei jyōyū sanbatsu" (Preface to the *Orchid Pavilion Gathering*), in *Shodō zenshū*, vol. 17, pp. 154–56.
7. See Chiang I-han, "*Record of Miao-yen Monastery*, A Calligraphic Handscroll by Chao Meng-fu (1254–1322)," *National Palace Museum Quarterly* 10, no. 3 (Spring 1976): 59–80.
8. See Ma Tsung-ho, *Shu-lin tsao-chien* (Collected writings on calligraphy) (1936; repr. ed., Taipei: Shang-wu yin-shu-kuan, 1965), vol. 2, *chüan* 10, p. 260a.
9. Ibid., vol. 2, *chüan* 10, p. 259b.
10. For the story of Hsieh K'un, see Richard B. Mather, trans., *A New Account of Tales of the World* (Minneapolis: University of Minnesota Press, 1976), pp. 253–54.
11. See Chu-tsing Li, *Autumn Colors on the Ch'iao and Hua Mountains*.
12. See Wen C. Fong and Marilyn Fu, *Sung and Yüan Paintings* (New York: The Metropolitan Museum of Art, 1975), pp. 88–91.
13. Reproduced in Wango H. C. Weng and Yang Boda, *The Palace Museum: Treasures of the Forbidden City* (New York: Harry N. Abrams, 1982), p. 192, pl. 95.
14. See Ts'ao P'ei-lien, ed., *Ch'ing-pi-ko ch'üan-chi* (The complete collected works of the Pure and Secluded Pavilion [of Ni Tsan]), Yüan-tai chen-pen wen-chi hui-k'an, vol. 10 (Taipei: Kuo-li chung-yang t'u-shu-kuan, 1970), *chüan* 11/7b–11a, pp. 488–95. For modern studies on Ni Tsan, see Huang Miao-tzu, "Tu Ni Yün-lin chuan cha-chi" (Notes on reading Ni Tsan's biography), in *Chung-hua wen-shih lun-ts'ung* (Collected essays on Chinese literature and history) (Peking: Chung-hua shu-chü, 1962), 3rd ser., pp. 247–72; biography and chronology of Ni Tsan in Chang Kuang-pin, ed., *Yüan ssu-ta-chia* (The four great masters of the Yüan) (Taipei: National Palace Museum, 1975), pp. 20–27, 87–198.
15. Ts'ao P'ei-lien, ed., *Ch'ing-pi-ko ch'üan-chi*, *chüan* 11/8b, p. 490.
16. Ibid., *chüan* 11/9a–9b, pp. 491–92.
17. Ibid., *chüan* 11/11a, p. 495.
18. See Ts'ao P'ei-lien, ed., "Yün-lin i-shih" (Anecdotes of Ni Tsan), in *Ch'ing-pi-ko ch'üan-chi*, *chüan* 11/5a, p. 483.
19. Chang Tuan, "Yün-lin Ni hsien-sheng mu-piao" (Epitaph of Yün-lin, Master Ni), in Ts'ao P'ei-lien, ed., *Ch'ing-pi-ko ch'üan-chi*, *chüan* 11/11a, p. 495.
20. It is possible that Ni Tsan, indeed, had blue or green eyes. In a poem on a painting by Ni dated 1363, a friend of Ni's wrote: "Master Ni Tsan who has green pupils" (ibid., *chüan* 8/26b, p. 400).
21. "Lacquer-tree nursery" and "wild horses" are allusions to Chuang-tzu; see Kuo Ch'ang-fen, comp., *Chuang-tzu chi-shih* (Collected annotations of Chuang-tzu) (1894; repr. ed., Taipei: Shih-chieh shu-chü, 1967), *chüan* 1, p. 3.
22. A version of Ni Tsan's portrait with Chang Yü's eulogy is described in Ts'ao P'ei-lien, "Yün-lin i-shih," *chüan* 11/2b, p. 478.
23. Ts'ao P'ei-lien, ed., *Ch'ing-pi-ko ch'üan-chi*, *chüan* 11/8a, p. 489.
24. Chou Nan-lao, "Yüan ch'u-shih Yün-lin hsien-sheng mu-chih-ming" (Tomb epitaph for the Yüan dynasty recluse Master [Ni] Yün-lin), in Ts'ao P'ei-lien, ed., *Ch'ing-pi-ko ch'üan-chi*, *chüan* 11/9a, p. 491.
25. T'ao Tsung-i, "Ch'en kung-tzu" (Young gentleman Ch'en), in *Cho-keng lu* (Notes taken after setting aside the plow), Ts'ung-shu chi-ch'eng chien-pien, vol. 83 (Taipei, 1965–66), *chüan* 24, p. 347.
26. See Huang Miao-tzu, "Tu Ni Yün-lin chuan cha-chi," p. 256.
27. Ts'ao P'ei-lien, ed., *Ch'ing-pi-ko ch'üan-chi*, *chüan* 11/7b, p. 488.
28. Chou Nan-lao, "Yüan ch'u-shih Yün-lin hsien-sheng mu-chih-ming," *chüan* 11/8b, p. 490.
29. Ni Tsan, "Ch'iao-hai shih-chi hsiao-yin" (Introduction to collected poems by [Ch'in] Ch'iao-hai), in Ts'ao P'ei-lien, ed., *Ch'ing-pi-ko ch'üan-chi*, *chüan* 10/3b–4a, pp. 444–45.
30. Ni Tsan, "Cho-i-chai shih-kao hsü" (Preface to collected poems of the Cho-i Studio [by Chou Cheng-tao]), dated 1373, in Ts'ao P'ei-lien, ed., *Ch'ing-pi-ko ch'üan-chi*, *chüan* 10/1b, p. 440.
31. Ibid., *chüan* 10/1a–2a, pp. 439–41.
32. Ni Tsan, preface to "Yü-pu-ch'i yung" (Chanted poetry on Yü-pu-ch'i [in Chekiang]), in Ts'ao P'ei-lien, ed., *Ch'ing-pi-ko ch'üan-chi*, *chüan* 4/2a–2b, pp. 145–46.
33. Ni Tsan, "Shu-huai" (Speaking my thoughts), in Ts'ao P'ei-lien, ed., *Ch'ing-pi-ko ch'üan-chi*, *chüan* 1/10b–11a, pp. 48–49.
34. Chang Yü, "T'i Yün-lin shih-chi" (Colophon to Ni Tsan's collected poems), in Ts'ao P'ei-lien. ed., *Ch'ing-pi-ko ch'üan-chi*, *chüan* 12/1a, p. 517.
35. Ts'ao P'ei-lien, ed., *Ch'ing-pi-ko ch'üan-chi*, *chüan* 12/4b, p. 534; Huang Miao-tzu, "Tu Ni Yün-lin chuan cha-chi," p. 259.
36. Ni Tsan, "Ching-shih" (On becoming aware), in Ts'ao P'ei-lien, ed., *Ch'ing-pi-ko ch'üan-chi*, *chüan* 8/8b, p. 364.
37. Ni Tsan, "Feng-yü" (Wind and rain), in Ts'ao P'ei-lien, ed., *Ch'ing-pi-ko ch'üan-chi*, *chüan* 5/28a, p. 239.
38. See Chang Kuang-pin, ed., *Yüan ssu-ta-chia*, p. 156.
39. Ni Tsan, "Liu-jih t'i" (Composed on the sixth day [of the lunar month]), in Ts'ao P'ei-lien, ed., *Ch'ing-pi-ko ch'üan-chi*, *chüan* 8/8b, p. 364.
40. Ni Tsan, "Pieh Lu shih nu" (Farewell to a daughter of the Lu family), in Ts'ao P'ei-lien, ed., *Ch'ing-pi-ko ch'üan-chi*, *chüan* 8/2b, p. 352.
41. Ni Tsan, "Chi Han Po-ch'ing" (Poem to Han Po-ch'ing), in Ts'ao P'ei-lien, ed., *Ch'ing-pi-ko ch'üan-chi*, *chüan* 8/3a, p. 353.
42. Ni Tsan, "Shun-ni" (Fair or foul), in Ts'ao P'ei-lien, ed., *Ch'ing-pi-ko ch'üan-chi*, *chüan* 8/2b, p. 352.
43. Ni Tsan, "Tsa-fu" (Miscellaneous poem), in Ts'ao P'ei-lien, ed., *Ch'ing-pi-ko ch'üan-chi*, *chüan* 7/11a, p. 315.
44. Ni Tsan, "Chih-cheng i-wei su-i shih" (Chih-cheng era, i-wei year [1355], poem on man in white), in Ts'ao P'ei-lien, ed., *Ch'ing-pi-ko ch'üan-chi*, *chüan* 1/2a, p. 31.
45. Ni Tsan, "Yü Ch'en Shu-fang" (Letter to Master Ch'en), in Ts'ao P'ei-lien, ed., *Ch'ing-pi-ko ch'üan-chi*, *chüan* 10/18a, p. 473.
46. Ni Tsan, preface to "T'i Chi-chao Chiang-chün i-hsiang" (Colophon to posthumous portrait of [Ni Tsan's wife] Chiang Yüan-chao), in Ts'ao P'ei-lien, ed., *Ch'ing-pi-ko ch'üan-chi*, *chüan* 7/21a, p. 335.
47. Ni Tsan, "Ch'iao k'o chu shih" (Tall evergreens, bamboo, and rocks), in Ts'ao P'ei-lien, ed., *Ch'ing-pi-ko ch'üan-chi*, *chüan* 6/9b, p. 258.

48. Chou Nan-lao, "Yüan ch'u-shih Yün-lin hsien-sheng mu-chih-ming," in Ts'ao P'ei-lien, ed., *Ch'ing-pi-ko ch'üan-chi*, *chüan* 11/9b, p. 492.
49. Cheng Yüan-yu, *Ch'iao-Wu chi* (Collected works of sojourning at Suchou), Yüan-tai chen-pen wen-chi hui-k'an, vol. 9 (Taipei: Kuo-li chung-ying t'u-shu-kuan, 1970), *chüan* 7/1a–b, pp. 233–34.
50. Ni Tsan, "Tsa-chu" (Miscellaneous writings), in Ts'ao P'ei-lien, ed., *Ch'ing-pi-ko ch'üan-chi*, *chüan* 10/8b, p. 454.
51. See [*Ch'in-ting*] *San-hsi-t'ang fa-t'ieh* (Rubbings of the Ch'ien-lung emperor's collection of masterpieces of ancient calligraphy kept at the Hall of Three Rarities), in Liang Shih-cheng et al., comps., *Yü k'o San-hsi-t'ang shih-ch'ü-pao-chi fa-t'ieh* (1747; repr. ed., Shanghai: Chung-hua t'u-shu-kuan, 1909), *chüan* 1, p. 3a.
52. Ma Tsung-ho, *Shu-lin tsao-chien*, vol. 2, *chüan* 10, p. 259b.
53. A famous record of Lu Heng's association with scholar-artists and poets is a handscroll, *T'ing-yü-lou t'u* (The Listening-to-Rain Pavilion), by Wang Meng, dated 1365, which was mounted with poems and colophons (dated 1348) written for Lu by Chang Yü, Ni Tsan, and fifteen other well-known poets and scholars of the time, including Chou Po-ch'i (d. ca. 1367), Chang Yü (1333–1385), Kao Ch'i (1336–1374), and the monk Tao-yen (Yao Kuang-hsiao, 1335–1419). See Ts'ao P'ei-lien, ed., *Ch'ing-pi-ko ch'üan-chi*, *chüan* 12/5a–14b, pp. 525–44; Pien Yung-yü, *Shih-ku-t'ang shu-hua hui k'ao* (Classified record of calligraphy and painting of Shih-ku Hall) (Taipei: Cheng-chung shu-chü, 1958), vol. 4, *chüan* 21, pp. 283–88.
54. Huang Kung-wang, *Hsieh shan-shui chüeh* (Secrets of landscape painting), in Yü Chien-hua, ed., *Chung-kuo hua-lun lei-pien* (Classified compilation of writings on Chinese painting) (Hong Kong: Chung-hua shu-chü, 1973), vol. 2, p. 696.
55. Ni Tsan, "Shun-ni," in Ts'ao P'ei-lien, ed., *Ch'ing-pi-ko ch'üan chi*, *chüan* 8/2b, p. 352.
56. Ching Hao, *Pi-fa chi* (Notes on brush method), in Yü Chien-hua, ed., *Chung-kuo hua-lun lei-pien* (Classified compilation of writings on Chinese painting) (Hong Kong: Chung-hua shu-chü, 1973), vol. 1, p. 607; see Richard Barnhart, *Wintry Forest, Old Trees: Some Landscape Themes in Chinese Painting* (New York: China Institute of America, 1972), pp. 14 ff.
57. Tu Fu, "Ch'un wang" (Looking forward to spring), in *T'ang shih san-pai-shou* (Three hundred poems of the T'ang dynasty) (1763; repr. ed., Hong Kong: Shih-chieh t'u-shu kung-ssu, n.d.), p. 142.
58. Ni Tsan, "Ku-mu chu shih ping fu" (Old trees, bamboo, rocks, and poem), in Ts'ao P'ei-lien, ed., *Ch'ing-pi-ko ch'üan-chi*, *chüan* 8/16b, p. 380; for another poem written for Kung-yüan, see ibid., *chüan* 3/6b, p. 104.
59. Huang Kung-wang, *Hsieh shan-shui chüeh*, p. 697.
60. Ni Tsan, "Wei Fang Yai hua shan chiu t'i" (Inscription for Fang Yai), in Ts'ao P'ei-lien, ed., *Ch'ing-pi-ko ch'üan-chi*, *chüan* 2/4a, p. 69.
61. See National Palace Museum, Taipei, comp., *Ku-kung shu-hua lu* (A descriptive catalogue of the painting and calligraphy in the National Palace Museum) (Taipei: National Palace Museum, 1965), vol. 3, *chüan* 6, pp. 20–21.
62. Ibid., p. 21.
63. Ibid.
64. For publication of Ts'ao Chih-po's fan painting at Princeton, see Chu-tsing Li, "Rocks and Trees and the Art of Ts'ao Chih-po," *Artibus Asiae* 23, no. 3/4 (1960): 153–92.
65. Huang Kung-wang, *Hsieh shan-shui chüeh*, vol. 2, p. 698.
66. National Palace Museum, comp., *Ku-kung shu-hua-lu*, vol. 3, *chüan* 6, pp. 20–21.
67. Ibid., p. 21.
68. Ni Tsan, "T'i-hua" (Colophon on a painting), in Ts'ao P'ei-lien, ed., *Ch'ing-pi-ko ch'üan-chi*, *chüan* 9/15b, p. 434.
69. Ni Tsan, "T'i *Shih-tzu-lin t'u*" (Inscription on the *Lion Grove Garden* painting), in Ts'ao P'ei-lien, ed., *Ch'ing-pi-ko ch'üan-chi*, *chüan* 9/11b, p. 426; see Tung Ch'i-ch'ang, *Hua-yen* (The eye of painting), I-shu ts'ung-pien, vol. 12 (Taipei: Shih chieh shu-chü, 1962), p. 52.
70. Tung Ch'i-chang, *Hua-yen*, p. 45.
71. Ni Tsan, "Ta Chang Tsao-chung shu" (Answering Chang Tsao-chung's letter), in Ts'ao P'ei-lien, ed., *Ch'ing-pi-ko ch'üan-chi*, *chüan* 10/7a–b, pp. 451–52.
72. Ch'ien Po, preface, in Ts'ao P'ei-lien, ed., *Ch'ing-pi-ko ch'üan-chi*, p. 1.
73. Anonymous, "Chin-ling ch'ung-ssu hsien-hsien chuan" (Biographies of worthies of Chin-ling), in Ts'ao P'ei-lien, ed., *Ch'ing-pi-ko ch'üan-chi*, *chüan* 11/1b, p. 476, and *chüan* 11/12a, p. 497.
74. Ibid., *chüan* 4/12b, p. 498.
75. Ts'ao P'ei-lien, ed., *Ch'ing-pi-ko ch'üan-chi*, addenda, p. 681.
76. Ibid., p. 599.
77. See comments by Wu K'uan, dated 1491, in "Yün-lin i-shih," in Ts'ao P'ei-lien, ed., *Ch'ing-pi-ko ch'üan-chi*, *chüan* 11/3a–b, pp. 479–80.
78. Ts'ao P'ei-lien, ed., *Ch'ing-pi-ko ch'üan-chi*, prefaces, pp. 9–11.

# 4 *Ming Dynasty Revivalism*

As THE DYNASTY that restored Chinese rule after the Mongol conquest, the Ming imperial government officially espoused a policy of revivalism, which permeated the political, cultural, and intellectual life of the period. By early Ming times landscape painting had become inextricably bound to Sung and Yüan models. While amateur painters in the Lake T'ai area continued to work in the late Yüan recluse-artist's calligraphic idiom, professional painters gathered at the court under the patronage of early Ming emperors restored the realistic and monumental styles of the Sung period. The continued development of the Sung and Yüan brush idioms during the following two centuries inspired a passionate concern with method, the codification of techniques, and the understanding and mastering of painting in a systematic manner. Reacting to technically proficient but superficial painters, Ming scholar-artists, under the influence of the Neo-Confucian School of the Mind, sought creative truth, not only in pictorial forms, but also within their own psyches. While inferior painters became captives of their craft, the superior ones achieved a tremendous range of flexibility, intensively studying ancient styles of calligraphy, painting, and poetry, and practicing Ch'an meditation and other philosophical disciplines.

As Ming landscape art evolved, painters and painting critics debated and struggled with issues of imitation and self-expression, rebellion and authenticity. But arguments about methods, models, schools, and inspiration only led to increasing fragmentation and extreme polarization of views and approaches, resulting in endless rivalry and partisan polemics. In describing the eccentric and fantastic painters of late Ming times, James Cahill (1967, 1982) successfully portrayed a picture of conflict, discord, and breakdown in late Ming China that seems to mirror his perception of our own modern-day world.[1] Nevertheless, at the end of the Ming period, painters and theorists began to devise unique strategems to achieve a new integration.

## *The Last of the Recluse Painters*

Huang Kung-wang's (1269–1354) *Dwelling in the Fu-ch'un Mountains*, dated 1350 (cf. fig. 67), represents the acme of naturalism in Yüan landscape art. In the 1360s and 1370s, at the end of the Yüan dynasty and the beginning of the Ming, landscape painting exhibited a new expressionist style and a growing tendency to display brushwork and surface abstraction. Wang Meng's (ca. 1308–1385) remarkable *Dwelling in the Ch'ing-pien Mountains* (*Ch'ing-pien yin-chü t'u*), dated 1366 (fig. 119), has been described by Max Loehr as a picture that "seems not so much to describe a passage of mountain scenery as to express a terrible occurrence . . . an eruptive vision."[2] Finding the painting "decidedly unintelligible in its presentation of space and form, disturbingly unnatural in its lighting," James Cahill regards the work "as the product of some extraordinary burst of creative genius that evidently proved unrepeatable."[3]

The stylistic genesis of this painting can nevertheless be traced to several sources, all of them lying outside the concern for naturalistic representation. First is Kuo Hsi's *Early Spring* of 1072 (cf. fig. 49), which seems to owe its inspiration more to psychological projection—images seen in the clouds, on a blank piece of silk, or on a battered, uneven plaster wall—than to a season in nature. In the Yüan dynasty many leading painters had an active interest in Taoism: according to Taoist beliefs in geomancy (*feng-shui*; wind and water), a powerful life-energy pulsates through mountain ranges and rivers and streams in patterns known as *ch'i-mo* (breath-veins).[4] Two examples of this interest in the concept of *feng-shui*, contemporary with Wang Meng's *Dwelling in the Ch'ing-pien Mountains*, are *Cloudy Mountains* (*Yün-shan t'u*) by the Taoist painter Fang Ts'ung-i (ca. 1300–1378), dated in the late 1360s (The Metropolitan Museum of Art; fig. 120), which has mountains that resemble a dragon ascending into the clouds; and Hsü Pen's (1335–1380) *Streams and Mountains* (*Ch'i-shan t'u*), dated 1372 (Cleveland Museum of Art; fig. 121), in which the mountain forms also reflect this concept of breath-veins. In Wang Meng's masterpiece as well as Fang's and Hsü's paintings, the charged brushwork, with ink dots and lines rolled up and swept along in endless whirling vortexes, describes not only the natural forms of peaks and valleys, but also the surging supernatural energies that pulsate through them.

Wang Meng, a native of Wu-hsing, and Hsü Pen, who had painted his *Streams and Mountains* while visiting Wu-hsing, most likely knew the handscroll attributed to the Northern Sung master Yen Wen-kuei (fl. ca. late 970s–ca. 1030) *A Buddhist Monastery in Autumn Mountains* (cf. fig. 64), which was then in the collection of Shen Po-hsüan in Wu-hsing. The serpentine, dragonlike mountain forms of the late Yüan clearly owed their schematized mountain folds to the archaistic formula, which through surface patterns had given landscape painting an expressive coherence and logic as compelling as any offered by naturalism. In their works Wang Meng and Hsü Pen showed great creative ambition in resurrecting the monumental style of the Northern Sung—an ambition that was shared, in a different way, by Ni Tsan (1301–1374) late in his life (cf. fig. 118). Whereas Ni Tsan maintained his sense of self in his stylistic transformation, always tempering and moderating his feelings, Wang Meng and Hsü Pen exploited the monumental idiom for melodramatic effect. This literal borrowing of the earlier style provoked Ni's remark that he had "attained the ideas of Ching [Hao] and Kuan [T'ung]" in a way that "Wang Meng and others could [not] have imagined in their dreams."

In different ways the intensely expressive works of Ni Tsan, Wang Meng, and Hsü Pen accurately convey the psychic unease of the artists during the anxiety-filled years at the end of the Yüan and the beginning of the Ming periods. The first Ming emperor Chu Yüan-chang (r. 1368–98), a man of humble origins who was extremely suspicious and vindictive, harbored an intense dislike for the arrogant Chiang-nan intellectuals, whom he blamed for the

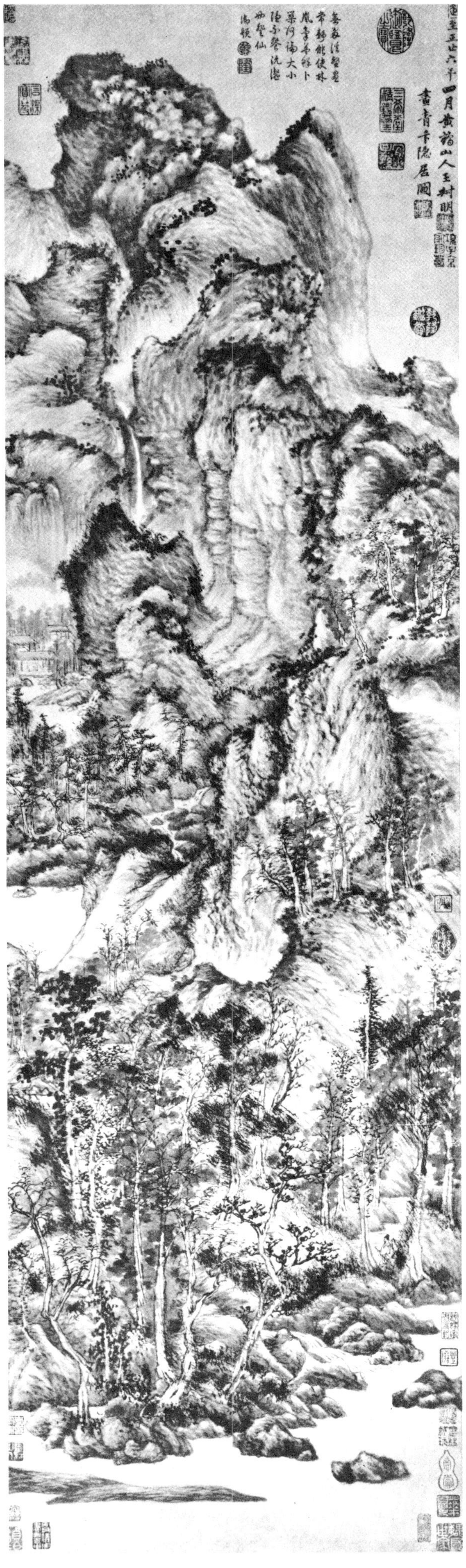

Fig. 119. Wang Meng, *Dwelling in the Ch'ing-pien Mountains* (*Ch'ing-pien yin-chü t'u*). Dated 1366. Hanging scroll, ink and color on paper. 141.0 x 42.2 cm (4 ft. 7 1/2 in. x 16 5/8 in.). Shanghai Museum

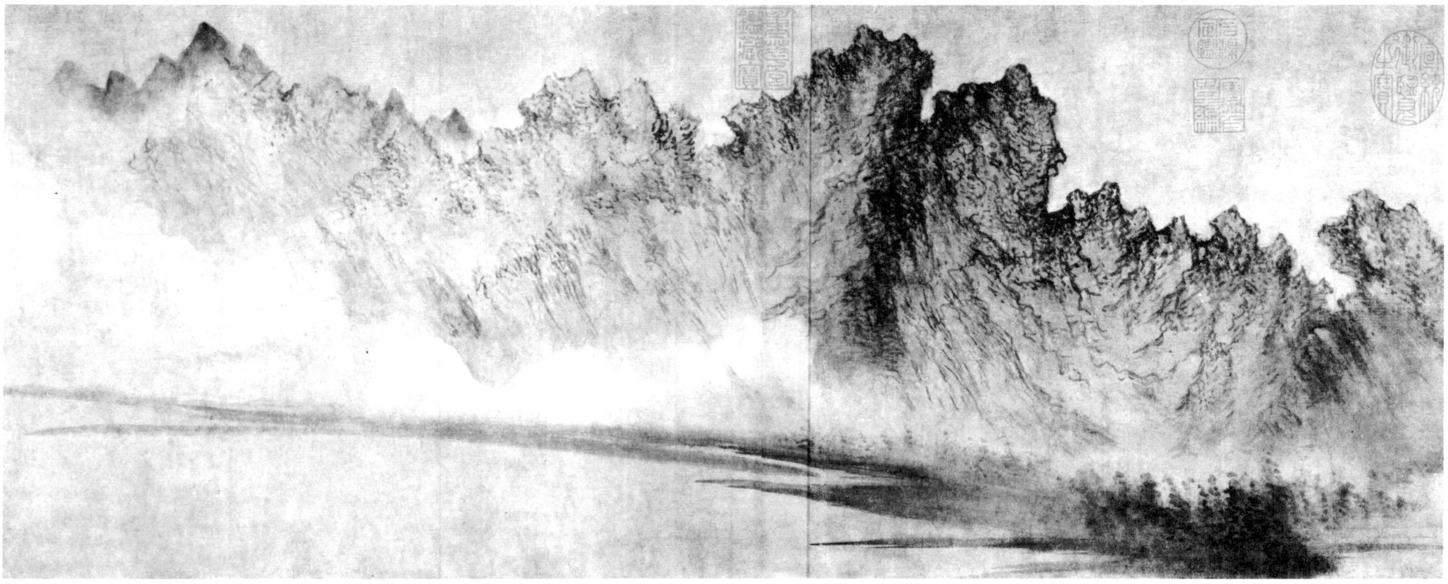

Fig. 120. Fang Ts'ung-i, detail, *Cloudy Mountains* (*Yün-shan t'u*). Undated, late 1360s. Handscroll, ink and light color on paper. 26.3 x 144.5 cm (10$^{1}/_{8}$ in. x 4 ft. 8$^{3}/_{4}$ in.). The Metropolitan Museum of Art, New York

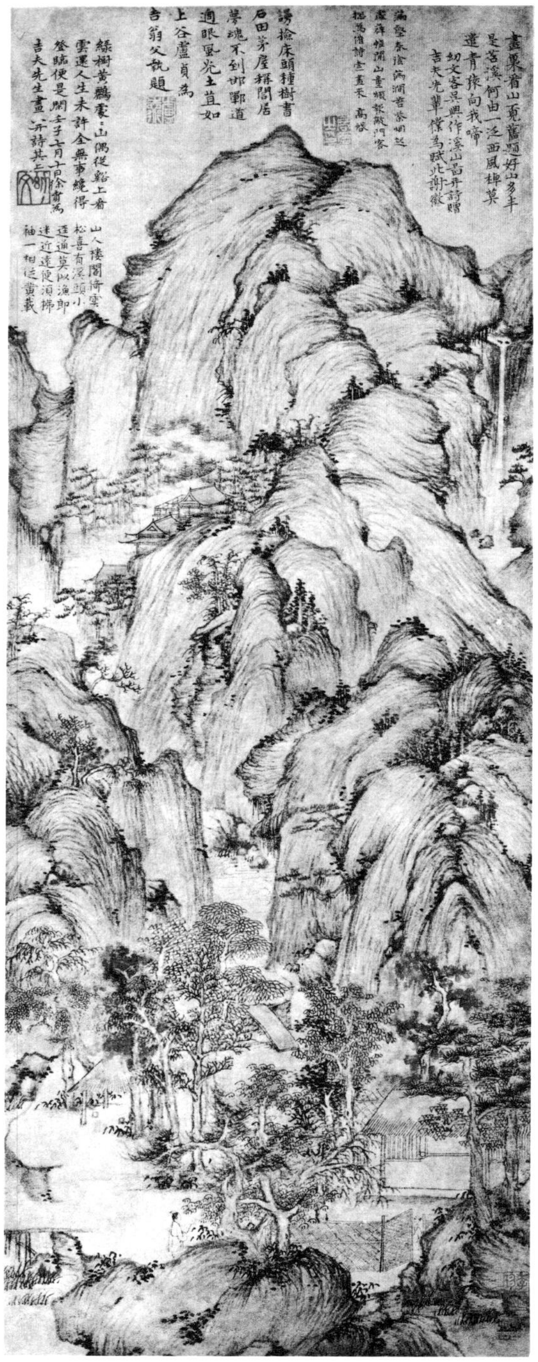

Fig. 121. Hsü Pen, *Streams and Mountains* (*Ch'i-shan t'u*). Dated 1372. Hanging scroll, ink on paper. 67.9 x 26.0 cm (26$^{3}/_{4}$ x 10$^{1}/_{4}$ in.). Cleveland Museum of Art

stubborn resistance of his archenemy Chang Shih-ch'eng during the protracted siege of Su-chou in 1367. Summoned to the new capital, Nanking, to serve, such leading Chiang-nan painters as Shen Chu (fl. ca. 1370), Chou Wei (fl. ca. 1370), and Chao Yüan (fl. ca. 1360–75) were put to death, in one way or another, for incurring the emperor's wrath. Other notable Chiang-nan artists—Wang Meng, Hsü Pen, Ch'en Ju-yen (ca. 1331–1371), among others—also died tragically. By about 1385 an entire generation of Chiang-nan scholar-artists had disappeared from the scene, effectively bringing to an end the burst of brilliant creativity in late Yüan landscape art.

A small hanging scroll painting on silk, by an unidentified artist, *Hermitage under Pine Trees* (*Sung-feng shu-wu*), in the Edward L. Elliott Family Collection at Princeton (no. 11), is evidently a work produced in the Chiang-nan region in the late 1360s or the early 1370s. The painting, of a secluded hermitage hidden behind tall pine trees under a towering mountain peak, follows a compositional scheme similar to Wang Meng's *Dwelling in the Ch'ing-pien Mountains* of 1366; the central peak, with its surging, overlapping folds, once again recalls the archaistic mountain forms in the handscroll *A Buddhist Monastery*. Although the painting exhibits knowledge of three-dimensional structure in the mountain and although the tree forms are typical of those of the fourteenth century, the painter chose to develop the composition in other ways: he divided the vertical picture plane geometrically into well-defined, carefully balanced units and devised intricate formal interplays among shapes, textures, and light and shade patterns throughout the painting. In the two equal halves of the picture surface the mountains occupy the upper half, and trees the lower; the jagged silhouette of the peak above is echoed by the twisted trunk and branches of the ancient pine below; the zigzag pattern of the waterfall in the upper right is answered by a similar pattern of the shoreline of the mountain stream in the lower left corner; the texture pattern of the mountains contrasts with the foliage patterns of the trees, yet the mountains and the trees are united by the carefully clustered round moss dots. In thus dealing with the problems of surface organization through patterns, shapes, stylized brushstrokes, and two-dimensional textures, the anonymous late fourteenth-century painter prefigured important landscape developments during the Ming period.

The first of the Ming painters who carried on in the Chiang-nan recluse tradition could scarcely have expected better treatment from their emperor than their late Yüan predecessors had received. The life and work of Wang Fu (1362–1416), who lived in early Ming times but was temperamentally a typical late Yüan painter, represent the transformation that took place within the Chiang-nan scholar-artist tradition at the beginning of the fifteenth century.

Born in Ni Tsan's hometown of Wu-hsi in 1362, the year before Chang Shih-ch'eng proclaimed himself prince of Wu in Su-chou, Wang Fu was almost six years old when the first Ming emperor ascended the throne in Nanking in early 1368. After passing his first degree in 1376 and seeking employment in Nanking two years later, he became implicated in some misadventure, most likely the same famous treason case of Hu Wei-yung in 1380 that reportedly caused over the years the deaths of more than 15,000 unfortunate souls, including Wang Meng,[5] and was banished to the northern border post of Ta-t'ung, in Shansi, where he endured a life of hardship for twenty years. In 1399 or 1400 he was allowed to return to Wu-hsi. He went to Nanking in 1403 to serve as a calligrapher at the Imperial Palace Library, and in 1413 and 1414 he attended the Yung-lo (Ming Ch'eng-tsu) emperor's (r. 1403–25) retinue during the emperor's visits to Peking. He died in Peking in 1416.

During his childhood, in about 1370, Wang Fu saw in the Wu-hsi home of a P'an Sung-ch'üan a painting by Ni Tsan, then the most famous living scholar-artist in Chiang-nan. Young Wang Fu was so impressed by the painting that nearly forty years later, while serving as a calligrapher in Nanking in 1408, he could still recall the composition, executing a copy from memory for one of P'an's sons, a physician in Nanking. On this painting, entitled *Remembering Ni Tsan's "Wu-t'ung Tree and Bamboo by a Thatched Pavilion"* (*I Ni Yün-lin wu-chu ts'ao-t'ang t'u*), now at The Art Museum, Princeton University (no. 13), Wang Fu's inscription reads, in part:

> When I was a boy I once saw in the home of the venerable [P'an] Sung-ch'üan a painting by Master Ni Yün-lin [Ni Tsan], *Wu-t'ung Tree and Bamboo by a Thatched Pavilion* [*Wu chu ts'ao-t'ang t'u*], done in color and inscribed with a poem:
>
> > Sparse *wu-t'ung* leaves bring drops of morning dew,
> > Hanging vines shade the green pond.
> > In a spotless pavilion in the wilderness,
> > I read a book on a long autumn day.
>
> There were a few more words in a colophon with a date, which I can no longer recall. Critics of the time considered it a work of the untrammeled class [*i-p'in*]. This was almost forty years ago, and no one knows where the painting is today. Meanwhile, both Master Ni and the venerable old gentleman [Sung-ch'üan] have passed away. Yet the wonderful way the painting conveyed its ideas, whenever I think of it, is still vivid in my eyes. . . .

Today, while on vacation with some free time, I sat at my desk with an inkstone, and did this work on paper in imitation [of Ni Tsan], which I will present to K'o-ch'eng. Although my work can never approach [Ni Tsan's] in resonance and untrammeled purity, it may preserve some of his compositional features.

On the first day of the tenth lunar month of the *wu-tzu* year, the sixth year of the Yung-lo era [October 19, 1408], Wang Meng-tuan [Wang Fu] wrote this.

This work by Wang Fu, which exemplifies early Ming scholar-painting, clearly sets the direction of development, in content as well as in style, for scholar-painting during the Ming period. A serious, self-motivated, and inner-directed work, the scholar's painting expressed the artist's mind and soul. Though freely bestowed upon men of like minds, it was never to be possessed, either through purchase or by force, by unworthy admirers—among them the rich and powerful who often desired such works for reasons repugnant to the artist. One anecdote about Wang Fu, reminiscent of the sort of stories told about Ni Tsan, relates that one night while living in Nanking Wang heard beautiful flute music being played next door and painted a bamboo scroll for the flutist. The man turned out to be a wealthy merchant, who, delighted by the unexpected gift, made the unhappy mistake of offering Wang a lavish gift of silks in exchange for another painting. Deeply offended, Wang not only refused, but also retrieved his original gift and tore it up.[6]

On special occasions, as with this work done for Doctor P'an, the scholar-painter produced a work expressly for a friend, to communicate special sentiments or thoughts. In this case he frequently added an inscription or colophon with a poem or remarks explaining the circumstances that gave rise to such sentiments. The poem or written remarks enhance the viewer's understanding of the intent (*chih*) of the painting, but the painter also had to communicate through his painting style. In this work, since Wang Fu was "remembering" Ni Tsan, he used his version of the Ni Tsan idiom to identify Ni's special qualities, a method he was able to employ whenever an evocation of Ni Tsan seemed appropriate, although Ni may not be directly mentioned in the title or colophon. Indeed Wang Fu appears to have so closely identified himself with Ni Tsan that his feelings were best expressed through Ni's images.

Wang Fu was the first to encounter the dilemma that confounded every later painter working in Ni Tsan's style: it could too easily lend itself to oversimplification or exaggeration. In order to succeed, Wang wisely chose to err equally in each direction. Instead of painting with a variety of texture strokes and dry washes (*jan*), and blurring and blending (*hu-t'u ch'i-pi*) them as only Ni Tsan could, Wang Fu built his forms (fig. 122) with a single type of brushstroke: an angular, "oblique" stroke done with the brush tilted at a sharp angle, frequently with a flicking motion. To achieve Ni's lonely and desolate feeling, Wang exaggerated the attenuated forms of the trees, dramatizing the mood of alienation with harsh angular strokes.

Wang's rock and tree forms and his treatment of spatial relationships are highly realistic, but, like the painter of *Hermitage under Pine Trees* of roughly the same time, Wang divided his design into well-defined

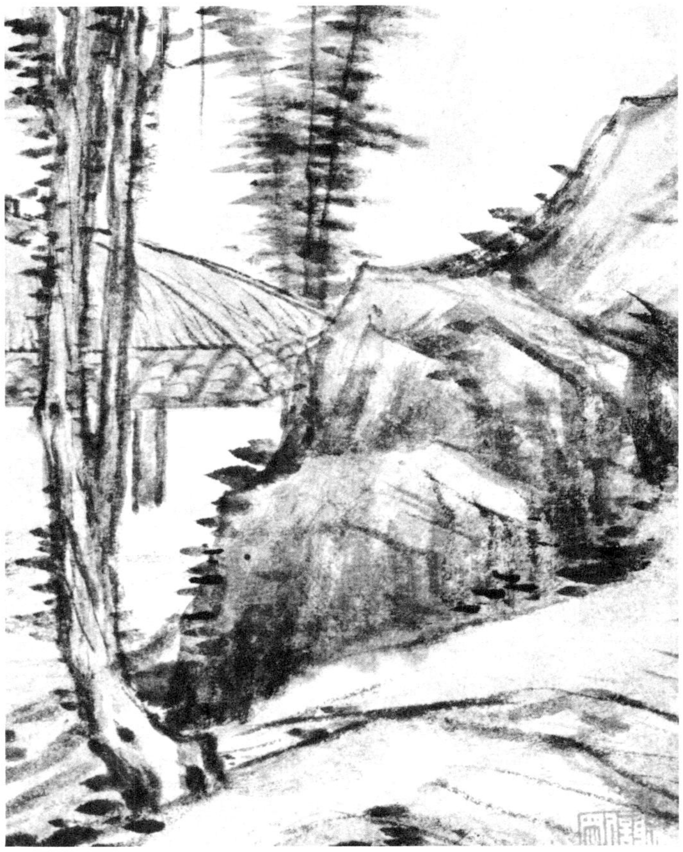

Fig. 122. Wang Fu, detail, *Remembering Ni Tsan's "Wu-t'ung Tree and Bamboo by a Thatched Pavilion" (I Ni Yün-lin Wu chu ts'ao-t'ang t'u)*, no. 13

formal units that balance the picture plane geometrically. In Ni Tsan's compositions (cf. figs. 108, 118), the foreground shoreline, the river, and the distant shore progress from front to back in separate horizontal stages; they derive from the panoramic scheme of *Wintry Groves and Layered Banks* attributed to Tung Yüan (cf. fig. 32). Ni's foreground elements remain a self-contained statement: starting at the water's edge at the bottom of the picture, they constitute the beginning of the pictured world, a realm distinctly separate from the viewer's world. Similarly Ni's background elements, while receding in depth along a continuous ground plane, are conceived as a far-distance statement, with forms that begin and end in the world of the landscape itself. In Wang Fu's work the tree branches, slopes, and shorelines intersect the borders of the picture at carefully measured points, and diagonal lines of the slope and the shore form a V at the bottom of the painting, echoed and counterbalanced by the inverted V of the treetops. The foreground elements of slope and shore have become triangular segments cut off by the lower borders of the painting. The painter's consciousness of the frame of the painting makes it part of the viewer's world.

Representation of space had ceased to be a challenge, and the early Ming painter turned his attention to surface organization and the rich interplay of brushstroke and ink, line and mass, surface and depth—creating brushwork and texture patterns that are visually absorbing and emotionally expressive.

## *The Era of the Professional Painter*

Despite Wang Fu's recognized achievement as a painter, he was employed as an official calligrapher at the Imperial Palace Library during the Yung-lo era. The painting specialists recruited under imperial patronage during the fifteenth century were required to be professional craftsmen able to fulfill the needs of the official Ming taste, which called for a return to the Sung monumental manner.

The so-called Ming Painting Academy (Hua-yüan) enjoyed powerful support during the reign of the artist-emperor Hsüan-te (Ming Hsüan-tsung; r. 1426–35), and remained strong through the Hung-chih reign of Emperor Ming Hsiao-tsung (1488–1505).[7] Reviving certain practices of the Sung Painting Academy developed under the artist-emperor Sung Hui-tsung (r. 1101–25), Ming emperors rewarded outstanding court painters with official titles; but Ming Academy painters were part of the inner palace service staff (*nei-kuan*), and did not enjoy the same rank as court officials. Working mostly in two of the inner palace service buildings, the Hall of Benevolence and Wisdom (Jen-chih-tien) and the Hall of Martial Brilliance (Wu-ying-tien), the painters reported to the palace eunuchs and received the same titles and pay as palace guards.[8]

Sung Academy painters had maintained a system of training and promotion through different academic ranks; Ming palace painters never fostered a cohesive academic goal or standard. Recruited from all parts of the country—many from the commercially prosperous coastal regions of Chekiang, Fukien, and Kuangtung provinces—these artists represented the ablest of the professional painters of the time. At the imperial palace they served every visual, didactic, and decorative need of the emperor and his vast palatial estate, adorning his chambers with religious and historical illustrations, birds and flowers, landscapes, architectural ornaments, and any other subject the court commanded them to paint.

One of the leading landscape masters during the Hsüan-te era was Li Tsai (fl. ca. 1426–36), a painter from P'u-t'ien, Fukien. A handscroll dated 1424, illustrating T'ao Ch'ien's (365–427) "Homecoming" ("Kuei-ch'ü-lai-ts'u"), which Li painted in collaboration with Ma Shih and Hsia Chih (both early 15th century), now in the Liaoning Provincial Museum, shows the return to the Southern Sung style in both figure and landscape art. In one of the scenes, "Sitting by a Limpid Stream Composing Poems" ("Lin ch'ing-liu erh fu-shih"; fig. 123), Li Tsai's portrayal of the seated poet T'ao Ch'ien recalls the standing portrait of Li Po by Liang K'ai (fl. early 13th century), in the Tokyo National Museum (fig. 124). Liang K'ai captured the walking poet both as a luminous source of divine inspiration and as a vividly volumetric and real human form in a radically simplified brush drawing that combines definition and modeling in each

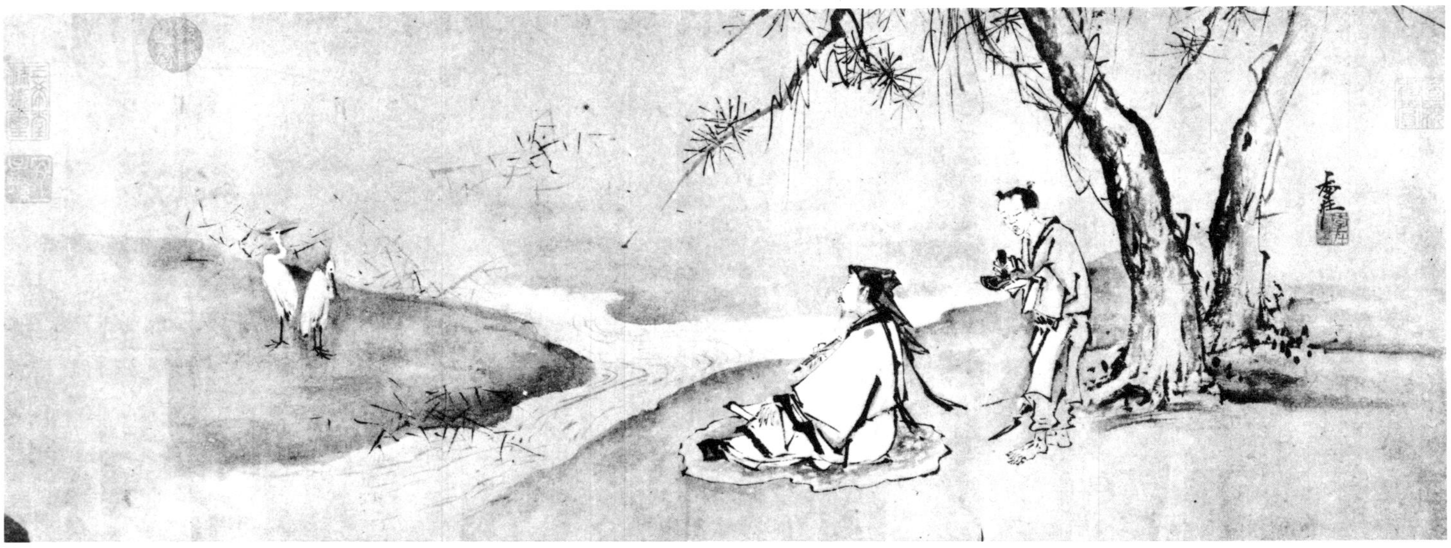

Fig. 123. Li Tsai, "Sitting by a Limpid Stream Composing Poems," detail, *T'ao Yüan-ming's Ode on "Homecoming"* (*Kuei-ch'ü lai-hsi*). Dated 1424. Handscroll, ink and light color on paper. 28.0 x 74.0 cm (11 x 29 1/8 in.). Liaoning Provincial Museum

Fig. 123a. Detail, fig. 123

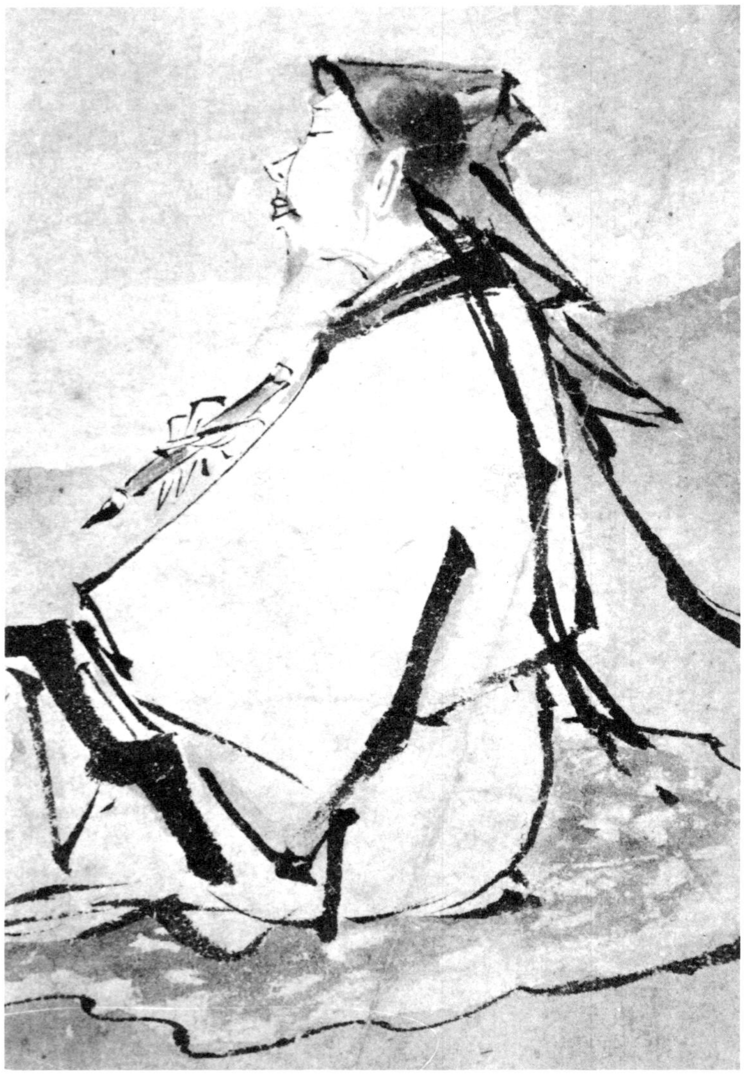

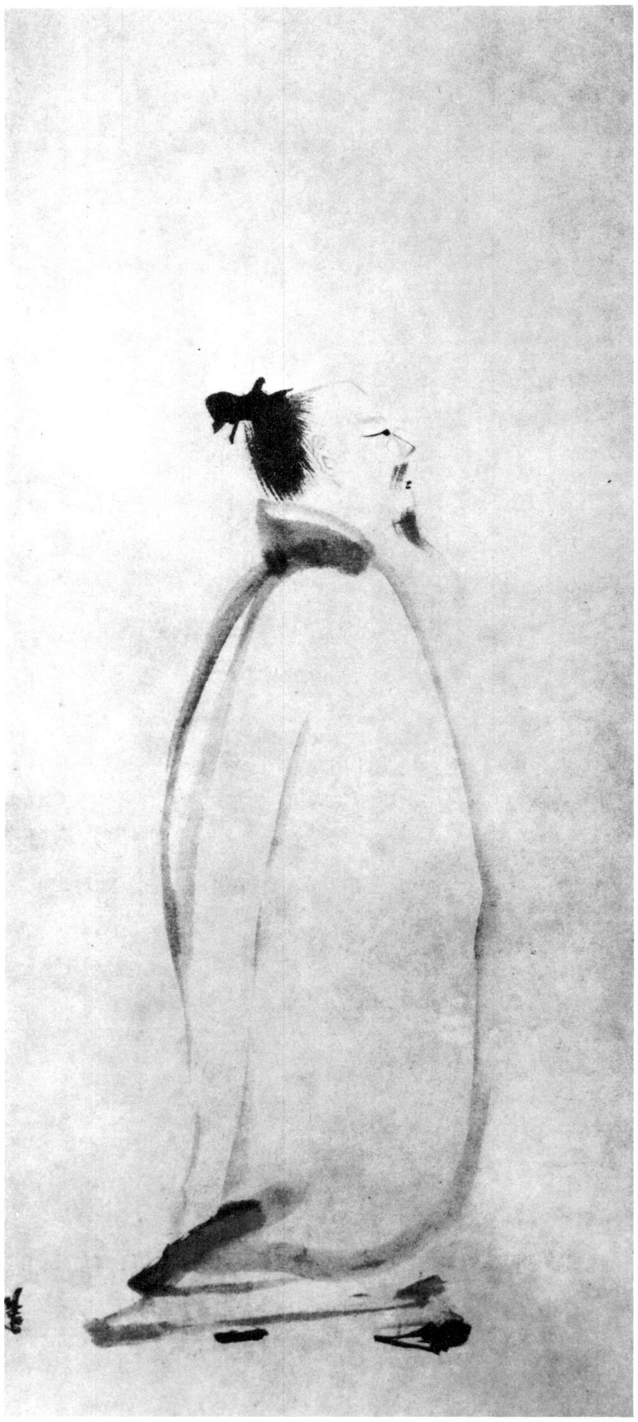

Fig. 124. Liang K'ai, *Li Po Chanting a Poem* (*Li Po hsing yin t'u*). Undated, early 13th century. Hanging scroll, ink on paper. 80.8 x 30.4 cm (31 3/4 x 12 in.). Tokyo National Museum

brushstroke. Li Tsai, by contrast, tended to stress, beneath the convention of a simple brush style, representational realism, using ink-wash modeling (fig. 123a). In describing the landscape setting for the figures, Li Tsai placed the river diagonally across the horizontal composition so that the seated poet on the right gazes into the far distance to the left; the space thus created is physically measured, cut off, and framed by the four borders of the composition.

In "Clouds Rising through the Peaks" ("Yün wu-hsin i ch'u hsiu"; fig. 125), another section of the same handscroll, Li Tsai adopted the early thirteenth-century Academy painter Hsia Kuei's ax-cut (*fu-p'i*) idiom; boldly applied brushstrokes, now clearly treated as formulas, create strong surface patterns (fig. 125a). Again, the seated poet in the right-hand corner stares into the distance to the left, and, with the distant peaks on the left brought forward into the picture plane, the scenery is once again measured and bounded by the frame. In Hsia Kuei's one-corner composition *Sailboat in the Rain* (cf. fig. 54) the fore-

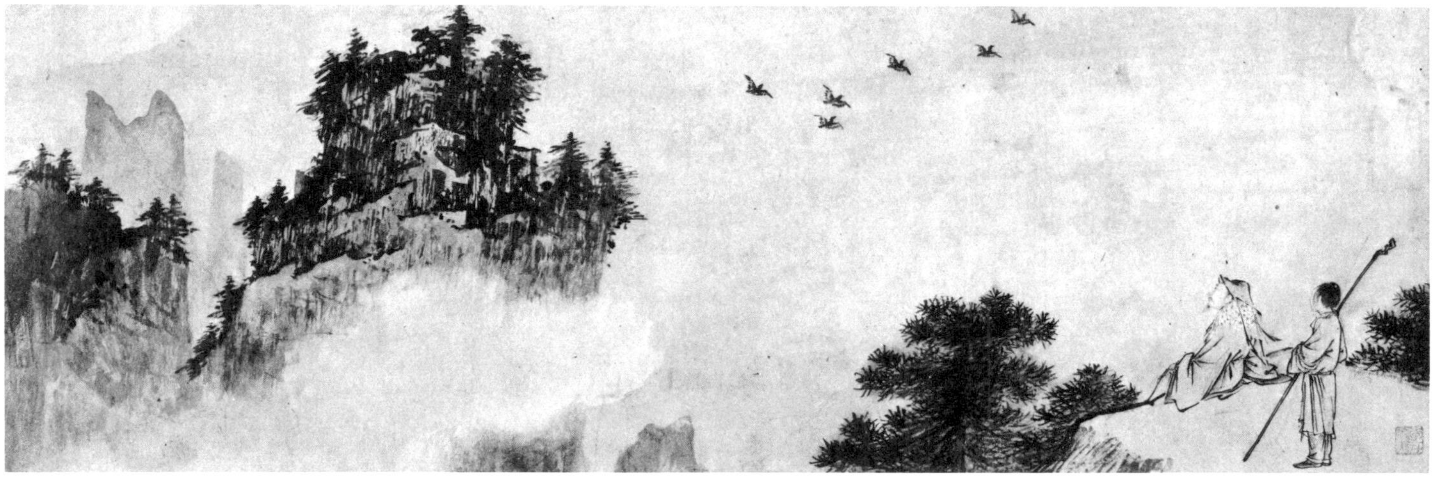

Fig. 125. Li Tsai, "Cloud Rising through the Peaks," detail, *T'ao Yüan-ming's "Homecoming"* (*Kuei-ch'ü lai-hsi*). Handscroll, ink and light color on paper. Dated 1424. 28.0 x 83.0 cm (11 x 32⅝ in.). Liaoning Provincial Museum

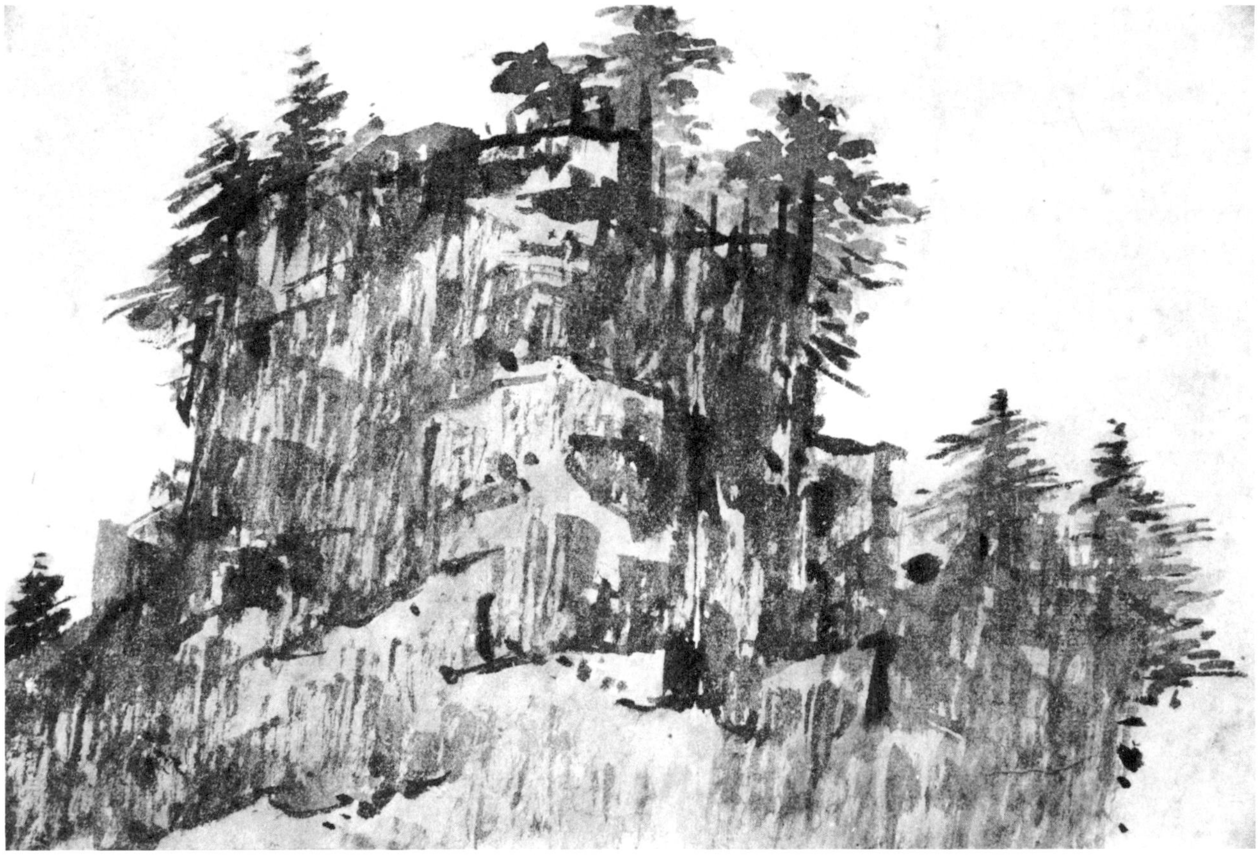

Fig. 125a. Detail, fig. 125

ground shore, the river, and the shoreline beyond the river all lie parallel to the picture plane. The composition is much the same flat-distance scheme as the eighth-century *Hawk and Ducks* (cf. fig. 18): the elements in the three superimposed planes, all viewed from the front, are held in a dynamic momentum and tension, pushing and pulling toward the two sides of the horizontal plane. Li Tsai divided his compositions diagonally into opposing triangular patterns. With all of the elements turned to the side and placed in the same foreground plane, the opposing diagonal forces are carefully balanced within the picture surface.

Upon hearing the works of one of the early Ming palace painters compared to those by the Southern Sung academicians Hsia Kuei and Ma Yüan (fl. ca. 1190–1264), the Yung-lo emperor is said to have complained that the simplified styles of Ma and Hsia represented merely "fragments of mountains and left-over waters, a reflection of the partial empire of the Southern Sung."[9] Clearly, as a symbol of the restored empire, Ming Academy landscape painting had to substitute fullness for emptiness, monumental grandeur for simplicity, and engagement for retreat.

By all accounts the most accomplished and esteemed painter of the mid-fifteenth century was Tai Chin (1388–1462) from Ch'ien-t'ang (Hang-chou prefecture in Chekiang province), who was regarded as the founder of the Che School of painting.[10] Son of a professional painter and, according to a late seventeenth-century tradition, also trained as a silversmith,[11] Tai Chin followed his father to the capital in the early 1420s. Having studied in the professional painting studios in Hang-chou, he was equally accomplished in figural and landscape art, commanding a wide repertory of styles and subject matter. He was presented to the Hsüan-te emperor through the introduction of a eunuch named Fu, but fell victim to the jealousies of powerful Academy painters, who effectively prevented him from a successful career at the palace. He nevertheless enjoyed wide esteem among the leading scholar-officials in the capital: the well-known calligrapher and bamboo painter Hsia Ch'ang (1388–1470), later minister of the Court of Imperial Sacrifices, for example, praised Tai as "a gentleman of wide and elegant learning."[12] According to one recent study, in about 1441 Tai returned to Hang-chou,[13] where he lived as a professional painter and died in 1462.

An outstanding and typical work in the Hsia Kuei idiom by Tai Chin is an unsigned hanging scroll on silk, *Returning Late from a Spring Outing* (*Ch'un-yu wan-kuei*), in the National Palace Museum, Taipei (fig. 126). To achieve the smooth and rich patterns favored by his wealthy patrons, Tai worked mostly on silk, the traditional medium of professional painters. In this painting evening mist suffuses the valley, rising through the verdant hills. A mildly intoxicated, slightly disheveled gentleman (fig. 126a)—no doubt a retired, successful scholar-official—returning late from a spring outing, knocks on the gate of his walled country estate in the lower right corner; behind him a valet holds his tired donkey, and trailing farther behind, on the road lined with blossoming peach trees at the other end of the bridge, servants slowly carry his folded parasol, empty picnic baskets, and portable stove; inside the gate a servant holding a lantern rushes across the front courtyard to answer the master's knock. In the distance farmers resting hoes on their shoulders return along a dike to their thatched cottages among the weeping willows, where a woman tends her chickens. The serenity of the landscape, combined with apt descriptive details, celebrates the good life of a prosperous era; the scene seems to exude a soft, scented air of contentment.

Compared to Ma Yüan's *Banquet by Lantern Light* (*Hua-teng shih-yen t'u*), also in the National Palace Museum, Taipei (fig. 127), Tai Chin's painting is at once more realistically descriptive and more sumptuously decorative. Instead of a concentrated poetic vision, Tai Chin preferred a profusion of genre details: the bedraggled donkey would be quite out of place in an elegant Southern Sung painting, for example. The figures in Tai's landscapes, always vividly drawn, are animated earthlings carrying out their daily lives. Tai's use of the Ma Yüan–Hsia Kuei idiom as a calligraphic formula is both felicitous and masterly: virtuoso brushwork, silky ink wash, and tasteful touches of color give the painting the rich, smoothly finished look of a tapestry. Instead of the stepped progression into depth seen in Southern Sung compositions, Tai used a continuous diagonally receding ground plane, tilted upward into the two-dimensional picture plane. In place of the three-dimensional background mountain of Yüan paintings (cf., e.g., fig. 118), Tai painted his

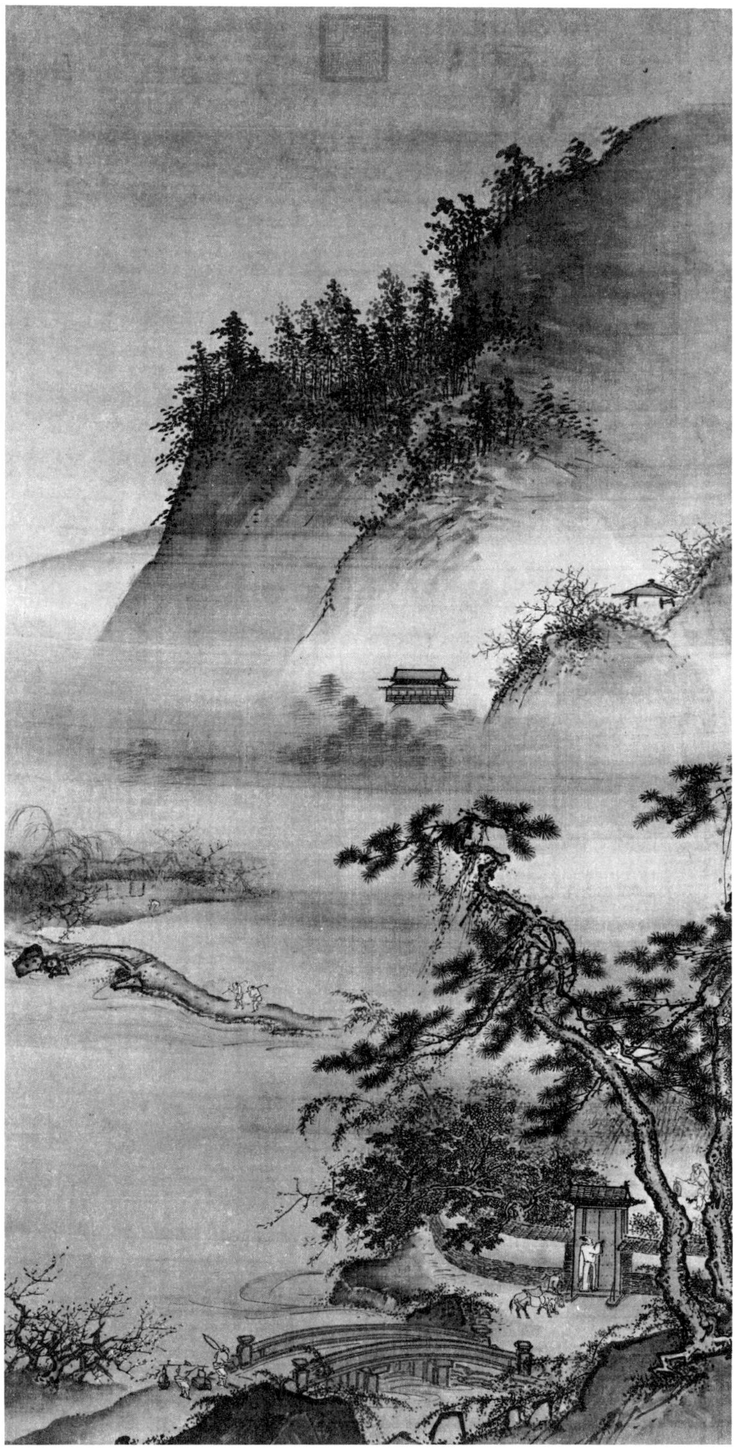

Fig. 126. Tai Chin, ***Returning Late from a Spring Outing*** (*Ch'un-yu wan-kuei*). Undated, ca. 1440. Hanging scroll, ink and light color on silk. 167.9 x 83.1 cm (5 ft. 6 1/8 in. x 32 3/4 in.). National Palace Museum, Taipei

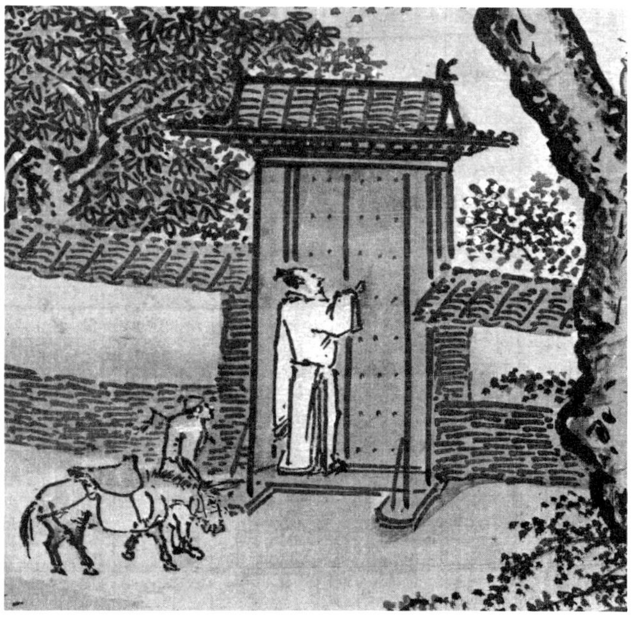

Fig. 126a. Detail, fig. 126

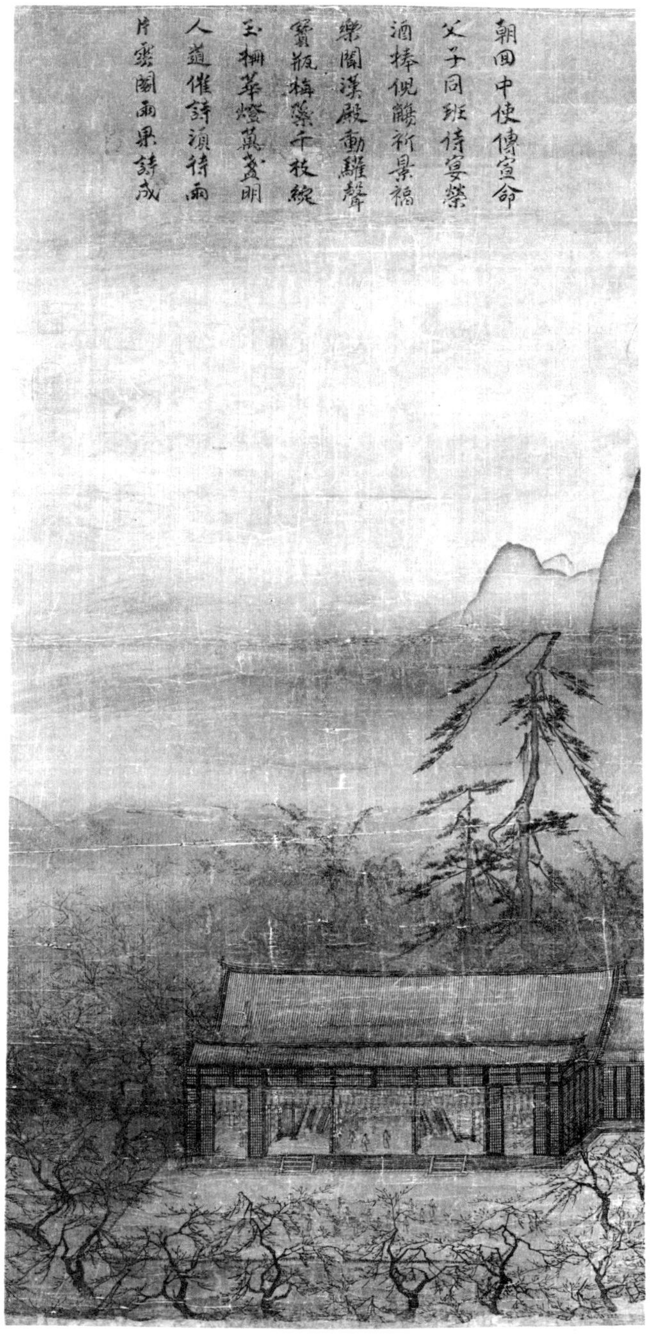


Fig. 127. Ma Yüan, ***Banquet by Lantern Light*** (*Hua-teng shih-yen t'u*). Undated, early 13th century. Hanging scroll, ink and color on silk. 111.9 x 53.5 cm (3 ft. 8 in. x 21 in.). National Palace Museum, Taipei

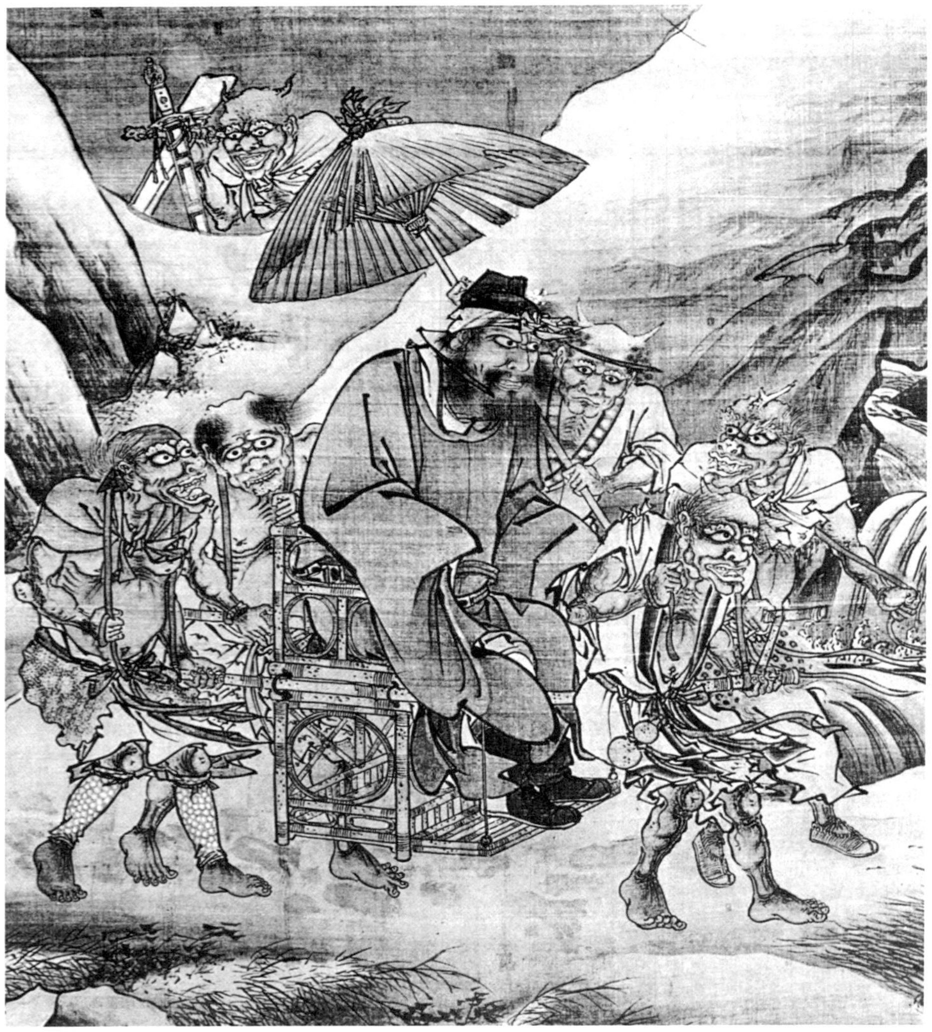

Fig. 128. Tai Chin, *A Nocturnal Outing of the Demon Queller Chung K'uei* (*Chung K'uei yeh-yu t'u*). Undated, ca. 1450. Hanging scroll, ink and color on silk. 189.7 x 120.2 cm (6 ft. 2⅝ in. x 3 ft. 11⅜ in.). Palace Museum, Peking

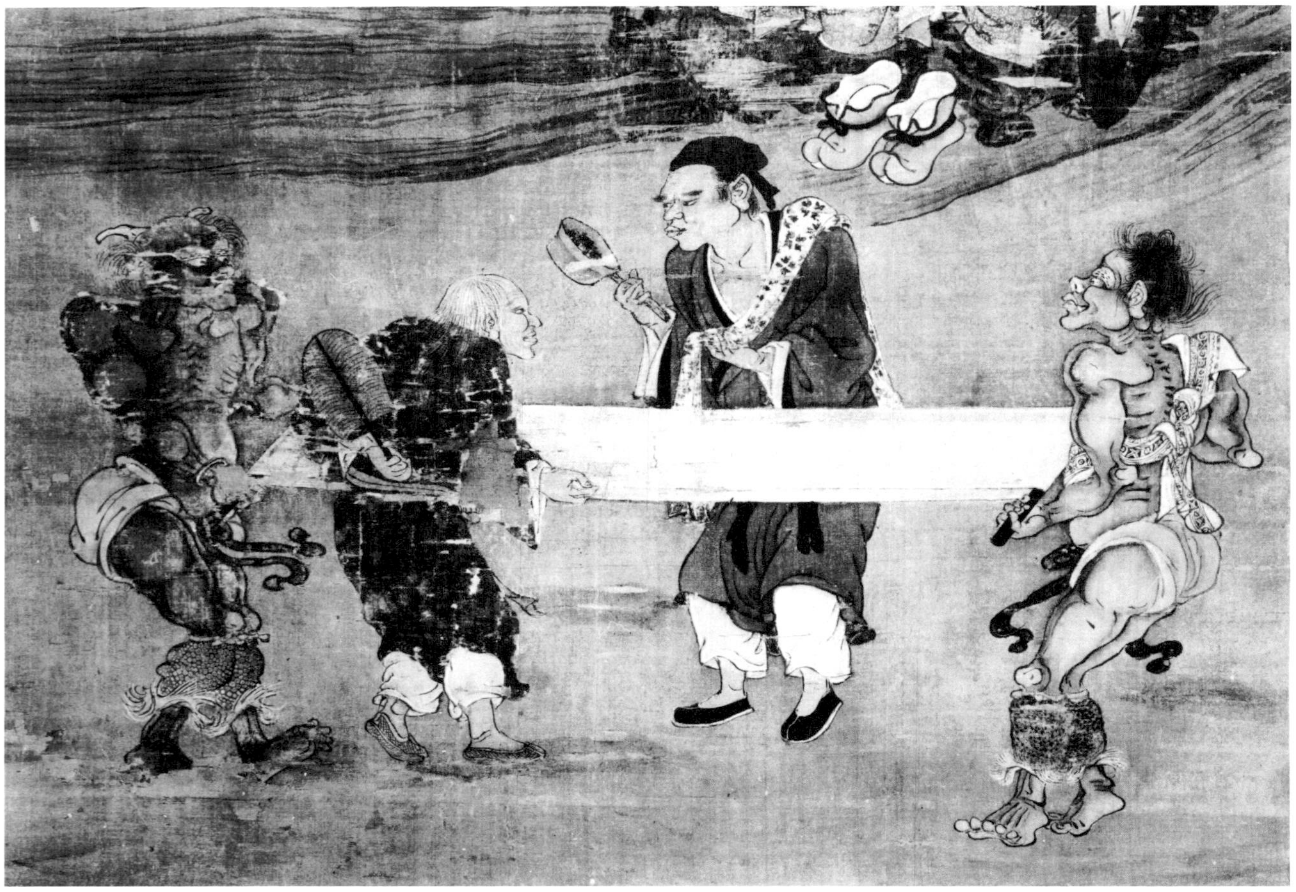

Fig. 129. Chou Chi-ch'ang, detail, one of *Five Hundred Lohans* (*Wu-pai lo-han t'u*). Dated 1178–81. Hanging scroll, ink and color on silk. Daitoku-ji, Kyoto

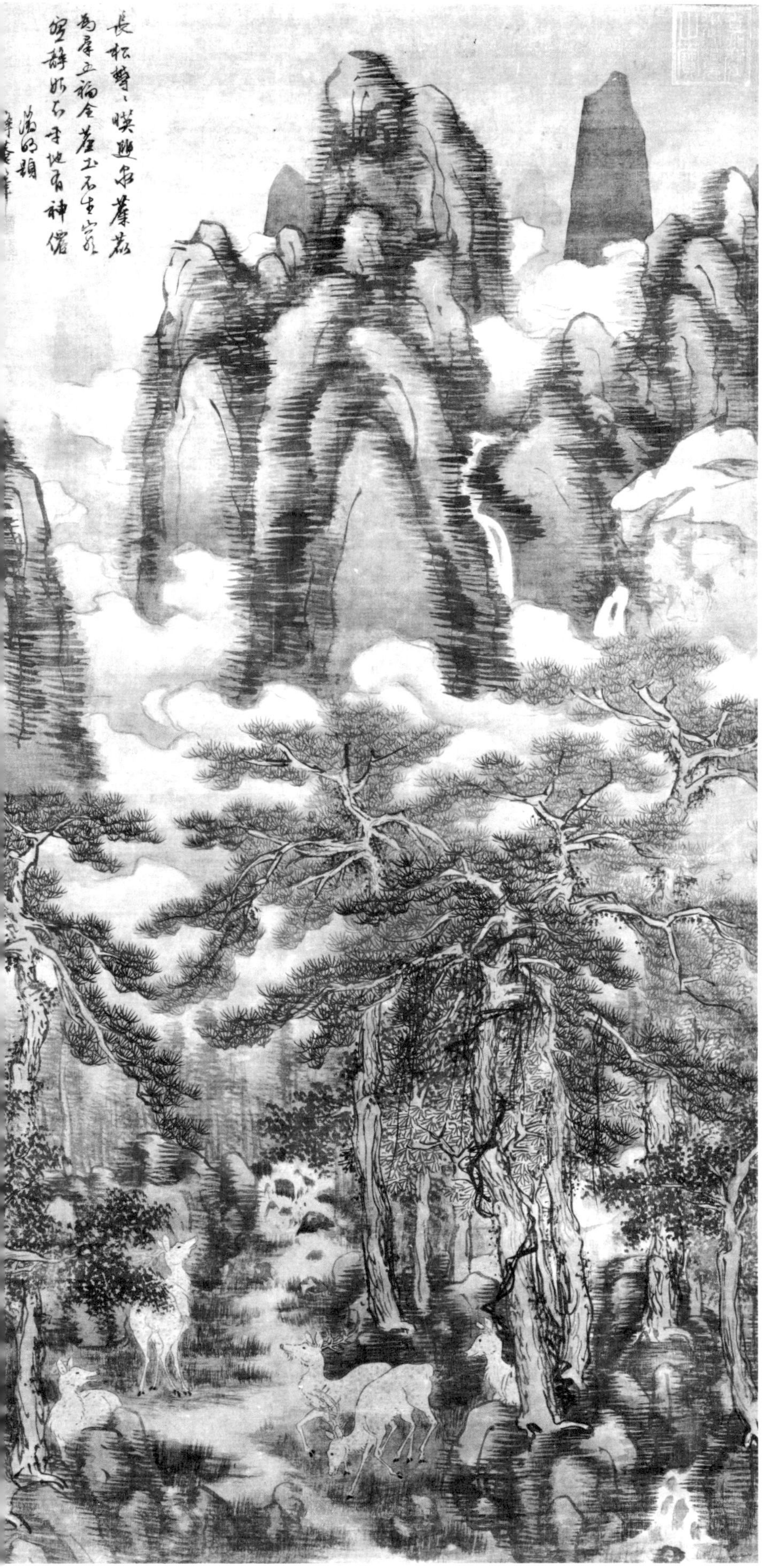

Fig. 130. Tai Chin, *Five Deer under Tall Pine Trees* (*Ch'ang-sung wu-lu*). Undated, ca. 1460. Hanging scroll, ink and color on silk. 142.5 x 72.4 cm (4 ft. 8 1/8 in. x 28 1/2 in.). National Palace Museum, Taipei

mountain peaks to rise like a flat screen in the picture plane, obstructing the view and thereby directing attention to the graceful and often intricate surface patterns.

A diligent student of ancient models, Tai was equally conversant in other Sung Academy styles. In narrative subjects, such as *Six Buddhist Patriarchs* (*Ta-mo liu-tai tsu-shih t'u*), now in the Liaoning Provincial Museum, and *Seeking the Tao in Cave Paradise* (*Tung-t'ien wen-tao t'u*), in the Palace Museum, Peking,[14] he used the precise descriptive technique of the early thirteenth-century academician Liu Sung-nien (ca. 1150–after 1225); in large landscape compositions depicting the four seasons, he adopted the monumental manner of the Northern Sung masters Kuo Hsi and Li T'ang (ca. 1070s–ca. 1150s).

In the hanging scroll *A Nocturnal Outing of the Demon Queller Chung K'uei* (*Chung K'uei yeh-yu t'u*), in the Palace Museum, Peking (fig. 128), Tai Chin painted a folklore subject in the popular style of religious representations. Tai's depiction of demon figures may be compared to those by the Southern Sung religious painter Chou Chi-ch'ang in *Five Hundred Lohans* (*Wu-pai lo-han t'u*), dated 1178 (fig. 129). The vivid theatricality of Tai's drawing, in carrying on the realism of the Sung professional painting tradition, also suggests a relationship to the newly risen popular dramas of the Yüan and the quasi-religious cycles of plays and novels, such as *The Journey to the West* (*Hsi-yu chi*) by Wu Ch'eng-en, of the Ming period.[15] Tai's virtuoso landscape setting, in the ax-cut (*fu-p'i*), devil-face (*kuei-mien*), and crab-claw (*hsieh-chao*) idioms of Li T'ang and Kuo Hsi, while serving the theatrical representation in a functional way, testifies to the high standards of popular illustrations of the time.

A totally different style is seen in Tai Chin's *Five Deer under Tall Pine Trees* (*Ch'ang-sung wu-lu*), in the National Palace Museum, Taipei (fig. 130), an unsigned work with an inscription by Wen Cheng-ming (1470–1559) identifying its painter as Tai Chin. A stylistic confirmation of the attribution may be found in a comparison with two recently published signed works by Tai in the Palace Museum, Peking—an album leaf, "Three Egrets under Pine Trees" ("San lu t'u"), and a handscroll representing Yang Wei-chen's (1296–1370) *Elegant Gathering under Mount Nan-p'ing at West Lake, Hang-chou* (*Nan-p'ing ya-chi t'u*; dated

1462).[16] The unusual feature shared by these three works is the use of round brushstrokes (*yüan-pi*) in a loose and untrammeled manner. The exuberantly full composition of *Five Deer* is built primarily of two contrasting types of brushstrokes: the mountain, tree, cloud, and deer forms are first drawn with a round curling brushstroke in a grass-script manner; after modeling with a light ink wash, the mountains are finished by a layer of long horizontal dots, applied with great verve and enthusiasm. This seemingly eccentric technique represents Tai Chin's homage to the late eleventh-century amateur landscape style of Mi Fu (1052–1107), whose renowned Mi dot idiom was transmitted through the works of the early Yüan scholar-painter Kao K'o-kung (1248–1310). In reducing landscape painting to pure brushstroke idioms, Tai Chin the professional painter added a dimension to his art: beyond pictorial representation, he shared the rising critical interest among late fifteenth-century scholar-painters and theorists in the purely formal problems of style in painting.

## *Two Philosophers of the School of the Mind*

In their quest for objective truth Northern Sung thinkers had proposed that, while the highest reality is *li* (the metaphysical principles that underlie the physical universe), objective principles and the subjective mind are neither discrete nor mutually exclusive. While in theory principles constitute a world of their own, in reality they can be found only within concrete objects, and then apprehended only through the mind of the experiencing self. Two thinkers, Ch'en Hsien-chang (1428–1500) and Wang Shou-jen (Wang Yang-ming; 1472–1529), developed the Neo-Confucian School of the Mind (*hsin-hsüeh pai*).

Born in 1428 to a well-to-do family in Hsin-hui, Kuangtung province, Ch'en Hsien-chang attained his second provincial degree in 1447, but twice, in 1448 and 1451, failed to pass the metropolitan examination in the capital. After visiting for some months in 1454 with the Neo-Confucian scholar Wu Yü-pi (1392–1469) in Kiangsi, he returned home, determined to become a sage. For several years, he assiduously studied Confucian and Neo-Confucian texts. Then, convinced that learning depended on personal insights, or "self-acquired" (*tzu-te*) knowledge, he embraced the Buddhist and Taoist practices of meditation, and devoted himself to "quiet sitting" (*ching-tso*) as a method of self-cultivation. He started teaching in his native village of Pai-sha. In 1466 he again went to Peking, and in 1469 failed a third time to pass the metropolitan examination. Returning home he concentrated on teaching and study and achieved renown as a teacher and thinker. In 1482 he went to Peking for the last time. The emperor granted him an honorary position at the Han-lin Academy, but he begged to return, pleading that he was in ill health and that his aging mother needed him at home. He died in 1500. In 1584, by imperial decree, a tablet in his honor was placed in the official temple of Confucius. Only four Ming scholars were so honored.[17]

Ch'en Hsien-chang's philosophy centered on the cultivation of the inner self through freedom, independence, and spontaneity. The Sung Neo-Confucian scholars Ch'eng I (1033–1107) and Chu Hsi (1130–1200) had defined the metaphysical *li* as "what is beyond shapes" (*hsing-erh-shang*) and the physical *ch'i* (ether) as "what is within shapes" (*hsing-erh-hsia*) and had considered the mind (*hsin*) as ether. By emphasizing the objective, empirical side of knowledge, Chu Hsi's "investigation of things leading to extension of knowledge" (*ko-wu chih-chih*) taught that the mind could reach out toward the object. Chu Hsi believed that though the mind may contain the *li*, it may not be equated with it. In other words, he considered the equation of principle with nature (*hsing*)—a designation for principle as contained by the mind—to be correct, but that equation of the principle with the mind to be wrong.[18] Ch'eng I's elder brother Ch'eng Hao (1032–1085), followed by Lu Chiu-yüan (1139–1193), on the other hand, seeing little distinction between mind and nature—therefore, between mind and principle—emphasized the union of the mind with all things through spiritual cultivation. Ch'en Hsien-chang, who began studying Chu Hsi's approach under Wu Yü-pi, discovered truth through the intuitive method of Lu Chiu-yüan. Only through long years of solitary struggle and "quiet sitting" did Ch'en learn to understand the principle through personal experience and direct observation, by what he called *t'i-jen wu-li* (a personal experience of the principles of things).[19] Yet Ch'en never went as far as Lu Chiu-yüan in equating mind with principle. Ch'en did not deny the objective existence of the principle; he merely insisted on the union of the subjective and the objective through self-acquired knowledge: through quiet meditation, he believed, the mind becomes one with the universe, "perfectly forming one body with all things" (*hun-jan yü wu t'ung-t'i*).[20]

Besides his roles as a teacher and thinker, Ch'en Hsien-chang was also a gifted poet and calligrapher. Known for his individualistic style of grass, or cursive, script, he is said to have used, in his later years, a coarse brush made of straw or rush (*mao-lung*). In a handscroll by Ch'en, *Poems on Plum Blossoms* (*Mei-hua ping chung tso*), written in 1491, in the John B. Elliott Collection at The Art Museum, Princeton University (no. 16), the rough and natural brushstrokes, made with a stiff and blunt-tipped brush, illustrate perfectly Ch'en's statement "My learning is based on the natural."[21] For Ch'en an empty and detached mind acquired through "quiet sitting" was essential both for understanding and for creativity. Though similar to the Taoist concept of something self-existing and self-perpetuating, Ch'en's naturalism, as pointed out by Jen Yu-wen (1970), was Confucian in content and dynamic in principle.[22] To Ch'en the essential characteristic of nature was "growth and growth, transformation and transformation" (*sheng-sheng hua-hua*), and he proposed that "utmost nothingness possesses utmost activity" (*chih-wu yu chih-tung*). In the Elliott scroll myriad variations multiply from the same simple, blunt, and straightforward brushwork, as quiescence and utter self-possession give rise to infinite movement and activity. Ch'en's calligraphy owes no allegiance to any particular ancient model; it shares the spiritual inheritance of the Ch'an Buddhist masters, who strove for intuitive self-enlightenment.

Wang Shou-jen (Wang Yang-ming), born in 1472 in Yü-yao, Chekiang province, son of a successful scholar-official, was twenty-eight at the time of Ch'en Hsien-chang's death. Although there is no record of any formal contact between these two great thinkers, Wang must have been influenced by Ch'en or Ch'en's followers. From an early age, Wang's interests were wide ranging, from knight errantry—horsemanship, archery, military strategy—to Taoism, Buddhism, and literary pursuits; but in his study of Neo-Confucian thought, he experienced a personal development similar to Chen's. For nearly ten years, between 1489 and 1498, he struggled with the doctrine espoused by Chu Hsi of the "investigation of things" (*ko-wu*), the idea that all things, including a single blade of grass or a tree, must embody within them the supreme principle. In one exercise, he investigated and pondered over a piece of bamboo until he became ill from the effort; then, in 1508, while living in exile in northern Kueichou, he suddenly realized that "to understand the truth of the sages, one's own nature is self-sufficient." From then on, "he taught his students exclusively about extending one's innate intuitive knowledge " (*chih liang-chih*).[23]

Passing the metropolitan examination in 1499 (having failed it in 1493 and 1496), Wang enjoyed an exceptionally fruitful political and military career. In 1506 he was exiled to Kueichou for having raised his voice against a powerful eunuch. While in exile he formulated the epoch-making theory that "knowledge and action are one" (*chih-hsing ho-i*): "Knowledge is the beginning of action, and action the completion of knowledge."[24] In 1510 he was recalled to service, and for the next dozen years he played an important role in the political and military affairs in the south. He suppressed banditry in four successful campaigns in 1517 and 1518 in modern Fukien, Kiangsi, and Kuangtung provinces, putting down the rebellion of Prince Ning in 1519 in Kiangsi. As governor of Kiangsi, he repaired flood damage and lifted the tax burden of the people. After his father died in 1522, Wang Shou-jen remained at home and devoted himself to lecturing and writing. In 1527 he was called once again to lead pacification campaigns against aboriginal rebels in Kuangsi. By the conclusion of that campaign, he was exhausted and ill; he died on his homeward journey in early 1529. In 1584 his tablet was ordered by imperial decree to be placed in the official Confucian temple.

Wang Shou-jen's doctrine of extending intuitive knowledge into action gave Ming thought a dynamic purpose. Since he based many of his ideas on the Ch'an Buddhist doctrine of sudden enlightenment, and since he frequently borrowed Buddhist idioms in his teachings, orthodox Confucianists attacked him vigorously for spreading "false learning." In the second half of the sixteenth century, some of Wang's followers, who indulged in extreme hedonistic behavior in the name of intuitive knowledge, were denounced as "crazy Ch'an" Buddhists. As a philosophy of action, Wang's teaching became popular in Edo and Meiji Japan (17th–19th centuries), as well as in twentieth-century Republican China.

A handscroll that preserves three family letters by Wang Shou-jen, addressed to a nephew named Cheng Pang-jui (personal name, Pao-i), now in the John B. Elliott Collection at Princeton (no. 22), bears at the beginning a portrait of the philosopher-soldier-statesman seated at his desk, brush in hand, with the recipent of the letters, respectfully attending to one side. The portrait is done in the plain-line drawing (*pai-miao*) style by an anonymous early fifteenth-century painter. The letters date from 1523–25;[25] they were mounted as a scroll after Wang's death in 1529 by Cheng, the owner of the letters, who both commissioned the portrait and requested the colophons by four of Wang's distinguished pupils, Huang Wan (1480–1554), Hsiao Ching-te (fl. 16th century), Huang Hung-kang (1492–1561), and Yeh Liang-p'ei (*chin-shih*, 1523), the third of which is dated 1531. The portrait shows Wang with a lean face and a full beard, seated slightly stooped, with a scroll-like backrest wedged between his body and the curved back of the chair; always frail, Wang had to be carried in a sedan chair during his last campaign just before he died. Wang's fine calligraphy, done in a highly cultivated running-script style in the manner of the *Preface to the Sacred Teaching in Wang Hsi-chih's Style* by Huai-jen, depicts the philosopher and man of action as an artist of uncommonly refined but conservative taste and temperament.

## *The Scholar-Amateur*

Born in 1427 to an established scholar-gentry family in Su-chou, the center of the scholar-painting tradition in the late Yüan period, Shen Chou (1427–1509) inherited much of his artistic and social lifestyle from family tradition. His great-grandfather Liang-ch'en is said to have been a friend of Wang Meng. His grandfather Ch'eng was called up for government service during the Yung-lo era (1403–24), but resigned soon afterward to pursue the quiet life of retirement at home. Shen Chou's father, Heng-chi, and elder uncle, Chen-chi, had studied classics and painting with Ch'en Chi, son of another well-known late Yüan painter Ch'en Ju-yen (ca. 1331–1371); Ch'en Chi, who excelled in bamboo painting, had taught Hsia Ch'ang, the scholar-official and bamboo painter from Su-chou who had befriended Tai Chin. Ch'en Chi's son Ch'en K'uan taught Shen Chou. Ch'en K'uan owned a number of important Yüan paintings, including Huang Kung-wang's *Stone Cliff at the Pond of Heaven* (*T'ien-ch'ih shih-pi*) and Wang Meng's *Heavy Snow at Mount T'ai* (*T'ai-tsung mi-hsüeh*), which was painted for Ch'en Ju-yen in 1370.[26] To celebrate the birthday of his teacher Ch'en K'uan, in 1467, Shen Chou painted the large hanging scroll *Towering Mount Lu* (*Lu-shan kao*; now in the National Palace Museum, Taipei) in the Wang Meng style. Following the examples of his grandfather, father, and uncle, the gentle, even-tempered Shen Chou stayed away from official examinations and government service, preferring a quiet life of reading and painting in retirement. Upon the death of his father in 1477 (when Shen was already fifty), he pleaded that he had to stay home in order to care for his aging mother. Although the exact reasons for Shen Chou's reluctance to serve are not clear, it is highly possible that the violent deaths of Wang Meng, Ch'en Ju-yen, and other Su-chou artists and intellectuals in the early Ming years persuaded generations of the Shen family to avoid the center of trouble.

According to Shen Chou's illustrious pupil Wen Cheng-ming (1470–1559), the master specialized in small pictures until he was forty, in about 1466. In the 1470s and 1480s Shen imitated and experimented with a wide range of Sung and Yüan styles, including a large silk hanging scroll in the archaic blue and green idiom, *Hsieh An and His Ladies in the Eastern Mountain* (*Hsieh An tung-shan t'u*), dated 1480 (Wango H. C. Weng collection), which follows a similar composition by Tai Chin.[27] Following in the tradition of the Su-chou painters, however, Shen, who was also renowned for his calligraphy in the Huang T'ing-chien

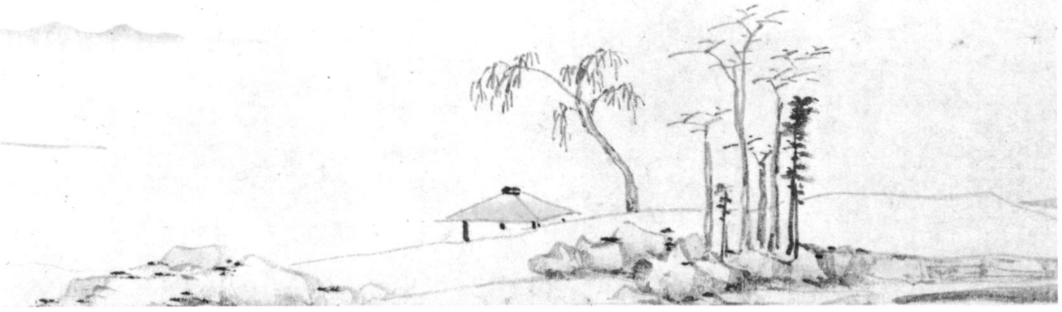

Fig. 131a. Shen Chou, detail, *Autumn Colors among Streams and Mountains* (*Ch'i-shan ch'iu-se*). Undated, ca. 1480. Handscroll, ink on paper. 19.8 x 640.2 cm (7¾ in. x 21 ft.). The Metropolitan Museum of Art, New York

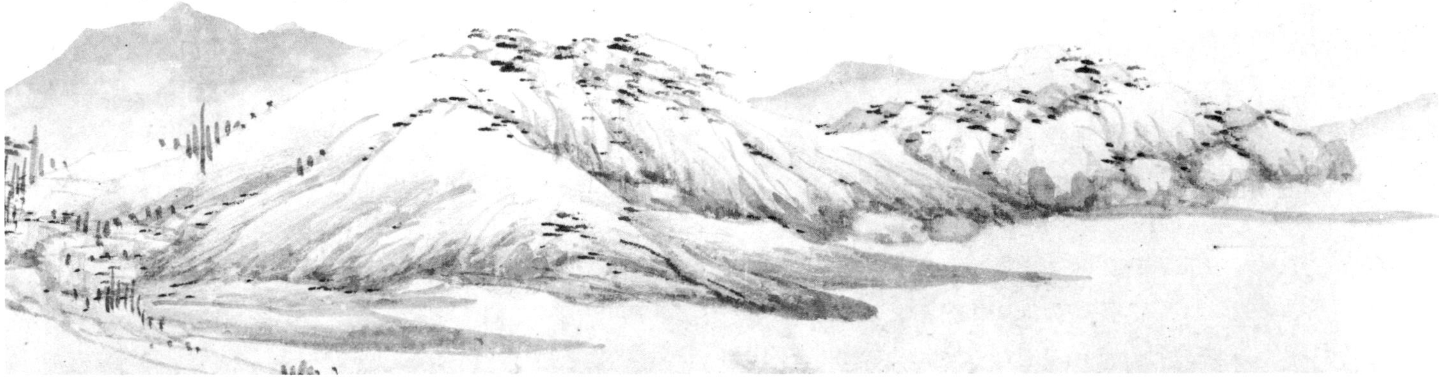

Fig. 131b. Shen Chou, detail, *Autumn Colors among Streams and Mountains*

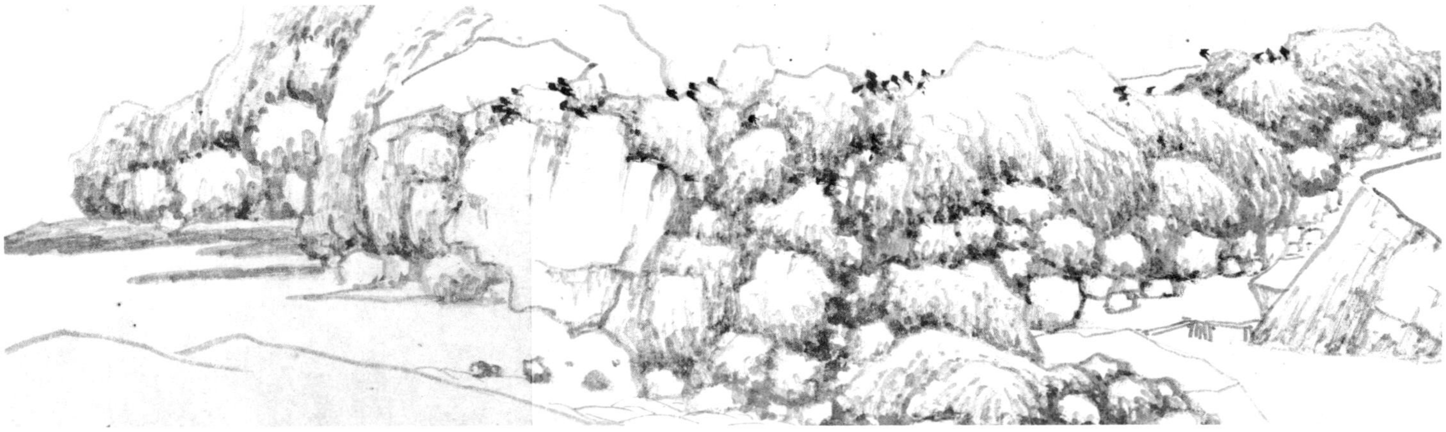

Fig. 131c. Shen Chou, detail, *Autumn Colors among Streams and Mountains*

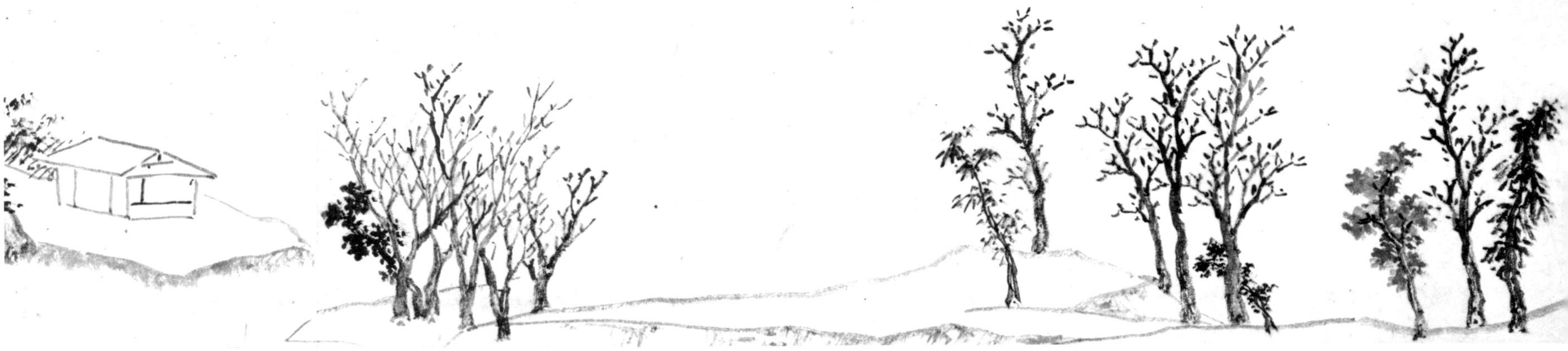

Fig. 131d. Shen Chou, detail, *Autumn Colors among Streams and Mountains*

style, was most comfortable with the calligraphic landscape idioms of the late Yüan masters.

In a long handscroll, *Autumn Colors among Streams and Mountains* (*Ch'i-shan ch'iu-se*), done about 1480, now in The Metropolitan Museum of Art, New York (figs. 131a–d), Shen explored four Yüan painters' landscape idioms—those of Ni Tsan, Huang Kung-wang, Wang Meng, and Wu Chen (1280–1354)—as related brush styles varying in expressive qualities; he moved from one to the next in rapid, smooth-flowing shifts. In a colophon appended to the handscroll Shen commented, "Ni Tsan's method is sparse [*lüeh*], but mine is complex [*fan*]. Yet though his method is sparse, his meaning is ample. This is why he is said to be inimitable."[28] Beginning with the familiar Ni Tsan motifs of sparse trees, barren rocks, and an empty pavilion (fig. 131a), Shen developed Ni's angular texture strokes (as seen in Wang Fu's *Remembering Ni Tsan's "Wu-t'ung Tree,"* dated 1408; cf. no. 13) into a more complex, longer texture pattern that reflects the style of Huang Kung-wang and an expansive shift in mood (fig. 131b). Then, turning his brushtip inward to form round, dense, curling, and stippling texture strokes, Shen created rock forms that contain the same controlled energy as those by Wang Meng (fig. 131c). Finally, in the last section of *Autumn Colors*, he used simple round brushstrokes to represent rolling shores and blunt and stubby trees, evoking the serene and melancholy mood of Wu Chen (fig. 131d). By practicing the different brush idioms of the Yüan painters one after another in the long handscroll format, Shen Chou succeeded in treating the theme of autumn mountains in a wide range of moods and interpretations. Similarly, in an album of twenty-two leaves, painted over a period of five years for a man named Chou Wei-te and completed in 1482 (now in the Chung-hsing-lu collection), Shen Chou used the album format to explore, develop, and expand on a full range of Sung and Yüan manners in a succession of individual but related compositions.[29]

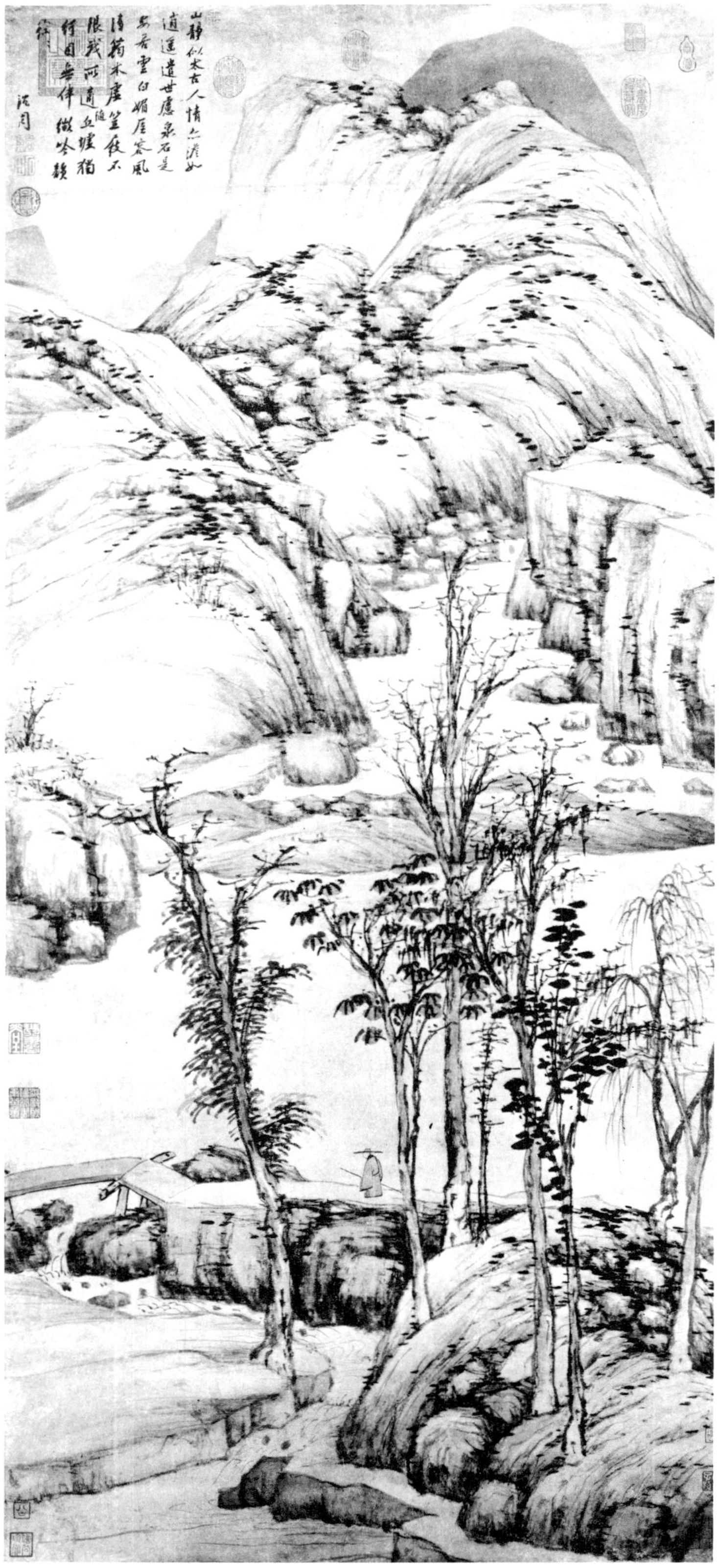

Fig. 132. Shen Chou, *Walking with a Staff* (*Ts'e-chang t'u*). Undated, ca. 1485. Hanging scroll, ink on paper. 159.1 x 72.2 cm (5 ft. 2⅝ in. x 28⅜ in.). National Palace Museum, Taipei

In an important hanging scroll in the National Palace Museum, Taipei, *Walking with a Staff* (*Ts'e-chang t'u*), painted about 1485 (fig. 132), Shen Chou used the Ni Tsan idiom to develop a poetic vision entirely his own. Though immediately recognizable as a work after Ni Tsan, the painting uses more than just Ni Tsan's brush method. Confronted with his need for a richer language to communicate his "meaning," Shen borrowed Huang Kung-wang's fuller hemp-skin texture pattern to re-create a quiet, seemingly austere landscape. Extending Wang Fu's ideas of formal interplay of brushstrokes and surface patterns (cf. no. 13),

Shen Chou treated individually realistic landscape forms in compositions made of carefully constructed contrasts and balances, in which brush patterns mirror, echo, and interlock. In comparing Shen Chou's *Walking with a Staff* with a composition by Ni Tsan, Jon Bourassa (1981) observed that "Shen's work is a balance of . . . parts which are held together more by artistic devices than through conformity to natural order."[30]

In the upper left corner of *Walking with a Staff*, Shen Chou inscribed a poem:

The mountain is quiescent as if in remote antiquity;
Man's feelings are tranquil and harmonious.
In blissful leisure, forgetting all worldly care,
I live peacefully among streams and rocks.
White clouds enhance the beautiful cliffs;
A fresh breeze sweeps through the empty bamboo and trees.
My sun hat and clogs do not restrain me
From exploring any hillocks and wild land—
Walking alone without a companion,
Lightly humming a poem, with a slow and gentle rhythm.

The poem and the painting describe perfectly the lifestyle and approach of Shen Chou, who depicted himself in the painting as gently reciting a verse while walking with a staff through serene mountain surroundings. Although there was no personal contact between Shen Chou and Ch'en Hsien-chang, who were exact contemporaries, Shen's painting parallels Ch'en's philosophical teaching. In imitating earlier styles, Shen did not copy, but instead depended on intuitive knowledge self-acquired through quiet meditation.

In an essay entitled "Night Vigil" ("Yeh-tso"), inscribed above a well-known painting of the same title, dated 1492 (now in the National Palace Museum, Taipei), Shen Chou wrote of waking one cold night, sitting quietly with a flickering lamp under a pale moon, and hearing sounds he had never heard before. He reflected that he had always sought knowledge through books, and had never achieved a state of outward quiescence [*wai-ching*] and inward repose [*nei-ting*], but that on that particular night he had "acquired sounds and colors through a quiescent and reposeful state of mind." Once possessed, these sounds had the effect of

> cleansing man's mind, spirit, and feelings, and helping him to express and realize his intent [*chih*] and meaning [*i*]. . . . Tonight's sounds and colors are no different from those of other nights, yet upon reaching my ears and eyes, they suddenly and wondrously become one [*ho*] with me. . . . When the sounds die down, and the colors disappear, my intent, brimming and overflowing, alone remains. What is this so-called intent? Is it, indeed, within me, or outside me? Is it found in external things, or is it expressed only when interacting with things? . . . Through mental fasting [*chai-hsin*] and sitting alone [*ku-tso*] by the light of a bright candle deep into the night, I must pursue the principles of affairs and things, as well as the wondrous workings of the mind and the body; by using this method for self-cultivation and responding [*ying*] to things, I shall surely acquire [*te*] understanding.[31]

Central to Shen Chou's beliefs, as to Ch'en Hsien-chang's, was the concept *te*, which means, as a verb, "to acquire," and, as a noun, "acquisition" or "insight." Instead of bookish knowledge or learning, Shen Chou sought intuitive response (*ying*) and understanding, when the mind becomes one (*ho*) with things; this intuitive approach applies to Shen's understanding of nature, as well as to his study of the ancient masters' brush styles. Ch'en Hsien-chang had spoken of *kan-ying*, impression and response; as explained by Jen Yu-wen (1970), Ch'en believed that "when the subjective mind is impressed or stimulated by objective phenomena, natural feelings are aroused and natural and proper responses are expressed."[32] Stimulated by the sounds and colors in a proper way, Shen Chou spoke of "expressing and realizing his intent and

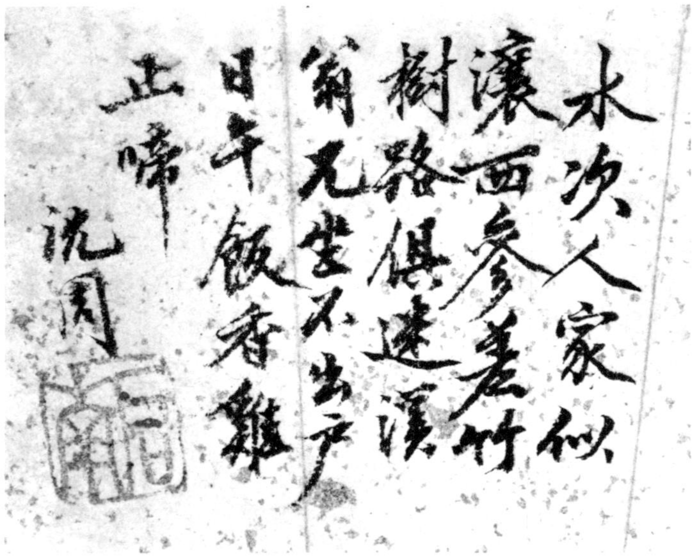

Fig. 133a. Shen Chou, detail of inscription, *Home by the Stream* (*Shui tz'u jen-chia*), no. 14A

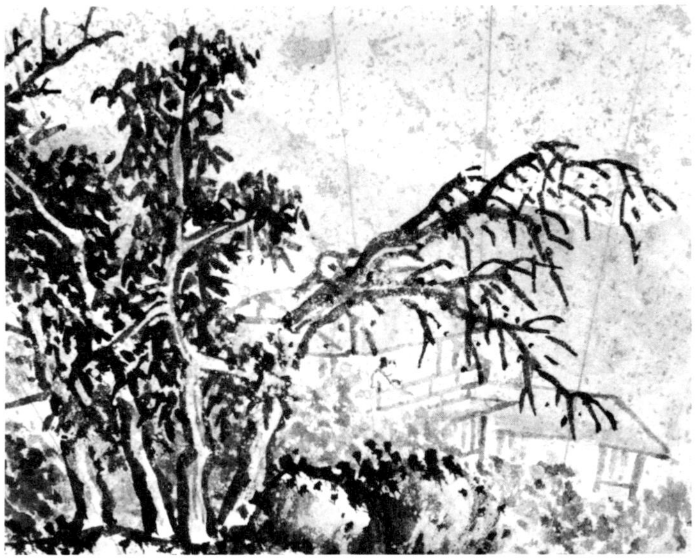

Fig. 133b. Shen Chou, detail, *Home by the Stream* (*Shui tz'u jen-chia*), no. 14A

meaning." The purpose of poetry and painting, for Shen Chou, was to "speak one's intent" (*yen-chih*). This intent is expressed only when it interacts with things through mental fasting and quiet meditation, as taught by the third-century B.C. mystic Chuang-tzu.[33] Ch'en Hsien-chang spoke of quiescence as a dynamic principle, a preparation for action. Shen Chou saw it as a means of acquiring understanding and of fully expressing his intent and meaning.

In *Walking with a Staff*, the mountain is "quiescent." Because the artist's feelings are "plain and harmonious," his drawing naturally expresses a quiet feeling. Even the bamboos and trees are described by the artist as empty or vacant (*hsü*), the precondition for receptiveness and creativity. James Cahill (1978) wrote, "Such drawing, rather than analyzing and defining the objects of the picture intellectually, from outside, seems to become the brush-equivalent of those objects, identical with them."[34] Sung painters sought nature in art; Shen Chou *became* nature in his painting.

The philosopher-artist's spirit of quiescence permeates every one of Shen's works. In a fan painting, *Home by the Stream* (*Shui-tz'u jen-chia*), painted about 1490, in the Edward L. Elliott Family Collection (no. 14A) Shen's inscription reads:

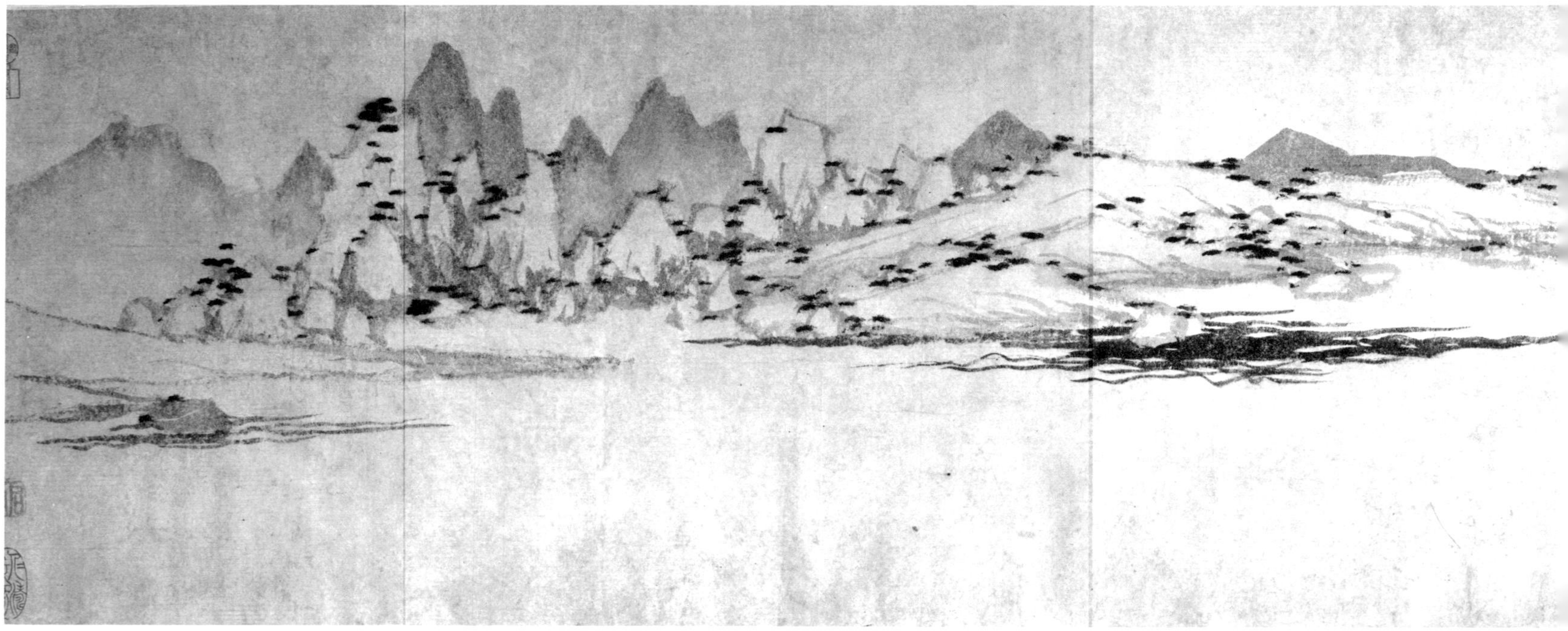

A home by the stream faces water flowing west,
Bamboos and trees, high and low, obscure mountain paths.
Watching the stream an old man sits, seldom leaving his door,
At noon he smells a delicious meal and hears the rooster crowing.

Just as the poem expresses total contentment, so is the painting a masterly lesson in compositional stability and repose. In the 1490s Shen Chou increasingly preferred the strong and firm brush idiom of Wu Chen, striving for utmost simplicity and clarity, and greater strength in surface design. Shen's trees (fig. 133a) resemble well-formed characters: individual brushstrokes in his painting, like those in his calligraphy (fig. 133b), which follows Huang T'ing-chien's style, reflecting Huang's precept of "driving every stroke with full force" (*pi-chung yung-li*).[35] Chiang Chao-shen (1976) links Shen's blunt and stiff brushwork with the Southern Sung–Che School tradition and sees it as evidence of Shen's effort to reconcile the Southern Sung and Yüan styles.[36] In the Princeton fan painting a strong, bare-branched tree occupies the center of the composition, bending over and sheltering the two-storied building in which the gentleman-scholar is seated. Resembling wrought-iron grillwork, the tree is done in round and blunt seal-script brushwork (cf. fig. 87). This and other trees, two of them covered with foliage done in short ax-cut strokes, all heavily brushed in dark ink, serve as a foil in the left-hand foreground. The stream in the right foreground runs diagonally to the left, into the distance. The interlocked diagonal shorelines are bounded and set off by the horizontal range of distant mountains, done in a smooth, light ink wash; three contrasting, dark patches of mountain peaks, closely hugging the light-colored mountain silhouette, stretch horizontally across the picture plane, further enhancing the stability of the composition.

In a handscroll *Saying Farewell: In the Style of Ni Tsan* (*Fang Yün-lin Sung-pieh*), painted about 1500, in The Art Museum, Princeton University (fig. 134), Shen Chou followed the Ni Tsan idiom once again. The broad river runs diagonally from lower left to upper right, separating the foreground in the lower right corner from the distant shoreline in the upper left. The Ni Tsan idiom is an ideal choice for the scene: in front is a cottage under some sparse trees; nearby two friends stand by the foreground shore bowing to each other to say farewell, while a small boat waits to ferry the traveler to some distant shore. Compared to Tai Chin's *Returning Late from a Spring Outing* (cf. fig. 126), Shen's painting has little descriptive content. As a more severe kind of imaginative triumph, the work shows landscape elements merely as brisk and impulsive brushwork, and it succeeds as no representational description can in conveying the extremes of

Fig. 134. Shen Chou, *Saying Farewell: In the Style of Ni Tsan* (*Fang Yün-lin Sung pieh*). Undated, ca. 1500. Handscroll, ink on paper. 163.0 x 29.0 cm (5 ft. 4 1/8 in. x 11 3/8 in.). The Art Museum, Princeton University

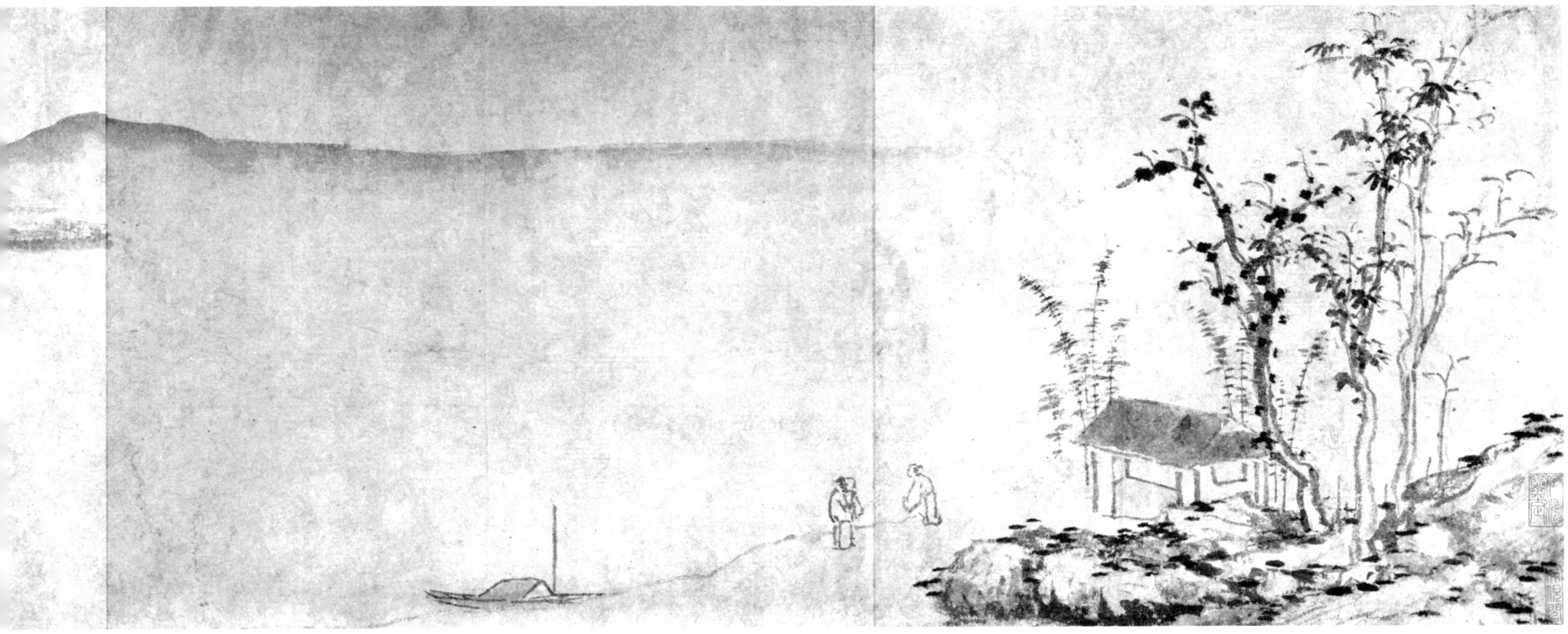

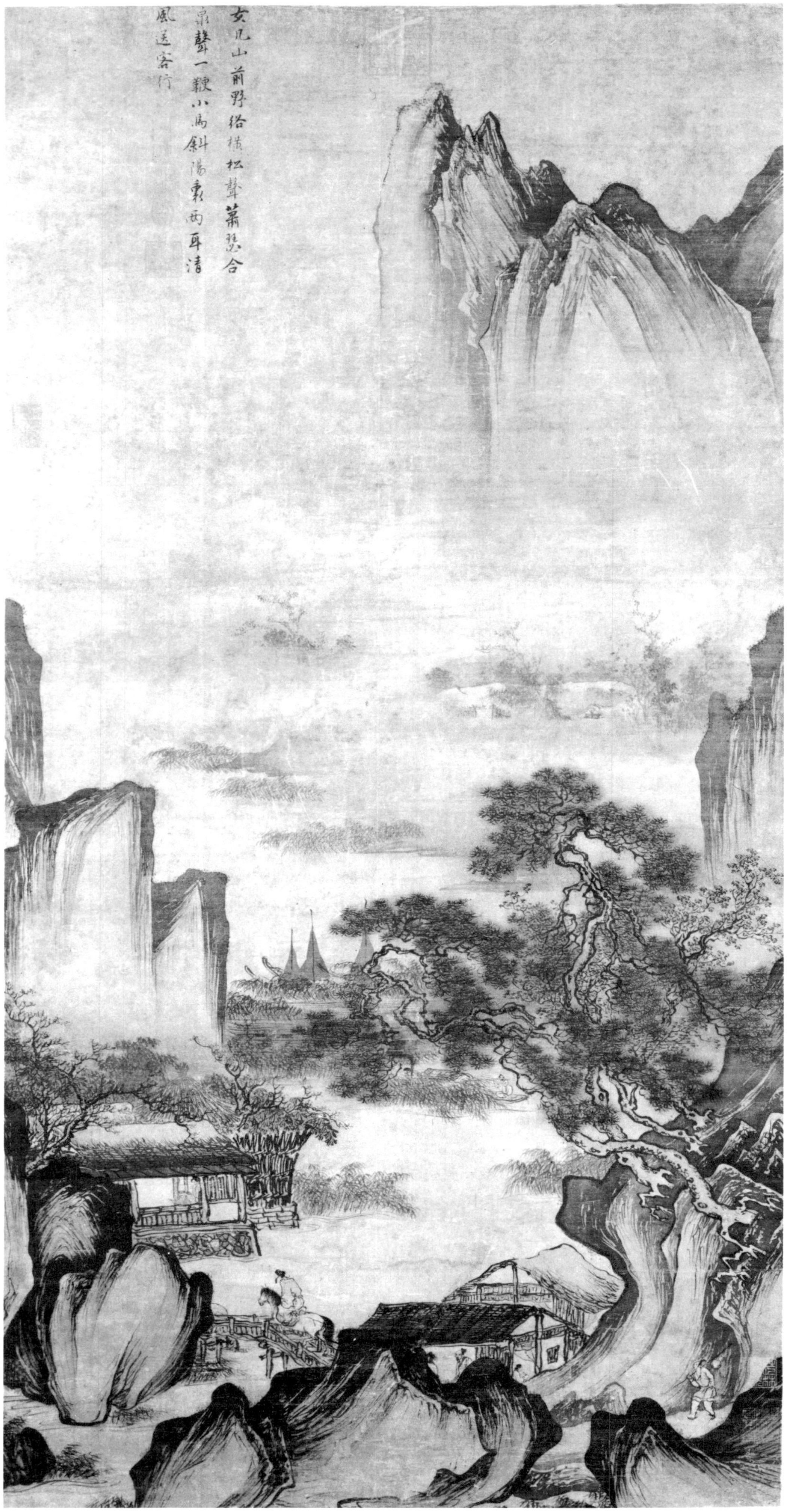

Fig. 135. T'ang Yin, *Seeing Off a Guest on a Mountain Path* (*Shan-lu sung-k'o*). Undated, ca. 1505–10. Hanging scroll, ink and light color on silk. 118.0 x 61.0 cm (3 ft. 10½ in. x 24 in.). The Art Museum, Princeton University

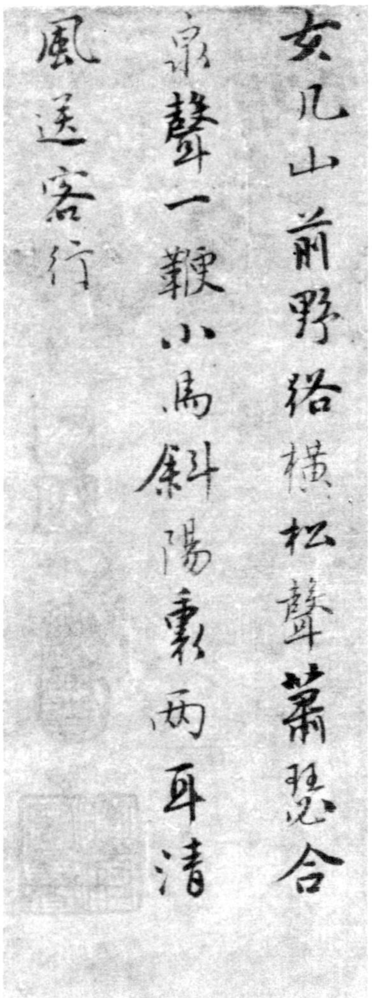


Fig. 135a. Detail of inscription, fig. 135

feeling—sorrow, regret, urgency, and delay—between two parting friends. Shen Chou enriches the sparse style of Ni Tsan with the long hemp-skin texture pattern of Huang Kung-wang, the dense and curling strokes of Wang Meng, and the round, stubby ones of Wu Chen. The outwardly quiet scenery bristles with powerful pincerlike brushstrokes, sprinkled dots, and ink dabs, all of which, applied with passion and speed, manifest control, precision, and ease. As a meditation on style, the painting displays Shen Chou's ability to achieve richness in sparseness, activity through quiescence. In "acquiring" and transforming the various brush idioms of the Yüan masters into his own style, he painted neither to please others nor merely to be stylish, but in quiet assertion of his natural unalienable selfhood.

## *A Professional Amateur*

Tai Chin and Shen Chou represent antithetical approaches to painting of the second half of the fifteenth century, Tai the professional and Shen amateur ideals. The two modes merged in the life and art of the early sixteenth-century Su-chou painter T'ang Yin (1470–1524).

Son of a merchant, T'ang Yin spent a profligate youth indulging in drinking and debauchery, but because of his literary talent was nevertheless befriended by Wen Lin (1445–1499), the father of Wen Cheng-ming, and other prominent scholars and officials in Su-chou. Placing first in the provincial examination in Nanking in 1498, he became involved in an examination scandal in the capital in the following year, thereby forfeiting forever an official career.[37] Disgraced and impoverished he turned to writing and painting for a living, and led the life of a dissolute artist. He is said to have started painting at the age of seventeen. His early works, influenced by Shen Chou, resemble those of the young Wen Cheng-ming, but later he studied under the leading Su-chou professional painter Chou Ch'en (ca. 1450–1535). In his popular paintings of beautiful women, T'ang Yin was also influenced by such professional painters as Wu Wei (1459–1508) and Tu Chin (fl. ca. 1465–1500), whom he met in Nanking in 1498.[38] T'ang Yin died in 1524.

Fig. 135b. Detail, fig. 135

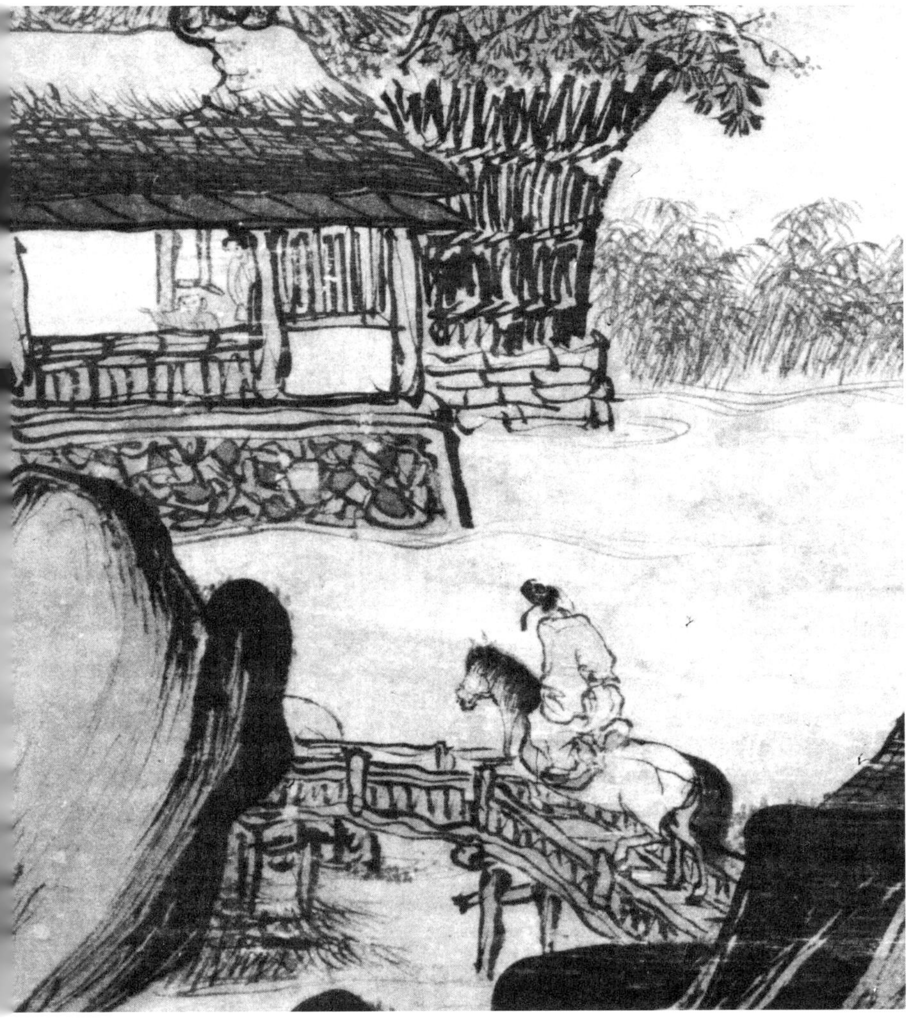

A silk hanging scroll, *Seeing Off a Guest on a Mountain Path* (*Shan-lu sung-k'o*), in the DuBois Schanck Morris collection in The Art Museum, Princeton University, bears an old attribution to the late Northern Sung master Li T'ang (fig. 135). The false attribution was based on a questionable cipher by the Sung emperor Hui-tsung, as well as fake imperial seals of the Hsüan-ho (1119–25) and Shao-hsing (1131–62) eras. Shen C. Y. Fu has identified this painting as a genuine work by T'ang Yin.[39] The composition, previously known by a typical Sung title, *Travelers among Streams and Mountains* (*Ch'i-shan hsing-lü t'u*), has been renamed, according to the sense of the poem, and is inscribed at the top with a poem (fig. 135a):

> In front of Mount Nü-chi, traversed by
> wild paths,
> The sound of whispering pines mixes with that
> of a waterfall.
> Striking his pony once, he rides into the sunset.
> With wind in my ears, I see my guest on his way.

The elegant calligraphy, which is executed in the square running-script style of Yen Chen-ch'ing (709–785; cf. fig. 69), though not signed, is clearly from T'ang Yin's hand; it compares closely with T'ang's *Odes to Fallen Flowers* (*Lo-hua shih*), dated about 1505, in the John B. Elliott Collection at Princeton (cf. no. 20). According to Chiang Chao-shen's study of T'ang Yin's life and art (1976), after T'ang returned home from disgrace in Peking in 1499—when he was about thirty—he worked vigorously in Chou Ch'en's Southern Sung Academy idiom, while writing his calligraphy in the square and level manner of Yen Chen-ch'ing, until about 1506, when he was about thirty-seven, when he switched his writing style to the more elongated, diagonal manner of Li Yung (678–747; cf. fig. 93).[40] In *Seeing Off a Guest*, which can be dated to about 1505–10, cottages at the mouth of a mountain inlet overlook a shallow bay; two men, a woman, and a child stand at the windows watching a guest riding off over a bridge; above the cottages great pine trees lean over the side of a cliff on the right; fishing boats rest at anchor in the bay; and, beyond the distant shoreline, silhouettes of other cottages are faintly visible under a tall mountain largely obliterated by mist. The painting, done in the Li T'ang–Hsia Kuei ink-wash style, is a romantic evocation of the monumental Sung landscape tradition.

A similar composition by T'ang Yin is seen in a painting, in the Shanghai Museum, entitled *Spring Visit to Mount Nü-chi* (*Ch'un-yu Nü-chi-shan*; fig. 136), which is the first of a superb series of four scrolls representing landscapes of the four seasons.[41] On the painting, T'ang's signed poem (fig. 136a), in calligraphy closely resembling that on the Princeton scroll, reads:

> Spring snow atop Mount Nü-chi is melting;
> Tender branches sprout from the roadside apricot trees.
> As I promised to visit here on this day,
> I carry my wine and my lute over a rustic bridge.

T'ang Yin wrote easily and was said to have turned out reams of poems, often playful in tone and sprinkled with lively colloquial expressions. But here he borrowed an old poem, attributed to the T'ang poet Yang Shih-e (*chin-shih*, 785), and found in Kuo Hsi's *Lofty Aims in Forests and Streams* (*Lin-ch'üan kao-chih chi*). Yang's original poem, as recorded by Kuo Hsi's son Kuo Ssu, is entitled, "Looking at Mount Nü-chi" ("Wang Nü-chi-shan"), and it reads:

> Spring snow atop Mount Nü-chi is melting;
> Tender branches sprout from the roadside apricot trees.
> I wish to visit there, yet do not know when;
> Looking at it in vexation, I turn my carriage around at a rustic bridge.[42]

This adaptive type of poetic borrowing illustrates T'ang Yin's working method. Located in Honan in northern China, Mount Nü-chi was probably no more than a name to T'ang Yin, yet a series of monumental compositions by him, of which the Shanghai and Princeton paintings are the earliest extant examples, bear poetic inscriptions specifically referring to it. Apparently T'ang's inspiration for this theme was Kuo Hsi's treatise on painting, in which the author credits Yang Shih-e's poem "Looking at Mount Nü-chi" as one of the many ancient verses that inspired his paintings. In re-creating a monumental landscape composition in the Northern Sung grand manner, T'ang appropriately found his inspiration in a poem that had stirred a Northern Sung master, rather than referring to a poem of his own. Yet he rewrote the second half of the poem, redirecting the mood from quiet contemplation to active participation, thereby providing a strong narrative focus—similar to that of Tai Chin's *Returning Late from a Spring Outing* (cf. fig. 126). A clearly defined story line was apparently important to art patrons of his time. Thus, while Yang Shih-e's poem voices the wistful sentiment "I wish to visit there, yet do not know when; / Looking at [the mountain] in vexation, I turn my carriage around at a rustic bridge," T'ang Yin's verse pledges the more specific promise "to visit here on this day," and the painting pictures his spring visitor followed by his servant carrying wine and his lute over a rustic bridge.

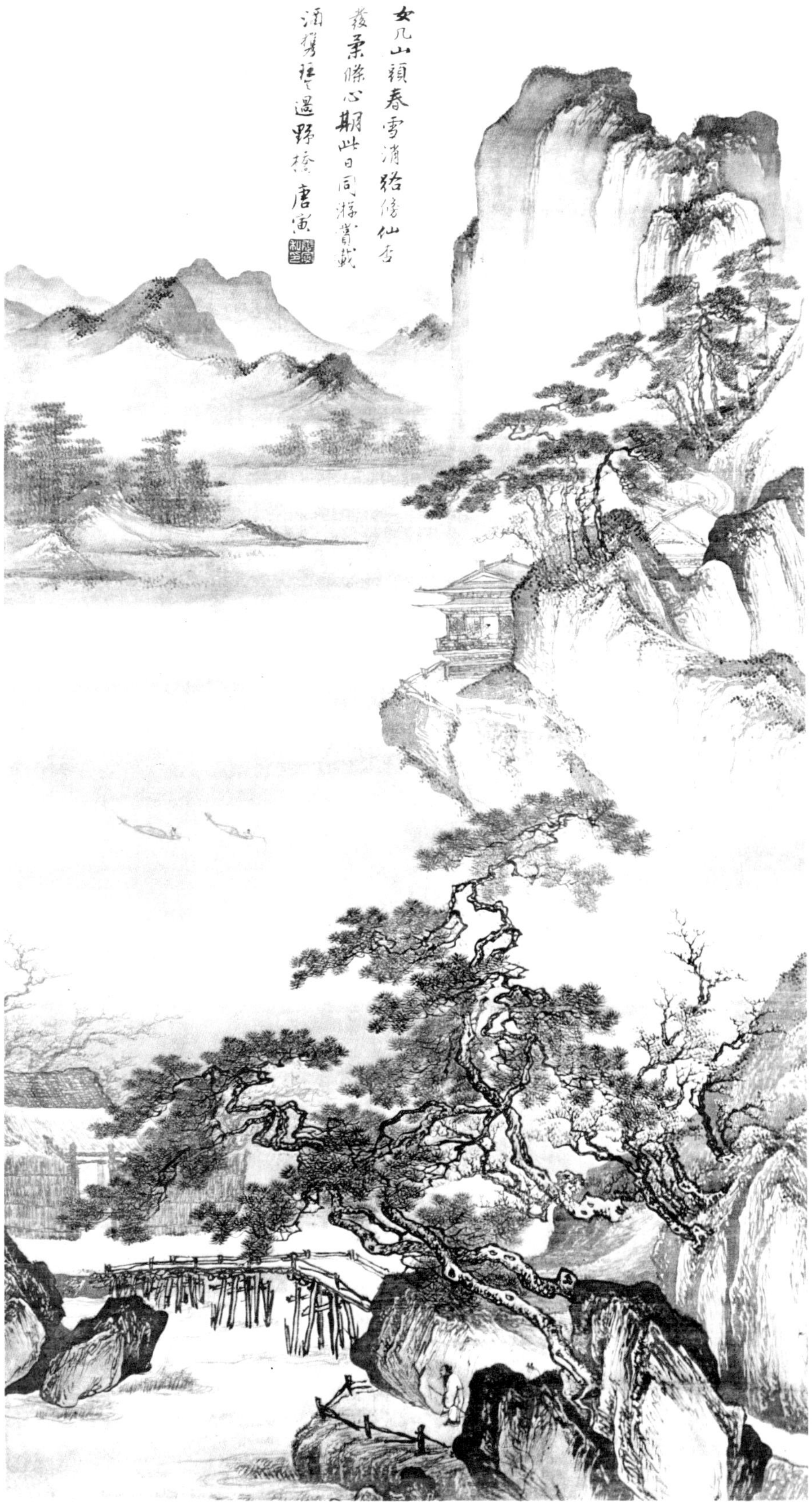

Fig. 136. T'ang Yin, *Spring Visit to Mount Nü-chi* (*Ch'un-yu Nü-chi-shan*). Undated, ca. 1505. Hanging scroll, ink and colors on silk. Shanghai Museum

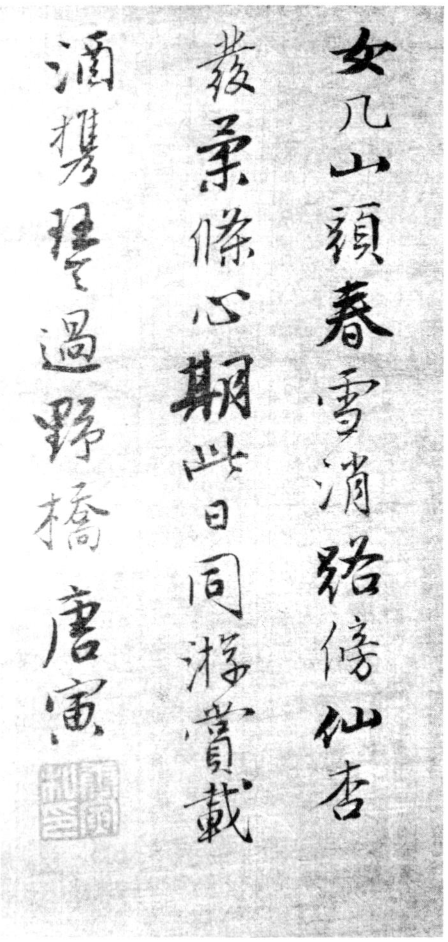


Fig. 136a. Detail of inscription, fig. 136

In *Spring Visit*, T'ang repeats a V-shaped mountain motif three times along the right-hand border. As the first of a series of four scrolls (meant to be hung from right to left), this composition, with its heavily weighted right side, is followed by one weighted on the left side, which has boulders ringing the lower edge on three sides of the composition; the third scroll shows a pond in the foreground and boulders ranging across the middle of the picture, and is followed by the final, winter scene, representing a snowy peak, in the Fan K'uan (ca. 960–1030) idiom, rising in a straight vertical plane in the left half of the painting.[43]

*Seeing Off a Guest* was clearly painted after *Spring Visit*. The artist repeated the magnificent group of pine trees as the dominant motif (fig. 135b), but rearranged the landscape elements: scallop-shaped boulders now ring the lower edges of the picture, and the cottages and the "rustic bridge" are made to follow the circular edge of the bay in the foreground, while faraway mountains, half hidden in the mist in the upper right corner, circle back into view on the opposite side. In thus clarifying and further developing the monumental composition, T'ang Yin established a poetic theme with Mount Nü-chi as the subject matter. Setting the scene with the first two lines, "In front of Mount Nü-chi, traversed by wild paths, / The sound of whispering pines mixes with that of a waterfall," his poem goes on to describe the activities depicted in his painting.

In *Whispering Pines on a Mountain Path* (*Shan-lu sung-sheng*; in the National Palace Museum, Taipei), which according to Chiang Chao-shen may be dated to 1516 (fig. 137), T'ang Yin continues with the Mount Nü-chi theme:

> In front of Mount Nü-chi, traversed by wild paths,
> The sound of the whispering pines harmonizes closely with that of the waterfall.
> As I listen quietly with total attention,
> I feel the spirit of Tao rising within me.

In this imposing composition, T'ang combines elements from *Spring Visit* and *Seeing Off a Guest*: the foreground boulders stand away from the lower border to form a more tightly knit mass in the middle distance; the great pine trees now grow from the left; and the earlier V-shaped mountain motif has become a commanding central massif, reminiscent of the great central peaks found in the Northern Sung landscapes by Fan K'uan (cf. fig. 48) and Li T'ang (cf. fig. 50).

Clearly, what distinguishes T'ang Yin from the common professional painter is his ability to exploit fully the formal and expressive potential of his paintings. When Chou Ch'en, T'ang's teacher, was asked why his art was not the equal of his pupil's, Chou replied, "Compared to Master T'ang, I lack only a few thousand volumes of books."[44] Such a statement, though perhaps apocryphal, reaffirms the accepted notion that fine art, as a product of learning, belonged to the privileged domain of a scholar. With its technical virtuosity, T'ang Yin's painting has a visual impact that never fails to amaze and impress; combined with his poetry, it conveys a spirit that is engaging and fun-loving, yet often deeply melancholy.

In technical brilliance and lightninglike intelligence, T'ang Yin had no equal. In mastering the ancient brush idioms, he pushed the resources of painting to their natural limits—and beyond. The secret of his extraordinarily versatile brushwork lies in his training in calligraphy, particularly in the fluid, running script style of Li Yung, which he favored in his later years. His brushstrokes move like quicksilver and bursts of flame, spinning out densely intertwining tree branches; turning angular, ax-cut beginnings into thin, round, and wet hemp-fiber strokes; and freely juxtaposing scribbled wire-mesh patterns with flat ink-wash areas. His ink technique has a deeply sensuous quality: rich charcoal blackness is daringly contrasted with an abundance of silky transparent gray. The effective use of languid ink wash heightens the dynamic energy of his brushwork. In *Traveling by Donkey with Poetic Thoughts* (*Ch'i-lü shih-i*), in the Shanghai Museum (fig. 138), although the landscape forms nearly fill the composition, the painting, because of the contrasting use of ink tones, does not look full. The mountains almost seem to rock and sway in sympathy with the emotion of the poem, which expresses the grief and desperation of a poverty-stricken, failed scholar:

> Failing despite my begging, I bundle up my books and return home,
> Riding a mule again up the blue hills.
> My face covered with wind, frost, and dust,
> I meet my country wife, dressed in straw.

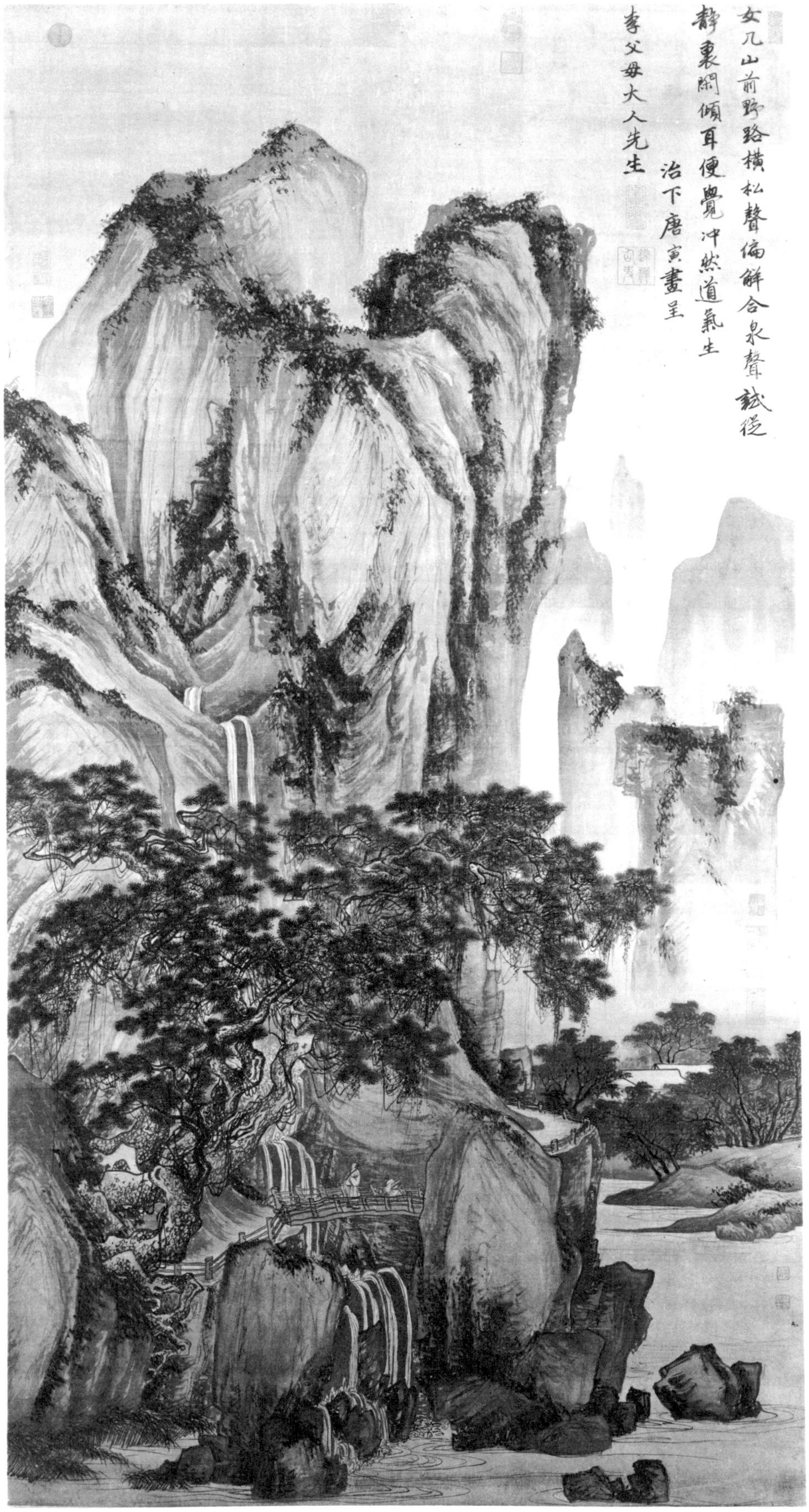


Fig. 137. T'ang Yin, *Whispering Pines on a Mountain Path* (*Shan-lu sung-sheng*). Undated, ca. 1516. Hanging scroll, ink and light color on silk. 194.5 x 102.8 cm (6 ft. 4 5/8 in. x 3 ft. 4 1/2 in.). National Palace Museum, Taipei

Every element of this painting—brushwork, contrasting ink tones, and composition—has been carried to an expressive extreme, yet such excesses are essential to T'ang Yin's style. The work seems to stand, as the artist often did in life, on the very edge of decorum, hanging precariously only to be saved from glib theatricality at the last moment by intensity and sincerity of emotion and an infallible sense of style and elegance.

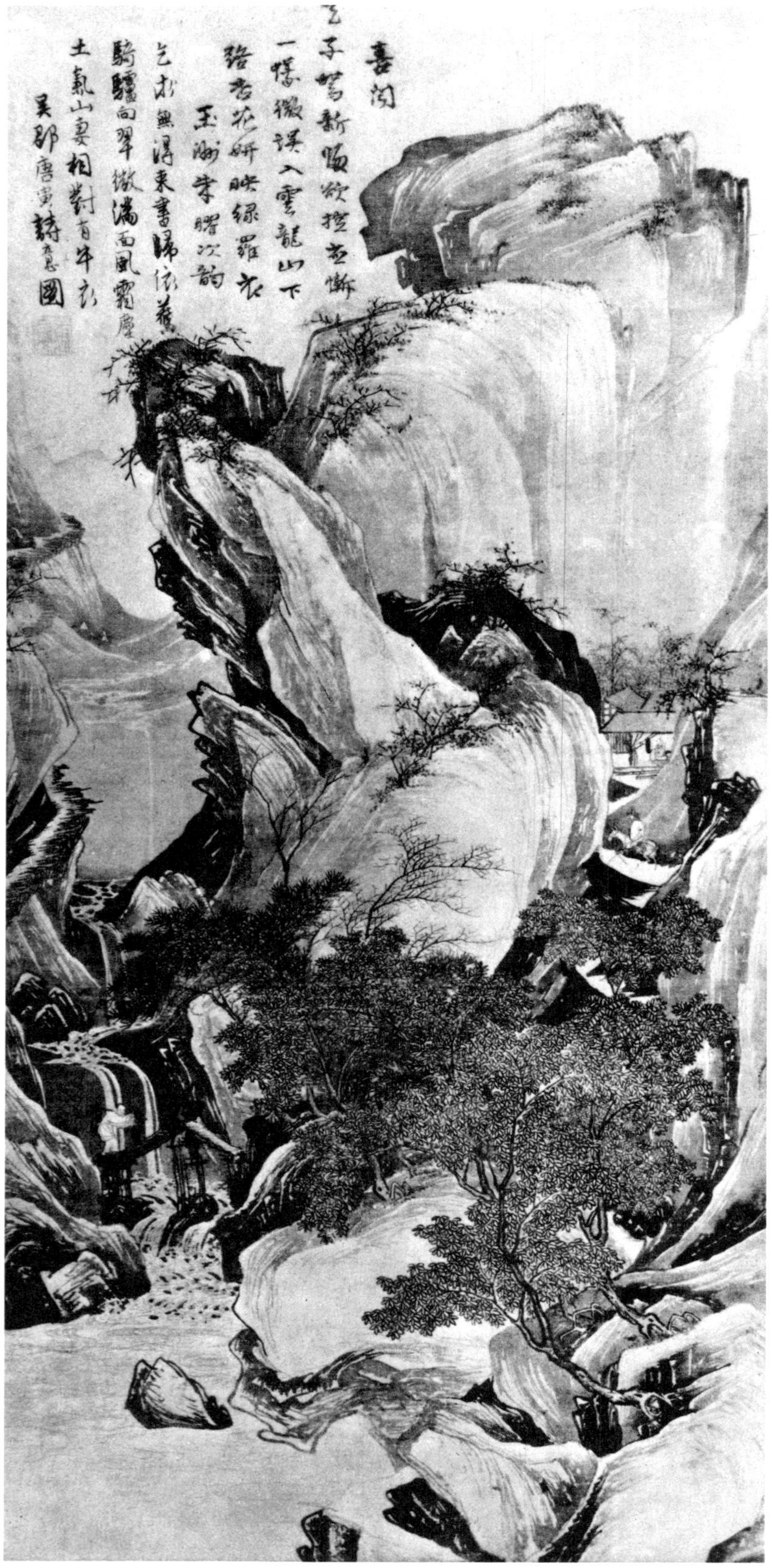

Fig. 138. T'ang Yin, *Traveling by Donkey with Poetic Thoughts* (*Ch'i-lü shih-i*). Undated, ca. 1510. Hanging scroll, ink on paper. Shanghai Museum

## *Painting Criticism: Toward a Synthesis*

Painting criticism, which flourished after the mid-Ming period, followed closely the development in Ming literary criticism. From the beginning of the dynasty to the end of the Ch'eng-hua era (1465–87), poetry and prose writing continued in the Sung and Yüan traditions. At the beginning of the sixteenth century, a time of peace and prosperity, Emperor Ming Hsiao-tsung (Hung-chih, r. 1488–1506) ruled as perhaps the most humane of the Ming emperors. Hung-chih's senior grand secretary Li Tung-yang (1447–1516), a leading poet and calligrapher, dominated the literary world by sponsoring a generation of younger literary talents. One of these followers, Li Meng-yang (1427–1529), a close friend of Wang Shou-jen's, became the leader of the literary revival (*fu-ku*) movement that swept the country in the early years of the sixteenth century.

Protesting against the ornate style in contemporary poetry and the so-called examination hall style (*t'ai-ko t'i*) in prose writing, Li Meng-yang argued that the proper model for prose should be the high prose style of the Ch'in and Han dynasties and for poetry the style of the High T'ang. Li took up the ideas of the Southern Sung critic Yen Yü (1180–1235), who, in comparing poetry with Ch'an Buddhism, spoke of sudden enlightenment (*tun-wu*) and of following the primary principle (*ti-i i*)—or the Great Vehicle (Mahayana)—which Yen compared to the poetry of the Han, Wei, Tsin, and High T'ang.[45] For Li Meng-yang the choice of the right models, like that of the primary principle, was simply a matter of setting for oneself the highest possible standards.

In discussing the problem of following models, Li stressed the importance of methods: "In the creations of the ancient master builders . . . every hall was different, and every door was not alike; yet in executing the square and the circle, no one could avoid using the ruler and the compass. . . . The ruler and the compass represent the methods [*fa*]." By "methods" Li had meant fundamental standards, rather than techniques and styles. While styles may change, standards can never be abandoned: "If someone can do without the ruler and the compass, he must still be able to execute the square and the circle, then he may forget about [the ruler and the compass]."

As the leader of the early seven masters (*ch'ien-ch'i-tzu*)—beside Li the others were Ho Ching-ming (1483–1521), Hsü Chen-ch'ing (1479–1511), Pien Kung (1476–1532), K'ang Hai (1475–1540), Wang T'ing-hsiang (1474–1544), and Wang Chiu-ssu (fl. ca. 1508)—Li Meng-yang saw the imitation of ancient models as taking place in a dualistic—indeed paradoxical—situation of continuity and change:

> [The great buildings of the past] were sometimes huge, sometimes grand and solitary, sometimes ornate, and sometimes remote and lonely. . . . Yet large or small, they never failed to conform to [the rules of] the square and the circle. . . . As long as they shared these common rules, [different works] could be individually lonely or remote, ornate or grand, or solitary or huge. After staying the same for a while, [the forms] began to shift and change, turning into [different styles]. . . . Such is the essence of transformation [ *pien-hua*]. Thus, without any attempt to adhere to the same methods, these same methods shall prevail; and without any attempt to be different, everyone shall speak in a different manner.[46]

Under the influence of the Neo-Confucian School of the Mind, the revivalists agreed that the "truth" of an ancient master was discovered only in one's own mind. By the second half of the sixteenth century, when Wang Shih-chen (1526–1590) succeeded Li Meng-yang and Li P'an-lung (1514–1570) as the leader of literary society—Li P'an-lung and Wang Shih-chen were among the later seven masters (*hou-ch'i-tzu*)—it was commonly accepted that the proper way to imitate was through individual transformation ( *pien*). To achieve correspondence (*ho*) with an ancient model, one must first learn departure (*li*) from it, or as Wang Shih-chen explained,

> If one's own method corresponds [*ho*; with the ancient method], one must try his best to express himself; if one's method departs [*li*; from the ancient method], one must concentrate on returning [to the ancient method]. When there is departure in correspondence, and correspondence in departure, one will then attain enlightenment [*wu*].[47]

Toward the end of the sixteenth century, during the Wan-li era (1573–1619), the revivalist doctrine of the later seven masters was vigorously attacked by antirevivalists led by the Yüan brothers of the Kung-an (Hunan) School. The Yüan brothers were not only great admirers of the paramount individualist Li Chih

(1527–1602), who had advocated the truth (*chen*) of the "childlike mind" (*t'ung-hsin*) uncontaminated by learning, but were also profoundly interested in the vernacular literature of popular theater and novels. Arguing that the truth of literature lies in the newness of "transformation," Yüan Hung-tao (1568–1610) pointed out that "there is no literature that survives a hundred years without change. As there are originators, there will be those at the end of a stream, and because of those at the end of a stream, there will again be originators." Rather than seeing change as a way to return to the old, Yüan insisted on change in order to be "true" to oneself: "If my face cannot resemble your face, how can I make it resemble some ancient master's face?" In other words, he concluded, "an able painter follows things [in nature], not people; an able scholar follows his own mind, not the Tao [of some ancient sages]; an able poet follows the myriad phenomena around him, not some earlier poet."[48]

Throughout the fifteenth century Ming painters had continued in the Sung and Yüan landscape styles without much theoretical discussion. While the Painting Academy and Che (Hang-chou) School professional painters worked proficiently in the Southern Sung ink-wash tradition, bringing new triumphs of realism, monumentality, and craftsmanlike perfection to their works, the amateur painters of the Wu (Su-chou) School carried on the calligraphic brush tradition of the late Yüan recluse-painters of that region, cultivating restraint and naturalness in their art as valuable qualities of the scholar and gentleman.

Although the professional and the amateur painters followed different earlier models, no overt preference for one set of ancient styles over another had been expressed by writers before the middle of the sixteenth century. In a poem describing how he "tried to follow the strengths of many recent painters [of the early Ming] as well as the ancient masters," Tu Ch'iung (1397–1474), a Su-chou scholar-painter and an older contemporary of Shen Chou's, contrasted Wang Wei's (699–759) ink-wash painting with the gold and green style of the two Lis: Li Ssu-hsün (651–716) and his son Li Chao-tao (fl. ca. 670–730). While pointing out that "Ma [Yüan] and Hsia [Kuei] had formed their own stiff and hard manner, quite different from the [strange and eccentric] school [of Mi Fu and Mi Yu-jen (1072–1151)]," and placing all the Yüan painters he named in Wang Wei's school, Tu mentioned, along with Wang Wei and the Mi tradition, a number of Northern and Southern Sung painters—Ching Hao (fl. ca. 870–930), Kuan T'ung (fl. ca. 907–23), Kuo Chung-shu (ca. 910–977), Tung Yüan (fl. 937–76), Chü-jan (fl. ca. 960–80), Wang Shen (1036–after 1089), Li T'ang, and Yen Tzu-p'ing (fl. ca. 1164–81)—whose stylistic lineages Tu did not attempt to classify definitively.

While the calligraphic styles of the four great masters of the late Yüan—Huang Kung-wang, Wu Chen, Ni Tsan, and Wang Meng—could be demonstrably related to Tung Yüan's hemp-fiber texture strokes, it was neither easy to characterize all other Northern Sung painters by definite texture patterns nor possible to trace simple lineages among them. Unlike the poetry critics, who could point to the works of a single period, the High T'ang, as the ideal model or primary principle that embodied all the methods and rules, the painting critics could use neither Sung nor Yüan painting as their exclusive model; instead they had to follow one theoretical tradition, which they called the Southern School, that might be proven to be superior to all others.

By the middle of the sixteenth century, painting criticism was enlivened by rival opinions championing respectively for the professional and the amateur schools of painters. In 1545 Li K'ai-hsien (1502–1568), a scholar, dramatist, poet, and a northerner, from Shantung, wrote *Painting Classifications of the Chung-lu Academy* (*Chung-lu hua-p'in*), in which Tai Chin was placed in the first rank while Shen Chou was relegated to the fourth (out of six).[49] In his *History of Painting in the Wu Prefecture during Our Illustrious [Ming] Dynasty* (*Kuo-ch'ao Wu-chün tan-ch'ing chih*; preface dated 1563), Wang Chih-teng (1535–1612), a native of Su-chou, rated Shen Chou as the principal artist in the divine class and Wen Cheng-ming in the excellent class.[50] Ho Liang-chun (1506–1573), another Wu scholar from Hua-t'ing, Kiangsu, and author of *Painting Discussions at the Four Friends' Studio* (*Ssu-yu-chai hua-lun*; completed in the 1560s), viewed Tai Chin as "the best among the professional painters," but, as a professional, somehow "limited by his personal qualities." Ho saw as the "correct," or Orthodox, tradition (*cheng-mo*) the succession of painting styles from the Northern Sung masters through Chao Meng-fu (1254–1322), Kao K'o-kung, and the four great masters of the late Yüan, to Shen Chou and Wen Cheng-ming, namely the Wu School.[51]

At the end of the sixteenth century, another scholar-artist from Hua-t'ing, Mo Shih-lung (ca. 1538–1587), a friend and older fellow townsman of Tung Ch'i-ch'ang's (1555–1636), began to apply lessons of Ch'an Buddhism to the study of painting. By analogy to Ch'an Buddhism, which was divided into a Southern and a Northern School, respectively representing the "sudden awakening" (*tun-wu*) and "gradual awakening" (*chien-wu*) approaches to enlightenment, Mo Shih-lung suggested that landscape painting could also be divided into Southern and Northern Schools—the Southern made up of scholar-painters who "entered the land of Tathagata Buddha in a single leap," the Northern by professional painters who "became Bodhisattvas only after a long and meritorious record of hardship."[52] Tung Ch'i-ch'ang began to sort out the problem, accepting Tu Ch'iung's and Ho Liang-chun's list of "correct" painters as the Southern School:

> In Ch'an Buddhism there is a Southern and a Northern School, which first separated in the T'ang period; in painting a similar division into a Southern and a Northern School also appeared in the T'ang period. But the people involved were not divided between southerners and northerners. The Northern School followed Li Ssu-hsün, father and son, who painted landscapes with colors; their manner was transmitted in the Sung period by Chao Kan (fl. ca. 961–76), Chao Po-chü [fl. ca. 1120–62], [Chao] Po-su down to Ma [Yüan], Hsia [Kuei], and others. The Southern School began with Wang Mo-chieh [Wang Wei], who first used a light ink-wash technique, transforming the outline method; it was transmitted by Chang Ts'ao (late 8th century), Ching [Hao], Kuan [T'ung], Tung [Yüan], Chü[-jan], Kuo Chung-shu, Mi father and son [Mi Fu and Mi Yu-jen], down to the four great masters of the Yüan. . . .[53]

Although the "Southern School" theory, as such, was incomplete (it did not deal fully with Li Ch'eng and Fan K'uan), illogical (it did not refer to a Southern style of painting), and historically without justification (therefore meaningless), it nevertheless provided the painters with a brilliant focus and a well-defined approach. Tung's message was plain: if a painter were only to stress "sudden awakening" by following the Southern School tradition of Tung Yüan, Chü-jan, and the four Yüan masters, his painting would naturally be truthful and life-enhancing.[54]

For the scholar-painters "sudden awakening" had long meant awakening to the ancient methods. In their heated polemics against professional painters of the Che School, the issue that most troubled the scholars was neither the difference in their respective models, nor the social status of the professional painter, but a wild, seemingly pretentious and uncontrolled approach in some of the middle and late Ming professional painting. Beginning in the late fifteenth century, a number of painters, inspired by Taoist ideas of freedom and individuality, had adopted the words *k'uang* ("wild" or "crazy") and *ch'ih* ("foolish" or "stupid") as parts of their artistic names. Shih Chung (Hsü Tuan-pen; 1437–ca. 1520), a musician and painter born in Nanking, called himself Ch'ih-weng, "Old Fool." On *Bare Trees and Rocks* (*K'u-mu shih t'u*), dated 1506, in the Edward L. Elliott Family Collection at The Art Museum, Princeton University (no. 17), the artist wrote:

> Old Fool freely lets his brush write forests and streams,
> A useless failure now in his seventieth year.
> He has experienced all the [romantic] moonlight in snow and flowers in the breeze.
> In old age he is too poor to buy more flowers.

Outwardly a dullard (he reportedly did not learn to talk until he was seventeen), Shih Chung did not pursue an official career, and he disguised his personal disappointments and sorrows with drinking, and "wild" and

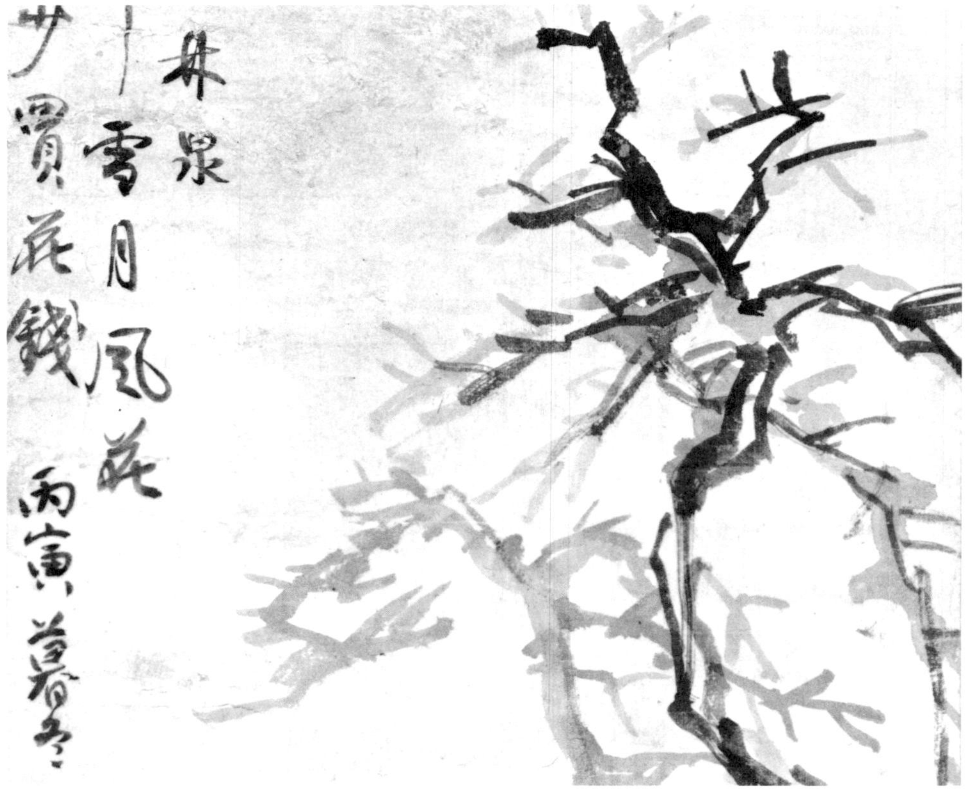


Fig. 139. Shih Chung, detail, *Bare Trees and Rocks* (*K'u-mu shih t'u*), no. 17

"foolish" behavior. In both calligraphy and painting, Shih's rough and unkempt brushwork (fig. 139), reflecting a stubborn, nonconformist personality, closely parallels Ch'en Hsien-chang's blunt and "natural" calligraphic style (cf. no. 16): individual brushstrokes, simple, direct, and unmodulated, enter and exit, twist and turn in an abrupt, insolent manner in both artists' works. Shih's unbridled vitality contrasts sharply with the manner of his contemporary Shen Chou (cf. figs. 133a, b), a model of cultured strength, civility, and balance. Yet Shih Chung, a talented poet and songwriter, was acquainted with Shen Chou, and the literary and artistic establishment accepted his eccentricities as a recognized form of nonconformity, the reverse side—even the necessary counterpart—of Confucian probity and earnest pursuit for truth. Shih

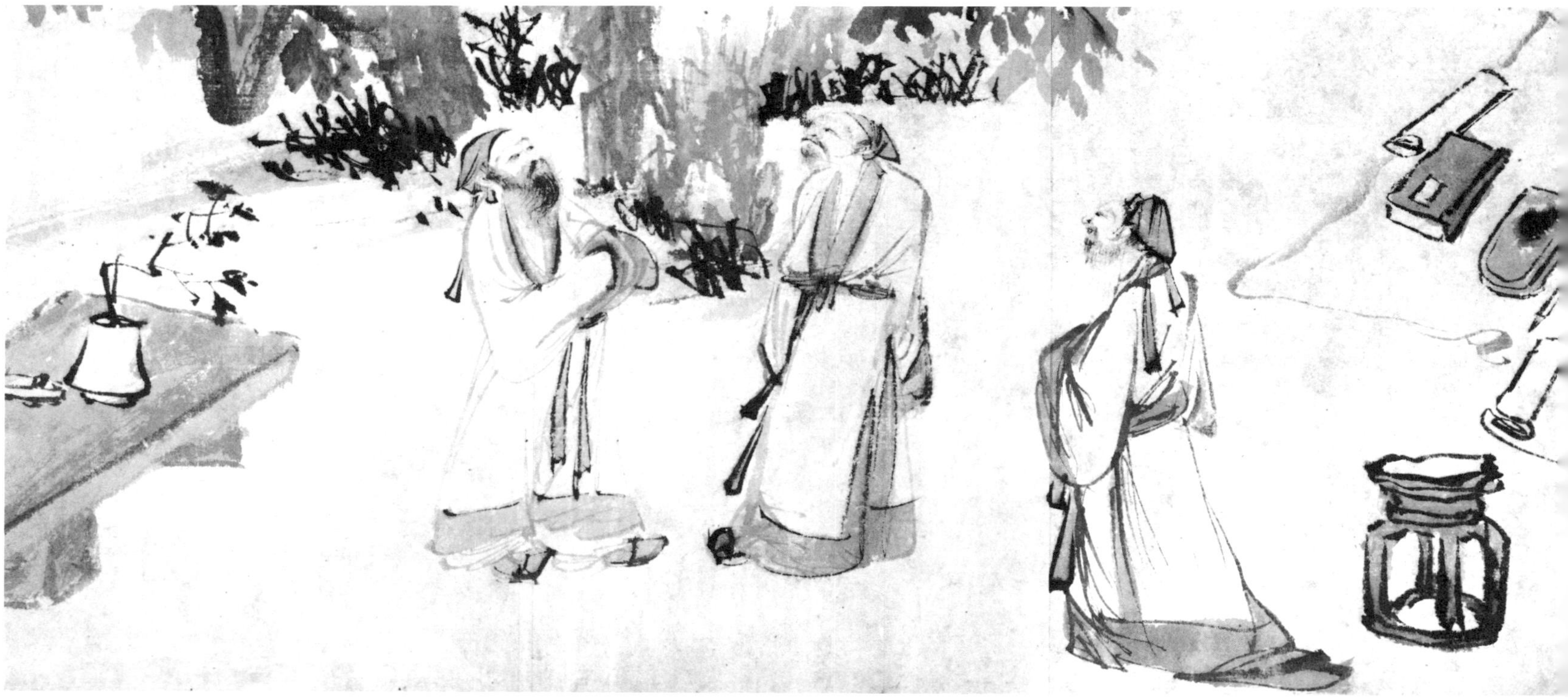

Fig. 140. T'ang Yin, detail, *The Lofty Scholars* (*Kao-shih t'u*). Undated, ca. 1520. Handscroll, ink on paper. 23.7 x 195.8 cm (9 3/8 in. x 6 ft. 5 1/8 in.). National Palace Museum, Taipei

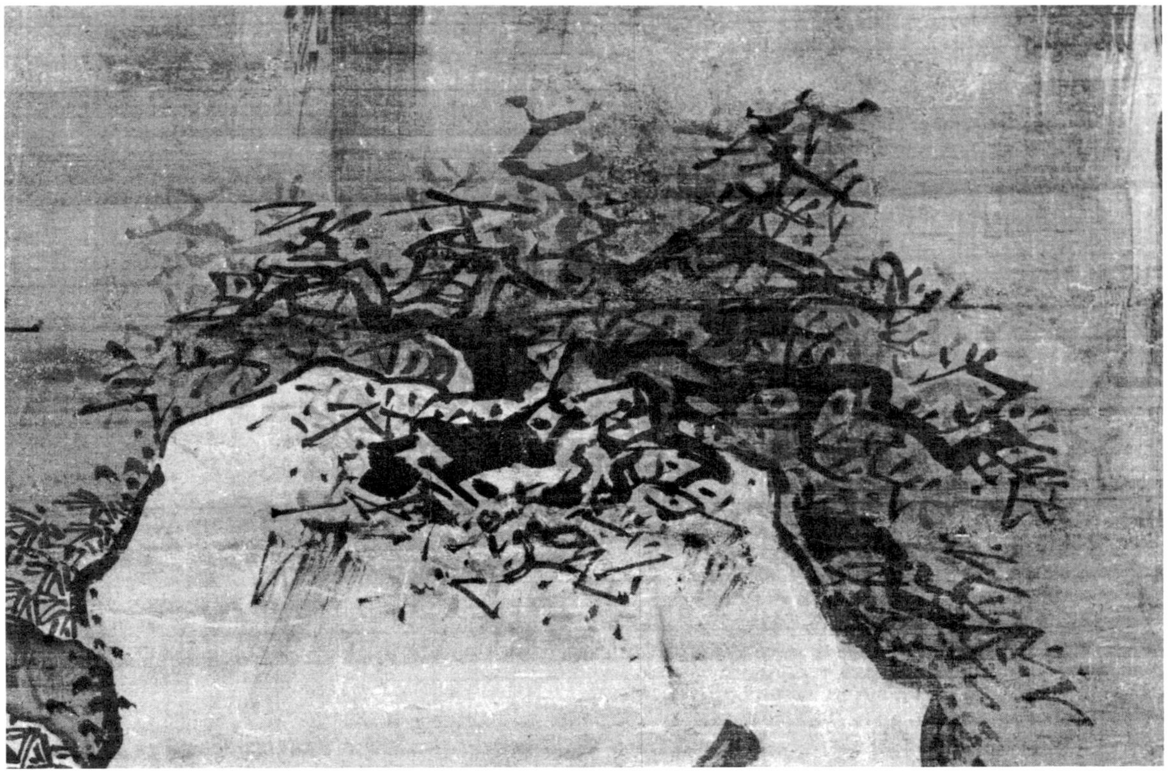

Fig. 141. Wang E, detail, *Winter in the Mountains* (*Tung-ching*). Undated, ca. 1500. Hanging scroll, ink and light color on silk. 183.0 x 104.0 cm (6 ft. x 3 ft. 5 in.). The Art Museum, Princeton University

Chung's "type" appears in a handscroll entitled *The Lofty Scholars* (*Kao-shih t'u*; fig. 140), datable to about 1520, by T'ang Yin, another nonconformist. James Cahill (1978) described the scholars as "not so much 'noble' as pompous, with their upturned faces and strutting demeanors."[55] As talented failures, the arrogant scholars became an increasingly familiar feature of late Ming culture and society, and their affected rudeness seemed to lend, if nothing else, certain poetic dignity to a life otherwise characterized by frustration.

Many professional painters who had aspired to the same values as the scholar-painters probably felt like failed scholars. Yet their attempts to mimic eccentric "scholarly" lifestyles and painting techniques met with violent condemnation from the gentleman-scholars. When striving for a spirit of freedom in their works, Ming Painting Academy and Che School professional painters, who did not have the scholar's benefit of years of training in fine calligraphy, often adopted a reckless kind of virtuoso brushwork that in fact looked very much like Shih Chung's (fig. 141; cf. fig. 139). In the late sixteenth century increasingly rough and crude brushwork in certain Che School paintings led to stern censure by scholar-critics, who called them the "evil," "aberrant," or "heterodox" (*hsieh-hsüeh*) school, "reaching pretentiously for an attitude of wildness [*t'u-ch'eng k'uang-t'ai*] but achieving nothing."[56]

If uncouth and coarse techniques merely offended, the idea that they might represent serious art proved positively threatening to Orthodox scholar-critics. In the intellectual context of the late sixteenth century, the commonly recognized issue was *pien*, or transformation. Change there must be, so everyone agreed, but was it to be change merely for the sake of newness—the untested and the unknown—or change as a necessary means for *fu-ku*, or return to ancient verities?

Successful answers to this question, both theoretical and stylistic, were provided by Tung Ch'i-ch'ang, whose proposal of a revolutionary revivalism—a Great Synthesis (*ta-ch'eng*) of the Sung and Yüan methods achieved through intuitive understanding—along with radical technical innovations, opened up a new direction, with vastly expanded new horizons for painting. By equating painting with calligraphy and turning landscape elements into diagrammatic formulas and pure, abstract brushwork, he revitalized landscape painting. By the time a new generation of talented artists took over under a new dynasty, in the second half of the seventeenth century, brilliant new landscape styles emerged. Yet no painter of that prolific new era could look back and say that he might have done the same without Tung Ch'i-ch'ang.

## NOTES

1. See James Cahill, *Fantastics and Eccentrics in Chinese Painting* (New York: Asia House Gallery, 1967); James Cahill, *The Compelling Image: Nature and Style in Seventeenth-century Chinese Painting* (Cambridge, Mass.: Harvard University Press, 1982).
2. Max Loehr, "Studie über Wang Meng (die Datierten Werke)," *Sinica* 14, no. 5/6 (1939): 273–90.
3. James Cahill, *Hills beyond a River: Chinese Painting of the Yüan Dynasty, 1279–1368* (New York and Tokyo: Weatherhill, 1976), p. 122.
4. For a discussion of *feng-shui* and its relation to painting, see John Hay, "Huang Kung-wang's *Dwelling in the Fu-ch'un Mountains*, The Dimensions of a Landscape" (Ph.D. diss., Princeton University, 1978).
5. See Hok-lam Chan, "Hu Wei-yung," in L. Carrington Goodrich and Chaoying Fang, eds., *Dictionary of Ming Biography: 1368–1644* (New York and London: Columbia University Press, 1976), vol. 1, pp. 638–41.
6. The story is found in *Ming-shih* (History of the Ming dynasty) as cited in Osvald Sirén, *Chinese Painting: Leading Masters and Principles* (New York: Ronald Press, 1956), vol. 4, p. 119.
7. For a discussion of the Ming Painting Academy, see Harrie Vanderstappen, "Painters at the Early Ming Court (1368–1435) and the Problem of a Ming Painting Academy," *Monumenta Serica* 15 (1956): 259–301; 16: 316–46; Suzuki Kei, "Min no ga-in sei ni tsuite" (A study on the organization of the Ming Painting Academy), *Bijutsushi* 15, no. 4/60 (1966): 95–106; Suzuki Kei, *Mindai kaiga shi kenkyū: Seppa* (A study of Ming dynasty painting history: the Che School) (Tokyo: University of Tokyo Press, 1968), esp. pp. 137–48, 151–83.
8. Today, the Wu-ying-tien (Hall of Martial Brilliance) in the former imperial palace compound in Peking is occupied by the Committee for the Preparation of Exhibitions of Archaeological Relics of the State Administrative Bureau of Museums and Archaeological Data (Kuo-chia wen-wu shih-yeh kuan-li chü).
9. Yeh Sheng, "Ch'ang-ling so shang shu-hua-chia" (Calligraphers and painters appreciated by the Yung-lo emperor), in *Shui-tung jih-chi* (Diary of east of the river), Chung-kuo shih-hsüeh ts'ung-shu, vol. 25 (1680; repr. ed., Taipei: Hsüeh-sheng shu-chü, 1965), *chüan* 3, p. 11b.
10. For Tai Chin, see Suzuki Kei, *Mindai kaiga shi kenkyū: Seppa*, pp. 15–37, 151–62; Ch'en Fang-mei, *Tai Chin yen-chiu* (A study of Tai Chin) (Taipei: National Palace Museum, 1981); Mo I-ch'in, "Tai Chin yü Che-p'ai" (Tai Chin and the Che School), *Ku-kung po-wu-yüan yüan-k'an*, no. 4 (1981): 3–15.
11. See Ch'en Fang-mei, *Tai Chin yen-chiu*, p. 11.
12. Ibid., pp. 33–34.
13. Ibid., pp. 45 ff.
14. For an illustration of *Six Buddhist Patriarchs*, see Liaoning Provincial Museum, ed., *Liao-ning-sheng po-wu-kuan ts'ang-hua chi* (Catalogue of the painting collection in the Liaoning Provincial Museum) (Peking: Wen-wu ch'u-pan-she, 1962), vol. 2, pl. 15; for *Seeking the Tao in Cave Paradise*, see *Ku-kung po-wu-yüan yüan-k'an*, no. 4 (1981): 44.
15. For a recent translation of Wu Ch'eng-en, *Hsi-yu chi*, see Anthony C. Yu, *The Journey to the West* (Chicago: University of Chicago Press, 1976).
16. See Mo I-chin, "Ming-tai kung-t'ing yüan-t'i yü Che-p'ai hui-hua" (Ming dynasty Che School painting), *I-yüan to-ying* 13 (1981): 35–37, pls. 20–22.
17. See Jen Yu-wen, "Ch'en Hsien-chang's Philosophy of the Natural," in William Theodore de Bary, ed., *Self and Society in Ming Thought* (New York: Columbia University Press, 1970), pp. 53–92; Huang P'ei and Julia Ching, "Ch'en Hsien-chang," in L. Carrington Goodrich and Chaoying Fang, eds., *Dictionary of Ming Biography*, vol. 1, pp. 153–56.
18. For recent discussions of Chu Hsi's philosophical system, see Mou Tsung-san, *Hsin-t'i yü hsing-t'i* (Mind and human nature) (Taipei: Cheng-chung shu-chü, 1969), vol. 3, esp. pp. 130–54; and Wei-ming Tu's review of Mou Tsung-san's work, "*Hsin-t'i yü hsing-t'i*" (Mind and human nature), *Journal of Asian Studies* 30, no. 3 (May 1971): 642–47.
19. Jen Yu-wen, "Ch'en Hsien-chang's Philosophy of the Natural," p. 72.
20. Ibid., p. 85.
21. Ibid., p. 64.
22. Ibid., pp. 66–69.
23. See Tang Chun-i, "The Development of the Concept of Moral Mind from Wang Yang-ming to Wang Chi," in William Theodore de Bary, ed., *Self and Society in Ming Thought*, pp. 100–108.
24. See Wing-tsit Chan, "Wang Shou-jen [Wang Yang-ming]," in L. Carrington Goodrich and Chaoying Fang, eds., *Dictionary of Ming Biography*, vol. 2, pp. 1408–16.
25. For an alternative date, 1515–16, see Chiang I-han, "P'u-lin-ssu-tun ta-hsüeh mei-shu-kuan ts'ang Wang Yang-ming san-cha chüan" (Wang Yang-ming's three letters in the collection of The Art Museum, Princeton University), *Ming-pao yüeh-k'an* 10, no. 1 (January 1975): 58–65.
26. Pien Yung-yü, *Shih-ku-t'ang shu-hua hui-k'ao* (Classified record of calligraphy and painting of Shih-ku Hall) (Taipei: Cheng-chung shu-chü, 1965), vol. 4, *chüan* 21, p. 299.
27. Osvald Sirén, *Chinese Painting: Leading Masters and Principles*, vol. 6, pl. 177.
28. Roderick Whitfield, *In Pursuit of Antiquity: Chinese Paintings of the Ming and Ch'ing Dynasties from the Collection of Mr. and Mrs. Earl Morse* (Princeton: The Art Museum, 1969), pp. 50–51.
29. For a discussion of Shen Chou's album painted for Chou Wei-te, see James Cahill, *Parting at the Shore: Chinese Painting of the Early and Middle Ming Dynasty* (New York and Tokyo: Weatherhill, 1978), pp. 88–89.
30. Jon Bourassa, "The Life and Work of the Literati Painter Yao Shou (1422–95): The Early Years," in *Suzuki Kei sensei kanreki-kinen: Chūgoku ega-shi ron* (Celebrating Professor Suzuki Kei's sixtieth birthday: collected essays on Chinese painting history) (Tokyo: Yoshikawa, 1981), pp. 101–2.
31. National Palace Museum, Taipei, comp., *Ku-kung-shu-hua lu* (A descriptive catalogue of the painting and calligraphy in the National Palace Museum) (Taipei: National Palace Museum, 1965) vol. 3, *chüan* 5, pp. 295–96; for an alternative translation, see James Cahill, *Parting at the Shore*, p. 90.
32. Jen Yu-wen, "Ch'en Hsien-chang's Philosophy of the Natural," p. 73.
33. Ch'ien Mu, "Jen-chien-shih" (Chapter on human world), in *Chuang-tzu tsuan-chien* (Notes and commentaries to Chuang-tzu) (Hong Kong: Tung-nan yin-wu ch'u-pan-she, 1957), p. 30.
34. James Cahill, *Parting at the Shore*, p. 91.
35. Huang T'ing-chien, *Shan-ku t'i-pa* (Colophons by Huang T'ing-chien), I-shu ts'ung-pien, vol. 22 (Taipei: Shih-chieh shu-chü, 1962), *chüan* 5, pp. 49–51.
36. Chiang Chao-shen, *Kuan-yü T'ang Yin te yen-chiu* (A study of T'ang Yin) (Taipei: National Palace Museum, 1976), p. 23.
37. For a sensitive study of T'ang Yin's biography, see ibid., esp. pp. 1–52, 129–44.
38. James Cahill, *Parting at the Shore*, p. 195.
39. Shen C. Y. Fu, while a graduate student at Princeton University in the early 1970s, identified *Shan-lu sung-k'o* and another painting in the Du Bois Schank Morris collection at The Art Museum, Princeton University (47–245) as works by T'ang Yin.
40. See Chiang Chao-shen, *Kuan-yü T'ang Yin te yen-chiu*, pp. 99–100.
41. The complete set of four hanging scrolls is illustrated in *T'ang Liu-ju hua-chi* (A collection of T'ang Yin's paintings) (Shanghai: Shanghai jen-min mei-shu ch'u-pan-she, 1960), pls. 22–25.
42. Kuo Hsi and Kuo Ssu, *Lin-ch'üan kao-chih chi* (Collection of *Lofty Aims in Forests and Streams*), in Yü Chien-hua, ed., *Chung-kuo hua-lun lei-pien* (Classified compilation of writings on Chinese painting) (Hong Kong: Chung-hua shu-chü, 1973), vol. 1, p. 641.
43. For an illustration, see *T'ang Liu-ju hua-chi*, pls. 22–25.
44. Sun Tsu-pai, "Ch'ien-yen: T'ang Yin chuan-lüeh ho i-shu chien-chieh" (Foreword: a brief introduction to T'ang Yin's biography and his art), in *T'ang Liu-ju hua-chi*, p. 2.
45. See Kuo Shao-yu, *Chung-kuo wen-hsüeh p'i-p'ing shih* (History of Chinese literary criticism) (Shanghai: Chung-hua shu-chü, 1961), pp. 238 ff.
46. Ibid., pp. 301–2.
47. Ibid., p. 323.
48. Ibid., pp. 372–73.
49. Li K'ai-hsien, *Chung-lu hua-p'in* (Painting classifications of the Chung-lu Academy), I-shu ts'ung-pien, vol. 12 (1545; repr. ed., Taipei: Shih-chieh shu-chü, 1962), pp. 55–56.

50. Wang Chih-teng, *Kuo-ch'ao Wu-chün tan-ch'ing chih* (History of painting in the Wu prefecture during our illustrious [Ming] dynasty), in *Hua-shih ts'ung-shu* (Compendium of painting histories) (1563; repr. ed., Taipei: Wen-shih-che ch'u-pan-she, 1974), vol. 3, pp. 1, 3.
51. Ho Liang-chün, *Ssu-yu-chai hua-lun* (Painting discussions at the Four Friends' Studio), I-shu ts'ung-pien, vol. 12 (Taipei: Shih-chieh shu-chü, 1962), p. 39.
52. Tung Ch'i-ch'ang, *Hua-yen* (The eye of painting), I-shu ts'ung-pien, vol. 12 (Taipei: Shih-chieh shu-chü, 1962), p. 43. According to Tung it was Mo Shih-lung who "divided the *tun* (sudden) and the *chien* (gradual) into the Southern and the Northern schools," p. 46.
53. Ibid., p. 24.
54. According to Tung, artists who "express joyfulness in painting" can expect to live very long lives, whereas hardworking professional painters often die young; ibid., pp. 23–24.
55. James Cahill, *Parting at the Shore*, p. 199.
56. See Richard Barnhart, "The 'Wild and Heterodox School' of Ming Painting," in Susan Bush and Christian Murck, eds., *Theories of the Arts in China* (Princeton: Princeton University Press, 1983), p. 365.

# 5 *The Great Synthesis*

THE SEVENTEENTH CENTURY opened in China during the twenty-eighth year of the reign of the Ming Wan-li emperor (Shen-tsung; r. 1573–1619) and closed in the thirty-eighth year of the reign of the Ch'ing K'ang-hsi emperor (Sheng-tsu; r. 1662–1721). Historians have long argued that the fall of the Ming had begun during the Wan-li reign, one of the worst periods in Chinese imperial history; the K'ang-hsi period, under Manchu rule, was among the most brilliant.

Reacting against the rigors of the stern, legalistic rule of the senior grand secretary Chang Chü-cheng (1525–1582), during which Ming China saw ten years of national security and prosperity, the young Wan-li emperor, then twenty years old, recovered the reins of government upon Chang's death in 1582, and abandoned himself to the pursuit of pleasures and mindless enrichment of his private coffers. Beginning in 1589 and continuing for more than twenty-five years, the emperor altogether avoided participating in court audiences, leaving government affairs either unattended or in the hands of the palace eunuchs. With intensifying struggles between court officials and eunuchs on the one hand, and the various factions of officials on the other, survival and longevity alone were deemed achievements.

For wealthy art lovers and collectors in the prosperous Chiang-nan region the late Ming era proved to be the best of times. Throughout the sixteenth century, private individuals amassed large fortunes in Chiang-nan through commerce, trade, and great holdings of farmland. Since emperors after the Hung-chih era (1488–1505) showed little interest in the arts, the collecting of fine ancient calligraphy and painting became the unchallenged domain of well-to-do retired scholar-officials and their families, who customarily built garden villas, libraries, and art collections. During this period, Hsiang Yüan-pien (1525–1590) assembled the greatest private painting and calligraphy collection in Chinese history. A native of Hsiu-shui (Chia-hsing), Chekiang province, and the youngest son of a wealthy family, Hsiang shunned an official career, but managed to achieve prominence through his collection. Hsiang's nearly exact contemporary Wang Shih-chen (1526–1590), a native of T'ai-ts'ang, near Su-chou, then the leader of literary society, was another ardent art lover and collector; Wang was also a distinguished compiler of writings on art. Other important Chiang-nan collectors included Ho Liang-chun (1506–1573), Ku Cheng-i (fl. ca. 1575–96), Mo Shih-lung (ca. 1538–1587), and Tung Ch'i-ch'ang (1555–1636), who lived in or near Hua-t'ing, modern Kiangsu province. Another flourishing commercial and art center was Hui-chou, Anhui, where Wang Tao-k'un (1525–1593; see no. 24) and Chan Ching-feng (fl. ca. 1570–95) lived and collected.

These great private art collections of the late sixteenth and early seventeenth centuries served to stimulate knowledge and creation of art at a time when the art of painting was losing vitality. For all its many-faced splendors, Ming revivalism as seen in the works of Tai Chin (1388–1462), Shen Chou (1427–1509), and T'ang Yin (1470–1524) had been one of continuation and development of the Sung and Yüan brush idioms. Now, in the twilight of the conservative Ming culture, the works produced in the traditional painting centers of Wu (Su-chou) and Che (Hang-chou) were—in the words of a Wu critic, Ku Ning-yüan (fl. ca. 1640)—like "spent arrows at the end of their flight."[1] During that time scattered bursts of creative energy, as seen in the archaistic works of Wu Pin (fl. ca. 1583–1626) and Ch'en Hung-shou (1599–1652), flourished in isolation, but, stranded by the receding tide of the old-style Ming revivalism, even these artists seemed to turn in upon themselves, reveling in eccentricity, and nostalgically, almost pathetically, clinging to archaic manners.[2] It was Tung Ch'i-ch'ang, the learned conservative-radical, who changed the fundamental nature of Ming painting and of Ming-style revivalism by advocating a total new transformation of the way of looking at ancient models as well as the very method of painting landscapes.

Then came the Manchu conquest in 1644 and a radical change in the political, social, and intellectual climate. From the outset of their southern campaign after taking Peking on June 4, 1644, the Manchus had effectively combined terror tactics with compromise, using Chinese generals to fight the war against the Southern Ming troops and welcoming members of the old social elite into local governments. After quelling the dangerous rebellion of the southern feudatories in 1681, the energetic K'ang-hsi emperor made six "southern inspection tours" (*nan-hsün*) through Chiang-nan in order to cement relations with the traditionally proud and independent southern scholar and gentry classes. Extending special courtesy to the local elite the emperor made ceremonial visits to the Ming imperial tombs in Nanking and granted two personal audiences (in 1684 and 1691) to the monk-painter Tao-chi (1642–1707), a member of the Ming imperial family.[3]

A venerable living symbol of continuity in the scholar-artist's world was Wang Shih-min (1592–1680) of T'ai-ts'ang, northeast of Su-chou, whose grandfather Wang Hsi-chüeh (1534–1611) was the Ming Wan-li emperor's senior grand secretary (at the end of the sixteenth century) and whose son Wang Shan (1645–1728) would rise to be the K'ang-hsi emperor's grand secretary (1717–23). Tutored in his youth by Tung Ch'i-ch'ang, Wang Shih-min was the leader of the so-called four Wangs; the other three were Wang Chien (1598–1677), Wang Hui (1632–1717), and Wang Yüan-ch'i (1642–1715). The first of these three, also from T'ai-ts'ang, was a great-grandson of Wang Shih-chen, the leader of the revivalist later seven masters in the 1570s; the last was Wang Shih-min's grandson. The four Wangs, together with Wu Li (1632–1718) and Yün Shou-p'ing (1633–1690), were known as the six great Orthodox masters. Wang Hui and Wu Li were born in Ch'ang-shu, near T'ai-ts'ang, and Yün came from Wu-chin, just northwest of Wu-hsi.

A remarkable cultural experiment took place in T'ai-ts'ang in the middle decades of the seventeenth century. Of like mind and purpose, the two older Wangs adopted the brilliant, younger Wang Hui, and together the three men carried out a systematic program of stylistic reconstruction in landscape painting. Basing their project on Tung Ch'i-ch'ang's notion of a Great Synthesis, they went beyond his narrow range of Tung Yüan–Chü-jan–Huang Kung-wang idiom to attempt a new synthesis of the so-called Southern School and Northern School styles. The vision they shared was bold and exciting: as Wang Hui demonstrated in his paintings, the art of ancient times had unity and completeness. Through a Great Synthesis, the student could find himself in a new realm of experiences.

Equally as remarkable as their artistic achievements were the human values fostered by these artists. An extraordinarily warm collaborative spirit blessed the T'ai-ts'ang experience: gone were the late Ming fragmentation and bitter rivalry; friends acting in a common bond of knowledge and mutual understanding generously praised and supported one another. Wang Chien discovered Wang Hui, but finding that the young man's talent taxed his own abilities as a mentor, he relinquished his role to Wang Shih-min. Both older Wangs soon became content to play the role of admirers and commentators, as Wang Hui surpassed their own achievements. Much of the older Wangs' extant writings consist of eulogistic colophons praising Wang Hui's paintings. Just as moving was the lifelong friendship between Wang Hui and Yün Shou-p'ing, who is said to have abandoned landscape in favor of flower painting, in deference to Wang Hui's genius in the landscape genre. Yün's writings chronicled Wang Hui's artistic triumphs. For his own part, Wang Hui was modest, sensitive, and earnestly appreciative. Although Wang Shih-min sometimes exploited his role as Wang Hui's mentor, always pressing him for more paintings, Wang Hui never refused or complained.

During these same years a galaxy of brilliant painters appeared in other orbits, beyond the environs of Su-chou—in Anhui and Kiangsi provinces, and in Nanking and Yang-chou in Kiangsu province. Many Ming loyalists had taken refuge in Buddhist priesthood and had chosen to devote themselves to painting because painting, unlike scholarship or literature, required physical action as well as thought. Hung-jen (1610–1663), Kung Hsien (ca. 1619–1689), Chu Ta (1624–1705), and Tao-chi all developed highly individualistic styles, but all three shared Tung Ch'i-ch'ang's goal in painting of holding the universe in their hands.[4]

## *Tung Ch'i-ch'ang: An Intuitive Leap*

A native of Shanghai, near Hua-t'ing, in the prefecture of Sung-chiang (modern Kiangsu province), Tung Ch'i-ch'ang was born in 1555 to a commoner family of moderate means. As a talented young scholar, he was hired as a private tutor by such prominent men as Lu Shu-sheng (1509–1605), president of the Board of Rites in Hua-t'ing, and Hsiang Yüan-pien, a wealthy art collector in Chia-hsing.[5] Passing the metropolitan *chin-shih* examination in 1589, he was selected to serve as a bachelor of the Han-lin Academy, and, in the following year, was appointed a compiler of history. He returned home in 1591, and in 1594 was summoned once more to Peking as one of the tutors of the heir apparent, Chu Ch'ang-lo (1582–1620). Refusing an appointment to a provincial post in 1599, Tung pleaded illness and retired to his home, emerging briefly in 1604 as a commissioner of education in Hu-kuang, only to retire again a year later in 1605. For the next seventeen years he lived at home. Summoned in 1620 by his prince, now Emperor Kuang-tsung (r. 1620), he was preparing to leave for the capital when the new emperor died, by poisoning, just thirty days after ascending the throne. In 1622 Tung was recalled to Peking by the succeeding emperor, Ming Hsi-tsung (r. 1620–27), and given the post of director of the Court of Sacrificial Worship. He was sent to compile materials at the southern capital, Nanking, as one of the directors for the compilation of the "veritable records" (*shih-lu*) of the reign period of the Ming Wan-li emperor, and he returned to Peking in early 1624 with a compilation of 300 manuscript volumes of archival materials. Receiving an honorific appointment as the president of the Board of Rites in Nanking in 1625, he quietly resigned and returned home in the following year. In 1631, at the age of seventy-seven, he was again called to Peking, this time by the last official Ming emperor, Ssu-tsung, who named him head tutor of the heir apparent. In 1634 Tung returned once more to Hua-t'ing, where he died two years later.

Tung Ch'i-ch'ang achieved recognition as a teacher, imperial tutor, examiner, and compiler of dynastic history. A cautious man, he carefully avoided politics, choosing to retire from office in 1599, when his influence with the crown prince began to cause jealousy and fear among his colleagues, and again in 1624, when the purge of the Tung-lin scholars by the powerful eunuch Wei Chung-hsien (1568–1627) persuaded him to leave Peking and to take up a sinecure position in Nanking. But Tung's life was never far from peril. His tenure as the education commissioner in Hu-kuang was cut short in 1605 by a student riot. And in 1616, after he had spent eleven years tending to family interests and building up his estate until it was one of the finest in Hua-t'ing, he saw his fine home razed to the ground, and valuable art collections looted by a rioting mob reacting to high-handed behavior by some of his family members.

Having feasted and trained his eye on the fine works of calligraphy and painting in Hsiang Yüan-pien's home, Tung had decided to form his own painting collection. In 1590, barely one year after he earned his *chin-shih* degree, he acquired a major painting, Chao Ling-jang's (fl. ca. 1070–1100) *River Village on a Clear Summer Day* (*Chiang-hsiang ch'ing-hsia*), now in the Museum of Fine Arts, Boston.[6] Beginning in 1591, while on home leave in Chiang-nan, he "began to search seriously for the splashed-ink [*p'o-mo*] works of the four [Yüan] masters"—Huang Kung-wang (1269–1354), Wu Chen (1280–1354), Ni Tsan (1301–1374), and Wang Meng (ca. 1308–1385).[7] In 1596 he acquired Huang Kung-wang's masterpiece, *Dwelling in the Fu-ch'un Mountains* (cf. fig. 67).[8] In 1597 he added to his collection two major works by (or attributed to) Tung Yüan (fl. ca. 937–76), *Hsiao and Hsiang Rivers* (cf. fig. 33) and *Residents of the Capital City* (*Lung-hsiu chiao-min t'u*; now in the National Palace Museum, Taipei).[9]

Tung needed only a painting by Wang Wei to lead the grand parade of the Southern School stylistic development. In 1595, when he was serving as a tutor to the crown prince in Peking, he heard of a newly discovered Wang Wei painting, *Rivers and Mountains after Snow* (*Chiang-shan hsüeh-chi t'u*; fig. 142), in Feng K'ai-chih's collection in Hang-chou.[10] He managed to persuade Feng to have the scroll brought to Peking for him to examine, whereupon he composed a long colophon discussing Wang Wei's style. He kept the scroll with him for nine months, returning it personally on a special visit to Feng's home in Hang-chou in the summer of 1596. In 1604, en route to serve as the educational commissioner in Hu-kuang, Tung stopped at the Buddhist monastery Chao-ch'ing-ssu on West Lake, and saw the scroll once more.[11] His encounter with and ruminations over this important scroll attributed to Wang Wei represented a major episode in his efforts to reconstruct the Southern School tradition.

Growing up in the intellectual climate of late sixteenth-century Ming China, Tung Ch'i-ch'ang was deeply influenced by the radical individualistic philosophy of Li Chih (1527–1602) and the antirevivalist figures of the Kung-an School of poetry, the three Yüan brothers. During the late 1590s, while serving as tutor to the crown prince in Peking, Tung became close friends with the Yüan brothers through their common interest in Ch'an Buddhism and shared admiration for Li Chih. Tung first met Li in early 1598 in a temple outside Peking, and despite the differences in their ages and positions, they took an instant liking to each other and became fast friends.[12]

Yet, unlike Li Chih and the Yüan brothers, Tung never denied the importance of ancient models. Significant differences existed between their respective areas of concern, painting and poetry. Whereas the target of the Yüan brothers' attack was imitation in poetry, the object of Tung's criticism was the lack of discipline and purpose in late Ming painting. By the late 1590s Tung had largely formulated his theory about the Northern and Southern schools of painting. It was not so much the intense radicalism of Li Chih and the Yüan brothers that influenced his thinking as their intuitive approach. Inspired by their doctrine of the mind—Li Chih's innate, childlike mind (*t'ung-hsin*)—Tung adopted an instinctive method of battling the shopworn conventions of late Ming painting.

Aware that yesteryear's innovation becomes today's convention, Tung chided contemporary painters who followed the Ma Yüan–Hsia Kuei idiom:

> Hsia Kuei followed Li T'ang, further simplifying his style, creating what the sculptors call a pared-down sketch. His idea was to avoid the narrow path of tracing and imitation. He made landscapes fade and diminish, incorporating the ink play of the two Mis [Mi Fu (1052–1107) and Mi Yu-jen (1072–1151)] in his brushwork. [Hsia Kuei] tried to destroy the [square] *ku* [ritual bronze beaker; i.e., an established method] in order to achieve a roundness [a less formal approach]; now [the Ming imitators of the Hsia Kuei idiom] are carving roundness back into a *ku*![13]

Tung's prescription for avoiding "the narrow path of tracing and imitation" was to treat painting as calligraphy:

> When a scholar turns to painting, he should apply to it the methods of writing unusual characters in the grass [cursive; *ts'ao*] or clerical [*li*] script, making his trees resemble curved iron bars, and mountains look as if they were drawn in the sand [with deep and round brushstrokes]. The narrow path of [seductive] sweetness and vulgarity should be avoided absolutely. His painting will then have a scholarly breath [*shih-ch'i*]. Otherwise, even if a work shows high technical competence, it already falls into the pernicious ways of a professional craftsman; it is then beyond all hope and remedy. If a painter could only free himself from the bondage [of craftsmanship], he would be like a fish escaping the net.[14]

Reducing landscape painting to pure brushwork, Tung argued:

> If one thinks of strange scenery, then painting is not the equal of real landscape; but if one considers the wonders of brush and ink, then landscape can never equal painting.[15]

Freed from the constraints of representation, the painter could produce bold brush drawings that were projections of the images in his own mind. And, in order to capture what Yen Yü (1180–1235) called "flavors beyond tastes" and "images beyond images," he should avoid descriptive details. As Tung put it, "In painting it is better to be obscure [*an*] than to be obvious [*ming*]. To be obvious is to trace all the sharp edges and corners of a *ku*; to be obscure is to hide behind clouds of mist."[16]

To the question "What if scholar-painters 'hiding behind clouds and mist' were simply bad amateurs?" Tung provided this answer: "To prevent impostors from mingling in their midst, scholar-painters should first learn to exhaust the limits of workmanship and technical skills, making creation their teacher and friend."[17] Paraphrasing the Southern Sung writer Chao Hsi-ku (ca. 1190), Tung intoned that every scholar-painter "must read ten thousand books and travel ten thousand miles."[18] A painter had to study not only ancient models, but also nature:

> The painter who models himself after ancient masters already belongs [in the Buddhist sense] to the Upper Vehicle. Advancing one more step, he must model himself after heaven and earth. . . . After he becomes familiar with nature, he will transmit the spirit [of the landscape]. To transmit the spirit there must be form. When the form, the mind, and the hand are in total accord, each forgetting the other's separate existence, then the spirit [of the landscape] will reside in a painting.[19]

In treating nature and ancient models as his two teachers, Tung approached both with the same desire for sudden awakening. He saw painting history as an enduring effort to restore simplicity and truth to art. Combining the notion of truth (*chen*), as advocated by Li Chih, with the earlier revivalists' arguments about correspondence (*ho*) and departure (*li*) in imitation, he defined the difference between mere copying and insightful imitation:

> While copying or tracing [a style] is easy, spiritual communion [with an old master] is difficult to express. Chü-jan followed Tung Yüan, Mi Fu followed Tung Yüan, Huang Kung-wang followed Tung Yüan, and Ni Tsan followed Tung Yüan. Although all of them followed the same Tung Yüan, each of them produced something different. When an ordinary painter copies and produces something that looks like any other copy, how can his work be passed on to future generations?[20]

Since the truth of an old master is discovered only in one's own mind, fidelity to the old means fidelity to one's own inner self. Thus the proper way to imitate or to seek correspondence is to transform, since the only way to be ancient is to endow the old with compelling new significances.

In collecting the old masters' works, Tung carefully read each painting for its stylistic connection and assiduously searched for the missing links that would make such connections manifest and complete: the paintings in his collections illustrated painting history, as he perceived it, in terms of a Southern School, with its proper, orthodox (*cheng*) succession from Wang Wei to the late Yüan masters. In colophons inscribed on a large album of copies of Sung and Yüan compositions, called *Within Small See Large* (*Hsiao-chung hsien-ta*; now in the National Palace Museum, Taipei), Tung wrote about the evolution of Sung and Yüan styles, frequently employing Ch'an Buddhist terminology to describe the artistic inner process of "awakening."[21] On the copy of Huang Kung-wang's *Summer Mountains* (*Hsia-shan*; Leaf 9), he commented, "When Huang Kung-wang copies Tung Yüan, he remains Huang Kung-wang; thus, one might say, he combines the best of the Sung and the Yüan." In describing Huang's deep understanding of Chü-jan (Leaves 8, 12), he quoted Chang Yü's (1283–1350) characterization of Huang as "the rapidly progressing Buddhist mystic [*dhātu*] who modeled himself after Chü-jan," implying that Huang had experienced a sudden awakening upon entering into Chü-jan's mind, as if "in one single leap." On the Wu Chen-style painting (Leaf 11), he wrote that "Chü-jan's mantle and alms bowl were inherited by Wu Chen; this work [by Wu] should not be looked upon as a Yüan painting, for it has attained the *san-mei* (samadhi; Buddhist meditation) of a lofty Northern Sung master"; and on Wang Meng's work after Tung Yüan (Leaf 10): "The brushwork derives entirely from Tung; it is a masterpiece by Wang before he achieved his transformation away from Tung."

Tung's method of authenticating ancient paintings was intuitive and pragmatic rather than—in the modern sense—historical and analytic, and on the whole his attitude toward traditional attributions was respectful. About disparate attributions to Tung Yüan, he commented:

> Both Tung Yüan's *Shu River* [*Shu-chiang t'u*] and his *Hsiao and Hsiang Rivers* [*Hsiao-Hsiang t'u*] are in my collection, but their brush methods look as if they were from two different hands. I own several other works by Tung Yüan, and not two of them look alike. Truly we might call [Tung Yüan] the [mysterious] dragon in painting.[22]

The dragon, symbol of nature's elemental forces, is known in Chinese mythology for its capacity for infinite and unpredictable transformations. To say that Tung Yüan either had or was capable of having many transformations was to acknowledge both his personal power as a painter and his historical influence. Since all major works attributed to Tung Yüan, whether painted by him or not, had affected and represented historical transformations, Tung Ch'i-ch'ang perceived them all as "truths" in his painting history.

In reconstructing the Southern School stylistic tradition, Tung Ch'i-ch'ang took the draping hemp-fiber (*p'i-ma*) calligraphic texture stroke as the principal technical clue. As he recounted in his long colophon dated 1595, on *Rivers and Mountains after Snow* (*Chiang-shan hsüeh-chi t'u*) attributed to Wang Wei (now in the Ogawa Family collection; fig. 142), he knew exactly what he expected of the scroll even before he saw it: "Is it possible that in a former life I had entered [Wang] Wei's studio and watched him paint . . . so I was able to recognize his style?" he asked.[23] He exaggerated his powers of premonition, since he did not find exactly what he was looking for in the scroll. The rock forms of *Rivers and Mountains*, done in thin

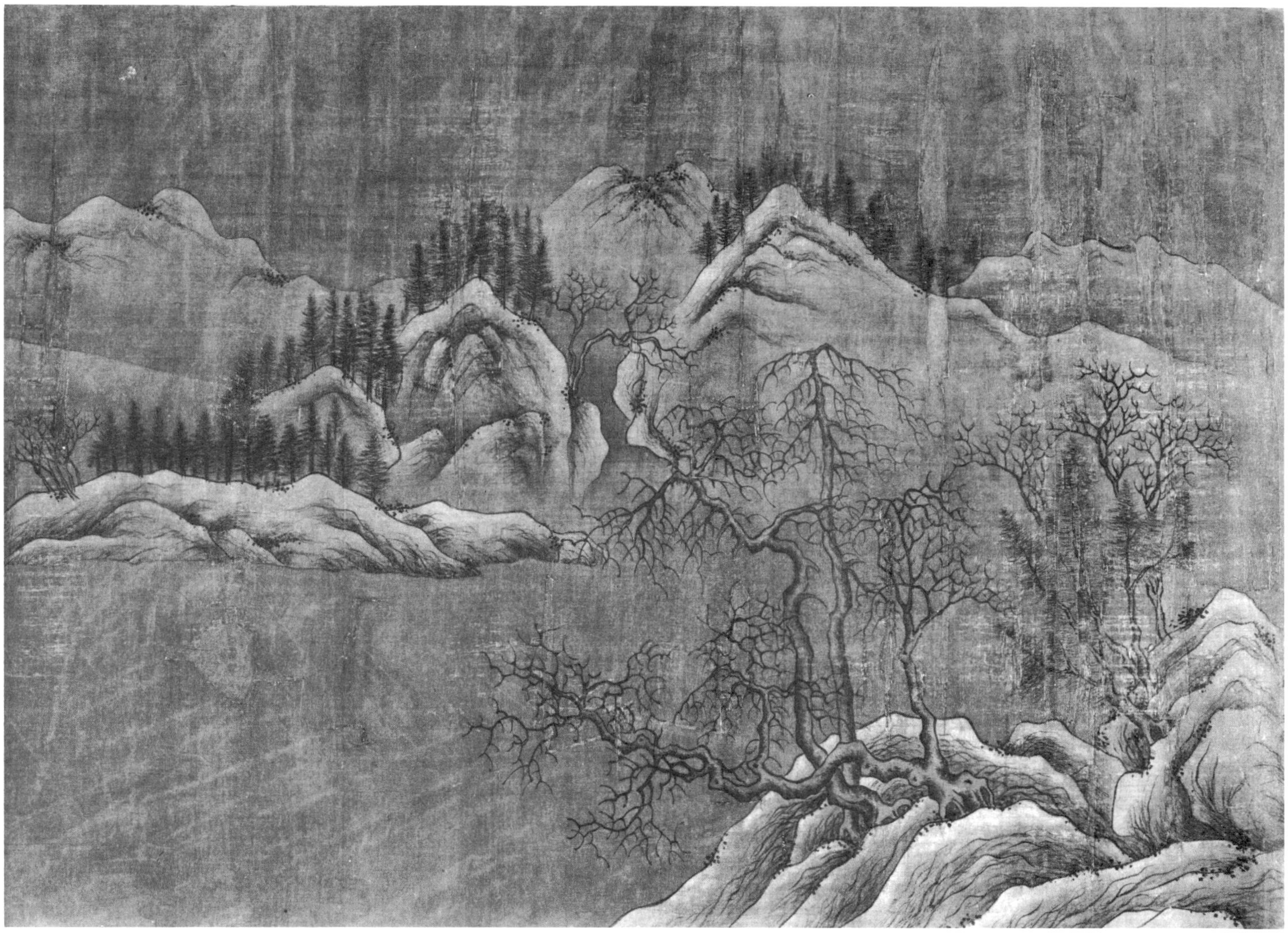

Fig. 142. Attributed to Wang Wei, detail, *Rivers and Mountains after Snow* (*Chiang-shan hsüeh-chi t'u*). Undated, copy ca. 1100(?). Handscroll, ink on silk. 28.4 x 171.5 cm (11 1/8 in. x 5 ft. 7 1/2 in.). Ogawa Family collection

contour lines and wirelike modeling strokes, could not easily be reduced to a simple calligraphic formula, so he resorted to generalizing statements: "When it comes to texture methods, every master from the T'ang through the Sung followed a special tradition. . . . It is like the five branches of Ch'an Buddhism: as soon as a word or phrase is uttered, we know immediately to which branch the speaker belongs." In a later colophon that he wrote about the attributed Wang Wei handscroll, he added, "Beginning with Wang Wei, a landscape painter employed both texture strokes and ink washes. . . . Once the basic method was formulated [by Wang Wei], it was not difficult [for later painters] to imitate and improvise."[24]

Thus Tung Ch'i-ch'ang the connoisseur was inseparable from Tung the painter: he studied the old masters' works from the creative vantage point of a painter, and he painted to relive and embrace painting history through the lifelong experience of a connoisseur. As a creative principle, Tung's art historical theory of a proper, orthodox stylistic lineage was synthetic rather than dogmatic. Just as the Mahayanist (Great Vehicle) Buddhists never declared the Hinayanas (Small Vehicles) false, but merely treated them as lesser truths to be embraced by the Great Truth, Tung taught that all ancient styles must be reunited in a "Great Synthesis" (*ta-ch'eng*) in which the best of each artist's style could be plucked from history and integrated into works in which the whole exceeded the sum of the parts. For level distance scenery he chose Chao Ling-jang; for stacked-up mountains and peaks, Chiang Shen (ca. 1090–1138); for texture strokes, he advised following Tung Yüan's hemp-skin technique as well as the dotted texture pattern of *Hsiao and Hsiang Rivers*. He recommended the methods of Tung Yüan and Chao Meng-fu for trees, and the rocks found in the Great General Li Ssu-hsün's *Waiting for the Ferry at the Autumn River* (*Ch'iu-chiang tai-tu t'u*), and those in Kuo Chung-shu's snow scene. He identified two Li Ch'eng (919–967) painting methods, an ink-wash style painted in a small format, and a blue and green style, and advocated both. "Having gathered [all these styles] into a Great Synthesis," he concluded, "the painter may then come out with inventions of his own."[25]

Tung's own insistence on his method as sudden awakening is compelling, but, without reference to the paintings he produced according to his theories, his advice has no meaning. Far from slavishly dabbling in earlier styles, Tung stripped himself "stark naked"—as his radical friend Li Chih had advised—in order to resolve the apparent paradoxes of transformation versus correspondence, nature versus ancient masters, Northern versus Southern schools, in a single intuitive leap. In the end the intellectual edifice built by Tung the theorist served only to guide and justify the revolution and reconstruction in painting led by Tung the painter. And, as a painter, Tung never needed, never wanted, and never succumbed to any doctrine but his own acute instincts.

Tung's stylistic development began with analysis and criticism of late Ming painting. Ming painting, he complained, was flat, because, in contrast to the ancient masters, his contemporaries paid too little attention to representing concave and convex forms in nature, with the result that their paintings failed to look "lively from all sides."[26] In addition, it was too fussy, an amalgam of piled-up bits, rather than a composition of three or four large divisions (*fen*) and gatherings (*ho*), in which "the principal requirement is to develop the momentum [*shih*] of the composition."[27]

Tung aimed to restore simplicity and substance to painting by building a style based on new technical principles. Whereas others of his time merely borrowed "skins and hairs" from ancient models, he analyzed the fundamental structures, the "bones" of the ancient styles, reducing them to bare essentials and making them work for him.

When he started to paint, he at first followed the Huang Kung-wang style. In a colophon dated November 26, 1596, inscribed on Huang Kung-wang's *Fu-ch'un* scroll, he wrote ecstatically:

> I remember when I was in the capital, after morning audiences, I used to chase after the censor-adviser Chou, asking to see this scroll. It was like visiting a great treasure trove, going there empty and returning full. I used to think how lucky I was to enjoy such a wonderful day, nourishing both my

> mind and my spleen. . . . Now I have acquired the scroll. . . . It is my teacher! It is my teacher! [The wonders of] any single mountain and all five [cosmic] peaks are all gathered here![28]

Throughout the late 1590s and the 1600s, as seen in extant works of this period, Tung refined and simplified his rendering of the Huang Kung-wang style, until he successfully reduced it to a diagrammatic formula: "In painting, mountains must show concave and convex forms. One begins by outlining the mountains first according to their outward forms and momentum (*shih*), then, within the outlined forms, applying straight texture strokes. This is the method of Huang Kung-wang."[29] In the short handscroll by Tung, *River and Mountains on a Clear Autumn Day* (*Chiang-shan ch'iu-chi*), painted in the 1610s (now in the Cleveland Museum of Art; fig. 143), he employs this new Huang Kung-wang formula of filling mountain outlines with straight texture strokes. The smooth bare rocks are conceived as abstract cubic masses (fig. 143a). Following the recognized Northern Sung composition, such as can be seen in *Wintry Groves and Layered Banks* attributed to Tung Yüan (cf. fig. 32), Tung Ch'i-ch'ang separated the mountains into three promontories lying diagonally across the picture plane. The trees, of several species each described by a particular brush formula, are carefully combined so that they range across the foreground in a rising and falling pattern (fig. 143b). In his writings Tung equated the drawing of trees with calligraphy, emphasizing that, "as in calligraphy, one concentrates one's power on the turning strokes. One must guard especially against letting a stroke go in one direction without checking it." Even branches and leaves had to show "four sides."[30]

These graphic patterns Tung manipulated as formal elements in abstract space, according to his new compositional ideas. Borrowing from ancient calligraphic criticism the concept of *shih* (kinetic force or momentum; discussed in chapter II) Tung saw landscape composition as abstract design with "rising-and-falling" (*ch'i-fu*), "opening-and-closing" (*fen-ho* or *k'ai-ho*), and "void-and-solid" (*hsü-shih*) movements:

> If a painter can both open [*fen*; divide] and close [*ho*] a composition, if his texture method is able to carry out all that he intends, then his painting will easily look convincing from all sides. . . . Only when a painter subtly weighs the void [*hsü*] against the solid [*shih*], and presents both aspects with feeling, will his painting naturally appear exciting.[31]

On one level, Tung Ch'i-ch'ang seemed to set aside the flat decorative surface treatment of the Ming in favor of the earlier, idealized tripartite composition of the Northern Sung. But the visual structure of his compositions is in fact radically new. His analytical landscape forms introduced totally new design possibilities. The cubically constructed masses, while implying volumes, are placed against space that is completely flat and neutral. The principles of void and solid, rising and falling, and opening and closing, which naturally tend to emphasize lateral movements along the picture plane, create free interplay and fusion between elements in back with those in front.

Until that moment, a sequential arrangement of elements along the vertical picture plane had been the standard composition of Chinese landscape paintings. In the Northern Sung period, painters used a systematic diminution of elements along the vertical plane to mark the three-stepped progression into depth. During the Yüan period, they learned to describe a continuous ground plane, gently tilting upward; and in the Ming period, having probed as deeply into the picture as possible, they returned to a flat and continuous decorative surface. In the paintings of these periods, vertical superimposition and lateral juxtaposition of elements was the rule, while overlapping and fusion was the exception. Tung Ch'i-ch'ang's cubic masses and overlapping foliage patterns, full of subtle effects of optical fusion and distortion, finally broke down the traditional vertical, sequential treatment. In Tung's paintings, objects appear to jump back and forth in all parts of the picture. Elements of the near, the middle, and the far distances are collapsed and pushed together. Continuous breath-force (*ch'i-shih*) movements now circulate and undulate palpably through the interconnected landscape forms. Tung Ch'i-ch'ang saw painting compositions neither as pictorial repre-

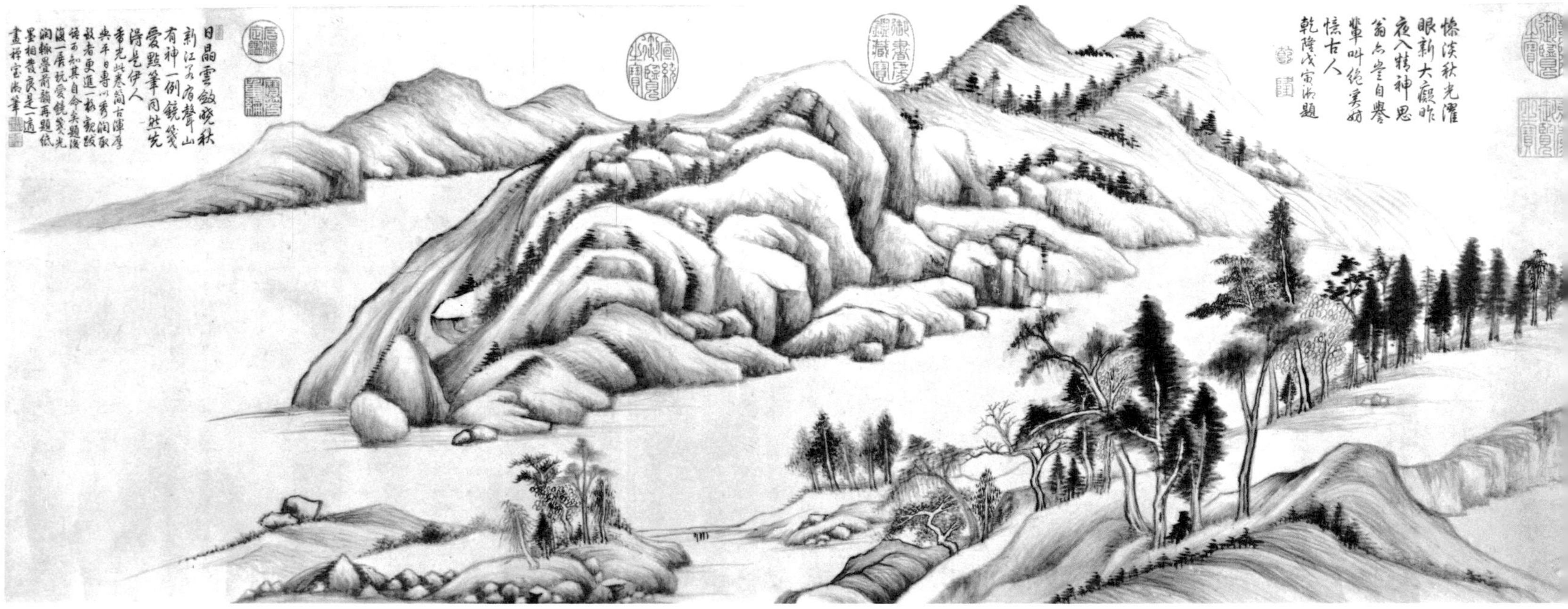

Fig. 143. Tung Ch'i-ch'ang, *River and Mountains on a Clear Autumn Day* (*Chiang-shan ch'iu-chi*). Undated, ca. 1610s. Handscroll, ink on paper. 38.4 x 136.8 cm (15 1/8 in. x 4 ft. 5 1/2 in.). Cleveland Museum of Art

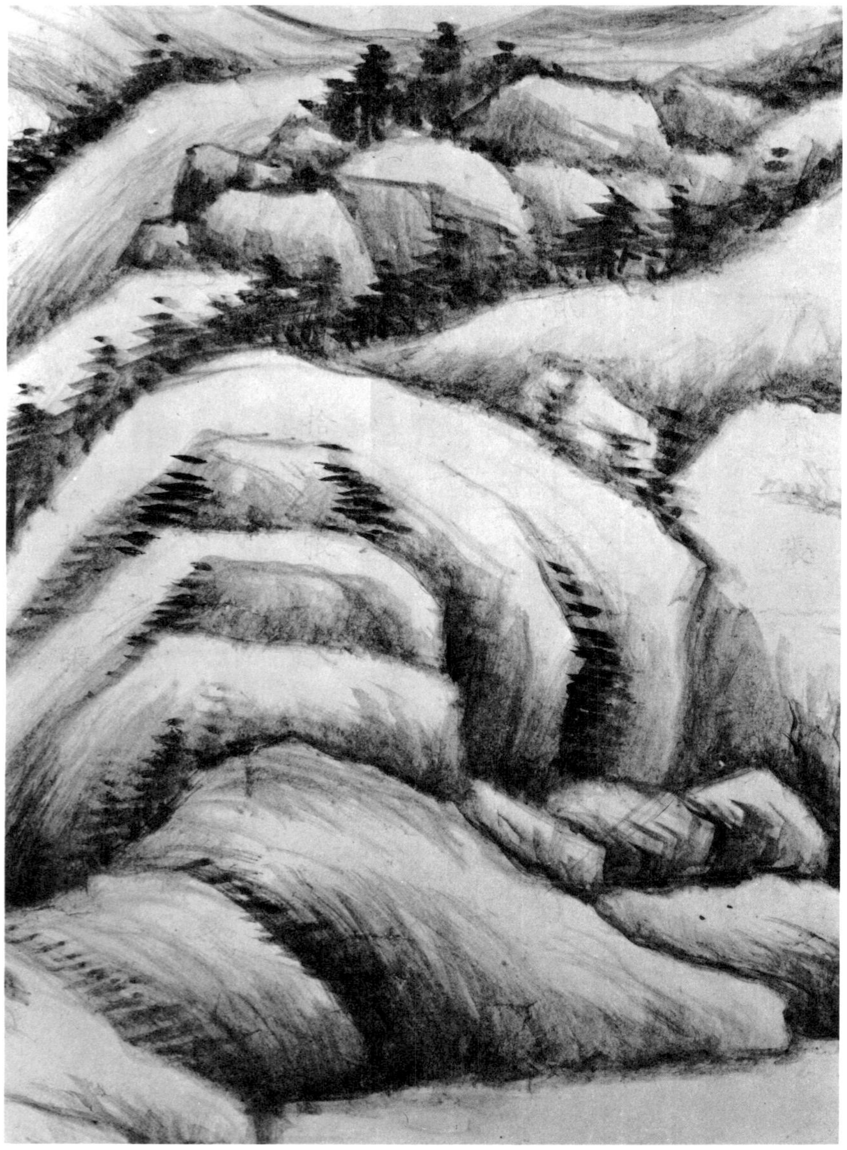

Fig. 143a. Detail, fig. 143

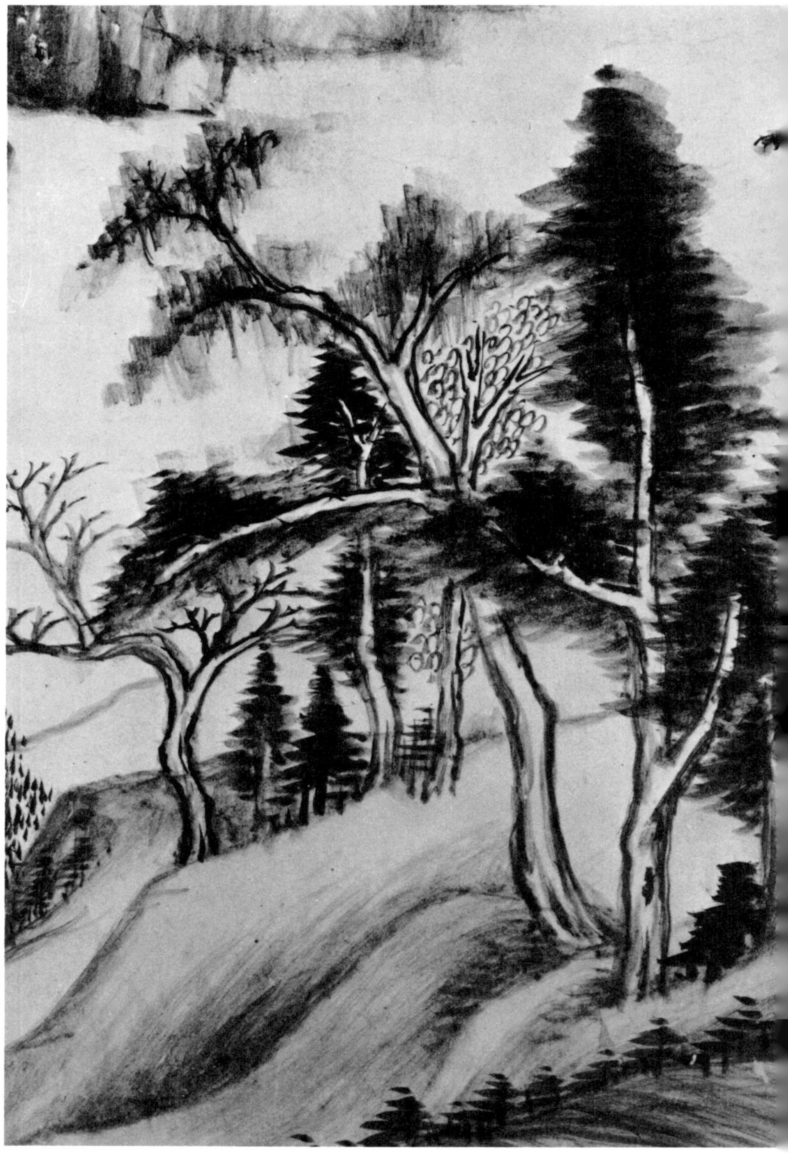

Fig. 143b. Detail, fig. 143

sentation nor as surface patterns, but as calligraphy: large, abstract characters written with sweeping, coming-and-going brush movements.

Tung recorded that he took up calligraphy seriously in about 1571 (when he was sixteen), first following Yen Chen-ch'ing (709–785), then the styles of Chung Yu (A.D. 151–230) and Wang Hsi-chih (ca. 307–ca. 365), which he felt he could not perfectly master. Then, for twenty years, he studied the Sung masters, finally succeeding in capturing "some moments of understanding."[32] He became a great admirer of Mi Fu, who was both a profound student of ancient calligraphy and a writer of great individuality. As he had insisted with painting, Tung maintained that "no calligrapher could imitate ancient styles without individual transformation"[33]:

> Ch'ien Mu-fu (fl. ca. 1100) once chided [Mi Fu] for writing too much like a "carved painting," and advised that he should rely principally on momentum [*shih*]. [Mi] was suddenly awakened [*wu*], so he completely discarded what he had learned, and produced designs of his own. He was like a Ch'an Buddhist after enlightenment, tearing off his flesh to return to his mother, breaking his bones to return to his father, shouting at his Buddha and cursing at his ancestors, totally changing his earlier appearance.[34]

Tung self-consciously compared himself with Chao Meng-fu (1254–1322), referring to himself as possessing "the [best] eye of the last three hundred years"—that is, since Chao.[35] He insisted, however, that Chao was much inferior to Mi Fu because Chao's writing lacked the force and momentum Tung considered to be crucial to calligraphy: "Chao's writing is too ripe and therefore vulgar." "My own writing," he added, "takes up where Chao Meng-fu left off, but mine has a somewhat raw quality."[36]

In a large handscroll, *Calligraphy in the Styles of the Four Sung Masters* (*Fang Su Huang Mi Tsai hsing-shu*) by Tung Ch'i-ch'ang, in the John B. Elliott Collection at The Art Museum, Princeton University (no. 26), Tung transcribed four pieces of writing by Su Shih (1036–1101), Huang T'ing-chien (1045–1105), Mi Fu, and Ts'ai Hsiang (1012–1067). One of the two seals by Tung, "Ta-tsung-po chang," refers to his honorific title as the president of the Board of Rites, thus dating the scroll to after 1625. Although the four sections of the scroll purport to follow four different styles, they all reflect Tung's own strongly individualistic manner. The third section, after Mi Fu, is done in large and bold characters: "Every character [by Mi Fu]," Tung once remarked, "could be enlarged and used in a signboard. Master Mi himself said, 'Large characters should look like small ones.' In essence, every character should have momentum."[37] Like Mi, Tung was an expert in fine, small-size writing; in the Elliott scroll, the large characters have the flexibility and subtle details of small writing, yet individual brushstrokes are fully imbued with power and momentum. For Tung Ch'i-ch'ang, now in his seventies, writing such a scroll was a pure pleasure, an opportunity to savor the delights of accidental correspondences with the ancient masters (cf. figs. 144 a,b) he had studied and knew so intimately. Such spontaneous correspondences offered a chance meeting between the mind and some ancient model, and they were perfectly transmitted by the hand through the unconditioned response of the brush, paper, and ink. In studying Mi Fu, Tung sought to capture not merely Mi's forms, but Mi's "moments of understanding"; thus the lessons he learned from ancient models were

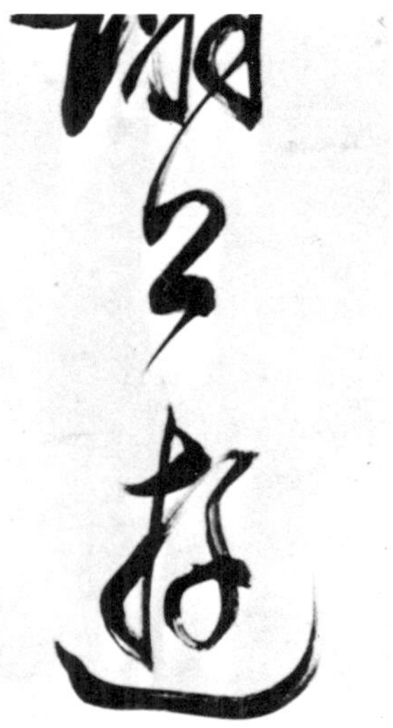

Fig. 144a. Tung Ch'i-ch'ang, detail, *Calligraphy in the Styles of the Four Sung Masters* (*Fang Su Huang Mi Ts'ai hsing-shu*), no. 26

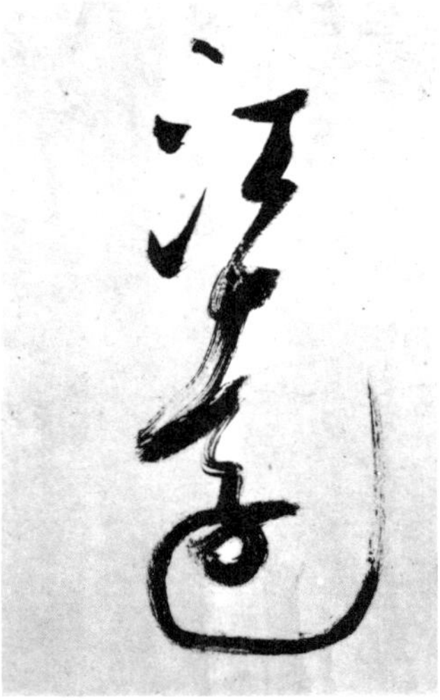

Fig. 144b. Mi Fu, detail, *Sailing on the Wu River* (*Wu-chiang chou chung shih*). Undated, ca. 1100. Handscroll, ink on paper. 31.3 x 559.8 cm (12 3/8 in. x 18 ft. 4 3/8 in.). John M. Crawford, Jr., collection

insights, rather than forms and techniques. Having awakened to the importance of momentum in Mi's writing, he was able to execute Mi's "square and circle" (Li Meng-yang's metaphor; cited in chapter 4) by ignoring Mi's ruler and compass. The key lies in the *wu-hsing*—the *hsing* (nature) for *wu* (awakening)—and not slavish imitation. Tung Ch'i-ch'ang was gifted with an uncommon *wu-hsing*, which gave him the best eye for connoisseurship and creativity in calligraphy and painting.

In an eight-leaf album, dated 1630 and therefore executed when Tung was seventy-five years old (seventy-six *sui*), formerly in the Edward L. Elliott Family Collection and now at The Metropolitan Museum of Art, New York (figs. 145a–d), Tung Ch'i-ch'ang interpreted the entire spectrum of Sung and Yüan painting styles in a set of contrasting brushstroke methods, while also depicting actual landscapes. In a colophon at the end of the album the master summed up his career:

> From the fourth month of the *ting-chou* year [1577], when I started to paint, until now, the *keng-wu* year [1630], fifty-three years have passed. Although the true style of my painting is not yet established, still the time I have spent is longer than any other painter. In ancient times the Lord Buddha, after preaching for forty-nine years, still had not turned the Wheel of the Law. Am I not like Buddha? If so, some later critic may indeed argue [as Mi Fu did about Li Ch'eng] that "there is no true Tung Ch'i-ch'ang!"

Tung's lament that his true style was "not yet established" reflected proper modesty on his part, but the colophon left no doubt that, after a lifetime of study, Tung fully expected to turn the Wheel of the Law in painting.

In the 1630 album, Tung took as his point of departure the early and late styles of Ni Tsan, which he rendered as pure calligraphic abstractions of earlier Sung styles. Tung began to study Ni Tsan in the early 1580s, when he gained access to the collection of Hsiang Yüan-pien, who had a special passion for Ni Tsan. Among Ni's extant dated works, the following bear Hsiang's collector's seals: *Water Bamboo Hermitage* (*Shui-chu chu*), dated 1343, now in the Municipal Collection, Peking; *Portrait of Yang Chu-hsi* (*Yang Chu-hsi kao-shih hsiao-hsiang*; collaborative work with the portraitist Wang I), dated 1363, in the Palace Museum, Peking; *Evening Tide on the River Sandbar* (*Chiang-chu mu-ch'ao*), dated 1363, in the John M. Crawford, Jr., collection; *Lion Grove Garden* (*Shih-tzu-lin t'u*), dated 1371, in the Palace Museum, Peking (?); and *Woods and Valleys of Mount Yü* (*Yü-shan lin-ho*), dated 1372, in The Metropolitan Museum of Art, New York.

Judging from Tung's dated comments, it appears that he did not fully grasp Ni Tsan's stylistic development until after he had acquired some major works by Ni in the 1610s and 1620s. In 1599 Tung saw, in the collection of his good friend Ch'en Chi-ju (1558–1639), Ni's *Autumn Clearing over a Fishing Lodge* (*Yü-chuang ch'iu-chi*; now in the Shanghai Museum), which bears an inscription by Ni, dated 1372, that dates the painting to 1355; Tung's brief colophon merely quotes Ku Cheng-i's (fl. ca. 1575–96) opinions about Ni Tsan, and (Tung perhaps not having read Ni's own inscription carefully) praises the work as "a masterpiece of [Ni's] later years."[38] In 1602 Tung wrote a colophon for Ni's *Six Gentlemen* of 1345 (cf. fig. 108); he noted that in this painting, Ni had modeled himself after Huang Kung-wang.[39] In a colophon written about 1603, on an album by Shen Chou, Tung stated, "In modeling himself after Tung Yüan in his earlier years, Ni Tsan followed the example of Huang Kung-wang."[40] In 1603 Tung inscribed Ni's *Autumn Woods and Mountain Colors* (*Ch'iu-lin shan-se*), writing that "Ni Tsan originally modeled himself after Tung Yüan, but in later years he transformed himself and painted small pictures in Kuan [T'ung's; fl. ca. 907–23] style."[41] In 1616 Tung painted a scroll "after Ni Tsan's fine style";[42] about 1625, after he was made president of the Board of Rites in Nanking, he did a painting "after Kuan T'ung" (using a seal alluding to his recently acquired high rank), and wrote on the painting, "Ni Tsan, after painting *Lion Grove Garden*, said that he had captured the ideas of Ching Hao and Kuan T'ung. Now I use Kuan [T'ung's] brushwork to write Ni Tsan's mountains. I only regret that old master [Ni] could not see me doing this!"[43] Meanwhile, in about 1620, Tung had acquired Ni's beautiful early work, *Water Bamboo Hermitage*;[44] also about 1620 he inscribed on Ni's *Painting Manual* (*Hua-p'u*; cf. figs. 113–15), and on Ni's *Pine Grove and Pavilion* (*Sung-lin*

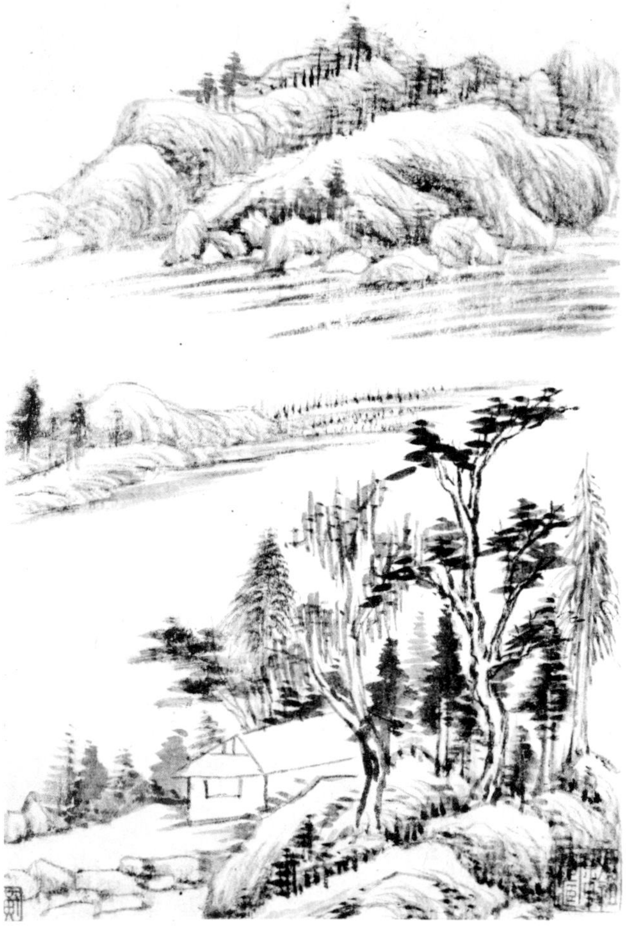

Fig. 145a. Tung Ch'i-ch'ang, album leaf 1 of *Eight Landscapes*. Dated 1630. Ink on paper. 24.5 x 16.0 cm ($9^{5}/_{8}$ x $6^{3}/_{8}$ in.). The Metropolitan Museum of Art, New York

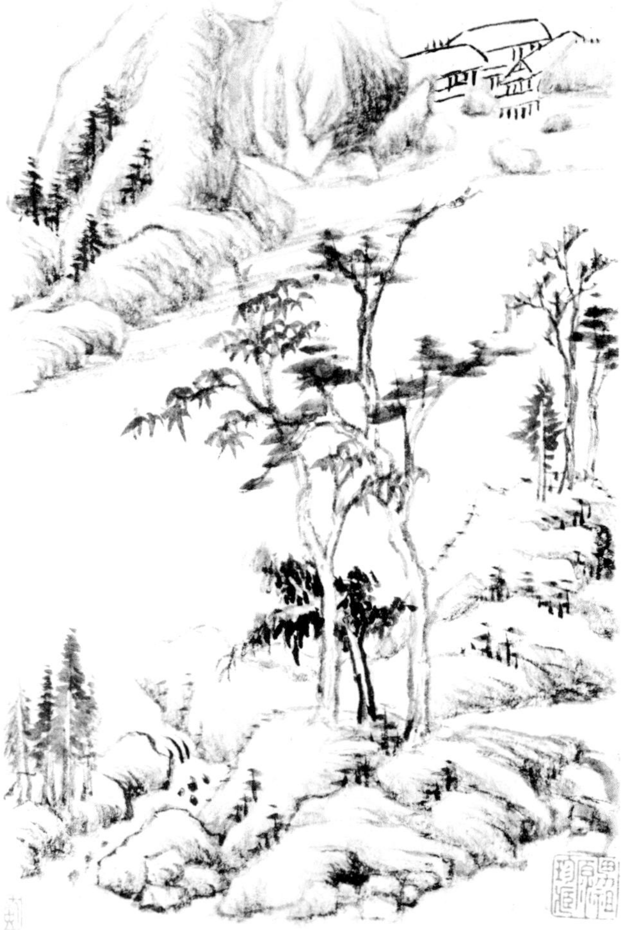

Fig. 145b. Tung Ch'i-ch'ang, album leaf 2 of *Eight Landscapes*

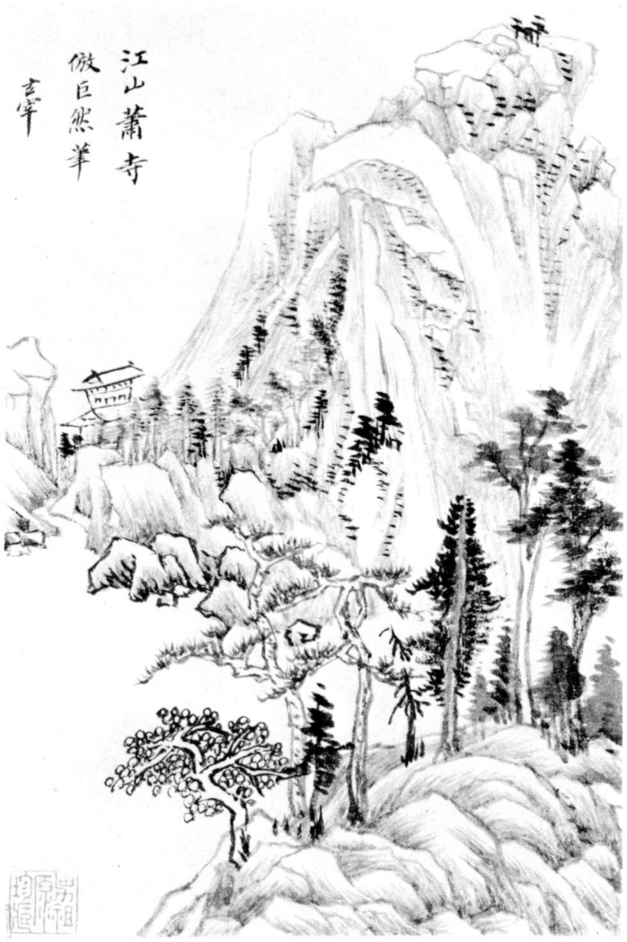


Fig. 145c. Tung Ch'i-ch'ang, album leaf 3 of *Eight Landscapes*

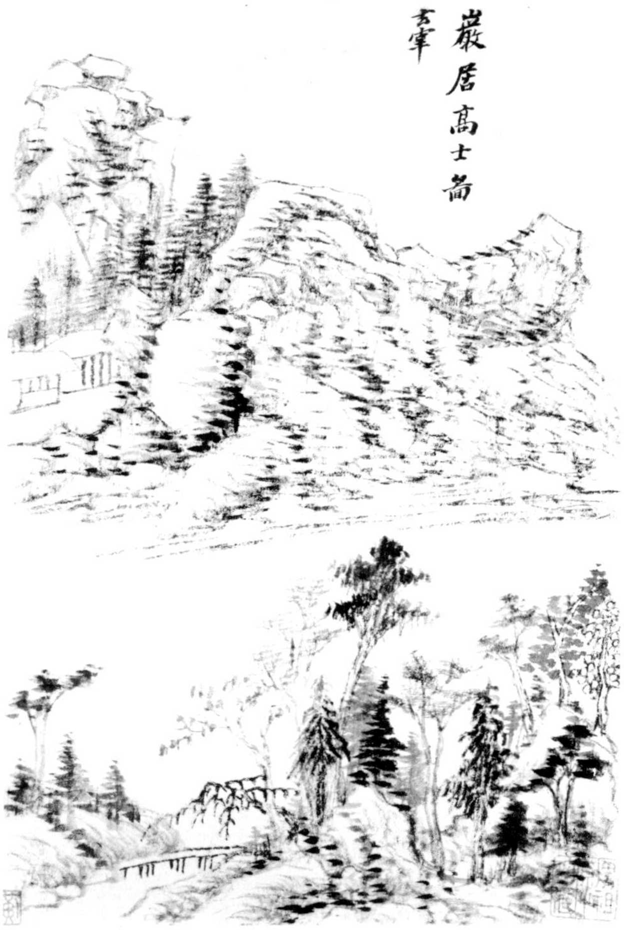

Fig. 145d. Tung Ch'i-ch'ang, album leaf 4 of *Eight Landscapes*

*t'ing-tzu*) of 1354, both in the National Palace Museum, Taipei.[45] And in about 1625, he painted *After Ni Tsan's "Hills and Valleys of Shan-yin"* (*Fang Ni Tsan Shan-yin ch'iu-ho t'u*), in the National Palace Museum, Taipei (fig. 146), and made the following remarks:

> Some time ago I had borrowed [Ni's *Hills and Valleys at Shan-yin*] to study, but failed to make a sketch. Now I try to re-create it with the help of Chü-jan's *Snow Clearing over the Mountain Pass* [*Kuan-shan hsüeh-chi*].[46]

This summary of Tung Ch'i-ch'ang's collecting experiences with Ni Tsan shows that it was not until the mid-1620s, when he was well into his sixties, that he finally gained a complete understanding of Ni's style. By that time he had become so enamored of Ni Tsan that he repeatedly tried to re-create Ni, the late Yüan master, through Chü-jan and Kuan T'ung, the two "patriarchs" of the tenth century, and conversely, through Ni, to re-create Chü-jan and Kuan T'ung, all in "a single intuitive leap."

In the album of 1630, Tung started with what he regarded as the early and late styles of Ni Tsan's art—an earthen landscape with round, parallel hemp-fiber brushstrokes, and a rocky landscape with angular, oblique "folded-ribbon" (*che-tai*) brushstrokes. He wrote to one side of the second leaf: "These two leaves represent the marrow of Ni Tsan's painting" (figs. 145a, b). Then, proceeding with the round method, he re-created the late tenth-century Southern masters Tung Yüan and Chü-jan (fig. 145c), and with the angular method, the early tenth-century Northern masters Ching Hao (fl. ca. 870–930) and Kuan T'ung (fig. 145d). In the remaining two leaves he combined the round and angular techniques to create scenic compositions.

In this Great Synthesis of Sung and Yüan paintings, Tung's basic method was the diagrammatic formula of filling "the outlined forms [with] straight texture strokes," which he had earlier extracted from the style of Huang Kung-wang. He then amplified this simple straight texture stroke (*chih-ts'un*), the archetype of all texture patterns, inventing a range of calligraphic texture methods that served as the alphabet of a new pictorial language. In the second half of the seventeenth century, while the Orthodox masters went on to systematize the Great Synthesis, the Indi-

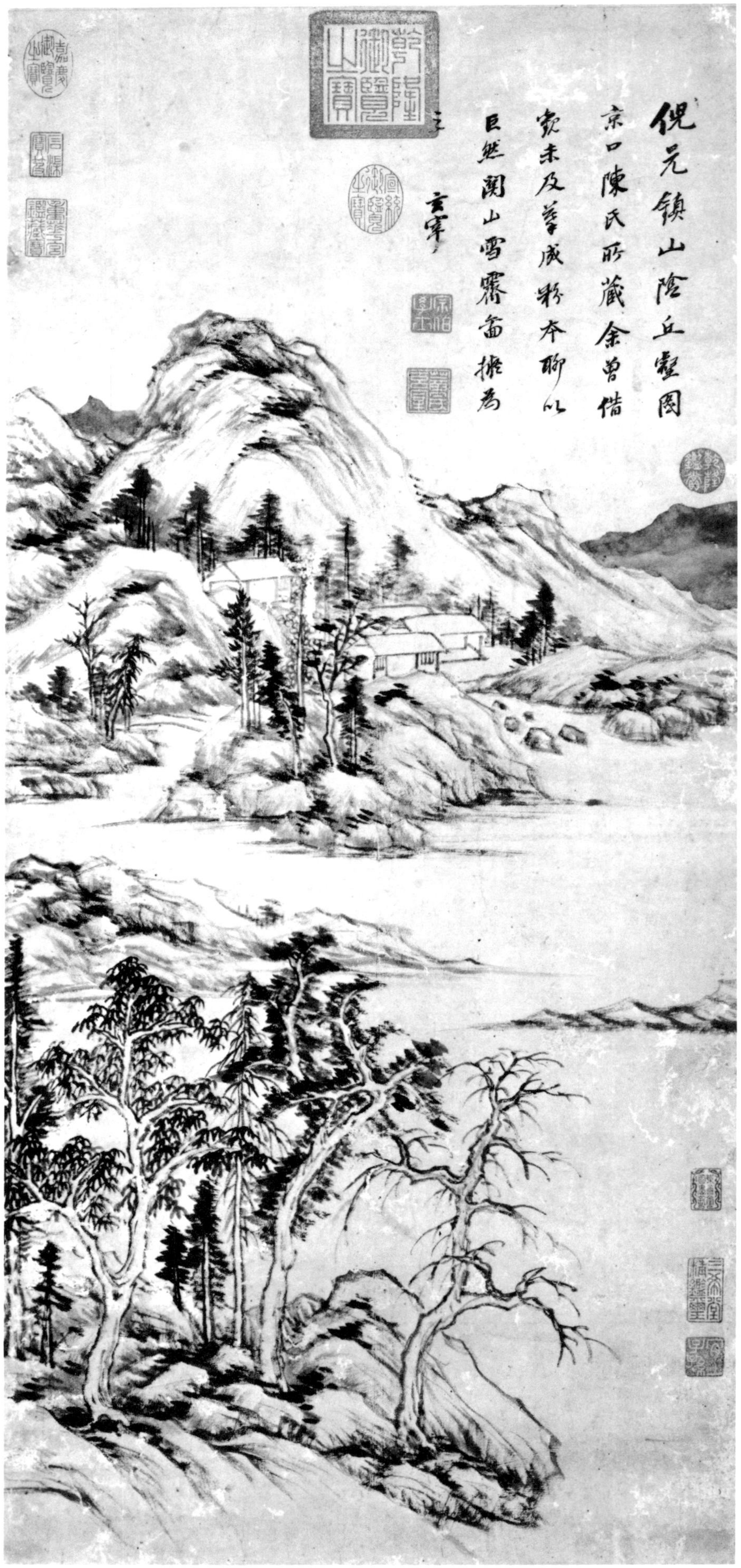


Fig. 146. Tung Ch'i-ch'ang, *After Ni Tsan's "Hills and Valleys of Shan-yin"* (*Fang Ni Tsan Shan-yin ch'iu-ho t'u*). Undated, ca. 1625. Hanging scroll, ink on paper. 96.9 x 45.1 cm (3 ft. 2 1/8 in. x 17 3/4 in.). National Palace Museum, Taipei

vidualist masters began to base their art on observation of nature, rather than study of earlier art, and to personalize their styles. In both these endeavors Tung's new approach to brush vocabulary proved indispensable.

## *Wang Shih-min's* Within Small See Large *Album*

Tung Ch'i-ch'ang's appointment, in 1594, as a tutor to the heir apparent came about through the efforts of his mentor Wang Hsi-chüeh (1534–1611), grand secretary to the Ming Wan-li emperor. From the late 1590s through the 1630s, Tung spent much time at his home in Hua-t'ing, and he frequently visited his mentor's home in T'ai-ts'ang. He was asked to tutor Wang's grandson Wang Shih-min, a particularly fortunate young man whose grandfather gave him everything he wanted. The young Wang resided in a separate estate, and was encouraged in his love for antiquities: "Whenever Wang Shih-min found a well-known masterpiece, he acquired it without considering the cost."[47]

As a student of painting, Wang had the best of instructors: Yün Shou-p'ing, in *Colophons of the Ou-hsiang Studio* (*Ou-hsiang-kuan hua-pa*), reported that when Wang Shih-min started to paint as a child, his grandfather asked Tung Ch'i-ch'ang to make models of trees and rocks for him. Tung did so, "illustrating Wang Wei's *Wang-ch'üan Villa*, the styles of Ching Hao, Tung Yüan, Mi Fu, Fan K'uan, and Li Ch'eng, giving the young man a range of tree and rock methods, their texturing, rubbing, outline, and ink wash to copy, each with a few words explaining the important principles."[48]

Besides illustrations of techniques, Wang Shih-min made copy books showing famous Sung and Yüan landscape compositions. A large album of twenty-two paintings (each 27⁵/₈ x 15⁷/₈ inches), entitled *Imitating Sung and Yüan Masters, Copies in Reduced Size, Paintings with Colophons* (*Fang Sung-Yüan-jen shu-pen hua-pa*), in the National Palace Museum, Taipei,[49] is also known by four large characters by Tung Ch'i-ch'ang, each filling a whole leaf, reading, "Within Small See Large" ("Hsiao-chung hsien-ta"). Following this "title" are twenty-two reduced but exactly rendered copies of well-known compositions by or attributed to eleven leading Sung and Yüan masters: Li Ch'eng (Leaf 1; cf. fig. 42), Fan K'uan (Leaf 2; fig. 147a), Tung Yüan (Leaf 3), Chao Meng-fu after Tung Yüan (Leaf 4), Chü-jan (Leaf 5; fig. 147b), Chao Meng-fu (?) (Leaf 6), Kao K'o-kung (Leaf 7), Huang Kung-wang (Leaves 8, 9, 12, 13, 16, 18), Wang Meng after Tung Yüan (Leaf 10), Wu Chen (Leaves 11, 15; fig. 147c; cf. fig. 37), Wang Meng (Leaves 14, 19), Wang Shen (Leaf 17), and Ni Tsan (Leaves 20–22). In eighteen instances the painting on the left-hand leaf is complemented on the right-hand leaf by an inscription signed by Tung Ch'i-ch'ang and accompanied by his seals; the inscriptions sometimes give the title and attribution of the original composition; argue for the attribution; comment on the style, source, and derivation; report the provenance and recent history of the work; and, in eight instances, record the dates of either Tung's personal experiences acquiring or parting with these paintings, or the writing of the inscriptions.

These carefully executed reduced copies, done in the late 1620s, are in fact not Tung Ch'i-ch'ang's work, but Wang Shih-min's. The album agrees with the description of an oversize album of models that Wang Shih-min was said to have made and to have carried around with him:

> [Wang Shih-min] once selected among ancient works some of the most successful in methods and in breath [*ch'i*], twenty-four in all, made reduced copies of them, and had them mounted into a giant album. He took this album with him wherever he went, to serve as his models. Thus, in his works, every compositional detail, every outline, texture, and ink wash had its origin in an ancient source.[50]

As tutor to the young Wang Shih-min, Tung helped to form the younger man's collection, passing on some of the ancient paintings in his own collection and advising Wang on the purchase of others. As Wang Shih-min made the copies as a record for study, Tung transcribed the titles and inscriptions he composed for the original works.

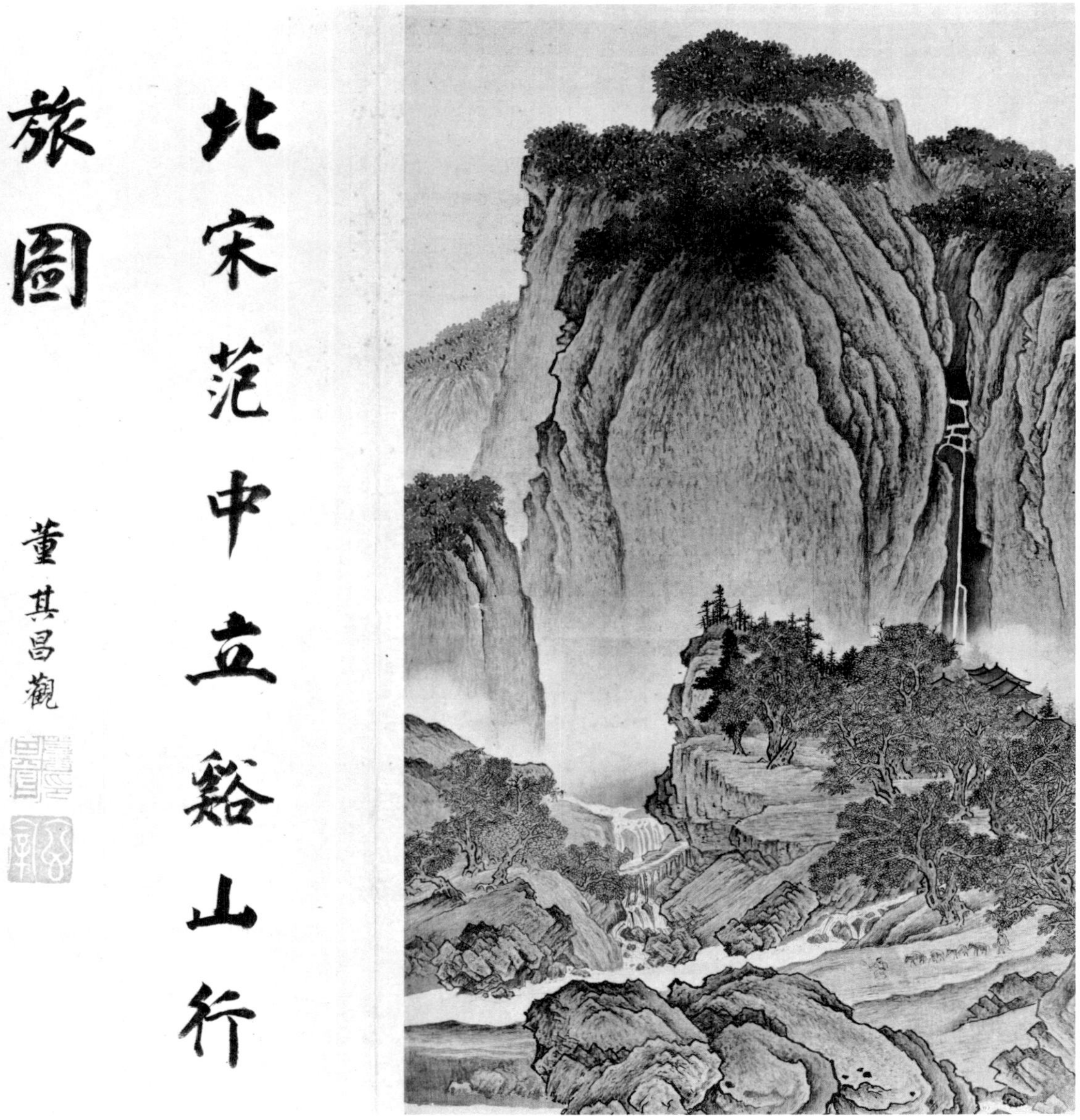


Fig. 147a. Wang Shih-min, "After Fan K'uan's 'Travelers among Streams and Mountains,'" and inscription by Tung Ch'i-ch'ang. Undated, late 1620s. Album leaf 2 of *Within Small See Large* (*Hsiao-chung hsien-ta*), ink and light color on silk. 70.2 x 40.2 cm ($27\frac{5}{8}$ x $15\frac{7}{8}$ in.). National Palace Museum, Taipei

The album provides valuable evidence for Tung's own collecting activities from the late 1590s through the 1620s. In 1598 he inscribed on the *Snow Scene* (Leaf 1; cf. fig. 42), which he attributed to Li Ch'eng, rather than Fan K'uan. Leaf 16 reproduces a composition by Huang Kung-wang,[51] acquired through exchange in 1599 and inscribed in 1600. Leaf 4 reproduces a painting described as by "Chao Meng-fu after Tung Yüan," acquired in 1607. Leaf 18 shows a Huang Kung-wang composition, seen and inscribed in 1614, which, Tung's inscription points out, "compares closely with the *Fu-ch'un* mountain scroll in [his] own collection," while Leaf 8 reproduces the well-known *Thick Woods in a Steep Valley* (*Tou-ho mi-lin*) by Huang.[52] In the inscription accompanying Leaf 8, Tung noted that he had known the work since his early days in Peking in the early 1590s. The painting subsequently entered the collection of Ku Cheng-i. Although Tung had long since acquired most of the works by Huang in Ku's collection, Ku had withheld this particular painting. Tung finally succeeded in purchasing it in 1620, presumably from Ku's descendants. In the mid-1620s, Tung acquired three important works by Wang Meng: *An Elegant Gathering among Forests and Streams* (*Lin-ch'uan ch'ing-chi*), dated 1367, by Wang (Leaf 14), which Tung compared favorably with Wang's *Dwelling in the Ch'ing-pien Mountains* of 1366 (cf. fig. 119), he purchased from a Tsou family in Su-chou in 1625; Wang Meng's *After Tung Yüan's "Travelers in Autumn Mountains"* (*Fang Tung Yüan Ch'iu-shan hsing-lu t'u*; Leaf 10), which he compared, in his inscription, with Tung Yüan's composition by the same title also in his collection, was inscribed in 1627; and Leaf 19 copies Wang's *Spring Dawn over Mount*

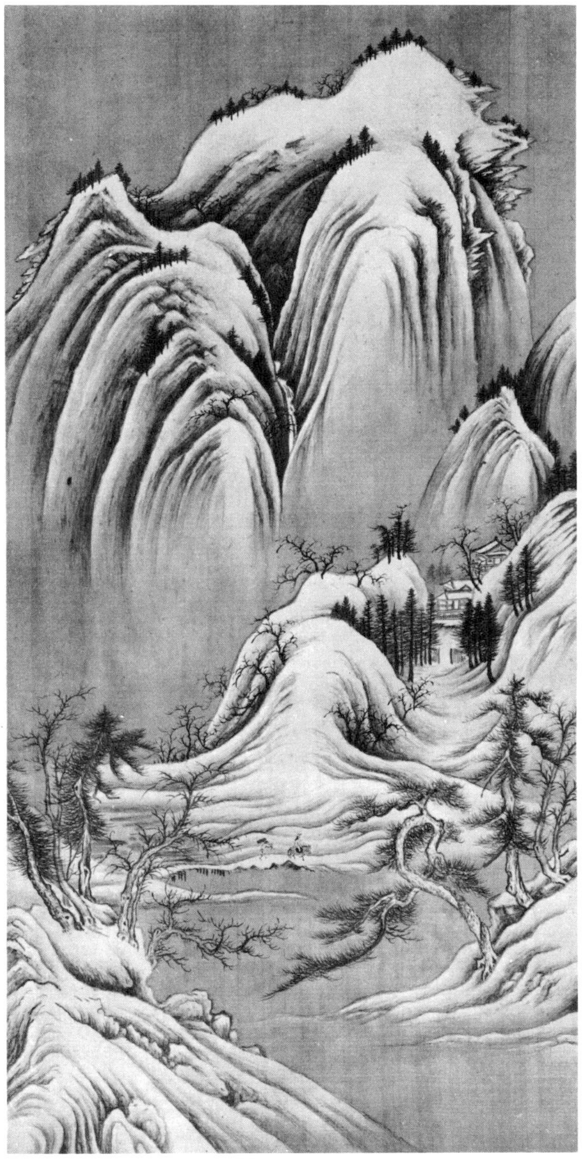

Fig. 147b. Wang Shih-min, "After Chü-jan's 'Snow Scene.'" Album leaf 5 of *Within Small See Large* (*Hsiao-chung hsien-ta*), ink on silk

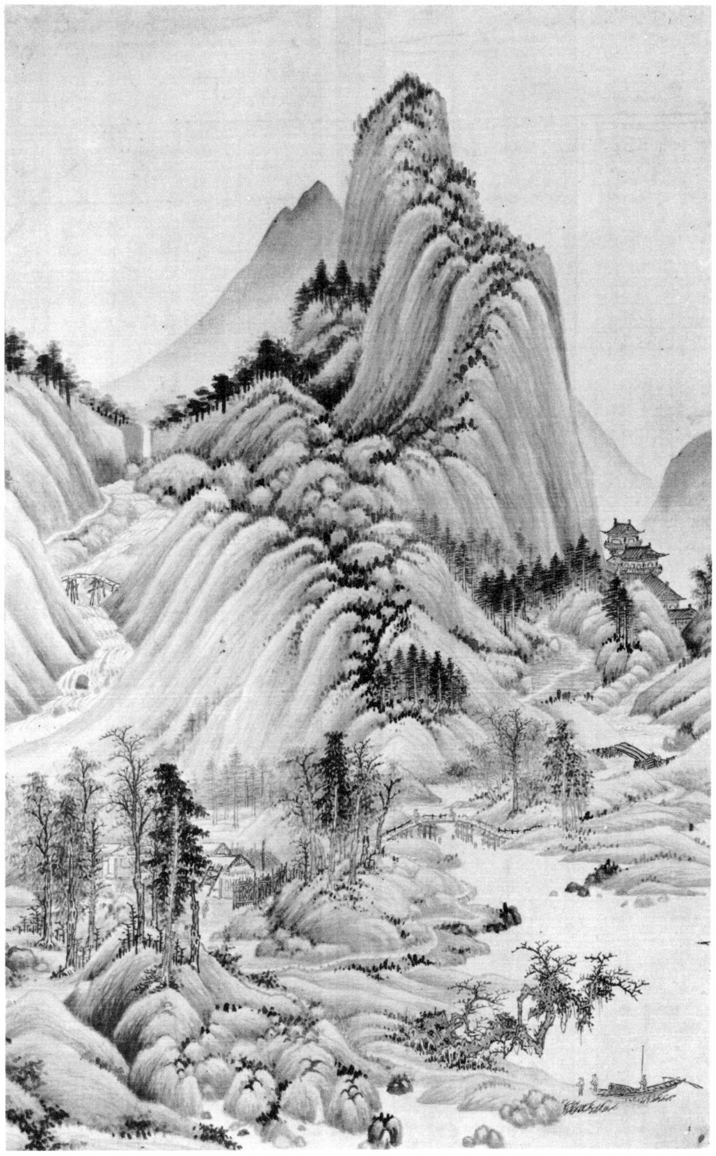

Fig. 147c. Wang Shih-min, "After Wu Chen." Album leaf 11 of *Within Small See Large* (*Hsiao-chung hsien-ta*), ink and light color on silk

*Tan-t'ai* (*Tan-t'ai ch'un-hsiao*; now in the National Palace Museum, Taipei), which he had bought in 1626 and gave to Wang Shih-min in 1627.[53] Presumably by 1627 or slightly later, when Wang Shih-min made these copies and Tung transcribed the inscriptions, all of these paintings, as well as the others shown in the album, had entered Wang Shih-min's collection.

This album was a prime source for Sung and Yüan models throughout the seventeenth century, not only for Wang Shih-min and his friend Wang Chien, but also for Wang Hui, Wu Li, and others lucky enough to have access to it.

## *Wang Hui: The Two Wings of Painting*

Wang Hui was born in Yü-shan (Mount Yü), a village near Ch'ang-shu, north of Su-chou, on April 10, 1632. Ch'ang-shu was the birthplace of Huang Kung-wang, whose tomb was located on the south side of Mount Yü. Like Wang Shih-min's family, Wang Hui's, though not related, originally came from T'ai-yüan, Shansi, in north China, moving to the south during the Mongol invasion in the late thirteenth century. Wang Hui's great-grandfather Wang Po-ch'en, grandfather Wang Tsai-shih, father Wang Huan-lung, and uncle Huan-ao were all painters, specializing in landscapes and birds and flowers.[54] Wang Hui's family was poor, but even as a child he played by drawing on the wall with a reed. His first teacher was a local painter by the name of Chang K'o. In 1651, at the age of nineteen, young Wang Hui was discovered by

Wang Chien, who introduced him, more than a year later, to Wang Shih-min. Astounded by the young man's natural talent, Wang Shih-min housed young Wang Hui at Hsi-t'ien, his country villa in the western suburb of T'ai-ts'ang, brought out all his treasured ancient paintings for him to study and copy, and introduced him as his protégé to other leading collectors.

A sense of how Wang Hui was viewed by his peers is best provided by Wang Shih-min, who wrote a long colophon on a snow scene painted by Wang Hui in the late 1660s:

> In recent years there have been as many painters as trees in a forest. . . . As for the kind of painter who has not been seen in the last 500 years, there is only our Wang Hui, one person, that is all. . . . He is like a student of Ch'an Buddhism who has achieved total awakening: by understanding one thing, he understands a hundred things. This is known as "entering into the Land of Tathagata Buddha in one single leap.". . .
>
> I have long had an obsession for the Tao of painting. Unfortunately, my natural endowment is dull and inferior, and moreover I have been hampered by the cares of worldly affairs. I have not been able to study diligently, and I have accomplished little. As for my other painter friends, known to me throughout my life, most of them have not been able to free themselves from prevailing fashions. I have always thought that such was the fault of our time. Little did I expect that in my declining years I would meet someone like Wang Hui. As I watch him, some ancient master suddenly appears before my eyes. Is this not a great good fortune?[55]

Wang Hui lived and worked for nearly thirty years in the company of Wang Shih-min and Wang Chien. (Wang Chien died in 1677 and Wang Shih-min in 1680.) Starting with the styles of Huang Kung-wang and Wang Meng, Wang Hui first mastered a Great Synthesis of Sung and Yüan styles through the Yüan calligraphic idiom. Then, in the 1680s, he made major efforts toward re-creating a monumental landscape style, by producing long handscrolls incorporating the Northern Sung idioms of Chü-jan, Fan K'uan, and Yen Wen-kuei (fl. ca. 970–1030).

Soon after the end of the rebellion of the Three Feudatories in 1681, the Ch'ing K'ang-hsi emperor started to consolidate his rule in the south. After his successful first southern inspection tour in 1684, he began to make plans for a second, which took place in 1689. New maps of the empire were ordered, and Sung Chien-chai, a powerful eunuch, recommended that Wang Hui be made a *tai-chao* (painter-in-waiting).[56] By 1691 Wang Hui found himself in Peking, supervising the creation of a record of the second imperial southern inspection journey of 1689. Breaking down the journey into episodes, Wang Hui designed a series of twelve massive handscrolls, known as *The Southern Inspection Tour Paintings* (*Nan-hsün t'u*). He painted most of the landscapes himself, in the monumental Northern Sung idioms he had perfected in the late 1680s, but left the figures, architectural drawings, and more routine work to his assistants. Upon the completion of the project in 1698, Wang Hui was granted an audience with the delighted emperor, who bestowed on him a scroll, personally inscribed "The landscape is clear and radiant" ("Shan-shui ch'ing-hui"), a quotation from the fourth-century poet Hsieh Ling-yün. Thus honored, Wang Hui returned home in November 1698, henceforth adopting the name Ch'ing-hui chu-jen (Master of the Clear and Radiant Hall). When he died in his birthplace, Yü-shan, on November 15, 1717, he was the most renowned painter in the south.

One of Wang Hui's early works, *After Chü-jan's Brushwork* (*Fang Chü-jan pi-i*), dated 1664, in the Earl Morse collection at The Art Museum, Princeton University (fig. 148), marks a transitional period, when Wang began to break away from Tung Ch'i-ch'ang's style to create a new style of his own. The immediate model for *After Chü-jan* was the *Snow Scene* (*Hsüeh-t'u*) attributed to Chü-jan, as known from Wang Shih-min's *Within Small See Large* album (Leaf 5; cf. fig. 147b). Wang Hui's painting was a birthday gift dedicated to "the venerable old Master Hsiu." Before the dedication, he wrote a couplet of two four-word phrases: "Mountains [and] streams round [and] full, / Grass [and] trees resplendent [and] lush." Wang took

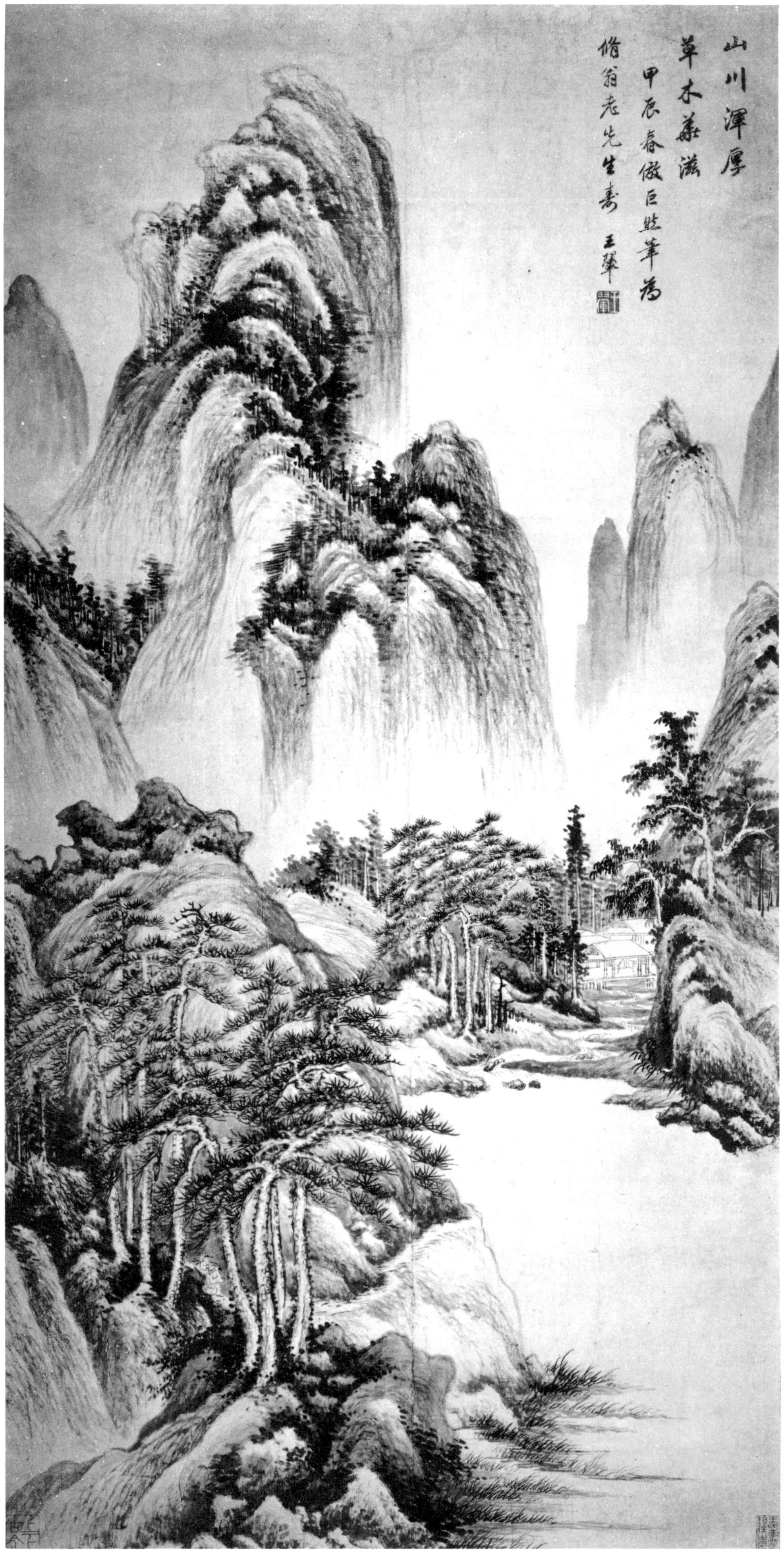


Fig. 148. Wang Hui, *After Chü-jan's Brushwork* (*Fang Chü-jan pi-i*). Dated 1664. Hanging scroll, ink on paper. 131.0 x 65.5 cm (4 ft. 3⅝ in. x 25¾ in.). The Art Museum, Princeton University

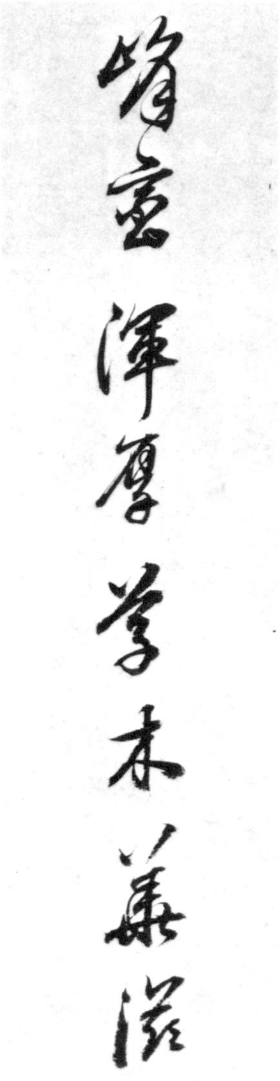


Fig. 149a. Tung Ch'i-ch'ang, detail of colophon, late 1620s, to album leaf 8 of Wang Shih-min's *Within Small See Large* (*Hsiao-chung hsien-ta*), ink on paper

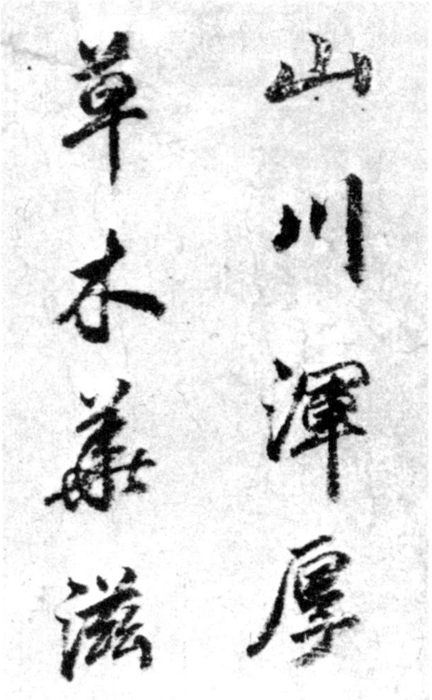


Fig. 149b. Wang Hui, detail of inscription, fig. 148

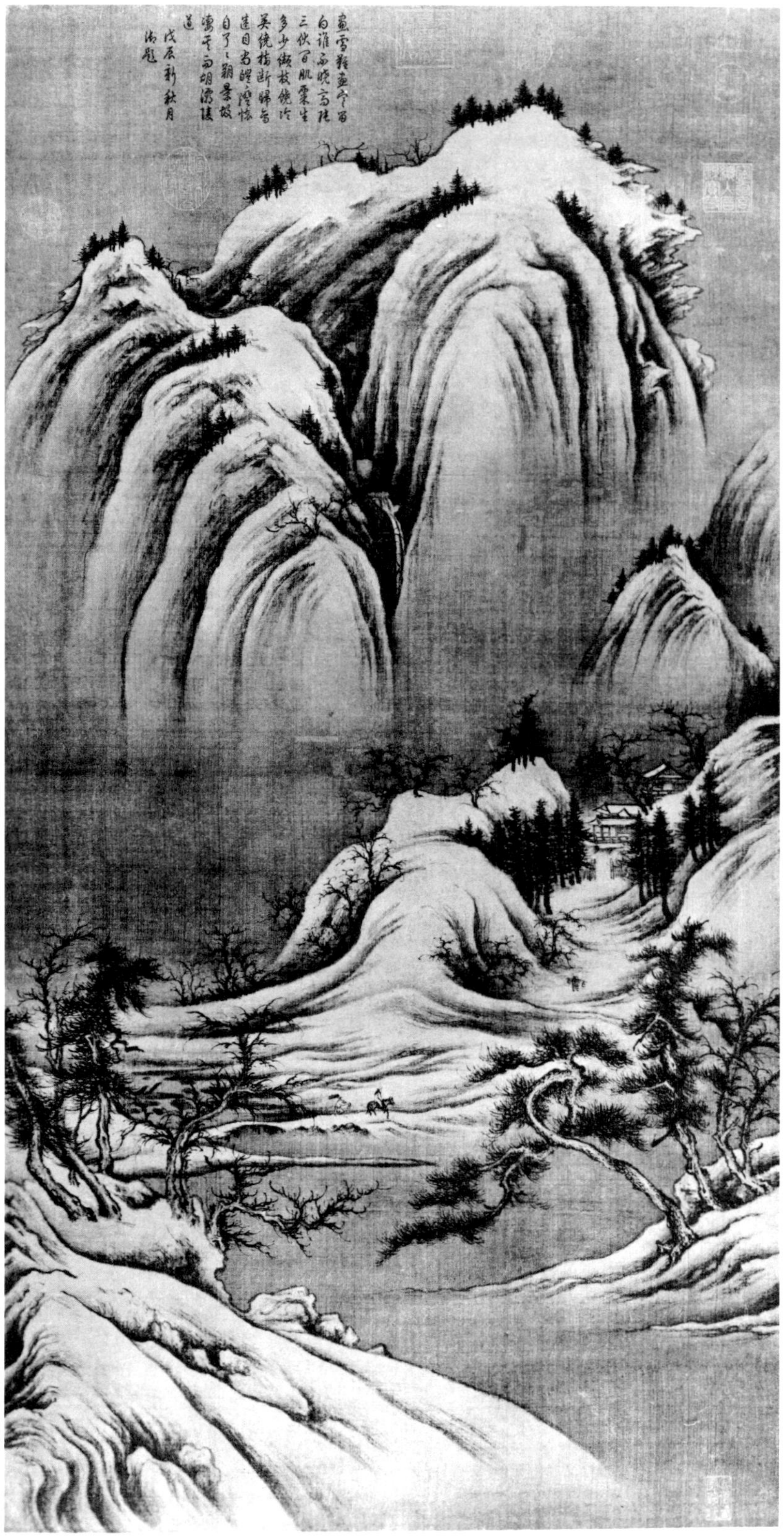

Fig. 150. Attributed to Chü-jan, *Snow Scene* (*Hsüeh-t'u*). Undated, copy ca. 1100(?). Hanging scroll, ink on silk. 103.6 x 52.5 cm (3 ft. 4¾ in. x 20⅝ in.). National Palace Museum, Taipei

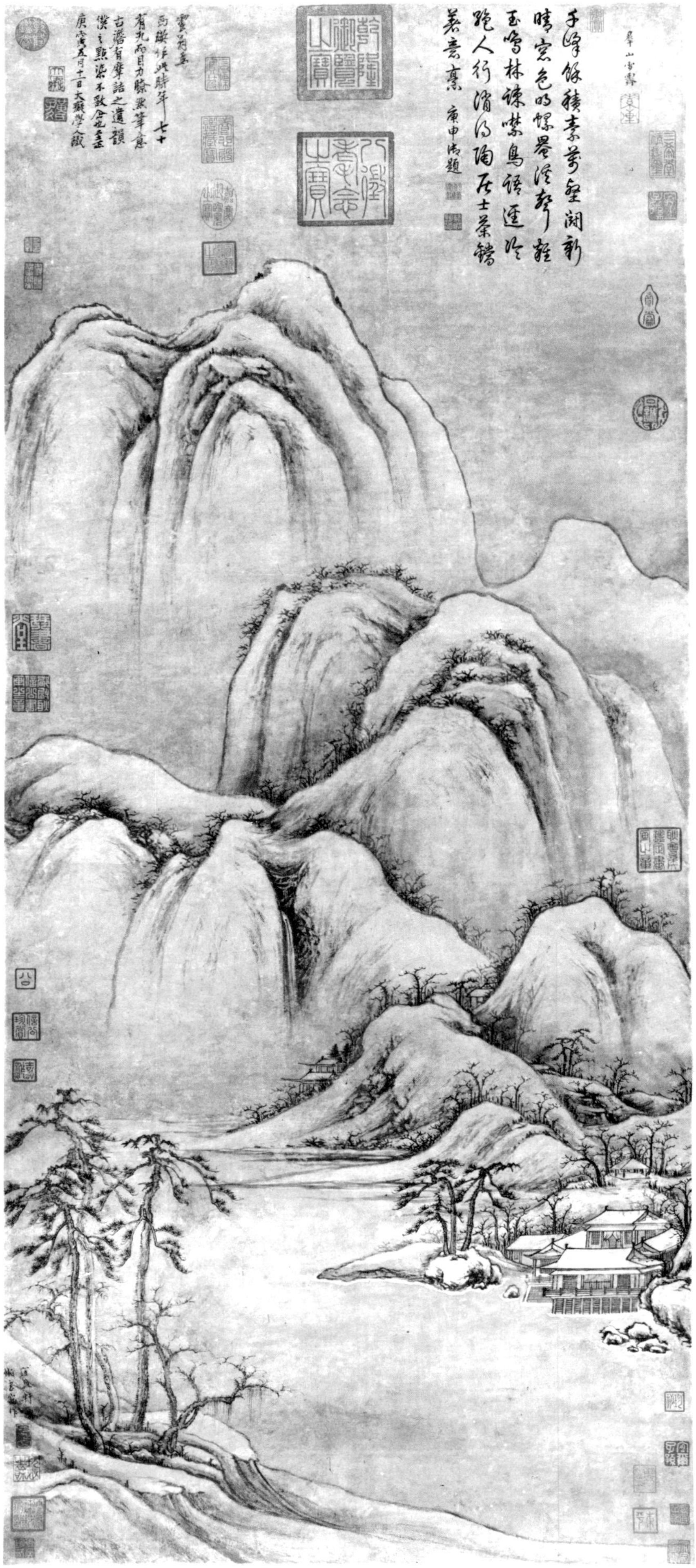

Fig. 151. Ts'ao Chih-po, *Mountain Peaks in Clearing after Snow* (*Ch'ün-shan hsüeh-chi*). Dated 1350. Hanging scroll, ink on paper. 129.7 x 56.4 cm (4 ft. 3 in. x 22¼ in.). National Palace Museum, Taipei

these two lines, originally part of Chang Yü's description of a painting by Huang Kung-wang, from Tung Ch'i-ch'ang's colophons in Wang Shih-min's *Within Small See Large* album (Leaves 8, 12; cf. figs. 149a, b). The use of this quotation on Wang Hui's painting had several levels of meaning. First, as the painting was meant to be a birthday present, the quotation was a felicitous eulogy, comparing the recipient's good health to luxuriant mountains and streams. Second, the words seemed to speak for the artist's own pride and satisfaction in his rich native land of Chiang-nan. Such praise no doubt would have pleased even the K'ang-hsi emperor, newly ascended to the throne in 1662. Finally, and most important, the colophon paid homage to Tung Ch'i-ch'ang, who, through Wang Shih-min, was Wang Hui's true teacher. For Wang Hui, this eight-word epithet, more than actually describing a landscape that is "round and full" and "resplendent and lush," characterized a rich and splendid painting style. Huang Kung-wang, according to Tung Ch'i-ch'ang, had "expressed joyfulness in painting."[57] Remembering Tung's words—"If one considers the wonders of brush and ink, then [real] landscape can never equal painting"—Wang Hui now created a "round and full" painting style with a "resplendent and lush" brushwork.

Wang Hui did not copy the Sung composition. Freely adapting elements from Wang Shih-min's copy in the *Within Small See Large* album, he enlarged the group of pine trees in the foreground on the left, linking them diagonally with the smaller pine forest in the middle distance, which in turn he related rhythmically with the great serpentine movement of the central peak in the background. In the drawing of the mountain form, he followed Tung Ch'i-ch'ang's graphic formula of filling the outlined forms with straight texture strokes. Individual brushstrokes rather than representing forms now conveyed the life and energy of the landscape; the brushstrokes grew and expanded continuously until the whole became a great flowing pattern of billowing eddies and countereddies.

A series of datable Yüan, Ming, and Ch'ing compositions derived from the original Sung *Snow Scene* attributed to Chü-jan, now in the National Palace Museum, Taipei (fig. 150), illustrates the successive changes in compositional structure in landscape painting since the Sung period. While Tung Ch'i-ch'ang's attribution of the *Snow Scene* to Chü-jan has been challenged, the composition, which relates closely to the opening section of the handscroll *Rivers and Mountains after Snow* attributed to Wang Wei (cf. fig. 142), shows the typical early Northern Sung three-stepped progression into depth.[58] In *Mountain Peaks in Clearing after Snow* (*Chün-shan hsüeh-chi*) by Ts'ao Chih-po (1272–1355), which is dated 1350 by an inscription by Huang Kung-wang, in the National Palace Museum, Taipei (fig. 151), the expanded mountains of the middle distance now move back diagonally into space, along a continuously receding ground plane; Ts'ao's treatment of space indeed closely resembles Huang Kung-wang's in the latter artist's *Fu-ch'un* scroll, also dated 1350 (cf. fig. 67). In Wang Shih-min's copy the mountain forms occupy the front of the picture plane; they relate to the frame of the composition in a manner typical of late Ming painting, as sweeping, zigzagging surface patterns.

In Tung Ch'i-ch'ang's renderings of the Chü-jan theme, as seen in his *Hills and Valleys of Shan-yin*, dated about 1625 (cf. fig. 146), and the leaf evoking Chü-jan's style in the album dated 1630 (cf. fig. 145c), the energized calligraphic texture strokes give the landscape elements a totally new appearance; rather than modeling and describing forms, the bluntly assertive calligraphic brushstrokes build forms that fully express the kinetic energies of the brushwork; the forms are no longer flat, they project and recede, and move with great dynamic force (*shih*) in abstract space.

Finally, in Wang Hui's *After Chü-jan*, the kinetic forces of the texture strokes have been totally marshaled in an orderly fashion to create an imposing design of billowing and undulating forms. The calligraphic formula of filling outlined forms with texture strokes now brings the painter to the center of the act of painting: in the words of the colophon to the ancient treatise on calligraphy, Lady Wei's *Battle Array of the Brush* (*Pi-ch'eng-t'u*), "the paper is the battlefield, the brush is sword and lance, . . . the heart and mind are the general, skill is the general's lieutenant."[59] "Wang Hui once told me," reported Wang Yüan-ch'i, "that in executing a composition, whether in a coarse or fine style, the painter must first see in front of him the basic outlines of entering and exiting."[60] Remarking that "in [landscape] painting one needs only to pay attention to the breath-force [*ch'i-shih*], the general outlines of the design," Wang Yüan-ch'i credited Wang Hui with the discovery of what was called the "dragon vein" (*lung-mo*) principle in composition:

> Although dragon veins that open and close, rise and fall in a composition had been present in ancient paintings, they were never clearly pointed out. Now that Wang Hui has made them clear, all students know what to follow. . . . The dragon vein marks the breath-force of a painting; its starting point may be oblique or symmetrical, rounded or fragmented, broken or continuous, hidden or apparent. This is the basic principle. . . . While the overall composition has opening and closing movements, individual sections of the composition also have their own openings and closings; and while there are overall risings and fallings, there are also individual risings and fallings. . . . If the dragon, in its many oblique or frontal, unified or broken, obscured or apparent, interrupted or continuous positions, is lively and vivid, the painting will be true.[61]

With Wang Hui's dragon-vein principle, which fully developed Tung Ch'i-ch'ang's idea of momentum, compositional unity in landscape painting now depended not so much on the balance and harmony of the parts, as in works of the earlier periods, as on the kinetic energy and tension—the momentum generated by individual brushstrokes within the organic pictorial structure.

Wang Hui used a new Chü-jan model in *After Chü-jan's "Mist Floating on a Distant Peak"* (*Fang Chü-jan Yen-fou yüan-hsiu t'u*), dated 1672, in the Earl Morse collection at The Art Museum, Princeton University (fig. 152).[62] The painting on silk shows a great heaving abstract mountain mass, with round calligraphic brushstrokes executed in abstract arcs, circles, and dots; the only natural elements are a few vertical trees in the lower portion of the composition, which serve to point out the direction of the dragon-vein movements. Again, Wang Hui did not copy his model precisely. An identical composition attributed to Chü-jan (fig. 153) in the Fuji-Yūrinkan Museum, in Kyoto, is a replica of Wang Hui's *Mist Floating*.[63] The model for both paintings seems to be *Seeking the Tao in Autumn Mountains* attributed to Chü-jan (cf. fig. 35), or a close replica of that composition.

Colophons by Wang Hui and his teachers Wang Shih-min and Wang Chien, accompanying *Mist Floating* of 1672, spoke of an exciting stylistic discovery. "This painting," wrote Wang Hui, "does not make use of any paths, streams, houses, temple buildings, boats, or bridges. It depends entirely on broad and heroic compositional forces." Wang Shih-min found "a primordial breath [*yüan-ch'i*] filling this composition," and Wang Chien called the work "a living reincarnation of Chü-jan."

Fully conscious of the significance of his stylistic experiments, Wang Hui described his method in two of the seals on these paintings: in the lower left corner of *After Chü-jan* the artist's seal reads, "I travel up and down through past and present" ("Shang-hsia ku-chin"), and above *Mist Floating* one seal reads, "Why not this way?" ("Yu-ho pu-k'o"). In *Mist Floating* Wang Hui finally discovered the archetype of the Southern School style: no descriptive details intruded; abstract brushwork and breath-forces prevailed. Wang-Hui realized that the secret of the Southern School style—calligraphic brushwork—was a Yüan rather than Sung legacy. "I must use the brush and ink of the Yüan," it came to Wang Hui suddenly, "to move the peaks and valleys of the Sung, and infuse them with the breath-resonance [*ch'i-yün*] of the T'ang. I shall then have a work of the Great Synthesis."[64]

Wang Hui disagreed with Tung Ch'i-ch'ang's dictum that "in painting it is better to be obscure than to be obvious": "Painting has its obvious and obscure aspects," he concluded. "These are like the two wings of a bird; neither should be used singly at the expense of the other. When the obvious and the obscure are equally perfected, a spirited breath [*ch'i*] will emerge."[65]

In an album of twelve leaves entitled *In Pursuit of Antiquity* (*Chü-ku*), dated 1673 and dedicated to Wang Shih-min, now in the Earl Morse collection at The Art Museum, Princeton University (figs. 154a,b), Wang Hui presented a brilliant display of his Great Synthesis of the "two wings" of painting, the "obscure" and

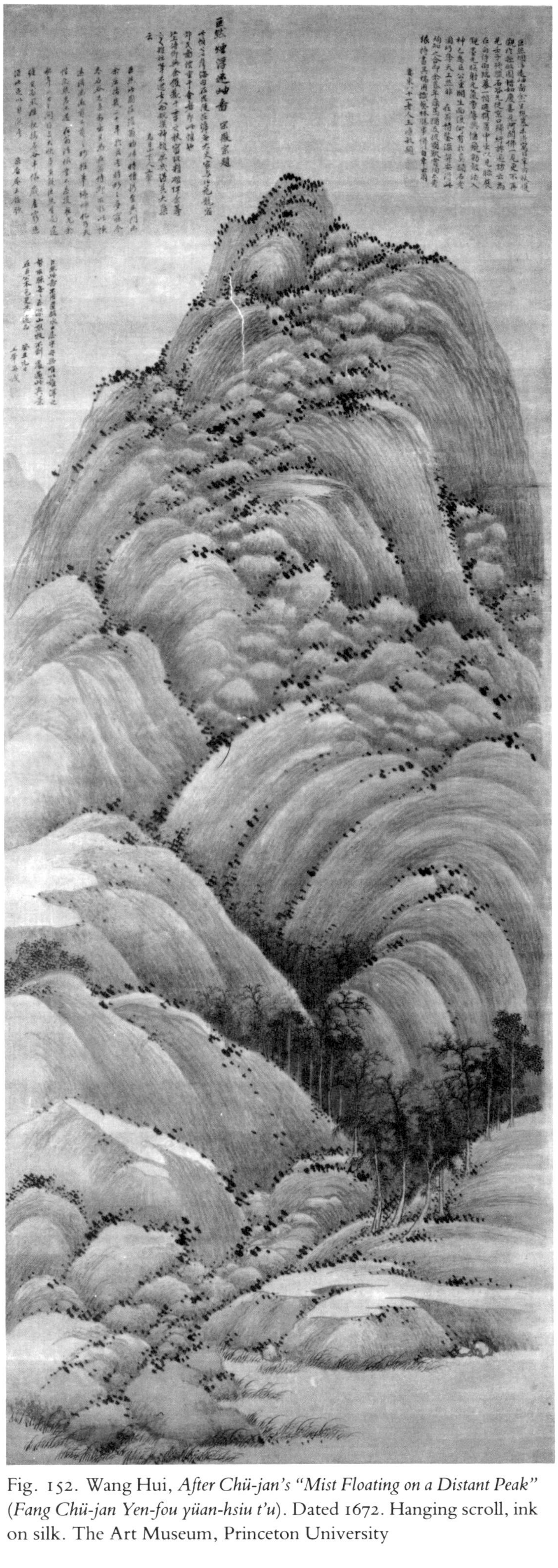

Fig. 152. Wang Hui, *After Chü-jan's "Mist Floating on a Distant Peak"* (*Fang Chü-jan Yen-fou yüan-hsiu t'u*). Dated 1672. Hanging scroll, ink on silk. The Art Museum, Princeton University

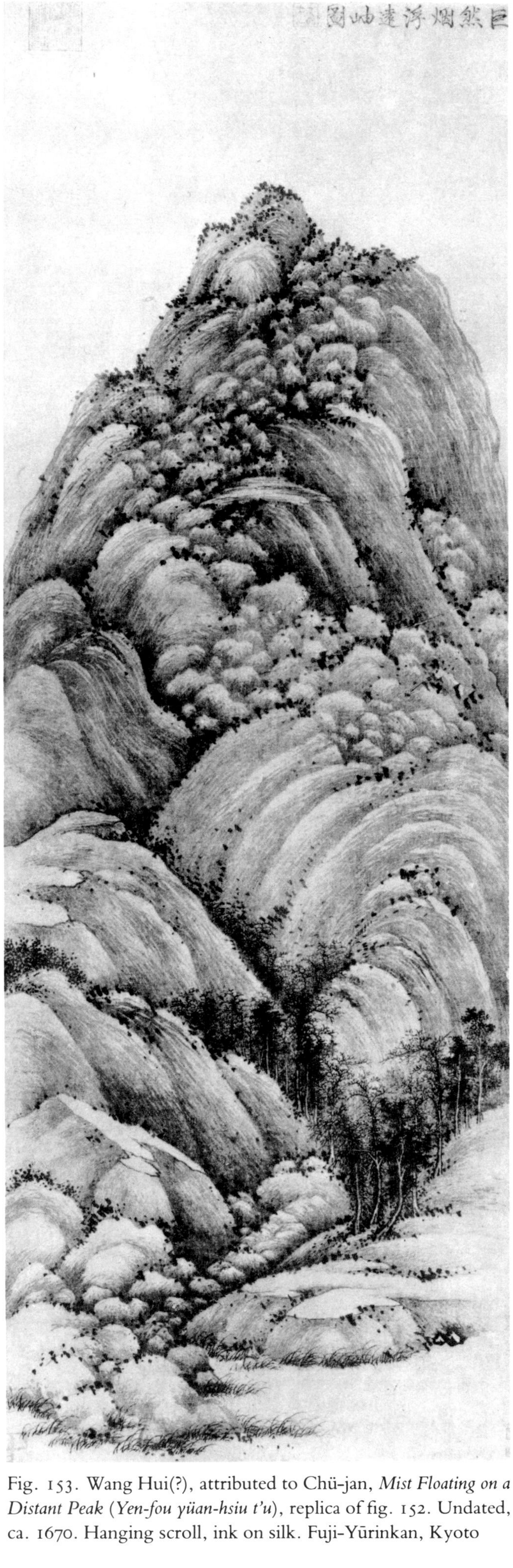


Fig. 153. Wang Hui(?), attributed to Chü-jan, *Mist Floating on a Distant Peak* (*Yen-fou yüan-hsiu t'u*), replica of fig. 152. Undated, ca. 1670. Hanging scroll, ink on silk. Fuji-Yūrinkan, Kyoto

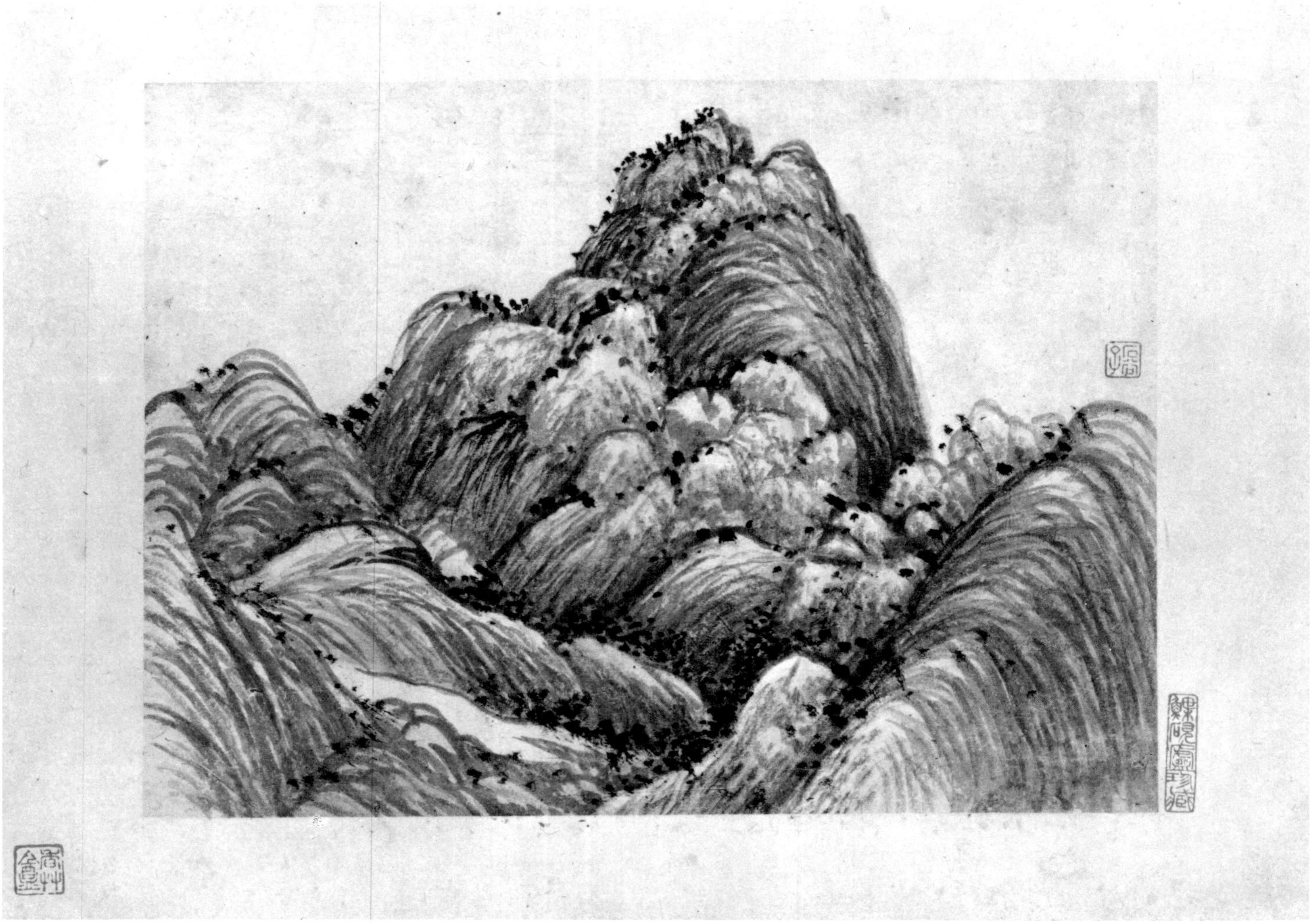

Fig. 154a. Wang Hui, "After Chü-jan." Dated 1673. Album leaf 1 of *In Pursuit of Antiquity* (*Ch'ü-ku*), ink on paper. 21.9 x 31.0 cm ($8^5/_8$ x $12^1/_4$ in.). The Art Museum, Princeton University

the "obvious." The album opens with the Chü-jan formula (fig. 154a), the archetypal host peak flanked by two guest peaks, done in semicircular round brushstrokes and round dots: not a single tree or blade of grass interferes with the abstract design. Developing from this, the pure Southern School style, he re-created with increasing descriptiveness the "cloudy mountains" (*yün-shan*) of Mi Fu and Kao K'o-kung, and a series of different but related hemp-fiber texture landscapes representing Tung Yüan, Huang Kung-wang, and Wang Meng. The remaining six leaves are devoted to more descriptive and decorative styles: that of Li Ch'eng (cf. fig. 42), that of Kuo Hsi (ca. 1010–ca. 1075; two leaves), that of Ts'ao Chih-po, and two landscapes with colors. Leaf 3 (fig. 154b), a charming spring scene of a boy and his buffalo by a stream, is done in a simple ink-wash style with soft greens and browns, its gentle lyricism deriving, through T'ang Yin, from the Southern Sung Academy style.

The wide range of styles covered in this album greatly impressed Wang Hui's contemporaries: "I am fond of Wang Hui's works in the styles of Ni [Tsan], Huang [Kung-wang], and Ts'ao Chih-po," wrote Liu Yü (fl. ca. 1660–90) in a colophon above Leaf 8, a colorful blue and green landscape, "but these fine and ornate pictures lean in an entirely different direction. If these too can be included in Wang Wei's Southern School, what more can one ask?"[66]

Throughout the 1660s and 1670s, Wang Hui's virtuoso accomplishments dazzled his friends and admirers. Yün Shou-p'ing, who witnessed "several transformations" in Wang Hui's paintings, proclaimed that each time he reached "a new summit."[67] Through Wang's Great Synthesis, Yün observed, a new unity was achieved among "even styles that had always been considered incompatible."[68]

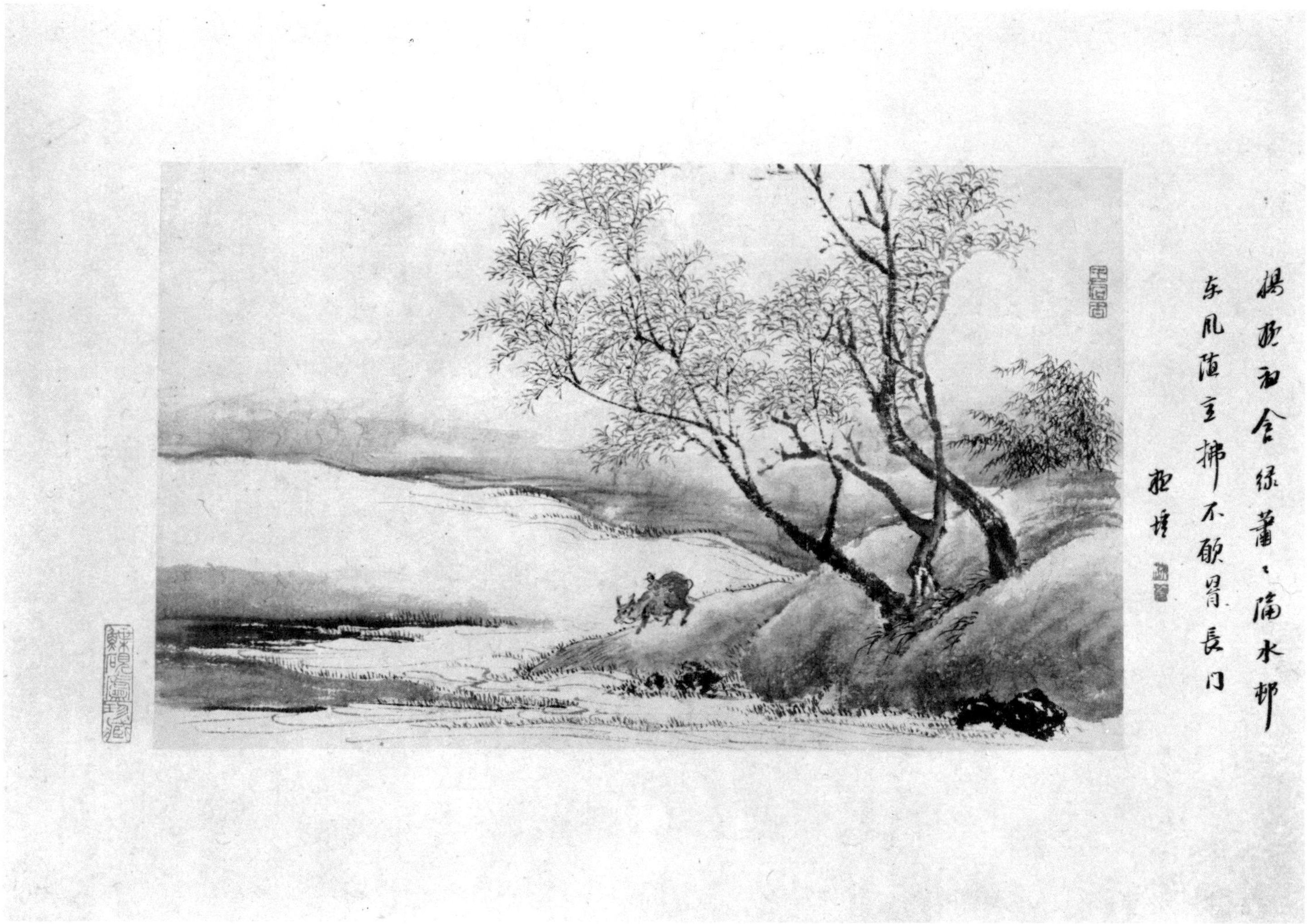

Fig. 154b. Wang Hui, "Herd Boy" ("Mu-t'ung"). Dated 1673. Album leaf 3 of *In Pursuit of Antiquity*, ink and light color on paper. 17.6 x 29.8 cm (6 7/8 x 11 3/4 in.)

Yet Wang Hui's very success in conquering new stylistic territory seemed to inhibit his potential. After Wang Shih-min died in 1680 and Wang Hui the brilliant student became a successful master, his own process of transformation came to an end. While the great imperial commission to lead the southern inspection tour project in the 1690s boosted his career, it did not give impetus to his painting. His redoubled efforts to persist in the path of imitating the ancients yielded, in the end, to the temptation to imitate himself.

One aspect of Wang Hui's work seldom mentioned by his contemporaries, but one of great value and interest to modern art historians, is his activity as a forger. As early as 1669 Chou Liang-kung (1612–1672), a well-known connoisseur and collector of contemporary paintings, had noted that "people of Wu [around Su-chou] often asked [Wang Hui] to paint, then mounted his works as antique paintings to deceive collectors."[69] Chou reported these circumstances matter-of-factly; Wang was young and poor, and, as Chou pointed out, "what he painted may adequately compete with the works of ancient masters." Today, the Sung and Yüan paintings forged by Wang Hui appear striking for their departure from the original models; they succeed as independent creations. In these interesting works, executed mostly in the late 1660s and early 1670s, Wang was just as concerned with stylistic innovations as he was in works done under his own name.

A replica attributed to Fan K'uan of his masterpiece *Travelers among Streams and Mountains* in the National Palace Museum, Taipei (cf. fig. 48), known simply as *Travelers* (*Hsing-lü t'u*; fig. 155), in the same museum, leads the list of extant possible Wang Hui forgeries. A smaller painting than the original, the

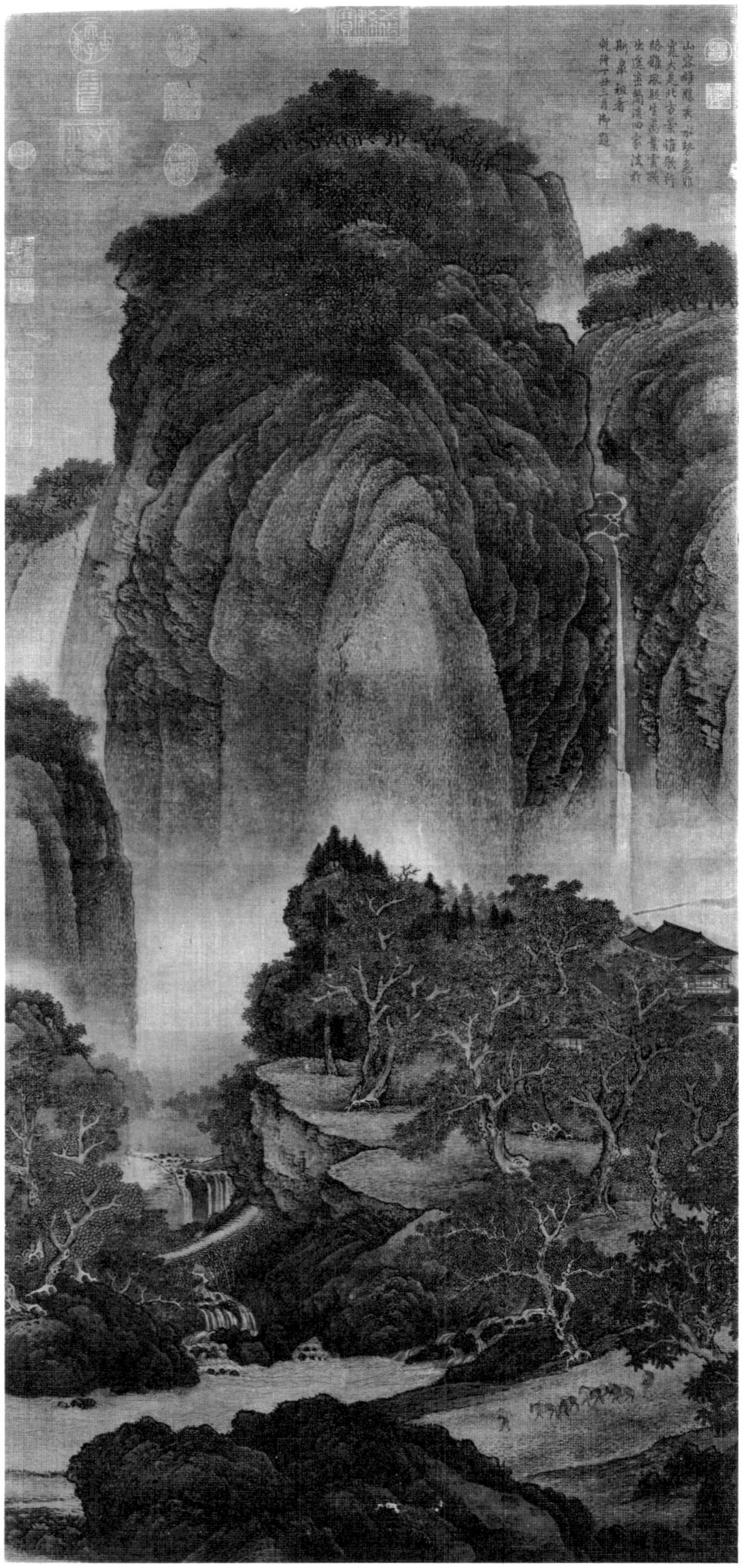

Fig. 155. Forgery by Wang Hui, formerly attributed to Fan K'uan, *Travelers* (*Hsing-lü t'u*). Hanging scroll, ink on silk. Undated, ca. 1670s. 155.3 x 74.4 cm (5 ft. 1 1/8 in. x 29 1/4 in.). National Palace Museum, Taipei

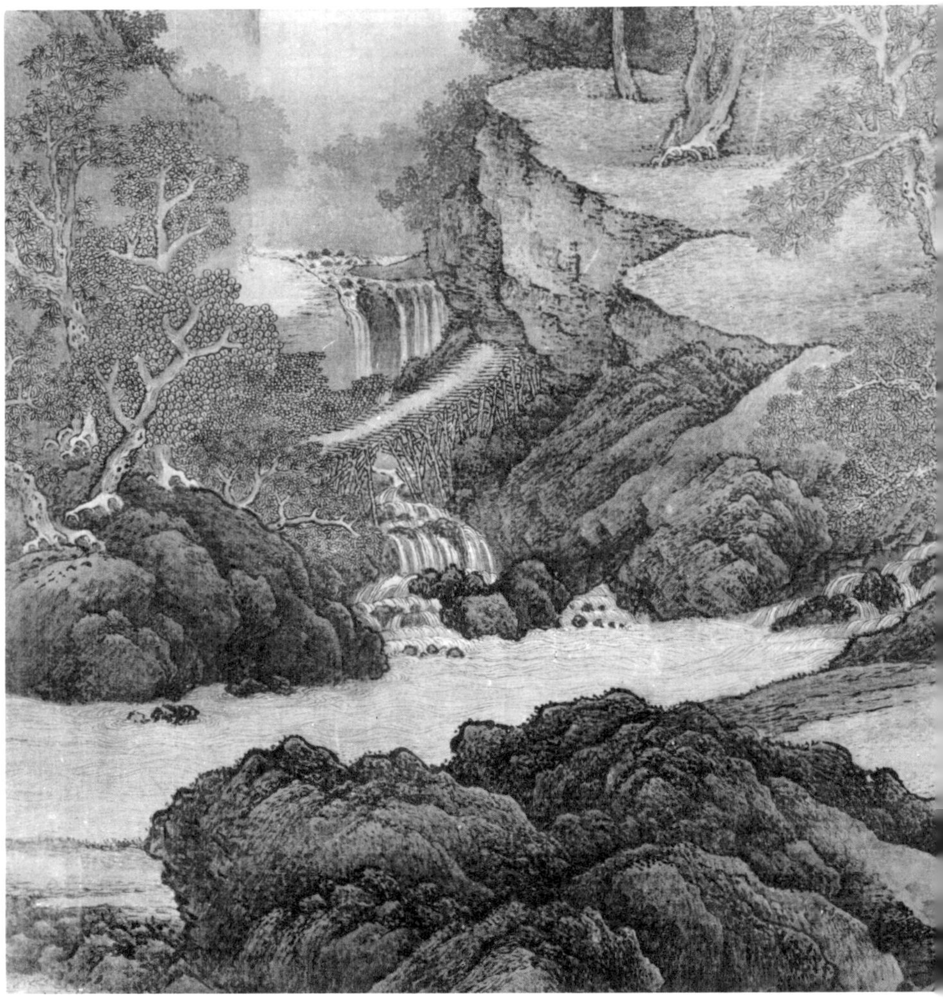

Fig. 155a. Detail, fig. 155

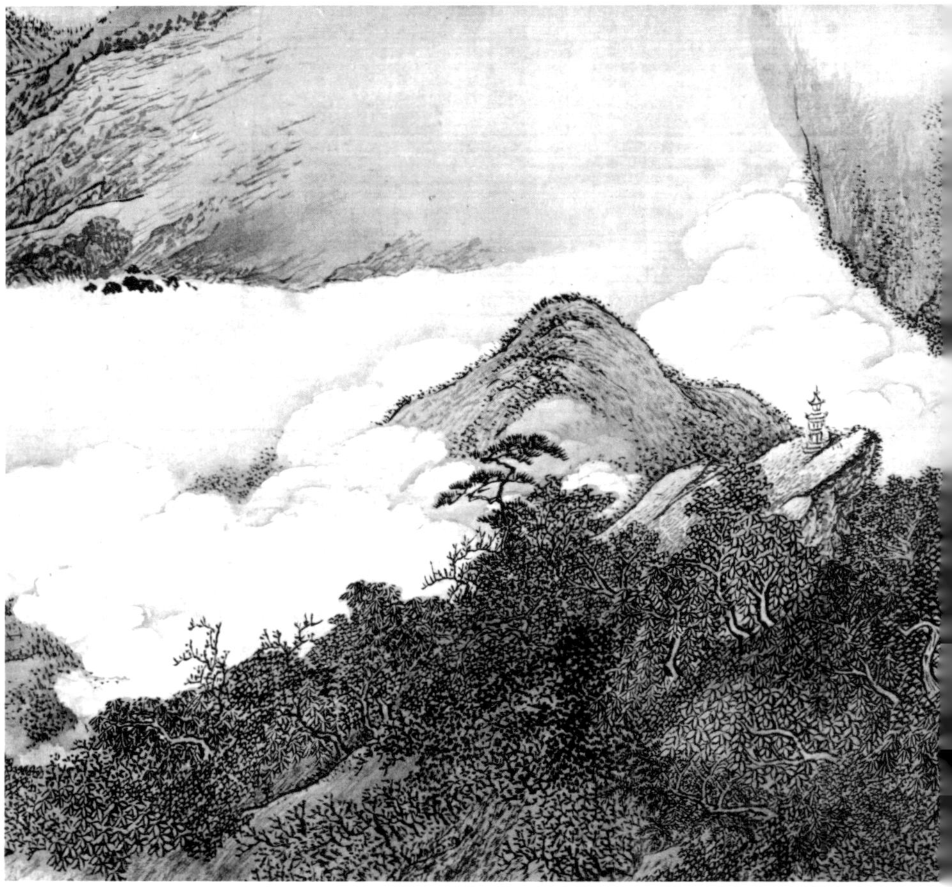

Fig. 156. Wang Hui, detail, *Colors of Mount T'ai-hang* (*T'ai-hang shan-se*). Dated 1669. Handscroll, ink and color on silk. 23.5 x 209.4 cm (9 1/4 in. x 6 ft. 10 1/2 in.). The Metropolitan Museum of Art, New York

hanging scroll *Travelers* shows on its mounting two colophons (cut out and preserved from a previous mounting), one dated 1671 by Wang Shih-min, and the other dated 1696 by Sung Chün-yeh (fl. ca. 1660–1710), who was a pupil of Wang Hui's and later a coeditor, under Wang Yüan-ch'i, of the K'ang-hsi imperial encyclopedic work *Manual on Calligraphy and Painting of the P'ei-wen Studio* (*P'ei-wen-chai shu-hua-p'u*; completed 1708). Wang Shih-min's colophon reported that "six-tenths [of his ancient painting collection] had come from Tung Ch'i-ch'ang," but that, by the time of his writing the colophon, in 1671, "only one- or two-tenths of it remained," then, "recently, going through some old trunks, [he] brought out Fan K'uan's *Travelers*" and had it remounted, writing a few words to mark the occasion. Sung Chün-yeh, in 1696, inscribing on the scroll sixteen years after the elder Wang's death, recounted that he had a chance to view the painting at Wang's old studio, "a bamboo house with paper windows," in the company of Wang Hui, who, moved by Sung's appreciation of "this authentic work by Fan K'uan, a rare treasure of the world," made a small copy and "presented it to [Sung] to reward [his] enthusiasm."[70]

In 1696 at Wang Shih-min's old home, Sung Chün-yeh could not have seen the original Fan K'uan, which had long before been sold to the famous collector Liang Ch'ing-piao (1620–1691). Most likely Wang Shih-min, having sold the original work to Liang in about 1671, had commissioned Wang Hui to produce a replacement, which he had mounted as Fan K'uan's *Travelers*. (The abridged name *Travelers* may have been Wang Shih-min's subtle way of differentiating a copy from the original.)

Around 1670 Wang Hui worked in the Fan K'uan raindrop (*yü-tien*) idiom. His superb handscroll *Colors of Mount T'ai-hang* (*T'ai-hang shan-se*), formerly in the Earl Morse collection and now in The Metropolitan Museum of Art, New York (fig. 156), was painted in the fall of 1669. In creating the *Travelers* attributed to Fan K'uan, Wang Hui worked not from the original Fan K'uan, but from Wang Shih-min's copy in the *Within Small See Large* album (cf. fig. 147a). A comparison of the sizes of these three works tells us something about the problems faced by the forger: the original Fan K'uan is more than 6 feet in height, the *Travelers* is just over 5 feet, and Wang Shih-min's reduced copy is less than half the size of the *Travelers*.

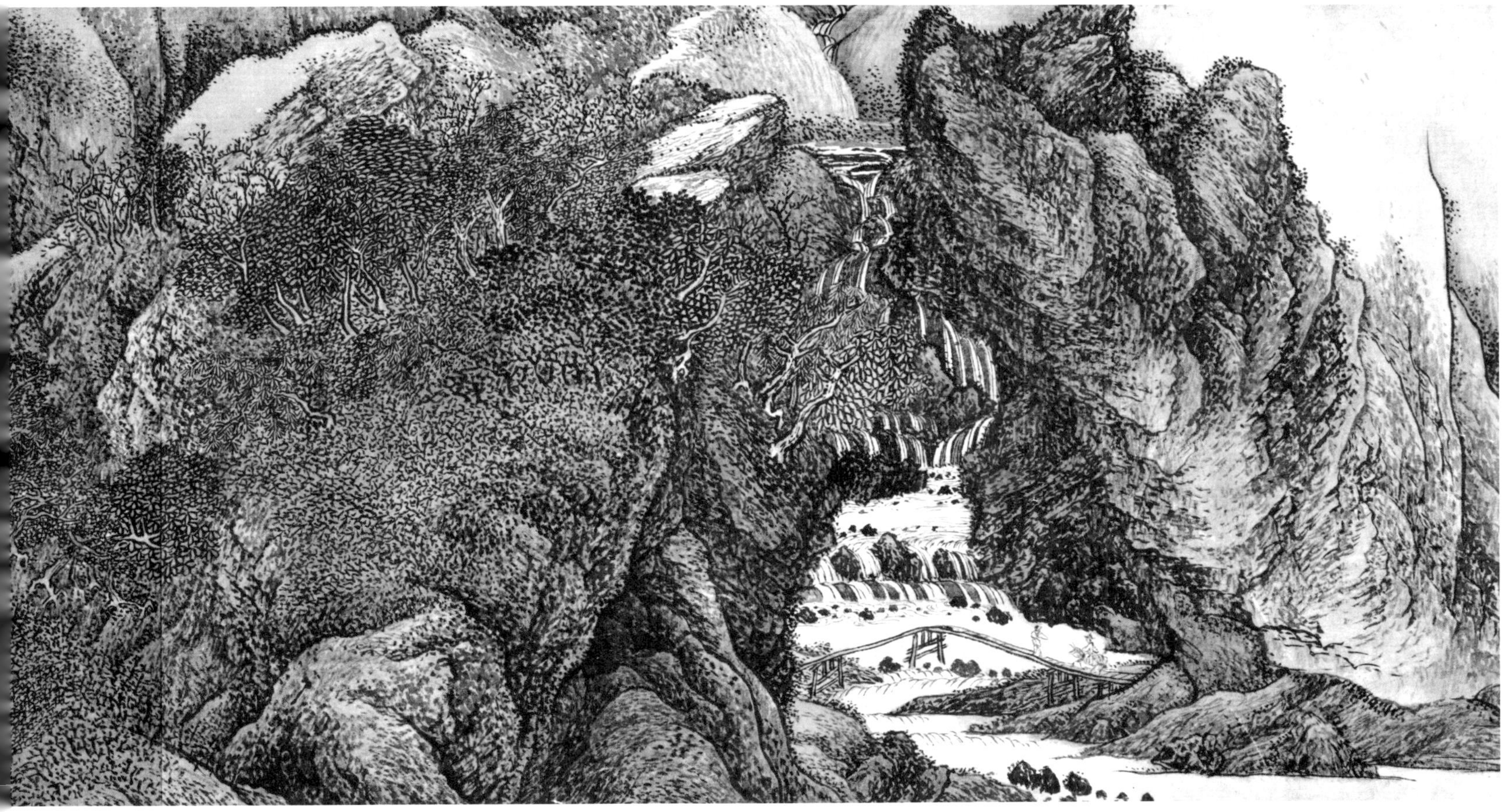

To enlarge from the small model, with the limited information it afforded, to a composition more than twice the model's size, Wang Hui wisely avoided repeating its simplified outlines and forms. Instead he worked with energized raindrop texture dots (fig. 155a), building small billowing rock forms into a large composition. Whereas Fan K'uan created a heroic image from large, carefully defined parts, without subordinating the parts to an organic whole, Wang Hui constructed an integrated composition from kinetic brushstrokes, producing large, continuous breath-force and dragon-vein movements.

Because of this bold approach Wang Hui's *Travelers* replica carries the same conviction as its Sung predecessor. "Filled with mist and clouds, and thickly amassed trees," reported Sung Chün-yeh, Wang's copy "arrested eyes and made hearts tremble." Some decades after Sung wrote those words, when both the original Fan K'uan and the replica had found their way into the Ch'ing Ch'ien-lung emperor's (Kao-tsung; r. 1736–95) collection, the former, recorded in the first series of the imperial catalogue, *Treasured Boxes of the Stony Moat* (*Shih-ch'ü pao-chi*), in 1744, passed virtually unnoticed by the emperor, while he chose the latter to be inscribed with a poem, dated 1757, which concludes with these lines: "The simple and plain methods of the four [Yüan] masters / All look to this as their first ancestor."[71] In comparison to Wang Hui's work, Fan K'uan's masterpiece probably appeared rather too cool, remote, and unfamiliar to eighteenth-century taste.

Other Wang Hui forgeries owned by the Ch'ien-lung emperor (National Palace Museum, Taipei) included *After Fan K'uan's Mount Lu* (*Mo Fan K'uan Lu-shan t'u*) attributed to the early Southern Sung master Chiang Shen.[72] Treating it as a variation on the Fan K'uan theme, Wang Hui imagined in this painting how a Southern Sung painter might have followed and imitated Fan's style. A second group dealt with the Li Ch'eng idiom, another important concern of Wang Hui's around the 1670s. An album leaf, *Jasper Peaks and Gem Trees* (*Yao-feng ch'i-shu*), attributed to Li Ch'eng, in the National Palace Museum, Taipei,[73] follows closely the brushwork and forms of Wang Hui's handscroll *After Li Ch'eng's "Snow Clearing"* (*Fang Li Ch'eng Hsüeh-chi t'u*), dated 1667 (fig. 158), while the large hanging scroll *Dense Snow on the Mountain Pass* (*Kuan-shan mi-hsüeh*) attributed to Hsü Tao-ning (ca. 1000–after 1066), also in the National Palace Museum, Taipei (fig. 157), appears to be a work by the same hand: the convoluted mountain forms, together with sinuous trees, thrust forward dramatically in one single dragon-vein movement.

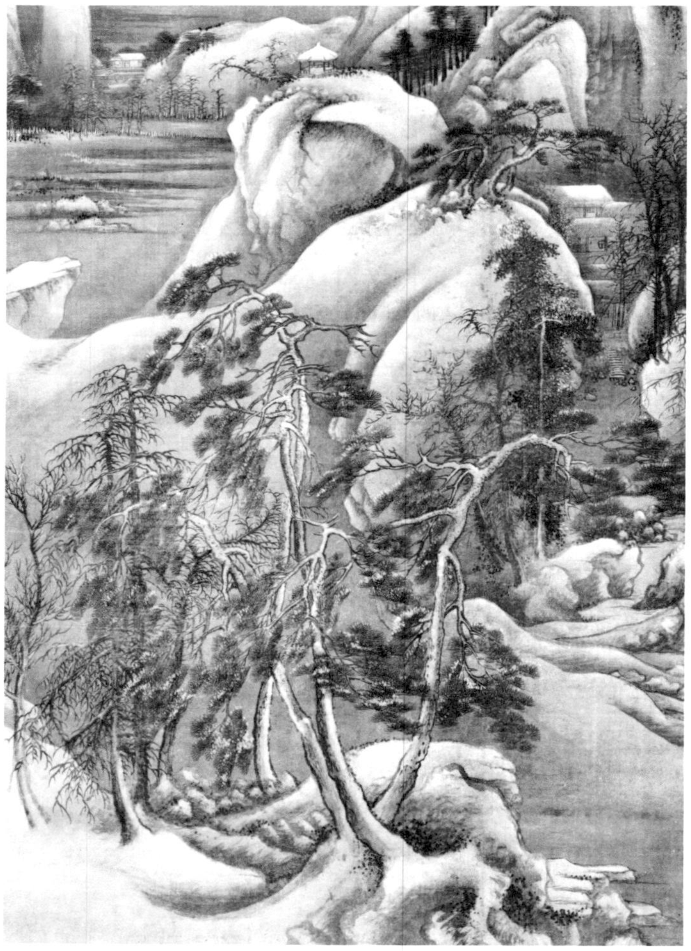

Fig. 157. Forgery by Wang Hui, formerly attributed to Hsü Tao-ning, detail, *Dense Snow on the Mountain Pass* (*Kuan-shan mi hsüeh*). Undated, ca. 1670. Hanging scroll, ink and color on silk. 121.3 x 81.3 cm (3 ft. 11¾ in. x 32 in.). National Palace Museum, Taipei

Wang Hui also forged Yüan styles. *Monastery in Autumn Mountains* (*Ch'iu-shan hsiao-ssu*) attributed to Wang Meng, dated 1362, in the National Palace Museum, Taipei (fig. 159), exhibits the same brush techniques and compositional principles as Wang's *After Chü-jan* of 1664 at Princeton (cf. fig. 148): the large pine trees in the foreground of *Monastery in Autumn Mountains* (fig. 159a) are especially similar to those in *After Chü-jan*, and the smaller ones above, leaning to one side, are pulled in toward the center, as part of the S-curve, dragon-vein movement winding through the composition.

*Landscape after Wu Chen* attributed to Hsü Pen (1335–1380), in the National Place Museum, Taipei

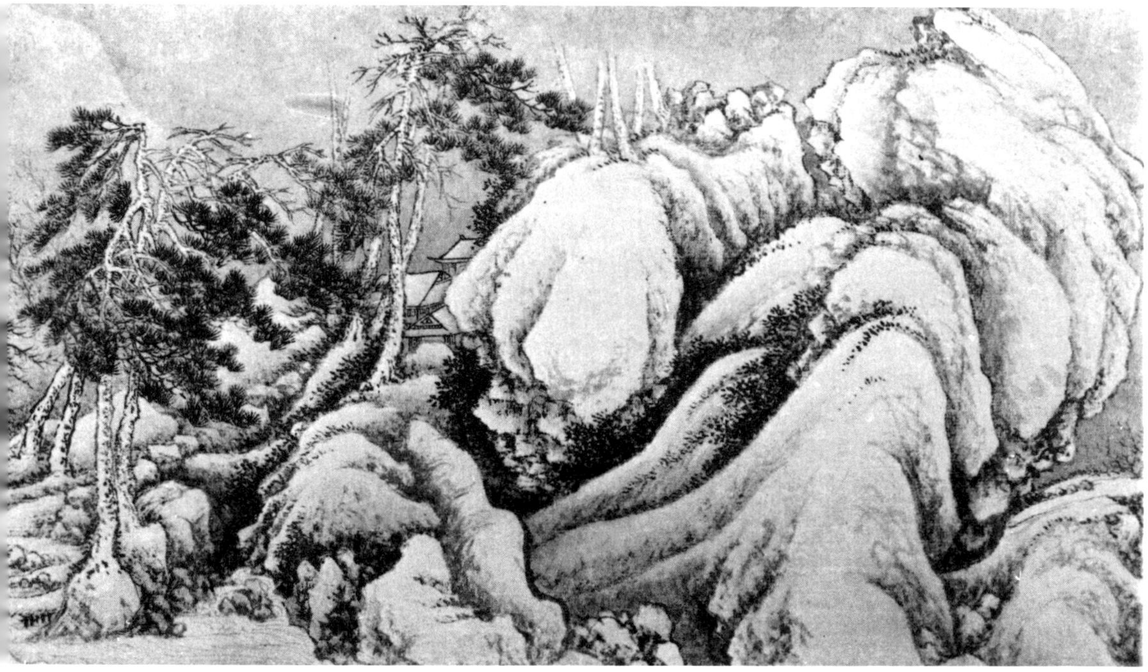

Fig. 158. Wang Hui, *After Li Ch'eng's "Snow Clearing"* (*Fang Li Ch'eng Hsüeh-chi t'u*). Dated 1667. Handscroll, ink on paper. National Palace Museum, Taipei

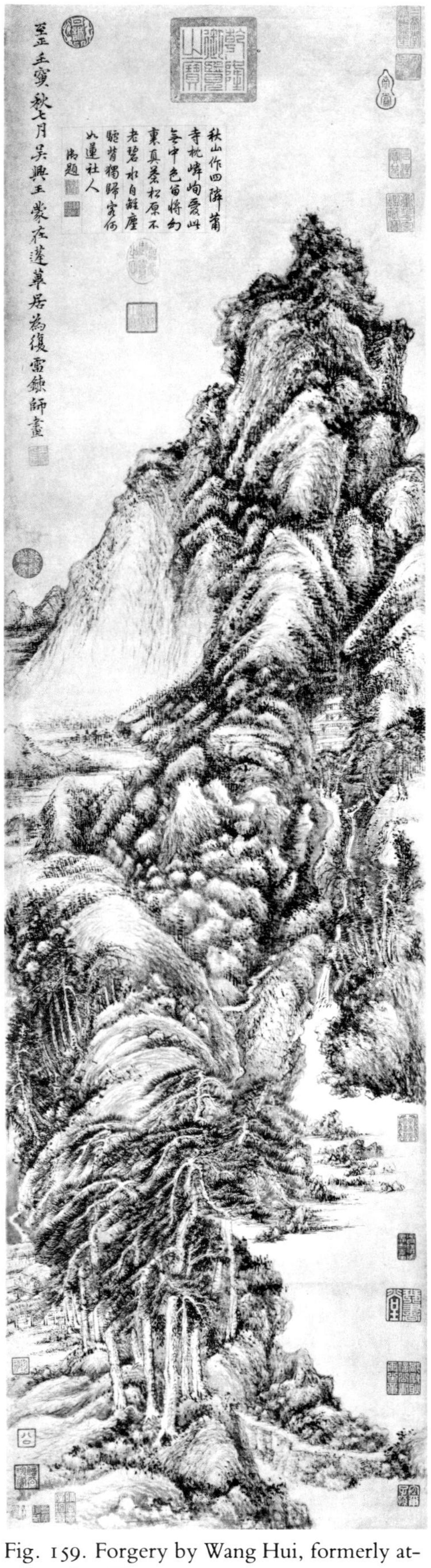

Fig. 159. Forgery by Wang Hui, formerly attributed to Wang Meng, *Monastery in Autumn Mountains* (*Ch'iu-shan hsiao-ssu*). Ca. 1670s (dated 1362). Hanging scroll, ink on paper. 142.4 x 38.5 cm (4 ft. 8 in. x 15 1/4 in.). National Palace Museum, Taipei

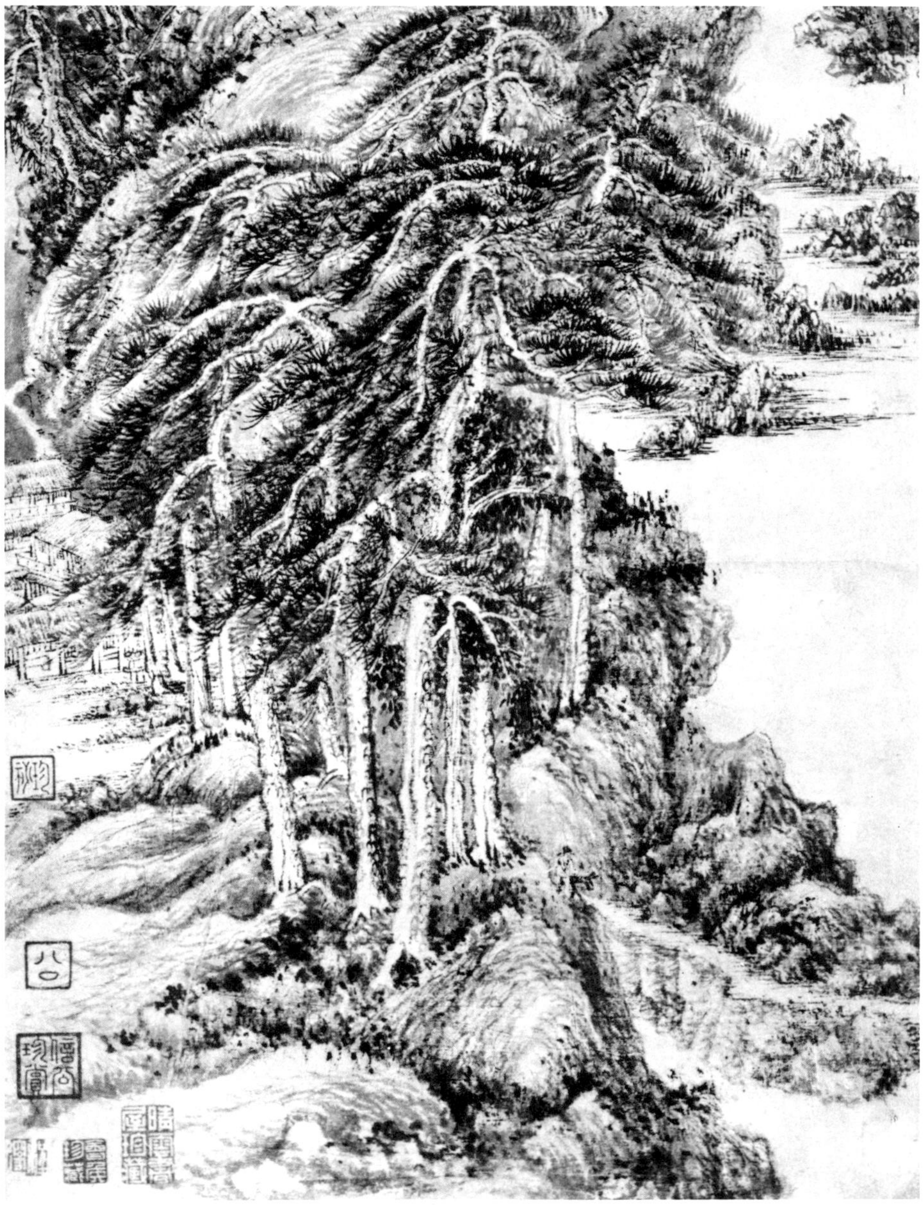

Fig. 159a. Detail, fig. 159

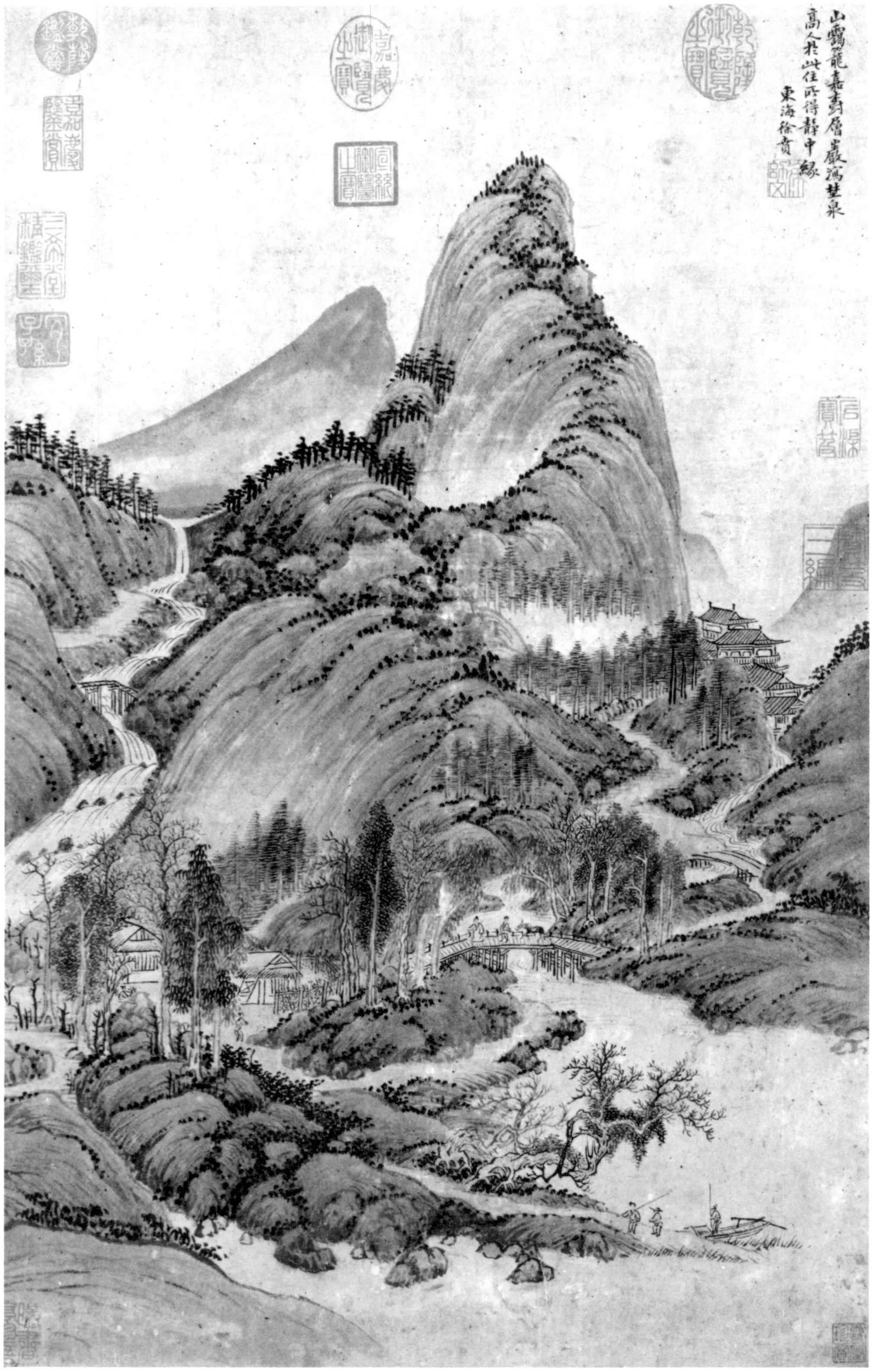


Fig. 160. Forgery by Wang Hui, formerly attributed to Hsü Pen, *Landscape after Wu Chen* (*Fang Wu Chen shan-shui*). Undated, 1670s. Hanging scroll, ink and light color on paper. National Palace Museum, Taipei

(fig. 160), is a work by Wang Hui based on Leaf 11 of Wang Shih-min's *Within Small See Large* album (cf. fig. 147c): while Wang Shih-min's copy still retains the Yüan compositional motifs of a well-defined foreground and an extended middle distance, Wang Hui's rendering, with its linked elements, single-mindedly emphasizes the S-curve of the central mountain range. The rounded arches, with neatly arranged hemp-fiber texture strokes and sprays of dots, closely resemble elements in Wang Hui's copy, dated 1673, now at the Freer Gallery of Art, Washington, D.C., of Huang Kung-wang's *Fu-ch'un* scroll.[74]

Thus, during the late 1660s and early 1670s, while perfecting his Great Synthesis of the Sung and Yüan landscape styles, Wang Hui apparently was also able to supply complete historical collections of Sung and Yüan paintings on demand.

## *Kung Hsien: Silent Poetry*

The burgeoning of painting talents in the middle of the seventeenth century, which reflected the dislocation of career patterns among the scholar class during the years of the Manchu conquest, led to a wider use of painting for expressive purposes. While Orthodox School masters such as Wang Hui celebrated the new era of peace under the Manchu rule, the Ming loyalists—known as the *i-min*, or "leftover citizens"—withdrew to become recluse poets or painters, reliving the experiences of those who endured the reign of the Mongols three centuries earlier. Referring to painting as "silent poetry" (*wu-sheng-shih*), they used it not only to lodge protest and bear witness, but also as a psychological self-defense against an increasingly turbulent and menacing world.

One such painter was Kung Hsien, who suffered a bitter life and died tragically. Although many of his poems remain, they offer little information about his early life; Chiang I-han (1981) suggests that Kung may have wished to forget his past.[75] Growing up in Nanking, he was apparently acquainted at an early age with such active political figures as Yang Wen-ts'ung (1597–1646) and Fang Wen (1612–1669), and may have become involved in the vicious factional struggles at the southern Ming court of Prince Fu, in Nanking, after the Manchus took Peking in 1644. Fang Wen, a lifelong friend of Kung's, was a zealous member of the Fu-she (Revival Society), an activist student party that succeeded the Tung-lin Academy scholars in opposition to officials associated with the powerful eunuch Wei Chung-hsien (d. 1627). Yang Wen-ts'ung, though associated with the Fu-she scholars, was a brother-in-law of Ma Shih-ying (1591–1646?), who was a close ally of Juan Ta-ch'eng (1587?–1646), who in 1639 was the target of a vicious attack by the Fu-she. In 1644 Ma was the principal supporter of Prince Fu, and Juan, on becoming president of the Board of War and grand guardian of the heir apparent, ordered wholesale arrest of the members of the Fu-she. About this time, Kung Hsien left Nanking for Yang-chou, after mentioning in a poem that "eight members of [his family] all died early."[76] In May 1645 Yang-chou fell to the Manchu forces, who in punishing the city for its stubborn resistance, led by the Ming loyalist general Shih K'o-fa (*chin-shih*, 1628), carried out a ten-day massacre. Kung Hsien escaped to Hai-an, T'ai-chou, where he served as a tutor to a family named Hsü for about five years, returning to Yang-chou in 1650 or 1651, briefly visiting Nanking in about 1655. Sometime in the mid-1660s he moved back to Nanking, first living under Mount Chung, calling himself a "monk who sweeps fallen leaves" (*sao lo-yeh seng*), and in 1668 acquiring a small plot of land under Mount Ch'ing-liang, where he finally built a home of his own, the Half-acre Garden (Pan-mu-yüan). There he lived in apparent peace for about twenty years, making occasional trips to Yang-chou to visit old friends. In the fall of 1689 the noted dramatist K'ung Shang-jen (1648–1718) visited Kung Hsien in Nanking. Shortly thereafter, Kung sent K'ung a letter expressing fear of persecution by an unnamed powerful person; soon afterward he died mysteriously. In a colophon to K'ung's poems lamenting Kung's death, Tsung Yüan-ting (1620–1696) wrote that Kung Hsien had died "at the hands of someone who had used violence to force him to write."[77] Apparently, as with Ni Tsan, the proud artist had refused to work for someone he despised and had been severely beaten. Kung Hsien, unlike Ni, did not survive the ordeal.

A brooding man, to judge by his poems and paintings, Kung Hsien was by nature a loner and an eccentric who had difficulty in getting along with people. Choosing reclusion as a way of life, he depended on painting for his livelihood. In a poem entitled "A Hundred Bitternesses" ("Pai-k'u"), he complained, "Even in old age I have to struggle to live."[78] Teaching painting, Kung Hsien left behind a series of sketchbooks dating from the 1650s to the 1680s. Made for beginning students, each of these illustrated step by step his methods of painting trees and rock and mountain forms and of creating compositions. For more than thirty years he developed and perfected a personal style, a dense yet translucent brushstroke and ink-dot technique that enabled him to express grief and emotion with extraordinary intensity and lyric feeling.

To express a strong sense of dislocation and alienation in their works, many Ming loyalist painters around 1650 had adopted the dry-brush manner of Ni Tsan. As James Cahill has demonstrated (1970), one

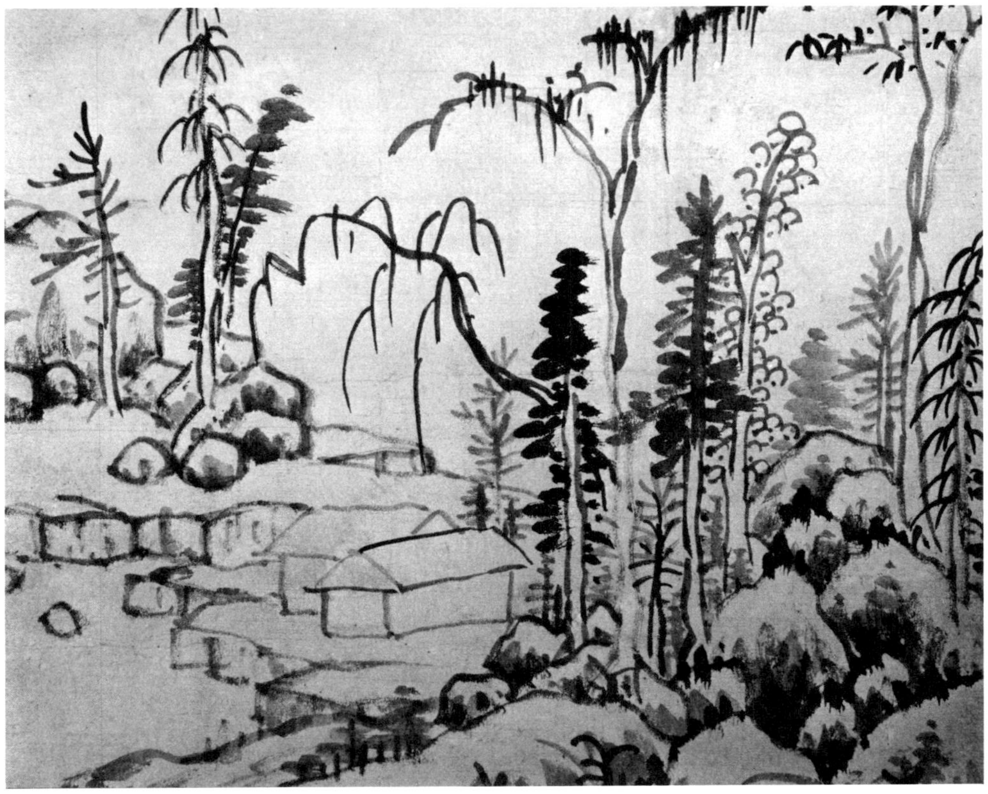

Fig. 161. Yün Hsiang, *Landscape* (*Shan-shui*). Undated, ca. 1650. Hanging scroll, ink on paper. Fuji-Yūrinkan, Kyoto

painter who had a special effect on early Kung Hsien was Yün Hsiang (1586–1655), who was from Wu-chin in the Lake Tai region and worked in Nanking.[79] Yün Hsiang's brushwork (fig. 161) produced flat forms; his round, single outlines done with a centered brushstroke made forms look empty, and when he used fused dry brushstrokes they rendered only textured surfaces. Rejecting the scribbling quality of late Ming scholar-painting in favor of a more monumental style, Kung Hsien began by inventing his own techniques. He wanted his forms to look substantial and solid. "A centered brush makes a round brushstroke," he wrote. "When the brushstroke is round, the breath [*ch'i*] will be thick and substantial [*hou*]."[80]As he demonstrated in an early sketchbook, he discovered in the 1650s that merely by repeating round brush outlines with lighter dry strokes, softening and blurring them, he could make the forms look well modeled and three-dimensional.[81] He approached his technical problems systematically, analyzing every problem in several steps. He first drew rounded boulders with round outlines (fig. 162a), repeating them three or four times in lighter ink, which, he explained, eliminated the need for texture strokes (*ts'un*). In another leaf (fig. 162b), he showed how to develop texture modeling with dry brushstrokes and ink wash, adding that the dry strokes should be applied first, followed by lighter-toned wet ones, so that rocks would look rich and full outside and full of "bone structure" inside. For foliage Kung showed how to produce deep and rich effects by applying up to six or seven separate layers of dots, broader texture strokes, and ink wash. The combination of dry modeling and wet ink wash enabled Kung to achieve, in the 1660s and 1670s, a landscape style of extraordinary density and substance—as Cahill calls it, "a completely convincing alternate world"[82]—best seen in his well-known *Thousand Peaks and Myriad Ravines* (*Ch'ien-yen wan-ho*), datable to the 1670s, in the Charles A. Drenowatz collection.

Building from dry to wet, sparse to dense, from rock outlines to bone structure, surface, and volume, Kung Hsien reconstructed a monumental style of landscape in order to master his own synthesis of the Sung and Yüan brush idioms. On a hanging scroll, *Landscape*, in the Honolulu Academy of Art, dated just a few months before his death in 1689, the artist wrote:

> In painting one must first synthesize [*tsung-li*] all Sung and Yüan methods, then, relaxing, one may create works in a simplified untrammeled manner [*i-p'in*]. [This way] a painting of a few sparse brushstrokes will embody all Six Principles. It will have a cultured breath [*wen-ch'i*] and a good

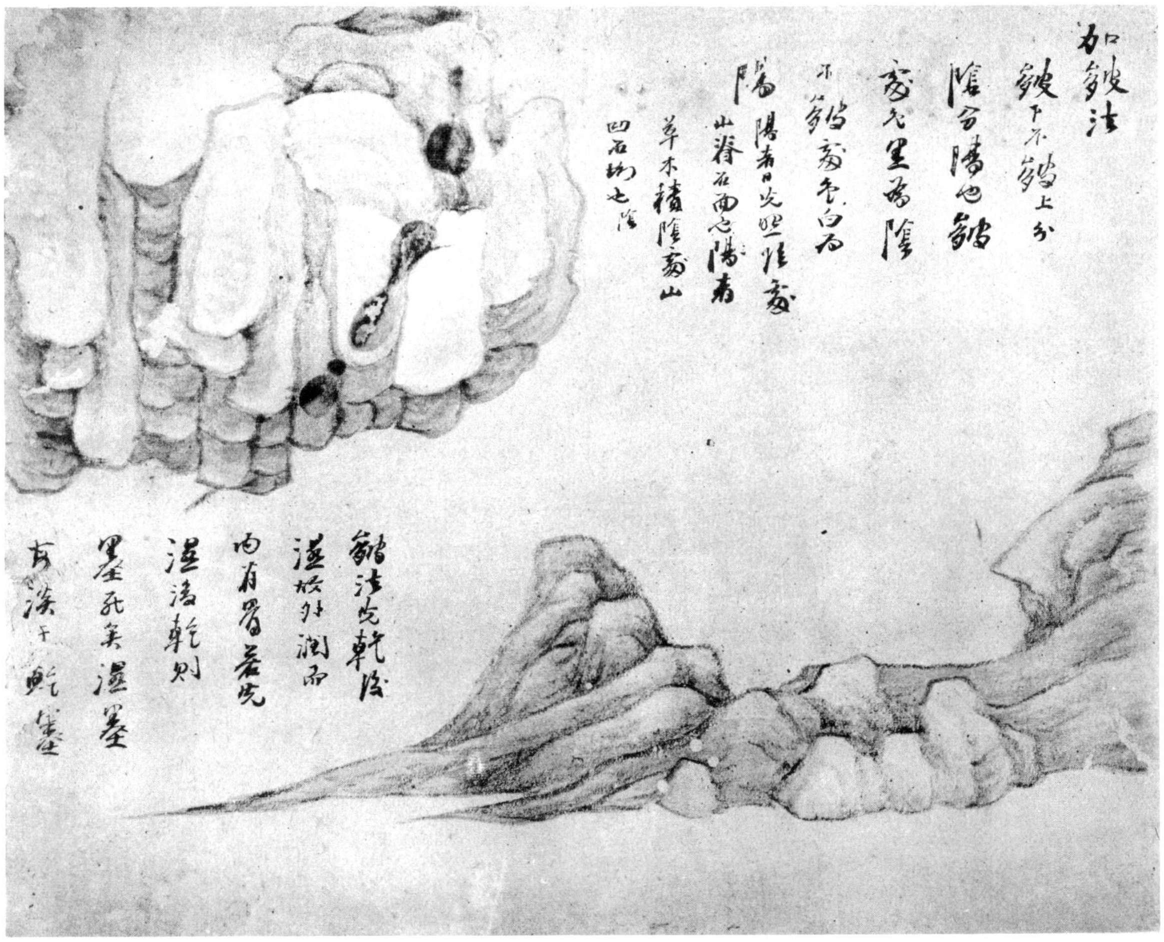

Fig. 162a. Kung Hsien, album leaf 4 of *Sketchbook* (*Shou-t'u kao*). Undated, ca. 1650s. Ink on paper. Provenance unknown

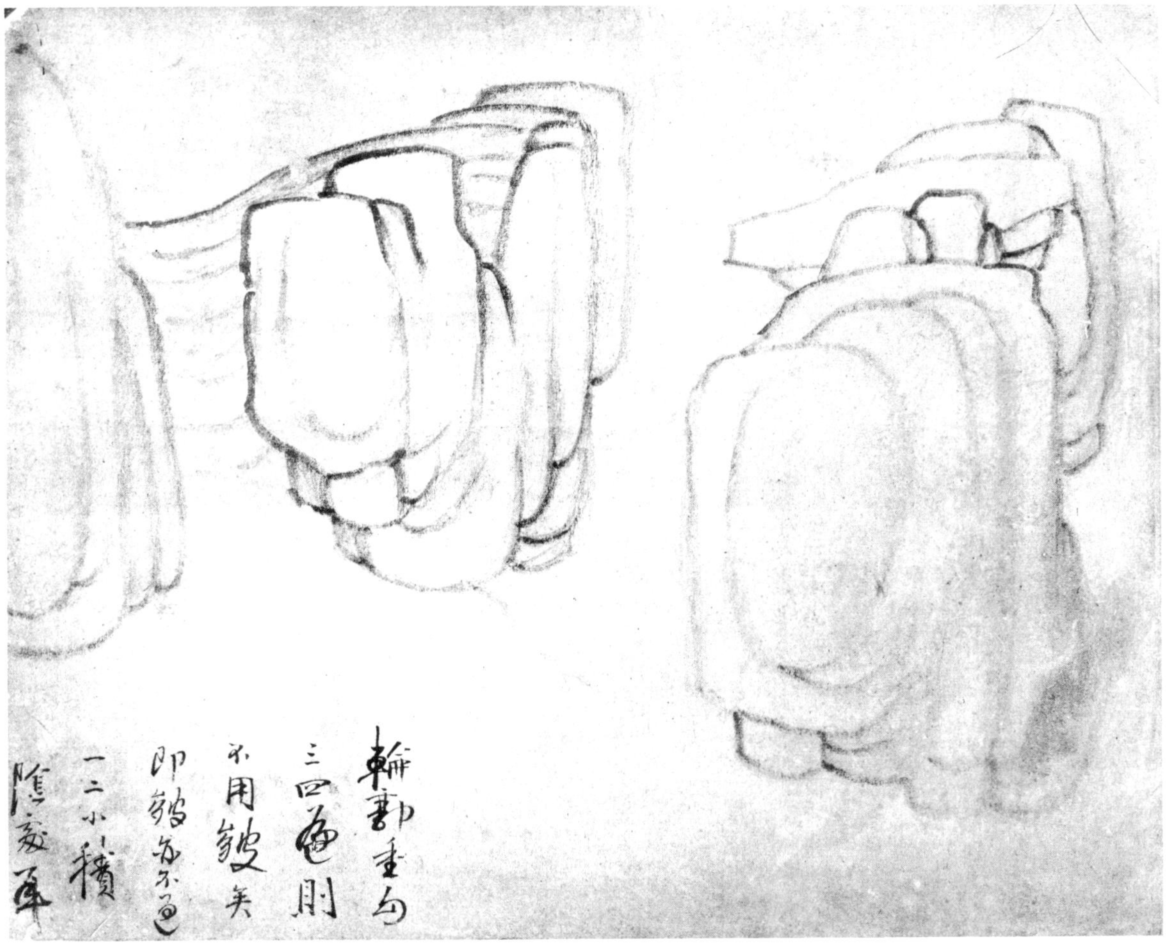

Fig. 162b. Kung Hsien, album leaf 5 of *Sketchbook*. Undated, ca. 1650s

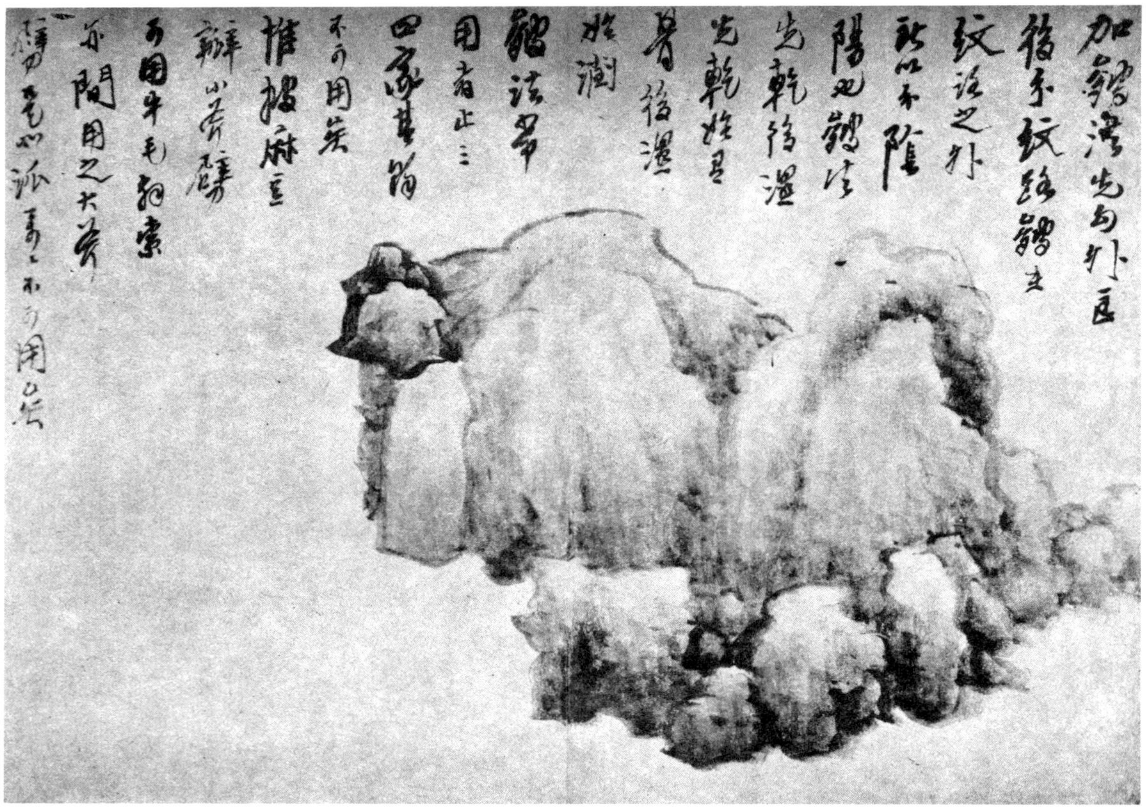

Fig. 163a. Kung Hsien, album leaf 10 of *Sketchbook*. Undated, 1680s. Ink on paper

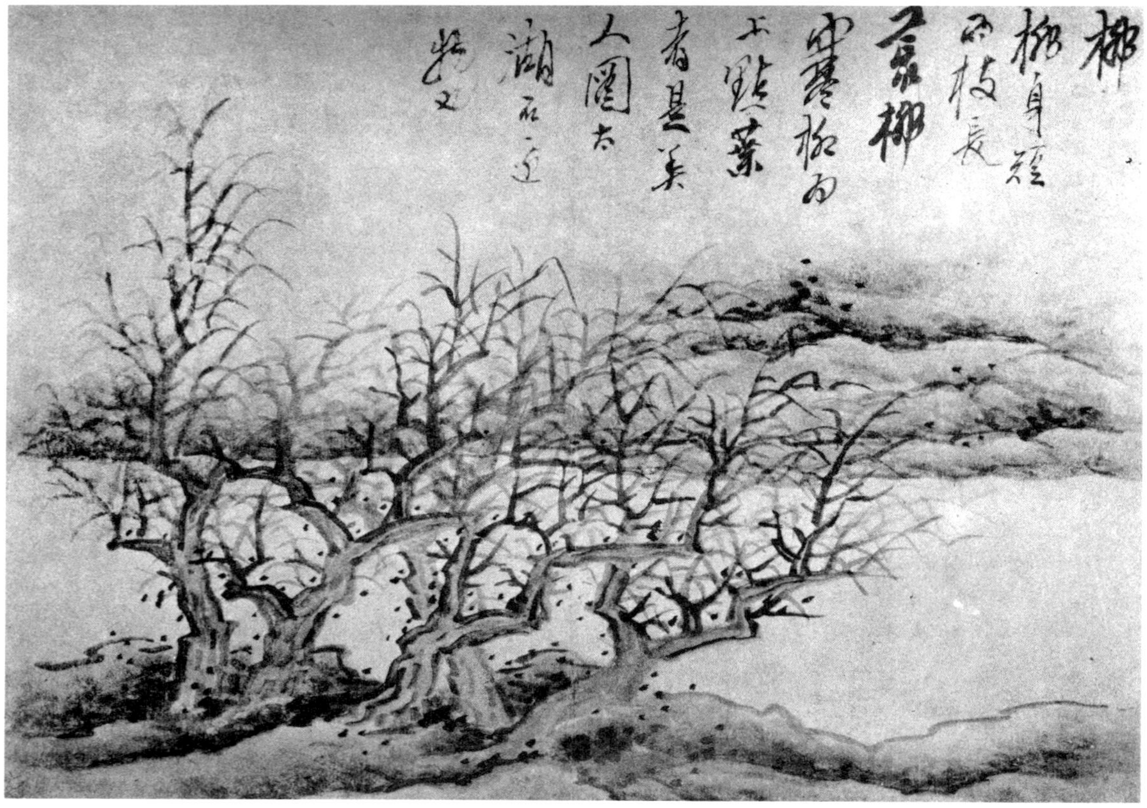

Fig. 163b. Kung Hsien, album leaf 15 of *Sketchbook*. Undated, 1680s

painting style [*hua-ko*]. . . . Wang Fu [1362–1416] and Shen Chou [1427–1505], in their later years, while playing with the Ni [Tsan]–Huang [Kung-wang] style, had rested on the foundation of the Tung [Yüan]–Chü-[jan] manner. These men are my teachers.[83]

In his late style of the 1680s, Kung's brush technique became mature and vigorous; he fashioned rock forms with a calligraphic formula of brisk outlines, modeled with layers of soft, mottled ink dots. "Before adding texture strokes," he explained in the sketchbook of the 1680s (fig. 163a),

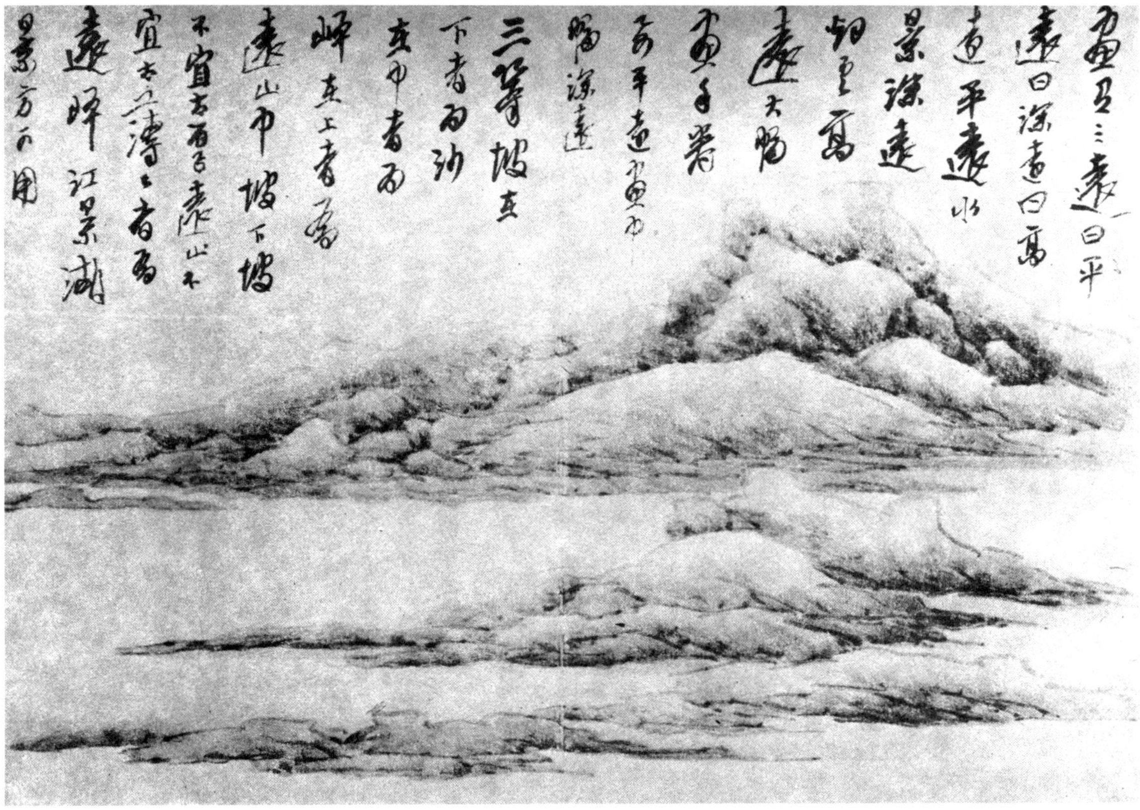

Fig. 163c. Kung Hsien, album leaf 12 of *Sketchbook*. Undated, 1680s

one must first make outlines, then interior fissure lines, adding texture strokes beside a fissure line to differentiate the shaded [*yin*] from the lighted [*yang*] areas. . . . There are only three or four frequently usable texture methods; the rest should not be used. Mostly I use the hemp-fiber [*p'i-ma*], bean-shaped [*tou-p'an*], and small ax-cut [*hsiao-fu-p'i*] patterns, occasionally mixing them with the cow-hair [*niu-mao*] and unraveled-rope [*chien-so*]. As for the large ax-cut pattern, it belongs to the Northern School, and it should never be touched.

Although Kung spoke as a follower of Tung Ch'i-ch'ang's Southern School theory, he showed little interest in reconstructing ancient models. Instead of painting in a wide variety of texture idioms, he concentrated on developing one specific texture method as his personal, individual style. To a question posed by a friend who was a Buddhist monk—"How do you show mountains, rivers, and the great earth in painting?"—his answer was, "It has to do with the beginnings of the universe, and this is why the painters can know no limits."[84]

In *An Immortal's Abode above the Clouds* (*Hsien-chia yün-chü*), a hanging scroll probably made in the mid-1680s, in the Edward L. Elliott Family Collection at The Art Museum, Princeton University (no. 37), Kung Hsien used elements from his sketchbook in a painting on a favorite theme: a peaceful hermitage far away from the contentions of the world. His poem on the painting reads:

Outside the immortal's abode clouds rise besides mountain peaks.
He erects a spacious pavilion to live above the clouds.
The Queen Mother of the West often sends him the bluebird messenger;
He opens and carefully reads her letters written in purple ink.

The tall composition shows the panoramic deep, flat-distance view, in which small cottages dot the open landscape. The artist borrowed two elements illustrated in his sketchbook, a row of ancient willow trees in the foreground (fig. 163b) and receding sandbanks in the far distance (fig. 163c). To express his loneliness and isolation, he painted the willow trees as rugged and leafless; in his sketchbook he called them wilderness willows (*huang-liu*), or cold-weather willows (*han-liu*). In the middle distance he placed two rocky islands,

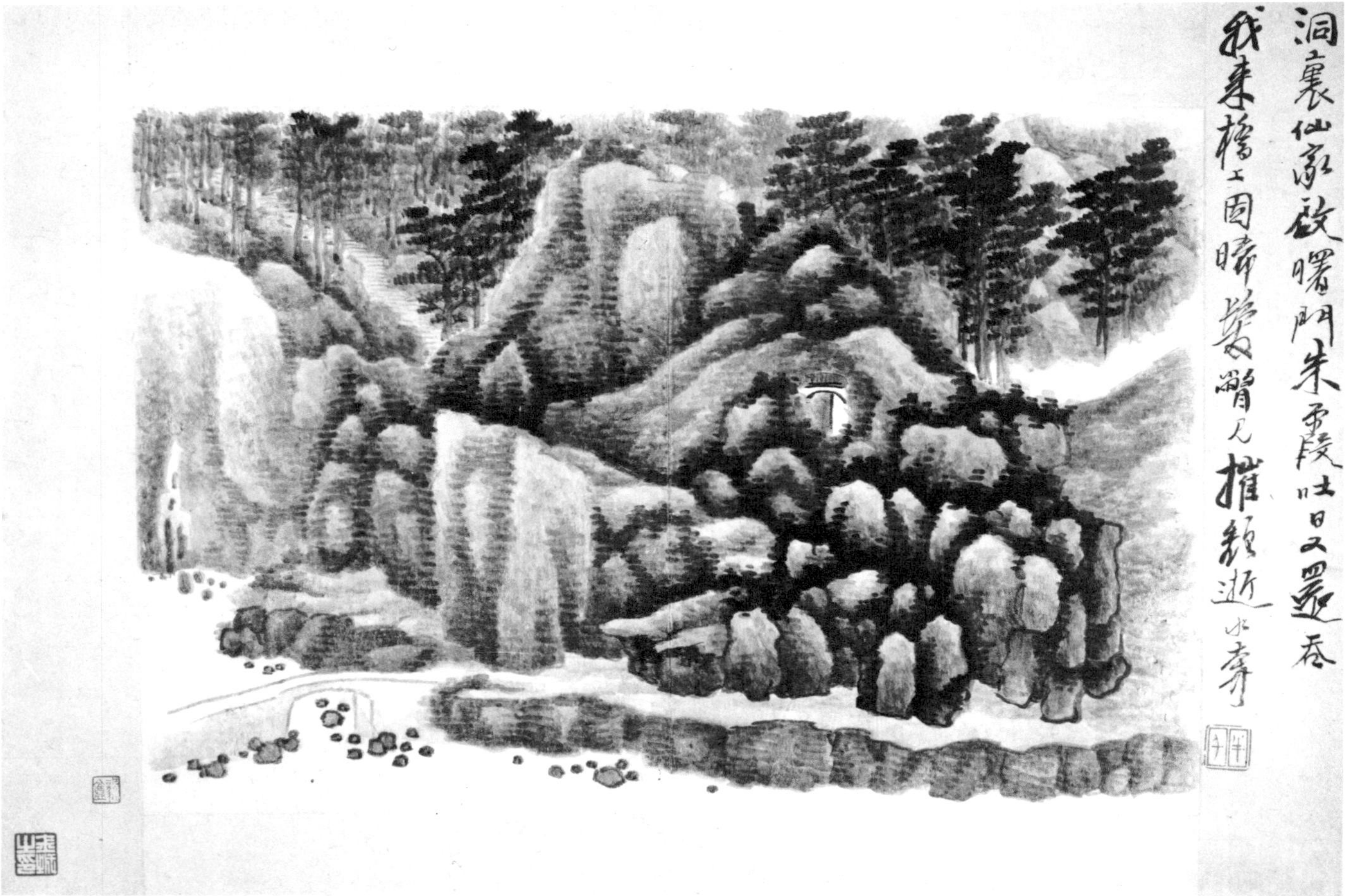

Fig. 164a. Kung Hsien, "The Immortal's Cave Dwelling." Dated 1688. Album leaf 8 of *Landscapes*, ink on paper. The Metropolitan Museum of Art, New York

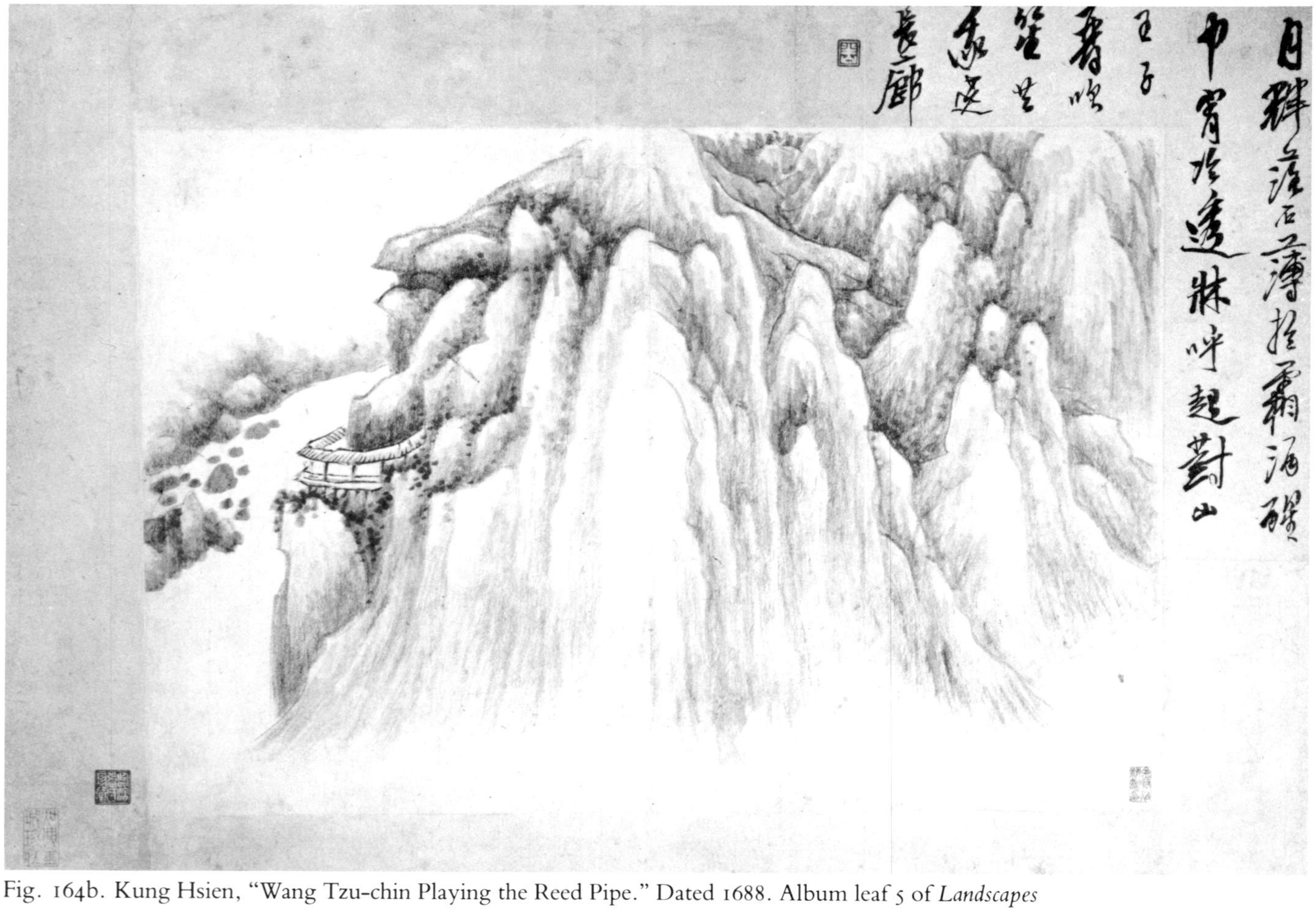

Fig. 164b. Kung Hsien, "Wang Tzu-chin Playing the Reed Pipe." Dated 1688. Album leaf 5 of *Landscapes*

surrounded by thick mist, which the sketchbook explained: "In painting cloudy mountains, the clouds must appear thick [*hou*]. For thirty years I tried to awaken to a method without success, then an old master pointed out to me, 'If the mountains are thick, the clouds will look thick.' "[85]

In the late 1680s Kung Hsien, now nearing seventy, continued to express bitterness and alienation in his paintings and poems. In a remarkable album of sixteen leaves dated 1688 (now in The Metropolitan Museum of Art, New York) Kung treated the album leaves as a series of mood poems, matching paintings and words. The poems express the artist's anguish: the successive visual images, some dark and morose, others gentle and lyrical, act as stunning settings for the poet's soliloquy. On "The Immortal's Cave Dwelling" (fig. 164a), the poem reads:

> The immortal in the cave opens his gate at dawn,
> Vermilion clouds disgorge the sun, then swallow it again.
> As I walk up the bridge to dry my hair,
> I glimpse my ravaged hairline in the flowing stream.

The voice is the more haunting for being addressed to no one but the poet himself, and the painting, reflecting the poem's mood, is dense and dark: the piled-up rocks and trees, built with thick layers of ink dots, carry a heavy emotional overtone as the bleak setting of a once ambitious man regretting his wasted life.

"Wang Tzu-chin Playing the Reed Pipe" (fig. 164b), from the same album, shows a dramatic view of a mountaintop as a prototypical triangular mountain symbol, as is accompanied by another emotion-laden verse:

> Moonlight falling on bare rocks, thinner than frost.
> Awaking from a drunken sleep at midnight, I feel cold penetrating my bed.
> I call out to Wang Tzu-chin [an immortal musician] on the other side of the mountain,
> Please play the reed pipe and stroll with me around the long walkway.

In keeping with the plea expressed in the poem and in contrast to Wang Hui's mountain symbol (cf. fig. 154a), Kung Hsien's painting seems lively and impassioned. Just as his brushwork, in luminous rich ink, alternates between intensity and languor, his spectacular daring and physical control offset his introspective mood.

## *Tao-chi: Return to the Primordial Oneness*

Tao-chi (also known as Yüan-chi or Shih-t'ao) was born in 1642 in Kuei-lin, Kuangsi province, as Chu Jo-chi, a tenth-generation descendant of Tsan, the prince of Ching-chiang (enfeoffed 1403–9), and a thirteenth-generation descendant of Chu Hsing-lung (d. 1344), the eldest brother of the founding Ming emperor Chu Yüan-chang.[86] Soon after Prince Fu fled Nanking on June 3, 1645, in the face of advancing Manchu troops, young Jo-chi's father, Chu Heng-chia, proclaimed himself a "protector of the realm" (*chien-kuo*), but in three months' time was defeated and killed by a cousin and another pretender, Prince T'ang of Fu-chou. Young Chu Jo-chi was saved by a family servant, who fled with the boy to Ch'üan-chou (Ch'ing-hsiang hsien), at the northern tip of Kuangsi. When the Manchu forces captured Ch'üan-chou two years later, the servant and his young master sought refuge in the Buddhist church: Jo-chi became Yüan-chi or Shih-t'ao, and his companion and "elder brother" took the name Ho-t'ao.

In 1650 the young mendicant monk, accompanied by his faithful friend, left Ch'üan-chou, traveling on foot and by boat northeast along the Hsiang River, then east through northern Hunan, Kiangsi, and Anhui, finally arriving in the Chiang-nan area. There, at Mount K'un, Sung-chiang, Kiangsu, Tao-chi became the disciple of a powerful Ch'an Buddhist priest, Lü-an Pen-yüeh (d. 1676). On a large handscroll, *Sixteen Lohans* (*Shih-liu lo-han*), dated 1667, now in The Metropolitan Museum of Art, New York (fig. 165),

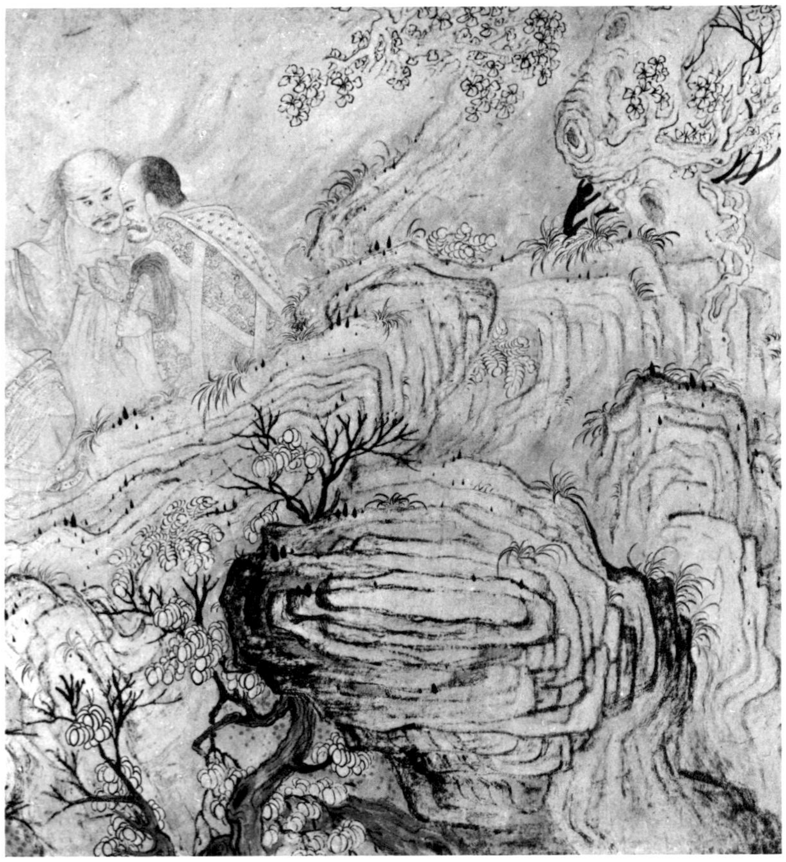

Fig. 165. Tao-chi, detail, *Sixteen Lohans*. Dated 1667. Handscroll, ink on paper. 47.0 x 599.4 cm (18½ in. x 19 ft. 8 in.). The Metropolitan Museum of Art, New York

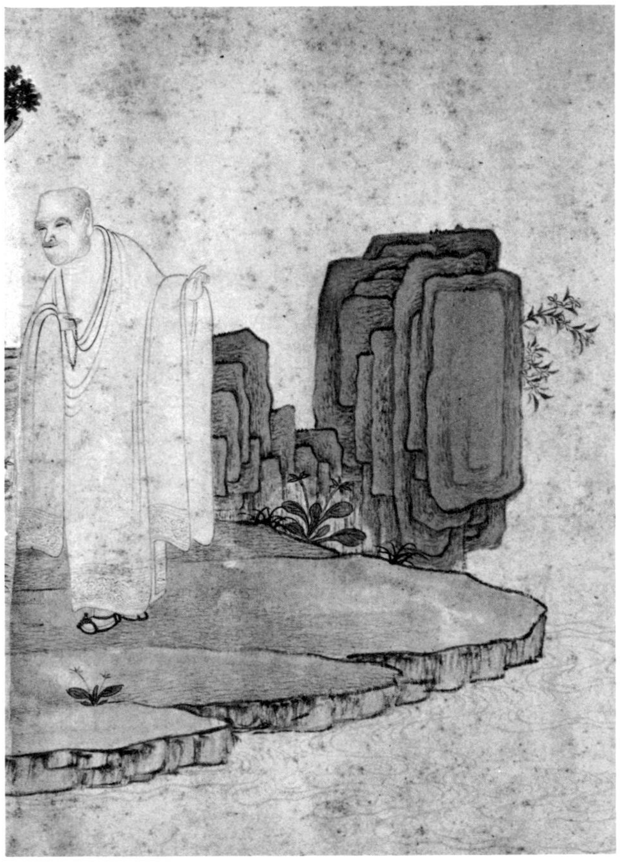

Fig. 166. Wu Pin, detail, *Sixteen Lohans*. Dated 1591. Handscroll, ink and color on paper. 32.4 x 414.3 cm (12¾ in. x 13 ft. 7⅛ in.). The Metropolitan Museum of Art, New York

Tao-chi, then twenty-five, proudly signed himself "grandson of T'ien-t'ung Min [Mu-ch'en, Lü-an's master], son of Shan-kuo Yüeh [Lü-an], Shih-t'ao, Chi." Between 1659 and 1661, Mu-ch'en Tao-min (1596–1674), accompanied by Lü-an, had served and received honors from the first Ch'ing emperor, Shih-tsu (Shun-chih; r. 1644–61).[87]

About 1665 Lü-an sent Tao-chi away to resume his wandering life. From the late 1660s through the 1670s, he and Ho-t'ao stayed in the area of Hsüan-ch'eng, Anhui. Then, in 1680, he moved on to Nanking. At the Ch'ang-kan (Pao-en) monastery, he found his first real home, a small house that he named I-chih-ko (Pavilion of a Single Plum Branch). A monk largely by circumstance, Tao-chi enjoyed his associations in the secular world, and he was spurred on by his talent and ambition. In December 1684, during the Ch'ing K'ang-hsi emperor's first southern visit, Tao-chi, because of his Ming lineage, was granted an audience with the emperor at the Ch'ang-kan monastery. By early 1687 he had moved on to Yang-chou, the lively metropolis of commerce and art north of the the Yangtze River. In the spring of 1689 he had a second interview with the K'ang-hsi emperor in Yang-chou. Late that year, the restless monk-painter set out for the capital, Peking, where he enjoyed the company of the nobles and grandees at court.

Returning from Peking to Yang-chou in late 1692, Tao-chi continued his wandering life for four more years. "My hair is white, and I am still without a home," he lamented in a poem dated 1695.[88] Finally, in late 1696, he built a retreat, Ta-ti-t'ang (Great Cleansing Hall), in Yang-chou. By that time, tired of wandering, bored with priesthood, and perhaps embarrassed in retrospect by his old worldly ambitions, he decided to shed his Buddhist garb, grow his hair, and "wash away" (*ta-ti*) all past mistakes and spiritual failings. Ceasing his peripatetic life, he settled down, concentrating on painting and on finishing his treatise, *Recorded Sayings on Painting* (*Hua-yü lu*), around 1700. He died in Yang-chou in 1707.

Tao-chi stated that he first painted orchids at the age of thirteen or fourteen, or around 1655.[89] His early artistic education, therefore, took place in Chiang-nan. By the time he painted *Sixteen Lohans* in 1667, in

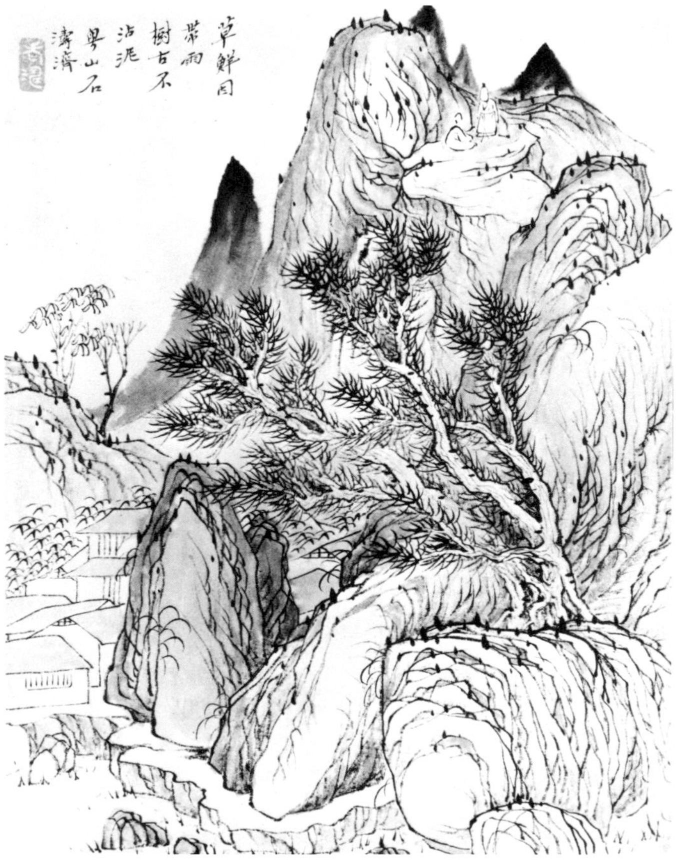

Fig. 167. Tao-chi, album leaf 6 of *Album of Landscapes*. Dated 1673. Ink on paper

Anhui, his personal style had been fully formed. Both Shen C. Y. Fu and James Cahill have suggested that Tao-chi during the late 1660s and 1670s was influenced by the Anhui masters such as Ch'eng Chia-sui (1565–1643) and Hung-jen (1610–1663), who had painted in Ni Tsan's dry-brush manner.[90] In his inscription on *Sixteen Lohans*, Tao-chi's Anhui friend Mei Ch'ing (1623–1697) identified Tao-chi's model as Li Kung-lin (ca. 1049–1106), the Northern Sung master of the plain-line drawing (*pai-miao*) brush style. Throughout the 1670s, as seen in his dated works of 1672, 1673, 1677, and 1678,[91] which were done mostly in the plain-line drawing style, Tao-chi acknowledged his debt in a seal, "Ch'ien-yu Lung-mien" ("Before me there was Lung-mien [Li Kung-lin]").

Yet Tao-chi probably never saw an original work by that Sung master. Unlike the erudite scholar-artists of the Orthodox School, Tung Ch'i-ch'ang and the four Wangs, who were reared and trained with the aid of the best available ancient works, Tao-chi, the unschooled monk, was largely self-taught. He apparently took his early training from popular late Ming sources, such as the figure paintings and woodblock illustrations by Wu Pin (fl. ca. 1583–1626), Ch'en Hung-shou (1599–1652), and Ting Yün-p'eng (ca. 1584–1638). Instead of the typical late Ming flat iron-wire (*t'ieh-hsien*) drawings and abstract surface patterns (fig. 166), however, Tao-chi used an energized calligraphic brushwork, enlivening his forms with palpable breath and momentum (figs. 165, 167).

A calligrapher of exceptional skill, as well as an extraordinary draftsman, Tao-chi delighted in the equivalencies between painting and calligraphy, developing painting styles through calligraphy and vice versa, engendering an astonishing variety of contrasting and complementary brush techniques. To allow full play to the metamorphic powers of his brush style, Tao-chi frequently employed the album format, which provided him with the opportunity of treating a large theme with not one image, but a whole series of images. Often working with as many as eight or twelve leaves, he dealt with a wide range of themes: pleasant outings; journeys; specific sites; flowers and fruit; landscapes and flowers in different seasons of the year; illustrations of recent or ancient poems; meditations on, or experiments with, brush and ink techniques; ancient styles; and art criticism. Avoiding conventional treatment of these themes, he interpreted every subject in an intensely personal way, making associations on multiple levels and in different directions: past and present, autobiographical and philosophical, formal and metaphysical.

After moving from Anhui to Nanking in 1680, Tao-chi began to sell his paintings, but at first had little success. Toward the end of the *jen-hsü* year, in early 1683, he completed a ten-leaf album at his studio Single Plum Branch during a snowstorm.[92] The words and images of these album leaves project a compelling emotional quality that vividly conveys the presence of the artist and involves the viewer in the issues and thoughts that concerned him. On Leaf 9, a flowering plum branch, he confesses his one source of pleasure—painting plum trees: "My regulated verse is not refined; the end of each year is difficult to pass, / Only my plum blossoms give me satisfaction, year after year." Leaf 1 shows an old hut surrounded by piled-up boulders and two plum trees, and an inscription: "I cultivate plum blossoms and prefer to live all alone."

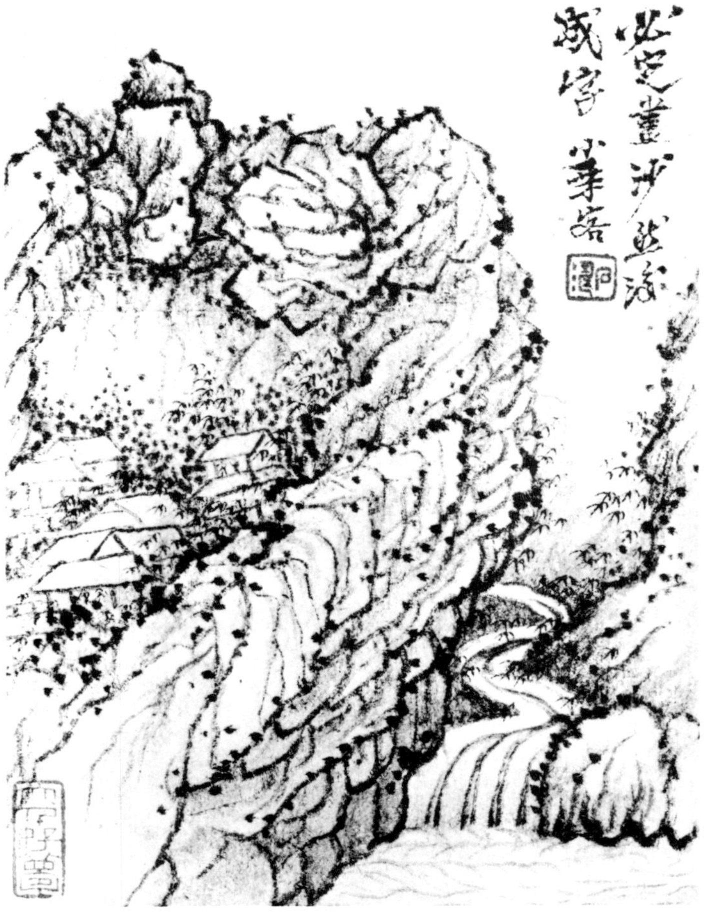

Fig. 168a. Tao-chi, "A Secluded Dwelling by a Mountain Chasm" ("Yen-ho yu-chü"). Dated 1682–83. Album leaf 7 of *Album of Landscapes and Flowers*, ink on paper. Provenance unknown, formerly Ta-feng-t'ang collection

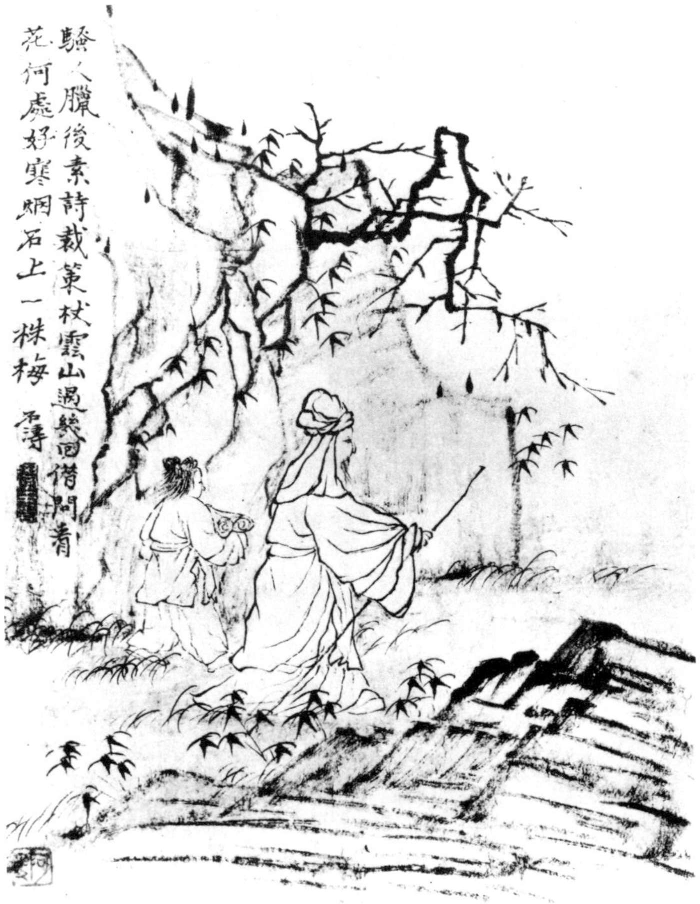

Fig. 168b. Tao-chi, "Searching for Plum Blossoms" ("T'an-mei t'u"). Dated 1682–83. Album leaf 2 of *Album of Landscapes and Flowers*

On Leaf 7 of the 1682–83 album, "A Secluded Dwelling by a Mountain Chasm" ("Yen-ho yü-chü"; fig. 168a), Tao-chi gives this advice for producing calligraphic effect in landscape painting: "Draw as if writing in the sand, / Then painting shall be like a written character." By repeating a single dry centered outline stroke over and over, and by modeling the rock form—as Kung Hsien had taught—by repeating the outline a second time with a lighter dry stroke, Tao-chi made rock forms seem to expand. His round brushstrokes, in the lotus-leaf-vein (*ho-yeh*) or unraveled-rope (*chieh-so*) texture pattern, and round dots created a large semicircle of mountain forms bending around the composition, filling the space inside the ring on the left with houses, and to the right with a mountain cascade. As a calligraphic design, the brush formula harnessed an overabundance of restless energy, converting it into majestically flowing breath-force movements, and, as landscape, the technique transmogrified the mountains into fantastic shapes and forms that suggest the supernatural and the divine.

In Leaf 2 of the same album, "Searching for Plum Blossoms" ("T'an-mei t'u"; fig. 168b), the artist, followed by his page, strides along in snow with a walking staff, looking for plum blossoms. His poem reads:

> The sorrowful poet, after the winter solstice, ponders over his plain verse;
> Waving his staff, how many times has he walked past the cloudy mountain?
> "Please sir," he asks, "where may I find some good flowers?"
> Behind the cold mist, above the cliff, is one branch of plum blossoms.

The angular boulders in the foreground, composed of square brushstrokes, set off the figures, the cliff, and the plum branch, done in swirling round strokes. Through the round brushwork, the painter expresses the poet's oneness with his surroundings: the patterns of drapery folds, rock fissures, and branches

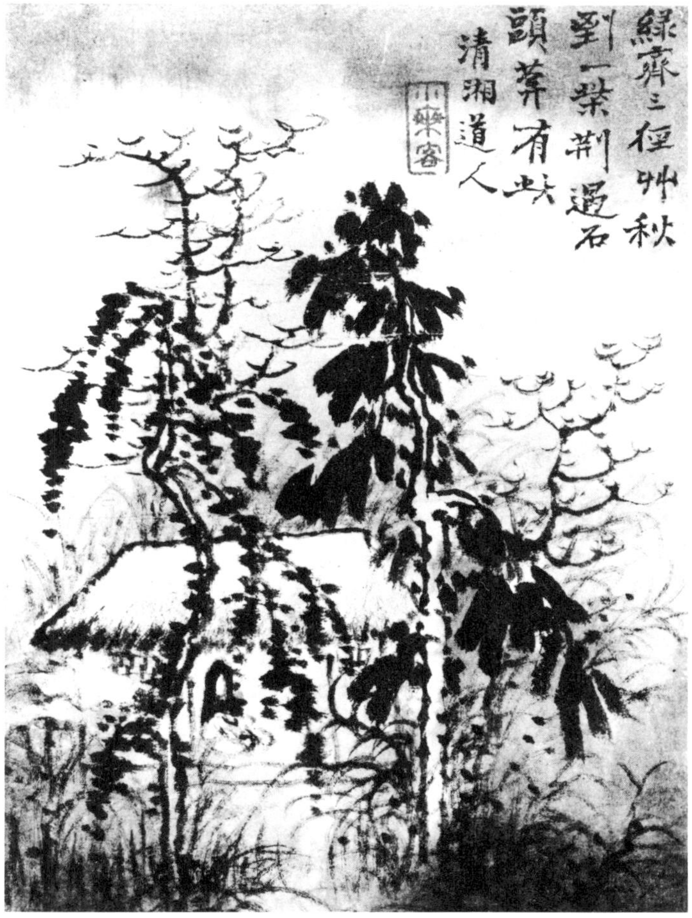

Fig. 168c. Tao-chi, "Stone Temple" ("Shih-t'ou-an t'u"). Dated 1682–83. Album leaf 4 of *Album of Landscapes and Flowers*

echo and interact. In his *Recorded Sayings on Painting*, while discussing the relationship between poetry and painting, Tao-chi pointed out that, more than literal correspondences, intuitive response could project imagery beyond description.[93] The artist's self-portrait, totally absorbed and merged into the surroundings, speaks volumes more than could be expressed in words.

The theme of the "sorrowful poet" (*sao-jen*) is taken up again in Leaf 8, *Melancholy Thoughts on the Hsiao and Hsiang Rivers*, now in the Edward L. Elliott Family Collection at The Art Museum, Princeton University (no. 44). This popular theme in landscape painting held a special significance for Tao-chi, ever since he first traveled on the Hsiao and Hsiang rivers as a boy in 1650, fleeing from his home province. His earliest extant work, an album leaf dated 1657, published in China,[94] represents a young monk in a boat on the river reading "Encountering Sorrow" ("Li-sao"), the famous ancient poem by China's archetypal "sorrowful poet," Ch'ü Yüan (343?–278 B.C.). Having lost the affection of his prince, Ch'ü Yüan wrote romantic and mournful poems, and drowned himself in the Mi-Lo River, a tributary of the Hsiang. The orphaned Tao-chi, now deprived of a rightful ruler, could only feel permanent sorrow.

On the Princeton leaf the artist wrote, "There are those special melancholy thoughts on the Hsiao and Hsiang rivers" ("Pieh-shih Hsiao-Hsiang i-tuan ch'ou"). More than a past journey or old pains remembered, the painting reflected a permanent condition of his mind, with indications of things to come. These "special melancholy thoughts" had caused an unalterable ambivalence in his nature: by the end of the 1680s, he would journey to Peking to curry favor with the new rulers, only to withdraw suddenly to reassert his allegiance to the Ming in the last years of his life. Because these "melancholy thoughts" could be neither appeased nor forgotten, they were the more calmly recollected. As opposed to the aggressive brush method of "A Secluded Dwelling," the soft moist landscape of "Melancholy Thoughts" is depicted with gentle, descriptive brushwork and ink wash; in an apparent reference to the "wild geese descending" section of the well-known theme Eight Views of the Hsiao and Hsiang Rivers (cf. no. 4), tall reeds and tree foliage rustling in the wind turn into a flock of birds in X-shaped brushstrokes.

The artist's calligraphy carefully matches the mood of the subject: the characters are in a subdued, archaizing clerical script. Along with Ni Tsan's popular painting style, Ni's reclusive, archaizing calligraphy style was also much in favor in the seventeenth century, and Tao-chi was its most accomplished practitioner. Retracing Ni Tsan's sources, Tao-chi adopted as his basic form the archaic regular script of Chung Yu (cf. fig. 107), who was also Li Kung-lin's calligraphic model. Stressing rectilinearity, he also adopted the solemn, monumental style of the clerical script; and, in a relaxed mood, combining the clerical with the more recent running style elements of the T'ang and Sung calligraphers, he wrote in a running-clerical manner similar to Ni Tsan's. By boldly exaggerating the contrasting clerical and regular elements, Tao-chi created a highly expressive calligraphy style that was widely emulated by the so-called Eight Eccentrics of the eighteenth century (cf. no. 48).

Carrying forth his stylistic experiments, Tao-chi painted, in the album of 1682–83, two examples of a familiar theme, an old house behind tall trees; one of them, "Stone Temple" ("Shih-t'ou-an t'u"; Leaf 4; fig. 168c), the polar opposite of his dry-brush style, features a great jumble of branches and leaves in wild, dark ink blotches. In an inscription dated 1685 on a renowned handscroll by Tao-chi in the wild manner, entitled *Ten Thousand Ugly Ink Dots* (*Wan-tien o-mo*), in the Su-chou Museum, the artist made clear his iconoclastic intentions: "Ten thousand dots of ugly ink, to make old Mi [Fu] die of vexation, / Lots of stringy, flaccid strokes, to make Tung Yüan fall down with laughter!"[95] Having developed his own special range of dry and wet styles, Tao-chi felt no desire to acknowledge any ancient master whose style his chanced to resemble: "Modern man, ancient man, who followed whose style? I enter and I exit, I let all other men's styles churn about under my brushtip," he wrote on "Cloudy Mountain" ("Yün-shan t'u"), Leaf 5 of his 1682–83 album. In two other leaves of the same album, he commented on paintings of his time: he remarked on Leaf 3 that painters of the Yün-chien School (followers of Tung Ch'i-ch'ang, such as Chao Tso; fl. ca. 1630–50) tended to paint in a wet style that was overly polished, therefore "vulgar"; on Leaf 6 he observed sadly that little could be expected from traditional painters—like Wang Hui, for instance—because all they knew was to try to "do interesting things with their brushwork."

While in Peking between 1690 and 1692, Tao-chi collaborated on paintings with both Wang Yüan-ch'i and Wang Hui.[96] By that time, however, he had become unalterably opposed to the Orthodox School method of painting by imitating ancient styles; "In this field," he wrote in a colophon dated 1694, "those who entered through the proper school will not achieve anything special."[97] After settling down in Yang-chou in late 1696, he made his full statement on the art of painting. His *Recorded Sayings on Painting*, completed about 1700, has been regarded by many modern scholars as the most original and systematically comprehensive theory of painting written since the Northern Sung dynasty.[98] Tao-chi vehemently advocated that the painter assert selfhood (*wo*) and avoid imitation. In so doing, he accepted many of the ideas and echoed the rhetoric of the late Ming antirevivalist and individualist thinkers.

*Recorded Sayings* opens with Tao-chi's theory of *i-hua*—literally, the single stroke, or painting of oneness—which Chou Ju-hsi (1969) translates as "the primordial line":

> In primeval antiquity there was no method, while primeval simplicity was intact. Once primeval simplicity disappeared, method was established. How was method established? It began with the primordial line [*i-hua*]. The primordial line is the basis of all things and the root of a myriad phenomena. . . . Now painting springs from man's mind [*hsin*]. . . . This primordial line which encompasses the infinity of creation . . . awaits man to grasp and take from it. . . . If a painter knows how to fall in and use this primordial line in a concrete though small way. . . people will now know how his paintings are done, and no painting will go against the dictates of his mind [or heart].[99]

Tao-chi probably developed his idea of *i-hua* from a discussion between his Ch'an master Lü-an Pen-yüeh and a master named Hsiu from the Pao-en Temple in Nanking. "Take the word *one* [written as a single horizontal stroke] and add no more to it," Hsiu reportedly said and then asked, "What do you have?" Lü-an answered, "The design is complete."[100] For Lü-an, "one" completed the transition from nothing to everything: before "one" nothing existed; after "one" followed creation, a "complete" design. As an artist, Tao-chi intuited this oneness of creation through the act of painting. More than the teachings of the past, his actions taught him to "create a method from no method, and use this method to embrace [*kuan*; string together] all methods." In painting, Tao-chi expanded his single-line brush methods into a broad range of complex techniques, producing his own Great Synthesis. By asserting selfhood and following his own mind (*hsin*)—as taught by the Neo-Confucian School of the Mind—he produced the painting of oneness. "Therefore I say," he quoted Confucius at the close of the chapter on *i-hua*, "my Tao is that of an all-embracing oneness [*i-i-kuan-chih*]."[101]

After establishing method in his first chapter, Tao-chi expounded the need to "understand method" (*liao-fa*) in chapter II. Using the familiar metaphor of the ruler and the compass, he explained that method must serve rather than enslave the painter:

> If the world knows only the ruler and the compass, but not the principles of the rotations of heaven and earth, then heaven and earth will tie people up with methods, and people will blind themselves by becoming servants to methods. . . . This is why if there is the method and he does not understand [how to use] it, he will then be hindered by the method.[102]

Chapter III stresses "transformation" (*pien-hua*). Paraphrasing the late Ming antirevivalist Yüan Hung-tao (1568–1610), Tao-chi wrote: "I am what I am and must always remain myself. . . . The beards and eyebrows of the ancients cannot grow on my face; the lungs and bowels of the ancients cannot be placed in my stomach. . . . How can I follow any ancient style without transforming it?"[103] Chapter IV, entitled "Respecting One's Own Response" ("Tsun-shou"), again emphasizes the importance of following one's own mind: "Painting responds to ink, ink responds to brush, brush responds to my wrist, my wrist responds to my mind."[104] Chapter V discusses the use of "brush and ink" (*pi-mo*), and chapter VI explains that the secret of using brush and ink lies in the "turning of the wrist" (*yün-wan*), which depends on one's ability to master transformation. In chapter VII, "Cosmic Atmosphere" ("Yin-yün"), the author returns to the primordial line: "From one comes a myriad of things, and from a myriad of things I must come back to one. By transforming a single stroke into the cosmic atmosphere, all things under heaven may be accomplished."[105] In Tao-chi's painting, single brushstrokes magically change from lines into surfaces and then into dots, constantly growing and expanding as they overlap, crisscross, and interpenetrate—until suddenly they coalesce into the cosmic atmosphere that represents the textures and substances of real landscapes.

Chapters VIII through XIV deal successively with technique and various methods of painting particular subjects: "Mountains and Rivers" ("Shan-ch'üan"), "Texture Methods" ("Ts'un-fa"), "Compositional Divisions" ("Ching-chieh"), "Compositional Types" ("Hsi-ching"), "Forests and Trees" ("Lin-mu"), "The Sea and the Waves" ("Hai-t'ao"), and "The Four Seasons" ("Ssu-shih"). In these sections Tao-chi the painter analyzed the landscape structure, gave his principles of organizing nature, described his brushwork systems and compositional schemes, and explained the interactions between nature and his art.

"Mountains and rivers are the forms and dynamic forces [*hsing-shih*] of heaven and earth," he declared in chapter VIII. Since individual mountains and peaks are but small segments of reality, according to Tao-chi, the painter must grasp larger principles and methods of transformation. In a passage reminiscent of the early tenth-century painter Ching Hao's discussion of substance and ornament in landscape painting, Tao-chi recommended that the painter use "principles of painting [*hua-chih-li*] and methods of brushwork [*pi-chih-fa*] to deal respectively with the substance [*chih*] and the ornament [*shih*] of heaven and earth."[106] He matched five sets of natural phenomena with their pictorial equivalents:

> Wind and rain, dark and light—these are the atmospheric qualities of mountains and rivers; sparse and dense, deep and far—these are the simplified patterns of mountains and rivers; crisscrossing, taking in and letting out—these are the rhythms of mountains and rivers; yin and yang, heavy and light—these show the spiritual concentration of mountains and rivers; waters and clouds, gathering and dispersing—these represent the linkages of mountains and rivers; [mountains] crouching and leaping, facing each other or placed back to back—these describe the alternating between action and retreat of mountains and rivers.

By merging himself with what he paints through *i-hua*, Tao-chi claimed, "I am able to embrace both the forms and the spirit of mountains and rivers. . . . Mountains and rivers seek me out to speak for them. They are born of me, and I of them. I gather up all strange mountain peaks and make them the rough draft of my paintings."[107]

In "Texture Methods," Tao-chi named thirteen texture patterns: curling clouds (*chüan-yün*), ax-cut (*fu-p'i*), hemp-fiber (*p'i-ma*), unraveled rope (*chieh-so*), devil face (*kuei-mien*), skeletal (*k'u-lu*), firewood (*lüan-ch'ai*), sesame seed (*chih-ma*), gold and green (*chin-pi*), jade dust (*yü-hsieh*), pellet holes (*tan-wo*), alum head (*fan-t'ou*), and boneless (*mo-ku*). "Because real mountain peaks are different physically, and each has a different face," he explained, "only when a real peak becomes a texture pattern will the texture pattern help the peak grow. . . . Without becoming a real peak, how does the texture method show its transformation? Without becoming the texture pattern, how does the mountain peak reveal itself?"[108]

In "Compositional Divisions," Tao-chi discussed the traditional division of the picture plane into "three layers"—the ground, the trees, and the mountains—and "two sections"—scenery below and mountains above. And in "Compositional Types" he laid out six compositional schemes:

> The scenery below is springlike, while the mountain above remains wintry;
> The trees below are wintry, while the mountain above is springlike;
> Hanging scenery: upright trees with an overhanging mountain, or an upright mountain with dangling trees;
> Borrowed scenery; a bare mountain made lively by man-made garden details;
> Cut-off scenery: either the top or the bottom, or both, of the trees and mountains are cut off;
> Thrilling and steep mountains, as on the immortals' islands.[109]

In "Forests and Trees" and "The Sea and the Waves," he explained that he drew trees "mostly with the same method as drawing rocks," and since, for him, all elements in painting shared the same principles, "mountains are like the sea, and the sea is like the mountains." He noted, moreover, that in drawing trees as well as other elements, he aimed for a raw (*sheng*) and pungent (*la*) quality in his brushwork.[110]

Chapters XV and XVI, "Away from the Dust of the World" ("Yüan-ch'en") and "Escaping from the Common" ("T'o-su"), deal with the cultivation of the right state of the mind while painting. Reflecting on the Taoist philosopher Chuang-tzu's teaching of "fasting of the mind" (*hsin-chai*), Tao-chi believed that "by leaving things to becloud themselves, and the dust of the world to mix by itself, my mind will be free from trouble." And, echoing one of Ching Hao's so-called Six Essentials, he spoke of the importance of concentrated thought (*ssu*) in landscape painting: "When thoughts are concentrated, the mind [or heart] reaches its mark and is joyful. Then painting will penetrate into the essence of the smallest things."[111]

Chapter XVII, "Combining with Calligraphy" ("Chien-tzu"), restates the belief that painting and calligraphy were one and the same, inspiring Tao-chi to attain new heights in painting with words and images: "The primordial line lies at the foundation of calligraphy and painting, which, in turn, represent the standards and variations of the primordial line."[112]

Finally, in chapter XVIII, "Nourishing and Drawing from the Repository" ("Tzu-jen"), Tao-chi turned to the broader uses and meanings of landscape painting. Brushwork, for Tao-chi, meant life (*sheng-huo*) and self-cultivation (*meng-yang*), while landscape made manifest for him everything he valued in life—position (*wei*), spirit (*shen*), change (*hua*), love (*jen*), movement (*tung*), quietude (*ching*), ritual (*li*), harmony (*ho*), respectfulness (*chin*), wisdom (*chih*), beauty (*wen*), martial strength (*wu*), virtue (*te*), righteousness (*i*), courage (*yung*), justice (*p'ing-i*), perceptiveness (*ch'a*), purity (*shan*), and purpose (*chih*). "I depend neither on mountain nor on water, neither on brush nor on ink, neither on past nor on present nor on any ancient sages," he concluded. "I depend only on what I am able to nourish and draw upon myself!"[113]

In a late work by Tao-chi, a large hanging scroll of about 1700 entitled *An Ancient House under Tall Pine Trees* (*Ch'ang-sung lao-wu*), in the John B. Elliott Collection at The Art Museum, Princeton University (no. 45), the artist returned to his favorite theme of a man sitting, gazing out of a house surrounded by mountains. The landscape is composed of familiar elements that appeared frequently in the artist's earlier works: the man in the house behind tall pine trees and distant peaks that are reminiscent of the Mount

Huang region in Anhui. The inscription above the landscape repeats a colophon found on an earlier painting by Tao-chi dated 1679 (fig. 169).[114] The inscription reads:

> An angry lion tearing at a rock,
> A thirsty steed galloping to a spring,
> Wind and rain gathering,
> Mist and clouds in a myriad shapes,
> Sublime and unworldly,
> Calm, steady, and straightforward.
> I apply these feelings with my brush and ink,
> But express myself beyond brush and ink.
> Will not the connoisseur upon seeing this die
> of laughter?

The first two lines of this statement are from an eighth-century critique of the work of a leading T'ang dynasty calligrapher, Hsü Hao (703–782). An admirer of Hsü Hao's, the great Northern Sung calligrapher Huang T'ing-chien (1045–1105), often quoted these lines to describe calligraphic works that he liked.[115] Now Tao-chi, who admired Huang T'ing-chien's work, borrowed these phrases as the theme of his painting, which he equated with calligraphy. Treating painting as calligraphy in *An Ancient House*, Tao-chi rearranged the familiar motifs of mountains and trees in a new design, "writing" strong and strange-looking rock and tree forms powerfully and expressively (fig. 170). Isolated in his studio in Yang-chou during his final years, he appears to have abandoned by this time the painting of actual landscapes, carrying to its logical conclusion Tung Ch'i-ch'ang's injunction "If one considers the wonders of brush and ink, then landscape can never equal painting."[116] "My brush can overturn the forces of mountains and rivers," he wrote in *Recorded Sayings*. "While real peaks cannot change the functions of my texture strokes, my texture strokes can develop special forms and forces for the mountains."[117]

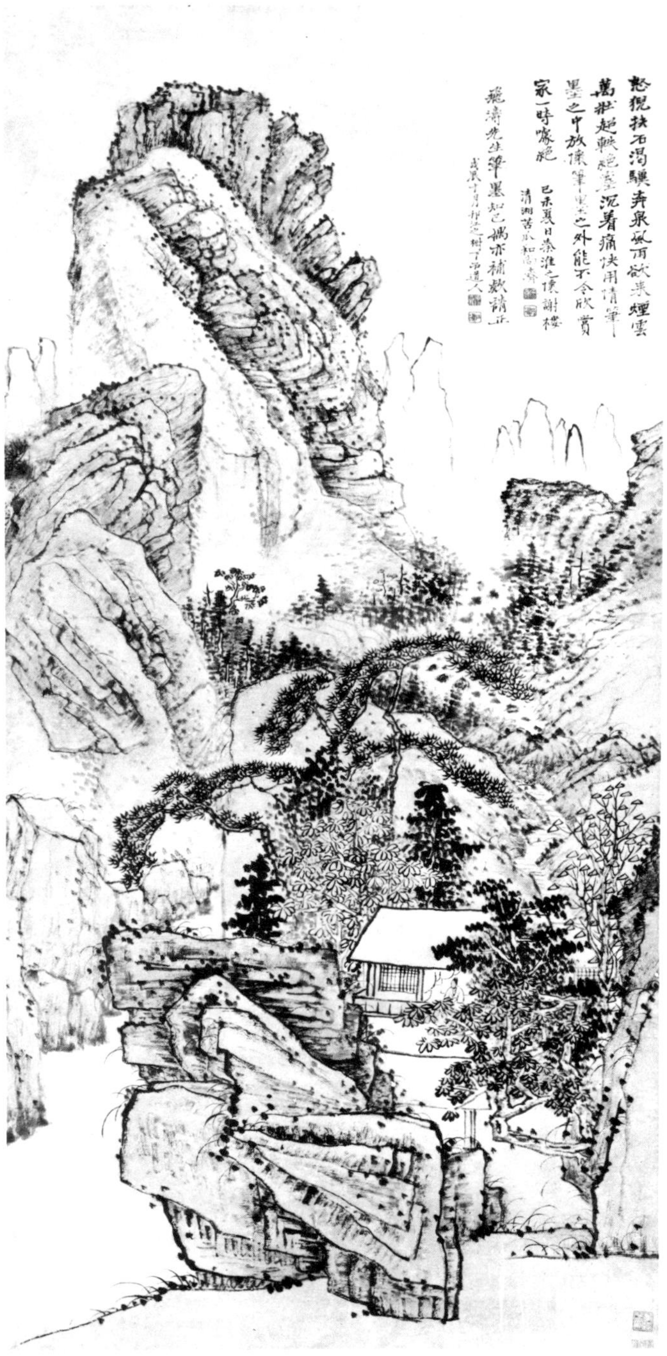

Fig. 169. Tao-chi, *Landscape for Fei-t'ao*. Dated 1679. Hanging scroll, ink on paper. 108.0 x 52.0 cm (3 ft. 6 1/2 in. x 20 1/2 in.). Freer Gallery of Art, Washington, D.C.

Yet the result Tao-chi tried to achieve in his late works was not representation of nature or expressive brushwork, or even an outpouring of emotion, but the spirit of oneness of creation experienced through the act of painting: "I apply these feelings with my brush and ink, / But express myself beyond brush and ink." "Before I was fifty," he wrote in *Recorded Sayings*, "I had not yet detached myself from the womb of mountains and rivers."[118] In the early 1700s, on reaching sixty, Tao-chi declared his independence of nature: "Even if my brush does not resemble brush and my ink does not resemble ink and my painting does not resemble painting, I make sure that my self [*wo*] is always present in my work."[119]

In spite of his theoretical writings Tao-chi's was not a theoretical art. His *Recorded Sayings* merely represented a rational effort at the end of his career to explain his art, which, being intuitive in approach, remained largely inexplicable. Tao-chi saw himself at the center of a holistic universe, the origin of himself

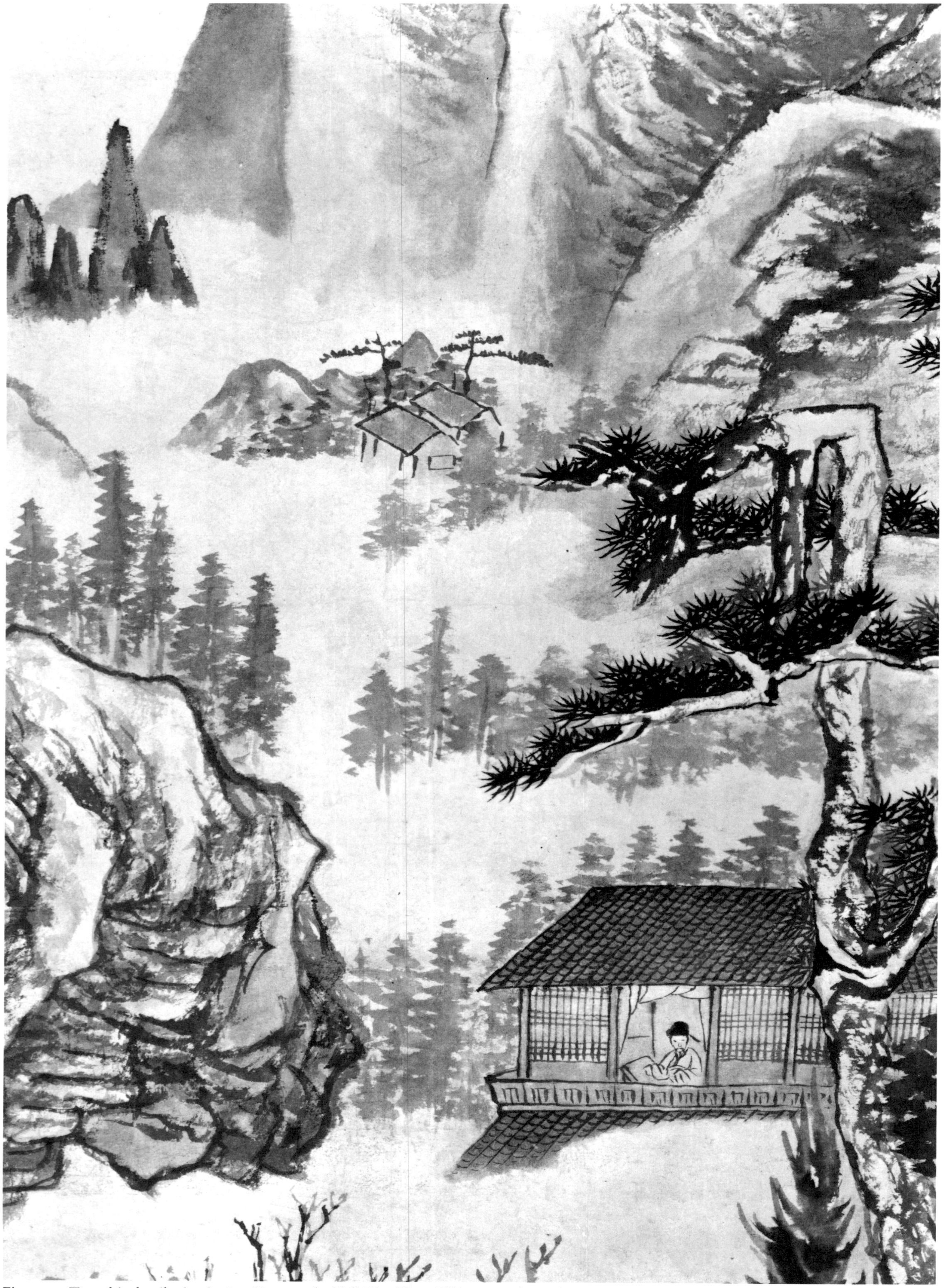

Fig. 170. Tao-chi, detail, *An Ancient House under Tall Pine Trees* (*Ch'ang-sung lao-wu*), no. 45

and the world, the past and the present. In response to this wholeness, he wielded his brush in a style that embraced or replaced all earlier methods and styles.

When Tao-chi's *Ancient House under Tall Pine Trees* is compared with Fan K'uan's *Travelers among Streams and Mountains* (fig. 48), the differences in their technique and approach to landscape are vast and obvious. Yet both works convey a compelling sense of the artist's exultation before nature's forms and principles that binds them to the great tradition of Chinese landscape art. For a handscroll of about 1700, Tao-chi composed a poem that sums up his relationship to his art:

> Beating drums with a cypress-wood stick,
> Or writing calligraphy with a sheep-hair brush,
> What matters most is the satisfaction of the moment,
> And never mind success or failure in the eyes of posterity.
> But unless the painter has the hand [of General Kuan Yü; d. A.D. 219] that can kill and break through the passes,
> How dare one play with a painting brush![120]

From landscape decorations on objects preserved in the Shosōin Treasury, Nara, to the works of Tao-chi, Chinese landscape painting developed from the building of its vocabulary in the eighth century to the formation of a final synthesis in the early eighteenth century. Unique among the world's great artistic expressions was the special position held by painting and calligraphy in the daily lives of the Chinese and in their culture. Because of the picturelike quality of the Chinese written language, and the close affinity between Chinese painting and beautiful writing, calligraphy and painting were natural, as well as useful and necessary, skills for the Chinese. It was with more truth than hyperbole that Tao-chi observed that "in everything bestowed by heaven, and with every person of greater or lesser talent, there is nothing that is not marked by the presence of calligraphy and painting."[121]

In the history of Chinese landscape painting, styles became more and more complex, until overspecialization brought on an inevitable decline from which renewal was possible only through radical simplification and a new synthesis. Unlike the Europeans and Americans, who saw human life directed either by divine providence or by scientific progress, the Chinese viewed historical change as essentially random and unpredictable, governed only by cyclical laws of waxing and waning, growth and decline, fragmentation and reintegration. Under stressful conditions, the only reliable individual recourse for survival, as the lives of leading Chinese scholar-artists such as Ni Tsan and Tao-chi have shown, was to pursue equilibrium and stability directed from within.

The deaths of Tao-chi, Wang Hui, and the other great early Ch'ing painters in the early decades of the eighteenth century marked the beginning of the end of the great tradition in Chinese landscape painting. During the eighteenth century, under the reigns of the Yung-cheng (Shih-tsung; r. 1722–35) and Ch'ien-lung emperors, many able painters worked at the court in the north and in the commercial centers, most notably Yang-chou, in the south, but none of these quite matched the stature and accomplishments of their great seventeenth-century predecessors, whose styles and theories they emulated. In the nineteenth and twentieth centuries China's protracted struggle for modernization finally destroyed the Great Synthesis that Wang Hui and Tao-chi worked successfully to achieve. Once again, the Chinese painter's world is in turmoil and transition, but this time with no promise of a new synthesis in sight. This, however, is a topic for another book.

NOTES

1. Ku Ning-yüan, "Kuo-ch'ao hua-p'ing" (A critical evaluation of Ming painting), in Wang Yüan-ch'i et al., comps., *P'ei-wen-chai shu-hua p'u* (Manual on calligraphy and painting of the P'ei-wen Studio) (1708; repr. ed., Taipei: 1969), *chüan* 18, p. 12b.
2. Wen C. Fong, "Archaism as a Primitive Style," in Christian F. Murck, ed., *Artists and Traditions: Uses of the Past in Chinese Culture* (Princeton: The Art Museum, 1976), pp. 89–109.
3. Wen C. Fong, *Returning Home: Tao-chi's Album of Landscapes and Flowers* (New York: George Braziller, 1976), pp. 20 ff.
4. Tung Ch'i-ch'ang, *Hua-yen* (The eye of painting), I-shu ts'ung-pien, vol. 12 (Taipei: Shih-chieh shu-chü, 1962), p. 23.
5. For the biography of Tung Ch'i-ch'ang, see Nelson Wu, "Tung Ch'i-ch'ang (1555–1636): Apathy in Government and Fervor in Art," in Arthur Wright and Denis Twichett, eds., *Confucian Personalities* (Stanford: Stanford University Press, 1962), pp. 260–382; Hironobu Kōhara, ed., *Tō Kishō no shoga* (Tung Ch'i-ch'ang: the man and his work) (Tokyo: Nigen-sha, 1981), esp. vol. 2, pp. 159–218.
6. For reproductions of Tung's colophons, dated 1596, on Chao Ling-jang's scroll, see Hironobu Kōhara, ed., *Tō Kishō no shoga*, vol. 2, pl. 32; Tung Ch'i-ch'ang, *Hua-yen*, pp. 37–38.
7. For Tung's colophon on *Residents of the Capital City* (*Lung-hsiu chiao-min t'u*), attributed to Tung Yüan, see National Palace Museum, Taipei, comp., *Ku-kung shu-hua lu* (A descriptive catalogue of the painting and calligraphy in the National Palace Museum) (Taipei: National Palace Museum, 1965), vol. 3, *chüan* 5, p. 19.
8. For an illustration of Tung's colophon, dated 1596, on *Dwelling in the Fu-ch'un Mountains*, see Hironobu Kōhara, ed., *Tō Kishō no shoga*, vol. 2, pl. 33; and National Palace Museum, comp., *Ku-kung shu-hua lu*, vol. 2, *chüan* 4, p. 134; see also Celia C. Riely, "Tung Ch'i-ch'ang's Ownership of Huang Kung-wang's *Dwelling in the Fu-ch'un Mountains*," *Archives of Asian Art* 28 (1974–75): 57–76.
9. In reference to the *Hsiao and Hsiang Rivers* scroll, see Tung Ch'i-ch'ang, *Hua-yen*, pp. 36–37; for this scroll and for *Residents of the Capital City*, see National Palace Museum, comp., *Ku-kung shu-hua lu*, vol. 3, *chüan* 5, p. 19.
10. Wen C. Fong, "*Rivers and Mountains after Snow (Chiang-shan hsüeh-chi)* attributed to Wang Wei (A.D. 699–759)," *Archives of Asian Art* 30 (1976–77): 6–33.
11. Ibid., pp. 11 ff.
12. Nelson Wu, "Tung Ch'i-ch'ang (1555–1636)," p. 280.
13. Tung Ch'i-ch'ang, *Hua-yen*, p. 37.
14. Ibid., p. 18.
15. Ibid., p. 25.
16. Ibid., p. 45.
17. Ibid., p. 22.
18. Ibid., p. 53.
19. Ibid., p. 27.
20. Ibid., p. 40.
21. *Fang Sung-Yüan-jen shu-pen hua pa [Hsiao-chung hsien ta]* (Imitating Sung and Yüan masters, copies in reduced size, paintings with colophons [within small see large]), in National Palace Museum, comp., *Ku-kung shu-hua lu*, vol. 4, *chüan* 6, pp. 71–75.
22. Tung Ch'i-ch'ang, *Hua-yen*, p. 50.
23. Wen C. Fong, "*Rivers and Mountains after Snow*," p. 15.
24. Ibid., pp. 17–18.
25. Ibid., p. 18.
26. Ibid., pp. 17, 19.
27. Ibid., p. 28.
28. Hironobu Kōhara, *Tō Kishō no shoga*, vol. 2, pl. 33; National Palace Museum, comp., *Ku-kung shu-hua lu*, vol. 2, *chüan* 4, p. 134.
29. Tung Ch'i-ch'ang, *Hua-yen*, p. 21.
30. Ibid., p. 20.
31. Ibid. p. 19.
32. Tung Ch'i-ch'ang, *Hua-ch'an-shih sui-pi* (Notes written at the Painting Meditation Studio), I-shu ts'ung-pien, vol. 28 (Taipei: Shih-chieh shu-chü, 1968), p. 3; for Tung's study of Wang Hsi-chih, see p. 5.
33. Tung Ch'i-ch'ang, *Jung-t'ai chi* (Notes from Jung-t'ai), Ming-tai i-shu-chia chi hui-k'an, vols. 11–14 (1630[?]; repr. ed., Taipei, 1968), *chüan* 2, p. 3a.
34. Ibid., *chüan* 2, p. 42a.
35. Ibid., *chüan* 2, p. 7a.
36. Ibid., *chüan* 2, pp. 3b, 7a.
37. Ibid., *chüan* 2, p. 3a; *chüan* 3, p. 6a.
38. Li Tso-hsien (*chin-shih*, 1835), *Shu-hua chien-ying* (Reflections on painting and calligraphy) (Taipei: Han-hua wen-hua shih-yeh ku-fen yu-hsien kung-ssu, 1971), vol. 2, *chüan* 20, pp. 8a, b.
39. P'ang Yüan-chi, *Hsü-chai ming-hua lu* (Supplement to annotated catalogue of P'ang Yüan-ch'i's art collection) (1909; 1924; repr. ed., Taipei: Han-hua wen-hua shih-yeh ku-fen yu-hsien kung-ssu, 1971), *chüan* 9, p. 5.
40. National Palace Museum, comp., *Ku-kung shu-hua lu*, vol. 4, *chüan* 6, p. 35.
41. An Ch'i, *Mo-yüan hui-kuan lu* (A comprehensive record of ink acquaintances: a catalogue of An Ch'i's collection of calligraphy and painting), Kuo-hsüeh chi-pen ts'ung-shu, vol. 155 (Taipei: Shang-wu yin-shu-kuan, 1968), *chüan* 5, pp. 18–19.
42. Pien Yung-yü, *Shih-ku-t'ang shu-hua hui-k'ao* (Classified record of calligraphy and painting) (Taipei: Cheng-chung shu-chü, 1958), vol. 4, *chüan* 30, p. 532.
43. Ibid., p. 533.
44. Chang Ch'ou, *Ch'ing-ho shu-hua fang* (Painting and calligraphy barge at Ch'ing-ho) (1616; repr. ed., Taipei: Hsüeh-hai shu-chü, 1975), *chüan* 11, p. 40.
45. National Palace Museum, comp., *Ku-kung shu-hua lu*, vol. 3, *chüan* 5, p. 204; vol. 4, *chüan* 6, p. 22.
46. Ibid., vol. 3, *chüan*, 5, pp. 406–7.
47. See Wang Shih-min's biography in Chang Keng, *Kuo-ch'ao hua-cheng lu* (History of painting during the Ch'ing dynasty) (preface dated 1735), in *Hua-shih ts'ung-shu* (Compendium of painting histories) (Taipei: Wen-shih-che ch'u-pan-she, 1974), vol. 3, *chüan* 1, p. 1b.
48. Yün Shou-p'ing, *Nan-t'ien hua-pa* (Yün Shou-p'ing's colophons on paintings), I-shu ts'ung-pien, vol. 25 (Taipei: Shih-chieh shu-chü, 1976), *chüan* 3, p. 96.
49. National Palace Museum, comp., *Ku-kung shu-hua lu*, vol. 4, *chüan* 6, pp. 71–75.
50. Chang Keng, *Kuo-ch'ao hua-cheng lu*, *chüan* 1, p. 16.
51. National Palace Museum, comp., *Ku-kung shu-hua lu*, vol. 4, *chüan* 6, p. 74.
52. Ibid., pp. 73–75.
53. Ibid. A hanging scroll entitled *Spring Dawn over Mount Tan-t'ai* (*Tan-t'ai ch'un-hsiao*) attributed to Wang Meng is now in the National Palace Museum, Taipei; see National Palace Museum, comp., *Ku-kung shu-hua lu*, vol. 4, *chüan* 8, *chien-mu* (supplementary list), p. 67.
54. For Wang Hui's biography, see Huang Shu-lin, "Wang Keng-yen hsien-sheng mu-chih-ming" (Wang Hui's tomb epitaph), in *Wang shih chia-ch'eng* (Records of the Wang family), *chüan* 10, pp. 50a–53a; Shen Te-ch'ien (167?–1769), "Wang Hui mu-chih-ming" (Wang Hui's tomb epitaph), in *Kuo-ch'ao ch'i-hsien lei-cheng chu-pien* (Biographies of notables of the Ch'ing dynasty), 1st. ser. (1884–90; repr. ed., Taipei: Wen-hai ch'u-pan-she, 1966), *chüan* 431, pp. 26a–27b; Chang Keng, *Kuo-ch'ao hua-cheng lu*, *chüan* 2, pp. 1a–b.
55. Wang Shih-min, *Hsi-lu hua-pa* (Wang Shih-min's colophons on paintings), in Ch'in Tsu-yung, ed., *Hua-hsüeh hsin-yin* (Insights from painting studies), Kuo-hsüeh chi-pen ts'ung-shu, vol. 15 (Taipei: Shang-wu yin-shu-kuan, 1968), *chüan* 3, pp. 72–73.
56. See Wang Hui's own preface to *Ch'ing-hui tseng-yen* (Writings presented to Wang Hui), ed. Hsü Chung-hsüan (1714; repr. ed., Feng-yü-lou, 1911), pp. 1b–2a.
57. Tung Ch'i-ch'ang, *Hua-yen*, p. 24.
58. See Richard Barnhart, "The 'Snowscape' Attributed to Chu-jan," *Archives of Asian Art* 24 (1970–71): 6–22; and Wen C. Fong, "*Rivers and Mountains after Snow*," pp. 25 ff.

59. Wang Yüan-ch'i et al., comps., *P'ei-wen-chai shu-hua-p'u, chüan* 3, p. 1b; see Richard Barnhart, "Wei Fu-jen's *Pi Chen T'u* and the Early Texts on Calligraphy," *Archives of Chinese Art Society of America* 18 (1964): 13–25.
60. Wang Yüan-ch'i, *Yü-ch'uang man-pi* (Jottings done beside a rain-splashed window), in Ch'in Tsu-yung, ed., *Hua-hsüeh hsin-yin, chüan* 7, p. 174.
61. Ibid., pp. 165–66.
62. See Roderick Whitfield, *In Pursuit of Antiquity: Chinese Paintings of the Ming and Ch'ing Dynasties from the Collection of Mr. and Mrs. Earl Morse* (Princeton: The Art Museum, 1969), pp. 114–16.
63. See *Yūrin taikan* (Illustrated catalogue of the Chinese art objects in the Fuji-Yūrinkan Museum) (Kyoto: Fuji-Yūrinkan Museum, 1929–49), vol. 3, pl. 12.
64. Wang Hui, *Ch'in-hui hua-pa* (Wang Hui's colophons on paintings), in Ch'in Tsu-yung, ed., *Hua-hsüeh hsin-yin, chüan* 4, p. 100.
65. Ibid.
66. Roderick Whitfield, *In Pursuit of Antiquity*, p. 124.
67. Yün Shou-p'ing, *Nan-t'ien hua-pa, chüan* 2, p. 69; Yün Shou-ping, *Ou-hsiang-kuan hua-pa* (Colophons of the Ou-hsiang Studio), in Ch'in Tsu-yung, ed., *Hua-hsüeh hsin-yin, chüan* 5, p. 22.
68. See Chang Keng, *Kuo-ch'ao hua-cheng lu*, vol. 2, pp. 1a–b.
69. Chou Liang-kung, *Tu-hua lu* (Record of reading paintings), I-shu ts'ung-pien, vol. 14 (Taipei: Shih-chieh shu-chü, 1968), *chüan* 1, sec. 2, p. 20.
70. National Palace Museum, comp., *Ku-kung shu-hua lu*, vol. 3, *chüan* 5, p. 37.
71. *Shih-ch'ü pao-chi ch'u-pien* (Treasured boxes of the stony moat), Ch'ien-ch'ing-kung, 2nd. ser. (Taipei: Ku-kung po-wu-yüan, 1971), *chüan* 2, p. 292.
72. National Palace Museum, Taipei, comp., *Ku-kung ming-hua san-pai chung* (Three hundred masterpieces in the National Palace Museum, Taipei) (Taipei: National Palace Museum, 1959), vol. 3, pl. 100; National Palace Museum, comp., *Ku-kung shu-hua lu*, vol. 3, *chüan* 5, p. 75.
73. National Palace Museum, comp., *Ku-kung ming-hua san-pai chung*, vol. 2, pl. 62; found in an album called *Li-tai hua-fu chi-tse* (Collection of paintings from successive dynasties), as recorded in National Palace Museum, comp., *Ku-kung shu-hua lu*, vol. 4, *chüan* 6, pp. 178–79.
74. For an illustration, see Hsin-chung Lovell, "Wang Hui's *Dwelling in the Fu-ch'un Mountains*: A Classical Theme, Its Origins and Variations," *Ars Orientalis* 8 (1970): 217–42.
75. Chiang I-han, "Kung Hsien te chia-shih, sheng-p'ing, chi chiao-yu: Kung Hsien yen-chiu chih-i" (Kung Hsien's family background, his life, and his friends: a study of Kung Hsien), *Hua-kang i-shu hsüeh-pao* 1 ( June 1981): 213–44.
76. Quoted in Wang Shih-ch'ing, "Kung Hsien te Ts'ao-hsiang-t'ang chi" (Poetry collections of Kung Hsien's Fragrant Grass Hall), *Wen-wu* 1978, no. 5: 46.
77. Chiang I-han, "Kung Hsien te chia-shih sheng-p'ing, chi chiao-yu": 234–35; also, Liu Wang-chi, "Kung Hsien," in *Chung-kuo ming-hua-chia ts'ung-shu* (A collection of famous painters in Chinese history) (Hong Kong: Chinese Calligraphy and Painting Institute, 1970), pp. 1109–10.
78. Quoted in Marc Wilson, "Kung Hsien: Theorist and Technician in Painting," *The Nelson Gallery and Atkins Museum Bulletin* 4, no. 9 (May–July 1969): 9.
79. James Cahill, "The Early Styles of Kung Hsien," *Oriental Art* 16, no. 1 (Spring 1970): 51–71; see also Shen C. Y. Fu, "An Aspect of Mid-seventeenth-century Chinese Painting: The 'Dry Linear' Style and the Early Work of Tao-chi," *Journal of the Institute of Chinese Studies of the Chinese University of Hong Kong* 8, no. 2 (December 1976): 604–15.
80. Szechuan Provincial Museum, comp., *Kung Pan-chien shan-shui-hua k'o-t'u kao: Sze-ch'uan-sheng po-wu-kuan teng shou-ts'ang* (Kung Hsien's sketchbooks for instructing students: based on works in the Szechuan Provincial Museum and other collections) (Ch'eng-tu: Sze-ch'uan jen-min ch'u-pan-she, 1981), pp. 38, 75.
81. See James Cahill, "Early Styles of Kung Hsien," p. 59; William Wu, "Kung Hsien's Style and His Sketchbooks," *Oriental Art* 16, no. 1 (Spring 1970): 74.
82. James Cahill, *The Compelling Image: Nature and Style in Seventeenth-century Chinese Painting* (Cambridge, Mass.: Harvard University Press, 1982), p. 183.
83. For an illustration of the Honolulu hanging scroll by Kung Hsien, dated 1689, see Osvald Sirén, *Chinese Painting: Leading Masters and Principles*, vol. 6, pl. 366.
84. Szechuan Provincial Museum, comp., *Kung Pan-chien shan-shui-hua k'o-t'u kao*, pp. 37, 74.
85. Ibid., pp. 28, 30.
86. For Tao-chi's biography, see Wen C. Fong, *Returning Home: Tao-chi's Album of Landscapes and Flowers*, esp. pp. 15–26. Important new documentary evidence establishing Tao-chi's birthdate as 1642 was published in Wang Shih-ch'ing, "Tsa-feng-wen-chi chung yü kuan Shih-t'ao te shih-wen" (Texts bearing upon Shih-t'ao [Tao-chi] in the Tsa-feng Literary Collection), *Wen-wu* 1979, no. 12: 43–48; see also Hsü Pang-ta, "Shih-t'ao sheng-tsu hsin ting" (Newly determined birth and death dates for Shih-t'ao [Tao-chi]), *Mei-shu-chia* 2 (1978): 2–8. Chinese writers traditionally call the artist by his *hao* Shih-t'ao, while writers outside China, choosing to refer to all Chinese artists by their proper names, call him Tao-chi. It has been pointed out that Tao-chi, meaning "the Monk Chi," first appeared only in Chang Keng's biography of the artist of about 1735 and that to be accurate we should call him either Chu Jo-chi (his secular given name) or Yüan-chi (his Buddhist given name). I have continued to use Tao-chi because it is the most familiar to Western readers.
87. I-ting, "*Po-yu-chi* tso-che Mu-ch'en Min" (Mu-ch'en Min, author of the *Collection of the Northern Journey*), in I-lin ts'ung-lu, vol. 3 (Hong Kong: Shang-wu yin-shu-kuan, 1962), pp. 146–50.
88. See Fu Pao-shih, *Shih-t'ao shang-jen nien-p'u* (Chronology of Shih-t'ao [Tao-chi]), Chung-kuo li-tai ming-jen nien-p'u hui-pien, 1st ser., vol. 7 (1948; repr. ed., Taipei, 1971), p. 76.
89. See poem by Tao-chi as cited ibid., p. 41.
90. Shen C. Y. Fu, "An Aspect of Mid-seventeenth-century Chinese Painting," p. 588; James Cahill, *The Compelling Image*, p. 196.
91. The 1672 hanging scroll *Watching a Waterfall from a Stone Bridge* is reproduced in James Cahill, ed., *Shadows of Mt. Huang: Chinese Painting and Printing of the Anhui School* (Berkeley: University Art Museum, 1981), p. 133, fig. 18. The 1673 album is reproduced in Hsieh Chih-liu, ed., *Shih-t'ao hua-chi* (Paintings by Shih-t'ao [Tao-chi]) (Shanghai: Shanghai jen-min mei-shu-kuan ch'u-pan she, 1960), pls. 36–39; and Victoria Contag, *Die Beiden Steine: Beitrag zum Verstandnis des Wesens Chinesischer Landschaftsmalerei* (Braunschweig: Verlagsanstalt Hermann Klemm, 1950), pl. 2. The 1677–78 album illustrating Su Shih's poems, in the P. C. Wong [Huang] collection in Hong Kong, is reproduced in Chang Wan-li and Hu Jen-mou, comps., *Li-tai ming-hua-chia tso-p'in hsüan-chi* (Selected painting and calligraphy of Shih-t'ao [Tao-chi]) (Hong Kong: K'ai-fa, 1969), vol. 6, pls. 124, 138.1–9.
92. Reproduced in Chang Yüan (Chang Ta-ch'ien), *Ta-feng-t'ang ming-chi* (Masterpieces from the Ta-feng-t'ang collection) (Tokyo: Benridō, 1955), pp. 24–28.
93. Yü Chien-hua, "Ssu-shih" (Four seasons), in *Shih-t'ao Hua-yü lu* (Shih-t'ao's [Tao-chi's] *Recorded Sayings on Painting*) (Peking: Jen-min mei-shu ch'u-pan-she, 1962), p. 58.
94. Reproduced in *Wen-wu* 1962, no. 12: 43, pl. 1.
95. For a discussion of this work, see James Cahill, *The Compelling Image*, p. 202.
96. For Tao-chi's collaborative painting with Wang Yüan-ch'i, see Osvald Sirén, *Chinese Painting: Leading Masters and Principles*, vol. 6, pl. 391a; and with Wang Hui, see *Exhibitions of Paintings of the Ming and Ch'ing Periods* (Hong Kong: The Urban Council and The Min-chiu Society, 1970), no. 51.
97. The colophon is found on an album dated 1694, now in the Los Angeles County Art Museum; see discussion in Marilyn and Shen Fu, *Studies in Connoisseurship: Chinese Paintings from the Arthur M. Sackler Collection in New York and Princeton* (Princeton: The Art Museum, 1974), p. 52.
98. Yü Chien-hua groups the eighteen chapters of *Hua-yü lu* under three general topics: the first seven deal with general principles, the next seven are concerned with concrete methods, and the last four turn to broader applications of painting; see Yü Chien-hua, ed., *Shih-t'ao Hua-yü lu*, pp. 81–88.
99. For an alternative translation, see Ju-hsi Chou, "In Quest of the Primor-

dial Line: The Genesis and Content of Tao-chi's 'Hua-yü lu'" (Ph.D. diss., Princeton University, 1969), p. 108; see also pp. 109–17.

100. Yü Chien-hua, ed., *Shih-t'ao Hua-yü lu*, p. 16.
101. See Cheng Cho-lu, *Shih-t'ao yen-chiu* (A study of Shih-t'ao [Tao-chi]), (Peking: Jen-min mei-shu ch'u-pan-she, 1961), pp. 49–50.
102. Yü Chien-hua, ed., *Shih-t'ao Hua-yü lu*, p. 20.
103. Ibid., p. 23.
104. Ibid., p. 28.
105. Ibid., p. 39.
106. Ibid., p. 40.
107. Ibid., p. 42.
108. Ibid., p. 45.
109. Ibid., p. 51.
110. Ibid., p. 53.
111. Ibid., p. 60.
112. Ibid., p. 62.
113. Ibid., p. 68.
114. See Richard Edwards, ed., *The Painting of Tao-chi, 1641–ca. 1720* (Ann Arbor: Museum of Art, University of Michigan, 1967), no. 3, pp. 74, 101.
115. Huang T'ing-chien, *Shan-ku t'i-pa* (Colophons by Huang T'ing-chien), I-shu ts'ung-pien, vol. 22 (Taipei: Shih-chieh shu-chü, 1962), *chüan* 4, p. 38; *chüan* 5, p. 43.
116. Tung Ch'i-ch'ang, *Hua-yen*, p. 25.
117. Yü Chien-hua, ed., "Chien-tzu" (Combining with calligraphy), in *Shih-t'ao Hua-yü lu*, p. 62, and "Ts'un-fa" (Texture strokes), p. 45.
118. Yü Chien-hua, ed., "Shan-ch'uan" (Mountains and rivers), *Shih-t'ao Hua-yü lu*, p. 42.
119. Yü Chien-hua, ed., "Yin-yun" (Cosmic atmosphere), *Shih-t'ao Hua-yü lu*, p. 38.
120. Reproduced in Li Yeh-shuang, *Shih-tao te shih-chieh* (The world of Shih-T'ao [Tao-chi]) (Taipei: Hsiung-shih mei-shu yüeh-k'an-she, 1973), pp. 86–87.
121. Yü Chien-hua, ed., "Chien-tzu," *Shih-t'ao Hua-yü lu*, p. 63.

# II

## *Eight Views of the Hsiao and Hsiang Rivers by Wang Hung*

ALFREDA MURCK

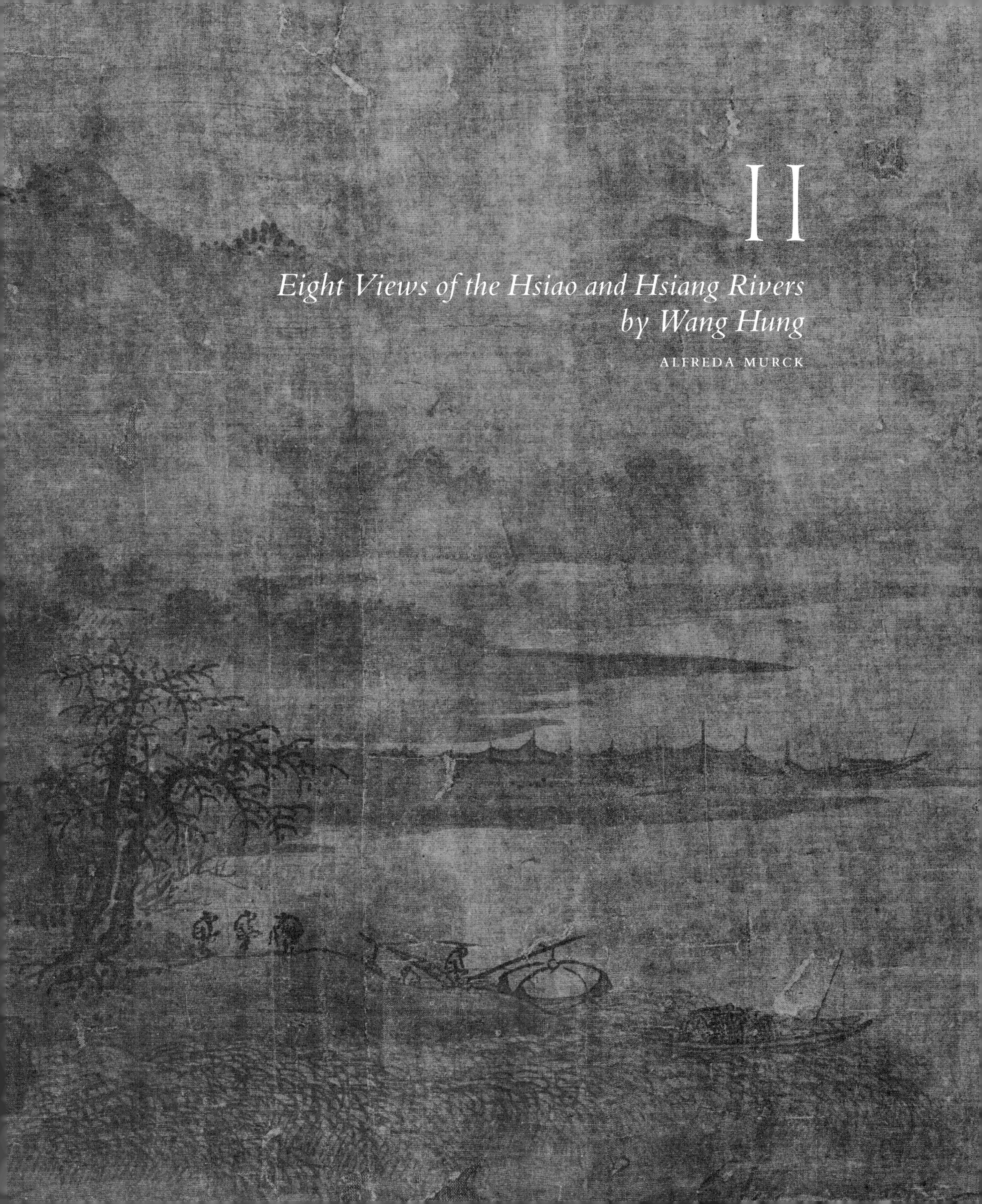

IN THE HISTORICAL RECORD Wang Hung deserves to be called obscure. That he existed at all is known only from a brief mention by Hsia Wen-yen (fl. 14th century) in an art historical text completed in 1365 and from a small signature that appears on "Night Rain," a section of the handscrolls *Eight Views of the Hsiao and Hsiang Rivers* in the Edward L. Elliott Family Collection (no. 4; figs. 1, 2). Hsia Wen-yen describes Wang as a native of Shu (Szechuan province) who painted in the Fan K'uan style during the Shao-hsing era (1131–62).[1] The Elliott paintings fit stylistically with Wang Hung's period of activity—the mid-twelfth century—and are the earliest extant set of a theme that was to become one of the most popular in Sung dynasty painting.[2]

## *The Hsiao and Hsiang Region*

Some 500 miles south of K'ai-feng, the Northern Sung dynasty capital, the Hsiao and Hsiang rivers flow through the modern province of Hunan (south of the lake), which takes its name from sprawling Lake Tung-t'ing at its northern edge. The vast marshy basin of Tung-t'ing is fed by dozens of rivers which originate in the southern mountains. One of the wettest regions of China, with an annual rainfall of over 52 inches, Hunan's landscape is transformed season by season. Following the heavy summer rains, rivers and lakes rise dramatically in summer and autumn, sometimes flooding, and recede to reveal shores and islets in the winter. The Yangtze River, just a few miles north of the lake, is linked to Tung-t'ing by riverlets and canals, which facilitate transportation and contribute to the seasonal flooding.

The Hsiang River originates south of Hunan in Kuangsi province and winds its way northward to Tung-t'ing. The first large river to join the Hsiang is the Hsiao, which has already traveled more than 200 miles from its origin at Mount Chiu-i. The Hsiao-Hsiang River technically identifies only the stretch from this point of convergence to the river's juncture with another major tributary, the Cheng River, at Heng-yang city, 250 twisting miles to the north, after which the river is called the Cheng-Hsiang. The Hsiao and Hsiang river region, both in paintings and poems on the Eight Views theme, however, signifies the entire landscape from the lush hills of the south to the low-lying marshy basin of the north. The geography exemplifies the ancient concept of mountains and marshes as places of retreat and reclusion.

In addition to the luxuriant beauty of the landscape, the Hsiao-Hsiang region had considerable literary and historical appeal as well. It emerges dramatically in the historical record during the first millennium B.C. as the state of Ch'u, a semi-Chinese kingdom with a tradition of shamanism. The Ch'u kingdom ultimately controlled almost half of the Chinese empire and attempted to conquer the rest. Despite a remarkably stable royal house and an effective administration, Ch'u was defeated in 221 B.C. by the Ch'in, the state that succeeded in unifying China. Hsiao-Hsiang never again became a political or cultural center, but it retained a reputation for distinction and excellence in the arts. Whereas north China came to be identified with the sober intellectuals who formed the Confucian tradition of social responsibility and decorum, the southern state of Ch'u gave rise to a freewheeling, less restrictive tradition of Taoism. Most indelibly associated with the region is the man who is thought to have written the mournful, fantastic, and often erotic poems collectively called *The Songs of the South* (*Ch'u Tz'u*): Ch'ü Yüan (343?–278 B.C.).[3]

A statesman of wisdom and ability, Ch'ü Yüan composed court documents with speed and literary polish. Envious of Ch'ü's talents a colleague slandered him to the king, and Ch'ü fell from favor; his attempts to offer advice about foreign policy met with banishment. Proclaiming his honesty in the face of a corrupt world, he wrote long sorrowful poems. And then, in grief and shame over his fate, he drowned himself in the Mi-Lo, a river in northern Hunan that flows into Lake Tung-t'ing (fig. 3). In the most

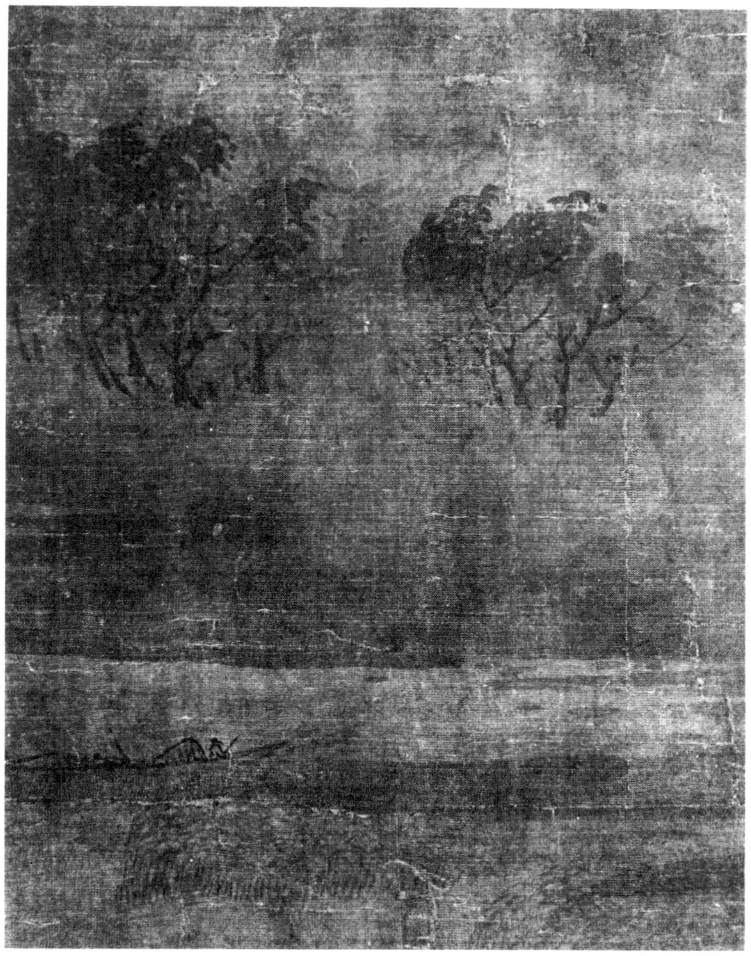

Fig. 1. Detail, "Night Rain on Hsiao and Hsiang"

Fig. 2. Signature of Wang Hung, detail, "Night Rain on Hsiao and Hsiang"

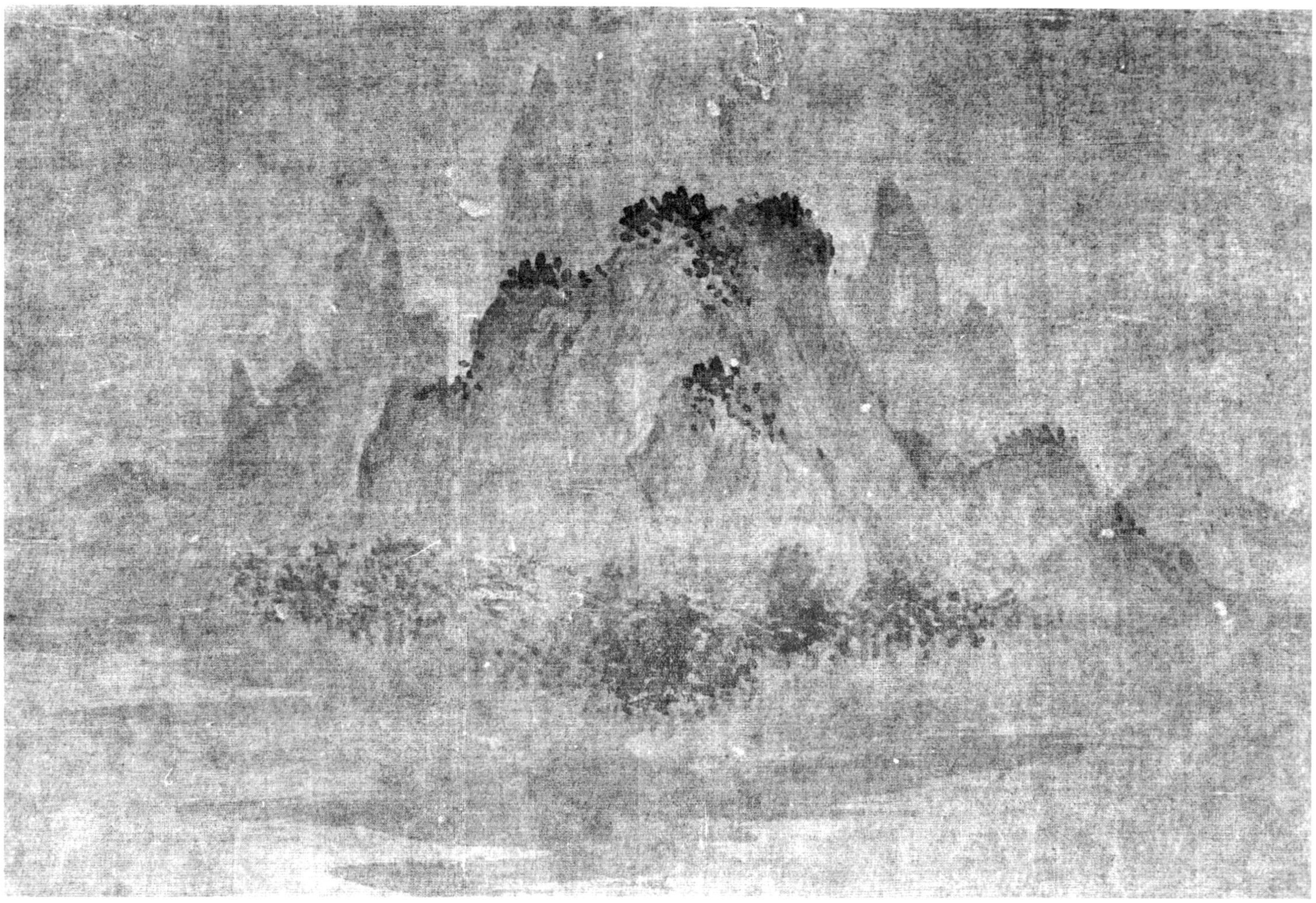

Fig. 3. Detail, "Autumn Moon over Lake Tung-t'ing"

renowned of his laments, "Encountering Sorrow" ("Li sao"), the poet is a magician who travels far and wide in an unsuccessful search for a wise ruler. His spirit journey ends in complete disillusionment with the worlds both of men and of gods.

Although partly apocryphal, the story of Ch'ü Yüan lived through his poems and he became a powerful symbol for those who strove to serve intelligently and honestly in the face of corruption. Ssu-ma Ch'ien, a great historian of the second century B.C. and Ch'ü's biographer, recorded that he wept when he read the poems and visited the place where Ch'ü had leapt into the river. Ch'ü Yüan's tragic story was of vital relevance to officials, who had to deal with the delicate matter of service in the civil bureaucracy. Since sound advice ill received could mean severe punishment, banishment, or death, political survival often hinged on the ability to select the most propitious moment to present a suggestion. Fascinated with Ch'ü Yüan, later poets addressed verses to him and dropped them into the Mi-Lo River. A festival for the propitiation of dragons became an annual commemoration of Ch'ü; it is celebrated to the present day.

*The Songs of the South* and the many romantic aspects of the Ch'ü Yüan legend add a bittersweet dimension to the Hsiao-Hsiang region. And while this literary legacy belonged to China as a whole, there is every reason to suppose that its aura was more potent for the scholar traveling the lakes and rivers of the Hsiao and Hsiang.

## *Sung Ti and the Eight Views*

About 1090 the statesman Shen Kua (1029–1093) compiled a monumental survey of science and humanities based on decades of observations and notes taken during his extensive travels. Among his notes is the following entry: "Sung Ti, the assistant secretary to the director [of the Bureau of Public Revenues] was an excellent painter. His most fully realized paintings were his level-distance landscapes."[4] Then appears the earliest list of the evocative, atmosphere-filled paintings that we now call *Eight Views of the Hsiao and Hsiang Rivers*:

Wild Geese Descending to Sandbar
Returning Sail off Distant Shore
Mountain Market, Clear with Rising Mist
River and Sky in Evening Snow
Autumn Moon over Lake Tung-t'ing
Night Rain on Hsiao and Hsiang
Evening Bell from Mist-shrouded Temple
Fishing Village in Evening Glow.

Shen Kua continues, "These are called the *Eight Views*. They are widely known among connoisseurs." The shorthand title that Shen Kua uses for the set of paintings, Eight Views, came to be closely associated with Sung Ti, and he is traditionally credited with the creation of the theme.[5]

Sung Ti lived from about 1015 to about 1080.[6] From a family of scholars, including several amateur painters, Sung and his brother Sung Tao were friendly with the eminent scholar and statesman Ssu-ma Kuang (1019–1086). Sung Ti and Sung Tao passed the imperial examination at the same time and went on to serve in various posts. In 1062 Sung Ti served as a reader for a palace examination, an honor that was reserved for scholars of distinction. At about that time he received a post in the regional office of the Ministry of Transportation in Ch'ang-sha—in the heart of the Hsiao-Hsiang region. His official duties must have required him to travel throughout the area: a local history for the province records that in 1063 Sung Ti visited Tan-shan Yen, a mountain in Yung-chou prefecture that lies at the point where the Hsiao flows into the Hsiang. It was at this time, during the Chia-yu era (1056–63), that Sung Ti painted eight scenes on the walls of the Eight Views terrace overlooking Ch'ang-sha. Sung Ti left the area by 1067, possibly as early as

1065, when he traveled with the preeminent Neo-Confucian philosopher and official Chou Tun-i (1017–1073) to Mount Lu, in modern Kiangsi province. In 1074 Sung Ti's career came to an unhappy end. A fire in the building of the Financial Commission, where he was then serving, was held to be his responsibility, and Sung Ti was banished. For reasons of health he requested an official leave to go to Loyang, where he became Ssu-ma Kuang's neighbor.[7] In his bitterness and humiliation Sung Ti must have felt a spiritual kinship with Ch'ü Yüan and other officials who had struggled to work conscientiously in a conflict-ridden bureaucracy. As Ch'ü Yüan triumphed through his poems, so Sung Ti ultimately achieved a reputation and a measure of lasting fame through his paintings.

In the absence of any surviving paintings by Sung Ti, all that remains as evidence of his talent is the praise of contemporary scholars and connoisseurs. Kuo Jo-hsü (fl. ca. 1075) wrote about Sung Ti and his brother at the end of their lives: "Both are excellent painters of landscapes with wintry forests, to which they impart elegance of mood and peacefulness in forms. The present age holds them in exceptionally high esteem."[8] Mi Fu (1052–1107) grouped Sung Ti together with two other distinguished civil servants, Yen Su, an executive of the Ministry of Rites, and Liu Ming-fu, academician of the Lung-t'u Pavilion. His choice of peers for Sung Ti reflects not only their mutual status as officials but also their common interest in the landscape style of the great tenth-century master Li Ch'eng (919–967): "Compared to the other two gentlemen, Fu-ku [Sung Ti] painted with an especially meticulous beauty. His pine branches were not three-dimensional, but were particularly clear, fine, and elegant."[9] The elegance and precision of Sung Ti's painting derived not only from a study of Li Ch'eng, but also from his careful observation of visual phenomena. Like his contemporary Kuo Hsi (ca. 1010–ca. 1090), Sung Ti is said to have taken inspiration from the irregular shapes and textures of an old wall. The story, recorded by Shen Kua in *Notes Written in Meng-ch'i* (*Meng-ch'i pi-t'an*), says that he advised a struggling artist that he could put more natural energy into his somewhat stale painting by draping a length of silk over a rough wall and letting it conform to the uneven surface. By observing it in different lights, morning and evening, the artist would begin to perceive a landscape of natural irregularity emerging from the highs and lows, the twists and turns. The painter is said to have taken his advice and thereafter improved daily.[10]

The *Painting Catalogue of the Hsüan-ho Era [1119–1125] (Hsüan-ho hua-p'u)* lists only one painting by Sung's elder brother, Sung Tao—a picture of pine and bamboo. As the authors noted, the reputation of Sung Ti far surpassed that of his brother. Thirty-one paintings are listed, and Sung Ti is praised for the poetic quality of his work: "He conveyed ideas lofty and mysterious, like a poet ascending the heights and composing verse."[11] Many of the titles, such as *Ancient Pine*, *Snowy Mountains*, *Twin Pines against Mountain Peak*, or *Small Wintry Forest*, confirm Mi Fu's record that Sung Ti's art drew upon that of Li Ch'eng. Other titles repeat the themes of the Eight Views: *Distant Shores, Journeying Sails*; *Range of Peaks, Distant Shores*; *Evening Clouds over the River*; and, more specifically, *Autumn Evening at Hsiao and Hsiang*. An entry that reads "Eight Views" is possibly a set of eight Hsiao and Hsiang paintings; the compilers of the catalogue were probably employing the abbreviation established by Shen Kua forty years before.

The success of Sung Ti's *Eight Views of the Hsiao and Hsiang Rivers* was immediate and far-reaching. As Shen Kua noted, the paintings circulated among the elite of society, even capturing the attention of the emperor. Emperor Sung Hui-tsung (r. 1101–25), known for his love of refined painting, is said to have commissioned the court painter Chang Ch'ien (fl. early 12th century) to travel by boat through the Hsiao-Hsiang region and record the scenery in eight scenes.[12]

The emperor himself painted a set of Eight Views and is said to have inscribed his sixth section with the following comment: "Having looked over Sung Ti's *Eight Views* I playfully took up my brush and made these. I call them *Eight Scenic Places*."[13] This note appears in a brief book of miscellany dated 1139 by the scholar Chang Ch'eng (d. 1139). Chang records another set of scrolls with imperial inscriptions and unusually large seals, suggesting that the idea had become so fashionable that forgers may have been creating artful copies to meet public demand: "I also saw a painting dealer display twelve scenes in twelve scrolls.

Each scroll used a sheet of Kuan-yin paper over 5 feet long. The titles were 'Clouds at Dawn Revealing the Sun'; 'Evening Rain on River at Dusk'; 'Fishing Village with Smoke at Day Break'; 'River Village, Clouds in Evening Sky'. . . ." Chang inexplicably lists fourteen titles, all poetic and similar in vein to Sung Ti's titles but broader in scope, giving more emphasis to spring and dawn. "Each scene carried a title written by the emperor and an imperial seal reading 'Imperial Painting Treasure.' The seal impression 5 inches wide was magnificent! It shows the emperor's keen enthusiasm."[14]

In their appraisal of Sung Ti's *Eight Views*, however, the critics did not always respond with as much enthusiasm. Teng Ch'un (fl. mid-12th century) disparaged Sung Ti's paintings as overly dark and dismal. Speculating that the ink-saturated scenes were painted first and that the titles were added later, he wrote: "Sung Ti's *Eight Views* are all evening scenes. 'Evening Bell from Mist-shrouded Temple' and 'Night Rain on Hsiao and Hsiang' are practically impossible to represent. The sound of a bell cannot be pictured. How much less Hsiao and Hsiang at night! Add to that the depiction of rain and what could possibly be seen? Most likely Fu-ku [Sung Ti] painted and afterward the titles were determined. The paintings are merely summary sketches of enveloping clouds, gloomy and dull."[15] In the thirteenth century Chao Hsi-ku reiterated this opinion: "Sung Fu-ku [Sung Ti] painted *Eight Views of the Hsiao and Hsiang Rivers*. Originally they had no predetermined titles. Later people gave them names such as 'Autumn Moon over Lake Tung-t'ing'; painters today who first choose titles are not scholar-gentlemen."[16]

The seemingly irrelevant question of whether the titles or the paintings came first was actually crucial to the then emerging ideal of spontaneous creativity. To have the subject matter of paintings dictated by set titles was thought to inhibit the painter's creative process. These ideas on painting developed from late Northern Sung essays about the creative process, most notably from the writings of Su Shih (1036–1101), one of the greatest poets and intellectuals of the eleventh century. Su Shih and Sung Ti were friends—Su, inscribing a painting by Sung Ti's nephew, reminisced that in former days he had traveled with Sung Ti[17]—and their friendship undoubtedly gave both of them an opportunity to explore their thoughts and theories on the relationship between poetry and painting.

## *Poetry in Painting*

Since it seemed wrong to many thinkers in the eleventh century that painting had never achieved the status of poetry, they set about to define the features that would qualify painting for the kind of admiration reserved for literature. Very naturally they used the aesthetic criteria established for poetry in looking at the possibilities of painting.[18] The idea that painting could share the values and status of poetry was thus a topic of absorbing interest among Sung Ti's peers, and Su Shih was its most articulate spokesman.

Su Shih traveled in the Hsiao-Hsiang region—which he called by its ancient name, the Southern Kingdom—in 1059, with his father, Su Hsün (1009–1066), and his brother, Su Ch'e (1039–1112), both distinguished scholars. Inspired by "the beauty of the mountains and rivers, the rusticity of local customs, and the traces of worthy and superior men," the three men passed their leisure hours on the boat writing poetry.[19] They selected and preserved one hundred poems in an anthology entitled *The First Collection from a Journey South* (*Nan-hsing ch'ien-chi*). In his preface Su Shih explained the importance of participating in *wen*, for Su a broad concept that embraced history, classics, literature, calligraphy, and painting—here best translated as "culture." He stated that the compositions of the greatest value are those the author feels compelled to compose. For him the creation of literature was not merely an opportunity to display one's ability, but an inevitable outpouring that could be checked no more than the inexorable flow of a river. The benefits of participating in *wen* could apply to painting as well as poetry. As he explained in a poem, the two pursuits are united in their source of inspiration:

To discuss paintings in terms of formal resemblance
Is a view comparable to a child's;
To compose poems that must be a particular poem
Is to completely misunderstand poetry;
The one fundamental rule in poetry and painting:
Natural talent and fresh originality.[20]

This sentiment must be considered in the context of Su Shih's primary aesthetic, which was based on a mastery of tradition. Only with a full understanding of the past, he argued, could the painter or poet harness spontaneity and integrate his own creativity with the inherited culture.

Su Shih's thoughts on the close parallels between painting and poetry are best known from his celebrated couplet on the convertibility of the poetry and painting of the great T'ang dynasty master Wang Wei (699–759): "Savoring Wang Wei's poems, one finds painting in them; / Contemplating Wang Wei's paintings, there are poems."[21] This idea was an eleventh-century interpretation; Wang Wei himself thought of the two disciplines as separate realms: "In this life I have usurped the fame of a poet; / In a former existence I must have been a painter."[22]

In a demonstration of his theory on the complementary nature of painting and poetry, Su Shih composed three poems that describe how Su had watched Sung Ti painting the composition *Evening View of Hsiao and Hsiang*.[23] Rather than merely describe the landscape—which would have been antithetical to his principle of engaging in *wen* with originality—Su Shih commented on the literary meanings as well as on the painter's method. The poems speak of Sung Ti's love of the Southern Kingdom and of mountains emerging from clouds beneath Sung Ti's spontaneously moving brush. Su commented on Sung Ti's working in an almost trancelike state, forgetting hand and brush, so that the paintings came from his memory. Some scholars have interpreted this remark to mean that Sung Ti worked in an autosuggestive manner,[24] but in light of Su Shih's essays on the importance of an unforced and natural participation in *wen*, it is more correctly understood as praise for Sung Ti's spontaneous participation in the act of painting, without any intention or ambition to create Art.[25] In one poem he describes a dispirited gentleman who tries to find solitude among the ancient misty trees of a remote river village. Su, who had firsthand knowledge of the dangers of politics, could be alluding to his own political misfortunes or those of Ch'ü Yüan or Sung Ti. The final poem interweaves allusions to the injustices of politics with images of Sung's intricate painting:

Close advisers to the emperor when counted are few,
Clouds and clear sky are naturally unequal.
Paths uncoiling run to the distant mountain,
Waters converging flow to the nearby stream.

Sung Ti most likely shared Su Shih's commitment to *wen* as the vehicle for self-expression and self-cultivation. Responding to Su's poetic couplet "Paths uncoiling run to the distant mountain,/Waters converging flow to the nearby stream," Sung Ti commented, "You, Sir, are also a fine painter."

## *Painting as Poetry*

Shen Kua's list of titles for Sung Ti's *Eight Views of the Hsiao and Hsiang* have some of the qualities of a poem. Instead of describing each part of the day, or every season, the titles evoke evening scenes and autumnal settings with just enough references to spring, sun, and clear weather to create a poetic tension of opposites. Far from serving merely as casual labels of Sung Ti's misty landscapes, the titles represent a set of variations on a selected theme: the illusory beauty of a watery world in transformation at the ends of days and years.

One of the most popular poetic forms at the time of Su Shih and Sung Ti was the *lü-shih* (regulated verse). Each *lü-shih* is eight lines in length, with either five characters or seven characters per line. Within the poem the lines are paired as couplets: line 1 with 2, line 3 with 4, and so on. In addition the two middle couplets (lines 3–4 and 5–6) must be parallel: they must match, character for character, in combinations of sameness, likeness, difference, and antithesis.[26] The lines by Su Shih cited above are an example: a description of paths receding into the distance in a motion of uncoiling is juxtaposed with the image of streams flowing together into the foreground. A further parallelism exists in the contrast of mountain, emblematic of height and solidity, with water, representing low places and fluidity. Similarly the eight titles of the Hsiao-Hsiang paintings imitate the structure of a regulated verse, with a pattern of parallels in the two central pairings.

| *Literal translation of titles of Sung Ti's Eight Views* | *Characteristics that suggest poetic parallelism* |
|---|---|
| *p'ing-sha yen-lo*<br>level sand, geese descending | low, descending, evening |
| *yüan-p'u fan-kuei*<br>distant shore, sail returning | distance, coming, evening |
| *shan-shih ch'ing-lan*<br>mountain market, clear vapor | mountain (hence: height and the south of the Hsiao-Hsiang region), daytime, clear weather, warm, vapor rising |
| *chiang-t'ien mu-hsüeh*<br>river sky, evening snow | river (hence: lowness and the north of the Hsiao-Hsiang region), evening, cloudy weather, cold, snow falling |
| *Tung-t'ing ch'iu-yüeh*<br>Tung-t'ing, autumn moon | water name: lake at north, time word: autumn (night implied), clear weather, moon rising |
| *Hsiao-Hsiang yeh-yü*<br>Hsiao Hsiang, night rain | water name: rivers at south, time word: night, cloudy weather, rain falling |
| *yen-ssu wan-chung*<br>mist temple, evening bell | temple (hence: mountain height), sound of bell (hence: personal reflection), evening |
| *yü-ts'un lo-chao*<br>fishing village, descending light | fishing village (hence: water, low), light, ending of day |

The juxtapositions favored in poetry are drawn from the dual cosmic principles of yin and yang. Through the description of the ceaseless interaction of these active and inactive forces, the poet could express the fullness of nature, the infinite variety of the universe.[27] Inherent in the yin-yang concept is the inequity of the two polar opposites; asymmetry is natural in the ever-shifting relationships. In the titles, while the height and solidity of mountains is contrasted with the lowness and fluidity of water, the balance tilts unevenly toward darkness and low-lying watery places. This unequal contrast is particularly evident in the central pairs ("couplets" 2 and 3). "Clear" is juxtaposed with inclement weather, and the opposite motions of rising and falling appear in the second couplet, in vapor rising from a mountain and snow falling into a river, and in the third couplet, in the moon implicitly rising and the rain explicitly falling. The second couplet juxtaposes warm with cold and activity with stillness, the sunny day at the market and the snowy evening along the river. The mountain market suggests the south of the region in contrast to the river-crossed north, which is in turn implied by river-sky-evening snow. This pattern emerges even more emphatically in the following pair of titles, where Lake Tung-t'ing, in the north of the region, is set against the Hsiao-Hsiang River, in the south of the region (and here the name seems to apply to a specific locale in contradistinction to its generic use in the set's title).

## *The Poetry of Monk Hui-hung and the Paintings of Wang Hung*

Not long after Shen Kua listed Sung Ti's titles for the Eight Views, a Ch'an Buddhist monk named Hui-hung (1071–1128), composed eight poems on the theme, following the order of Shen Kua's list. A precocious youth, Hui-hung caught the attention of the literary community at an early age. At fourteen he took the Buddhist name of Te-hung and became a disciple of the Ch'an master San-feng Ching. Despite his relative youth, Hui-hung seems to have made the acquaintance of Su Shih and Huang T'ing-chien (1045–1105), and his poetry owes a great deal to their influence. The Ch'an precept that experience should be valued over the written word apparently did not inhibit Hui's development as a poet: his prodigious literary output is preserved in six different collections.[28]

Hui-hung was prompted by the comment of a fellow monk to compose verses on the Eight Views of the Hsiao and Hsiang: "Sung Ti painted Eight Views of excellent quality. People say he creates language without sounds. Monk Yen playfully said that I make pictures with sounds. Therefore I have taken each scene and composed a poem."[29] Whether or not Hui-hung ever saw Sung Ti's actual paintings, he followed the sequence of titles in Shen Kua's list.

Mounted in two handscrolls, the eight Wang Hung paintings are now in a different order from that given by Shen Kua and followed by Hui-hung, but the grouping of the paintings in pairs corroborates that they must originally have been in the order of Sung Ti's titles and Hui-hung's poems. The four pairs, or "couplets," are arranged as follows:

| *Shen Kua's List of Sung Ti's titles* | *Present Wang Hung sequence* |
|---|---|
| Wild Geese Descending to Sandbar<br>Returning Sail off Distant Shore | Night Rain on Hsiao and Hsiang<br>Autumn Moon over Lake Tung-t'ing |
| Mountain Market, Clear with Rising Mist<br>River and Sky in Evening Snow | Wild Geese Descending to Sandbar<br>Returning Sail off Distant Shore |
| Autumn Moon over Lake Tung-t'ing<br>Night Rain on Hsiao and Hsiang | Evening Bell from Mist-shrouded Temple<br>Fishing Village in Evening Glow |
| Evening Bell from Mist-shrouded Temple<br>Fishing Village in Evening Glow | Mountain Market, Clear with Rising Mist<br>River and Sky in Evening Snow |

When photographs of Wang Hung's eight scenes are rearranged as pairs according to the order of Shen Kua's list, a new pattern emerges (fig. 4). Viewing the compositions from right to left as one would if unrolling a handscroll, the first pair—"Geese Descending" and "Returning Sail"—have an opposite but complementary structure: the void with distant mountains at the right of "Geese Descending" gives way to a hill with trees, while "Returning Sail" begins with hills and trees at the right and trails off into the void with distant mountains. When placed together the hills and trees meet in the center, not in any literal continuation of one landscape into the next, but in a complement of forms. The continuation of design seems even more deliberate in the two "couplets" that lie at the center of the "poem." The expanse of water at the left of "Mountain Market" flows into the still river at the right of the snow scene, and the swelling earthen hills at the left of "Autumn Moon over Lake Tung-t'ing" match the hill with stream that lies at the right of "Night Rain." Since the parallelism of regulated verse cannot be repeated for more than two couplets, the last pair of paintings—"Evening Bell" and "Evening Glow"—do not show clear continuity of design. As in many poems, the mood shifts in these last paintings to a more introspective and personal tone. The most dense and complicated of the eight compositions, "Evening Bell," provides an eloquent summation before the poem's conclusion, the quiet ending of the day in "Fishing Village."

The rearrangement of the paintings in the scroll helps to explain the problematic position of the scroll's signature, the only known example of Wang Hung's writing, at the right-hand edge of "Night Rain."

Fig. 4. Wang Hung, *Eight Views of the Hsiao and Hsiang Rivers*, no. 4, regrouped according to Sung Ti's list (from right to left, top to bottom)

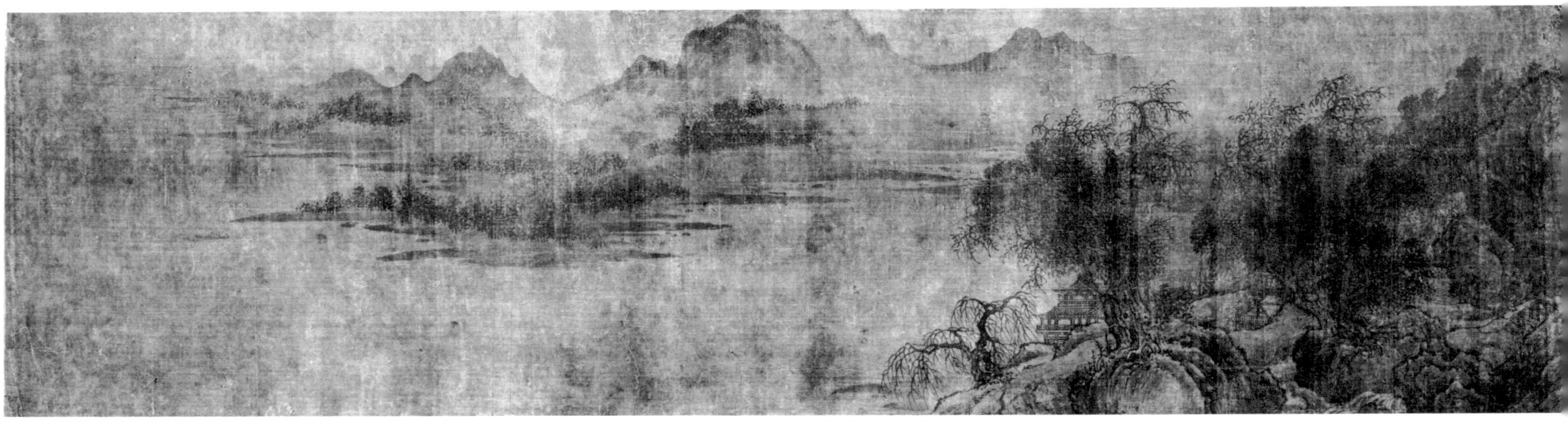

2. "Returning Sail off Distant Shore"

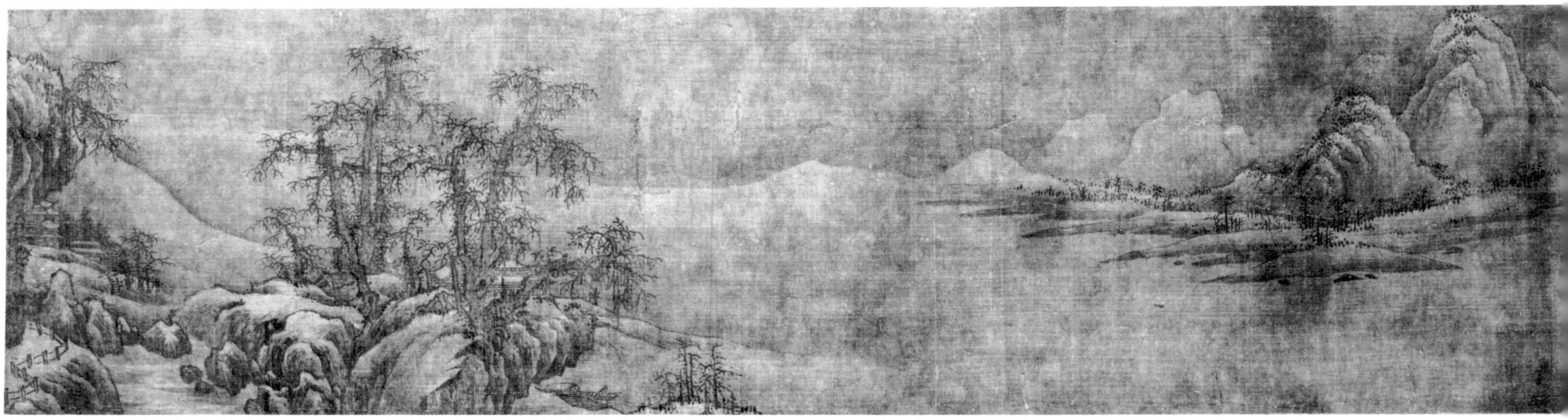

4. "River and Sky in Evening Snow"

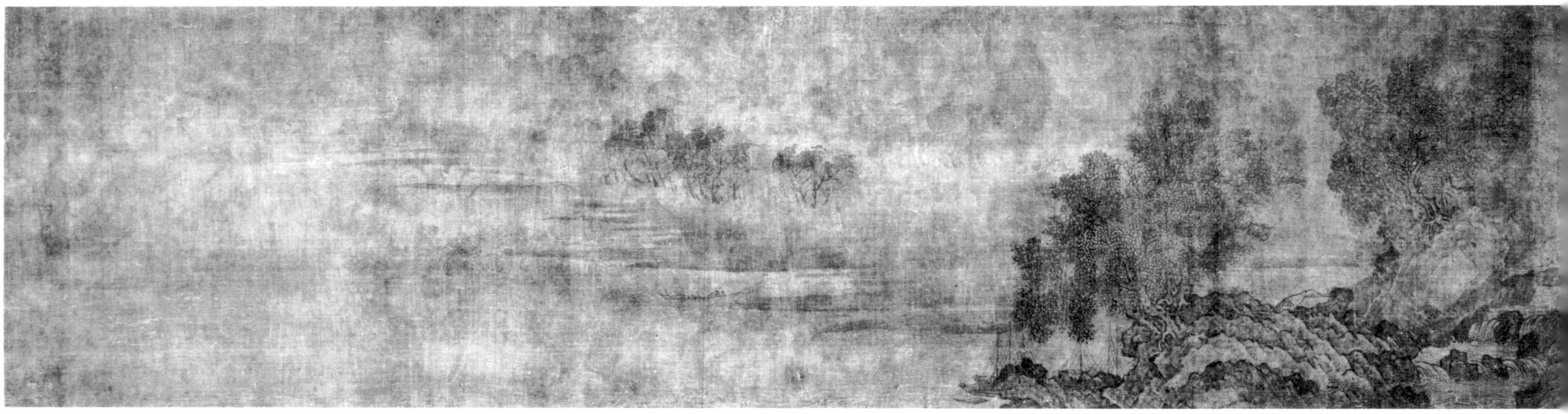

6. "Night Rain on Hsiao and Hsiang"

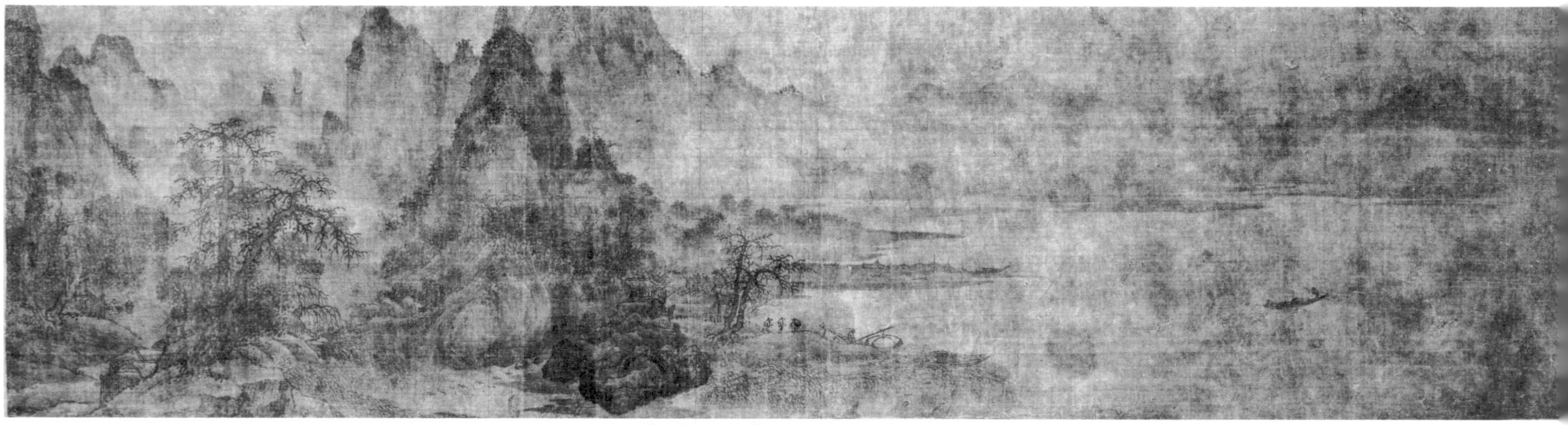

8. "Fishing Village in Evening Glow"

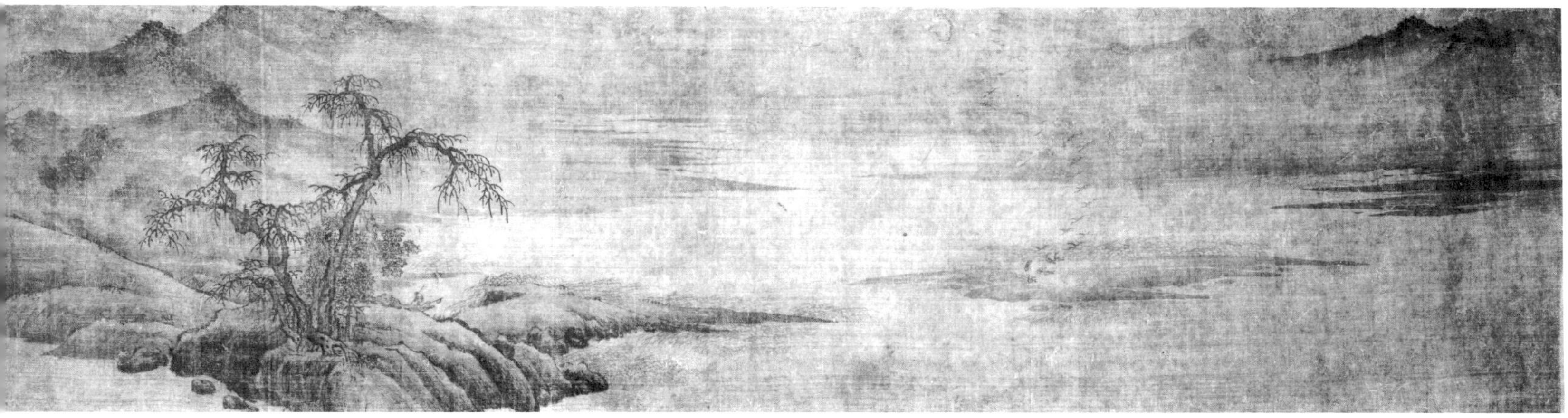

1. "Wild Geese Descending to Sandbar"

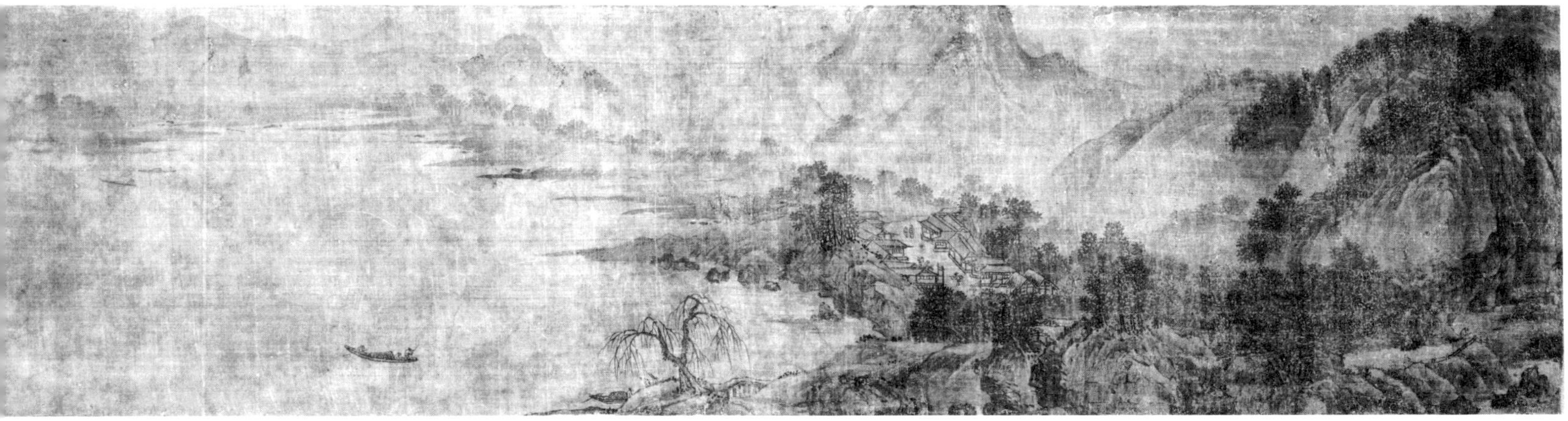

3. "Mountain Market, Clear with Rising Mist"

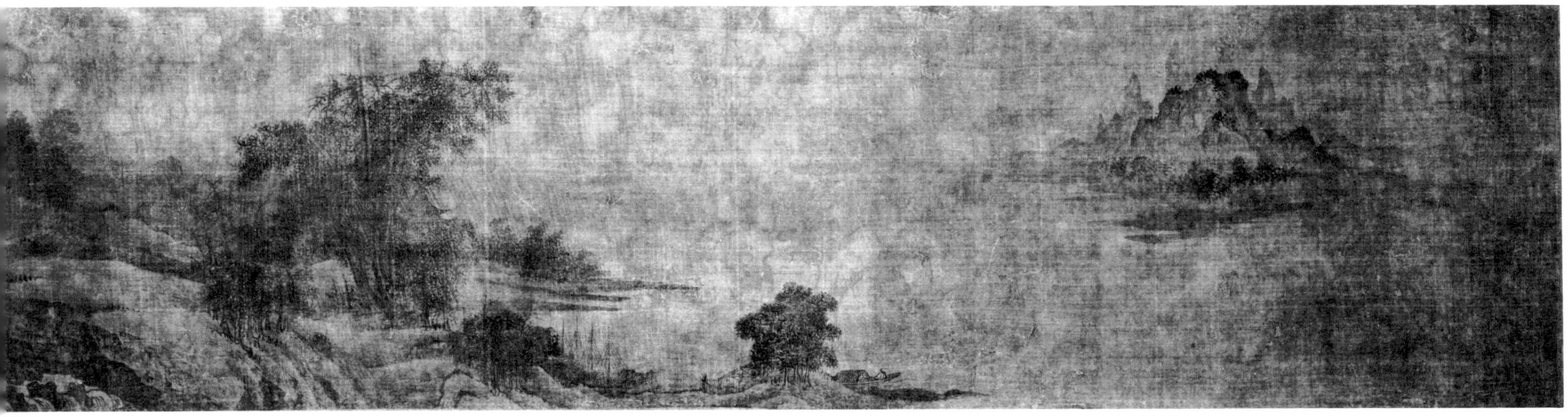

5. "Autumn Moon over Lake Tung-t'ing"

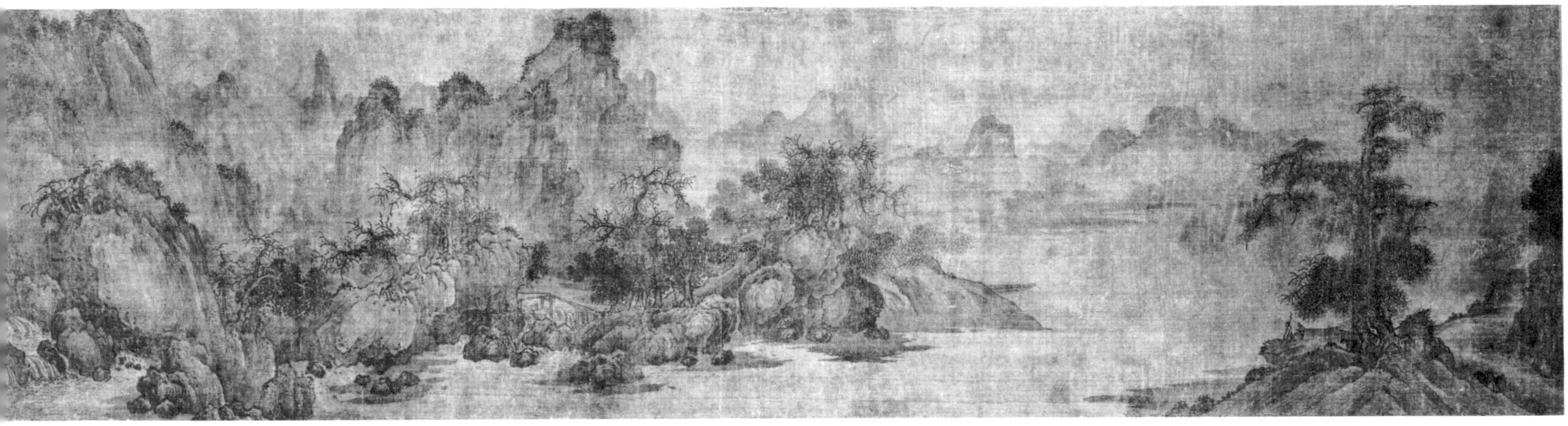

7. "Evening Bell from Mist-shrouded Temple"

While it cannot be authenticated by comparison with other signatures, several factors argue for its authenticity. First, no physical evidence such as a brushstroke encroaching on damaged silk nearby clearly disqualifies it. Second, signatures in small neat characters without prefatory comment, title, or verb frequently appear on twelfth-century paintings. A less positive factor is the very obscurity of the painter, whose name would have been a poor choice for any later owner wishing to enhance the pedigree of his scroll. Yet the ordering of the Wang Hung set may solve the puzzle. As noted above, Emperor Sung Hui-tsung is said to have inscribed the sixth section of his *Eight Scenic Places*. If the Wang Hung paintings are rearranged according to the Shen Kua list, "Night Rain" is the sixth painting, suggesting that Wang Hung followed imperial precedent. Later convention established the beginning or end of the scroll as the appropriate location for a signature. The present physical sequence of the painting may have resulted when discomfiture with a signature on the sixth painting prompted an owner to have "Night Rain" mounted at the beginning of the set; if this hypothesis is true, "Autumn Moon" and "Night Rain" would have been moved from the position of the third couplet to the front of the set and reversed. Then, to observe the convention of placing the snow scene at the end of a series, "Evening Snow" and "Mountain Market" would have been shifted from the position of the second couplet to the end.

The artistic tradition of the *Eight Views* began with paintings by Sung Ti, with thematic titles, possibly original, but first recorded a few years later by Shen Kua. Those titles were then transposed into a set of poems by Hui-hung, perhaps twenty or thirty years later, and subsequently back into paintings by Wang Hung. The ancestral line is unfortunately incomplete; undoubtedly other sets of paintings and poems, which may have been known to Wang Hung, intervened in this sequence. Nevertheless a correspondence exists between Hui-hung's poems and Wang Hung's paintings. In the following comparison, the poems and paintings will be discussed in the original order of Shen Kua's list, which was probably also the original order of Wang Hung's paintings.

The correspondence is not always a precise one: what the poet Hui-hung could describe that the painter Wang Hung could not was a progression through time as well as through space. Toward this end Hui-hung chose to ignore some of the rules of regulated verse. He discarded the conventional rhyming pattern at the end of every second line, and while he always maintained eight lines of seven characters each, he did not always make the central couplets, lines 3–4 and 5–6, parallel. Instead of character-for-character matching, he often turned to a personal reflection in the third couplet, a comment on his own past or present activity. His unorthodox approach allowed him freedom to describe a series of events. He provided journeys through time and space in which the landscape, weather, and time of day are always in transition.

### 1. Wild Geese Descending to Sandbar

Hui-hung's poem "Geese Descending" describes an autumnal evening with noisy geese flapping and calling. Having finally settled down, they are frightened into flight by the sound of a flute:

> The lake's autumn colors of burnished bronze,
> Late afternoon sun, white sand, nebulous light:
> Fluttering, about to land, still more calling and crowding,
> By fives, by tens, among dense rushes;
> Not yet returned to Hsi-hsing, melancholy unto old age,
> A cloudless evening sky, the heaven as if swept;
> At the wind-borne sound of a flute, they rise alarmed,
> Writing cursive script in space like Wang Hsi-chih.

Unable to depict all of the poem's events in one painting, Wang Hung appears to have chosen to illustrate the first half of the poem, the geese descending to the glistening sandbar. In the sort of subtle nuance favored by twelfth-century court painters, Wang Hung may be hinting that the fisherman we see

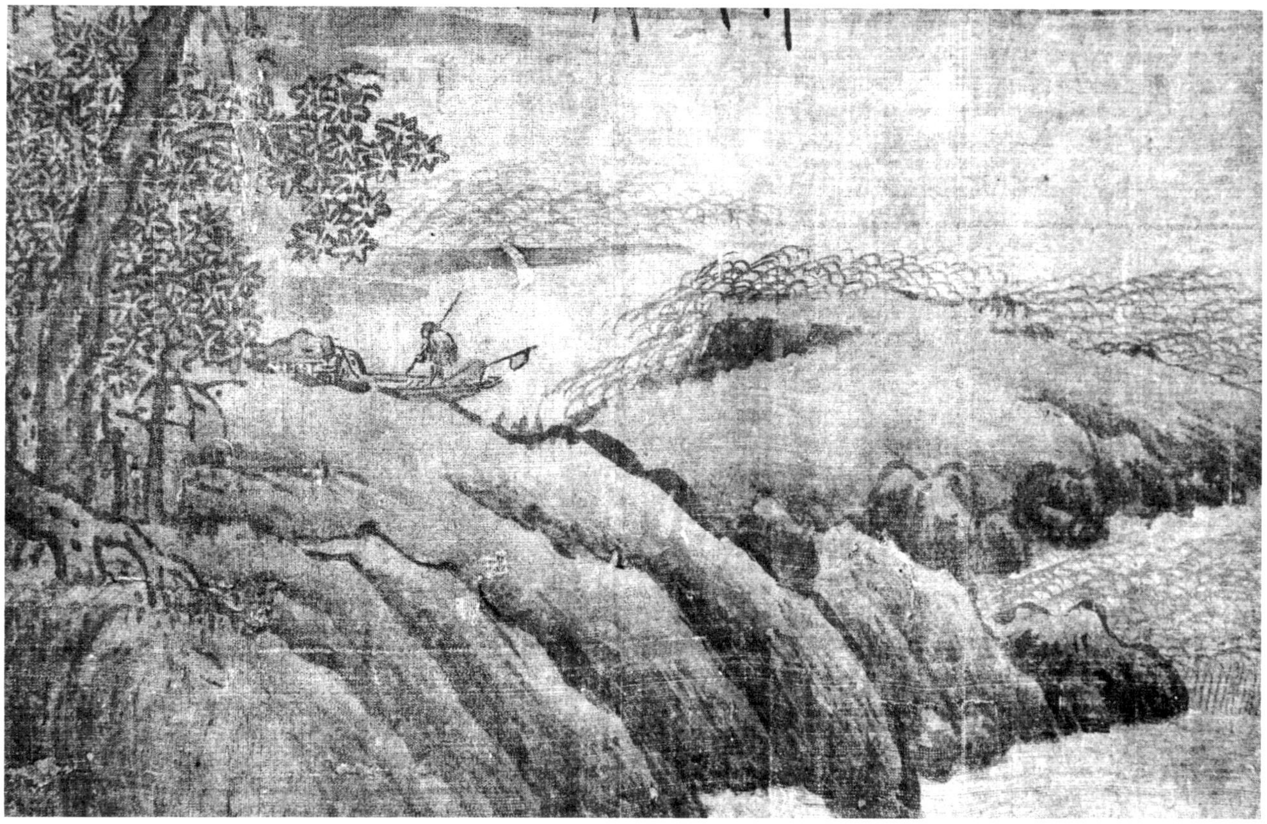

Fig. 5. Detail, "Wild Geese Descending to Sandbar"

mooring his boat is also the flute player who in a few moments will startle the geese (fig. 5). Through the quiet fisherman Wang Hung emphasizes the third couplet of the poem, the moment of melancholy reflection on the place to which the poet/fisherman has not yet been able to return. In his last line Hui-hung imagines that the geese are writing script in imitation of one of the fathers of Chinese calligraphy, Wang Hsi-chih (ca. 307–ca. 365). Wang Hung's pale ink washes (now, along with the silk, somewhat darkened) capture the impression of light filtered through evening haze. With firm black strokes he conveys a contrast between the methodical fisherman and the anxious gaggle of geese. The thick brushwork of the leafless tree, the expansive vista, and the soft earthen banks owe more to the river landscapes of Tung Yüan (fl. 937–76) than to Fan K'uan (ca. 960–1030), whose style Wang is said to have followed.[30]

## 2. Returning Sail off Distant Shore

The lyrical mood of "Geese Descending" is transformed into a more intense meditation in "Returning Sail." From his pavilion the poet watches the pattern of waves on the surface of the water, a scene that recalls lines from an essay by Su Hsün on the nature of *wen*.[31] Basing his discussion on the *Book of Changes* (*I-ching*), Su Hsün described the interaction of wind across water as the most perfect example of something being created out of the unintended and perfectly spontaneous interaction of two contrasting but complementary things. The wind crosses over the water creating ripples. In Hui-hung's poem,

> An easterly breeze suddenly turns into a whirlwind.
> I sit watching patterns of waves, like fine silk gauze;
> Setting sun illuminates the horizon, White Isle lies crosswise.
> The river's current swallows the sky, a distant traveler's sailboat;
> Leaning on a railing, threads of thoughts tangled in the wind,
> Over a vast expanse, I suspect I see a wild duck or goose.
> Gradually aware of a mast emerging through the glare,
> This time—adding or detracting—you must rely on the poet's vision.

Here Wang Hung re-created the poem's details exactly: the painting shows a gentleman leaning on the railing of a waterside pavilion (fig. 6). If we follow the man's gaze out across the water, we struggle with him to perceive correctly the sail of the distant boat near the far shore. Hui-hung's line "Over a vast expanse, I suspect I see a wild duck or goose" alludes to an anecdote about two gentlemen who saw a wild goose in the sky. Deceived by the distance, one said it was a duck, the other said a martin. The story was cited in a debate between Buddhists and Taoists to illustrate that the same truth can have different interpretations. As a Ch'an Buddhist Hui-hung would have been concerned with the illusory nature of reality. At the same time, he also seems to use the story for its literal meaning, the unreliability of visual perception. In the poem, as the distant object moves, the poet realizes it is a sail and asks the viewer to imagine with him the eerie outline of a boat barely visible in the hazy glare of sun and water.[32]

### 3. Mountain Market, Clear with Rising Mist

The title of this scene is often translated "mountain village in clearing rain." But *shan-shih* is a mountain market and *ch'ing-lan* is more literally given as a clear day with vapor. The idea is not simply that a rainstorm has passed, but that in sunlight the saturated landscape has begun to release wraiths of steam.

> Last night's rain is letting up, mountain air is heavy,
> Steam rising, sun and shadow, shifting light amid trees;
> The silkworm market comes to a close, the crowd thins out,
> Roadside willows by the market bridge: golden threads play;
> Whose house with flower-filled plot is across the valley?
> A smooth-tongued yellow bird calls in spring breeze;
> Wine flag in hazy distance—look and you can see:
> It's the one west of the road to Che Tree Ridge Valley.

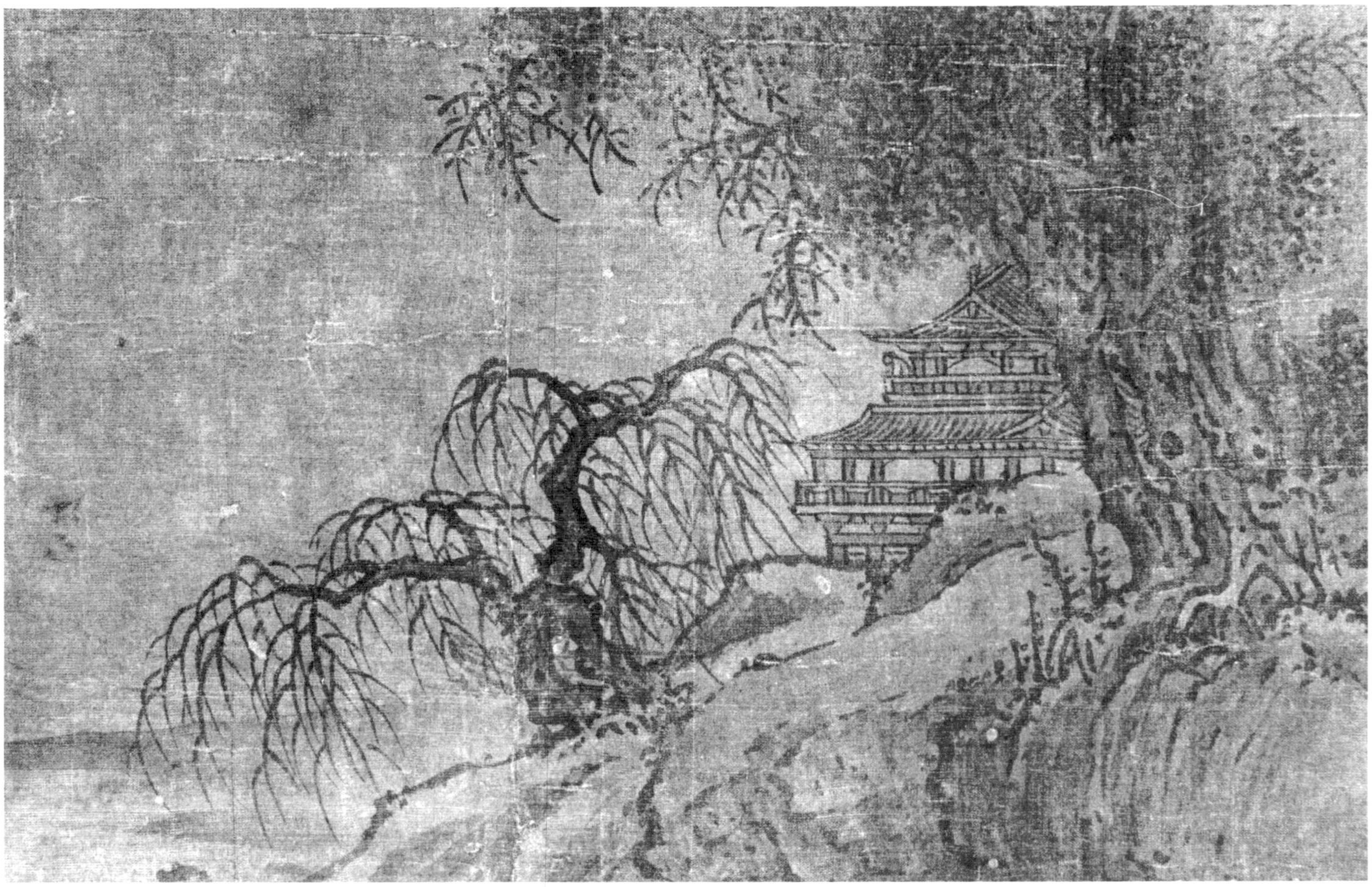

Fig. 6. Detail, "Returning Sail off Distant Shore"

Wang Hung captured the heavy atmosphere of the warm and humid day in a convincing visualization of Hui-hung's poem (fig. 7). The hillside house at the right with clearing may only vaguely suggest the house with flower-filled plot that Hui-hung wonders about in the fifth line, but the wine-shop flag so difficult for Hui-hung to see is unquestionably present in the palest of ink on the small tree-lined ridge to the left of center. Hui-hung reinforces the suggestion that the trade at this market is in silkworms by mentioning the *che* tree: *che* leaves were used to feed just-hatched silkworms. Hui-hung's poem encompasses an entire day, from hazy morning to the close of the market and the poet's thoughts of wine. Despite the temporal limitations of his medium, the painter succeeds in suggesting the scope of the day's activities: a single figure rounds the bend at the far right, the boats arrive at the willow tree landing, and a few merchants gather in the market. The two figures walking up the hill at the bottom of the village became a permanent bit of iconography for "Mountain Market," most memorably pictured enveloped in mist in a brilliant ink-splash version of the scene by Yü-chien (fl. mid-13th century; fig. 8).[33]

### 4. River and Sky in Evening Snow

Probably the best-known poem about a snowstorm is by Liu Tsung-yüan (773–819):

> Birds of a thousand hills flown away;
> Men along myriad paths gone without a trace;
> In a solitary boat an old man with rush cape and hat,
> Alone, fishing in the snow of an icy river.[34]

In the first line of his poem, Hui-hung alludes to Liu Tsung-yüan, creating a scene of similar quietude:

> Dark ink-splashed clouds, all returning birds are gone,
> Pure spirits suddenly make river and sky snowy;

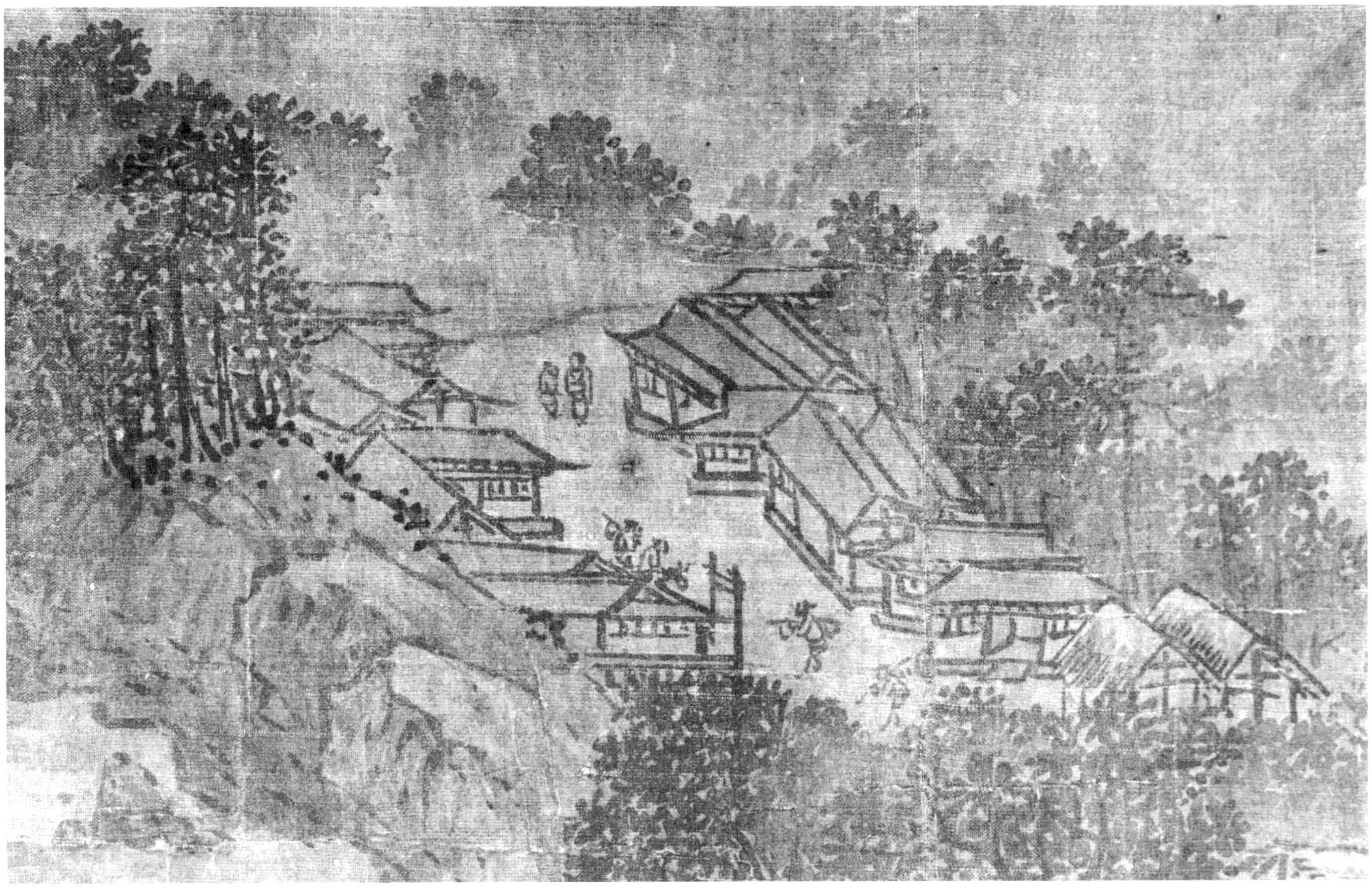

Fig. 7. Detail, "Mountain Market, Clear with Rising Mist"

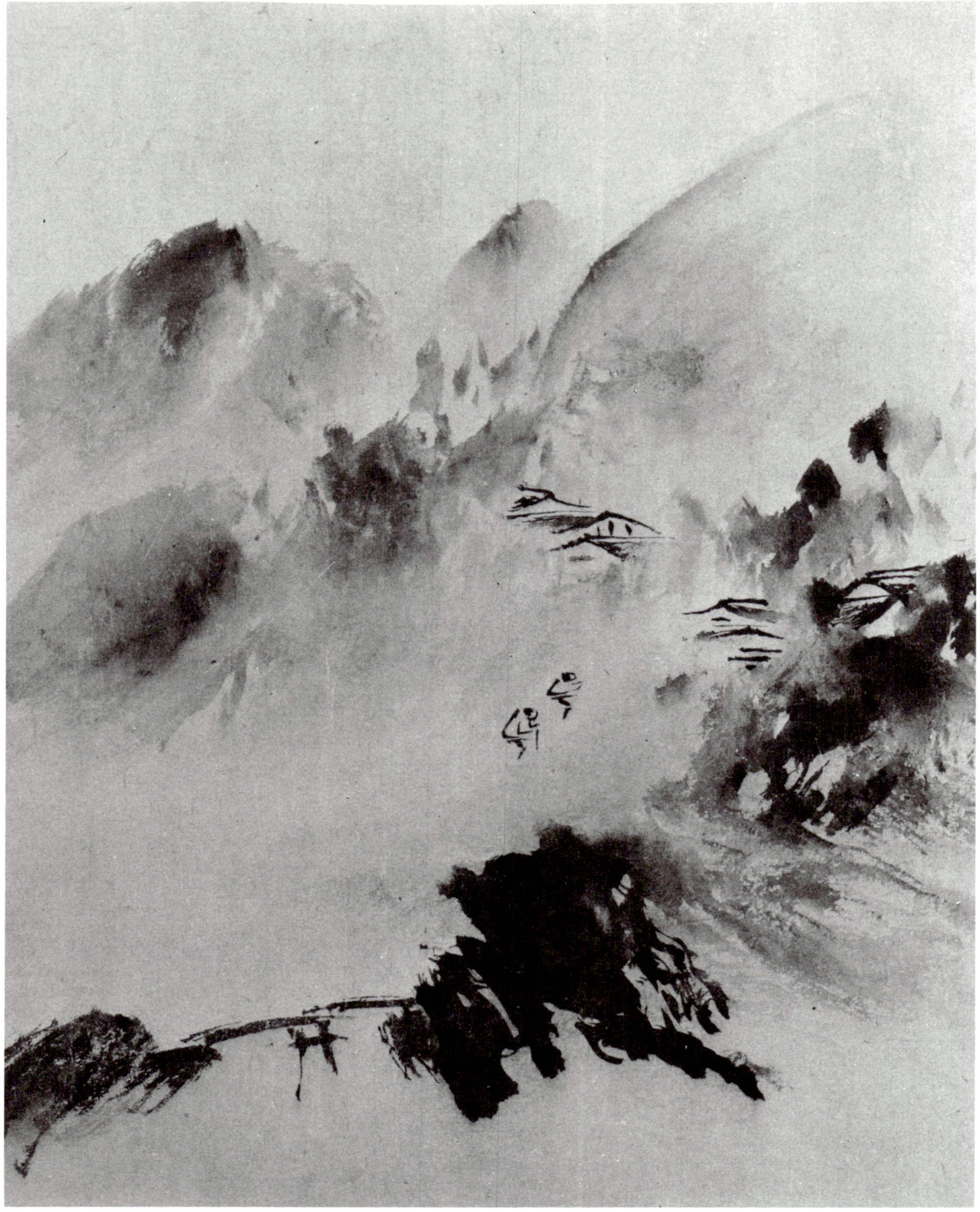

Fig. 8. Yü-chien, detail, *Mountain Market, Clear with Rising Mist* (*Shan-shih ch'ing lan*). Undated, mid-13th century. Hanging scroll (originally one of Eight Views), ink on paper. 33.0 x 83.1 cm (13 x 32 3/4 in.). Idemitsu Art Museum, Tokyo

or Tokyo National Museum? see p.59

A stream's beauty manifest, thick snow sifting wildly,
Ten thousand silent trees, made peaceful by the cold;
In a solitary boat lying listening: patter on door and window.
Rising to look: the night clearing, then a brilliant moon;
Startled that green hills are entirely whisked away,
But feeling still more that spring pastels have been returned.

As the night passes the storm clears and the poet is astonished that the dark mountains have disappeared, but under a bright moon the glistening snow reminds him of a spring landscape. In Wang Hung's painting the river stretches broad and still in the cold; the horizon is barely distinguishable. The man seated in the small boat, who appears to be the thoughtful poet, also recalls the fisherman of Liu Tsung-yüan's poem (fig. 9). The rough earthen banks at the left, with their sloping surfaces, share characteristics with the great boulders that line the shores of the long snowscape *Streams and Hills under Fresh Snow* ascribed to Kao K'o-ming (fl. 1st half 11th century) in the John M. Crawford, Jr., collection,[35] providing another reference to Northern Sung style.

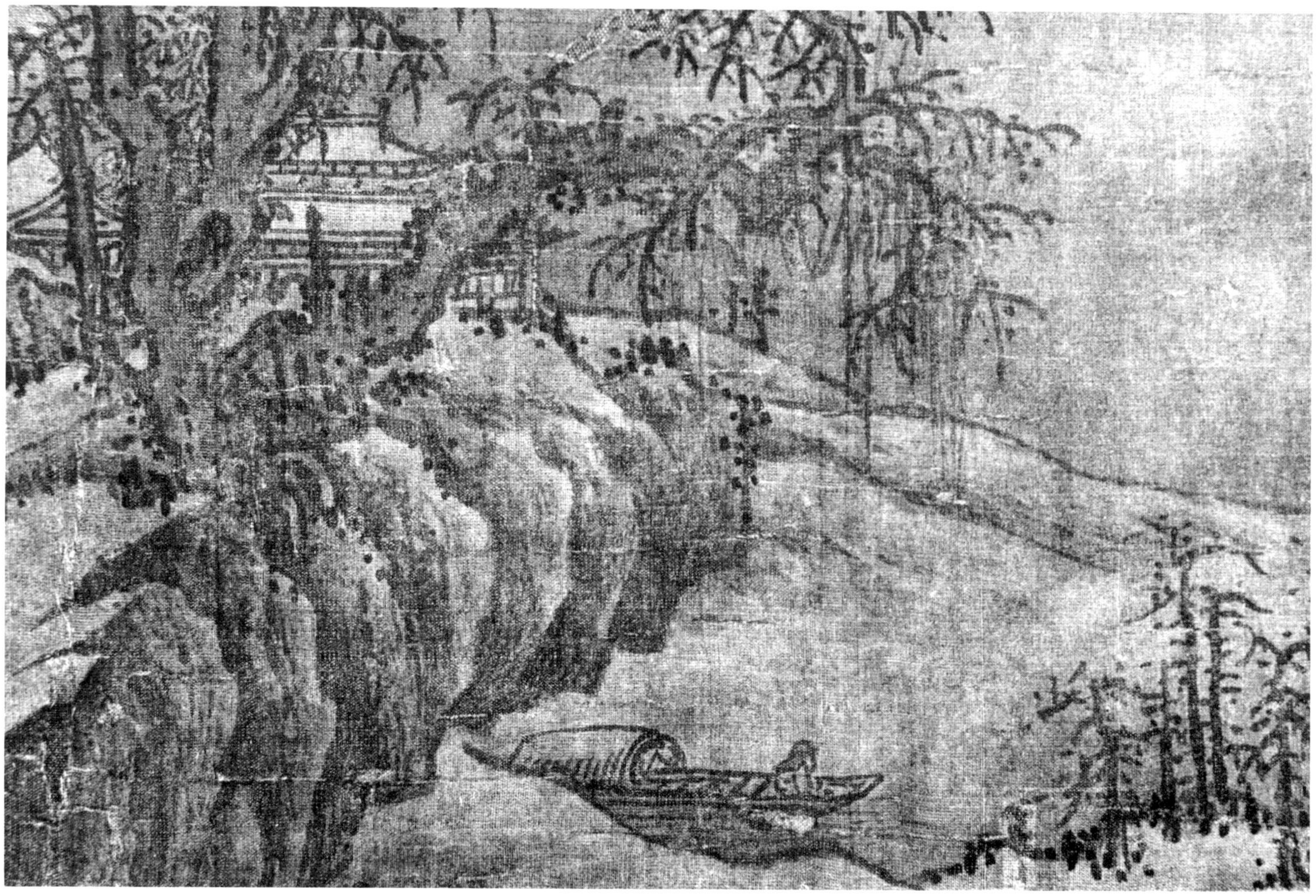

Fig. 9. Detail, "River and Sky in Evening Snow"

One late twelfth-century author described the profound expression that a refined and educated painter could give to the *Eight Views of the Hsiao and Hsiang Rivers*: "In 'Autumn Moon over Lake Tung-t'ing' there is no moon. In 'River and Sky in Evening Snow' there is no snow. He depicts only the limpid quality of moonlight and the bitterness of cold."[36] This understated approach was Wang Hung's as well: the most memorable aspect of the scene is the aura of perfect calm.

### 5. Autumn Moon over Lake Tung-t'ing

The mottled silk of the Wang Hung painting hints that the sphere of a moon may have been present, but a careful examination suggests that—as in the twelfth-century author's description—the moon was not painted. In Hui-hung's poem however, it is a palpable presence:

> Fragrance of oranges everywhere, green and yellow coming out,
> At sunset mooring boat at the bramble gate;
> Lapping waves, and a moon like a handsome woman,
> The waves boast as if playing with beauty;
> Deep night the Milky Way without clouds,
> High winds beat water into white confusion;
> At the fifth night watch, someone plays a painted bugle.
> Throwing on clothes, I rise to look: below, a golden basin.

From mooring the boat at sunset to the rising of the moon, the poet is conscious of the colorful beauty of the lakeside haven. As night passes the stars are clear in a cloudless sky. At the fifth watch (that is, between four and six in the morning), he rises at the sound of a horn and sees the moon reflected like a gold basin in the lake. In a second set of Hsiao-Hsiang poems, Hui-hung emphasized the color of the moonlight and changed the title accordingly to "Autumn Color over Tung-t'ing."

Wang Hung includes in his picture a scholar resting on his elbow in a small boat moored near a humble hut by the foreground trees. Regrettably the painting is damaged in the area of his face, but he appears to be gazing out at the moonlit scene and the great looming mountain across the water, which may represent Mount Chün, the well-known peak on the north shore of Lake Tung-t'ing. The tumbling stream at the left seems to flow from a similar stream at the right of the following scene, "Night Rain on Hsiao and Hsiang."

### 6. Night Rain on Hsiao and Hsiang

Hui-hung's poem opens with his departure from the Yüeh-lu Academy, a school established by the Sung government in the K'ai-pao era (968–76). On Mount Yüeh-lu at the north end of the Heng range, the academy was about three miles from the west bank of the Hsiang River as it passes Ch'ang-sha. With over one thousand scholars in residence, Yüeh-lu became one of the four great academies under the Sung.

> Porch windows of Yüeh-lu Hall were just before my eyes,
> Clouds appeared and suddenly rolled up the picture;
> Gentle wind creating white-topped waves,
> Lower the sails, stop at the shore—tonight I'll lodge at a fishing village;
> Among dense reeds fires are lit, the evening meal prepared,
> In the middle of the lake there seem to be fish;
> Intensely moved by the pure state and the ordinary affairs of life,
> Under my leaking thatched roof, chanting alone, I'm oblivious to dawn.

Given the topic of his poem, Hui-hung's vision of fish in the lake may have been inspired by the splash of raindrops, suggesting open mouths at the surface of the water. Teng Ch'un's criticism of Sung Ti's paintings included a condemnation of the common artisans who used gimmicks in a literal illustration of the scene: "They used torches to illuminate hawsers and lamps glaring from boats. These pictures are superficial and offensive. As representations they are worse than unsuccessful. It has been said in ridicule that all one has to do is cut off a length of several feet of black silk to hang up in his hall, and he is well on the way to fame."[37]

In a close parallel to "Autumn Moon," Wang Hung placed the scholar on his boat in the middle of the scene, presumably chanting his poem. This, the most mist-obscured scene of the set, owes a debt to the art of Mi Yu-jen (1072–1151). The wind-bent trees with simple trunks of two strokes are paraphrases from the motifs of Mi Yu-jen, who was himself fascinated with the Hsiao and Hsiang region.[38]

### 7. Evening Bell from Mist-shrouded Temple

> Ten years on dusty roads with carriages and horses,
> Late in the year the traveler's mind distracted by ten thousand thoughts;
> Suddenly startled by a sound: a bell, from where?
> A temple in a misty village in the remotest possible place;
> Far beyond the stream a dwelling visible between tall bamboo.
> Wanting to summon the small boat, but no one is there to ferry me;
> A gaunt figure leaning on a wisteria staff, a west wind at his back,
> A returning monk enters the mist and vines, and disappears.

The correspondence of this poem to Wang Hung's illustration is particularly close. The figure standing at the right is the traveler who has been jolted by the sonorous tones of the temple bell (fig. 10). Faithful to the poem, a cluster of dwellings is pictured across the stream behind the bluff at the center of the painting. In a

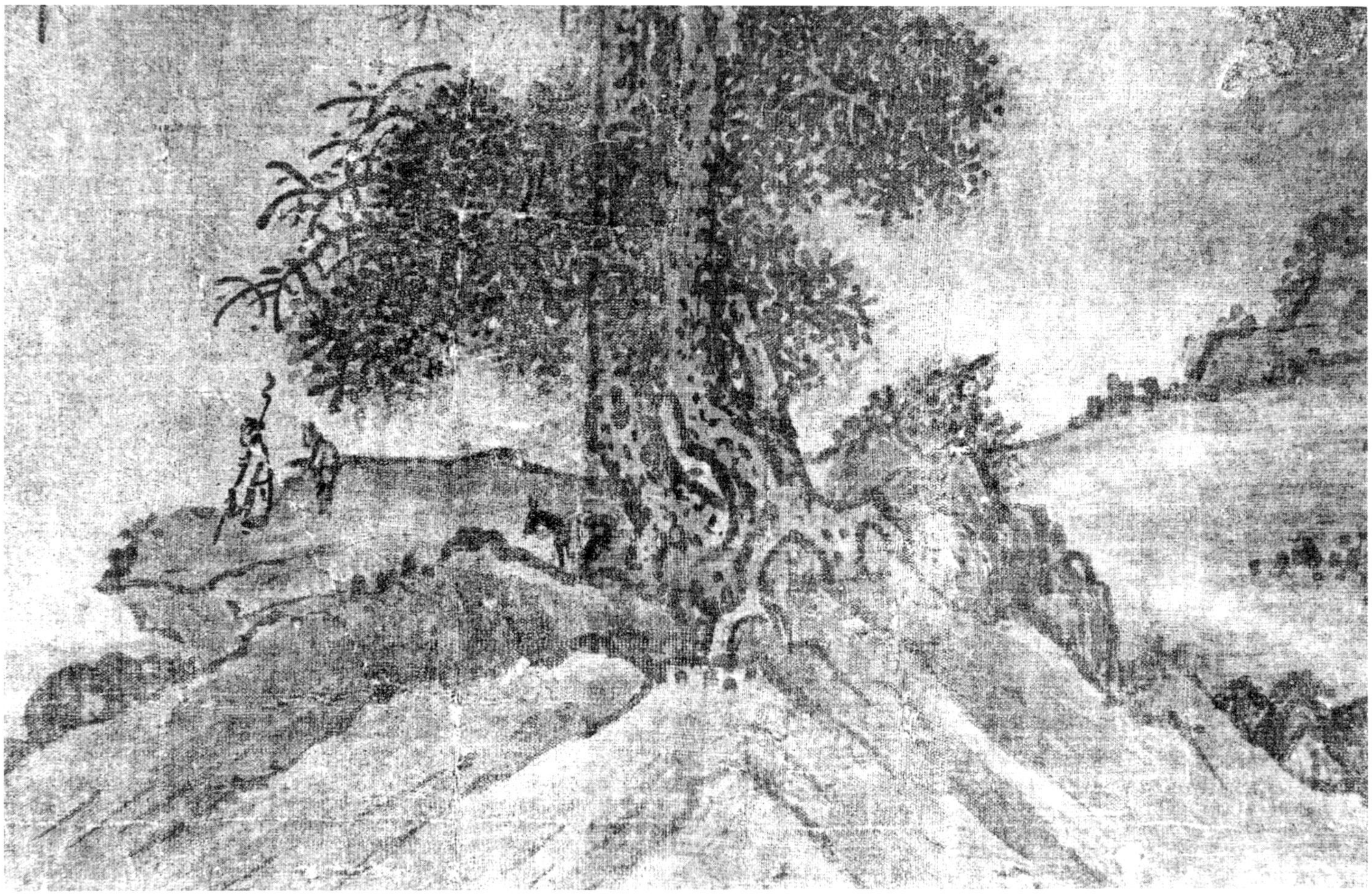

Fig. 10. Detail, "Evening Bell from Mist-shrouded Temple"

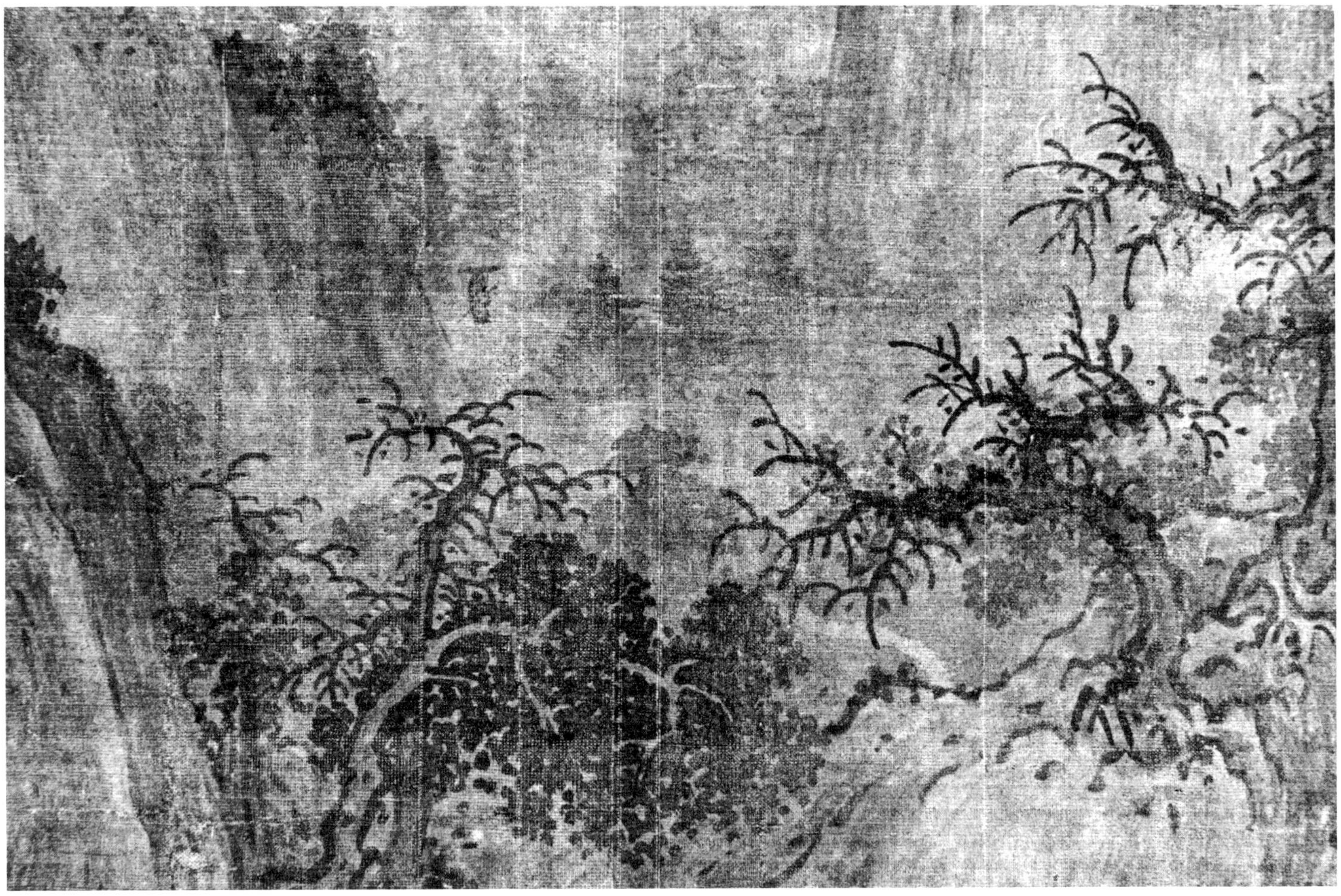

Fig. 11. Detail, "Evening Bell from Mist-shrouded Temple"

particularly felicitous detail, the bamboo that parts to reveal the dwelling lies on the traveler's line of sight to the dwelling, not on our line of sight. The little ferry boat that the traveler wishes to summon rests in the water beyond the shoulder of the hill near the dwelling. The remote temple is barely visible in Wang Hung's painting, duly shrouded with mist in the steep valley at the left, where a monk can barely be discerned climbing the hill (fig. 11). Perhaps it was unclear to Wang Hung which figure in Hui-hung's poem leans on the length of wisteria, the traveler or the monk, for he shows both of them grasping a twisted staff.

The Eight Views very possibly were understood by Buddhists as a progression from an unenlightened state to an enlightened state, in a cycle comparable to the Ten Ox Herding pictures. In Hui-hung's poems such a progression can be interpreted from his images of flighty, easily distracted geese (the wayward mind) to a gradual focusing on truth, to a moment of awakening, followed by a return to the mundane world of fishermen and the pungent smell of wine. Hui-hung composed a second set of poems on the same titles, and, exercising the liberty of the poet, he arranged them in a somewhat different order. "Evening Bell from Mist-shrouded Temple"—its startling bell signifying a spiritual awakening that comes after a long journey—nevertheless remains in the penultimate position. On *Eight Views* painted by Chiang Shen (1090–1138), known only from a record of the inscription by Cheng Chü-fu (fl. 14th century), "Evening Bell" is also in the seventh position and is followed by "Evening Snow," perhaps to convey the ineffable calm that follows enlightenment.[39] The seventh position for the "Evening Bell" scene may refer to the Buddhist concept of eight levels of consciousness. At the seventh level the ego emerges and the fundamental error of perception occurs. It is consequently at this level that the fundamental correction, or transformation, must also take place. Through a purification of one's perceptions an enlightened, egoless vision of the world is possible.

8. Fishing Village in Evening Glow

Jade-green reeds whistling, the wind sighs,
Sandy village lanes are bright, scattering remnants of sun;
Beyond a bamboo fence millet is steaming, the fragrance drifts about,
Opposite the gate, hanging up fishing nets, silver shimmering.
Poling boats gradually near the Peach Blossom Inn,
Assaulting the nose the pungent fragrance of heady liquids;
Hoisting a basket with you: ample for our intoxication,
Lying gazing at river and hills, the reds and greens blur.

In this poem Hui-hung seems to take the role of a fisherman and helps as well as observes the labor. After stowing their gear and lifting up the basket of fish, the fishermen turn to their reward in a nearby wine shop. Clearly a basket of fish bought an adequate amount of wine, for the verse ends with the poet in an inebriated haze. The title of this poem is the only one that uses a word for light, and it is the diminishing light of the end of the day (fig. 12).

In creating *Eight Views of the Hsiao and Hsiang Rivers*, Wang Hung composed with an awareness of visual and emotional dynamics. He combined blunt, sometimes coarse brushwork with ink wash of every gradation to achieve an accomplished structuring of space and forms. Inspired by the art of poetry, he developed a pictorial set of contrasts and parallelisms, while at the same time brilliantly conveying the idea of a journey through the paintings from right to left. The figure in "Geese Descending" is leaving his boat toward the left, in the same direction that our eye is moving. As if to reinforce the theme of journey, the painter opens the second scene, "Returning Sail," with a figure crossing a bridge, and the third scene, "Mountain Market," with a figure rounding a bend. "Mountain Market" shows people traveling by foot and boat from all directions and is the most activity-filled of the scenes. In contrast, the following "Evening Snow" and "Autumn Moon" contain solitary figures in muted silence, both seated in their small boats, pausing for a time in their journeys. In "Night Rain" the man in the small boat sings loudly into the storm.

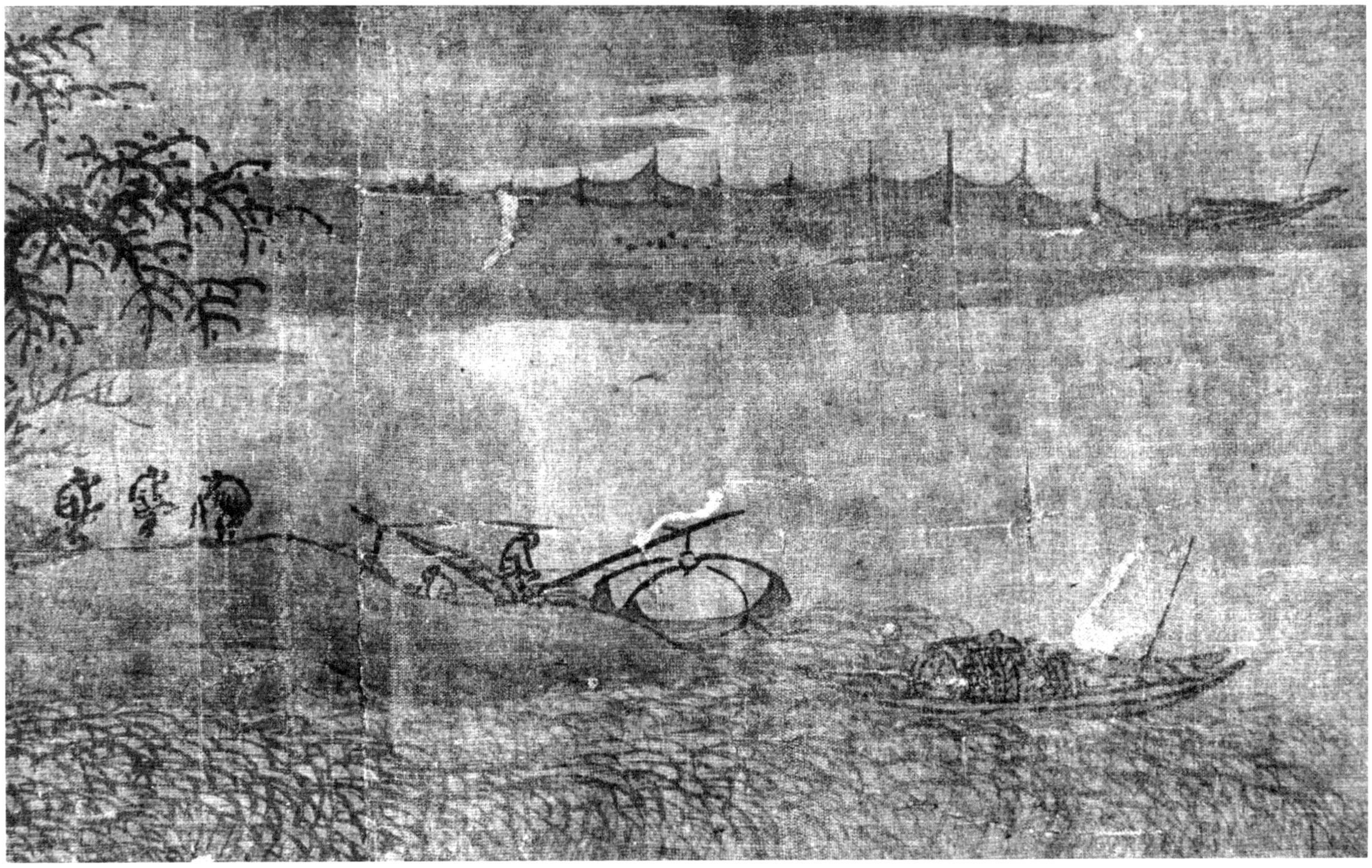

Fig. 12. Detail, "Fishing Village in Evening Glow"

A peaceful stillness suffuses "Evening Bell," as the traveler stands beneath ancient pines and, looking at the empty boat, longs to cross the stream. The concentration of boulders, cliff faces, and twisting trees form a wild landscape that intensifies the stillness of the lone monk climbing the hill. The density of the landscape in "Evening Bell" does not prepare us for the serene calm of "Fishing Village." The still face of a lake is disturbed only by the small skiff moving toward shore. The curves of coves and banks, and the rhythm of the line of fishing nets hung up to dry slow the cadence of viewing and instill an aura of serenity. The depiction of fishermen bringing in their catch is so evocative that one almost expects to hear the distant music of their voices. A crescendo of mountain peaks seems to create an echo up the misty valley, resonating until we see the man seated by his brazier. The traveler is at home, no longer adrift. He sits in a posture of meditation, facing right toward the beginning of the series, his back to the trees and mountains that definitively end the set (fig. 13).

The interest at the end of the Northern Sung in poetry and painting is well documented. At Emperor Sung Hui-tsung's court, painters competed to give subtle visual expression to a poetic line or couplet. Emperor Sung Kao-tsung (r. 1127–62) in Southern Sung drove the relationship between painting and poetry to a new and literal extreme in his massive court project to illustrate the *Classic of Poetry (Shih-ching)*.[40] More modest attempts to express poetry through painting also became popular, but the tendency seems to have been to make the implicit relationship explicit by inscribing poetic lines of the painting.[41] Indeed Wang Hung's paintings each carry a gourd-shaped seal reading "imperially inscribed," suggesting that they may originally have been accompanied by poetic inscriptions. Painting in this milieu, Wang Hung tried to capture the spirit of the Hsiao-Hsiang region, not by depiction of actual scenery but through thoughtful compositions filled with an abundance of ordinary detail and the mist-veiled beauty of its landscape of lakes and rivers. More important, he was attempting to express in visual terms the qualities and structures of poetry, as well as the themes of change, evanescence, and the journey—themes that apply equally to the landscape and to human life.

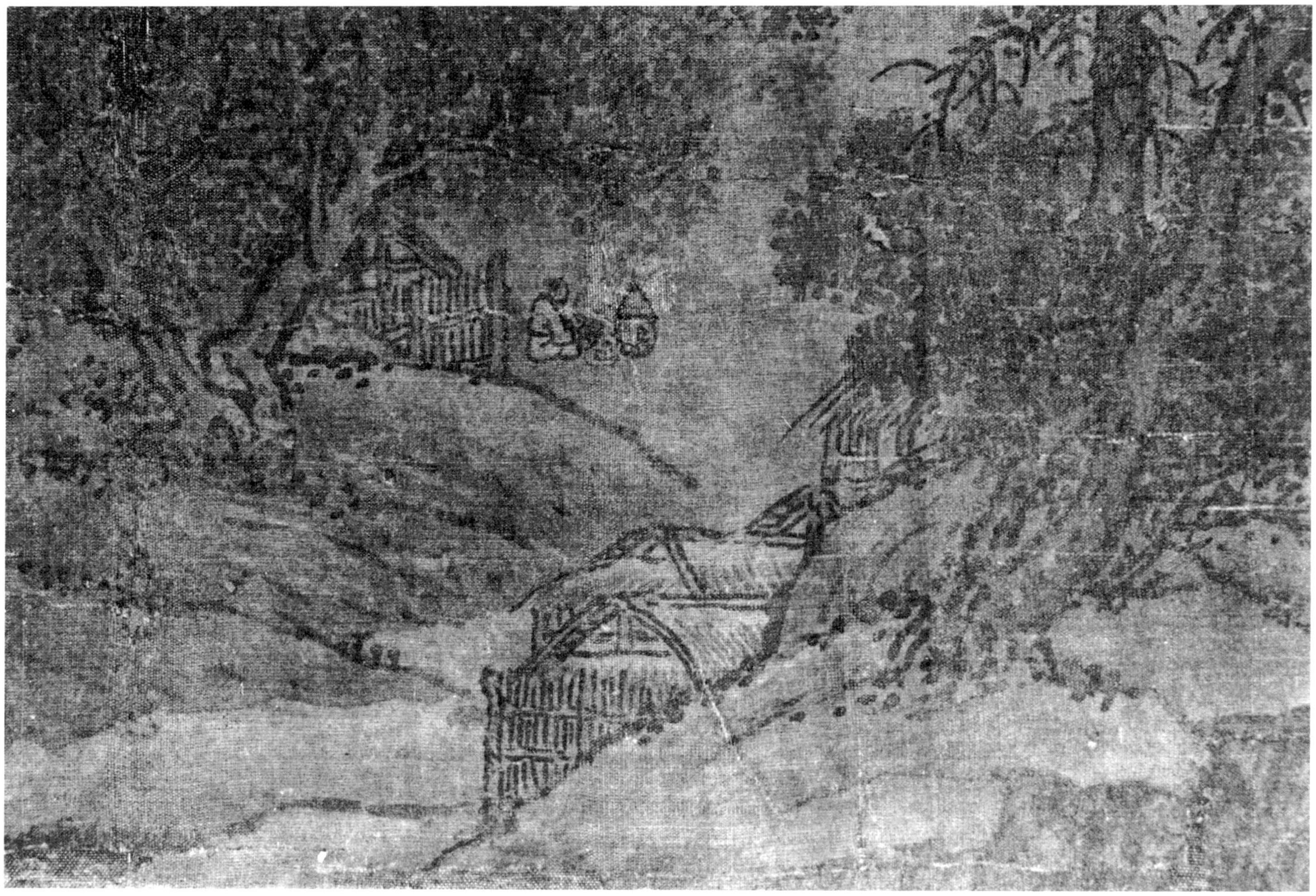

Fig. 13. Detail, "Fishing Village in Evening Glow"

Later artists occasionally painted the Eight Views of the Hsiao and Hsiang Rivers, but the popularity of the subject dramatically declined in China after the fall of the Sung dynasty in 1279. Its loss of favor cannot be explained by the political cataclysm of the Mongol conquest, for the Yüan dynasty witnessed a renewed interest in the relationship between poetry and painting. If paintings of the Eight Views of Hsiao and Hsiang did not imitate the structure of poetry, it may have been this very format of multiple paintings that doomed it. For a scholar practicing Su Shih's concept of spontaneous creation fueled by the exhilaration of the moment, a cumbersome cycle of eight paintings may have seemed a laborious exercise. And the predetermined titles came to be seen as the confines and distance of another's inspiration. Combined with an emphasis on the expressiveness of calligraphic brushwork, Su Shih's principles led to a new aesthetic and a different way of relating poetry and painting. Wang Hung stands close to the beginning of this complicated evolution, exploring the Hsiao-Hsiang theme at a moment when it still presented an invigorating challenge.

NOTES

1. Hsia Wen-yen, *T'u-hui pao-chien* (Treasured mirror of painting), in *Hua-shih ts'ung-shu* (Compendium of painting histories) (1365; repr. ed., Taipei: Wen-shih-che ch'u-pan-she, 1974), vol. 2, p. 89.
2. The author wishes to thank the following friends and colleagues for comments on this paper: Richard Barnhart, Peter Bol, Wen Fong, Kao Yu-kung, Christian Murck, and Paul Watt.
3. David Hawkes, *Ch'u Tz'u: The Songs of the South* (London: Oxford University Press, 1959; Boston: Beacon Press, 1962).
4. Shen Kua, *Meng-ch'i pi-t'an chiao-cheng* (Notes written in Meng-ch'i), ed. Hu Tao-ching (1088–93; repr. eds. Shanghai, 1956; Taipei, 1961), *chüan* 17, pp. 9–10.
5. For a biography of Sung Ti and a thorough discussion of the origins of the Hsiao-Hsiang theme, see Shimada Shujiro, "Sō Teki to Shōshō hakkei" (Sung Ti and the *Eight Views of the Hsiao and Hsiang Rivers*), *Nanga Kansho* 104 (1941): 6–13. For discussions of the theme's history in Japan, see Watanabe Akiyoshi, *Shōshō hakkei zu* (*Eight Views of the Hsiao and Hsiang Rivers*), Nihon no bijutsu, no. 124 (Tokyo: Shibundō, 1976); Richard Stanley-Baker, "Mid-Muromachi Paintings of the Eight Views of Hsiao and Hsiang" (Ph.D. diss., Princeton University, 1979); Barbara Brennan Ford, "The Eight Views of Hsiao and Hsiang in Muromachi Painting" (M.A. thesis, Columbia University, 1973).
6. Shimada Shujiro ("Sō Teki to Shōshō hakkei," p. 8) inferred Sung Ti's dates from those of Sung Tao (1013–1083). See Ch'ang Pi-te et al., comp., *Sung-jen chuan-chi tz'u-liao so yin* (Index to biographical materials of Sung figures) (Taipei: Ting-wen, 1974), vol. 1, pp. 749–50, which mistakenly lists two Sung Taos in the eleventh century. Shimada's citation of a Ssu-ma Kuang poem addressed to Sung Tao, using the style name Shu-ta and referring to him as Sung Ti's brother, demonstrates that the two Sung Taos are the same person.
7. Shimada Shujiro, "Sō Teki to Shōshō hakkei," p. 9.
8. Kuo Jo-hsü, *T'u-hua chien-wen chih* (Experiences in painting), in *Hua-shih ts'ung-shu* (Taipei: Wen-shih-che ch'u-pan-she, 1974), vol. 3, pp. 5–6. For a slightly different translation, see Alexander C. Soper, *Kuo Jo-hsü's Experiences in Painting* (Washington, D.C.: American Council of Learned Societies, 1951), p. 45.
9. Mi Fu, *Hua-shih* (Painting history), I-shu ts'ung-pien, vol. 10 (Taipei: Shih-chieh shu-chü, 1975) pp. 9, 24. Like Liu Ming-fu, Yen Su was also an academician of the Lung-t'u Pavilion.
10. Shen Kua, *Meng-ch'i pi-t'an chiao-cheng*, *chüan* 17, p. 10.
11. *Hsüan-ho hua-p'u* (Painting catalogue of the Hsüan-ho era [1119–25]), in *Hua-shih ts'ung-shu* (1120; repr. ed. Taipei: Wen-shih-che ch'u-pan-she, 1974), vol. 1, pp. 129–30.
12. The earliest record of this commission does not appear until the fourteenth century: Hsia Wen-yen, *T'u-hui pao-chien*, p. 89. Without explaining why, Hsia reports that the artist was seized and was forced to stay in the Hsiang River region.
13. Chang Ch'eng, *Hua-lu kuang-i* (Miscellaneous record on painting), I-shu ts'ung-pien, vol. 10 (1139; repr. ed., Taipei: Shih-chieh shu-chü, 1975), p. 174.
14. Ibid.
15. Teng Ch'un, *Hua-chi* (A continuation of painting history), in *Hua-shih ts'ung-shu* (1167; repr. ed., Taipei: Wen-shih-che ch'u-pan-she, 1974), vol. 1, p. 317. Translation adapted from Alexander C. Soper, *Kuo Jo-hsü's Experiences in Painting*, p. 157, n. 429.
16. Translated in Susan Bush, *The Chinese Literati on Painting: Su Shih (1037–1101) to Tung Ch'i-ch'ang (1555–1636)*, Harvard-Yenching Institute Studies, no. 27 (Cambridge, Mass.: Harvard University Press, 1971), p. 113, no. 179.
17. The comment was inscribed on Sung Tzu-fang's painting and is in Su Shih, *Tung-p'o t'i-pa* (Colophons by Su Shih), I-shu ts'ung-pien, vol. 22 (Taipei: Shih-chieh shu-chü, 1962), *chüan* 5, pp. 98–99.
18. For an informative survey of Northern Sung attitudes toward painting, see Susan Bush, *The Chinese Literati on Painting*, pp. 22–82.
19. For a thorough examination of Su Shih's thoughts on culture, see Peter Kees Bol, "Culture and the Way in Eleventh-century China" (Ph.D. diss., Princeton University, 1982), esp. pp. 134–35.
20. Su Shih, *Chi-chu fen-lei Tung-p'o hsien-sheng shih* (Annotated poetry of Master Tung p'o), Ssu-pu ts'ung-k'an ch'u pien so pen (Taipei: Shang-wu yin-shu-kuan, 1967), vol. 5, *chüan* 11, p. 29a.
21. Hans H. Frankel, "Poetry and Painting: Chinese and Western Views of their Convertibility," *Comparative Literature* 9, no. 4 (Fall 1957): 289–307. This pioneering article is an excellent introduction to the subject.
22. Ibid., p. 289.
23. The poems are recorded in Su Shih, *Tung-p'o hsü-chi* (Supplementary writings of Su Shih), Ssu-pu pei-yao (Taipei: Chung-hua shu-chü, 1965), *chüan* 2, pp. 5–6.
24. Richard Stanley-Baker, "Mid-Muromachi Paintings," p. 18.
25. Peter Kees Bol, "Culture and the Way," pp. 126–37.
26. For a more detailed description of regulated verse, see Hans H. Frankel, *The Flowering Plum and the Palace Lady: Interpretations of Chinese Poetry* (New Haven: Yale University Press, 1976), pp. 213–15; James Robert Hightower, "Some Characteristics of Parallel Prose," in John L. Bishop, ed., *Studies in Chinese Literature*, Harvard-Yenching Institute Studies, no. 21 (Cambridge, Mass.: Harvard University Press, 1966), pp. 108–39.
27. For a lucid discussion of the phenomenon, see Andrew H. Plaks, *Archetype and Allegory in the "Dream of the Red Chamber"* (Princeton: Princeton University Press, 1976), esp. pp. 43–53, 146–211.
28. Most notably *Leng-chai yeh hua* (Night conversations from a cold studio), which was assembled from 1111 to 1128, and *Shih-men wen-tzu ch'an* (Meditations on literature of Stone Gate).
29. Hui-hung, *Shih-men wen-tzu ch'an* (Meditations on literature of Stone Gate), Ssu-k'u ch'üan-shu chen pen (1776; repr. ed., Taipei: Shang-wu, 1980), *chüan* 8, p. 6. Hui-hung composed a second set of poems of four lines of seven characters each (*chüan* 15, p. 32).
30. See *Summer Mountains*, Shanghai Museum, handscroll, in Richard Barnhart, *Marriage of The Lord of the River: A Lost Landscape by Tung Yüan*, *Artibus Asiae* Supplementum 27 (1970): fig. 3. Wang Hung does not include the spiky reeds that frequently grow in the Tung Yüan landscapes, but rather depicts the water rushes in pale curving strokes that suggest softly rippling grass.
31. See Peter Kees Bol, "Culture and the Way," pp. 130–32.
32. Liang Hsiao-tzu, ed., *Nan-Ch'i shu* (History of southern Ch'i) (Peking: Chung Hua, 1972), *chüan* 54, p. 935 (s.v. biography of Ku Huan).
33. See Tokyo National Museum, comp., *Sōgen no kaiga* (Chinese paintings of the Sung and Yüan dynasties) (Kyoto: Benridō, 1962), pls. 121, 123.
34. Liu Tsung-yüan, "Chiang-hsüeh" (River snow), in *T'ang-shih san-pai shou* (Three hundred poems of the T'ang) (Taipei: Wen-yüan, 1965), p. 296.
35. See Laurence Sickman, ed., *Chinese Calligraphy and Painting in the Collection of John M. Crawford, Jr.* (New York: Pierpont Morgan Library, 1962), pl. 2.
36. Tseng Min-hsing (1120?–1175), *Tu hsing tsa-chih* (Thoughts on waking alone), *chüan* 1, cited by Shimada Shujiro, "Sō Teki to Shōshō hakkei," p. 12.
37. Teng Ch'un, *Hua-chi*, vol. 1, p. 317; translation adapted from Alexander C. Soper, *Kuo Jo-hsü's Experiences in Painting*, p. 157, n. 429.
38. *Cloudy Mountains* (The Metropolitan Museum of Art, New York), in Wen C. Fong and Marilyn Fu, *Sung and Yüan Paintings* (New York: The Metropolitan Museum of Art, 1973), pl. 6. For a discussion of Mi Yu-jen and the Hsiao-Hsiang theme, see Howard Rogers, "Cloudy Mountains," no. 24, in Wai-kam Ho et al., *Eight Dynasties of Chinese Painting* (Cleveland: Cleveland Museum of Art and Indiana University Press, 1980), pp. 42–44.
39. Ch'en Pang-yen (1603–1647), comp., *Li-tai t'i-hua shih lei* (Poetic inscriptions on paintings through the ages), Ssu-k'u ch'üan-shu (Taipei: Shang-wu yin-shu-kuan, 1980), *chüan* 39, pp. 2–3.
40. See Julia K. Murray, "Sung Kao-tsung, Ma Ho-chih, and the Mao 'Shih' Scrolls: Illustrations of the *Classic of Poetry*" (Ph.D. diss., Princeton University, 1981).
41. See Hsü Pang-ta, "Nan-Sung ti-hou t'i hua shu k'ao pien" (Authentication of the postscripts by Southern Sung emperors and empresses), *Wen-wu* 1981, no. 6: 52–64.

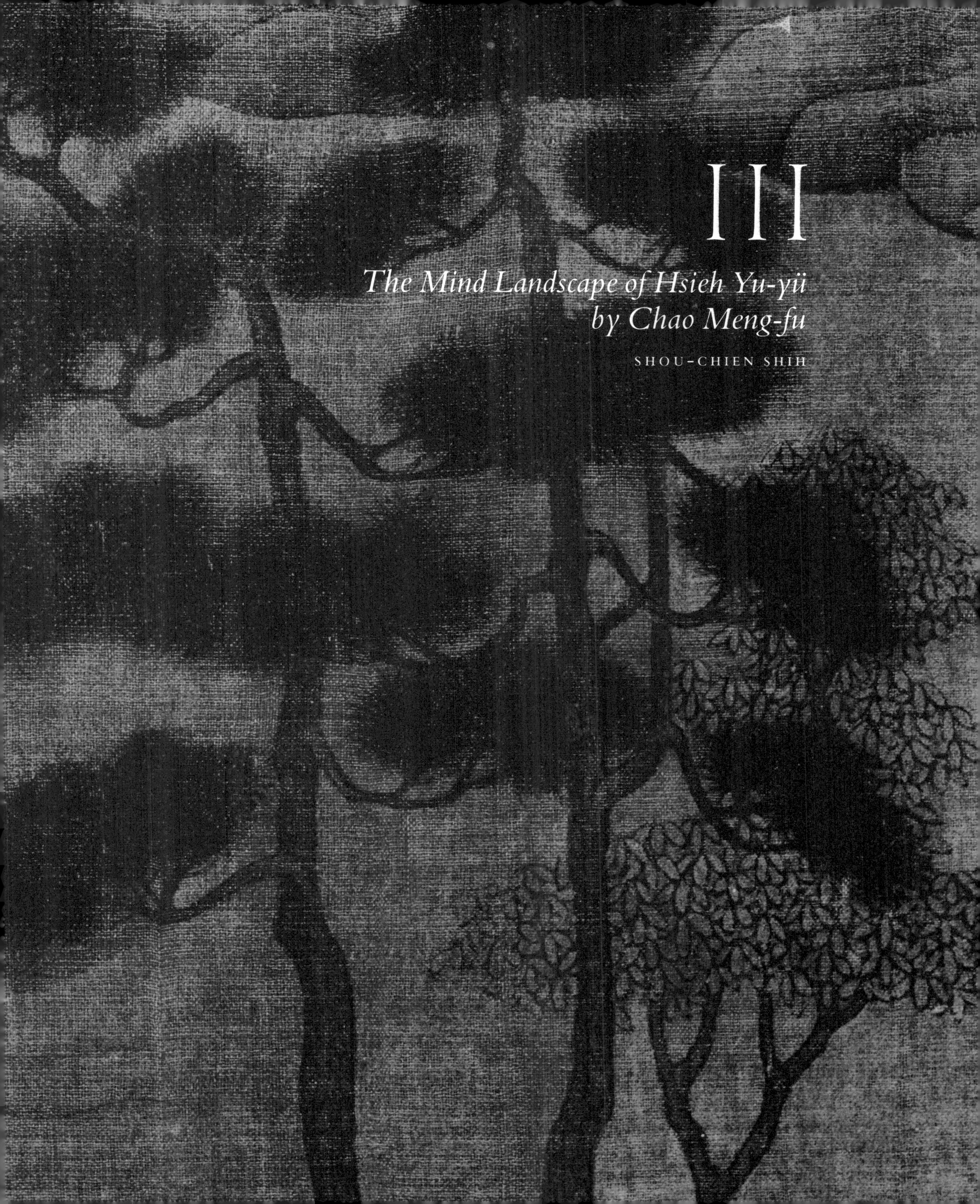

# III

## *The Mind Landscape of Hsieh Yu-yü by Chao Meng-fu*

SHOU-CHIEN SHIH

THE FIRST IMPRESSION of *The Mind Landscape of Hsieh Yu-yü*, a handscroll by Chao Meng-fu (1254–1322) now in the Edward L. Elliott Family Collection (no. 6),[1] is of a luxuriant landscape composed of strange cloudlike rock formations, piled layer upon layer to create an enormous mountain. The handscroll is painted in the archaic blue and green style, originally in a heavy application of bright malachite and azurite pigments that have since faded to somber, though still elegant, tones. The composition centers on the mountain that parallels the picture plane across the middle ground. Receding at each end of the composition and rising from the river that runs across the bottom of the scroll, the mountain extends beyond the silk to close off the view into the distance. Several groups of pine trees are placed at approximately equal intervals horizontally along the picture, and, to the left of the center of the scroll, a small flat area is outlined by closely piled boulders. In this "space cell," to use Ludwig Bachhofer's term, the recluse Hsieh K'un (Hsieh Yu-yü; 280–322) sits on a mat in a relaxed pose, gazing into the river. The mat is a tiger skin, the traditional symbol of wild, uncorrupted nature. The pose, the flowing stream, the space cell, and the overall soft-toned backdrop of the mountain all contribute to an otherworldly atmosphere of peace and purity, representing the hermit's aloof spiritual state—his "mind landscape." It is a scene immediately distinguishable from everyday experience—especially the harsh everyday experience prevalent at the time of its painter, Chao Meng-fu.

A descendant of the Sung royal line, Chao Meng-fu was twenty-five years old when the Yüan Mongols defeated the Sung dynasty in 1279. Under Mongol rule China suffered not only from the chaotic aftermath of war but also from the incompetent fiscal policies of the invaders. In an attempt to legitimize their dynasty and to stabilize the government, the Yüan leaders tried to coax the Sung aristocrats into rejoining government service. Many refused, believing that such participation would betray their moral integrity, but Chao, convinced that accepting an official position would be the best means of restoring order and preserving Chinese traditions that the Mongols might otherwise destroy, chose to serve at court. At the end of 1286 he accepted the emperor's summons and went to Peking; six months later he took on his duties as a division chief in the Ministry of War. The decision was undoubtedly difficult for him—it remained a controversial issue in subsequent histories for many centuries—and not only in moral terms; Chao was an accomplished painter, calligrapher, and poet, and, despite his royal upbringing, he was not immune to the appeal of the life of a recluse—contemplating nature in a secluded setting and pursuing the cultivation of the mind. To resolve the conflict between these contradictory aims, Chao Meng-fu opted to follow the modified type of eremitism known as *ch'ao-yin* (reclusion at court), performing his public and official duties while keeping his private life and inner thoughts separate and intact.

In his public role Chao Meng-fu worked courageously for a better, more humane government. He raised his voice against the powerful Uighur minister Sengge, for example, charging that Sengge's corrupt economic policies were harming the Chinese people as well as their culture. His protest did not arise from personal political ambition or loyalty to a particular ruler; rather he acted out of a deep concern for humanity. Sengge was finally condemned to death in 1291, and Chao Meng-fu went on to work for the reinstatement of the civil service recruitment examination, which was finally restored in 1315.[2]

Despite these impressive achievements in his public life, Chao continued to value his role as a spiritual recluse. He once expressed his philosophy of life in a eulogy for a friend whose name remains unknown (the original manuscript is in the National Palace Museum, Taipei):

> Do not seek riches in making a living.
> Do not seek glory in serving as an official.

In order to feel content in your own mind remain unperturbed, without desire for riches
and glory, and your neighbors will praise your goodness.
This is what "reputation" means.
Why must one seclude himself in craggy caves, conceal his footsteps in forest and mountains,
in order to have achieved purity [*ch'ing*]?[3]

The idea of remaining a recluse while serving at court had already had a long tradition in Chinese history by the time of Chao Meng-fu. Traditionally the recluse was a literati who renounced civil service, the career of the educated, withdrawing to devote himself entirely to self-cultivation, especially artistic and scholarly pursuits. Although the decision to diverge from the norm always entailed giving up the unchallenged social status and secure livelihood enjoyed by most literati, the recluse's seemingly untrammeled way of life had a genuine attraction of its own. It not only provided the possibility of escape from the political dangers inherent in public life, especially in time of social and political turmoil, but it also came to be regarded as an ideal, a practice thought to further communion between the human spirit and nature. Freedom from responsibilities of power, fame, and wealth, and a return to pristine nature certainly had a philosophical foundation in Chinese cultural history—in the writings of Lao-tzu and Chuang-tzu, the two patriarchs of Taoism, for example—but the ideal of the recluse was in opposition to orthodox state Confucianism, which insisted that public service is the first responsibility of the educated class. Partly because of this conflict with state Confucianism and partly because of the physical and other hardships the recluse inevitably faced, new, modified types of eremitism developed—*ch'ao-yin*, the "reclusion at court" later practiced by Chao Meng-fu, and *shih-yin* (reclusion at market). Instead of physical detachment from political and social life, these new forms of reclusion required only spiritual independence. This compromise way of life gained many proponents, and by the early fourth century Wang K'ang-chü went so far as to declare that the ability to combine the two patterns of life successfully was a higher achievement than to pursue a secluded life of enlightenment alone.[4]

Another fourth-century follower of *ch'ao-yin* was the subject of Chao Meng-fu's painting—Hsieh K'un, an important government official of the Eastern Tsin dynasty. His story, recorded in *A New Account of Tales of the World* (*Shih-shuo hsin-yü*) by Liu I-ch'ing (403–444), offers many parallels with Chao Meng-fu's life.

Hsieh K'un's time, like the Yüan, was a period of great turmoil. In 317 the Tsin government lost half of its territory to northern barbarians and was forced to move the capital south from Ch'ang-an across the Yangtze River to Nanking. In their makeshift court the newly recovered government had to confront not only the military threat from northern China but also the internal conflicts between the original oligarchy and local elites. Some military commanders at the front even became powerful enough to challenge the authority of the weakened central government.

In his official capacity Hsieh K'un was less concerned with the imperial family than with a private campaign to restore traditional political morality. Therefore, whatever the dynasty's difficulties, Hsieh K'un insisted that appropriate respect should be paid to the emperor. When the ambitious commander-in-chief Wang Tun refused to go to the Tsin court to swear his fealty to the emperor, Hsieh K'un argued eloquently to persuade him to change his mind. Although his plea did not sway Wang, it earned Hsieh a reputation as "an official who does his duty thoroughly."[5]

The cultivation of an independent spirit, however, rather than successful performance of official duties, was Hsieh's ultimate aspiration. Once, when he was asked by the crown prince, Ssu-ma Shao (299–325), to compare himself with Yü Liang (289–340), a contemporary with an equally excellent reputation as an official, Hsieh K'un replied, "As for sitting in ceremonial attire in the temple or hall and making the hundred officials keep to the rules, I am no match for Liang. But when it comes to '[living in seclusion on] a single hill' or '[fishing in] a single stream,' I consider myself superior to him."[6] To effect a compromise between his desire to become a hermit and his self-appointed mission to revive political morality in his troubled time, Hsieh K'un set up a clear distinction between his public and private life. While serving the state honestly and devotedly, he behaved unconventionally outside of court in order to free his mind from "unnatural" restrictions, return to nature, and achieve spiritual inviolability.

*A New Account of Tales of the World* asserts that Hsieh K'un consciously modeled himself on the most celebrated hermit figures in Chinese history, the Seven Sages of the Bamboo Grove: Chi K'ang, Juan Chi, Juan Hsien, Shan T'ao, Liu Ling, Hsiang Hsiu, and Wang Jung. Active about fifty years before Hsieh K'un's time, these literati were renowned for their dissolute behavior. Said to sit around naked with their hair unkempt, they exemplified extreme eccentricity. Hsieh K'un is said to have displayed his own unconventional nature by teasing a girl who was weaving next door until she became so annoyed that she broke his teeth. As with anecdotes of the Seven Sages, this tale was considered to be evidence of Hsieh's unfettered mind. And, also in the tradition of the Seven Sages, Hsieh K'un's legend became a model for later scholar-painters wishing to break with convention.

Ku K'ai-chih (ca. 344–ca. 406), a painter-official of the later Eastern Tsin period, also chose a life that balanced public duties with private nonconformity. In his time political persecution was common, and unguarded remarks invariably had tragic consequences, but Ku managed to speak his mind without repercussions by playing the fool. When Huan Hsüan, an ambitious warlord and rebel, removed the paintings from a cabinet that Ku had entrusted to him and returned the empty cabinet, Ku commented to his friends that the paintings were so divine that they had disappeared like Taoist immortals.[7] Such behavior earned Ku a reputation for eccentricity that was accepted as part of his artistic personality, but he may well have consciously chosen to act strangely as a self-protective guise.

Born after Hsieh K'un's time, Ku clearly admired the celebrated recluse. As recorded in *A New Account of Tales of the World*, Ku painted a portrait of Hsieh K'un, placing the recluse among crags and rocks. The use of landscape elements in a portrait was an innovation that Ku explained by quoting Hsieh's remark that his "single hill" and "single stream" were superior to Yü Liang's. "Therefore," Ku is reported to have said, "this gentleman should be placed among hills and streams."[8]

Although Ku's portrait of Hsieh K'un no longer existed in Chao Meng-fu's day, it was an art historical legend, and the description of Ku K'ai-chih's portrait as well as the stories of Hsieh K'un and Ku K'ai-chih contributed to Chao's choice of subject for *The Mind Landscape of Hsieh Yu-yü*. The colophons on the handscroll confirm that Chao made a parallel between his life and that of his predecessors, and they provide valuable information that helps to date the painting.

## *The Seals and Colophons*

At the lower left-hand corner of *The Mind Landscape of Hsieh Yu-yü* is Chao Meng-fu's seal, primary evidence that Chao Meng-fu is the painter of this handscroll. (Neither an inscription by the artist nor the seals from later collectors appear on the painting itself.) Following the painting are twelve colophons by later literati written on two sections of paper. The first paper includes eight colophons written by the literati of the fourteenth century and two by early seventeenth-century scholars. The second paper, separated from the first by a piece of silk, consists of two colophons by the mid-nineteenth-century collector Lo T'ien-ch'ih.

By the seals and colophons we can partially reconstruct the handscroll's history of ownership. The author of the first colophon, Chao Yung (ca. 1290–ca. 1360), the second son of Chao Meng-fu, states that the painting was treasured in the collection of a monk named Wu-yen, and that his colophon was written at the monk's request. Wu-yen was quite active in the late fourteenth century in the Su-chou area, where he befriended such prestigious literati as K'o Chiu-ssu (1290–1343) and Ku Ying (1310–1369) in the literary gatherings patronized by Ku. Since Chao Yung had social connections with the members of Ku's literary circle, he was acquainted with Wu-yen. The idea of inviting Chao Yung, himself a well-known painter and calligrapher in his own right, to inscribe a colophon on his late father's painting must have been irresistible. After Wu-yen the painting came into the possession of an unknown collector, who brought it in 1391 to the county school of Chien-ning (present Fukien province) to be examined by the four scholars who jointly composed the third colophon. Thereafter the history of the handscroll is unknown until 1607, when, as Ch'en Chi-ju's colophon informs us, it was in the collection of Hsiang Meng-huang, brother of the great collector Hsiang Yüan-pien (1525–1590). In the seventeenth century the handscroll was for a time owned by the famous collector Liang Ch'ing-piao (1620–1691), several of whose seals appear on the colophon. Liang was one of the foremost connoisseurs of his time, renowned for the high standard of his painting collection; he also owned another masterpiece by Chao Meng-fu, *Autumn Colors on the Ch'iao and Hua Mountains* (*Ch'iao-Hua ch'iu-se*; now in the collection of the National Palace Museum, Taipei). In the mid-nineteenth century Lo T'ien-ch'ih came into possession of the *Mind Landscape*; it bears several of his seals. Lo also inscribed the handscroll twice, first in 1846 and then in 1847. The handscroll recently came into the Edward L. Elliott Family Collection from the C. C. Wang collection.

Written in two lines, Chao Yung's colophon points out that the *Mind Landscape* was painted in Chao Meng-fu's early years. This colophon is not dated, but judging from the calligraphic style it was probably written around 1360.

After Chao Yung's colophon, the late Yüan dynasty painter Ni Tsan (1301–1374) inscribed a seven-character poem:

> This was Hsieh Yu-yü, who should be portrayed among the hills and cliffs;
> But at the Gull-Wave Pavilion [Chao Meng-fu's retreat], as the moon set, the window
> that opened to the night was empty.
> No one really understood the seemingly idiotic behavior of Hu-t'ou [Ku K'ai-chih].
> Handling his brush in front of the ink pond, he used painting to amuse himself.[9]

Probably written in the 1360s, Ni Tsan's poem not only identifies the portrait of Hsieh K'un by Ku K'ai-chih as the stylistic model of this painting, but it also alludes to the painting's underlying motivation. Subtle political overtones include the reference to the setting moon, a metaphor for the fall of the Sung dynasty. The "empty" window symbolizes Chao Meng-fu's sense of isolation from his friends after deciding to terminate his reclusive life and accept a position in the Yüan court. With these images Ni Tsan showed his sympathy toward Chao's inner conflict—between his urgent sense of responsibility toward society and his desire to follow the inner pursuits of a recluse. For Ni Tsan, Ku K'ai-chih's "seemingly idiotic behavior" had a parallel in Chao Meng-fu's controversial decision; both were conscious responses to unique situations confronted by sensitive minds and were little understood by their contemporaries. For both Ku K'ai-chih and Chao Meng-fu, painting was the only way to "amuse"—as Ni Tsan put it—and express themselves.

In contrast to Ni Tsan's reflective poem, the third colophon is a simple record by four literati of their viewing of the painting, dated 1391. These three colophons are on a single piece of paper, which, in the seventeenth century, was moved from its original location following the colophons by Yao Shih, Wang Ch'i, Teng Yü, Yü Chi, and Sung Wu. The transposition of colophons was probably intended to increase the commercial value of the handscroll: Chao Yung's identification of the scroll as an early work of his father's is the scroll's most impressive piece of documentation, perhaps even more valuable for the collector than the beautiful calligraphy itself; and the colophon of Ni Tsan, who was admired as a great painter and a recluse, also adds to the value of the work. The change in sequence of colophons was surely complete by the time of Liang Ch'ing-piao, since he placed his seal on the seam joining the two papers.

The present order of the colophons by Chao Yung, Ni Tsan, and the four literati of 1391 disrupts the historical progression, which originally began with the colophon of Chao Meng-fu's lifetime friend Yao

Shih (d. ca. 1318), one of the Eight Talents of Wu-hsing. Like Ni Tsan's colophon, Yao Shih's is a poem in seven-character verse. It reads:

> Though sullied by yellow dust and born with the talent for serving in government hall
> and state temple,
> With his dashing, elegant nature and charming, romantic style, no one was his equal;
> Speech with unworldly purity [Hsieh K'un] and the painting of magnificent quality
> [Ku K'ai-chih's portrait of Hsieh], the one as well the other, have been admired and
> appreciated generation after generation,
> And the girl at the loom [the weaver whom Hsieh K'un teased], to her regret, has been
> a topic for a thousand years.

The similarity between Hsieh and Chao is also the subject of the next colophon, written by Wang Ch'i (fl. ca. 1290–1310), a close friend of the early Yüan scholar-poet Yao Sui (1238–1313) and probably a friend of Chao Meng-fu's. Wang's colophon, in the form of a short essay, reads:

> When Ku Ch'ang-k'ang [Ku K'ai-chih] painted Hsieh Yu-yü's portrait, he positioned him among crags and rocks. People asked him the reason. He replied, "Yu-yü himself claimed that his 'single hill' and 'single stream' were superior [to Yü Liang's]; therefore this gentleman should be placed among hills and streams." Although his [Hsieh's] character as a recluse was so refined and elegant that it deserves to be admired, he could also remain faithful as a minister. At that time few among his colleagues could emulate him [in terms of fidelity]. Several hundred years later, it is the old gentleman of the Pine-Snow Studio [Chao Meng-fu's studio], whose mind and spirit could really understand this and translate it into painting. It is both highly appropriate in its design and extremely wonderful in its artistic idea. Were Ch'ang-k'ang reborn today, he would nod his head in agreement when he saw this painting.

The colophons by Yao Shih and Wang Ch'i provide the most important information for establishing a date for *The Mind Landscape of Hsieh Yu-yü*. As Wang Ch'i suggests, Chao Meng-fu may be seen—and, more important, probably saw himself—as the early Yüan period counterpart of Hsieh K'un. Chao's depiction of Hsieh K'un was probably a conscious attempt to identify himself with an appropriate role model, rather than an arbitrary choice of subject. Other recluses whom he might have painted, such as T'ao Ch'ien (365–427), who refused to serve in government because he despised the politics of his day, were not as close to Chao Meng-fu's own sympathies. Both Yao Shih and Wang Ch'i's interpretations of the handscroll imply it was painted while Chao Meng-fu was serving in the Yüan government. Chao Yung's declaration that this painting was one of his father's early works, in combination with the subject of the painting, a statement about the alternatives of service or retreat, suggests that *The Mind Landscape of Hsieh Yu-yü* was painted shortly after Chao Meng-fu decided to accept the summons of the Yüan government in 1286.

Wang Ch'i's colophon is followed by those of Teng Yü (fl. early 14th century), Yü Chi (1272–1348), and Sung Wu (1260–ca. 1340). Both Yü Chi and Sung Wu were well-known writers a generation younger than Chao Meng-fu, who had received encouragement from Chao because of their literary talent. The two colophons following Sung Wu's both date from the beginning of the seventeenth century. Ch'en Chi-ju's (1558–1639) one-line colophon of 1607 simply records the date and the place of his viewing. Tung Ch'i-ch'ang's (1555–1636) colophon is longer and more detailed.

Tung was probably the most influential art critic in Chinese history. By the time he contributed his colophon to the *Mind Landscape*, he had already carefully studied Chao Meng-fu's *Autumn Colors on the Ch'iao and Hua Mountains*, which, he wrote, "captures the refinement of T'ang without its minutiae, grasps the vigor of Northern Sung without its harshness," pronouncing it "the greatest brush masterpiece in the whole life of Wen-min [Chao Meng-fu's posthumous name]."[10] When he first viewed the *Mind Landscape*,

Tung Ch'i-ch'ang apparently failed at first to recognize it as a work by Chao Meng-fu because its style differed so greatly from *Autumn Colors on the Ch'iao and Hua Mountains*. Tung admits in his colophon that had it not been for the Yüan colophons, he would have mistakenly attributed the painting to Chao Po-chü (fl. ca. 1120–62), another descendant of the Sung imperial clan known for his revival in the mid-twelfth century of the blue and green style of landscape painting, because of the "unnatural" quality of the draftsmanship.

Tung Ch'i-ch'ang's confusion can be understood when the painting style of the Elliott handscroll is compared with that of the *Autumn Colors* scroll. Unlike the *Mind Landscape*, Chao's *Autumn Colors* shows an open landscape with a convincing receding ground plane. Color is used only lightly in *Autumn Colors*, and the painting is more representational, with a greater sense of depth and volume than in the *Mind Landscape*. If the style of *Autumn Colors* was intended to be "modern," then the style of the *Mind Landscape* was designed to be "archaic." As discussed in the Yüan colophons, Chao Meng-fu wished to recreate an Eastern Tsin dynasty portrait; it seems natural that he would have used an Eastern Tsin dynasty style. Since Ku K'ai-chih's original portrait of Hsieh K'un was no longer available in the thirteenth century, in trying to recreate an "authentic" portrait of Hsieh K'un, Chao first had to solve two problems: he had to interpret the original fragmentary literary account describing this official-recluse, and he had to translate these abstract ideas into a pictorial language.

## *A New Painting Style*

In the traditional approach of learning ancient classics by a thorough study of later commentaries, Chao Meng-fu seems to have reconstructed Ku K'ai-chih's portrait of Hsieh K'un from examination of texts and of related paintings dated from the fourth century to the thirteenth century. The study of the tradition did not lead him to create a pastiche of paintings from the more recent T'ang and Sung periods. Instead he returned to the origins of the tradition, where the purest expression of the hermit ideal was presumably to be found. Choosing an appropriate role model, Hsieh K'un, Chao found a solution that differed from that of many of his Sung forerunners who depicted classical themes. Chao revived an old style but infused it with new meaning.

Since Chao Meng-fu followed the original literary description of Ku K'ai-chih's painting, his interpretation was faithful to the tradition he cherished. His placement of Hsieh K'un in the space cell, edged by rocky hills and bordered in front by a stream, for instance, is a direct illustration of the *New Account of Tales of the World* anecdote about Ku K'ai-chih's ingenious design of Hsieh K'un's portrait: Ku painted Hsieh K'un among crags and rocks because Hsieh said he excelled among hills and streams.

Chao's interpretation, furthermore, must have derived from his own study of copies of Ku K'ai-chih's works as well as others from Ku's period. A set of pictures on clay bricks, recently excavated from the Nanking area, depicts the Seven Sages of the third century A.D. and another recluse, Jung Ch'i-ch'i, from the fifth century B.C.[11] The portrait of Juan Chi (210–263) provides one possible source for the *Mind Landscape*. Here the subject sits in a pose similar to that of Chao Meng-fu's Hsieh K'un, and the tiger skin in the portrait bears a strong resemblance to that in the *Mind Landscape* (fig. 1).

Dated to the late fourth or early fifth century, the Nanking clay pictures very possibly imitate a well-known version by an ancient master on silk or paper. Several painters had used the Seven Sages as a subject before Ku K'ai-chih's time, and Ku K'ai-chih was aware of them.[12] Nevertheless the most plausible source of the Nanking pictures is Ku K'ai-chih. He was certainly the most important painter in Nanking in the late fourth century, he was prolific, and his admiration for the Seven Sages is well known. The notion can further be supported by a list drawn up by Chang Yen-yüan (fl. ca. mid-9th century), which specifically attributes two portrait paintings of Jung Ch'i-ch'i and Juan Hsien, who also appear in the Nanking brick version, to Ku K'ai-chih.[13]

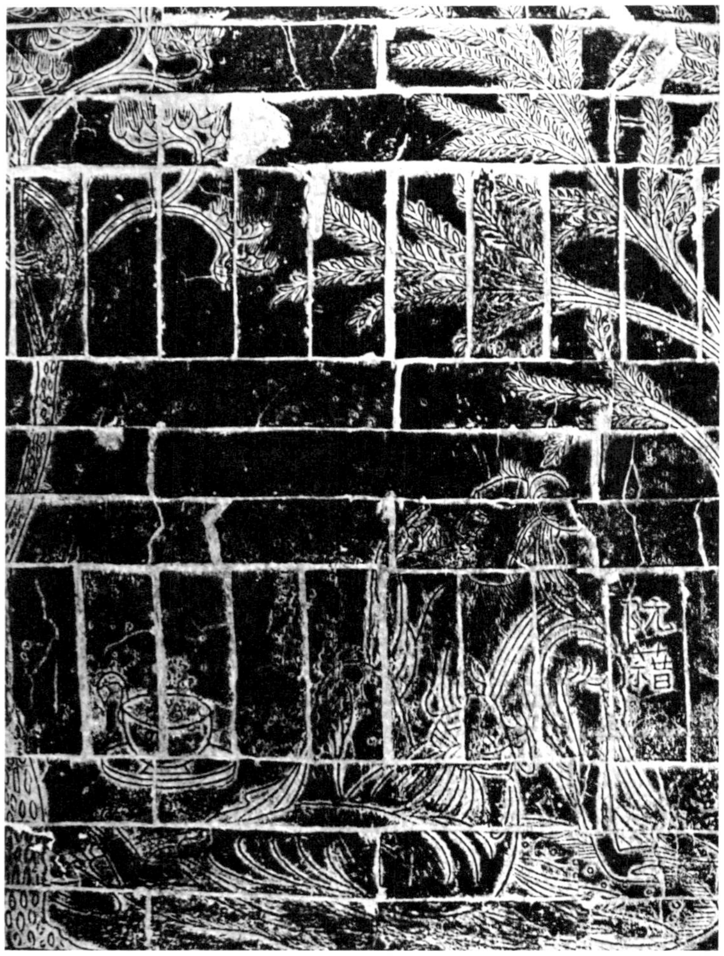


Fig. 1. Anonymous, portrait of Juan Chi, detail, *Seven Sages of the Bamboo Grove and Jung Ch'i-ch'i* (*Chu-lin ch'i-hsien yü Jung Ch'i-ch'i*). Late 4th–early 5th century. Rubbing from impressed clay bricks. Measurements unknown. Tomb at Hsi-shan-ch'iao, Nanking

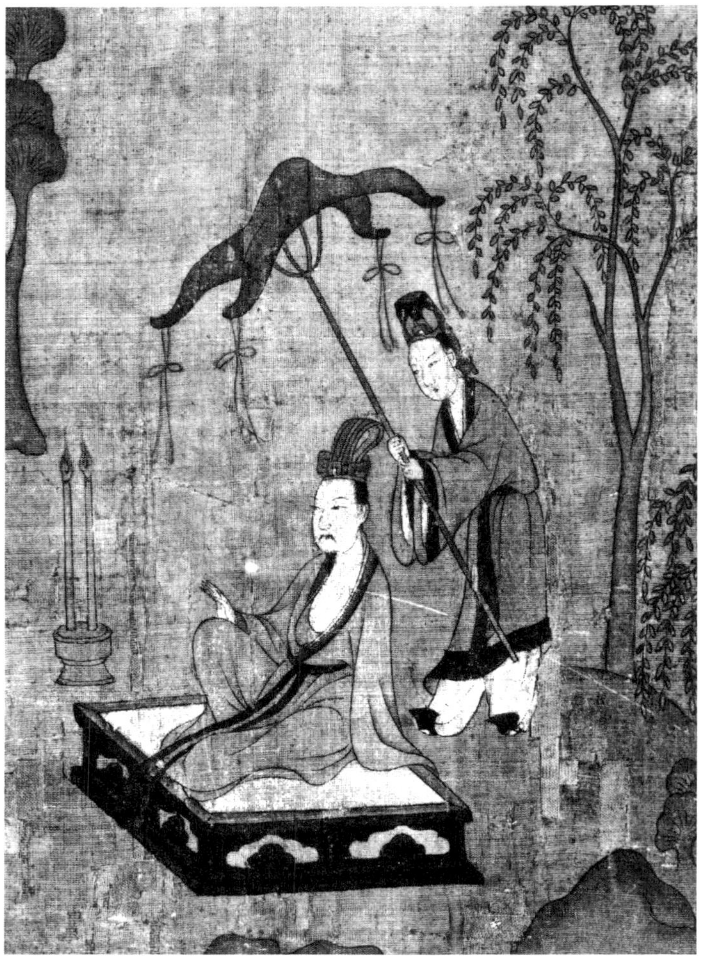

Fig. 2. Attributed to Ku K'ai-chih, detail, *Nymph of the Lo River* (*Lo-shen fu*). Undated, late 4th century. Handscroll, ink and color on silk. 27.1 x 572.8 cm ($10^{5}/_{8}$ in. x 18 ft. $9^{1}/_{2}$ in.). Palace Museum, Peking

Several similarities between the *Mind Landscape* and *The Seven Sages of the Bamboo Grove* indicate that Chao Meng-fu was inspired by a personal acquaintance with the ancient painting. There is no evidence showing the existence of any Six Dynasties version of the painting in the early Yüan period, but the collector Wang Hu-ch'en owned a T'ang copy of *The Seven Sages of the Bamboo Grove*, and Chao may well have seen it. Wang served as an official in Su-chou from 1278 to 1283 and in Chen-chiang afterwards, and apparently had good relations with artists in the Hang-chou and Wu-hsing areas.[14] His collection was always available to art enthusiasts, and Chao Meng-fu, as the leading figure of the Wu-hsing literati, would have been a most welcome guest. Chao's *Mind Landscape of Hsieh Yu-yü* may thus have been inspired by an acquaintance with the archaic representation of *The Seven Sages of the Bamboo Grove*, possibly painted by Ku K'ai-chih, through T'ang copies like the version in Wang Hu-ch'en's collection.

Another possible source of the thematic type of recluse painting was another painting attributed to Ku K'ai-chih, *Nymph of the Lo River* (*Lo-shen fu*; fig. 2). Representing one scene from the poem composed by Ts'ao Chih (192–232), the painting depicts the poet seated on a platform surrounded by landscape motifs—a mountain, a stream, and trees. Although the position of the poet's legs recalls that of Juan Chi's in the Nanking bricks, the pose of this figure—leaning on the left hand, with torso held straight—is generally more formal. Although *Nymph of the Lo River* omits the tiger skin, it provides the first complete prototype depiction of a seated gentleman in a landscape setting. At least two copies of Ku's *Nymph of the Lo River* were extant in Chao's time. One had been removed from the Sung imperial collection to the Yüan court in 1276 after the fall of Hang-chou; according to the Yüan art historian T'ang Hou (fl. ca. early 14th century), the second was in a private collection in the south.[15]

Chao Meng-fu was familiar with at least one of the versions of this famous painting. On one of the three versions of the *Nymph of the Lo River* known today, a copy in the Palace Museum, Peking (the other two are in the Liaoning Provincial Museum and the Freer Gallery, Washington, D.C.), probably datable to the twelfth century, Chao Meng-fu's seal appears in the lower right corner of the painting silk.[16]

Chao Meng-fu's *Mind Landscape* painting also shows some resemblance to one of the scenes in a late copy of a T'ang painting, *The Ten Views of the Thatched Hut* (*Ts'ao-t'ang shih-chih t'u*; fig. 3), attributed to the hermit Lu Hung (fl. 1st half 8th century), which depicts the scenic surroundings of Lu's retreat. The fifth scene, "Cloud-Brocade Water Flowing" ("Yün-chin-tsung"), shows a rocky cliff on the water's edge where the hermit spends his time listening to the flowing water. The bare rocks that occupy a large part of the composition and the abundant streams that flow into each other recall the scenery surrounding the figure of Hsieh K'un in Chao Meng-fu's painting. Although no literary evidence suggests that Chao Meng-fu was acquainted with the *Ten Views* painting, he must have known similar renderings of the hermit theme through copies by Sung artists. Among these copies, one by Li Kung-lin (ca. 1049–1106) was in the collection of Wang Chih (late 13th century), who was, like Wang Hu-ch'en, one of the most important collectors of the early Yüan period.[17] As Wang's close friend, Chao Meng-fu no doubt had many chances to see paintings in Wang's collection, including Li Kung-lin's copy of *The Ten Views of the Thatched Hut*. Chao could also have seen a copy executed by Lin Yen-hsiang (fl. ca. 1140), which was known to collectors in southern China in the late thirteenth century.[18] This is suggested by the appearance, recorded in literary sources, of one of Chao's seals on another copy of Lu Hung's painting, now unfortunately inaccessible.[19]

Another possible source is a fan painting of a seated hermit attributed to Ma Ho-chih (*chin-shih*, 1131, d. ca. 1190), the leading artist in the early Southern Sung painting academy (fig. 4), which shows a hermit

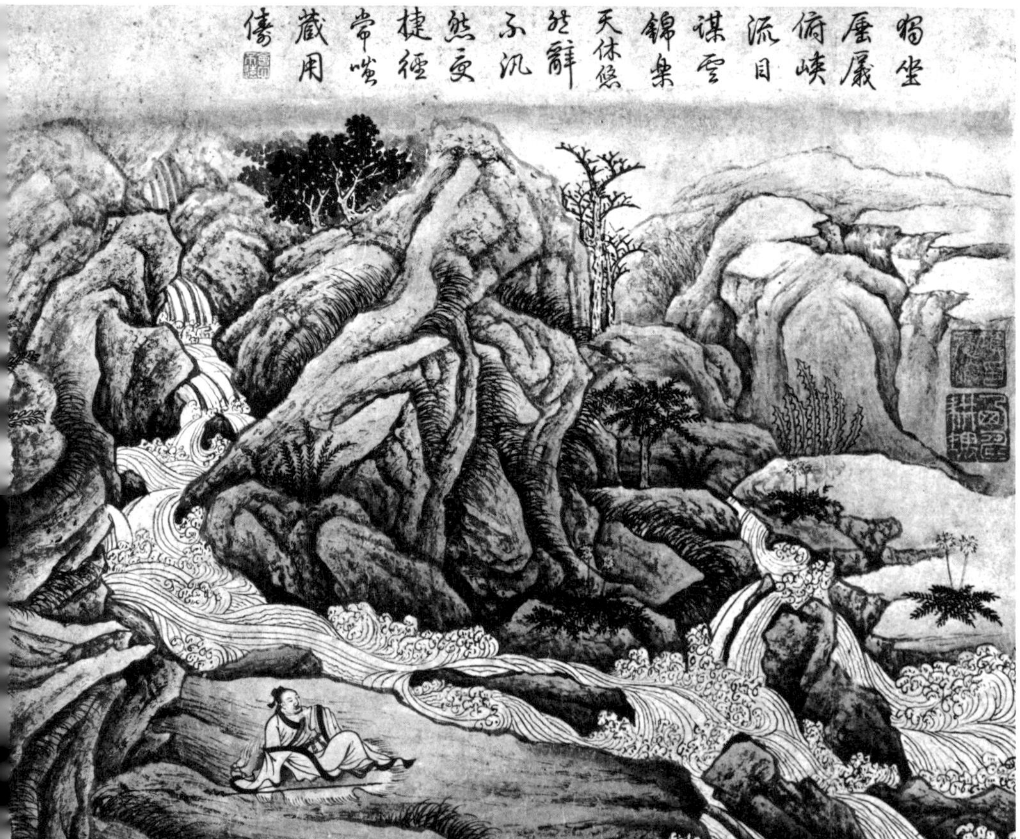

Fig. 3. Attributed to Lu Hung, detail, *The Ten Views of the Thatched Hut* (*Ts'ao-t'ang shih-chih t'u*). Undated, early 8th century. Handscroll, ink on paper. 29.4 x 60.0 cm (11 5/8 x 23 5/8 in.). National Palace Museum, Taipei

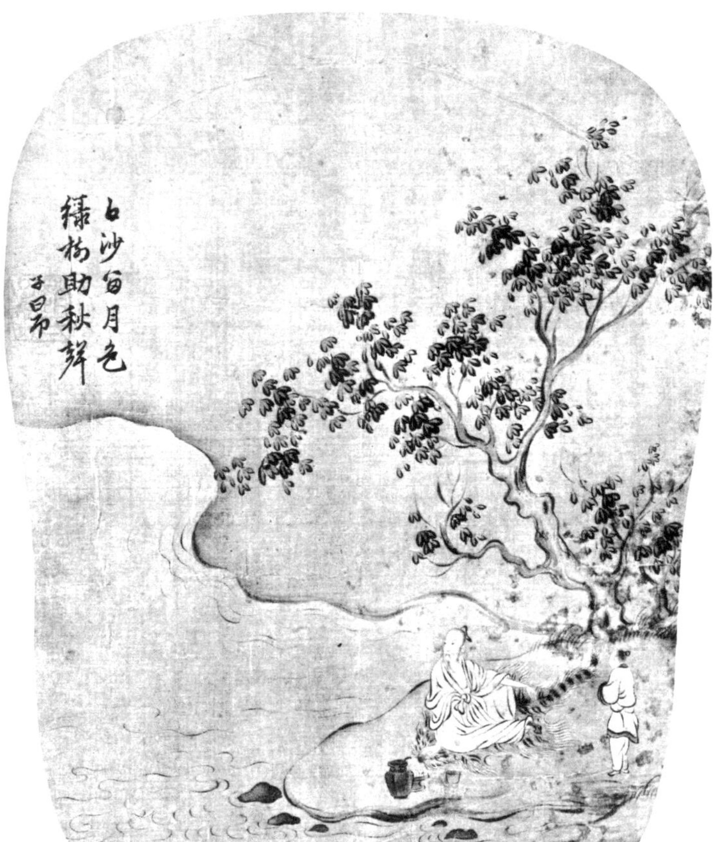

Fig. 4. Ma Ho-chih, *Hermit on Tiger Skin* (*Yüeh-she ch'iu-sheng*). Undated, mid-12th century. Gourd-shaped fan, ink and color on silk. 30.0 x 22.0 cm (11 3/4 x 8 5/8 in.). Liaoning Provincial Museum

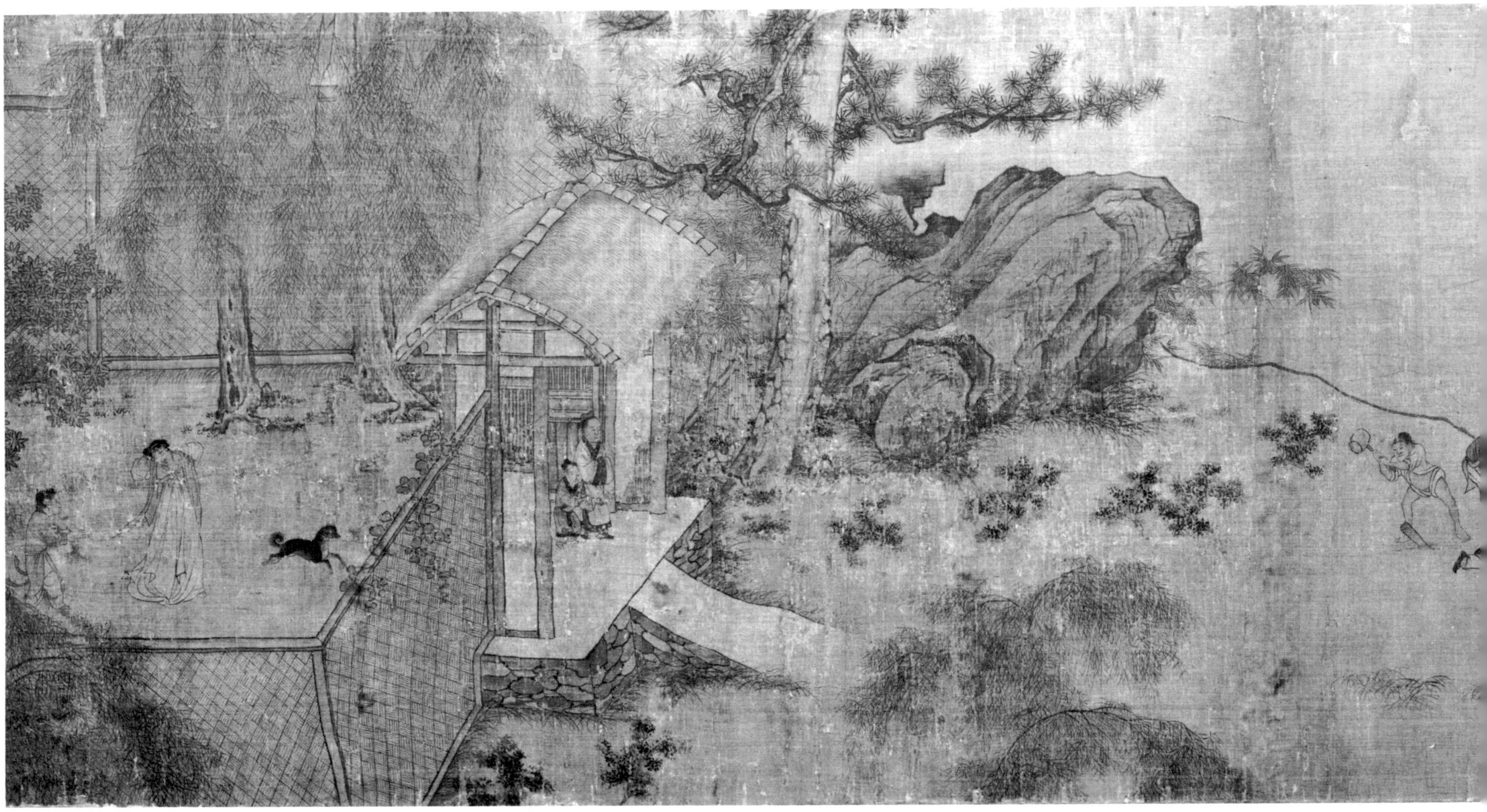

Fig. 5. Attributed to Li Kung-lin, detail, *T'ao Yüan-ming Returning Home* (*Yüan-ming kuei-yin t'u*). Undated, late 11th century. Handscroll, ink and light color on silk.

sitting in a relaxed pose, on a tiger skin beside a flowing stream, motifs that also appear in Chao's handscroll. That the shared elements in these two paintings do not result from mere coincidence is proven by the existence of a two-line poem inscribed on the Liaoning fan by Chao Meng-fu. The lines read:

> The color of moonlight stays on the white sand,
> The music of autumn is supplemented by the green willow.

They are actually derived from a poem entitled "The House on the Wang River" ("T'i Wang-hsi-kuan") by the T'ang poet Li Po, with only one character, *liu* (willow), replacing the original *chu* (bamboo). The style of the calligraphy is close to that of another piece of writing entitled *A Letter to Hsien-yü Shu*, datable to 1286–87, in the collection of the National Palace Museum, Taipei,[20] and therefore very close to the approximate date of the *Mind Landscape* handscroll. The inscription confirms Chao's knowledge of the Liaoning painting in particular, and to the seated hermit theme of Southern Sung painting in general, in his reconstruction of the classic image of Hsieh K'un.

Chao Meng-fu's study of the traditional representation of the hermit theme played a decisive role in his development of the iconography of Hsieh K'un's *Mind Landscape*. From Ma Ho-chih of the Southern Sung, the eremitic theme may be traced back to Lu Hung of the T'ang period and finally to the classic master Ku K'ai-chih of the fourth century. Chao Meng-fu chose the phrase "should be placed among the hills and streams" from *A New Account of Tales of the World* as the essential feature of Ku's portrait of Hsieh, because that image fitted easily into the painting tradition of seated hermit representation.

In the process of enlivening the old pictorial tradition concerning reclusion, Chao Meng-fu created a new illustrative form. From the two main types of Chinese eremitism, one derived from *The Seven Sages of the Bamboo Grove* and the other from T'ao Ch'ien, developed two separate painting traditions, the "iconic" and the "narrative." The iconic type, exemplified by *The Seven Sages of the Bamboo Grove*, refers to no known sequence of anecdotes and indicates no narrative elements of time and place. As with religious icons

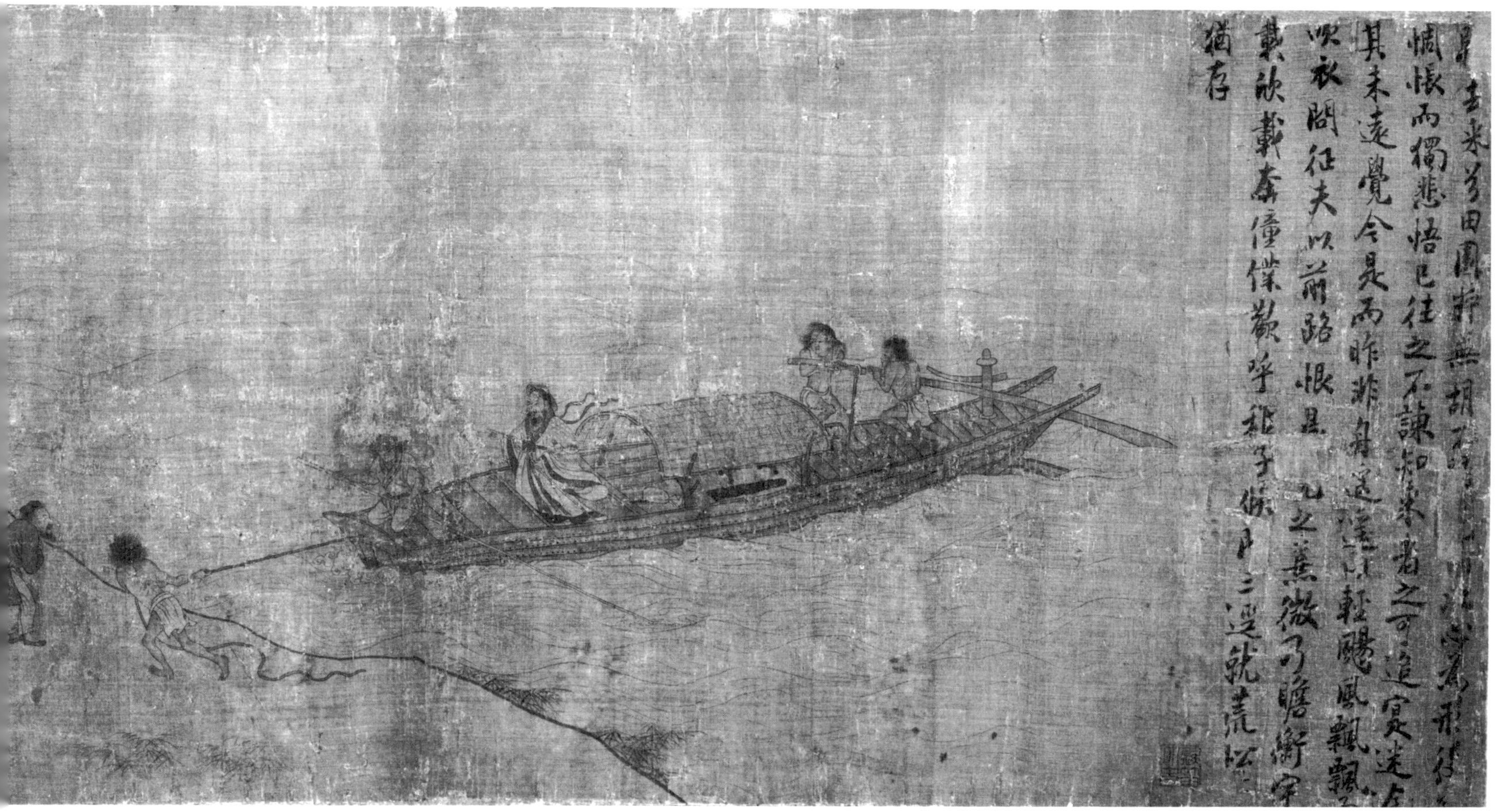

37.0 x 518.5 cm (14 5/8 in. x 17 ft. 1/4 in.). Freer Gallery of Art, Washington, D.C.

this type of image seldom includes sufficient details to permit one subject to be distinguished from another. Since only vague, generalized props and facial characteristics were depicted, explanatory cartouches had to be included for identification of the figures. By Chao Meng-fu's time the iconic hermit representation—the hermit posed under a tree, or the seated hermit in a landscape or garden setting—had developed into a popular genre of Chinese figure painting.[21]

In narrative paintings of hermits, the painter included elements that identified it as a particular scene from a story or anecdote about a legendary or historical recluse. This "narrative" type of representing the theme of reclusion was first developed in paintings depicting T'ao Ch'ien. T'ao's long narrative poem "Homecoming" ("Kuei-ch'ü-lai ts'u") has long been considered by scholars in China and Japan to be one of the most important literary sources of eremitism. Scholars, especially in the Sung period, praised T'ao Ch'ien as an ideal recluse; the famous historian Ou-yang Hsiu (1007–1072) considered T'ao's "Homecoming" to be the best poem in the history of Chinese literature. Also in the eleventh century Li Kung-lin produced his celebrated handscroll illustrating T'ao Ch'ien's "Homecoming," which became a model for later paintings. Although Li Kung-lin's original is no longer extant, several early copies show that it offered an alternative to the iconic tradition by presenting a series of scenes, each evoking a specific line or couplet of the poem (fig. 5). In the narrative painting tradition, whether or not the appropriate section of the text precedes each scene, the painter essentially functions as a storyteller, and the painting serves as an illustration of the literary work.

Neither "iconic" nor "narrative" accurately characterizes Chao Meng-fu's *Mind Landscape of Hsieh Yu-yü*. Chao certainly absorbed certain influences from the iconic illustration type, but his handscroll also reveals narrative qualities never found in iconic depictions. The painting originates in the conversation between Hsieh K'un and Ssu-ma Shao popularized by *A New Account of Tales of the World*, but instead of mapping out the story scene by scene, Chao interpreted only the last section of the anecdote, using it to suggest the entire text. Chao's handscroll implies every nuance of Hsieh K'un's experience in a single scene without limiting it to a depiction of a particular place and time, as is usually the case in a narrative painting. In effect, Chao Meng-fu invented a combination type of hermit picture.

Unlike the iconic type, this new combination type does not rely on cartouches or inscriptions to identify its subject but on the viewer's familiarity with the literary text. The very specific formal relationship between the seated hermit and the landscape around him provides the clue that helps viewers associate it with the anecdote about Hsieh K'un. This new type is less concerned with illustrating a story than with depicting an abstract idea, a certain state of mind. Chao's painting does not attempt to present a pictorial biography enumerating the details of Hsieh K'un's life, but to summarize the significance of reclusion.

The appearance of this combined form owed its origins mainly to the specific subject matter, and it was subject matter of supreme personal significance for Chao Meng-fu. Through Hsieh K'un's image he intended to portray his own feelings on the ideal of reclusion. For this purpose the iconic approach would have been too general to convey his specific message, and the narrative approach, too restricted. So he modified the narrative mode, adopting the traditional setting to establish the identity of Hsieh K'un, and at the same time rendering his central figure on the iconic tradition. By so doing he created a new "lyric" type of hermit picture that would give full expression to his profound personal identification with Hsieh K'un.

This type of painting marked an innovative departure in late thirteenth-century Chinese art. Certainly classical texts had long been used to convey highly valued concepts, and Chao Meng-fu was not the first to imbue narrative representation with an expressive quality. As early as the late eleventh and twelfth centuries, Li Kung-lin and his major follower, Ma Ho-chih, had achieved expressive interpretations of their narrative subjects; Li Kung-lin's illustration (now in The Art Museum, Princeton University) of the *Classic of Filial Piety* (*Hsiao-ching*) and Ma Ho-chih's several sets of illustrations of the *Classic of Poetry* (*Shih-ching*) are admirable contributions to this tradition. Ma Ho-chih, for example, successfully expressed the people's hope for the arrival of the true king of virtue from the *Classic of Poetry*. His illustrations thus served to praise the newly founded Southern Sung dynasty, then challenged by a puppet government supported by the Tartars.[22] But Chao Meng-fu added a fresh element to this tradition: whereas Li Kung-lin and Ma Ho-chih had used their expressive styles to interpret traditional, external subjects, he subordinated classical subjects to the expression of his own emotions. Ma Ho-chih illustrated in his *Classic of Poetry* handscroll theories about ideal government, but in the Elliott handscroll Chao Meng-fu acted as a detached observer of his own attitudes through identification with the fourth-century court recluse Hsieh K'un. To accomplish this end Chao Meng-fu originated the *hsieh-i* (writing-idea) approach, the expression of emotion in painting, for the narrative tradition, an innovation that shaped all later artistic development in China.

## *Emotion in Painting*

The new task for the artist—to express emotion in painting—required Chao Meng-fu and the others who followed this approach to reconsider available stylistic vocabularies. The representational style, primarily aimed at successful three-dimensional illusion, had been continually refined by Southern Sung artists until it reached its height of development in Chao's day. But for Chao's purposes the archaistic Six Dynasties style, characterized by schematic forms and unrealistic space, was more suitable, not only because the subject of Hsieh K'un was an archaic one, but also because the archaic style allowed the artist the psychological distance he needed to detach himself from the real world and invent a reclusive paradise. For the first time in Chinese painting history, a painter revived an earlier stylistic tradition instead of trying to achieve the most realistic representation possible.

In the Elliott handscroll individual motifs and overall structure have a distinct archaistic flavor. Instead of using well-articulated rock forms, for example, like those in other twelfth-century landscape paintings in the blue and green manner, such as Chao Po-chü's *Autumn Colors on Rivers and Mountains* (*Chiang-shan ch'iu-she*; fig. 6) and Wang Hsi-meng's *A Thousand* Li *of Rivers and Mountains* (*Ch'ien-li chiang-shan*; fig. 7),

Fig. 6. Chao Po-chü, detail, *Autumn Colors on Rivers and Mountains* (*Chiang-shan ch'iu-she*). Date unknown. Handscroll, ink and color on silk. Measurements unknown. Palace Museum, Peking

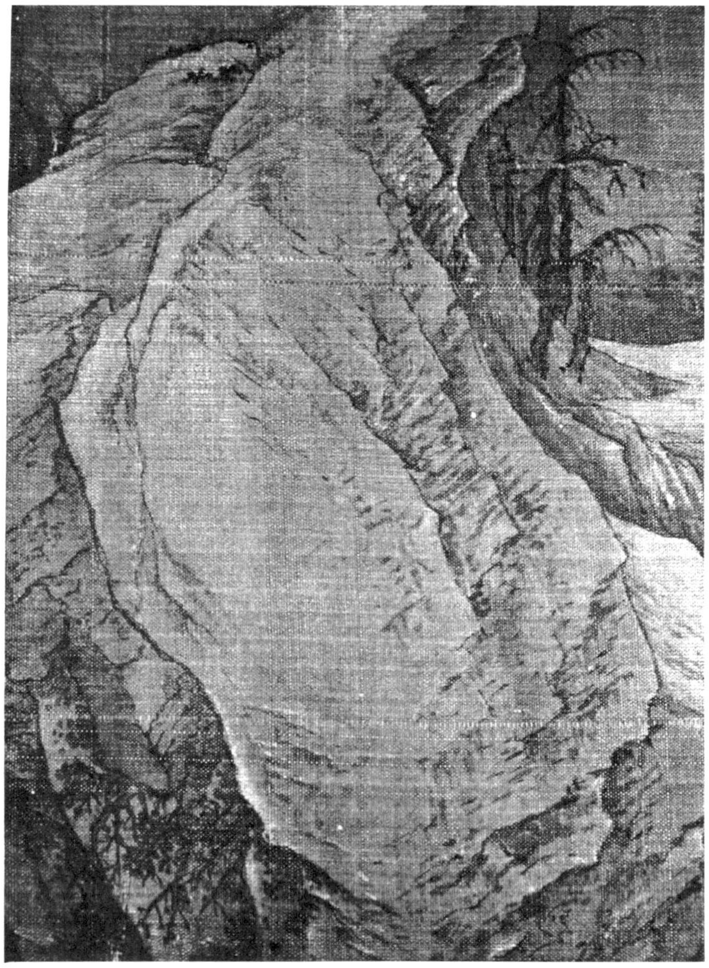

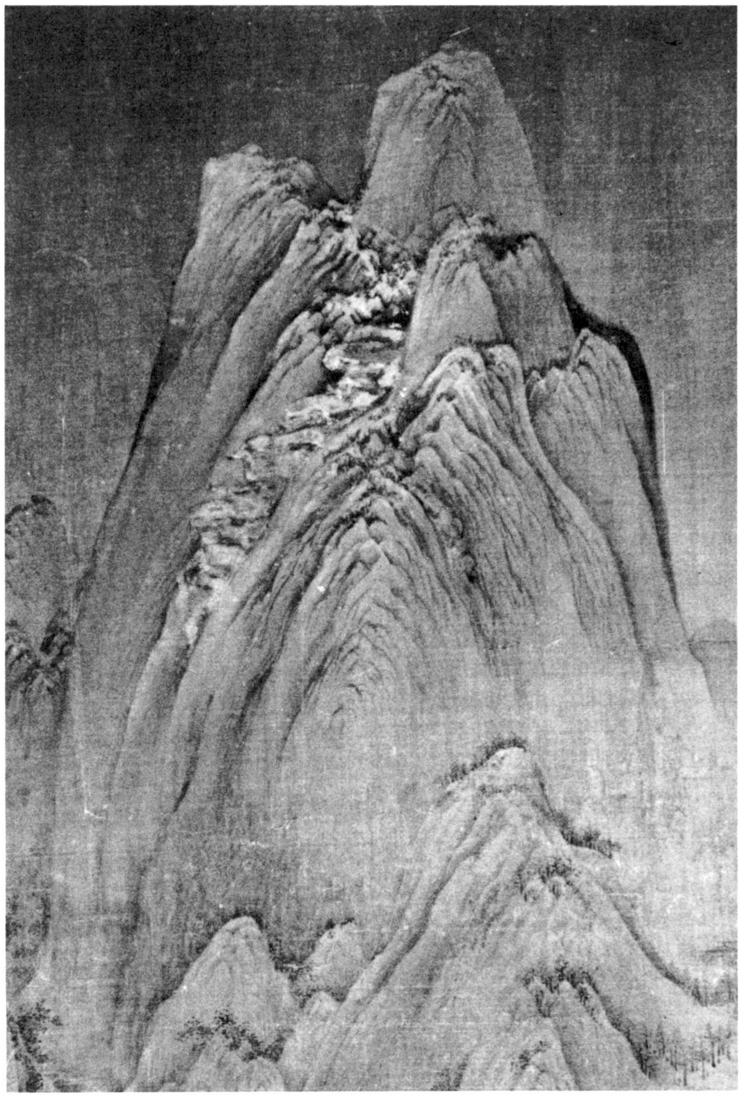

Fig. 7. Wang Hsi-meng, detail, *A Thousand* Li *of Rivers and Mountains* (*Ch'ien-li chiang-shan*). Dated 1113. Handscroll, ink and color on silk. 51.5 x 1,191.5 cm (20¼ in. x 39 ft. 1⅛ in.). Palace Museum, Peking

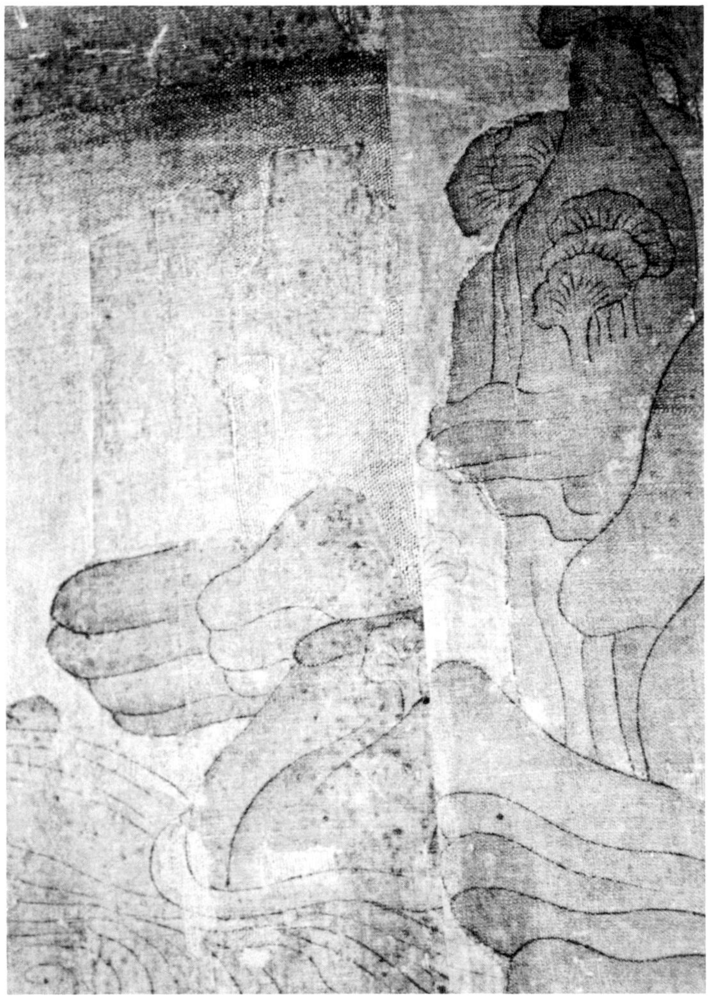

Fig. 8. Attributed to Ku K'ai-chih, detail, *Nymph of the Lo River* (*Lo-shen fu*). Undated, late 4th century. Handscroll, ink and color on silk. 27.1 x 572.8 cm (10⅝ in. x 18 ft. 9½ in.). Palace Museum, Peking

both now in the collection of the Palace Museum, Peking, Chao Meng-fu drew his rocks without texture strokes, describing the surface of the rocks only with pigment. The soft round edges of his rocks give them a cloudlike appearance. The direct source for such rock formations, as the colophons of this handscroll suggest, is the work of Ku K'ai-chih, particularly *Nymph of the Lo River*. Chao's indebtedness to this painting, especially to the Peking version which he knew, is also revealed by his use of almost identical landscape motifs that appear in the Peking version (fig. 8). In both handscrolls, for example, the rock forms as well as the edges of the riverbank are defined by curving outlines. Even in the piling of rocks to form a mountain, the paintings have a striking similarity.

The space cell is another archaic stylistic allusion. It is not dependent on brushstrokes, but rather on the configuration of the rocks and the tilting-up of the ground plane at an unnatural angle. An early example of this spatial structure can be found in the wall painting illustrating the Mahāsattva Jātaka story in Cave 428 in Tun-huang, dated on the basis of stylistic analysis to the third quarter of the sixth century (fig. 9). Chao Meng-fu borrowed several other compositional devices from the art of the fifth and sixth centuries for his *Mind Landscape*: the use of tall trees spaced at even intervals across the foreground, the naïve disproportion of the figure in comparison with trees and hills—all are archaic compositional elements also seen in the Nanking *Seven Sages of the Bamboo Grove* bricks. All of these elements make the style of Chao Meng-fu's *Mind Landscape* far closer to that of its archaic prototypes than to that of its immediate predecessors, such as Ma Ho-chih's fan painting of the seated hermit—in spite of their shared subject matter. Chao Meng-fu certainly knew that every period has a particular "structure" for presenting artistic forms; he fully discussed this idea in his theory of calligraphy in his *Thirteen Colophons to the Preface to the Orchid Pavilion Gathering* (*Lan-t'ing shih-san pa*).[23] In re-creating a long-lost classic painting and revealing himself through the painting, he rejected, no doubt consciously, the sophisticated illusionistic structure developed by twelfth- and thirteenth-century landscape painters.

Like Chinese poets, who favored the use of classical allusions to convey certain specific sentiments, Chao sought to express his desire to retreat into seclusion by adopting a style from the past. The archaistic rock forms, the mountain formation, and the awkward spatial setting all detached the artist from the real world in which he was reluctantly involved and plunged him back into the time of Ku K'ai-chih and of Hsieh K'un and T'ao Ch'ien. Just as paintings of horses by Han Kan (fl. ca. 740–56) typify the T'ang dynasty, a time of military power achieved through strong cavalry, Ku K'ai-chih's work exemplifies the golden age of eremitism. Perhaps this is the main reason that the Elliott handscroll, a work belonging to the general category of blue and green landscape painting, bears no relationship to any work attributed to Li Ssu-hsün (651–716) or Li Chao-tao (fl. ca. 670–ca. 730), the acknowledged masters of this genre.

Chao also demonstrated emotion through a highly expressive brush style. Calligraphy has long been referred to as an artist's "mind print." Literati artists believe that a superbly executed brushstroke is not only a gesture of abstract beauty or the reflection of careful training, but also a revelation of the writer's state of mind. To a painter seeking various expressive qualities in his painting, calligraphic technique was obviously not a tool to be overlooked. In the late eleventh century, Li Kung-lin experimented with this calligraphic approach to painting; his followers Ch'iao Chung-ch'ang (fl. 1st half 12th century) and Ma Ho-chih carried on his example in the twelfth century; and Chao Meng-fu adopted the calligraphic approach in the thirteenth century.

The draftsmanship of the Elliott handscroll is characterized by absolutely disciplined lines of constant thickness. As shown on the outlines of the rocks, these brushlines are executed with a small brush handled with constant controlled pressure on the tip. In this style the beginnings and the endings of the brushstrokes are invisible because the artist consciously concealed the tip of the brush to achieve the archaic flavor of the seal script (*chuan-shu*).

The seal script is the earliest form among the five popularly practiced script forms of Chinese calligraphy, and therefore has been considered as the archaic style since at least A.D. 240–48, the approximate date

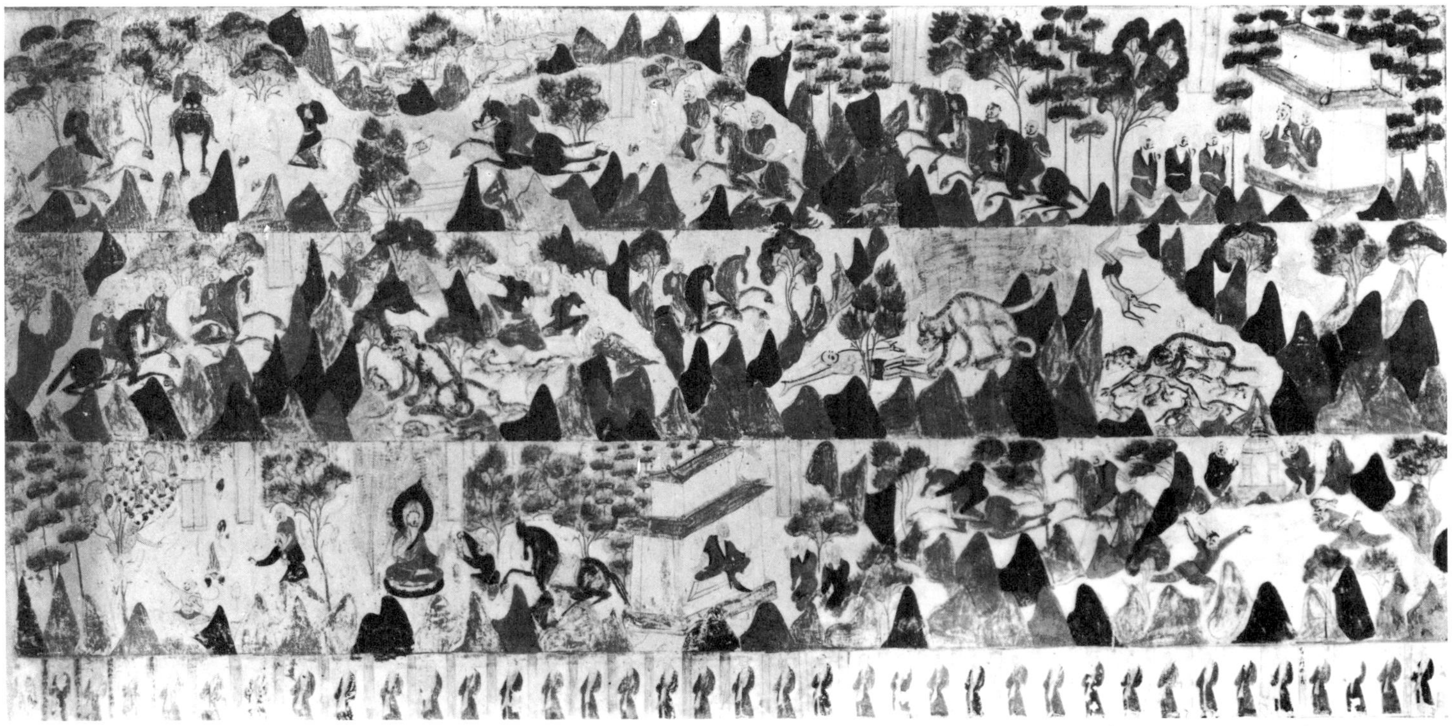

Fig. 9. Anonymous, detail, *Mahāsattva Jātaka*. Undated, 3rd quarter 6th century. Wall painting. Cave 428, Tun-huang, Kansu province

of the carving of the *Three Styles of the Stone Classics*, attributed to Han-tan Ch'un.[24] In the Yüan period the seal script enjoyed great popularity in the "archaistic" movement and played an important role as part of the revival of the past. Chao Meng-fu was the pioneer of the revitalization of this archaic writing form. His achievement, exemplified by the six-character frontispiece to his *Record of the Miao-yen Monastery* (*Hu-chou Miao-yen-ssu chi*; no. 7), had a decisive influence on his followers, among them the well-known calligraphers Chao Yung, Chao Meng-fu's son and author of the first colophon on the *Mind Landscape*, and Yü Ho (fl. ca. 1330–60).[25] Ku K'ai-chih's brushwork has been characterized as the style of *kao-ku yu-ssu* (archaic floating silk), which, as the term suggests, features very thin, refined brushlines. Chao Meng-fu used the seal script technique in *The Mind Landscape of Hsieh Yu-yü* in order to recapture Ku's archaic floating-silk brush mode. As a result *The Mind Landscape of Hsieh Yu-yü* not only re-creates Ku K'ai-chih's masterpiece, it also presents Chao Meng-fu himself in the guise of an ancient master, holding a conversation across time with Ku K'ai-chih.

The Elliott handscroll was apparently the first product of this calligraphic interpretation on ancient styles in Chao Meng-fu's artistic career. In *Autumn Colors on the Ch'iao and Hua Mountains* (see page 70), produced later in 1296, he applied constantly changing pressure and round brushlines in well-controlled rhythms derived from regular script (*k'ai-shu*), imitating the draping hemp-fiber (*p'i-ma*) brush mode of the tenth-century master Tung Yüan (fl. 937–76). In another handscroll entitled *Twin Pines against a Flat Vista* (*Shuang-sung p'ing-yüan*; page 104), Chao used techniques from running script (*hsing-shu*) and grass script (*ts'ao-shu*), which employ the tip as well as the sides of the brush at a faster speed, to interpret landscape motifs in the Li Ch'eng (919–967)–Kuo Hsi (ca. 1010–ca. 1090) tradition.[26] While Chao became technically proficient in every calligraphic style of the past, he also created a distinct personal style, applying the flying white (*fei-pai*) technique of the grass script to the depiction of rock surfaces in such works as *Bamboo, Rocks, and Orchid* (*Chu shih yu-lan*; fig. 10).

Although Chinese artists and art critics of the thirteenth century had already developed the concept by which various stylistic schools are classified by different brush modes, Chao Meng-fu's *Mind Landscape of Hsieh Yu-yü* represents the first attempt to translate systematically a particular brush mode into calligraphic language. As a result of this innovation, the past could more successfully be reconstructed and invigorated.

The different script styles were thought by literati to convey particular qualities. Grass script, for

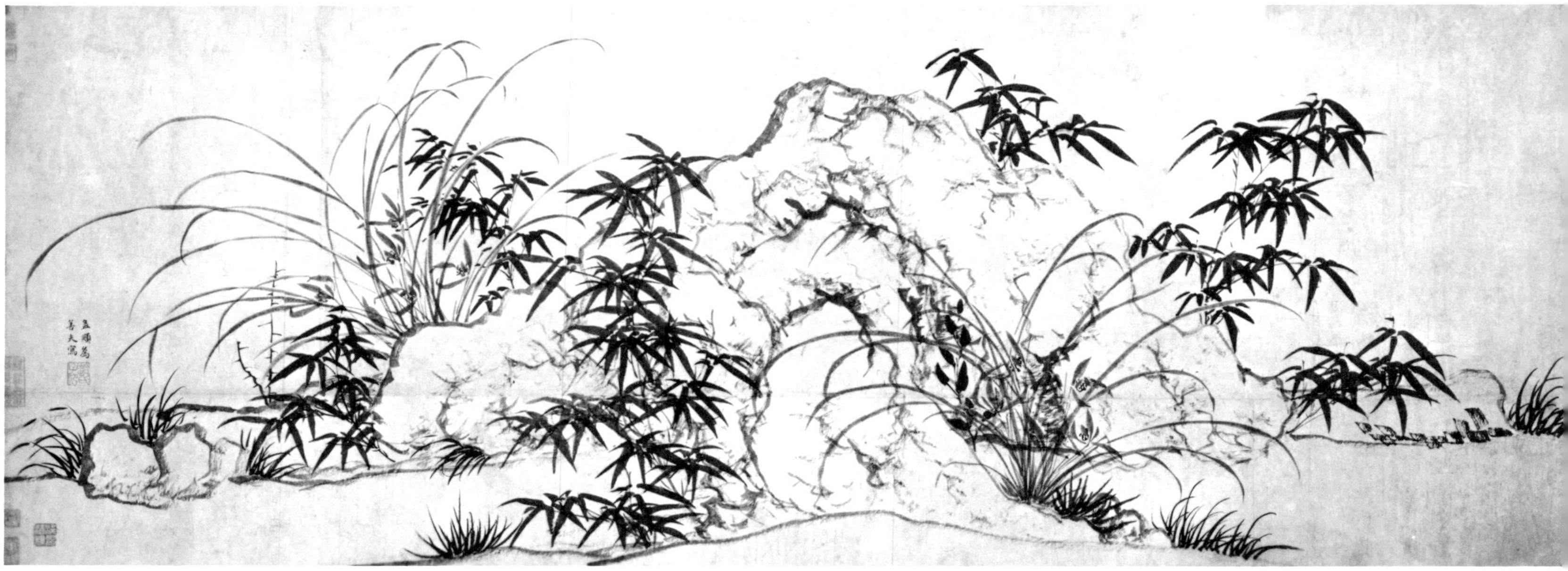

Fig. 10. Chao Meng-fu, *Bamboo, Rocks, and Orchid* (*Chu shih yu-lan*). Undated, late 13th–early 14th century. Handscroll, ink on paper. 50.5 x 144.1 cm (19⅞ in. x 4 ft. 8¾ in.). Cleveland Museum of Art

example, conveys heroic or unconventional qualities, while seal script suggests remoteness and refinement. In Chao's handscroll, as objective reality gives way to expressionism, the draftsmanship does not aim to give the illusion of space and three-dimensional landscape forms. Although Chao never uses his brushwork to create purely abstract forms, as Ming painters later would do, his brushstrokes are more lyrical than those of Sung painters. Stroke by stroke, rock by rock, layer by layer, Chao Meng-fu built up shapes with seal script strokes, constructing a unified, oblique, and at the same time otherworldly "purified" landscape.

By rendering his blue and green landscape with thin wavy and swelling brushlines, Chao Meng-fu established a new tradition in blue and green landscape painting. Later literati painters favored Chao Meng-fu's style for the graceful beauty of its controlled brushwork and its somber coloring. The painter Yün Shou-p'ing (1633–1690) summed up the importance of Chao Meng-fu's style for later landscape painters in his colophon for a handscroll, also in the blue and green manner, by the Southern School painter Wang Hui (1632–1717):

> The blue and green style underwent a great change in the hands of Chao Meng-fu. Eliminating traces of the stiff portrayals by Sung artists, he instead reinvested the style with profundity, making it attractive and at the same time extremely elegant and graceful. It so sparkles with spiritual vitality that it catches viewers' eyes immediately. This is what people mean by the phrase "after brightness reaches the extreme, it spontaneously returns to blandness and naturalness." Without doubt Chao Meng-fu was truly the teacher of the painters of later centuries. . . .[27]

Yün Shou-p'ing's phrase "eliminating traces of the stiff portrayals by Sung artists" refers to the most controversial issue in seventeenth-century art circles: the theory of the divergence of the Southern and Northern schools. As the major proponent of this theory, Tung Ch'i-ch'ang rediscovered the style of Wang Wei (699–759), the patriarch of the Southern School, or the Orthodox tradition, by the wavy and swelling brush mode he observed in Chao Meng-fu's blue and green style. In 1595 Tung wrote a colophon on a painting by Wang Wei, expressing his joy at discovering the stylistic connection between Wang Wei's work and an unidentified blue and green landscape painting by Chao Meng-fu that he had seen in a private collection.[28] Tung Ch'i-ch'ang's painstaking effort to reconstruct an orthodox lineage of blue and green painters was not wholly successful; when he wrote his colophon on *The Mind Landscape of Hsieh Yu-yü* he failed to see the connection between that painting and paintings by any classic masters in his prescribed lineage, not to mention Wang Wei. That task was left to the Orthodox School masters of the next generation to accomplish. By that time Chao's handscroll had already had a significant influence on Orthodox School painters who practiced the blue and green manner.

One example of Chao Meng-fu's influence can be seen in Wang Chien's (1598–1677) small blue and green work *Landscape after Chao Meng-fu* (*Fang Chao Meng-fu shan-shui*; fig. 11), showing a hermit in a natural setting—an homage to *The Mind Landscape of Hsieh Yu-yü*. Although Wang Chien follows a typical seventeenth-century compositional structure, he uses the same kind of wavy brush technique that Chao Meng-fu used, to describe swelling rock contours and to model sinuous interiors.[29] Interpreting his own mind landscape, Wang Chien used Chao's brushwork in a similar expressive way and carried on the tradition of paintings depicting the theme of eremitism.

The brush technique first developed in the Elliott handscroll, as imitated by Wang Chien and others, forged a new link between historically conscious painters of the seventeenth century and the patriarchs in the orthodox lineage. Impressed by its refinement and expressiveness, Wang Chien and his colleagues thought this kind of brushwork successfully conveyed the spirit of classic masters like Wang Wei and Tung Yüan. Thus, they believed, the best way to paint in the blue and green style of Wang Wei or Tung Yüan was to adopt Chao Meng-fu's brush technique. With this notion there emerged a new school as well as a new style: the Orthodox, Southern School of blue and green landscape painting. To found a school of painting was probably not Chao Meng-fu's intention, but his synthesizing technique and style marked an important event in the history of Chinese painting.

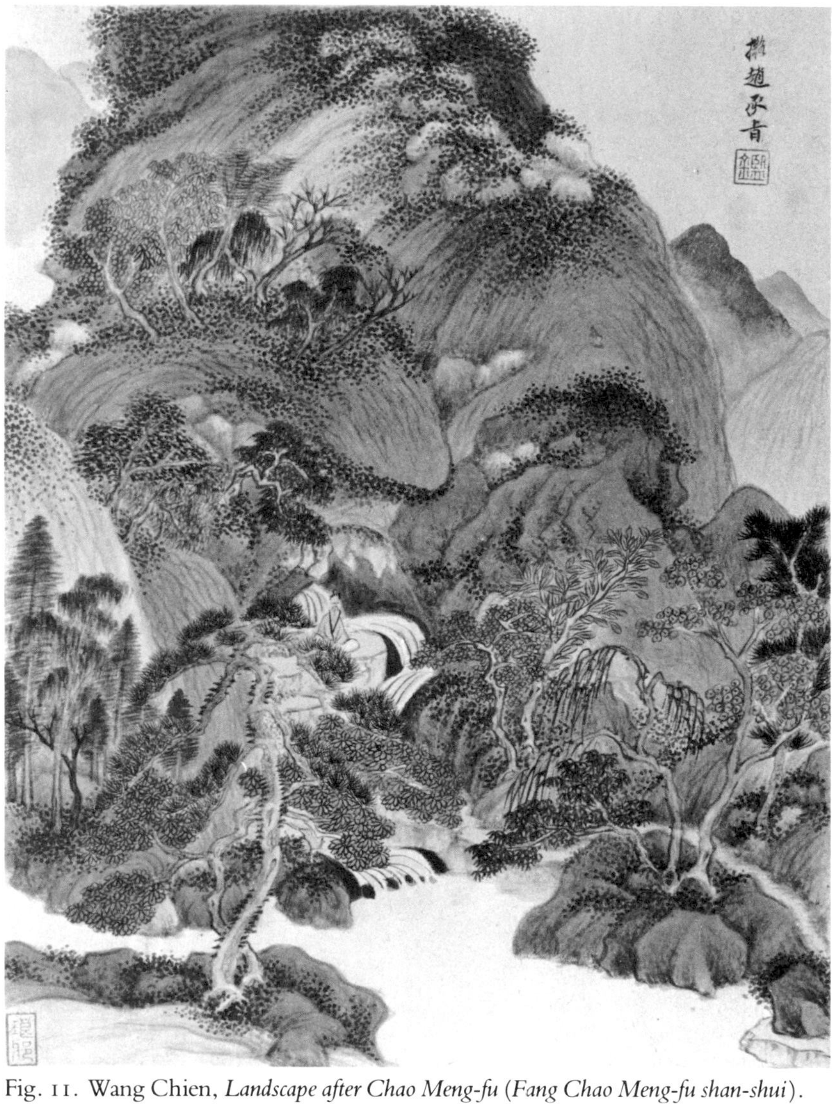

Fig. 11. Wang Chien, *Landscape after Chao Meng-fu* (*Fang Chao Meng-fu shan-shui*). Undated, 17th century. Album leaf, ink and color on paper. 33.1 x 25.7 cm (13 x 10⅛ in.). Private collection

## NOTES

1. Studies of this handscroll can be found in Sherman E. Lee and Wai-kam Ho, *Chinese Art under the Mongols: The Yüan Dynasty (1279–1368)* (Cleveland: Cleveland Museum of Art, 1968), pp. 90–91; James Cahill, *Hills beyond a River: Chinese Painting of the Yüan Dynasty, 1279–1368* (New York and Tokyo: Weatherhill, 1976), pp. 40–41; and Richard E. Vinograd, "Some Landscapes Related to the Blue-and-Green Manner from the Early Yüan Period," *Artibus Asiae* 41, no. 2/3 (1979–80): 101–31.

   According to Pien Yung-yü, in *Shih-ku-t'ang shu-hua hui k'ao* (Classified record of calligraphy and painting) (Taipei: Cheng-chung shu-chü, 1956), *chüan* 4, pp. 119–20, there was another version of the scroll, which had two inscriptions by Chao Meng-fu himself. Unfortunately the version is now lost and this claim cannot be verified.
2. Yang Tsai, "Ta Yüan ku Han-lin-hsüeh-shih ch'en-chih jung-lu-tai-fu chih-chih-kao chien pei kuo-shih Chao kung hsing-chuang" (The biography of the late Master Chao), in Chao Meng-fu, *Sung-hsüeh-chai wen-chi* (The collected works of Chao Meng-fu), Ssu-pu ts'ung-k'an (Taipei: Shang-wu yin-shu-kuan, 1967), pp. 124–25.
3. National Palace Museum, Taipei, comp., *Ku-kung shu-hua lu* (A descriptive catalogue of the painting and calligraphy in the National Palace Museum) (Taipei: National Palace Museum, 1965), vol. 1, p. 245.
4. Wang Yao, "Lun hsi-ch'i yin-i chih feng" (Discussion of the tradition of longing for reclusion), in *Chung-ku wen-hsüeh shih lun-chi* (Essays on the history of Chinese medieval literature) (Shanghai: Ku-tien wen-hsüeh ch'u-pan-she, 1956), pp. 49–68. For a discussion of reclusion in the Yüan period, see Frederick W. Mote, "Confucian Eremitism in the Yüan Period," in Arthur F. Wright, ed., *The Confucian Persuasion* (Stanford: Stanford University Press, 1960), pp. 202–40.
5. Liu I-ch'ing, *Shih-shuo hsin-yü* (A new account of tales of the world), Ssu-pu ts'ung-k'an (Taipei: Shang-wu yin-shu-kuan, 1967), *chüan* 6, p. 41.
6. Richard B. Mather, trans., *A New Account of Tales of the World* (Minneapolis: University of Minnesota Press, 1976), pp. 253–54.
7. Liu I-ch'ing, *Shih-shuo hsin-yü*, *chüan* 7, p. 33.
8. Ibid., p. 34.
9. Translation of the first part of Ni Tsan's poem by Wai-kam Ho, in Sherman E. Lee and Wai-kam Ho, *Chinese Art under the Mongols*, pp. 90–91.
10. Chu-tsing Li, *The Autumn Colors on the Ch'iao and Hua Mountains: A Landscape by Chao Meng-fu*, *Artibus Asiae* Supplementum 21 (1964): 94, 98.
11. Alexander C. Soper, "A New Chinese Tomb Discovery: The Earliest Representation of a Famous Literary Theme," *Artibus Asiae* 24, no. 2 (1961): 79–86; Nagahiro Toshio, "Shih-so kan no Chikurin Shichiken to Eikei-ki no gazu" (On the mural engravings of the Seven Sages of the Bamboo Grove and Jung Ch'i-ch'i, dating between the Tsin and Sung dynasties), *Kokka* 867 (August 1963): 15–21; Ch'en Chih, "Tui-yü Nan-ching Hsi-shan-ch'iao Nan-ch'ao mu chuan-k'e Chu-lin-ch'i-hsien t'u te kuan-chien" (Concerning the southern dynasty brick engraving of the Seven Sages of the Bamboo Grove from Hsi-shan-ch'iao, Nanking), *Wen-wu* 1961, no. 10: 47–48.
12. Chang Yen-yüan, *Li-tai ming-hua chi* (Record of famous painters of successive dynasties), in *Hua-shih ts'ung-shu* (Compendium of painting histories) (Taipei: Wen-shih-che ch'u-pan-she, 1974), vol. 1, *chüan* 5, pp. 70, 72.
13. Ibid., p. 69.
14. Chou Mi, *Yün-yen kuo-yen lu* (Clouds and mist drifted before the eyes), Mei-shu ts'ung-shu, 2nd ser., vol. 2 (Shanghai: Shen-chou kuo-kuang she, 1928), *chüan* 1, p. 45a.
15. Wang Yün, *Shu-hua mu-lu* (Catalogue of painting and calligraphy), Mei-shu ts'ung-shu, 4th ser., vol. 6 (Shanghai: Shen-chou kuo-kuang she, 1928), p. 6a; T'ang Hou, *Ku-chin hua-chien* (Survey of paintings of ancient and contemporary periods), Mei-shu ts'ung-shu, 3rd ser., vol. 2 (Shanghai: Shen-chou kuo-kuang-she, 1928), pp. 1a–b.
16. There is a piece of Chao Meng-fu's calligraphy, dated 1299, immediately following the painting on the Peking handscroll. According to the Palace Museum, however, the calligraphy is a forgery. The authenticity of Chao's seal, on the other hand, seems not to be in doubt; see Palace Museum, Peking, ed., *Chung-kuo li-tai hui-hua: Ku-kung po-wu-yüan ts'ang-hua chi* (Chinese paintings in the collection of the Palace Museum) (Peking: Palace Museum, 1978), vol. 1, appendix, pp. 2–3. For the Liaoning version, see *Liao-ning sheng po-wu-kuan ts'ang-hua chi* (Catalogue of the painting collection in the Liaoning Provincial Museum) (Peking: Wen-wu ch'u-pan-she, 1962), pp. 1–2. For the Freer Gallery version, see Thomas Lawton, *Freer Gallery of Art, Fiftieth Anniversary Exhibition, II: Chinese Figure Painting* (Washington, D.C.: The Smithsonian Institution, 1973), pp. 18–29.
17. Chou Mi, *Yün-yen kuo-yen lu*, *chüan* 1, p. 43a.
18. Ibid., *chüan* 2, pp. 73a–81a; Chuang Shen, "T'ang Lu Hung *Ts'ao-t'ang shih-chih t'u* chuan k'ao" (A study of *The Ten Views of the Thatched Hut* by Lu Hung of the T'ang dynasty), in *Chung-kuo hua-shih yen-chiu hsü chi* (Essays on Chinese painting history, a sequel) (Taipei: Shang-wu yin-shu-kuan, 1961), pp. 161–62.
19. Chuang Shen, "T'ang Lu Hung *Ts'ao-t'ang shih-chih t'u* chuan k'ao," pp. 149–50.
20. National Palace Museum, Taipei, comp., *Ku-kung fa-shu* (Collection of calligraphy in the National Palace Museum) (Taipei: National Palace Museum, 1974), vol. 17, pp. 14–15. Actually Hsien-yü Shu was not the recipient of this letter, but the misleading title has been used since the eighteenth century and has been retained by the museum as the official title of the work.
21. See Ellen Johnston Laing, "Neo-Taoism and the *Seven Sages of the Bamboo Grove* in Chinese Painting," *Artibus Asiae* 36, no. 1/2 (1974): 5–54.
22. Wen C. Fong and Maxwell K. Hearn, "Silent Poetry: Chinese Paintings in the Douglas Dillon Galleries," *The Metropolitan Museum of Art Bulletin* 39, no. 3 (Winter 1981–82): 18–19.
23. For Chao Meng-fu's *Lan-t'ing shih-san pa* (Takashima collection, Japan), see *Shoseki meihin sōkan* (A collection of calligraphy masterpieces) (Tokyo: Nigen-sha, 1964), vol. 9.
24. The attribution has remained controversial. A third-century calligrapher, Wei Chi, has been suggested as another possible inscriber of the work. Neither attribution can be proven. See Kanda Kiichiro et al., eds., *Shodō zenshū* (Reproductions of well-known works of calligraphy) (Tokyo: Heibon-sha, 1965), vol. 3, pp. 168–69, pls. 65–67.
25. Shen C. Y. Fu et al., *Traces of the Brush: Studies in Chinese Calligraphy* (New Haven: Yale University Art Gallery, 1977), pp. 45–47, pl. 15a.
26. Wen C. Fong and Marilyn Fu, *Sung and Yüan Paintings* (New York: The Metropolitan Museum of Art, 1973), pp. 88–91.
27. Yün Shou-p'ing, *Ou-hsiang-kuan chi* (The collected works of Yün Shou-p'ing) (Taipei: Hsüeh-hai ch'u-pan-she, 1972), *chüan* 12, pp. 22a–b.
28. Wen C. Fong, "*Rivers and Mountains after Snow* (*Chiang-shan hsüeh-chi*) attributed to Wang Wei (A.D. 699–759)," *Archives of Asian Art* 30 (1976–77): 13–15.
29. Ibid., 16–17.

# IV

*Catalogue*

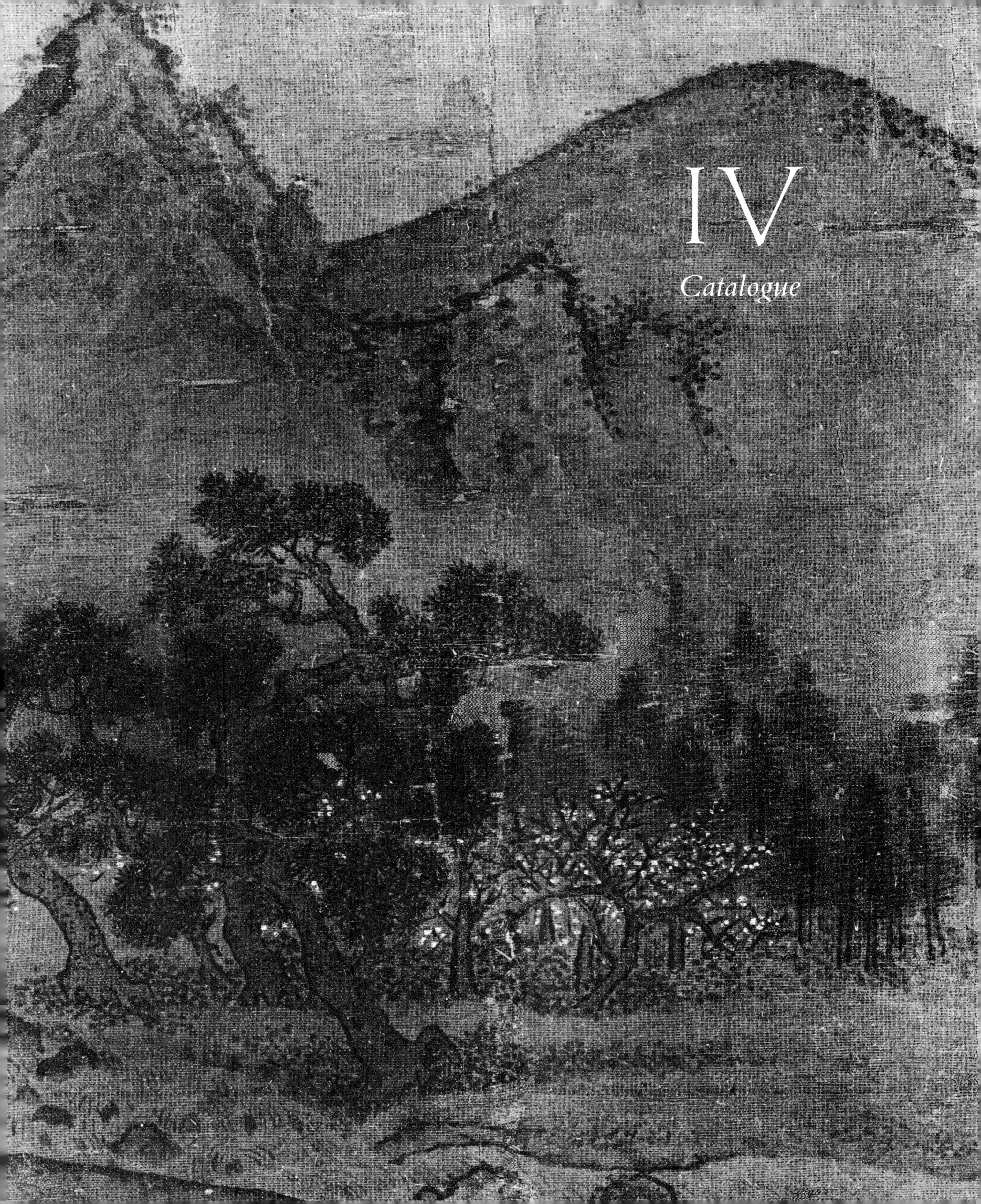

# 1 Huang T'ing-chien (1045–1105)

## *Scroll for Chang Ta-t'ung (Tseng Chang Ta-t'ung ku-wen t'i-chi)*

Dated 1100
Handscroll, ink on paper
Calligraphy: 34.2 x 54.0 cm (13 1/2 in. x 18 ft. 2 1/8 in.); colophons: 33.7 x 205.0 cm (13 1/2 in. x 6 ft. 8 1/2 in.)

CALLIGRAPHY: prose, 171 characters in 46 columns of running script.

ARTIST'S SIGNATURE: Fu-weng.

COLOPHONS (from right to left):

1. Wang To (1592–1652): prose, 61 characters in 3 columns of regular script. Signature: On the day after the Lantern Festival [fifteenth day of the first lunar month] of the *ping-hsü* year [1646], Wang To from western Honan inscribed this.
2. Wu K'uan (1435–1504): prose, 77 characters in 7 columns of running script. Signature: Wu K'uan. Seal: Wu Yüan-po yin (square relief).
3. Li Tung-yang (1447–1516): prose, 57 characters in 7 columns of free-form running script. Signature: Li Tung-yang inscribed this. Seal: Hsi-ya (tall rectangle relief).
4. Mo Shao-te (fl. early 19th century): prose, 127 characters in 6 columns of regular script. Signature: On the fourth day after the great snow of the *jen-shen* year of the Chia-ch'ing era [1812], Mo Shao-te from An-ting [in Hopei province] appreciated and cautiously inscribed this. Seal: Shao-te (double seal, square, half relief, half intaglio).
5. Chang Yüan (Chang Ta-ch'ien; 1899–1983): prose, 422 characters in 32 columns of running script. Signature: Chang Ta-ch'ien, Yüan. Seals: Chang Yüan chih yin-hsin (square intaglio); Ta-ch'ien-chü-shih (square relief); Pai-sui ch'ien-ch'iu (square relief).

COLLECTORS' SEALS:
Emperor Sung Kao-tsung (r. 1127–62), 8 seals.
Yang I-ch'ing (1454–1530), 1 seal.
Chou Hsiang-yün (fl. 20th century), 7 seals.
Chang Yüan, 14 seals.
5 unidentified seals.

John B. Elliott Collection (L180.69)

PUBLISHED: Fushimi Chūkei, "Kō Teiken sho zō Chō Daidō kan" (Huang T'ing-chien's scroll for Chang Ta-t'ung), *Shohin* 150 (1964): 1–16, pls. 1–28; Richard Barnhart, "Chinese Calligraphy—the Inner World of the Brush," *The Metropolitan Museum of Art Bulletin* 30, no. 5 (April–May 1972): 231, 232, figs. 1, 2; Shen C. Y. Fu, "Huang T'ing-chien's Calligraphy and His Scroll for Chang Ta-t'ung: A Masterpiece Written in Exile" (Ph.D. diss., Princeton University, 1976); Shen C. Y. Fu et al., *Traces of the Brush: Studies in Chinese Calligraphy* (New Haven: Yale University Art Gallery, 1977), p. 245, pl. 6; Nakata Yūjirō and Fu Shen, eds., *Obei shūzō Chūgoku hōsho meisekishū* (Masterpieces of Chinese calligraphy in American and European collections), vol. 1 (Tokyo: Chūōkōron-sha, 1981), pp. 66–77, 139, pls. 59–66.

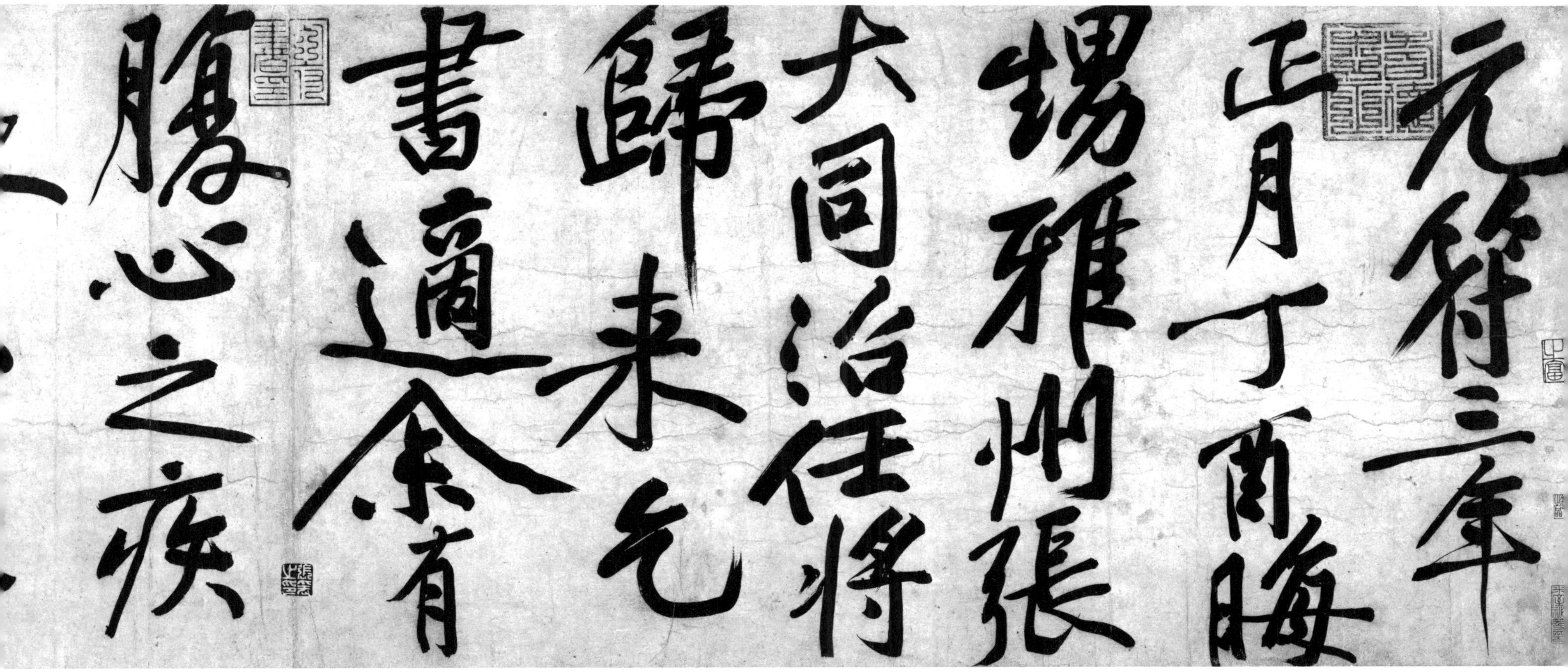
元符三年
正月丁酉晦
錫雅州張
大同治任將
歸來乞
書適余有
腹心之疾

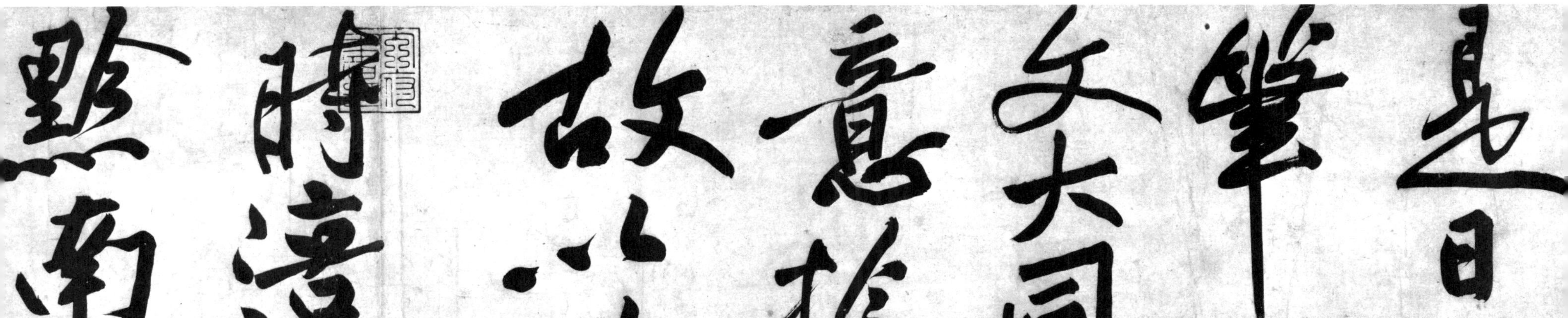
是日小間試
筆書此
大同有
意於古文
故以此遺之
時涪翁自
黔南遷

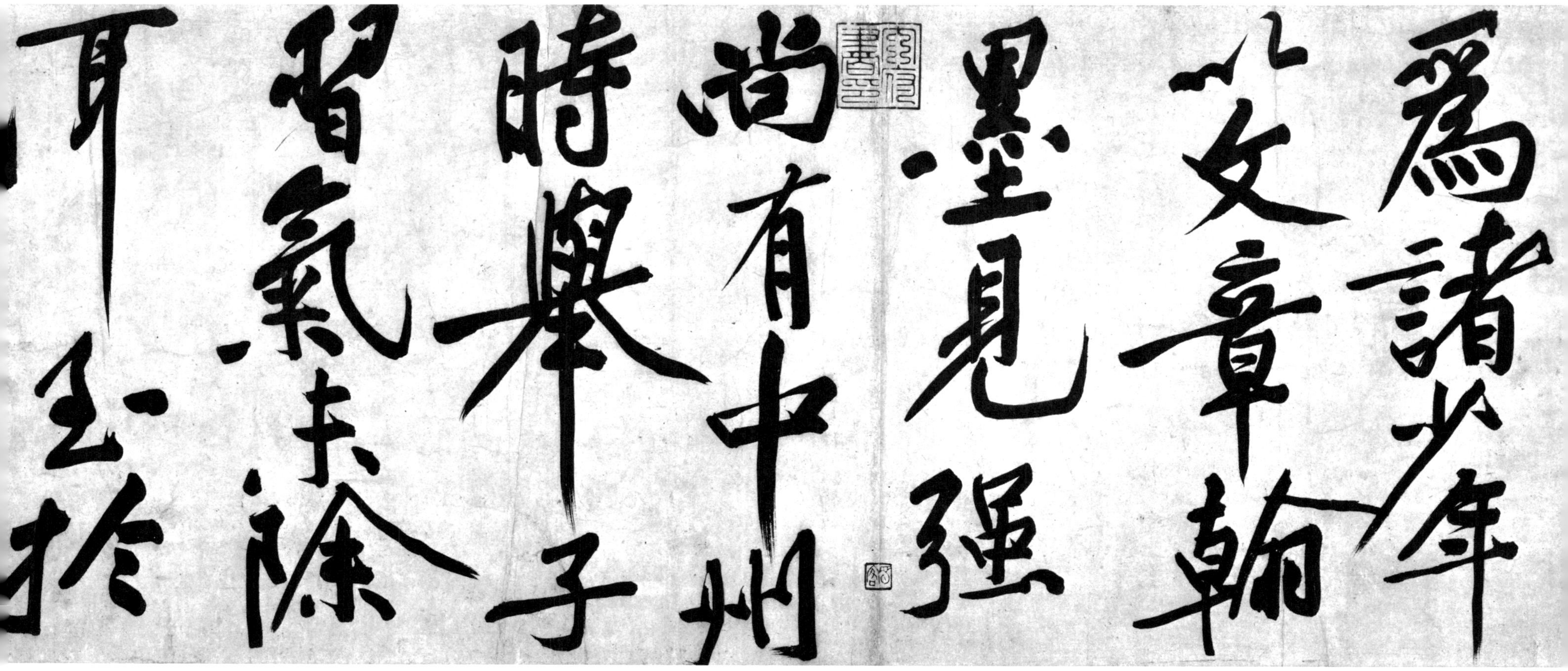
爲諸少年
以文章翰
墨見强
尚有中州
時舉子
習氣未除
耳至於

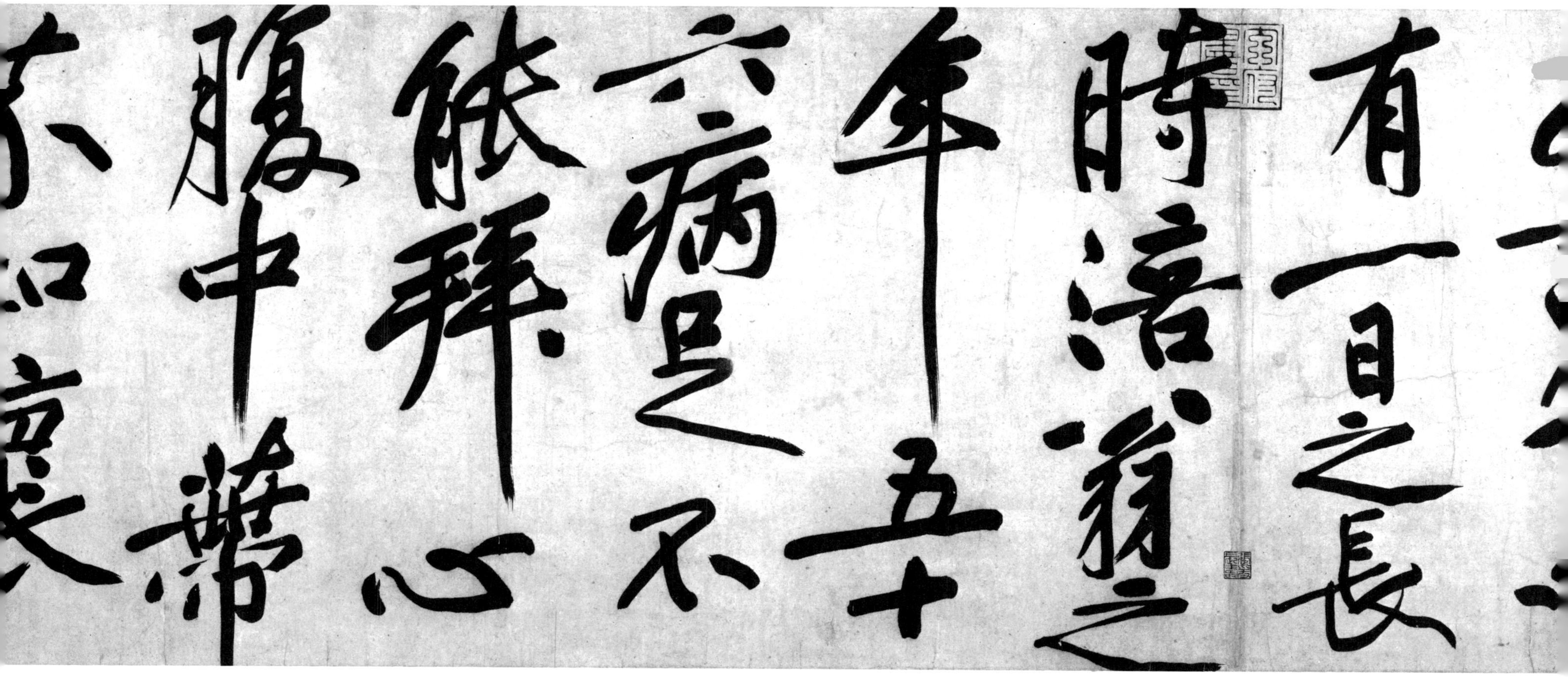
有一日之長
時諸翁之
年五十
亦病足不
能拜心
腹中蔕

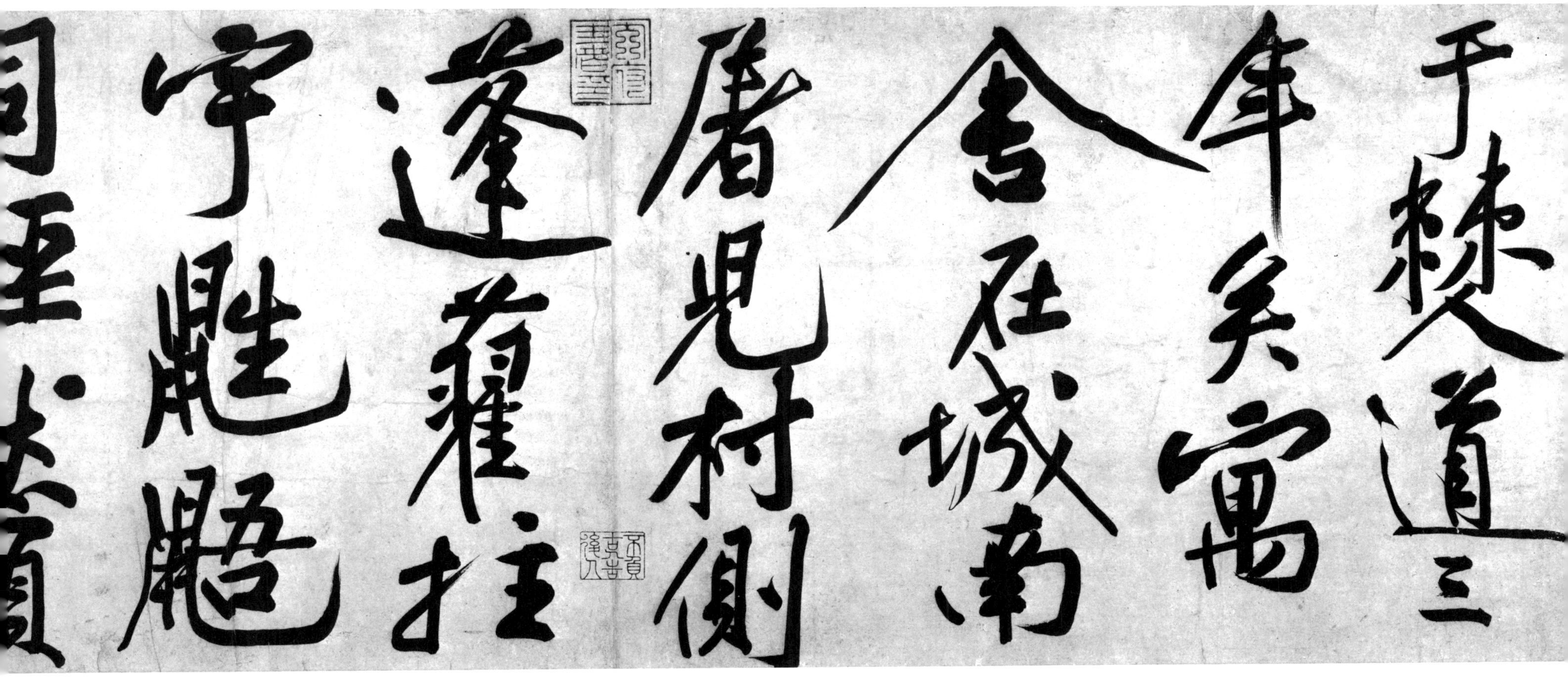

三年矣寓
舍在城南
屠兒村側


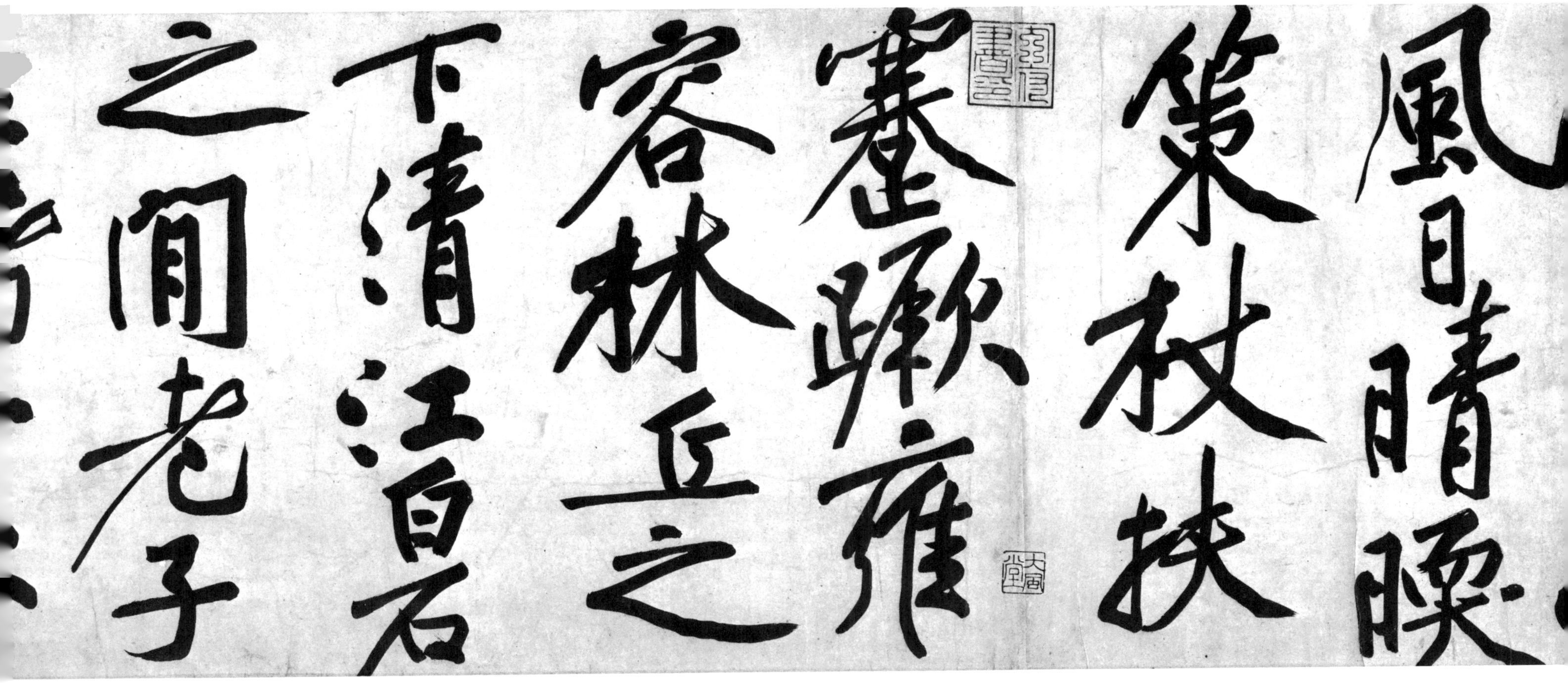

風日晴暖
策杖扶
下清江白石
之間老子

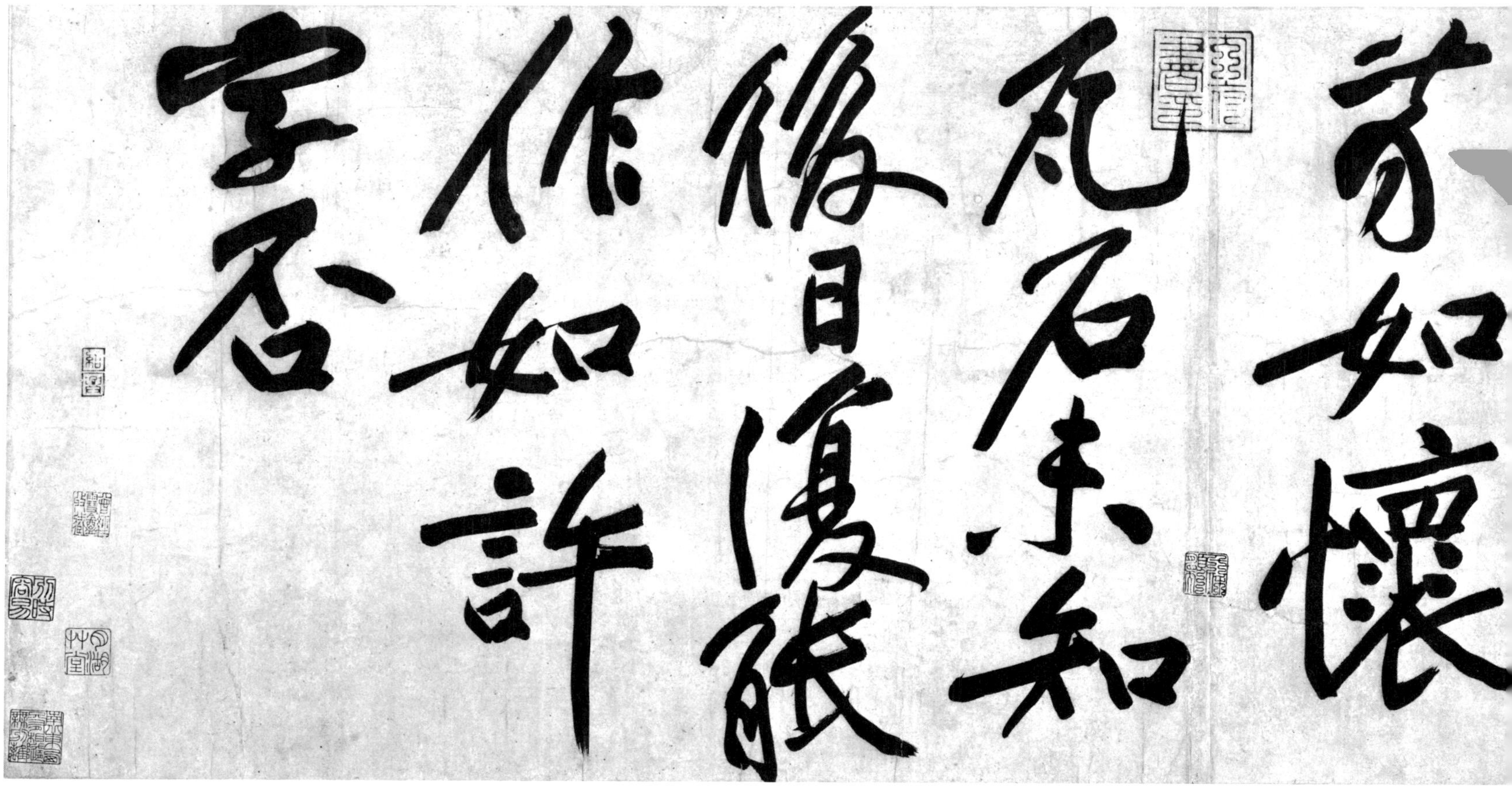

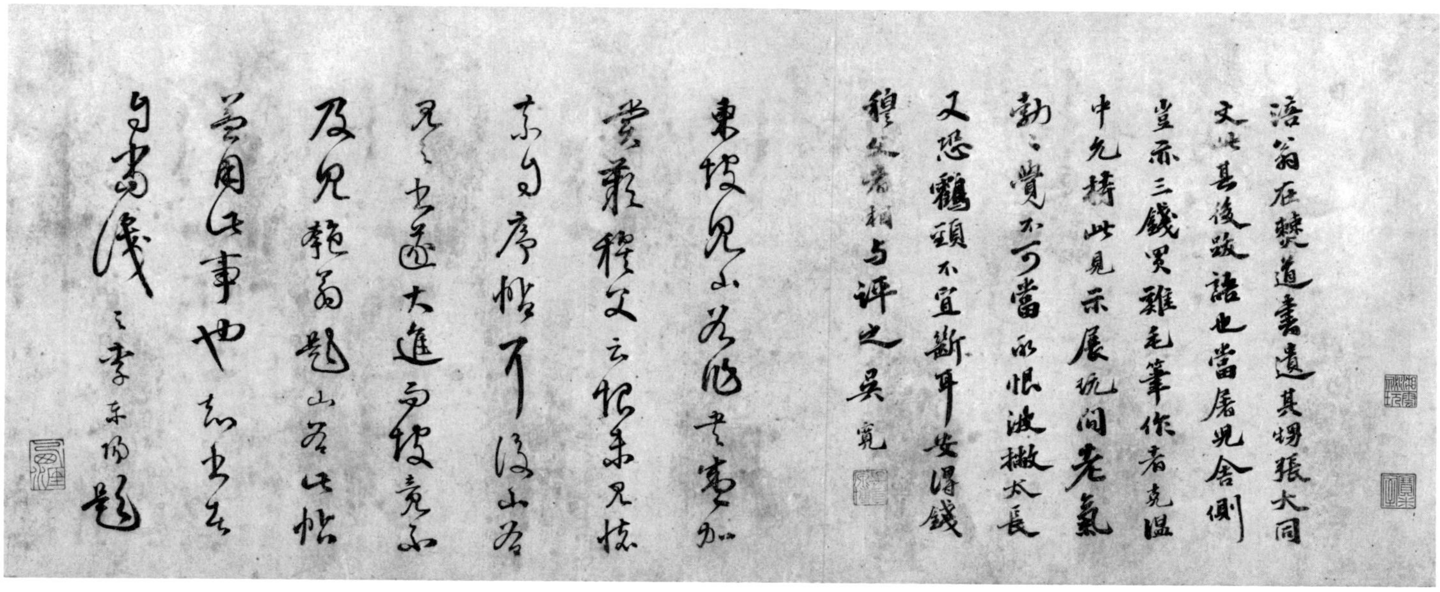

Li Tung-yang

Wu K'uan

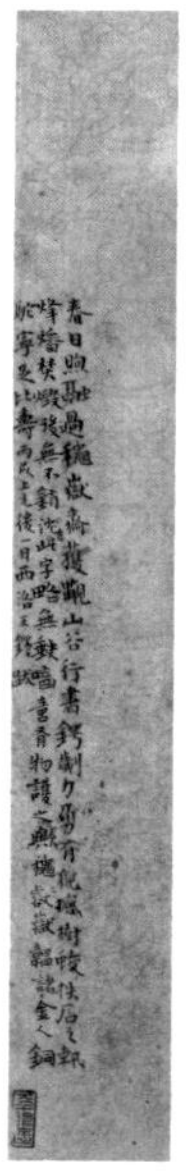

Wang To

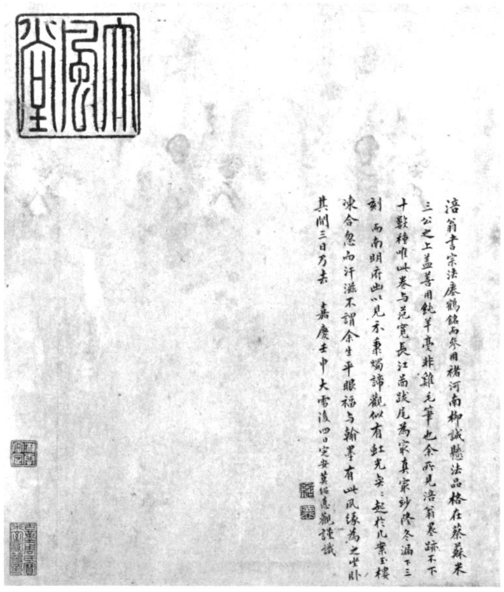

Mo Shao-te

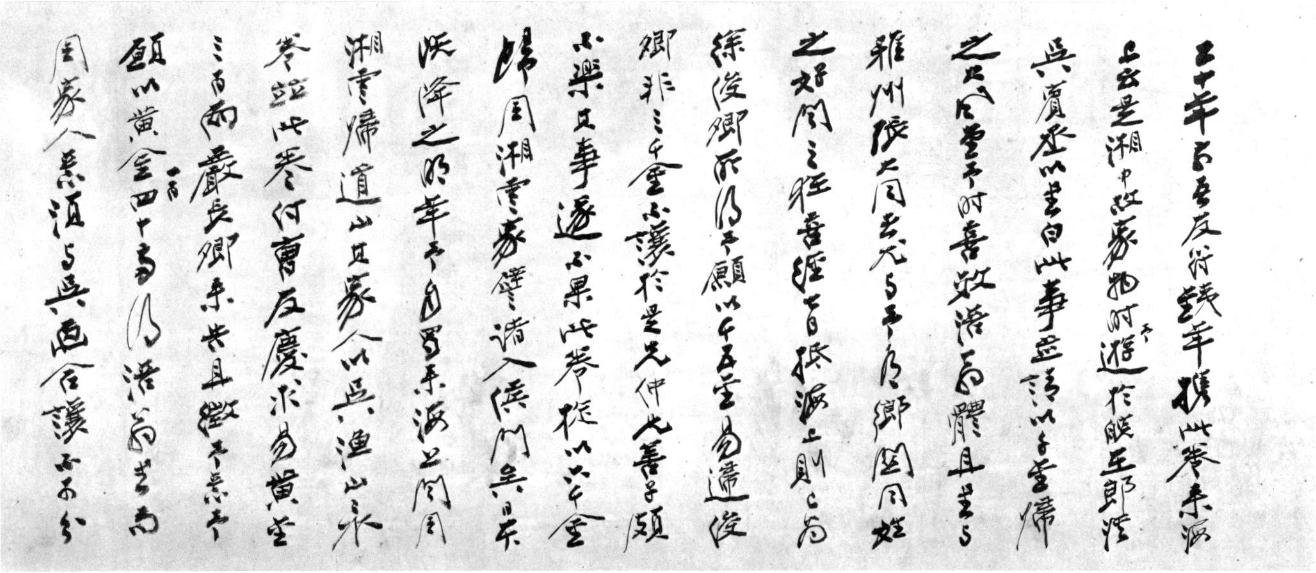

Chang Yüan (Chang Ta-ch'ien)

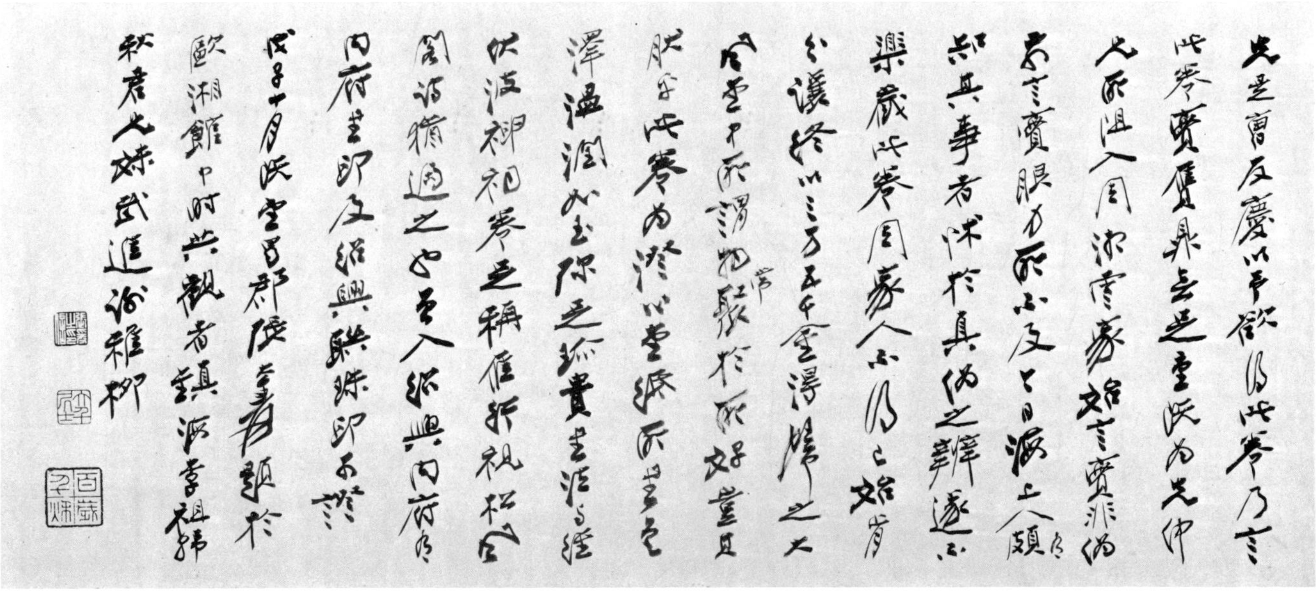

Chang Yüan (Chang Ta-ch'ien)

# 2 Mi Fu (1052–1107)

## *Three Letters (San cha)*

Ca. 1093–94
Album of three leaves (A–C), ink on paper
A: 31.7 x 33.0 cm (12 1/2 x 13 in.); B: 30.9 x 40.6 cm (12 1/8 x 16 in.); C: 31.7 x 39.7 cm (12 1/2 x 15 5/8 in.)

CALLIGRAPHY: Leaf A, "Abundant Harvest" ("Sui-feng t'ieh"): prose, 62 characters in 7 columns of running script. Leaf B, "Escaping Summer Heat" ("T'ao-shu t'ieh"): prose, 73 characters in 8 columns of running script. Leaf C, "Hasty Reply before Guests" ("Tui k'o ts'ao-ts'ao t'ieh"): prose, 65 characters in 9 columns of running script (for translations of the calligraphy, see pages 87–88).

ARTIST'S SIGNATURES: I, Fu, bow my head and ask to speak again (A–C).

ARTIST'S SEAL: Yü-hsiung hou-jen (square relief; A).

COLLECTORS' SEALS:
Ming imperial seal, 1 half seal.
Wang Ssu-jen (1575–1646), 1 seal.
Ch'en Hung-shou (1599–1652), 2 seals.
Kuan Ssu (fl. 1600–30), 3 seals.
Tung Wen-chi (*chin-shih*, 1649), 2 seals.
An Ch'i (1683–1744), 4 seals.
Chou P'u-hsin (modern), 21 seals.
Ch'en Kuo-chao (dates unknown), 3 seals.
Fei Chao-k'un (dates unknown), 8 seals.
Liu Hsün-hou (dates unknown), 1 seal.
Liu Yün-lung (dates unknown), 8 seals.
Lü Shan-t'ao (dates unknown), 1 seal.
Lü Yin-nai (dates unknown), 2 seals.
Unidentified owners, 23 seals.
11 unidentified seals.

John B. Elliott Collection (L176.70)

PUBLISHED: Shen C. Y. Fu et al., *Traces of the Brush: Studies in Chinese Calligraphy* (New Haven: Yale University Art Gallery, 1977), pp. 101, 148–49, 246–47, pls. 9a, b, c; Nakata Yūjirō and Fu Shen, eds., *Obei shūzō Chūgoku hōsho meisekishū* (Masterpieces of Chinese calligraphy in American and European collections), vol. 1 (Tokyo: Chūōkōron-sha, 1981), pp. 140–41, pls. 74–76; Nakata Yūjirō, *Bei Futsu* (Mi Fu) (Tokyo: Nigen-sha, 1982), vol. 1, pp. 217–18; vol. 2, pls. 110–115; Suzuki Kei, comp., *Chūgoku kaiga sōgō zuroku: daiikkan, Amerika–Kanada hen* (Comprehensive illustrated catalogue of Chinese paintings: volume 1, American and Canadian collections) (Tokyo: University of Tokyo Press, 1982), pp. 156–57, pl. A17–105.

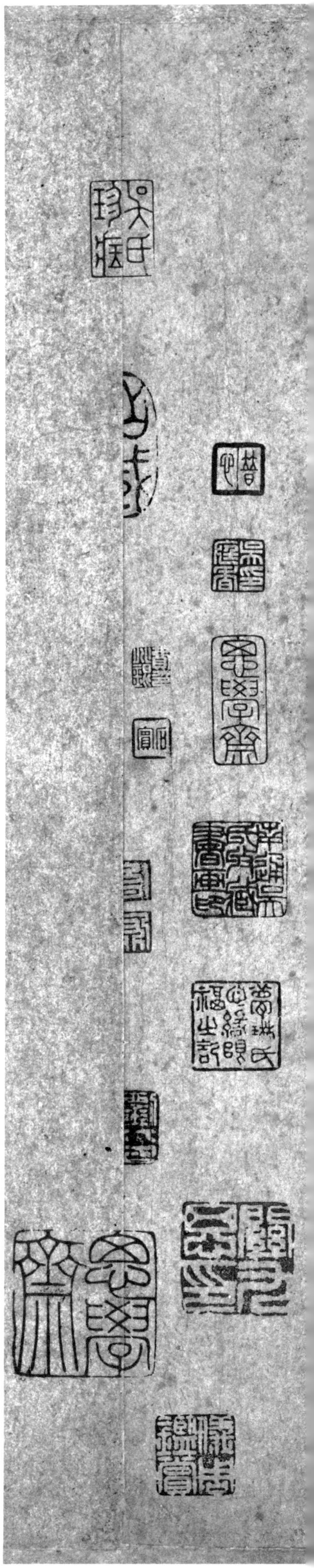

Leaf A, "Abundant Harvest" ("Sui-feng t'ieh")

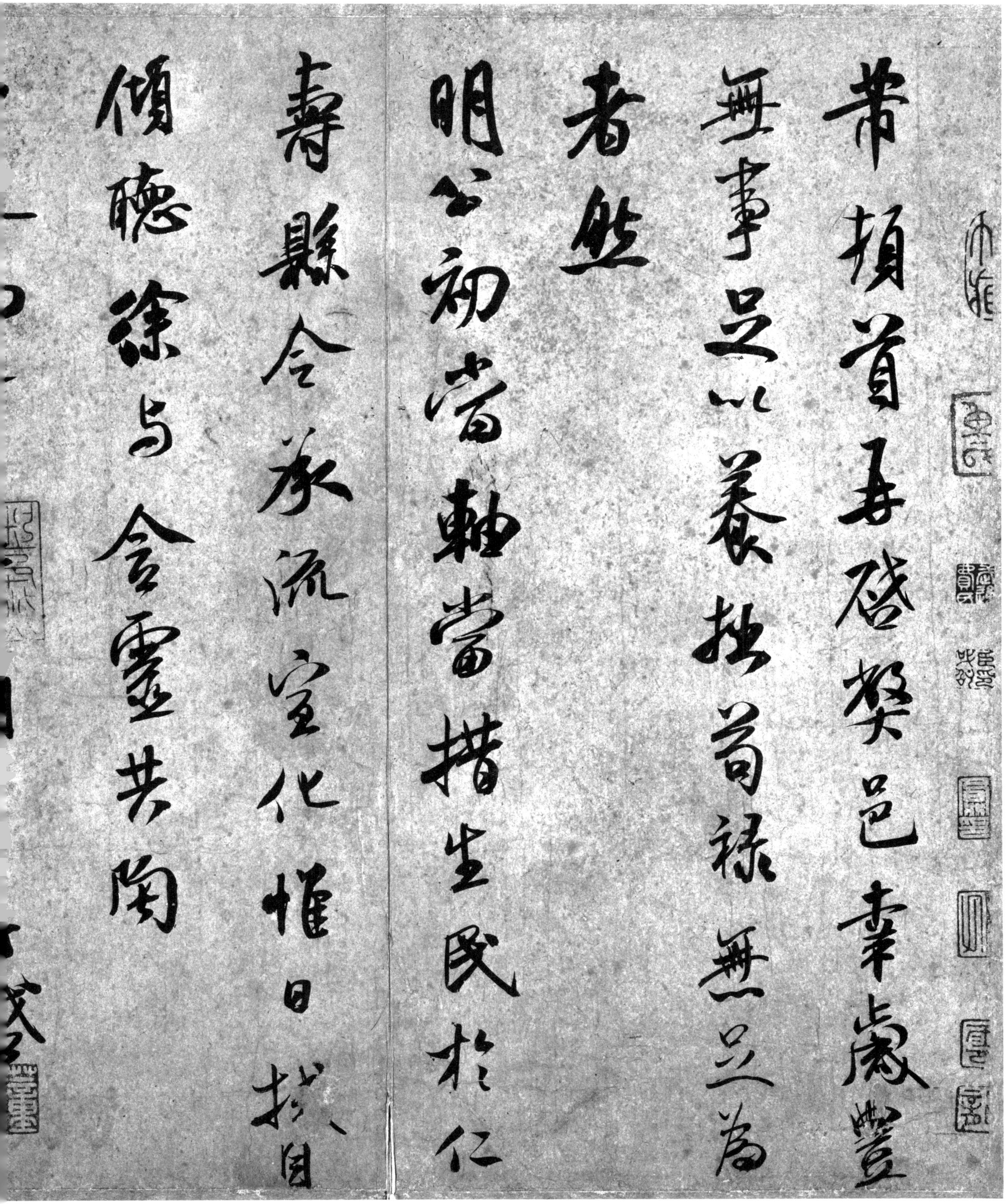
芾頓首再啓黎邑幸歲豐
無事足以養拙苟祿無足為
者然
明公初當軸當措生民於仁
壽縣令承流宣化惟日拭目
傾聽餘與含靈共陶

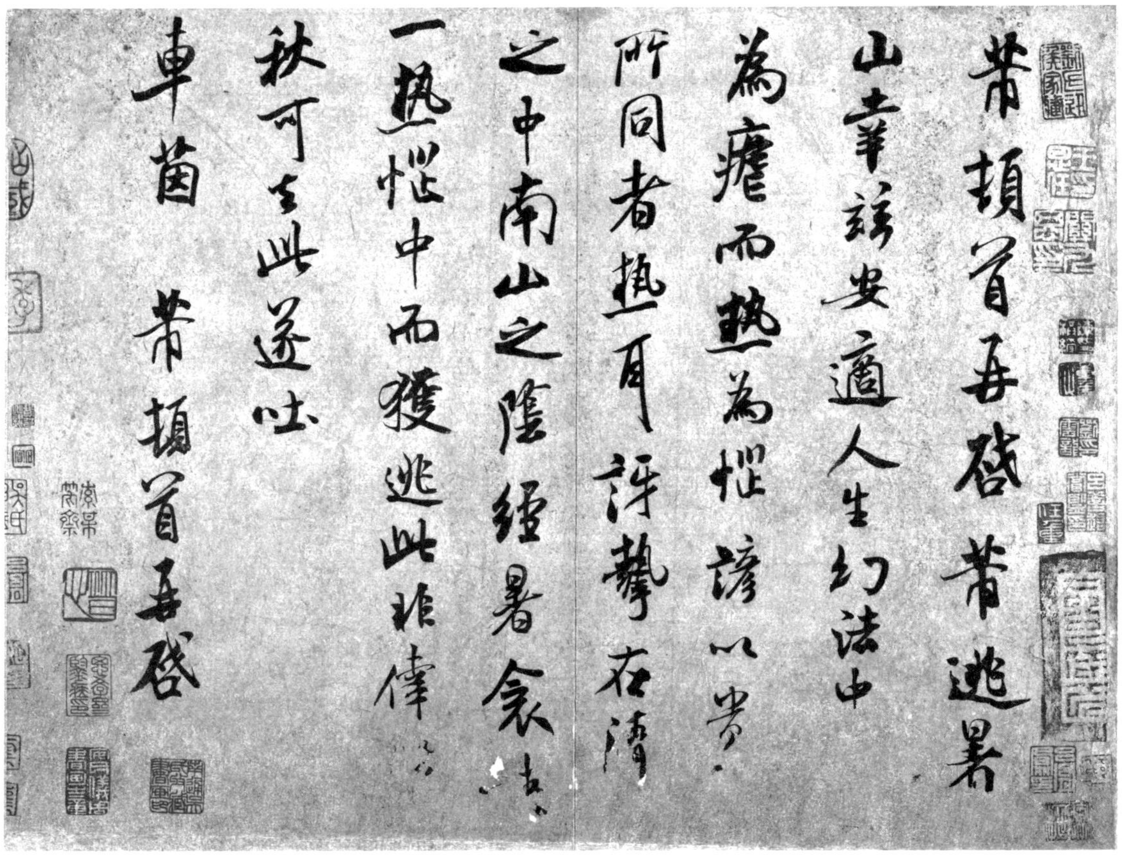

Leaf B, "Escaping Summer Heat" ("T'ao-shu t'ieh")

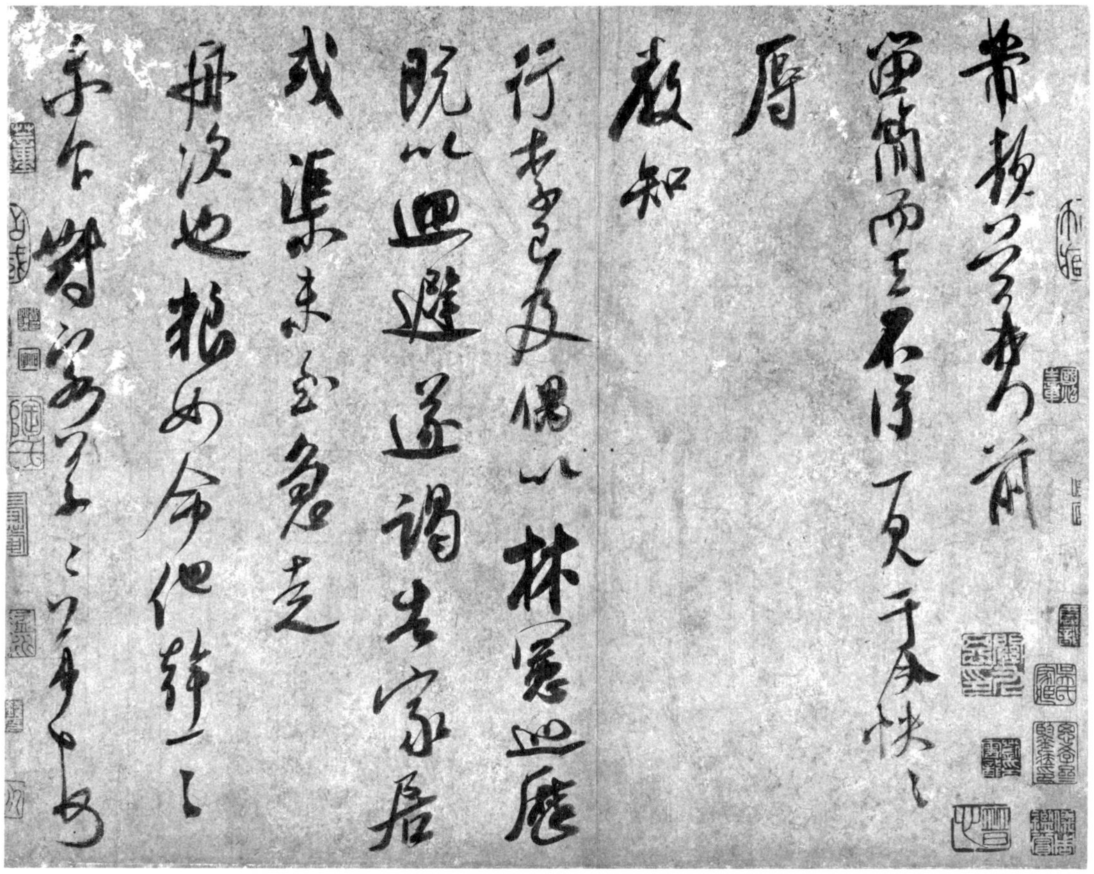

Leaf C, "Hasty Reply before Guests" ("Tui k'o ts'ao-ts'ao t'ieh")

# 3 Anonymous

## *Landscape in the Style of Fan K'uan (Fang Fan K'uan shan-shui)*

Ca. 1150
Round fan mounted as a hanging scroll, ink and light color on silk
23.9 x 25.5 cm (9 3/8 x 10 in.)

No artist's signature or seals.

COLLECTORS' SEALS:

1. Huang Li-chai (dates unknown): Kuan-chung Huang Li-chai ts'eng kuan (square intaglio; lower right, silk mounting).
2. Unidentified owner: Ch'ing-ch'ün-i chien-shang (square relief; lower right, silk mounting).
3. Unidentified seal: Shih-[ ] (square relief; lower left, painting).

Edward L. Elliott Family Collection (L29.75)

PUBLISHED: Wen C. Fong, *Summer Mountains: The Timeless Landscape* (New York: The Metropolitan Museum of Art, 1975), pls. 34, 35; Ishikawa Jun et al., eds., *Bunjinga suihen* (Selection of the finest Chinese and Japanese literati paintings), vol. 2 (Tokyo: Chūōkōron-sha, 1977), pl. 40; Suzuki Kei, comp., *Chūgoku kaiga sōgō zuroku: daiikkan, Amerika–Kanada hen* (Comprehensive illustrated catalogue of Chinese paintings: volume 1, American and Canadian collections) (Tokyo: University of Tokyo Press, 1982), p. 129, pl. A17–044.

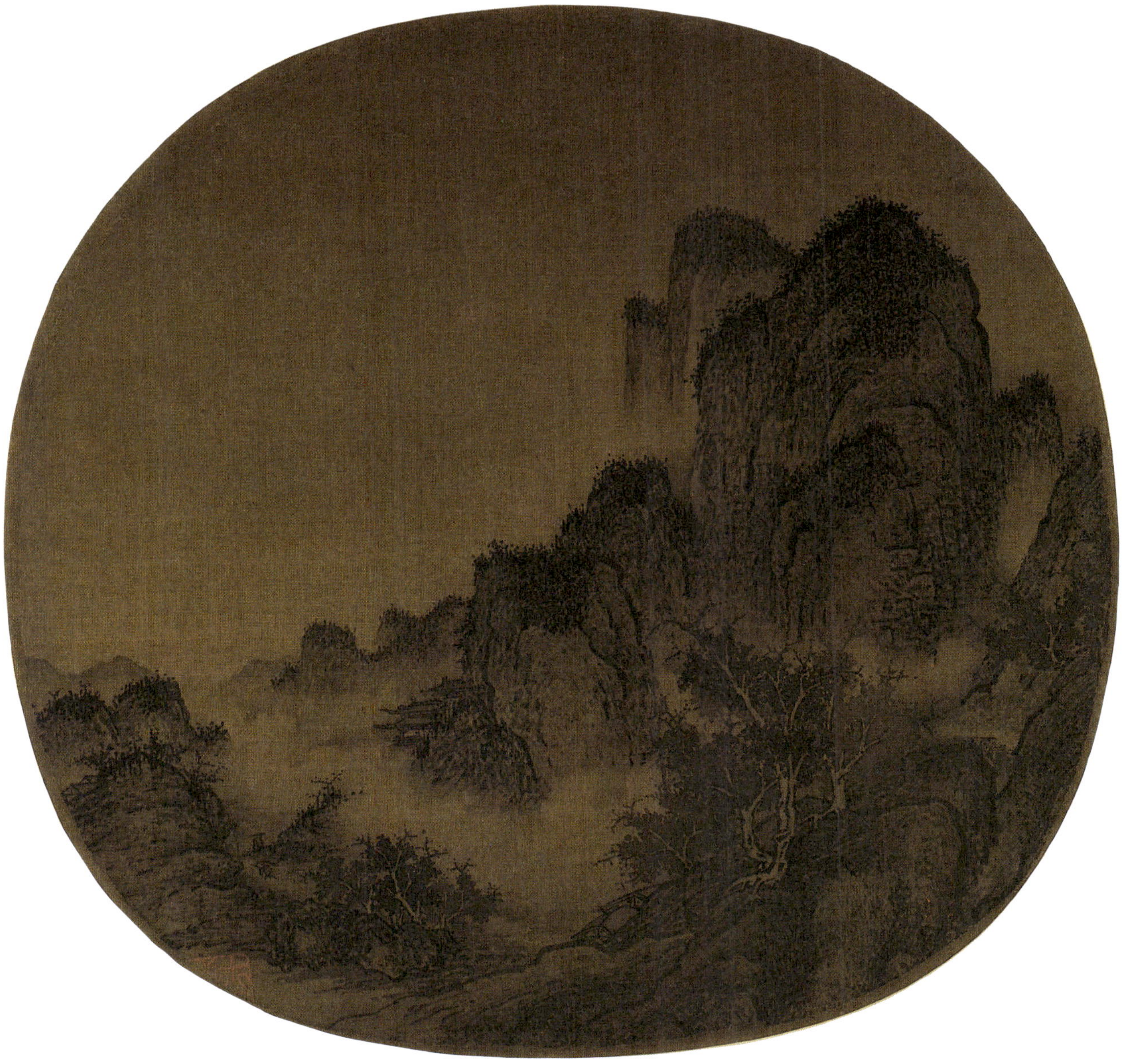

# 4 Wang Hung (fl. ca. 1131–61)

## *Eight Views of the Hsiao and Hsiang Rivers (Hsiao-Hsiang pa-ching)*

Ca. 1150
Two handscrolls (A,B), each with four sections of paintings and colophons, ink on silk
Frontispiece: 23.6 x 87.5 cm (9 1/4 x 34 1/2 in.); painting, average measurements, each section: 23.4 x 90.7 cm (9 1/4 x 35 3/4 in.); colophons, handscroll A: 23.4 x 165.7 cm (9 1/4 x 5 ft. 5 1/8 in.); handscroll B: 23.4 x 236.0 cm (9 1/4 x 7 ft. 8 7/8 in.)

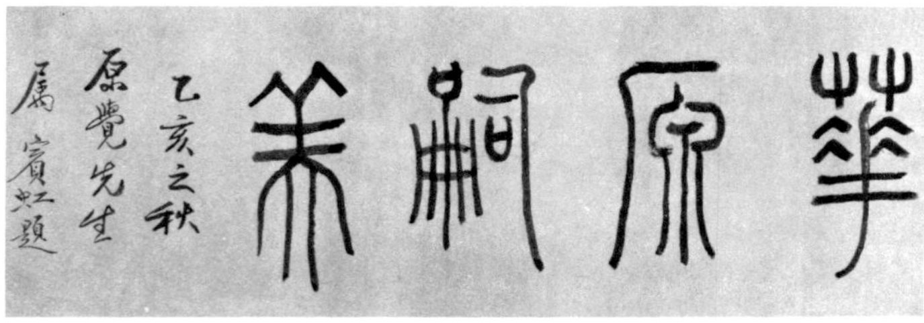

FRONTISPIECE, calligraphy by Huang Pin-hung (1864–1955) (4 character title in seal script): "Masterpiece in the Style of Fan K'uan [ca. 960–1030]" ("Hua-yüan ssu-mei"). Signature: In the autumn of the *i-hai* year [1935], Pin-hung inscribed this for Master Yüan-chüeh.

HANDSCROLL A (from right to left): "Night Rain on Hsiao and Hsiang" ("Hsiao-Hsiang yeh-yü"); "Autumn Moon over Lake Tung-t'ing" ("Tung-t'ing ch'iu-yüeh"); "Wild Geese Descending to Sandbar" ("P'ing-sha yen-lo"), "Returning Sail off Distant Shore" ("Yüan-p'u fan-kuei").

ARTIST'S SIGNATURE: Wang Hung (right, "Night Rain").

COLOPHONS (from right to left):

1. Yü Yün-wen (1511–1579): prose, 113 characters in 11 columns of regular script. Signature: In the fourth lunar month of the summer of the *jen-shen* year of the Lung-ch'ing era [1572], Yü Yün-wen wrote this. Seals: Chung-wei (tall rectangle intaglio); P'ai-ch'üeh chih-yang (tall rectangle intaglio).
2. Mo Shih-lung (ca. 1538–1587): prose, 111 characters in 10 columns of running script. Signature: Mo Shih-lung from Hua-t'ing [in Kiangsu province] inscribed this. Seals: Yün-ch'ing (square intaglio); Mo-sheng Ch'iu-shui (square intaglio).
3. Lo T'ien-ch'ih (1805–after 1847). Signature: On the twenty-first day of the tenth lunar month of the *ting-wei* year, the twenty-seventh year of the Tao-kuang era [1847], Sheng-hu, Lo T'ien-ch'ih, examined this scroll in the Chi-hsing Studio. Seal: Lo shih Liu-hu (square relief).
4. Huang Pin-hung: prose, 92 characters in 12 columns of running script. Signature: Pin-hung inscribed this.

HANDSCROLL B (from right to left): "Evening Bell from Mist-shrouded Temple" ("Yen-ssu wan-chung"); "Fishing Village in Evening Glow" ("Yü-ts'un lo-chao"); "Mountain Market, Clear with Rising Mist" ("Shan-shih ch'ing-lan"); "River and Sky in Evening Snow" ("Chiang-t'ien mu-hsüeh").

COLOPHONS (from right to left):

1. Kuei Tien (fl. late 19th–early 20th century): 7 character regulated verse in 8 lines, followed by a 23 character note, in 10 columns of running script. Signature: Kuei Tien from Nan-hai [in Kuangtung province] inscribed this in the sixth lunar month of the *jen-hsü* year [1922]. Seals: Kuei Nan-p'ing yin (square relief); Ju-[ ] hou-jen (tall rectangle relief).
2. Chou Tzu-ch'i (1871–1923): 5 character regulated verse, followed by rhymed prose, in 137 characters in 13 columns of regular script. Signature: Chou Tzu-ch'i from eastern Lu [Shantung province] respectfully inscribed this. Seal: Ch'i (round relief).
3. Chang Hsüeh-hua (fl. ca. late 19th century–after 1939): 7 character regulated verse in 8 lines, followed by a 10 character note, in 8 columns of free-form regular script. Signature: Chou Tao-jen, Chang Hsüeh-hua. Seal: Ts'u-ch'en yen-kuan (square relief).
4. Huang Wei-ts'ai (fl. late 19th–early 20th century): 7 character regulated verse in 8 lines in 8 columns of regular script. Signature: Tzu-ching, Huang Wei-ts'ai, inscribed this. Seals: Huang Wei-ts'ai yin (squat rectangle intaglio); Tzu-ching (square relief).
5. Shen Tse-t'ang (*chü-jen*, 1873): 7 character quatrain, followed by a 6 character note, in 9 columns of running script. Signature: In the eighth lunar month of the *jen-hsü* year [1922] Shen Tse-t'ang inscribed this. Seal: Shen Tse-t'ang yin (square intaglio).
6. Ling Ho (fl. late 19th–early 20th century): 7 character regulated verse in 8 lines, followed by a 6 character note, in 7 columns of running script. Signature: Ling Ho inscribed this. Seal: Meng-cheng (square relief).
7. Wu Shih-ch'ing (fl. late 19th–early 20th century): 7 character regulated verse in 8 lines in 10 columns of running script. Signature: Wu Shih-ch'ing inscribed this. Unidentified seal (square relief).
8. Li Ting-yüan (fl. late 19th–early 20th century): 5 character regulated verse in 8 lines, followed by a 31 character note, in 12 columns of regular script. Signature: Your junior, Li Ting-yüan, respectfully inscribed this.

9. Liang Ch'ing-kuei (1858–1931): 7 character quatrain in 5 columns of running script. Signature: Liang Ch'ing-kuei inscribed this. Seals: Liang Ch'ing-kuei yin (square intaglio); Hsiao-shan (square relief); Hao-hsüeh wei fu (tall rectangle relief).
10. T'ien-nan-tun-sou (fl. late 19th–early 20th century): two 5 character regulated verses, each in 8 lines, followed by 3 notes in 36 characters, in 18 columns of clerical and running script. Signature: T'ien-nan-tun-sou inscribed this.
11. Yang Sung-fen (fl. late 19th–early 20th century): 7 character regulated verse in 8 lines, followed by a 10 character note, in 17 columns of running script. Signature: Yang Sung-fen. Seal: Tzu-kuei (tall rectangle relief).
12. Lu Nai-t'ung (fl. late 19th–early 20th century): 7 character quatrain, followed by a 88 character note, in 22 columns of running script (dated 1925). Signature: Lu Nai-t'ung. Seal: Lu Nai-t'ung yin (square relief).
13. Ch'en Chih-nai (fl. late 19th–early 20th century): 7 character regulated verse in 8 lines, followed by 3 notes in 84 characters, in 20 columns of running script. Signature: In the fifth lunar month of the summer of the *jen-hsü* year [1922], your junior, Ch'en Chih-ting, wrote this. Seals: Chih-ting hsiao yin (tall rectangle intaglio); Yu-ssu [ ] [ ] shan [ ] yen (tall rectangle relief).
14. Wu Tao-jung (1852–1936): 8 characters in 1 column of running script. Signature: On the day before the Double Fifth Festival of the *kuei-hai* year [1923], Taoist Wu Tao-jung respectfully viewed this scroll. Seals: Yung-ch'un (square relief); Tao-jung ch'ang-shou (square intaglio).
15. Li Yüan-shih (fl. late 19th–early 20th century): On the Dragon Boat Festival of the *kuei-hai* year [1923], Li Yüan-shih viewed this.
16. P'an P'u (b. 1852): two 7 character quatrains, with a 10 character title, followed by a 6 character note, in 7 columns of running script. Signature: In the third lunar month of the spring of the *jen-hsü* year [1922], Pa-min-ch'iao-sou, P'an P'u, wrote this in the Ram City [Canton], in his seventy-first year [*sui*]. Seal: Men-sun hsin-yung chih yin (tall rectangle relief).
17. P'an Shih-ch'eng (*chin-shih*, 1832): prose, 268 characters in 21 columns of running script. Seal: P'an Teh-yü shou-ts'ang ku-chin chin-shih yin (square relief).
18. Lin Chih-chün (fl. late 19th century–before 1962): prose, 83 characters in 8 columns of running script. Signature: Lin Chih-chün inscribed this in his seventy-eighth year [*sui*], in the winter of the *ping-shen* year [1956].

COLLECTORS' SEALS:
Southern Sung imperial seal: Yü-shu (gourd-shaped relief; upper right, each section).
2 unidentified half seals (right edge, each section).
2 unidentified seals (right edge, "Night Rain").

Edward L. Elliott Family Collection (L117.71 a–b)

PUBLISHED: Lo Yüan-chüeh, *Sung Wang Hung Hsiao-Hsiang pa-ching t'u chüan* (An illustrated portfolio of the Sung dynasty Wang Hung scroll of *Eight Views of the Hsiao and Hsiang Rivers*) (Hong Kong, n.d. [1956?]); Suzuki Kei and Akiyama Terukazu, eds., *Chūgoku bijutsu* (Chinese art in Western collections) (Tokyo: Kōdan-sha, 1973), vol. 1, pls. 8, 9; Suzuki Kei, ed., *Suiboku bijutsu taikei* (Complete collection of ink paintings), vol. 2 (Tokyo: Kōdan-sha, 1974), pls. 8, 9; Watanabe Akiyoshi, *Shōshō hakkei zu* (*Eight Views of the Hsiao and Hsiang Rivers*), Nihon no bijutsu, no. 124 (Tokyo: Shibundō, 1976), pp. 24–25, pl. 22 ("Mountain Market," "Night Rain"); Ishikawa Jun et al., eds., *Bunjinga suihen* (Selection of the finest Chinese and Japanese literati paintings), vol. 2 (Tokyo: Chūōkōron-sha, 1977), p. 119, figs. 11–12; pls. 71, 72; Miyazaki Ichisada et al., *Sōgen no bijutsu* (Art of the Chinese Sung and Yüan dynasties) (Tokyo: Heibon-sha, 1980), p. 209, fig. 65; Suzuki Kei, comp., *Chūgoku kaiga sōgō zuroku: daiikkan, Amerika–Kanada hen* (Comprehensive illustrated catalogue of Chinese paintings: volume 1, American and Canadian collections) (Tokyo: University of Tokyo Press, 1982), pp. 136–37, pl. A17–066.

"Night Rain on Hsiao and Hsiang" ("Hsiao-Hsiang yeh-yü")

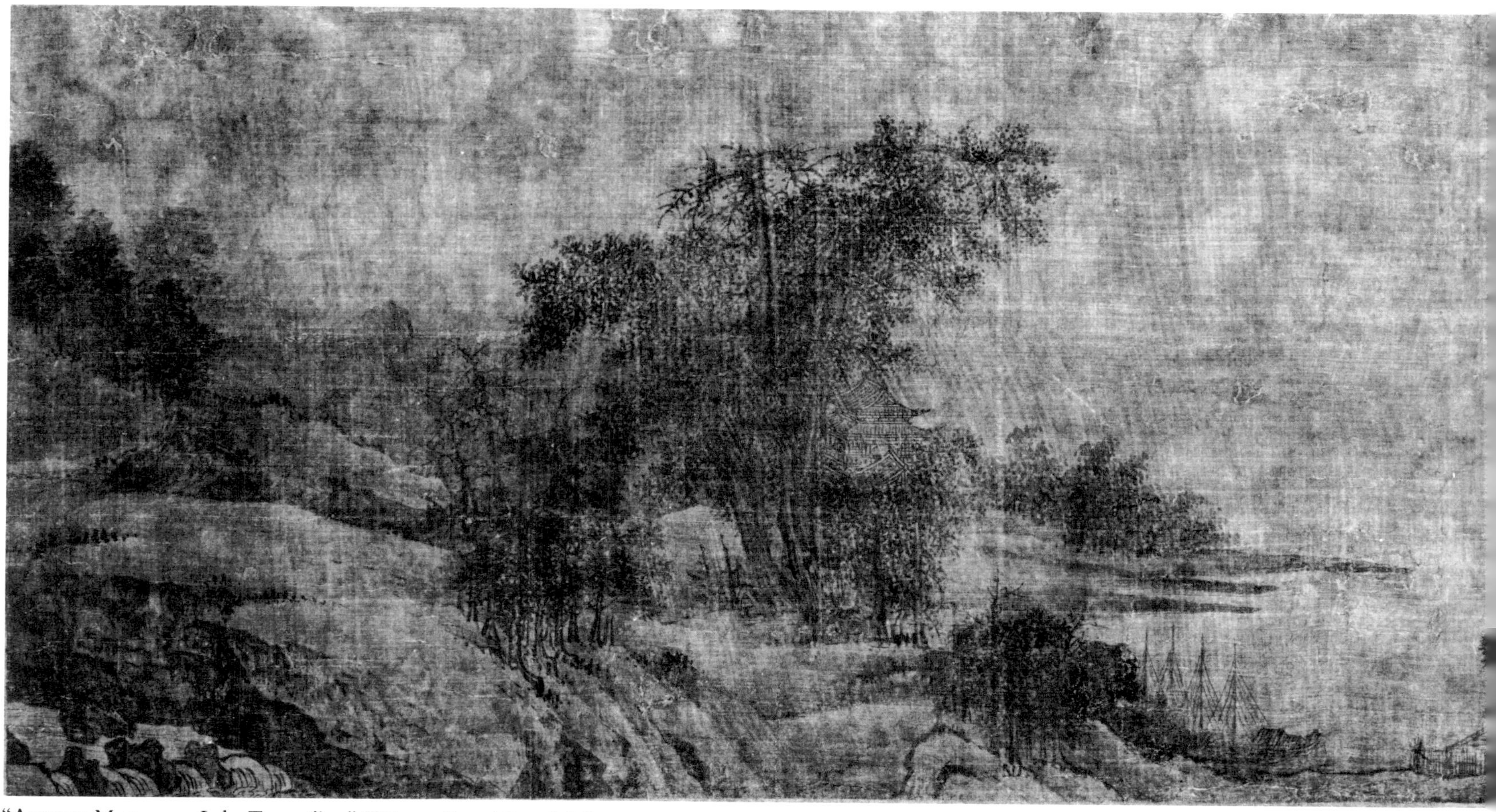
"Autumn Moon over Lake Tung-t'ing" ("Tung-t'ing ch'iu-yüeh")

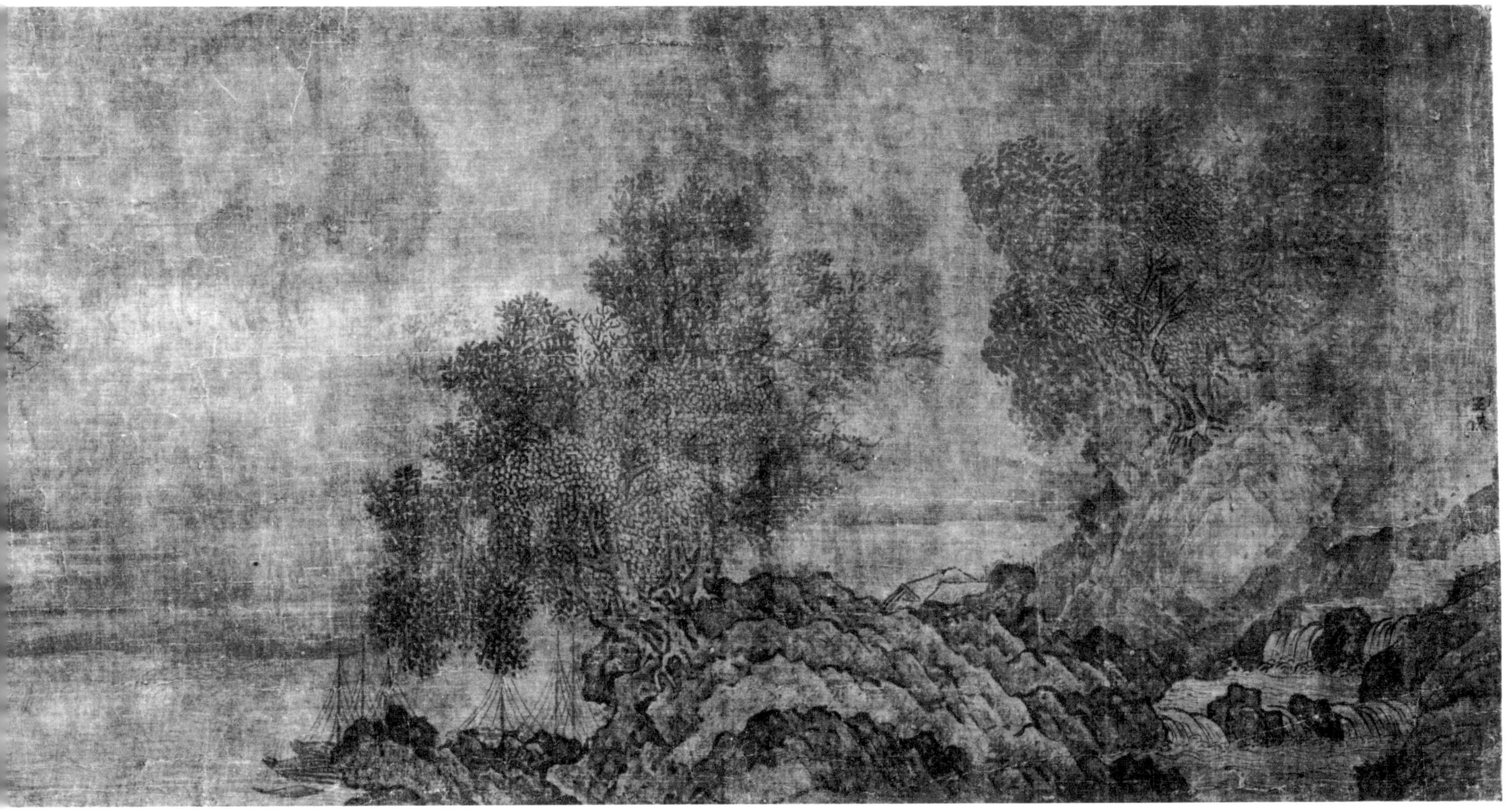

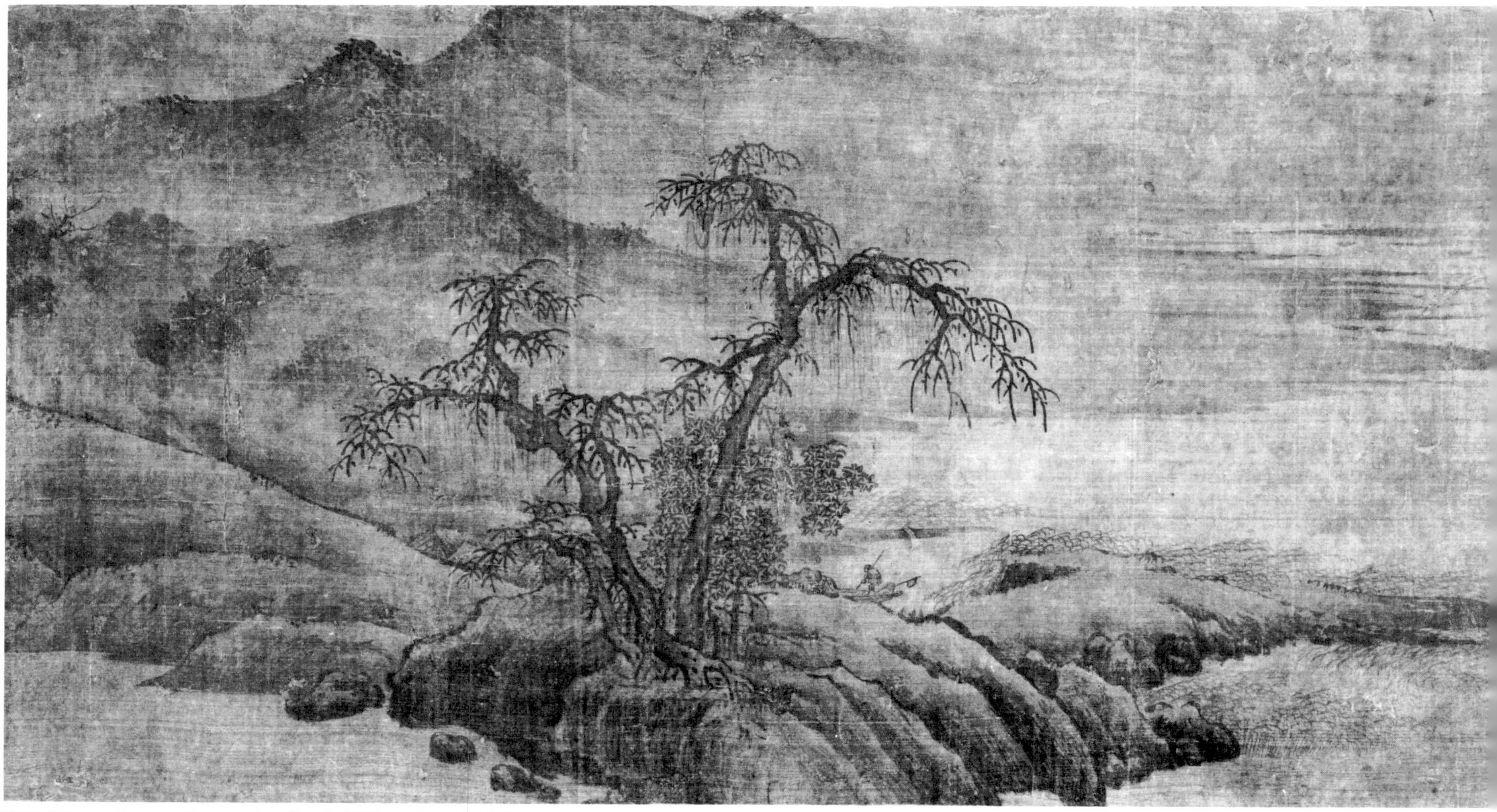
"Wild Geese Descending to Sandbar" ("P'ing-sha yen-lo")

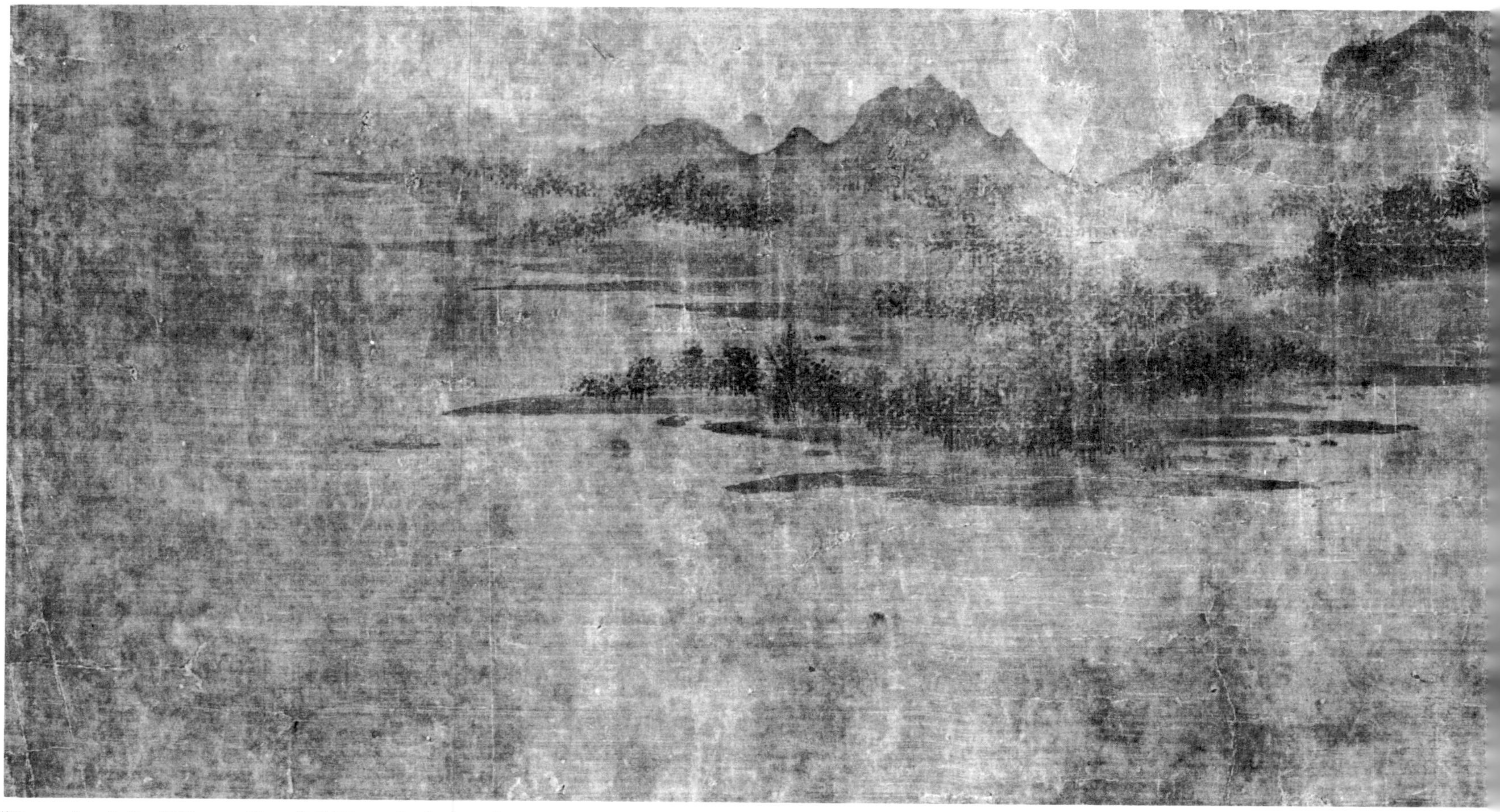
"Returning Sail off Distant Shore" ("Yüan-p'u fan kuei")

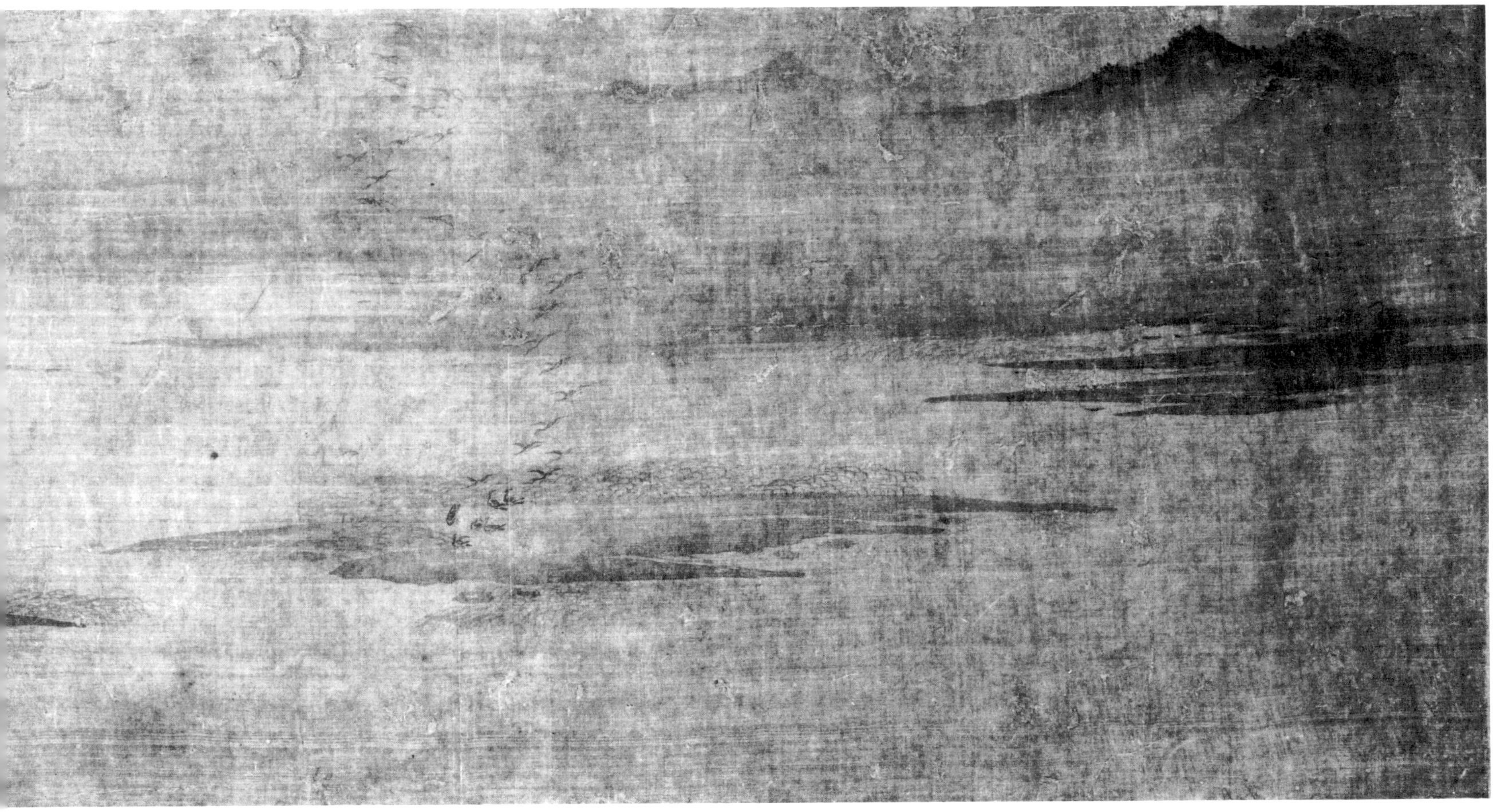

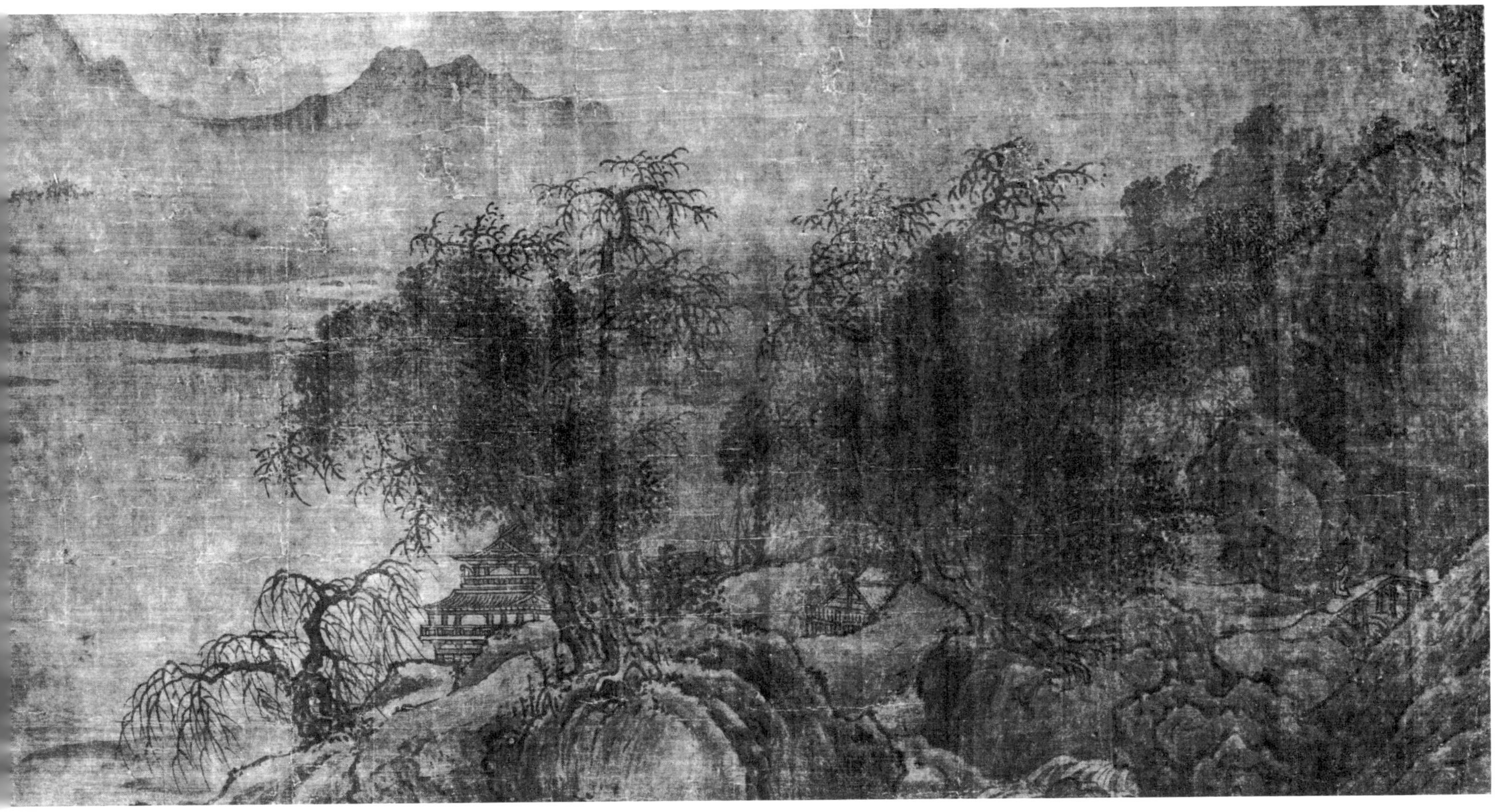

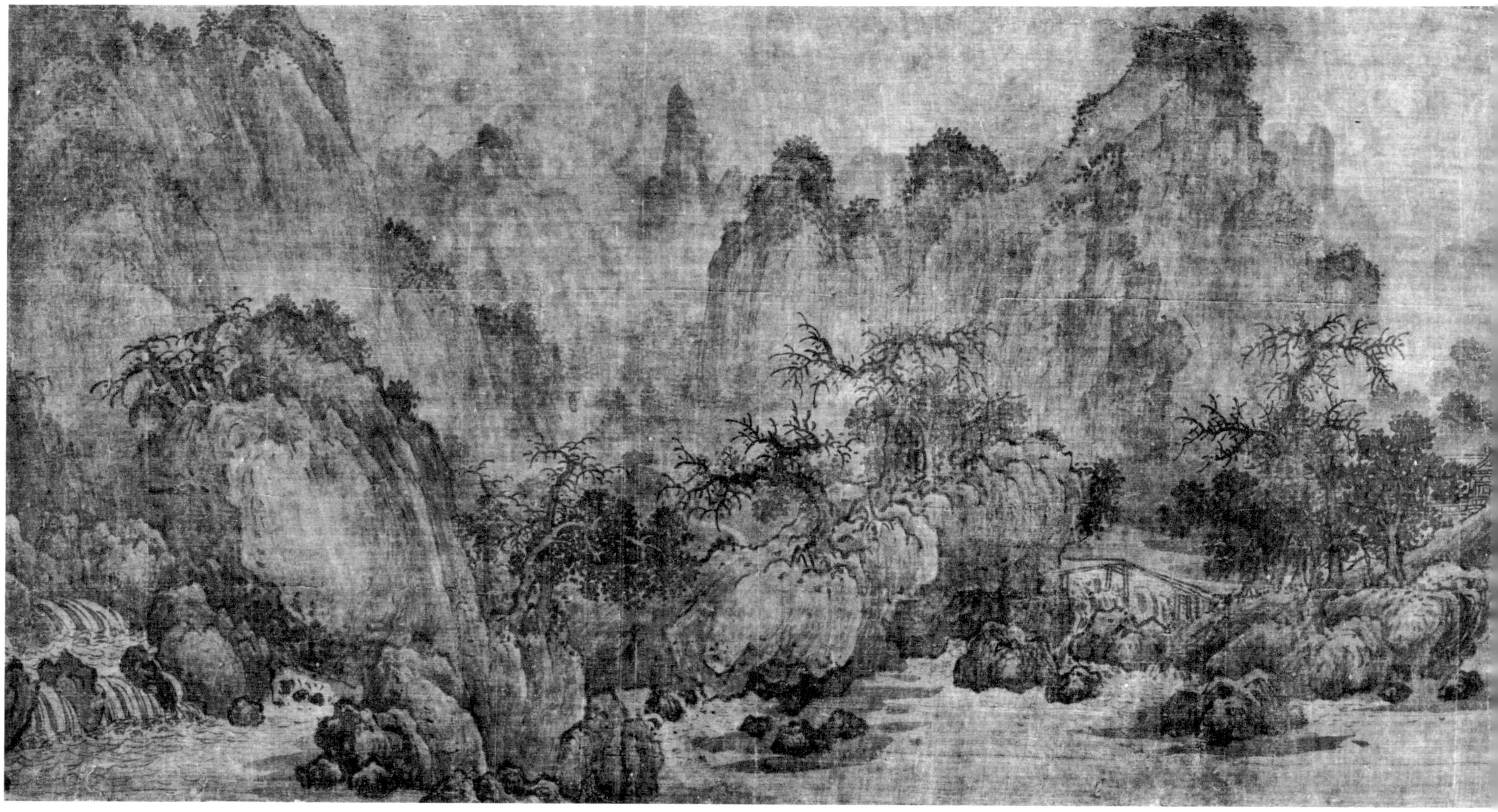
"Evening Bell from Mist-shrouded Temple" ("Yen-ssu wan-chung")

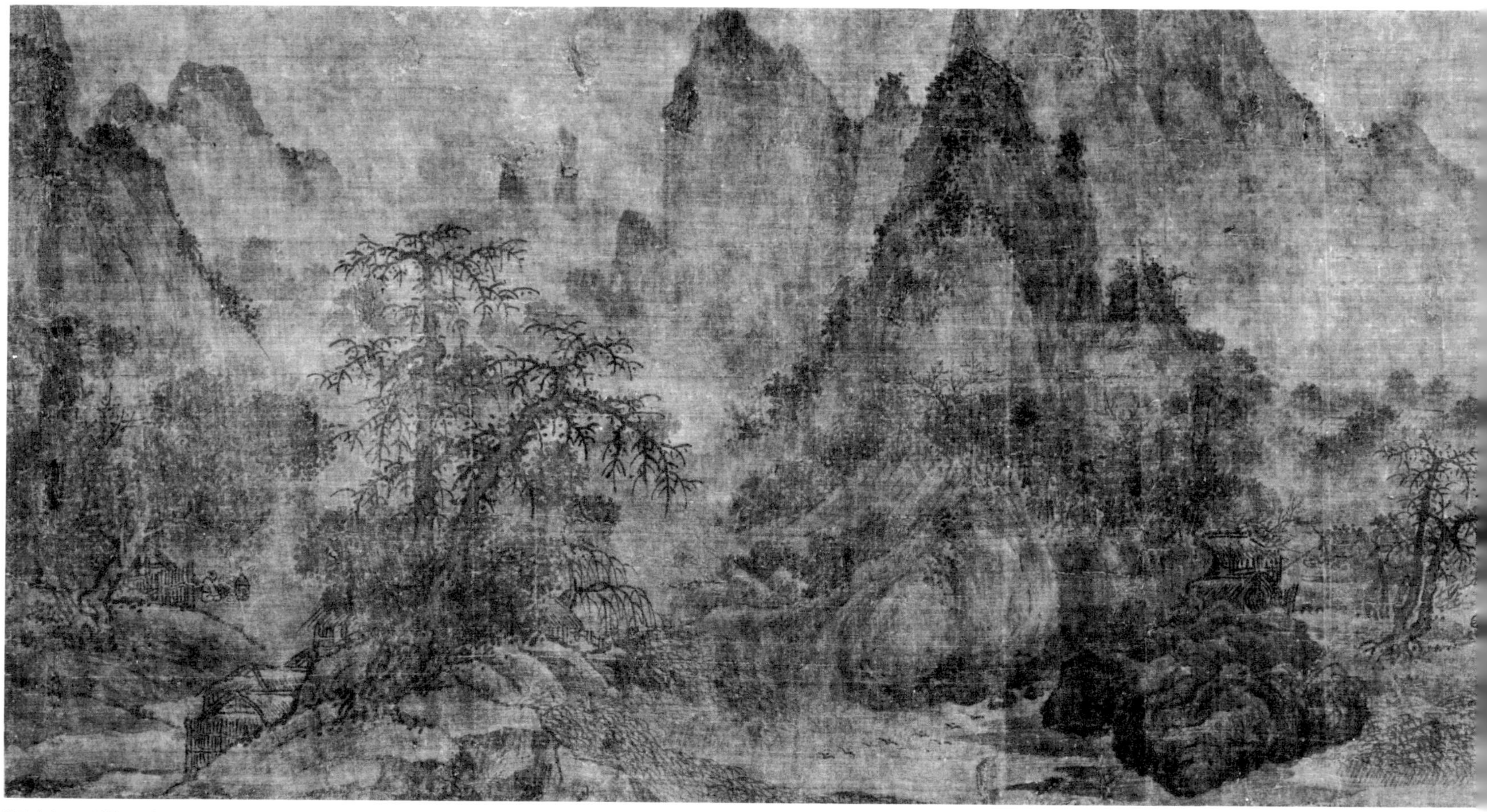
"Fishing Village in Evening Glow" ("Yü-ts'un lo-chao")

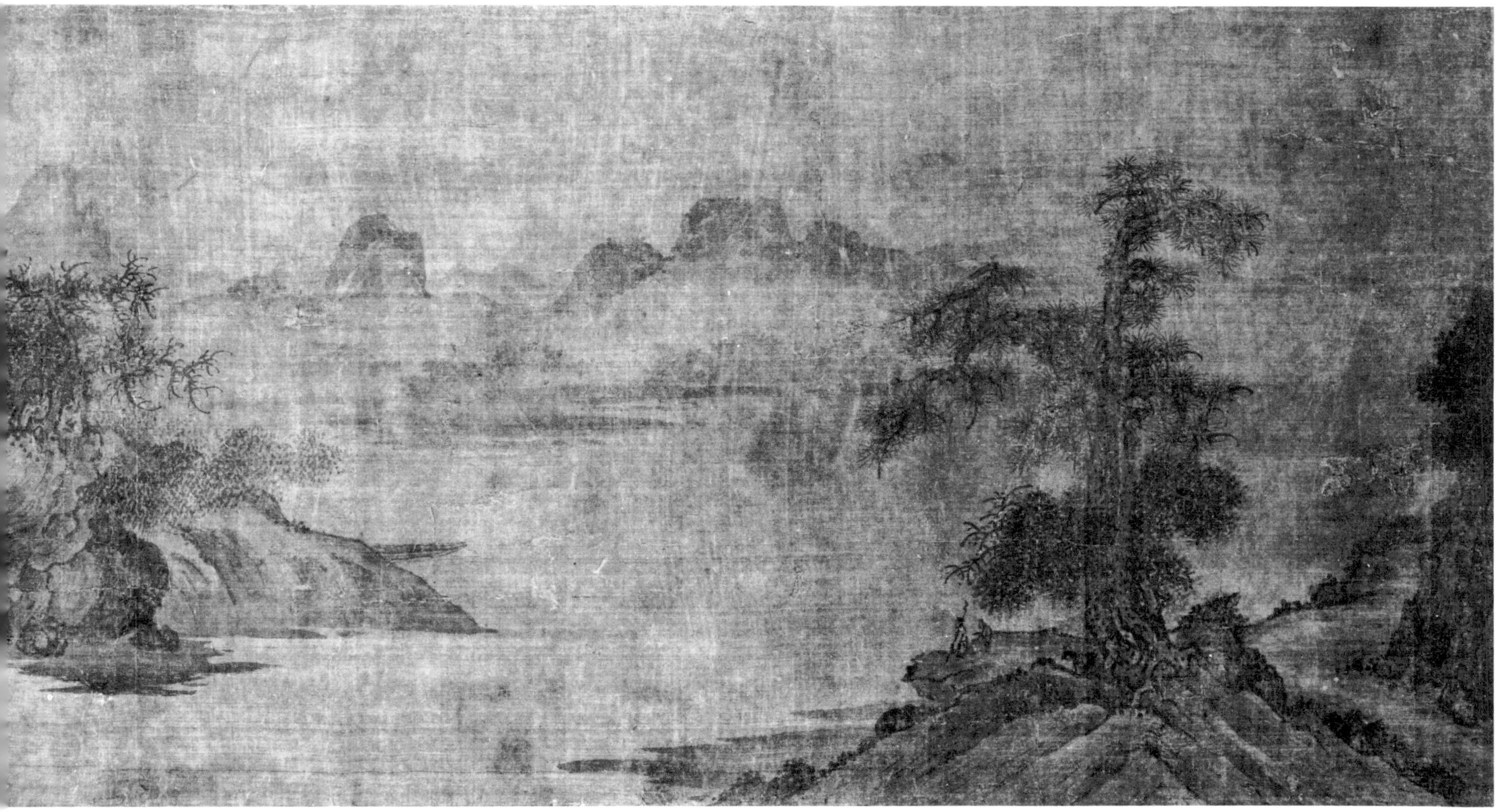

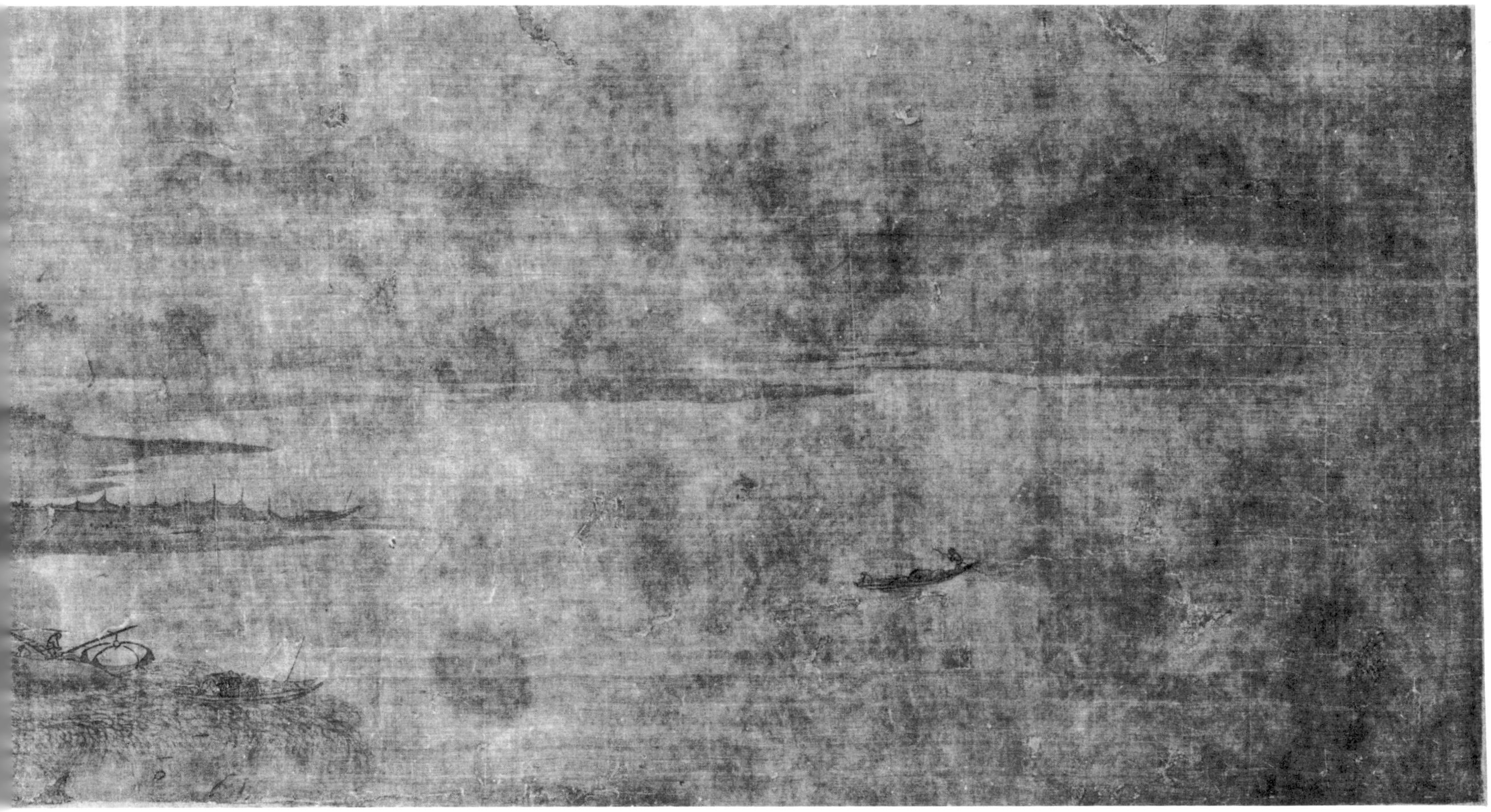

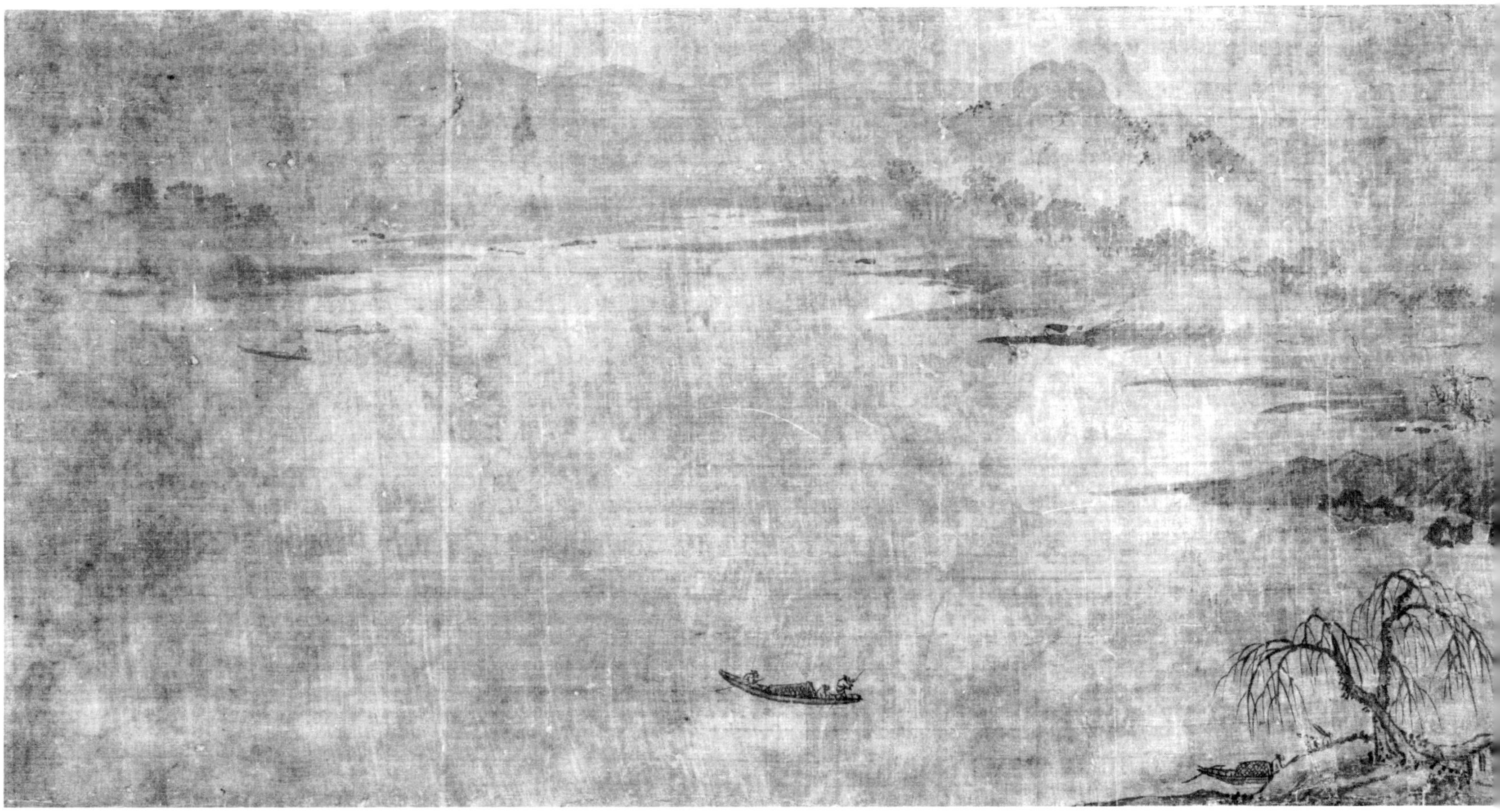
"Mountain Market, Clear with Rising Mist" ("Shan-shih ch'ing-lan")

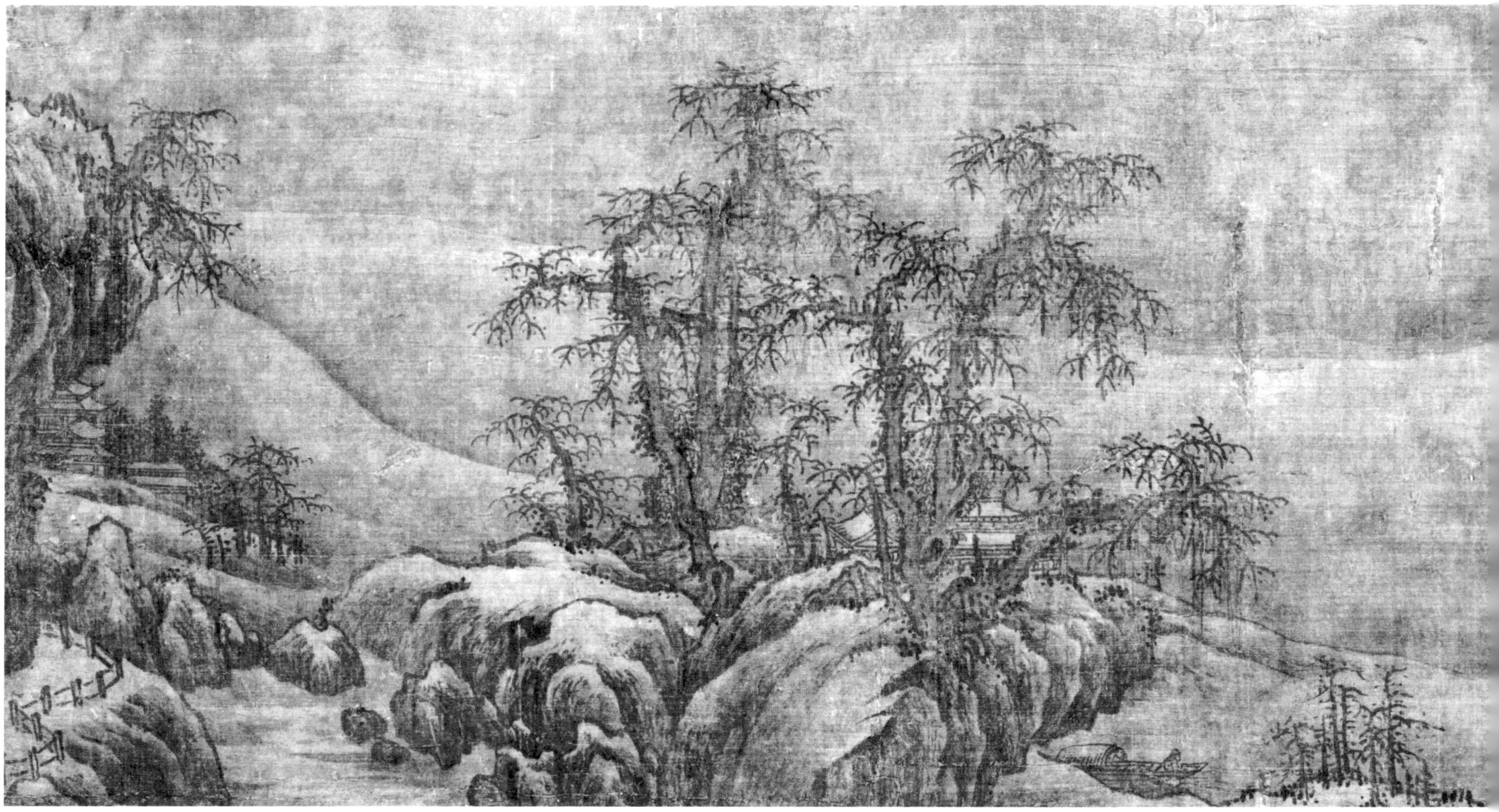
"River and Sky in Evening Snow" ("Chiang-t'ien mu-hsüeh")

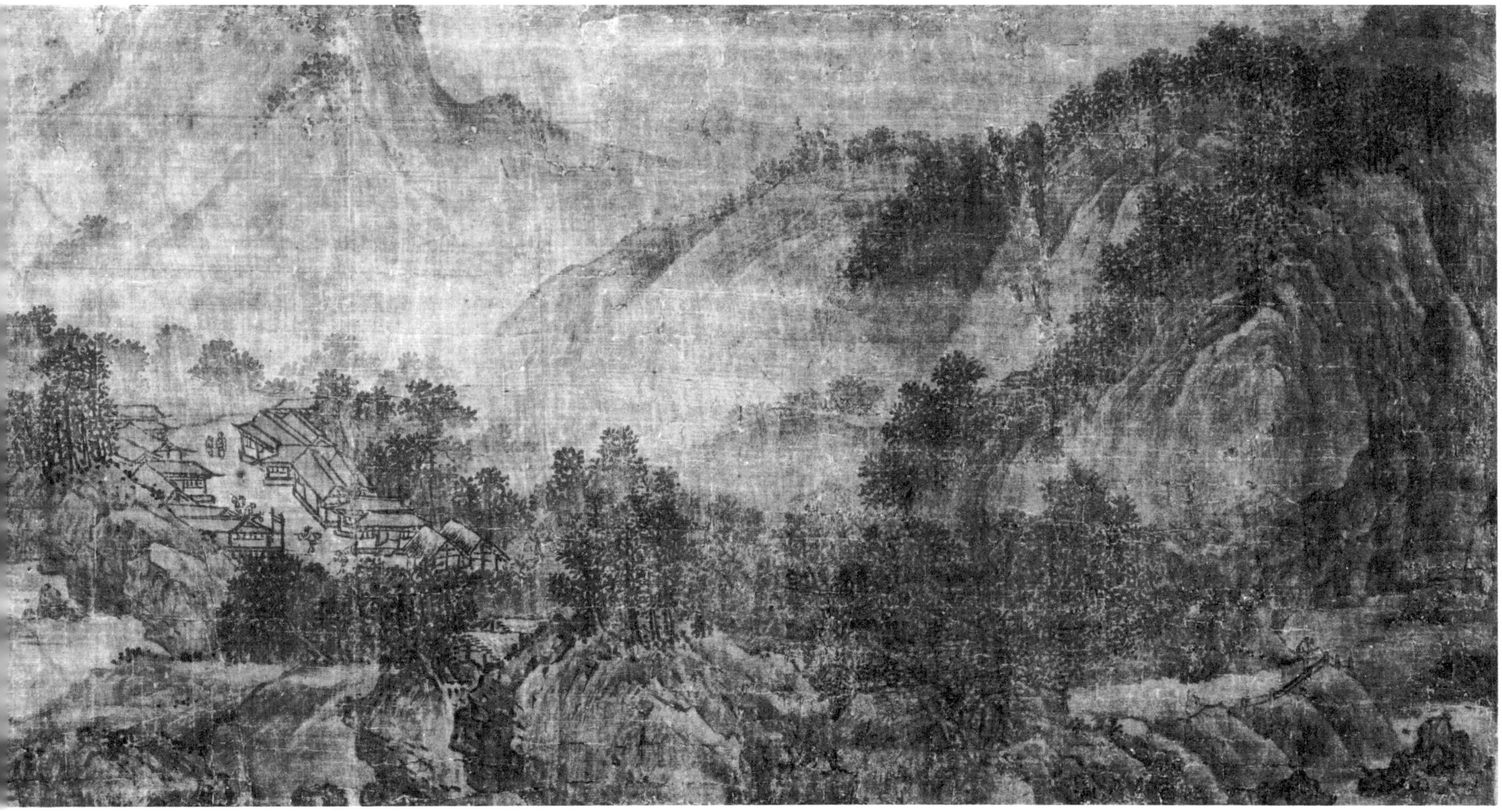

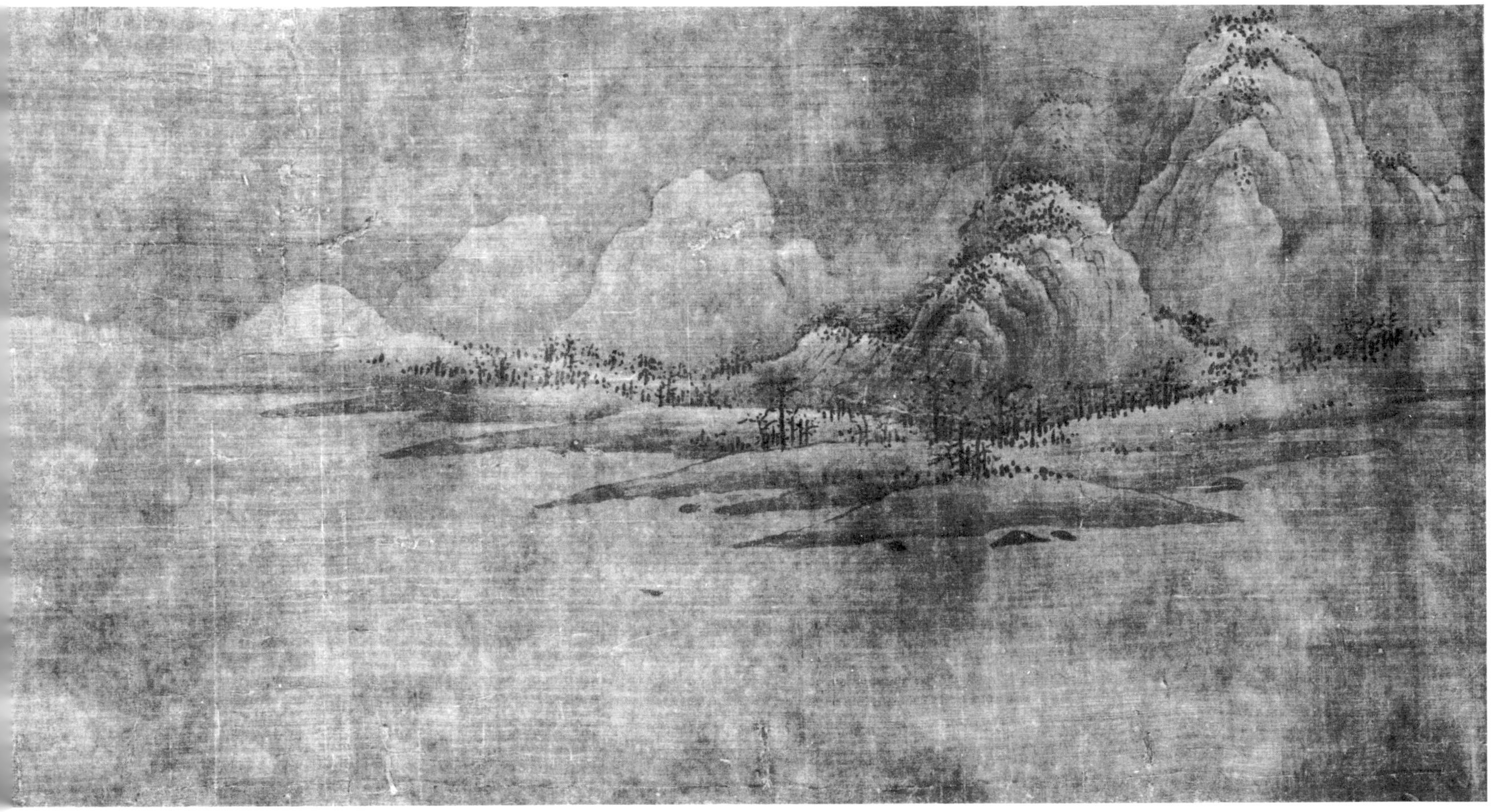

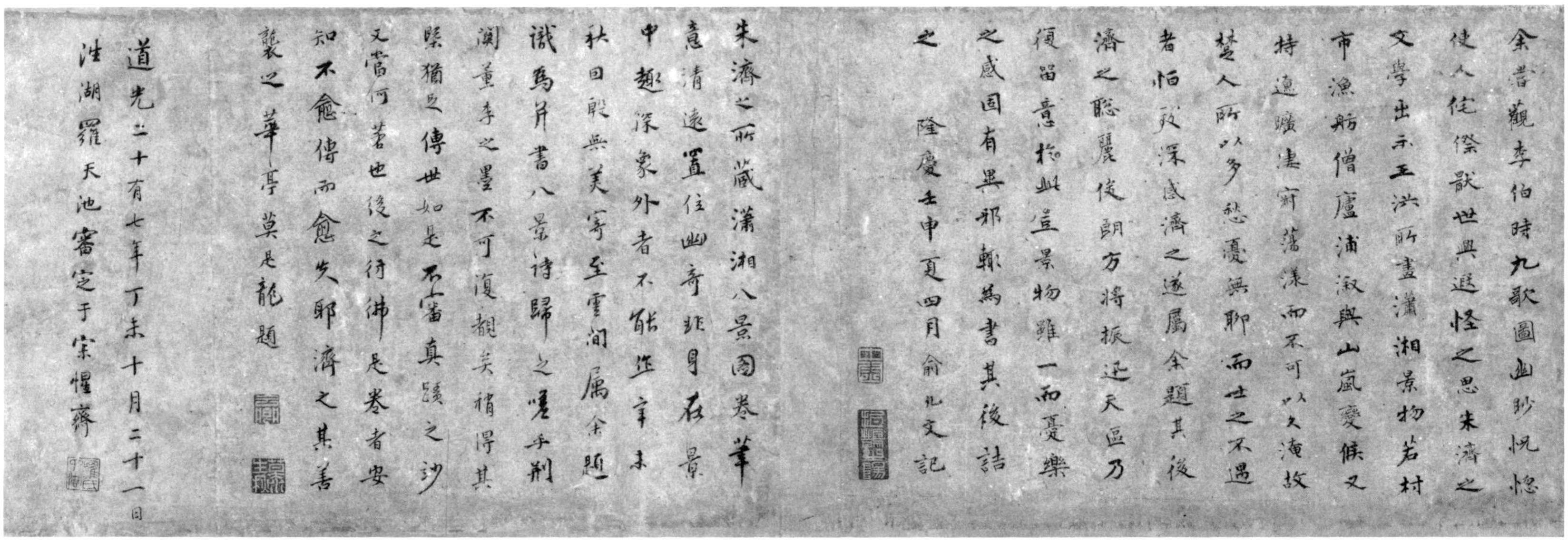

Lo T'ien-ch'ih Mo Shih-lung Yü Yün-wen

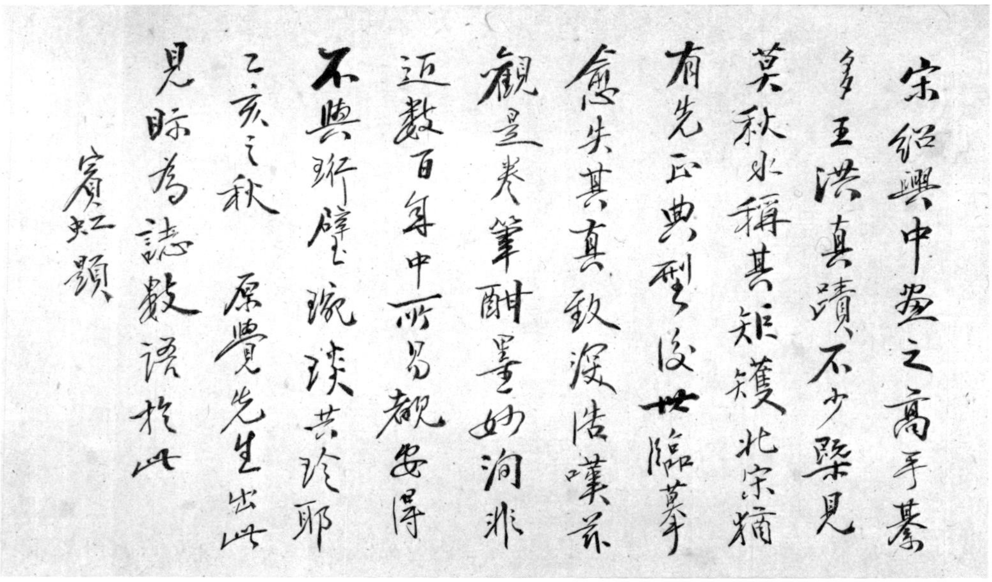

Huang Pin-hung

Chang Hsüeh-hua Chou Tzu-ch'i

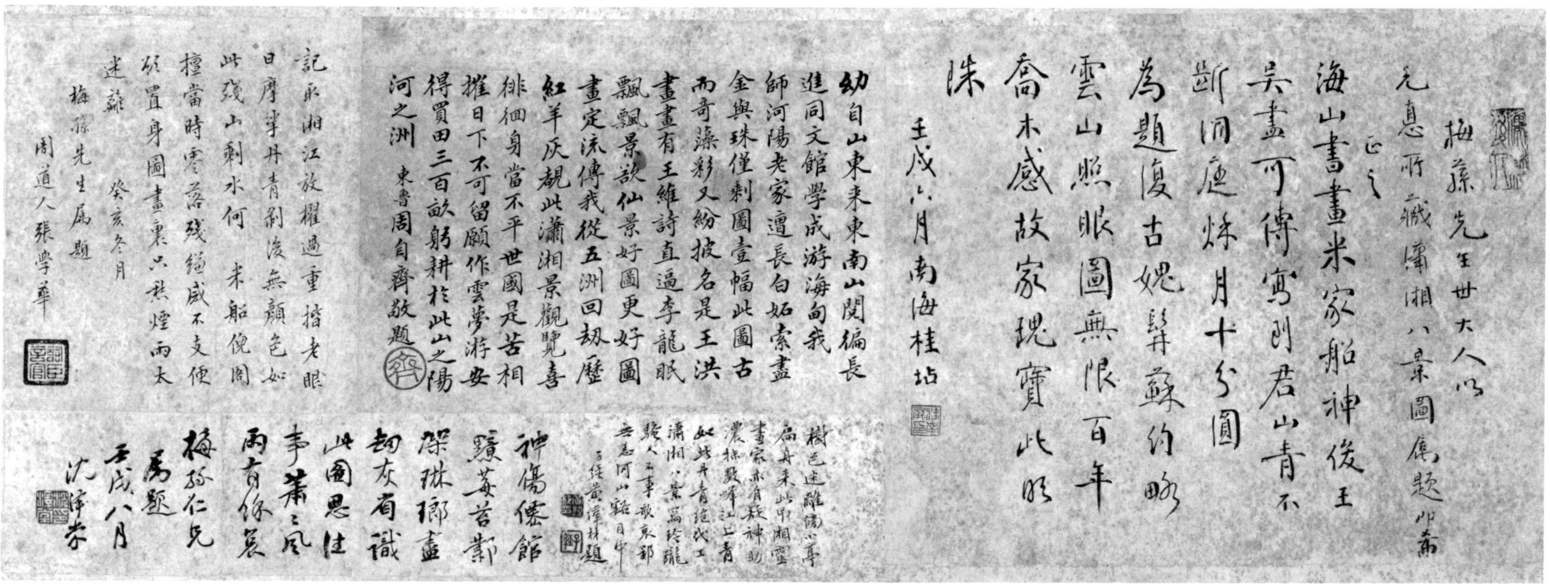

Shen Tse-t'ang Huang Wei-ts'ai Kuei Tien

Liang Ch'ing-kuei Li Ting-yüan Wu Shih-ch'ing

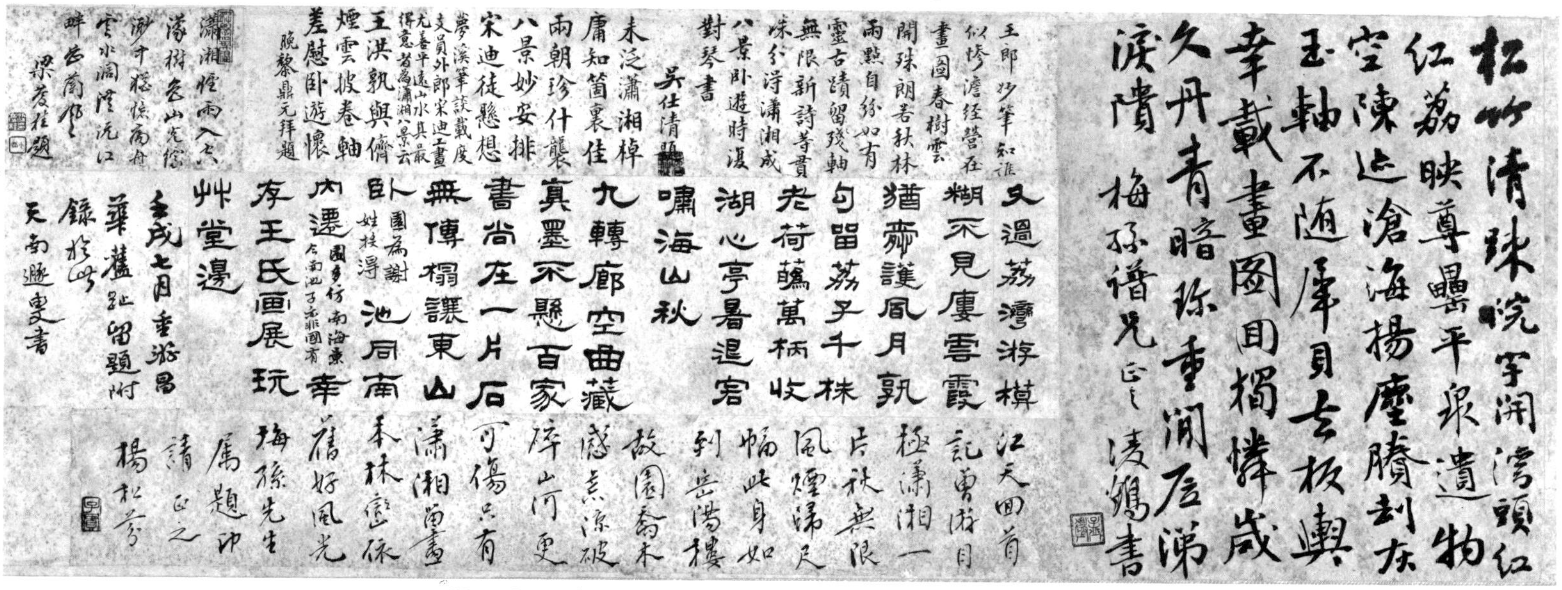

T'ien-nan-tun-sou Yang Sung-fen Ling Ho

Lu Nai-t'ung

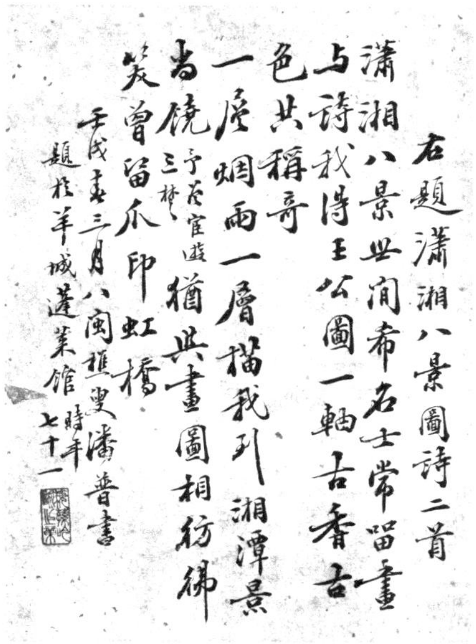

P'an P'u

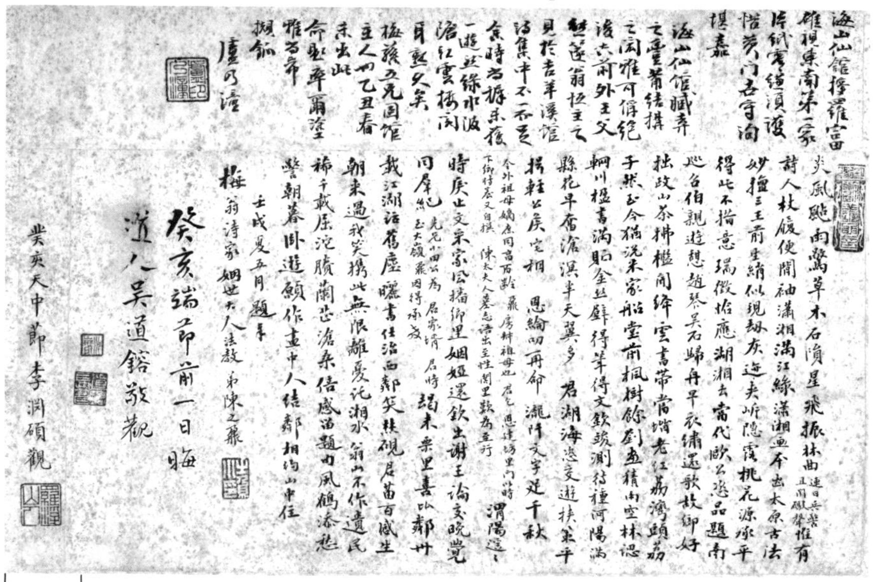

Wu Tao-jung Ch'en Chih-nai

Li Yüan-shih

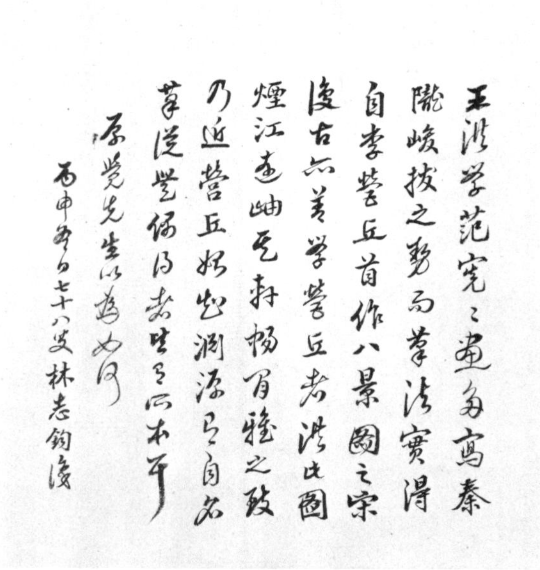

Lin Chih-chün

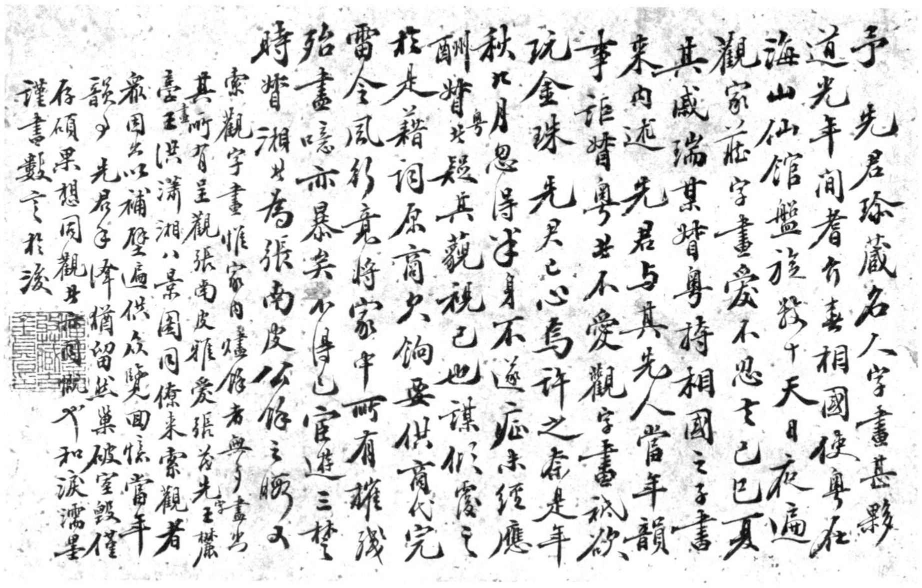

P'an Shih-ch'eng

# 5 Anonymous

## *Peach Blossoms by a Spring River (T'ao-hua ch'un-shui)*

12th century
Album leaf, ink and color on silk
19.6 x 21.3 cm ($7^{3}/_{4}$ x $8^{3}/_{8}$ in.)

No artist's signature or seal.

COLOPHON by Chang Yüan (Chang Ta-ch'ien; 1899–1983) (7 character title, followed by a 6 character note, in 1 column of running script): A Sung painting, *Peach Blossoms by a Spring River*, in the imperial collection during the Shao-hsing era (1131–62). Seals: Chang Yüan ssu-yin (square intaglio); Ta-ch'ien fu-ch'ang ta-chi (square intaglio).

COLLECTOR'S SEAL: Southern Sung imperial seal: Nei-tien mi-shu chih yin (square relief; upper right).

Edward L. Elliott Family Collection (L225.70)

PUBLISHED: Suzuki Kei, comp., *Chūgoku kaiga sōgō zuroku: daiikkan, Amerika–Kanada hen* (Comprehensive illustrated catalogue of Chinese paintings: volume 1, American and Canadian collections) (Tokyo: University of Tokyo Press, 1982), p. 142, pl. A17–075.

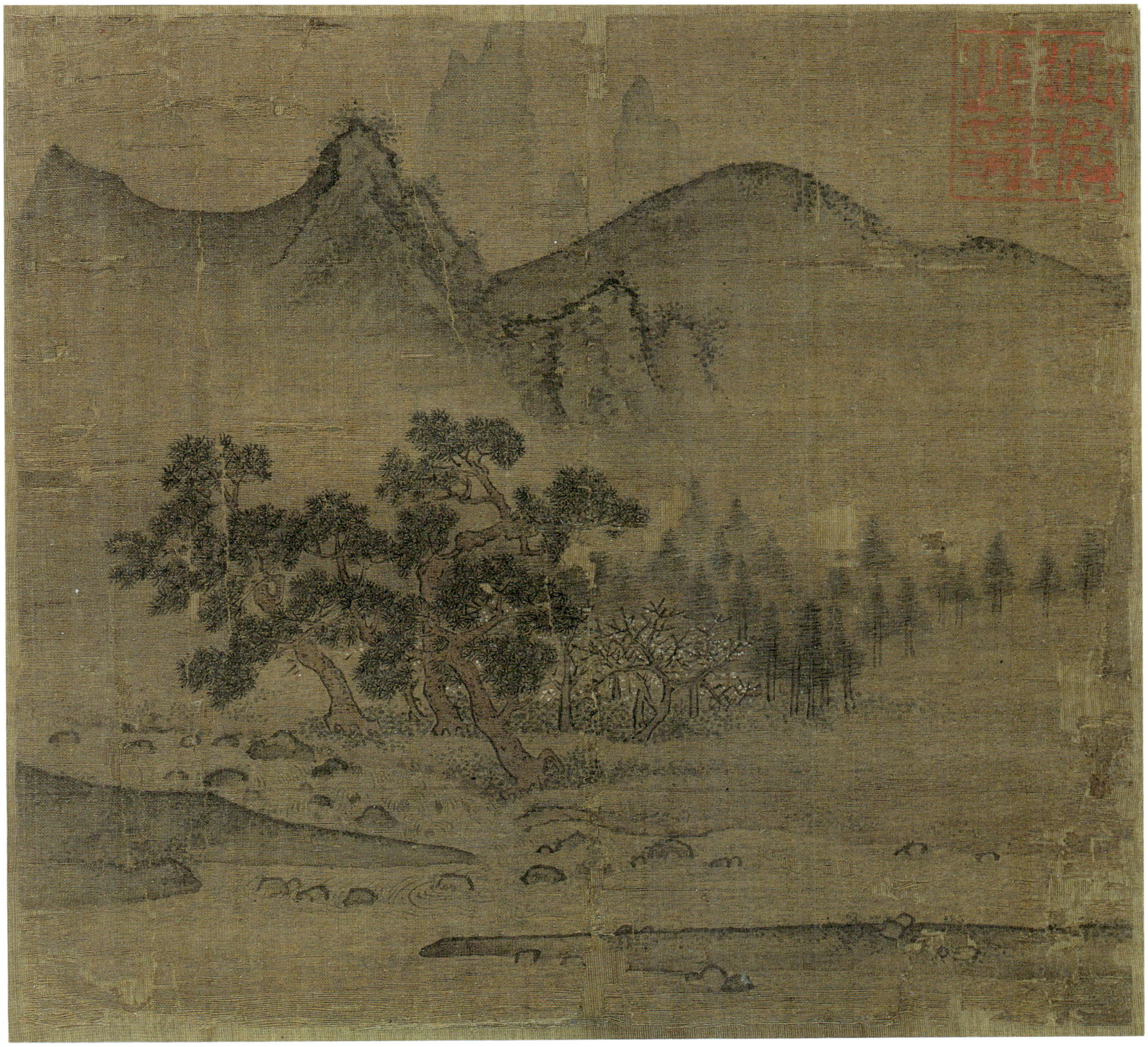

# 6 Chao Meng-fu (1254–1322)

## *The Mind Landscape of Hsieh Yu-yü (Yu-yü ch'iu-ho)*

Ca. 1287
Handscroll, ink and color on silk
Painting: 27.4 x 117.0 cm (10¾ in. x 3 ft. 10 in.); colophons: 27.4 x 214.3 cm (10¾ in. x 7 ft. ⅝ in.)

ARTIST'S SEAL: Chao shih Tzu-ang (square relief; lower left).

COLOPHONS (from right to left):

1. Chao Yung (ca. 1290–ca. 1360): prose, 38 characters in 2 columns of running script. Signature: Yung carefully inscribed this.
2. Ni Tsan (1301–1374): 7 character quatrain in 4 columns of regular script. Signature: Ni Tsan.
3. Chou Pin (fl. ca. late 14th century): prose, 35 characters in 3 columns of cursive script.
4. Yao Shih (d. ca. 1318): prose, 33 characters in 4 columns of running script. Signature: Yao Shih from Wu-hsing [in Chekiang province] inscribed this. Seal: Yün-an (square relief).
5. Wang Ch'i (fl. ca. 1290–1310): prose, 103 characters in 9 columns of cursive script. Signature: Wang Ch'i from eastern Lu [Shantung province]. Seals: San-huai-t'ang (tall rectangle intaglio); Lang-ya Wang shih (square relief).
6. Teng Yü (fl. early 14th century): 7 character quatrain in 4 columns of free-form running script. Signature: Teng Yü, Mu-chih. Seals: Lu-ling Teng hsüeh-shih chia (tall rectangle relief); Chüeh-fei-chai (square relief).
7. Yü Chi (1272–1348): 7 character quatrain in 2 columns of running script. Signature: Yü Chi. Seal: Yü Po-sheng fu (square relief).
8. Sung Wu (1260–ca. 1340): 6 character quatrain in 3 columns of regular script. Signature: Sung Wu. Seals: Wu I-shih Sung Tzu-hsü (square relief); Wan-hsiang ts'ui-han (square relief).
9. Ch'en Chi-ju (1558–1639): prose, 15 characters in 1 column of running script. Signature: In the *ting-hai* year of the Wan-li era [1587], Ch'en Chi-ju saw this at Hsiang Meng-huang's Wan-chüan Pavilion.
10. Tung Ch'i-ch'ang (1555–1636): prose, 48 characters in 6 columns of running script. Signature: On the last day of the ninth lunar month of the *chi-yu* year [1609], Tung Ch'i-ch'ang saw and inscribed this. Seal: Tung Hsüan-tsai (square intaglio).
11. Lo T'ien-ch'ih (1805–after 1847):
    a) Prose, 94 characters in 5 columns of running script. Signature: On the fifteenth day of the twelfth lunar month

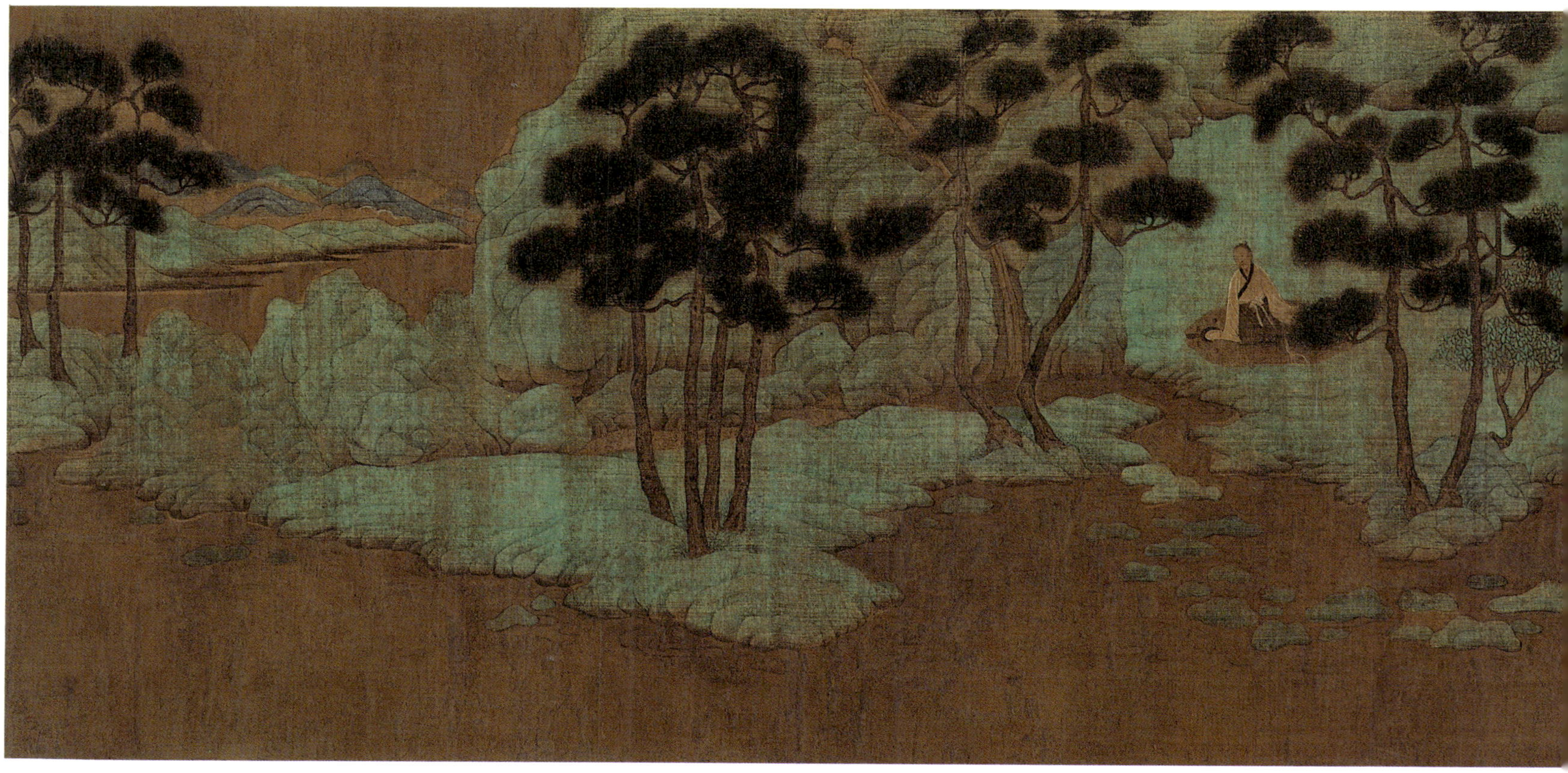

of the *ping-wu* year of the Tao-kuang era [1846], Lo T'ien-ch'ih saw this again, while temporarily residing at Master Yeh's Keng-hsia-hsi-kuan [Studio]. Seals: Liu-hu (tall rectangle relief); Lo (round intaglio).

b) Prose, 44 characters in 4 columns of running script. Signature: On the second day of the tenth lunar month of the *ting-wei* year [1847], [Lo] in the Chi-hsing Studio again inscribed this. Seal: Lo shih T'ien-ch'ih (square intaglio).

COLLECTORS' SEALS:

Liang Ch'ing-piao (1620–1691), 2 seals.
Lo T'ien-ch'ih, 4 seals.
Ch'en Ch'ing-ho (dates unknown), 1 seal.
Wang Chi-ch'ien (b. 1907), 8 seals.
Unidentified owners, 2 seals.
4 unidentified seals.

Edward L. Elliott Family Collection (L216.69)

PUBLISHED: Sherman E. Lee and Wai-kam Ho, *Chinese Art under the Mongols: The Yüan Dynasty (1279–1368)* (Cleveland: Cleveland Museum of Art, 1968), p. 90, fig. 17; Chu-tsing Li, "Stages of Development in Yüan Landscape Painting," *National Palace Museum Bulletin* 4, no. 2 (May–June 1969): fig. 1; Richard Barnhart, *Marriage of the Lord of the River: A Lost Landscape by Tung Yüan, Artibus Asiae* Supplementum 27 (1970): fig. 24; Suzuki Kei and Akiyama Terukazu, eds., *Chūgoku bijutsu* (Chinese art in Western collections) (Tokyo: Kōdan-sha, 1973), vol. 1, p. 21; Helmut Brinker, "Ch'an Portraits in a Landscape," *Archives of Asian Art* 27 (1973–74): 9, fig. 2; James Cahill, *Hills beyond a River: Chinese Painting of the Yüan Dynasty, 1279–1368* (New York and Tokyo: Weatherhill, 1976), pls. 10, 11; Wen C. Fong, *"Rivers and Mountains after Snow* (*Chiang-shan hsüeh-chi*) attributed to Wang Wei (A.D. 699–759)," *Archives of Asian Art* 30 (1976–77): 16, fig. 7; Ishikawa Jun et al., eds., *Bunjinga suihen* (Selection of the finest Chinese and Japanese literati paintings), vol. 3 (Tokyo: Chūōkōron-sha, 1979), pl. 64; Suzuki Kei, comp., *Chūgoku kaiga sōgō zuroku: daiikkan, Amerika–Kanada hen* (Comprehensive illustrated catalogue of Chinese paintings: volume 1, American and Canadian collections) (Tokyo: University of Tokyo Press, 1982), pp. 130–31, pl. A17–056; Richard M. Barnhart, *Along the Border of Heaven: Sung and Yüan Paintings from the C. C. Wang Family Collection* (New York: The Metropolitan Museum of Art, 1983), p. 112, fig. 49, pp. 114–15, fig. 50.

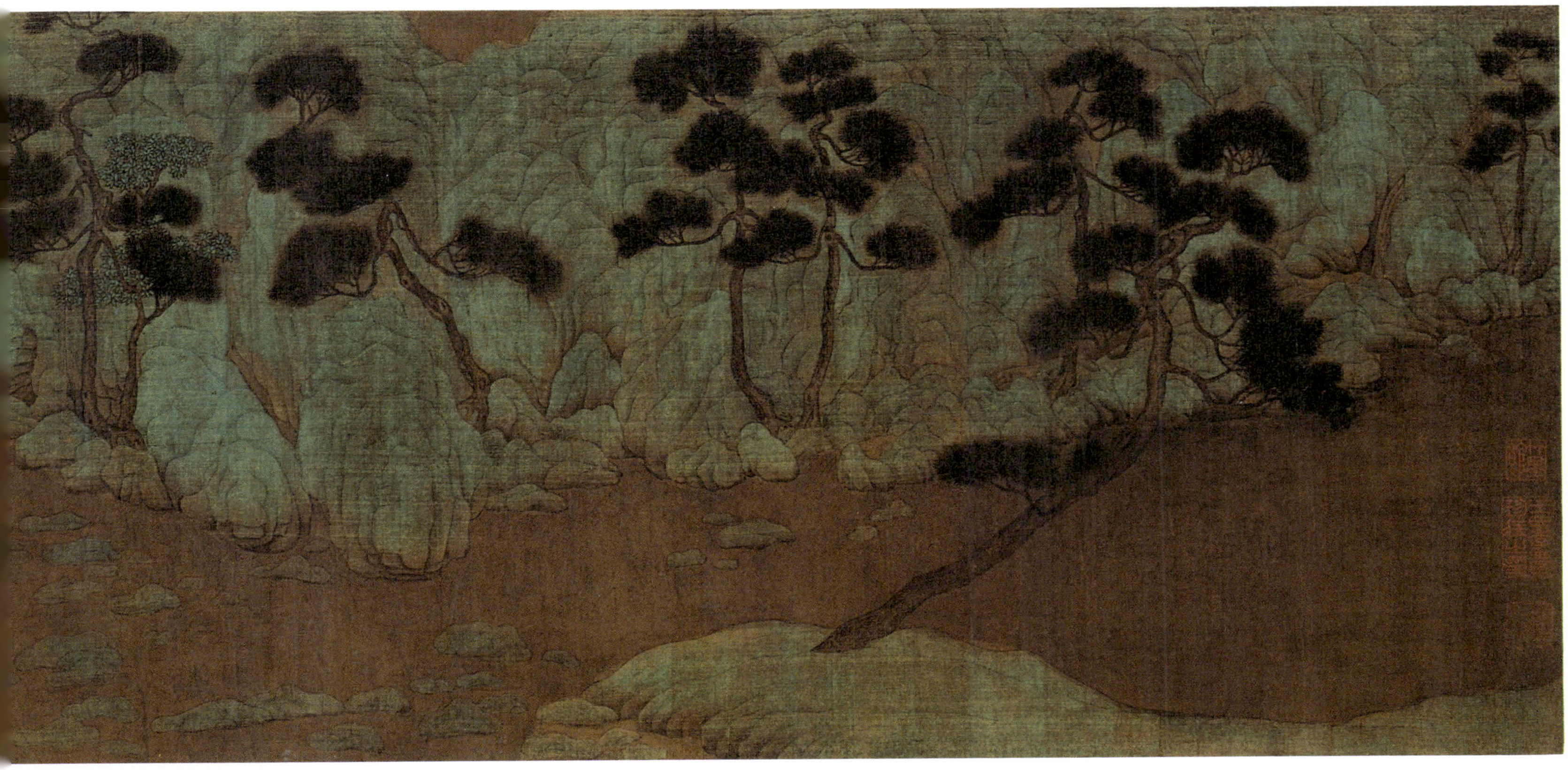

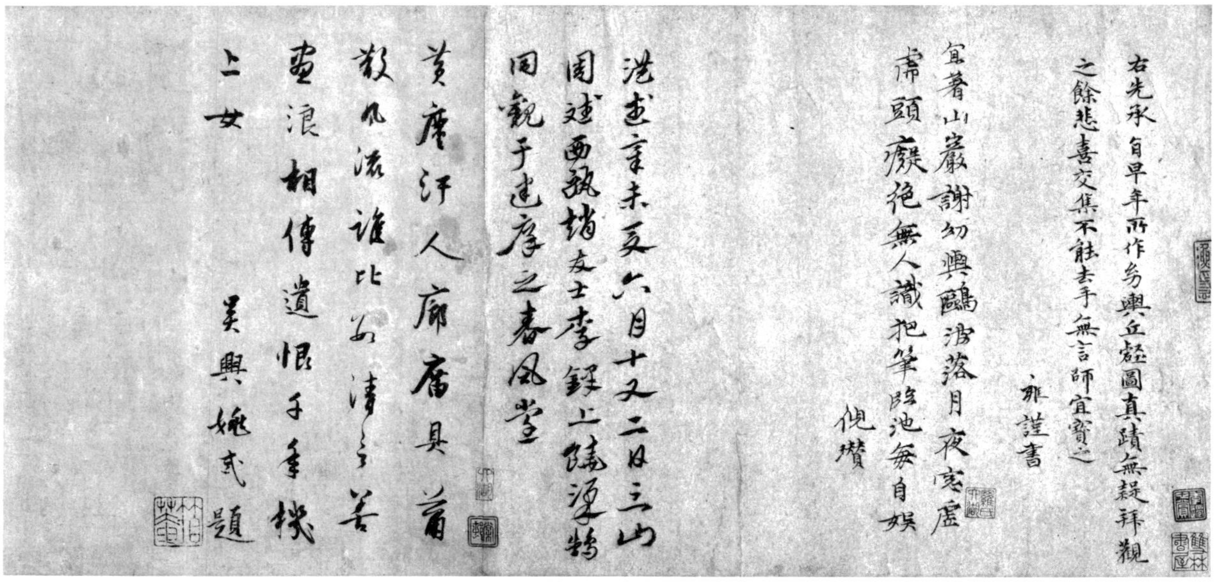

Yao Shih Chou Pin Ni Tsan Chao Yung

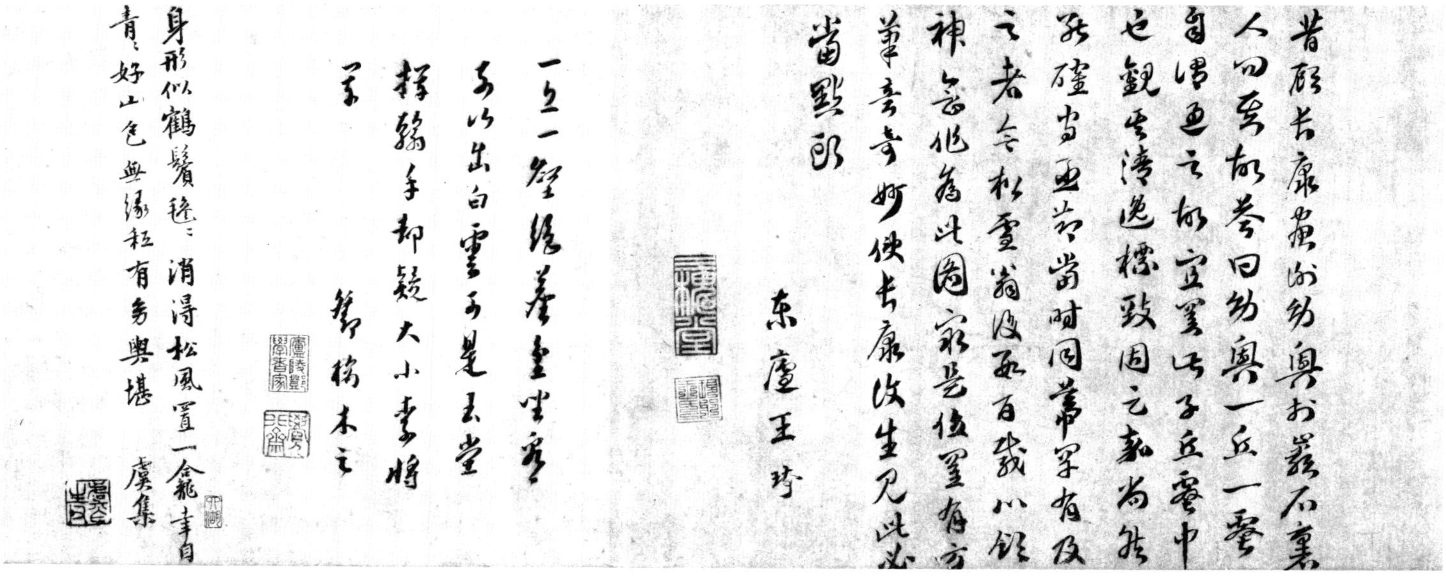

Yü Chi Teng Yü Wang Ch'i

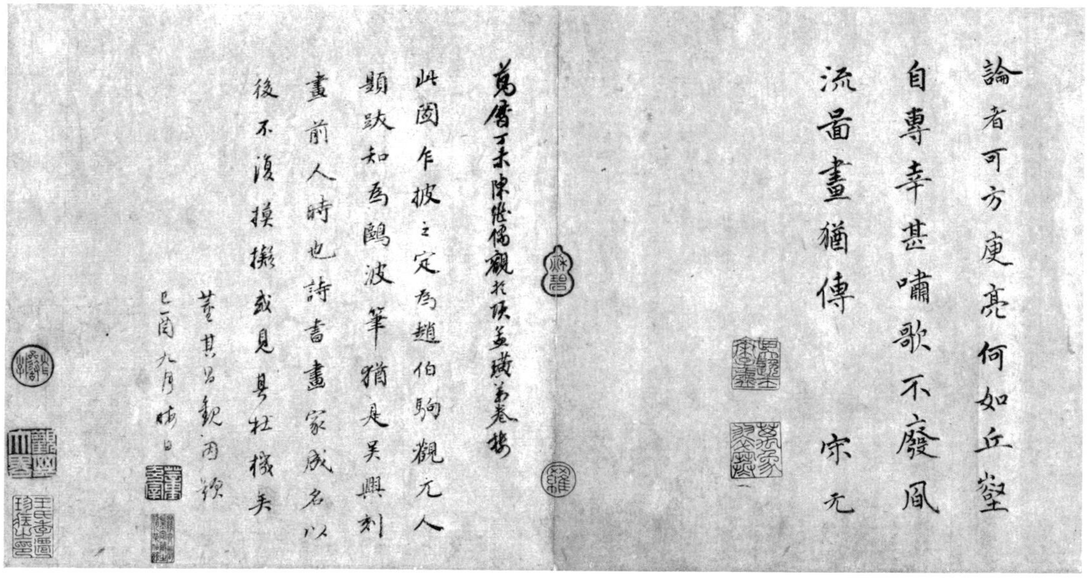

Tung Ch'i-ch'ang Ch'en Chi-ju Sung Wu

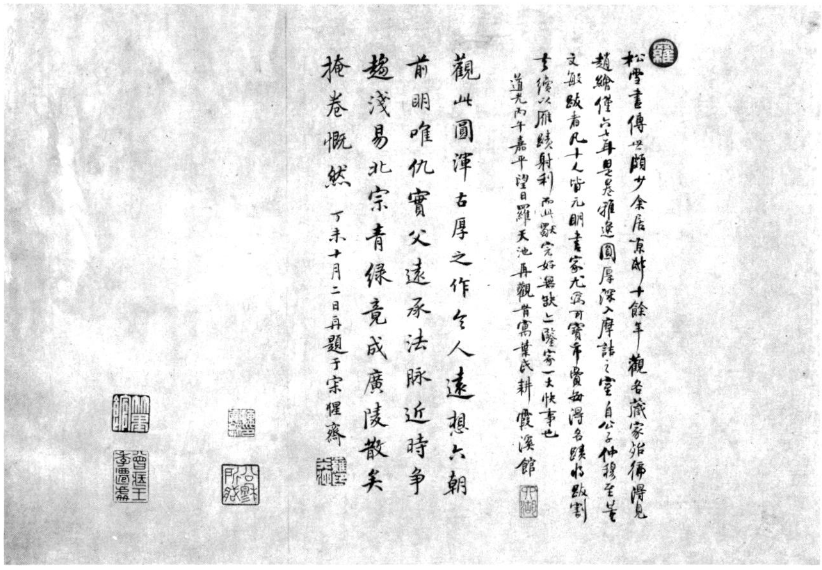


Lo T'ien-ch'ih (b)    Lo T'ien-ch'ih (a)

# 7 Chao Meng-fu (1254–1322)

## *Record of the Miao-yen Monastery (Hu-chou Miao-yen-ssu chi)*

Ca. 1309–10
Handscroll, ink on paper
Calligraphy: 34.2 x 364.5 cm (13 1/2 in. x 11 ft. 11 1/2 in.); colophons: 34.6 x 206.7 cm (13 5/8 in. x 6 ft. 9 3/8 in.)

CALLIGRAPHY: 6 character title in 3 columns of seal script, followed by a 783 character essay in 89 columns of regular script.

ARTIST'S SEALS: Sung-hsüeh-chai (tall rectangle relief; following the text and repeated twice on junctures of paper).

COLOPHONS:

1. Yao Shou (1422–1495):
   a) Prose, 96 characters in 9 columns of free-form running script. Signature: On the seventh day of the tenth lunar month of the *wu-tzu* year of the Ch'eng-hua era [1468], a guest in Yung-ning [in Kiangsi province] inscribed this. Seals: Kung-shou (square relief); Tzu-yu tan-ch'iu (square intaglio); Chia-shen chin-shih (square relief); Wan-chüan-lou (tall rectangle relief); Huai-chung-tzu (square relief).
   b) Prose, 102 characters in 9 columns of running script. Signature: On the twelfth day of the [tenth] lunar month [of the *hsin-mao* year of the Ch'eng-hua era (1471)], Shou wrote this by lamplight, while staying in the Chih Garden. Seals: Tan-ch'iu-tzu (tall rectangle relief); Yao shih Kung-shou (tall rectangle relief); Chia-ho Yao shih (square relief); Hsi-hsi chüan-yu k'o (square relief); Liang-ho-hsüan (tall rectangle relief); Hsin-yü (double seal, both square relief).
   c) Prose, 72 characters in 7 columns of running script. Signature: Kung-shou.
   d) Prose, 111 characters in 10 columns of running script. Signature: On the fifth day of the fourth lunar month of the *jen-yin* year [1482], I-shih, Yao Shou inscribed this.
2. Chang Chen (fl. mid-15th century): prose, 96 characters in 12 columns of running script (between Yao's first and second colophons). Signature: Chang Chen inscribed this.
3. Chang Chien (1853–1926): prose, 34 characters in 3 columns of regular script (dated 1909).
4. Wang T'ung-yü (1855–after 1932): prose, 213 characters in 13 columns of running script. Signature: On the [day of the] Midautumn Festival of the *jen-shen* year [1932], I had the opportunity to examine, appreciate, and inscribe this scroll, Wang T'ung-yü in his seventy-eighth year [*sui*]. Seal: Wang T'ung-yü yin (square intaglio); Sheng-chih i tzu Hsü-yüan (square relief).

COLLECTORS' SEALS:
Hsiang Yüan-pien (1525–1590), 46 seals.
Hsiang Sheng-mo (1597–1658), 22 seals.
Shen K'an (fl. 17th century), 1 seal.
Wan-yen Ching-hsien (fl. late 19th–early 20th century), 2 seals.
Chin Ch'üan-sheng (fl. late 19th–early 20th century), 2 seals.
Pao Hsi (fl. early 20th century), 4 seals.
Chin Ch'eng (1878–1926), 2 seals.
T'an Ching (fl. early 20th century), 10 seals.
Chang Heng (1915–1963), 2 seals.
Liu T'ing-chih (modern mounter), 1 seal.
Unidentified owners, 2 seals.

John B. Elliott Collection (L178.70)

PUBLISHED: Richard Barnhart, "Chinese Calligraphy—the Inner World of the Brush," *The Metropolitan Museum of Art Bulletin* 30, no. 5 (April–May 1972): 232, fig. 5; Richard Barnhart, "Li T'ang (c. 1050–c. 1130) and the Kōtō-in Landscapes," *The Burlington Magazine* 114, no. 830 (May–August 1972): 305–14, pls. 44, 45; Chiang I-han, "Chao Meng-fu shu, Hu-chou Miao-yen-shih chüan" (*Record of the Miao-yen Monastery*, a calligraphic handscroll by Chao Meng-fu), *National Palace Museum Quarterly* 10, no. 3 (Spring 1976): 59–81, pl. 1; Shen C. Y. Fu et al., *Traces of the Brush: Studies in Chinese Calligraphy* (New Haven: Yale University Art Gallery, 1977), pp. 169, 251, 252, pls. 15a, 15b; Nakata Yūjirō and Fu Shen, eds., *Obei shūzō Chūgoku hōsho meisekishū* (Masterpieces of Chinese calligraphy in American and European collections), vol. 3 (Tokyo: Chūōkōron-sha, 1981), pp. 23–37, 138, pls. 18–26; Suzuki Kei, comp., *Chūgoku kaiga sōgō zuroku: daiikkan, Amerika–Kanada hen* (Comprehensive illustrated catalogue of Chinese paintings: volume 1, American and Canadian collections) (Tokyo: University of Tokyo Press, 1982), pp. 130–31, pl. A17–055; Tseng Yu-ho Ecke, *The Art of Chinese Calligraphy, A History* (Honolulu: University of Hawaii Press, forthcoming).

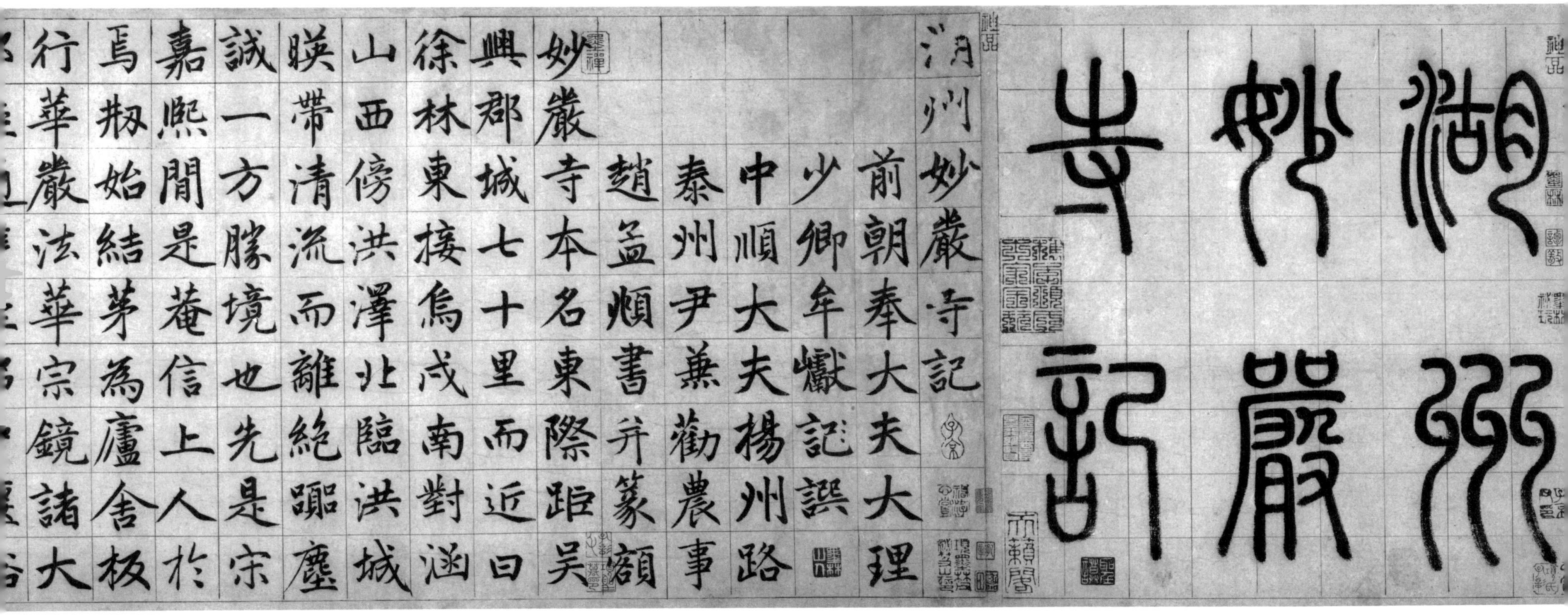
湖州妙嚴寺記
湖州妙嚴寺記
前朝奉大夫大理
少卿牟巘記譔
中順大夫楊州路
泰州尹兼勸農事
趙孟頫書幷篆額
妙嚴寺本名東際距吳
興郡城七十里而近曰
徐林東接烏戍南對涵
山西傍洪澤北臨洪城
暌帶清流而離絕蹋塵
誠一方勝境也先是宋
嘉熙間是菴信上人於
焉掀始結茅為廬舍板
行華嚴法華宗鏡諸大

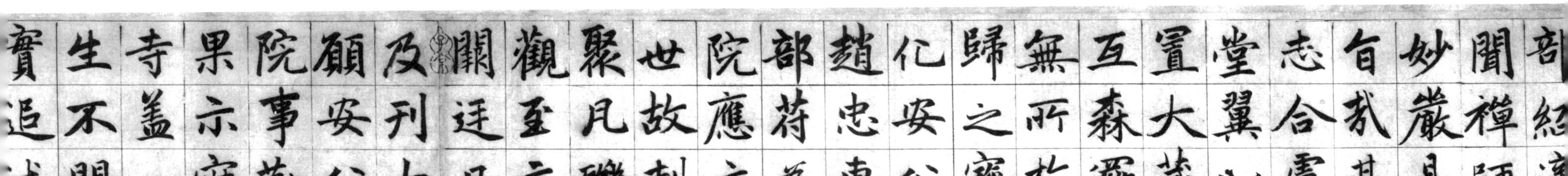
聞禪師飛錫至止遂以
妙嚴易東際之名深有
旨哉其徒古山道安同
志合慮募緣建前後殿
堂翼以兩廡莊嚴佛像
置大藏經琅函貝牒布
互森羅念里民之遺骨
無所於藏遂浚蓮池以
歸之寶祐丁巳是菴既
化安公繼之安素受知
趙忠惠公維持翊助給
部符為甲乙流傳朱殿
院應元寔為之記中更
世故封火洞然安公乃
聚凡礫掃煨燼一新舊
觀至元間兩詣
闕廷凡申陳皆為法門
及刊大藏經板卷滿所
願安公之將北行也以
院事勤重付屬如寧後
果示寂于燕之大延壽
寺蓋一念明了洞視死
生不間豪髮寧顧踐真
實追述前志再度一大

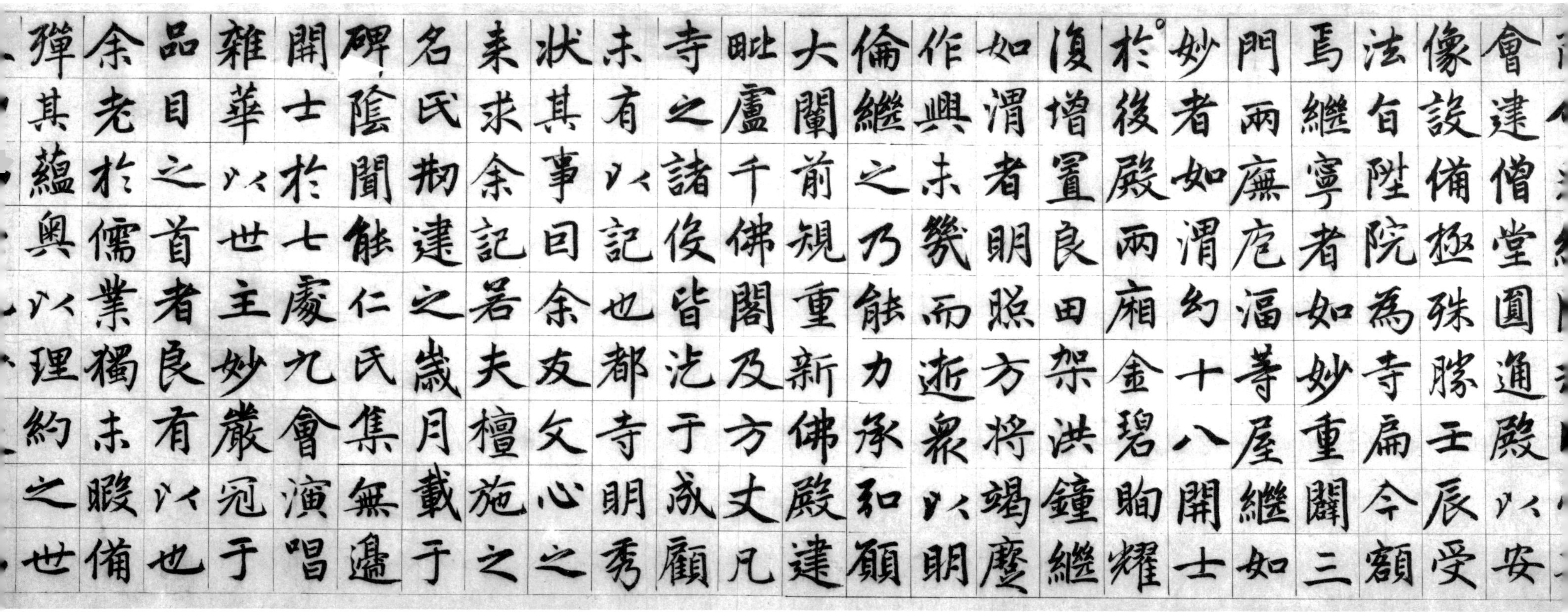

會建僧堂圓通殿以安
像設備極殊勝壬辰受
法旨陞院爲寺扁今額
焉繼寧者如妙重闢三
門兩廡庵湢等屋繼如
妙者如渭約十八開士
於後殿兩廂金碧昫耀
復增置良田架洪鐘繼
如渭者明照方將竭塵
作興未幾而逝衆以明
倫繼之乃能力承初願
大闡前規重新佛殿建
毗盧千佛閣及方丈凡
寺之諸役皆迄于成顧
未有以記也都寺明秀
狀其事因余友文心之
來求余記若夫檀施之
名氏刱建之歲月載于
碑陰聞能仁氏集無邊
開士於七處九會演唱
雜華以世主妙嚴冠于
品目之首者良有以也
余老於儒業獨未暇備
殫其蘊奧以理約之世

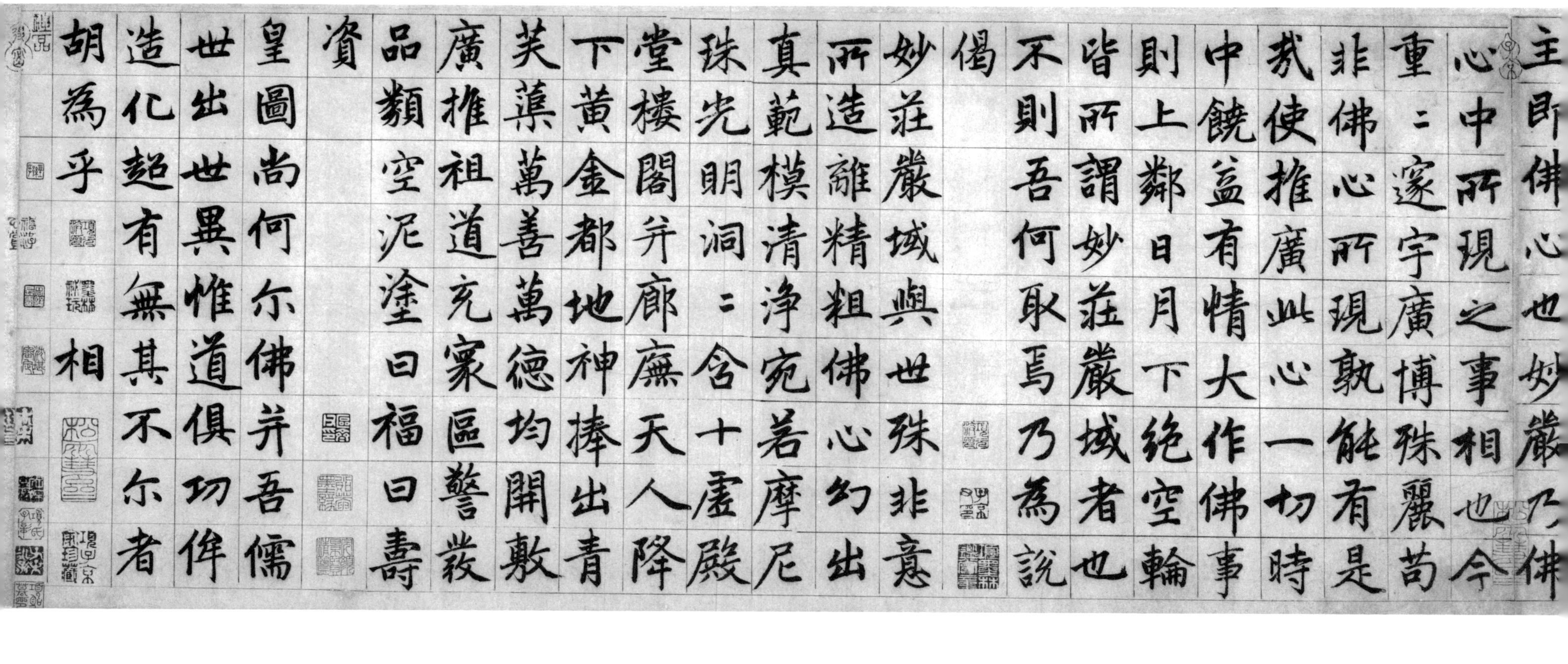

主即佛心也妙嚴乃佛
心中所現之事相也今
重重邃宇廣博殊麗苟
非佛心所現孰能有是
哉使推廣此心一切時
中饒益有情大作佛事
則上鄰日月下絶空輪
皆所謂妙莊嚴域者也
不則吾何取焉乃爲説
偈
妙莊嚴域與世殊非意
所造離精粗佛心幻出
真範模清淨宛若摩尼
珠光明洞洞含十虛殿
堂樓閣并廊廡天人降
下黄金都地神捧出青
芙蕖萬善萬德均開敷
廣推祖道充寰區警蔑
品類空泥塗曰福曰壽
資
皇圖尚何尒佛并吾儒
世出世異惟道俱切併
造化超有無其不尒者
胡爲乎相

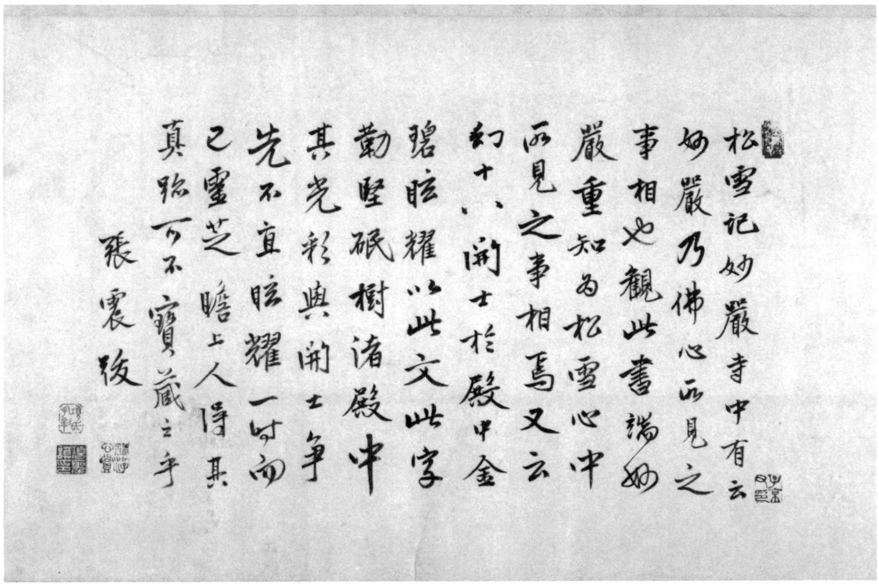

Chang Chen

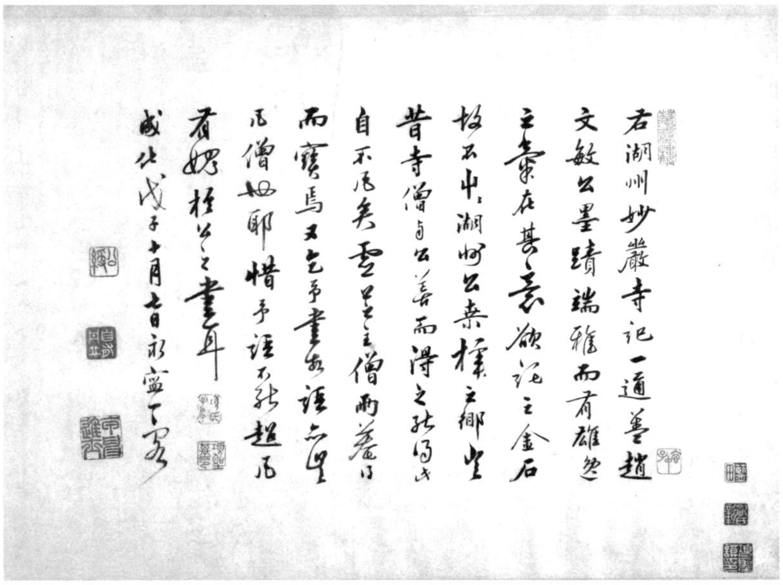

Yao Shou (a)

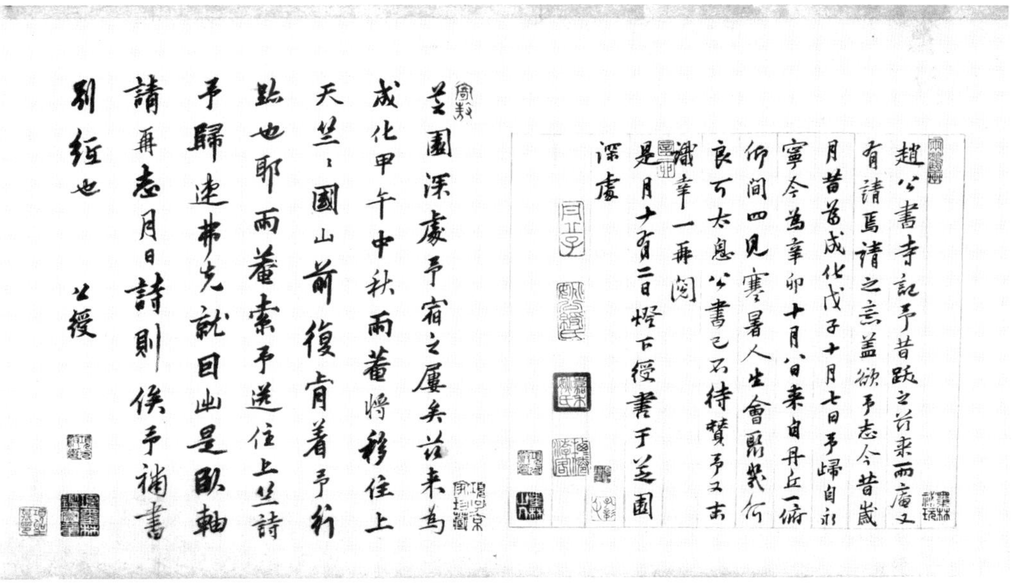

Yao Shou (c) Yao Shou (b)

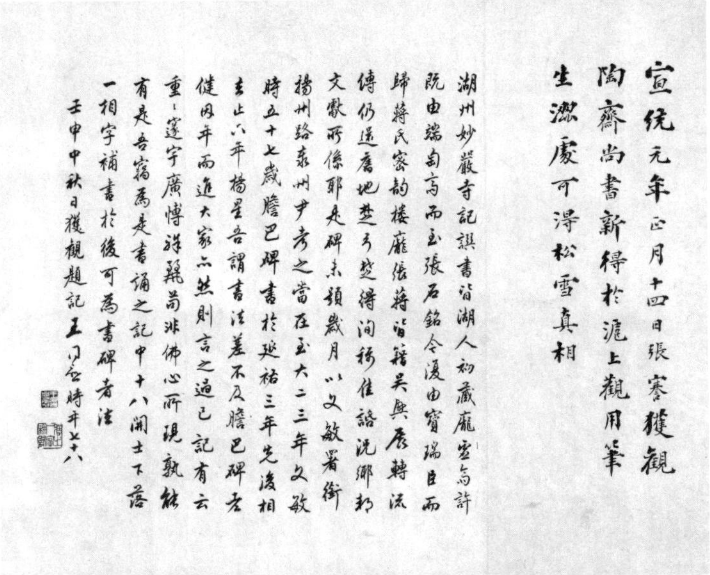

Wang T'ung-yü Chang Chien

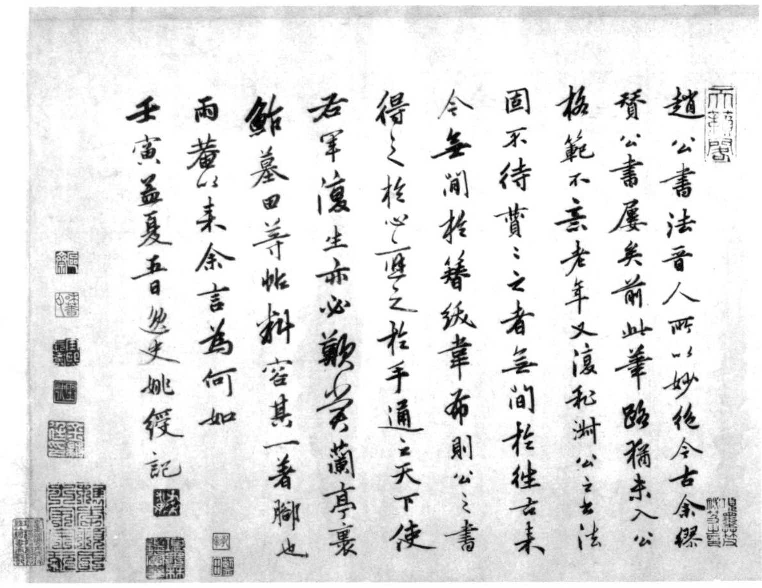

Yao Shou (d)

# 8 Anonymous

## *Pear Blossoms and Bird (Li-hua shan-ch'üeh)*

Ca. 1300
Hanging scroll, ink and color on paper
91.5 x 30.7 cm (36 x 12 in.)

No artist's signature or seals.

INSCRIPTION by emperor Ch'ing Kao-tsung (r. 1736–95): 7 character quatrain, followed by a 7 character note, in 4 columns of running script. Seals: Ch'ien-lung (double seal, square, half relief, half intaglio).

COLLECTORS' SEALS:

1. Hsiang Yüan-pien (1525–1590): Shen-p'in (tall rectangle relief; lower right); T'ien-lai-ko (tall rectangle relief; lower right); Tzu-ching (gourd-shaped relief; lower left); Hsiang Yüan-pien yin (square relief; lower left); Mo-lin-shan-jen (square intaglio; lower left).
2. Ch'ing emperors:
   a) Kao-tsung (r. 1736–95): Ch'ien-lung yü-lan chih pao (oval relief; upper right); Yang-hsin-tien chien-ts'ang pao (tall rectangle relief; upper right); Ch'ien-lung chien-shang (round intaglio; right); San-hsi-t'ang ching-chien hsi (tall rectangle relief; upper right); I tzu-sun (square intaglio; upper right); Shih-ch'ü pao-chi (square relief; upper left).
   b) Jen-tsung (r. 1796–1820): Chia-ch'ing yü-lan chih pao (oval relief; top); Shih-ch'ü chi-chien (square relief; right).
   c) Sun-ti (r. 1909–11): Hsüan-t'ung yü-lan chih pao (square relief; upper right).
3. Ch'en Jen-t'ao (1906–1968): Chin-kuei kuo-pao wu-shuang (oval relief; top); Chin-kuei pao-ts'ang Ch'en shih Jen-t'ao (double seal, round relief, square relief; left); Jen-t'ao ch'i-yüan (oval relief; lower left); Wu-shuang (square relief; lower left); Chin-kuei shih ching-chien hsi (square relief; lower left).

Edward L. Elliott Family Collection (L141.78)

PUBLISHED: Ch'en Jen-t'ao, *Chin-kuei ts'ang-hua chi* (Chinese paintings from the King Kwei [Chin-kuei] collection) (Hong Kong: T'ung-ying, 1956), vol. 1, pl. 1; Ch'en Jen-t'ao, *Chin-kuei ts'ang-hua p'ing-shih* (Annotated catalogue of Chinese paintings from the King Kwei [Chin-kuei] collection) (Hong Kong: T'ung-ying, 1956), vol. 1, pp. 1–4.

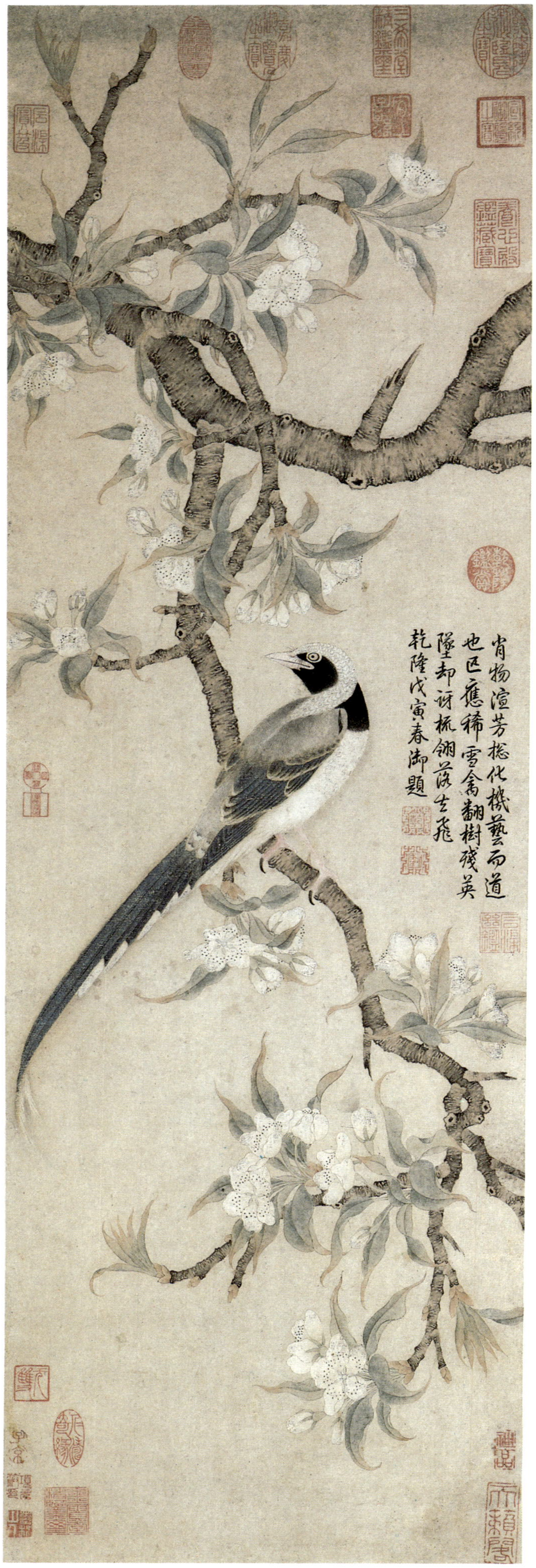

# 9 Hsüeh-ch'uang (P'u-ming; fl. first half 14th century)

## *Orchid, Bamboo, and Rock (Yu-lan chu shih)*

Ca. 1340
Hanging scroll, ink and light color on silk
34.0 x 86.1 cm (13 3/8 x 33 7/8 in.)

ARTIST'S SIGNATURE: Hsüeh-ch'uang.

ARTIST'S SEALS: Hsüeh-ch'uang (square relief); Wu-wai ch'ing-lo (square intaglio).

Edward L. Elliott Family Collection (L29.80)

PUBLISHED: Mayuyama Junkichi, ed., *Mayuyama, Seventy Years* (Tokyo: Mayuyama and Company, 1976), vol. 2, p. 83, pl. 169; Suzuki Kei, comp., *Chūgoku kaiga sōgō zuroku: daiikkan, Amerika–Kanada hen* (Comprehensive illustrated catalogue of Chinese paintings: volume 1, American and Canadian collections) (Tokyo: University of Tokyo Press, 1982), p. 129, pl. A17–037.

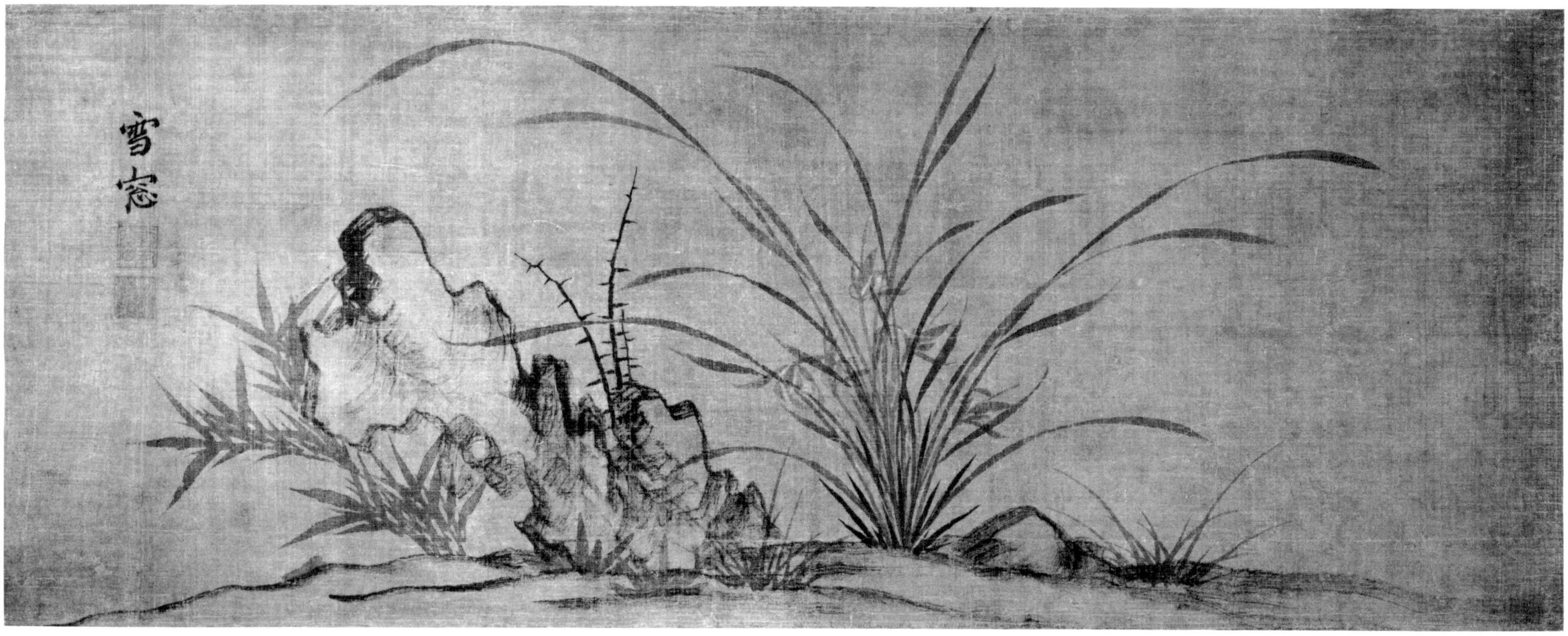

# 10 Ni Tsan (1301–1374)

## *Twin Trees by the South Bank (An nan shuang shu)*

Dated 1353
Hanging scroll, ink on paper
Painting: 56.0 x 27.0 cm (22 x $10\frac{5}{8}$ in.); colophons: 19.0 x 27.0 cm ($7\frac{1}{2}$ x $10\frac{5}{8}$ in.)

ARTIST'S INSCRIPTION: 13 character preface, followed by a 7 character quatrain, in 4 columns of regular script (for a translation of the inscription, see page 118).

ARTIST'S SIGNATURE: Ni Tsan, on the last day of the second lunar month of the thirteenth year of the Chih-cheng era [1353].

COLOPHONS (on a sheet of paper above the painting, from right to left):

1. Wen Cheng-ming (1470–1559): 7 character quatrain in 3 columns of running script. Signature: Cheng-ming. Seals: Wen Cheng-ming yin (square intaglio); Cheng-chung (square relief).
2. Chang Yüan (Chang Ta-ch'ien; 1899–1983): 107 character note in 6 columns of running script. Signature: In the second lunar month of the *hsin-mao* year [1951], Chang Yüan carefully inscribed this. Seal: Ta-ch'ien ching-yen (tall rectangle relief).

COLLECTORS' SEALS:
Chu Chih-ch'ih (fl. 16th century), 4 seals.
Chang Tai (1597–ca. 1684), 1 seal.
Liang Ch'ing-piao (1620–1691), 3 seals.
Pien Yung-yü (1645–1712), 2 seals.
Chang Shan-tzu (1882–1940), 1 seal.
Chang Yüan, 3 seals.
Ch'en Jen-t'ao (1906–1968), 3 seals.
Ch'i Keng (20th century), 1 seal.
Li Lin (20th century), 3 seals.
Li Chi-yün (20th century), 3 seals.
Unidentified owners, 5 seals.

Gift of Mr. and Mrs. Wen C. Fong in honor of Mrs. Edward L. Elliott (75-35)

PUBLISHED: Ishikawa Jun et al., eds., *Bunjinga suihen* (Selection of the finest Chinese and Japanese literati paintings), vol. 3 (Tokyo: Chūōkōron-sha, 1979), p. 124, fig. 16; Susan E. Nelson, "Rocks beside a River: Ni Tsan and the Ching-Kuan Style in the Eyes of Seventeenth-century Critics," *Archives of Asian Art* 33 (1980): 77, fig. 12; Richard M. Barnhart, *Along the Border of Heaven: Sung and Yüan Paintings from the C. C. Wang Family Collection* (New York: The Metropolitan Museum of Art, 1983), p. 156, fig. 73; Wen C. Fong, "*Twin Trees by the South Bank* by Ni Tsan," *Apollo* (forthcoming).

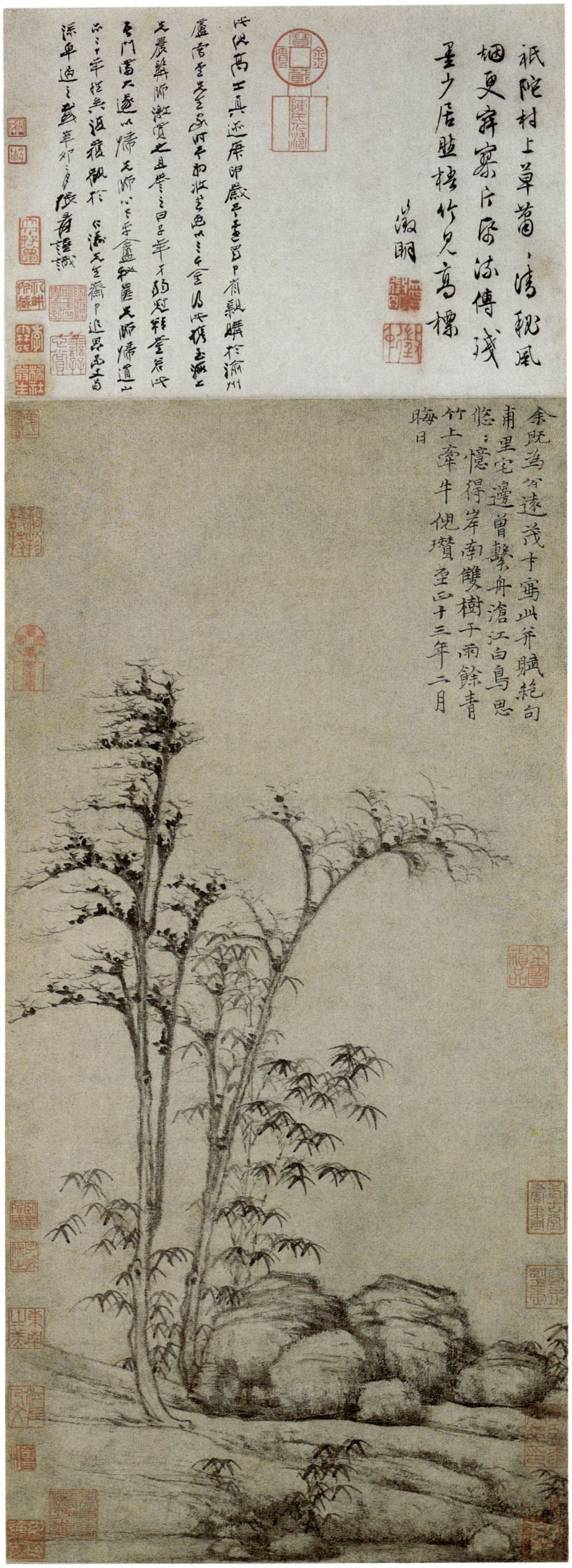

# 11 Anonymous

## *Hermitage under Pine Trees (Sung-feng shu-wu)*

Ca. 1360
Hanging scroll, ink and color on silk
80.3 x 30.3 cm (31 5/8 x 11 7/8 in.)

ARTIST'S INSCRIPTION (an area of replaced silk in the upper right [15.8 x 18.7 cm (6 1/4 x 7 3/8 in.)] suggests that the original inscription may have been cut off; the present one is a later interpolation [upper left, 10 characters in 1 column of regular script]): On *ku-jih* [the eighth day of the first lunar month] in the second year of the Chih-ta era [1309], Hsüeh-an playfully painted this.

ARTIST'S SEALS: Hsüeh-an (square intaglio); unidentified.

Edward L. Elliott Family Collection (L161.70)

PUBLISHED: Suzuki Kei, comp., *Chūgoku kaiga sōgō zuroku: daiikkan, Amerika–Kanada hen* (Comprehensive illustrated catalogue of Chinese paintings: volume 1, American and Canadian collections) (Tokyo: University of Tokyo Press, 1982), p. 128, pl. A17–032.

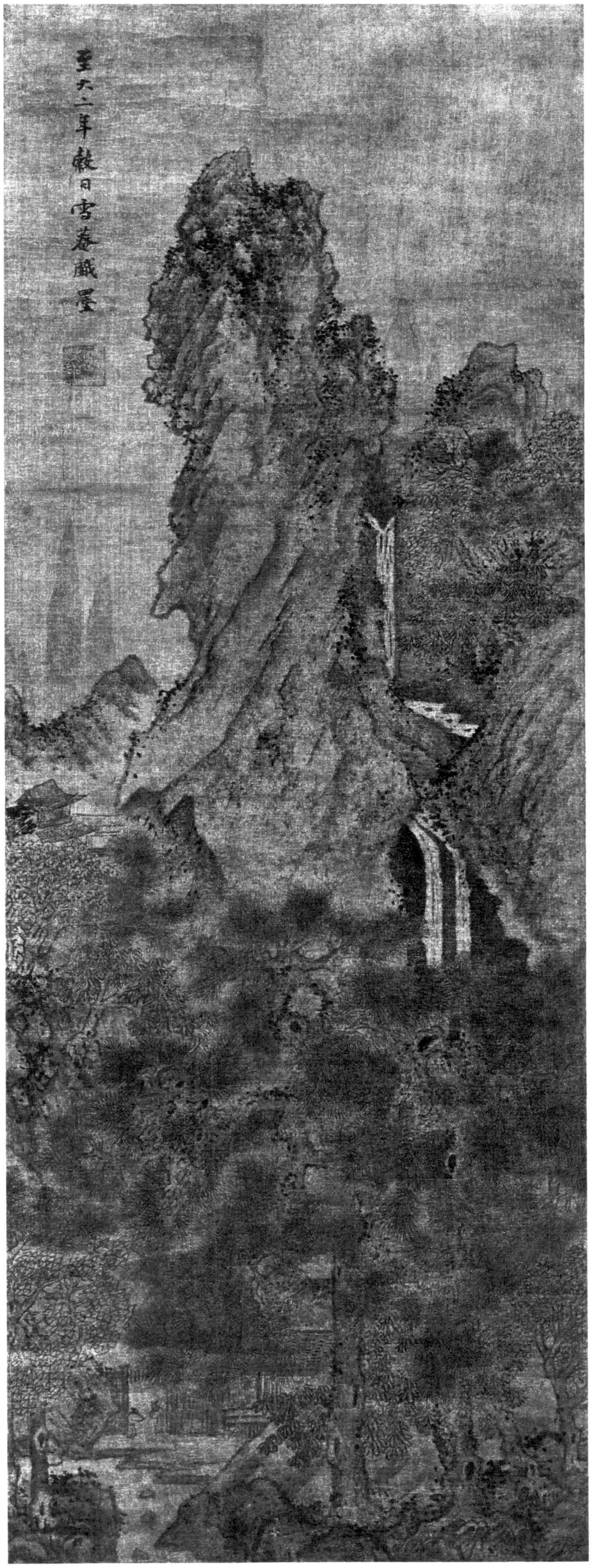

# 12 Sung K'o (1327–1387)

## *T'ao Ch'ien's Poems, and Bamboo and Rocks (Shu T'ao-shih chi chu shih hsiao-ching)*

Dated 1370
Handscroll, ink on paper
Calligraphy: 25.9 x 627.9 cm (10 1/8 in. x 20 ft. 7 1/4 in.); painting: 25.9 x 151.0 cm (10 1/4 in. x 4 ft. 11 1/2 in.)

CALLIGRAPHY (transcriptions of 28 poems by T'ao Ch'ien [365–427], in 4 script styles); for translations, see James Robert Hightower, *The Poetry of T'ao Ch'ien* (Oxford: Clarendon Press, 1970), pp. 11, 12, 22, 23, 25–28, 30, 31, 33, 35, 64, 65, 67–69, 74, 76, 79–83, 85–91, 93, 124–56:

1. Six 4 character verses, with titles and prefaces, in 66 columns of regular script: "Hovering Clouds" ("T'ing-yün"), "For the Lord of Ch'ang-sha" ("Tseng Ch'ang-sha-kung tsu-tsu"), "A Reply to Prefect Ting of Ch'ai-sang" ("Ch'ou Ting Ch'ai-sang"), "A Reply to Adviser P'ang" ("Ta P'ang ts'an-chün"), "An Exhortation to Farmers" ("Ch'üan nung"), "On Naming My Son" ("Ming tzu").
2. Three 5 character verses, with titles, in 25 columns of running script: "A Lament in the Ch'u Mode" ("Yüan shih Ch'u tiao shih P'ang chu-pu Teng Chih-chung"), "In Reply to Adviser P'ang" ("Ta P'ang ts'an-chün"), "Written on the First Day of the Fifth Month to Match a Poem by Secretary Tsai" ("Wu-yüeh tan tso ho Tsai chu-pu").
3. Nine 5 character verses, with titles, in 77 columns of draft cursive script: "On Moving Houses, Two Poems" ("I chü erh shou"), "To Match a Poem by Liu, Prefect of Ch'ai-sang" ("Ho Liu Ch'ai-sang"), "To Liu, Prefect of Ch'ai-sang" ("Ch'ou Liu Ch'ai-sang"), "A Reply to Secretary Kuo, Two Poems" ("Ho Kuo chu-pu erh shou"), "At General Wang's Party for Departing Guests" ("Yü Wang fu-chün tso ta k'o"), "A Farewell to Yin Ching-jen, Secretary at Chin-an" ("Yü Yin Chin-an pieh"), "To Clerk Yang" ("Tseng Yang ch'ang-shih").
4. Ten 5 character verses, with titles and prefaces, in 67 columns of cursive script: "At the Year's End, a Reply to the Attendant Chang" ("Sui-mu ho Chang ch'ang-shih"), "Reply to a Poem by Clerk Hu, to be Shown to Sheriff Ku" ("Ho Hu hsi-ts'ao shih Ku tsei-ts'ao"), "A Lament for My Cousin, Chung-te" ("Pei ch'ung-ti Chung-te"), "Poems after Drinking Wine" (7 poems) ("Yin chiu").

PAINTING: "Bamboo and Rocks."

ARTIST'S INSCRIPTIONS:

1. Prose, 48 characters in 5 columns of cursive script (between calligraphy and painting):

   In the ninth lunar month of the *keng-hsü* year [1370], I came to Yün-chien [in Kiangsu province] and stayed at Hsü Yen-ming's place. Yen-ming always admired my calligraphy, and because I lingered at his home for a long time, he therefore prepared this handscroll and asked me to write on it. In regular, running, draft cursive, and cursive scripts, I transcribed poems by T'ao [Ch'ien] and gave this scroll [to Yen-ming] as a present.

2. Prose, 96 characters in 4 columns of regular script (following painting):

   I came to Yün-chien to stay at Hsü Yen-ming's place. Day and night, I laughed and talked with him for over forty days. Yen-ming deeply loves my calligraphy; therefore I transcribed poems by T'ao Ching-chieh [T'ao Ch'ien] in four script types on this handscroll. There was much blank paper left, so I playfully made this small painting of bamboo and rocks. I have never mastered painting, but I nevertheless took up the brush again, and what I painted was cleansed of the meanness of the dusty world. Although common people may not appreciate this, connoisseurs will be able to assess its value. On the twenty-fourth day of the ninth lunar month of the *keng-hsü* year [1370], by lamplight, Sung K'o, Chung-wen, from Tung-Wu [eastern Kiangsu province] inscribed this.

3. Prose, 10 characters in 1 column of running script (end of scroll): In my forty-fourth year [*sui*], the *keng-hsü* year [1370], I made this.

ARTIST'S SIGNATURES: Sung K'o from Wu-chün [Kiangsu province] wrote this (beginning of the scroll); Sung K'o wrote this (end of the running script section); Sung K'o, Chung-wen fu, from Tung-Wu, again, inscribed this (between calligraphy and painting).

ARTIST'S SEALS: Tung-Wu-sheng (square relief; after all signatures, calligraphy); Sung Chung-wen (square relief; after the running script section); Sung Chung-wen (square intaglio; second inscription).

COLLECTORS' SEALS:
Wu Ping (fl. late 16th–early 17th century), 1 seal.
Pien Yung-yü (1645–1712), 4 seals.
Ch'ing emperors: Kao-tsung (r. 1736–95), 3 seals; Jen-tsung (r. 1796–1820), 1 seal; Sun-ti (r. 1909–11), 3 seals.
Ku Yün-t'ao (dates unknown), 1 seal.

Chou Chao-lü (dates unknown), 1 seal.
Sung Pang-i (dates unknown), 4 seals.
Unidentified owners, 4 seals.

John B. Elliott Collection (L45.73)

PUBLISHED: Wang Shih-chieh and Na Chih-liang, eds., *I-yüan i-chen* (A garland of Chinese paintings and calligraphy) (Hong Kong: K'ai-fa, 1967), vol. 2, pl. 37; Suzuki Kei, comp., *Chūgoku kaiga sōgō zuroku: daiikkan, Amerika–Kanada hen* (Comprehensive illustrated catalogue of Chinese paintings: volume 1, American and Canadian collections) (Tokyo: University of Tokyo Press, 1982), p. 132, pl. A17–059.

MEMBER OF A WEALTHY FAMILY in Ch'ang-chou (in Su-chou prefecture), Sung K'o was a large and forthright man with a broad range of talents; besides his mastery of painting and calligraphy, he was also skilled as an archer, swordsman, and rider.[1] In his youth he was spendthrift and overindulged in wine, but upon reaching maturity he gave up drinking and began to study military strategy, eventually going north to serve under a general in Yen (modern Hopei province), guarding China's frontier passes. Dissatisfied with this life, he returned to his native area some time before 1356, and soon thereafter the rebel leader Chang Shih-ch'eng asked Sung to join his government. Sung refused, retreating instead into a circle of literary companions known as the Ten Friends of the North Wall, which centered around the poet Kao Ch'i (1336–1374). In this state of semiretirement, which he spent in Su-chou and Sung-chiang (Yün-chien), Sung devoted himself to the study of ancient calligraphy, Chou bronzes, Han inkstones, and the lute. Filling at least ten sheets of paper a day with his calligraphy (one source claimed the number was 1,000),[2] Sung soon earned a reputation as a superlative calligrapher, and admirers daily flocked to his door. Weary of such constant social contact, Sung K'o became a recluse. His reclusive period ended shortly after the establishment of the Ming dynasty, when Chu Yüan-chang, the first Ming emperor, summoned Sung to court as a calligrapher-in-attendance and appointed him as deputy prefect of Feng-hsiang, in Shensi province.

Sung K'o, both because of his revival of archaic calligraphy styles and his frequent combination of poetry, calligraphy, and painting in single works, epitomized Yüan artistic ideals. And yet, Sung's calligraphy is more than a summation of fourteenth-century revival taste. By merging ancient and modern brushwork and by combining different script types within single works produced in one creative effort, Sung heralded new developments. He influenced Ming calligraphy, both the regular script (*chen-shu*) practiced at court and the cursive script (*ts'ao-shu*) of the Sung-chiang School calligraphers. Shen Tu (1357–1434) and Shen Ts'an (1379–1453), important Ming court calligraphers, based their regular script on Sung's style. His influence can also be detected in the cursive writing of the best-known Ming calligrapher, Chu Yün-ming (1461–1527), who wrote that Sung's calligraphy was "heavenly and not the result of human effort."[3]

The most active time of Sung's artistic career was about 1370, the date of *T'ao Ch'ien's Poems, and Bamboo and Rocks*. Works of this period display the full range of Sung's stylistic sources, including ancient, nearly contemporary, and contemporaneous models. In 1364 Sung K'o had obtained a rubbing of the *Preface to the Orchid Pavilion Gathering* (*Lan-t'ing-chi hsü*) by Wang Hsi-chih (ca. 307–ca. 365), which was made from the Ting-wu stone engraving (carved ca. 998–1061). He studied and wrote colophons for this piece during 1370 and in the same year transcribed Chao Meng-fu's *Thirteen Colophons to the Preface to the Orchid Pavilion Gathering* (*Lan-t'ing shih-san pa*), which provides historical and stylistic comments about Wang Hsi-chih. (Sung's copy of this work is in the Li Ch'i-yen collection, Hong Kong.) Wang's calligraphy is traditionally considered a source of Sung's style, and characteristics of Wang's style appear in most of Sung K'o's writings, but his influence is usually muted. *Poem on an Official Banquet (Kung-yen shih)*, a hanging scroll now in the National Palace Museum, Taipei, shows quite a direct link with Wang, following the style of Wang's *On the Seventeenth (Shih-ch'i t'ieh*; rubbing in Wango H. C. Weng collection). The last ten poems in the John B. Elliott Collection scroll bear a relationship to the same model.

Of greater significance to Sung K'o's stylistic development was Huang Hsiang (ca. 220–ca. 279), who copied the Han dynasty *Swiftly Completed Essay (Chi-chiu-chang)* in draft cursive script (*chang-ts'ao-shu*). Draft cursive—which features abbreviations within but no links between characters, wavelike diagonals that point toward the lower right, and stressed brushtip movement—had been out of fashion, except for brief interludes, since the Tsin dynasty. In the Yüan period Chao Meng-fu revived the script style, and by the time of Sung K'o it became even more popular than modern cursive script (*chin-ts'ao-shu*), the favorite type of the preceding dynasty. Sung was familiar with the *Swiftly Completed Essay* through copies made by Chao Meng-fu in 1306 and 1309 and through a copy that he considered to be an original work by Huang Hsiang.[4] In 1370 Sung K'o copied the *Swiftly Completed Essay* in pure draft cursive script.

Besides Chao Meng-fu, K'ang-li Nao-nao (1295–1345) and Jao Chieh (fl. ca. 1300–67), two other Yüan calligraphers who also wrote in draft cursive script, served as models for Sung K'o.[5] Jao Chieh was Sung's personal friend. His calligraphy in *Poem for Portrait of Monk Chung-feng* (*Chung-feng ch'an-shih hua-hsiang tsan*, 1365; the National Palace Museum, Taipei) resembles Sung's writing in the structure of its characters and its brushwork, but it is lackluster in comparison. Sung was also influenced by his contemporaries in his other cursive styles. Yang Wei-chen (1296–1370), for example, another personal friend, influenced Sung's wild cursive writing (*k'uang-ts'ao-shu*).

Sung also followed the archaic model of Chung Yu (A.D. 151–230). His interest in this Wei period calligrapher may have been stimulated by Ni Tsan (1301–1374), who patterned his regular script after Chung's. Ni Tsan and Sung no doubt knew each other, quite possibly through their mutual friend Chang Yü (1333–1385). Sung inscribed two of Ni's paintings, and Ni twice wrote about him, praising Sung's ability as a bamboo painter and his scholarly nature, which made him an ideal companion with whom to discuss the "heart of antiquity."[6]

*T'ao Ch'ien's Poems, and Bamboo and Rocks* is an excellent example of Sung K'o's ability to combine and transform his models in calligraphy. Although the exact date of his appointment as calligrapher-in-attendance is not known, this scroll was probably executed before Sung went to serve at the Ming court. It was painted as a gift in the Sung-chiang home of Hsü Yen-ming, who is mentioned by Sung in his inscription as an ardent admirer of his calligraphy and a generous host. In his inscription on the scroll, Sung stated that he wrote out T'ao Ch'ien's poems in *ssu-t'i* (four styles of calligraphy).

The scroll opens with six poems written in regular script (*chen-shu*), which is characterized by rectilinear, tightly structured, and unconnected characters. Since features of clerical script (*li-shu*)—such as wavelike diagonals and characters with loosely constructed outer frames over tight inner components—also occur in Sung's writing here, the script type is therefore more accurately described as protoregular script (*chin-li-shu*). The square proportions and clerical traits of the characters are reminiscent of the work of Chung Yu, as well as of Ni Tsan, but the linking of strokes within characters, especially in the fourth poem, represents a unique interpretation.

The script type changes at the seventh poem, with a shift in the poetic meter from four characters per line to five, to running script (*hsing-shu*), which continues through the ninth poem, where Sung has added his signature. As with his regular script, his running script was also modified; Sung adopted the wavelike diagonals of draft cursive, reflecting his taste for archaistic styles.

The last nineteen poems are written in variations of cursive script. Although Sung mentioned only draft cursive and cursive scripts in his inscription, these two are blended with each other and with wild cursive. Sung K'o called his cursive script *ts'ao-shu*, which usually signifies modern cursive writing, but while modern cursive is distinguished by quickly executed, well-articulated brushstrokes, much of the cursive writing in the Elliott scroll has vastly simplified forms with strings of linked characters and exaggerated loops within characters—all features of wild cursive script. The basis of this style was the writing of the monk Huai-su (725–785); others of Sung's works, such as *Poem by Tu Fu* (*Shu Tu Fu shih*; collection unknown) show even more of a debt to this model. In the Elliott scroll the modern and wild cursive elements are intermingled and fused with features of draft cursive script, such as flared diagonals and tapered endings on many strokes and the absence of connecting characters. This combination of draft, modern, and wild cursive brushwork presages the Ming synthesis of these three script types. The calligraphy in the Elliott scroll is fast but not glib. The dark uniform ink tones, even brush pressure, and wide, regular spaces between columns are brought to life by an imaginative mixture of angles and curves, of flared archaic-type strokes and modern well-articulated brushwork.

Although Sung K'o dismissed the painting in *T'ao Ch'ien's Poems, and Bamboo and Rocks* as something to fill "blank paper," it is actually an integral part of the scroll, a spontaneous expression of brush movement used to form a picture instead of characters. The motif of bamboo and rocks was a standard metaphor; since the Northern Sung period, ink bamboo had been associated with scholar-artists. Groves of bamboo represented a scholar-recluse's garden retreat; the plant itself, with its resilient nature, represented a scholar's mind and will. It was an image that Sung K'o frequently painted in casual brush play; Ming sources claim that Sung originated painting bamboo and rocks in vermilion ink when he worked in the Hall of Examinations during the early Ming era.[7] According to the story, Sung often picked up a brush dipped in the red ink used for annotating texts and quickly added a spray of bamboo to some official papers.

In this scroll the bamboo, done in black and gray ink, are quickly and playfully executed. They are much less realistic than the bamboo in his earlier paintings of similar compositions: one, dated 1369, now in the Freer Gallery of Art, Washington, D.C., and an earlier one, in the Cleveland Museum of Art (intended gift from the A. Dean Perry collection). His brushstrokes and the overall quality of the painting still follow the same sources evident in the earlier works: Ni Tsan, Hsü Pen (1335–1380), Chao Meng-fu, and Kuo Pi (1280–1335). (Sung K'o knew Ni Tsan and Hsü Pen personally. He had written inscriptions on or impressed his seal on works by both Chao Meng-fu and Kuo Pi.) But here the fluid brushstrokes function primarily as an expressive outlet and are therefore only loosely modeled upon the other painters' styles. The pictorial representation in the Elliott scroll parallels one meaning of the poems by T'ao Ch'ien; since T'ao was the paradigm of the scholar-recluse, the image of bamboo, combined with the poetry and calligraphy, characterizes the spirit of Yüan eremitism.

JAN STUART

NOTES

1. For a biography with comprehensive bibliography, see James J. Y. Liu, "Sung K'o," in L. Carrington Goodrich and Chaoying Fang, eds., *Dictionary of Ming Biography: 1368–1644* (New York and London: Columbia University Press, 1976), vol. 2, pp. 1223–24.
2. Wang Ao, ed., *Ku-su-chih* (Gazetteer of Su-chou prefecture, Kiangsu province) (1506; repr. ed., Taipei: Hsüeh-sheng shu-chü, 1965), *chüan* 56, p. 9.
3. Ch'en T'ien (*chin-shih*, 1886), ed., *Ming-shih chi-shih* (Record of Ming poetry), Kuo-hsüeh chi-pen ts'ung-shu, vol. 183 (Taipei, 1968), sec. *chia*, *chüan* 8, p. 175.
4. What Sung K'o accepted as an original Huang Hsiang work was probably a version copied by Yeh Meng-te (1077–1148) in 1120 from the supposedly authentic *Chi-chiu-chang* in emperor Sung Hui-tsung's Hsüan-ho calligraphy collection, catalogued in the *Hsüan-ho shu-p'u*, which was generally considered to be authentic. Sung's copy matches Yeh's in the textual lacunae and organization and in the size of the script. Yeh's may also have been the copy that Chao Meng-fu used. See Chang Heng, *Sung K'o shu chi-chiu-chang* (Sung K'o's transcription of the *Swiftly Completed Essay*) (Peking: Wen-wu ch'u-pan-she, 1960), intro.
5. Hsieh Tsin, *Ch'un-yü tsa-shu* (Random talks in spring rain: a discussion of calligraphy), I-shu ts'ung-pien, vol. 3 (Taipei: Shih-chieh shu-chü, 1973), *chüan* 1, p. 5.
6. Ch'en T'ien, ed., *Ming-shih chi-shih*, p. 176.
7. Ibid.

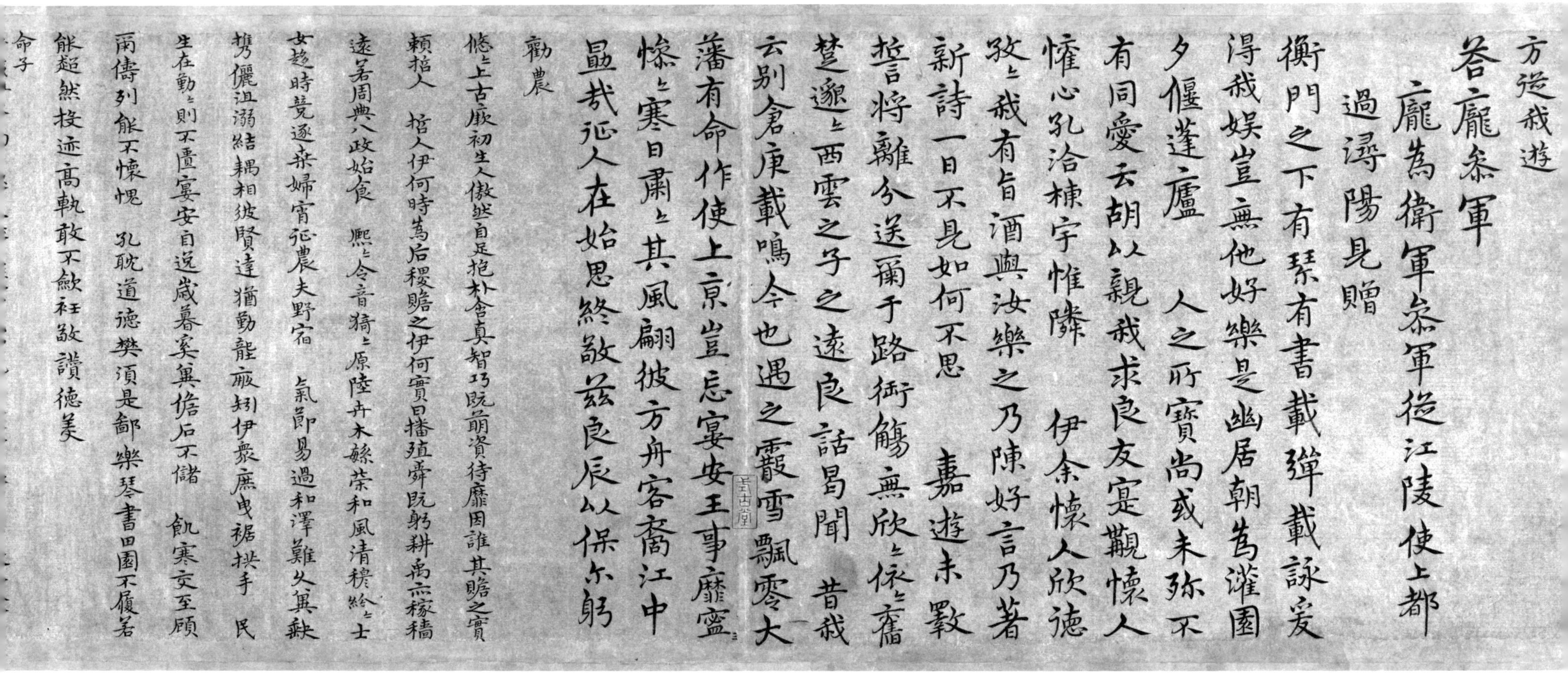
方從我遊
答龐參軍
龐為衛軍參軍從江陵使上都
過潯陽見贈
衡門之下有琴有書載彈載詠爰
得我娛豈無他好樂是幽居朝為灌園
夕偃蓬廬　人之所寶尚或未珍不
有同愛云胡以親我求良友寔覯懷人
懽心孔洽棟宇惟鄰　伊余懷人欣德
孜孜我有旨酒與汝樂之乃陳好言乃著
新詩一日不見如何不思　嘉遊未斁
誓將離分送爾于路銜觴無欣依依舊
楚邈邈西雲之子之遠良話曷聞　昔我
云別倉庚載鳴今也遇之霰雪飄零大
藩有命作使上京豈忘宴安王事靡寧
慘慘寒日肅肅其風翩彼方舟容裔江中
勗哉征人在始思終敬茲良辰以保爾躬
勸農
悠悠上古厥初生人傲然自足抱朴含真智巧既萌資待靡因誰其贍之實
賴哲人　哲人伊何時為后稷贍之伊何實曰播殖舜既躬耕禹亦稼穡
遠若周典八政始食　熙熙令音猗猗原陸卉木繁榮和風清穆紛紛士
女趍時競逐桑婦宵征農夫野宿　氣節易過和澤難久冀缺
攜儷沮溺結耦相彼賢達猶勤壟畝矧伊眾庶曳裾拱手　民
生在勤勤則不匱宴安自逸歲暮奚冀儋石不儲　飢寒交至顧
爾儔列能不懷愧　孔耽道德樊須是鄙董樂琴書田園不履若
能超然投迹高軌敢不斂衽敬讚德美
命子

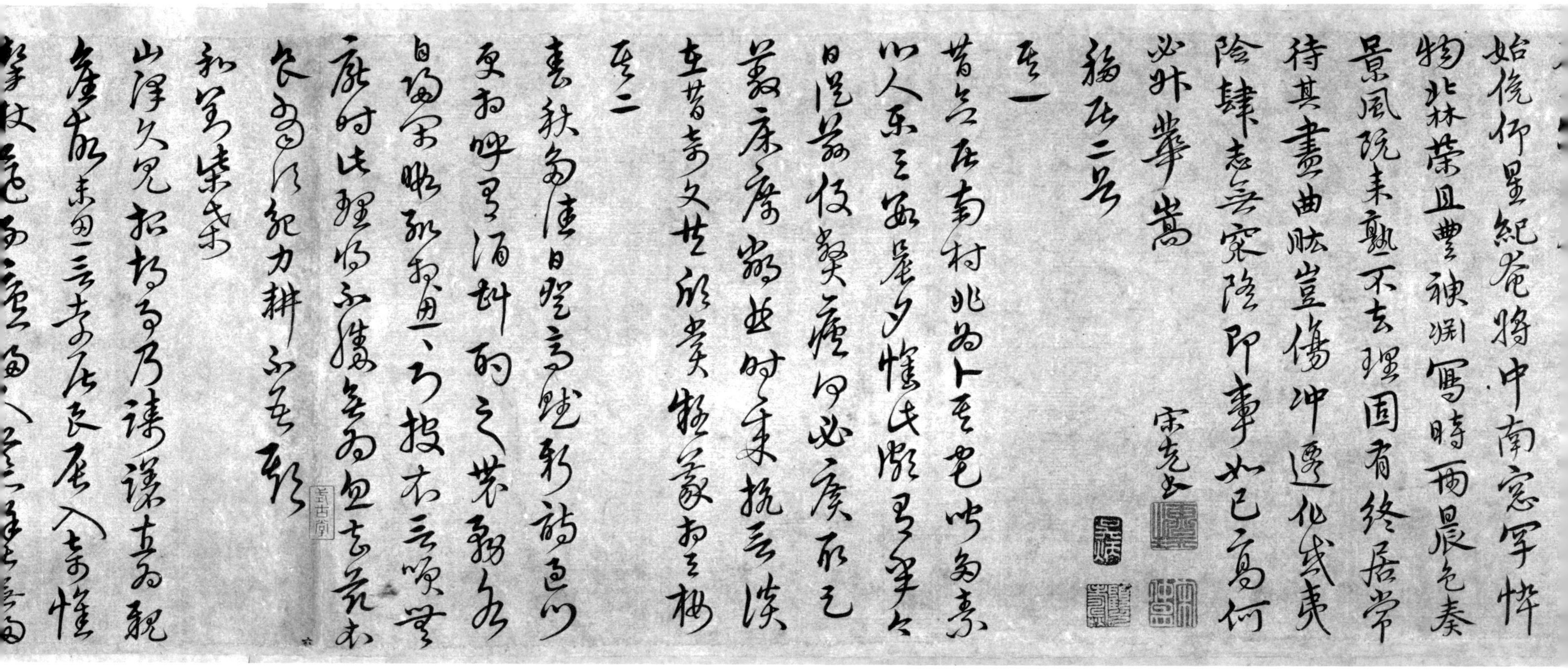
始俛仰星紀奄將中南窓罕悴
物北林榮且豐神淵寫時雨晨色奏
景風既來孰不去理固有終居常
待其盡曲肱豈傷沖遷化或夷
險肆志無窊隆即事如已高何
必升華嵩
宋克書

晉陶靖節先生詩

吴郡宋克書

停雲

停雲思親友也罇湛新醪園列初榮願言不
從嘆息彌襟

靄靄停雲濛濛時雨八表同昏平路伊阻靜寄
東軒春醪獨撫良朋悠邈搔首延佇 停
雲靄靄時雨濛濛八表同昏平陸成江有酒有酒閑
飲東窗願言懷人舟車靡從 東園之樹
枝條再榮競用新好以招余情人亦有言日
月于征安得促席說彼平生 翩翩飛鳥息我
庭柯斂翮閒止好聲相和豈無他人念子寔
多願言不獲抱恨如何

贈長沙公族祖

長沙公於余為族祖同出大司馬昭穆既遠
已為路人經過潯陽臨別贈此

同源分流人易世疏慨然寤歎念茲厥初禮服
遂悠歲月眇徂感彼行路眷然躊躇 於穆
令族允構斯堂諧氣冬暄映懷圭璋爰采春
花載警秋霜我曰欽哉實宗之光 伊余云
遘在長忘同笑言未久逝焉西東遙遙三湘滔滔
九江山川阻遠行李時通 何以寫心貽此話言
進簣雖微終焉為山敬哉離人臨路悽然
款襟或遼音問其先

酬丁柴桑

有客有客爰來爰止秉直司聰于惠百里飡勝如

命子

悠悠我祖爰自陶唐邈為虞賓歷世重光御龍勤夏豕韋翼商穆穆司徒厥族以昌
紛紛戰國漠漠衰周鳳隱於林幽人在丘逸虬繞雲奔鯨駭流天集有漢眷予愍
侯於赫愍侯運當攀龍撫劍夙邁顯茲武功書誓山河啟土開封亹亹丞相允迪
前蹤 渾渾長源蔚蔚洪柯群川載導眾條載羅時有語默運因隆窊
在我中晉業融長沙 桓桓長沙伊勳伊德天子疇我專征南國功遂辭歸臨寵
不忒孰謂斯心而近可得 肅矣我祖慎終如始直方二臺惠和千里於皇仁考
淡焉虛止寄跡風雲冥茲慍喜 嗟余寡陋瞻望弗及顧慚華鬢負影隻
立三千之罪無後為急我誠念哉呱聞爾泣 卜云嘉日占亦良時名汝曰儼字
汝求思溫恭朝夕念茲在茲尚想孔伋庶其企而 厲夜生子遽而求火凡百有
心奚特於我既見其生實欲其可人亦有言斯情無假 日居月諸漸免子
孩福不虛至禍亦易來夙興夜寐願爾斯才爾之不才亦已焉哉

怨詩楚調示龐主簿鄧治中

天道幽且遠鬼神茫昧然結髮念善
事僶俛六九年弱冠逢世阻始室
喪其偏炎火屢焚如螟蜮恣中
田風雨縱橫至收斂不盈廛夏日長
抱飢寒夜無被眠造夕思雞鳴及
晨願烏遷在己何怨天離憂悽目
前吁嗟身後名於我若浮烟慷
慨獨悲歌鍾期信為賢

答龐參軍

相知何必舊傾蓋定前言
有客賞我趣每每顧林園談諧無
俗調所說聖人篇或有數斗酒閒飲
自歡然我實幽居士無復東西
緣物新人惟舊弱毫多所宜
情通萬里外形跡滯江山君其愛
體素來會在何年

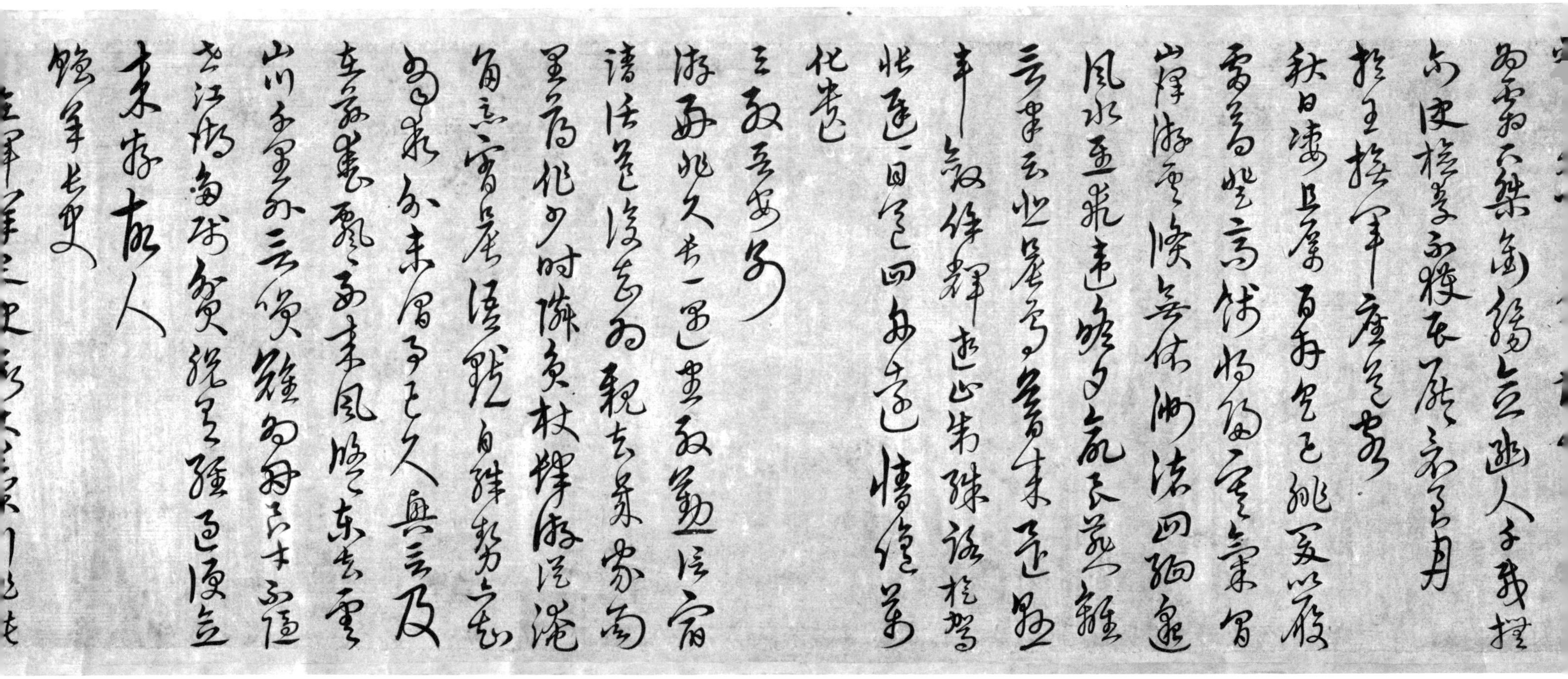

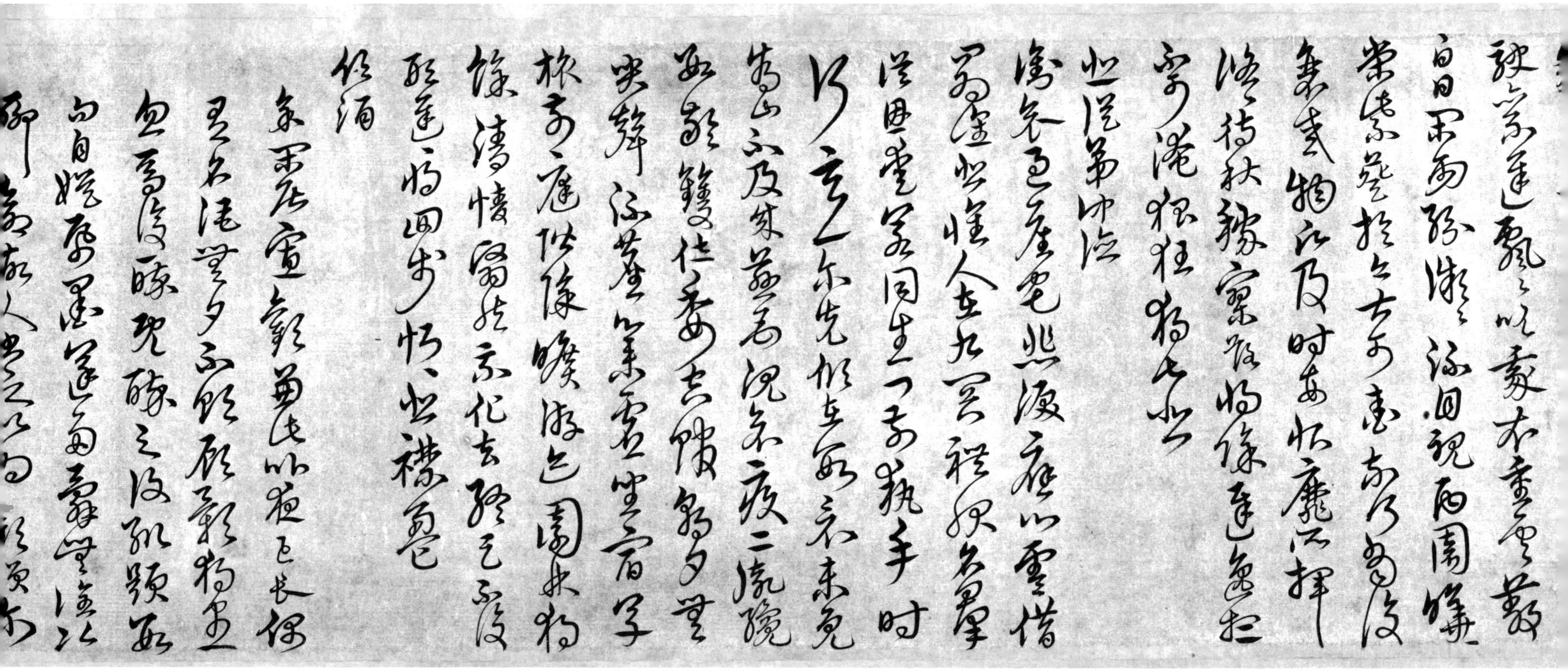

人昧兜夜接箒寸出已寸江禾
曉後庭蕭共風雅凄蕭寒
源祈執節弱如陰兆男登情々緣
若極々若年多果有其身纏耕
錢絲在用直比實不須去々面
年外多名同此日如
兩卷集來
家在宜人用時之四運周桐庭
鳥落蕉悲秋已先秋形葉勢
少墉嘉擬暮鳥如曉々秋不為
樂分思來景不知携家壺觴
下日煙遠將
和節至為二云
葛一堂秋林中支貯涼後悵風丹
時來四颯開衾襟自文淡冥々葉欲起
豈知蟬圍此隱思條消負露殘
依々堂已多稱一色己兆亡歎青
綠化菓陰一飄在目斟 弱之髮
秋偏學陰末朱青比多生之後來
卿用忘集聲色々盈自重悵六
一何凉
和渾圓三表清潔其秋兮為雲隱灑
豈殊氣色高風景激懷出洗年

其
三之
思生三春後悲秋空黃庭
雲陰多年我叙正秋古人重實
重面修止多人在年寄為出三
修心自寞河一家涼九城開己一
迷夜理丹霓比果為先菊迷負病
不稜傷語生鍾高出為秋少謹
謹多歌孫之角精爽久何如
悠悠送涼後擇涼共久庭暮翔為
多黃黃未一變秋思文娛清陰
殊少安人言運兜陰樵悵思代
六言中之言不靜
景蕭和殊出信
秋節悽盛人條謀哉此氣昭
旦兆六日葉蕭氣可三言素能叙
光涯自坂一色默寞寂寥穆淡旅
力出來聽向夕生風起空雲沒
多山原々氣蕭嚴殊々飛鳥邑
比生鮮出在坂伊秋虛應
形讀獸至雲為以承當氣家通
應收通惶後由化靈接已自凉
惶夜運接悲秋

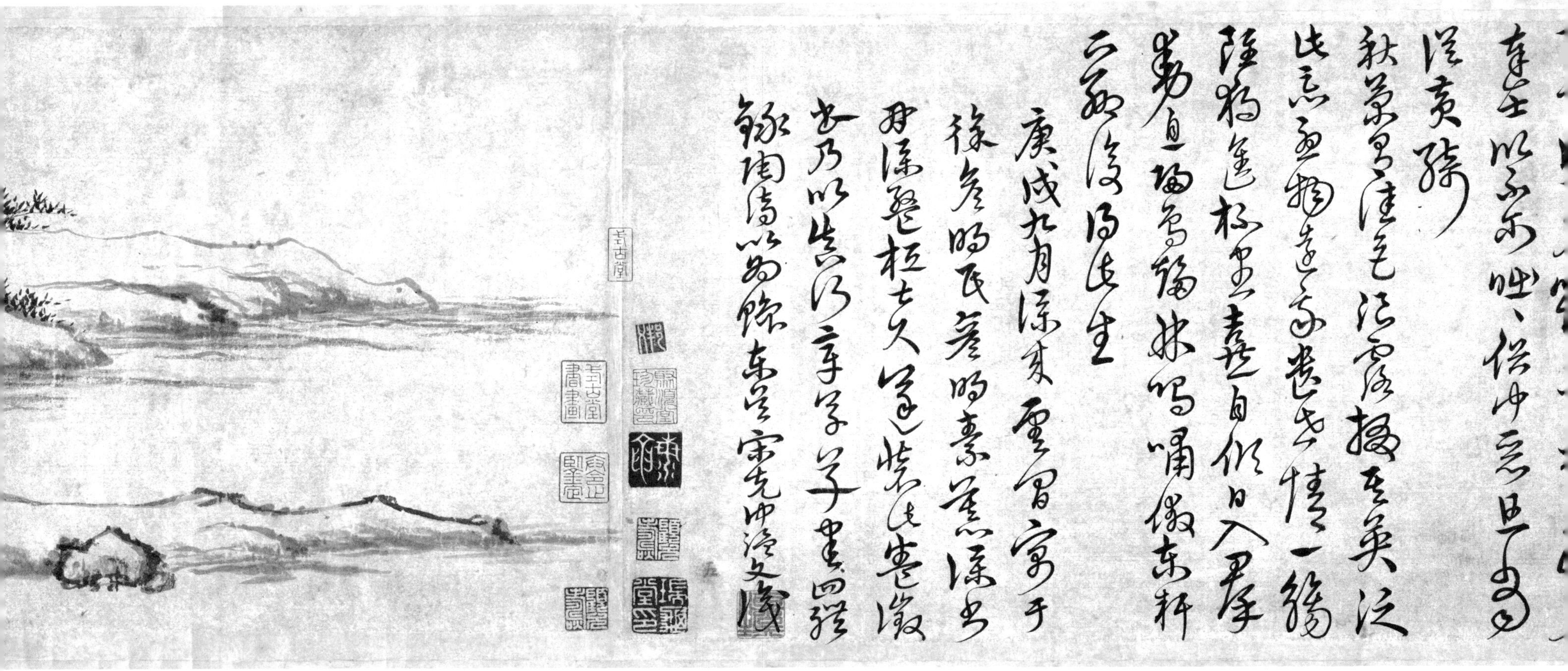

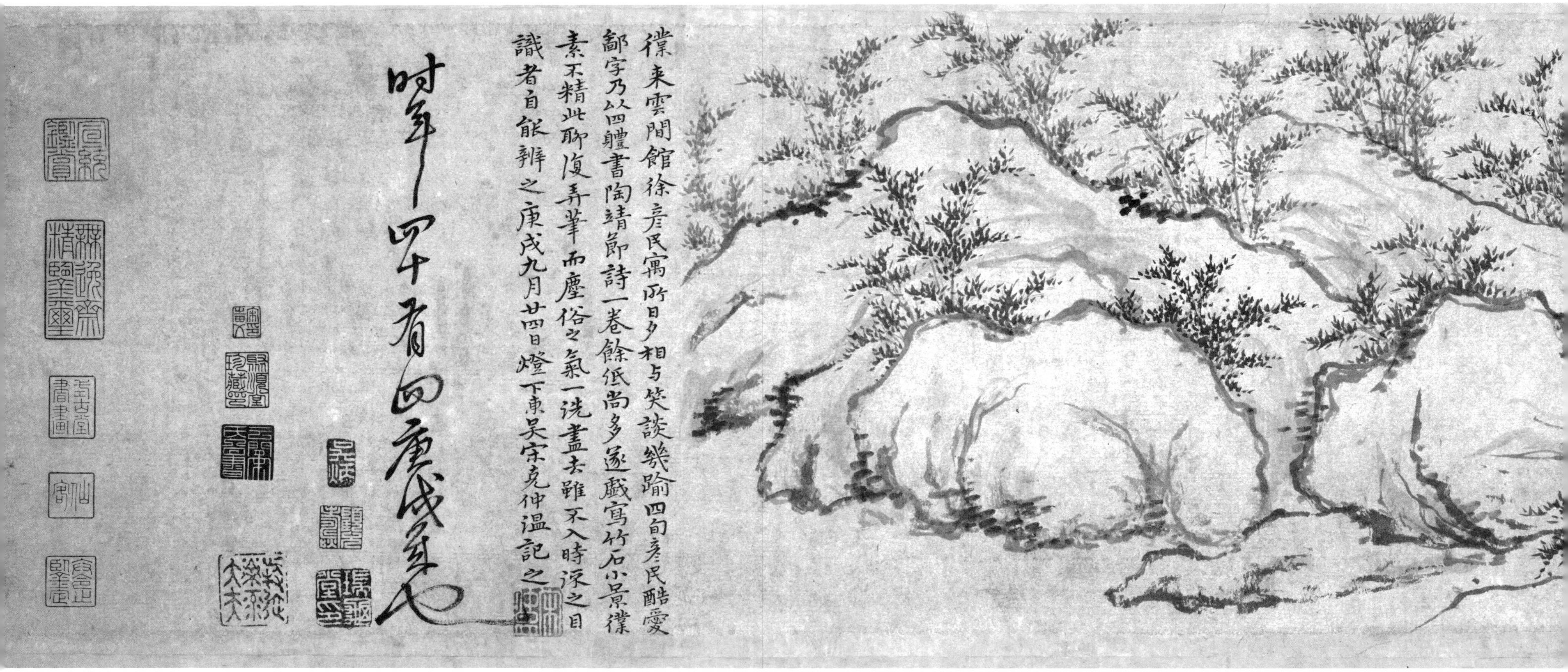
僕来雲閒館徐彥民寓所日夕相与笑談幾踰四旬彥民酷愛
鄙字乃以四體書陶靖節詩一卷餘紙尚多遂戲寫竹石小景僕
素不精此聊復弄筆而塵俗之氣一洗盡去雖不入時深之目
識者自能辨之庚戌九月廿四日燈下東吳宋克仲温記之

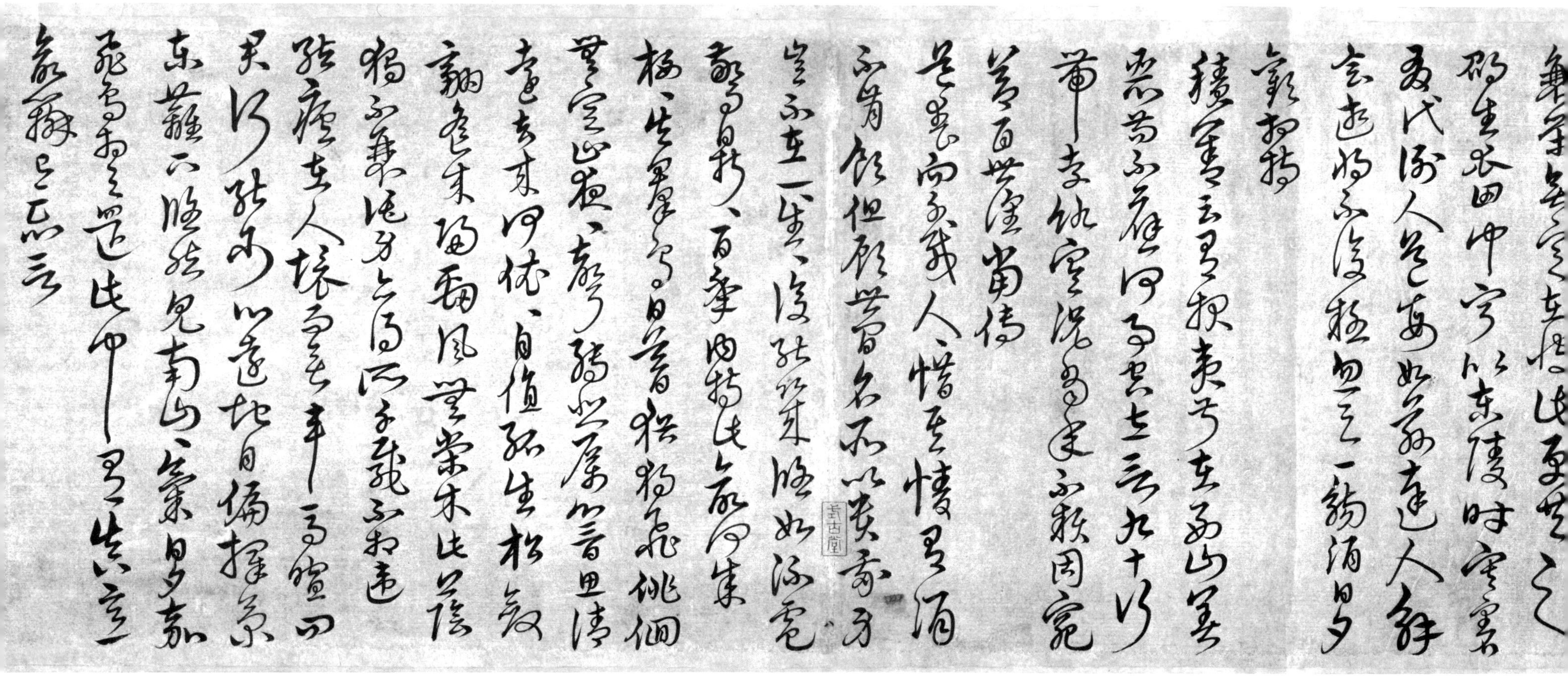

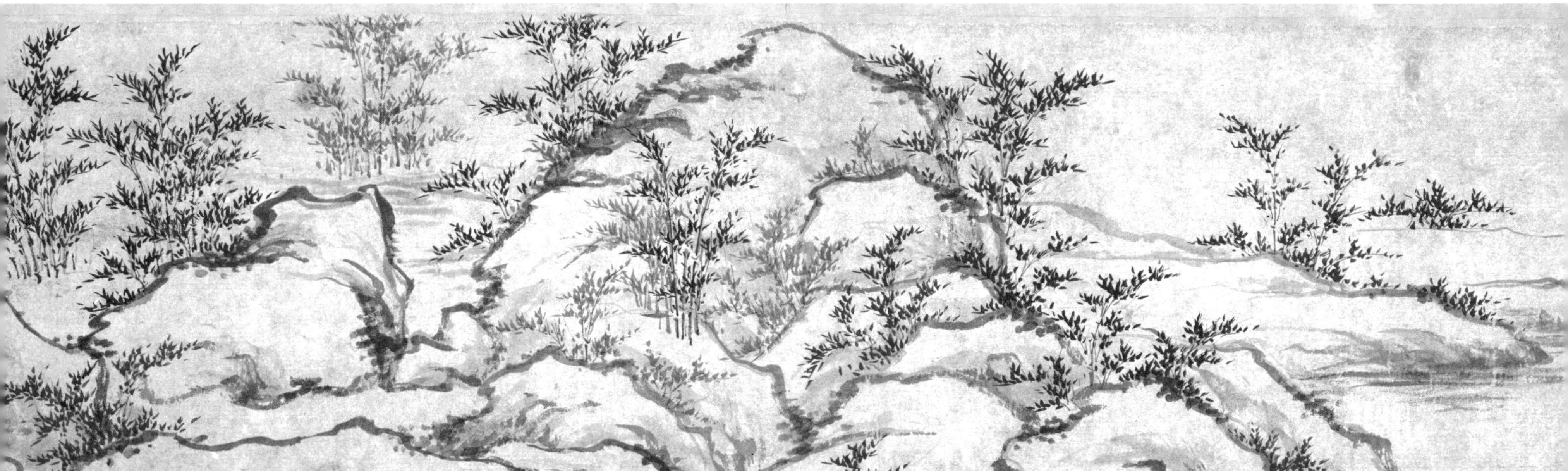

# 13 Wang Fu (1362–1416)

## *Remembering Ni Tsan's "Wu-t'ung Tree and Bamboo by a Thatched Pavilion"* *(I Ni Yün-lin Wu chu ts'ao-t'ang t'u)*

Dated 1408
Hanging scroll, ink on paper
74.9 x 29.9 cm (29 1/2 x 11 3/4 in.); colophon: 28.7 x 29.9 cm (11 1/4 x 11 3/4 in.)

ARTIST'S INSCRIPTION: prose, 224 characters in 15 columns of regular script (for a translation of the artist's inscription, see pages 133–34).

ARTIST'S SIGNATURE: On the first day of the tenth lunar month of the *wu-tzu* year, the sixth year of the Yung-lo era [1408], Wang Meng-tuan inscribed this.

ARTIST'S SEALS: Meng-tuan (square intaglio); P'o-yen-chai (square intaglio); Yu-shih-sheng (tall rectangle intaglio); Yu-hsi han-mo (square relief); Chiu-lung-shan-chung-tao-shih (damaged square intaglio).

COLOPHON by Shao Pao (1460–1527) (7 character quatrain, followed by a 16 character note, in 7 columns of running script; on a separate sheet of paper attached to the top of the painting):

> The recluse Yün-lin [Ni Tsan; 1301–1374] inscribed a poem on his painting.
> And the clarity of his painting was passed down to old Master Shih [Wang Fu].
> By the lonely thatched pavilion under bamboo and *wu-t'ung* trees,
> No one knows where to shoot wild geese.
>
> Fu-hsüan showed me this painting; my respect to those two masters [Ni Tsan and Wang Fu] is reflected in this verse. Signature: On the eleventh day of the tenth lunar month of the *keng-wu* year in the Cheng-te era [1510], Erh-ch'üan, Shao Pao inscribed this. Seal: Kuo-hsien (square relief).

COLLECTOR'S SEALS:
Hsieh Kang-kuo (dates unknown): Hsieh Kang-kuo yin (square intaglio; lower right, painting); Juan-[ ]-lou (square relief; lower right, painting); Tz'u-chou mi-chi (square relief; lower left, painting); Hsieh (round relief; lower right, colophon); K'uang-weng (square relief; lower right, colophon).

Gift of Mr. and Mrs. Wen C. Fong in honor of John B. Elliott (83-43)

Published: Kawai Senro et al., eds., *Shina nanga taisei* (Collection of Chinese paintings of the Southern School), vol. 1 (Tokyo: Kōbun-sha, 1936), pt. 9, pl. 102.

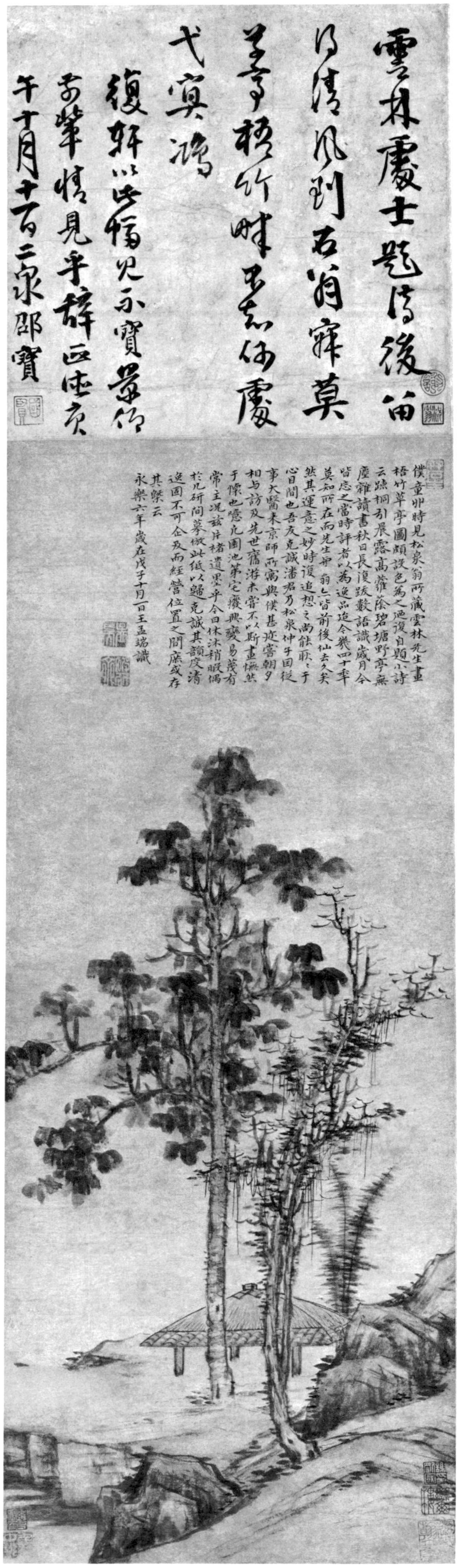

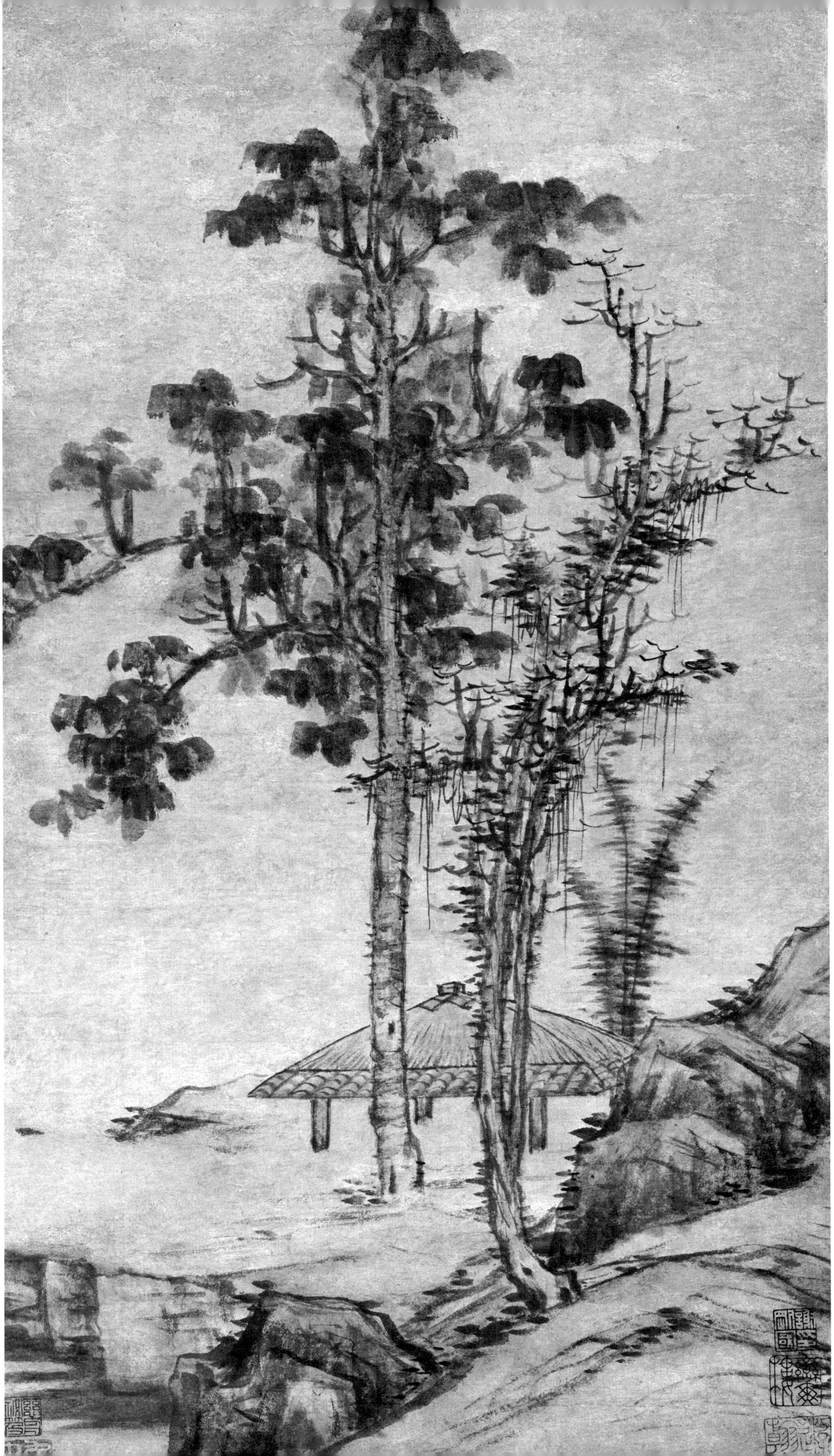

# 14 Shen Chou (1427–1509), Shao Pao (1460–1527)

## *Two folding fans mounted as album leaves*

Leaf A: Shen Chou (1427–1509)
*Home by the Stream (Shui tz'u jen-chia)*
Ca. 1490
Ink on gold-flecked paper
18.1 x 53.7 cm (7 1/8 x 21 1/8 in.)

ARTIST'S INSCRIPTION: 7 character quatrain in 6 columns of running script (for a translation of the artist's inscription, see page 149).

ARTIST'S SIGNATURE: Shen Chou.

ARTIST'S SEAL: Ch'i-nan (square relief).

COLLECTORS' SEALS: Unidentified owners: Ch'ang-chou Wang shih Hsin-yüeh-hsüan so ts'ang (square relief; lower right); Shao-shih shen ting (square relief; lower left).

Edward L. Elliott Family Collection (L173.70a)

PUBLISHED: Suzuki Kei, comp., *Chūgoku kaiga sōgō zuroku: daiikkan, Amerika–Kanada hen* (Comprehensive illustrated catalogue of Chinese paintings: volume 1, American and Canadian collections) (Tokyo: University of Tokyo Press, 1982), p. 145, pl. A17–083.

Leaf B: Shao Pao (1460–1527)
*Four-character Poem (Ssu-yen shih)*
Undated
Ink on gold-flecked paper
18.0 x 48.2 cm (7 1/8 x 19 in.)

CALLIGRAPHY (4 character quatrain, with a 4 character title, in 7 columns of free-form running script):

*Walking with a Green Staff (Ch'ing-li chang-lu)*
As the North Star shines tonight,
I grasp my staff to take a walk.
Thinking of men of the past,
My mind travels through thousands of years.

ARTIST'S SIGNATURE: Erh-ch'üan.

ARTIST'S SEAL: Erh-ch'üan (tall rectangle relief).

COLLECTOR'S SEAL: Unidentified owner: Shao-shih (oval relief; lower right).

Edward L. Elliott Family Collection (L173.70b)

Unpublished.

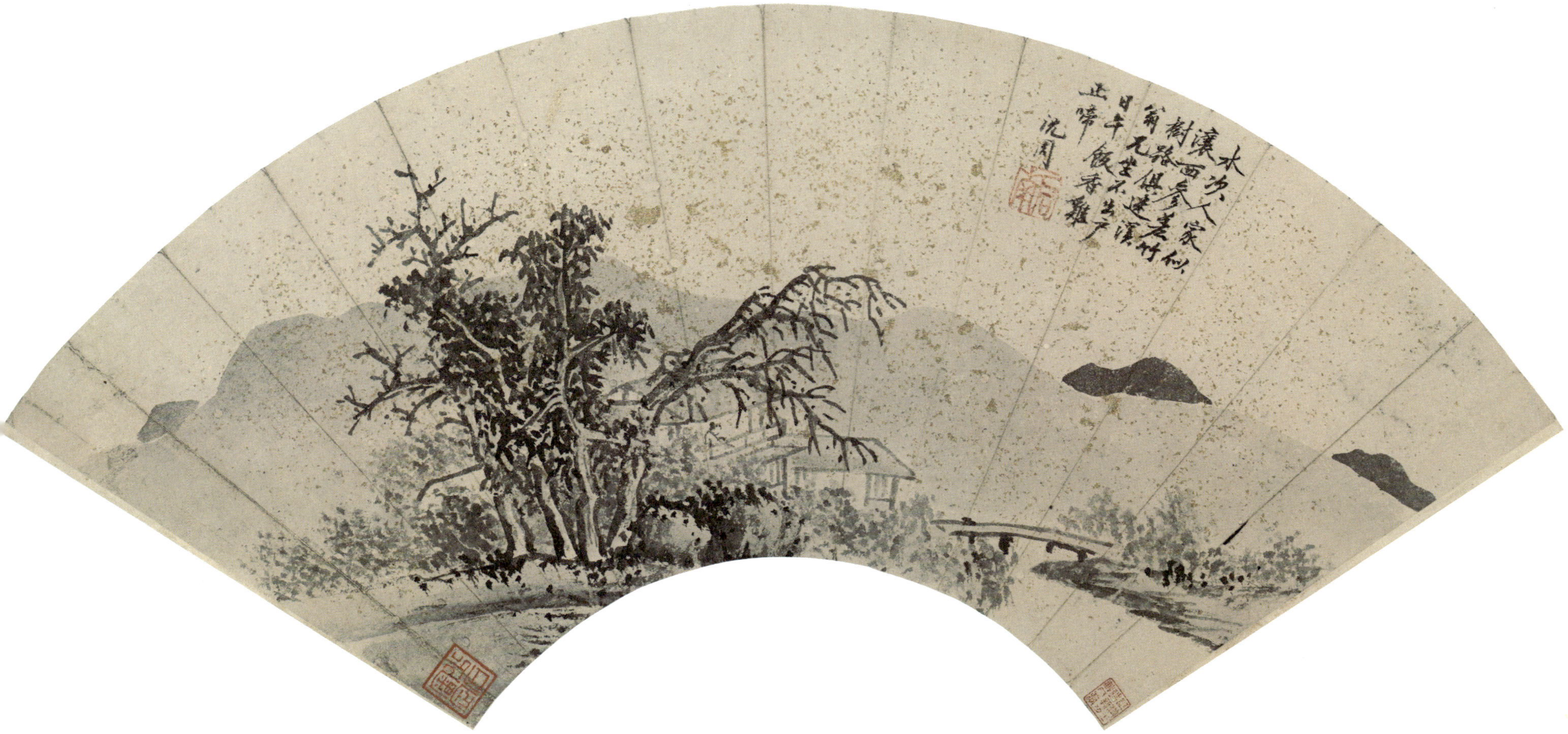

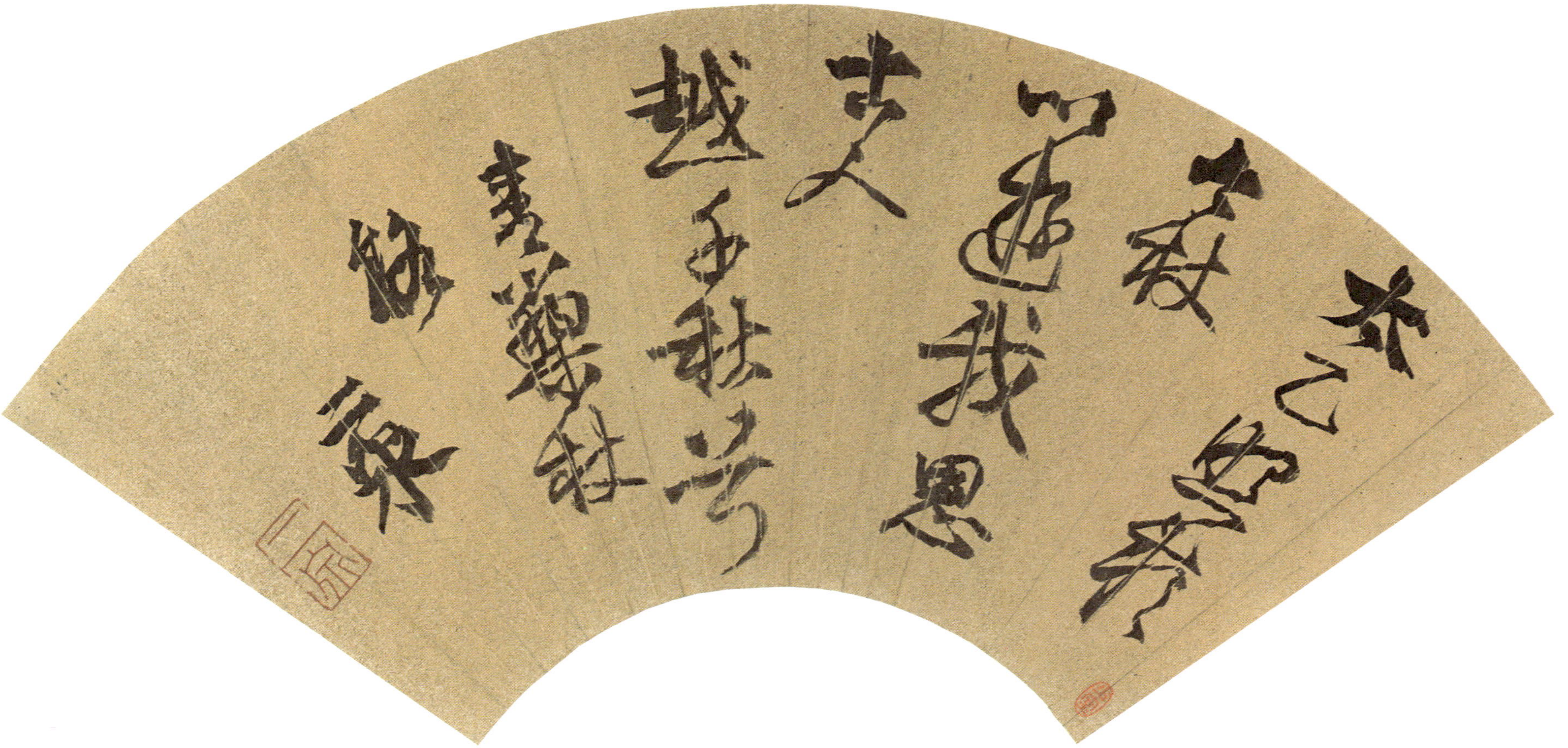

# 15 Shen Chou (1427–1509)

## *Farewell at a Spring River (Ch'un-chiang sung pieh)*

Dated 1499
Handscroll, ink and color on paper
Painting: 26.0 x 152.3 cm (10¼ in. x 5 ft.); colophons: 26.9 x 122.5 cm (10⅝ x 4 ft. ⅞ in.)

ARTIST'S SIGNATURE: Shen Chou of Ch'ang-chou made this in his seventy-third year [*sui*].

ARTIST'S SEAL: Ch'i-nan (square relief).

COLOPHONS (from right to left):

1. Wang Chih-teng (1535–1612): 79 characters in 8 columns of running script. Signature: Wang Chih-teng of T'ai-yüan [in Shansi province] inscribed this. Seals: Ch'ang-chih (gourd-shaped relief); Wang Chih-teng yin (square intaglio).
2. Chang Feng-i (1527–1613): 67 characters in 7 columns of running script. Signature: Chang Feng-i of Ch'ang-chou. Seals: Wo-kuo-nan-tzu (square intaglio); Chang Po-ch'ao shih (square intaglio).
3. Ch'iao Ch'ung-hsiu (fl. ca. early 18th century): 35 character note in 2 columns of running script. Signature: On the third day of the eighth lunar month of the Yung-cheng era [1735], Ku-weng inscribed this. Seal: Ch'ung-hsiu (tall rectangle intaglio).

COLLECTORS' SEALS:

1. Chu Chih-ch'ih (fl. ca. 16th century): Hsiu-ning Chu Chih-ch'ih chen-ts'ang t'u-shu (tall rectangle relief; lower right, painting); Chu Chih-ch'ih chien-shang (square relief; lower left, painting); Ti-i hsi-yu (square relief; lower left, painting).
2. Ch'iao Ch'ung-hsiu: Ch'iao Ch'ung-hsiu yin (square intaglio; lower right, silk mounting); Ch'iao-[ ] Ch'ung-hsiu (square relief; lower left, painting); Ku-weng (square intaglio; left edge, colophon).
3. Ma Chi-tso (modern collector): Ma Chi-tso chien-shang chang (tall rectangle relief; left edge, colophon).
4. Unidentified owners: Pao-ting-ko shu-hua chi (tall rectangle relief; left edge, colophon); Ch'ien-lin shan-ch'iao (square intaglio; left edge, colophon).

John B. Elliott Collection (L297.70)

PUBLISHED: Suzuki Kei, comp., *Chūgoku kaiga sōgō zuroku: daiikkan, Amerika–Kanada hen* (Comprehensive illustrated catalogue of Chinese paintings: volume 1, American and Canadian collections) (Tokyo: University of Tokyo Press, 1982), p. 134, pl. A17–062.

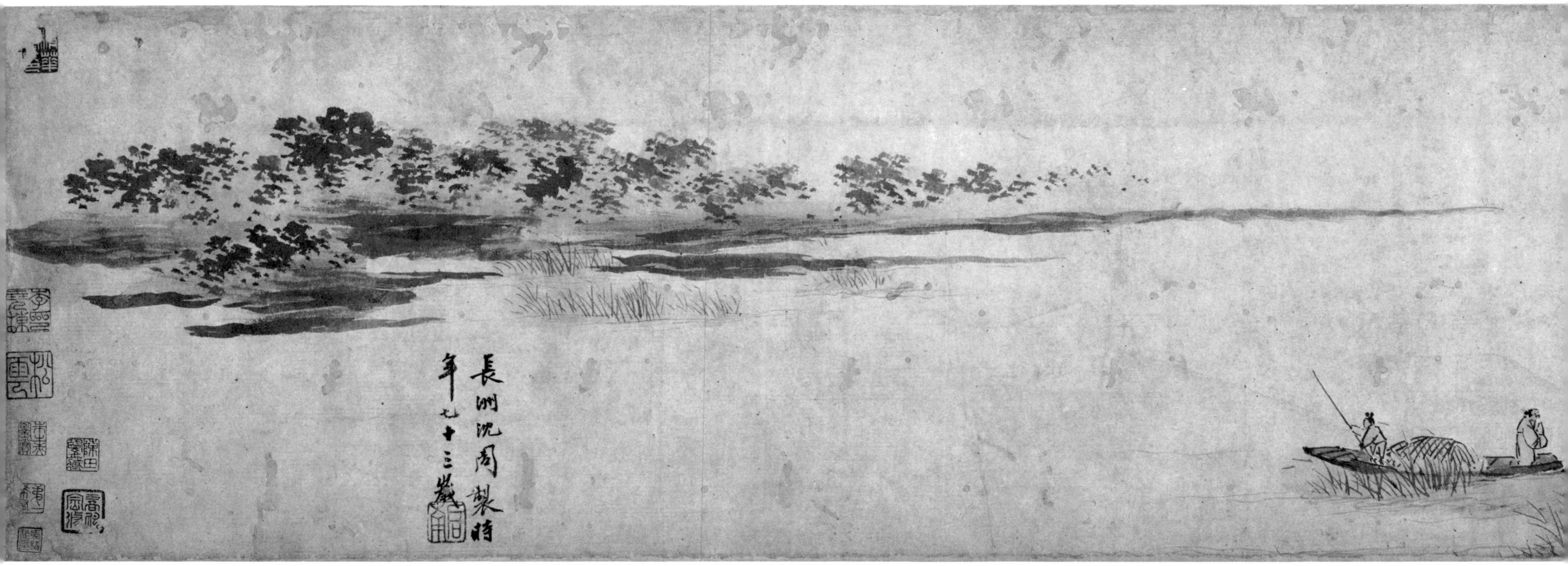

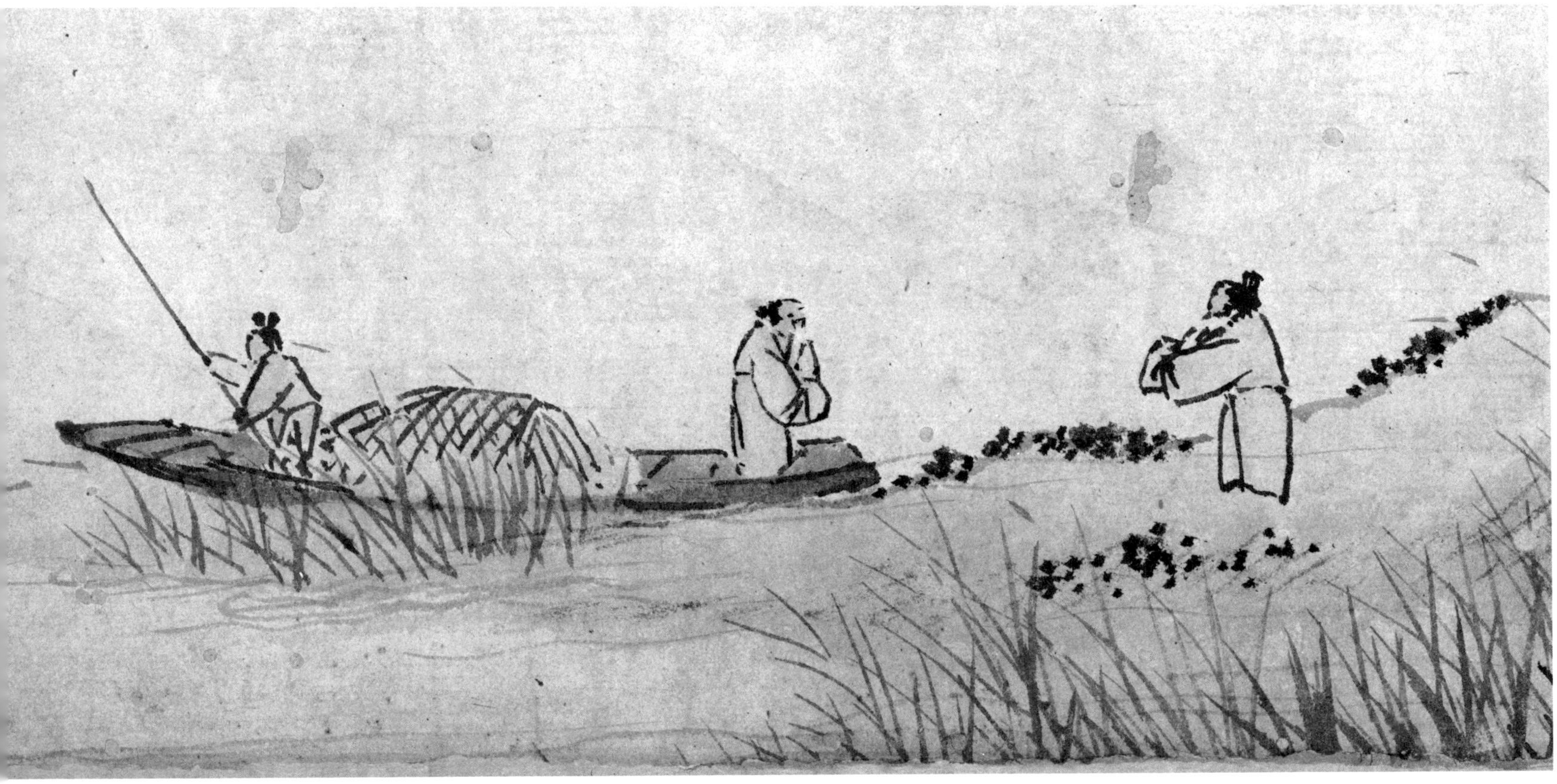

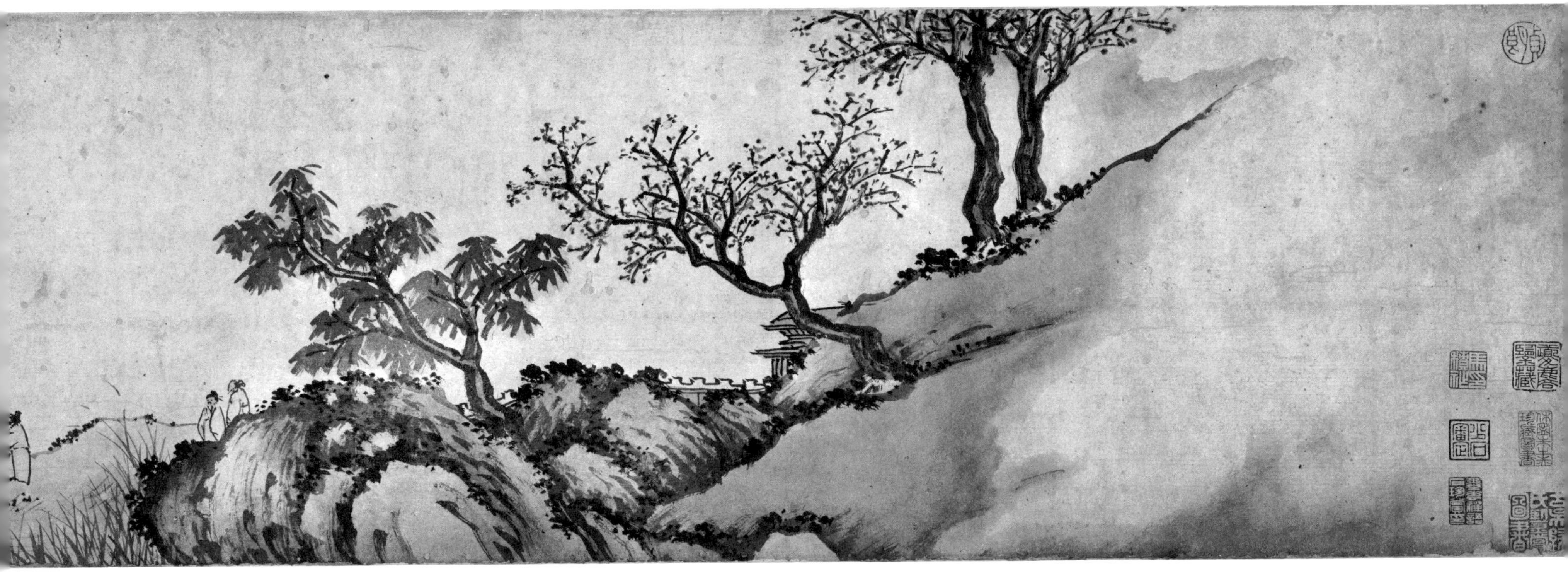

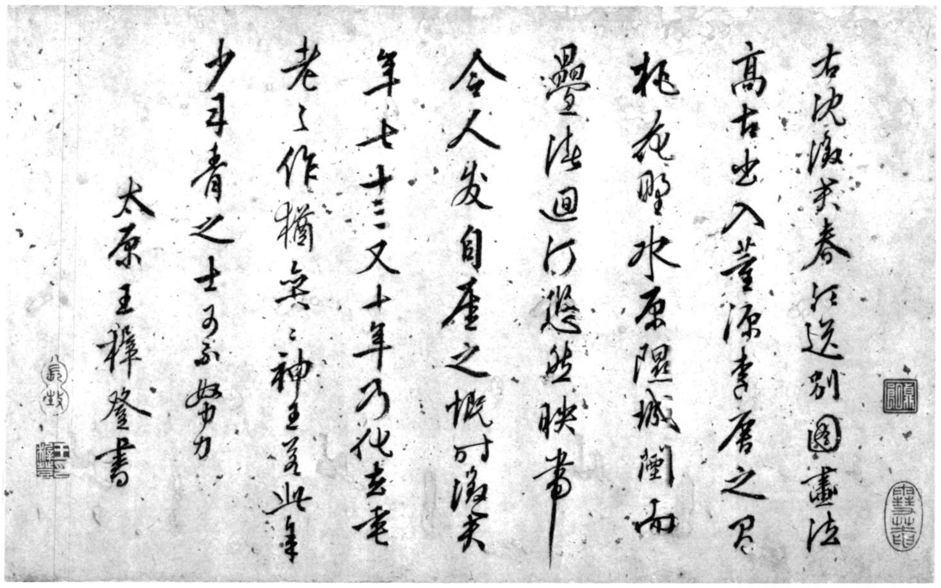

Wang Chih-teng

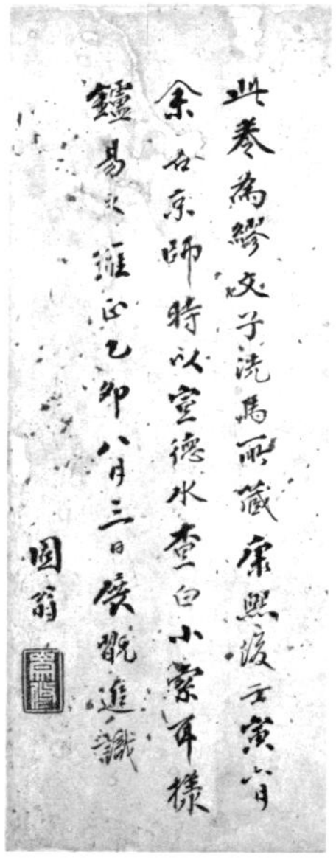

Ch'iao Ch'ung-hsiu

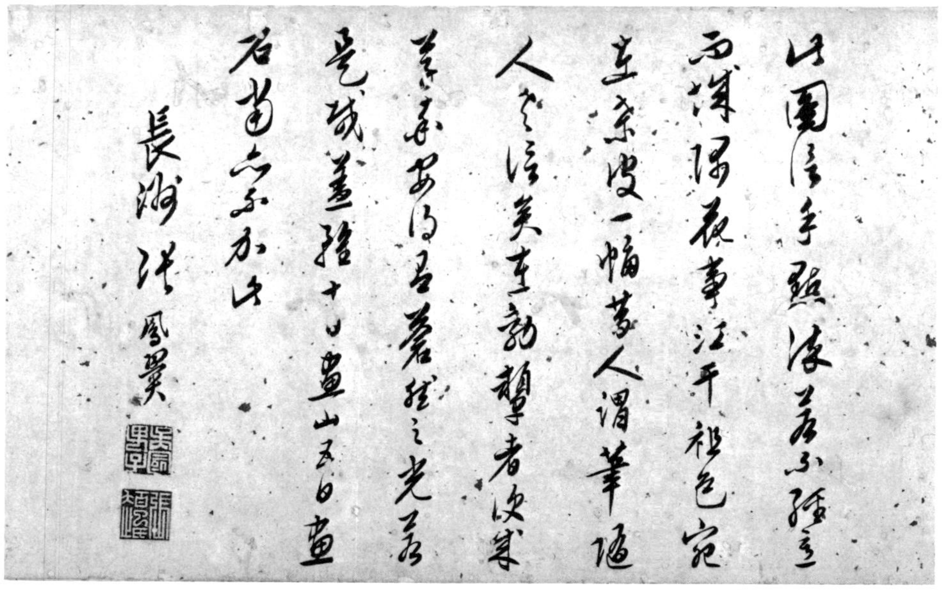

Chang Feng-i

# 16 Ch'en Hsien-chang (1428–1500)

## *Poems on Plum Blossoms (Mei-hua ping-chung tso)*

Dated 1491
Handscroll, ink on paper
30.5 x 897.4 cm (12 in. x 29 ft. 5 1/8 in.)

CALLIGRAPHY (nine 5 character regulated verses, each in 8 lines, with a 5 character title, followed by notes, totaling 383 characters in 99 columns of cursive script):

*Writing about Plum Blossoms While Ill*

Last year, boasting of my health,
I went to Mount Chi to search for plum blossoms.
Emptying many wine cups, I lingered there until the shadow of the cliff merged into darkness.
When I returned home, my clothes were damp with fragrant dew.
What direction does the Big Dipper point now?
Those branches facing south have already lost half their blossoms.
As I descend the reception room steps, my sons and daughters laugh at me, limping on old weak feet.

Solitary Islet, a seeming blur of snow,
Praised as a marvel over thousands of years:
Outsiders can never reach this place.
Few people know of its existence.
While I was both savoring the flowers' perfection and lamenting their coming decline, the buds had already opened more than halfway.
As I look back at the base of the west cliff,
The southerly branches reflect the beauty of the north-facing flowers.

Life is like flowing water.
Blossoms appear first on the southerly branches;
Facing their silhouettes I keep my distance.
Still, without even moving my seat closer I can smell the blossoms.
To prolong this moment I watch the moon a long while.
In homage I crawl slowly down the stairs
And sit among the flowers,
Afraid they will have lost their fragrance.
I support my weak body and finish this poem.

Everywhere tips of plum branches are bathed by moonlight.
Their images sparkle on the screen near my pillow.
Rivers and mountains are the Great Ultimate,
Grasses and flowers, too, have a pure existence.
The pavilion is so cold the blossoms' fragrance can barely penetrate,
But their vivid shadows seem to spread across the window screen.
The iciness of the cliff may block the passage of my crippled feet.
Still, supported by my bramble staff, I am in high spirits.

While I lean on an armrest, the sun begins its descent.
The east cliff is rich with blossoming flowers;
The lofty moon, so cold, shines alone.
During the night fragrance from nearby flowers entices me;
Pouring wine, I write so easily.
But how can it be simple to tune the lute's pure strings?
Where is Mount Lo-fu [metaphor for plum blossoms], for there in dreams spirits wander.

Among countless flowers on land and water,
The plum is spotlessly pure.
How can it be that wherever I stop to observe,
No one can be seen enjoying the blossoms?
The breeze wafts lightly through the walled village to the north.
Shining, the lonely moon illuminates southerly branches.
An old man, I sit directly in front of the trees
And try to infuse this poem with their spirit.

The mountain pavilion is nestled in a grove of plums,
Planted by myself, the Old Gentleman of the Mountain.
Their blossoms amuse me in my old age,
But without an audience they will still bloom.
Plum color so pure is reflected on my books,
And their fragrance suffuses the pool of ink from which I write.
So I will follow you, Master Plum,
And never serve the weedy underbrush.

Wind and moon are beyond rivers and mountains;
Heaven and earth are among the trees and grasses.
Fragments of plum shadows quiver on the blind as it is rolled up.
Resting chin in hand I inhale their subtle fragrance.
I suggested to my friends we have an immense acreage of plums,
An enchanted spot for chanting poems.
Although Mount Chung-nan [metaphor for eremitism] is dotted with white pavilions [to attract elegant guests],
Little Mount Lu will not turn out the same.

Where are there flowers unforgettable?
Chiang-men, from where the river flows.
Flower beds are totally exposed in the moonlight.
Not a petal is swept along by the current.
Soaring pines offer shelter and rows of pure bamboo
make nests for the birds.
White gulls holding blossoms in their beaks linger,
unwilling to leave,
And swoop down among the fishermen in straw raincoats.

ARTIST'S SIGNATURE: On the twenty-third day of the twelfth lunar month of the *hsin-hai* year of the Hung-chih era [1491], Shih-weng wrote these poems in the Hsiao-lu-kang Studio.

ARTIST'S SEAL: Shih-chai (square intaglio).

INSCRIPTION by T'ao Yün-ping(?) (dates unknown) (prose, 27 characters in 3 columns of free-form running script):

This scroll is in the collection of Yü Po-ch'ing. People from near and far know and admire this treasure. Although people tried to buy the scroll, offering a high price, none of them succeeded. Now I am lucky enough to appreciate this scroll; how could I say that such good fortune is easily achieved? Signature: [ ]-[ ] shu. Seal: T'ao shih Yün-ping [ ] (square relief).

COLOPHONS (from right to left):

1. Pao Chen (19th century?): prose, 122 characters in 10 columns of regular script. Signature: A later follower from Fan-ch'ang [in Honan province], Pao Chen, Fang-chin, inscribed this. Seal: Pao Chen yin (square intaglio).
2. Su T'ing-k'uei (ca. 1800–1871): 5 character regulated verse in 8 lines, followed by a 44 character note, in 16 columns of running script. Signature: Su T'ing-k'uei. Seals: Su T'ing-k'uei yin (square intaglio); Ch'-shih hou tso (square relief).

COLLECTORS' SEALS:
Weng Fang-kang (1733–1818), 1 seal.
Wu Hsi-tsai (1799–1870), 1 seal.
Tuan Fang (1861–1911), 1 seal.
Ho Yüan-yü (early 19th century Cantonese collector), 4 seals.
T'an P'ei (fl. late 19th–early 20th century), 1 seal.
Lien Ch'eng (dates unknown), 1 seal.
Kuan Ch'eng (dates unknown), 1 seal.
Yen Hai (dates unknown), 3 seals.
Unidentified owners, 5 seals.
1 unidentified seal.

Gift of John B. Elliott (80–43)

PUBLISHED: Shen C. Y. Fu et al., *Traces of the Brush: Studies in Chinese Calligraphy* (New Haven: Yale University Art Gallery, 1977), p. 262, pl. 30; Nakata Yūjirō and Fu Shen, eds., *Obei shūzō Chūgoku hōsho meisekishū* (Masterpieces of Chinese calligraphy in American and European collections), vol. 4 (Tokyo: Chūōkōron-sha, 1982), pp. 76–84, 136, 165–66, pls. 83–92.

CH'EN HSIEN-CHANG, better known by one of his sobriquets, Pai-sha-tzu, was a philosopher, educator, and calligrapher in Hsin-hui in Kuangtung province.[1] Although he passed the 1447 provincial examination, Ch'en never realized his ambition, in spite of numerous attempts, to succeed at the more important metropolitan examinations. Since the doors to a government career remained closed to him, he became both a student and a teacher of Neo-Confucianism, traveling to Kiangsi in 1454 to study under Wu Yü-pi (1392–1469). Under Wu's tutelage Ch'en developed his own philosophy, a syncretic blend of Confucianism, Buddhism, and Taoism united by the primary doctrine of naturalism, which was also the governing aesthetic of Ch'en's calligraphy.[2] "By practicing calligraphy," he explained, "I purify my mind, pacify my emotions, and cultivate my spirit. This is why I immerse myself in the art."[3]

Ch'en's broad stylistic range, which reached its zenith in his cursive script style, modeled after the Tsin dynasty masters, can be divided into three stages. The first phase covers his early forties into his early sixties (1467–87), when he modeled his writings on Chung Yu (A.D. 151–231), Wang Hsi-chih (ca. 307–ca. 365), Su Shih (1036–1101), Huang T'ing-chien (1045–1105), and Mi Fu (1052–1107).[4] At this time he also developed a personal style, represented by *Poem on New Year's Day* (*Yüan-tan shih-pi*), dated 1481.[5] In this composition each character tilts to the lower left and is energized by a lifting-and-pressing movement (*ch'i-fu*) of the brush. By manipulating the brush so that the tip is hidden, however, in the technique called *chung-feng*, Ch'en gave his characters smooth silhouettes, which soften the otherwise harsh effect of the piece.

These characteristics were further elaborated by his use of the *mao-lung* (literally, rush dragon, brush made of *miscanthus* rush), with which he began to experiment in his sixties. *Poems on Plum Blossoms* in The

Art Museum, Princeton, is representative of Ch'en Hsien-chang's later period. These poems were written during an illness when Ch'en was sixty-three, at the Hsiao-lu-kang Studio (built in 1489).[6] Because of the stiffness of the brush, the characters in this piece have severe silhouettes, and the brushstrokes show little thickening and thinning. Since rush is far less absorbent than the animal hair usually used for brushes, it created a contrast in tones. Even when fully loaded with ink, the rush brush could write only five or six characters at one time; within this group, the first character usually appears larger in scale, softer in silhouette, and moister in ink tone; the following characters seem smaller and stiffer, and are so dry that they appear in *fei-pai* (flying white), a stroke containing broken lines and uninked areas. Although they range in size, the characters are basically symmetrical, a feature that adds stability to the composition. As in his early writing, Ch'en used the *chung-feng* technique, and the roundness of the brushstrokes subdues the harsh effect. The blunt yet controlled brushwork creates a sense of momentum that is apparent in the sharp juxtapositions between light and dark, moistness and dryness, and solids and voids. Acknowledging this tension, Ch'en wrote that in his calligraphy style he always tried to achieve an effect of tranquility in dynamism: "Free yet not untrammeled, stable yet not stagnate—these are the principles I use to create a marvelous dynamic quality. [I am] neither disturbed by a sense of astonishment if the brush movement is fluid and controlled nor anxious if the brush seems to stick. Such mental stability gives my calligraphy an aura of tranquility."[7]

In the last stage of Ch'en's stylistic development, from 1494 to 1500, his style shifted from dynamic tranquility to heroic representation. His calligraphy on his parents' tomb stele, dated to 1497, and that for the Tz'u-yün temple, dated to 1499, both in his hometown,[8] strongly reflect the influences of Yen Chen-ch'ing (709–785) and Ou-yang Hsün (557–641). Nevertheless his energetic, unembellished brushwork breaks the rigid restrictions of T'ang aesthetic principles and conveys a sense of freedom. "My writing style," Ch'en wrote, "follows classic formulae, yet it is not confined by them. It looks free yet not uncontrolled; awkward yet rich in skill; straightforward yet full of subtlety."[9] The qualities found in Ch'en Hsien-chang's calligraphy are momentum and naturalism, both reactions against the Ming preference for the elegant and refined Chao Meng-fu (1254–1322) idiom.[10]

PAO-CHEN CH'EN

NOTES

1. For further biographical information, see Jen Yu-wen, *Pai-sha-tzu yen-chiu* (A study of Pai-sha-tzu) (Hong Kong: Chien shih Meng-chin shu-wu, 1970), pp. 26–43; Huang P'ei and Julia Ching, "Ch'en Hsien-chang," in L. Carrington Goodrich and Chaoying Fang, eds., *Dictionary of Ming Biography: 1368–1644* (New York and London: Columbia University Press, 1976), vol. 1, pp. 153–56.
2. Jen Yu-wen, "Ch'en Hsien-chang's Philosophy of the Natural," in William Theodore de Bary, ed., *Self and Society in Ming Thought* (New York: Columbia University Press, 1970), pp. 53–92.
3. Ch'en Hsien-chang, *Pai-sha-tzu ch'üan-chi* (The complete works of Pai-sha-tzu) (Hsin-hui, Kuangtung: Pi-yü-lou, 1771), *chüan* 2, p. 26b; for a reproduction of the calligraphy of the text, see Ch'en Ying-yao, *Pai-sha hsien-sheng i-chi* (Calligraphy of Master Pai-sha) (Hong Kong: Ch'en shih Keng-tu-t'ang, 1959), p. 39.
4. Jen Yu-wen, *Pai-sha-tzu yen-chiu*, pp. 336–39.
5. Ch'en Ying-yao, *Pai-sha hsien-sheng i-chi*, p. 8.
6. Juan Jung-ling, "Pai-sha hsien-sheng nien-p'u" (Chronology of Master Pai-sha), in Ch'en Ying-yao, ed., *Pai-sha hsien-sheng chi-nien chi* (Memorial essays for Master Pai-sha) (Hong Kong: Ch'en shih Keng-tu-t'ang, 1952), p. 39.
7. Ch'en Hsien-chang, *Pai-sha-tzu ch'üan-chi*, *chüan* 2, p. 26b.
8. Ch'en Ying-yao, *Pai-sha hsien-sheng i-chi*, pp. 43–44.
9. Ch'en Hsien-chang, *Pai-sha-tzu ch'üan-chi*, *chüan* 2, p. 26b.
10. Mai Hua-san, "Pai-sha shu-fa tui yü Ming-tai shu-feng chih ying-hs'iang" (The influence of Master Pai-sha's calligraphy in the Ming period), in Ch'en Ying-yao, ed., *Pai-sha hsien-sheng chi-nien chi*, pp. 53–54; Jen Yu-wen, *Pai-sha-tzu yen-chiu*, p. 339.

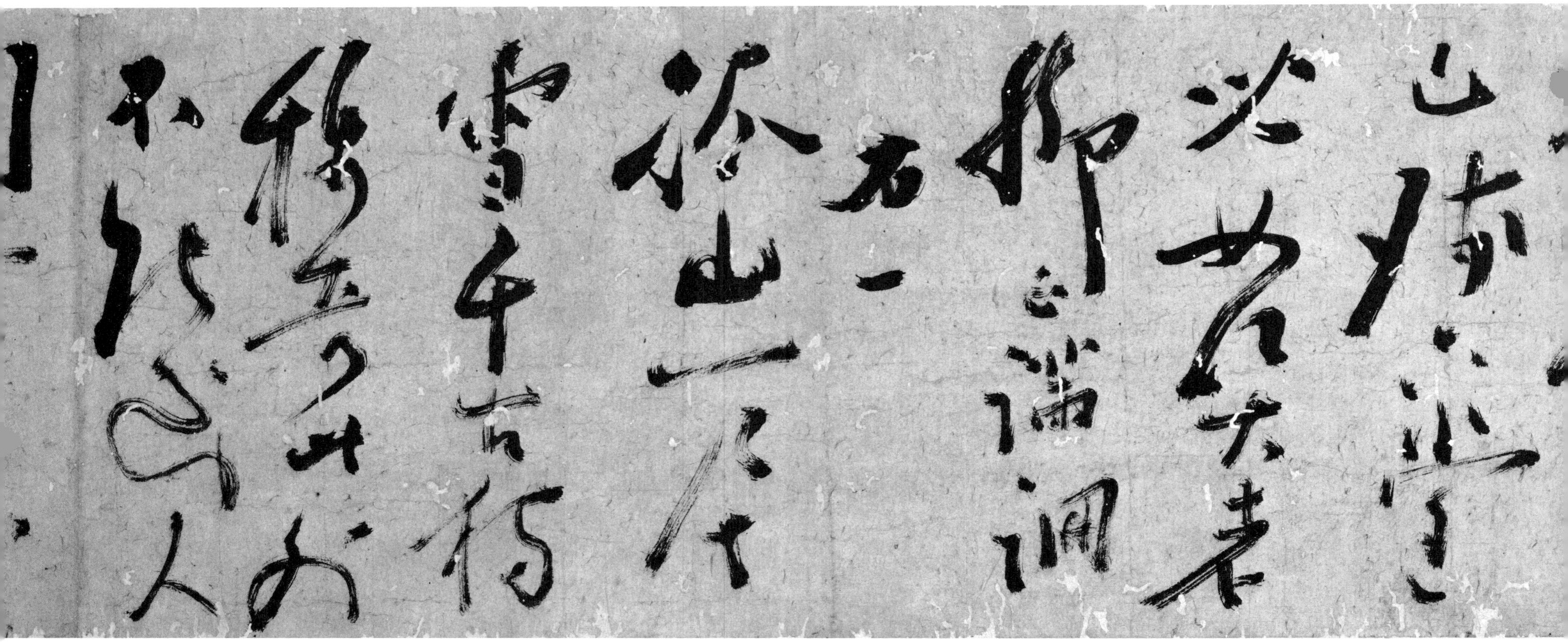

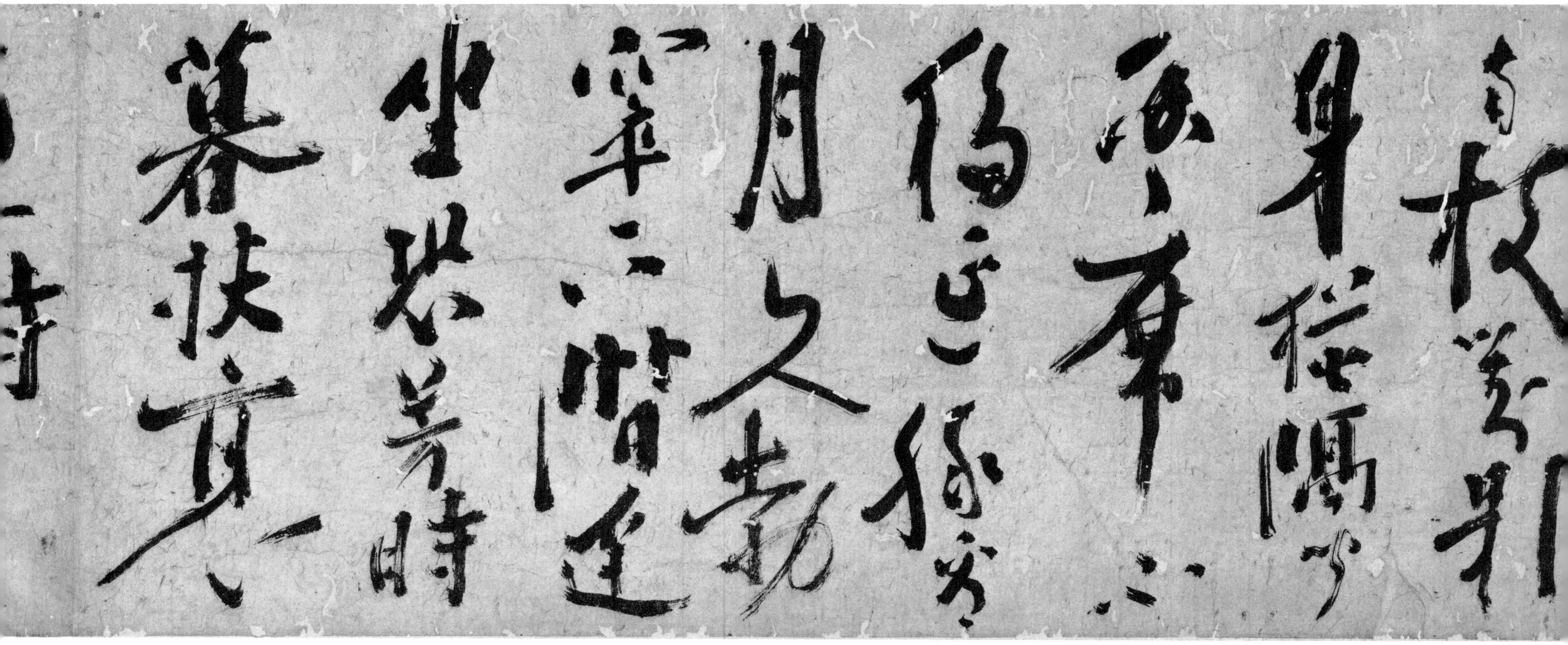

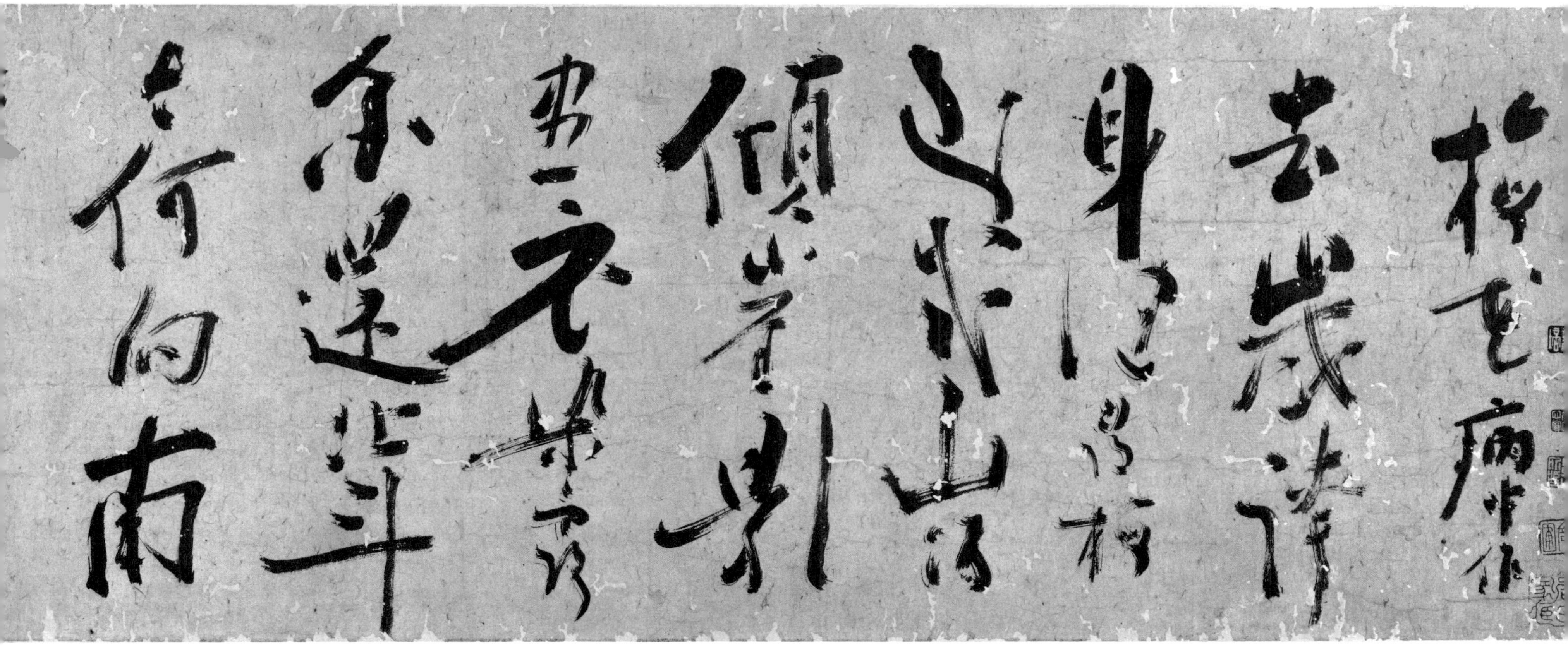

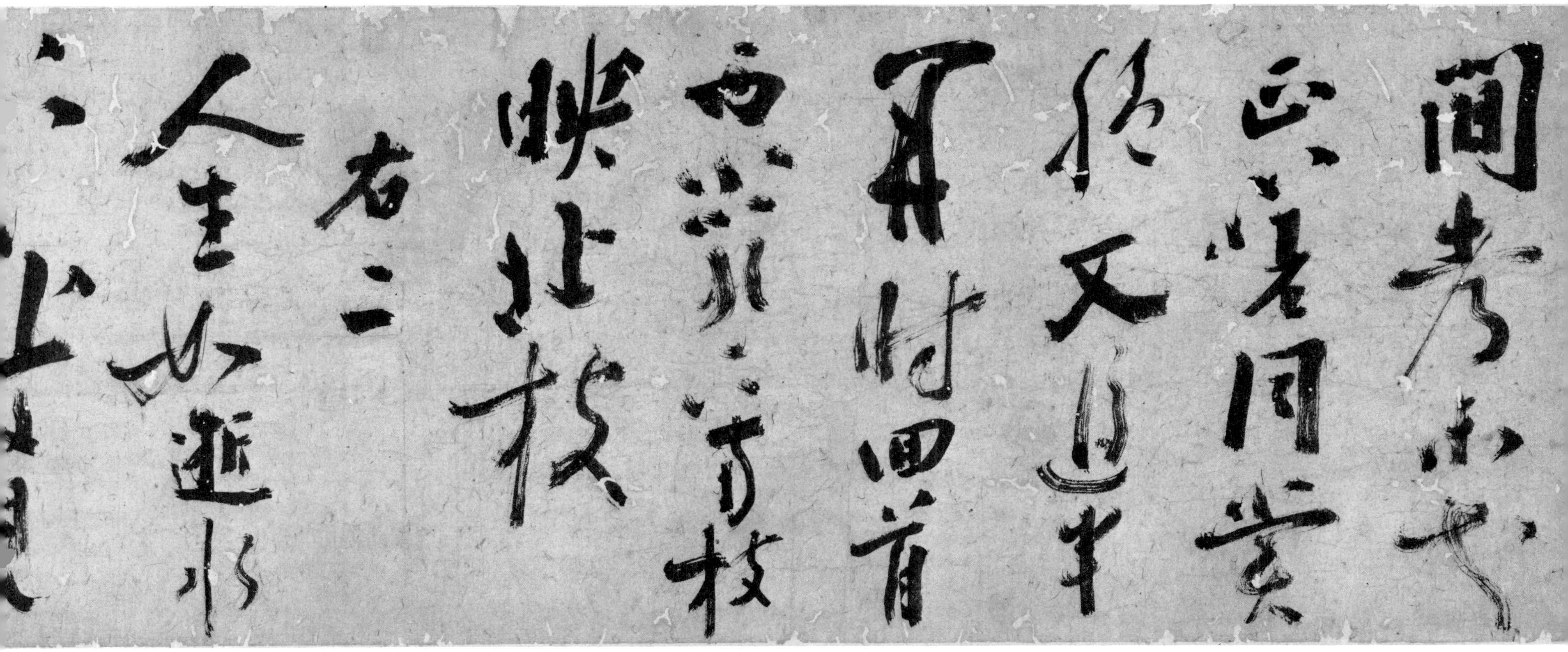

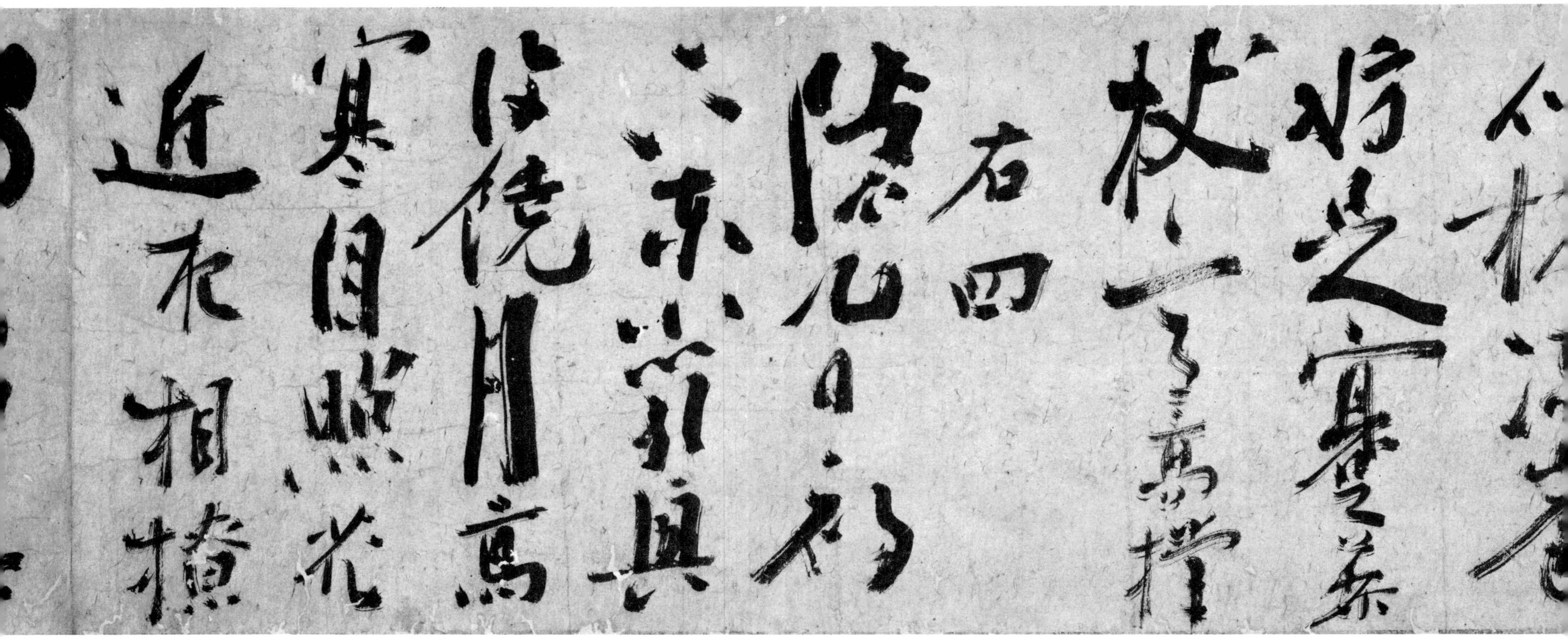

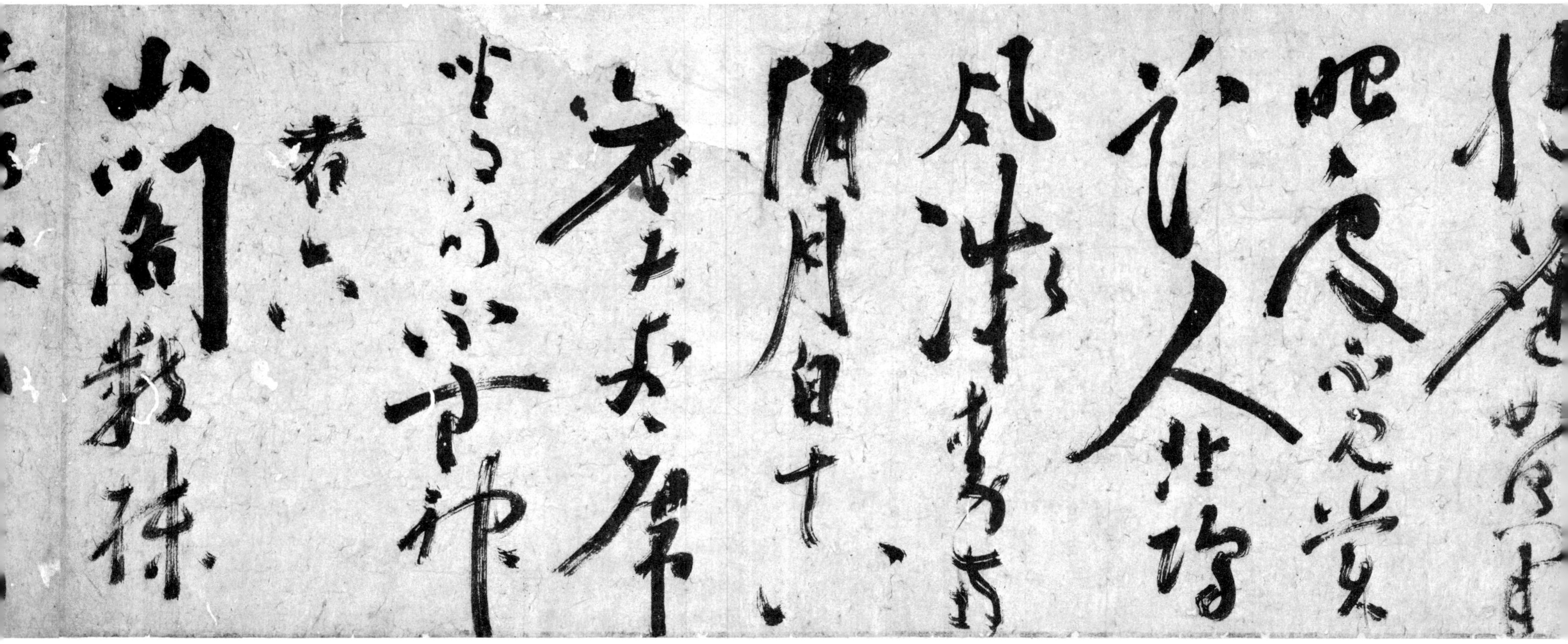

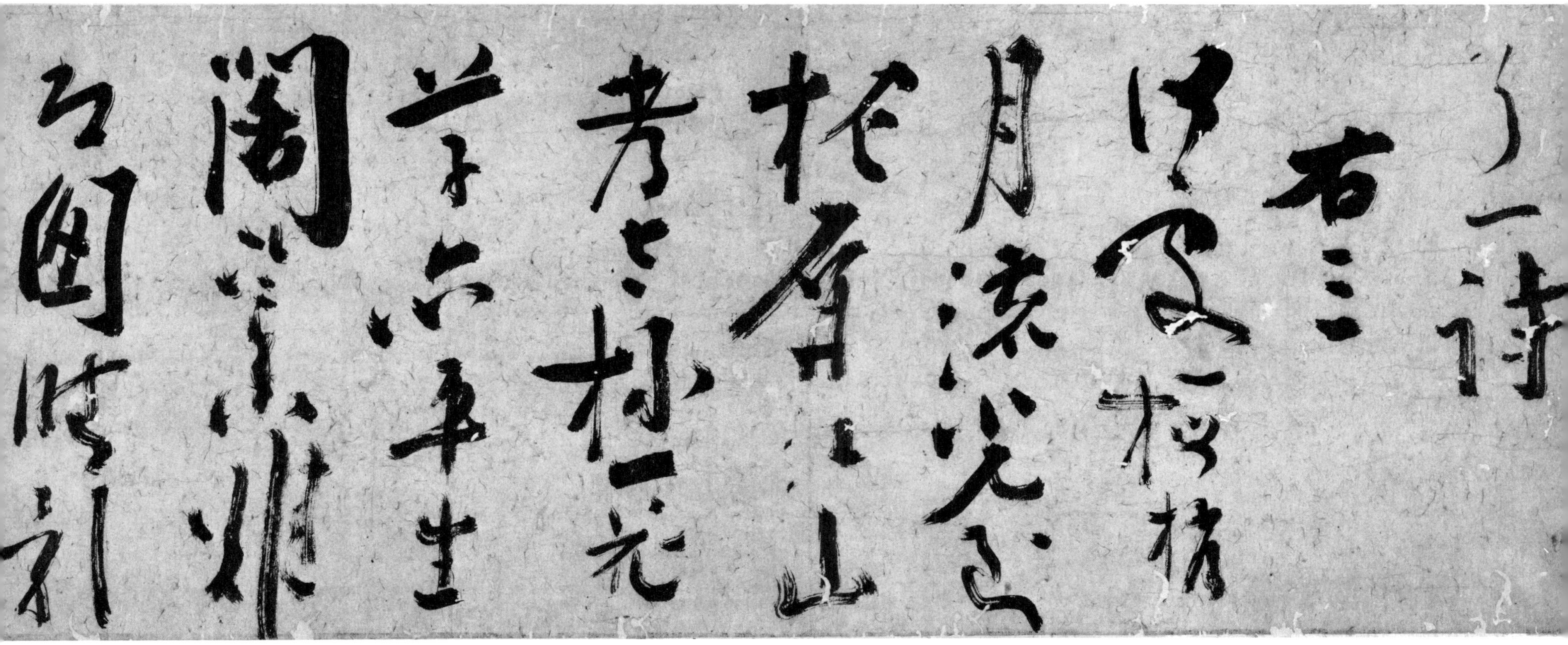

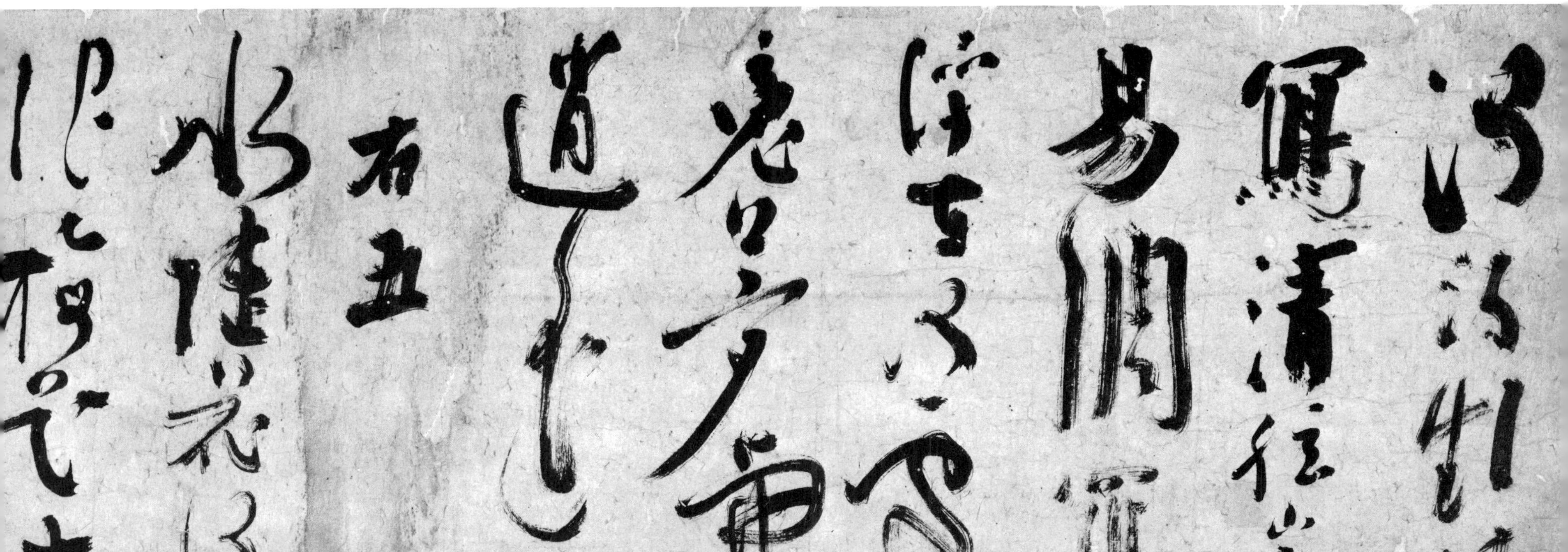

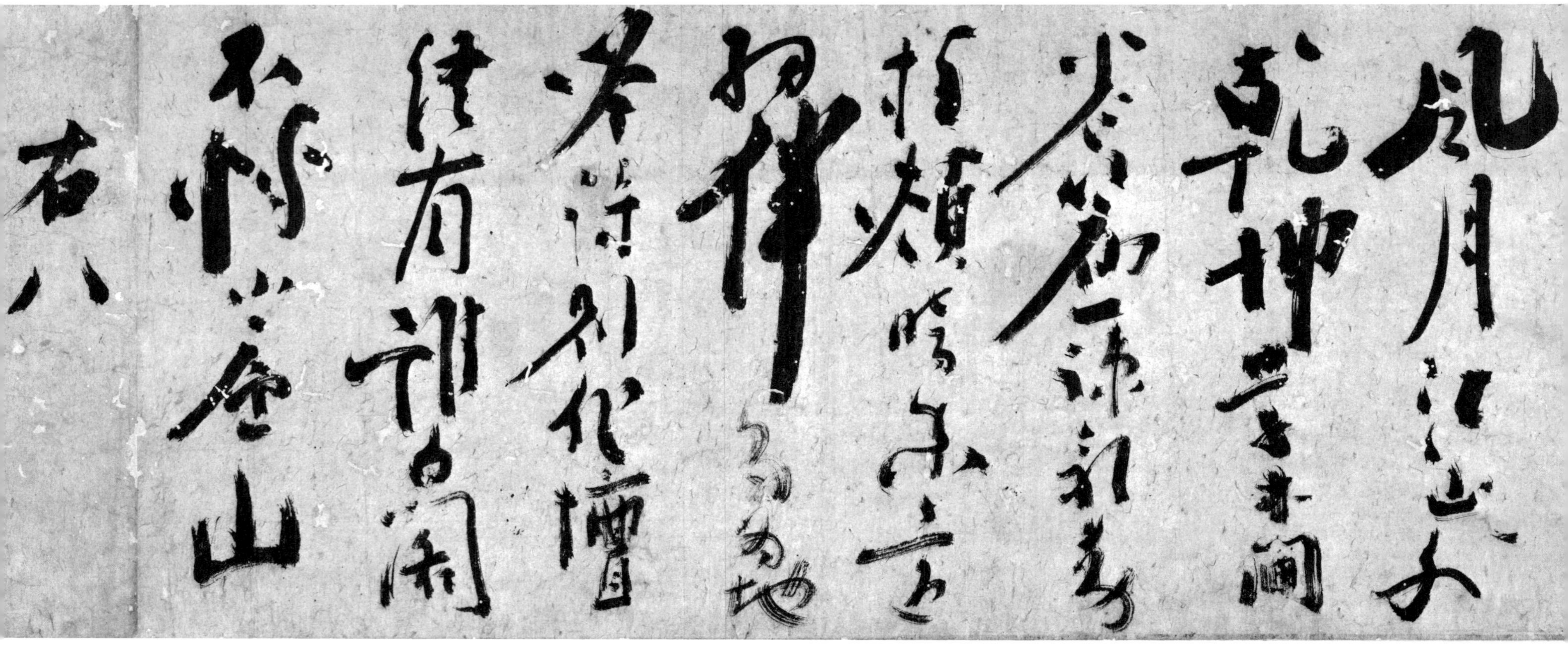

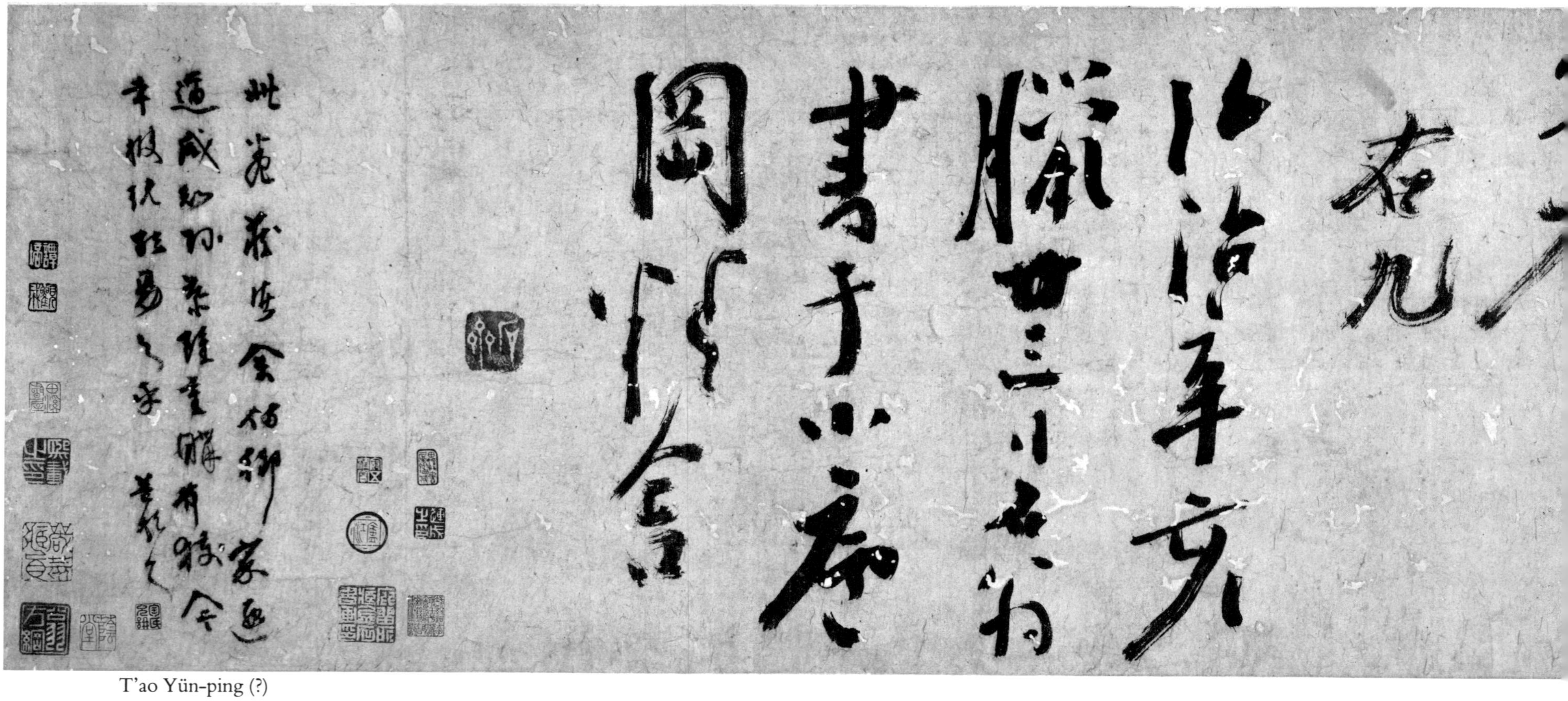

T'ao Yün-ping (?)

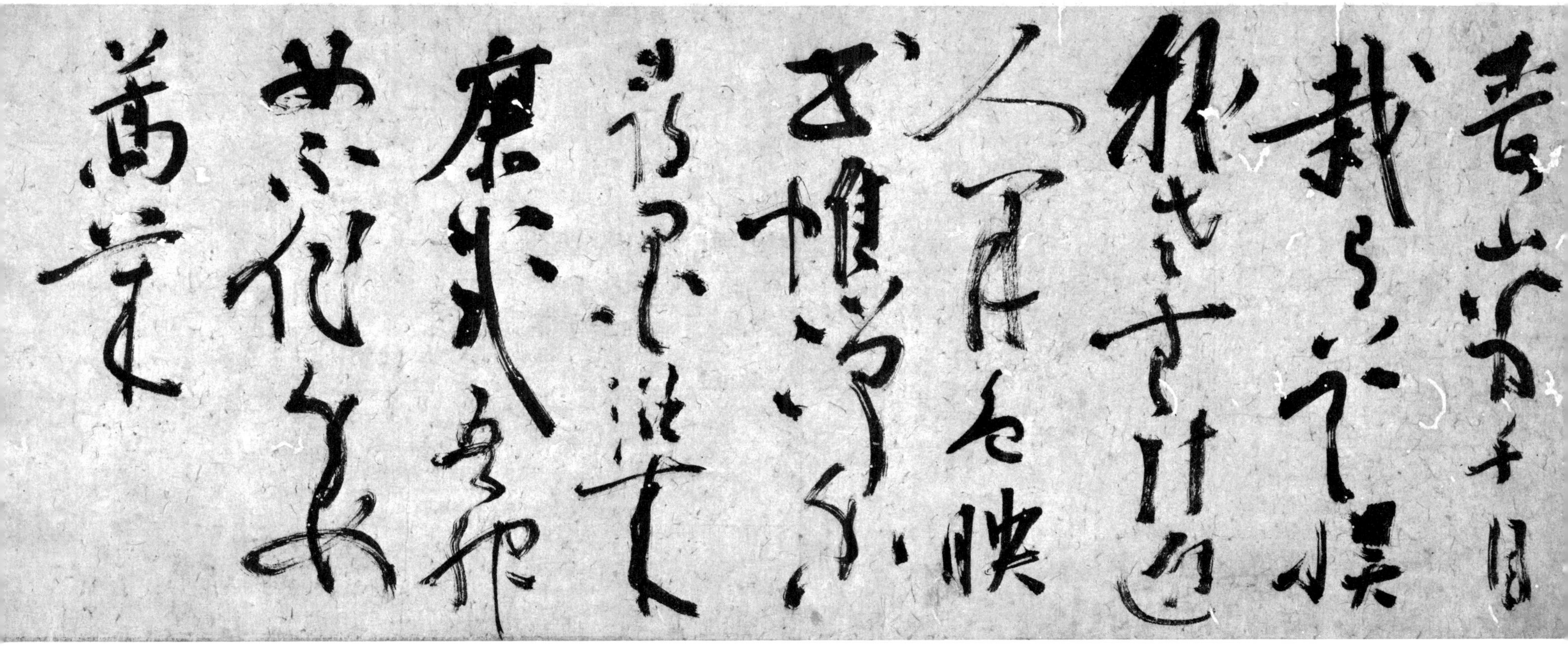

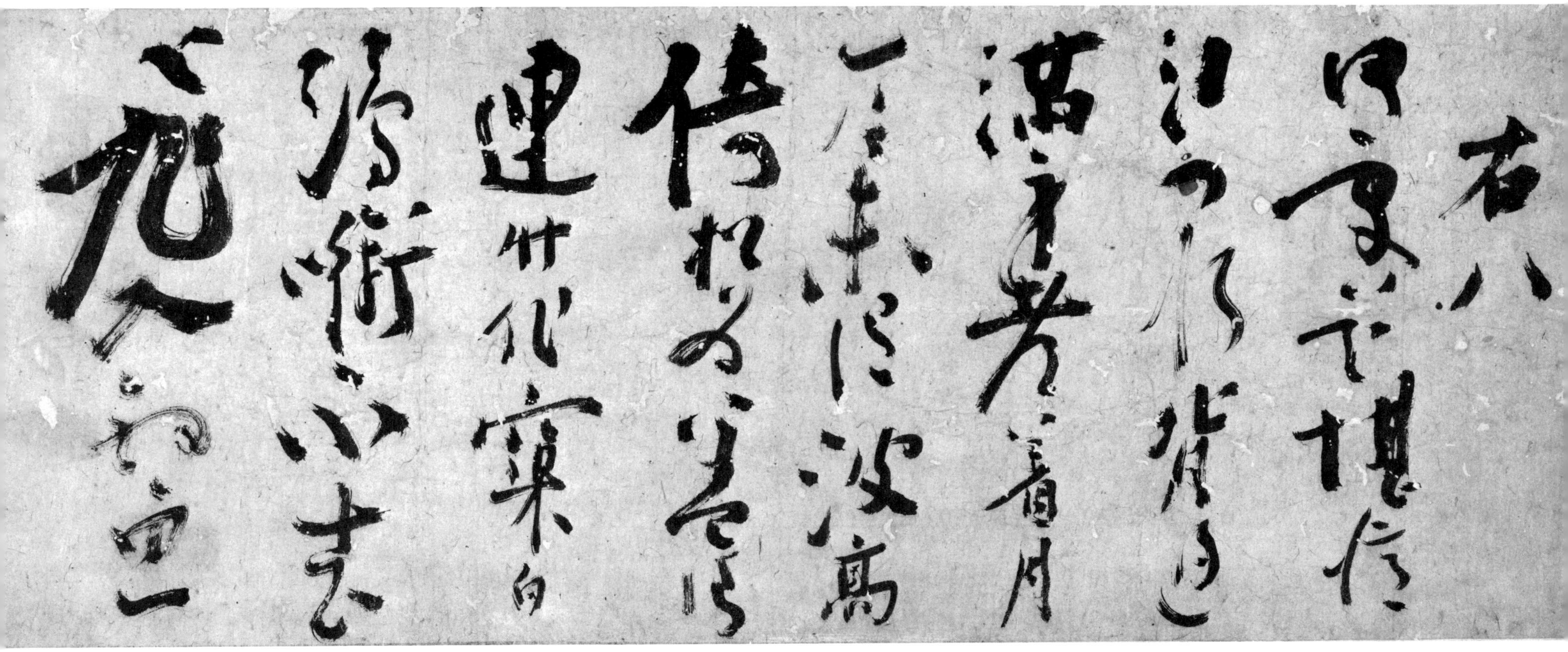

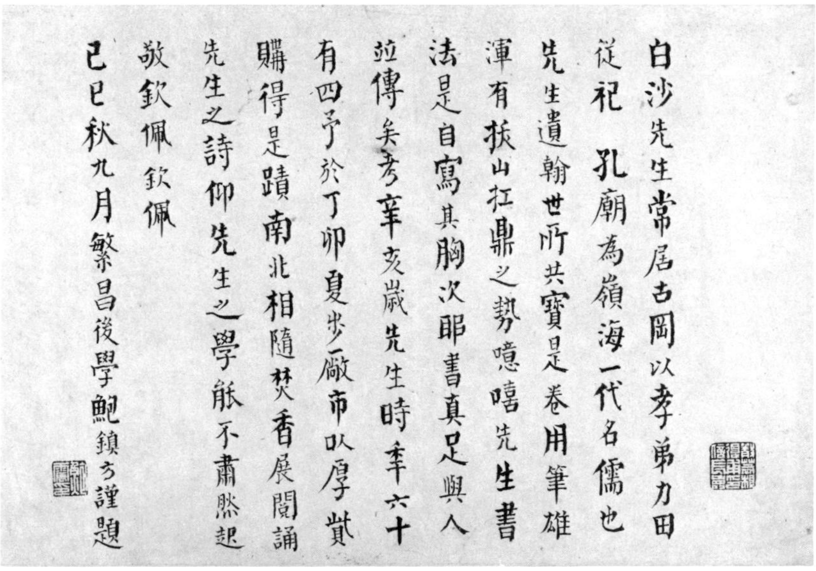


Pao Chen

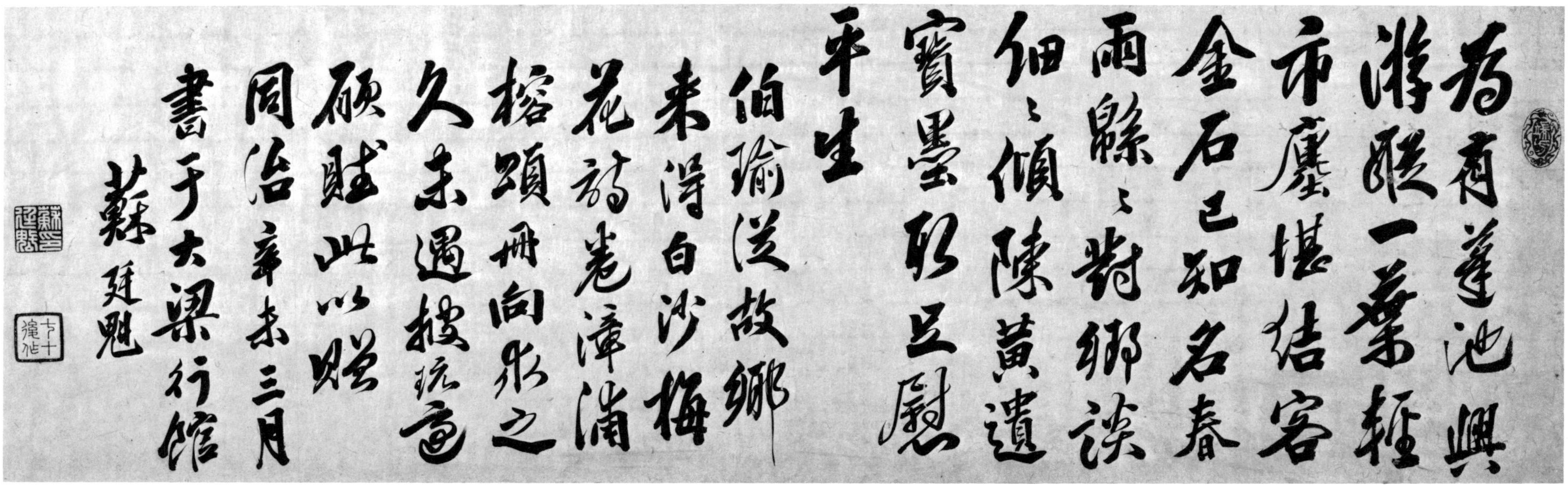

Su T'ing-k'uei

# 17 Shih Chung (Hsü Tuan-pen; fl. 1437–1520)

## *Bare Trees and Rocks (K'u-mu shih t'u)*

Dated 1506
Hanging scroll, ink on paper
80.5 x 30.7 cm (31$^{3}/_{4}$ x 12$^{1}/_{8}$ in.)

ARTIST'S INSCRIPTION: 7 character quatrain in 3 columns of running script (for a translation of the artist's inscription, see page 159).

ARTIST'S SIGNATURE: In the late winter of the *ping-yin* year [1506], Ch'ih-weng painted this.

INSCRIPTION by Fan Tseng-hsiang (1845–1931) (7 character regulated verse in 8 lines, followed by a 12 character note, in 7 columns of free-form regular script):

> His calligraphy is like his painting; his painting is like his calligraphy.
> His calligraphy, painting, and poem—all are expressive.
> He only began to speak when he was seventeen; how unusual that he had remained silent for sixteen years!
> When he reached seventy, his brushwork became mature, almost hoary.
> People said he was an old fool, but he laughed so hard that he fell over.
> When he painted trees and rocks in his old age they were strange and marvelous; his calligraphic brushstrokes looked like small entwined dragons.
> Remove their skin and hair [superficial aspects] and the bone and muscle [inner essence] will show through.
> This reflects the poems of the Ch'an monks, Han-shan and Shih-teh.
>
> Signature: On the ninth day of the *chia-yin* year [1914] my old friend Tung-hsüan asked me to inscribe this, Tseng-hsiang.

COLLECTORS' SEALS:

1. Ho Yüan-yü (early 19th century Cantonese collector): T'ien-hsi shu-wu (square relief; lower right).
2. Chiang Ku-sun (1901–1973): Chiang Tzu-i (square intaglio; lower right); Ku-sun chien-ts'ang (square intaglio; lower right); Tung-hsüan chien-shang (square relief; lower right); Lai-ku-t'ang (square intaglio; lower right); T'ai-ch'ang i-su (square intaglio; lower left).
3. Unidentified owner: [ ]-mei (square intaglio; lower right).

Gift of John B. Elliott (82–98)

PUBLISHED: Suzuki Kei, comp., *Chūgoku kaiga sōgō zuroku: daiikkan, Amerika–Kanada hen* (Comprehensive illustrated catalogue of Chinese paintings: volume 1, American and Canadian collections) (Tokyo: University of Tokyo Press, 1982), p. 127, pl. A17–015.

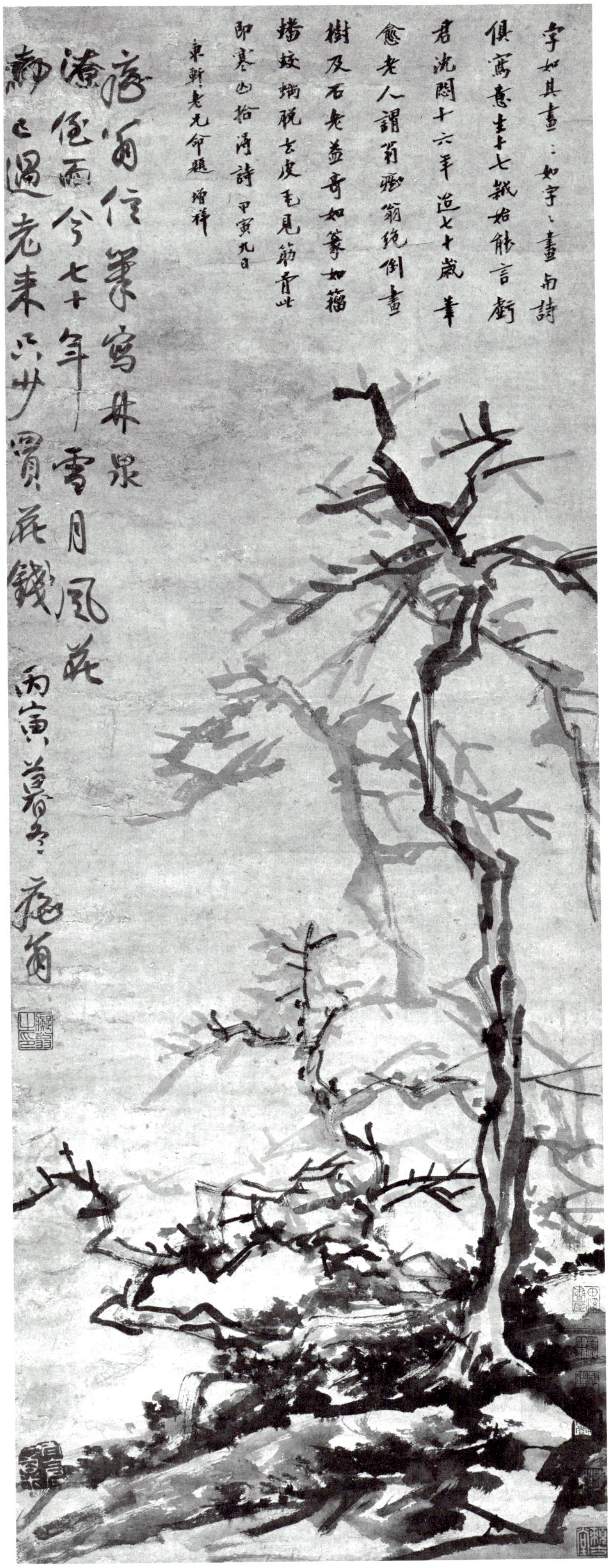

# 18 Lin Liang (fl. ca. 1450–1500)

## *Birds and Bamboo (Chu ch'in t'u)*

Ca. 1480
Hanging scroll, ink on silk
161.5 x 85.6 cm (5 ft. 3⁵/₈ in. x 33³/₄ in.)

ARTIST'S SIGNATURE: Lin Liang.

ARTIST'S SEAL: I-shan t'u-shu (square relief).

Edward L. Elliott Family Collection (L128.71)

PUBLISHED: Suzuki Kei, comp., *Chūgoku kaiga sōgō zuroku: daiikkan, Amerika–Kanada hen* (Comprehensive illustrated catalogue of Chinese paintings: volume 1, American and Canadian collections) (Tokyo: University of Tokyo Press, 1982), p. 161, pl. A17–114.

LIN LIANG (*tzu*, I-shan), a native of Nan-hai, Kuangtung province, was famous for his calligraphic bird and flower paintings. Lin began his painting career studying with artists whose identities remain unknown.[1] In 1455, working in Canton, he was discovered by Ch'en Chin, the administrative commissioner of Kuangtung. Probably through Ch'en's recommendation, Lin went to Peking as vice administrator of the Bureau of Construction in the Board of Works. Artistically talented and socially adept, Lin Liang was soon promoted to judge of the Embroidered-Uniform Guard in the Jen-chih Pavilion—then the highest rank for a court painter.[2] That Lin Liang had no rivals at court is confirmed by this poem by his contemporary Ch'iu Chün (1420–1495).

> In the front hall of the Jen-chih Pavilion is the painting academy.
> For painting a thousand bolts of silk come from the O [Goose] River
> [in Szechuan province] every year. . . .
> Painters compete with one another in ink and color paintings;
> Among them, who can surpass Lin I-shan from the Ram City [Canton]?[3]

Lin Liang became best known for his expressive birds, especially wild birds in their natural habitats. The energetic activity of birds and their vast and tranquil environment fascinated Lin, and he arranged the elements of his works to heighten that contrast. He usually used a diagonal composition, choosing his brushwork style, application of ink, and relative proportions according to this principle. *Birds and Bamboo* is a typical example of this style of painting; its diagonal composition suggests a sense of space and drama. Most of the birds fall in a zone stretching from the upper right to the lower left of the picture plane, which divides the composition into two triangles. The upper left triangle is densely filled with a cliff, abundant plants, two mynahs, and two condors. The lower right triangle is much sparser, containing only a heron, shrimp, and reeds to balance the composition. The plants and birds appear in the foreground, which links them intimately to the viewer.

Firm, vigorous brushstrokes and a variety of ink tones depict not only the shape and texture of the birds' feathers and their expressions, but also their quick movements. Lin's innovative brush techniques convey the spirit as well as the physical attributes of the birds. He created the landscape elements with bold, quick brushstrokes derived from ancient models. The wet triangular texture strokes used for the rocks are derived from works by Ma Yüan (fl. ca. 1190–1264) and Hsia Kuei (fl. 1st half 13th century); the two-dimensional silhouettes of the shadowy bamboo leaves recall the styles of Wang Fu (1362–1416; see no. 13) and Hsia Ch'ang (1388–1470); and the thickening-and-thinning brush technique seen in the resilient reeds is clearly derived from orchid paintings by Hsüeh-ch'uang (fl. 1st half 14th century; see no. 9) and Chao Meng-Fu (1254–1322).

The swift spontaneous brushwork that dominates the Edward L. Elliott Family Collection scroll is related to cursive script. The calligraphic quality of Lin's painting brought him recognition and praise from

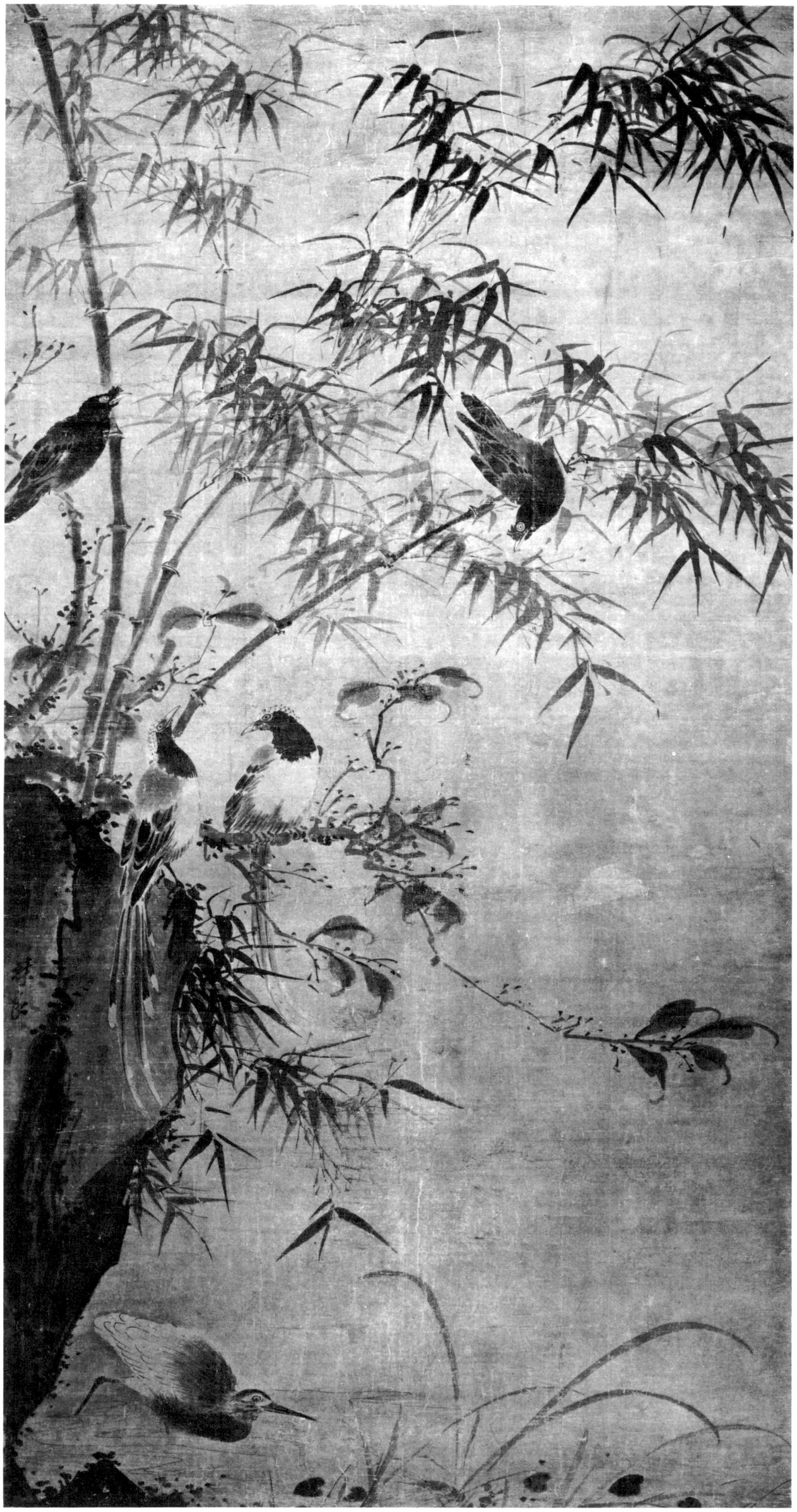

contemporary literati artists, including Ch'en Hsien-chang (1428–1500; see no. 16), Li Tung-yang (1447–1516), and Wu K'uan (1435–1504). Probably through Wu K'uan, who befriended Shen Chou (1427–1509) and Ch'en Yü (1440–1506; Ch'en Ch'un's grandfather), Lin became well-known in the Su-chou area. Chu Yün-ming (1461–1527), a noted Su-chou calligrapher, regarded Lin as the best artist in the genre of bird painting.[4] Lin Liang's calligraphic technique and his sensitivity in applying softly graded ink tones inspired the bird and flower genre of the Wu School painters, who worked in the Su-chou area from the sixteenth to the eighteenth century.

PAO-CHEN CH'EN

NOTES

1. For Lin Liang's biography, see Huang Tso, *Kuang-chou jen-wu chuan* (Biographies of men of Canton), Pai-pu ts'ung-shu chi-ch'en (1526; 1821–50; repr. ed., Taipei: I-wen yin-shu-kuan, n.d.), *chüan* 21, p. 5; Chü Ta-chün, *Kuang-tung hsin-yü* (A new account of tales of Kuangtung) (1700; repr. ed., Taipei: Hsüeh-sheng shu-chü, 1968), *chüan* 13, pp. 2–3; Li T'ien-ma, "Lin Liang nien-tai k'ao" (An investigation of Lin Liang's biography), in *I-lin ts'ung-lu*, vol. 3 (Hong Kong: Shang-wu yin-shu-kuan, 1962), pp. 35–38; Juan Yüan and Li Hung-pin, eds., *Kuang-tung t'ung-chih* (Gazetteer of Kuangtung province) (1864; repr. ed., Shanghai: Shang-wu yin-shu-kuan, 1934), *chüan* 326, p. 5545.
2. Suzuki Kei, "Min no gainsei ni tsuite" ( A study on the organization of the Ming Painting Academy) *Bijutsushi* 15, no. 4/60 (1966): 99; Huang Tso, *Kuang-chou jen-wu chuan*, p. 5.
3. Ch'iu Chün, *Ch'iung-t'ai hui-kao* (The collected writings of Ch'iung-t'ai), Ssu-k'u ch'üan-shu chen-pen ssu-chi, vol. 330 (1785; repr. ed., Taipei: Shang-wu yin-shu-kuan, 1973), *chüan* 6, p. 13b.
4. Chu Yün-ming, *Chu shih shih-wen chi* (The collected poetry and essays of Chu Yün-ming) (Taipei: Kuo-li chung-yang t'u-shu-kuan, 1971), *chüan* 1, pp. 33–34.

# 19 Anonymous

## *Searching for Demons on Mount Kuan-k'ou (Kuan-k'ou sou-shan t'u)*

Ca. 1500

Handscroll, ink on silk

Frontispiece: 47.9 x 117.0 cm ($18\frac{7}{8}$ in. x 3 ft. $10\frac{1}{8}$ in.); painting: 48.4 x 935.9 cm (19 in. x 30 ft. $8\frac{1}{2}$ in.); colophons: 48.7 x 98.3 cm ($19\frac{1}{8}$ in. x 3 ft. $2\frac{3}{4}$ in.)

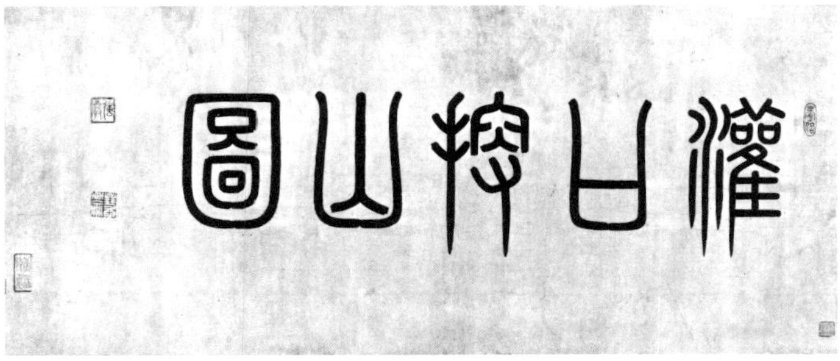

FRONTISPIECE: (anonymous 5 character title in seal script): "Searching for Demons on Mount Kuan-k'ou."

SIGNATURE (later interpolation): "Searching for Demons on Mount Kuan-k'ou." In the *ping-yin* year of the T'ai-ting era [1326] Ting Yeh-fu painted this.

LABEL by K'ang Yu-wei (1858–1927): prose, 23 characters in 1 column of running script (silk mounting before painting).

COLOPHONS:

1. Anonymous: prose, 33 characters in 1 column of free-form regular script (silk mounting after painting).
2. K'ang Yu-wei: prose, 129 characters in 6 columns of running script. Signature: On Buddha's birthday [the eighth day] of the fourth lunar month of the *wu-wu* year [1918], K'ang Yu-wei, Yu-wei fu, from Nan-hai [in Kuangtung province] inscribed this. Seal: K'ang Yu-wei yin (square intaglio); Wei-hsin pai-jih ch'u-shan shih-liu nien san chou ta-ti yu-pien ssu-chou ching san-shih-i kuo hsing liu-shih wan li (square relief).
3. Teng Erh-ya (1884–1954): prose, 369 characters in 21 columns of running script. Signature: Teng Erh-ya. Seals: Erh-ya (round relief); Erh-ya (square intaglio).

COLLECTORS' SEALS:

Southern Sung imperial seal, 1 seal (forgery).
Chia Ssu-tao (1213–1275), 2 seals (forgery).
Ming imperial seal, 2 seals (forgery).
Liang Ch'ing-piao (1620–1691), 9 seals (forgery).
K'ang Yu-wei, 3 seals.
Niu Yüan-lu (dates unknown), 1 seal.
Unidentified owner, 1 seal.
3 unidentified seals.

Gift of John B. Elliott (82–97)

PUBLISHED: Suzuki Kei, comp., *Chūgoku kaiga sōgō zuroku: daiikkan, Amerika–Kanada hen* (Comprehensive illustrated catalogue of Chinese paintings: volume 1, American and Canadian collections) (Tokyo: University of Tokyo Press, 1982), p. 148, pl. A17–091.

SEARCHING FOR DEMONS ON MOUNT KUAN-K'OU, a handscroll by an anonymous artist, illustrates the meritorious deeds of the god Erh-lang, the deified image of the ancient hero Li Ping. As the governor of Ch'eng-tu (in Szechuan province) during the third century B.C., Li Ping built the Tu-chiang dam and set up an irrigation system, thereby controlling the frequent floods that had plagued the region. Out of respect and gratitude the people idolized him as their tutelary deity. Gradually the image of Li Ping, who was revered for his mysterious power over water spirits, merged with that of the hunting deity Erh-lang, worshiped by the Chiang clan in west Szechuan for his control over mountain animals.[1] The Erh-lang cult became popular in Szechuan under the patronage of the Later Shu emperor, Meng Ch'ang (r. 934–65), and in 965, when the Sung dynasty conquered the kingdom, it adopted the cult, erecting temples for the god in K'ai-feng, the Northern Sung capital, and throughout China. Later, Erh-lang became identified with other figures, such as Kuan Hsing, the third son of Kuan Yü (d. A.D. 219), a general of the Shu-han state (A.D. 220–65) in Szechuan; Chao Yü, a virtuous governor of Chia-chou, Szechuan, of the Sui period (581–618); and Yang Chin, a eunuch at the Northern Sung court.[2] Whatever Erh-lang's mythological background, the deity was credited with having defeated a vicious flood-arousing dragon and other demonic creatures on Mount Kuan-k'ou, in Szechuan.

The story of Erh-lang's subduing a dragon and ridding Mount Kuan-k'ou of mountain demons was first illustrated by Kao I, who worked in K'ai-feng in the tenth century.[3] Although none of Kao I's original work still exists, a Southern Sung copy of his painting is now in the Steven Junkunc collection. The figure types in the Junkunc version served as models for those in a number of later copies, including a late Southern Sung copy in the Palace Museum, Peking,[4] and five Ming copies: one each in The Art Museum, Princeton University; the Lo Yüan-chüeh collection; the Freer Gallery of Art, Washington, D.C.;[5] and two in the Yünnan Provincial Museum.[6]

In both composition and iconography, the Princeton scroll is closest to the Junkunc version. The other versions differ from the Junkunc scroll either in composition or in iconography: for example, both the Peking and the Lo Yüan-chüeh compositions read from left to right; the Junkunc and Princeton versions read from right to left. The Peking and Freer versions lack the portrait of the deity. Finally most of the versions have incomplete narrative sequences and the order of elements in the sequences varies. The Princeton and Junkunc scrolls share the same pictorial episodes, with only slight variations in the sequence. The landscape elements are more elaborate in the Princeton version; the rocks and trees are tightly compressed into two parallel, horizontal registers. The zone between these acts as a kind of conduit, a "space channel" through which the activities of the figures flow. The Princeton version is more complete: it begins with a scene of Erh-lang's ghost soldiers taming snakes and a tiger; a similar but incomplete rendering of this episode appears in the middle of the Junkunc scroll. In the following scene in the Junkunc scroll, Erh-lang is dressed in chain-mail armor and a helmet in the manner of a T'ang *lokapāla* (a Buddhist guardian-king; fig. a); in the Princeton scroll he is represented as a Ming official, wearing a *pu-fu* (appliquéd robe) with a round collar, and a square design of a dragon embroidered on the front. The costume is borrowed from the conventions of the Ming period dramatization of Erh-lang's legend.[7] Erh-lang, seated in front of six attendants on a folding chair, leans to his right (the viewer's left) and casts his eyes toward the action in the rest of the scroll, as he listens to a soldier's report of victories over the demons of the sea and mountains.

The following scenes show various stages of the battle. Just to the left of Erh-lang two ghost soldiers rush to assist their comrades in an attempt to capture the ferocious dragon and writhing sea creatures. On the mountains and in the forest, ghost soldiers and wild animals engage in a desperate battle. Hordes of ghost soldiers, armed with swords and spears, try to kill or capture the horrified demonic animals, which include a squirrel, a monkey, and an antelope dressed as a human. Farther to the left, another group of

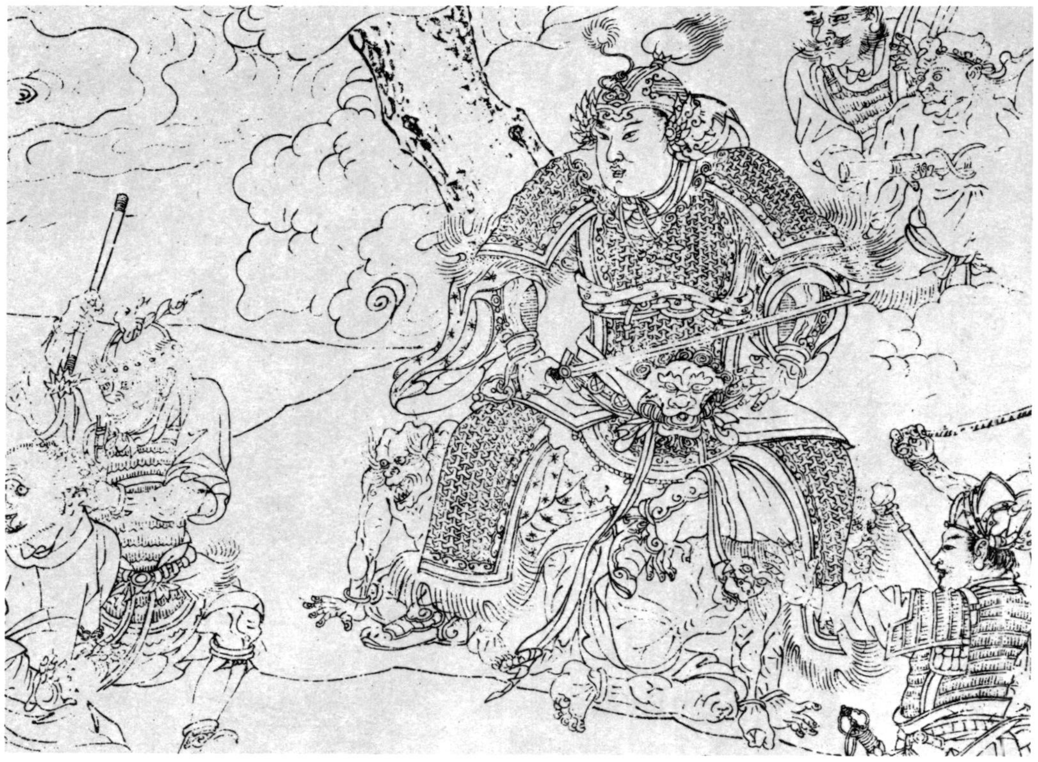

Fig. a. Attributed to Wu Tao-tzu, detail, *Searching for Demons on Mountains (Sou-shan t'u)*. Undated, ca. 13th century. Album leaf 41 of *The Ink Paintings by Wu Tao-tzu* (*Tao-tzu mo-pao*), ink on paper. Measurements unknown. Steven Junkunc collection

soldiers chases and shoots at two anthropomorphic female monkeys and a black rabbit, and in the next scene a muscular ghost soldier drags two other monkeys and their babies to the left. (This scene is omitted in the Junkunc version.) Next follows a heated life-and-death struggle in a forest; the demons are doomed to annihilation: poisonous snakes are stretched taut; an angry bull is pushed and pulled; a dog is thrown over the victor's shoulder; and a deer, a fox, and four frogs are snared and dragged away. In the next to last scene, three anthropomorphic female monkeys are pushed to the right by two soldiers, one of whom emits a flame that scorches a bat hovering in the air. The painting concludes with two soldiers who carry a defeated leopard hanging from a tree trunk supported on their shoulders.

In style the Princeton painting is a Ming adaptation of the Southern Sung court tradition, which uses ax-cut (*fu-p'i*) texture strokes and harsh angular outlines. These features are completely absent in works, such as the Junkunc scroll, that follow the Wu Tao-tzu (fl. ca. 710–60) tradition, which is characterized by fluid plain-line (*pai-miao*) drawing.

An inscription at the end of the scroll gives the date of the painting as 1327, which would place the painting in the Yüan dynasty, but the inscription is spurious. The apparel of the main figure and the painting style clearly date the painting to the Ming dynasty, and the imperial seal "Kuang-yün chih pao," used by the emperor Ming Hsüan-tsung (r. 1425–34), which appears on the top of the last section of the handscroll, is a forgery. The Princeton scroll must have been painted after the first half of the fifteenth century.

PAO-CHEN CH'EN

NOTES

1. Sang Hsiu-yün, "Li Ping yü Erh-lang-shen" (Li Ping and the deity Erh-lang), in *Chung-yang yen-chiu-yüan ch'eng-li wu-shih chou-nien chi-nien lun-wen chi* (Collected essays in celebration of the fiftieth anniversary of the Academia Sinica) (Taipei: Chung-yang yen-chiu-yüan, 1978), vol. 2, pp. 659–78.
2. Ibid.; Jung Chao-tsu, "Erh-lang-shen k'ao" (An examination of the deity Erh-lang), in Lou Tsu-k'uang et al., eds., *Chung-shan ta-hsüeh min-su ts'ung-shu* (Folklore series of Sun Yat-sen University), vol. 2 (1928; repr. ed., Taipei: Fu-lu t'u-shu kung-ssu, 1969), pp. 142–71; Huang Chih-kang, *Chung-kuo te shui-shen* (Chinese water gods and goddesses) (Hong Kong: Lung-men shu-tien, 1968), pp. 28–43.
3. Kuo Jo-hsü, *T'u-hua chien-wen chih* (Experiences in painting), in *Hua-shih ts'ung-shu* (Compendium of painting histories) (Taipei: Wen-shih-che ch'u-pan-she, 1974), vol. 3, p. 39.
4. Huang Miao-tzu, "*Sou-shan t'u*" (*Searching for Demons on Mountains*), *Ku-kung po-wu-yüan yüan-k'an* 3 (1980): 17–18; Chin Wei-no, "*Sou-shan t'u* te nei-jung yü i-shu piao-hsien" (The content and artistic representation of *Searching for Demons on Mountains*), *Ku-kung po-wu-yüan yüan-k'an 3* (1980): 19–22.
5. See Li Lin-ts'an, "*Sou-shan t'u* chüan te t'an-t'ao" (A study of *Searching for Demons on Mountains*), in *Chung-kuo ming-hua yen-chiu* (Studies of Chinese painting) (Taipei: I-wen yin-shu-kuan, 1973), vol. 1, pp. 217–20.
6. See Yang Fu and Kuo Tsung-hsüan, "Ming mo-pen *Sou-shan t'u* chi" (A note on the Ming copies of *Searching for Demons on Mountains*), *Ku-kung po-wu-yüan yüan-k'an* 4 (1980): 66–68.
7. See Chao Yüan-tu, ed., *Yüan Ming ku-pen tsa-chü* (Rare plays of the Yüan and Ming periods) (1615; repr. ed., Peking: Chung-kuo hsi-chü ch'u-pan-she, 1957), *chüan* 29, pt. 4, p. 9a.

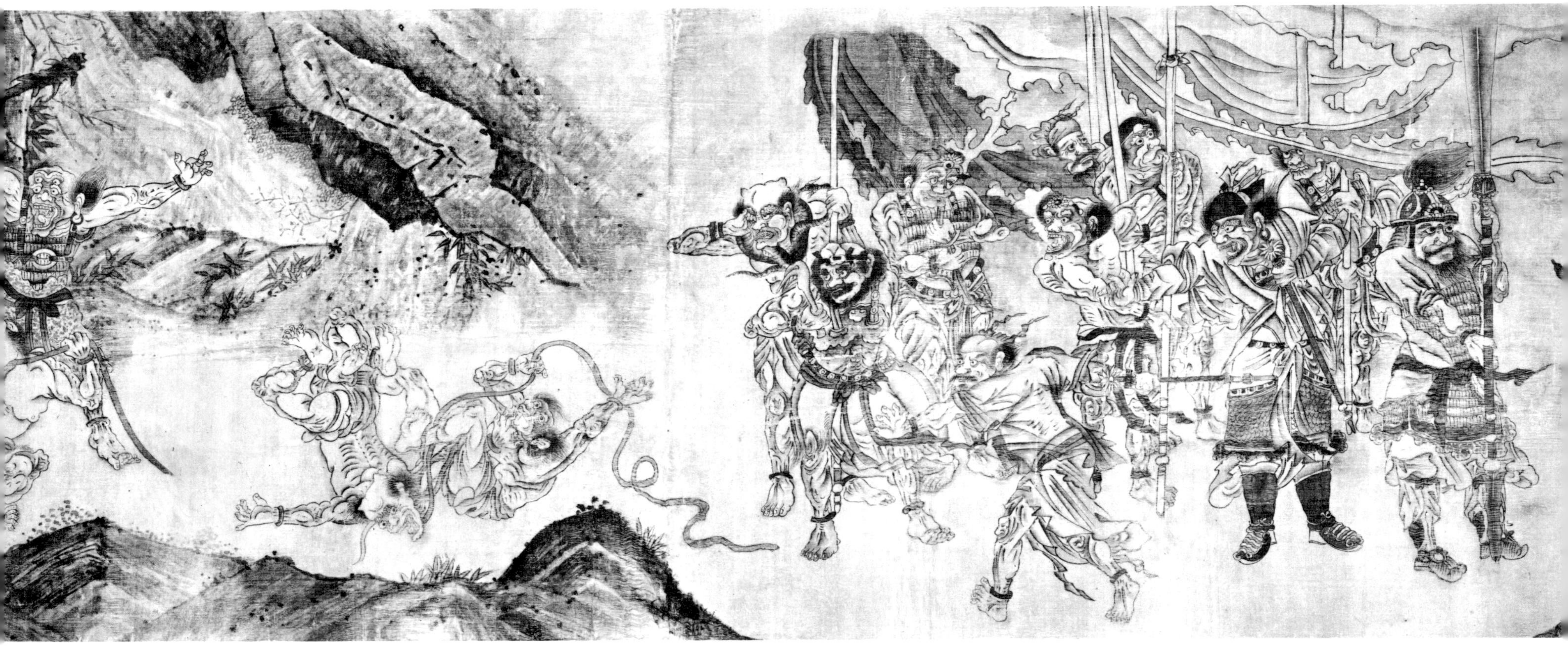

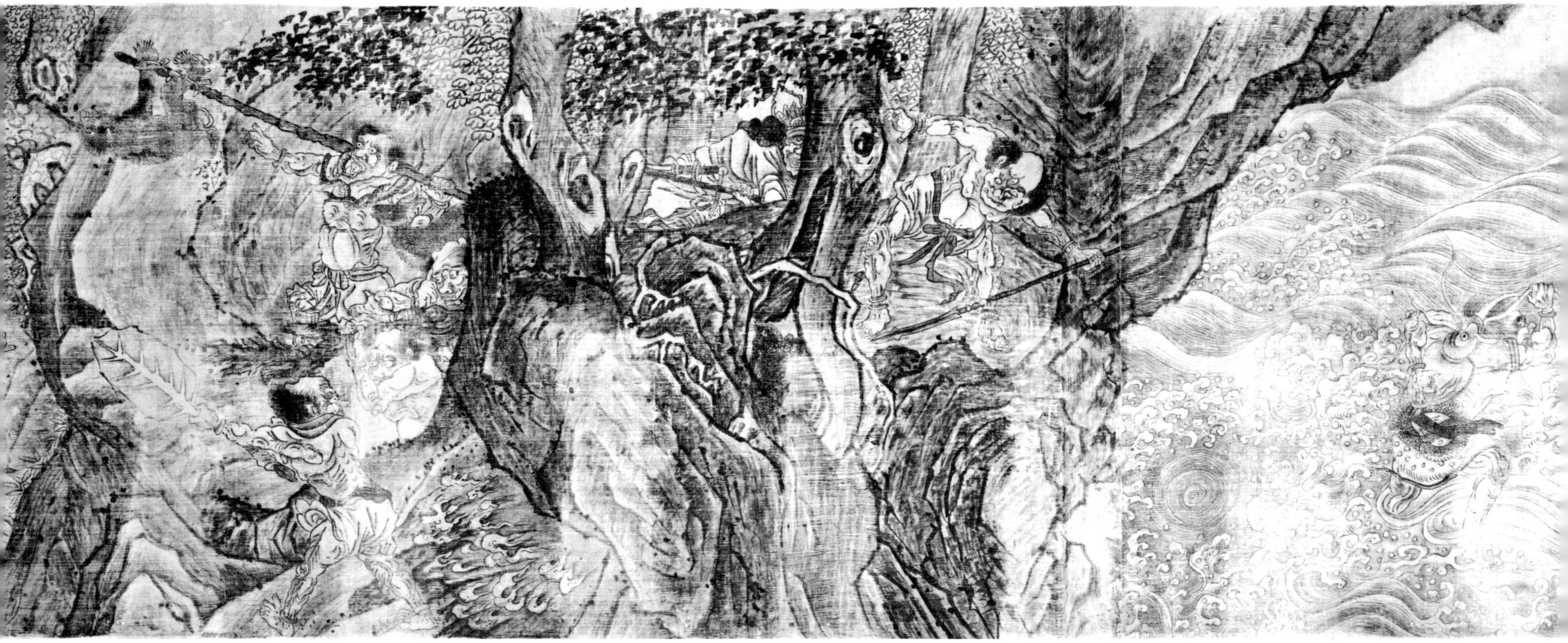

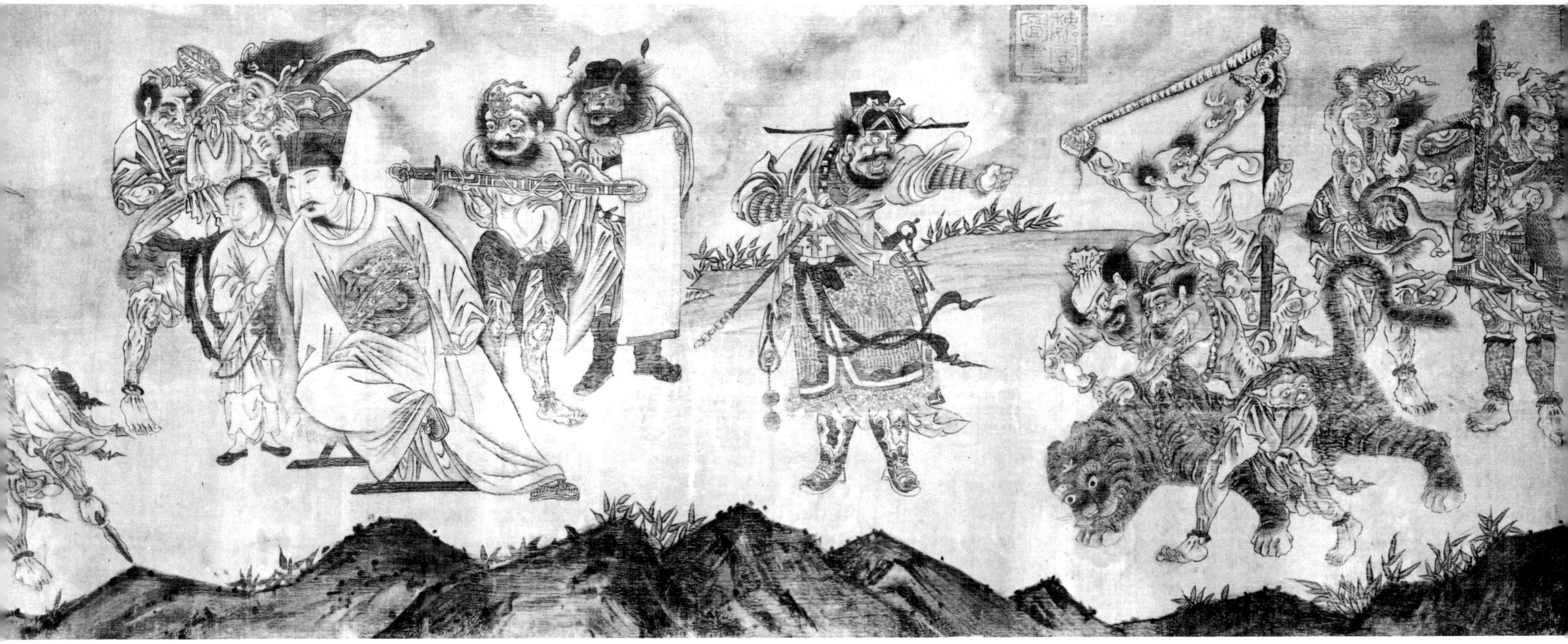

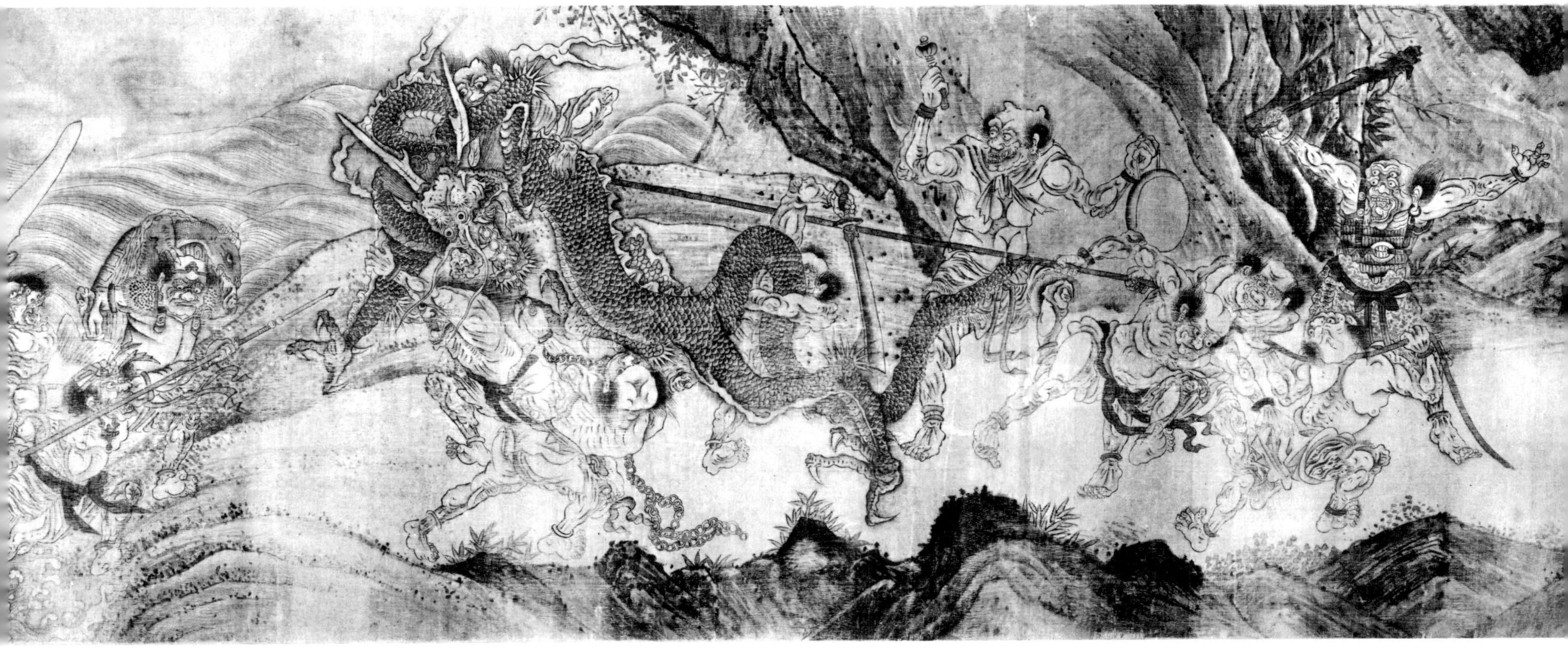

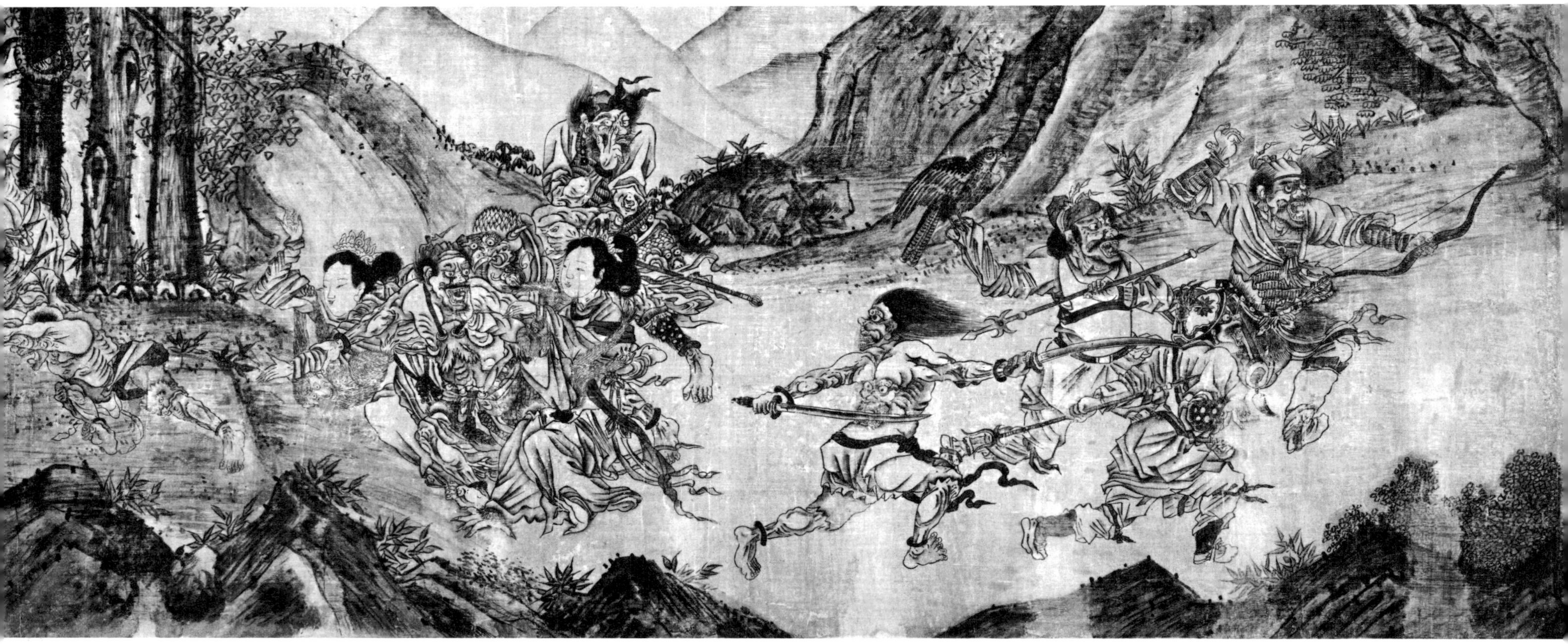

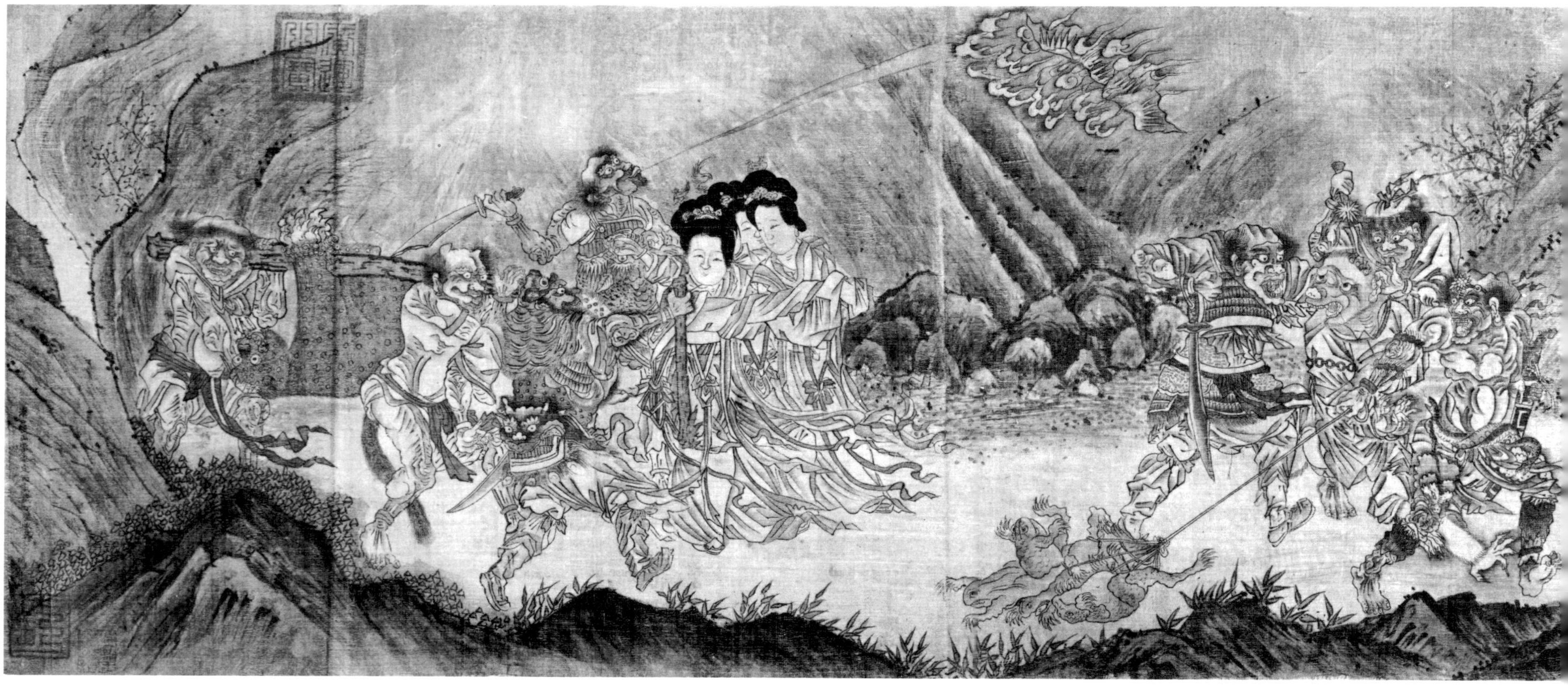

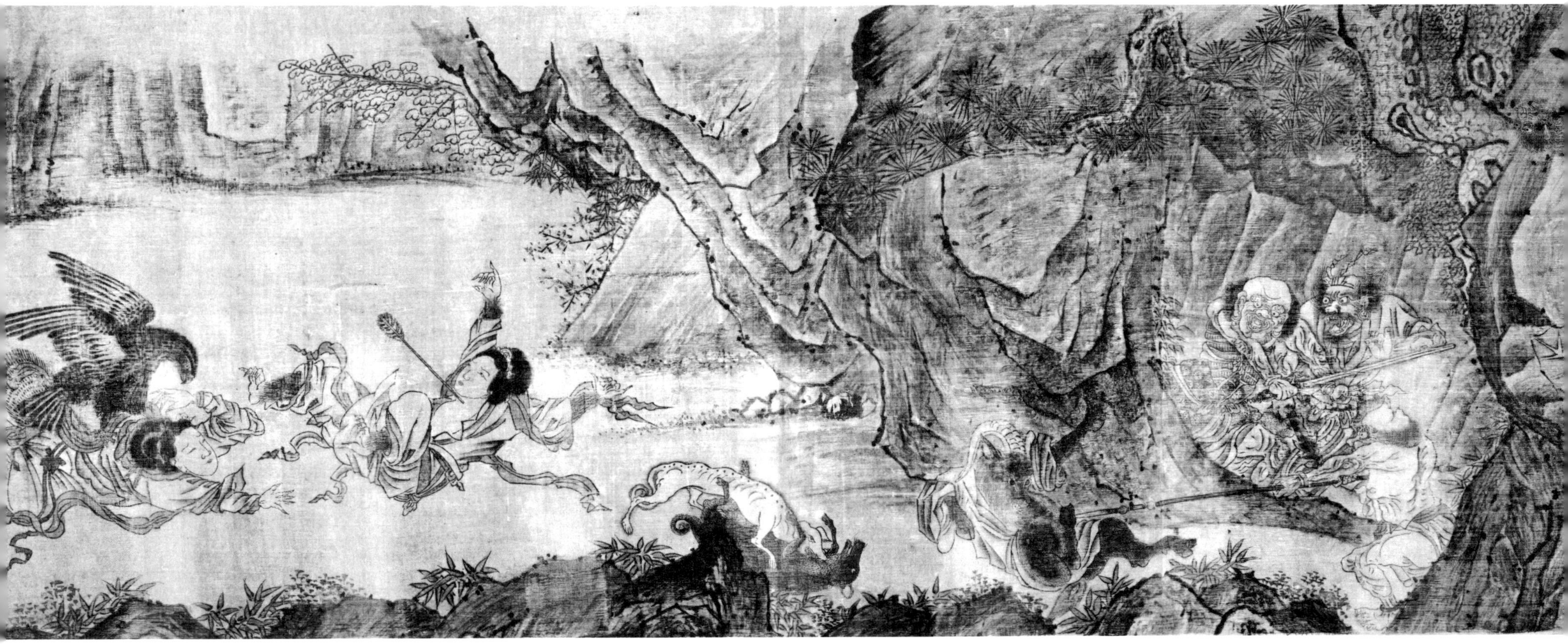

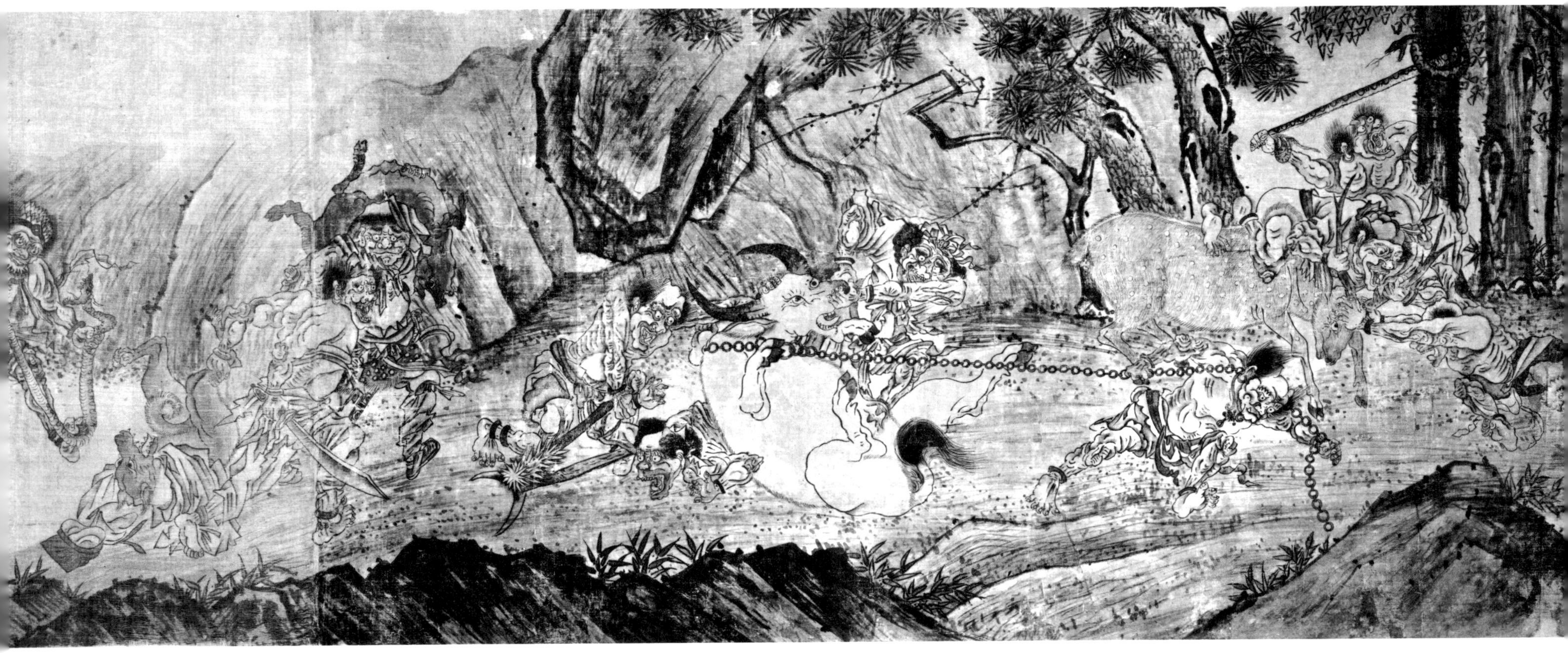

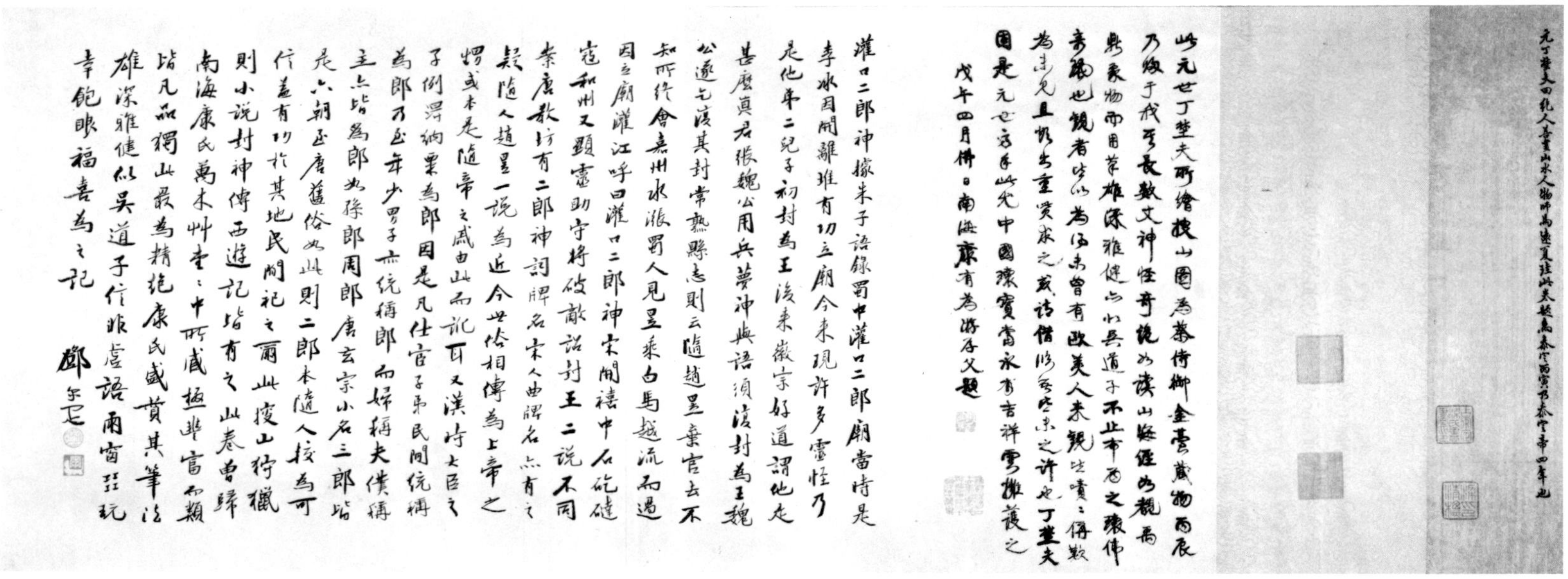

Teng Erh-ya K'ang Yu-wei Anonymous colophon

# 20 T'ang Yin (1470–1524)

## *Odes to Fallen Flowers* (*Lo-hua shih*)

Ca. 1505
Album leaves mounted as a handscroll, ink on paper
25.1 x 649.2 cm (9 7/8 in. x 21 ft. 11 1/2 in.)

CALLIGRAPHY: twenty-one 7 character regulated verses, each in 8 lines, in 147 columns of free-form regular script.

ARTIST'S SIGNATURE: T'ang Yin of Chin-ch'ang [Su-chou] drafted this.

COLOPHON by Ma Yüeh-kuan (1688–1755): 48 character note in 3 columns of free-form regular script. Signature: Ma Yüeh-kuan of Ch'i-shan [in Anhui province] inscribed this.

COLLECTORS' SEALS: Unidentified owners: Te-ta shen ting (square relief; lower right, calligraphy); Sung-chiang Li shih Chung-[ ] chen-ts'ang yin (square relief: lower left, calligraphy).

John B. Elliott Collection (L132.71)

PUBLISHED: Chiang Chao-shen, *Kuan-yü T'ang Yin te yen-chiu* (A study of T'ang Yin) (Taipei: National Palace Museum, 1976), pp. 98–99, pl. 33b; Nakata Yūjirō and Fu Shen, eds., *Obei shūzō Chūgoku hōsho meisekishū* (Masterpieces of Chinese calligraphy in American and European collections), vol. 5 (Tokyo: Chūōkōron-sha, forthcoming).

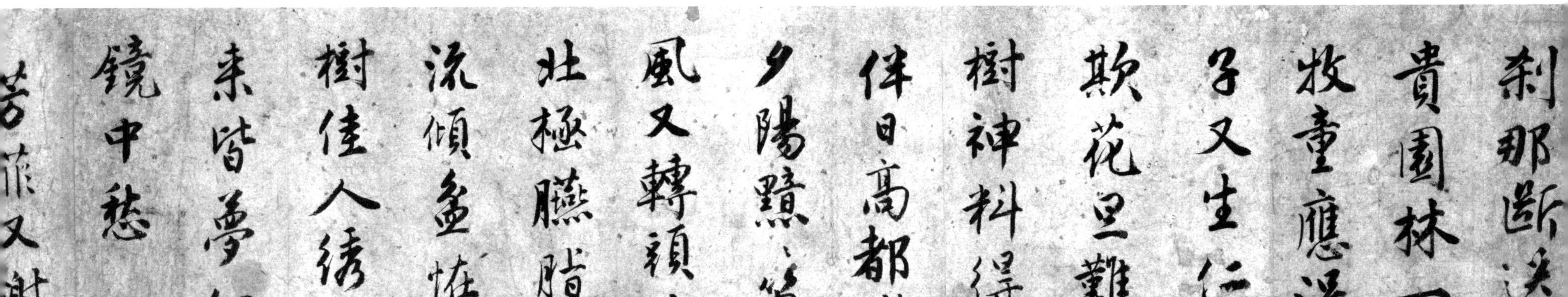

收難傳賒熏神國色
自來多命薄桃紅又
見一年春已無錦帳圍
金谷澤托青鞋緇麴
塵繞樹百田心語口明
年句曾是何人
天涯淹遠碧雲橫社
日園林紫燕輕飛葉
參差誰問渡杏花零
落憶題名月明犬吠村
中夜雨過鶯啼葉滿
城人不歸來春又去與
誰連臂唱盈盈
白華垂柳弄新晴紫
背浮萍田點生三月尋

帳多風燒燈坐盡千
金夜對酒空思一點
紅偏是東君向魚雁
心情說在雨聲中
蕉酒新啼滿袖痕憐
香惜玉此心存可憐
窓外風鳴樹孤負尊
前月滿軒葬井似嘶
亡國恨墜樓如報主
入恩長洲日暮生芳草
銷盡江淹黯黯魂
滿堂離笑强追陪別有
愁膓日九迴時節又驚
梁燕亂鉛華無素際
東淮香消衣常傷腰

芳菲又謝一年新
肱今無八斗陳命薄
錯拋傾國色緣輕不
遇買金人杜鵑啼血山
中夜蝴蝶遊魂葉底
春色即是空空是色
欲從調御懺貪嗔
坐看芳菲了悶中曲
教遮護層層風衛蜂
蜜熟香粘白梁燕巢
成濕補紅國色可憐
難再得酒杯何故不
教空悪觀馬足車輪
下丁庁西飛丁庁東

芳騎鳳侶一時齋唱
芳行收燈院落傷栖
燕細雨樓臺濕囀鶯莫
問東君訴恩慈自來
春夢不分明
催耕聲裏蜂柴門蝶
蒲香中蘿草園西子
歸湖餘有井照君出
塞尚留村春風院院深
籠鎖細雨絲絲歎斷魂
拾得球紅悪拋去也教
粘向阿威牆
春來嚇去匆匆刺眼
繁華轉眼空杏子單

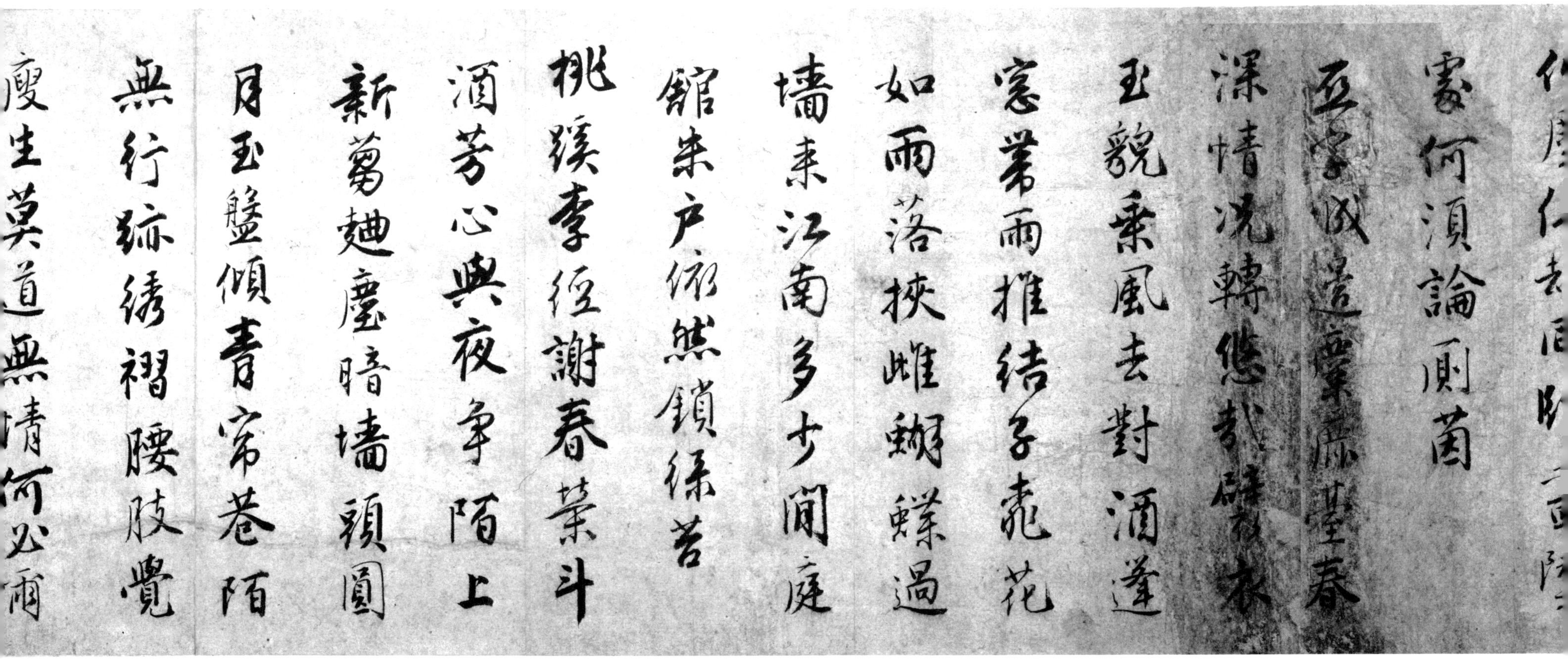
處何須論廁菌
深情況轉悠哉碎衣
玉貌乘風去對酒逢
窓帶雨推結子花
如雨落挾雌雄蝶過
墻來江南多少閒庭
館朱戶鄉然鎖綠苔
桃蹊李徑謝春葉斗
酒芳心與夜爭陌上
新蔦麴塵暗墻頭圓
月玉盤傾青帘巷陌
無行跡綉褶腰肢覺
瘦生莫道無情何必雨

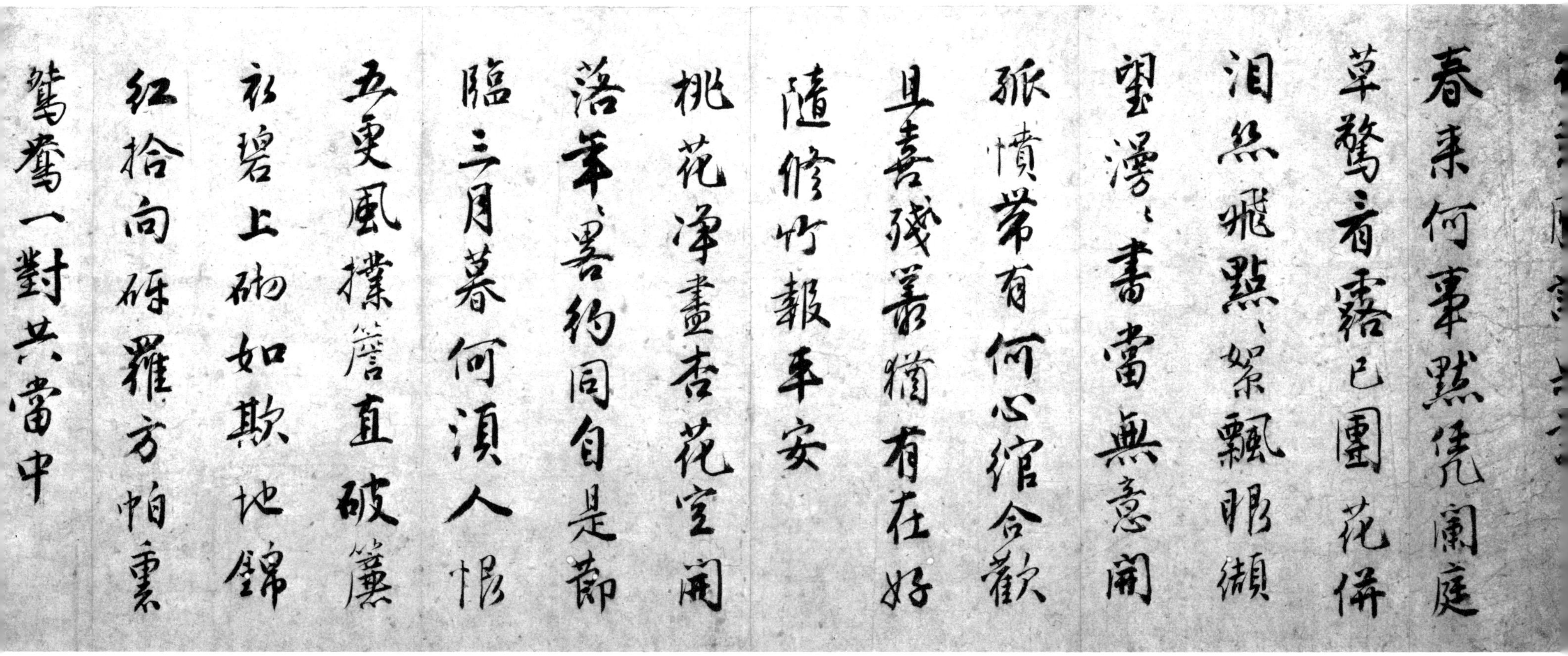
春來何事點凭闌庭
草鶯有露已團花併
泪絲飛點絮飄眼懶
望灣書當無意閑
孤憤常有何心綰合歡
且喜殘叢猶有在好
隨修竹報平安
桃花淨盡杏花空闌
落年年約同自是節
臨三月暮何須人悵
五更風撲簷直破簾
衫碧上砌如欺地錦
紅拾向砾羅方帕熏
鴛鴦一對共當中

瘦夢斷遼陽沒信來
門掩黃昏花落盡半
酥且薦掌中杯
貌嬌命薄兩難全鶯
老花毬謝些緣年長
盧姬悲晚嫁日高黃
鳥喚春眠人生自古稀
七十斗酒何論價十千
痛惜穠纖又逢暮好燒
銀燭覆觥船
花落花開總屬春開
時休羨落休嗔好知
青草枯髏塚就是紅
樓掩面人山後已教休
之藏宋陳迹此八頁中

瘦生莫道無情何必雨
自緣我輩正鍾情
惻惻悽悽憂自悞花枝
零落鬢絲添週遮燕
語春三月蕩漾波紋
日半簾病酒不堪朝
轉劃聽風且喜晚來
恬綠楊影裏蒼苔上
為惜殘紅手自拈
楊柳樓頭月半規笙
歌院裏夜深時花枝
灼灼難長好漏水丁丁不
肯遲金釧袖籠新藕
滑翠眉奩映小雛垂
亂青多少愁多少百

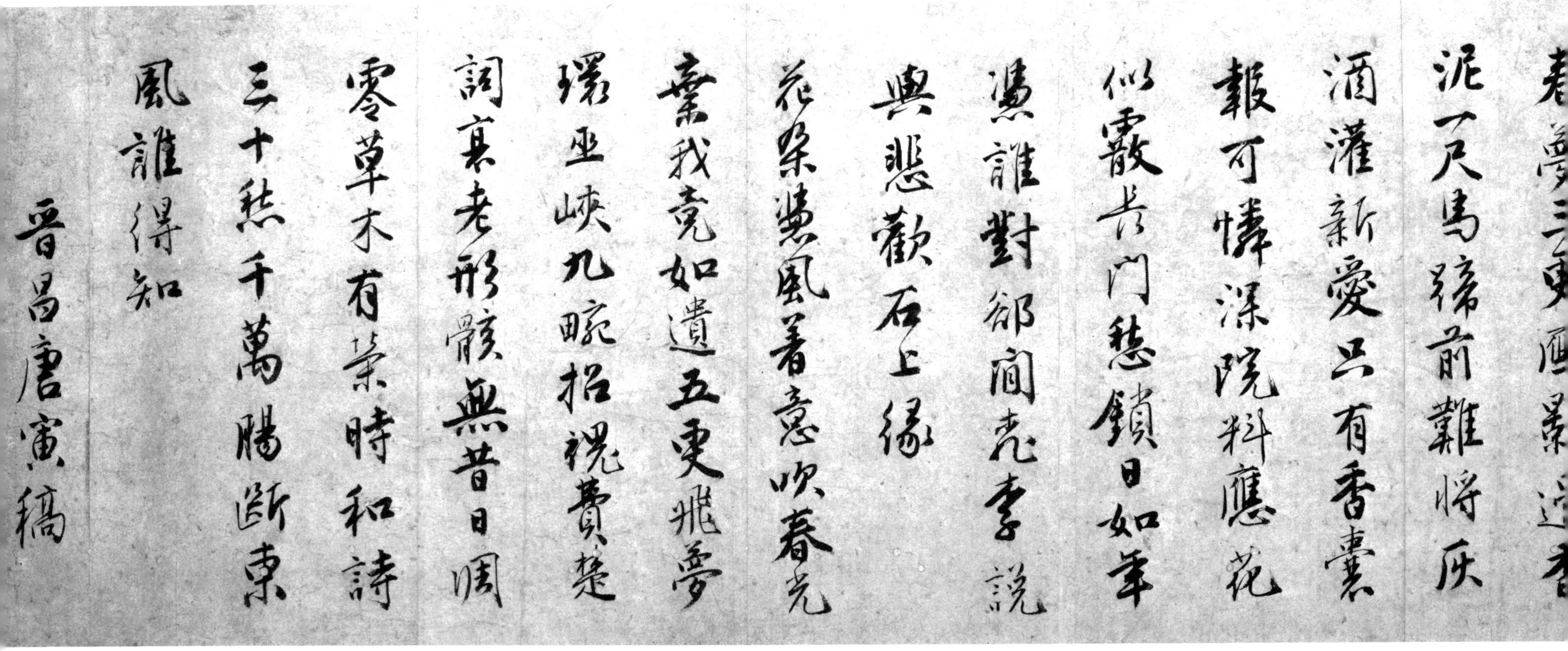


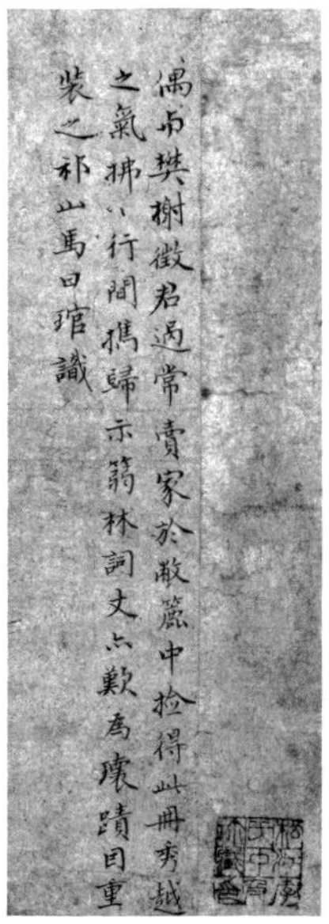
Ma Yüeh-kuan

# 21 Wen Cheng-ming (1470–1559)

## *Flowers, Landscapes, and Poems (Shih hua ts'e)*

Dated 1558
Eleven album leaves mounted as a handscroll: five leaves of painting (A–E) alternating with five leaves of calligraphy (AA–EE), followed by one leaf of colophons (F)
Painting, ink on paper; calligraphy, ink on gold-flecked paper
Painting, average measurements, each leaf: 30.9 x 52.8 cm (12 1/8 x 20 3/4 in.); calligraphy, average measurements, each leaf: 30.4 x 52.7 cm (12 x 20 3/4 in.)

PAINTING: Leaf A, "Narcissus"; Leaf B, "Wild Geese and Rushes"; Leaf C, "Plum Blossoms"; Leaf D, "Birds Perching on a Wintry Tree"; Leaf E, "Magnolia."

CALLIGRAPHY:
Leaf AA (7 character regulated verse in 8 lines in 8 columns of running script):

She stands in a gown with green collar and white sleeves, ever so graceful;
My eyes brightened when I saw her smiling face.
Fragrance empties out of jade petal cups made heavy by the morning dew.
Elegantly in the dawn's mist, she is reminiscent of the Nymph of the Lo River, with her gauze slippers stirring the dust.
On the riverbank by the old Han capital, Prince Ts'ao Chih took off his jade pendant and gave it to her.
In return the nymph, on a sandbar, shyly signaled her budding affection.
How regrettable that Prince Ch'en-ssu's [Ts'ao Chih's] talent to describe the nymph's charm ran dry;
And that I, who want to compose a poetic tribute to the narcissus blowing in the breeze, am incapable.

Leaf BB (7 character regulated verse in 8 lines in 8 columns of running script):

The sandy bank at the foot of the deserted slope is tinged yellow in the sunset.
For ten miles around, the water reeds are whitened by the new frost.
At sunset, over flat sandbars hang wisps of clouds.
Wild geese quietly fly over the endless river.
The water is cold and the heavens so distant; the west wind rushes by.
Footprints of the geese remain wet on the sand after the frost.
In the bright moonlight it is not surprising to see the geese alarmed and flustered,
Because along the lakes and rivers there is no safety from the hidden arrows of hunters.

Leaf CC (7 character regulated verse in 8 lines, including a crossed-out character, in 9 columns of running script):

In pure white her fairylike figure stands lightly under the trees.
By the water her unworldly elegance compares with a clear piece of jade.
Her gentle fragrance hangs in the wind and casually rustles the hair on my temples.
Slender shadows spread on the window screens in romantic moonlight.
Like signs of spring at Mount Lo-fu [metaphor for plum blossoms], she seems so far even dreams cannot reach her.
She is as pure as the chilly morning air at Mount Ku-yeh, where the snow melts.
Favoring solitude, she selects for herself a blossoming season different from that for all other flowers.
Never would she be attracted by the melody of a flute wafting from high up in a pavilion.

Leaf DD (7 character regulated verse in 8 lines, including a crossed-out character, in 8 columns of running script):

On a chilly plain in the clear autumnal sky the sun begins to sink,
Quietly the ravens go to roost.
Falling leaves from almost bare mulberry trees rustle in the misty sky.
The moon rises behind a mountain city covered with light frost.
The frost is pristine, the moonlight cold, and the trees abundant.
This is just the moment when the frightened birds calm down.
There may be people observing the Chang-jen star;
Breeze, do not disturb the bare branches.

Leaf EE (5 character regulated verse in 8 lines, followed by a 30 character note, in 10 columns of free-form running script):

The green *wu-t'ung* tree is already bare,
Streams flow slowly through icy valleys.
Alone I ramble along through the grays and yellows of the season,
Where there are no barking dogs or human footprints.
The morning sun shines into the forest.
So the gray mist suddenly vanishes.
Sometimes I see the wind from towering cliffs blow snow off the pine trees.

In spring of the *wu-wu* year [1558], I unexpectedly found several sheets of old paper. So I wet my brush to amuse myself in ink play and transcribed these previously done poems to match these paintings.

ARTIST'S SIGNATURES: Cheng-ming (AA–DD); Cheng-ming, in his eighty-ninth year [*sui*] (EE).

ARTIST'S SEALS: Wen Cheng-ming yin (square intaglio; A, AA, BB, E, EE); Wen Chung-tzu (square intaglio; AA, CC, DD); T'ing-yün (round relief; AA, BB, CC, DD, EE); Heng-shan (square relief; BB, C, CC, DD, EE).

COLOPHONS:

1. Lo Chen-yü (1866–1940): prose, 52 characters in 2 columns of running script. Signature: Lo Chen-yü from Shang-yü [in Chekiang province] examined these paintings at Cloud Window in the Ch'en-han Pavilion, [his] temporary residence in Higashiyama [in Kyoto]. The fourth lunar month of the *chia-yin* year of the Hsüan-t'ung era [1914]. Seal: Lo Chen-yü yin (square intaglio).
2. Naitō Kō (Naitō Kōnan; 1866–1934): prose, 57 characters in 3 columns of running script (dated 1915). Signature: Naitō Kō. Seal: Shin Kō (square, half relief, half intaglio); Hō-sa-an-shu (square relief).
3. Nagao Kō (Nagao Uzan; 1864–1942): prose, 66 characters in 4 columns of running script (dated 1915). Signature: Nagao Kō viewed and inscribed this. Seal: Uzan (square intaglio).

COLLECTORS' SEALS:

1. Ts'ao Ch'ao-nan (dates unknown): Ts'ao shih Ch'ao-nan (square intaglio; all except EE); Ts'ao-nan chien-shang (square intaglio; EE); Ch'iao-kuo shih-wan (tall rectangle relief; EE); Tzu-sun pao chih (square relief; B, E); Shang-chien-chia (square intaglio; EE).
2. Wang Erh-ju (dates unknown): Wang shih Erh-ju chien-shang (square relief; AA–EE).
3. Wang Ch'ing-hsün (20th century): Shang-hai Wang Ch'ing-hsün chia ts'ang kuo (square relief; CC, EE).
4. Unidentified owners: Yen-chou t'ai-shou (square intaglio, CC); Shu-i kuo yen (square relief; DD).

Gift of David L. Elliott (75–33)

PUBLISHED: Richard Edwards et al., *The Art of Wen Cheng-ming (1470–1559)* (Ann Arbor: The University of Michigan, 1976), pp. 199–203; Suzuki Kei, comp., *Chūgoku kaiga sōgō zuroku: daiikkan, Amerika–Kanada hen* (Comprehensive illustrated catalogue of Chinese paintings: volume 1, American and Canadian collections) (Tokyo: University of Tokyo Press, 1982), p. 126, pl. A16–073.

THE MOST INFLUENTIAL ARTIST in the Ming period,[1] Wen Cheng-ming (personal name, Pi; *tzu*, Cheng-chung) was the leader of the Wu School painters, a group of scholar artists centered in Su-chou from the sixteenth to the early eighteenth century, including such men as Ch'en Ch'un and Chü Chieh (see nos. 23, 25). A cautious, diligent, and erudite man, Wen cultivated his talents in poetry, painting, and calligraphy. Although he originally hoped for a career in government service and took the qualifying examinations ten times, he never succeeded in passing. Eventually he received a post at court through the recommendation of certain influential friends. In 1523 Wen took on the post of attendant in the Han-lin Academy, but in 1527, insulted because he was treated more as a painter than as a scholar, he resigned and returned to Su-chou. He lived there as an artist for the rest of his life.[2]

*Flowers, Landscapes, and Poems* combines the arts of poetry, painting, and calligraphy. Done in 1558, a year before Wen's death, the scroll demonstrates his finesse at creative adaptation of other masters' styles. The subject matter of Leaf A, a narcissus and an eroded Lake T'ai rock, is indicative of the same Ming literati taste apparent in Chinese garden designs. Wen Cheng-ming's depiction of the narcissus in *pai-miao* (plain-line drawing) is a technique that originated with Li Kung-lin (ca. 1049–1106) and was later reinterpreted through the style of Chao Meng-chien (1199–1267). Using calligraphic abbreviations, Wen transformed Chao's descriptive style into an expressive manner.

The reeds in Leaf B, "Wild Geese and Rushes," recall the brush idiom of Wu Chen (1280–1354), but the short, harsh brushstrokes derive more from Wen's own calligraphy. His "Plum Blossoms" (Leaf C) are innovative because of the sparseness of the composition, the thin and sharp delineation of the petals, and the boneless (*mo-ku*) ink strokes of the tree trunk, which lacks the usual moss found in paintings by the two master plum-blossom painters Ch'ao Pu-chih (1053–1110) and Wang Mien (1287–1359). Wen's personal devices served as a canon for later Wu School painters. The last two paintings (Leaves D, E) of the scroll reveal Wen's adaptation of brush idioms characteristic of Shen Chou (1427–1509). In Leaf D the hoary tree

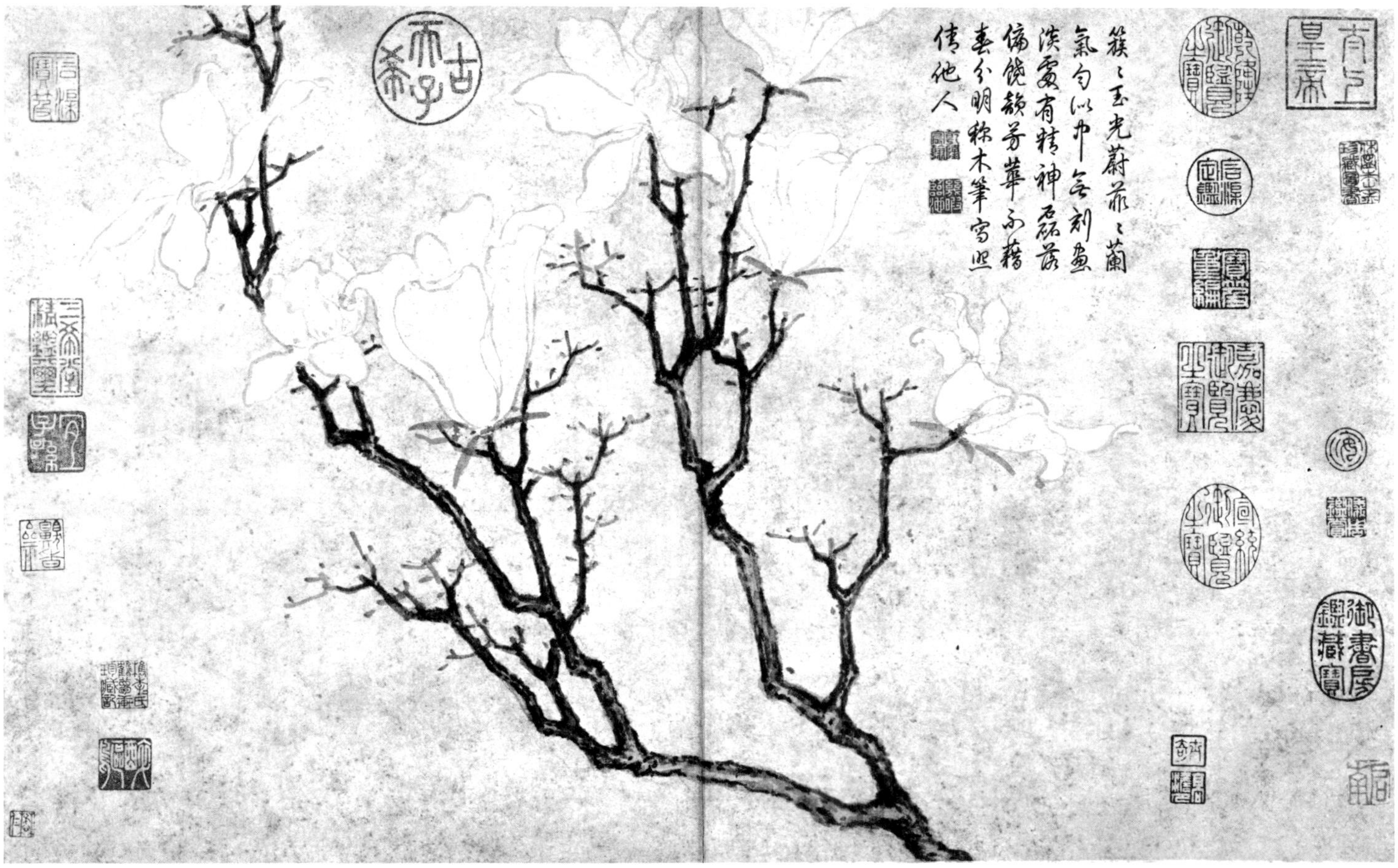

Fig. a. Shen Chou, Leaf 1, *Album of Sketches from Life* (*Hsieh-sheng ts'e*). Dated 1494. Album leaf, ink on paper. 34.6 x 57.2 cm ($13^{5}/_{8}$ x $22^{1}/_{2}$ in.). National Palace Museum, Taipei

trunk marked by dry, blunt texture strokes and wet moss relate to elements of such works by Shen Chou as *Juniper Trees* (*Ch'i-hsing-k'uai*; Nanking Museum). The simple outline drawing used to create form, the fragile twisting petals of the magnolia, which are then accentuated by faint ink wash surrounding their contour lines, is also typical of Shen Chou (fig. a). The brushwork in these two paintings, nevertheless, is subtler and more refined than that of Shen Chou, reflecting the careful, precise nature of the younger artist.

Each painting is followed by a poem written in running script after the model of Wang Hsi-chih (ca. 307–ca. 365) as known through a work by Huai-jen (fl. 7th century), *Preface to the Sacred Teaching* (*Sheng-chiao hsü*). Wen's characters are somewhat elongated, and the brushstrokes have smooth silhouettes and round heads and tails. These traits contrast with the style of Wen Cheng-ming's writing in works made before 1520, which were based on Chao Meng-fu's style. There the characters are square, and the brush-strokes begin and end in triangular points.

Pao-chen Ch'en

NOTES

1. For more biographical information, see: Chiang Chao-shen, *Wen Cheng-ming yü Su-chou hua-t'an* (Wen Cheng-ming and the Wu School painters) (Taipei: National Palace Museum, 1977); Richard Edwards et al., *The Art of Wen Cheng-ming (1470–1559)* (Ann Arbor: The University of Michigan, 1976).

2. Chiang Chao-shen, *Wen Cheng-ming yü Su-chou hua-t'an*, pp. 125–37; Li Shao-wen, "Contempt and Teasing," in *Huang-Ming shih-shuo hsin-yü* (A new account of tales of the world of the Ming dynasty), 1573–1620, Rare Book Division, Library of the National Palace Museum, Taipei, n. pag.

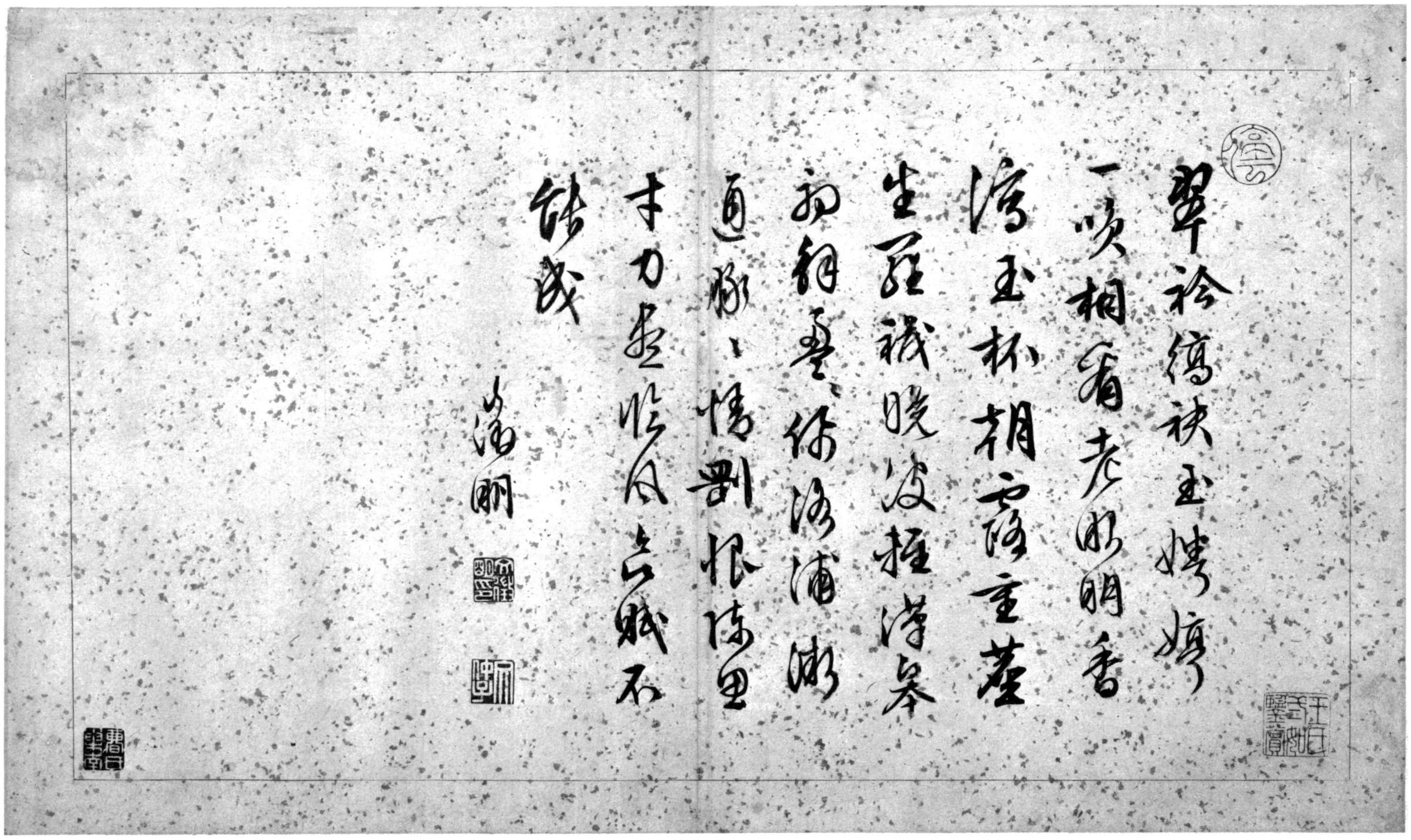

Leaf AA

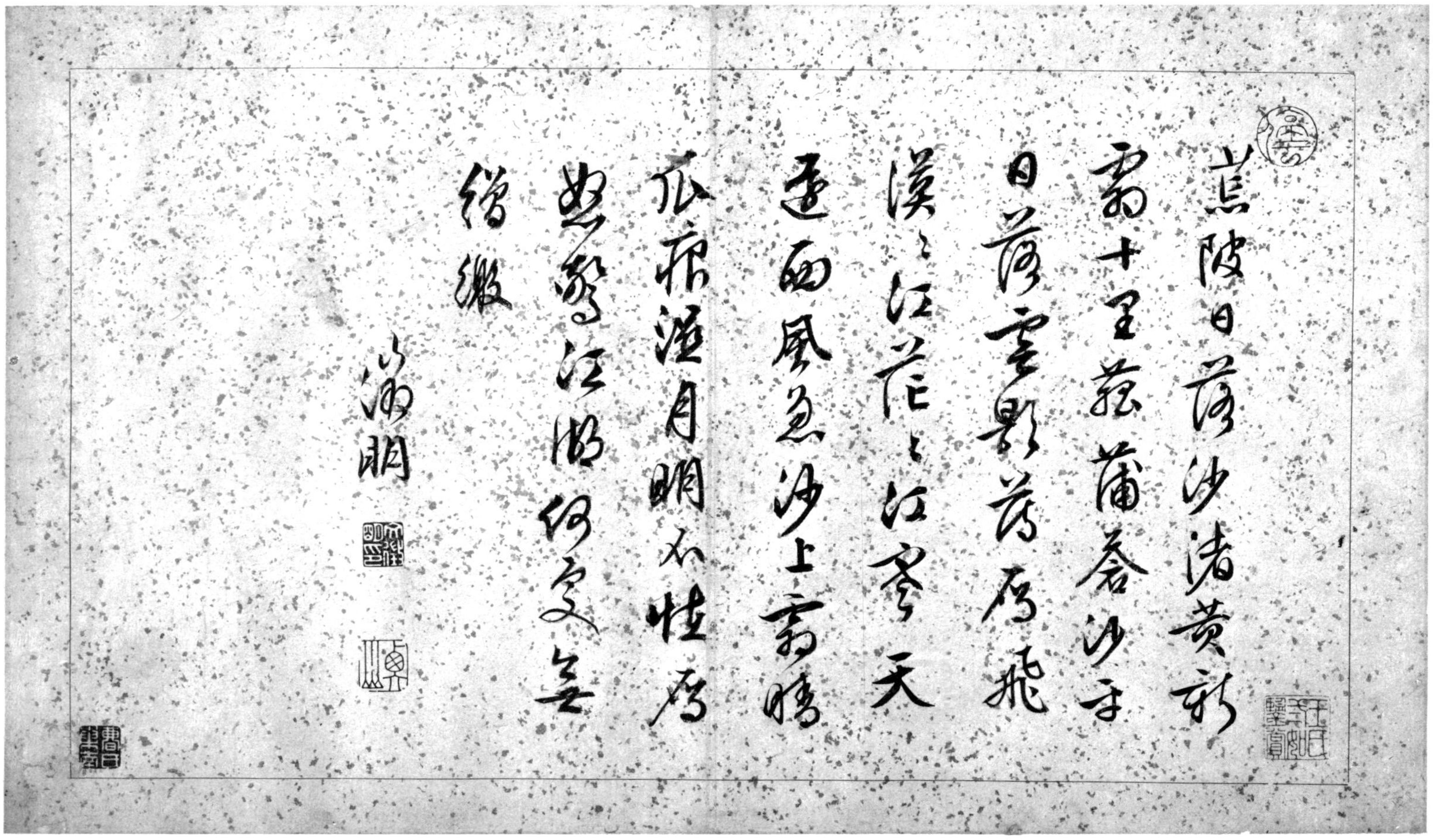

Leaf BB

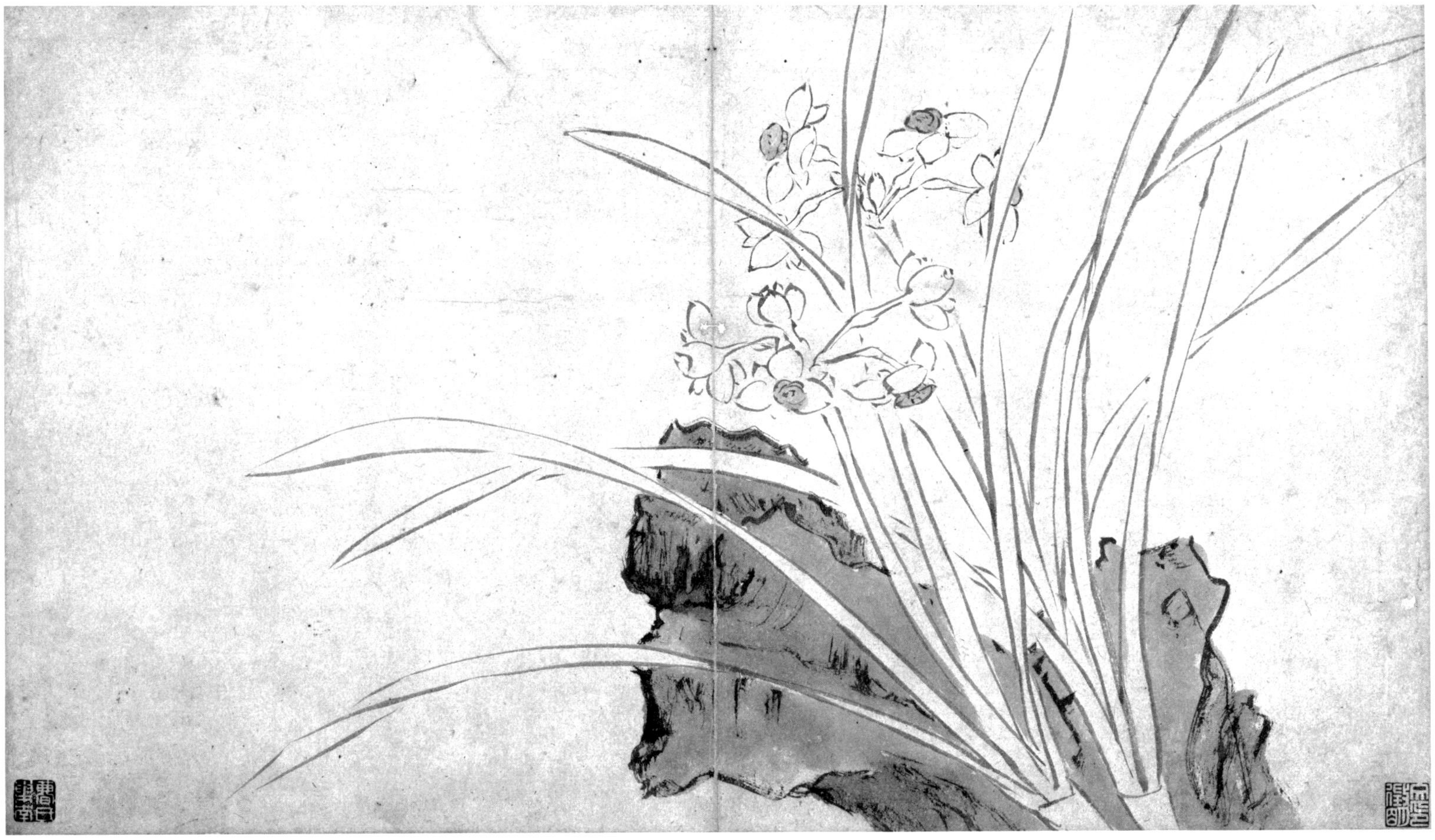
Leaf A, "Narcissus"

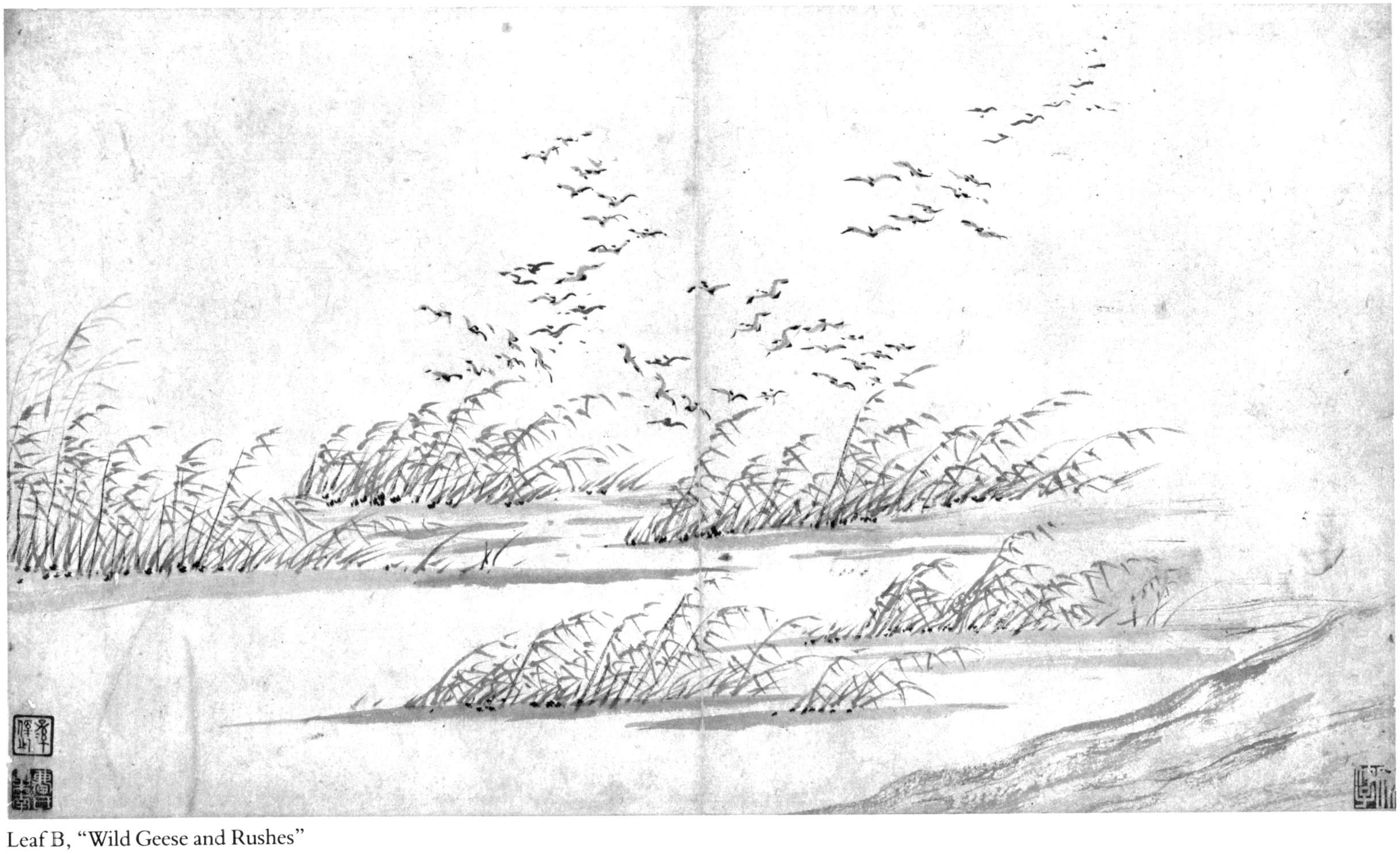
Leaf B, "Wild Geese and Rushes"

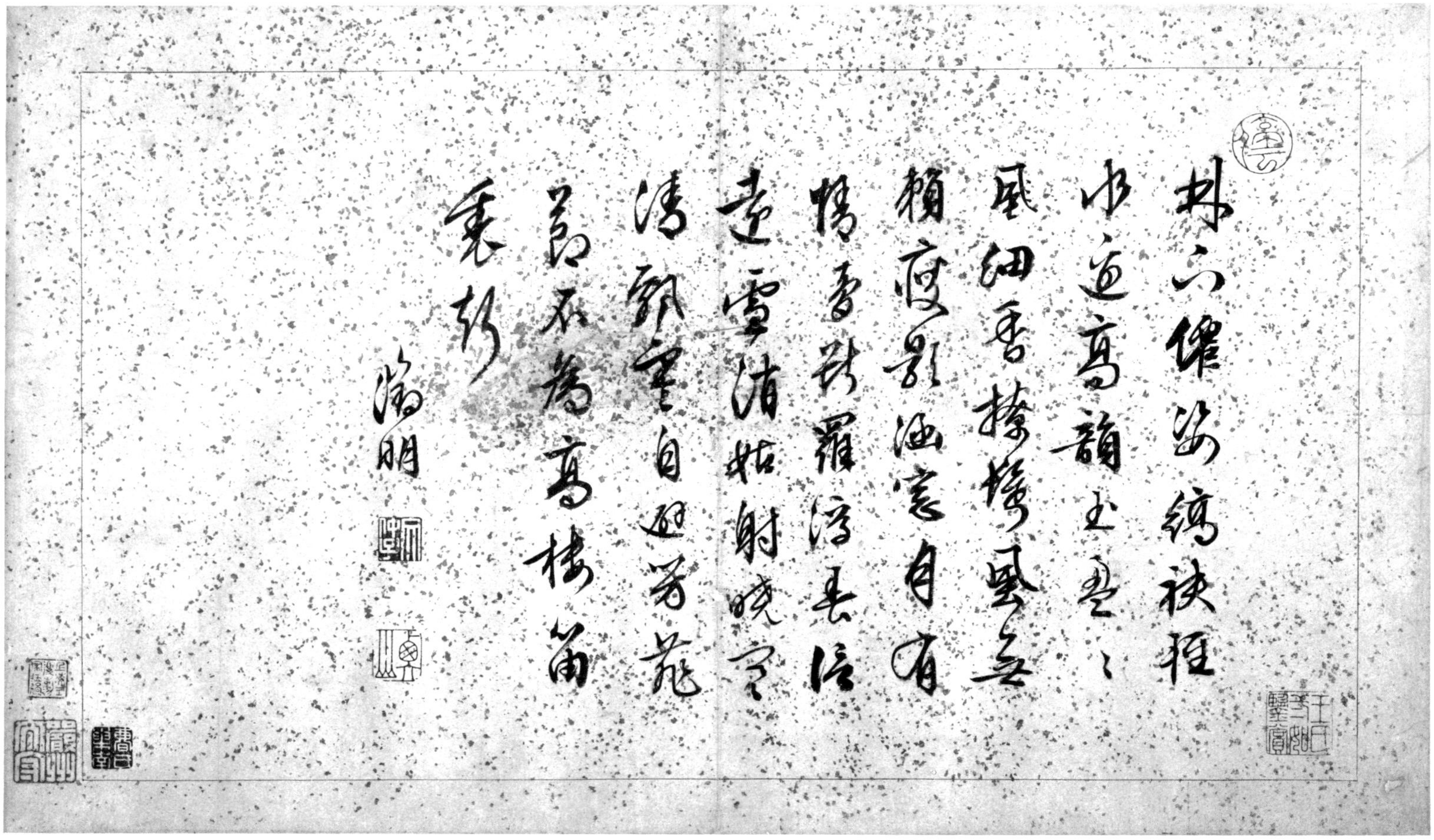

Leaf CC

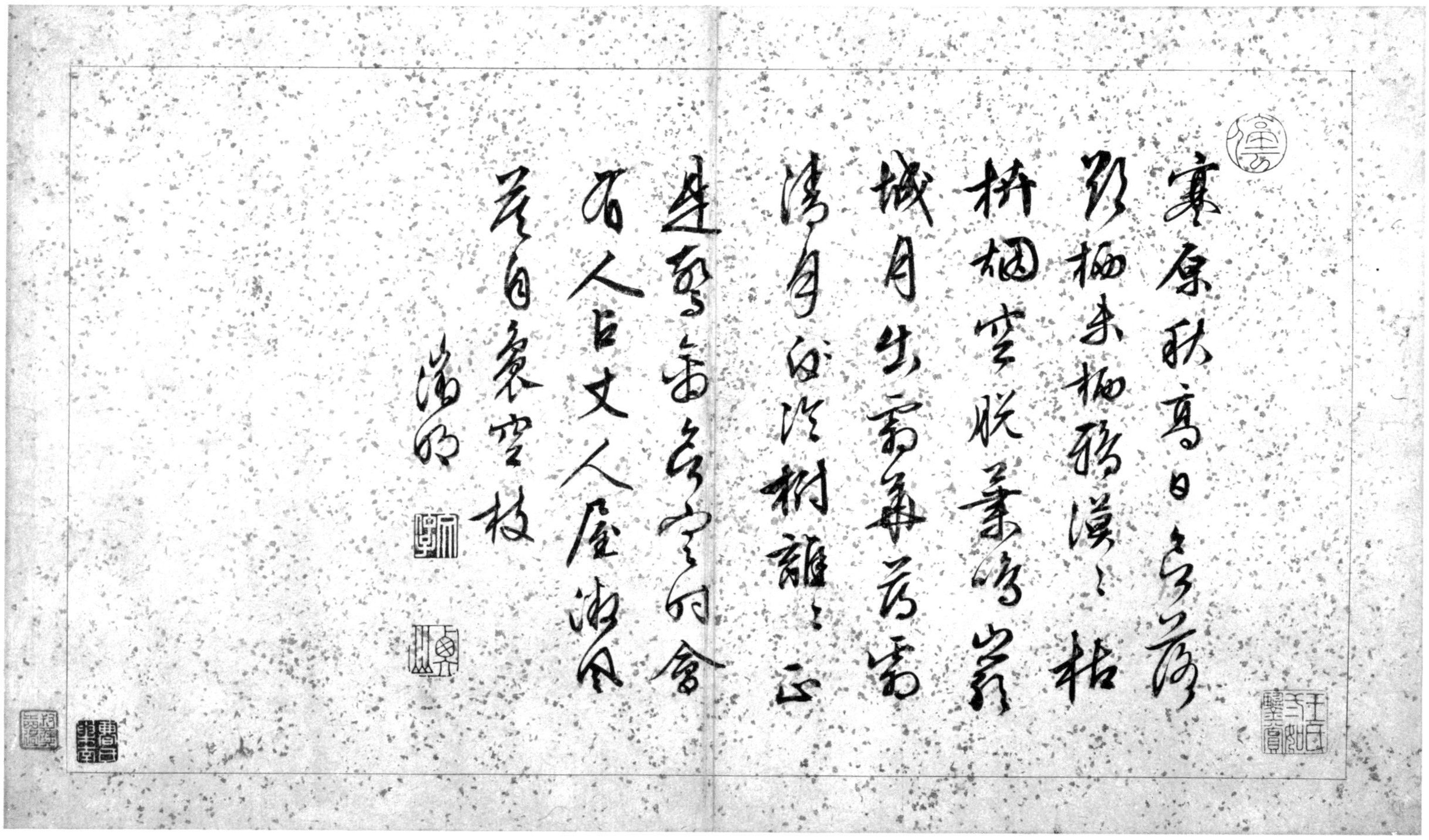

Leaf DD

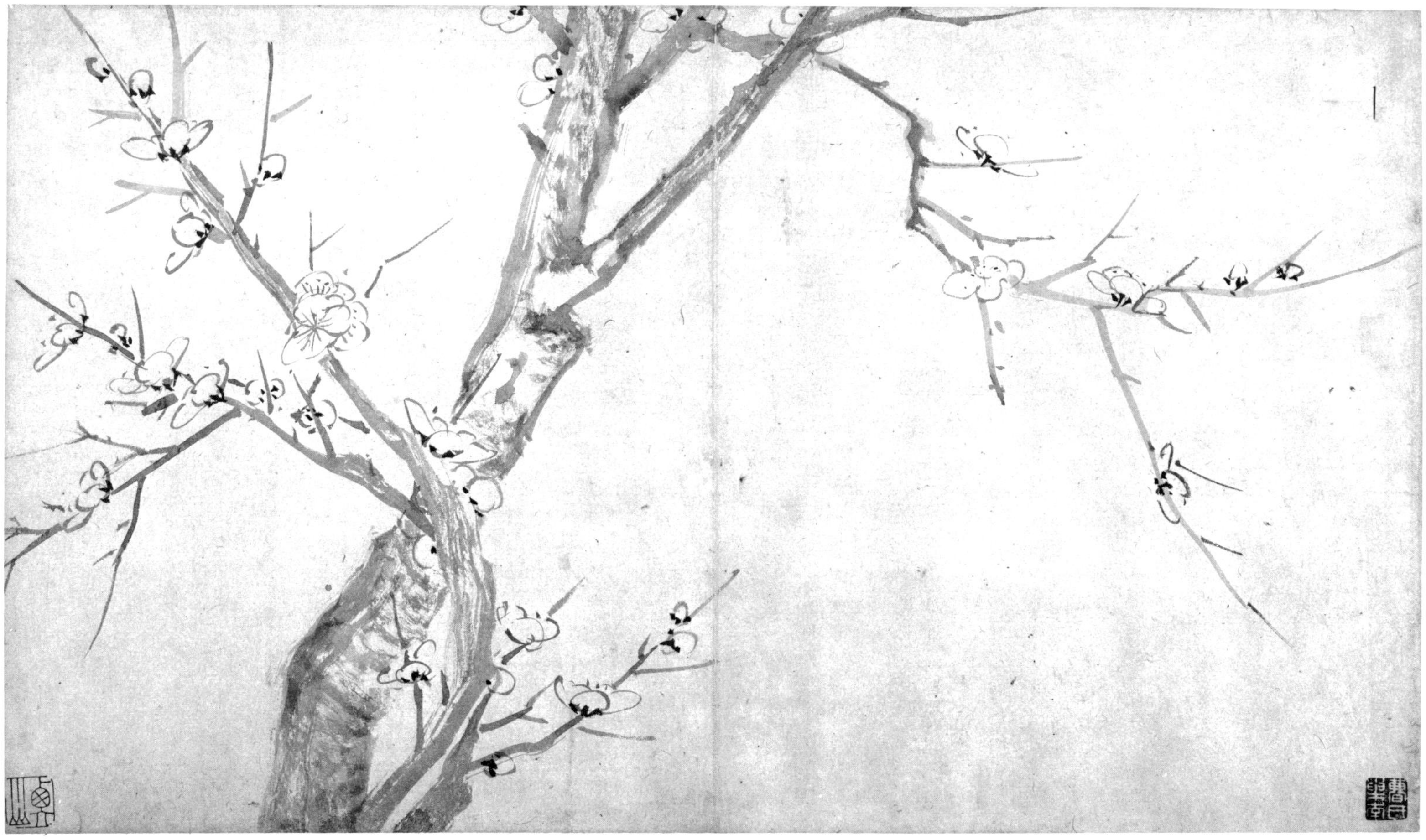

Leaf C, "Plum Blossoms"

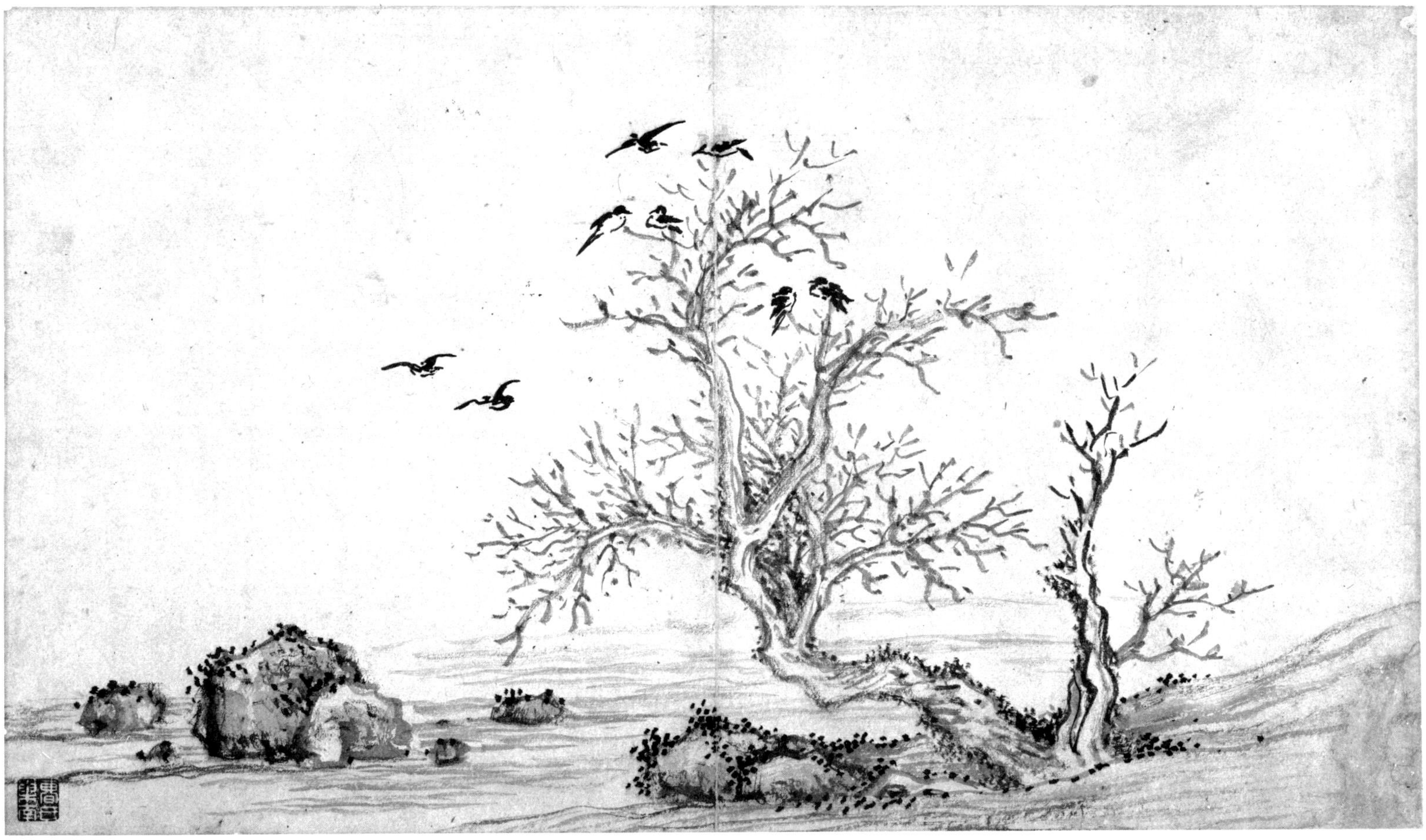

Leaf D, "Birds Perching on a Wintry Tree"

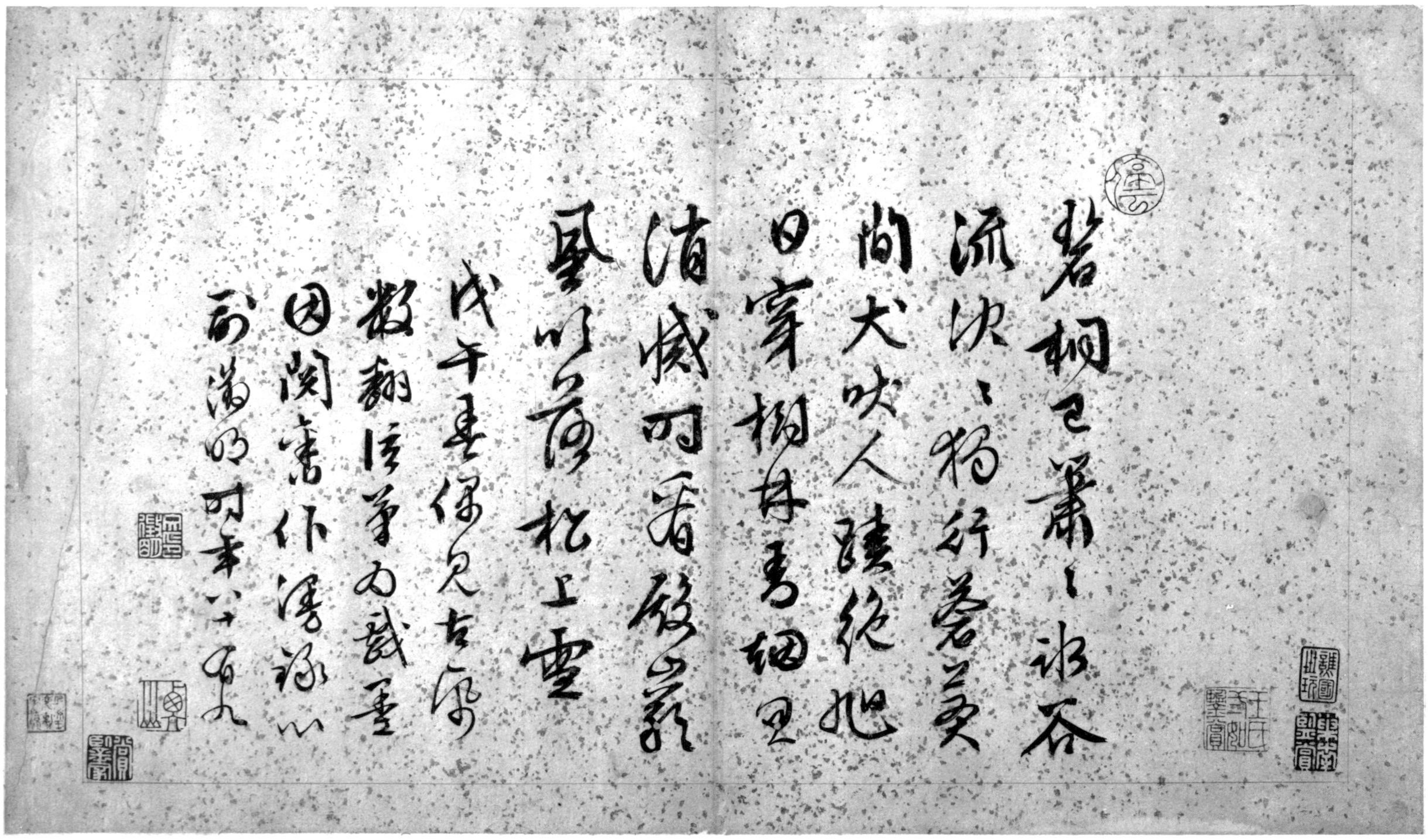

Leaf EE

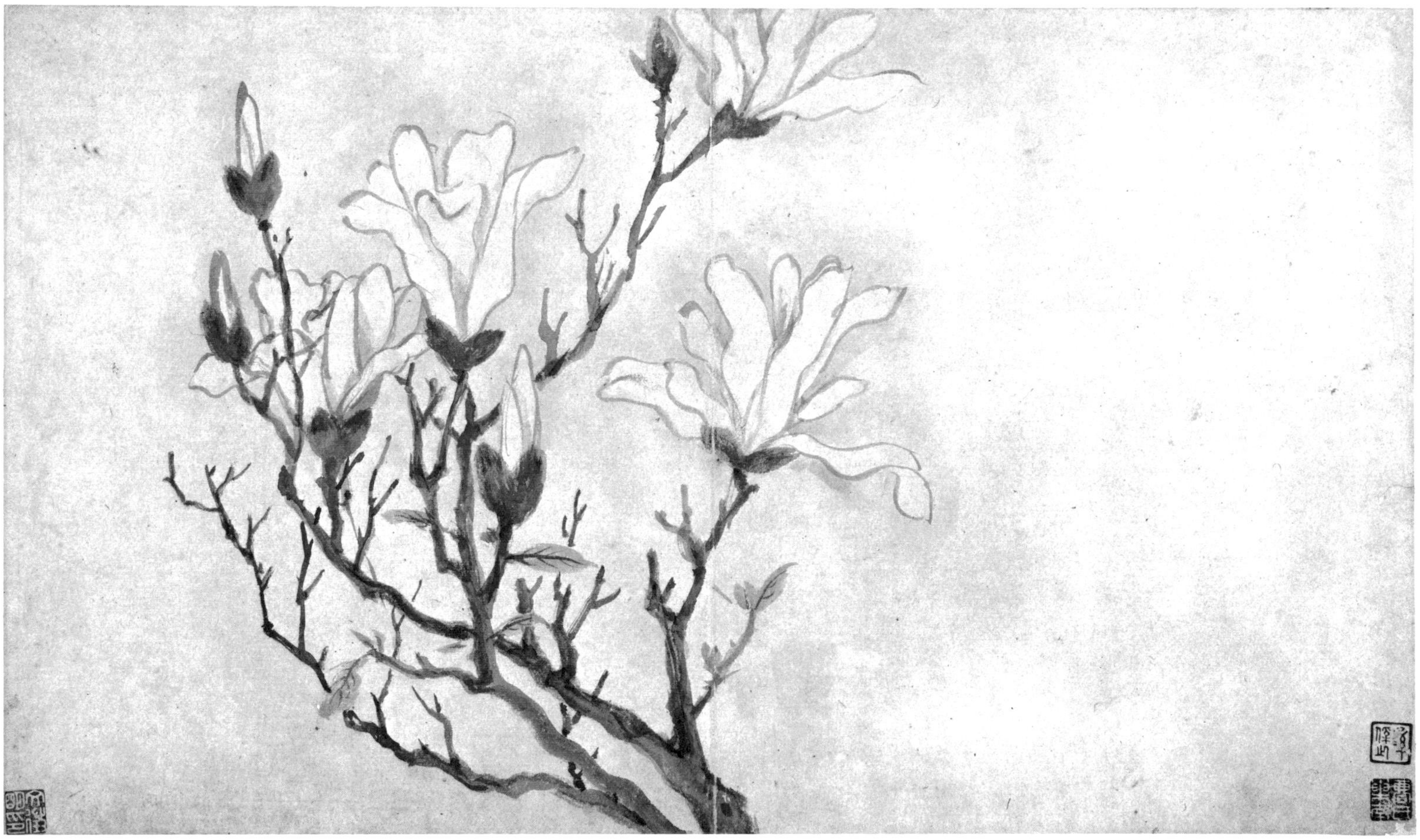

Leaf E, "Magnolia"

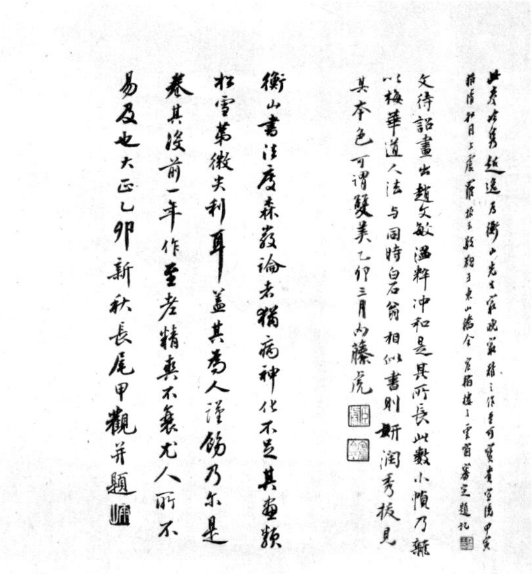


Nagao Kō (Nagao Uzan) — Lo Chen-yü — Naitō Kō (Naitō Kōnan)

# 22 Wang Shou-jen (Wang Yang-ming; 1472–1529)

## *Letters to His Nephew Cheng Pang-jui (Chih chih Cheng Pang-jui san cha)*

Ca. 1523–25
Handscroll, ink on paper
Painting: 24.3 x 43.0 cm (9 1/2 x 16 7/8 in.); calligraphy: 24.3 x 215.4 cm (9 1/2 in. x 7 ft. 5/8 in.); colophon: 24.0 x 292.8 cm (9 1/2 in. x 9 ft. 7 1/4 in.)

No inscription or signature on the painting.

CALLIGRAPHY (from right to left):

Letter 1 (prose, 181 characters in 21 columns of running script):

When the Wang-kuei Mountain Temple was being restored, I donated a beam specifically on behalf of my maternal grandfather and my second eldest maternal uncle. I heard that the community therefore had my name written on the beam. Since the temple has been so significant to the history of our community, why did you not go earlier to state your problem to the provincial governor? Instead, you waited until the Hsiang family had already bought the temple and then spoke out. By that time our fellow villagers had lost the chance to act. I have never before written memorials to be sent to a provincial governor. That is a well-known fact. Do please explain my position to my second eldest maternal aunt so she will not blame me. Since the temple must not be destroyed, our community should make a statement [to that effect] to the provincial governor. If the villagers would be willing to collect money to redeem the temple from the Hsiang family, I do not think that the provincial governor would disagree. Your aunt [Wang Shou-jen's wife] is still sick. Her medicine is of no use. My thanks to my second eldest maternal aunt who cared about my wife so much that she sent a messenger to see us. Yang-ming [Wang Shou-jen] sends this letter to his nephew Pao-i [Cheng Pang-jui]. You may also let our fellow villagers know [the contents of the letter].

Letter 2 (prose, 139 characters in 19 columns of running script):

Yang-ming wrote this for his talented nephew [Cheng] Pao-i. You may check your grandmother's lending account with the related documents, and then go with the man I sent to collect all the debts. Wrap the money and send it here so that your grandmother can save it. You must not spend it casually. This is what your grandmother repeatedly insisted on, and you must not disobey. Originally your grandmother wanted to go home because of this matter, and it was I who patiently asked her to stay. You can understand what this really means and must never let your grandmother blame me for mishandling her business. You should also take great care in dealing with everything concerning our family business. As for my niece, I will soon send somebody to bring her here to live with us. I will let you know in advance. On the third day of the fourth lunar month, Yang-ming wrote this for his talented younger brothers and nephews to read.

Letter 3 (prose, 88 characters in 12 columns of running script):

Once I sent a messenger to escort my second eldest maternal aunt here. However, because she had not yet recovered from an ailment, I did not force my invitation. Recently I heard that she had already recovered; therefore I sent a messenger especially to greet her and bring her here. When this letter reaches you I am hoping that she will bring her granddaughter so that we may all live together. The issue about the girl marrying into the Wang family must be discussed and a decision reached after their arrival; only then can we promise it. Do not worry, I will take care of everything. I will not discuss any details [in this letter]. Yang-ming wrote this for his nephew Pao-i to read. The sixteenth day of the tenth lunar month.

COLOPHONS (from right to left):

1. Huang Wan (1480–1554): prose, 110 characters in 11 columns of running script. Signature: Chiu-an-chü-shih, Huang Wan, inscribed this. Seal: Tsung-hsien (square relief).
2. Hsiao Ching-te (fl. 16th century): prose, 190 characters in 22 columns of running script. Signature: disciple Hsiao Ching-te respectfully wrote this. Seal: Kao-ku (square relief).
3. Huang Hung-kang (1492–1561): prose, 109 characters in 12 columns of running script. Signature: In the midsummer of the *jen-ch'en* year of the Chia-ching era [1532], disciple Huang Hung-kang respectfully wrote this colophon. Seal: Hung-sung (square relief).
4. Yeh Liang-p'ei (*chin-shih*, 1523): prose, 168 characters in 20 columns of running script. Signature: Yeh Liang-p'ei from T'ai-nan [in Shansi province?] wrote this. Seal: Ching-chih (square relief).

COLLECTORS' SEALS:

Chiang Pi (*chü-jen*, 1564), 1 seal.
Chang Wan-ch'en (fl. ca. late 17th century), 2 seals.
Yeh Kung-ch'o (1889–1968), 7 seals.

Wang Nan-p'ing (modern collector), 5 seals.
Unidentified owners, 2 seals.
2 unidentified seals.

Gift of Mrs. Edward L. Elliott (79–95)

PUBLISHED: Chiang I-han, "P'u-lin-ssu-tun ta-hsüeh mei-shu-kuan ts'ang Wang Yang-ming san-cha chüan" (Wang Yang-ming's three letters in the collection of The Art Museum, Princeton University), *Ming-pao yüeh-k'an* 10, no. 1 (January 1975): 58–65; Wang Nan-p'ing, ed., *Ming Ch'ing shu-hua hsüan-chi* (Selections of Chinese painting and calligraphy [15th–18th century]) (Hong Kong: Nan-hua yin-shua yu-hsien kung-ssu, 1975), p. 169; Suzuki Kei, comp., *Chūgoku kaiga sōgō zuroku: daiikkan, Amerika–Kanada hen* (Comprehensive illustrated catalogue of Chinese paintings: volume 1, American and Canadian collections) (Tokyo: University of Tokyo Press, 1982), p. 118, pl. A16–051; Nakata Yūjirō and Fu Shen, eds., *Obei shūzō Chūgoku hōsho meisekishū* (Chinese calligraphy in American and European collections), vol. 5 (Tokyo: Chūōkōron-sha, forthcoming).

WANG YANG-MING (personal name, Shou-jen), from Yü-yao, Chekiang province, was the most notable philosopher of the Ming dynasty. A holder of the *chin-shih* degree (1499), Wang was also a distinguished official and calligrapher. Beginning in 1505 Wang received students in Peking, instructing them in Neo-Confucian philosophy. His teaching was soon interrupted; in 1506 Wang was banished to Lung-ch'ang (northwest Kueichou) for having offended Liu Chin (d. 1510), a powerful eunuch. He spent two years (1508–9) there among the Miao and Yao tribesmen, subsisting on a meager diet and fighting continual sickness. Wang Yang-ming's response to this hostile environment was to emphasize "tranquility of the mind," and by so doing he reached "sudden enlightenment" in 1508. Thereafter he began to advocate that knowledge of the principle of things resides in the inner mind.[1] This theory opposed standard Neo-Confucianism as espoused by Chu Hsi (1130–1200), who held that knowledge was the result of the investigation of things. In 1509 Wang Yang-ming formulated his second theory, "the unity of knowledge and action." He defined knowledge as the beginning of action and action as the completion of knowledge. As his third principle, proposed in 1521, he stated that the mind is innately intelligent and pure and can be improved through self-cultivation, with actions reflecting the substance of the mind. Similarly he asserted that calligraphy is a "mind print," or "reflection," of man's inner substance.

In the tradition of Chinese calligraphy, Wang trained by copying classical models, eventually modifying them to form his own individual style: "I began the study of calligraphy by freely copying classical models, but what I learned was merely superficial likeness. Later I learned to hold my brush and never wrote quickly until I had my thoughts concentrated, my worries pacified, and the classical models excluded from my mind. In this way, I gradually came to understand the principles of calligraphy. . . ."[2]

Wang Yang-ming excelled in running script. His writing before 1520 reveals the influence of Wang Hsi-chih (ca. 307–ca. 365), Li Yung (678–747), and Huang T'ing-chien (1045–1105). In his *Account of the Unshabby Pavilion* (*Ho-lou-hsüan chi*), dated 1508–9 (fig. a), the left-hand components of each character are emphasized, causing most of the characters to tilt to the left, as they do in Huang T'ing-chien's style. The slender profiles of the characters, the relaxed brush movement, and the open spacing between words and columns recall the styles of Wang Hsi-chih and Li Yung. Wang Yang-ming's personal style is apparent in the round corners and fluid strokes of his characters. Using a pliant brush of weasel hair, Wang avoided much of the pressing and lifting movements with which most calligraphers finish a stroke. Instead he usually kept the brush on the paper, executing smooth turns that give his writing a natural appearance. Wang's serene state of mind in this period is reflected in his calligraphic style.

Between 1522 and 1526, Wang's situation changed drastically. His father died in 1522, and his first wife, Lady Chu, in 1525.[3] As head of the family, he became closely tied to his relatives; he supervised all family business, cared for Lady Chu during her illness, and arranged the marriage of his maternal niece. These events are the topics of *Letters to His Nephew Cheng Pang-jui* (personal name, Pao-i), whose grandmother was Wang's second eldest maternal aunt. Although the three letters are undated, they must have

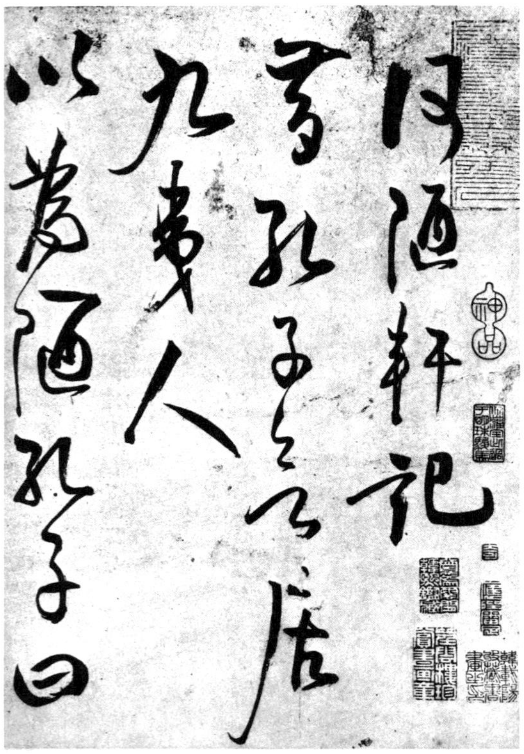

Fig. a. Wang Shou-jen, detail, *Account of the Unshabby Pavilion* (*Ho-lou-hsüan chi*). Ca. 1508–9. Handscroll, ink on paper. 29.8 x 679.2 cm (11¾ x 22 ft. 3⅜ in.). Tokyo National Museum

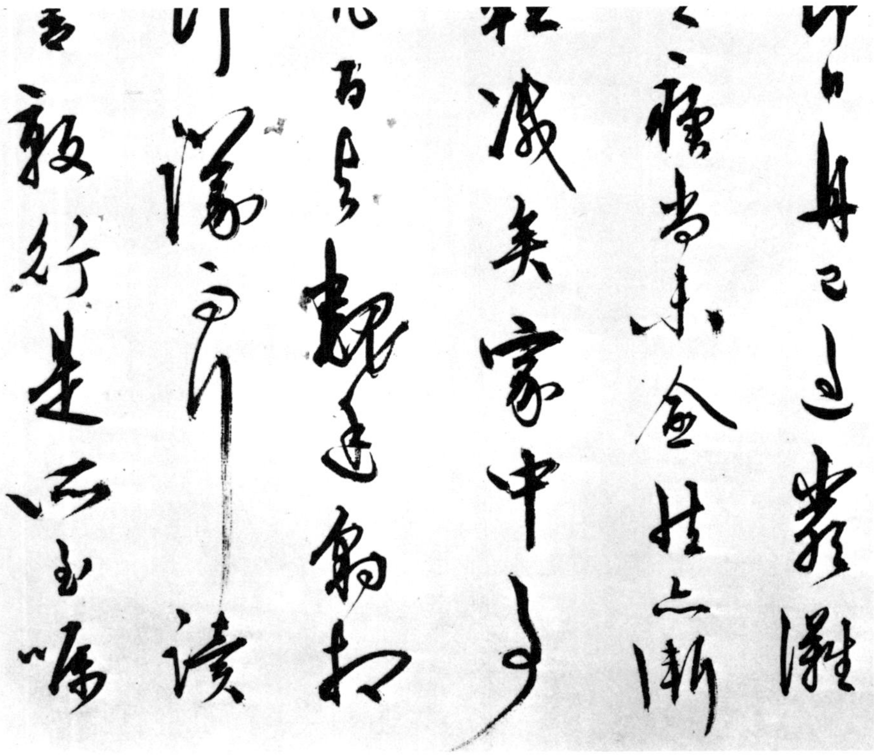

Fig. b. Wang Shou-jen, detail, *Letter to [Wang] Cheng-hsien* (*Yü Cheng-hsien shu*). Ca. 1527–28. Handscroll, ink on paper. Measurements unknown

been written before the death of his first wife. Judging from the letters' contents, they should be rearranged chronologically in the reverse of their present order.[4] The episodes covered took place between autumn 1523 and spring 1525. In the autumn of 1523, Wang wrote to invite his second eldest maternal aunt to come live with him (see translation of Letter 3). She did in fact join him for a year. The following spring (1524) she asked him to write to Cheng about the matter of a loan (see translation of Letter 2). Sometime after the writing of this letter, still in 1524, his aunt returned to Cheng's home. That winter Lady Chu became very ill, and his aunt became so concerned that she sent a messenger to ask after the ill woman. When Wang wrote to express his gratitude for her gesture, Lady Chu was already close to death (see translation of Letter 1); she died early in 1525.

The calligraphy of these letters reveals the writer's anxiety during this period. The characters are rectangular, with sharp, angular corners, and the brushwork is swift, showing evidence of having been executed with a blunt brush. Identical features also appear in his letters of 1527–28 to his adopted son, Wang Cheng-hsien (fig. b). Such qualities reflect the straightforwardness Wang acquired as he settled into old age.

The provenance of this scroll is complex. Sometime after Wang's death in 1529, Cheng Pao-i (Pang-jui) had the letters mounted as a handscroll, for some unknown reason in reverse chronological order. About 1523 Cheng asked Wang's disciples Huang Wan (1480–1554), Hsiao Ching-te (fl. 16th century), Huang Hung-kang (1492–1561), and Yeh Liang-p'ei (*chin-shih*, 1523) to write colophons on the endpaper attached to the mounted scroll. The frontispiece, which has a portrait of Wang and an attendant, was a later addition made before the scroll was collected by Chiang Pi (*chü-jen*, 1564),[5] whose seals are impressed on the junctures of the present scroll.

The portrait of Wang Yang-ming is a free interpretation of an original painting by an anonymous painter. Both Wang and his attendant (or Cheng Pang-jui?) are painted in plain-line drawing (*pai-miao*). Wang sits on the right, in an armchair with a tall scrolled cushion. He is dressed in the typical costume of a Ming scholar, with a high cap with ribbons, robe with V-shaped collar and billowing sleeves, long skirt, and flat-soled shoes. His face, with long beard, is thin yet lively. Wang is depicted raising his brush in order to dip it into the ink on the inkstone and write several more characters to complement those already brushed on the paper before him. Iconographically the portrait in The Art Museum, Princeton University, is related to two other versions: one is attributed to Ch'en Hung-shou (1599–1652), in the Fogg Art Museum, Cambridge, Massachusetts (fig. c);[6] the other version is in the Yamada Jun collection (fig. d). All three versions share similarities in the features of the figures and their costumes, suggesting that they were based on the same original model, a portrait from life of Wang Yang-ming.

PAO-CHEN CH'EN

NOTES

1. For further biographical information, see Wing-tsit Chan, "Wang Shou-jen," in L. Carrington Goodrich and Chaoying Fang, eds., *Dictionary of Ming Biography: 1368–1644* (New York and London: Columbia University Press, 1976), vol. 2, pp. 1409–16.
2. Ch'ien Te-hung et al., eds., *Wang Yang-ming ch'üan chi* (The complete works of Wang Yang-ming) (1595; repr. ed., Shanghai: Shih-chieh shu-chü, 1936), pp. 10–11.
3. Ch'ien Te-hung et al., eds., *Wang Yang-ming ch'üan chi*, pp. 651, 656 (chronology).
4. See Chiang I-han, "P'u-lin-ssu-tun ta-hsüeh mei-shu-kuan ts'ang Wang Yang-ming san-cha chüan" (Wang Yang-ming's three letters in the collection of The Art Museum, Princeton University), *Ming-pao yüeh-k'an* 10, no. 1 (January 1975): 58–65.
5. Chang Yüan-chieh, ed., *Yü-yao hsien-chih* (Local gazetteer of Yü-yao prefecture) (1899; repr. ed., Taipei, 1974), *chüan* 23, p. 21.
6. The Fogg painting is undated. It was misdated to 1646 in Wing-tsit Chan, "Wang Shou-jen," pl. 12, because the cyclical year *ping-hsü*, which corresponds to 1646, 1706, 1766, and so on, appears in the inscription by an eighteenth-century calligrapher, Chu Wen-cheng, and was mistaken for the execution date of the painting.

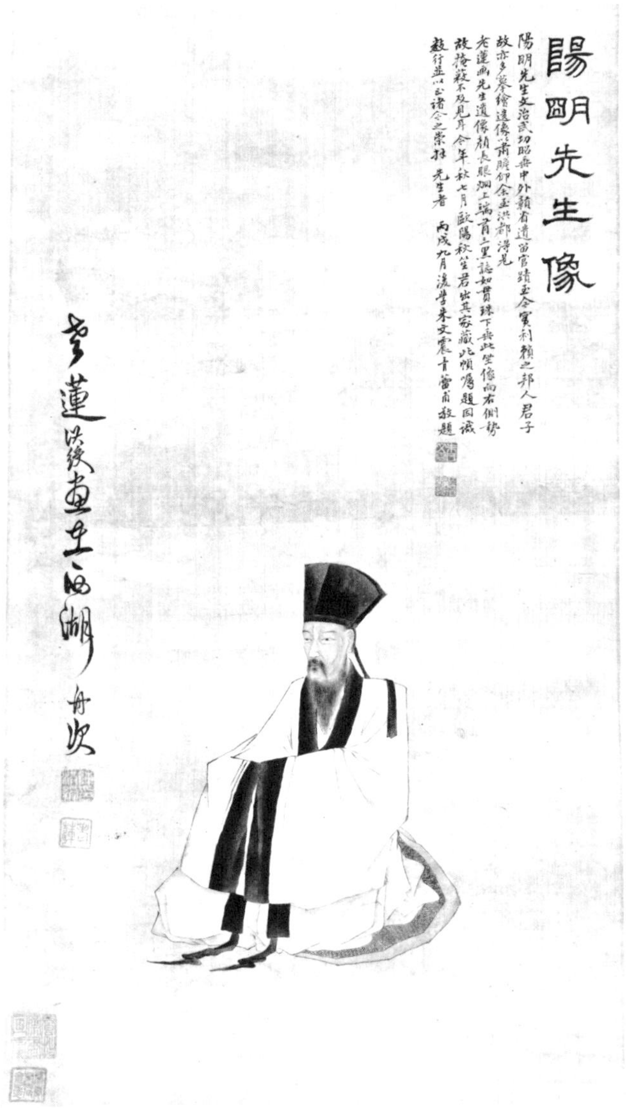


Fig. c. Attributed to Ch'en Hung-shou, *Portrait of Master Yang-ming* (*Yang-ming hsien-sheng hsiang*). Undated, 18th century (?).Hanging scroll, ink and color on silk. Measurements unknown. Fogg Art Museum, Harvard University, Cambridge, Massachusetts

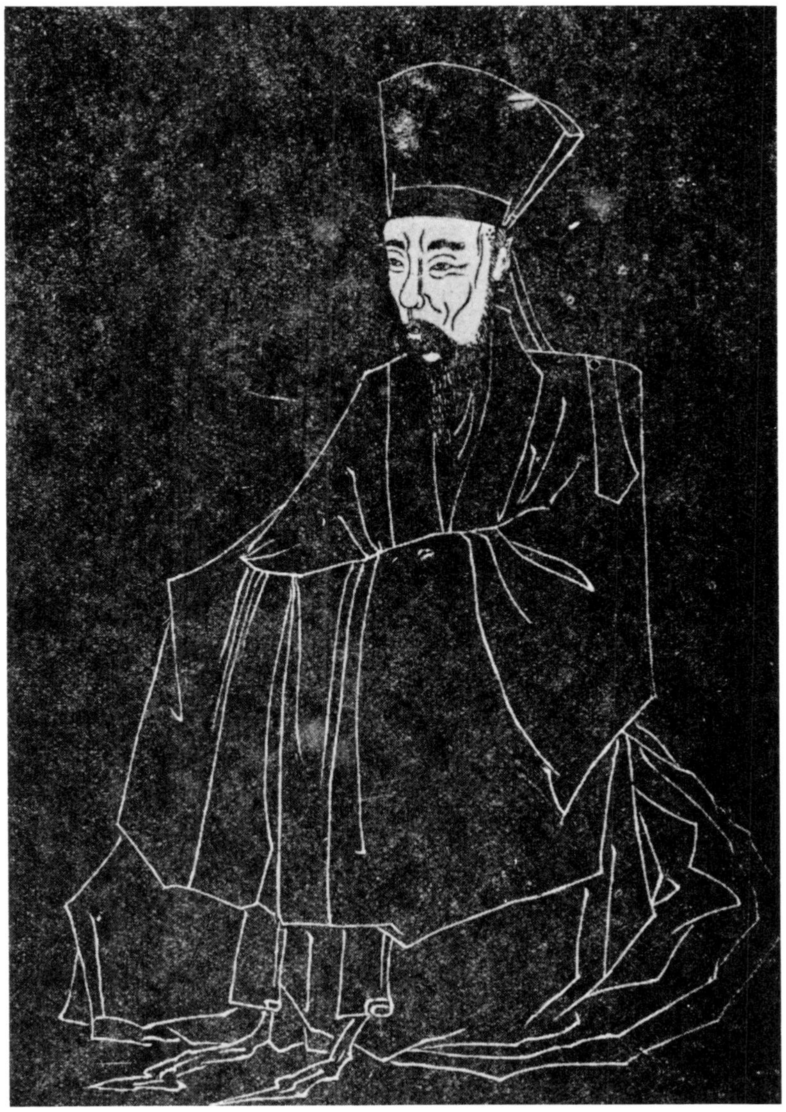

Fig. d. Anonymous, *Portrait of Master Wang Yang-ming* (*Wang Yang-ming hsien-sheng i-hsiang*). Undated, 16th century. Rubbing, hanging scroll, ink on paper. Measurements unknown. Yamada Jun collection

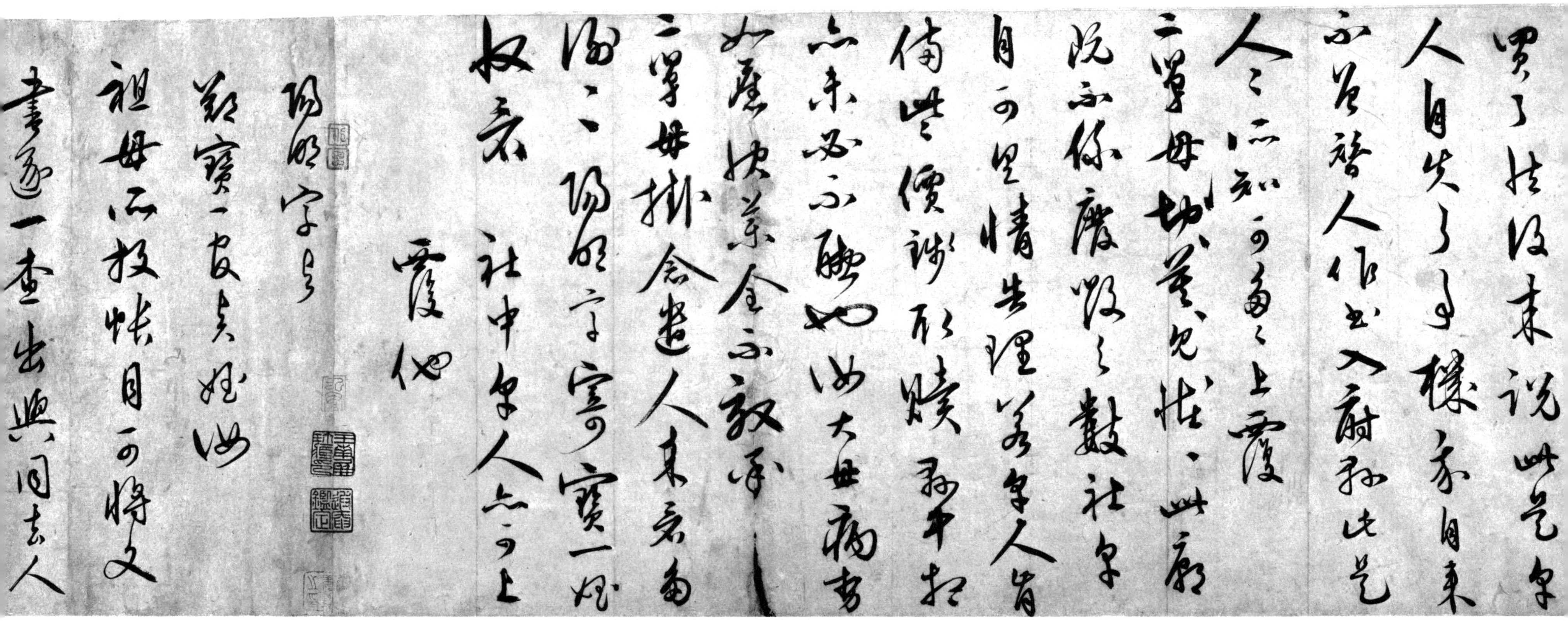

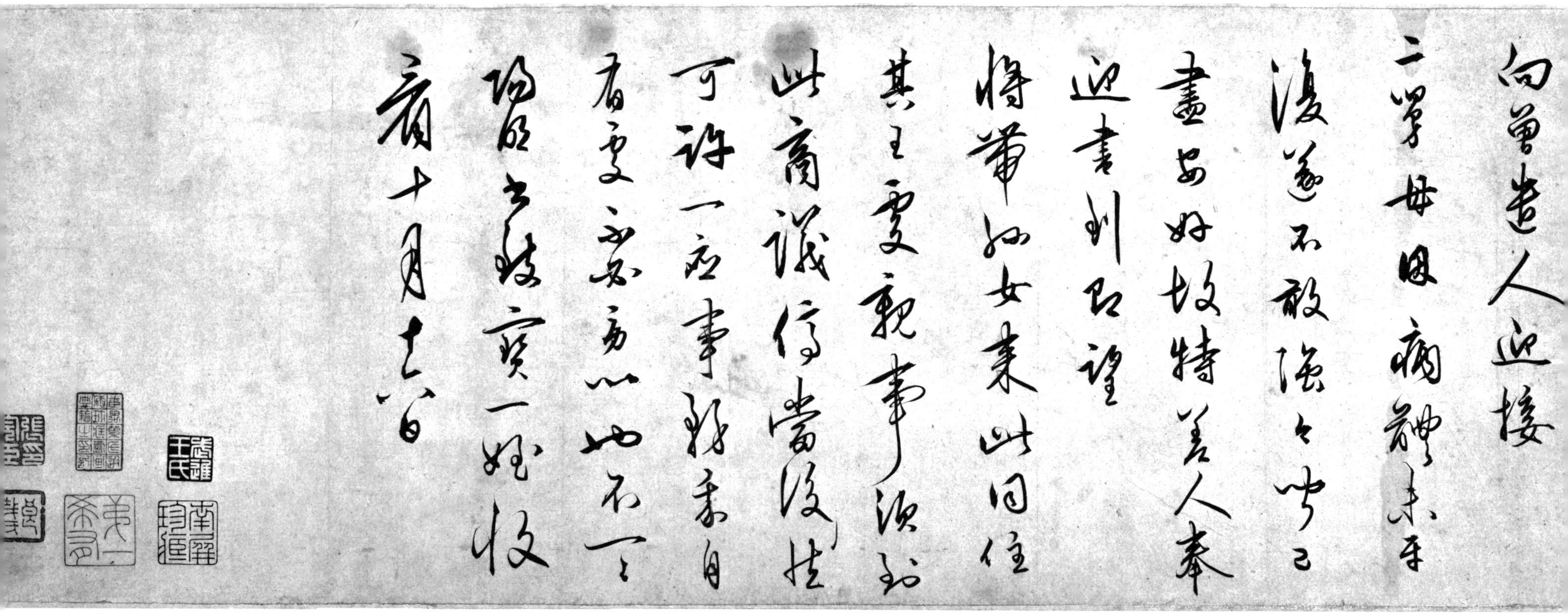

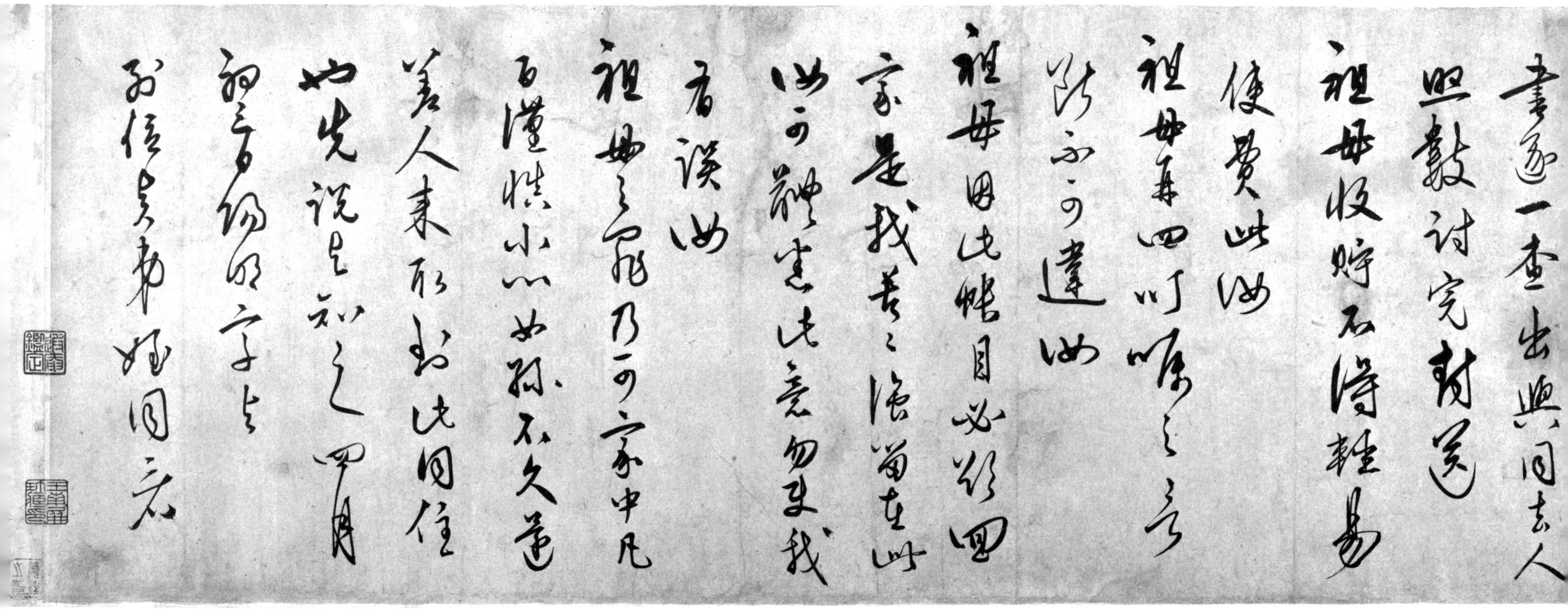

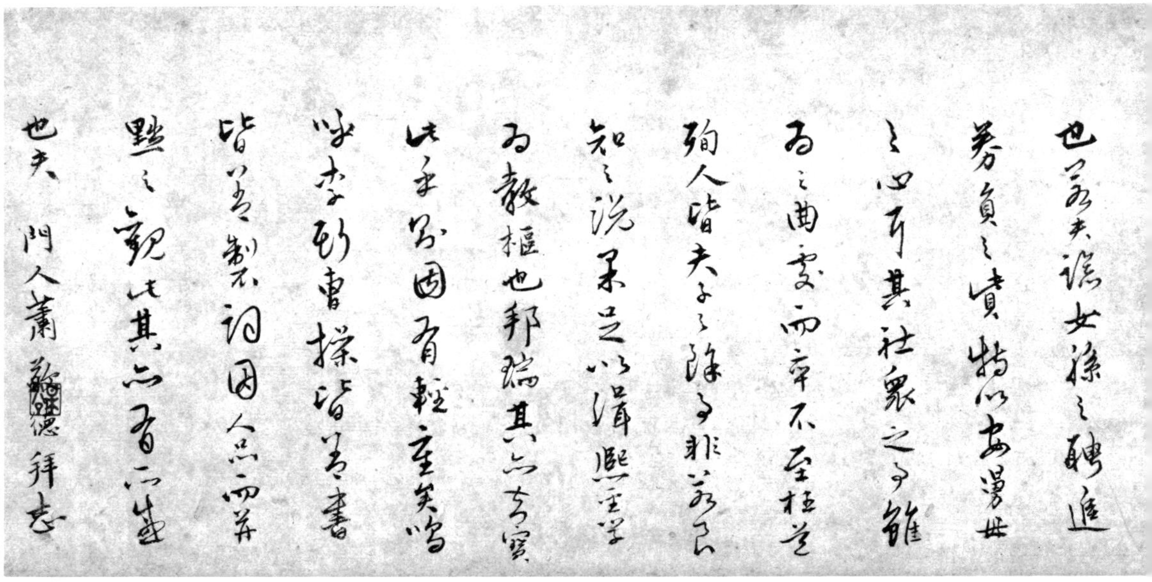

Hsiao Ching-te

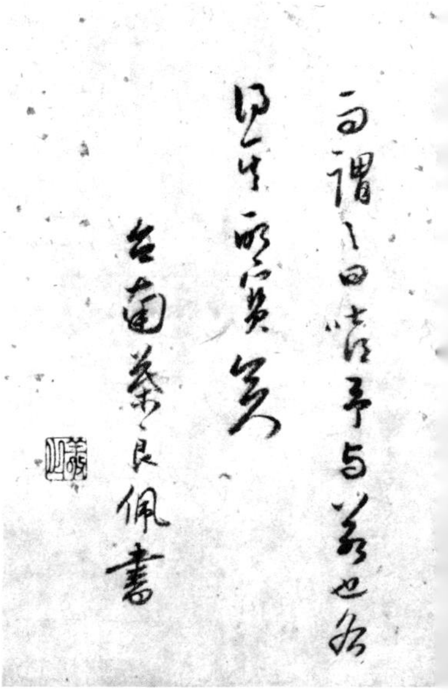

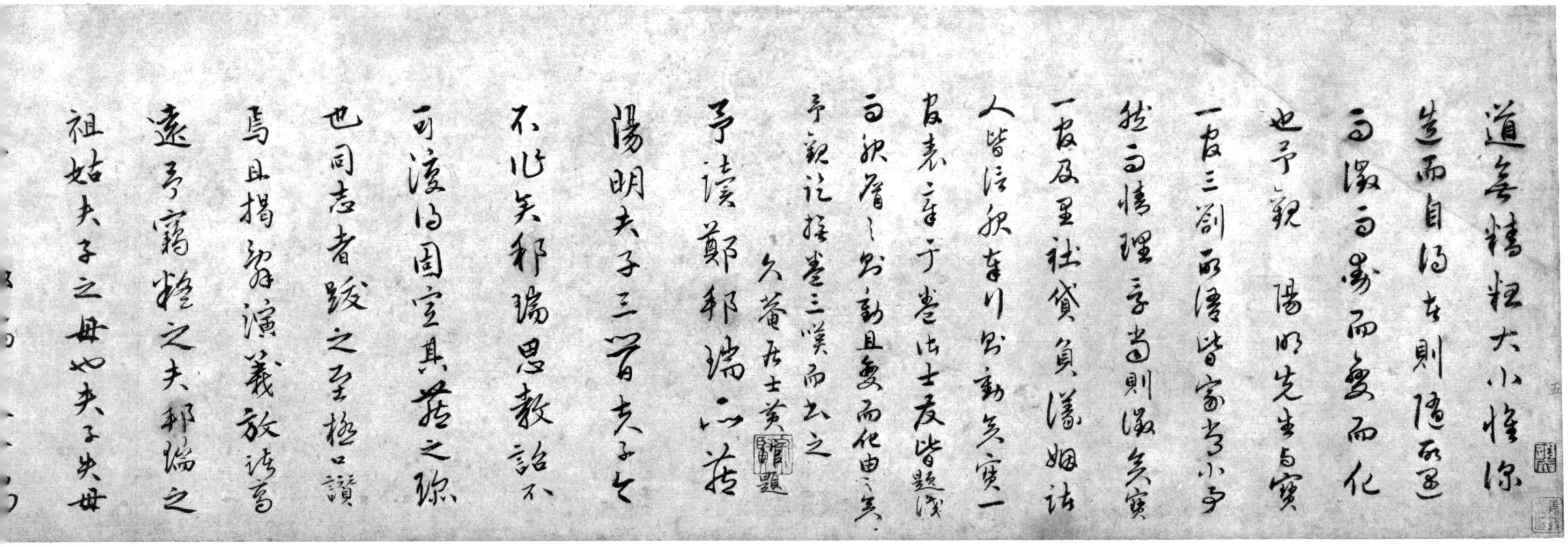

Huang Wan

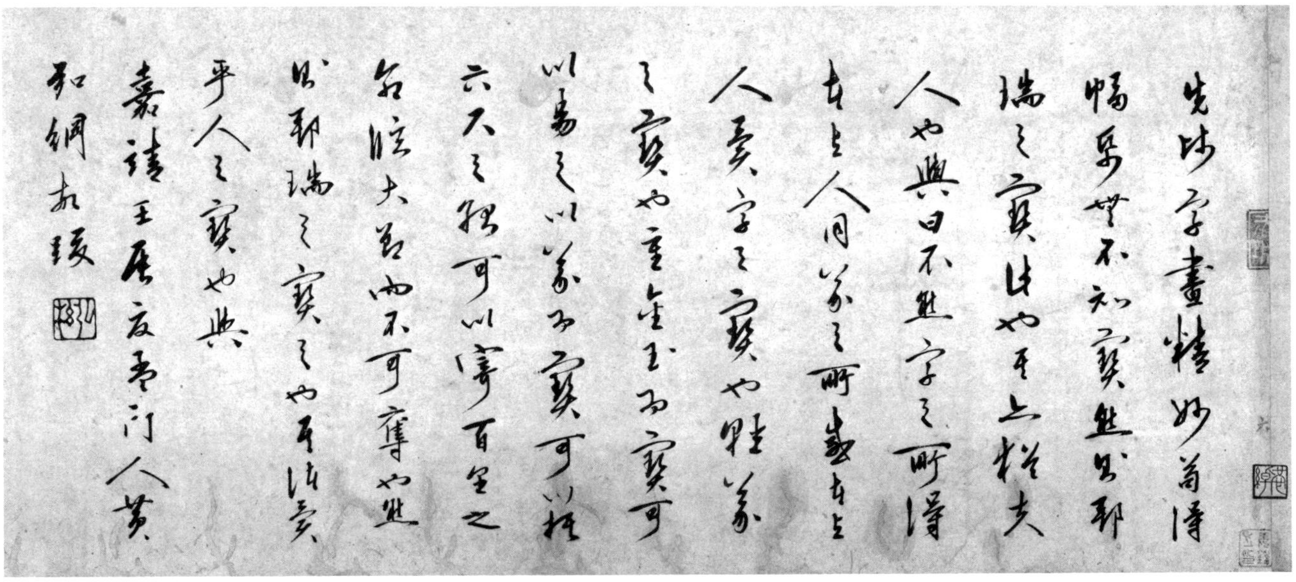

Huang Hung-kang

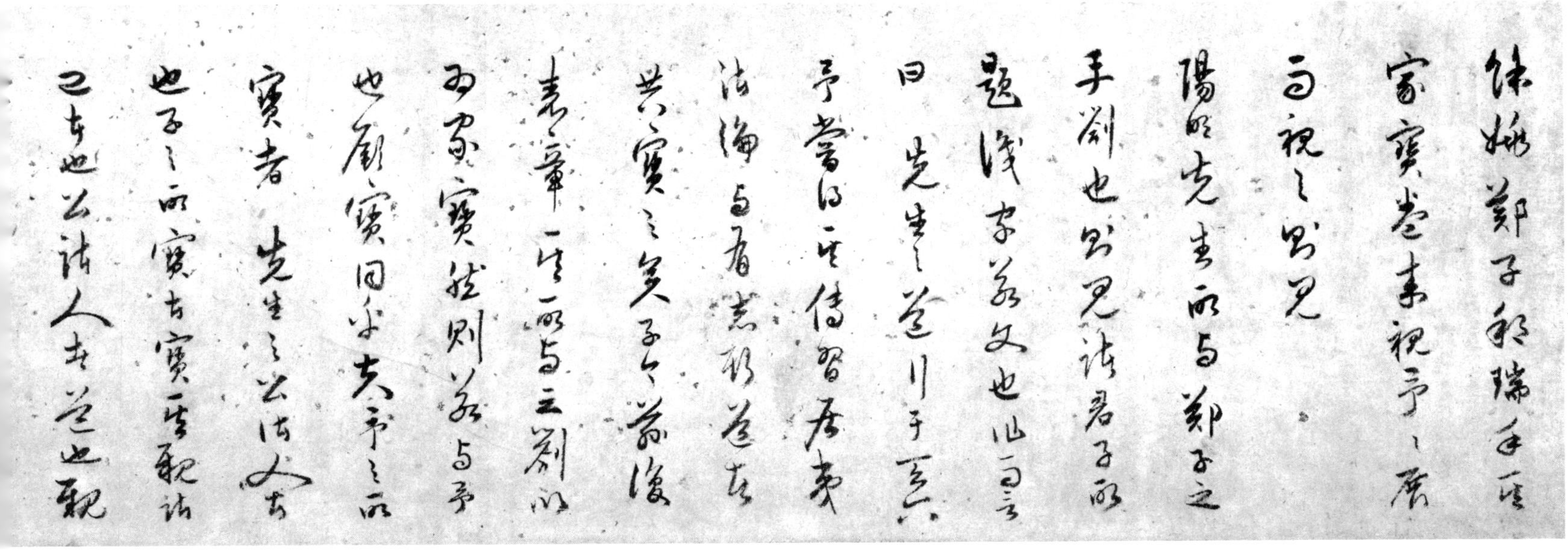

Yeh Liang-p'ei

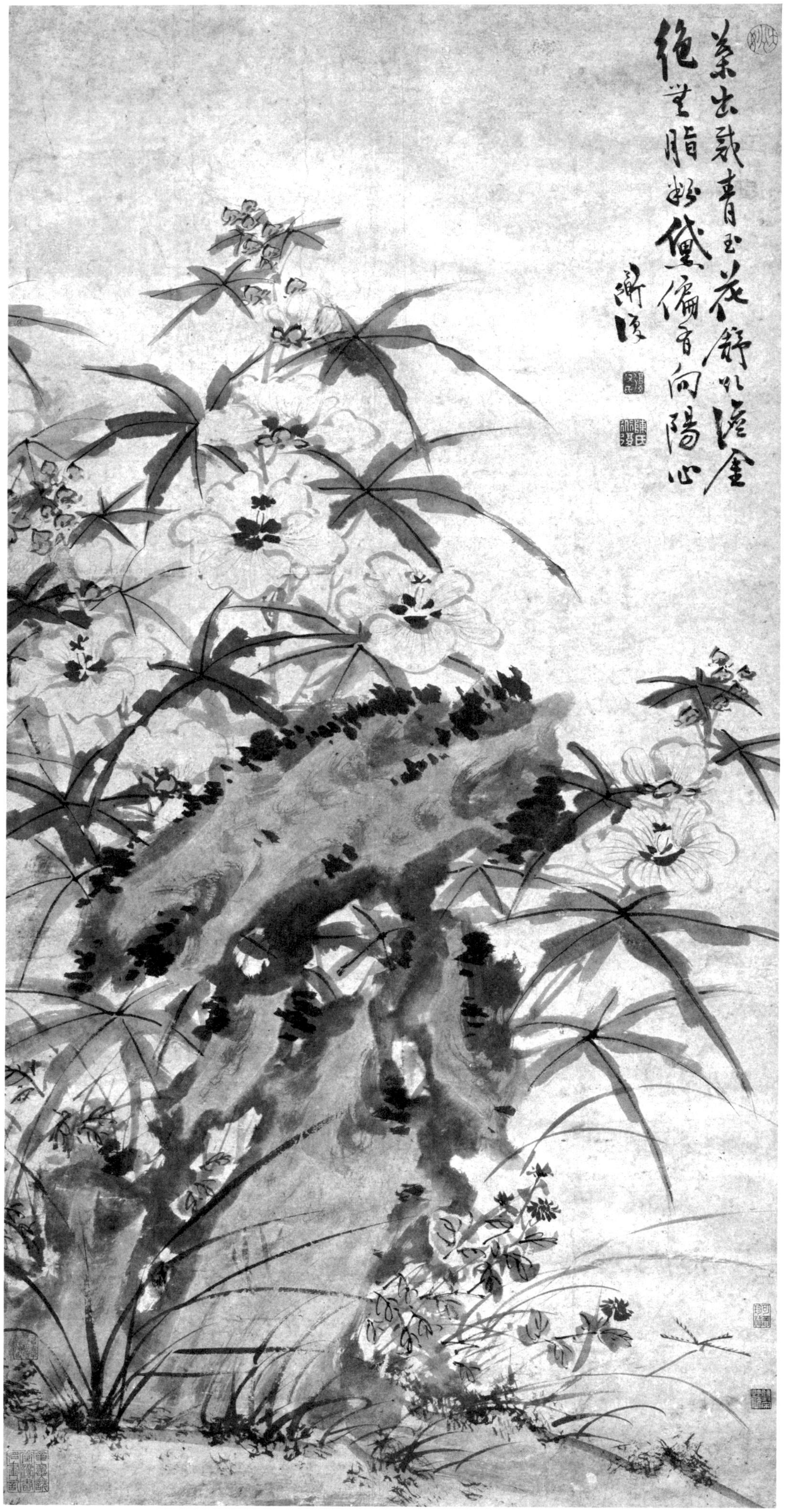

# 23 Ch'en Ch'un (1484–1544)

## *Mallows and Garden Rock (Ch'iu-k'uei hu-shih)*

Ca. 1541
Hanging scroll, ink on paper
116.8 x 60.0 cm (3 ft. 10 in. x 23 5/8 in.)

ARTIST'S INSCRIPTION (5 character quatrain in 2 columns of running script):

Leaves are like cut-outs of jade.
Flowers strive to outshine gold.
They are without a trace of makeup,
Just with their hearts toward the sun.

ARTIST'S SIGNATURE: Tao-fu.

ARTIST'S SEALS: Fu-fu shih (square intaglio); Ch'en shih Tao-fu (square intaglio); Ta-yao (round relief).

COLLECTORS' SEALS:

1. Ch'eng Po-fen (modern collector): K'o-an chen-mi (square relief; lower right); Shuang-Sung-lou (square intaglio; lower right).
2. Chang I (dates unkown): Chang I Sheng-t'ang fa-shu ming-hua chi (square relief; lower left); T'iao-shang Chang Pao-pai liu-lan so-chi (square relief; lower left).

Gift of Mrs. Edward L. Elliott (80–41)

PUBLISHED: Suzuki Kei, comp., *Chūgoku kaiga sōgō zuroku: daiikkan, Amerika–Kanada hen* (Comprehensive illustrated catalogue of Chinese paintings: volume 1, American and Canadian collections) (Tokyo: University of Tokyo Press, 1982), p. 161, pl. A17–112.

AS THE CHILD of a wealthy family in Ch'ang-chou (in Su-chou prefecture), Ch'en Ch'un (*tzu*, Tao-fu; *hao*, Pai-yang) was exposed to art through the Sung and Yüan painting collections of his grandfather, Ch'en Yü (1440–1506). Ch'en Yü was a close friend of Shen Chou's (1427–1509; see nos. 14A, 15), and Ch'en Ch'un's father, Yao (d. 1516), was intimate with Wen Cheng-ming (1470–1559; see no. 21). Ch'en Ch'un grew up in an environment well suited for the development of his wide-ranging talents in painting, calligraphy, and poetry.[1]

Ch'en Ch'un first studied painting with Wen Cheng-ming, and his works from this period exhibit the refined and subtle qualities of Wen's style. A rift developed between the two after the death of Ch'en's father in 1516, when Ch'en began to turn to Taoism and Buddhism, developing an unrestrained lifestyle that offended his conservative mentor and friend. In 1519 Ch'en left Su-chou to study at the Imperial Academy in Peking; when he returned in 1523 Wen Ch'eng-ming was no longer in Su-chou, having been summoned to Peking to serve at the Han-lin Academy.

Ch'en's journey to Peking, together with his Buddhist and Taoist inclinations, broadened his approach to art. Ch'en used his natural talents to liberate his painting style from Wen Cheng-ming's influence and looked to the expressive landscape and ink flower paintings of Shen Chou for models. In calligraphy, too, his style broadened and relaxed. After he reached the age of forty, he primarily used the rapid running and cursive scripts, rejecting the more meticulous regular script of his earlier pieces. The dynamic natural style of his later writings is based on the styles of Yang Ning-shih and Li Huai-lin (both fl. 10th century).

*Mallows and Garden Rock* shows the boldness and richness of Ch'en Ch'un's ink flowers in comparison with Wen Cheng-ming's (fig. a) or even Shen Chou's (fig. b). The subject matter of the Princeton painting reflects Ming literati taste: flowers grouped around an eroded, grotesquely shaped Lake T'ai rock is an arrangement borrowed from Chinese garden design. The painting's composition is daring, offering a close-up view of mallows, which occupy nearly three-quarters of the picture plane. The eye-catching effect of the painting is further enhanced by the strong contrast between the dark, solid rock against the light,

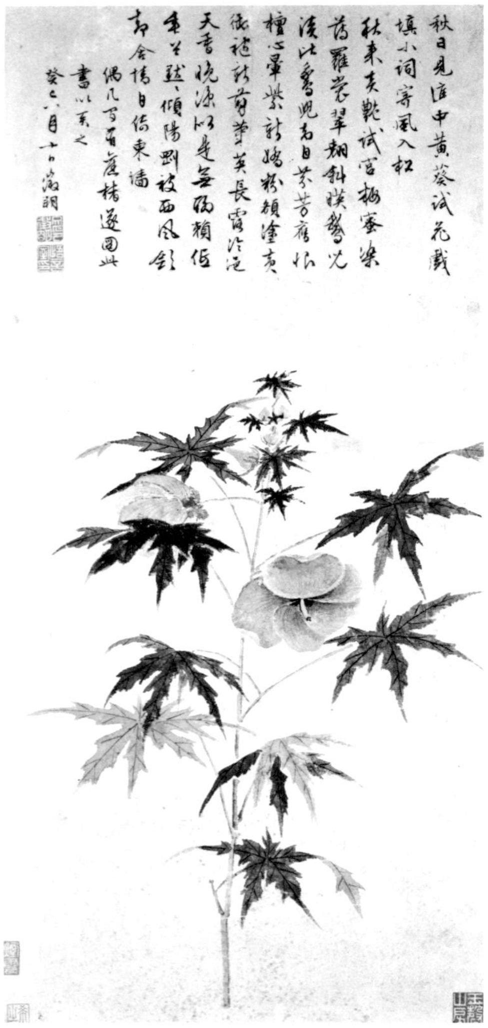

Fig. a. Wen Cheng-ming, *Mallows* (*Ch'iu-k'uei*). Dated 1533. Album leaf, ink on paper. 65.4 x 30.3 cm (25¾ x 11⅞ in.). National Palace Museum, Taipei

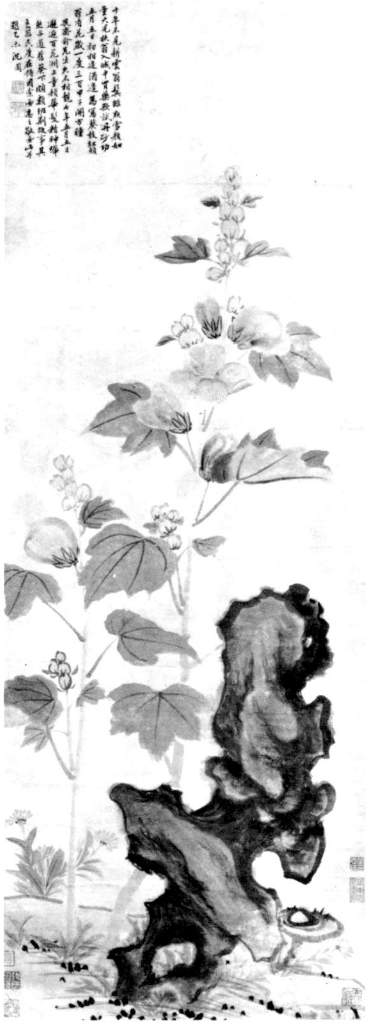

Fig. b. Shen Chou, *Rose Mallows* (*Shu-k'uei*). Dated 1475. Hanging scroll, ink and color on paper. 126.5 x 39.6 cm (4 ft. 1 in. x 15⅝ in.). Nelson Gallery–Atkins Museum, Kansas City

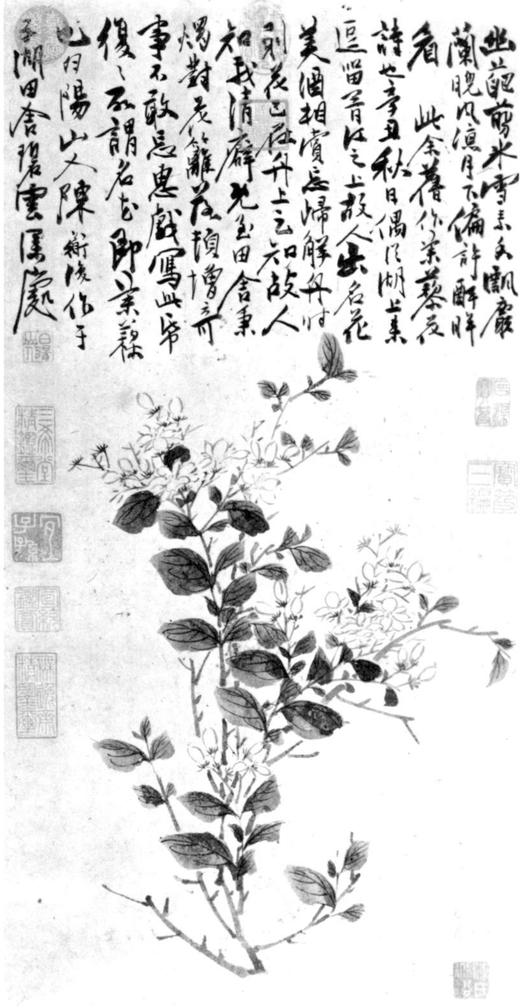

Fig. c. Ch'en Ch'un, *White Jasmine Flowers* (*Mo-li*). Dated 1541. Hanging scroll, ink on paper. 58.3 x 30.4 cm (23 x 12 in.). National Palace Museum, Taipei

fragile flowers and the smooth, curving blossoms next to pointed palmate leaves. Moist ink washes and spontaneous brushwork give the painting a three-dimensional presence.

The calligraphy in the upper right-hand corner of the painting conveys a simultaneously relaxed and dynamic impression through the elongated formation of individual characters, the asymmetrical composition, and the uneven yet decisive brushstrokes.[2] These features also characterize Ch'en Ch'un's inscription on *White Jasmine Flowers* (*Mo-li*), a piece dated to 1541 (fig. c). The stylistic similarities between these two writings indicate that the Princeton painting was also executed in 1541, when Ch'en Ch'un was fifty-seven.

Pao-chen Ch'en

NOTES

1. For further biographical information, see Ch'en Pao-chen, *Ch'en Ch'un yen-chiu* (A study of Ch'en Ch'un) (Taipei: National Palace Museum, 1978).
2. For the poem, see Ch'en Ch'un, *Ch'en Pai-yang chi* (The collected works of Ch'en Ch'un) (1615; repr. ed., Taipei: Hsüeh-sheng shu-chü, 1973), p. 226. Ch'en Ch'un often inscribed this poem on his paintings of mallows.

# 24 Wang Tao-k'un (1525–1593)

## *Landscape (Shan-shui)*

Dated 1585
Hanging scroll, ink on silk
151.0 x 57.8 cm (4 ft. $11\frac{1}{2}$ in. x $22\frac{3}{4}$ in.)

ARTIST'S SIGNATURE: In the autumn of the *i-yu* year [1585], Nan-min, Wang Tao-k'un painted this.

ARTIST'S SEALS: Wang Tao-k'un yin (square intaglio); Tzu Yü-ch'ing (square relief).

Edward L. Elliott Family Collection (L53.70)

PUBLISHED: Suzuki Kei, comp., *Chūgoku kaiga sōgō zuroku: daiikkan, Amerika–Kanada hen* (Comprehensive illustrated catalogue of Chinese paintings: volume 1, American and Canadian collections) (Tokyo: University of Tokyo Press, 1982), p. 129, pl. A17–042.

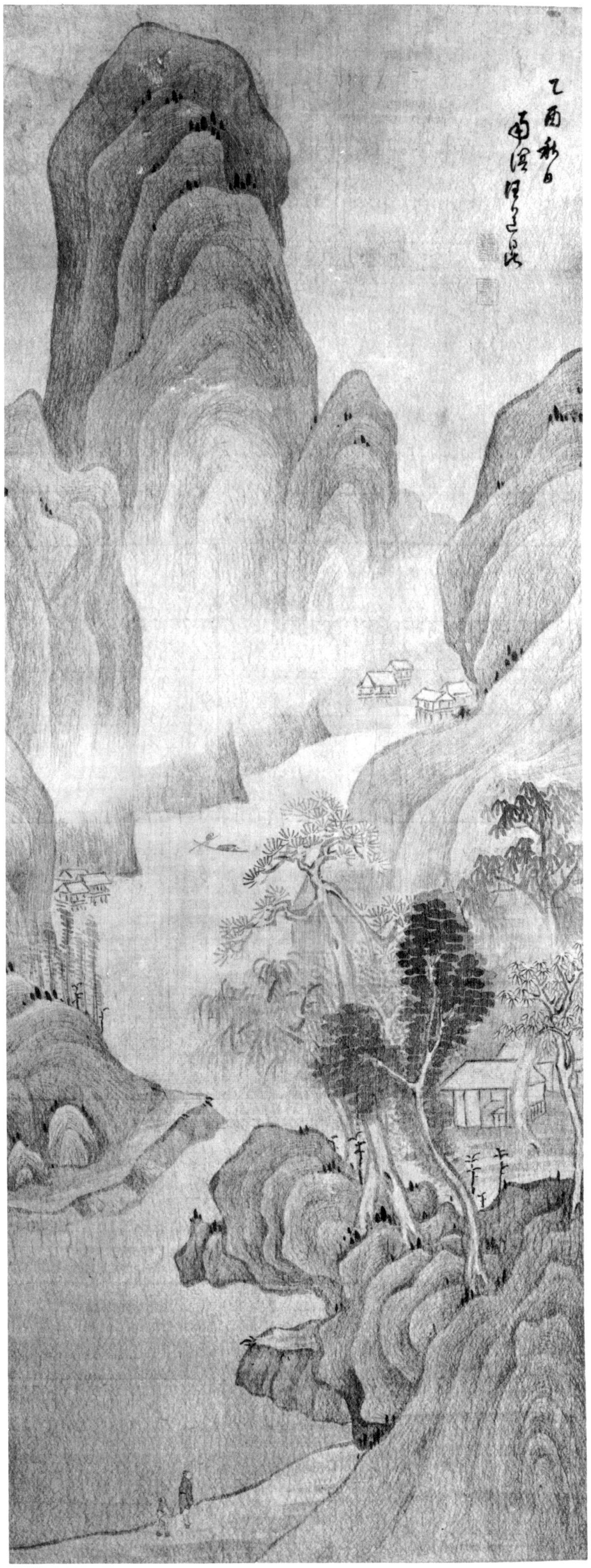

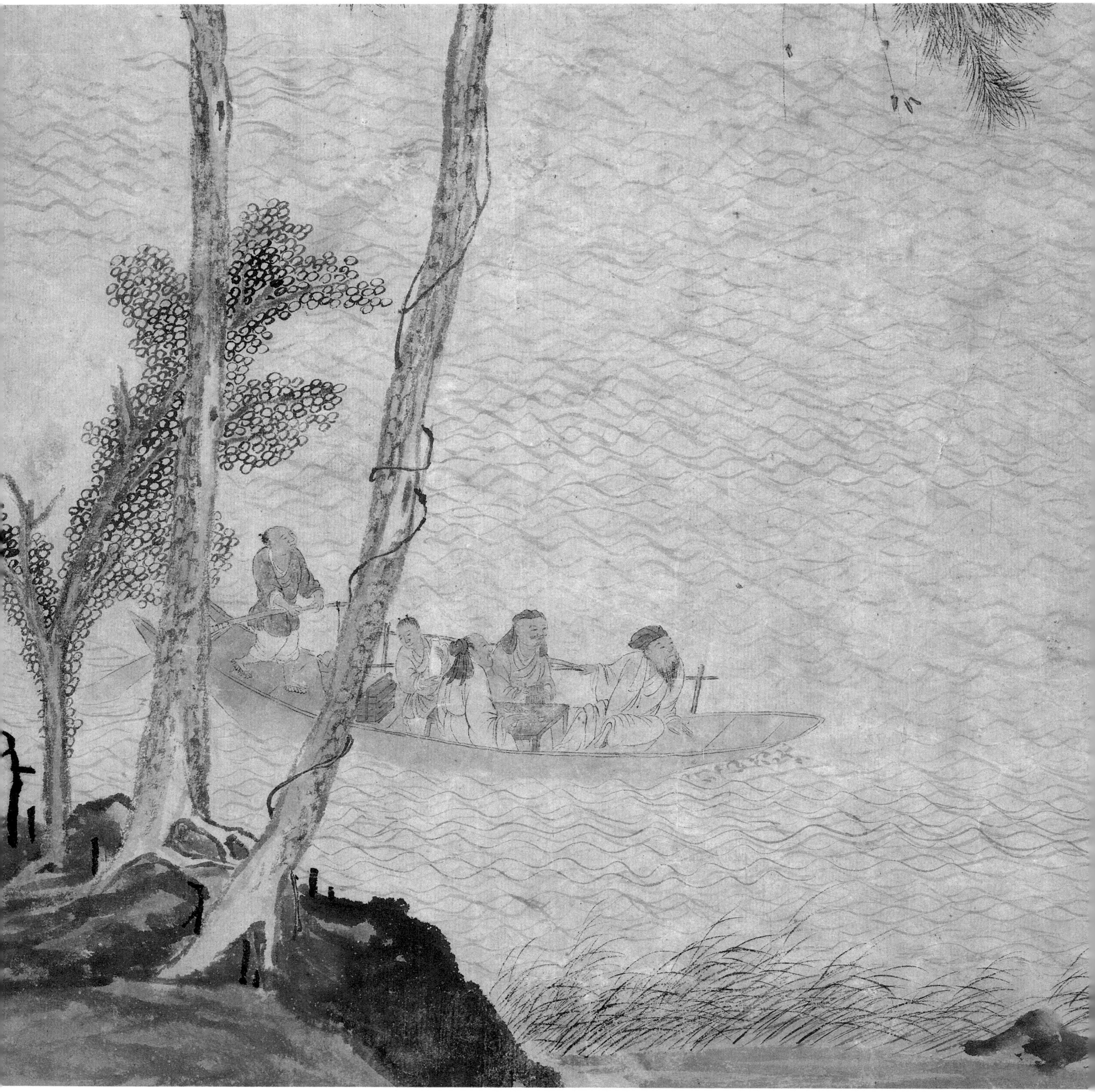

# 25 Chü Chieh (ca. 1531–1585)

## *Red Cliff (Ch'ih-pi yu)*

Dated 1575
Hanging scroll, ink and color on paper
90.0 x 40.7 cm (35½ x 16 in.)

ARTIST'S INSCRIPTION (3 character title in 1 column of clerical script): "Boating under the Red Cliff" ["Ch'ih-pi yu"].

ARTIST'S SIGNATURE: In the autumn of the *i-hai* year of the Wan-li era [1575], Chü Chieh painted this.

ARTIST'S SEAL: Chü Chieh yin (square intaglio).

COLLECTOR'S SEAL: Ma Chi-tso (modern collector): Ma Chi-tso yin (square relief; lower right).

Edward L. Elliott Family Collection (L225.70)

PUBLISHED: Suzuki Kei, comp., *Chūgoku kaiga sōgō zuroku: daiikkan, Amerika–Kanada hen* (Comprehensive illustrated catalogue of Chinese paintings: volume 1, American and Canadian collections) (Tokyo: University of Tokyo Press, 1982), p. 128, pl. A17–023.

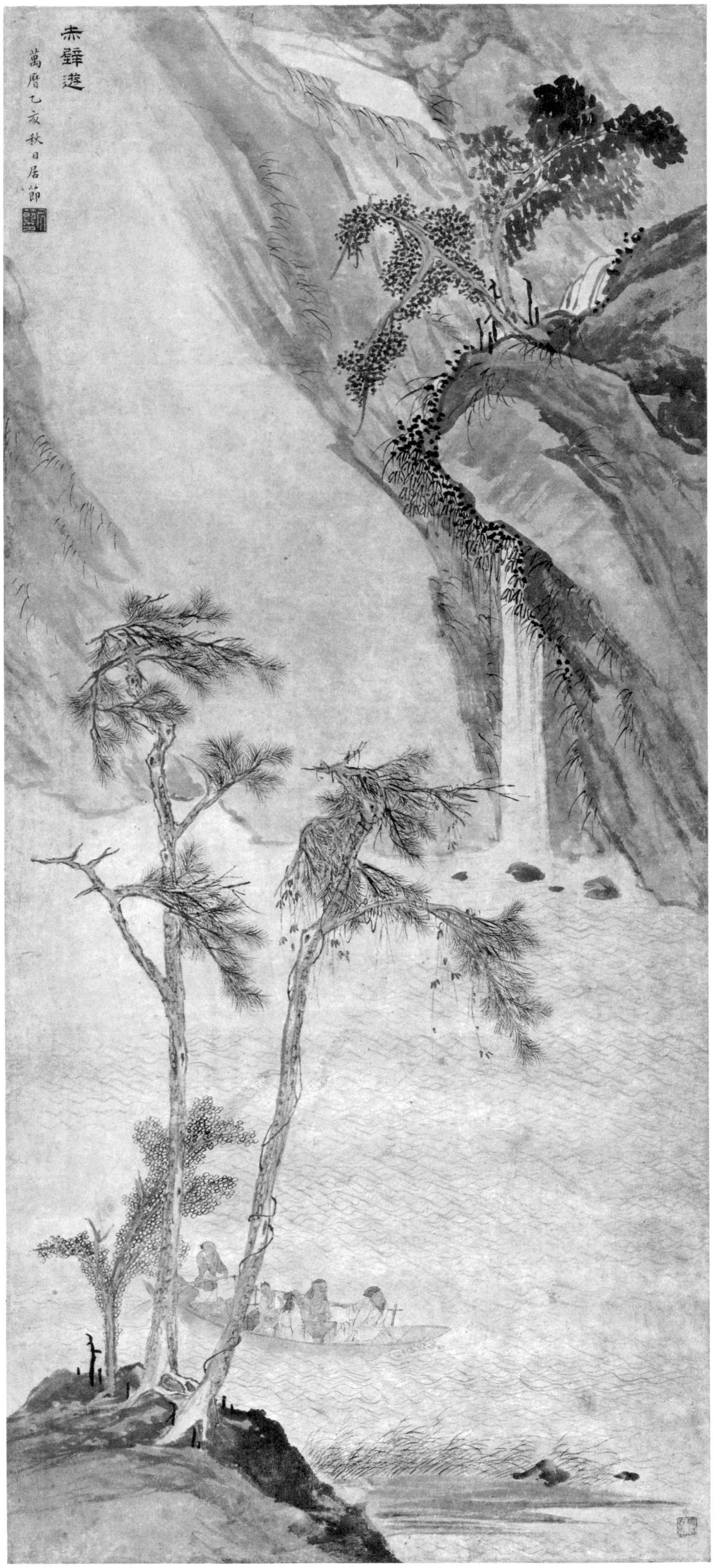

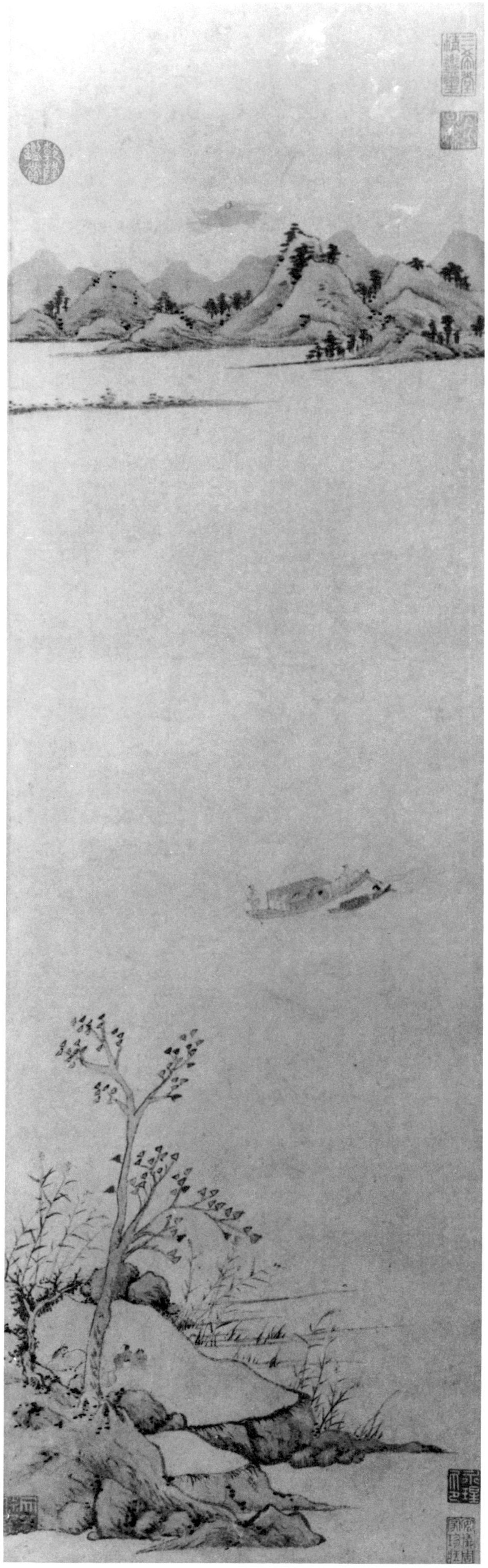

Fig. a. Wen Chia, detail, *Song of the Lute* (*P'i-p'a-hsing*). Dated 1563. Hanging scroll, ink and color on paper. 149.8 x 29.8 cm (4 ft. 11 in. x 11¾ in.). Osaka Municipal Museum of Fine Art

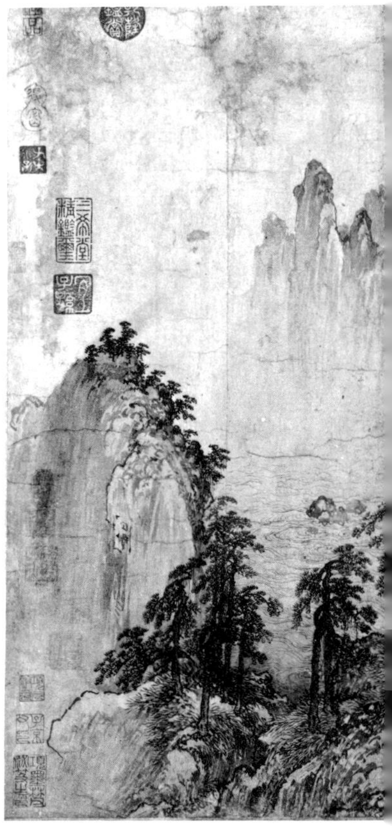

Fig. b. Wu Yüan-chih, *Red Cliff* (*Ch'ih-pi t'u*). Undated, ca. 1196. Handscroll, ink on paper. 50.8 x 136.4 cm (20 in. x 4 ft. 5¾ in.). National Palace Museum, Taipei

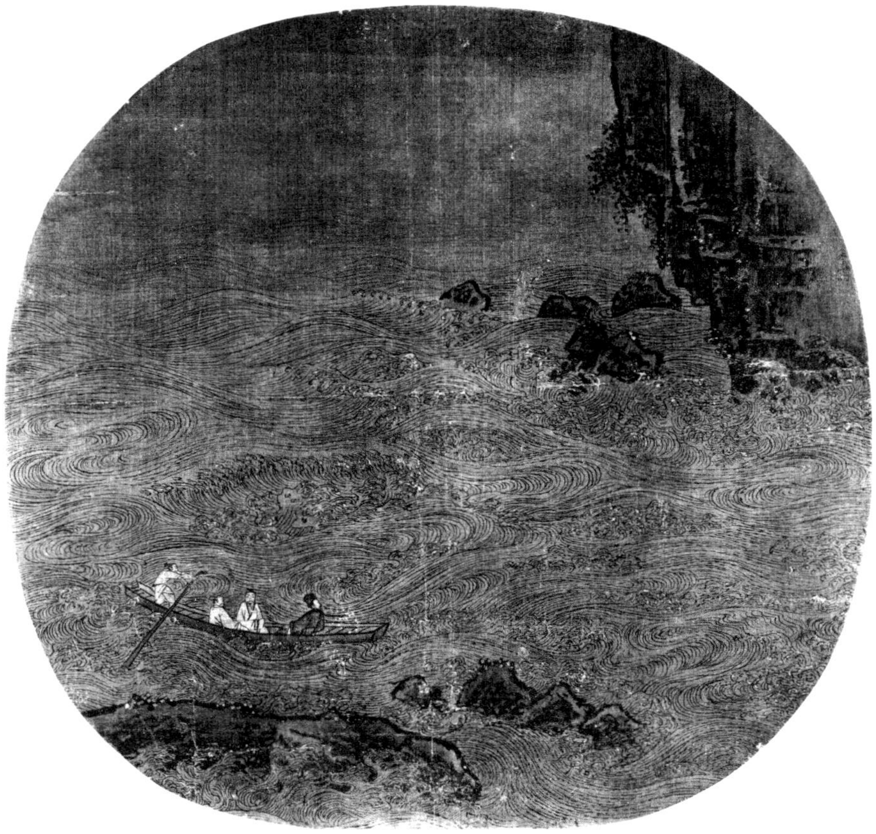

Fig. c. Li Sung, *Red Cliff (Ch'ih-pi t'u)*. Undated, late 12th–early 13th century. Album leaf mounted as a hanging scroll, ink and color on silk. 24.8 x 26.0 cm (9¾ x 10¼ in.). Nelson Gallery–Atkins Museum, Kansas City

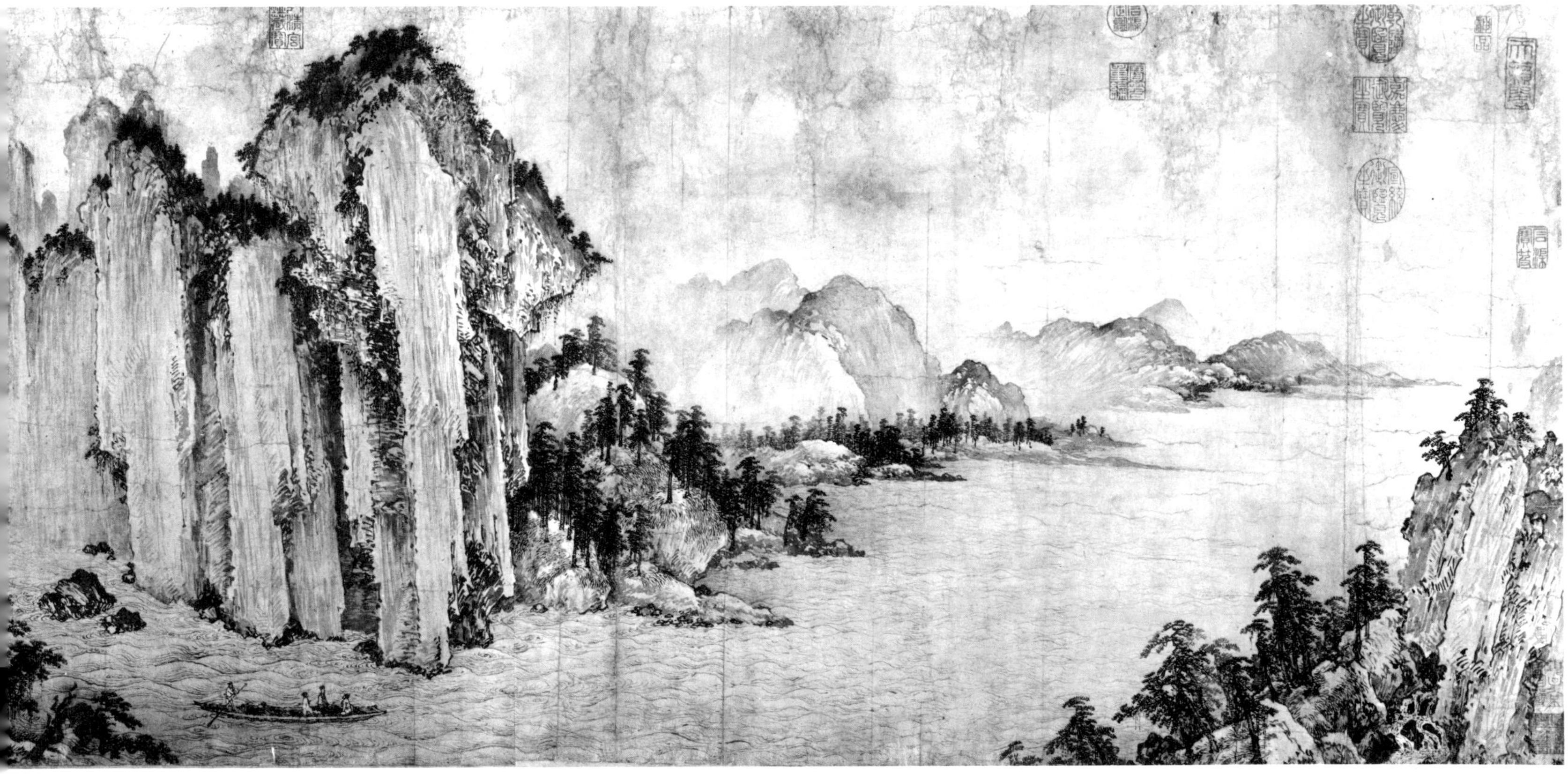

MOST MING PAINTERS from the Su-chou area worked in the orbit of Wen Cheng-ming (1470–1559). Chü Chieh (*tzu*, Shih-chen, Ping-chung; *hao*, Shang-ku) was no exception.[1] He studied painting with Wen's second son, Wen Chia (1501–1583), about 1541.[2] The landscape *Red Cliff* owes much to the Wen family style, especially the densely dotted tree foliage and the meticulously brushed figures.

The painting is a romantic narrative illustrating the prose poem of the same title by Su Shih (1036–1101). The scene depicts Su Shih's visit to the historic site of the Red Cliff (Ch'ih-pi), Hupei province, where the military alliance of Liu Pei (A.D. 162–223) and Sun Ch'üan (A.D. 182–255) defeated the army led by Ts'ao Ts'ao (A.D. 155–220) in A.D. 218. In this composition the foreground and background are split by a diagonally receding river; both banks tilt upward to the left. In the lower left triangle an earthen mound in the foreground supports a round-leafed deciduous tree and two pines, so tall that they overlap the base of the distant monumental cliff in the upper right. Behind the pines Su Shih, two friends, a serving boy, and an oarsman are boating on the river. A compositional type in which detailed figure activities appear in a lower corner, in contrast to simplified mountains in an upper corner, is common in Wu School paintings, typified by an example by Wen Chia, *Song of the Lute* (*P'i-p'a-hsing*; fig. a).

The figures are depicted by thin, refined iron-wire (*t'ieh-hsien*) brushstrokes while most of the landscape elements are represented with simple light, moist vegetable pigments in soft hues. The overall atmosphere appears warm and inviting, which contrasts with the dynamic and heroic expressions of the same subject matter by Wu Yüan-chih (fl. ca. 1190s; fig. b) and Li Sung (fl. 1190–1230; fig. c). Intimacy, subtlety, and lyricism were important aesthetic values for Wu School painters when interpreting romantic subject matter, such as the poems "Red Cliff" and "Song of the Lute."

PAO-CHEN CH'EN

NOTES

1. Hsü Hsin, *Ming hua-lu* (Record of Ming painters), Mei-shu ts'ung-shu, vol. 3 (Taipei: Kuang-wen shu-chü, 1963), pt. 7, p. 31.

2. Chiang Chao-shen, *Wen Cheng-ming yü Su-chou hua-t'an* (Wen Cheng-ming and the Wu School painters) (Taipei: National Palace Museum, 1977), p. 196.

# 26 Tung Ch'i-ch'ang (1555–1636)

*Calligraphy in the Styles of the Four Sung Masters (Fang Su Huang Mi Tsai hsing-shu)*

Undated
Handscroll, ink on paper
55.0 x 933.5 cm (21⅝ in. x 30 ft. 7½ in.)

CALLIGRAPHY:

1. Transcription of prose by Su Shih (1036–1101) in 14 columns of running script.
2. Transcription of a 7 character quatrain by Huang T'ing-chien (1045–1105) in 7 columns of running script.
3. Transcription of 2 poems by Mi Fu (1052–1107), 5 character regulated verse in 8 lines, followed by a 7 character quatrain in 22 columns of running script.
4. Transcription of a 7 character quatrain by Tsai Hsiang (1012–1067) in 6 columns of running script.

ARTIST'S INSCRIPTION: In the calligraphy styles of Su Shih, Huang T'ing-chien, Mi Fu, and Tsai Hsiang.

ARTIST'S SIGNATURE: Ch'i-ch'ang.

ARTIST'S SEALS: Hsüan-tsai shih (square relief); Ta-tsung-po chang (square intaglio).

COLLECTORS' SEALS:
Ts'ao Jung (1613–1685), 2 seals.
Ta Ch'ung-kuang (1623–1692), 1 seal.
Kao Shih-ch'i (1645–1704), 7 seals.
Emperor Ch'ing Kao-tsung (r. 1736–95), 11 seals.
Wu Jung-kuang (1773–1843), 1 seal.
Emperor Ch'ing Jen-tsung (r. 1796–1820), 4 seals.
Wu Yün (1811–1883), 3 seals.
Li Chia-fu (1839–1904), 1 seal.
Unidentified owner, 1 seal.

John B. Elliott Collection (L87.83)

PUBLISHED: *Fine Chinese Ceramics, Paintings and Works of Art* (New York: Christie, Manson and Woods International, 1983), pp. 252–56, no. 673.

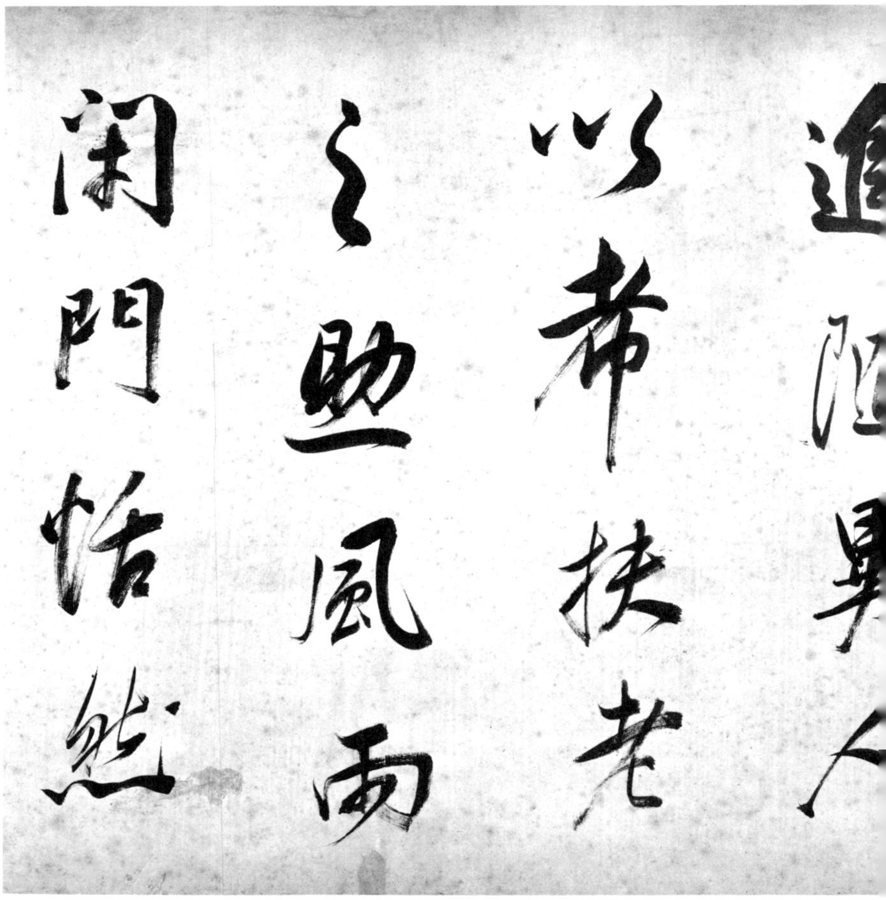

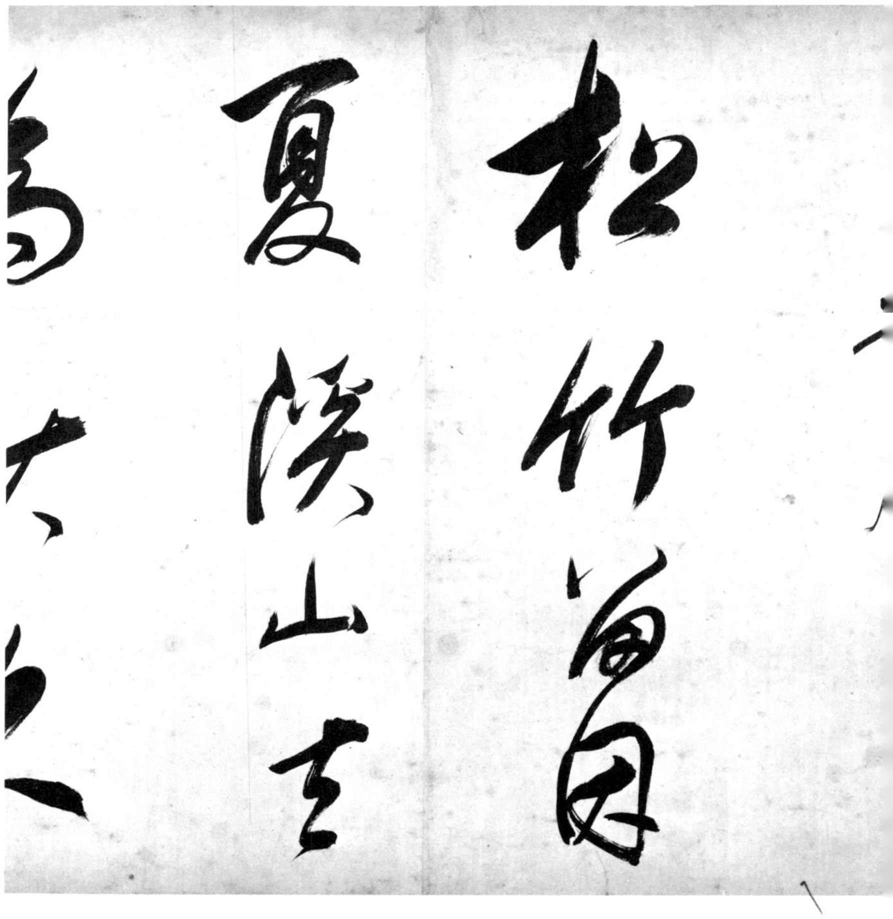

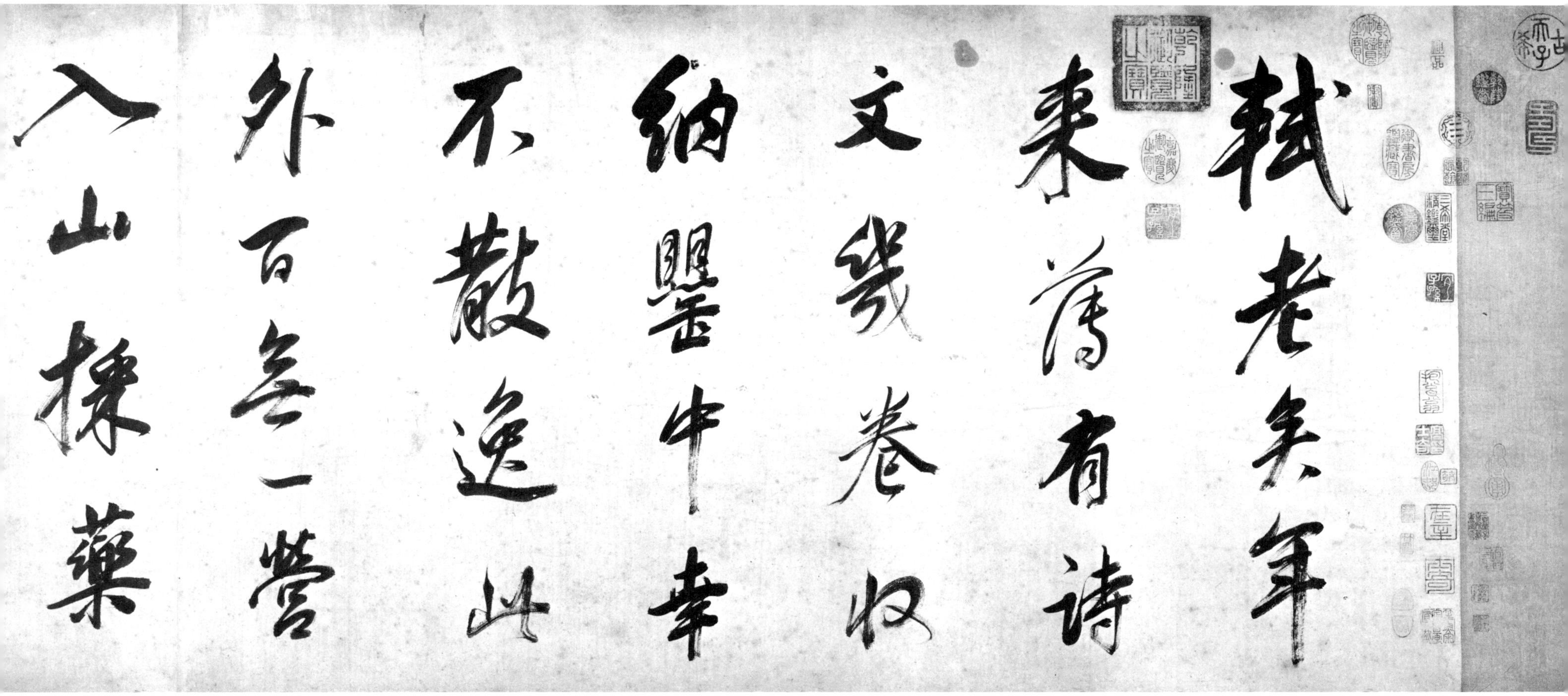
軾老矣年
來屢有詩
文幾卷收
納囊中幸
不散逸此
外百念一營
入山採藥

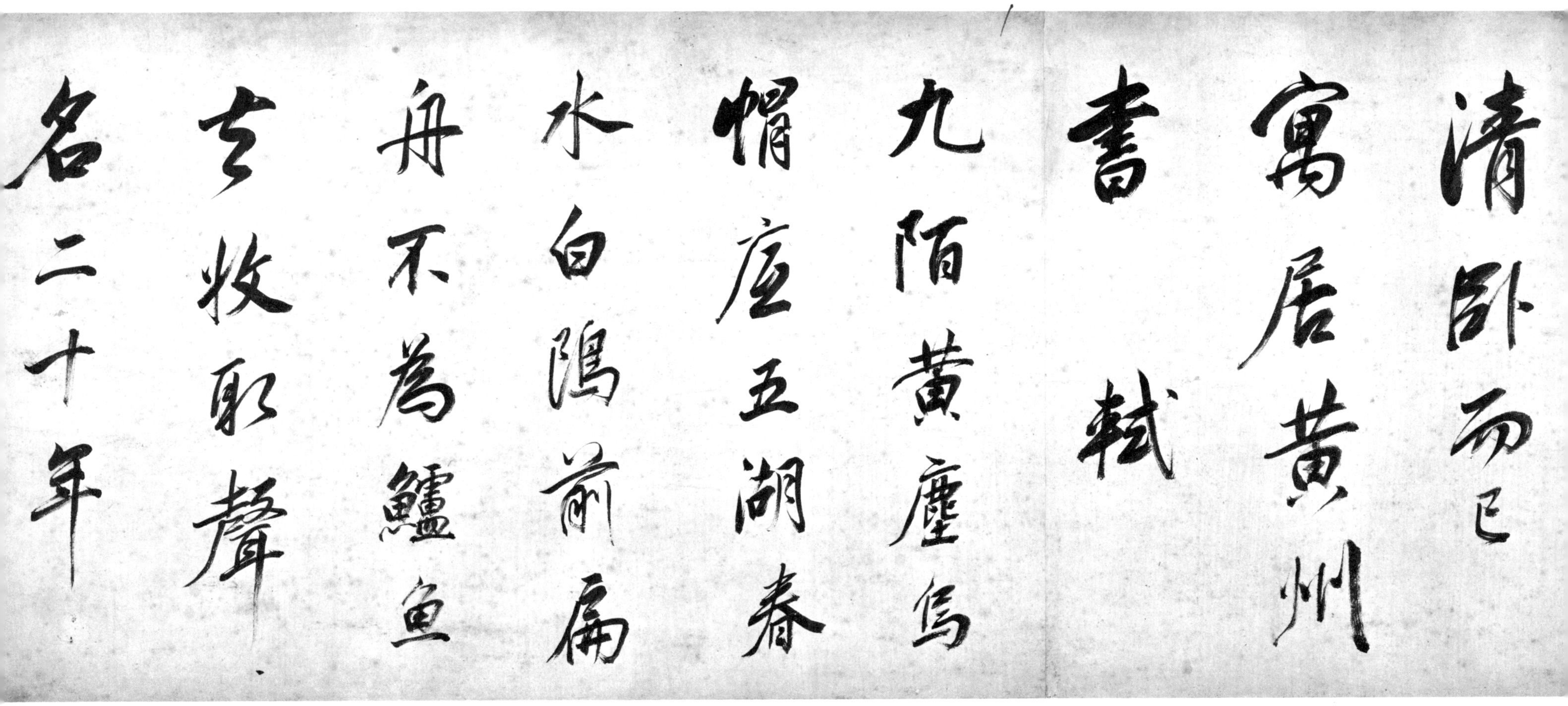
清卧而已
寓居黄州
書 軾
九陌黄塵烏
帽底五湖春
水白鷗前扁
舟不為鱸魚
去收取聲
名二十年

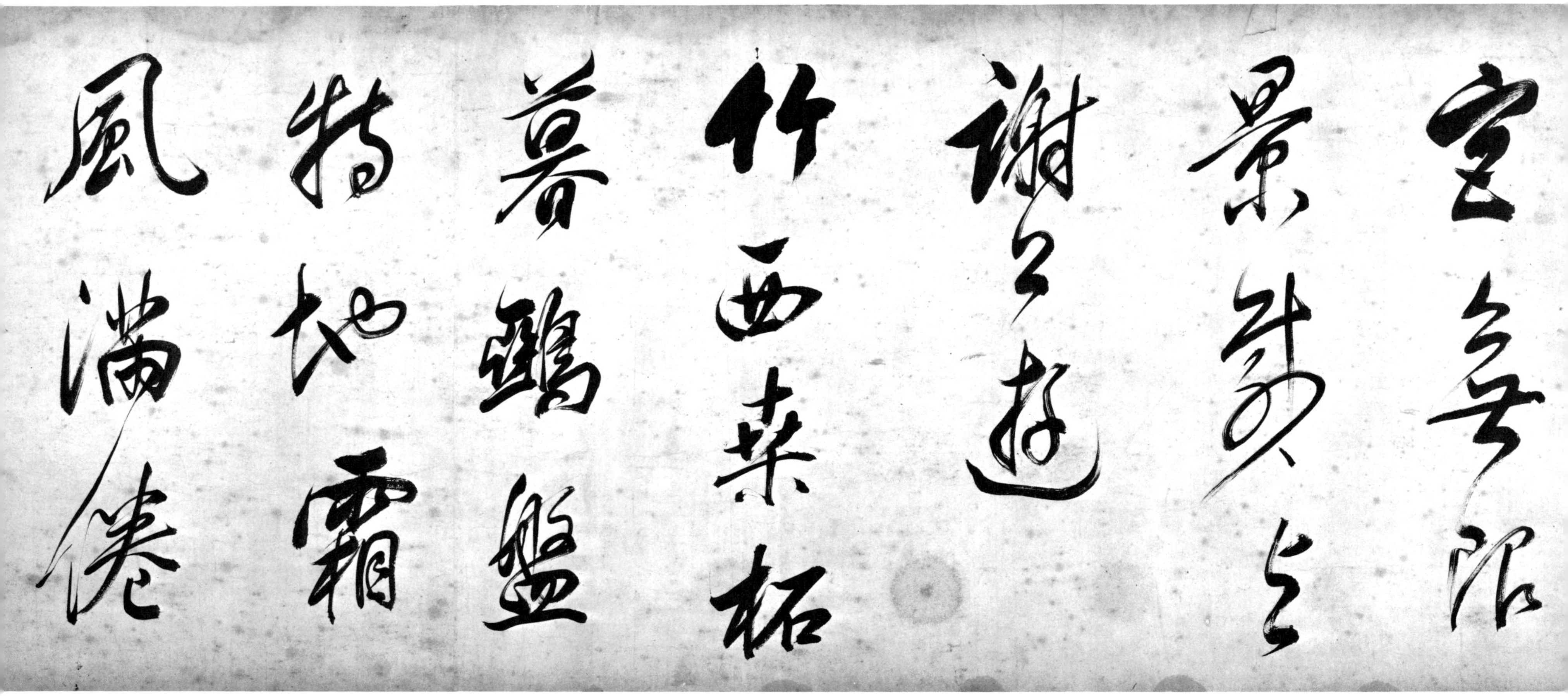

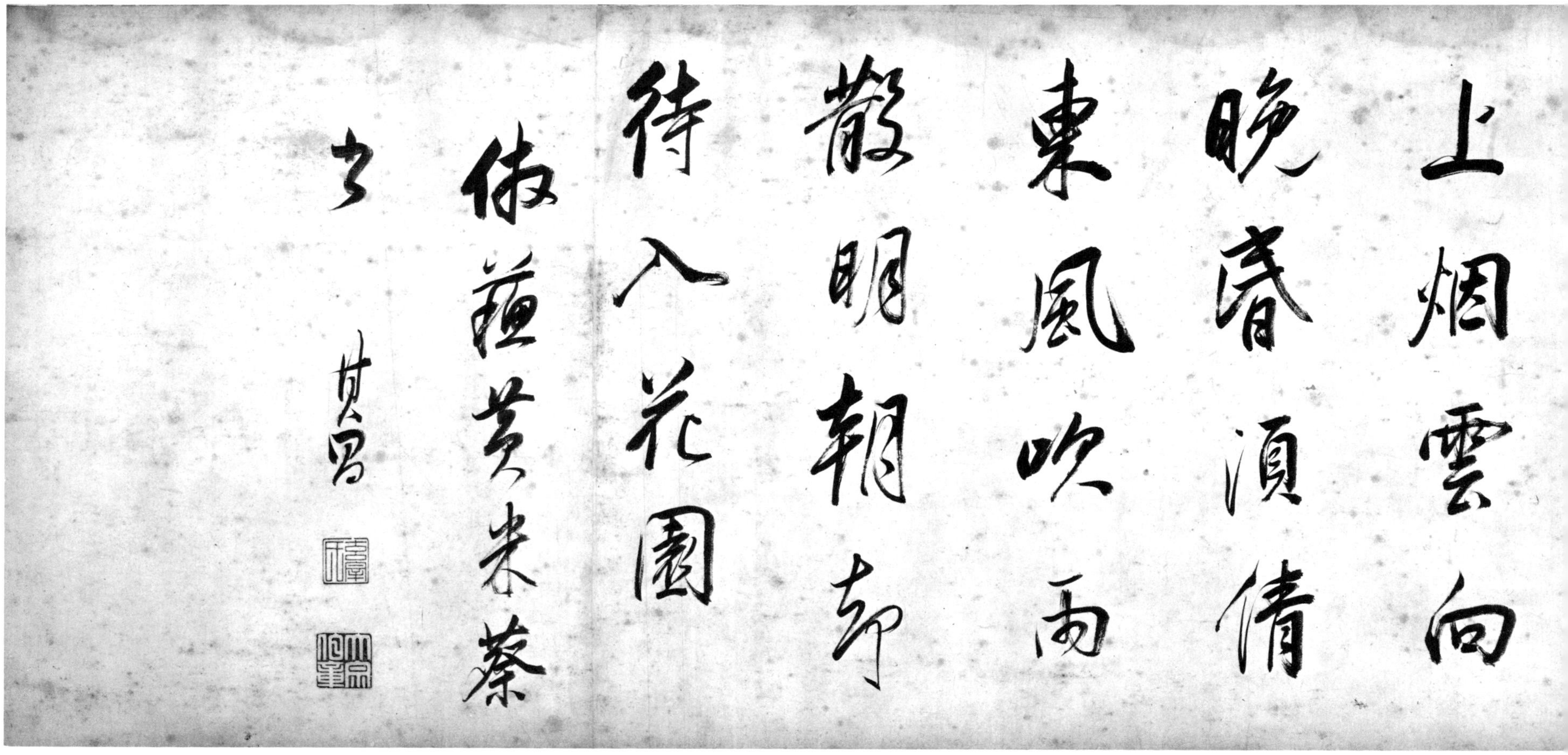
上烟雲向
晚春須倩
東風吹雨
待入花園
仿蘇黃米蔡
之
其昌

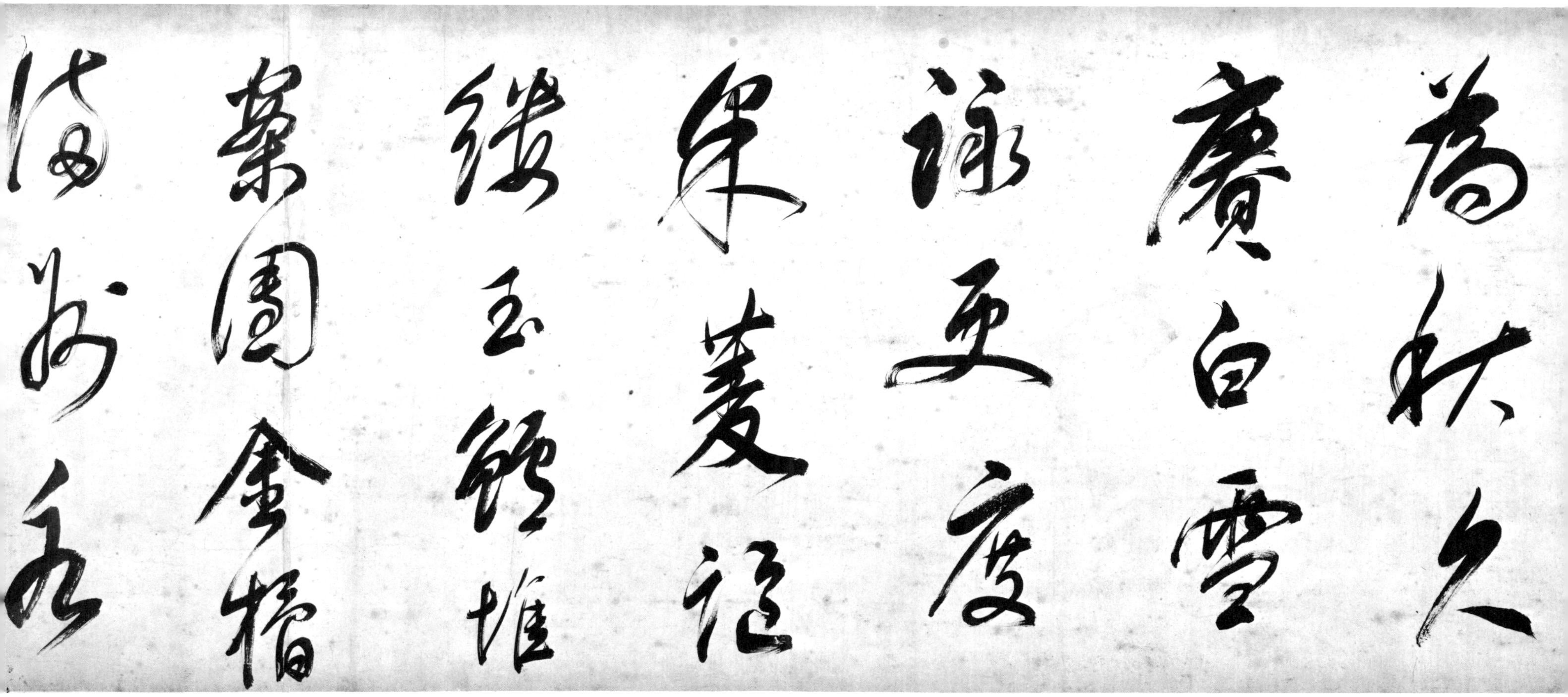

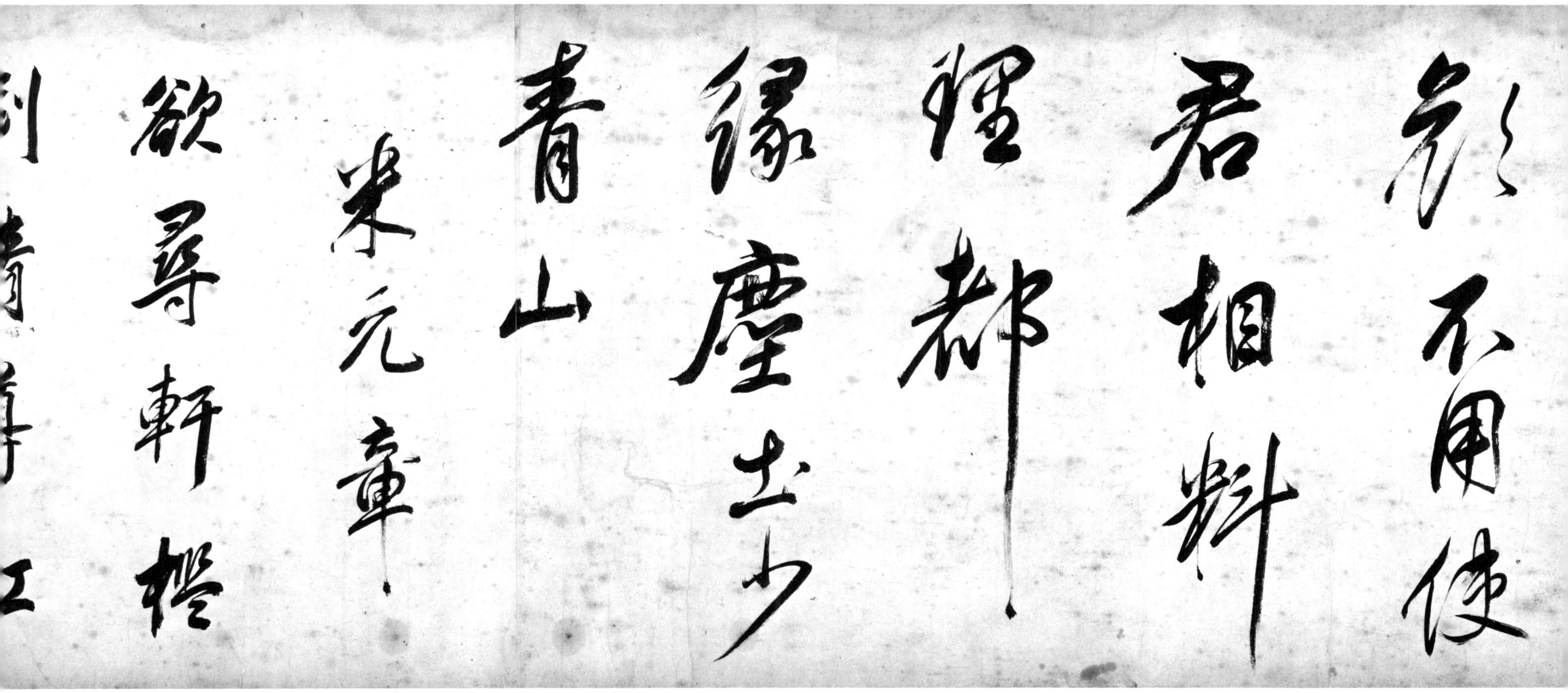
影不用使
君相料
理都
緣塵土少
青山
米元章
欲尋軒檻

# 27 Li Liu-fang (1575–1629)

## *Landscapes (Shan-shui ts'e)*

Dated 1625
Album of eight leaves (A–H), ink on gold-flecked paper
Average measurements, each leaf: 23.0 x 15.6 cm (9 x 6 1/8 in.)

ARTIST'S INSCRIPTION (11 characters in 2 columns of running script): On an autumn day in the *i-ch'ou* year [1625], while in the Chien-t'ui Studio in T'an-yüan, [Li Liu-fang] painted this.

ARTIST'S SIGNATURE: Li Liu-fang.

ARTIST'S SEALS: Li Liu-fang yin (square intaglio; all except B); Ch'ang-heng (square intaglio; all except B).

Edward L. Elliott Family Collection (L48.70)

PUBLISHED: Suzuki Kei, comp., *Chūgoku kaiga sōgō zuroku: daiikkan, Amerika–Kanada hen* (Comprehensive illustrated catalogue of Chinese paintings: volume 1, American and Canadian collections) (Tokyo: University of Tokyo Press, 1982), p. 158, pl. A17–106.

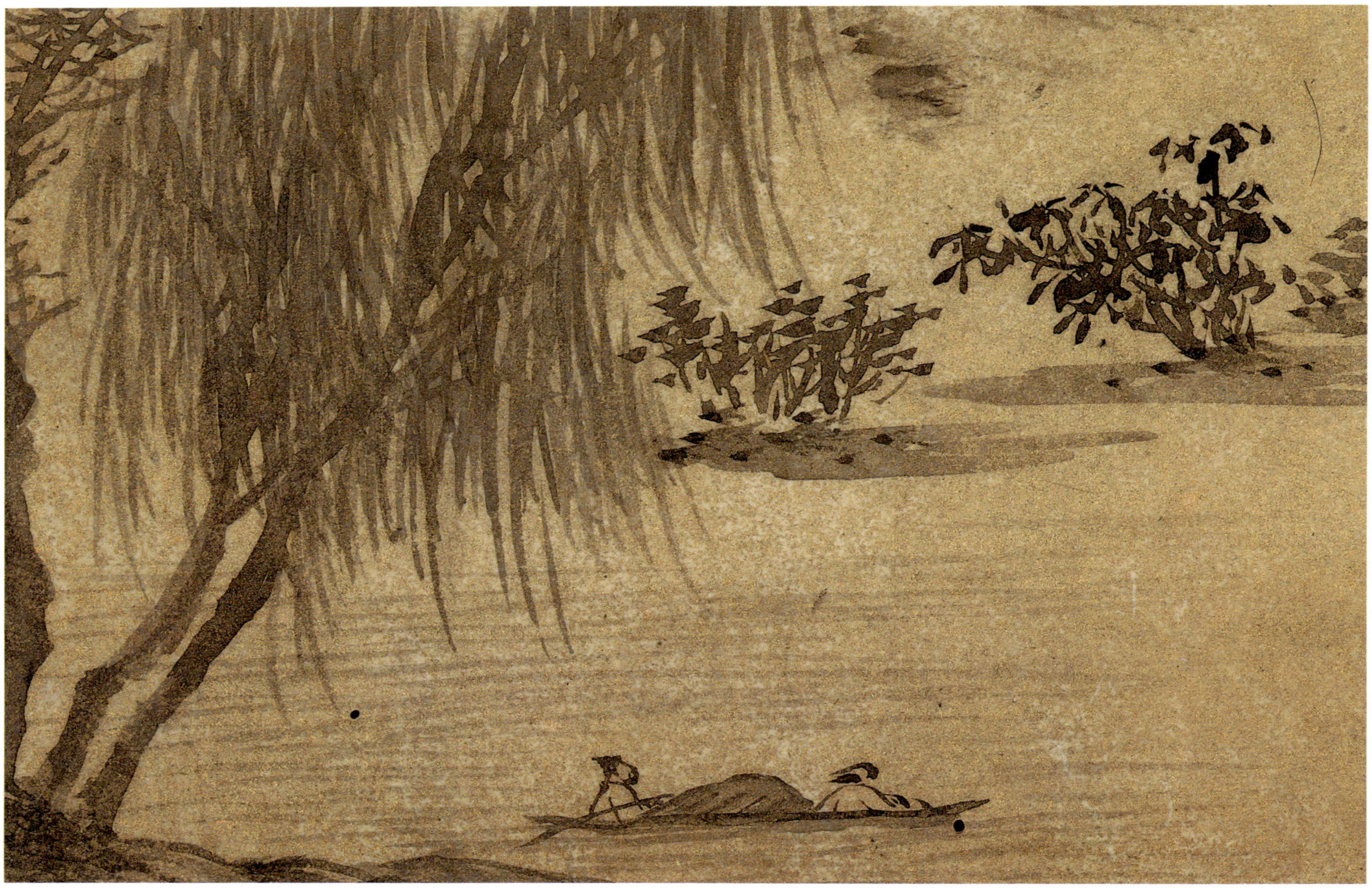

Leaf D, detail

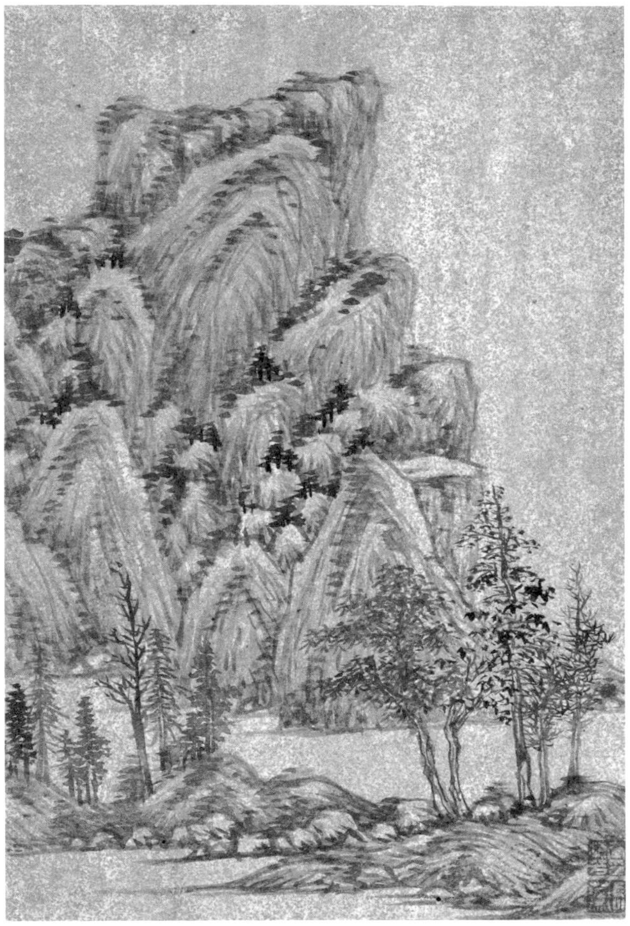

Leaf A

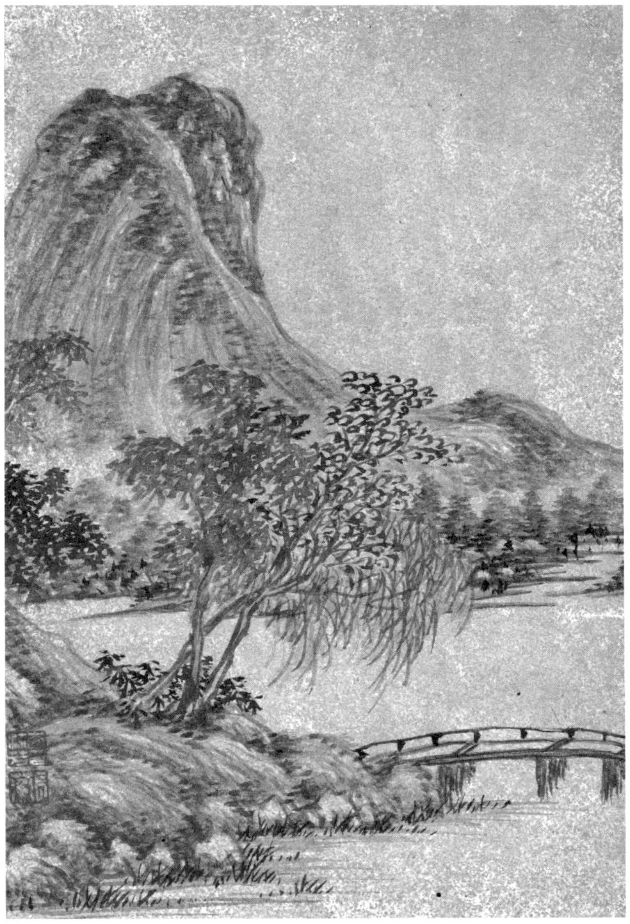

Leaf B

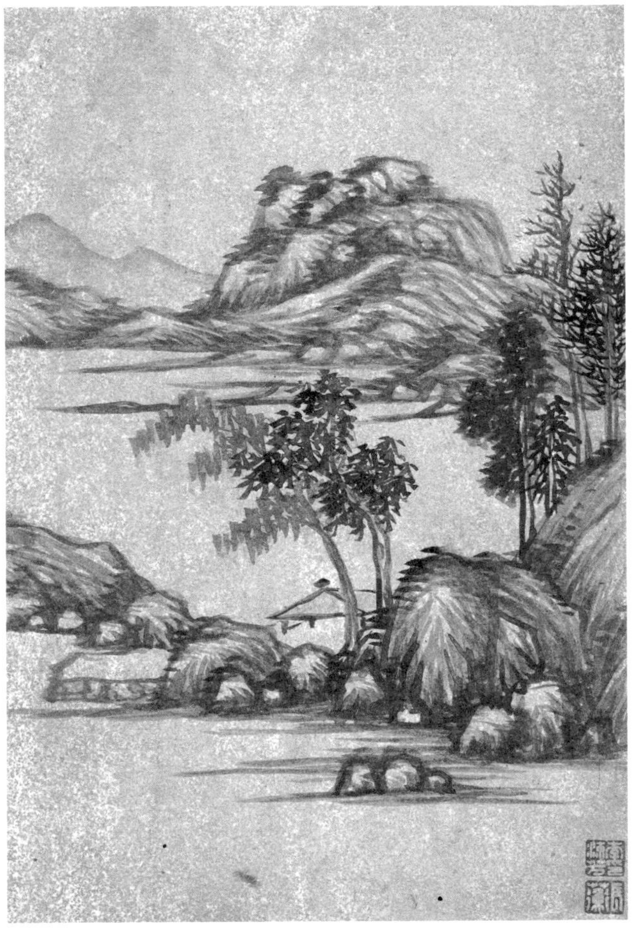

Leaf C

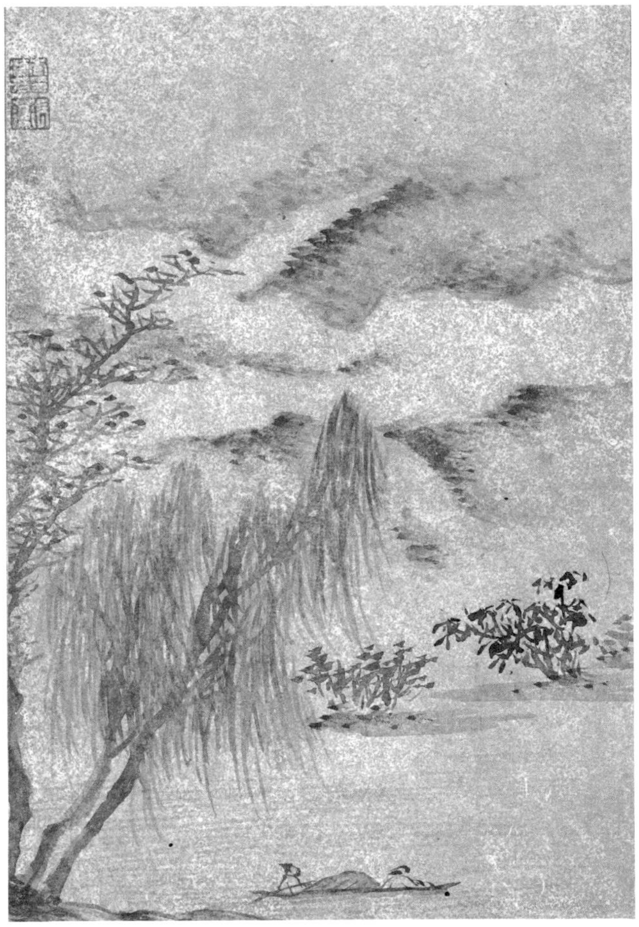

Leaf D

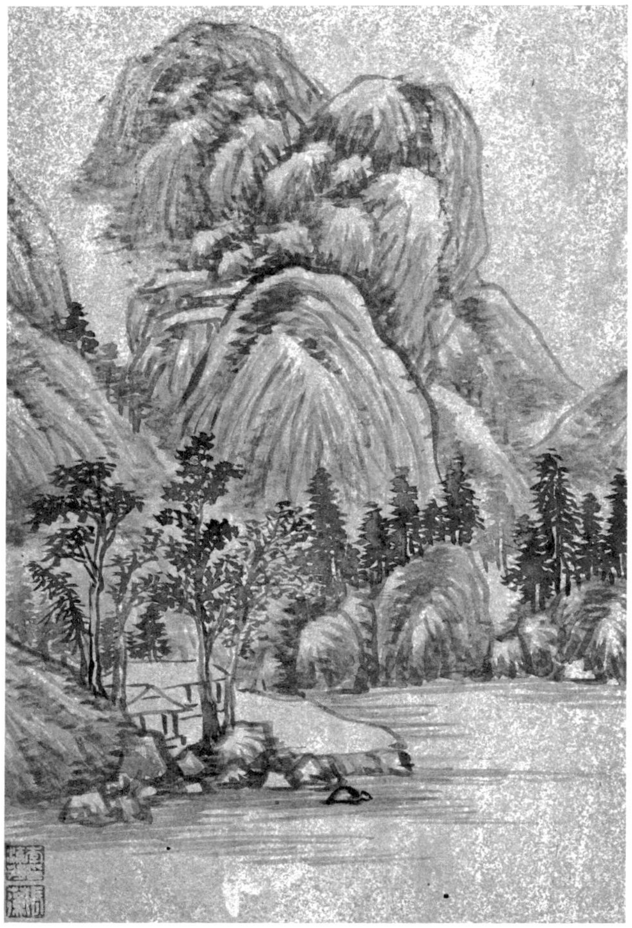

Leaf E

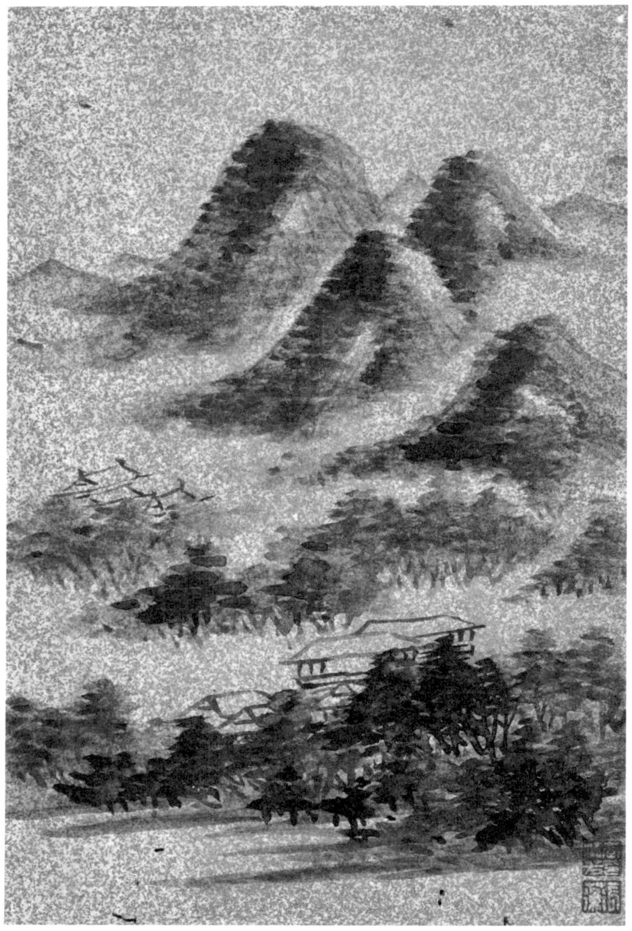

Leaf F

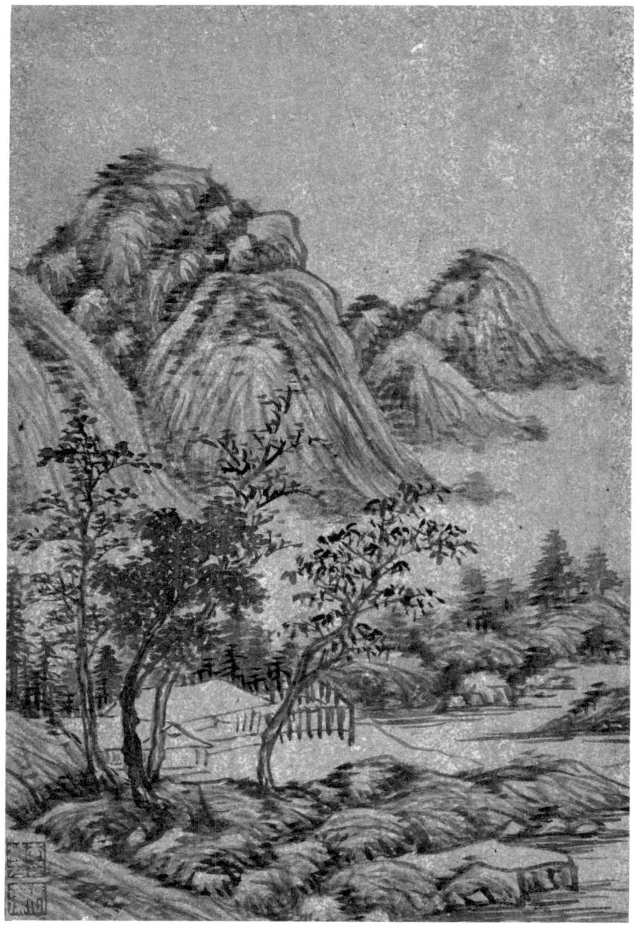

Leaf G

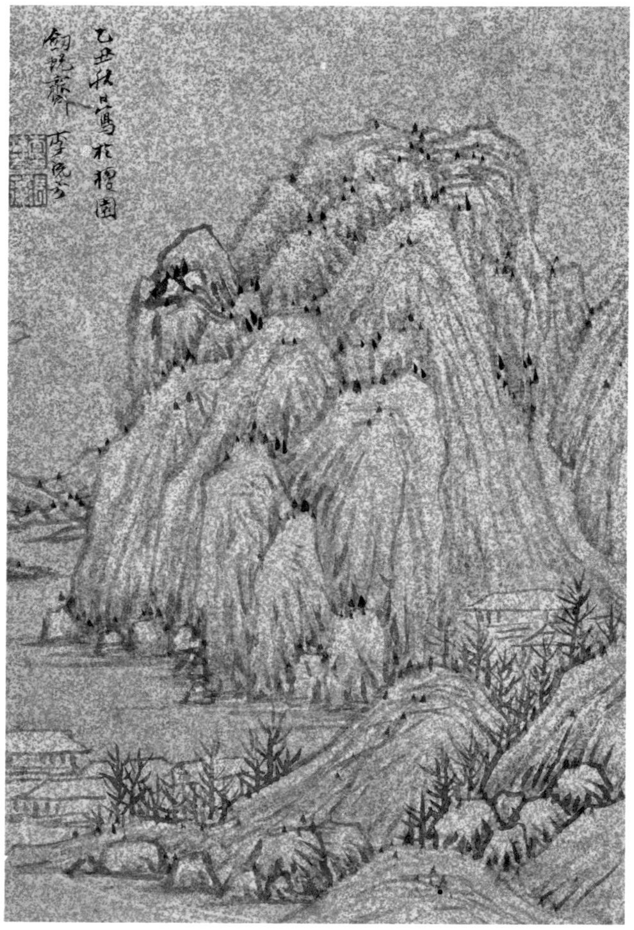


Leaf H

# 28 Wen Jen-kai (fl. late 16th century)

## *Landscapes after Sung and Yüan Masters (Fang Sung Yüan shan-shui ts'e)*

Dated 1584
Album of ten leaves of landscape painting (A–J) alternating with ten leaves of calligraphy (AA–JJ): painting (A,B, D–H, J), ink and color on silk (C,I), ink on silk; calligraphy, ink on gold-flecked paper
Average measurements, each leaf: 20.8 x 16.8 cm (8 1/8 x 6 5/8 in.)

PAINTING: Leaf A, "Boating under Willow Trees"; Leaf B, "Sailing on an Autumn River"; Leaf C, "Landscape in the Style of Wu Chen (1280–1354)"; Leaf D, "Landscape in the Style of Chao Meng-fu (1254–1322)"; Leaf E, "Landscape in the Style of Huang Kung-wang (1269–1354)"; Leaf F, "Landscape in the Style of Kao K'o-kung (1248–1310)"; Leaf G, "Landscape in the Style of Huang Kung-wang"; Leaf H, "Landscape in the Style of Wang Meng (1308–1385)"; Leaf I, "Landscape in the Style of Ni Tsan (1301–1374)"; Leaf J, "Snowscape."

ARTIST'S SIGNATURE: In the winter of the *chia-shen* year of the Wan-li era [1584], Wen Jen-kai from Ku-Wu [Chekiang province] made this (J).

ARTIST'S SEALS: Wen Jen-kai (tall rectangle relief; A, C, D, G, I); Wen Jen-kai yin (square intaglio; B, E); Wen Jen-kai (square intaglio; F, J); Chung-chi (double seal, both square relief; H).

COLOPHONS:
Leaf AA by Lü Kuang-shen (dates unknown): 7 character quatrain in 5 columns of free-form running script. Signature: Lü Kuang-shen. Seal: Tui-ming (square relief).

Leaf BB by Chu Keng (*chin-shih*, 1568): 7 character quatrain in 4 columns of cursive script. Signature: Chin-t'ing, Chu Keng. Seal: Shao-ch'in fu (square intaglio).

Leaf CC by Yang Wen-huan (dates unknown): 5 character quatrain in 3 columns of cursive script. Signature: Yang Wen-huan. Seals: Wen-huan (square relief); Yang Po-tzu yin (square intaglio).

Leaf DD by Lü Kuang-shen: 5 character quatrain in 4 columns of free-form running script. Signature: Lü Kuang-shen. Seal: Tui-ming (square relief).

Leaf EE by Yang Te-cheng (*chin-shih*, 1577): 5 character quatrain in 3 columns of cursive script. Signature: Ch'u-t'ing, Yang Te-cheng. Seal: Yang Te-cheng yin (square intaglio).

Leaf FF by Wang Huan (*chin-shih*, 1583): 7 character quatrain in 4 columns of running script. Signature: Wang Huan. Seals: Wang Huan (square relief); Ts'ui-wei-kuan yin (square intaglio).

Leaf GG by Shih K'o (*chin-shih*, 1571): 7 character quatrain in 4 columns of running script. Signature: Shih K'o. Seal: Ju-ho (square intaglio).

Leaf HH by Hu Shih-lin (dates unknown): 7 character quatrain in 4 columns of running script. Signature: Hu Shih-lin. Seal: Hu shih Ling-chao (square intaglio).

Leaf II by Chang Yüeh (*chin-shih*, 1559): 5 character quatrain in 4 columns of cursive script. Signature: Chang Yüeh. Seals: Ching-chai (square relief); Chang Chung-tzu chang (square intaglio).

Leaf JJ by Lü Kuang-shen: 7 character quatrain in 5 columns of cursive script. Signature: Tui-ming-shan-jen, Kuang-shen, inscribed this while drunk. Seals: Tui-ming (square relief); K'un-sun (tall rectangle intaglio).

Edward L. Elliott Family Collection (L234.70)

PUBLISHED: Ch'en Jen-t'ao, *Chin-kuei ts'ang-hua chi* (Chinese paintings from the King Kwei [Chin-kuei] collection) (Hong Kong: T'ung-ying, 1956), vol. 2, pl. 31 (Leaves H, J); Ch'en Jen-t'ao, *Chin-kuei ts'ang-hua p'ing-shih* (Annotated catalogue of paintings from the King Kwei [Chin-kuei] collection) (Hong Kong: T'ung-ying, 1956), vol. 2, pp. 152–55.

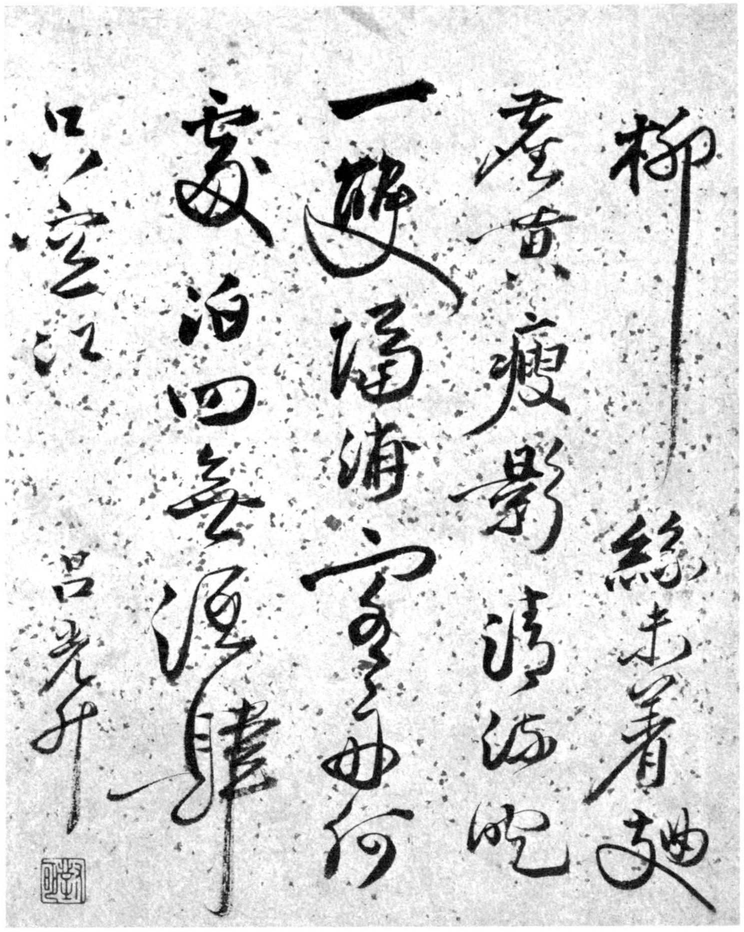

Leaf AA by Lü Kuang-shen

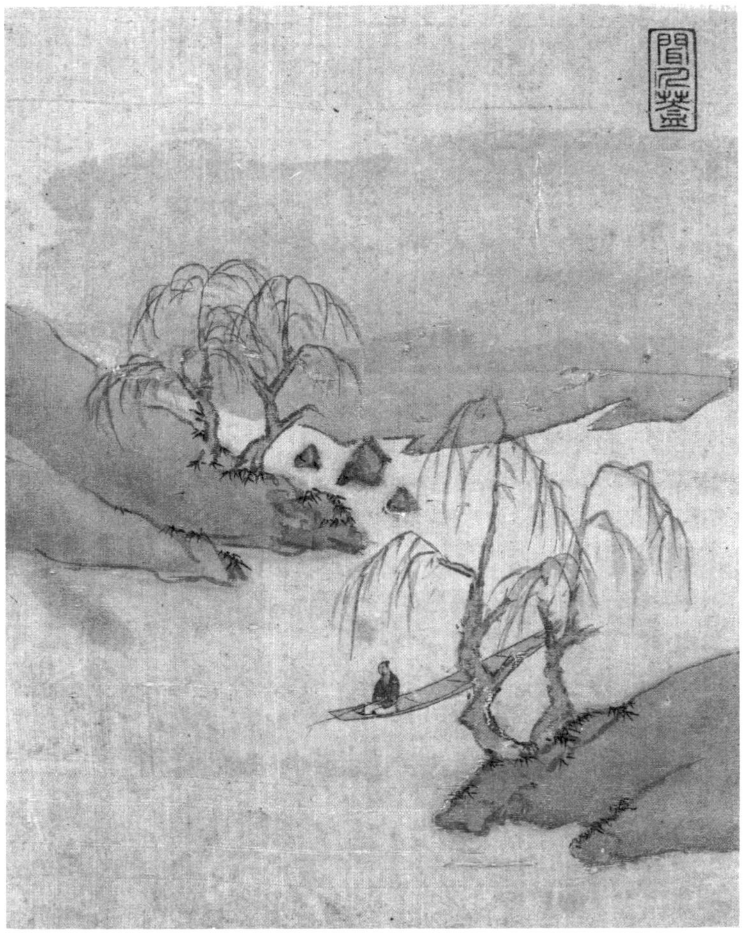

Leaf A, "Boating under Willow Trees"

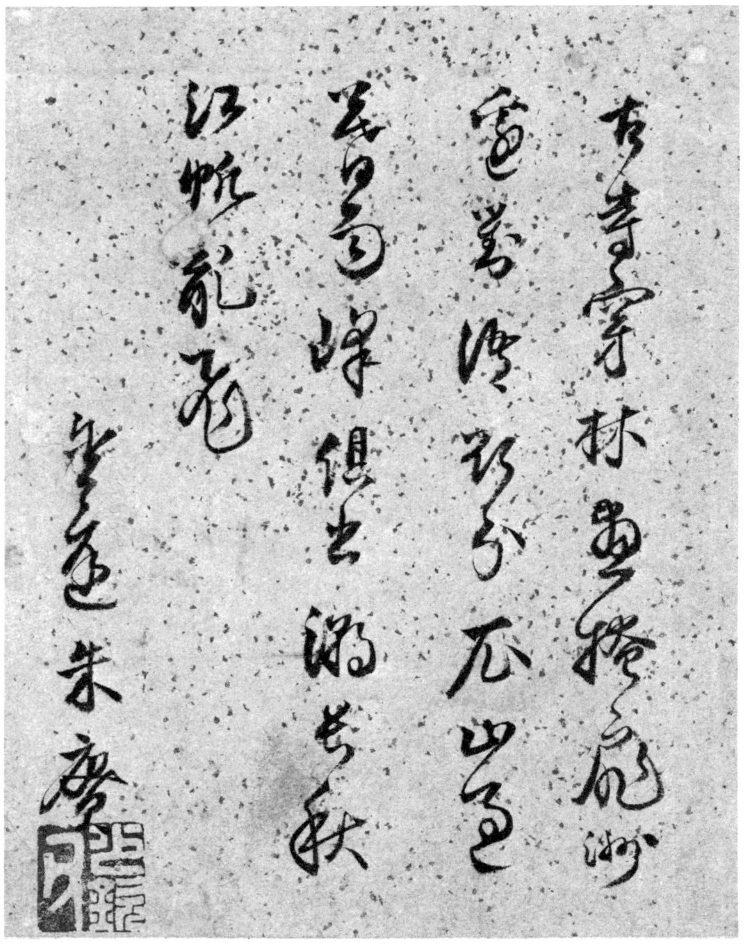

Leaf BB by Chu Keng

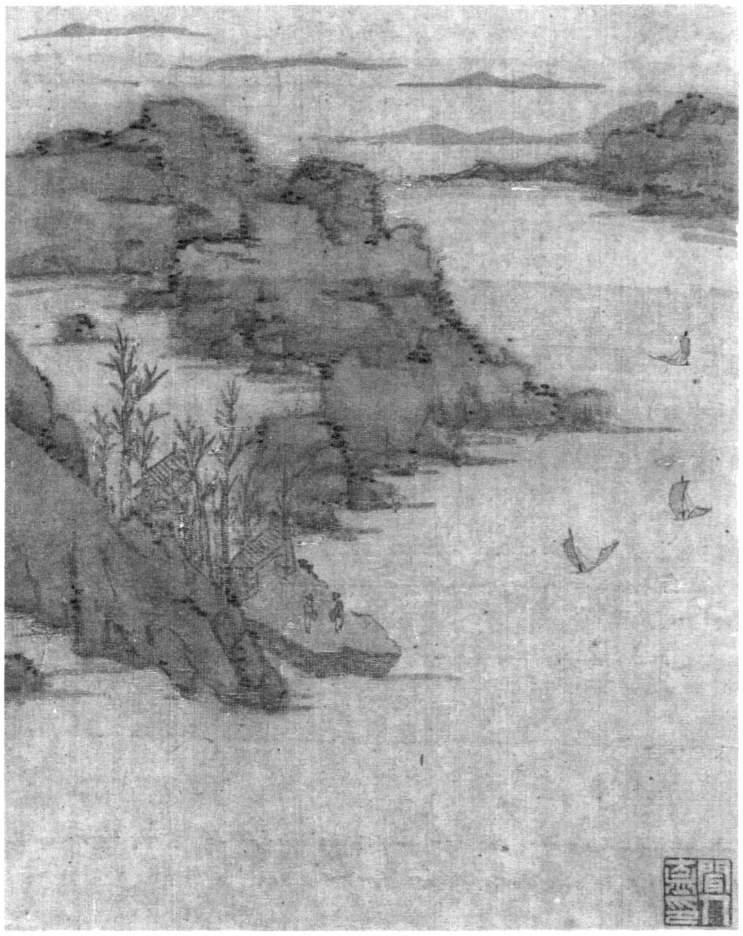

Leaf B, "Sailing on an Autumn River"

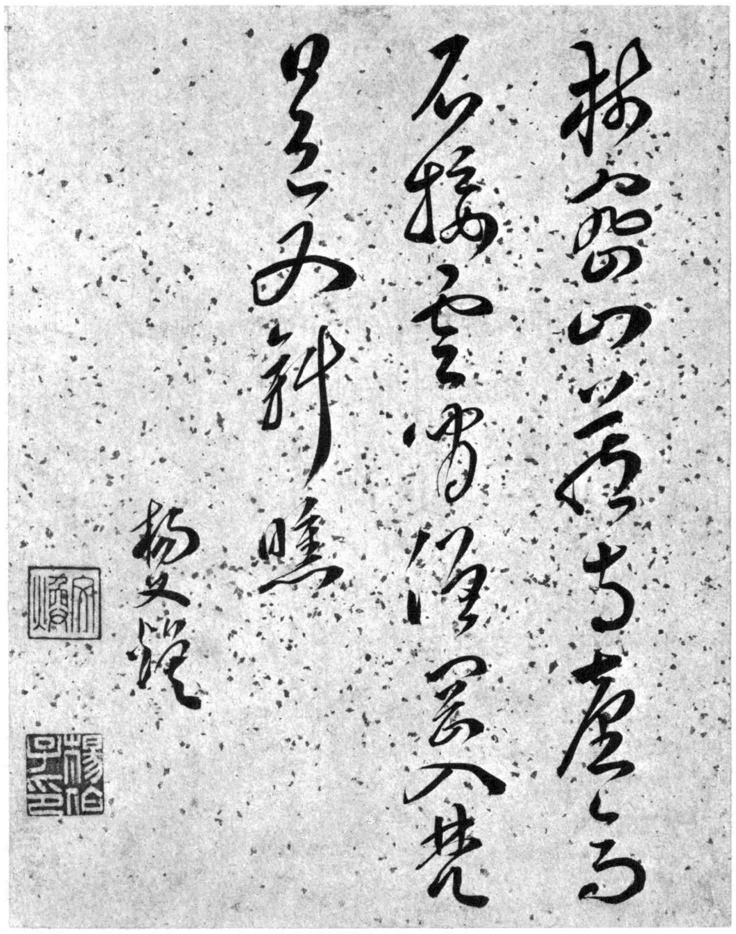

Leaf CC by Yang Wen-huan

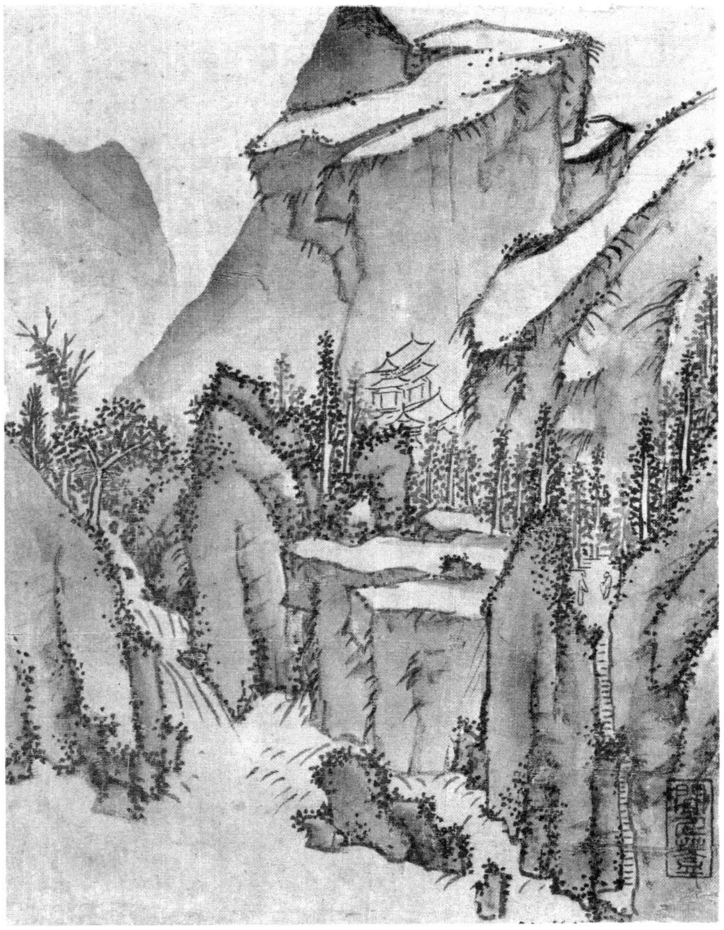

Leaf C, "Landscape in the Style of Wu Chen (1280–1354)"

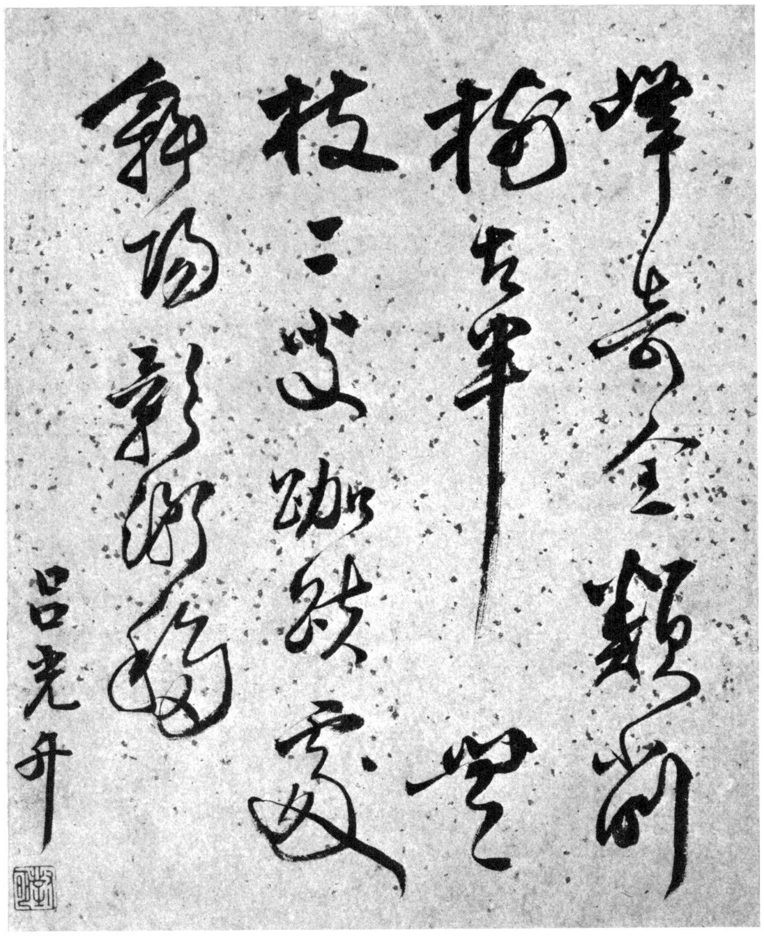

Leaf DD by Lü Kuang-shen

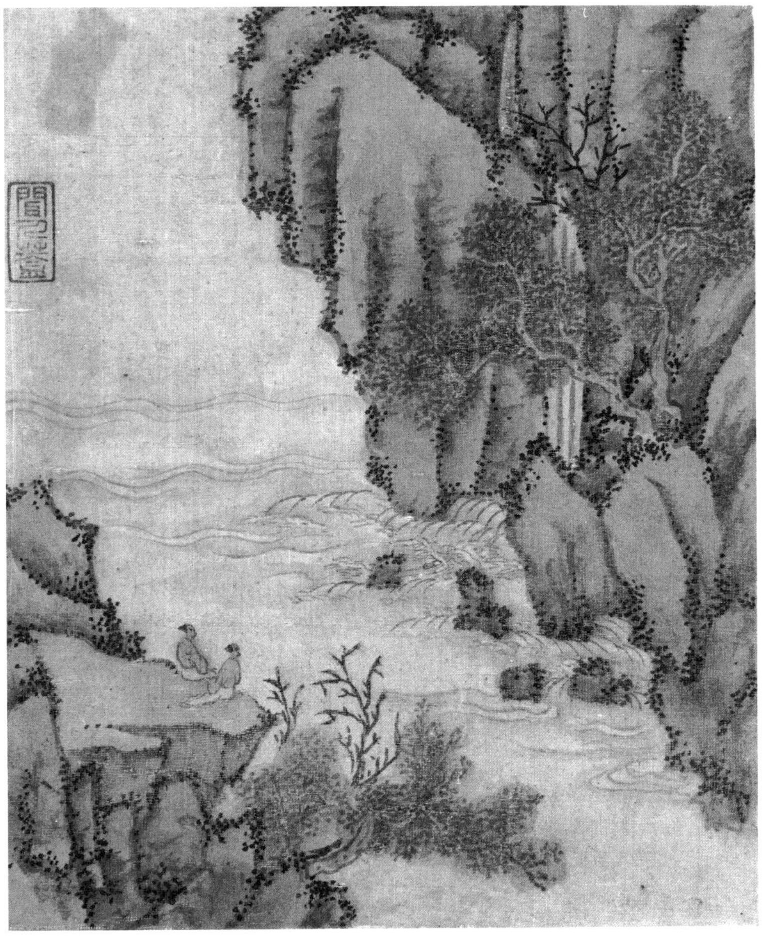

Leaf D, "Landscape in the Style of Chao Meng-fu (1254–1322)"

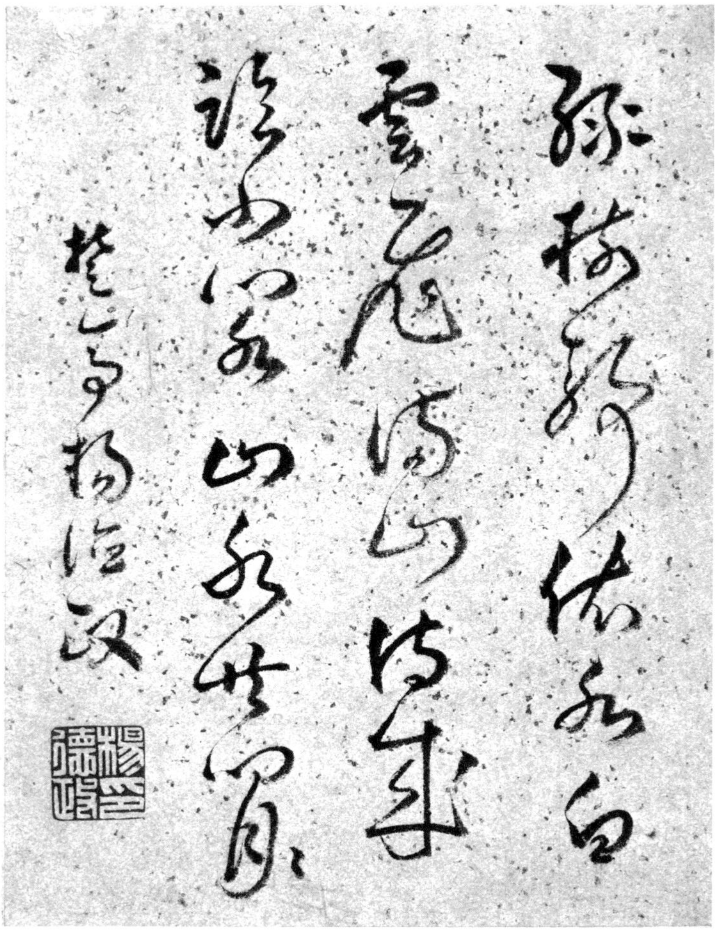

Leaf EE by Yang Te-cheng

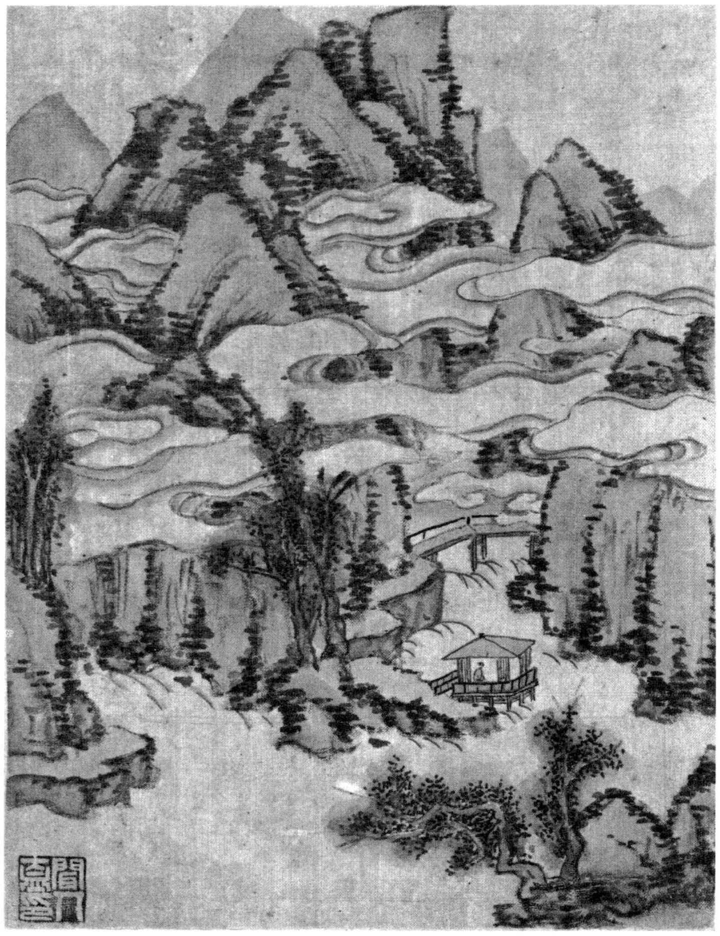

Leaf E, "Landscape in the Style of Huang Kung-wang (1269–1354)"

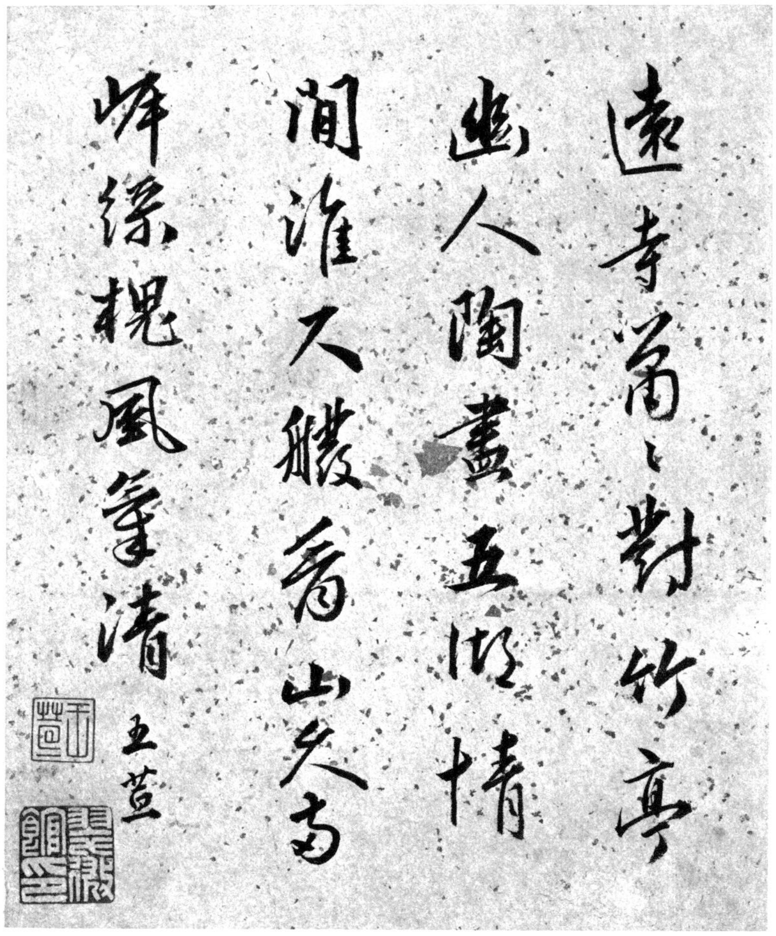

Leaf FF by Wang Huan

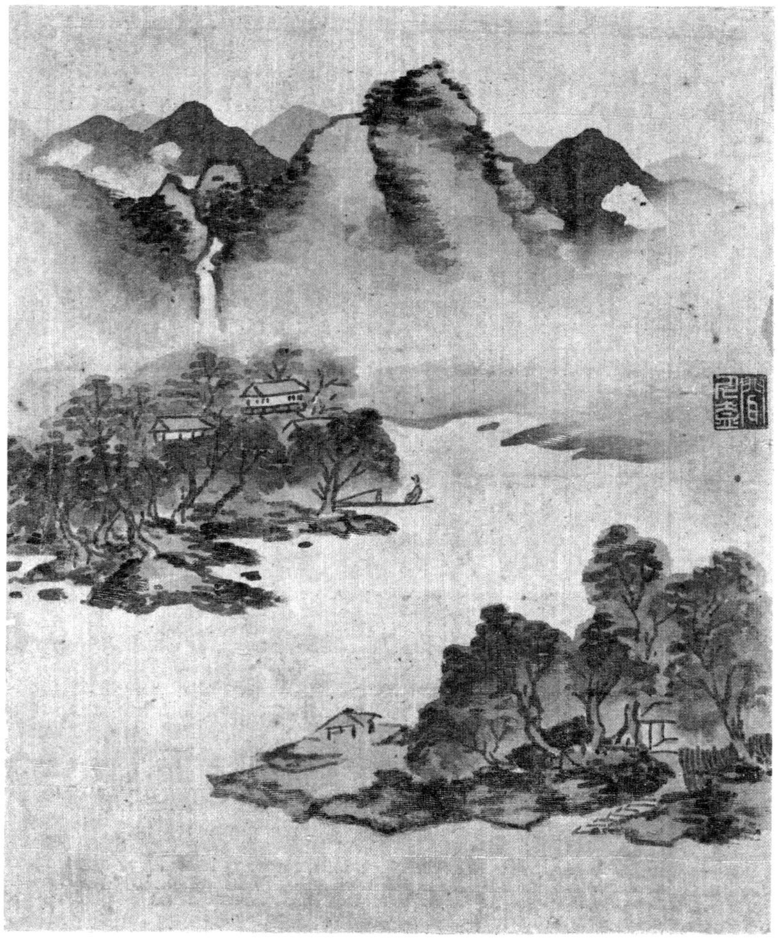

Leaf F, "Landscape in the Style of Kao K'o-kung (1248–1310)"

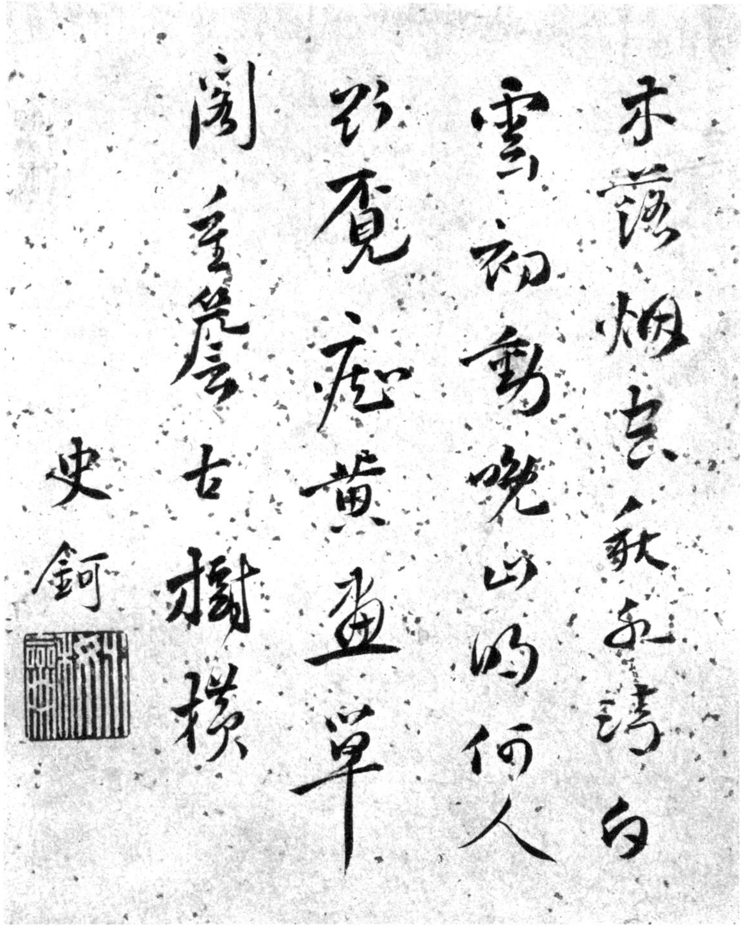

Leaf GG by Shih K'o

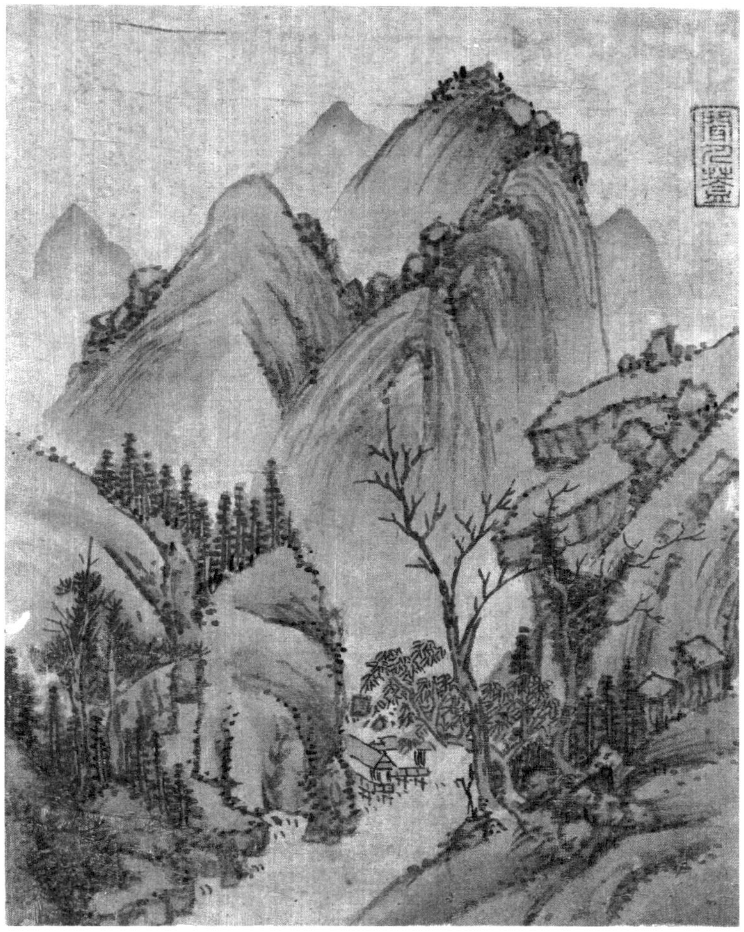

Leaf G, "Landscape in the Style of Huang Kung-wang (1269–1354)"

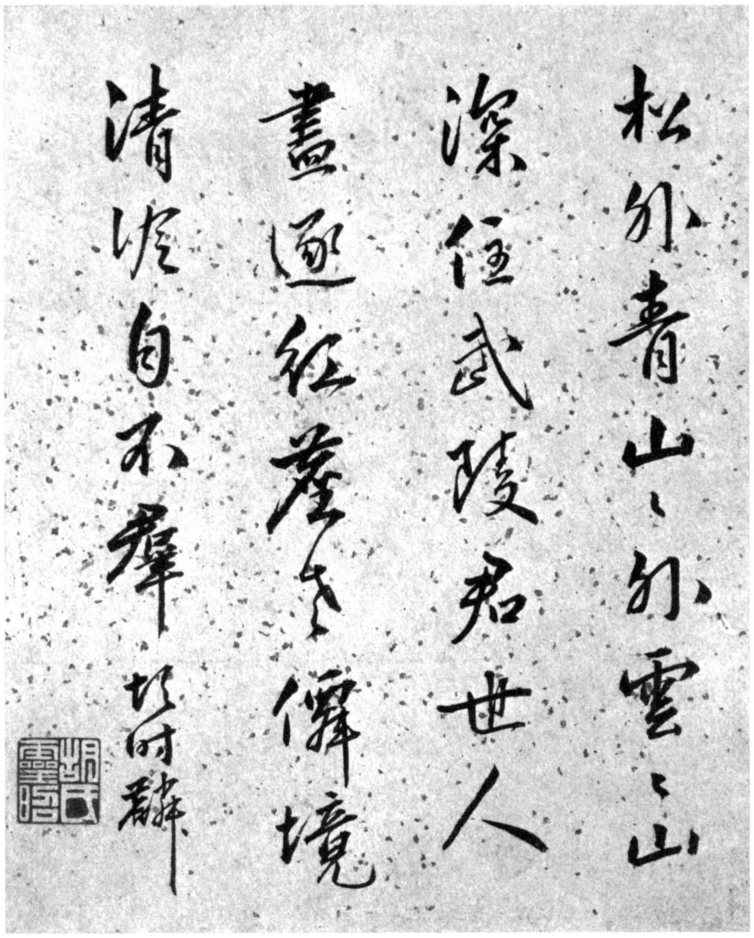

Leaf HH by Hu Shih-lin

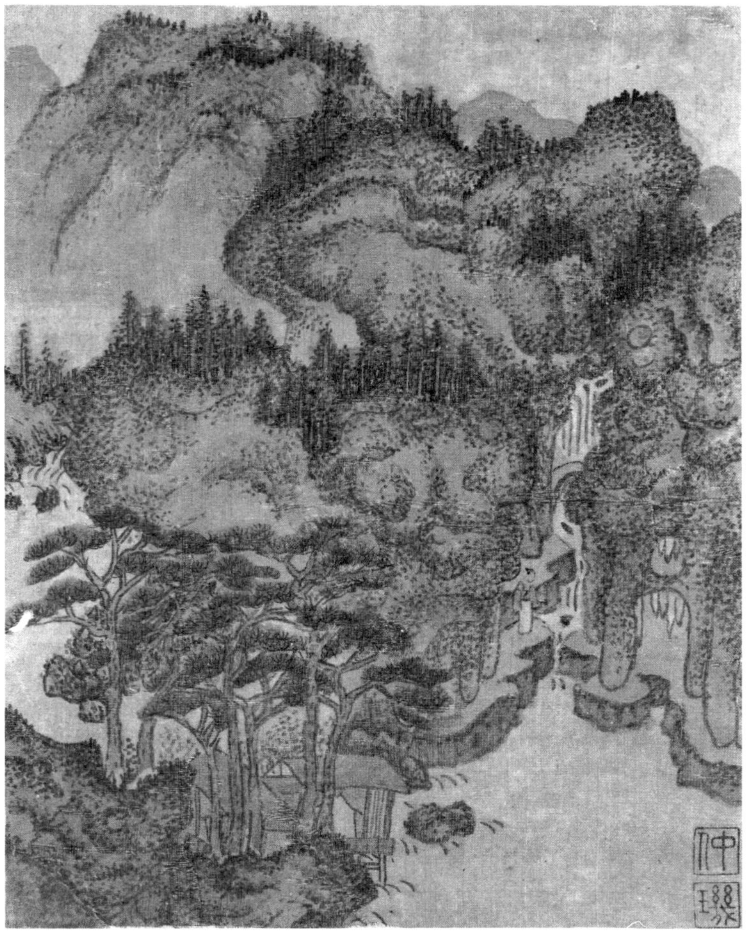

Leaf H, "Landscape in the Style of Wang Meng (1308–1385)"

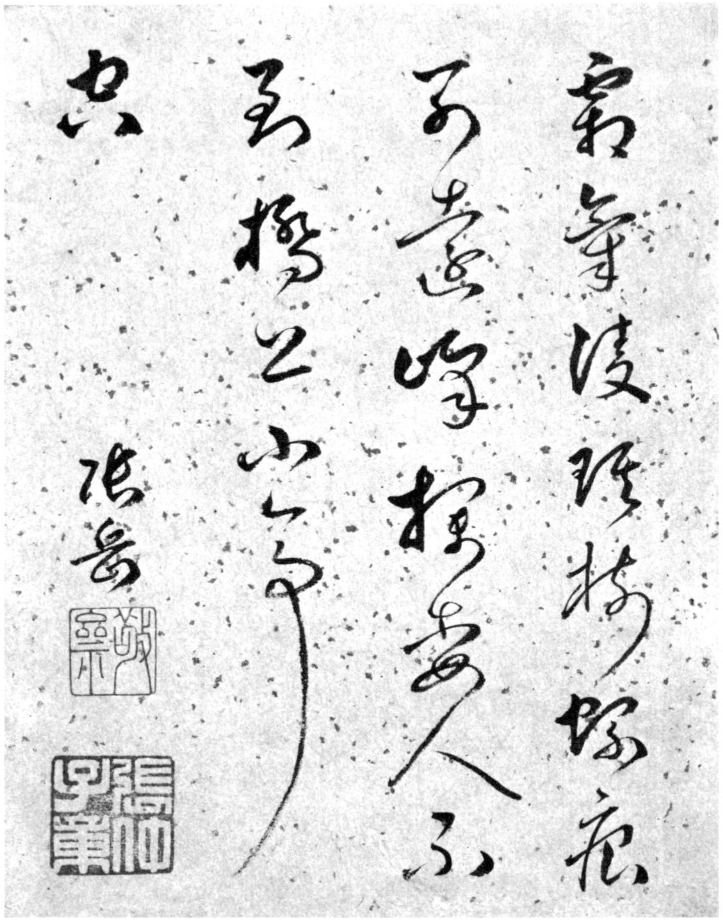

Leaf II by Chang Yüeh

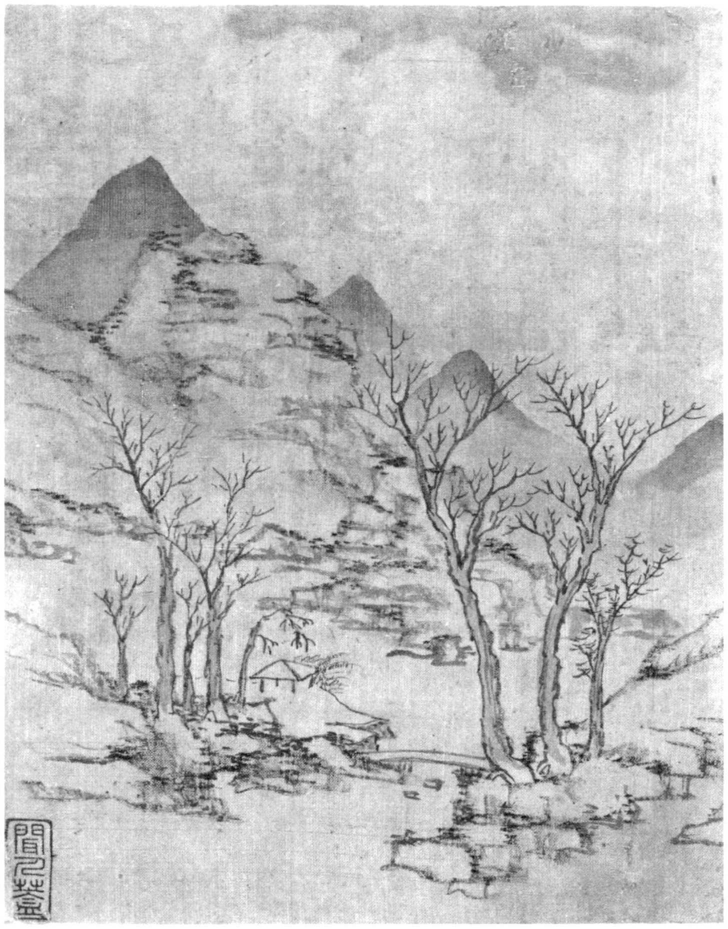

Leaf I, "Landscape in the Style of Ni Tsan (1301–1374)"

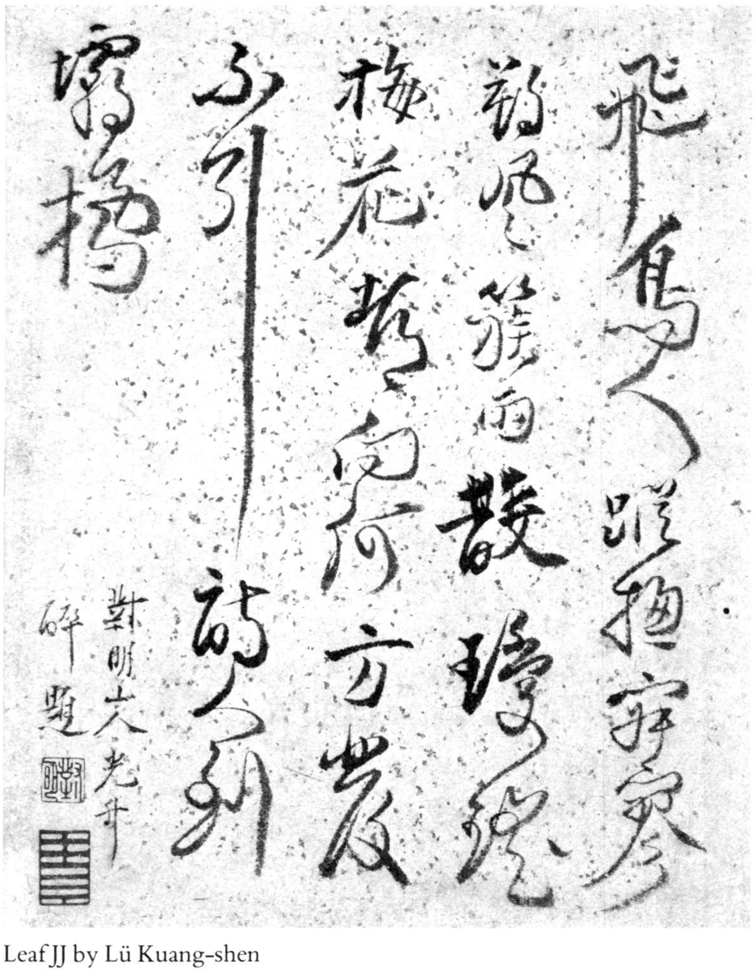

Leaf JJ by Lü Kuang-shen

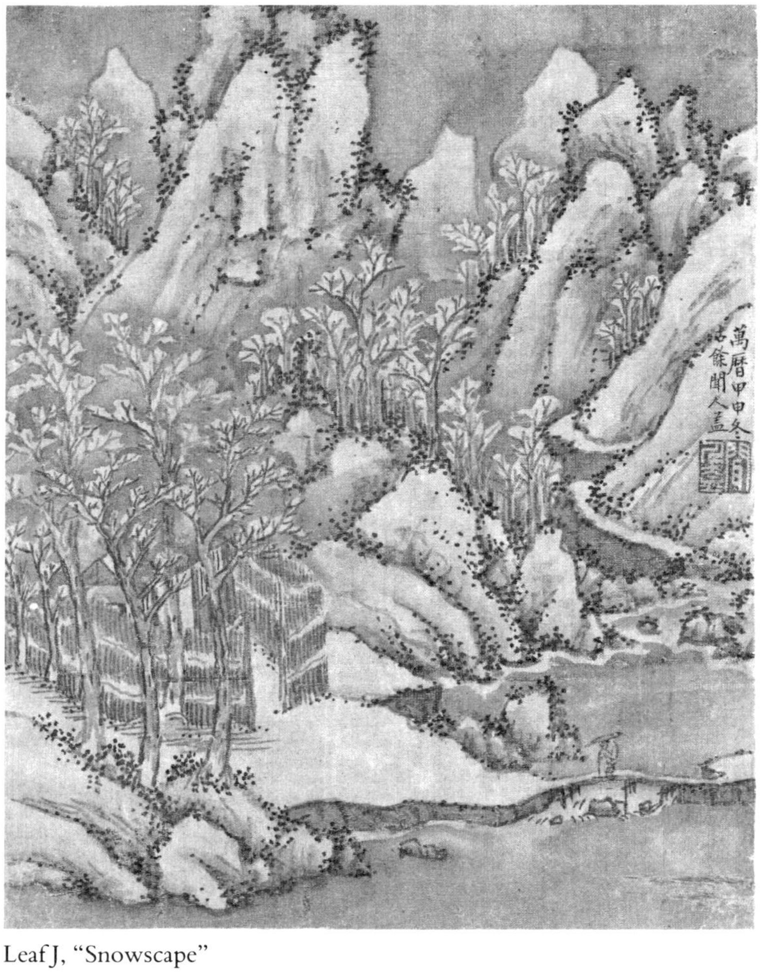

Leaf J, "Snowscape"

# 29 Feng K'o-pin (ca. 1575–after 1644)

## *Bamboo and Rocks (Chu shih t'u)*

Dated 1622
Handscroll, ink on paper
Frontispiece: 27.9 x 97.3 cm (11 in. x 3 ft. $2\frac{1}{4}$ in.); painting: 26.3 x 243.5 cm ($10\frac{3}{8}$ in. x 7 ft. $11\frac{7}{8}$ in.); colophons: 26.2 x 424.5 cm ($10\frac{3}{8}$ in. x 13 ft. $11\frac{1}{8}$ in.); 26.1 x 28.8 cm ($10\frac{1}{2}$ x $11\frac{3}{8}$ in.)

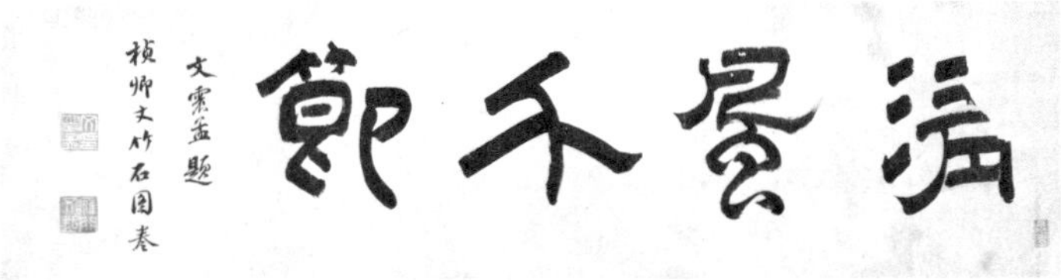

FRONTISPIECE, calligraphy by Wen Cheng-meng (1574–1636) (4 character title in seal script): "Clear Manner and Upright Character" ["Ch'ing-feng chieh-chieh"] (an oval-shaped damaged area appears near the character *ch'ing*). Signature: Wen Cheng-meng inscribed this handscroll, "Bamboo and Rocks," by Master Cheng-ch'ing.

ARTIST'S INSCRIPTION (prose, 19 characters in 2 columns of running script): In the *jen-hsü* year [1622], when I was in the capital, I copied the texture strokes of Tzu-yüan [Hsing T'ung; 1551–1612] when painting rocks, and the method of Li Hsi-chai [Li K'an; 1245–1320] for miniature bamboo.

ARTIST'S SIGNATURE: Feng K'o-pin from Pei-hai [in Shantung province].

ARTIST'S SEALS: Feng K'o-pin yin (square intaglio); Cheng-ch'ing (square relief); Chu-shih-shan-fang (tall rectangle intaglio).

INSCRIPTIONS (from right to left):

1. Wu Po-yü (*chin-shih*, 1613): 7 character regulated verse in 8 columns of running script. Signature: Wu Po-yü inscribed this. Seals: Wu Po-yü yin (square intaglio); Fu-sheng fu (square relief); Nan-i-t'ing (squat rectangle relief).
2. Ho K'o (*chin-shih*, 1616): 7 character quatrain in 3 columns of running script. Signature: Ho K'o inscribed this. Seals: Ho K'o yin (square intaglio); Mu-an (square intaglio).
3. Cheng Chih-hsüan (fl. late 16th–early 17th century): two 7 character quatrains, followed by a 23 character note, in 4 columns of regular script (dated 1623). Signature: Cheng Chih-hsüan inscribed this. Seal: Cheng Chih-hsüan yin (square intaglio).
4. Ho K'o: 7 character quatrain in 3 columns of running script. Signature: K'o again inscribed this. Seals: Ho K'o chih yin (square intaglio); Meng-tse (square relief).

COLOPHONS (mounted in 2 sections, from right to left):
Section I (10 colophons):

1. Wen Cheng-meng: prose, 161 characters in 16 columns of running script. Signature: On the tenth day after the Tuan-yang Festival of the *jen-hsü* year [1622], Wen Cheng-meng inscribed this. Seals: Wen Ch'i Cheng-meng (square intaglio); Ch'ing-yao-yü (square intaglio).
2. Hsing T'ai-chi (ca. late 16th–early 17th century): prose, 94 characters in 11 columns of cursive script. Signature: Hsing T'ai-chi from Ch'ing-yüan [in Shansi province]. Seals: T'ai-chi ssu yin (square intaglio); Ta-lai (square relief).
3. Fang K'o-chuang (ca. late 16th–early 17th century): prose, 46 characters in 4 columns of running script. Signature: The Garden Hermit, Fang K'o-chuang. Seals: Fang K'o-chuang yin (square intaglio); Tan-shih shih (square intaglio).
4. Ch'en Lieh (ca. late 16th–early 17th century): prose, 135 characters in 14 columns of free-form running script. Signature: Your friend, Ch'en Lieh. Seals: Ch'en Lieh chih yin (square intaglio); Tzu Kuang-ju (square intaglio).
5. Chao Ping-chung (b. 1570): prose, 63 characters in 6 columns of regular script. Signature: Chao Ping-chung. Seals: Chi-ch'ing shih (square intaglio); Ping-chung chih yin (square intaglio).
6. Yang Hung (ca. late 16th–early 17th century): prose, 40 characters in 4 columns of regular script. Signature: Inscribed by your companion in obtaining the *chin-shih* degree, Yang Hung from Wu-ling [in Hunan province]. Seal: Yang Hung chih yin (square intaglio).
7. P'an Tseng-hung (*chin-shih*, 1616): prose, 166 characters in 14 columns of running script. Signature: Chih-ti, P'an Tseng-hung, inscribed this. Seals: P'an Tseng-hung yin (square relief); Chao-tu fu (square intaglio).
8. Han Ching (*chin-shih*, 1610): 7 character regulated verse in 8 lines, followed by a 112 character note, in 18 columns of running script. Signature: Han Ching from western Wu [Kiangsu province]. Seals: Han Ching chih yin (square intaglio); Ch'iu-chung shih (square relief).
9. Huang Ju-heng (1558–1626): prose, 100 characters in 10 columns of running script. Signature: Huang Ju-heng from Wu-lin [Hang-chou]. Seals: Huang Ju-heng yin (square intaglio): Chen-fu shih (square intaglio).
10. Shen Yen (1566–1638): 7 character verse in 16 lines in 10 columns of running script. Signature: Shen Yen from western Wu [Kiangsu province] inscribed this. Seals: Shen Yen chih yin (square intaglio); Ho-shan (square intaglio).

Section II (two colophons):

1. Wang I-jung (1845–1900): prose, 19 characters in 2 columns of regular script. Seal: I-jung (tall rectangle intaglio).
2. Sheng Hsüan-huai (1844–1916): prose, 40 characters in 4 columns of running script. Signature: Chih-sou. Seal: Yü-chai (squat rectangle intaglio).

COLLECTOR'S SEALS: Sheng Hsüan-hai: Wu-chin Sheng Hsüan-huai shou-ts'ang shu-hua chi (tall rectangle relief; lower right, painting); Yü-chai ch'ing-chien (square intaglio; lower right, painting); Ku-lung-chieh-kuan (square intaglio; lower left, second colophon section).

Edward L. Elliott Family Collection (L295.70)

PUBLISHED: Suzuki Kei, comp., *Chūgoku kaiga sōgō zuroku: daiikkan, Amerika–Kanada hen* (Comprehensive illustrated catalogue of Chinese paintings: volume 1, American and Canadian collections) (Tokyo: University of Tokyo Press, 1982), p. 136, pl. A17–068.

FENG K'O-PIN (*tzu*, Cheng-ch'ing), a native of I-tu, Shantung province, was a scholar-official and a painter of monochrome bamboo studies. He received his *chin-shih* degree in 1622 and later became vice minister at the Court of Imperial Sacrifices. His painting talent was nurtured by his father, Feng Ch'i-cheng (fl. late 16th–early 17th century), who was a student of the Imperial Academy in Peking, a friend of Hsing T'ung's (1551–1612) and Tung Ch'i-ch'ang's (1555–1636), and a well-known painter of ink bamboo paintings in the style of Li K'an (1245–1320).[1]

Feng K'o-pin executed the monochrome handscroll *Bamboo and Rocks* while he was in the capital in 1622. In this composition five groups of rocks, loosely dispersed along a curving groundline, alternate with five inscriptions. Ming literati ink flower painters frequently employed the compositional device of interspersing landscape motifs and text against a blank background. The technique is an adaptation of a composition used by Wu Chen (1280–1354) in his *Fishermen* handscroll (now in the Shanghai Museum), which in turn originated in early narrative handscrolls, such as *Admonitions to the Court Ladies* (*Nü-shih chen*; see page 13), attributed to Ku K'ai-chih (ca. 344–ca. 406), and *Ode on the Red Cliff* (*Ch'ih-pi fu t'u*) by Ch'iao Chung-ch'ang (fl. 1st half 12th century).

Traditionally a monochrome rendering of bamboo and rocks symbolized an uncompromising Confucian gentleman. The genre flourished during the late eleventh century under the aegis of Su Shih (1036–1101) and Wen T'ung (1019–1079). Later painters reinterpreted the expressive and personal styles of these artists according to the aesthetic standards of their own times. Yüan masters, for example, preferred calligraphic abbreviation to meticulous description: Chao Meng-fu (1254–1322) stressed the pictorial effect of contrasting dense, wet bamboo silhouettes against crude, dry rock forms, while Wu Chen emphasized dark, rich, and vigorous brushwork. The emotional intensity of their brushstrokes reflected their ability to maintain their moral integrity under the reign of the Mongol conquerors. Ming literati, however, enjoyed a stable and wealthy society, and their interests turned to such leisurely pastimes as garden design. Miniature bamboo and rocks became favorites in their gardens, as well as in their paintings, and Feng K'o-pin's painting demonstrates this aspect of Ming literati taste rather than the traditional symbolism of bamboo as the unbending spirit.

The motifs in the painting were based on those of Hsing T'ung and Li K'an. In his inscription the artist indicates that he "copied the texture strokes of Tzu-yüan [Hsing T'ung] when painting rocks, and the method of Li Hsi-chai [Li K'an] for miniature bamboo." Feng undoubtedly had occasion to view Hsing's paintings, since Feng's father and Hsing were both officials from Shantung province serving in Peking and were known to be friends. In this painting Feng's rock motifs show a debt to Hsing's *Variegated Rocks* (*Wen-shih*; fig. a), dated 1611, which is probably a portrayal of Hsing's own garden, built in 1600.[2] Following Hsing's approach, Feng painted his rocks as if piling up individual shell-like boulders, each enclosed by a wobbly outline and filled in with layers of irregular concentric circles. In spite of the similarity in technique, the overall effects of the two painters' rocks are quite different. Hsing's rocks, described with

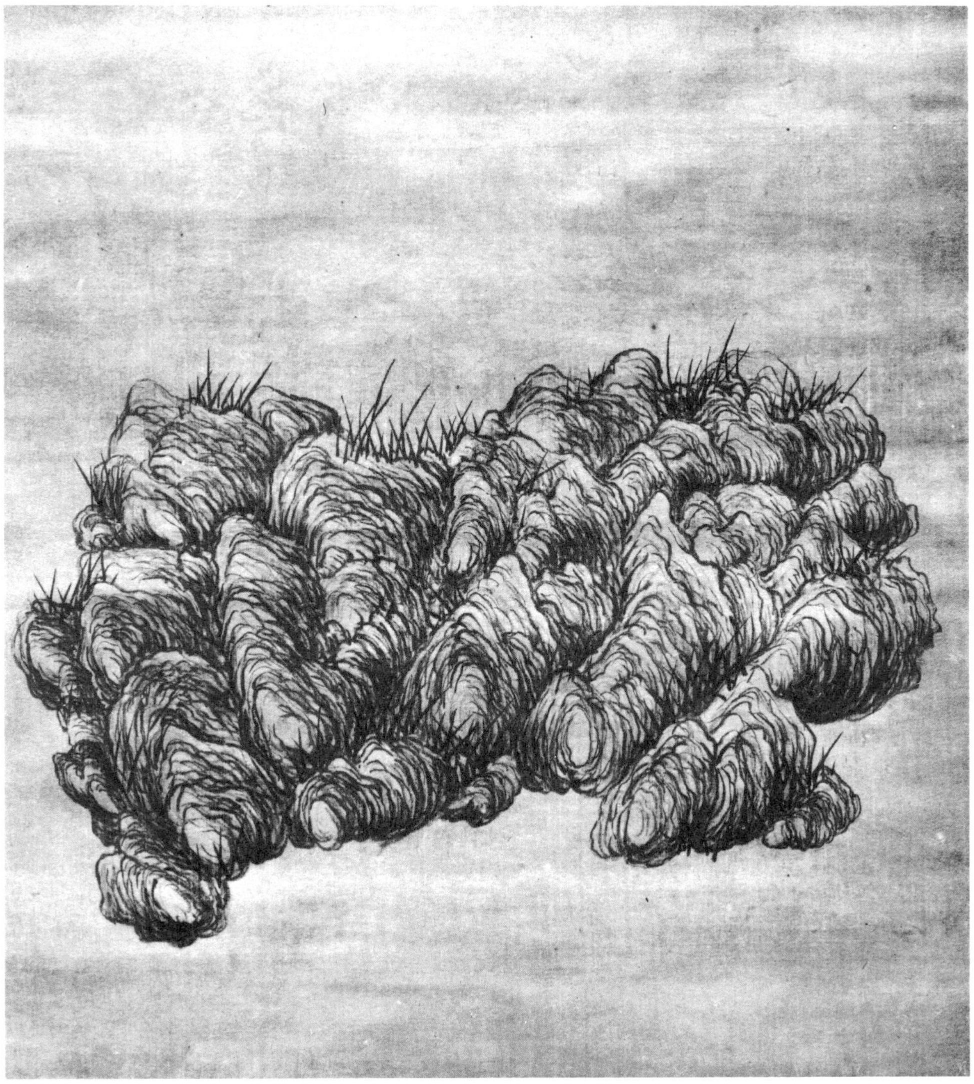

Fig. a. Hsing T'ung, detail, *Variegated Rocks* (*Wen-shih*). Dated 1611. Hanging scroll, ink on silk. 14.1 x 51.2 cm (5 1/2 x 20 1/8 in.). Osaka Municipal Museum of Fine Art

texture strokes, are hard and tight, whereas Feng's rocks, largely indicated by tonal ink washes and sparser texture strokes, appear soft and loose.

Feng's knowledge of Li K'an's miniature bamboo must have been transmitted to him through his father. Although none of Li's paintings of miniature bamboo is extant, his paintings of other subjects show the sharp silhouettes seen in Feng's bamboo shoots and the vigorous brushwork of his leaves.

After this painting was finished in 1622, Feng invited a group of his friends, led by Wen Cheng-meng (1574–1636), the great-grandson of Wen Cheng-ming, to add a frontispiece and colophons. In 1623 he asked another group of friends, including Wu Po-yü (*chin-shih*, 1613), Ho K'o (*chin-shih*, 1616), and Cheng Chih-hsüan (fl. late 16th–early 17th century), to add their inscriptions to the painting. Before it came to the Edward L. Elliott Family Collection, this handscroll passed through the collections of Wang I-jung (1845–1900) and Sheng Hsüan-huai (1844–1916), both of whom wrote their colophons on a separate sheet of paper attached after the section of Ming colophons.

PAO-CHEN CH'EN

NOTES

1. For further biographical information on both Feng K'o-pin and Feng Ch'i-cheng, see Mao Yung-po and Liu Yao-ch'un, eds., *Ch'ing-chou fu-chih* (Gazetteer of Ch'ing-chou) (1859; repr. ed., Taipei: Hsüeh-sheng shu-chü, 1970), *chüan* 45, p. 35b.
2. See Hsing T'ung, *Chieh-yüan chi* (Collected writings of Chieh-yüan) (preface by Ch'en Tzu-kao, 1617), photocopy in the Gest Oriental Library, Princeton University, *chüan* 1, pp. 1–11.

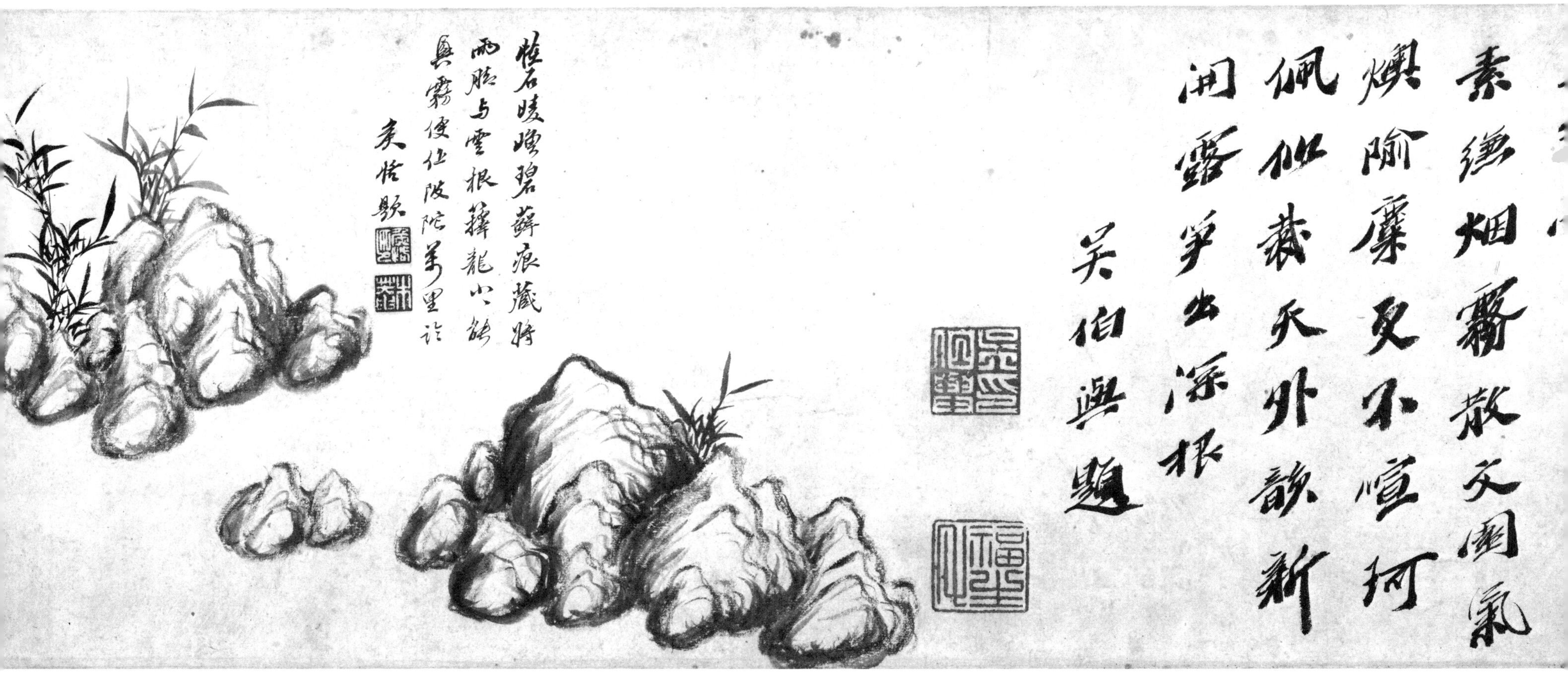
吴伯與題

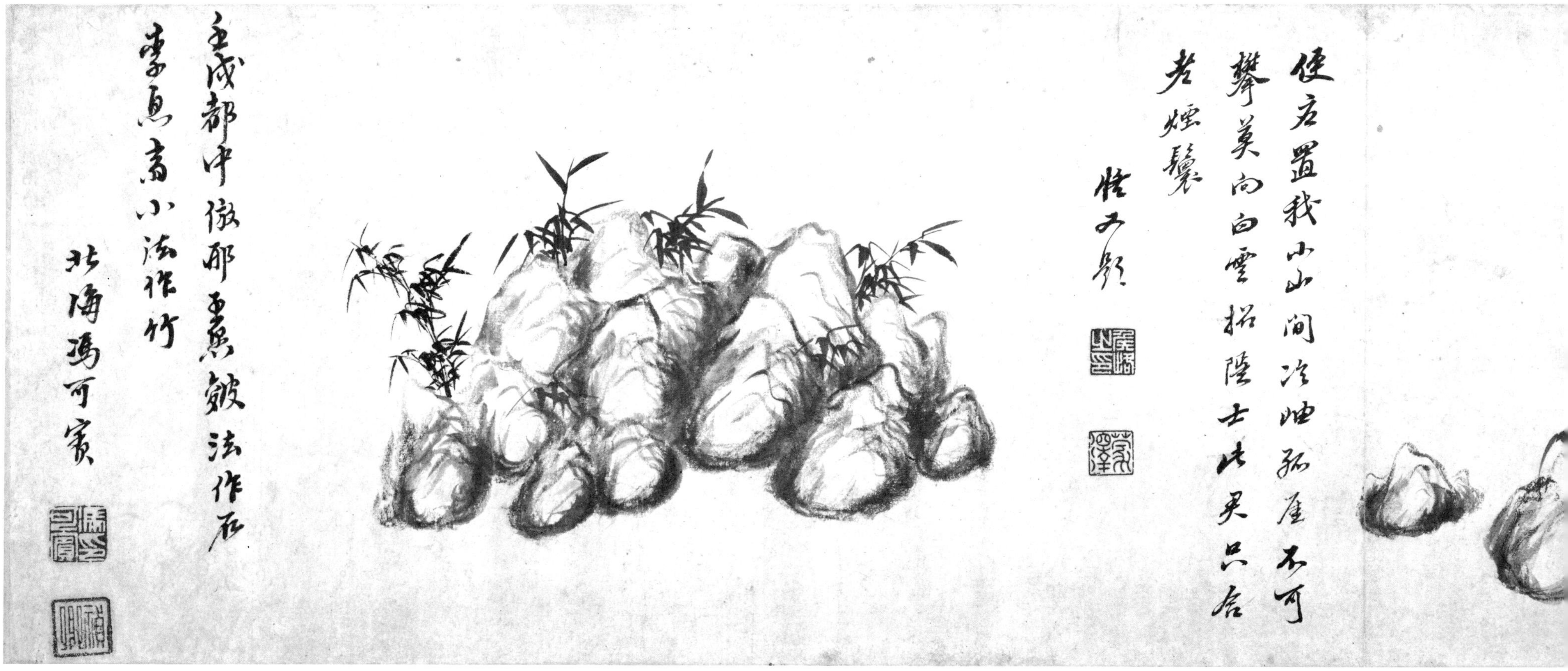
壬戌都中倣郭熙皴法作石
李息齋小法作竹
北海馮可賓

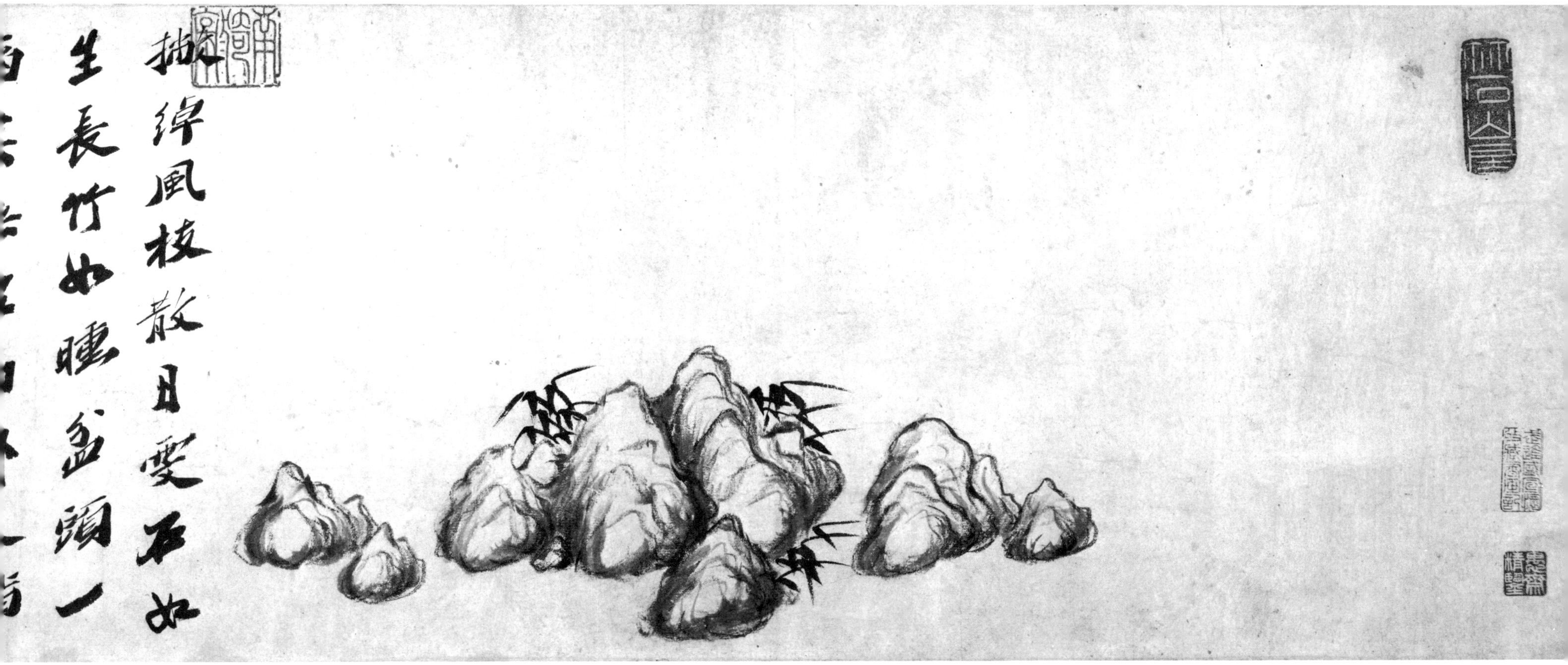

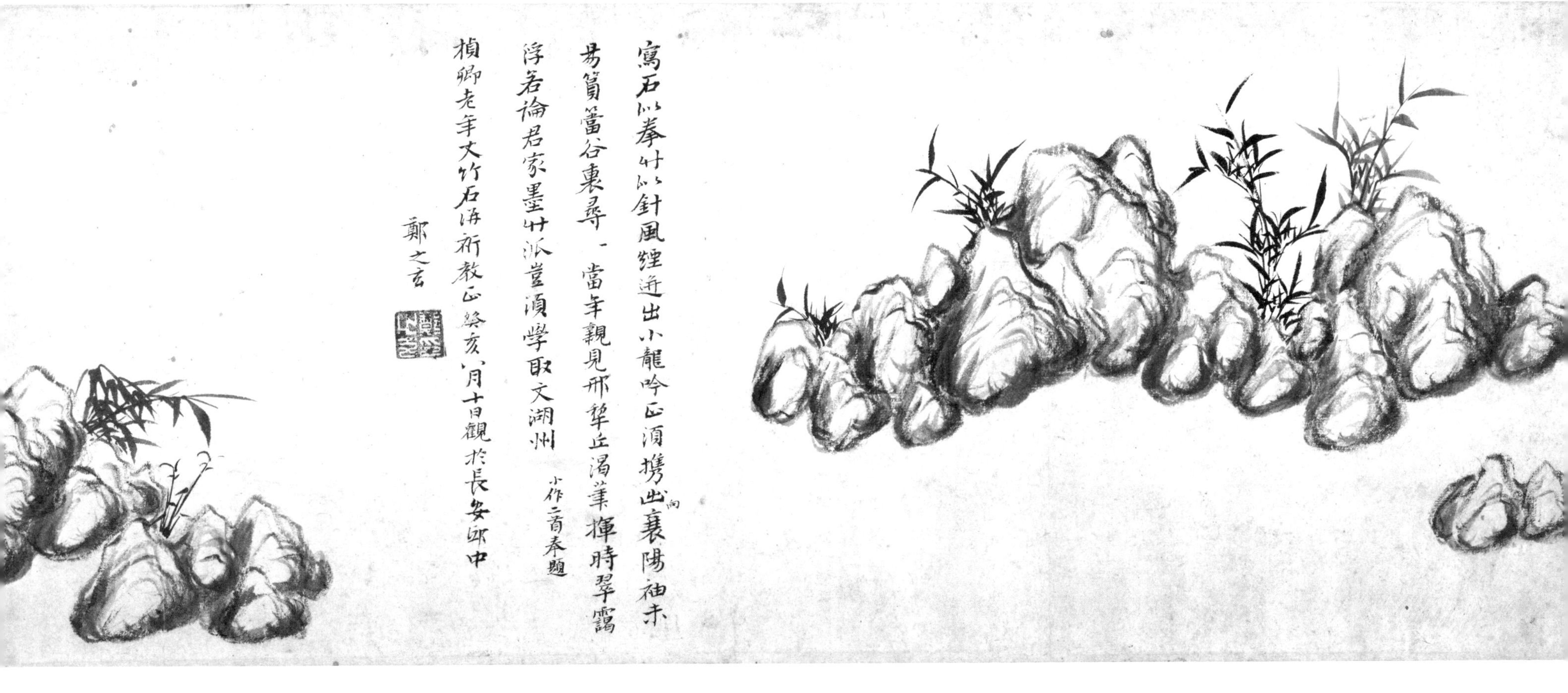
寫石以拳竹以針風纏迸出小龍吟正須携出向襄陽袖未
易篔簹谷裏尋 當年親見邢華丘渴筆揮時翠露
浮若論君家墨竹派豈須學取文湖州 小作二首奉題
楨卿老年文竹石海祈教正癸亥八月十日觀於長安邸中
鄭之玄

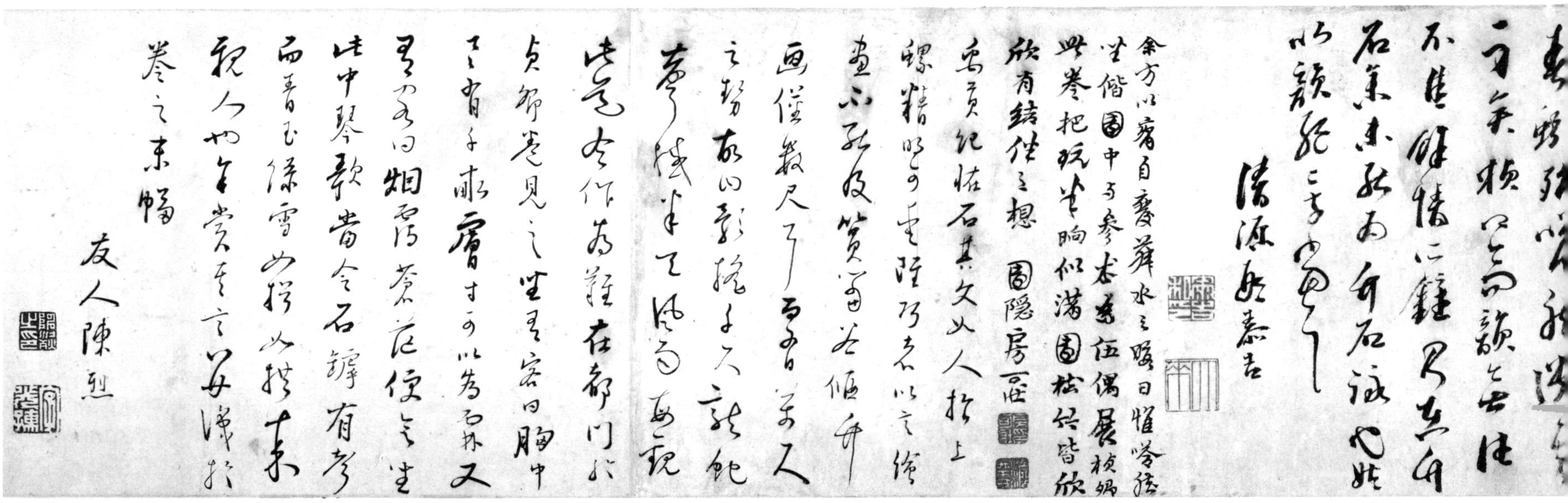

Ch'en Lieh    Fang K'o-chuang    Hsing T'ai-chi

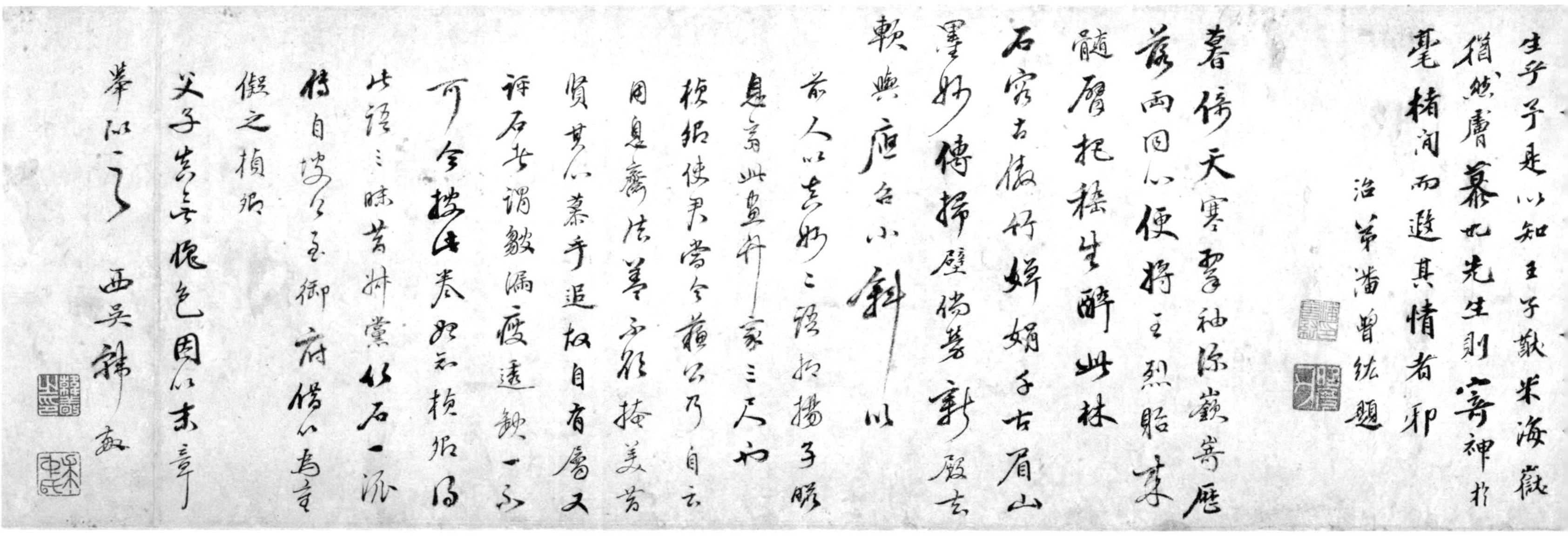

Han Ching

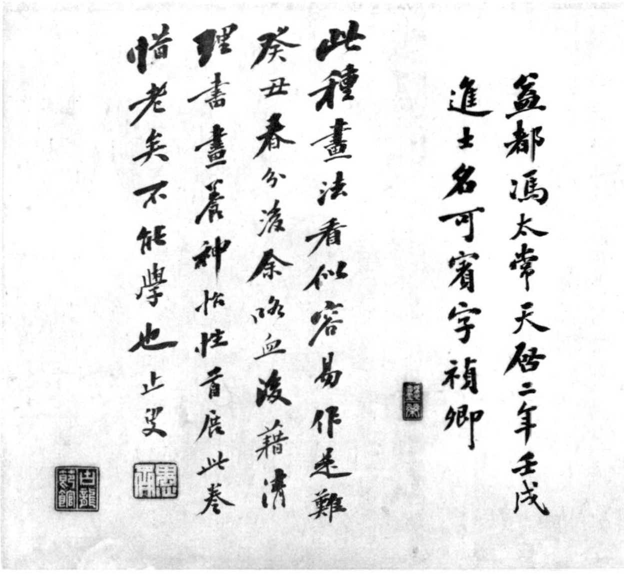

Sheng Hsüan-huai    Wang I-jung

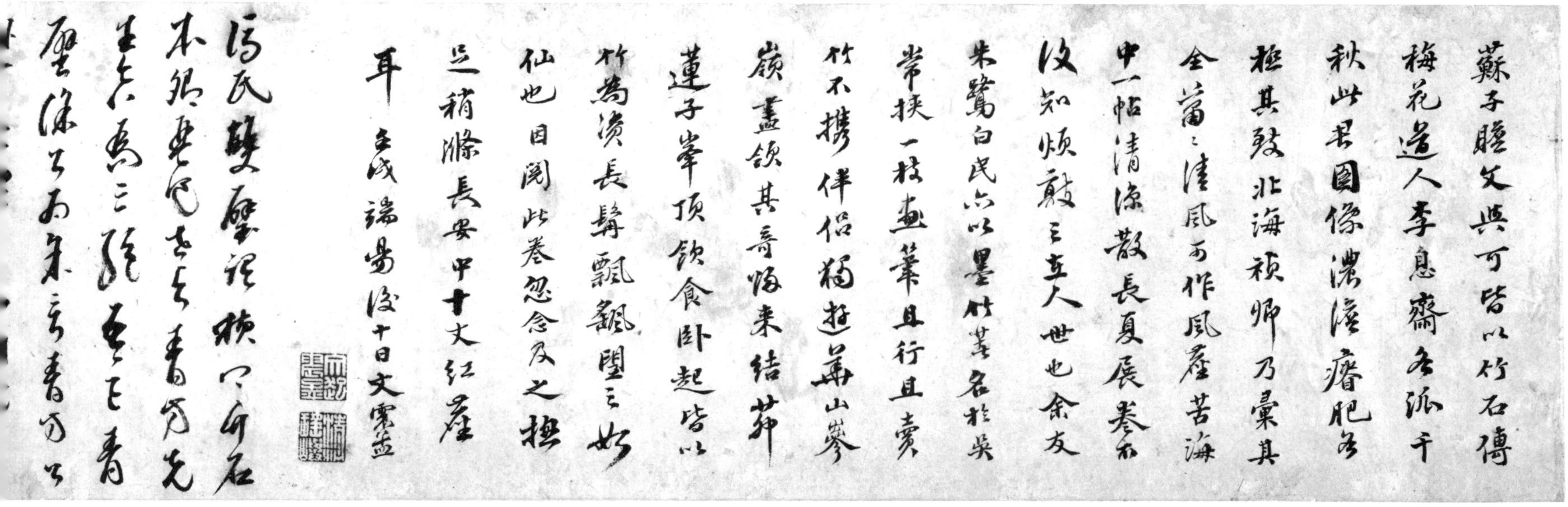

Wen Cheng-meng

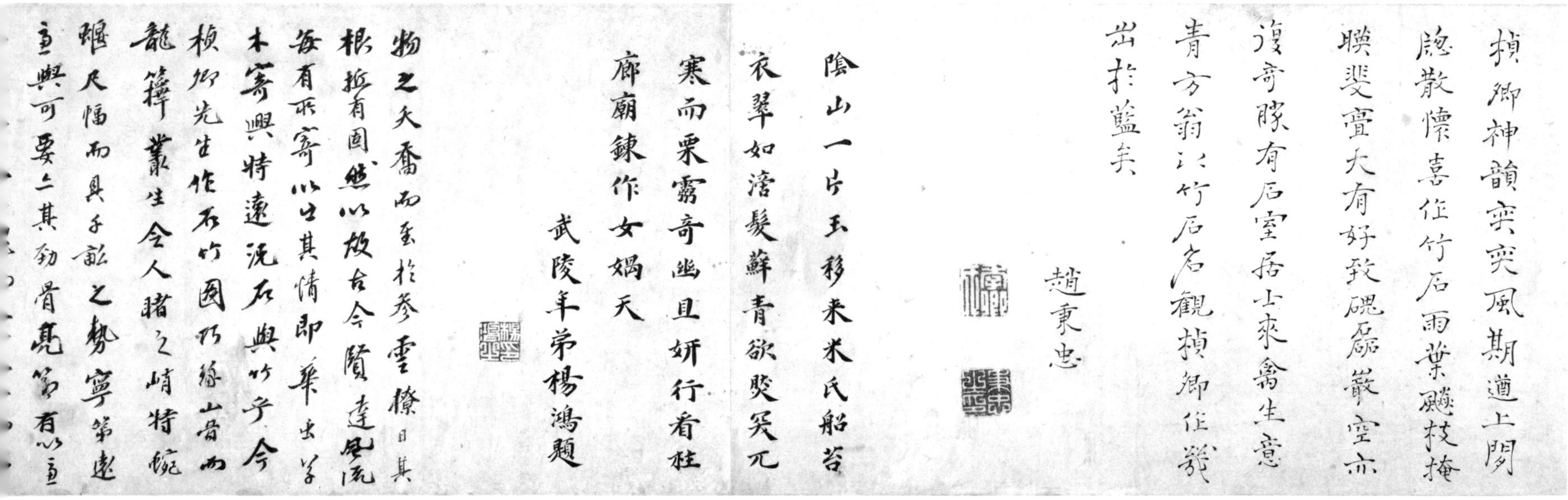

P'an Tseng-hung

Yang Hung

Chao Ping-chung

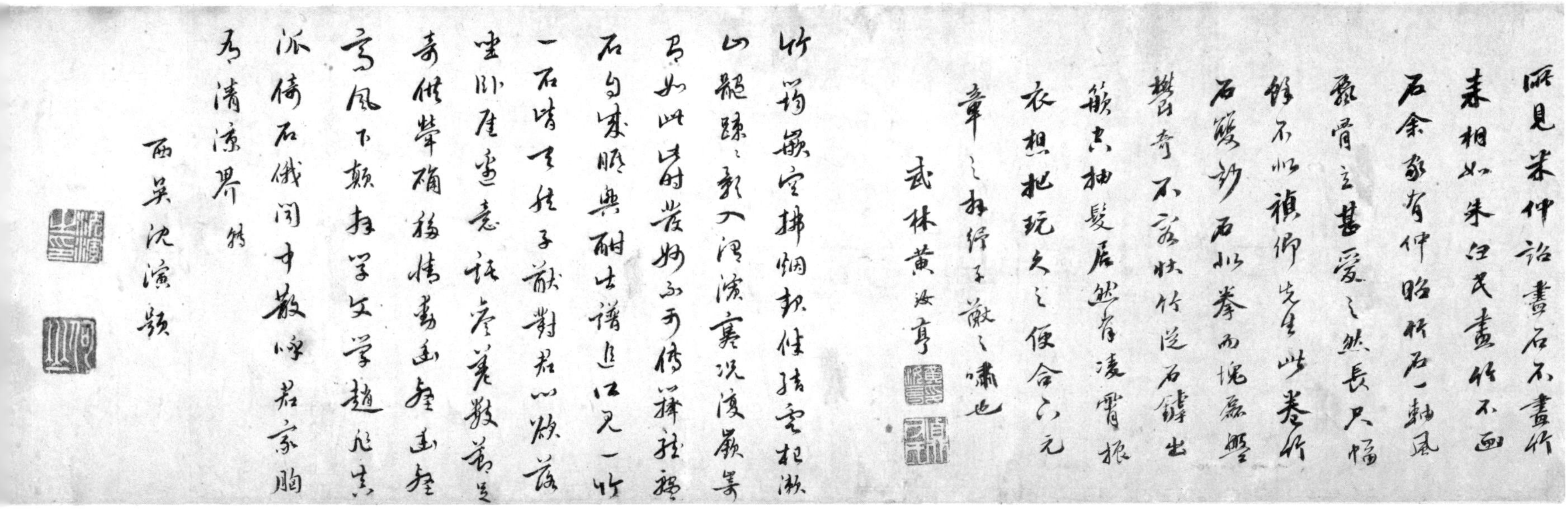

Shen Yen

Huang Ju-heng

# 30 Lan Ying (1585–after 1664)

## *Landscape in the Style of Huang Kung-wang (Fang Huang Kung-wang shan-shui)*

Dated 1624
Handscroll, ink and color on gold-flecked paper
Painting: 28.2 x 624.8 cm (11 1/8 in. x 20 ft. 6 in.); colophons: 28.2 x 76.4 cm (11 1/8 x 30 1/8 in.)

ARTIST'S INSCRIPTION (prose, 98 characters in 10 columns of running script):

> Huang Tzu-chiu [Huang Kung-wang; 1269–1354] painted a handscroll of the Fu-ch'un Mountains. The brushwork is blunt and moving, and the mountains, valleys, and villages are so marvelous that they make the painting look different from his other works. Meng-tse [ca. late 16th–early 17th century], a great man of letters, studied Huang Kung-wang's way of painting; furthermore he has a deep understanding of Huang's methods. While chanting poems, Meng-tse wetted his brush and sketched the two mountains, Mount Huang and Mount Po; drifting, transitory clouds seemed to swallow the peaks. The painting was treasured and Meng-tse did not feel like showing it to ordinary visitors. I made this painting especially for Master Meng-tse. I hope that Master Meng-tse will not tease me for showing off in front of an expert, but will rather teach me some clever techniques in order that Huang Kung-wang's style may be revived all over the world. How does this sound?

ARTIST'S SIGNATURE: In the fifth lunar month of the *chia-tzu* year [1624], Lan Ying, a student from Ch'ien-t'ang [in Chekiang province] painted this.

ARTIST'S SEALS: T'ien-shu (square relief); Lan Ying chih yin (square intaglio).

INSCRIPTION by Ch'eng T'ing-i (dates unknown) (7 character quatrain in 3 columns of running script):

> I built my house among layers of mountain peaks;
> Uncultivated acres of green with swift waterfalls.
> My robe's sleeves are cool to the touch.
> Marvelously Lan Ying painted this scroll.
> Whose fishing boats did he put on the mountain streams?

Signature: Hsüeh-yai, Ch'eng T'ing-i. Seal: P'ao-hsin (tall rectangle relief).

COLOPHONS (from right to left):

1. Hu Ch'ang-keng (dates unknown): prose, 105 characters in 7 columns of running script. Signature: Hu Ch'ang-keng inscribed this. Seals: Ch'ang-keng tzu Tzu-hsi (square intaglio); Mu-yen-chü-shih (square intaglio).
2. Ch'en Keng-ling (dates unknown): three 7 character quatrains, followed by a 43 character commentary, in 9 columns of running script. Signature: Ch'en Keng-ling from Ma-p'ing [in Hupei province]. Seal: Ch'en Hsia-ku (square intaglio).
3. Chou Chia-chün (dates unknown): two 7 character regulated verses in 13 columns of running script. Signature: On the first day of the twelfth lunar month of the *kuei-hai* year [1683], Chou Chia-chün saw this painting at the Old Straw Hut in Lan-ch'eng. Seal: Chia-chün ssu yin (square intaglio).

COLLECTORS' SEALS:
Ch'eng Po-fen (modern collector), 3 seals.
Unidentified owners, 8 seals.

Gift of John B. Elliott (76–41)

PUBLISHED: Suzuki Kei, comp., *Chūgoku kaiga sōgō zuroku: daiikkan, Amerika–Kanada hen* (Comprehensive illustrated catalogue of Chinese paintings: volume 1, American and Canadian collections) (Tokyo: University of Tokyo Press, 1982), p. 112, pl. A16–034.

TRADITIONAL CHINESE ART HISTORIANS have long regarded Lan Ying as the last master of the Che School, which revived the Southern Sung academic style in the Ming dynasty. But Lan Ying was more than an academic painter; he was a creative artist who molded the academic and the literati traditions of painting into an individual style.[1]

Lan Ying (*tzu*, T'ien-shu; *hao*, Tieh-fu) was a native of Ch'ien-t'ang, Chekiang. At first, under an unknown teacher, Lan trained to become a professional artist in the Southern Sung academic style, painting figures, architecture, and landscapes. When he was in his early twenties, he became fascinated by the amateur school of literati painters. He began to devote himself to the study of poetry and calligraphy, befriend scholars, and visit the private collections of Sun K'o-hung (1533–1611) and Tung Ch'i-ch'ang (1555–1636).[2] Probably influenced by Tung, Lan Ying thereafter modeled his style after those of the four Yüan masters: Huang Kung-wang (1269–1354), Wu Chen (1280–1354), Ni Tsan (1301–1374), and Wang Meng (1308–1385).

Lan Ying's paintings made before 1634 all share certain characteristics—smooth outlines, moist ink tones, and long center-tipped (*chung-feng*) brushwork. These are evident in his *Landscape in the Style of Huang Kung-wang*, dated to 1624. The painting is a panoramic horizontal view of a number of islands set in a vast river against a backdrop of distant mountain ranges. Riverside and mountain dwellings and small fishing boats are scattered across the landscape. This idiom is derived from Huang Kung-wang's *Dwelling in the Fu-ch'un Mountains* (*Fu-ch'un shan-chü t'u*; page 71). Lan Ying specifically mentions his affinity for this great Yüan master in his inscription at the end of the scroll (see translation).

The motifs of conical mountains, simple houses, forked trees, and small, loose boulders in the Lan Ying scroll all derive from Huang's painting vocabulary. Nonetheless Lan Ying gave these borrowed images a personal interpretation by compressing their forms, thereby creating a sense of spatial ambiguity. In Lan's painting the conical earthen mounds were first defined by distinct outlines and then rapidly filled in with long, slanted texture strokes. These soft earthen mounds are juxtaposed against clusters of jagged multifaceted rocks, which are derived from Huang's alum-head (*fan-t'ou*) rocks. Lan Ying's mountains appear tight, massive, and two-dimensional, a reflection of his preference for surface pattern over a clearly defined sense of volume and space.

In addition to the Huang Kung-wang style, which dominates the painting, Lan Ying has included motifs from other, disparate sources. The overlapping laterally arranged rocks that top the large earthen mounds in the middle section reflect the Che School tradition. The dense, sharp horizontal dots on the mountains' contours derive from the brushwork style of Mi Fu (1052–1107) by way of Tai Chin (1388–1462). Moreover the simplified trees, built up with two strokes for the tree trunks and dots for leaves, are elements from the style of Wu Chen. Lan's use of a thin wash of light vegetable pigment applied over nonabsorbent gold-flecked paper reflects his adoption of Ming literati taste, as represented in the works of Shen Chou (1427–1509; see nos. 14A, 15), Wen Cheng-ming (1470–1559; see no. 20), and Tung Ch'i-ch'ang. Under Lan Ying's direction all of these diverse elements were modified and orchestrated into a Huang Kung-wang style landscape. In his early work Lan Ying assimilated rather than transformed painting motifs from ancient masters.

In his sixties Lan Ying developed a mature individual style, adapting the styles of his predecessors into a manner of his own. He developed a highly individual visual language, at its height in *Autumn River* (no. 31). This painting has a composition reminiscent of those of Ni Tsan, who characteristically chose to emphasize the foreground view, eliminate the middle-ground motifs, and abbreviate the distant mountains. In the lower right section Lan Ying also adopted Ni Tsan's bare-tree motif and accompanied it with a Lake T'ai rock—a fashionable combination for garden designs. The simple fishing boat and pliant water reeds under the tall red-leaved maple tree recall the paintings of Wu Chen. The most important pictorial source for this painting, however, is Wang Meng; the coniferous and deciduous trees, the Lake T'ai rock, the distant mountain ranges covered with dense hairlike texture strokes, and blunt, "scorched ink" (*chiao-mo*) dots all resemble Wang's technique. Lan transformed these motifs by giving them short broken outlines and using dry ink and twisted, feathered texture strokes. As a result of these techniques, *Autumn River*, like most of Lan Ying's works, lacks clear spatial definition and formal cohesiveness. Stressing surface abstraction over a sense of three-dimensionality, Lan's painting takes classic Yüan models known for their subtle and placid spirit and charges them with energy—producing an anxious, restless landscape.

PAO-CHEN CH'EN

NOTES

1. Patricia Berger, "Lan Ying and the Chekiang Masters," in James Cahill, ed., *The Restless Landscape: Chinese Painting of the Late Ming Period* (Berkeley: Art Museum, University of California at Berkeley, 1971), pp. 133–35; Marilyn and Shen Fu, *Studies in Connoisseurship: Chinese Paintings from the Arthur M. Sackler Collection in New York and Princeton* (Princeton: The Art Museum, 1974), pp. 111–13; Yen Chüan-ying, *Lan Ying te fang-ku hui-hua* (Lan Ying and his paintings in the style of ancient masters) (Taipei: National Palace Museum, 1980), pp. 14, 86.

   Hu Sai-lan categorized Lan Ying as one of the transformation painters of the seventeenth century in *Wan Ming pien-hsing chu-i hua-chia tso-p'in chan* (Style transformed: a special exhibition of works by five late Ming artists) (Taipei: National Palace Museum, 1977), p. 7.
2. Yen Chüan-ying, *Lan Ying te fang-ku hui-hua*, pp. 1–14.

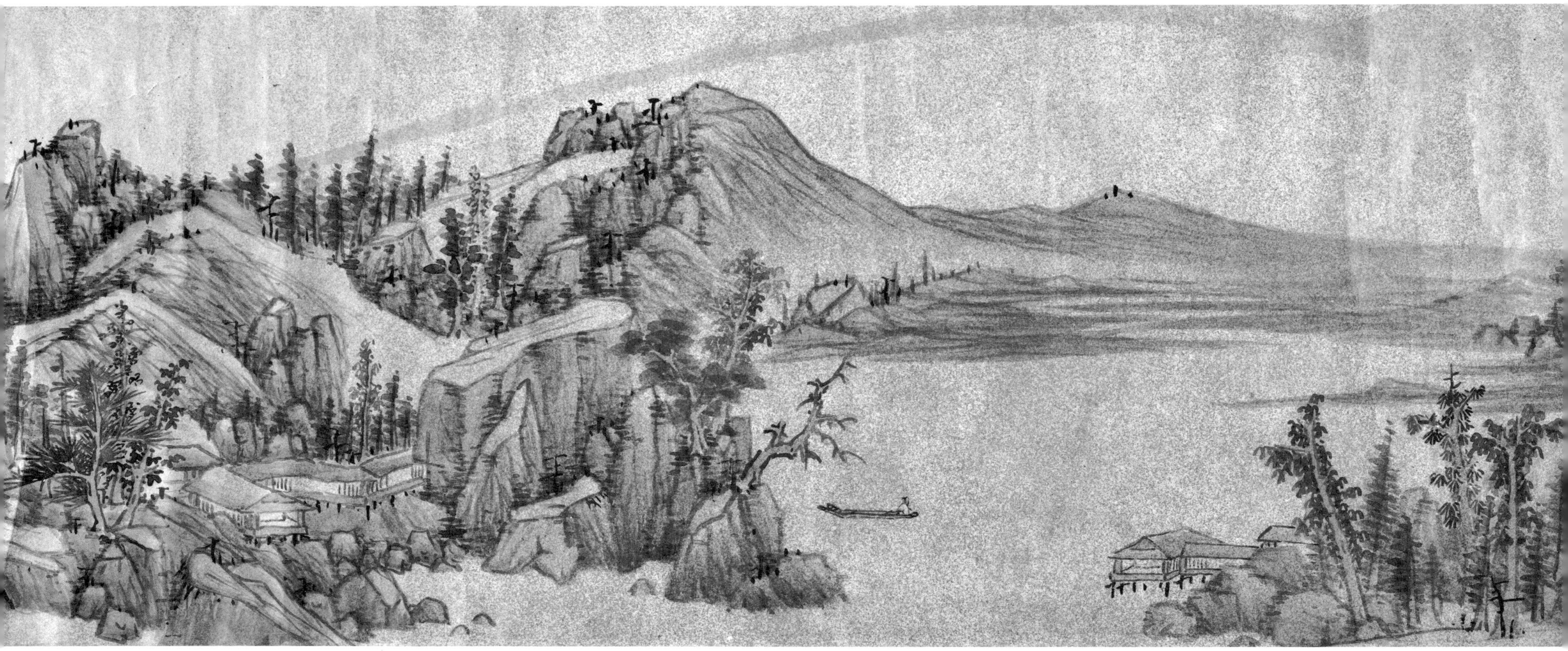

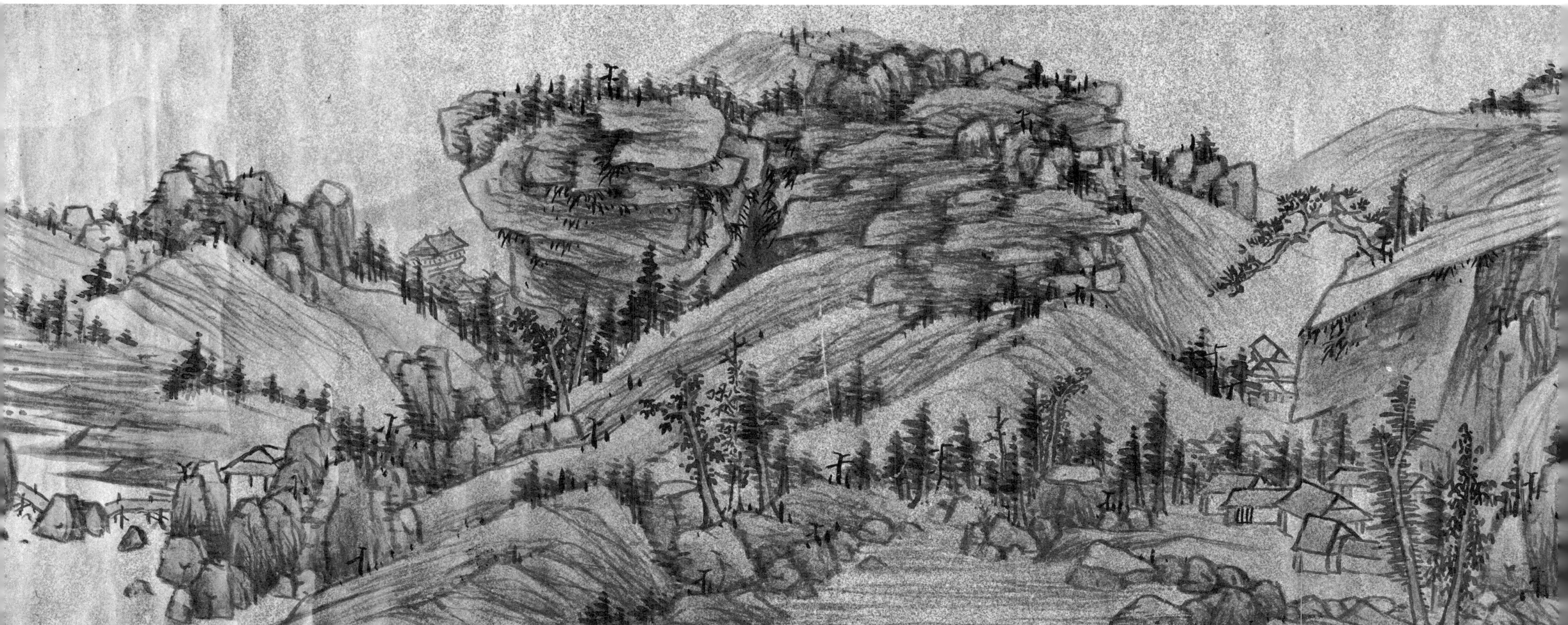

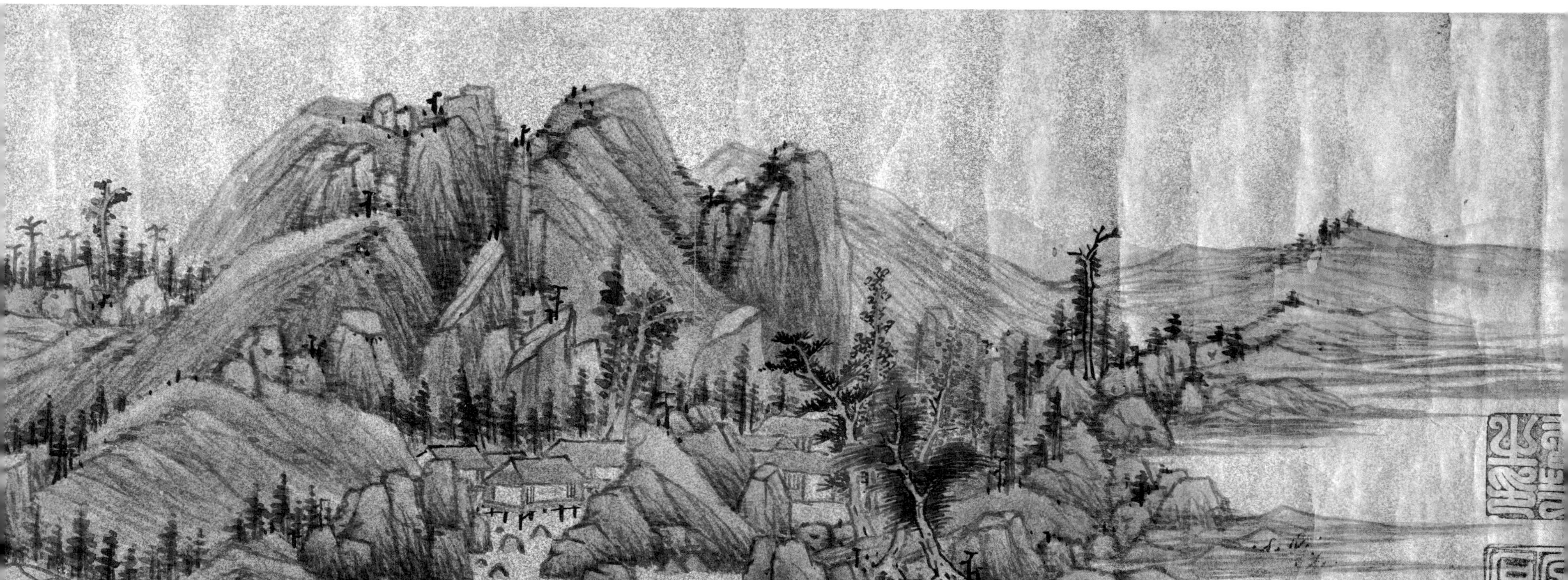

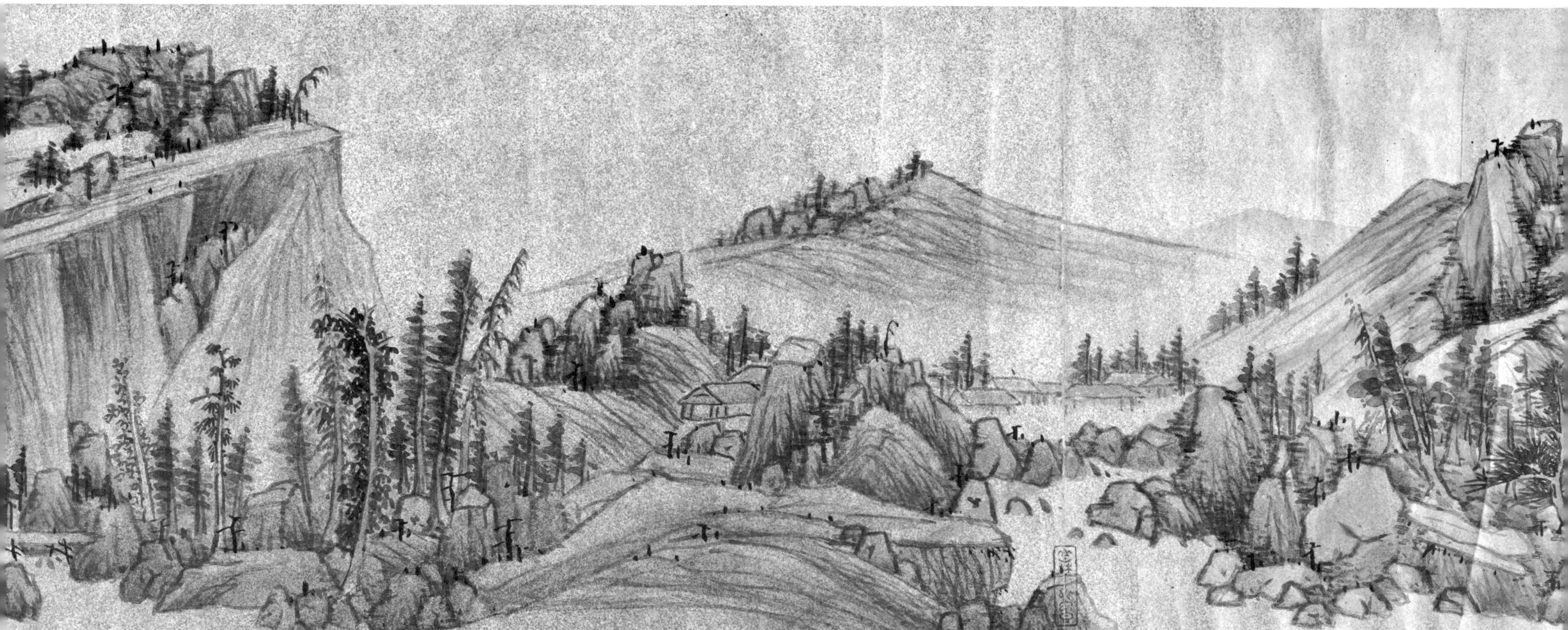

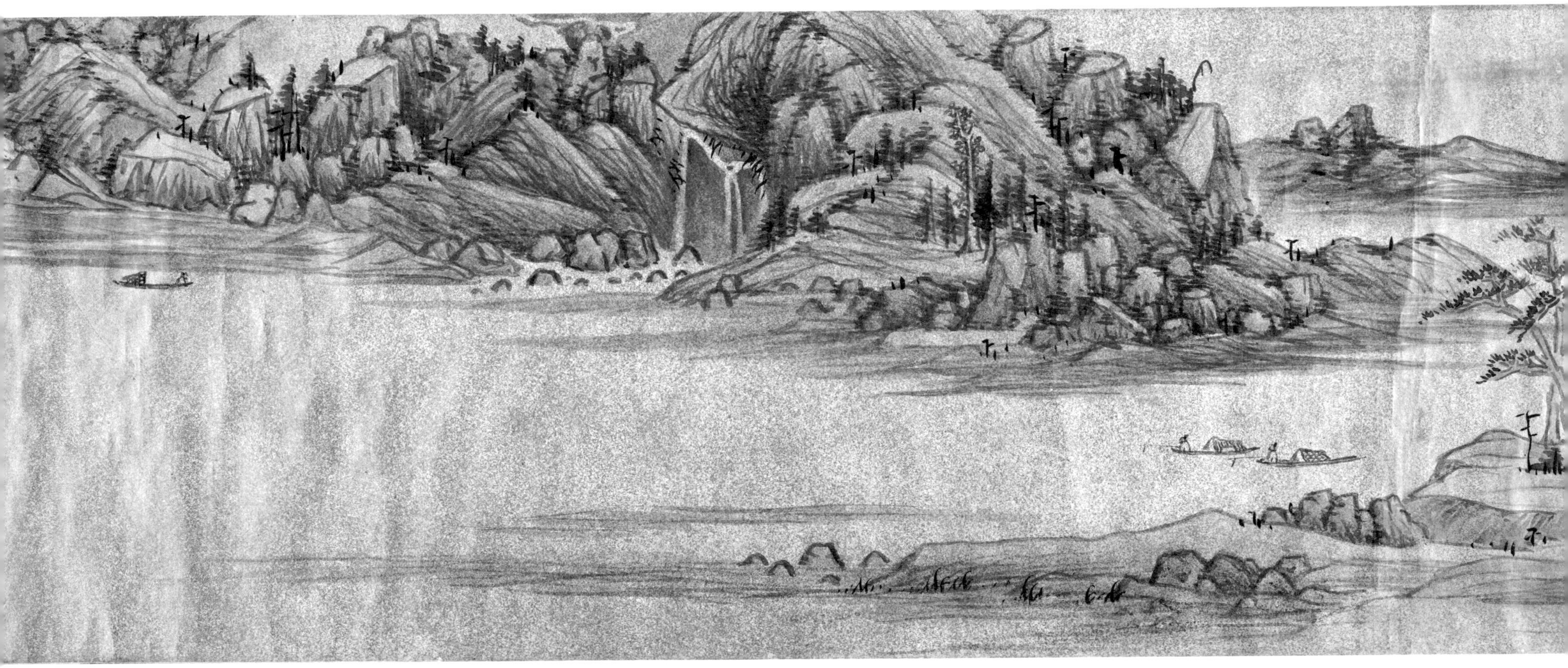

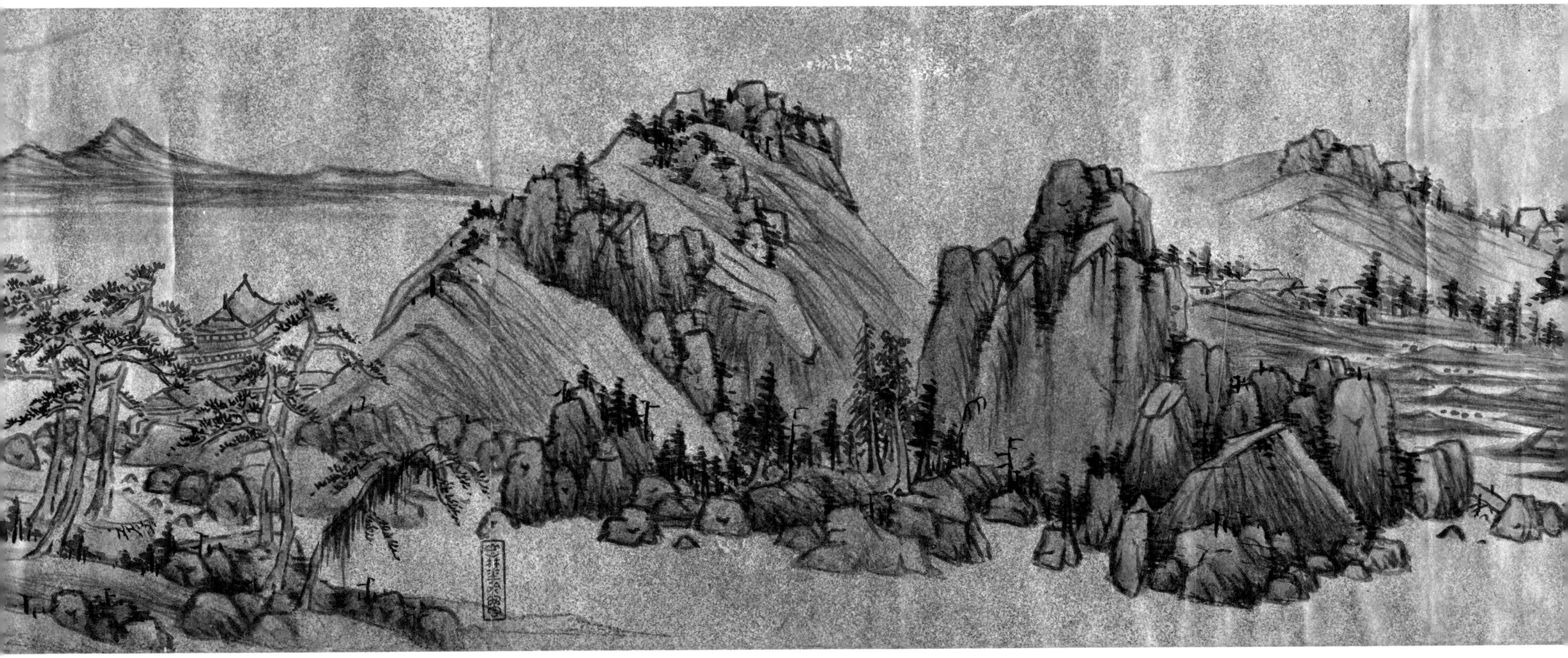

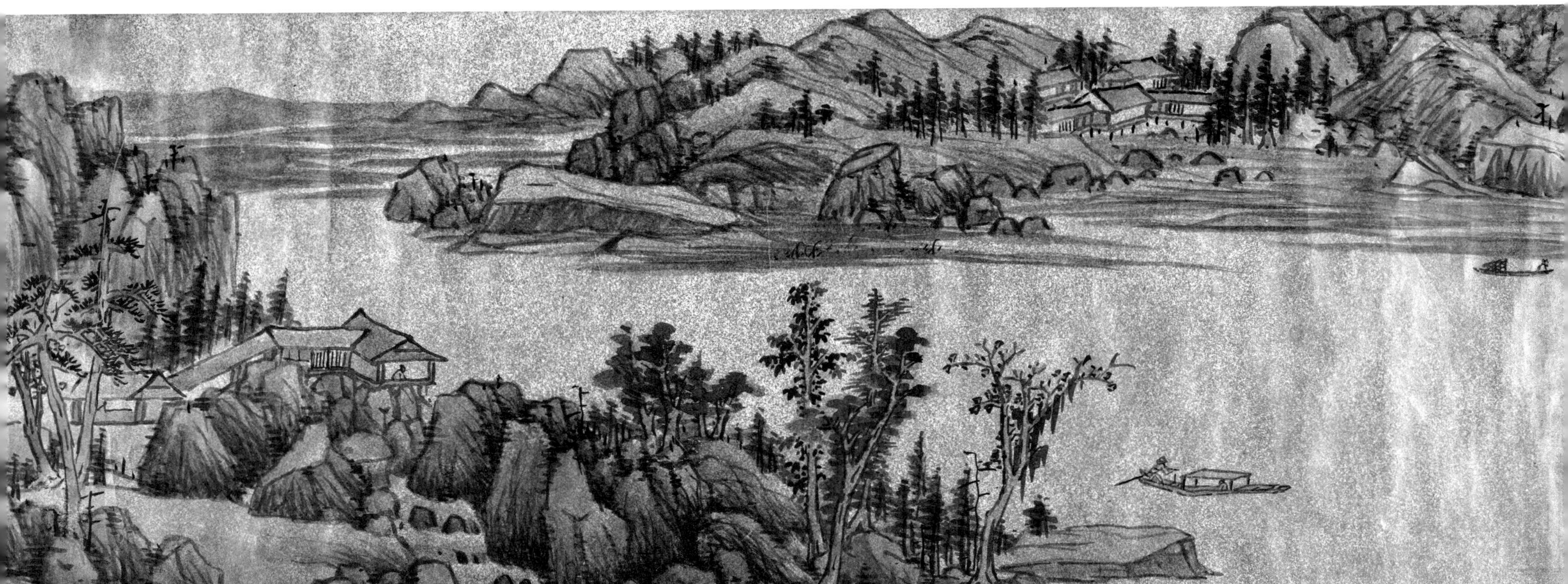

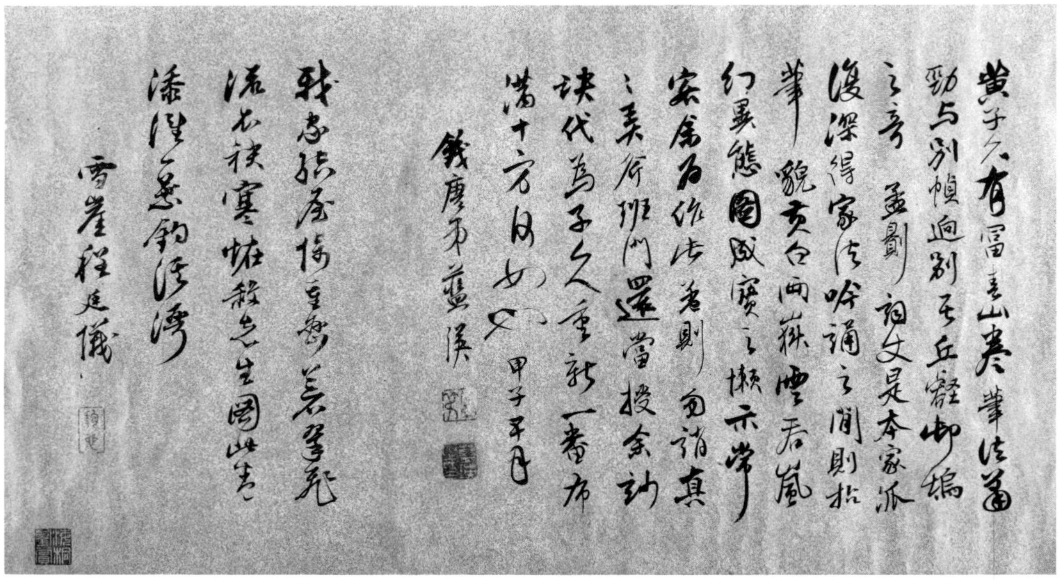

Inscription by Ch'eng T'ing-i　　Artist's inscription

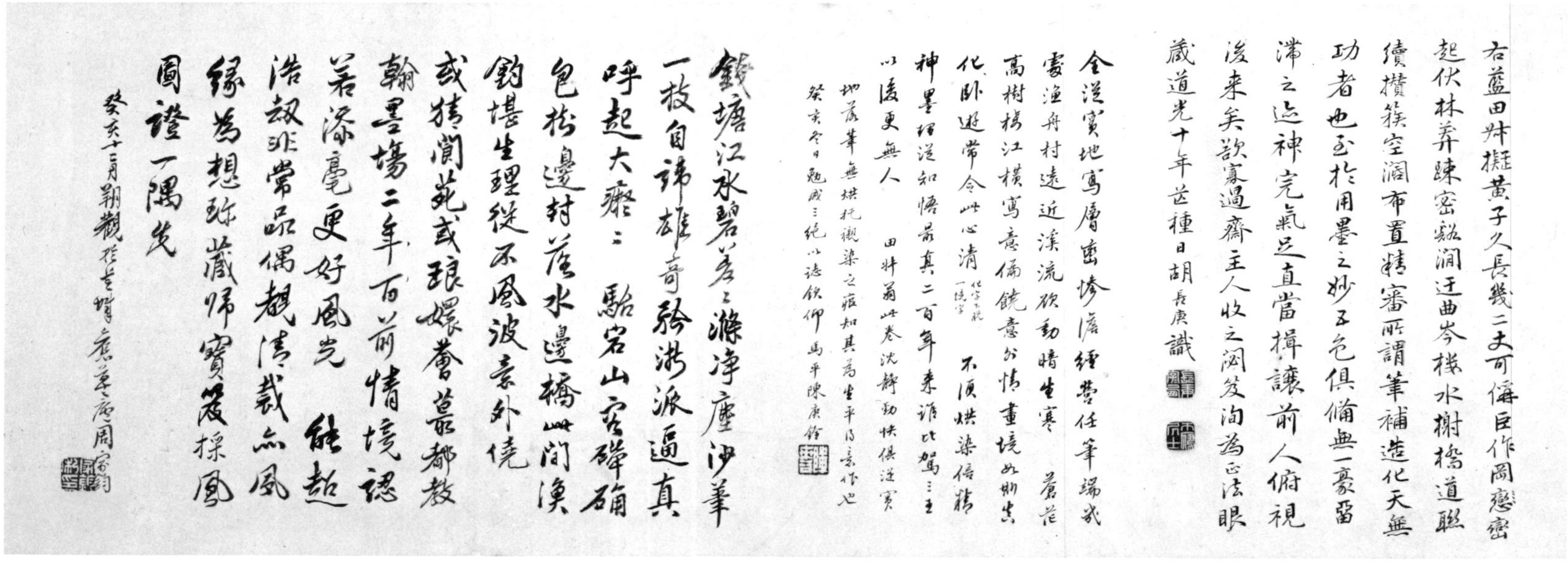

Chou Chia-chün　　Ch'en Keng-ling　　Hu Ch'ang-keng

# 31 Lan Ying (1585–after 1664)

## *Autumn River (I chiang ch'iu-shui)*

Dated 1640
Hanging scroll, ink and color on paper
95.5 x 37.8 cm (3 ft. 1⅝ in. x 14⅞ in.)

ARTIST'S INSCRIPTION (7 character quatrain, followed by a 23 character note, in 8 columns of running script):

Autumn river, clear and tranquil;
Thick dew-covered reeds at dusk.
Only those under the boat's thatched roof realize
That leaves, reddened and drunk from frost, have piled
up over half the boat.

In the winter of the *keng-ch'en* year [1640], while I painted this at Ch'ih-shang Garden, Erh-kung, my literary friend, often visited me and we engaged in intellectual conversations. Therefore I commemorate [those intimate times] and present the painting for his appraisal.

ARTIST'S SIGNATURE: Farmer from Mount Wu [Wu-shan-nung], Lan Ying.

ARTIST'S SEALS: Lan Ying chih yin (square intaglio); T'ien-shu (square relief); Tieh-fu (oval relief).

COLLECTORS' SEALS: Unidentified owners: Yen-pi chih yin (square intaglio; lower right); Yün-t'ing chen-ts'ang (square intaglio; lower right).

Gift of Mrs. Edward L. Elliott (81–44)

PUBLISHED: Suzuki Kei, comp., *Chūgoku kaiga sōgō zuroku: daiikkan, Amerika–Kanada hen* (Comprehensive illustrated catalogue of Chinese paintings: volume 1, American and Canadian collections) (Tokyo: University of Tokyo Press, 1982), p. 129, pl. A17–025; James Cahill, *The Distant Mountains: Chinese Painting of the Late Ming Dynasty, 1570–1644* (New York and Tokyo: Weatherhill, 1982), pl. 103; John Rosenfield et al., eds., "Art of Asia Acquired by North American Museums, 1982," *Archives of Asian Art* 35 (1982): 106, fig. 46.

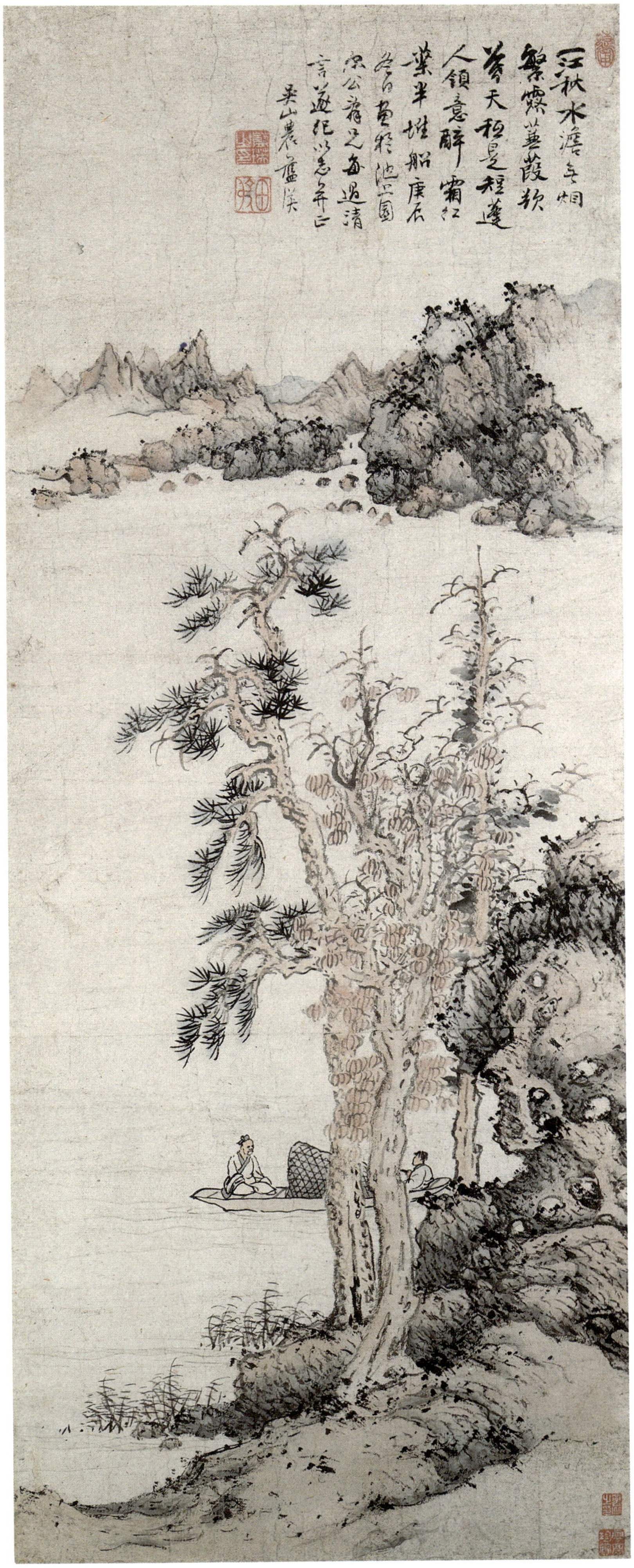

# 32 Shen Hao (1586–ca. 1661)

## *Landscapes after Sung and Yüan Masters (Fang Sung Yüan shan-shui ts'e)*

Dated 1652
Album of ten leaves, ink and color on paper (A–G, J); ink on paper (H, I)
Average measurements, each leaf: 29.7 x 24.2 cm (11 3/4 x 9 1/2 in.)

ARTIST'S INSCRIPTIONS:
Leaf A, "Landscape in the Style of Wen Cheng-ming (1470–1559)" (prose, 9 characters in 3 columns of regular script): [Wen] Cheng-ming's paintings in the style of Chao Meng-fu [1254–1332] look like this.

Leaf B, "Landscape in the Style of Lu Kuang (fl. mid-14th century)" (prose, 17 characters in 3 columns of cursive script): Paintings by Lu T'ien-yu [Lu Kuang] after Sung masters were mediocre. I painted the countryside of Min and Yüeh [Fukien and Kuangtung provinces] following his style.

Leaf C, "Landscape in the Style of Shen Chou (1427–1509)" (prose, 9 characters in 3 columns of running script): Playing the lute under the dew-covered *wu-t'ung* trees in the autumn, painted in the style of Shih-weng [Shen Chou].

Leaf D, "Landscape in the Style of Chao Ling-jang" (fl. ca. 1070–1100)" (prose, 12 characters in 3 columns of regular script): [Chao] Ling-jang's [technique], elegant and splendid, was heaven-sent. I painted this using the special traits of his style.

Leaf E, "Landscape in the Style of Li Kung-lin (1049–1106)" (prose, 16 characters in 2 columns of running script): The Nine Lakes area [in Fukien province] has many unusual trees. I remembered that Li Kung-lin had painted this theme, so I occasionally imitated his style.

Leaf F, "Landscape in the Style of Fan K'uan (ca. 960–1030)" (prose, 8 characters in 2 columns of running script): Done in the spirit of the painting of peach blossom wave on a remote cliff by Fan Hua-yüan [Fan K'uan].

Leaf G, "Landscape in the Style of Huang Kung-wang (1269–1354)" (prose, 7 characters in 2 columns of running script): Painted in the style of Tzu-chiu's [Huang Kung-wang's] paintings of fallen leaves in autumnal villages.

Leaf H, "Landscape in the Style of Tung Yüan (fl. 937–76)" (prose, 15 characters in 2 columns of running script): Paintings by Pei-yüan [Tung Yüan] of summer mountains after rain [are so marvelous that] the Great Mi [Mi Fu, 1052–1107] could not even reach such a level. Here I used the five colors of ink to improve this painting.

Leaf I, "Landscape in the Style of Ni Tsan (1301–1374)" (prose, 12 characters in 3 columns of regular script): The remote and sparse atmosphere in paintings by Yün-lin [Ni Tsan] can only be captured by those who master the spirit of Ch'an [Zen].

Leaf J, "Landscape in the Style of Kuo Hsi (ca. 1010–ca. 1090)" (21 characters in 5 columns of running script): "Ten Thousand Peaks in the Clearing after a Snow," in the style of Kuo Ho-yang [Kuo Hsi]. In the winter of the *jen-ch'en* year [1652], I painted these ten leaves in the manner of the ancient masters in order to express my profound and lofty ideas.

ARTIST'S SIGNATURE: Shen Hao (J).

ARTIST'S SEALS: Shen Hao chih yin (square, half relief, half intaglio; A, J); Shih-t'ien (oval relief; B); Shen Hao (square intaglio; C, H); Lang-ch'ien (square relief; D); Lang-chü (square intaglio; E); Lang-ch'ien (reversed square relief overlapping a Lang-chü seal as seen in E, I); Shih-t'ien (square relief; F, G, J); Shang-hsia ch'ien-nien (round relief; J).

COLLECTOR'S SEALS: Ma Chi-tso (modern collector): Chi-tso (square relief; A, D, G, I); Chi-tso ch'ang-shou (square intaglio; F); Ma Chi-tso chien-shang chang (tall rectangle relief; J).

Edward L. Elliott Family Collection (L230.70)

PUBLISHED: Suzuki Kei, comp., *Chūgoku kaiga sōgō zuroku: daiikkan, Amerika–Kanada hen* (Comprehensive illustrated catalogue of Chinese paintings: volume 1, American and Canadian collections) (Tokyo: University of Tokyo Press, 1982), p. 160, pl. A17–109.

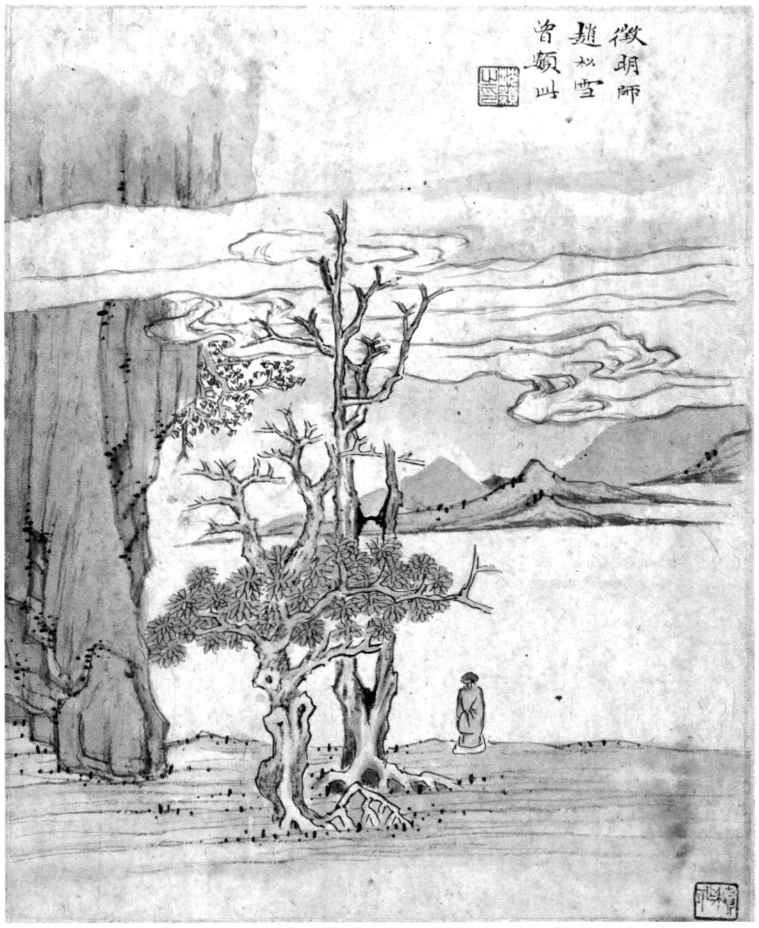
Leaf A, "Landscape in the Style of Wen Cheng-ming (1470–1559)"

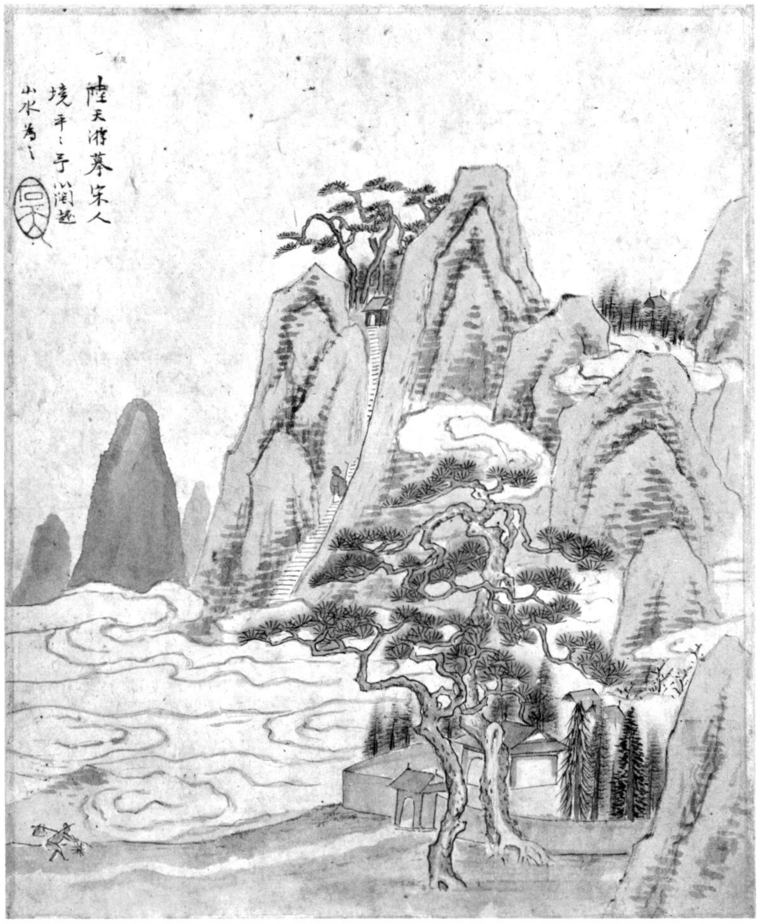
Leaf B, "Landscape in the Style of Lu Kuang (fl. mid-14th century)"

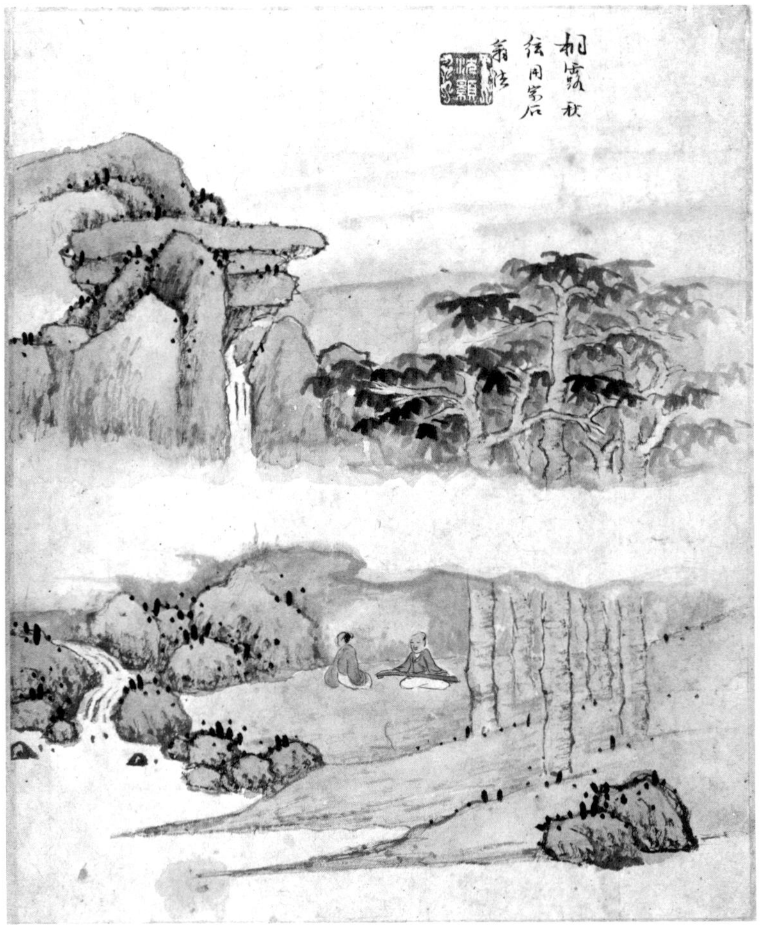
Leaf C, "Landscape in the Style of Shen Chou (1427–1509)"

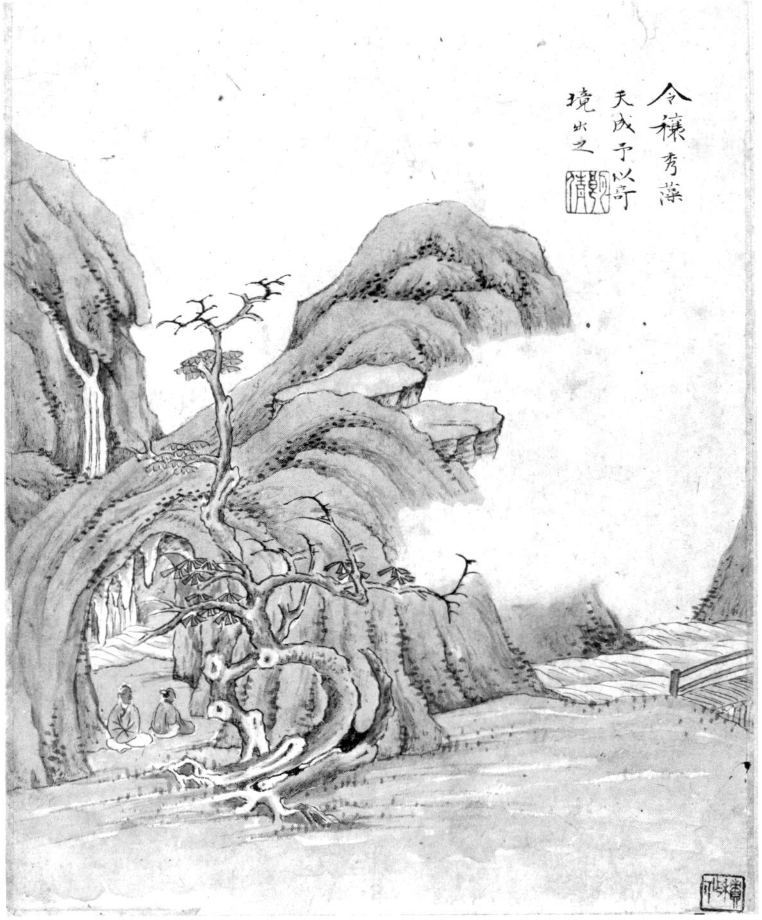
Leaf D, "Landscape in the Style of Chao Ling-jang (fl. ca. 1070–1100)"

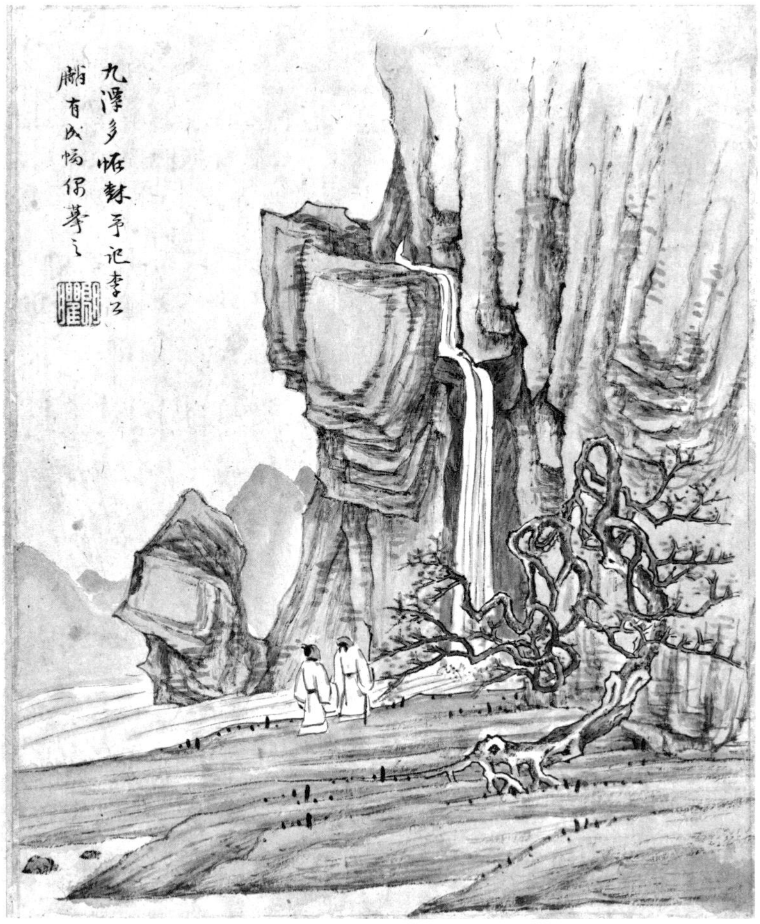

Leaf E, "Landscape in the Style of Li Kung-lin (1049–1106)"

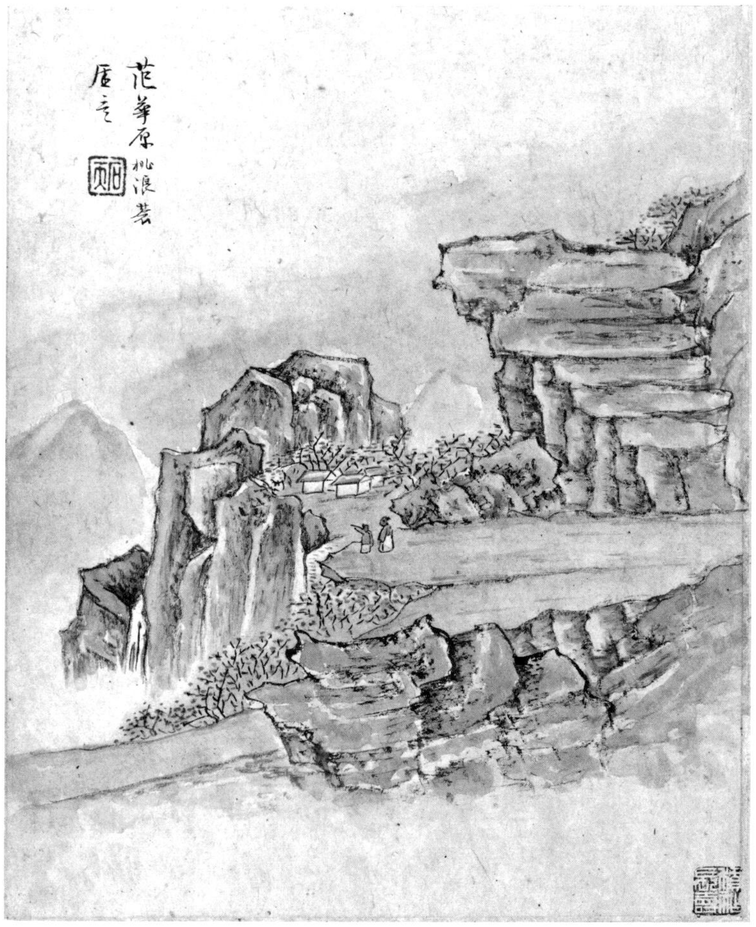

Leaf F, "Landscape in the Style of Fan K'uan (ca. 960–1030)"

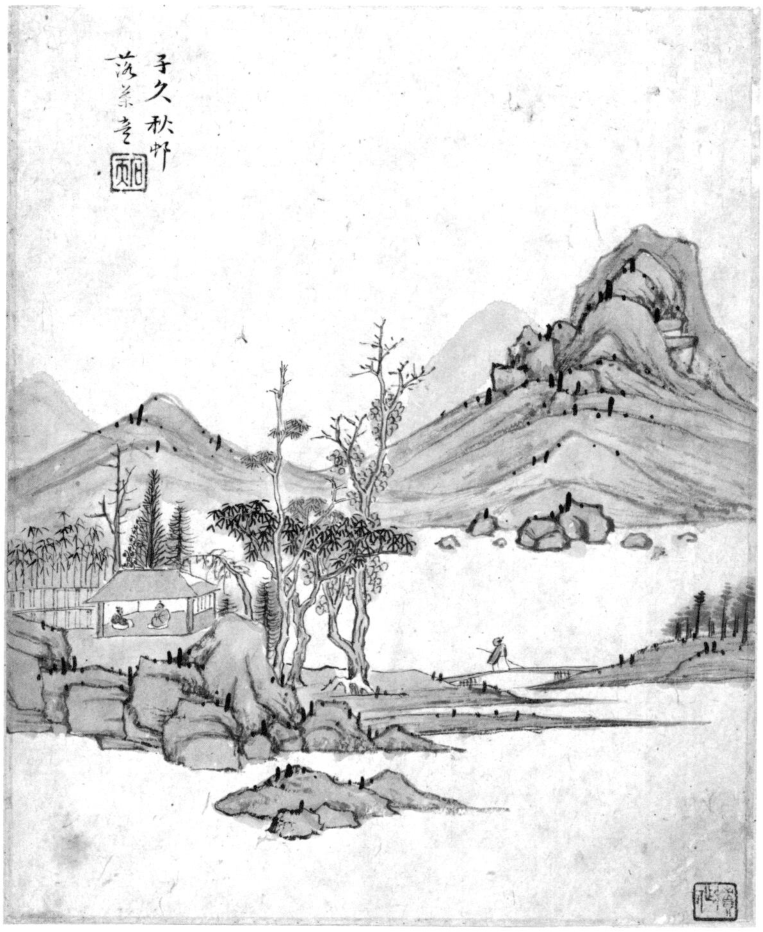

Leaf G, "Landscape in the Style of Huang Kung-wang (1269–1354)"

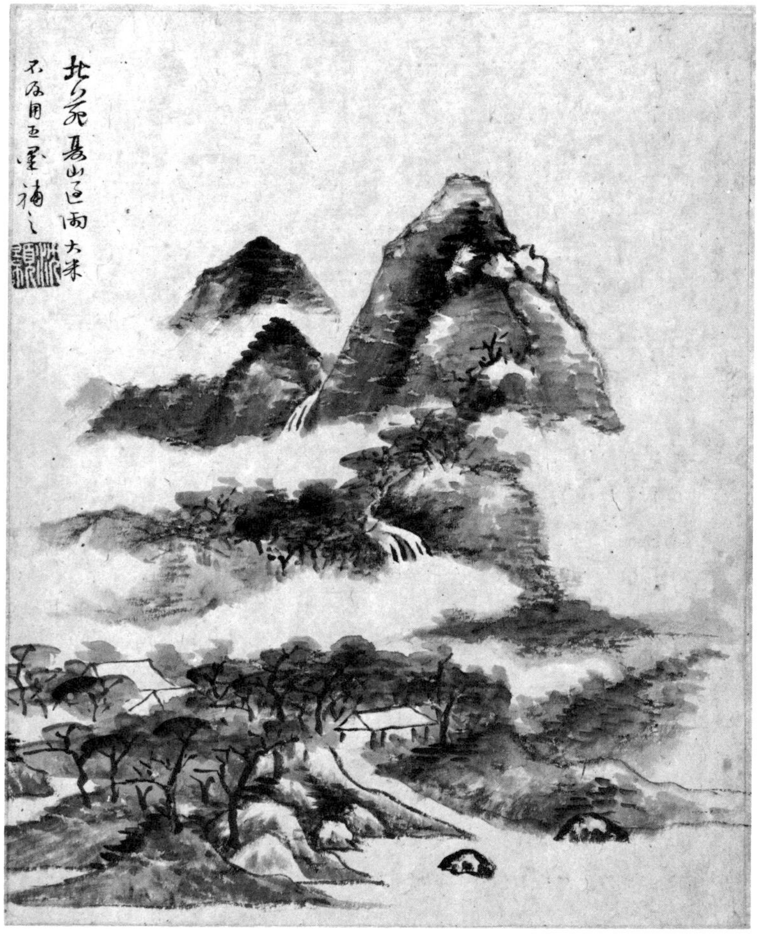

Leaf H, "Landscape in the Style of Tung Yüan (fl. 937–76)"

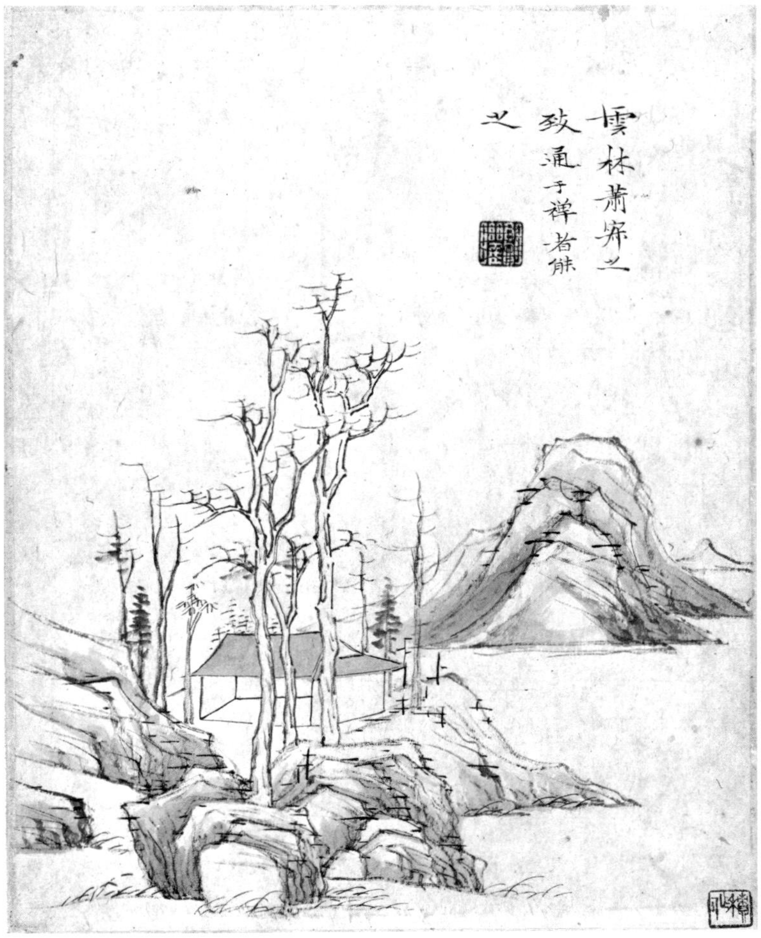

Leaf I, "Landscape in the Style of Ni Tsan (1301–1374)"

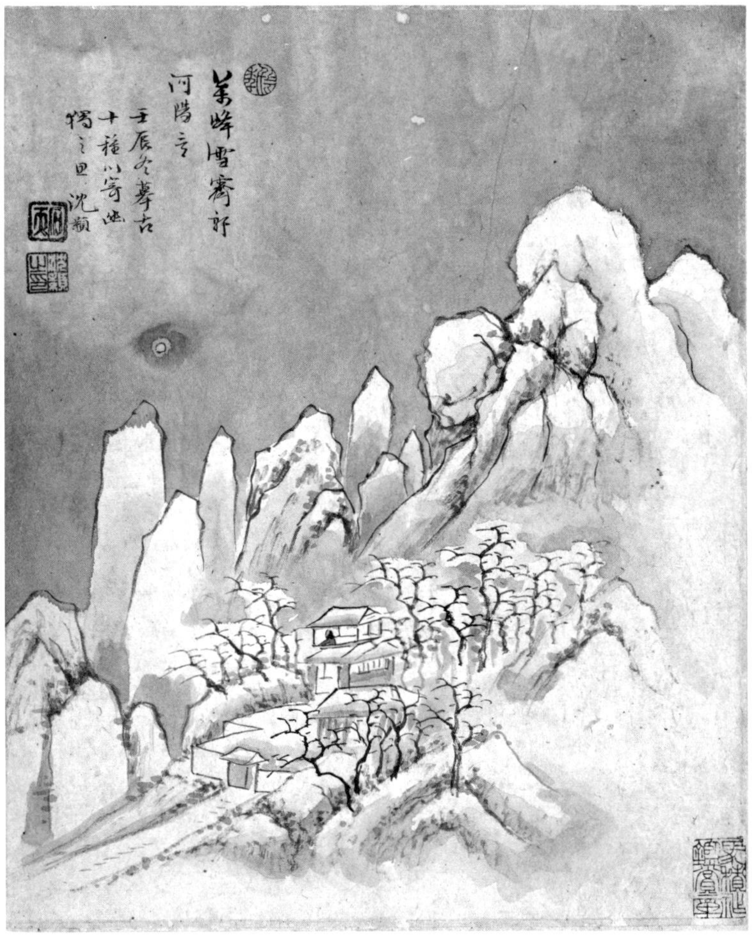

Leaf J, "Landscape in the Style of Kuo Hsi (ca. 1010–ca. 1090)"

# 33 Ch'en Hung-shou (1599–1652)

## *Five-character Poem (Wu-yen shih)*

After 1644
Hanging scroll, ink on paper
114.7 x 30.0 cm (3 ft. $9^{1}/_{8}$ in. x $11^{3}/_{4}$ in.)

CALLIGRAPHY (5 character quatrain in 2 columns of cursive script); translation by Adele Rickett, in Tseng Yu-ho Ecke, *Chinese Calligraphy* (Philadelphia: The Philadelphia Museum of Art; and Boston: Boston Book and Art, 1971), p. 73:

> How I love to wander in the hills,
> Drinking wine along the way.
> But of the moment, fleeting, what regret
> Such happiness can never be repeated.

ARTIST'S SIGNATURE: Hung-shou presented this to the son of [his] sworn brother Yin-jen, asking for his comments.

ARTIST'S SEALS: Ch'en Hung-shou yin (square relief); Chang-hou (square intaglio).

COLLECTORS' SEALS:
1. Chang Yüan (Chang Ta-ch'ien; 1899–1983): Chang Yüan chih yin (square intaglio; lower left); Ta-ch'ien-chü-shih (square relief; lower left).
2. Unidentified owner: K'ai-lo-t'ang ts'ang (square relief; lower left).

Gift of John B. Elliott (71–1)

PUBLISHED: Tseng Yu-ho Ecke, *Chinese Calligraphy* (Philadelphia: The Philadelphia Museum of Art; and Boston: Boston Book and Art, 1971), pl. 73; Suzuki Kei, comp., *Chūgoku kaiga sōgō zuroku: daiikkan, Amerika–Kanada hen* (Comprehensive illustrated catalogue of Chinese paintings: volume 1, American and Canadian collections) (Tokyo: University of Tokyo Press, 1982), p. 111, pl. A16–027; Nakata Yūjirō and Fu Shen, eds., *Obei shūzō Chūgoku hōsho meisekishū* (Chinese calligraphy in American and European collections), vol. 5 (Tokyo: Chūōkōron-sha, forthcoming); Tseng Yu-ho Ecke, *The Art of Chinese Calligraphy, A History* (Honolulu: University of Hawaii Press, forthcoming).

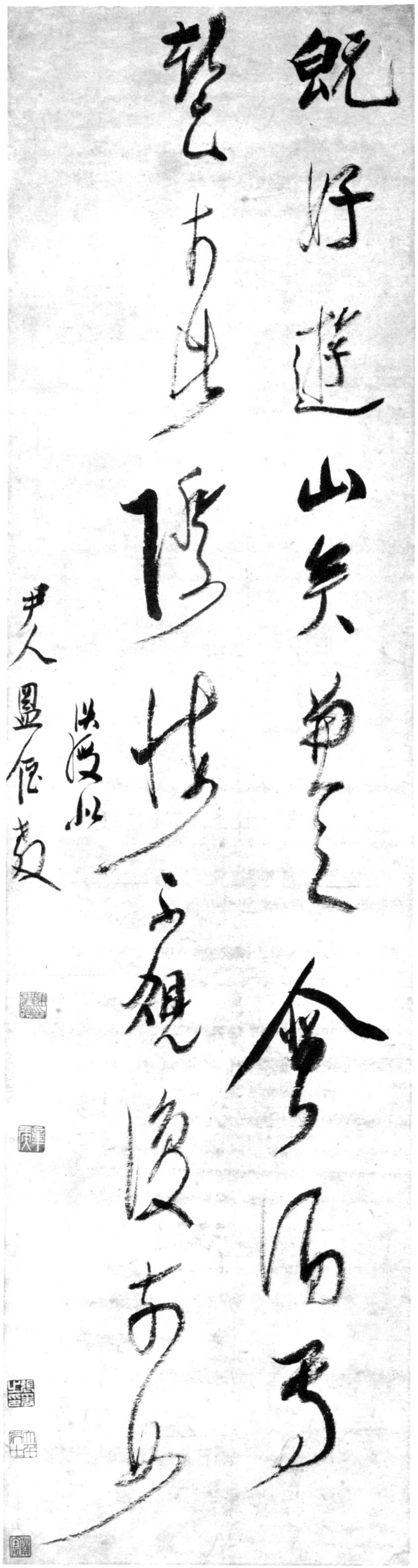

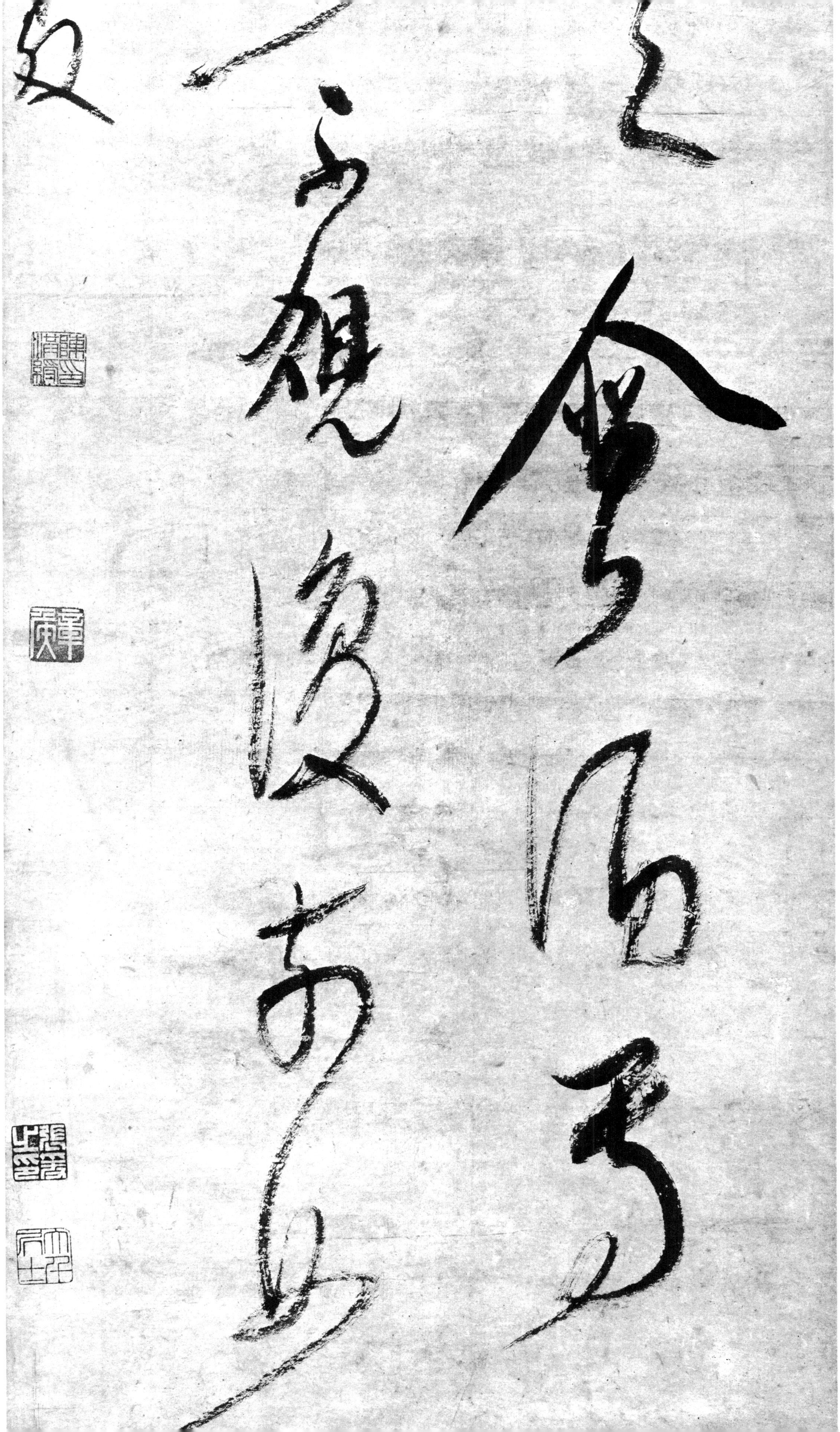

# 34 Pien Wen-yü (fl. ca. 1611–71)

## *Eight Views of West Lake (Hsi-hu pa-ching)*

Dated 1629
Album of ten leaves. Frontispiece (a,b): ink on gold-flecked paper, 27.5 x 36.6 cm (10⅞ x 14⅜ in.)
Painting (A–H): ink and color on silk; colophons on facing leaves (AA–HH): ink on gold-flecked paper, average measurements, each leaf; 22.8 x 15.6 cm (9 x 6⅛ in.)

FRONTISPIECE, calligraphy by Chang Kuo-shen (dates unknown) (4 character title in running script): "Scenes of Hang-chou" ("Wu-ling ching-wu"). Signature: Kuo-shen. Seal: Chang Kuo-shen yin (square intaglio).

ARTIST'S INSCRIPTIONS (2 character title in regular script): Leaf A, "Ku-shan"; Leaf B, "Ling-yin"; Leaf C, "T'ao-kuang"; Leaf D, "Ching-tz'u"; Leaf E, "Yün-chü"; Leaf F, "Fa-hsiang"; Leaf G, "Yen-hsia"; Leaf H, "Tuan-ch'iao."

ARTIST'S SIGNATURE: In the fourth lunar month of the *i-ssu* year [1629] I painted this album, *Eight Views of West Lake*, Pien Wen-yü (H).

ARTIST'S SEAL: Wen-yü (square intaglio; H).

COLOPHONS by Chang Kuo-shen:
Leaf AA: 5 character regulated verse in 8 lines in 5 columns of cursive script, quoted from a poem by Chang Yü (dates unknown). Signature: Kuo-shen transcribed this. Seals: Chang Kuo-shen yin (square intaglio); T'ien-kuan chih chang (square intaglio).

Leaf BB: 5 character verse in 14 lines (with one character missing) in 6 columns of cursive script, quoted from a poem by Lo Chia-ch'ang (dates unknown). Signature: Kuo-shen transcribed this. Seal: Chang shih Kuo-shen (square intaglio).

Leaf CC: 5 character regulated verse in 8 lines in 4 columns of cursive script, quoted from "On the T'ao-kuang Cliff" by Po Chü-i [722–846]. Signature: Kuo-shen transcribed this. Seal: Po-ch'i (square intaglio).

Leaf DD: prose, 51 characters in 5 columns of cursive script. Signature: Kuo-shen inscribed this. Seal: Chang Kuo-shen yin (square intaglio).

Leaf EE: 5 character regulated verse in 8 lines in 4 columns of cursive script. Signature: Kuo-shen. Seal: Shu-ch'ing shih (square relief).

Leaf FF: 7 character rhymed verse in 56 characters in 5 columns of cursive script, quoted from a poem by Liu Ta-yen (dates unknown). Signature: Chang Kuo-shen copied this. Seal: Chang shih Kuo-shen (square intaglio).

Leaf GG: prose, 76 characters in 6 columns of cursive script. Signature: Kuo-shen. Seal: Po-ch'i shih (square relief).

Leaf HH: prose, 54 characters in 5 columns of cursive script. Signature: Kuo-shen. Seal: Chang Kuo-shen Shu-ch'ing fu (squat rectangle relief).

COLLECTORS' SEALS:
1. Ch'en Jen-t'ao (1906–1968): Chin-kuei shih (tall rectangle relief; a).
2. Ch'en K'uei-lin (dates unknown): Pao-yü-ko shu-hua chi (tall rectangle relief; a).
3. Unidentified owners: Hsüeh lung-o (tall rectangle relief; a); Kung-ying chen-wan (square relief; a); Shao-shih shen-ting (square relief; A, D, E, H); Shao-shih chien-ts'ang (square relief; B, C, F, G).
4. Unidentified seal: [ ] t'ing-ch'iu-sheng-kuan (square intaglio; A).

Edward L. Elliott Family Collection (L233.70)

PUBLISHED: Ch'en Jen-t'ao, *Chin-kuei ts'ang-hua chi* (Chinese paintings from the King Kwei [Chin-kuei] collection) (Hong Kong: T'ung-ying, 1956), vol. 2, pls. 35, 36 (Leaves E, G); Ch'en Jen-t'ao, *Chin-kuei ts'ang-hua p'ing-shih* (Annotated catalogue of Chinese paintings from the King Kwei [Chin-kuei] collection) (Hong Kong: T'ung-ying, 1956), vol. 1, pp. 168–72; Suzuki Kei, comp., *Chūgoku kaiga sōgō zuroku: daiikkan, Amerika–Kanada hen* (Comprehensive illustrated catalogue of Chinese paintings: volume 1, American and Canadian collections) (Tokyo: University of Tokyo Press, 1982), p. 138, pl. A17–068.

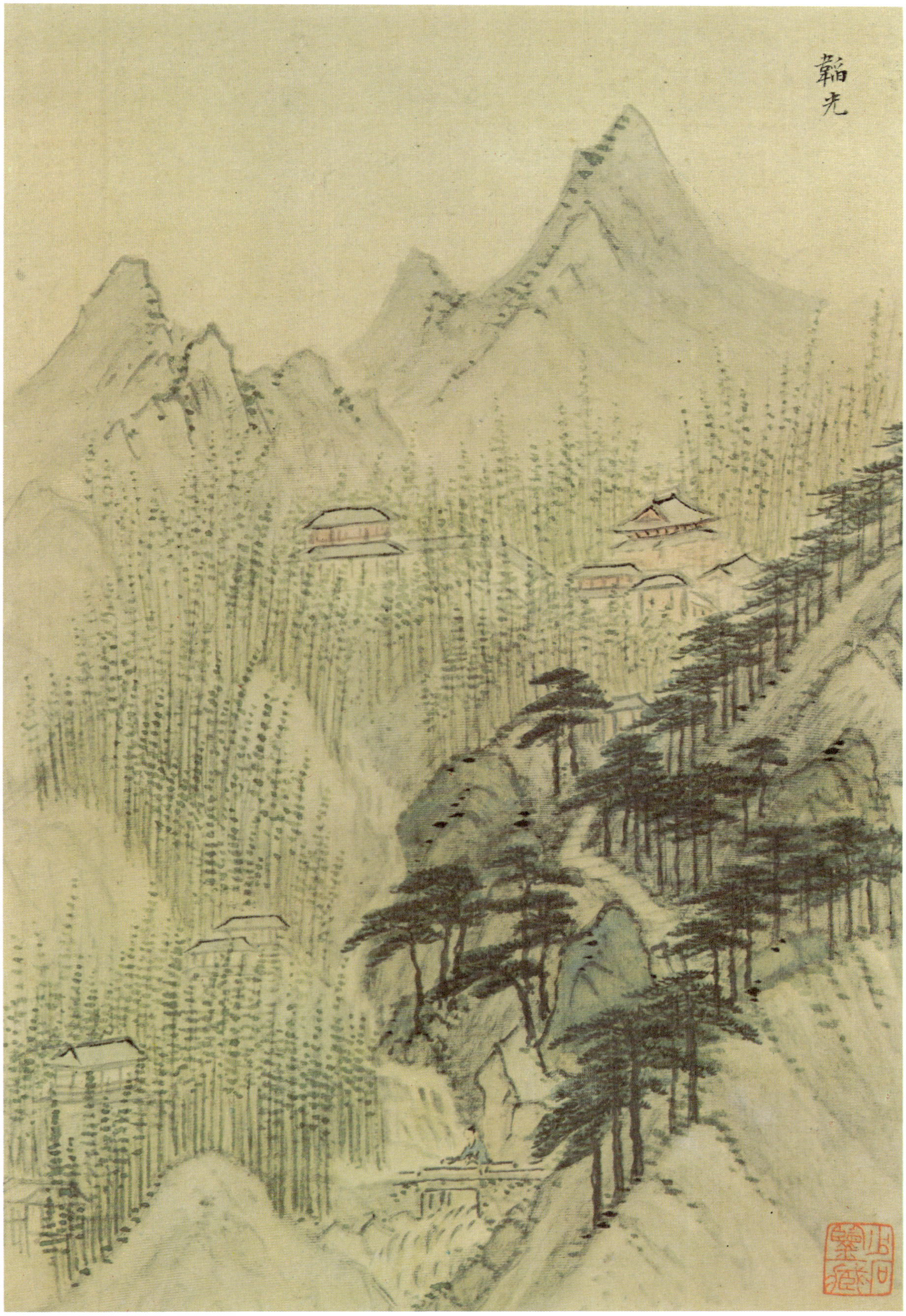


Leaf C, detail

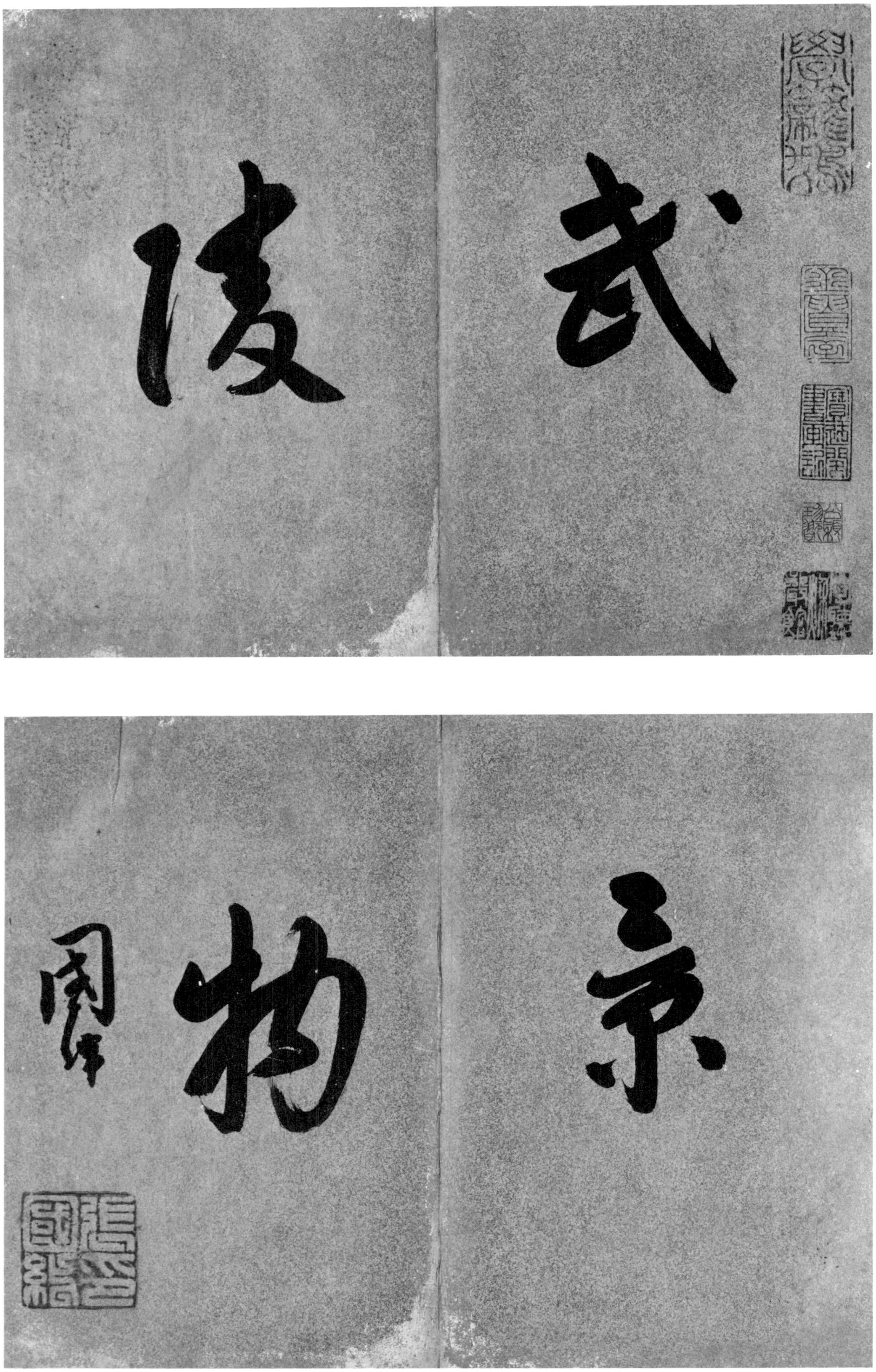

Frontispiece by Chang Kuo-shen

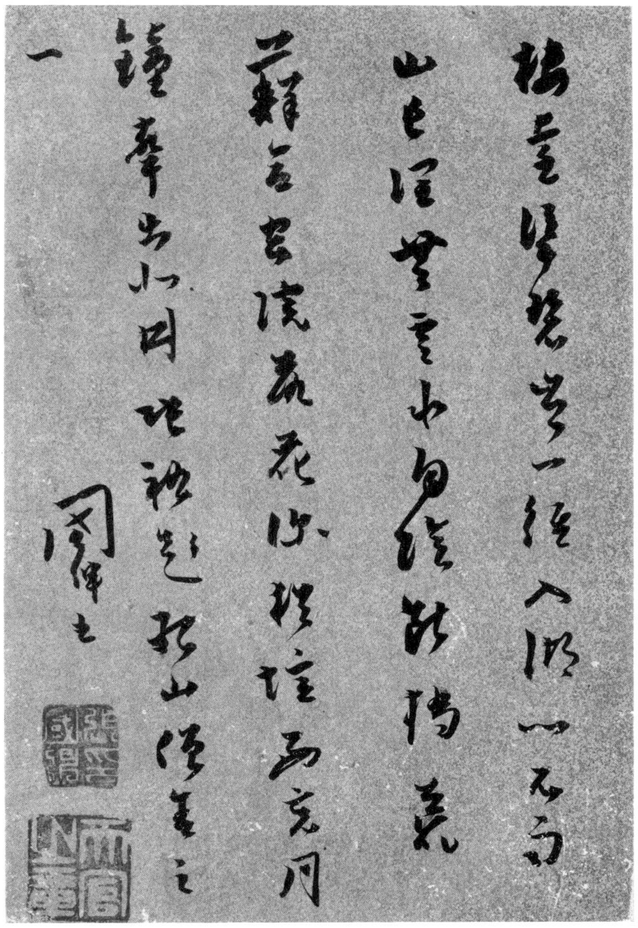

Leaf AA

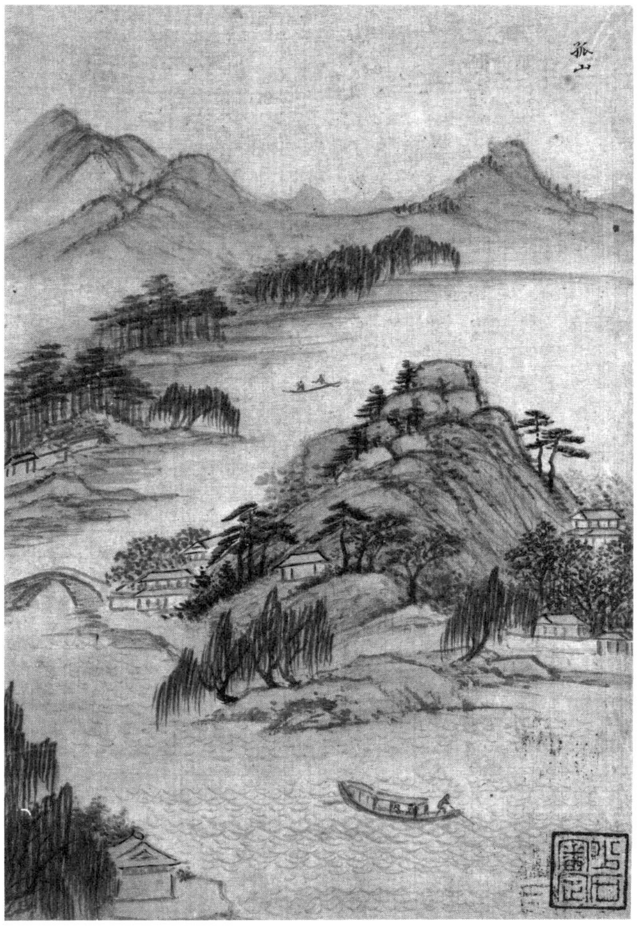


Leaf A, "Ku-shan"

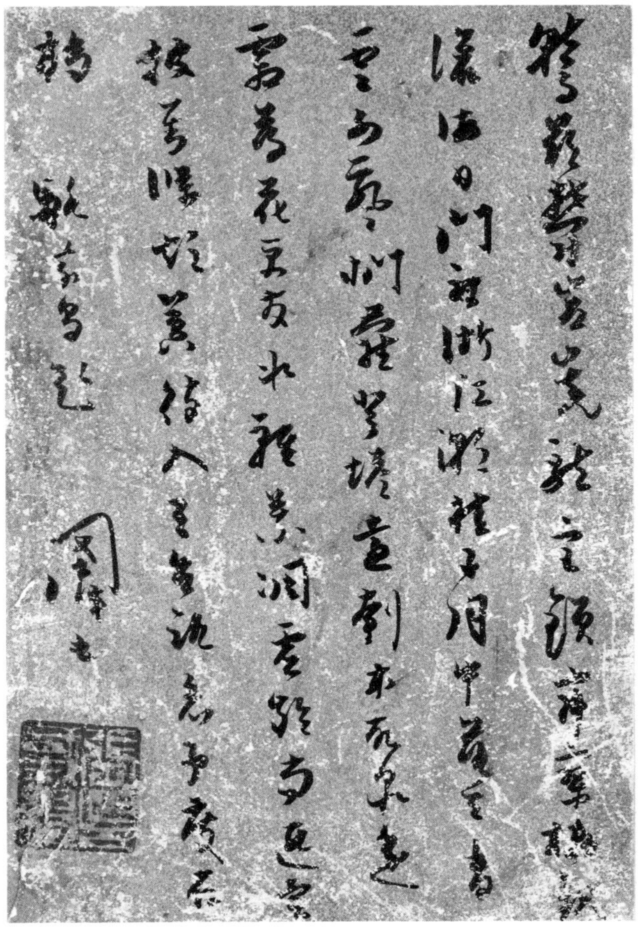

Leaf BB

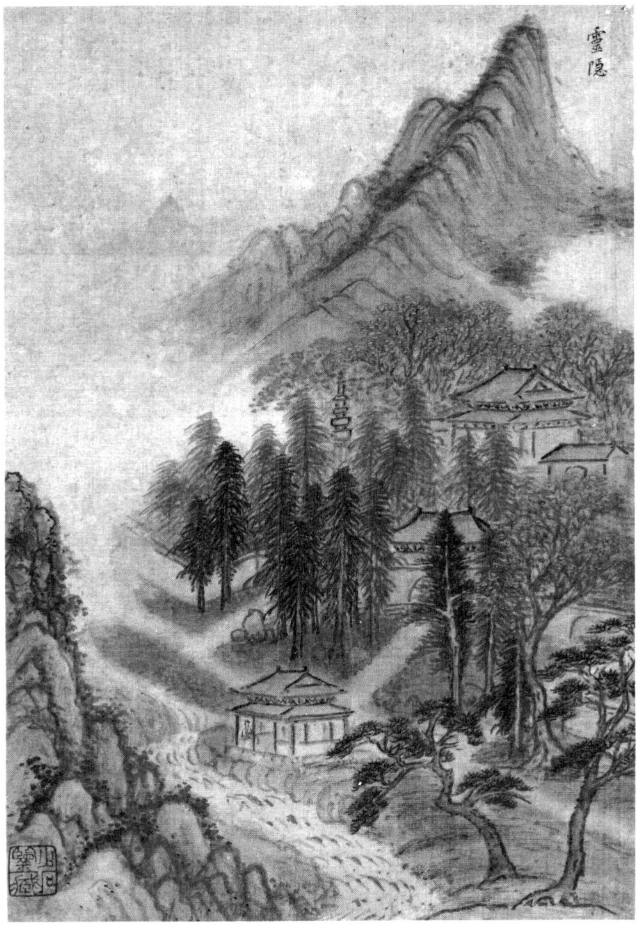


Leaf B, "Ling-yin"

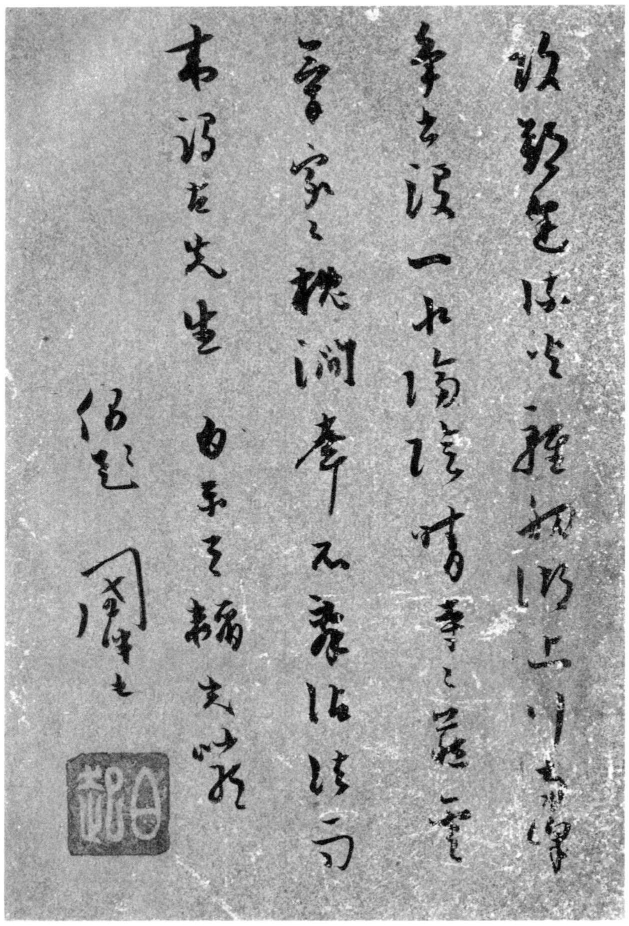

Leaf CC

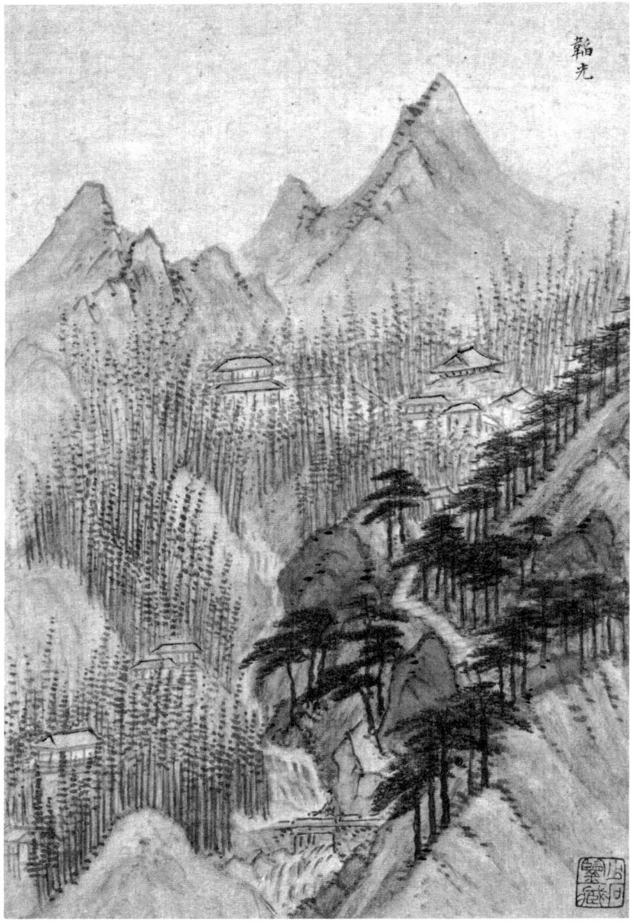

Leaf C, "T'ao-kuang"

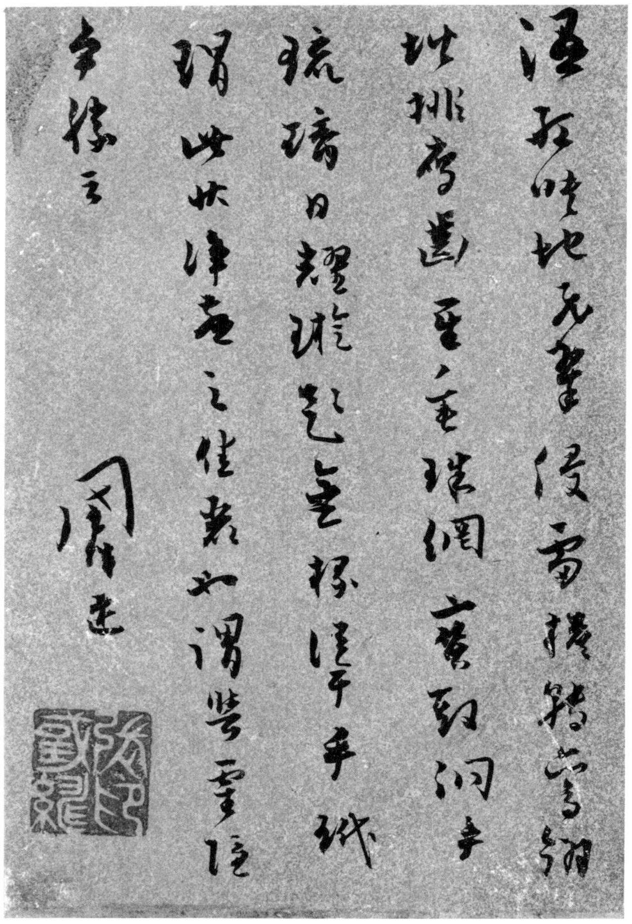

Leaf DD

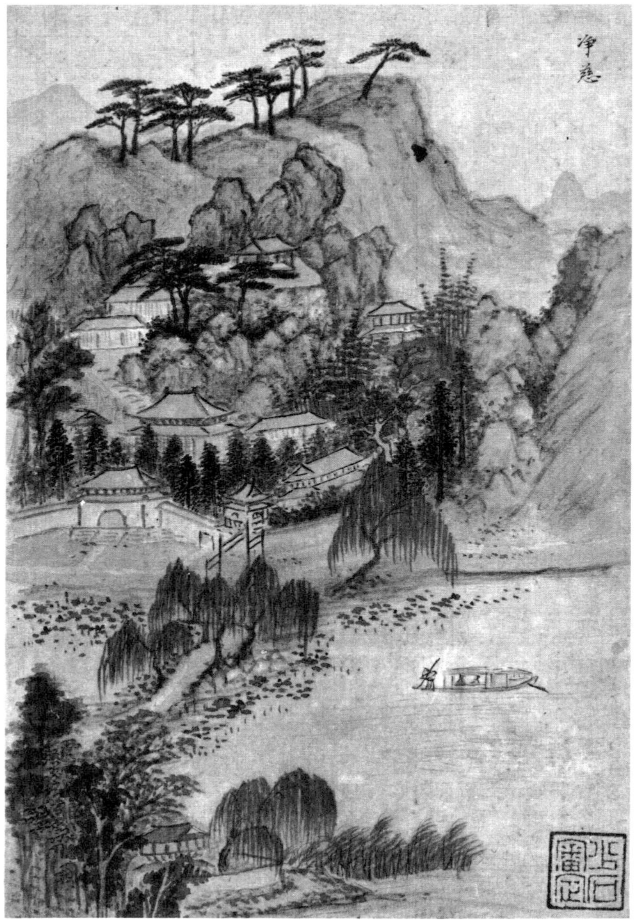

Leaf D, "Ching-tz'u"

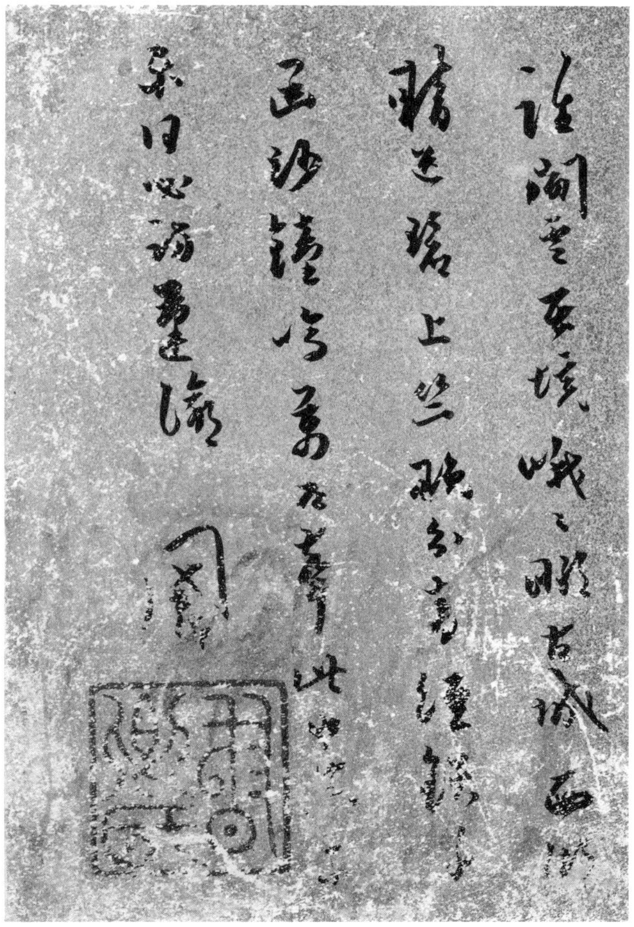

Leaf EE

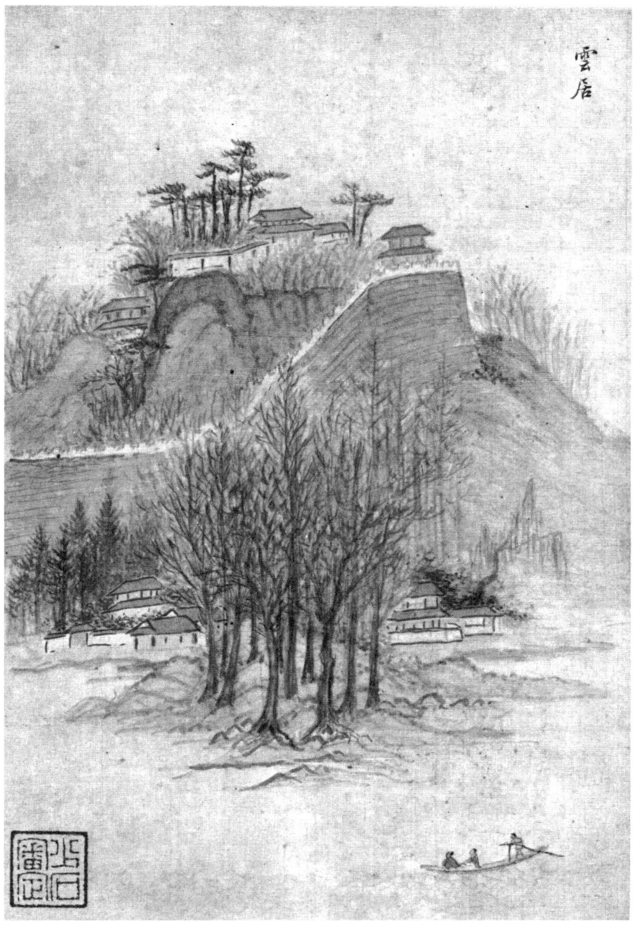


Leaf E, "Yün-chü"

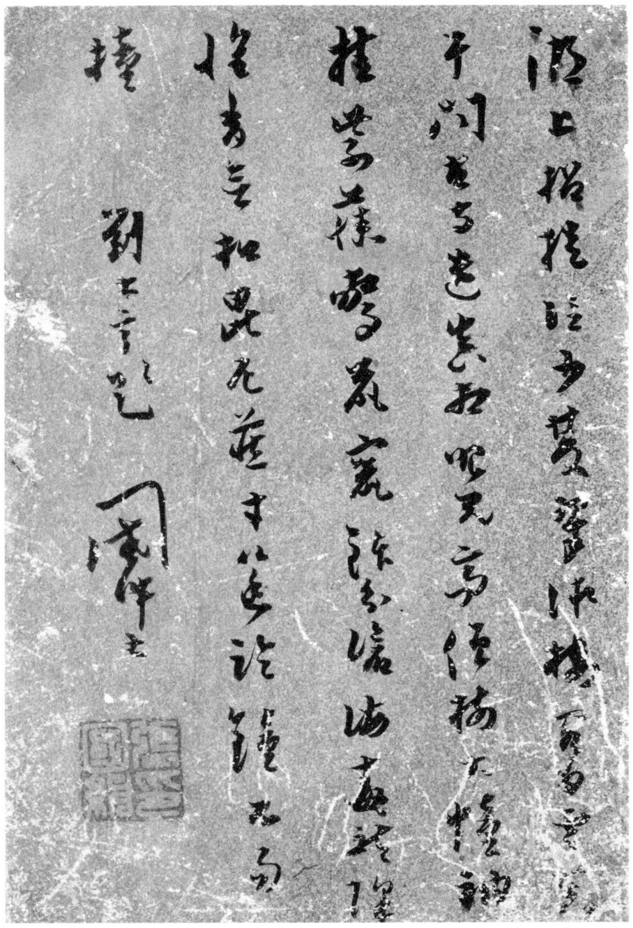

Leaf FF

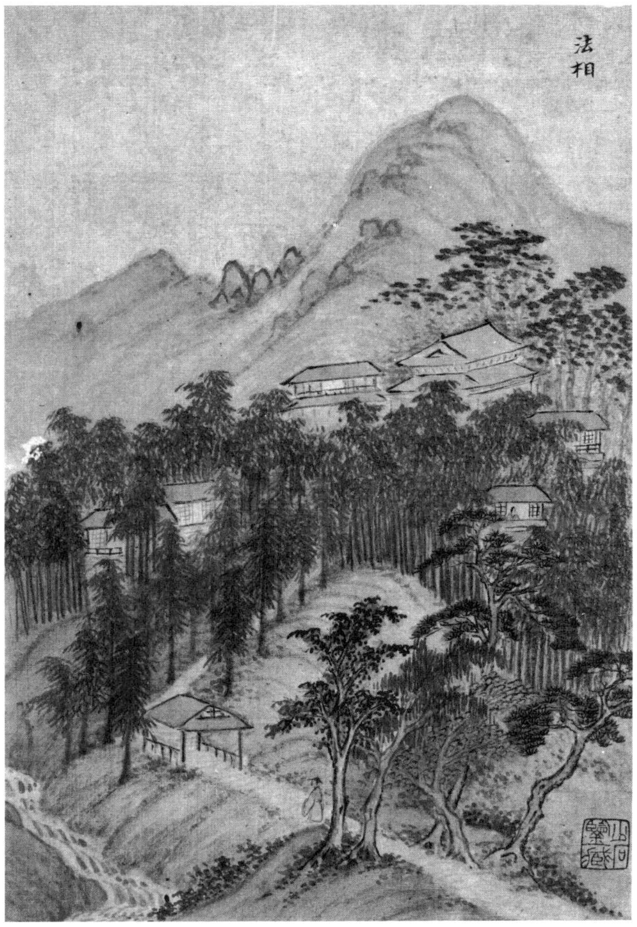


Leaf F, "Fa-hsiang"

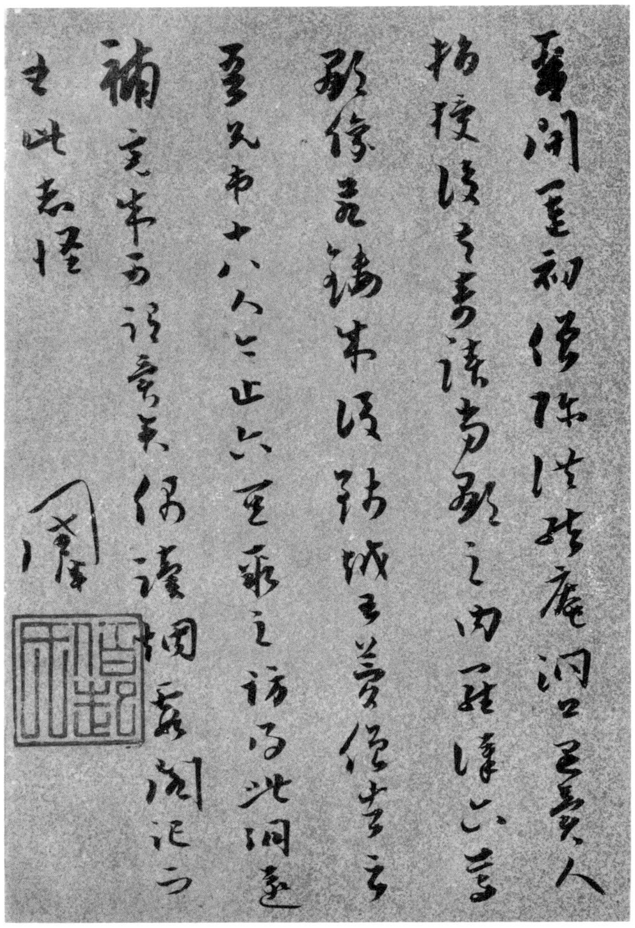

Leaf GG

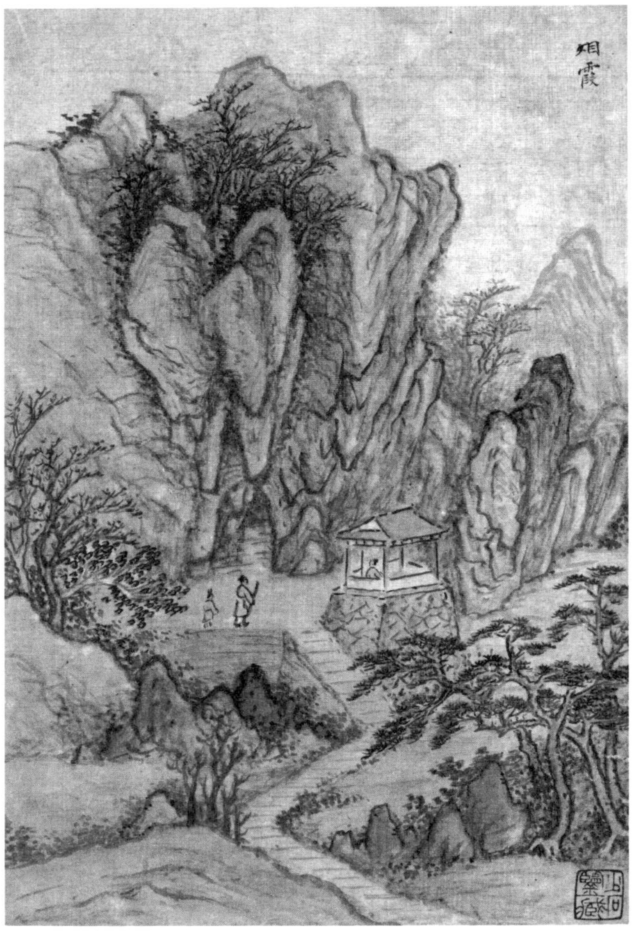

Leaf G, "Yen-hsia"

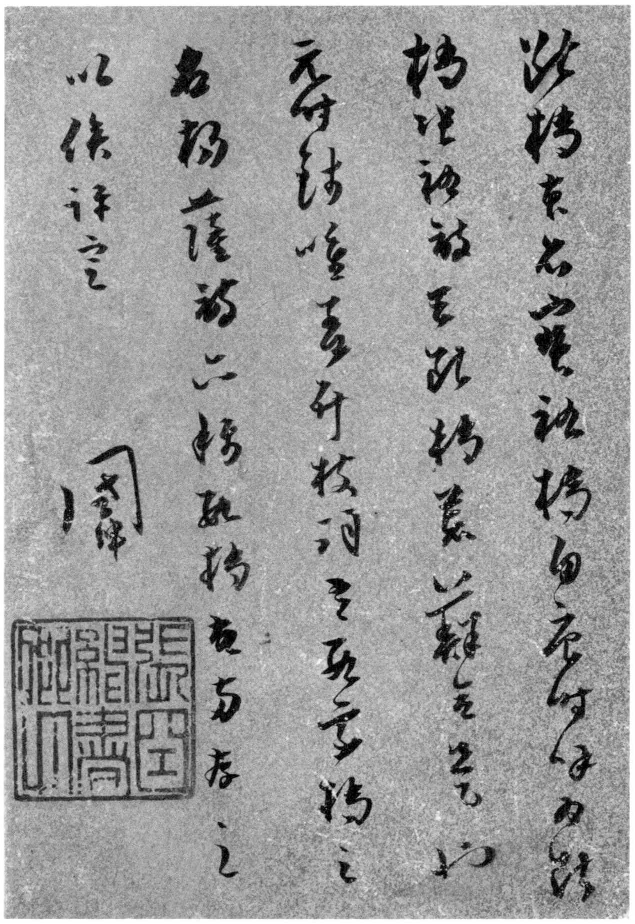

Leaf HH

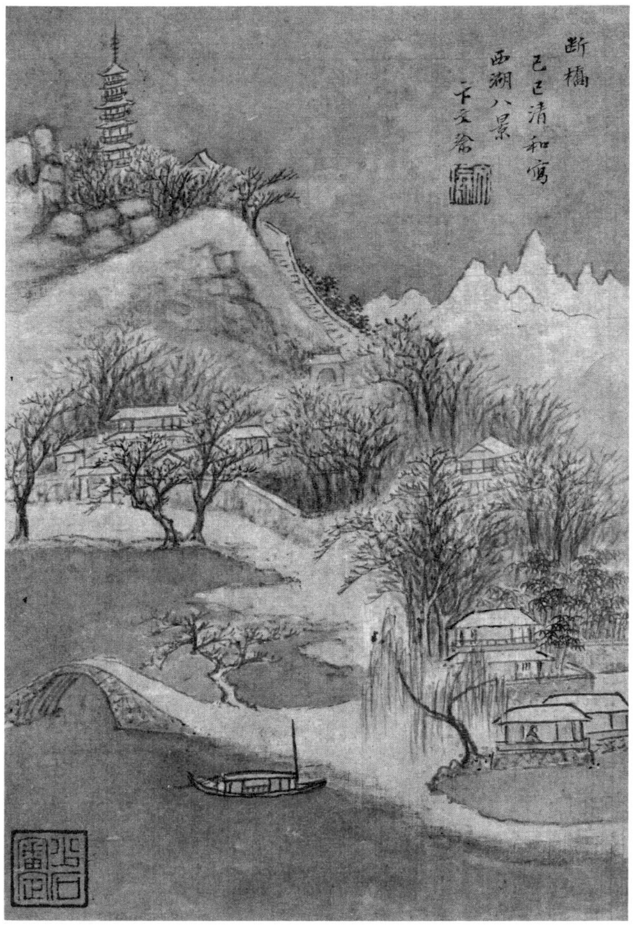

Leaf H, "Tuan-ch'iao"

# 35 Cha Shih-piao (1615–1698)

## *Landscape in the Style of Ni Tsan (Fang Ni Tsan shan-shui)*

Undated
Hanging scroll, ink on paper
204.4 x 75.4 cm (6 ft. $8\frac{1}{2}$ in. x $29\frac{5}{8}$ in.)

ARTIST'S INSCRIPTION (7 character quatrain, followed by a 7 character note, in 4 columns of running script):

> The heroic old pine exudes coolness in the evenings;
> Luxuriantly fragrant grasses carpet the pristine shore.
> With wooden staff I journeyed farther from home
> than I realized.
> It is best to view the green mountains from across
> the river.
>
> Painted for Wei-sheng, my respected friend.

ARTIST'S SIGNATURE: Cha Shih-piao.

ARTIST'S SEALS: Cha Shih-piao yin (square, half relief, half intaglio); Mei-huo shih i tzu yüeh Erh-chan (square relief).

COLLECTOR'S SEALS: Ch'eng Po-fen (modern collector): Ch'eng shih Po-fen (square relief; lower left); Ku-hsi Ch'eng shih Shuang-Sung-lou k'ao-ts'ang fa-shu ming-hua yin (tall rectangle relief; lower left); K'o-an chen-mi (tall rectangle relief; lower left).

Edward L. Elliott Family Collection (L1.70)

Unpublished.

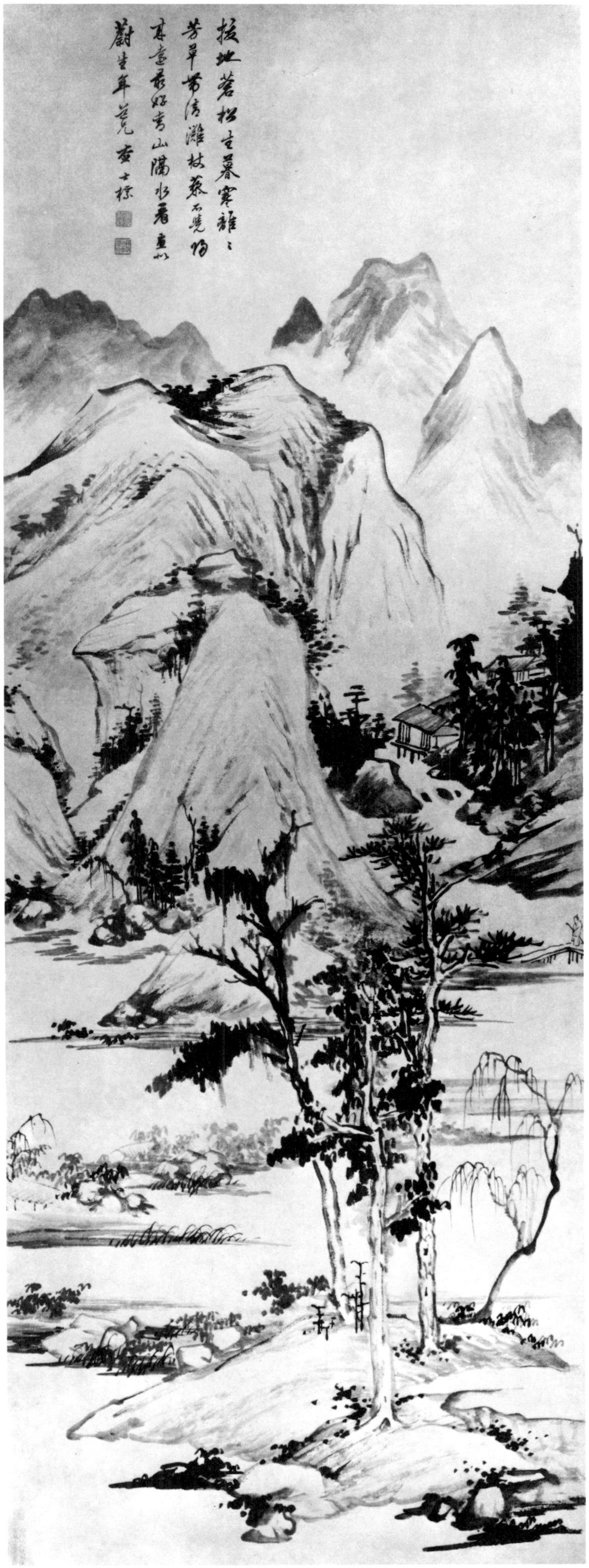

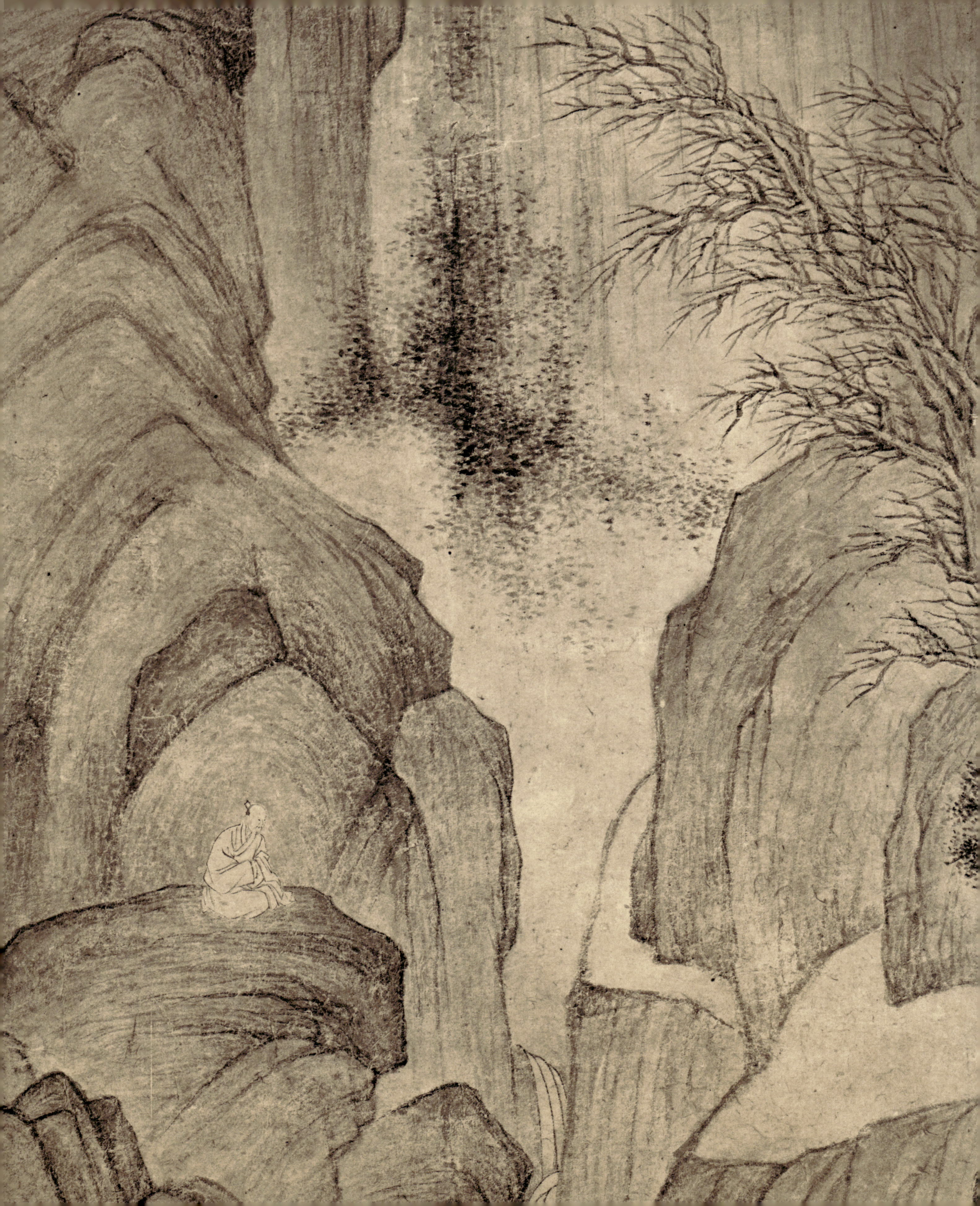

# 36 Chang Feng (d. 1662)

## *Listening to the Waterfall (Shih-yai t'ing ch'üan)*

Ca. 1658–60
Hanging scroll, ink on paper
94.3 x 40.9 cm (3 ft. 1 1/8 in. x 16 1/8 in.)

ARTIST'S INSCRIPTION (4 character regulated verse in 8 lines, in 2 columns of regular script):

> Looking up I see rocky cliffs; bending down I hear rushing water.
> The mountain trees are firm and upright; the valley flowers burst forth in a riot of brightness.
> The call of a yellow-plumed bird [pierces] ten thousand layers of gray mist.
> Those with tranquil hearts walk through the scenery, forever enjoying it.

ARTIST'S SIGNATURE: Chang Feng from Shang-yüan [in Kiangsu province] painted his ideas and inscribed this to amuse Master Shih-ch'ing.

ARTIST'S SEAL: Shang-yüan-lao-jen (square relief).

COLLECTOR'S SEALS: Ma Chi-tso (modern collector): Ma Chi-tso yin (square intaglio; lower left, painting); Chi-tso shen-ting (square relief; lower left, silk mounting); Ma shih shu-hua (square intaglio; lower left, silk mounting).

Edward L. Elliott Family Collection (L218.70)

PUBLISHED: Kawai Senro et al., eds., *Shina nanga taisei* (Collection of Chinese paintings of the Southern School), vol. 1 (Tokyo: Kōbun-sha, 1936), pt. 9, pl. 241; Ch'en Jen-t'ao, *Chin-kuei ts'ang-hua chi* (Chinese paintings from the King Kwei [Chin-kuei] collection) (Hong Kong: T'ung-ying, 1956), vol. 1, pl. 42; Ch'en Jen-t'ao, *Chin-kuei ts'ang-hua p'ing-shih* (Annotated catalogue of Chinese paintings from the King Kwei [Chin-kuei] collection) (Hong Kong: T'ung-ying, 1956), vol. 2, pp. 190–92; Suzuki Kei, comp., *Chūgoku kaiga sōgō zuroku: daiikkan, Amerika–Kanada hen* (Comprehensive illustrated catalogue of Chinese paintings: volume 1, American and Canadian collections) (Tokyo: University of Tokyo Press, 1982), p. 126, pl. A17–009.

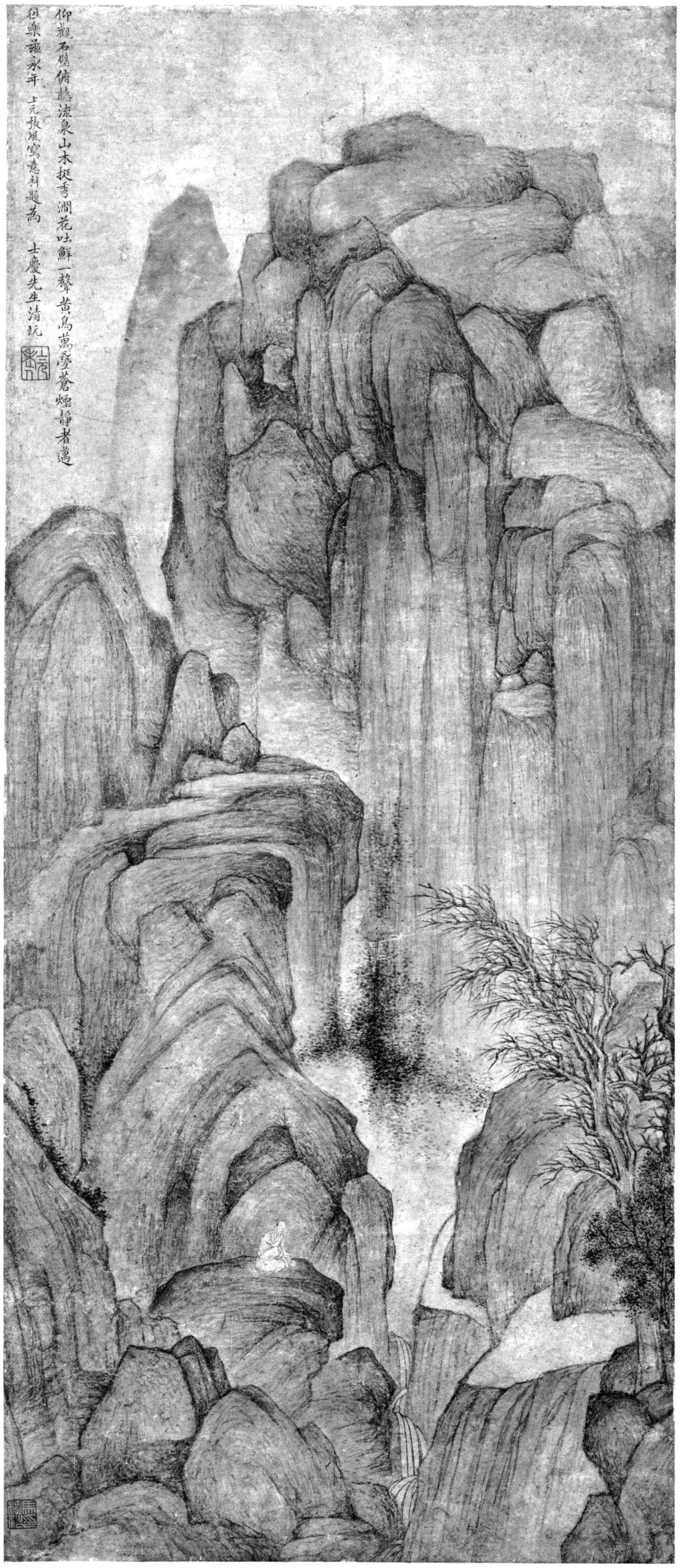

ALTHOUGH IN HIS YOUTH Chang Feng (*tzu*, Ta-feng; *hao*, Chen-hsiang fo-k'ung; Sheng-chou-tao-shih) started preparing for a traditional government career, even passing the entry level *chu-sheng* exams by the end of the Ming dynasty in 1644, he ultimately devoted himself to Buddhist, Taoist, and artistic pursuits. The chaotic state of the declining Ming dynasty left him little room to maneuver into officialdom; forced to abandon his official status, his elder brother, Chang I, a member of the Embroidered-uniform Guard, converted to Taoism. In Nanking, under his brother's influence, Chang Feng followed a similar path and developed eclectic talents as a classical scholar, seal carver, and landscape and figure painter.[1]

His landscapes exhibit two styles, an expressive and a descriptive manner.[2] In his paintings executed before 1650, the artist followed the lyrically expressive styles of Yüan literati painters, such as Huang Kung-wang (1269–1354) and Ni Tsan (1301–1374). Later criticizing his light, airy mode of this period in an album leaf dated 1644 (fig. a), Chang wrote, "It bothers me that my painting will never achieve a quality of paleness. Although I tried my best to achieve that quality in this painting, the brushwork ultimately looks overdone."

About 1650, Chang made the long journey to Peking and the surrounding region.[3] The monumentality of the northern Chinese mountains had a strong impact on his later style, which became heavier and more crowded. For models he turned to the Northern Sung masters as interpreted through Ming painters, especially the style of Li T'ang (ca. 1070s–ca. 1150s) as seen through T'ang Yin (1470–1524). *Listening to the Waterfall* is an example of this development in Chang's style.

In the compact composition, a man sits on a boulder above a cascading waterfall. Two groups of jagged rocks fill the foreground, a mountain rises on the left in the middle ground, and a towering wall of mountains completes the scene in the right background. This asymmetrical arrangement was the scheme preferred by Northern Sung monumental landscape painters. Except for a few trees and other vegetation in the fore- and middle grounds the mountains are bare. The barren rock faces are represented by dry outlines and modeling lines. Each rock is enclosed by a thin dark contour line and then filled in with long, densely packed hemp-fiber (*p'i-ma*) texture strokes in pale ink. Ink wash was used very sparingly to create shadows on the rock surfaces. This composition and its brushwork are reminiscent of T'ang Yin's *Late Spring in a Wooded Valley* (*Mu-ch'un lin-ho*; National Palace Museum, Taipei), which is characterized by application of hemp-fiber texture strokes of the Tung-Chü School to monumental mountains derived from the Fan K'uan–Li T'ang tradition. The

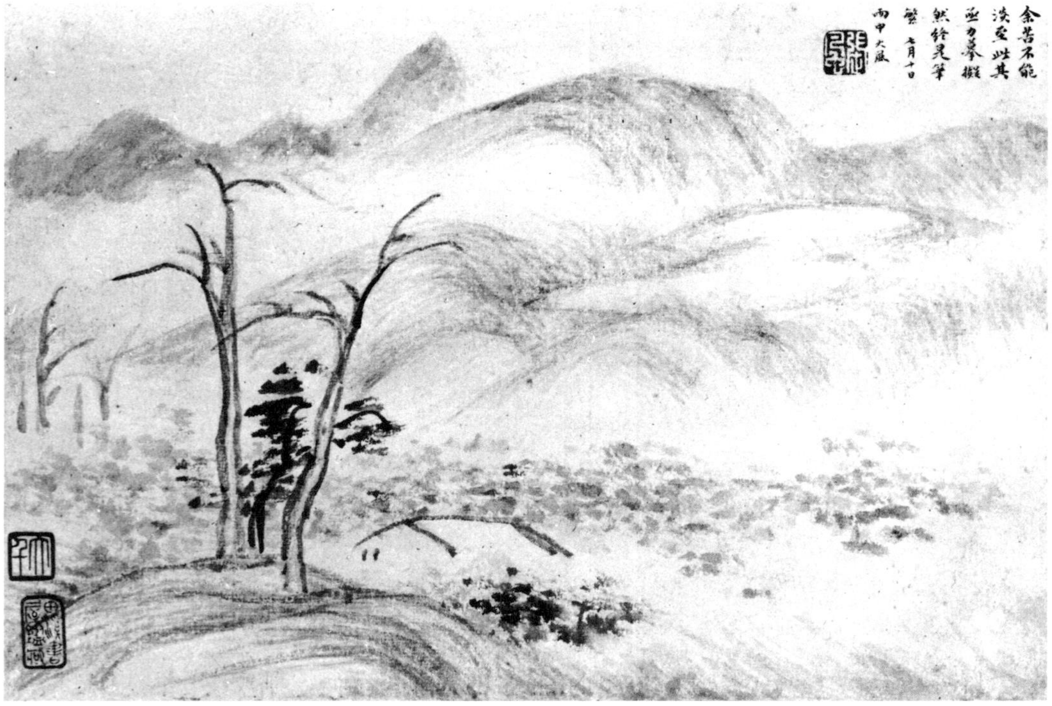

Fig. a. Chang Feng, *Landscape* (*Shan-shui*). Dated 1644. Album leaf 7 of *Landscapes* (*Shan-shui*), ink on paper. The Metropolitan Museum of Art, New York

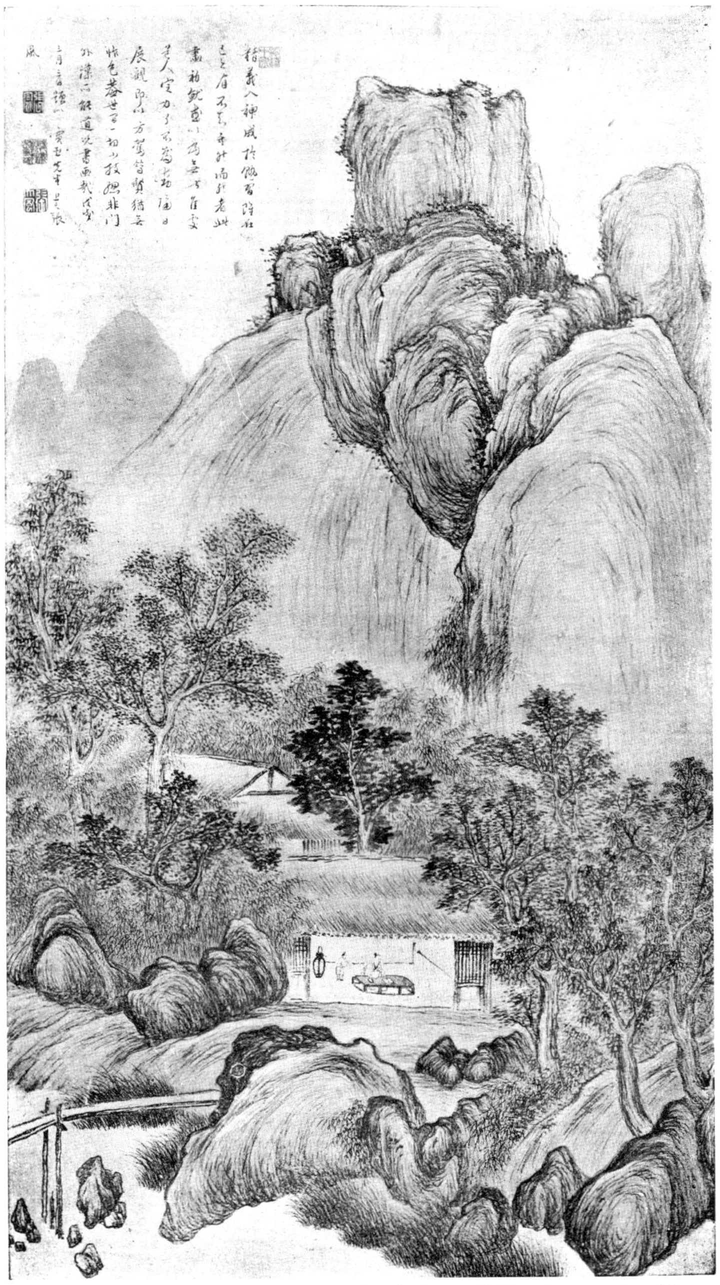

Fig. b. Chang Feng, *Reading in a Thatched Hut* (*Ts'ao-t'ang tu-shu t'u*). Dated 1658. Hanging scroll, ink on paper. Measurements unknown. Ti P'ing-tzu collection

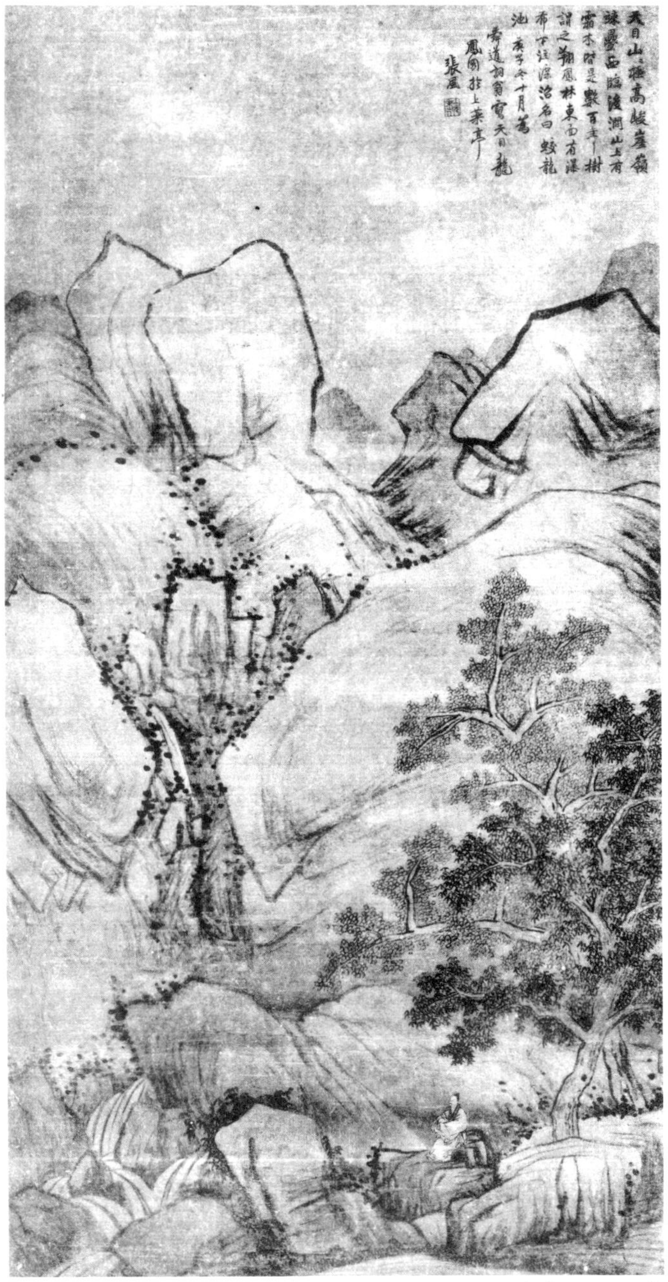

Fig. c. Chang Feng, *T'ien-mu Mountains' Dragon and Phoenix Peaks* (*T'ien-mu lung-feng t'u*). Dated 1660. Hanging scroll, ink on paper. Measurements unknown. Provenance unknown

overall effect of the Elliott hanging scroll is weighty, solemn, and remote. The regularity and stability of the calligraphy in the inscription echoes the architectonic structure of the painting.

The painting is undated, but the brushwork is close to that of another painting by Chang Feng, dated 1658 (fig. b), and is almost identical with that of a landscape dated 1660 (fig. c). *Listening to the Waterfall* must have been executed between 1658 and 1660.

PAO-CHEN CH'EN

NOTES

1. Jao Tsung-i, "Chang Feng and His Family," *Journal of The Institute of Chinese Studies of The Chinese University of Hong Kong* 8, no. 1 (1976): 51–70.
2. Shen C. Y. Fu, "An Aspect of Mid-seventeenth Century Chinese Painting: The 'Dry Linear' Style and the Early Work of Tao-chi," *Journal of The Institute of Chinese Studies of The Chinese University of Hong Kong* 8, no. 2 (1976): 579–615.
3. The *terminus ad quem* for Chang Feng's arrival in Peking must have been 1655, as suggested by An Chih-yüan, who saw Chang's calligraphy on a wall of a tavern; see An's colophon (dated 1665) to Chang's album leaves (dated 1644), now in The Metropolitan Museum of Art.

# 37 Kung Hsien (1619–1689)

## *An Immortal's Abode above the Clouds (Hsien-chia yün-chü)*

Ca. mid-1680s
Hanging scroll, ink on silk
176.3 x 53.4 cm (5 ft. 9³/₈ in. x 21 in.)

ARTIST'S INSCRIPTION: 7 character quatrain in 5 columns of running script (for a translation of the artist's inscription, see page 197).

ARTIST'S SIGNATURE: Kung Hsien painted and inscribed this.

ARTIST'S SEALS: Kung Hsien (square intaglio); Pan-ch'ien (square relief).

Edward L. Elliott Family Collection (L196.70)

PUBLISHED: Suzuki Kei, comp., *Chūgoku kaiga sōgō zuroku: daiikkan, Amerika–Kanada hen* (Comprehensive illustrated catalogue of Chinese paintings: volume 1, American and Canadian collections) (Tokyo: University of Tokyo Press, 1982), p. 129, pl. A17–049.

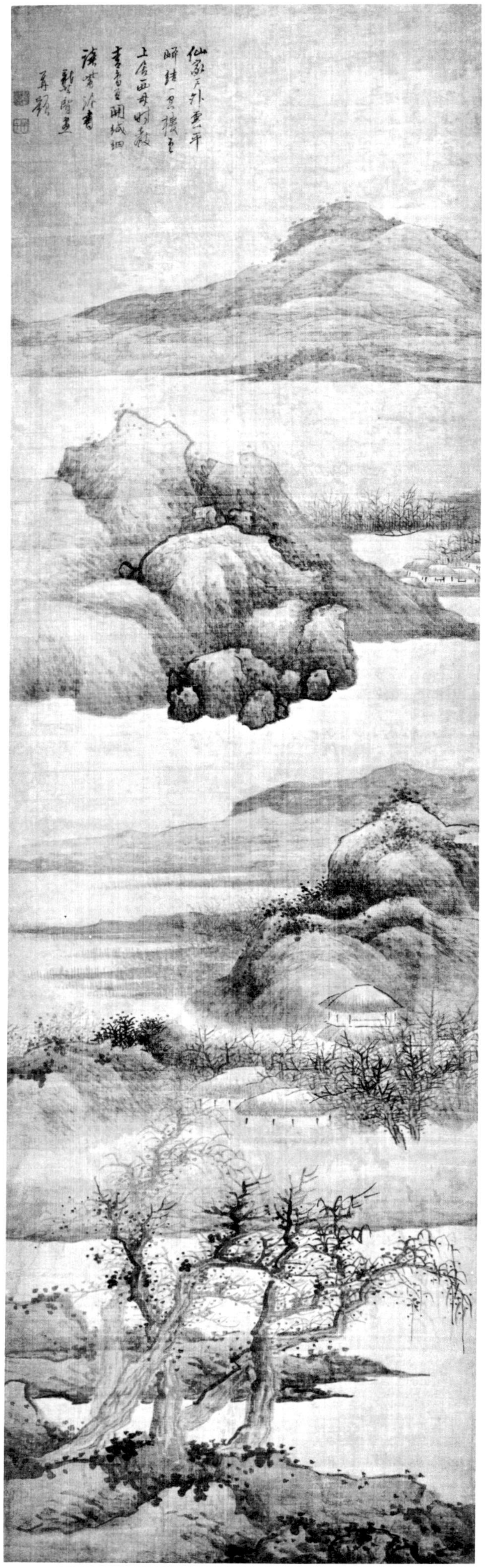

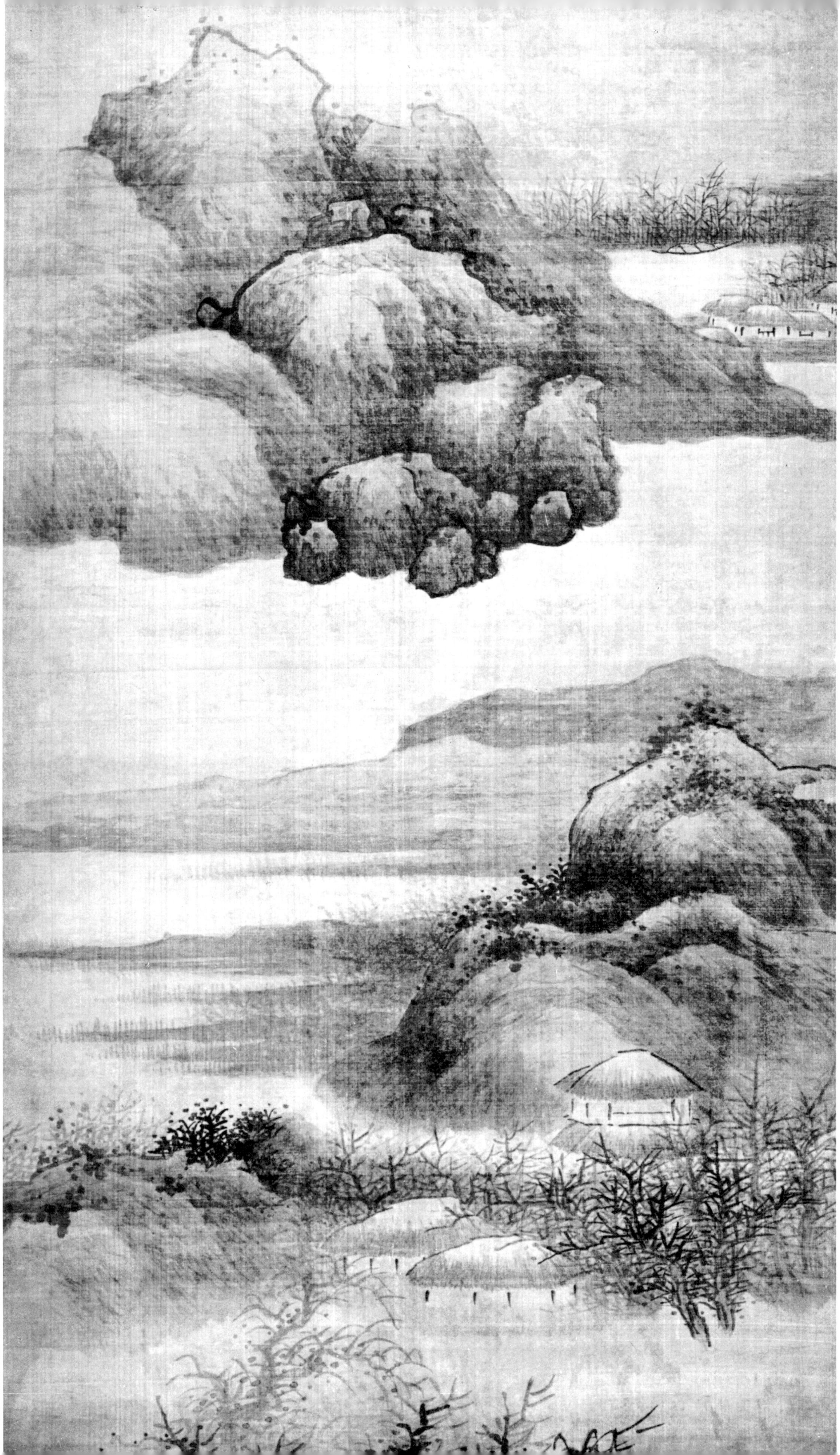

# 38 Hu Ta (Tien-tao-jen; fl. late 17th–early 18th century)

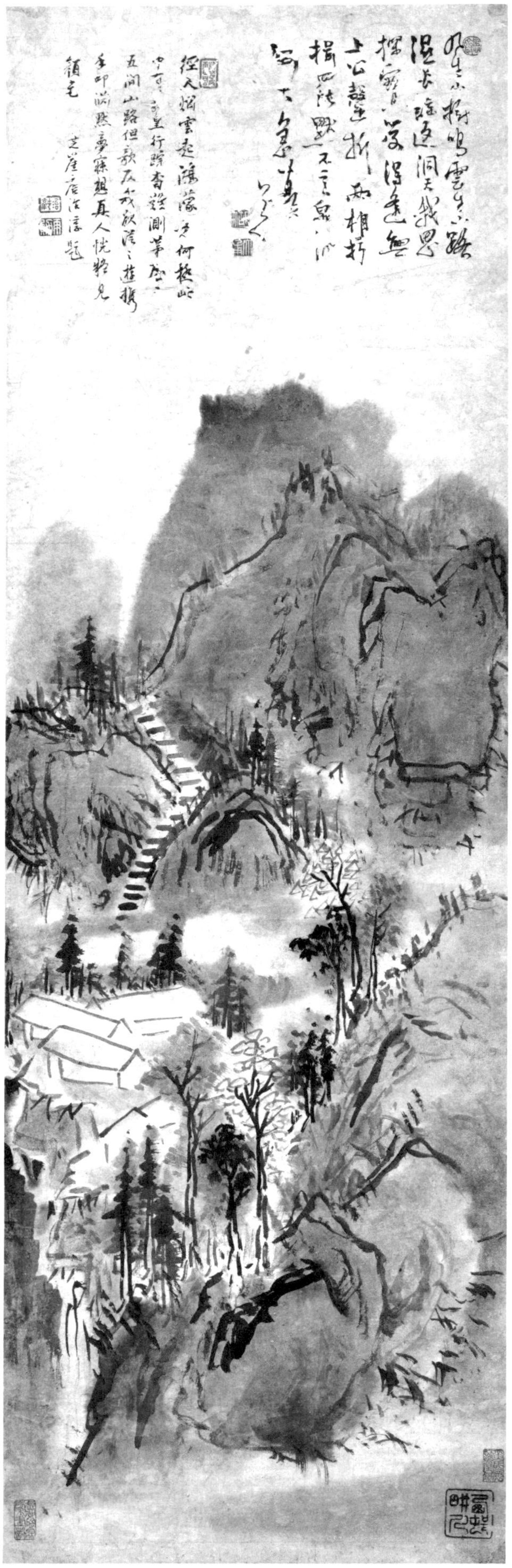

*Wind among Mountain Groves*
*(Feng sheng shan-shu)*

Undated
Hanging scroll, ink on paper
95.2 x 31.0 cm (3 ft. 1 1/2 in. x 12 1/4 in.)

ARTIST'S INSCRIPTION (5 character regulated verse in 8 lines in 6 columns of free-form running script; upper right):

The wind stirred and the mountain trees groaned,
Clouds rose and moistened the winding path.
With a loud yelp I returned to the mountain cave of the Taoist immortals;
There hoping to find the secret of their treasured scriptures,
By chance I met the revered Master Hsing-shang.
We bowed to each other, curving our backs like music stones [*ch'ing*].
Bowing we remained silent.
How swiftly the river flows!

ARTIST'S SIGNATURE: Tien-tao-jen.

ARTIST'S SEALS: Hu Ta (square intaglio); Ta-fu (square intaglio); Huan-chai (round relief).

INSCRIPTION by T'ang Chih-ch'un (dates unknown) (5 character regulated verse in 8 lines in 5 columns of running script; upper left):

Fog rises from below my feet on the path.
The spreading mist is so vast.
Mist covers immeasurable spaces.
Taoist immortals may be living here,
But their whereabouts are too hard to fathom.
They may live in small thatched huts scattered about, and pass the time singing and walking to and fro along the mountain path.
I wish I could follow them and with them reach inner peace through meditation.
Even in my dreams, I long to meet a Taoist immortal.
I can almost see his shining face.

Signature: T'ang Chih-ch'un from Chih-yai inscribed this.
Seals: Chih-ch'un (squat rectangle relief); Yü-hsün (squat rectangle intaglio); unidentified seal (tall rectangle relief; beginning of the inscription).

COLLECTORS' SEALS: Unidentified owners: Huang shih huai-hsüan-t'ang ts'ang (tall rectangle relief, yellow ink; lower right); Hsi-ts'un keng-jen (square relief; lower right); Ch'ang-chung wu-mei so ch'iu shu-hua chi (tall rectangle relief; lower left).

Edward L. Elliott Family Collection (L306.70)

PUBLISHED: Lao T'ien-pi, ed., *Ming i-min shu-hua lu* (Catalogue of calligraphy and painting by the Ming loyalists) (Hong Kong: Ho shih chih-lo-lou, 1962), p. 48 (text reference); Suzuki Kei, comp., *Chūgoku kaiga sōgō zuroku: daiikkan, Amerika–Kanada hen* (Comprehensive illustrated catalogue of Chinese paintings: volume 1, American and Canadian collections) (Tokyo: University of Tokyo Press, 1982),p. 128, pl. A17–032.

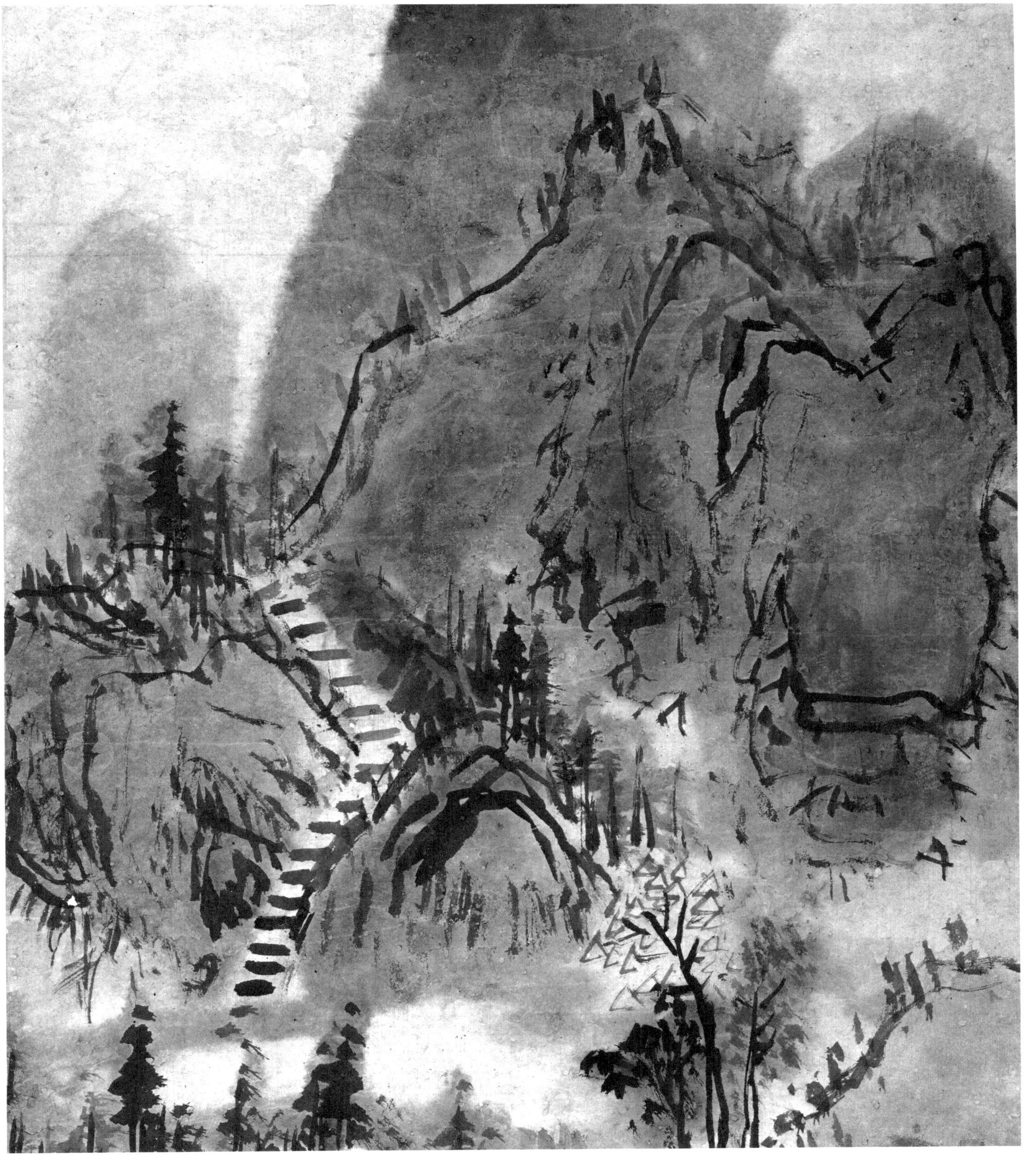

# 39 Chu Ta (Pa-ta-shan-jen; 1626–1705)

## *Papayas (Mu-kua)*

Ca. 1692
Album leaf mounted as a hanging scroll, ink and color on paper
20.0 x 14.6 cm (7⁷/₈ x 5³/₄ in.)

ARTIST'S SIGNATURE: Pa-ta-shan-jen painted this.

ARTIST'S SEAL: Hsüeh-hsüeh yung (tall rectangle relief).

Edward L. Elliott Family Collection (L81.83)

Unpublished.

A SCION of the Ming imperial family, the artist Chu Ta was born in Nan-ch'ang, Kiangsi province, in 1626. His name at birth was T'ung-hsin; Ta was his earliest sobriquet; and he adopted several others after the Manchu conquest of Ming China in 1644, when, to avoid political persecution, he became a Buddhist monk. Between 1648 and 1661 he took the names Hsüeh-ko, Ko-shan, and Lü. Between 1661 and 1687 he converted to Taoism, took the new name of Chu Tao-lang, and devoted himself to establishing a monastery, Ch'ing-yün-p'u, in Nan-ch'ang.[1] The name Ch'uan-ch'i also appears on some of his paintings before 1687.[2] Thereafter he usually signed himself either "Jo-chao" or "Pa-ta-shan-jen,"[3] the name most often used to identify him today.

Talented in poetry, calligraphy, and seal carving, Chu Ta became especially renowned for his painting. He was brought up in a family of artists: his grandfather Chu To-chen painted in the style of Mi Fu (1052–1107), and his father, Chu Mo-chin, followed the style of the late fifteenth- and early sixteenth-century Wu School masters. The sources for Chu Ta's paintings cover a broader range than his family influences. Before 1675 he modeled his landscape style and calligraphy on Tung Ch'i-ch'ang (1555–1636) and his bird and flower painting on Liang K'ai (fl. ca. 1201–1204), Mu Ch'i (fl. mid-13th century), and Lin Liang (fl. ca. 1450–1500).[4] Only a few of Chu Ta's paintings from this period are extant. They all feature simple forms and square brushwork (*fang-pi*) executed with an obliquely held brush. After 1675 Chu Ta's

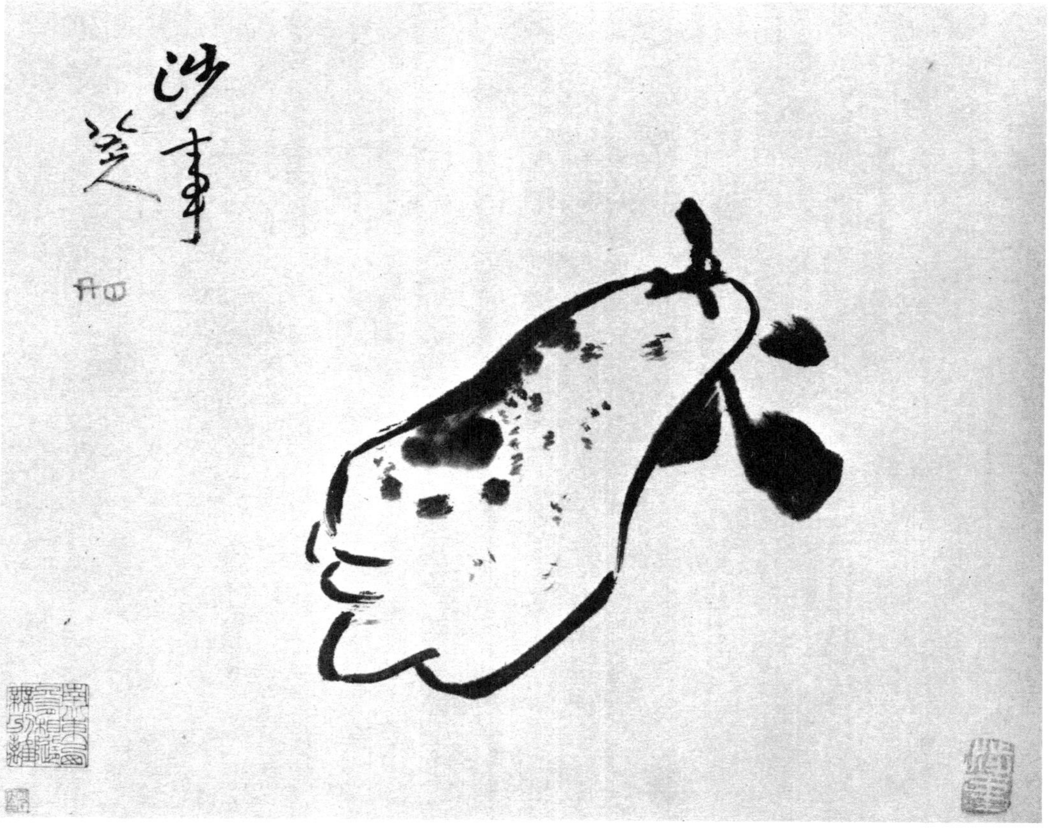

Fig. a. Chu Ta, *Buddha's Hand Fruit* (*Fo-shou*). Dated 1692. Album leaf 5 of *Flower, Fruit, Bird, and Insect Painting* (*Hua-niao shu-kuo ts'ao-ch'ung ts'e*), ink (?) on paper. Measurements unknown. Provenance unknown

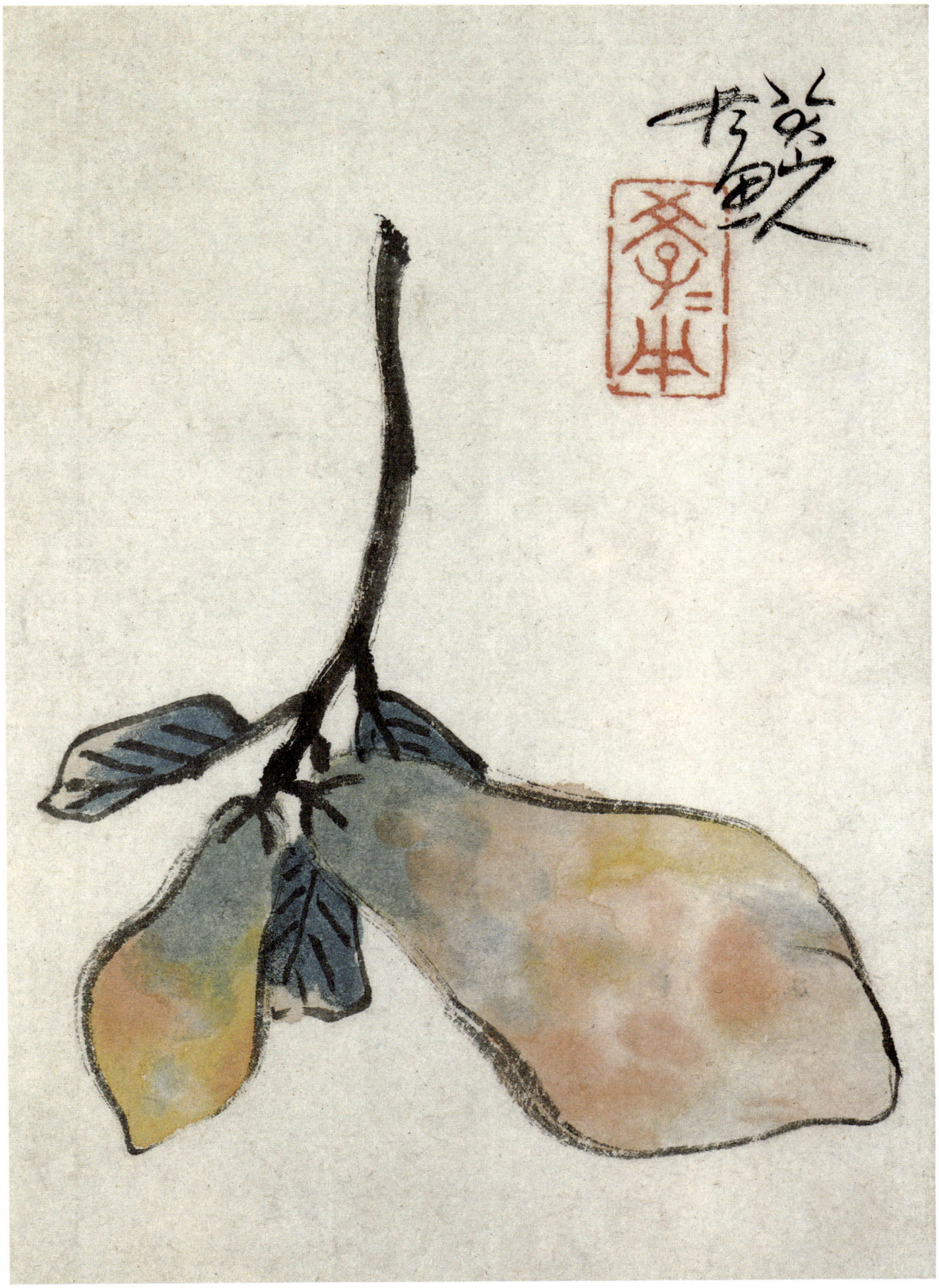

personal style became increasingly pronounced. Dynamic composition, sharp contrast between simplified forms, rich variation in ink tones, and bold and "round" brush technique (*yüan-pi*) were characteristic of this period.

*Papayas*, except for its relatively stable composition, corresponds to Chu Ta's later period. Rendered with assertive calligraphic strokes in dark ink, a branch with two hanging papayas and three small leaves is treated as a triangle, with one papaya pointing to the lower left and the other to the lower right. Round brushwork derived from seal script was used in the veins for the leaves. Cursive script brush techniques, such as flying white (*fei-pai*) and thickening-and-thinning brushstrokes, describe the contours of the papayas. In contrast to the bold outlines, the coloration of the painting is delicate and subtle. Light blue and green paint with orange and yellow vegetable pigments were applied in layered washes, giving the fruit a look of three-dimensionality. The crisp and elegant quality of this painting reflects the controlled sensitivity Chu Ta achieved late in life.

The Elliott painting is undated, but based on the style of the artist's signature in the upper right corner, which reads "Pa-ta-shan-jen hua" (Pa-ta-shan-jen painted this), it must have been executed before 1695. The character *pa* was composed of two angular hooks facing each other; this, along with the choice of the character *hua* as a suffix to the signature, were the hallmarks of Chu Ta's signature before 1695.[5] The similarity of subject matter, brushwork, and signature of Chu Ta's *Papayas* to his *Buddha's Hand Fruit* (*Fo-shou*; fig. a), dated to 1692, further suggests an approximate date in the early 1690s for the Edward L. Elliott Family Collection scroll.

PAO-CHEN CH'EN

NOTES

1. For more biographical information, see Wen C. Fong, "A Letter from Shih-t'ao to Pa-ta-shan-jen and the Problem of Shih-t'ao's Chronology," *Archives of the Chinese Art Society of America* 13 (1959): 22–53; Hsieh Chih-liu, *Chu Ta* (Shanghai: Shanghai jen-min mei-shu ch'u-pan-she, 1958); Chou Shih-hsin, ed., *Pa-ta-shan-jen chi ch'i i-shu* (Pa-ta-shan-jen and his art) (Taipei: I-shu t'u-shu kung-ssu, 1974), pp. 86–95.
2. Wen C. Fong, "A Letter from Shih-t'ao," p. 43.
3. Chu Ta's use of the sobriquet Pa-ta-shan-jen can be traced to as early as 1671, but he did not use it exclusively until 1689; see Chou Shih-hsin, ed., *Pa-ta-shan-jen chi ch'i i-shu*, p. 199; Wen C. Fong, "A Letter from Shih-t'ao," p. 42.
4. Wang Fang-yü, "On the Poems of Chu Ta," *National Palace Museum Quarterly* 11 (Autumn 1976): pt. 1, 37–46; Chou Shih-hsin, *Pa-ta-shan-jen chi ch'i i-shu*, pp. 133–34.
5. After 1695 Chu Ta signed his name as "Pa-ta-shan-jen hsieh" (Pa-ta-shan-jen wrote this); *hsieh* replaced *hua* as the suffix, and *pa* was simplified into two slashes facing each other. See Hsieh Chih-liu, *Chu Ta*, p. 15; Chou Shih-hsin, *Pa-ta-shan-jen-chi ch'i i-shu*, p. 202.

# 40 Ch'i Chai-chia (1630–1707)

*Landscape in the Style of Ni Tsan*
*(Fang Ni Tsan shan-shui)*

Dated 1681
Hanging scroll, ink on paper
78.0 x 35.0 cm ($30^{3}/_{4}$ x $13^{3}/_{4}$ in.)

ARTIST'S INSCRIPTION (prose, 9 characters in 2 columns of running script): I made and presented this to Master Tzu-hua, in the autumn of the *hsin-yu* year [1681].

ARTIST'S SIGNATURE: Ch'i Chai-chia.

ARTIST'S SEALS: Ch'i Chai-chia yin (square intaglio); Chih-hsiang shih (square relief).

COLLECTOR'S SEAL: Unidentified owner: Shou-ho-lo-chai shu-hua (square relief; lower right).

Edward L. Elliott Family Collection (L210.70).

PUBLISHED: Suzuki Kei, comp., *Chūgoku kaiga sōgō zuroku: daiikkan, Amerika–Kanada hen* (Comprehensive illustrated catalogue of Chinese paintings: volume 1, American and Canadian collections) (Tokyo: University of Tokyo Press, 1982), p. 127, pl. A17–011.

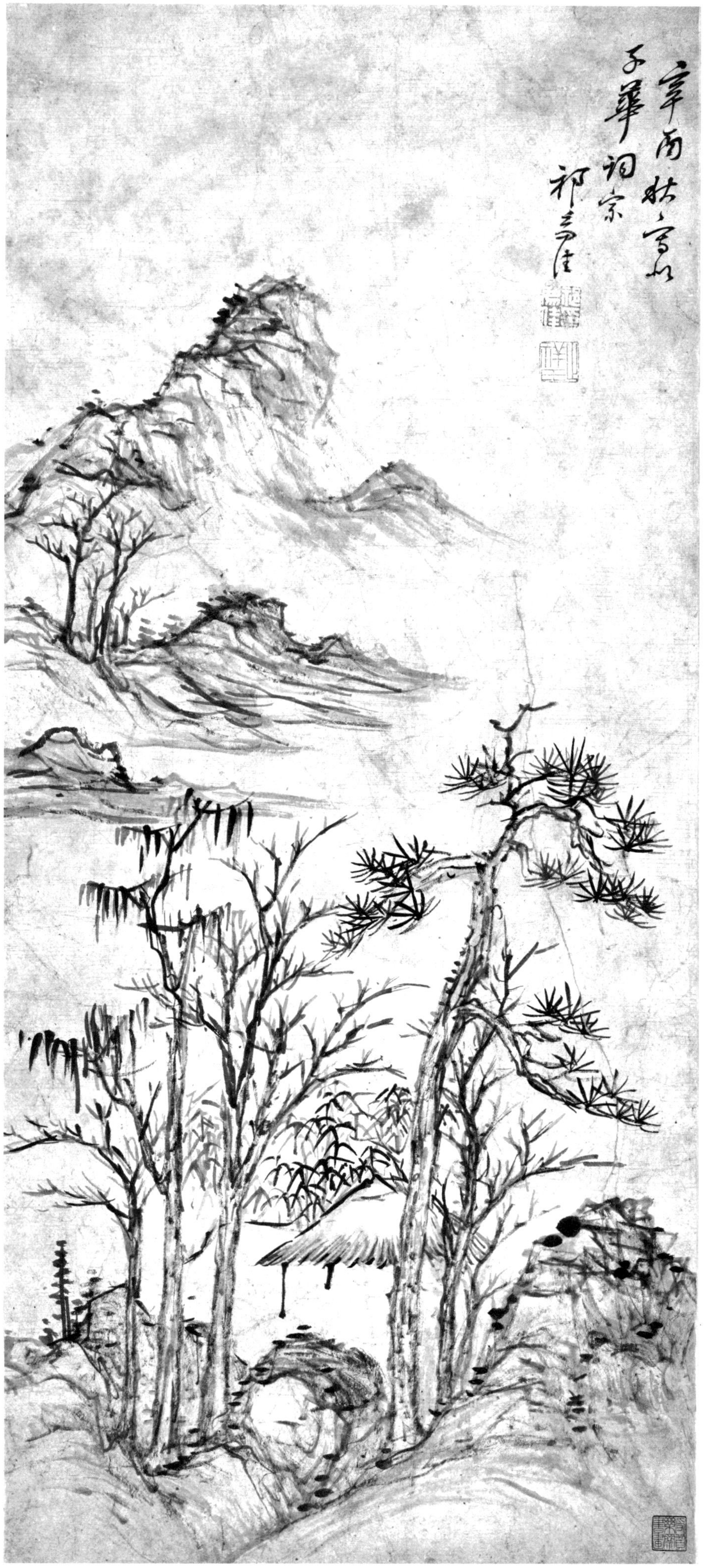

# 41 Wang Hui (1632–1717)

## *Landscapes after Sung and Yüan Masters (Fang Sung Yüan shan-shui ts'e)*

Dated 1712
Album of eight leaves, ink and color on paper (A–G); ink on paper (H)
40.3 x 32.7 cm (15⁷/8 x 12⁷/8 in.)

ARTIST'S INSCRIPTIONS:
Leaf A, "Landscape in the Style of Li Ch'eng (919–967)" (prose, 8 characters in 2 columns of regular script): "River Pass after Snow," after Li Ying-ch'iu [Li Ch'eng].

Leaf B, "Landscape in the Style of Fan K'uan (ca. 960–1030)" (5 character couplet, followed by a 4 character note, in 2 columns of regular script):

> Rain tinted green pours in the deep mountains.
> The old temple shades the flower-petal-red stream.
>
> After Fan Hua-yüan [Fan K'uan].

Leaf C, "Landscape in the Style of Wang Shen (1036–ca. 1080)" (prose, 8 characters in 2 columns of regular script): "Sailing from Chiao-men in the Morning," after Wang Chin-ch'ing [Wang Shen].

Leaf D, "Landscape in the Style of Ma Yüan (fl. ca. 1190–1264)" (prose, 7 characters in 2 columns of regular script): "Picking Water Chestnuts," after Ma Yao-fu [Ma Yüan].

Leaf E, "Landscape in the Style of Chao Po-chü (fl. ca. 1120–62)" (7 character couplet, followed by a 7 character note, in 3 columns of running script):

> There are endless clouds over myriad layers of blue mountains.
> There the immortals' moon-watching terrace is located.
>
> After Chao Po-chü's blue and green style.

Leaf F, "Bamboo Grove in the Style of Kuan Tao-sheng (1262–1319)" (prose, 22 characters in 3 columns of free-form regular script): Lady Kuan painted "The Bamboo Grove" and Chao Ch'eng-chih [Chao Meng-fu] wrote an account on it; these passed through many hands and were praised by all as two marvels.

Leaf G, "Landscape in the Style of Kao K'o-kung (1248–1310)" (5 character couplet, followed by a 13 character note, in 5 columns of regular script):

> Midrange mountain slopes emerge from mists of good omen.
> The central peak is surrounded by auspicious clouds.
>
> Following the brush technique of the Grand Secretary, Kao Yen-ching [Kao K'o-kung], and the expression that Huang Kung-wang [1269–1354] left behind.

Leaf H, "Copy of a Painting by Ni Tsan (1301–1374)":
1. Transcription of an inscription by Ni Tsan (7 character quatrain, followed by a 7 character note, in 4 columns of regular script; upper right):

> The mist over the sandbar gently veils the waves on the lake;
> In the sixth month a sensation of coolness arises from looking at images of light green.
> I especially love the giant banana leaves in front of my window.
> Like tall fans of green gauze, they sway in the wind.
>
> Written on the first day of the sixth lunar month of the *wu-shen* year [1368].

2. Transcription of a poem by Ni Tsan (7 character quatrain, followed by a 7 character note, in 4 columns of regular script; upper right):

> Dots of green moss seem about to creep onto my gown.
> Above the pond swollen with springtime waters, cranes and waterfowl soar.
> The desolate village is silent; visitors seldom come.
> There is only the studio boat moored by the bamboo gate.
>
> In the evening of the Double Seventh Festival, I casually wrote this poem to fill the paper, Tsan.

ARTIST'S SIGNATURE: In the summer of the *jen-ch'en* year of the K'ang-hsi era [1712], Wang Hui from Hai-yü [in Kiangsu province] copied this painting while in the Lai-ch'ing Studio.

ARTIST'S SEALS: Wang Hui chih yin (square intaglio; A, B, E–H); Shih-ku (square relief; F, H); Shih-ku-tzu (square relief; B, E, G); Wang Hui (tall rectangle relief; C, D); Shang-hsia ch'ien-nien (round relief, G).

COLLECTORS' SEALS:
1. Tsai Yüan (d. 1861): I-ch'in-wang pao (square relief; all).
2. Unidentified owners: Hsü shih mi-chi (square relief; F); Ming-shan-t'ang chen-ts'ang shu-hua yin-chi (tall rectangle relief; F).

Gift of Mrs. Edward L. Elliott (82–99)

Unpublished.

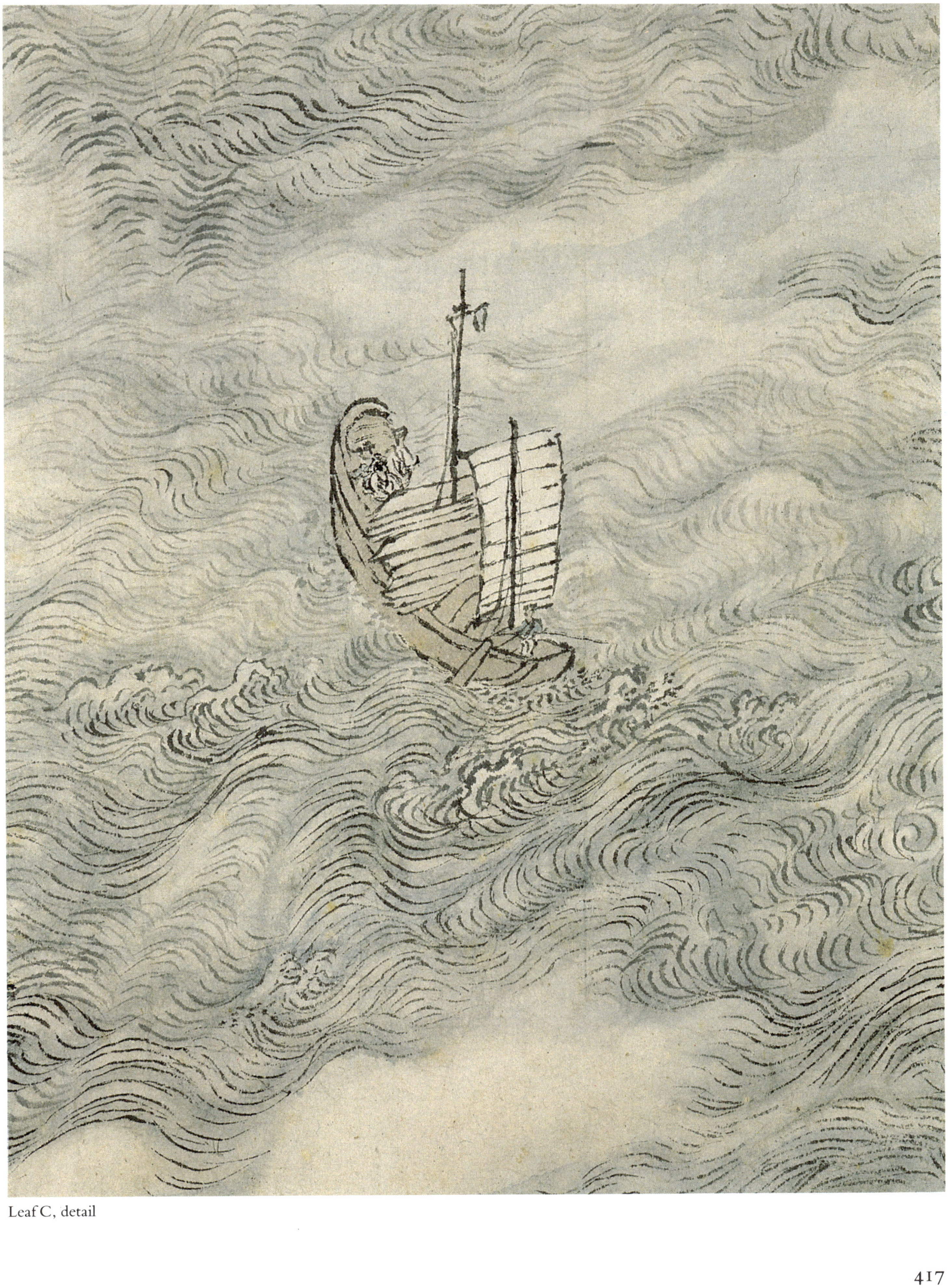

Leaf C, detail

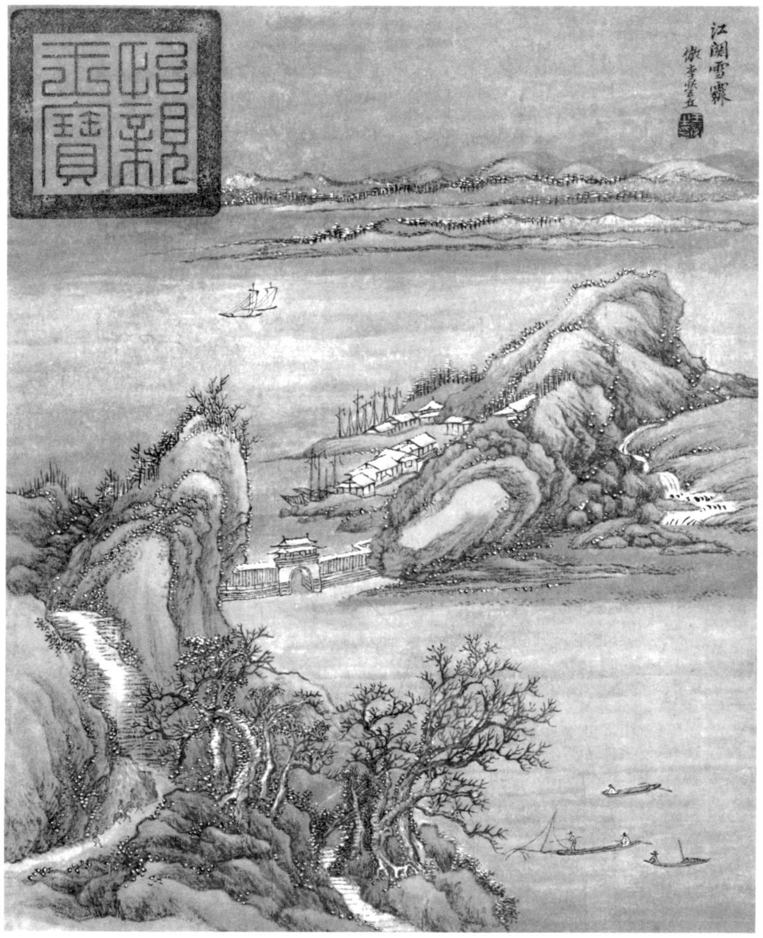

Leaf A, "Landscape in the Style of Li Ch'eng (919–967)"

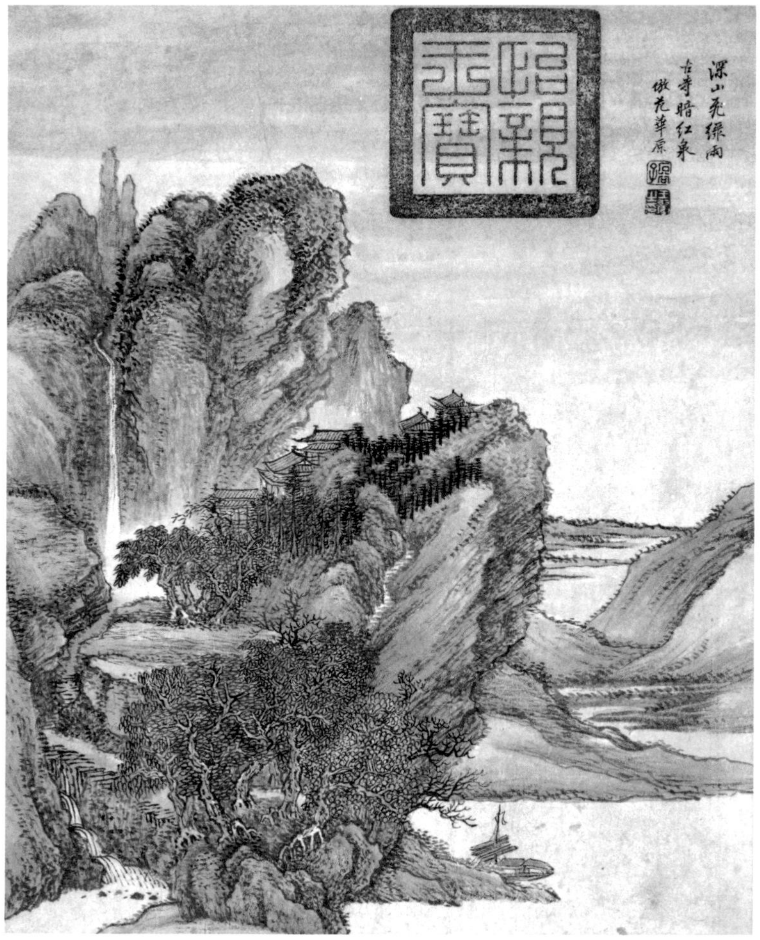

Leaf B, "Landscape in the Style of Fan K'uan (ca. 960–1030)"

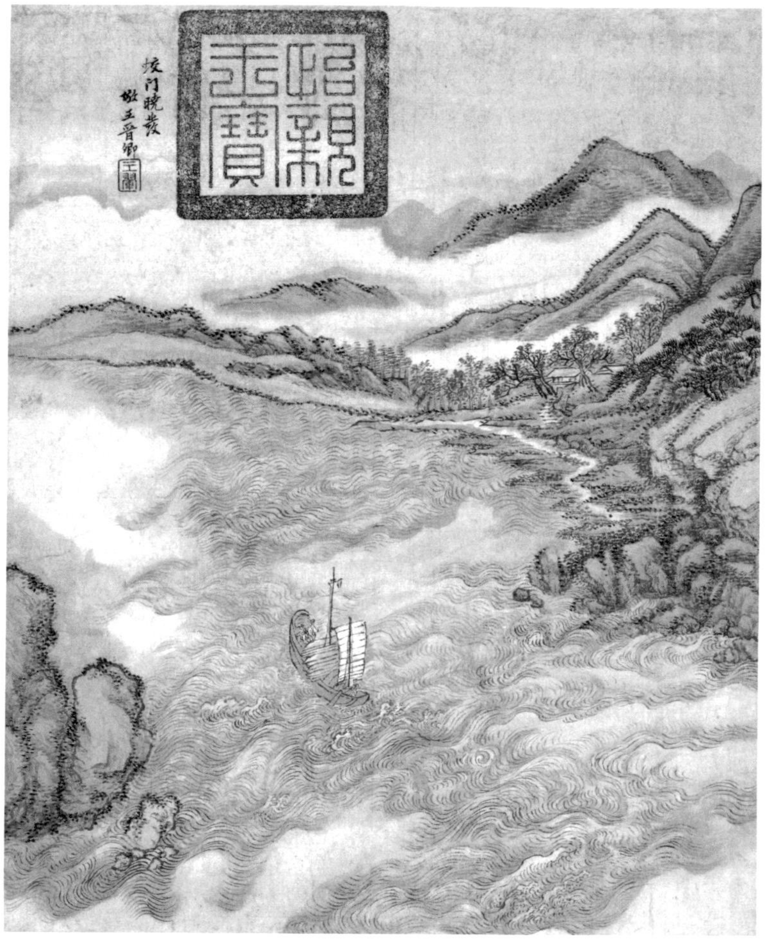

Leaf C, "Landscape in the Style of Wang Shen (1036–ca. 1080)"

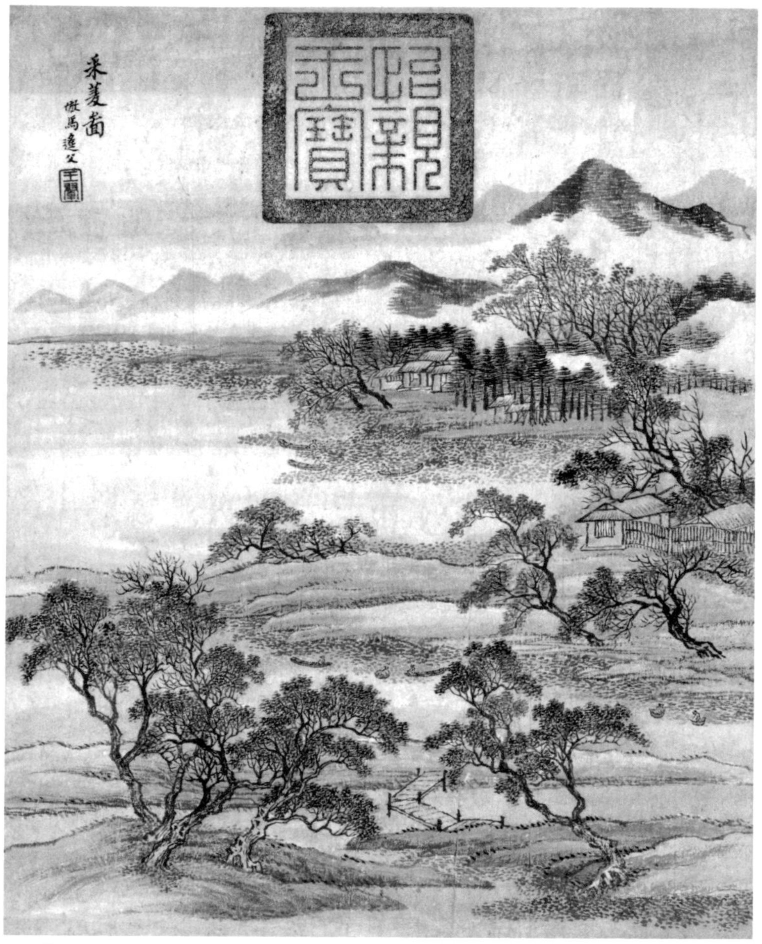

Leaf D, "Landscape in the Style of Ma Yüan (fl. ca. 1190–1264)"

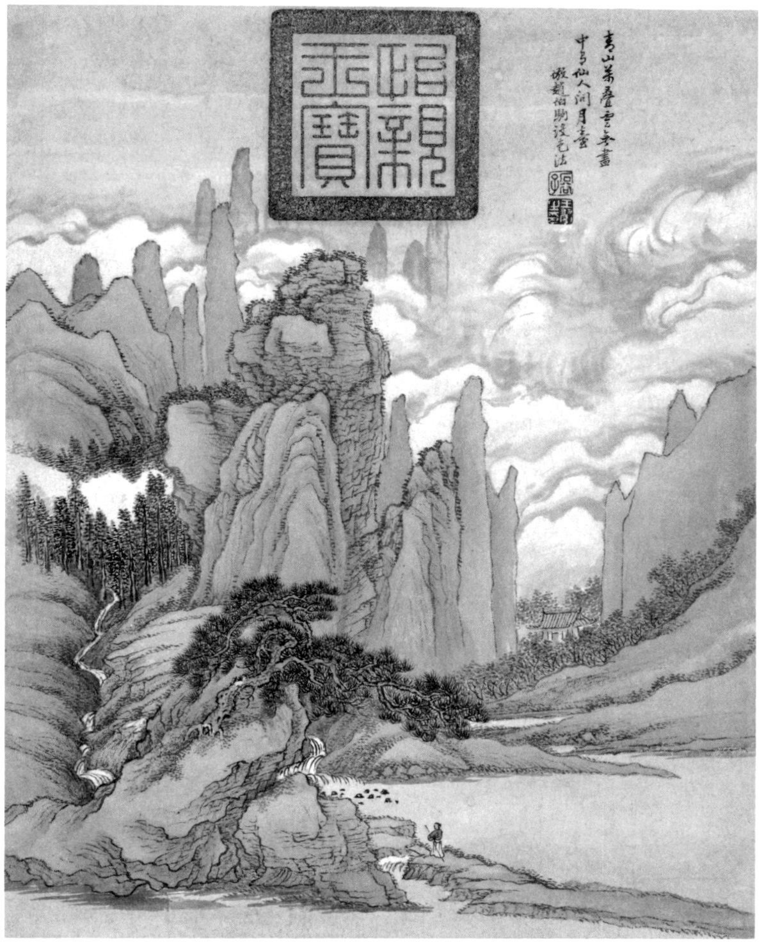

Leaf E, "Landscape in the Style of Chao Po-chü (fl. ca. 1120–62)"

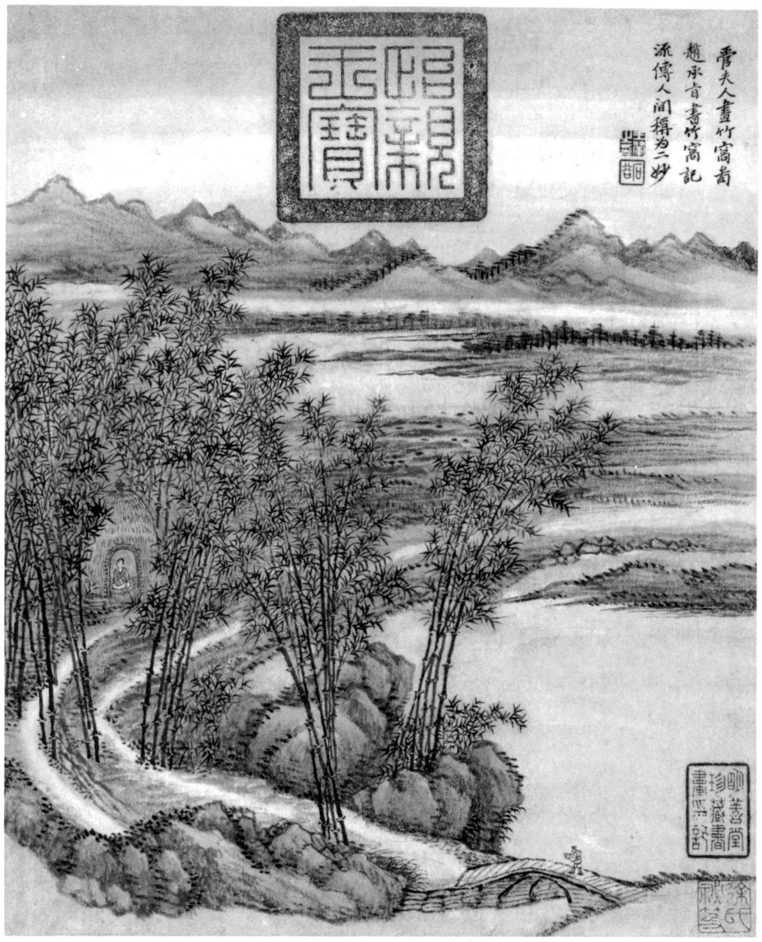

Leaf F, "Landscape in the Style of Kuan Tao-sheng (1262–1319)"

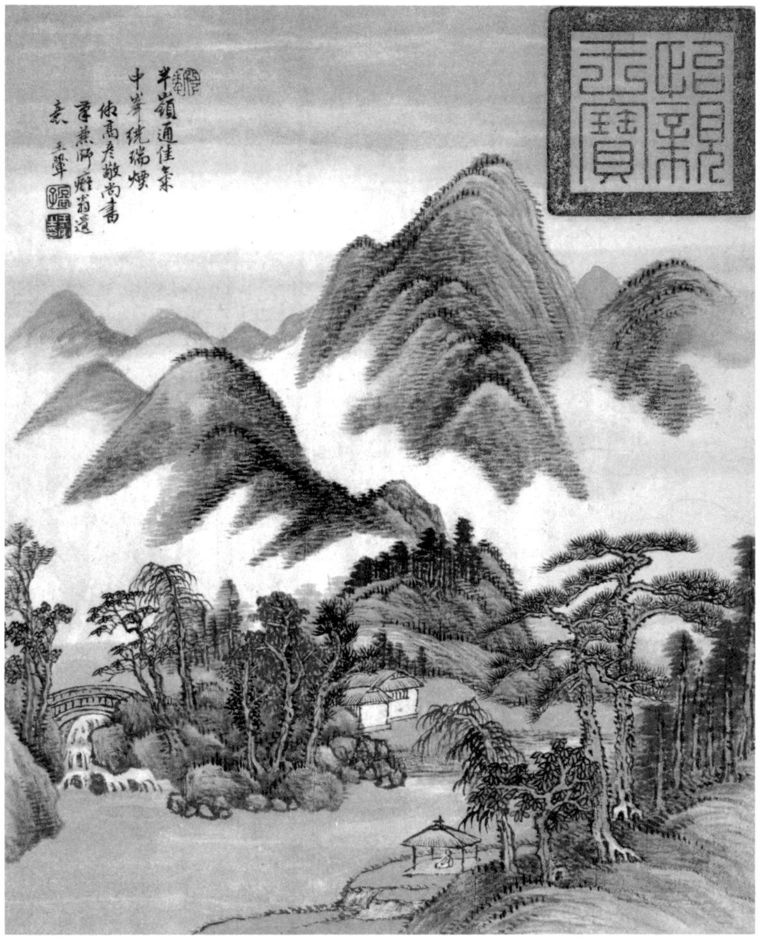

Leaf G, "Landscape in the Style of Kao K'o-kung (1248–1310)"

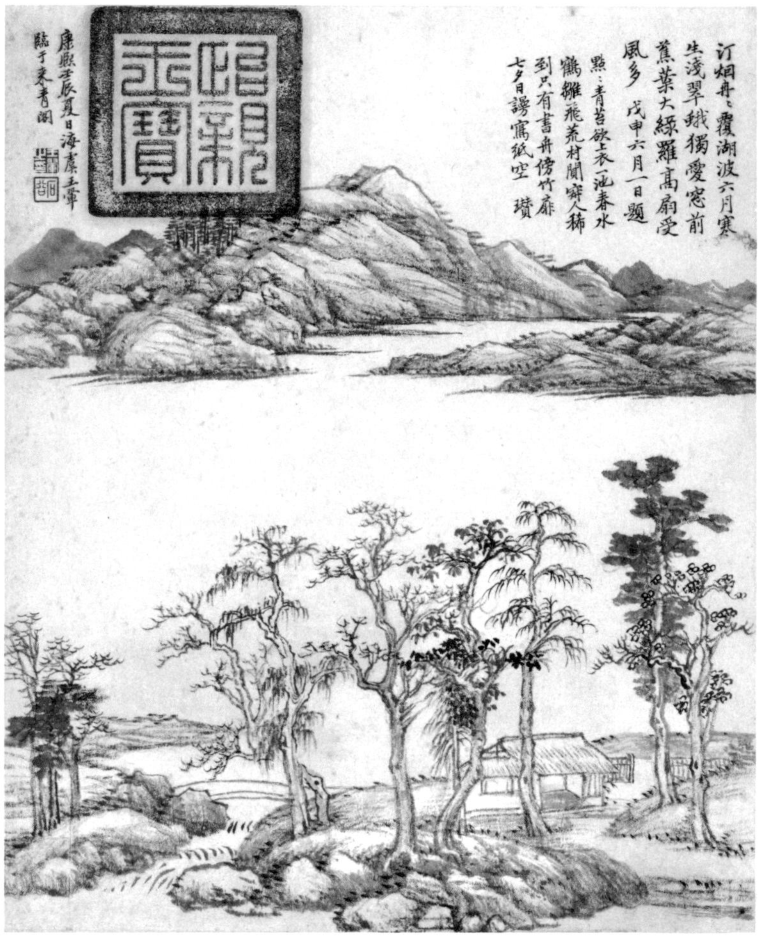

Leaf H, "Copy of a Painting by Ni Tsan (1301–1374)"

# 42 Yün Shou-p'ing (1633–1690)

## *Flowers, Landscapes, and Vegetables (Hua-hui shan-shui shu-kuo ts'e)*

Dated 1674

Album of eight leaves of painting (A–H) followed by one leaf with a colophon (I): painting (B, F, G, H), ink and color on paper (A, C, D, E), ink on paper; colophon, ink on gold-flecked paper

Painting, average measurements, each leaf: 26.4 x 59.4 cm ($10\frac{3}{8}$ x $23\frac{3}{8}$ in.); colophon: 27.9 x 62.1 cm (11 x $24\frac{1}{2}$ in.)

ARTIST'S INSCRIPTIONS:

Leaf A, "Landscape, Bamboo, Rock, and Bare Trees":
1. Prose, 100 characters in 6 columns of running script (right).
2. Prose, 34 characters in 4 columns of running script (left).

Leaf B, "River Landscape with Man in Boat in the Style of Tung Yüan (fl. 937–76)": 15 characters in 2 columns of running script (right).

Leaf C, "Cloudy Mountains in the Style of Mi Fu (1052–1107) and Mi Yu-jen (1072–1151)":
1. 5 character quatrain, followed by a 69 character note, in 8 columns of running script (right).
2. Prose, 17 characters in 2 columns of running script (left).

Leaf D, "Bamboo, Trees, and Rocks" (from right to left):
1. Prose, 24 characters in 3 columns of running script.
2. Prose, 39 characters in 3 columns of running script.
3. Prose, 89 characters in 6 columns of running script.
4. Prose, 85 characters in 4 columns of running script.

Leaf E, "Willows and Boatman in the Style of Ma Ho-chih (*chin-shih*, 1131, d. ca. 1190)": 7 character regulated verse in 8 lines, followed by 62 character note, in 11 columns of running script (left).

Leaf F, "Peony in the Style of Hsü Ch'ung-ssu (11th century)":
1. 7 character quatrain in 2 columns of running script (right).
2. Prose, 123 characters in 5 columns of running script (left).

Leaf G, "Lotus": 4 characters in 1 column of running script.

Leaf H, "Cabbages":
1. Prose, 26 characters in 5 columns of running script (right).
2. Prose, 39 characters in 4 columns of running script (left).

ARTIST'S SIGNATURES: Hsi-hsi kuo-k'o, Shou-p'ing (C); Shou (D); Nan-t'ien ts'ao-i, Shou-p'ing (E); On the second day of the twelfth lunar month, Shou-p'ing wrote this (F); Ts'ao-i-k'o, Shou-p'ing again inscribed this (F); Nan-t'ien ts'ao-i (G); Shou-p'ing wrote this by a lamp (H); Pao-yung-k'o (H).

ARTIST'S SEALS: Yüan-k'o (square relief; A–E); Tung-hsüan (tall rectangle relief; A, H); Cheng-shu (square relief; A, C, F); Cheng-shu (square intaglio; D); Shu-tzu (squat rectangle relief; A); Shou-p'ing (squat rectangle relief; A, D, E, H); Shou-p'ing (square intaglio; D, F); Yün Shou-p'ing yin (square intaglio; B, C); Yün-tsai (tall rectangle intaglio; C); Tung-yüan wai-shih (square intaglio; C); Shou-p'ing (square, half relief, half intaglio; D, E, F, G); Hsüan-shang (tall rectangle intaglio; E); Nan-t'ien hsiao-yin (square intaglio; G, H).

INSCRIPTIONS:

1. Kao Shih-ch'i (1645–1704):
   a) Prose, 14 characters in 3 columns of free-form regular script. Signature: Tu-tan-weng, Shih-ch'i (B).
   b) Prose, 50 characters in 5 columns of running script. Signature: On the third day after the Midautumn Festival of the *hsin-ssu* year [1701], Chiang-ts'un, Kao Shih-ch'i inscribed this (E).
   c) Prose, 22 characters in 2 columns of regular script. Signature: On the eighteenth day of the eighth lunar month

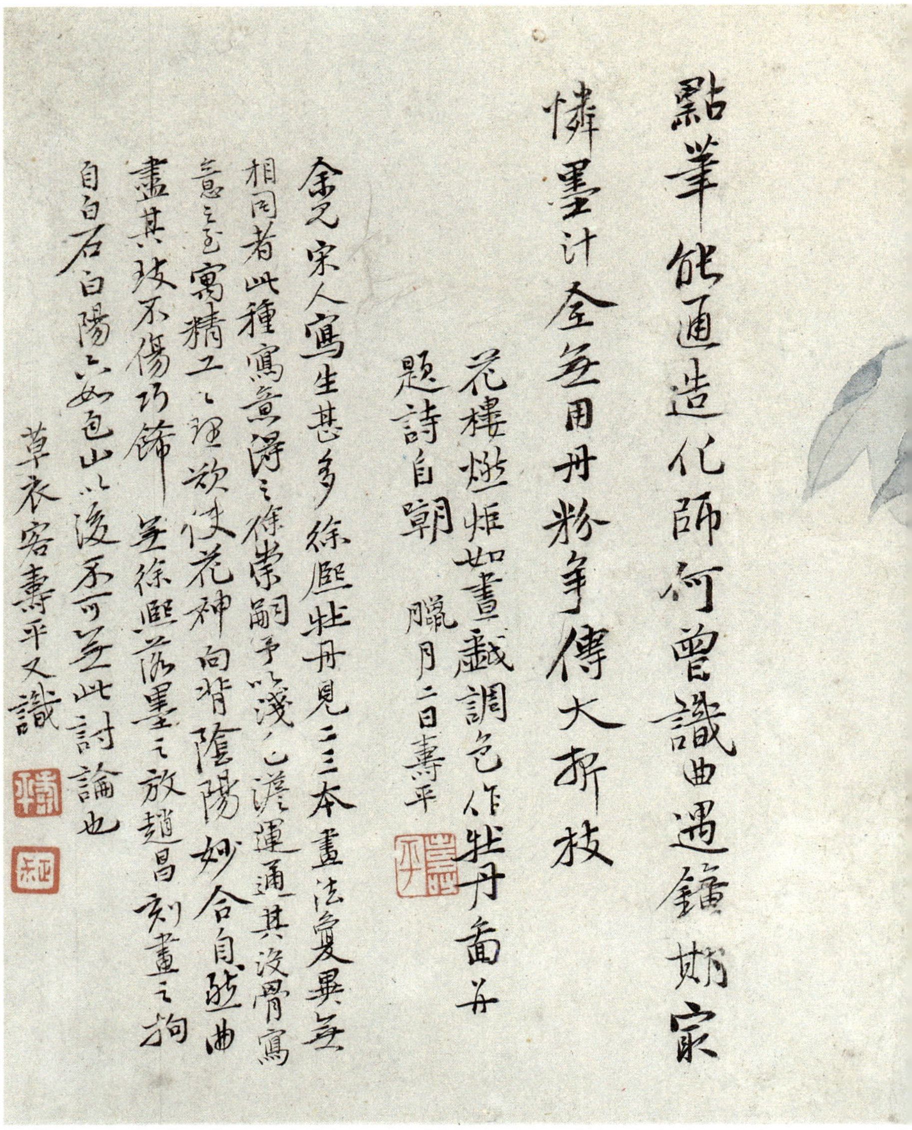

of the *hsin-ssu* year [1701], Tu-tan-weng, Kao Shih-ch'i, wrote this (H).

2. Chang Ying (1637–1708): prose, 7 character couplet in 2 columns of free-form regular script. Signature: Lo-p'u, Ying (H).

COLOPHON by Ho Shao-chi (1799–1873): prose, 118 characters in 11 columns of running script (I). Signature: Ho Shao-chi. Seal: Tzu-chen (square relief).

COLLECTORS' SEALS:
Fei Nien-tz'u (1855–1905), 11 seals.
Lin Hsiung-kuang (fl. ca. late 19th–early 20th century), 3 seals.
Chiang Piao (fl. ca. late 19th–early 20th century), 3 seals.
Unidentified owners, 6 seals.

Gift of David L. Elliott (75–29)

PUBLISHED: Suzuki Kei and Akiyama Terukazu, eds., *Chūgoku bijutsu* (Chinese art in Western collections) (Tokyo: Kōdan-sha, 1973), vol. 2, pls. 81, 82 (Leaves G, H); Kawakami Kei and Tsuruta Takeyoshi, *Chūgoku no meiga* (Famous Chinese paintings) (Tokyo: Sekaibunka-sha, 1977), p. 25 (Leaves G, H); Julia K. Murray, "An Album of Paintings by Yün Shou-p'ing, the Recluse of Nan-t'ien," *Record of The Art Museum, Princeton University* 37, no. 1 (1978): 3–25; Ishikawa Jun et al., eds., *Bunjinga suihen* (Selection of the finest Chinese and Japanese literati paintings), vol. 7 (Tokyo: Chūōkōron-sha, 1979), pls. 65–72; Suzuki Kei, comp., *Chūgoku kaiga sōgō zuroku: daiikkan, Amerika–Kanada hen* (Comprehensive illustrated catalogue of Chinese paintings: volume 1, American and Canadian collections) (Tokyo: University of Tokyo Press, 1982), p. 116, pl. A16–044.

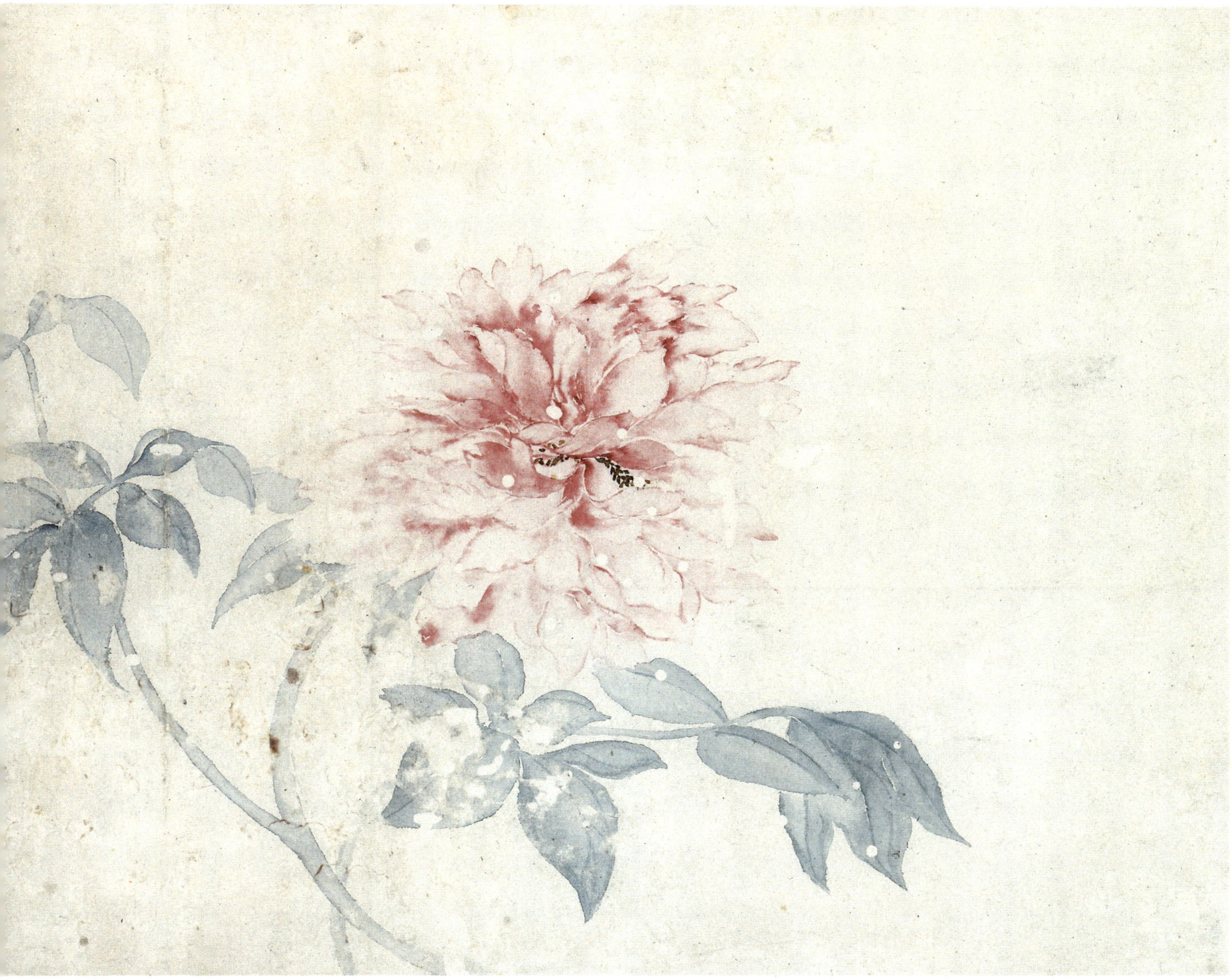

Leaf F, "Peony in the Style of Hsü Ch'ung-ssu (11th century)"

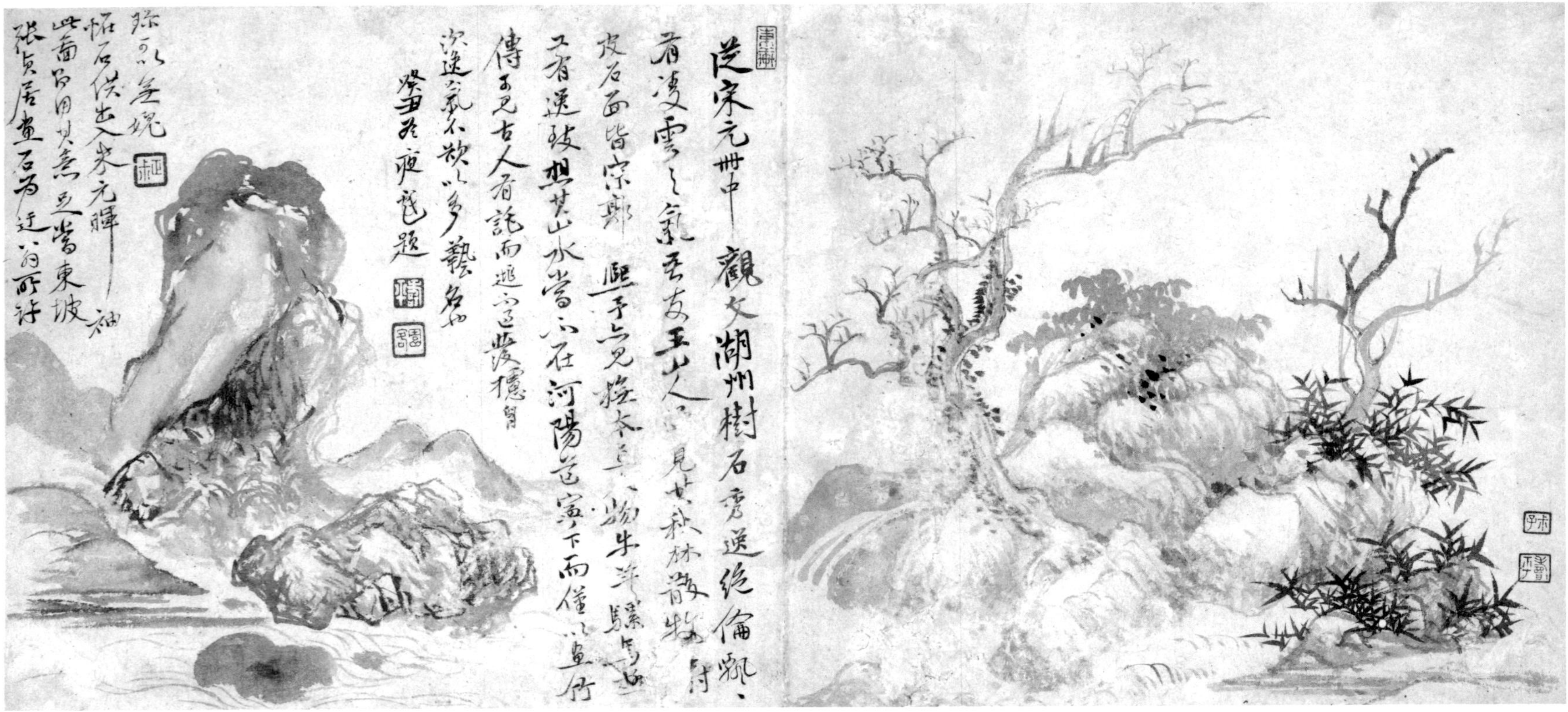

Leaf A, "Landscape, Bamboo, Rock, and Bare Trees"

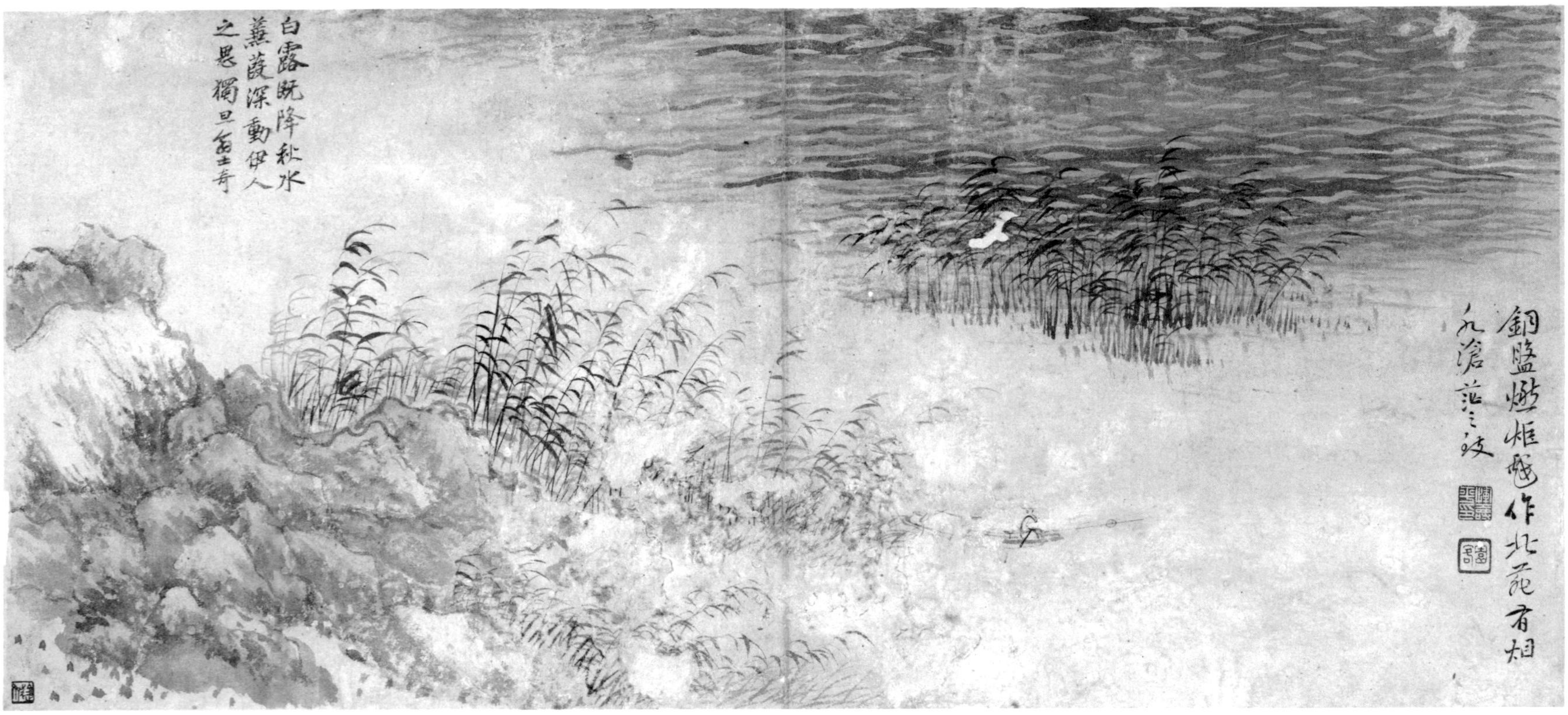

Leaf B, "River Landscape with Man in Boat in the Style of Tung Yüan (fl. 937–76)"

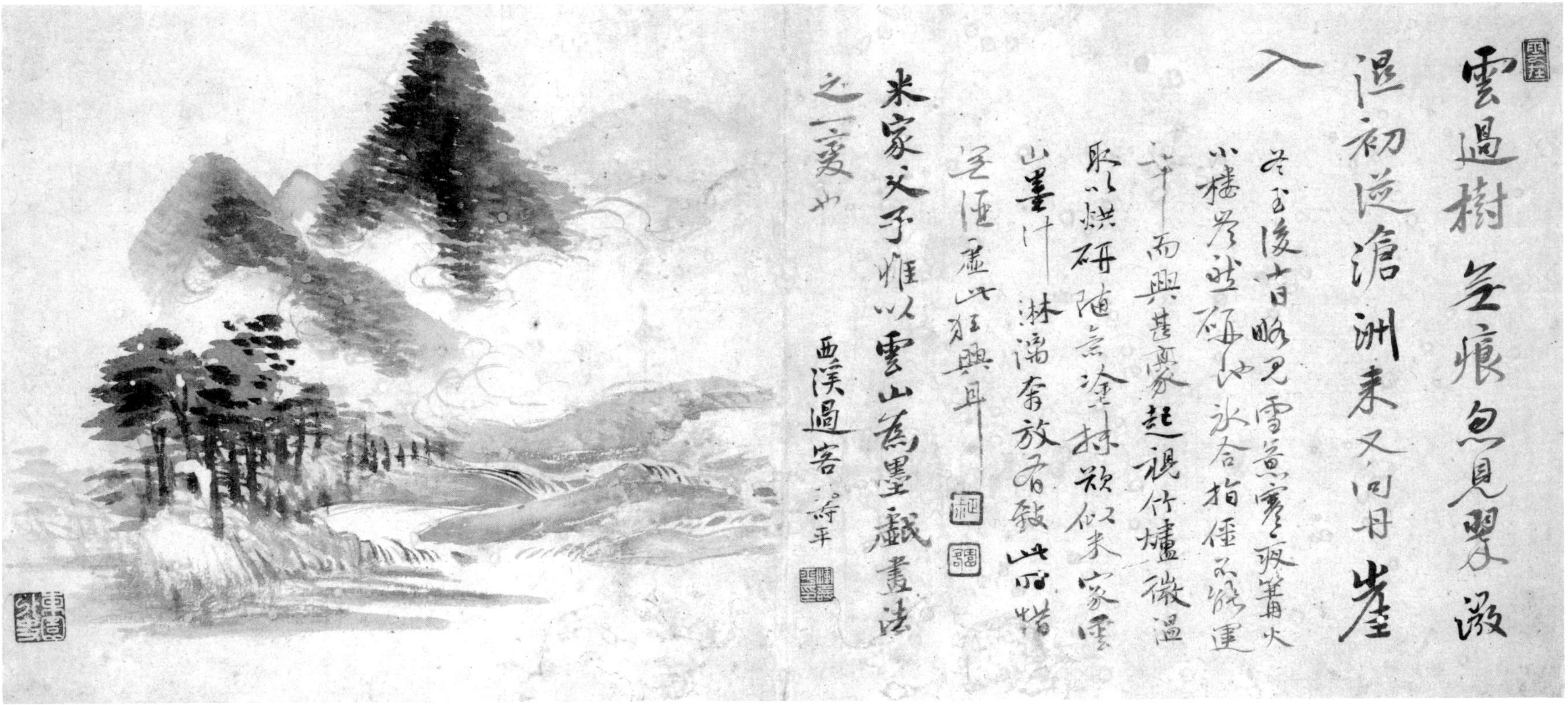

Leaf C, "Cloudy Mountains in the Style of Mi Fu (1052–1107) and Mi Yu-jen (1072–1151)"

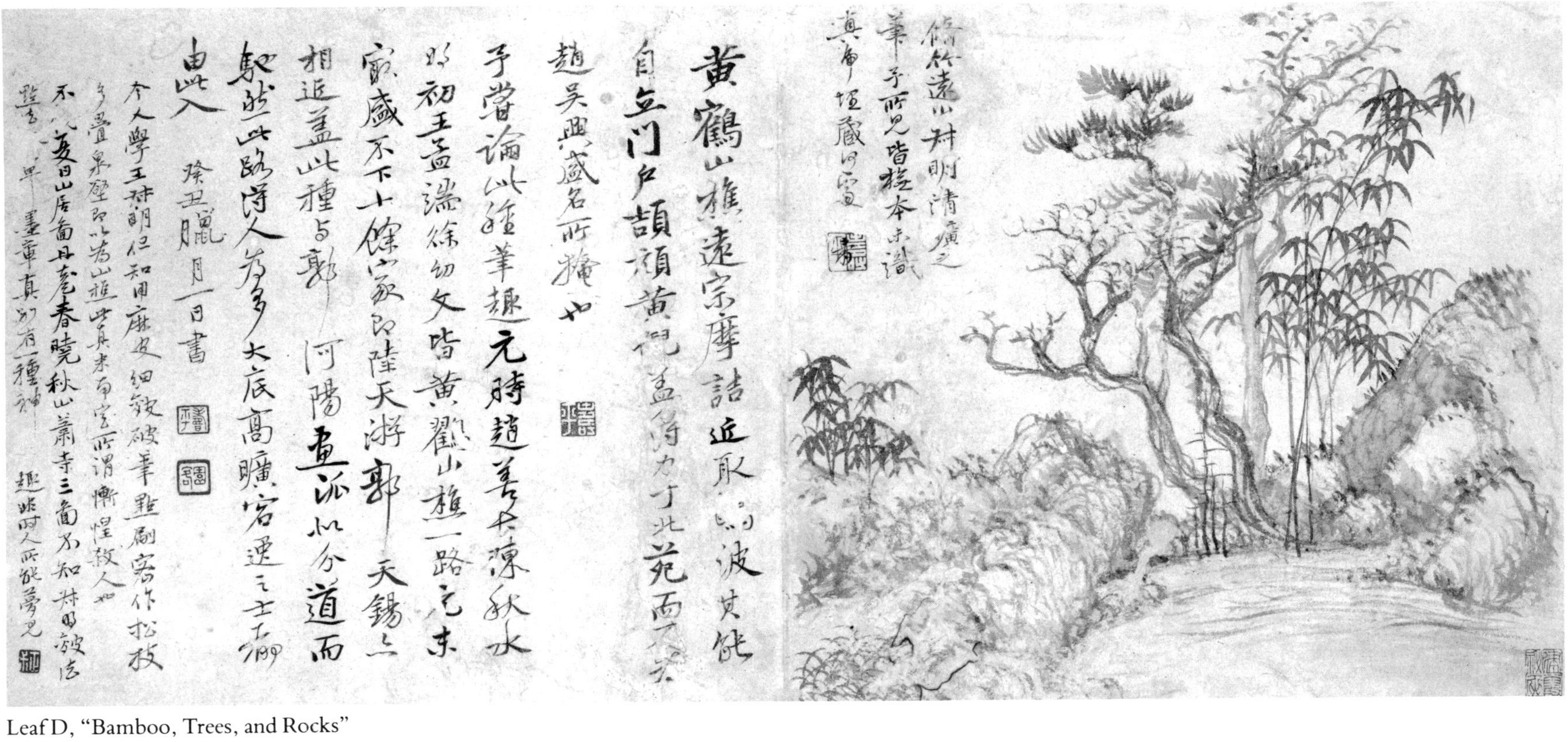

Leaf D, "Bamboo, Trees, and Rocks"

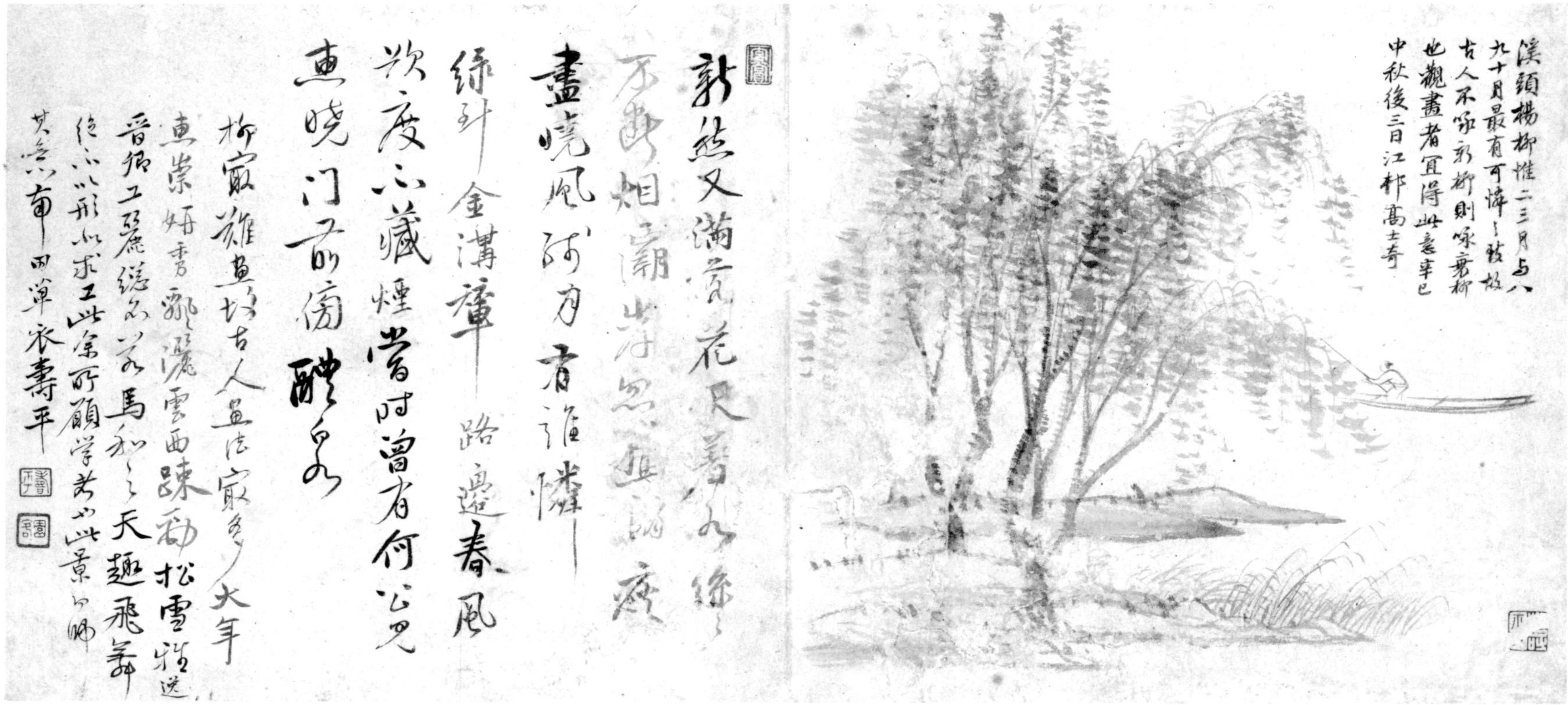

Leaf E, "Willows and Boatman in the Style of Ma Ho-chih (*chin-shih*, 1131, d. ca. 1190)"

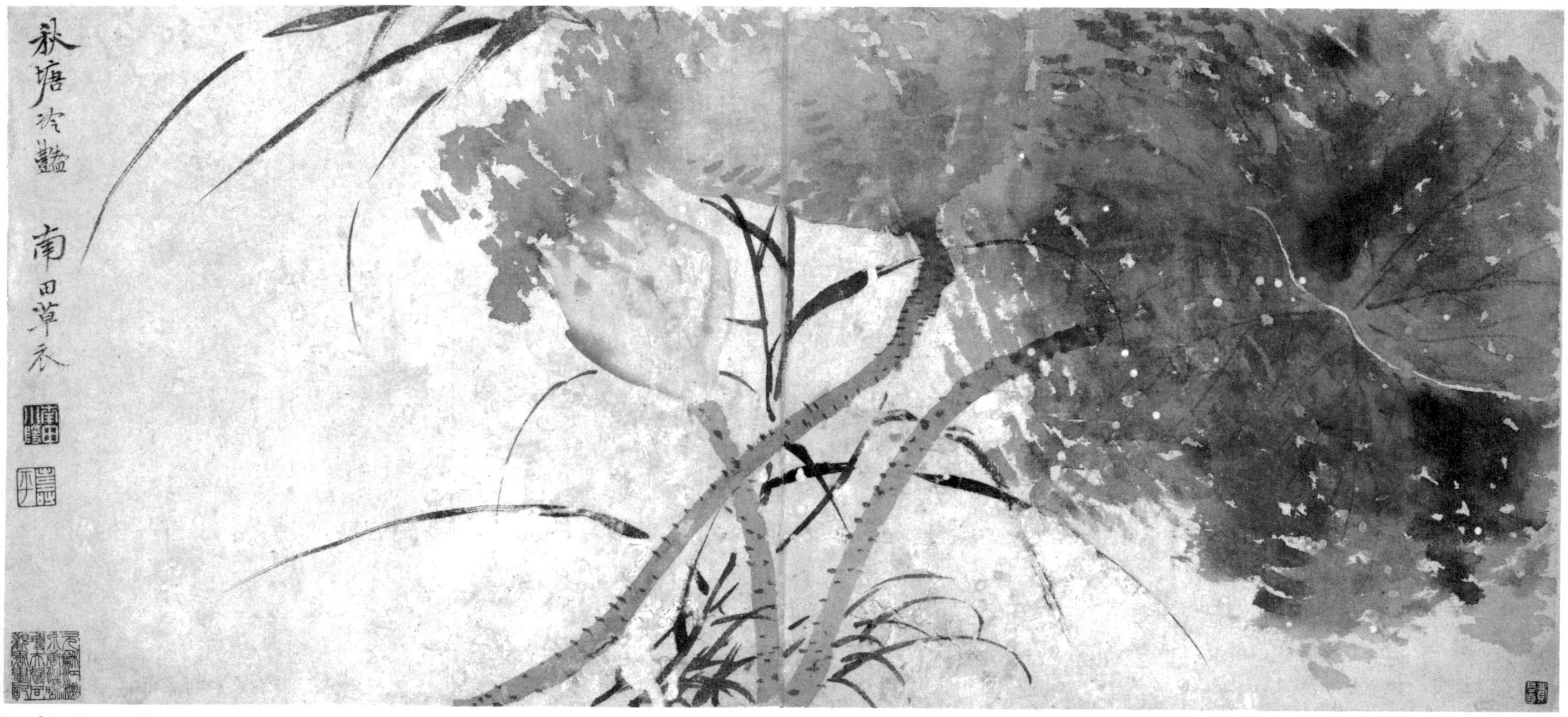

Leaf G, "Lotus"

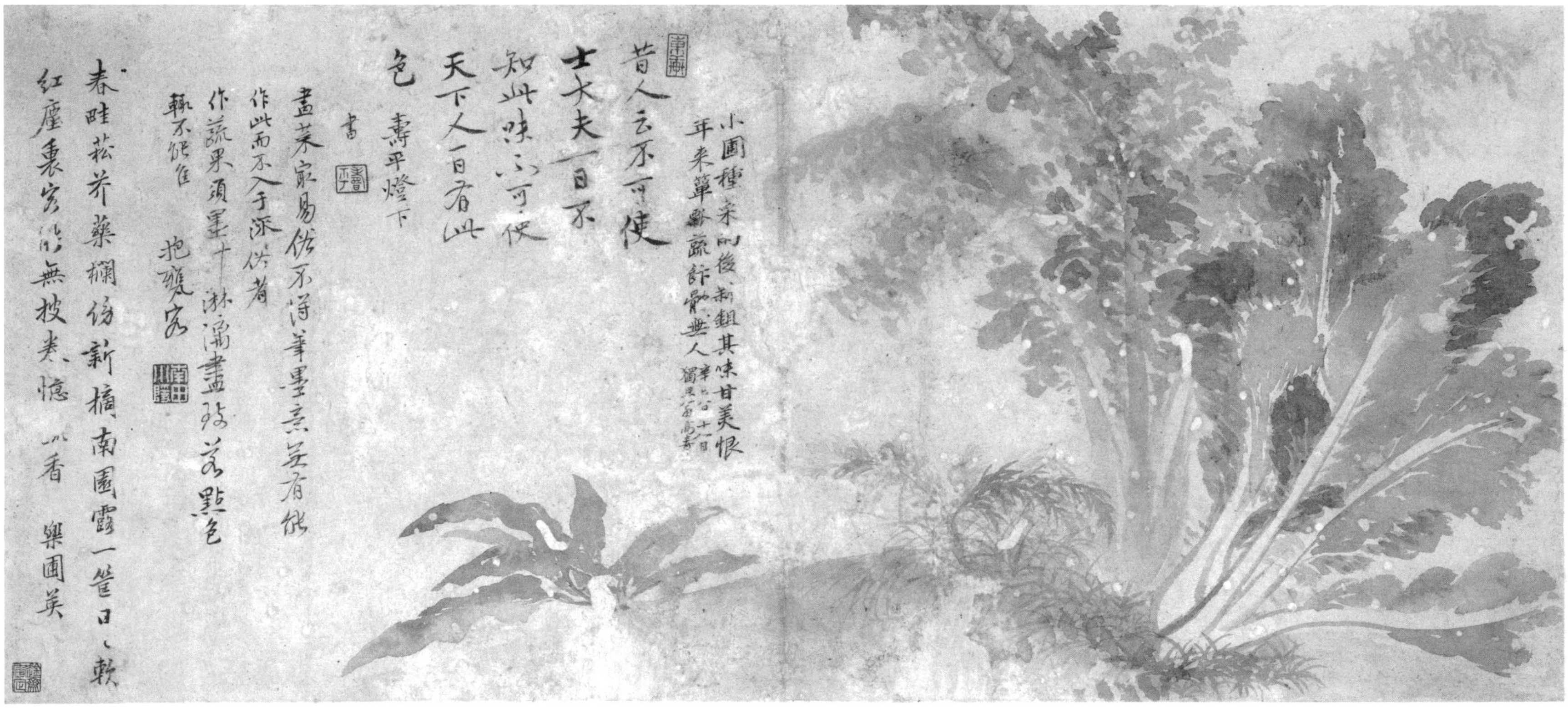

Leaf H, "Cabbages"

Leaf I, colophon by Ho Shao-chi

# 43 Sung Lo (1634–1713)

## *Landscape in the Style of Ni Tsan (Fang Ni Tsan shan-shui)*

Dated 1694
Hanging scroll, ink on silk
128.8 x 51.4 cm (4 ft. $2^{3}/_{4}$ in. x $20^{1}/_{4}$ in.)

ARTIST'S INSCRIPTION (prose, 134 characters in 7 columns of running script):

> I know how to paint, but I never paint casually. The deeper my knowledge about painting, the greater the difficulty of execution. Once in a while, when people ask me for a painting, I will give them an orchid and bamboo painting done in an expressive style that hides the awkwardness and vulgarity of my technique. At the end of autumn, in the *chia-hsü* year [1694], Master Kao Shih-ch'i [Kao Chiang-ts'un; 1645–1704] visited my office at Wu-men [Su-chou]. We discussed in detail "Six Principles of Painting" [by Hsieh Ho; fl. ca. 479–502], while looking at rare paintings, which had titles written in gold paste and were kept in jade-decorated cases. After the discussion I understood better than ever the essence of painting. Consequently I made this landscape in a free manner, following the styles of ancient masters, and then gave it to Master Kao as a farewell present. I dare to hope that this painting, a treasure of mine, will somehow serve as an amusing object capable of pleasing the connoisseur. Also present at this discussion were the famous painting masters, the esteemed Wu-mu-shan-jen [Wang Hui; 1632–1717] and the esteemed Ning-tu-shan-jen [Lo Mu; 1622–after 1704]. I recorded this account especially to express my simultaneous shame and happiness.

ARTIST'S SIGNATURE: Wei-an-chu-jen, Sung Lo.

ARTIST'S SEALS: Lo yin (square intaglio); Man-t'ang (square relief); K'uai-tsai-t'ang (tall rectangle intaglio).

COLLECTORS' SEALS:
1. Huang Chung-t'ao (dates unknown): Tseng tsai Huang Chung-t'ao ch'u (square intaglio; lower right).
2. Unidentified owners: Li-tsai chien-ting wu-shang miao-p'in (square intaglio; lower right); Tun-ch'iu i-feng chien-shang shu-hua yin (square intaglio; lower right); Tien-yün-ko (square intaglio; lower left); Wu-ling ch'ing-wan (square intaglio; lower left); Yüan-nung (square relief; lower left).

Edward L. Elliott Family Collection (L219.70)

PUBLISHED: Suzuki Kei, comp., *Chūgoku kaiga sōgō zuroku: daiikkan, Amerika–Kanada hen* (Comprehensive illustrated catalogue of Chinese paintings: volume 1, American and Canadian collections) (Tokyo: University of Tokyo Press, 1982), p. 128, pl. A17–026.

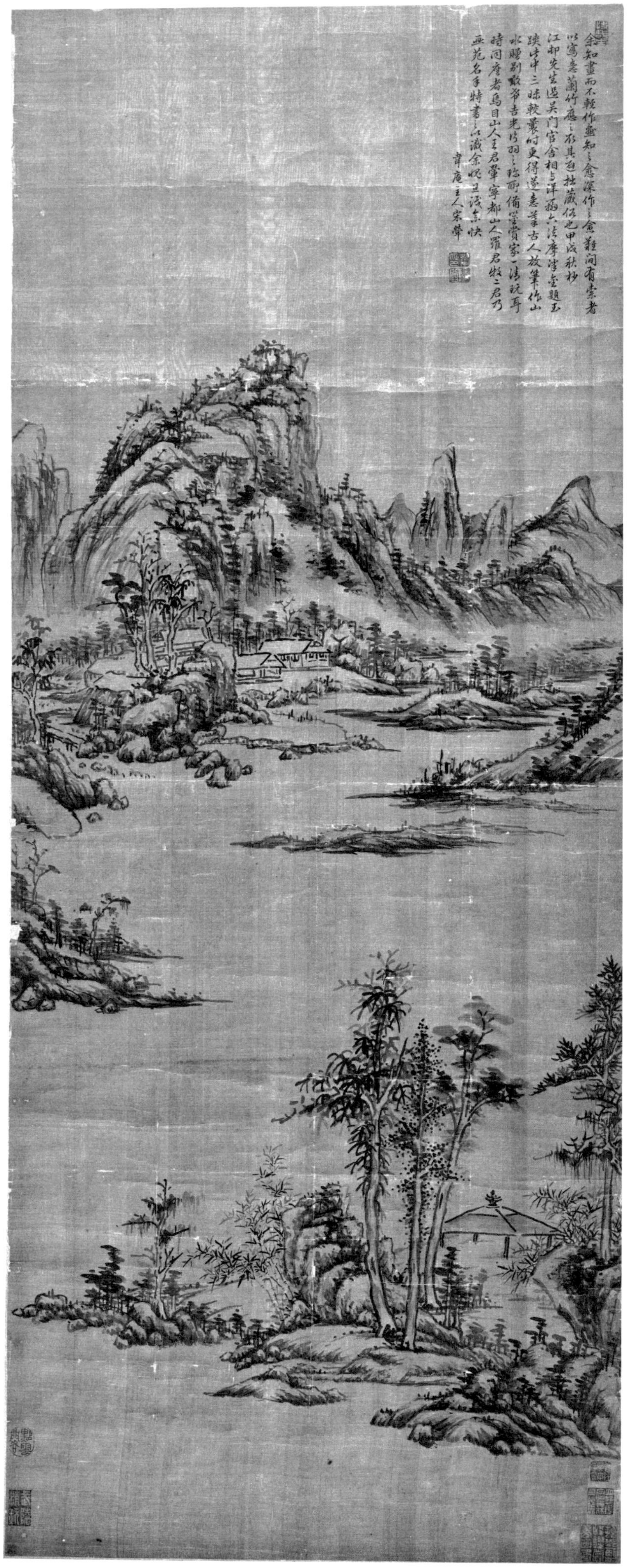

ALTHOUGH SUNG LO (*tzu*, Chung-mu; *hao*, Man-t'ang; Mien-chin-shan-jen; Hsi-p'i-chü-shih) was born in Shang-ch'iu, Honan province, he grew up in Peking. His father, Sung Ch'üan (1598–1652), a Ming official, surrendered to the Manchu conquerors in 1644 and received the post of grand secretary. In 1647 the emperor Ch'ing Shih-tsu (r. 1644–61) conferred upon Sung Lo, then just thirteen years old, the title of officer of the guards, a common honor for high officials' sons. In the following year Sung won the highest honors in a literary examination. In 1692 he was appointed governor of Kiangsu, which was the commercial as well as the artistic center of China at the time.[1]

Active in the artistic circle of Kiangsu, Sung Lo was an enthusiastic art patron, collector, and painter. Introduced by his friend Ts'ao Yin (1658–1712), Sung Lo must have known the art critic Chou Liang-kung (1612–1672) and the connoisseurs Kao Shih-ch'i (1645–1704) and Po-erh-tu (d. 1701). He would also have known the artists Tao-chi (1642–1707), Mei Ch'ing (1625–1697), Hung-jen (1610–1664), and Cha Shih-piao (1615–1698), all of the Anhui School; Kung Hsien (1619–1689) and K'un-ts'an (1612–ca. 1673) of the Nanking School; Fan I-chih (*chin-shih*, 1640; d. 1652), the Ming loyalist painter; and Wang Hui (1632–1717) and Yün Shou-p'ing (1633–1690), both of the Orthodox School.[2]

Sung's *Landscape in the Style of Ni Tsan* reveals an affinity with the Orthodox tradition of the four Yüan masters: Huang Kung-wang (1269–1354), Wu Chen (1280–1354), Ni Tsan (1301–1374), and Wang Meng (1308–1385), especially the styles of Huang Kung-wang and, as the title suggests, Ni Tsan. The principal features of Sung's painting are two land spits: the foreground and the distant ground are separated by a vast expanse of water, which zigzags from the bottom to the middle zone of the picture. The basic composition, as well as the foreground motif, were derived from Ni Tsan's scheme of a triangularly shaped foreground with an empty pavilion flanked by rocks and slender trees. Ni eliminated the middle ground, giving his paintings a spare and serene atmosphere. The motifs in the distant ground of Sung's painting show Huang Kung-wang's influence: the dense arrangement of simple houses, stylized trees constructed of horizontal strokes laid across vertical lines, hemp-fiber (*ma-p'i*) texture strokes delineating cone-shaped mountains topped by rocky plateaus, and clusters of small alum-head (*fan-t'ou*) rocks all reflect Huang's style. Nevertheless the painting also shows Sung Lo's personal interest in creating contrast: solid patches of trees and moss are accentuated against blank areas of the mountain. Sung encircled the compact mountain range with a veil of semitransparent haze. He executed his firm, elegant brushwork in rich, wet ink, in a range of tones. Sung's use of blank areas and atmospheric effects and his predilection for moist ink tones recalls the stylistic mannerisms of Tung Ch'i-ch'ang (1555–1636), widely adopted by seventeenth-century Orthodox painters for their landscapes in the style of Huang Kung-wang.

PAO-CHEN CH'EN

NOTES

1. Arthur Hummel, ed., *Eminent Chinese of the Ch'ing Period* (Washington, D.C.: United States Government Printing Office, 1943), pp. 689–90.
2. Jonathan D. Spence, "Tao-chi, An Historical Introduction," in Richard Edwards et al., *The Painting of Tao-chi* (Ann Arbor: University of Michigan, 1967), pp. 18–19.

# 44 Tao-chi (1642–1707)

## *Melancholy Thoughts on the Hsiao and Hsiang Rivers (Hsiao-Hsiang ch'ou)*

Dated 1682–83
Album leaf mounted as a hanging scroll, ink on paper
Leaf: 18.1 x 13.9 cm (7 1/8 x 5 1/2 in.)

ARTIST'S INSCRIPTION (prose, 7 characters in 2 columns of free-form regular script): There are those special melancholy thoughts on the Hsiao and Hsiang rivers.

ARTIST'S SIGNATURE: Hsiao-sheng-k'o [a Hinayana Buddhist].

ARTIST'S SEAL: Tien-seng (tall rectangle relief).

COLLECTOR'S SEAL: Chang Yüan (Chang Ta-ch'ien; 1899–1983): Ts'ang chih Ta-ch'ien (square intaglio; lower left).

Edward L. Elliott Family Collection (L82.83)

PUBLISHED: Chang Yüan (Chang Ta-ch'ien), *Ta-feng-t'ang ming-chi* (Masterpieces from the Ta-feng-t'ang collection) (Tokyo: Benridō, 1955), vol. 2, pl. 27b; *Shih-t'ao shan-shui wu-shang miao-p'in* (Masterpieces of landscape paintings by Shih-t'ao) (Taipei: Ya-yin-chai, n.d.), pl. 16.

ONE OF THE TRUE GENIUSES of Chinese painting history, Tao-chi was born Chu Jo-chi, a prince in the Ming imperial family in Kuei-lin, Kuangsi, in 1642.[1] Two years later the Ming dynasty fell, and in the ensuing war and chaos his father died and his family broke apart. Under a eunuch's protection the young prince converted to Buddhism and became a monk, taking as his personal names Shih-t'ao, Tao-chi, Yüan-chi, and K'u-kua-ho-shang. He then began a life of wandering.[2]

By 1682 Tao-chi had traveled to most of the scenic spots in the lower Yangtze River valley: he had journeyed to Hunan along the Hsiao and Hsiang rivers and had crossed Lake Tung-t'ing to visit Mount Lu in Kiangsi. Next he had visited Mount Huang in Anhui; then he had proceeded to West Lake in Hang-chou, and had finally come to rest in Nanking. The picturesque landscapes he saw and the painters he befriended —such as Mei Ch'ing (1625–1697) and Mei Keng (fl. ca. late 17th–early 18th century)—spurred his desire to paint. Through Mei Ch'ing, Tao-chi became familiar with works by the Anhui School artists, including Hung-jen (1610–1664), Ch'eng Sui (1605–1691), and Hsiao Yün-ts'ung (1596–1673). Under their influence Tao-chi developed a neat, dry, linear brushstroke quality, seen, for example, in his *Sixteen Lohans* (*Shih-liu lo-han*), dated to 1667 (The Metropolitan Museum of Art, New York; see page 200).

During the 1680s Tao-chi settled temporarily at the I-chih-k'o (Pavilion of a Single Plum Branch) in Nanking, where he met such artists as K'un-ts'an (1612–ca. 1673), Tai Pen-hsiao (1621–1691), K'ung Shang-jen (1648–1718), Kung Hsien (1619–1689), Cha Shih-piao (1615–1698), and the Manchu connoisseur Po-erh-tu (d. 1701). Through Po-erh-tu he received an imperial audience on the occasions of the emperor Ch'ing Sheng-tsu's (r. 1662–1772) southern journeys in 1684 and 1689. Fame, glory, and friendship surrounded Tao-chi in this period, but he could never forget his bitter experiences in early life. In a poem entitled "Song of My Life," written in 1687, Tao-chi lamented:

> All my life I have had noble aspirations
> To renounce this world of dust;
> After enduring separation from my family,
> I was confirmed in our true religion.
>
> Seeking the Tao was not an easy journey;
> Even in my dreams, I entrusted my soul to a close friend [Ho-t'ao];
> For thousands of *li* past the Hsiao and Hsiang rivers and Lake Tung-t'ing,
> We traveled on roads that stretched into the distance toward the lands of the immortals. . . .[3]

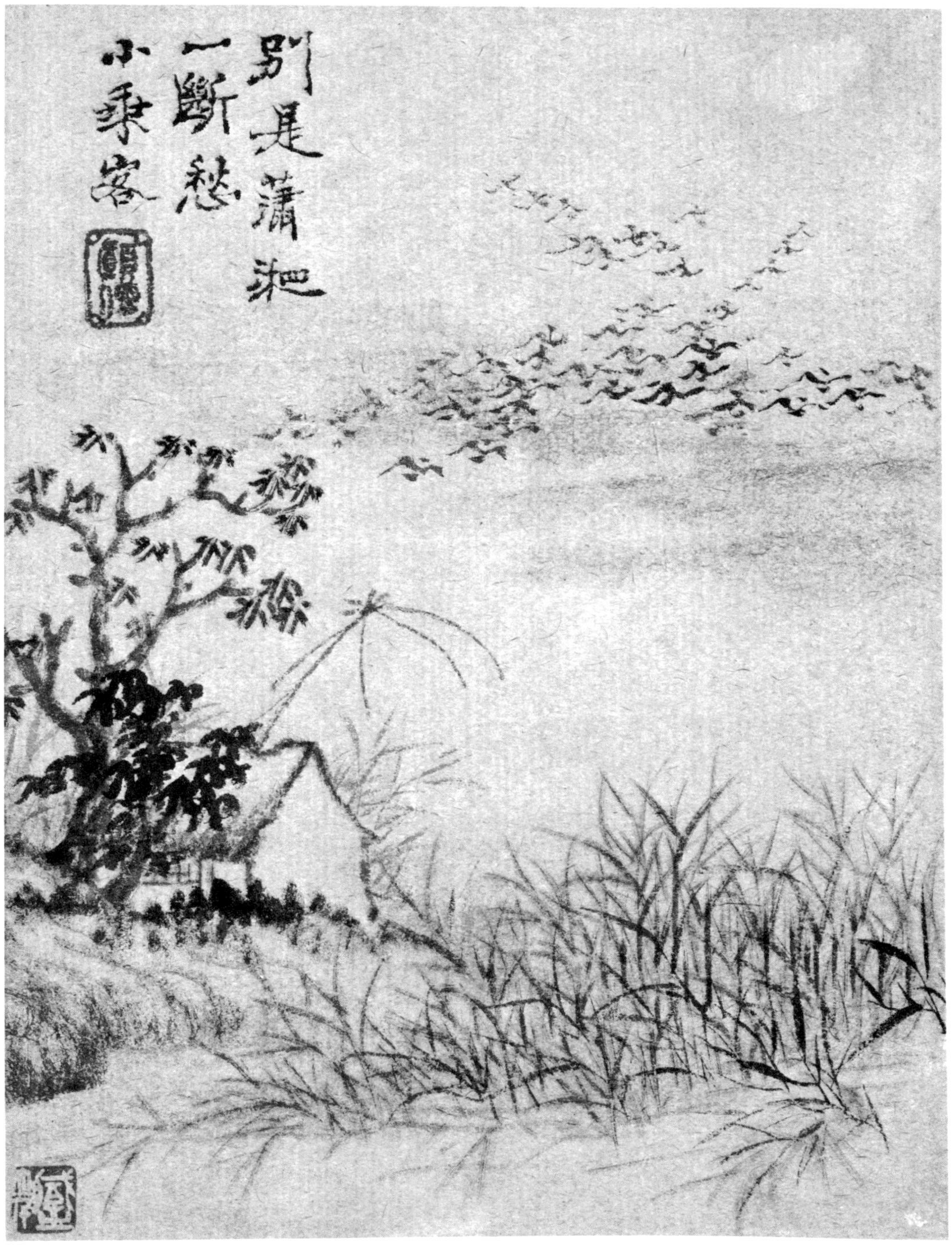
別是蒲杷
一斷愁
小乘客

The sad and lonely atmosphere of the poem is reflected in *Melancholy Thoughts on the Hsiao and Hsiang Rivers*, dated 1682–83. Although the painting conveys deep emotion, it is relatively simple. A fishing hut, partially hidden behind two sparsely leaved trees, sits on a riverbank fringed with reeds. A fishing net with its bottom submerged in the river is visible behind the hut. The water is delineated only by a few horizontal brushstrokes that suggest the surface of the water. A flock of wild geese flies overhead, depicted by assertive brushstrokes executed with a blunt, worn brush (*t'u pi*) in dark ink. Particularly in these brushstrokes in "scorched" ink (*chiao-mo*), the former prince discloses his private grief on viewing the picturesque landscape of a country no longer ruled by his family. A homeless monk who wandered along the rivers, Tao-chi resembled the migrating wild geese in the autumnal sky. The bleak atmosphere of the album leaf is heightened by the artist's autograph in the upper left: "There are those special melancholy thoughts on the Hsiao and Hsiang rivers." Following this inscription Tao-chi signed the painting with the epithet "a Hinayana Buddhist" and used a seal with the words "a lunatic monk," an epithet adopted for self-abasement.

About 1690, Tao-chi went to Peking, probably at the invitation of Po-erh-tu. Although praised by Wang Hui (1632–1717) and Wang Yüan-ch'i (1642–1715), who considered Tao-chi to be the best painter from the south, Tao-chi was unhappy in the capital. He left Peking in 1692 and went to Yang-chou, where he spent his late years as a professional painter. There he built the Ta-ti-t'ang, and about 1697 began to refer to himself as Ta-ti-tzu. In his 1699 letter to the painter Chu Ta (Pa-ta-shan-jen; see no. 39), asking for a painting for his Ta-ti-t'ang, Tao-chi wrote: "Please do not refer to me as a monk, for I am a man who keeps his hair and wears a hat."[4]

Unconcerned with fame and honor, Tao-chi led a serene life in his post-Peking years. His paintings of this period are characterized by fluid brushwork and moist, graded ink tones. *An Ancient House under Tall Pine Trees* (*Ch'ang-sung lao-wu*; no. 45) can be dated to this period on the basis of its style. The fantastic landscape has elements reminiscent of the region around Mount Huang, where Tao-chi lived in the 1670s. In a cloudy valley, in a multistoried building screened by two tall pines, a man sits reading; other trees are partially obscured by a huge rock near the water's edge. The pines have short needles and few branches, revealing their origin in the harsh climate of Mount Huang. The sea of clouds for which Mount Huang is known fills most of the valleys between the painting's rocky mountains. In the distance a tiny island with two small huts in front of two pines emerges from the sea. This remote and mysterious residence, a dwelling fit for immortals, is a common motif in most of Tao-chi's paintings of Mount Huang. To the left, beyond the island, a row of sharp triangular peaks looming above the clouds is Tao-chi's adaptation of a motif found in the paintings of Mei Ch'ing. The artist applied various modeling strokes to represent different rock textures, unified by a consistently moist treatment of graded ink tones. The foreground rocks were represented with the unraveled rope (*chieh-so*) and tiny raindrop (*yü-tien*) texture strokes; and the distant rocks show hemp-fiber (*ma-p'i*) texture strokes. The wet ink treatment reveals Tao-chi's debt to Tung Ch'i-ch'ang (1555–1636). Both the painting and the inscriptions in the upper right are smooth and fluid, reflecting the inner harmony that Tao-chi achieved in his late years. The poem of the inscription also appears on a landscape by Tao-chi in the C. C. Wang collection, which was executed in 1679.

PAO-CHEN CH'EN

NOTES

1. Wen C. Fong, "A Letter from Shih-t'ao to Pa-ta-shan-jen and the Problem of Shih-t'ao's Chronology," *Archives of the Chinese Art Society in America* 13 (1959): 22–53.
2. For further biographical information, see Cheng Cho-lu, *Shih-t'ao yen chiu* (A study of Shih-t'ao) (Peking: Jen-min mei-shu ch'u-pan-she, 1961); Li Yeh-shuang, *Shih-t'ao te shih-chieh* (The world of Shih-t'ao [Tao-chi]) (Taipei: Hsiung-shih mei-shu yüeh-k'an-she, 1973); Marilyn and Shen Fu, *Studies in Connoisseurship: Chinese Paintings from the Arthur M. Sackler Collection in New York and Princeton* (Princeton: The Art Museum, 1974), pp. 36–37, 168–73, 220.
3. English translation from Wen C. Fong, *Returning Home: Tao-chi's Album of Landscapes and Flowers* (New York: George Braziller, 1976), pp. 16–17; Chinese in Li Yeh-shuang, *Shih-t'ao te shih-chieh*, p. 21.
4. Wen C. Fong, "A Letter from Shih-t'ao," p. 24.

# 45 Tao-chi (1642–1707)

## *An Ancient House under Tall Pine Trees (Ch'ang-sung lao-wu)*

Ca. 1700
Hanging scroll, ink on paper
184.8 x 88.3 cm (6 ft. 3/4 in. x 33 3/4 in.)

ARTIST'S INSCRIPTION: prose poem, 52 characters in 4 columns of clerical and regular scripts (for a translation of the artist's inscription, see page 207).

ARTIST'S SIGNATURE: Asking Master Tzu-mo for his learned comment. Ch'ing-hsiang, Shih-t'ao, Chi, painted and inscribed this.

ARTIST'S SEALS: T'ou-pai i-jan pu shih tzu (tall rectangle intaglio); K'u-kua-ho-shang Chi hua-fa (oval intaglio); Hsia-tsun-che (tall rectangle relief).

COLLECTORS' SEALS:

1. Chou Huai-chung (dates unknown): Chou shih Huai-chung Chien-ts'ang (tall rectangle relief; lower right).
2. Sun Lien-shu (dates unknown): Lien-shu shen-ting (square relief; lower right); Hai-yang Sun shih Lien-shu chen-shang shu-hua yin-hsin (square relief; lower right).
3. Chang Yüan (Chang Ta-ch'ien; 1899–1983): Pieh-shih jung-i (square relief; lower left); Ta-ch'ien-chü-shih kung-ching pai shih chih i (square relief; lower left); Nan pei tung hsi chih yu hsiang-sui wu pieh-li (square relief; lower left); Ch'iu t'u pao ku-jou ch'ing (squat rectangle intaglio; lower left); Ti kuo chih fu (square relief; lower left); Ta-feng-t'ang Chien-chiang K'un-ts'an Hsüeh-ko K'u-kua mo-yüan (tall rectangle relief; lower left).

John B. Elliott Collection (L169.75)

PUBLISHED: Chang Yüan (Chang Ta-ch'ien), *Ta-feng-t'ang ming-chi* (Masterpieces from the Ta-feng-t'ang collection) (Tokyo: Benridō, 1955) vol. 1, pl. 35.

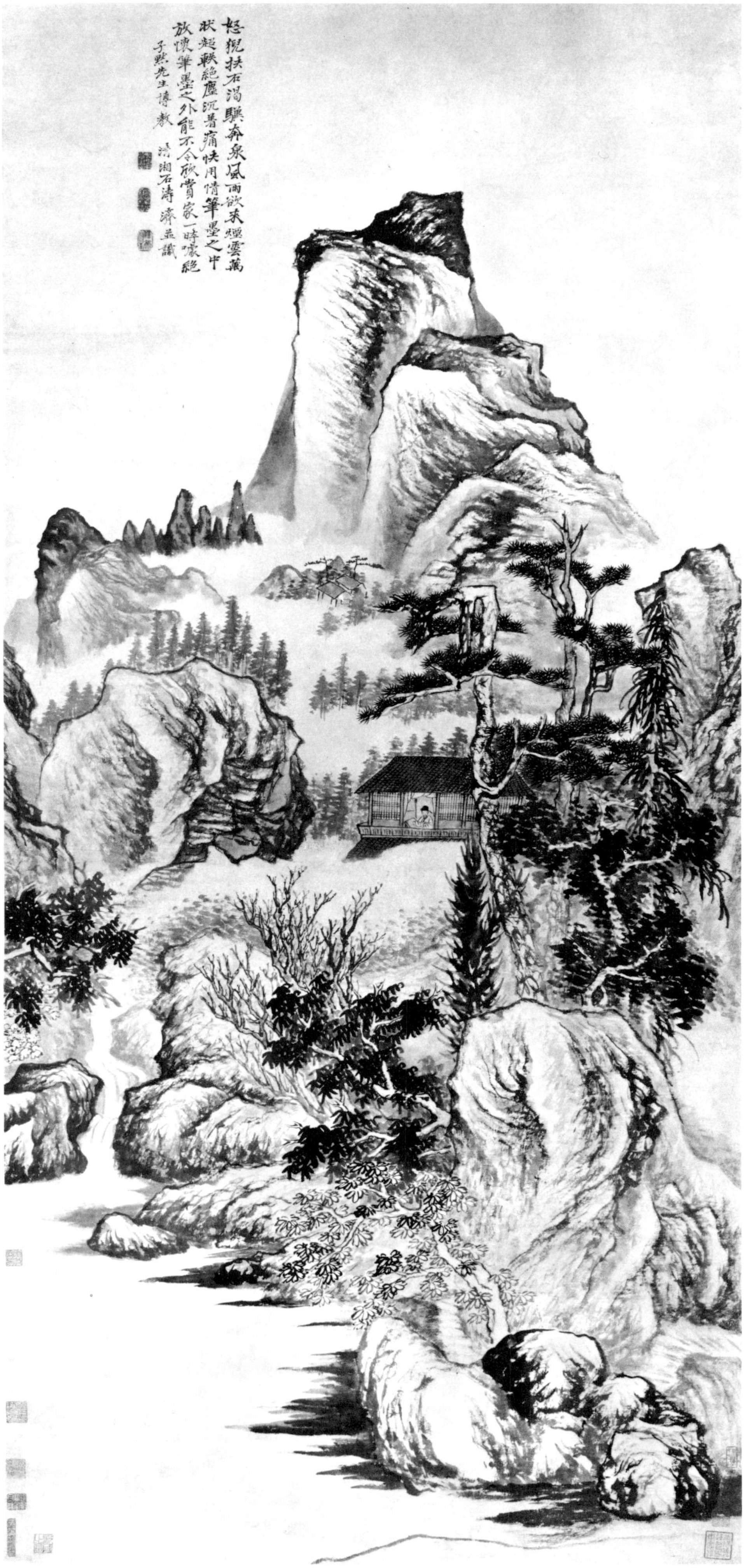

# 46 Kao Ch'i-p'ei (1672–1734)

## *Returning from Yeh-lang (Yeh-lang kuei-tu)*

Dated 1707
Handscroll, ink on paper
Painting: 27.9 x 190.8 cm (11 in. x 6 ft. 3 1/8 in.); calligraphy: 27.9 x 189.5 cm (11 in. x 6 ft. 2 5/8 in.)

FRONTISPIECE, calligraphy by Ch'en I-hsi (1648–1709) (7 character quatrain, followed by a 33 character note, in 9 columns of free-form running script):

When the poplar blossoms wither, the cuckoo will start to call.
On hearing that Yün-piao had passed through West Valley,
I transferred my sorrow to the bright moon,
Wishing that the wind would carry it west to Yeh-lang.

People of the ancient period considered the Yeh-lang district a remote and poor region. Their comments on it were plaintive and sorrowful. Yet I lived there for one year before returning home; what is to stop me from recording it all?

Signature: In the midwinter of the *ting-hai* year [of the K'ang-hsi era; 1707] I-hsi inscribed this. Seals: I-hsi (square intaglio); I chien han-mo (square relief); Pien-pi-lou (tall rectangle relief).

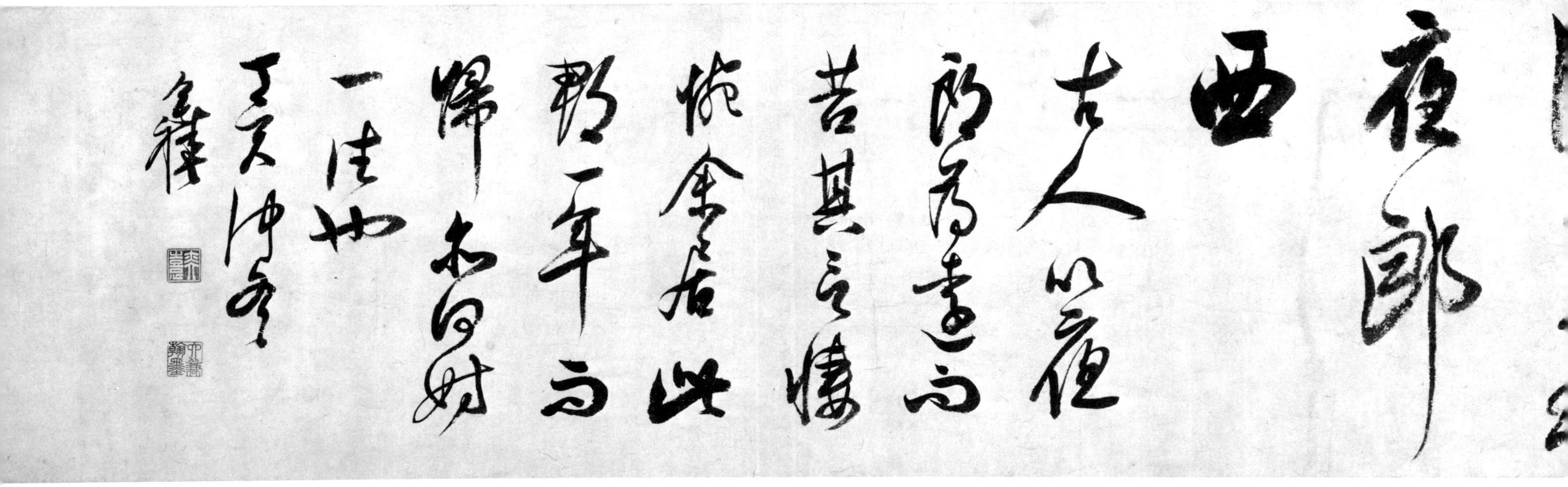

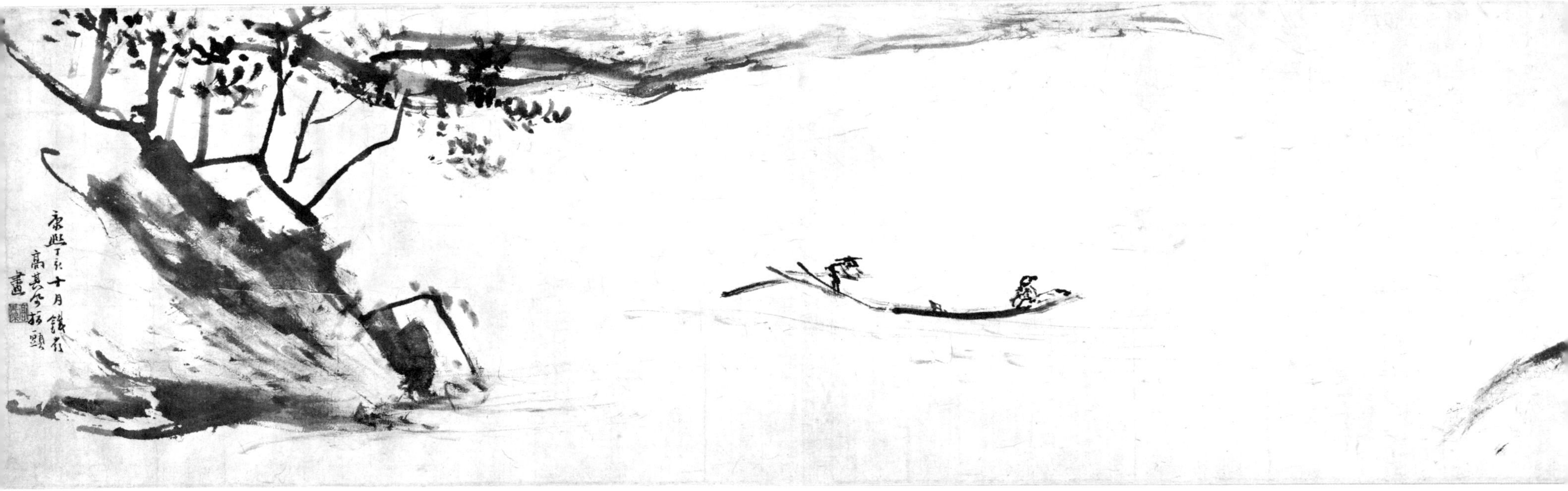

ARTIST'S INSCRIPTION (prose, 14 characters in 3 columns of running script): In the tenth lunar month of the *ting-hai* year of the K'ang-hsi era [1707], Kao Ch'i-p'ei from T'ieh-ling [in Liaoning province] painted this with the tips of his fingers.

ARTIST'S SEAL: Kao Ch'i-p'ei (square relief).

Edward L. Elliott Family Collection (L50.70)

PUBLISHED: Suzuki Kei, comp., *Chūgoku kaiga sōgō zuroku: daiikkan, Amerika–Kanada hen* (Comprehensive illustrated catalogue of Chinese paintings: volume 1, American and Canadian collections) (Tokyo: University of Tokyo Press, 1982), p. 146, pl. A17–087.

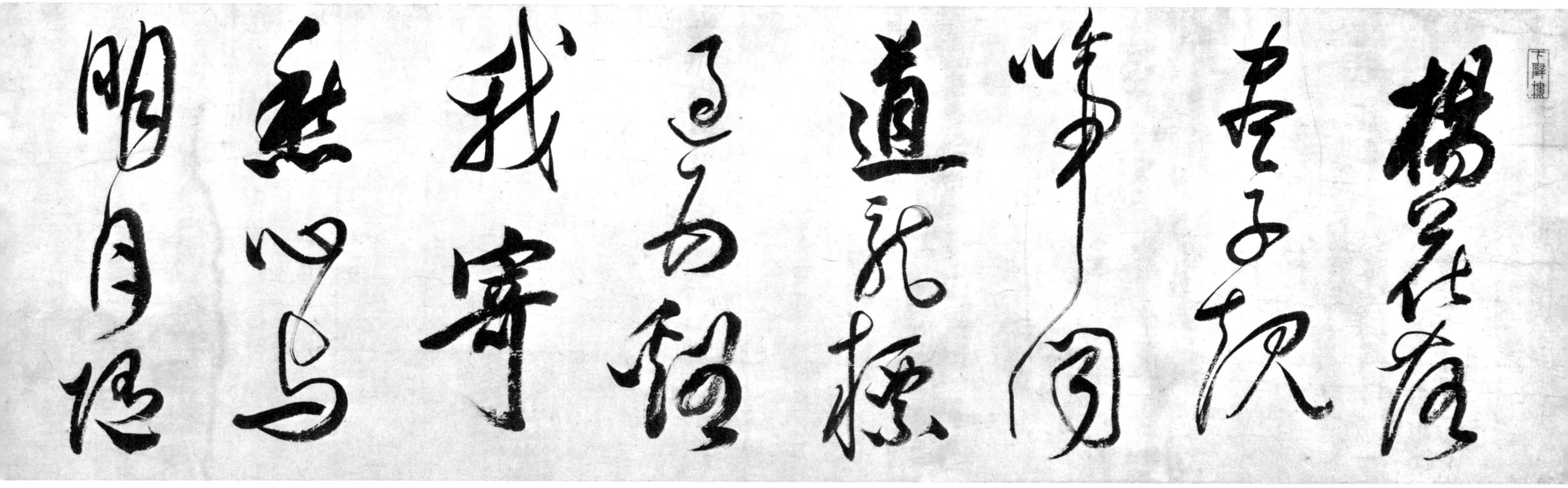

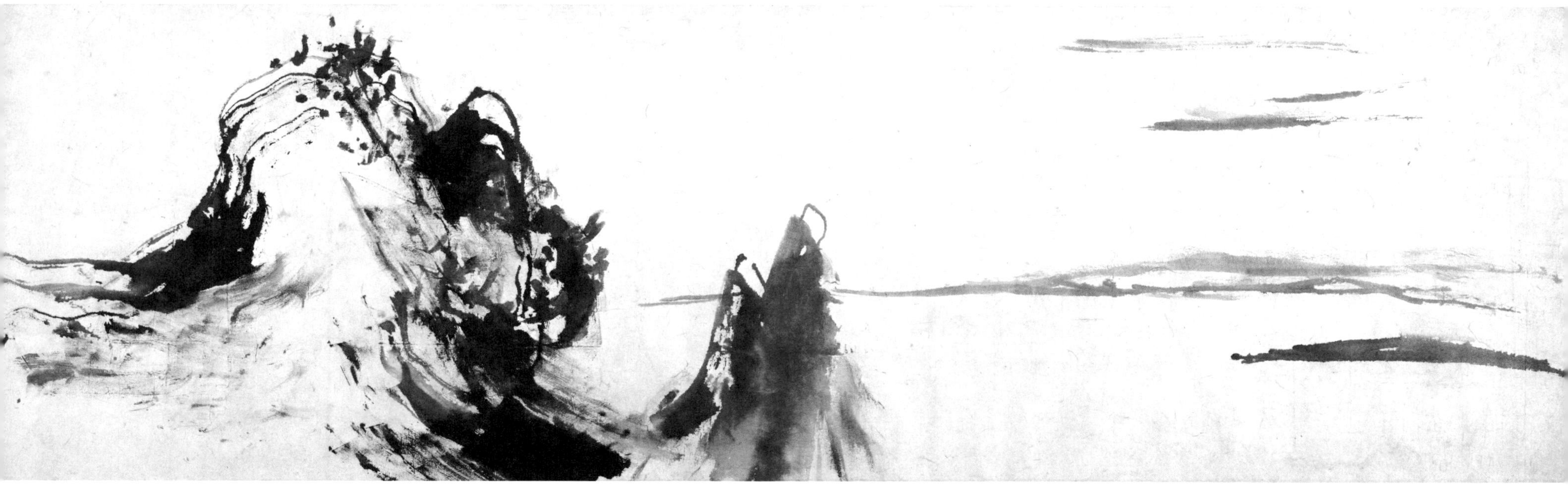

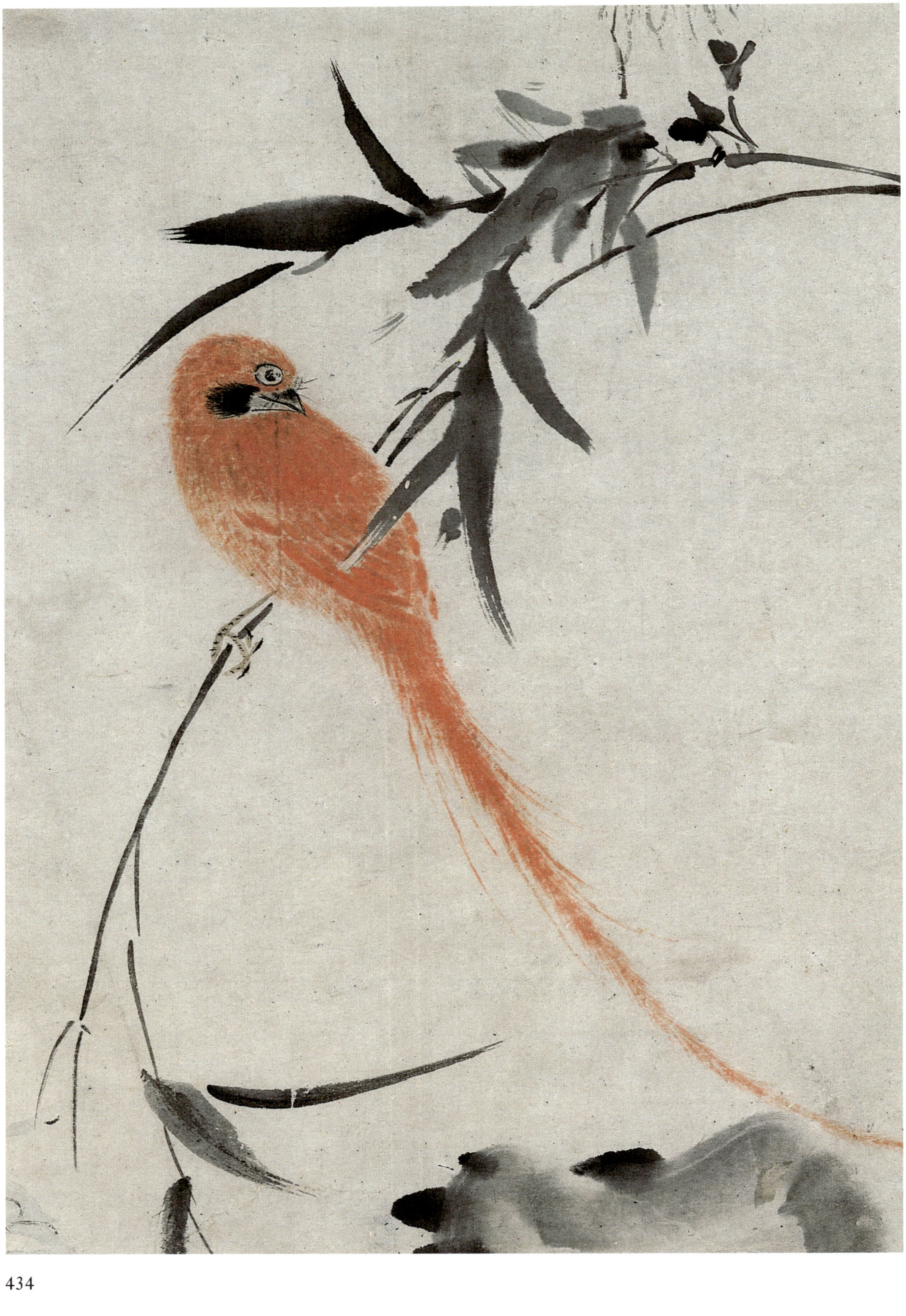

# 47 Hua Yen (1682–ca. 1765)

## *The Red Bird (Chu ch'üeh)*

Undated
Hanging scroll, ink and color on paper
126.8 x 59.5 cm (4 ft. 2 in. x 23³/₈ in.)

ARTIST'S INSCRIPTION (5 character verse in 3 columns of running script, totaling 50 characters; quoted from one of the "Drinking Wine" poems by T'ao Ch'ien [365–427]; translation from James Robert Hightower, *The Poetry of T'ao Ch'ien* (Oxford: Clarendon Press, 1970), pp. 133–34:

> The fall chrysanthemums have lovely colors.
> I pluck the petals that are wet with dew,
> And float them in this Care Dispelling Thing
> To strengthen my resolve to leave the world.
> I drink my solitary cup alone
> And when it's empty, pour myself another.
> The sun goes down, and all of nature rests
> Homing birds fly chirping toward the grove.
> I sit complacent on the east veranda,
> Having somehow found my life again.

ARTIST'S SIGNATURE: Hsin-lo-shan-jen painted this and transcribed T'ao Ch'ien's poem.

ARTIST'S SEALS: Hua Yen (square intaglio); Ch'iu-yüeh (square intaglio); Ch'iu-k'ung i ho (tall rectangle relief).

COLLECTORS' SEALS:

1. P'an shih-ch'eng (*chin-shih*, 1832): P'an Shih-ch'eng yin (square intaglio; lower left); Te-yü shen-ting (square relief; lower left corner).
2. Ch'en Yu-chou (dates unknown): Ch'en Yu-chou ts'ang (square intaglio; lower right).
3. Unidentified owners: Wu tzu-ch'i (oval intaglio; lower right).

Edward L. Elliott Family Collection (L197.70)

PUBLISHED: Ch'en Jen-t'ao, *Chin-kuei ts'ang-hua chi* (Chinese paintings in the King Kwei [Chin-kuei] collection) (Hong Kong: T'ung-ying, 1956), vol. 1, pl. 59; Ch'en Jen-t'ao, *Chin-kuei ts'ang-hua p'ing-shih* (Annotated catalogue of Chinese paintings from the King Kwei [Chin-kuei] collection) (Hong Kong: T'ung-ying, 1956), p. 239; Suzuki Kei, comp., *Chūgoku kaiga sōgō zuroku: daiikkan, Amerika–Kanada hen* (Comprehensive illustrated catalogue of Chinese paintings: volume 1, American and Canadian collections) (Tokyo: University of Tokyo Press, 1982), p. 129, pl. A17–048.

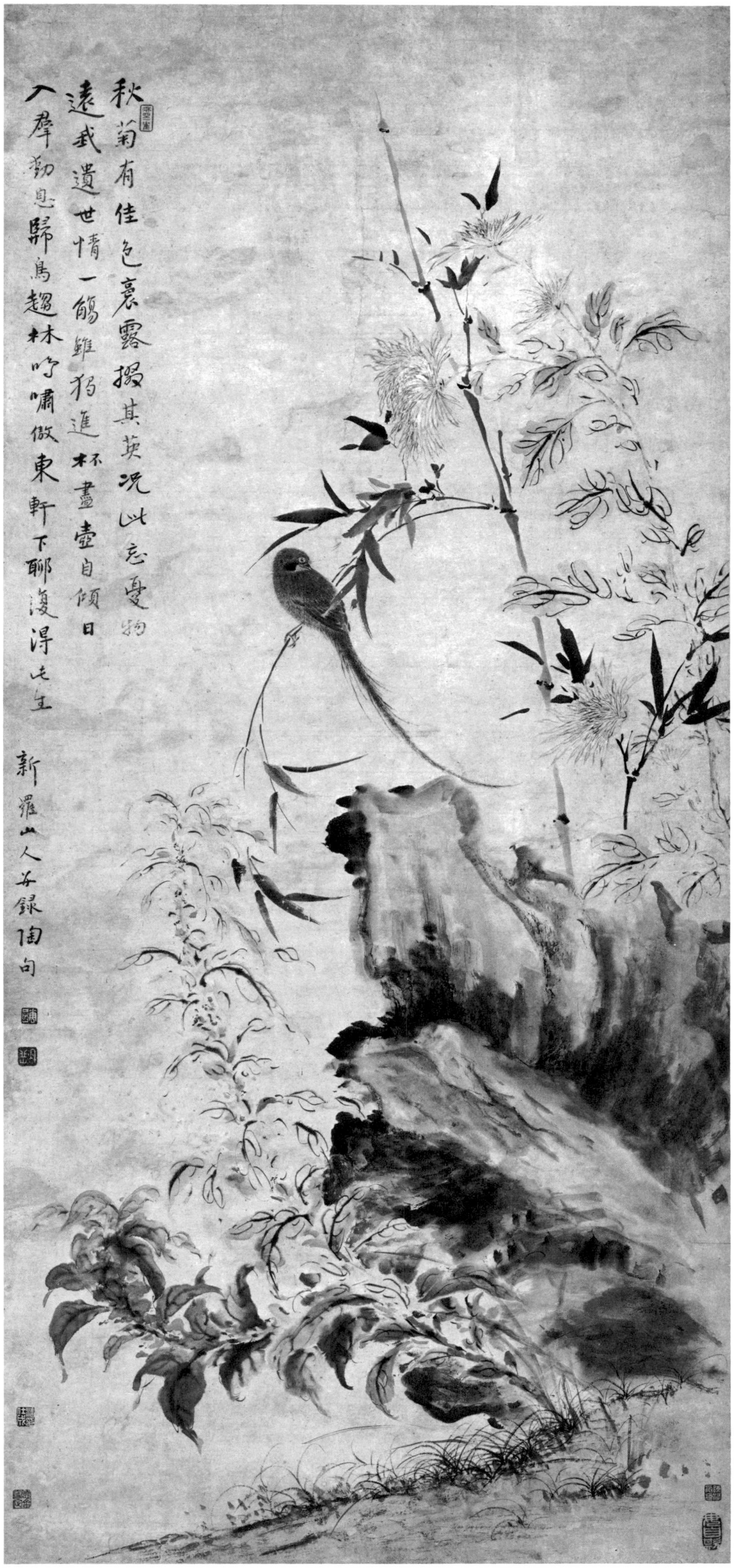

THE EIGHT ECCENTRICS of Yang-chou (Yang-chou-pa-kuai) is a nineteenth-century name given to a group of several masterful and innovative painters who were active in Yang-chou, Kiangsu province, between 1710 and 1765.[1] Of the many artists discussed as among the "Eight," six artists are consistently mentioned: Wang Shih-shen (nos. 48, 49, 50), Li Shan (nos. 51, 52), Chin Nung (no. 53), Huang Shen (nos. 54, 55), Cheng Hsieh (1693–1765), and Lo P'ing (1733–1799). Others sometimes included are Hua Yen (no. 47), Kao Hsiang (1686–ca. 1753), Li Fang-ying (1696–1754), Min Chen (fl. ca. 1730–90), and Kao Feng-han (1683–ca. 1747). One painter who, perhaps because of the relative scarcity of his works, is never included as one of the Eight Eccentrics, but who painted in a similar style and who influenced these painters, is Ch'en Chuan (no. 56). The "Eccentrics" name derived from the free and bold manner in which these painters worked, but it is somewhat misleading. None of them tried intentionally to create bizarre or eccentric effects in their paintings; rather they saw themselves as carrying on the *wen-jen* (literati) painting tradition in a changing time in history.

Between 1710 and 1765 Yang-chou was a wealthy community, culturally as well as materially. Strategically located on the Grand Canal just north of its intersection with the Yangtze River, it became the center of an important transportation network. After certain reforms in 1492, which made salt trading a profitable entrepreneurial venture, Yang-chou attracted a large number of new merchant settlers.[2]

Breaking the tradition-bound patterns of Chinese society, in which merchants were the lowest class, the salt merchants quickly gained upward social mobility, competing with the scholarly elite for prestige. Third- and fourth-generation merchant sons regularly took the civil service examinations and received degrees. With their increased social position and literati-style educations, the salt traders engaged in and patronized standard scholarly pastimes, hosting literary gatherings and collecting books and paintings. Not yet totally secure with their new status, the merchants eagerly tried to emulate all the accouterments of the literati lifestyle. While they did not necessarily conform to the true scholar-gentleman's code of social welfare and Confucian loyalty, they observed all the outward forms.

The eagerness with which the merchants welcomed painters and poets in Yang-chou was well received by many artists, another departure from tradition. The true literati of earlier days responded to such overtures by barring their doors. Yielding to economic pressures and political realities of eighteenth-century China, the scholar-artist had to accept the reshaping of traditional values. While the merchant class climbed steadily in the social order, the old scholar class experienced instability. Most of the scholars were no longer landed gentry, and without sources of private income they had to pass the *chin-shih* examination and take official positions to make a living. But since the Ch'ing government had a quota system, it was impossible for all who trained for degrees to receive them. Men who had practiced painting and calligraphy as avocations found themselves in the position of having to support themselves by selling their art. As a result, traces of bitterness and irony sometimes appear in the Yang-chou Eccentrics' paintings.

The artists mixed freely with their hosts at literary gatherings, in the grand private gardens of the patron-merchants. Usually the entertainment consisted of such traditional enjoyments as admiring antiquities and paintings, or competing in poetry-writing contests. Both groups saw themselves as continuing the patterns of the past and in most of their outward behavior tried to ignore the great social and economic upheaval taking place in Yang-chou.

Presentiments of the new commercial society did occasionally disturb the surface, however, as merchants, who had few opportunities for investment, sometimes indulged in bizarre escapades. One is said to have scattered 10,000 taels-worth of sheets of pure gold foil from a mountain into the trees and grasses. Another grew so fond of acquiring paintings that he offered to trade his daughter to Huang Shen in exchange for one of Huang's paintings.[3] Although such behavior met with greater tolerance than it would have earlier, most members of Yang-chou society maintained traditional standards and decorum.

The most characteristic common feature of the Eccentrics' style is an almost abstract treatment of calligraphic brushstrokes, pools of ink, and soft, rich colors. This characteristic, and a tendency to paint large-scale, close-up views of their subjects, became especially pronounced in the hands of the later Eccentrics. The development of this style essentially fell into three evolutionary stages: first, Ch'en Chuan, Hua Yen, Wang Shih-shen, and Kao Hsiang—influenced by individualist painters such as Tao-chi (nos. 44, 45) and Hu Ta (no. 38), who had both been active in Yang-chou—experimented with free brushwork and bold compositions. Li Shan, Chin Nung, Huang Shen, Li Fang-ying, and Cheng Hsieh further developed their manner. Finally the Yang-chou Eccentric style culminated with Chin Nung's student, Lo P'ing, who was known for his hauntingly strange paintings of ghosts and skeletons done with blurred, moist brushwork and splashy washes. He claimed to have painted these subjects from "real-life" encounters.

The Eight Eccentrics favored the painting of albums, a format that had steadily gained popularity since the time of Shen Chou (1427–1509). The album was well suited to these artists' interest in thematic musings on everyday objects, such as flowers, vegetables, birds, and insects. For the first time these motifs became more popular than paintings of landscapes. The Yang-chou artists transformed the manner of earlier bird and flower paintings by turning what had once been an analytic, carefully descriptive mode of painting into semi-abstract ink play.

The first and more conservative of the so-called Eight Eccentrics were Hua Yen and Ch'en Chuan. Whereas Ch'en formed a direct bridge between Tao-chi and the earlier Yang-chou style to Chin Nung, Huang Shen, and Li Shang, Hua Yen was more aloof from other Yang-chou painters and had a less direct influence on them.

One of the most versatile of the Eight Eccentrics, Hua Yen did not use the splashy techniques of the other Eccentrics, but his compositions were never dull. He was best known for the "humorous realism"[4] of his bird and animal studies, sometimes expressed in his choice of unorthodox subject matter, such as a wild animal fleeing a brushfire—other times appearing in the interjection of a note of whimsy into a relatively traditional composition. *The Red Bird* (no. 47) demonstrates this humorous touch in the bright, flat color of the bird, but it also shows Hua Yen's technical mastery with brush and ink and with color. The suffused blues and ink tones in the foliage to the left and the chrysanthemum blossoms in neat ink outlines with blue stems in the contourless boneless (*mo-ku*) style are refreshing in their coolness. The vermilion bird, perched elegantly and naturally on a curving stem of bamboo, is not at all eccentric. Hua's wash garden rocks also show consummate skill. So light that they hover cloudlike on the paper, they still manage to convey an appropriate sense of bulk and weight.

As a young man Ch'en Chuan studied with Mao Ch'i-ling (1623–1716), a renowned Chekiang scholar, an artist, and a former monk.[5] Ch'en followed the eremitic lifestyle of his mentor, even in Yang-chou, where Ch'en had to live by selling his paintings. His combination of a *wen-jen* lifestyle and a career as an artist influenced Chin Nung, Li Shan, and others of the Eccentrics.

*Plum Blossoms*, Ch'en's album in the Edward L. Elliott Family Collection (no. 56), was undoubtedly inspired by some of Tao-chi's plum paintings (Ch'en owned eleven paintings by Tao-chi). Although it is impossible to suggest a specific model, the album *Plum Branches: Poems and Paintings* (*Mei-hua-shih ts'e*), now at The Art Museum, Princeton University, is a possibility.[6] In general Ch'en Chuan's plums are less substantial and more abstract than Tao-chi's. The moist brushstrokes forming the branches, with puddles of different tones of ink suffused into each other, are more vehicles for ink play than convincing solid, three-dimensional branches. Inspired by the physical beauty of the plum as well as its symbolism of spiritual purity and refined, scholarly living, Ch'en drew the flowers from every possible vantage point. Although his album is painted from real observations of nature, in several leaves, such as Leaf C, Ch'en rearranged the natural, organic relationship of the twigs into a patterned geometric design. The painted image is only part of the total effect of Ch'en's album leaves. In Leaf C, for example, the atmosphere and relationship to an environment, lacking in the painting, are provided by the inscription, which describes a rising mist and the shimmering reflection of the plum blossoms in water. Ch'en thus involves the viewer's imagination in order to complete the scene.

Chin Nung's plum paintings represent a later development of the style developed by Ch'en Chuan. Chin did not begin to paint plums until 1736, the year he traveled to Peking in order to participate in the special *po-hsüeh* examination for which he had been recommended.[7] Chin was among the many who failed, but the trip to the capital gave him the opportunity to see several private painting collections. When he saw a plum blossom painting by Chao Meng-chien (1199–1267), Chin was deeply moved. This experience may have stimulated a more than avocational interest in painting. He began his artistic career relatively late in life, when he was nearly fifty, although he must have started painting earlier by practicing bamboo. Then he learned to paint plums and Buddhist subjects, and finally landscapes.

*Ink Plum* (no. 53) depicts a tree that sweeps across the paper in a grand gesture. Chin's choice of dark, moist ink wash for the main trunk and dry, sprightly calligraphic strokes for the twigs and flowers effectively contrasts age and strength with youth and delicacy. Heavy black ink dots along the trunk and branches stand in single file like parading soldiers, introducing a staccatto rhythm reminiscent of plum paintings by Wang Shih-shen.[8] Chin often said that Wang Mien (1287–1359) and Chao Meng-chien were his models for plums, but in this scroll he achieved a bold directness not even hinted at in the earlier painters' works.

Chin's plum is a stable, straightforward image: it is as if he took the entwined branches of a real tree and reconstructed them to suit his own vision. Many of his paintings have an architectonic construction that echoes his calligraphy style. The two-column signature on *Ink Plum* is typical of his script, which is archaistic. He not only recalls the flared diagonal brushstrokes of clerical script (*li-shu*), but he uses his brush like a chisel, as if he were cutting an ancient stone stele. His painting is entirely two-dimensional. The ink seems to rest on the surface of the paper without soaking into it, an effect also seen in Ch'en Chuan. A comparison between Leaf D of *Plum Blossoms* (no. 56) with a scroll by Chin in the Yale University Art Gallery (fig. a) shows Chin Nung's indebtedness to Ch'en Chuan. Leaf D is inscribed in a blank space left between the flowering twigs on the right and left sides of the picture. With the calligraphy directly between the plum branches, almost as if it were a part of the tree, the flowers and calligraphy read as an unbroken series of calligraphic brushstrokes, stressing the two-dimensional surface. Building upon this kind of vision, Chin Nung, in the Yale scroll, enclosed a bold, dark inscription on all four sides with silvery plum branches.

Although born in 1687, the same year as Chin Nung, Huang Shen developed a very different artistic temperament. Huang's father died while Huang was still young, and he had to enter a Buddhist monastery when he was eighteen or nineteen in order to support his mother. He studied painting with Shang-kuan Chou (1665–1750) and learned from him *kung-pi-hua*, a technique of precise line drawing, as well as various methods for painting figures, bird and flower motifs, and landscapes. By day he painted religious subjects for the temple in which he lived, and at night he practiced his own compositions.[9]

Huang's affiliation with Buddhism affected not only his choice of subject matter, but also his style. In *Man Appreciating an Ink Slab* (no. 55), the body of the man is represented by quick brushstrokes and dark and medium tone patches of ink; there is no anatomical description. The head is more fully described. The bulbous cranium is outlined with a single clear, steady stroke and the facial features are carefully but playfully described. The precedent for portraits with detailed heads and generalized, abstracted bodies goes back to Ch'an (Zen) painting, as practiced in the Sung and Yüan dynasties. Liang K'ai's thirteenth-century portrait of Li Po (now in the Tokyo National Museum; see page 136) is an example of a prototype. But Huang's figure injects more of a comical note into his painting than was present in the earlier works.

Huang liked to paint in the same quick manner he used for his calligraphy, which he modeled after the script style of Huai-su (725–785). As a young artist Huang saw a piece of Huai-su's calligraphy and suddenly had an awakening. Grabbing the brush and paper of a nearby shopkeeper, he started to paint, triumphantly slapping the table and exclaiming, "I've got the secret."[10] This treatment of painting as wild cursive calligraphy (*k'uang-ts'ao-shu*) led some traditional connoisseurs to comment that it was hard to

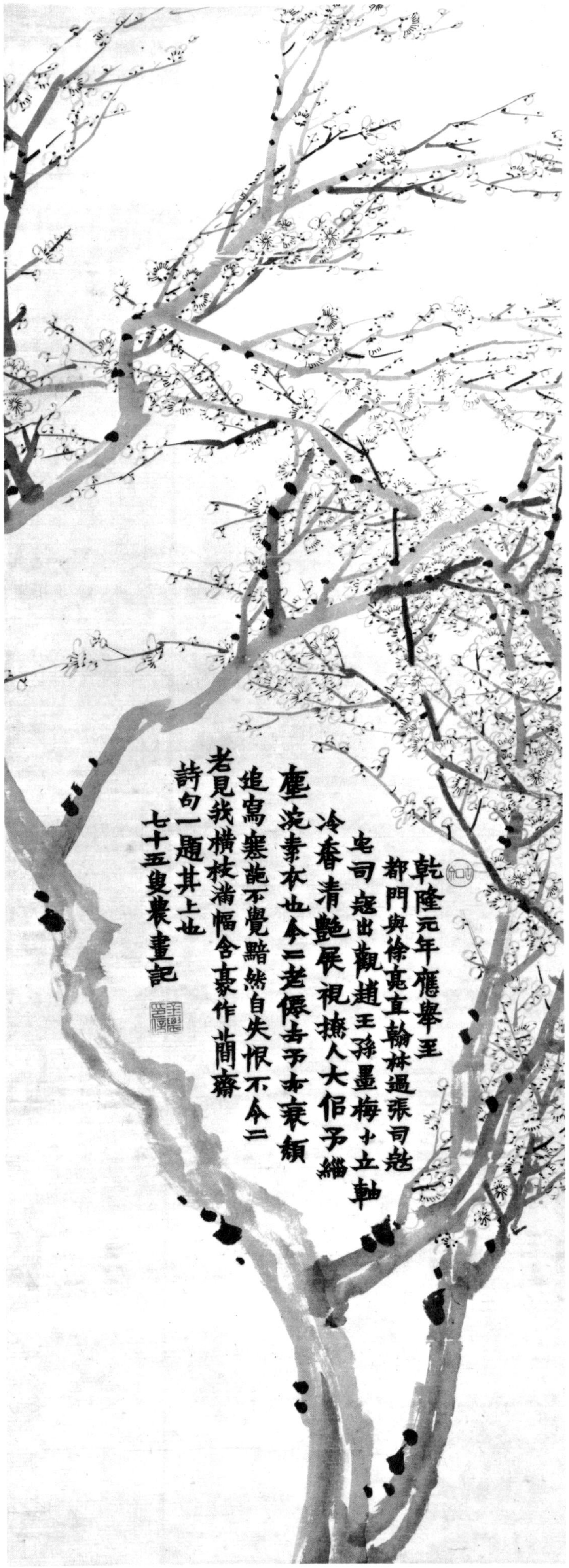


Fig. a. Chin Nung, *Plum Blossom and Calligraphy* (*Mo-mei*). Undated, ca. 1761. Hanging scroll, ink on paper. 116.2 x 41.6 cm (16³/₈ in. x 3 ft. 9³/₄ in.). Yale University Art Gallery, New Haven

Fig. b. Anonymous (academic style in the manner of Li Ti [fl. 1187]), *Bird on a Flowering Branch* (*Pai-mei yu-ch'in*). Undated, 12th century. Album leaf mounted as a hanging scroll, ink and color on silk. 23.8 x 24.5 cm (9³/₈ x 9⁵/₈ in.). Cleveland Museum of Art

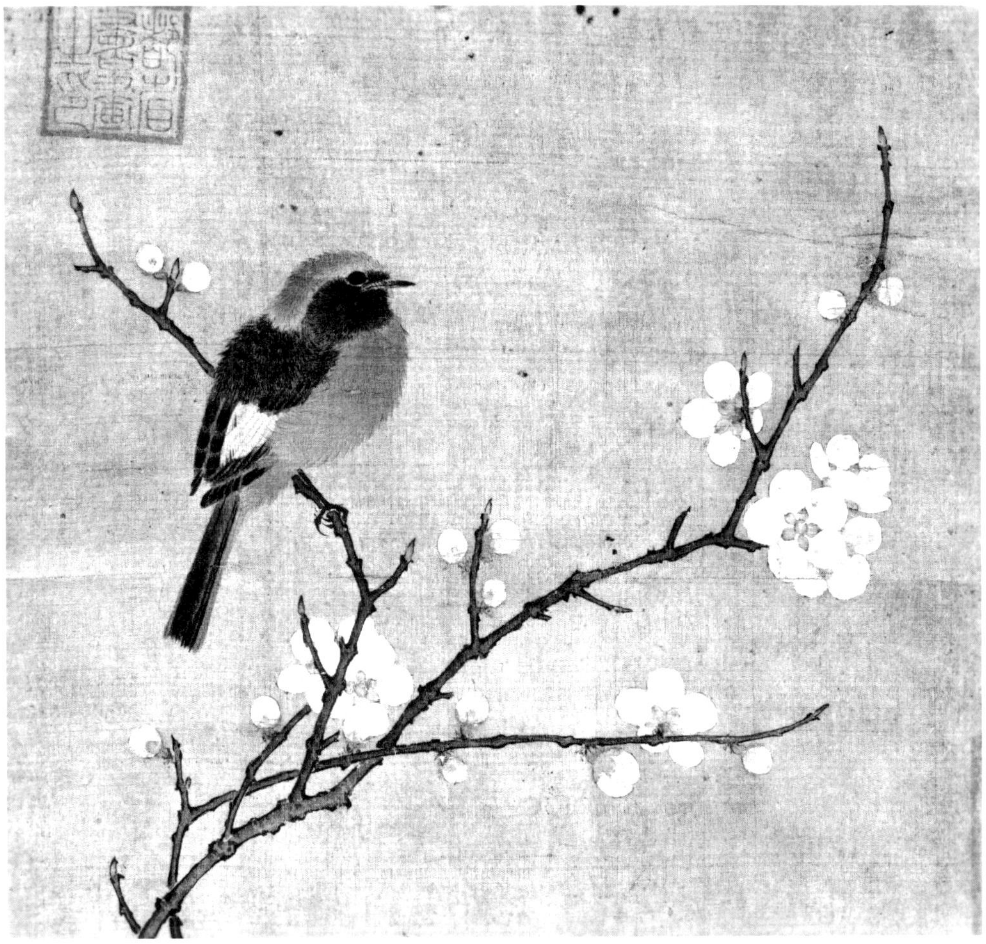

discern the forms in Huang's painting until one stepped back several feet. The silk worms on the mulberry leaves of Leaf G (no. 54), for example, are very loosely constructed, with ink-dot bodies and bright red mouths. The subject, traditionally associated with welcoming spring, here suggests a deeper meaning. The fat, humorous worms, taking gluttonous bites of juicy green leaves, almost seem a satirical observation on the affluent world of Yang-chou. In Leaf C, a painting of a grasshopper on a hawthorn branch, Huang devised a clever composition using the top and right borders of the album leaf as a frame, emphasizing the empty center of the album leaf. Although this picture bears no inscription, the lines, dots, and dabs of the dangling branch on the right edge, which compare closely with Huang's cursive calligraphy style, act as a substitute. Huang's painting and calligraphy are almost interchangeable.

Li Shan was fond of painting bird and flower albums. Although albums from the Sung dynasty were his distant prototypes, his style was very different. This is particularly clear when an anonymous album leaf in the style of Li Ti (fl. 1187), now in the Cleveland Museum of Art (fig. b), is compared with Leaf E of Li Shan's album *Birds and Flowers* (no. 51). The Cleveland leaf depicts a songbird on a flowering apricot branch, and the Princeton leaf shows three sparrows on a wand of blossoming plum. Both paintings are broken-branch (*che-chih*) compositions, in which a segment of nature is "broken" out of its context and scrutinized in a close-up view. The twelfth-century album has meticulous, tightly controlled brushwork. The branch has been outlined in ink, then filled in with color. Each feather of the bird is distinguishable, and the coloring and texturing of the different plumage sections is carefully reproduced. While the painter has not succeeded in giving the illusion of three-dimensional space, neither has he ignored it entirely. Li Shan observed none of the precision, and little of the concern for verisimilitude, of the Sung tradition, applying ocher color mixed with ink in rapid dabbing strokes and broad washes. In a sense the birds of Li's painting are caricatures of sparrows, but his light, playful brushwork suggests their impetuous and flightly nature. In keeping with the spirit of the brushwork, Li ignored the depiction of depth in his arrangement of plum branch and birds, concentrating instead on creating a pattern that fills the rectangular picture plane.

JAN STUART

NOTES

1. The term "Eight Eccentrics" first appeared in Li Yü-fen, *Ou-po-lo-shih shu-hua kuo-mu k'ao* (Records of paintings and calligraphy that have passed before my eyes), preface dated 1894 (Peking: Wen-k'uei-t'ang, Lung-fu-ssu, 1897), *chüan* 3, p. 24a. He defined the group as consisting of Wang Shih-shen, Li Shan, Chin Nung, Huang Shen, Cheng Hsieh, Lo P'ing, Kao Hsiang, and Li Fang-ying. The modern historian Ku Lin-wen defines the group as Wang Shih-shen, Huang Shen, Chin Nung, Kao Hsiang, Li Shan, Cheng Hsieh, Li Fang-ying, and Lo P'ing, in *Yang-chou pa-chia shih-liao* (Reference materials on the Eight Eccentrics of Yang-chou) (Shanghai: Shanghai jen-min mei-shu ch'u-pan-she, 1962). For a more thorough discussion of the different possible groupings, see Vicki F. Weinstein, "Painting in Yang-chou 1710–1765: Eccentricity or the Literati Tradition?" (Ph.D. diss., Cornell University, 1972), pp. 142–46.
2. See Ho Ping-ti, "The Salt Merchants of Yang-chou: A Study of Commercial Capitalism in Eighteenth-century China," *Harvard Journal of Asiatic Studies* 17 (June 1954): 130–68.
3. Ku Lin-wen, *Yang-chou pa-chia shih-liao*, p. 13.
4. Osvald Sirén, *Chinese Painting: Leading Masters and Principles* (New York: The Ronald Press, 1956), vol. 5, p. 247.
5. Biographies of both Ch'en Chuan and Mao Ch'i-ling appear in Arthur Hummel, ed., *Eminent Chinese of the Ch'ing Period* (Washington, D.C.: United States Government Printing Office, 1943), pp. 85–86, 563–65.
6. Marilyn and Shen Fu, *Studies in Connoisseurship: Chinese Paintings from the Arthur M. Sackler Collection in New York and Princeton* (Princeton: The Art Museum, 1974), pp. 294–301, no. 33.
7. For a discussion of the foundation of Chin's career as an artist, see Chu-tsing Li, "The Bamboo Paintings of Chin Nung," *Archives of Asian Art* 27 (1973–74): 53–75.
8. Wai-kam Ho et al., *Eight Dynasties of Chinese Painting* (Cleveland: Cleveland Museum of Art, 1980), p. 365, pl. 267.
9. Minor differences in biographical data occur among several sources, such as Ku Lin-wen, *Yang-chou pa-chia shih-liao*, p. 13; Wai-kam Ho et al., *Eight Dynasties*, pp. 367–68, no. 269; Vicki F. Weinstein, "Painting in Yang-chou," pp. 131–33.
10. Ku Lin-wen, *Yang-chou pa-chia shih-liao*, p. 12.

# 48 Wang Shih-shen (1686–1759)

## *Asking for Snow Water (Ch'i-shui t'u)*

Dated 1740
Hanging scroll, ink on paper
91.0 x 26.7 cm. (2 ft. 11 7/8 in. x 10 1/2 in.)

ARTIST'S INSCRIPTIONS:

1. 27 character preface, followed by a 7 character regulated verse in 8 lines, in 6 columns of running script (top).
2. 24 character preface, followed by a 7 character quatrain, in 8 columns of running script (bottom).

ARTIST'S SIGNATURES: Ch'ao-lin (top inscription); Your junior, Shih-shen, casually made this in the Ch'ing-shan-shu-wu [Studio] (bottom inscription).

ARTIST'S SEALS: Chin-jen Wang Shih-shen (square intaglio; top inscription); Chin-jen (oval intaglio; bottom inscription).

COLOPHONS (on paper mounting surrounding the painting, in chronological order):

1. Chiao Wu-tou (1680s–after 1760): 7 character verse in 12 lines, followed by a 5 character note, in 5 columns of running script (lower left). Signature: Wu-tou, Chiao Shih-chi, inscribed this in the Kua-lu Hut, in the ninth lunar month, in the autumn of the *keng-ch'en* year [1760]. Seals: Shih-chi (square intaglio); Wu-tou hsien-sheng (square intaglio).
2. Chin Nung (1687–1764): prose, 224 characters in 7 columns of regular script (lower right). Signature: In his seventy-fifth year [*sui*] Chin Nung, from Hang-chün [in Chekiang province] made this. Seal: Chin Chi-chin yin (square intaglio).
3. Cheng Hsieh (1693–1765): prose, 111 characters in 10 columns of running script (top). Seals: Cheng Pan-ch'iao (square intaglio); Hsieh ho chia chih yu yen (square intaglio); Ko ch'ui ku Yang-chou (tall rectangle relief).
4. Yang Fa (ca. mid-18th century): 5 character verse in 12 lines (excluding 2 crossed-out characters), followed by a 38 character note, in 3 columns of cursive script (upper left). Signature: On the twenty-fourth day of the twelfth lunar month of the *hsin-ssu* year of the Ch'ien-lung era [1762], in his seventieth year [*sui*], Yang Fa wrote this. Seals: Min-yün (square intaglio); Yang Fa (square intaglio).
5. Min Hua (ca. 1760): 5 character verse in 8 lines in 4 columns of running script (right). Signature: Yü-ching, Min Hua, inscribed this. Seal: Yü-ching (square intaglio).
6. Ch'en Liang (dates unknown): 7 character quatrain in 2 columns of running script (right). Signature: Tui-ou, Ch'en Liang. Seals: Tui-ou (square relief); Ch'en Liang chih yin (square intaglio).

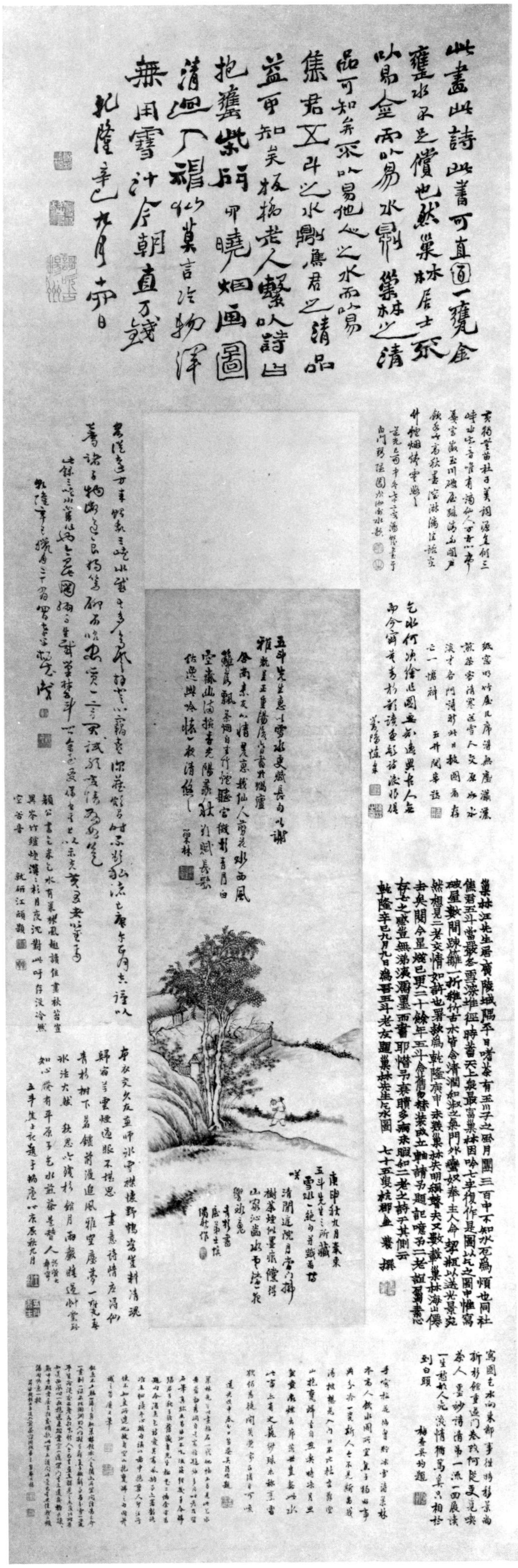

7. Wu Chün (dates unknown): 7 character verse in 8 lines in 5 columns of running script (lower right). Signature: Mei-ch'a, Wu Chün inscribed this. Seal: Sui-chou (square intaglio).
8. Chiang Ch'i (dates unknown): 5 character verse in 8 lines in 3 columns of regular script (left edge). Signature: Chiu-yen, Chiang Ch'i, inscribed this. Seals: Chiang Ch'i (square intaglio); Chih-shih (square relief).
9. Wu Ch'ing-p'eng (1786–1850s): three colophons, all on the mounting below the painting:
   a) 5 character quatrain in 8 columns of running script. Signature: On the vernal equinox of the *wu-shen* year of the Tao-kuang era [1848], Hu-an, Wu Ch'ing-p'eng, inscribed this. Seal: Wu Ch'ing-p'eng yin (square intaglio).
   b) Prose, 125 characters in 8 columns of running script. Signature: Hu-an inscribed this again. Seals: Hu-an (square relief); Wu Ch'ing-p'eng yin (square intaglio).
   c) 5 character verse in 26 lines, followed by a 15 character note, in 7 columns of running script. Signature: Hu-an wrote this again. Seals: Hu-an (square relief); Wu Ch'ing-p'eng (square intaglio).
10. T'ang I-fen (1778–1853): 7 character verse in 8 lines, followed by a 25 character note, in 7 columns of running script (upper right). Signature: In the midwinter of the *chi-yu* year of the Tao-kuang era [1849], T'ang I-fen, in his seventy-second year [*sui*], wrote this, following Mao-chou's *shui* rhyme scheme, in Ch'in-yin-yüan at Pai-men [Nanking]. Seal: Yü-sheng (double seal, both round relief).

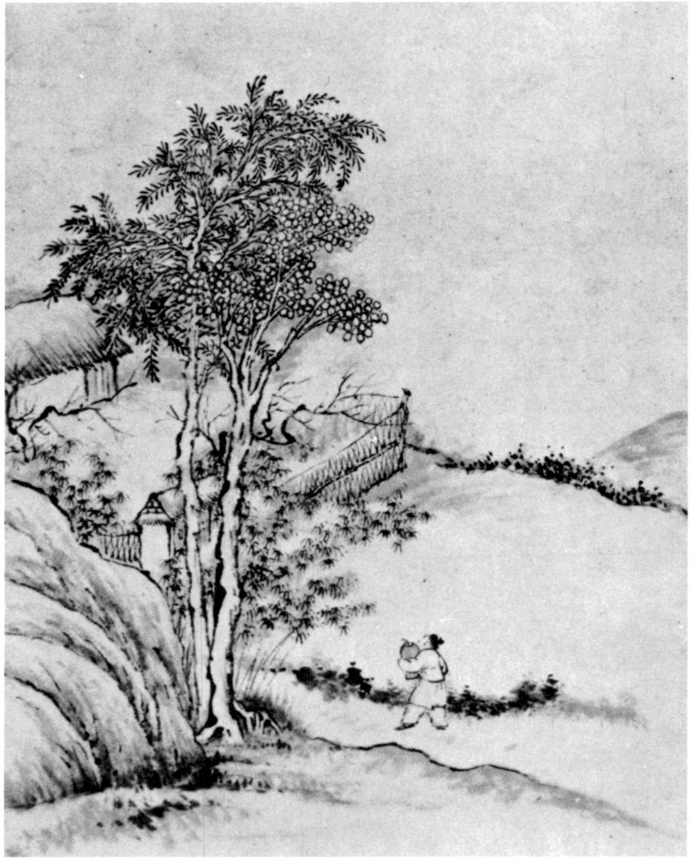

Gift of Mrs. Edward L. Elliott (79–13)

PUBLISHED: Alfreda Murck, "Wang Shih-shen's *Asking for Snow Water, Tributes to a Tea Drinker*," *Record of The Art Museum, Princeton University* 27, no. 2 (1978): 1–30; John Rosenfield et al., eds., "Art of Asia Acquired by North American Museums, 1980," *Archives of Asian Art* 34 (1981): 108, fig. 39; Suzuki Kei, comp., *Chūgoku kaiga sōgō zuroku: daiikkan, Amerika–Kanada hen* (Comprehensive illustrated catalogue of Chinese paintings: volume 1, American and Canadian collections) (Tokyo: University of Tokyo Press, 1982), p. 111, pl. A16–026.

# 49 Wang Shih-shen (1686–1759)

## *Bamboo and Orchid (Lan chu t'u)*

Undated
Hanging scroll, ink and color on paper
85.8 x 28.0 cm ($33^{3}/_{4}$ x 11 in.)

ARTIST'S INSCRIPTION (prose, 25 characters in 2 columns of regular script): I often paint orchids, pleased by their lack of pretentiousness. They are as pure and gentle as a recluse. Their fragrance is incomparable. Is the orchid not the king of flowers?

ARTIST'S SIGNATURE: Ch'ao-lin.

ARTIST'S SEALS: Chin-jen-fu (tall rectangle relief).

COLLECTORS' SEALS:

1. Ch'en Jen-t'ao (1906–1968): Chin-kuei pao-ts'ang Ch'en shih Jen-t'ao (double seal, round relief, square relief; upper left); Jen-t'ao chien-ting (tall rectangle relief; lower right).
2. Unidentified owners: Yung hsin shuang-hsüeh chien (tall rectangle intaglio; lower right); Tzu-t'eng-hua-kuan (square intaglio; lower left).

Edward L. Elliott Family Collection (L207.70)

PUBLISHED: Ch'en Jen-t'ao, *Chin-kuei ts'ang-hua chi* (Chinese paintings from the King Kwei [Chin-kuei] collection) (Hong Kong: T'ung-ying, 1956), vol. 1, pl. 62; Ch'en Jen-t'ao, *Chin-kuei ts'ang-hua p'ing-shih* (Annotated catalogue of Chinese paintings from the King Kwei [Chin-kuei] collection) (Hong Kong: T'ung-ying, 1956), Appendix, pp. 6–7; Suzuki Kei, comp., *Chūgoku kaiga sōgō zuroku: daiikkan, Amerika–Kanada hen* (Comprehensive illustrated catalogue of Chinese paintings: volume 1, American and Canadian collections) (Tokyo: University of Tokyo Press, 1982), p. 127, pl. A17–013.

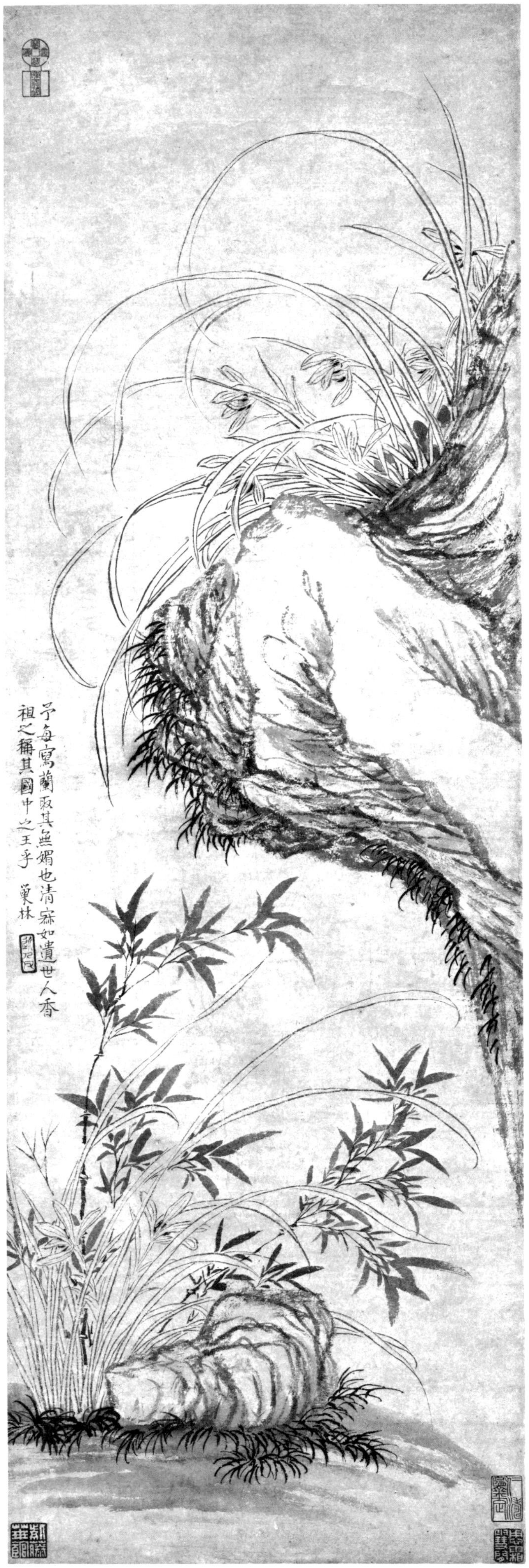

# 50 Wang Shih-shen (1686–1759), Kuan Hsi-ning (fl. ca. 1736–95), and Wu K'an (fl. ca. 1736–95)

## *Butterflies (Hua tieh)*

Dated 1741
Hanging scroll, ink and color on paper
122.5 x 43.7 cm (4 ft. 1/4 in. x 17 1/4 in.)

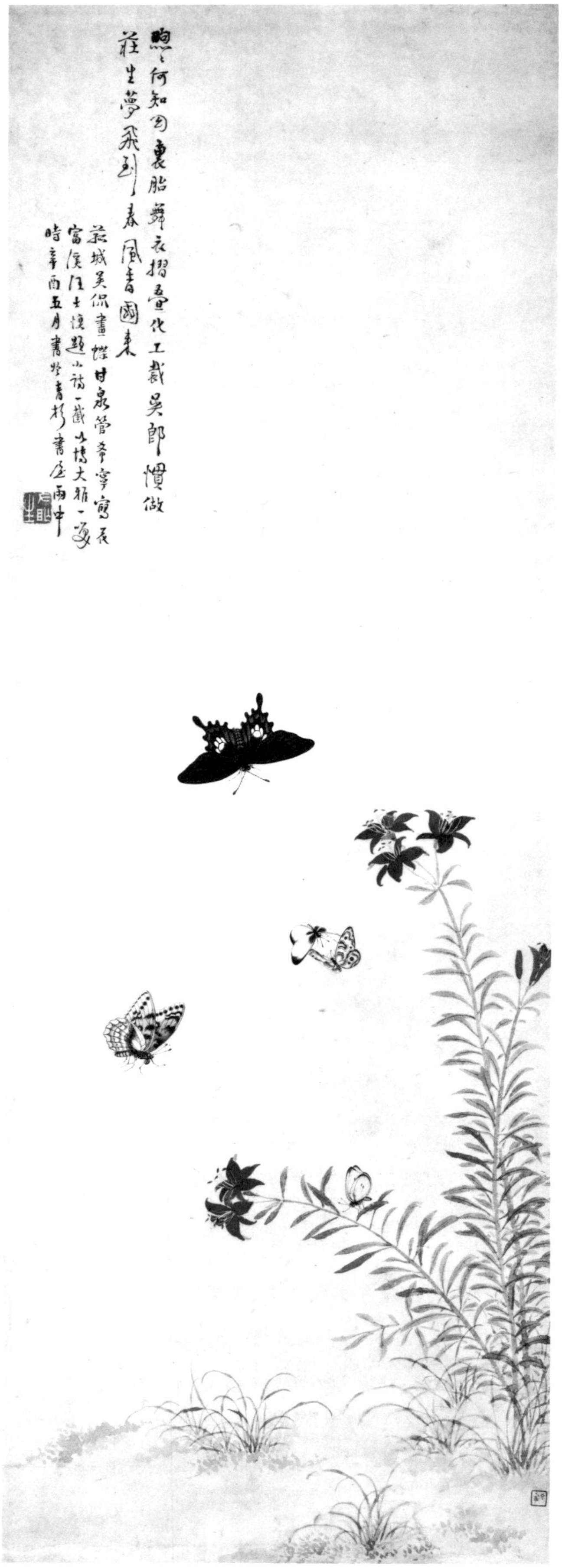

ARTISTS' INSCRIPTION (7 character quatrain, followed by a 42 character note, in 5 columns of running script):

> In cocoons as warm as sunshine, how can they realize that
> they are but embryos in an illusionary world?
> Their pleated dancing dresses are nature's work.
> The young men of Wu are used to dreaming like
> Chuang-tzu;
> And flying through the spring breeze to a fragrant
> kingdom.
>
> Wu K'an from Ku-ch'eng [in Chekiang province] painted the butterflies, Kuan Hsi-ning from Kan-ch'üan [in Shensi province] painted the flowers, and Wang Shih-shen from Fu-hsi [in Anhui province] inscribed a brief poem hoping to bring forth a smile from scholars. Written in the rain in the Ch'ing-shan-shu-wu [Studio] in the fifth lunar month of the *hsin-yu* year [1741].

ARTISTS' SEALS:
1. Wang Shih-shen: Tso-mang-sheng (square intaglio; upper left).
2. Kuan Hsi-ning: Hsi-ning (square relief; lower right).

Edward L. Elliott Family Collection (L323.70)

PUBLISHED: Suzuki Kei, comp., *Chūgoku kaiga sōgō zuroku: daiikkan, Amerika–Kanada hen* (Comprehensive illustrated catalogue of Chinese paintings: volume 1, American and Canadian collections) (Tokyo: University of Tokyo Press, 1982), p. 128, pl. A17–024.

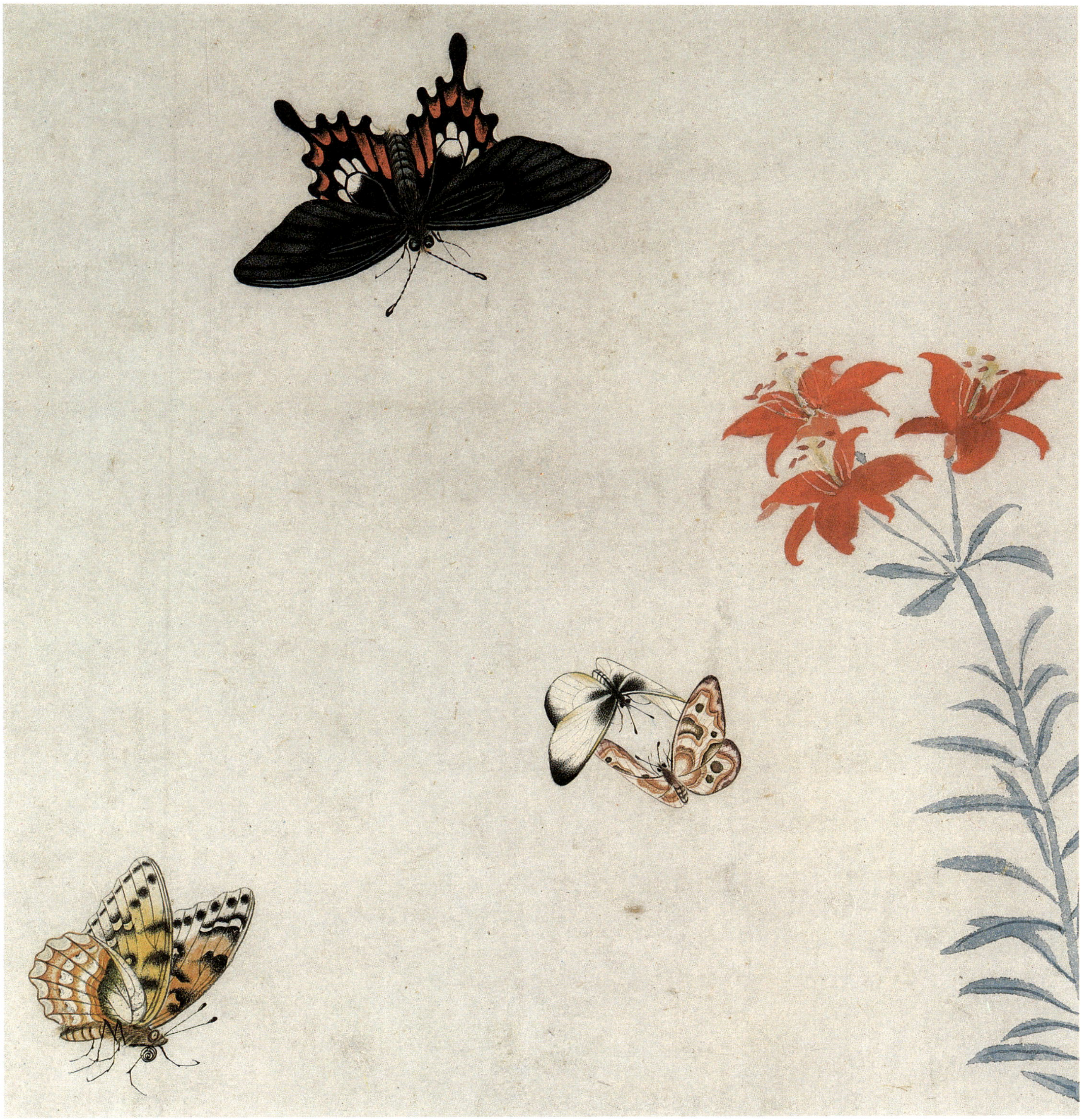

# 51 Li Shan (fl. ca. 1711–62)

## *Birds and Flowers (Hua-niao ts'e)*

Dated 1731
Album of twelve leaves (A–L), ink and color on paper
Average measurements, each leaf: 28.9 x 38.8 cm ($11^{3}/_{8}$ x $15^{1}/_{4}$ in.)

ARTIST'S INSCRIPTIONS:
Leaf A, "Orchids" (7 character quatrain in 3 columns of running script):

With fluid ink I paint the fragrant flowers.
What is lacking is a pot and then a stone wall to put it on.
I remember when the spring wind blew through the deep valleys;
Woodcutters carried home the orchids, as plentiful as grass.

Leaf B, "Magpie on a Bamboo Stalk" (prose, 40 characters in 5 columns of running script):

When the vexing heat of summer had dissipated and the autumn air was crisp, then I would often sit in my bamboo garden and enjoy the pure breeze blowing through the fence. I would feel relaxed. One day, by accident, I found a draft of a painting done by a Yüan dynasty artist, which was to be presented to the emperor; it was of four resting magpies. It pleased me so much that I made a copy.

Leaf C, "Magpie on a Willow Branch": no inscription.

Leaf D, "Narcissus, Wild Berries, and Bamboo Shoot" (4 characters in 1 column of running script): Felicitous offerings at New Year's.

Leaf E, "Birds" (7 character quatrain in 3 columns of running script):

When their feathers had not yet grown thick enough to be watertight,
Suddenly they flew toward the celestial city to show off their remarkable appearance.
But they could not fly into the imperial gardens filled with so many flowers,
Instead, as usual, they settled on wintry branches.

Leaf F, "Peony" (7 character couplet in 2 columns of running script):

I can paint a rough outline of its general shape;
It is like mashed watermelon pulp.

Leaf G, "Day Lily" (7 character couplet in 5 columns of running script):

Both its color and fragrance can be painted;
But its ability to forget the cares of mankind is difficult to illustrate.

Leaf H, "Cicadas" (7 character quatrain in 3 columns of running script):

Warm sunshine and soft clouds after a late spring rain,
Make me feel like gazing at the clear sky and listening [to the sounds of nature].
The magenta petals have all fallen, but pink ones will replace them;
Coming from a branch somewhere I hear the sound of cicadas chirping.

Leaf I, "Quail and Plants" (7 character quatrain, followed by a 5 character note, in 8 columns of running script):

Hidden among the grasses in patched robes,
With the coming of autumn they fatten themselves on grains and millet.
What is the purpose of competing with one another?
This only ends in frenzied, aimless flight.

Leaf J, "Two Perch Strung Together by a Willow Wand" (7 character quatrain in 4 columns of running script):

On the white-crested wave we always see the old man.
His home is his boat, blown by the wind.
He hooks a fresh perch three feet long;
His sons and grandsons fan the fire among the flowering reeds.

Leaf K, "Roses" (7 characters in 1 column of running script): Holding the brightness of all the months.

Leaf L, "Wisteria" (7 character quatrain in 12 columns of running script):

I mistake the golden bees and lavender butterflies,
Thinking they are wisteria that might have grown on T'ao Ch'ien's old bamboo fence.
A small plant, it has will and knows where to sprout,
Either in Buddhist monasteries or imperial gardens.

ARTIST'S SIGNATURES: Li Shan (A, B, D, G); Ao-tao-jen (C); Mo mo-jen, Li Shan (E); Fu-t'ang, Li Shan (H, J); Li Shan painted this in the autumn of the *hsin-hai* year [1731] (I); Li Shan made this (K); Fu-t'ang, Shan, painted this in the eighth lunar month of the ninth year of the Yung-cheng era [1731] (L).

ARTIST'S SEALS: Hui-t'ing (tall rectangle intaglio; A); Shan (square relief; B); Tsung-yang (square intaglio; B); Tsung-yang (squat rectangle intaglio; D, I); Tsung-yang (oval intaglio; C, G); Tsung-yang (square relief; E); Li Shan (square intaglio; F); Shan yin (square intaglio; H); Tiao-ch'ung-kuan (oval relief; J); Ao-tao-jen (oval relief; K); Tsung-yang (tall rectangle intaglio; L).

COLLECTOR'S SEALS: Unidentified owner: Hsiao-ho shen-ting (square relief; A); Ou-hua-hsiang-kuan (square intaglio; D).

Gift of John B. Elliott (76–42)

PUBLISHED: Suzuki Kei, comp., *Chūgoku kaiga sōgō zuroku: daiikkan, Amerika–Kanada hen* (Comprehensive illustrated catalogue of Chinese paintings: volume 1, American and Canadian collections) (Tokyo: University of Tokyo Press, 1982), pp. 143–44, pl. A17–077.

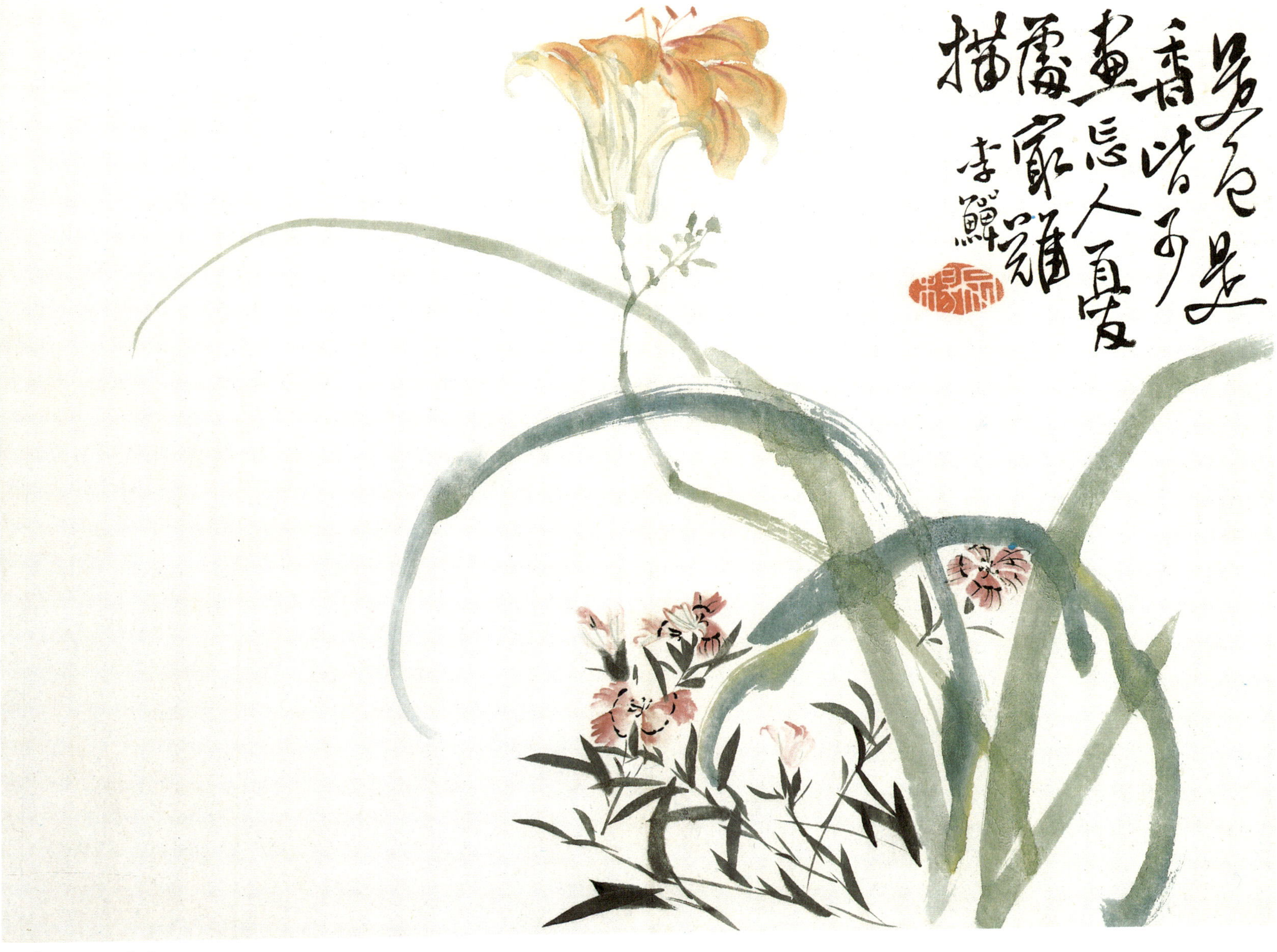

Leaf G, "Day Lily"

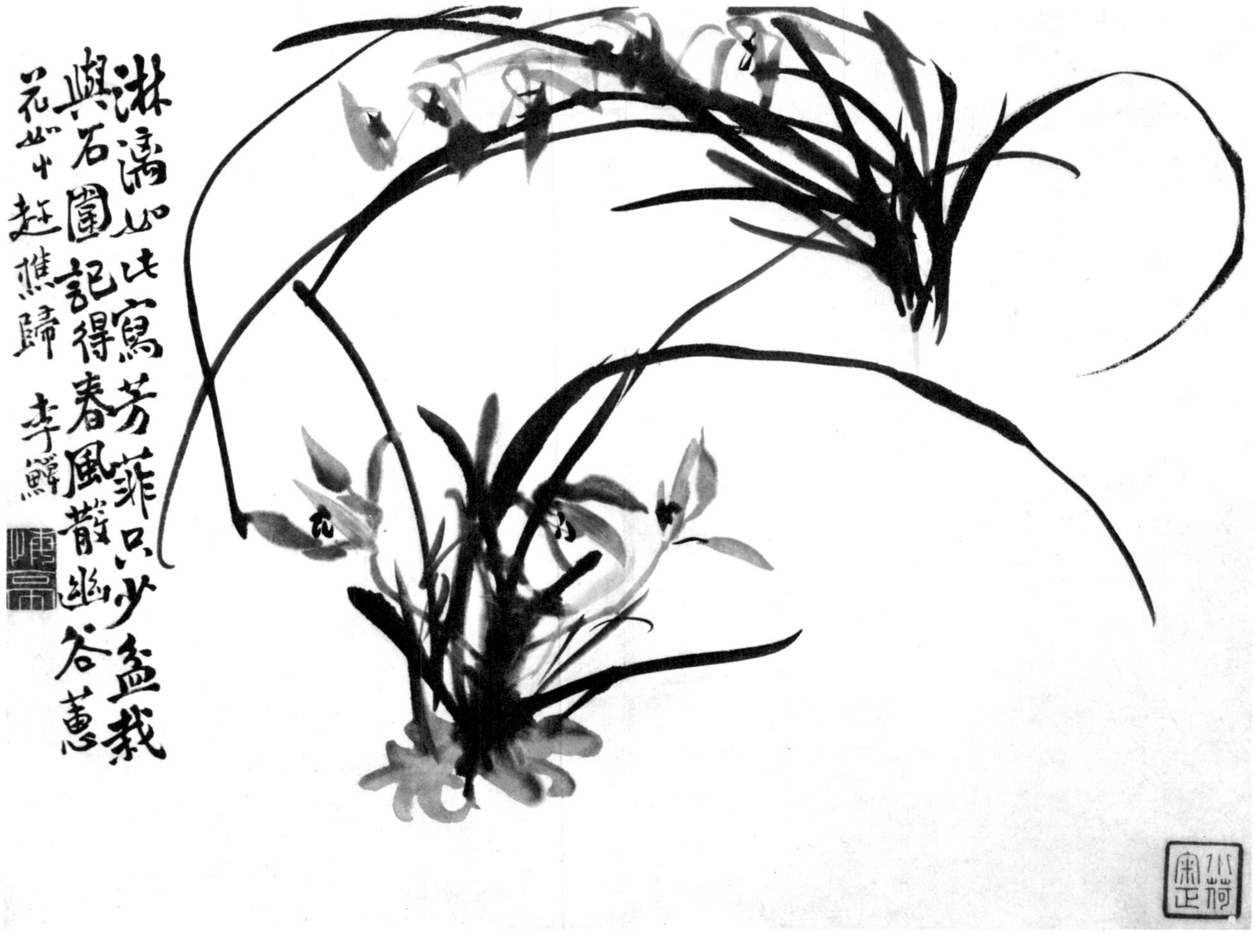

Leaf A, "Orchids,"

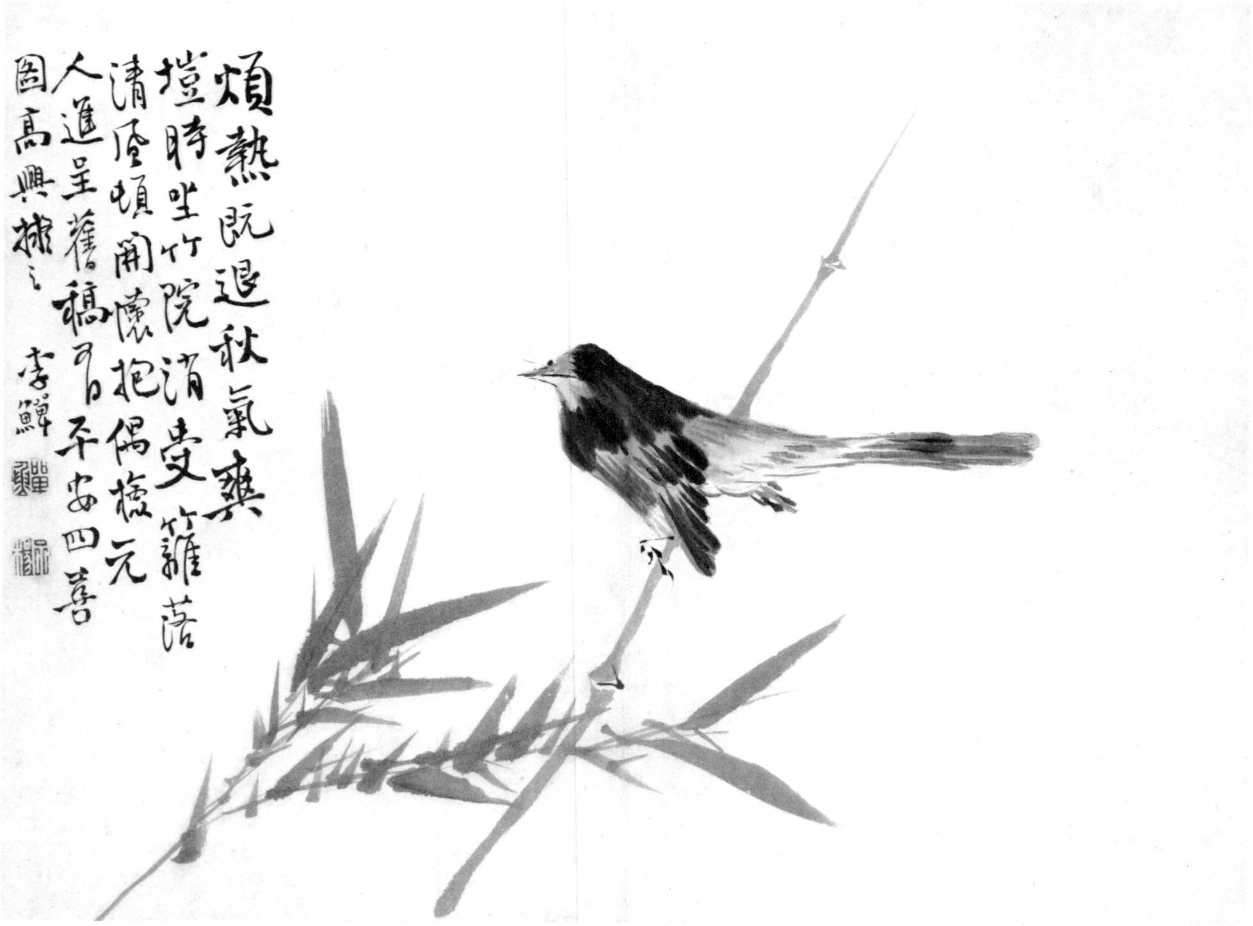

Leaf B, "Magpie on a Bamboo Stalk"

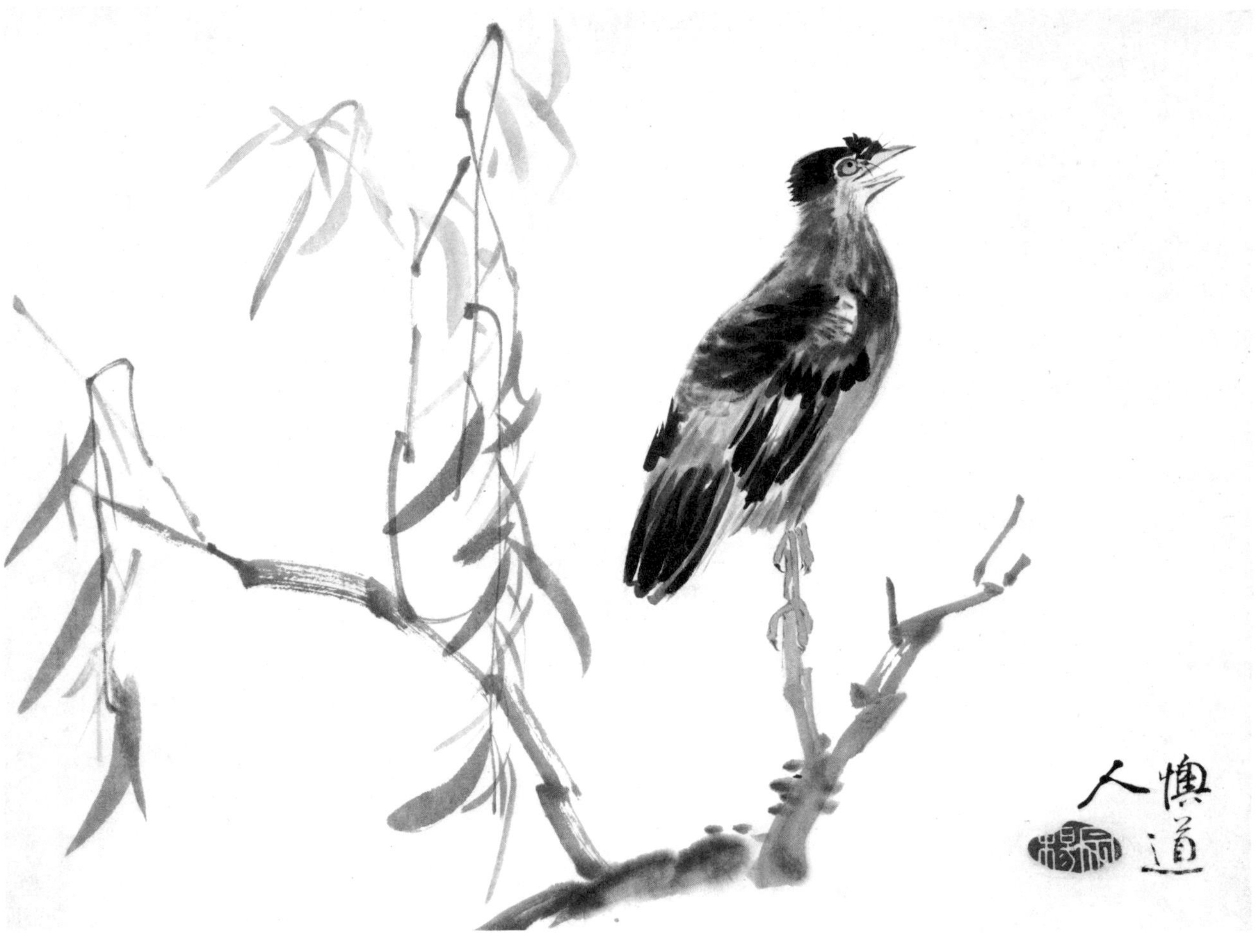


Leaf C, "Magpie on a Willow Branch"

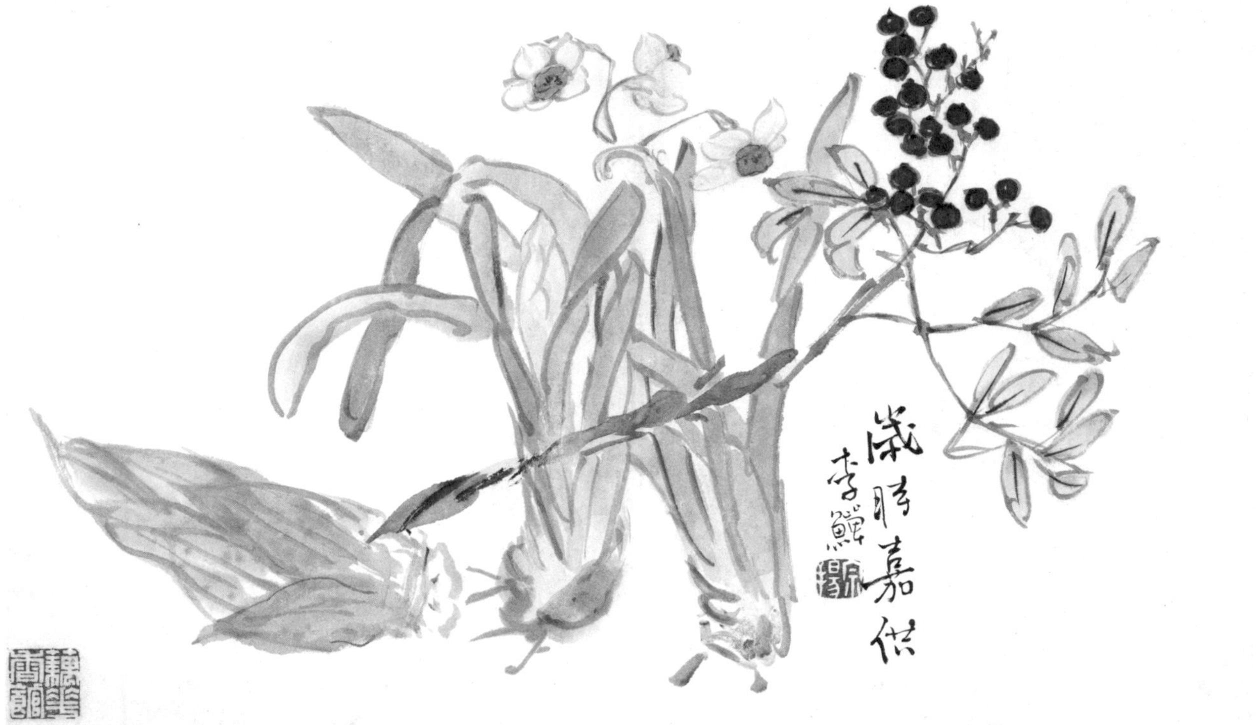


Leaf D, "Narcissus, Wild Berries, and Bamboo Shoot"

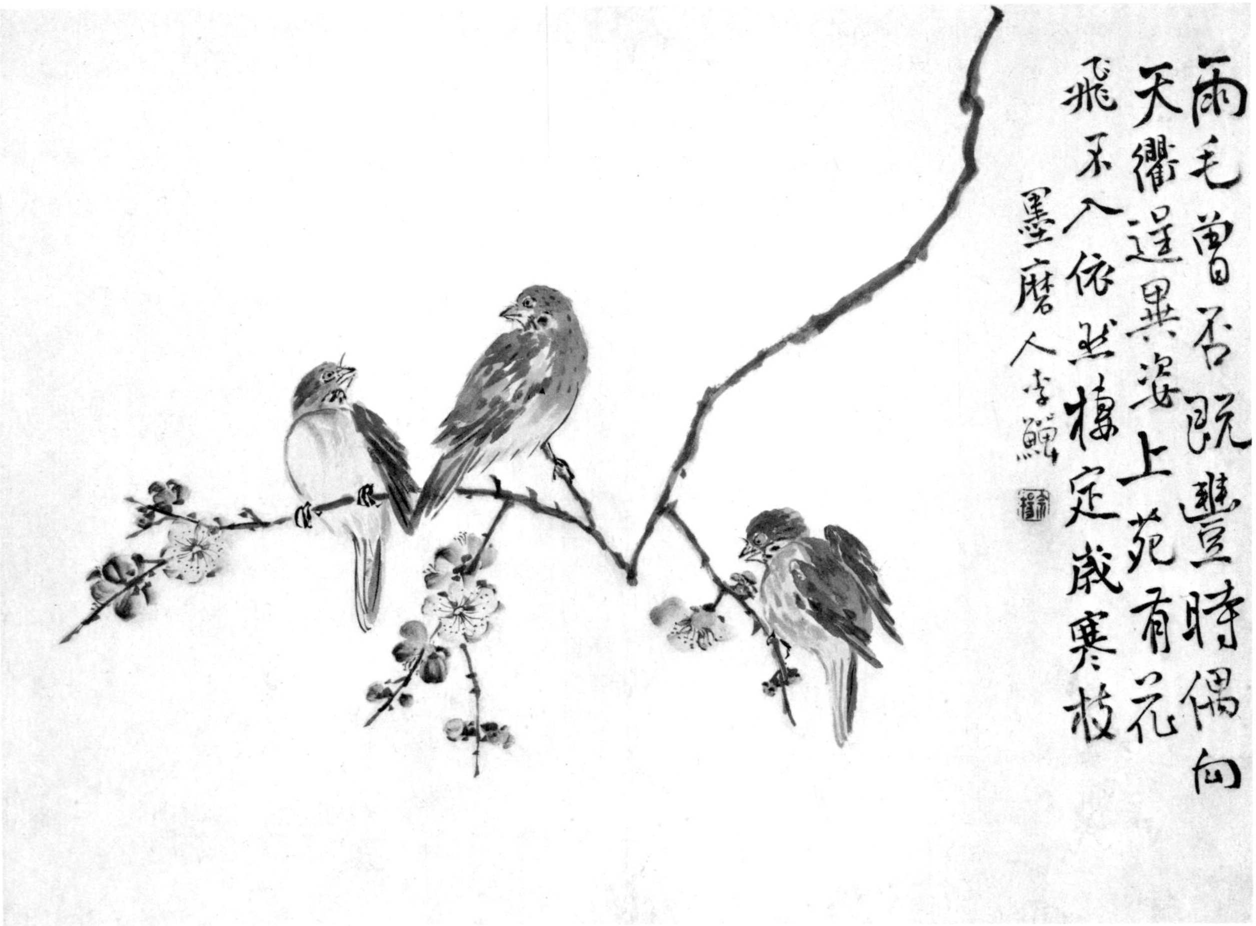

Leaf E, "Birds"

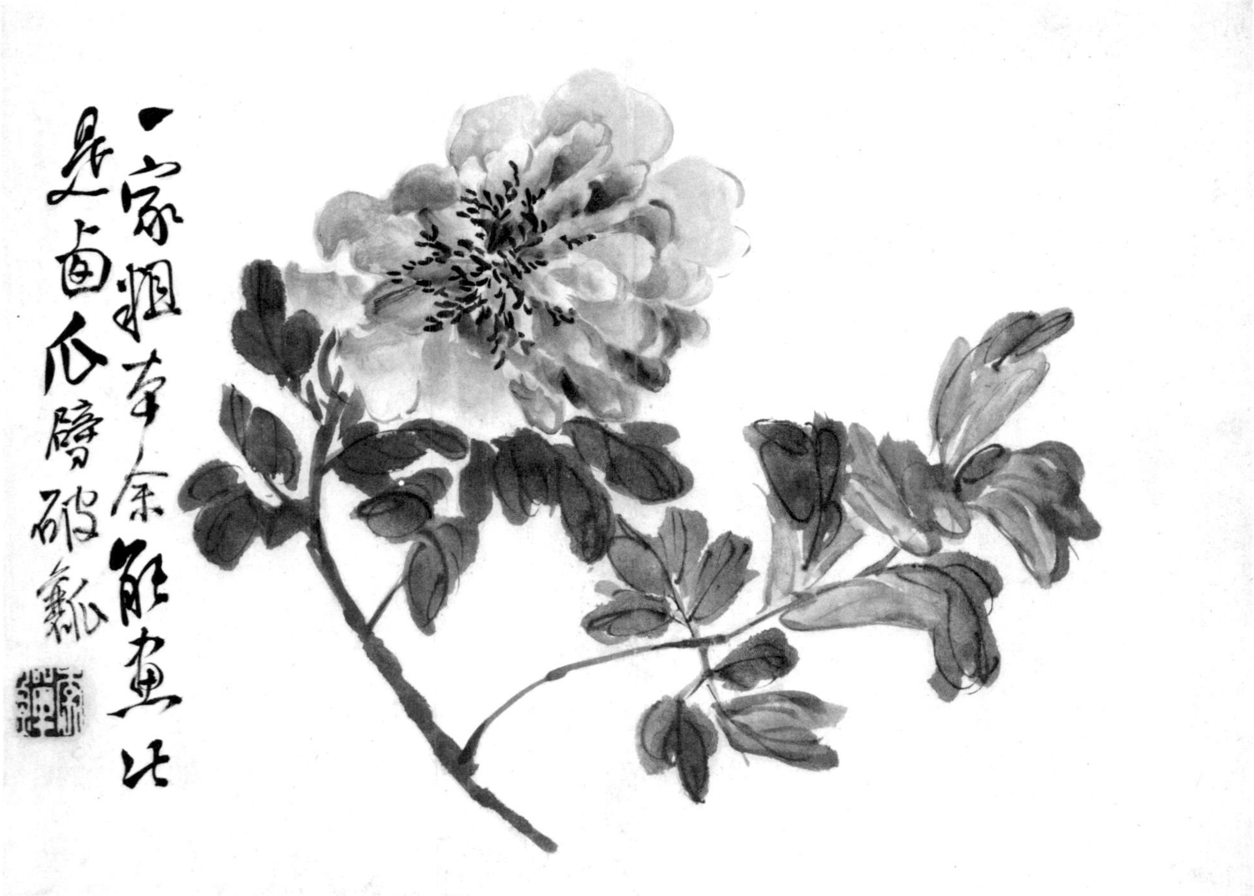

Leaf F, "Peony"

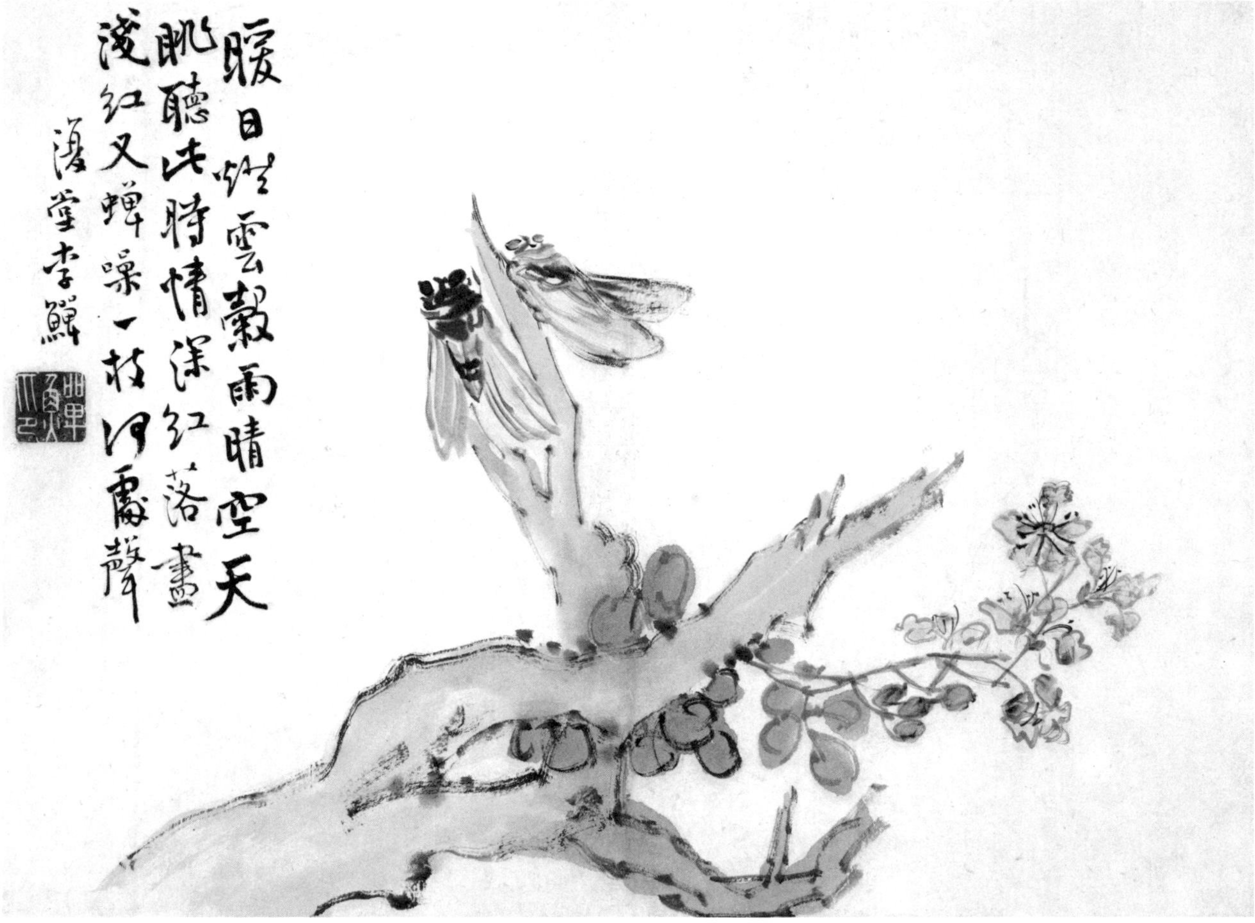

Leaf H, "Cicadas"

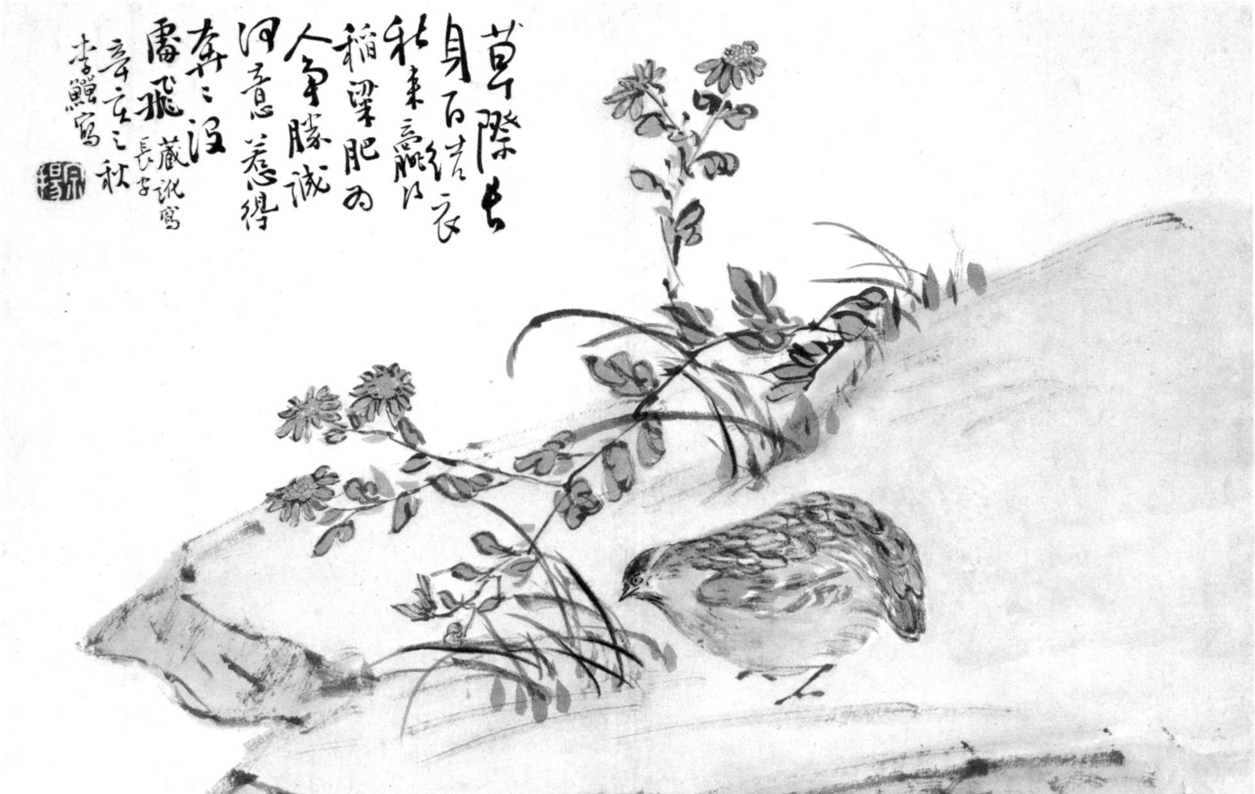

Leaf I, "Quail and Plants"

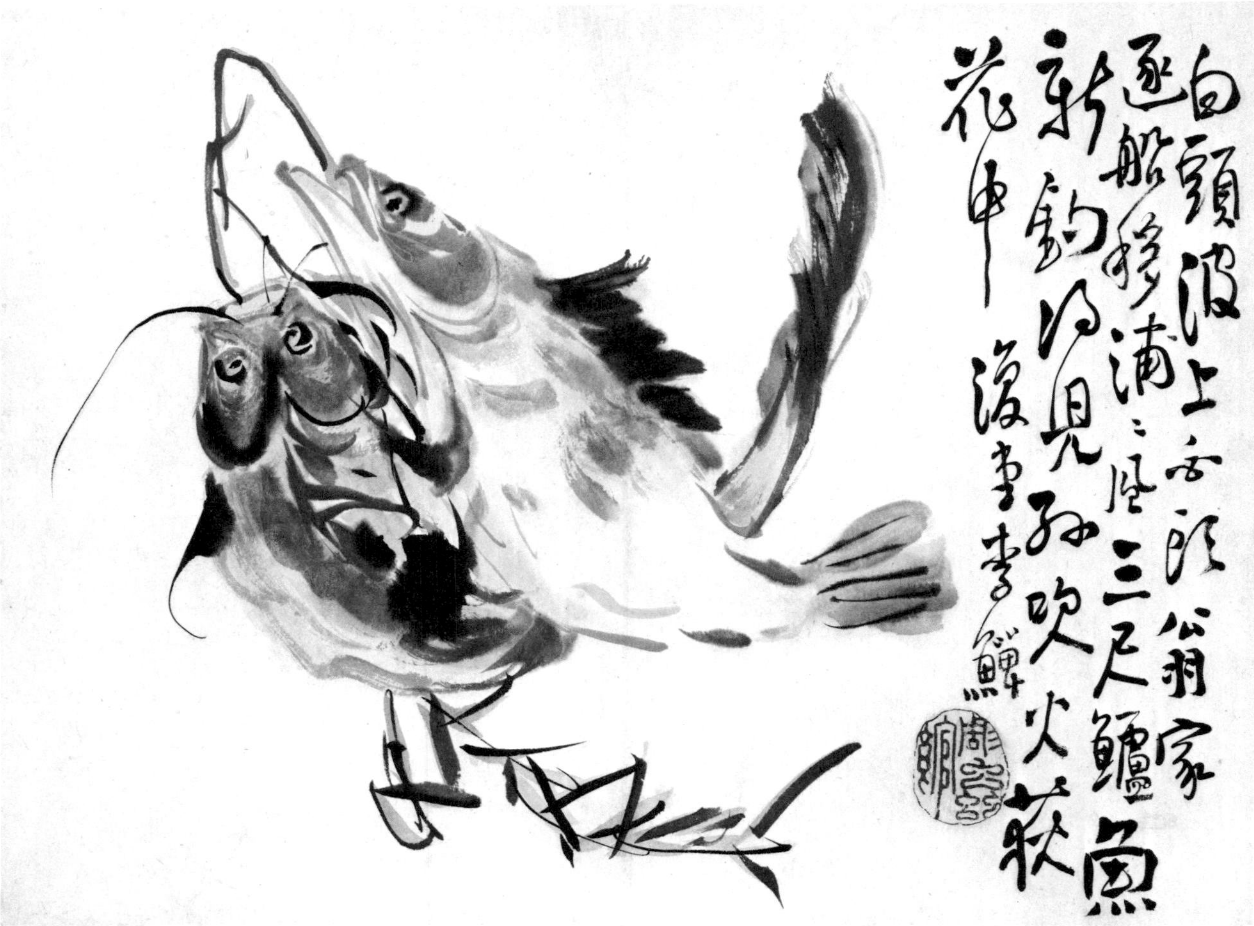


Leaf J, "Two Perch Strung Together by a Willow Wand"

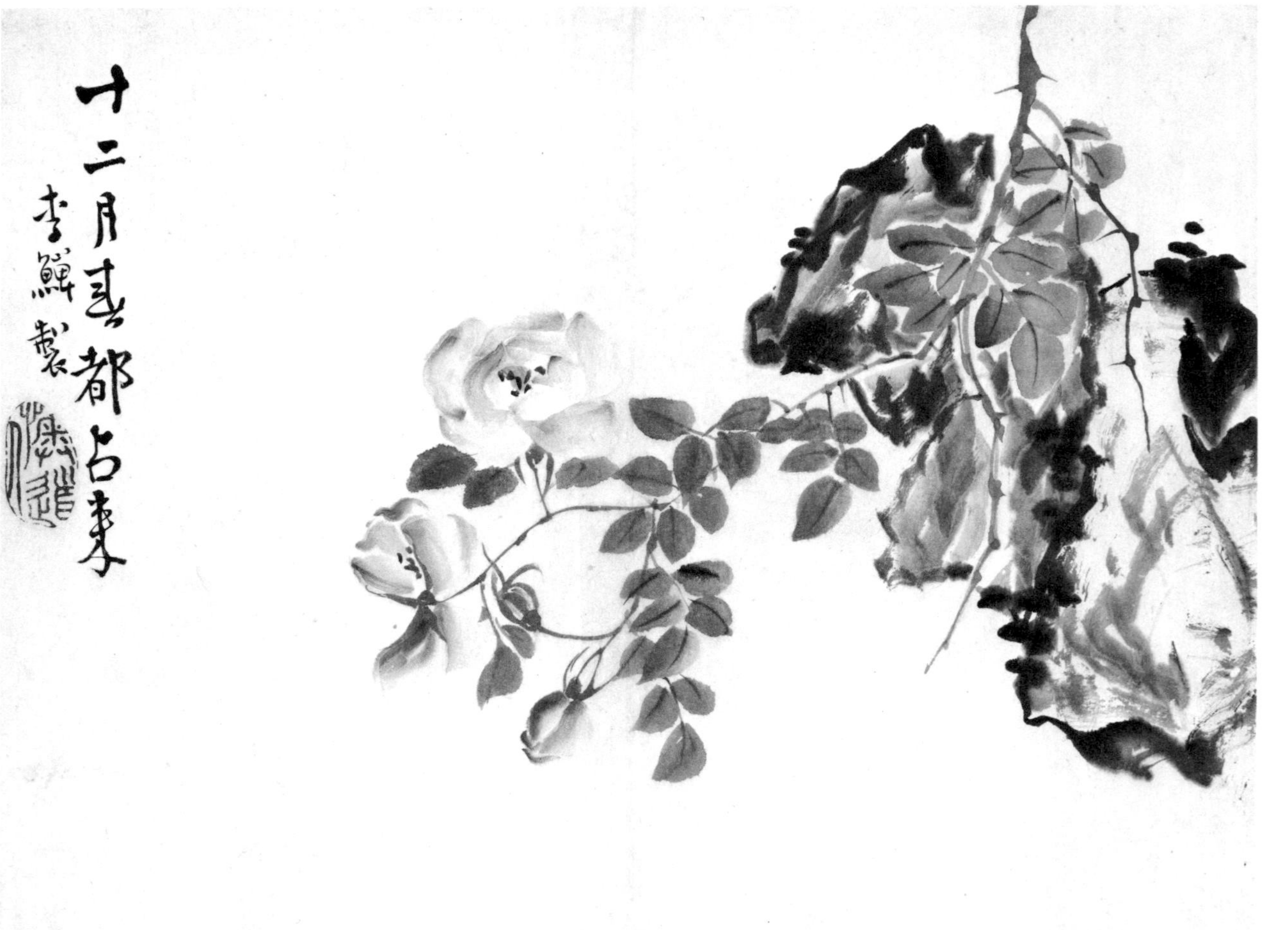

Leaf K, "Roses"

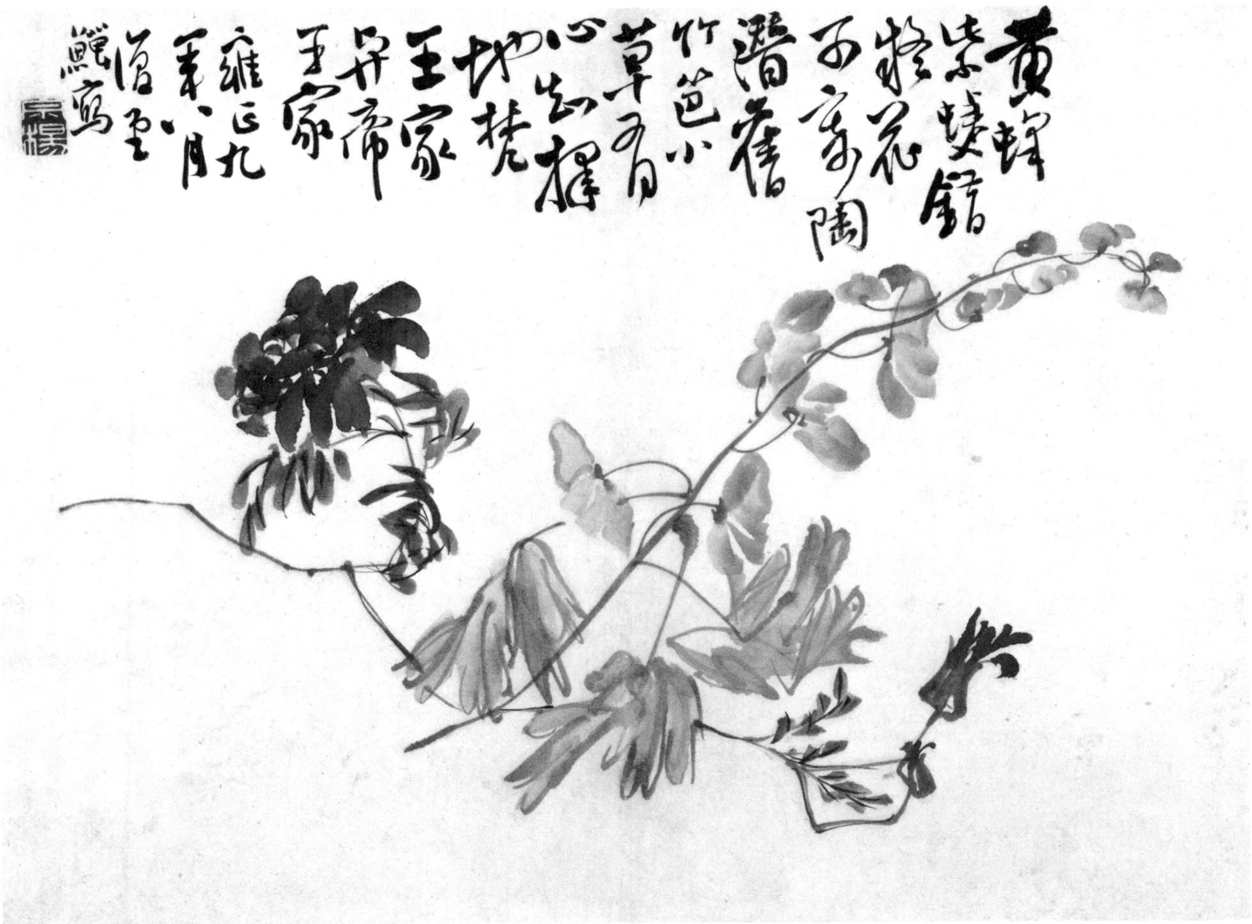

Leaf L, "Wisteria"

# 52 Li Shan (fl. ca. 1711–62)

## *Cock and Cockscomb (Kuan shang chia kuan)*

Dated 1754
Hanging scroll, ink and color on paper
176.0 x 47.3 cm (5 ft. 9 1/4 in. x 18 5/8 in.)

ARTIST'S INSCRIPTION (7 character quatrain in 2 columns of regular script):

> The *p'eng* [a mythical bird with a gigantic wingspread]
> soars above a trail of clouds, over vast seas and skies.
> Beyond the wind and clouds for ten thousand miles—
> a rare opportunity.
> Remain loyal like the sunflower, which always turns
> to the sun,
> And from now on official promotions will come one
> after the other.

ARTIST'S SIGNATURE: Fu-t'ang, Ao-tao-jen, Li Shan, made this in the intercalary fourth lunar month of the nineteenth year of the Ch'ien-lung era [1754].

ARTIST'S SEALS: Shan yin (square intaglio); Tsung-yang (square relief).

Edward L. Elliott Family Collection (L246.70)

PUBLISHED: Suzuki Kei, comp., *Chūgoku kaiga sōgō zuroku: daiikkan, Amerika–Kanada hen* (Comprehensive illustrated catalogue of Chinese paintings: volume 1, American and Canadian collections) (Tokyo: University of Tokyo Press, 1982), p. 126, pl. A17–008.

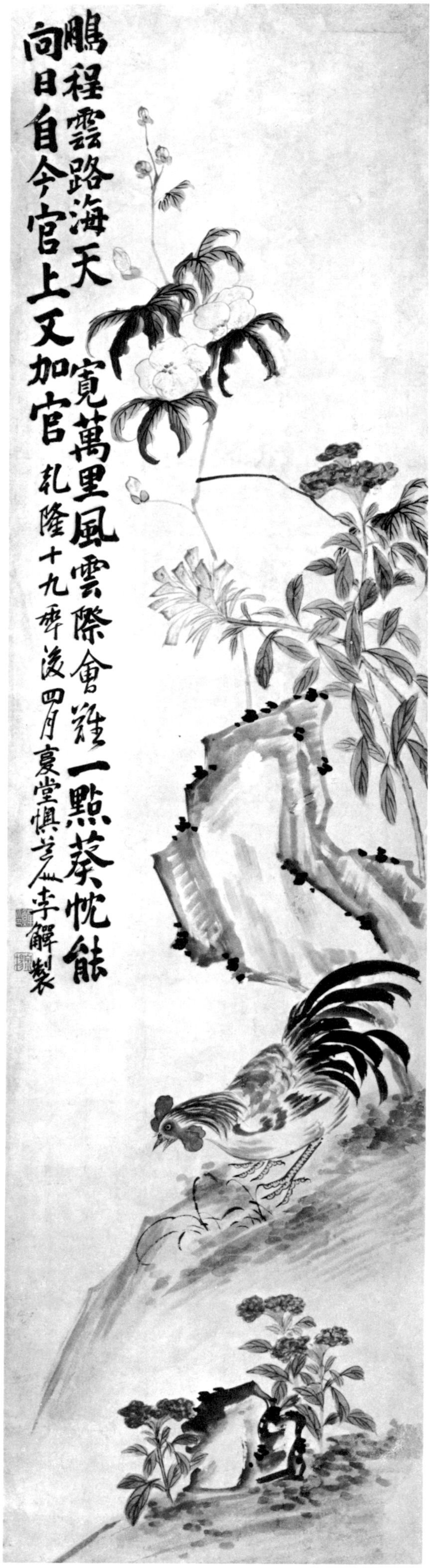

# 53 Chin Nung (1687–1764)

## *Ink Plum (Mo-mei)*

Undated
Hanging scroll, ink on paper
98.0 x 47.5 cm (3 ft. 2⅝ in. x 18¾ in.)

ARTIST'S SIGNATURE: Chi-liu-shan-min, Chin Nung, painted this in a temporary residence at Kuang-ling [Yang-chou, Kiangsu province].

ARTIST'S SEAL: Chin Nung yin-hsin (square relief).

Edward L. Elliott Family Collection (L198.70)

PUBLISHED: Suzuki Kei, comp., *Chūgoku kaiga sōgō zuroku: daiikkan, Amerika–Kanada hen* (Comprehensive illustrated catalogue of Chinese paintings: volume 1, American and Canadian collections) (Tokyo: University of Tokyo Press, 1982), p. 127, pl. A17–016.

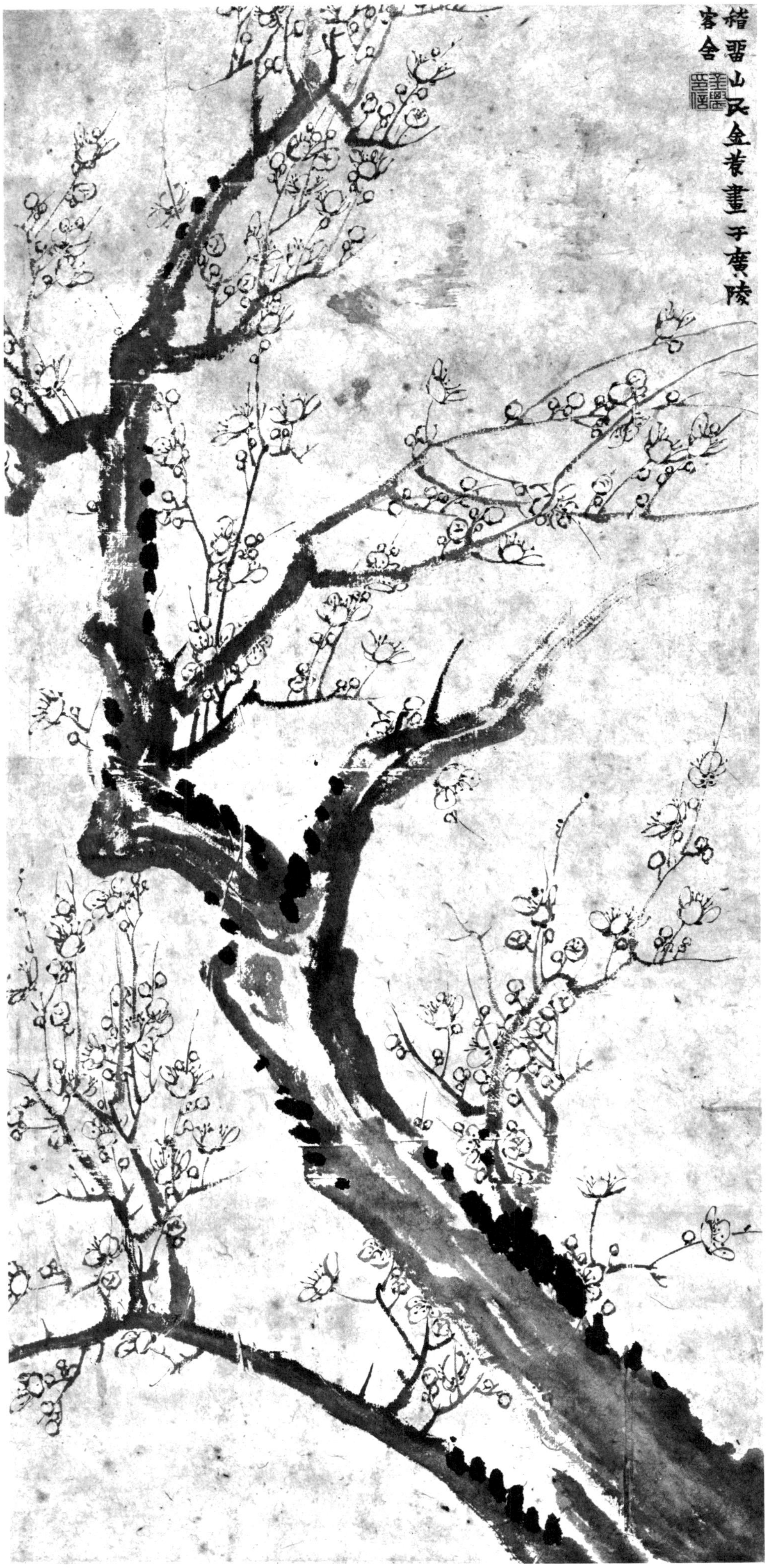

# 54 Huang Shen (1687–ca. 1768)

## *Figures, Flowers, and Insects*
## *(Jen-wu hua-hui ts'ao-ch'ung ts'e)*

Undated
Album of eight leaves: ink and color on paper (A-G); ink on paper (H)
Average measurements, each leaf: 23.3 x 32.5 cm ($9\frac{1}{8}$ x $12\frac{3}{4}$ in.)

ARTIST'S INSCRIPTIONS:
Leaf A, "Taoist Immortal": 4 character quatrain in 2 columns of cursive script.
Leaf B, "Cicada": 5 character regulated verse in 8 lines in 3 columns of cursive script.
Leaf C, "Grasshopper on a Hawthorn Branch": no inscription.
Leaf D, "Taoist Immortal Liu Hai Playing with a Toad": 4 character quatrain in 1 column of cursive script.
Leaf E, "Butterfly": 5 character quatrain in 2 columns of cursive script.
Leaf F, "Vegetables": prose, 9 characters in 3 columns of cursive script.
Leaf G, "Silkworms": 4 character quatrain in 2 columns of cursive script.
Leaf H, "Plum Blossoms": 7 character quatrain in 5 columns of cursive script.

ARTIST'S SIGNATURE: Ying-p'iao (H).

ARTIST'S SEALS: Huang Shen (double seal, both square intaglio; A–E); Shen (square relief; F); Huang Shen (square intaglio; H); Ying-p'iao (square relief; H); I-tsun ch'ang-[ ] (tall rectangle relief; F).

COLLECTORS' SEALS:
1. Pien Tzu-mu (dates unknown): Pien shih Tzu-mu shen-ting (tall rectangle relief; H); T'ing-hsüeh-an ch'ing-shang (tall rectangle relief; F, H); Tzu-mu shou-ts'ang (square relief; A, D).
2. Unidentified owner: Ai-sung pi ts'ung-tz'u (round relief; C).

Gift of John B. Elliott (76–43)

PUBLISHED: Suzuki Kei, comp., *Chūgoku kaiga sōgō zuroku: daiikkan, Amerika–Kanada hen* (Comprehensive illustrated catalogue of Chinese paintings: volume 1, American and Canadian collections) (Tokyo: University of Tokyo Press, 1982), p. 115, pl. A16–042.

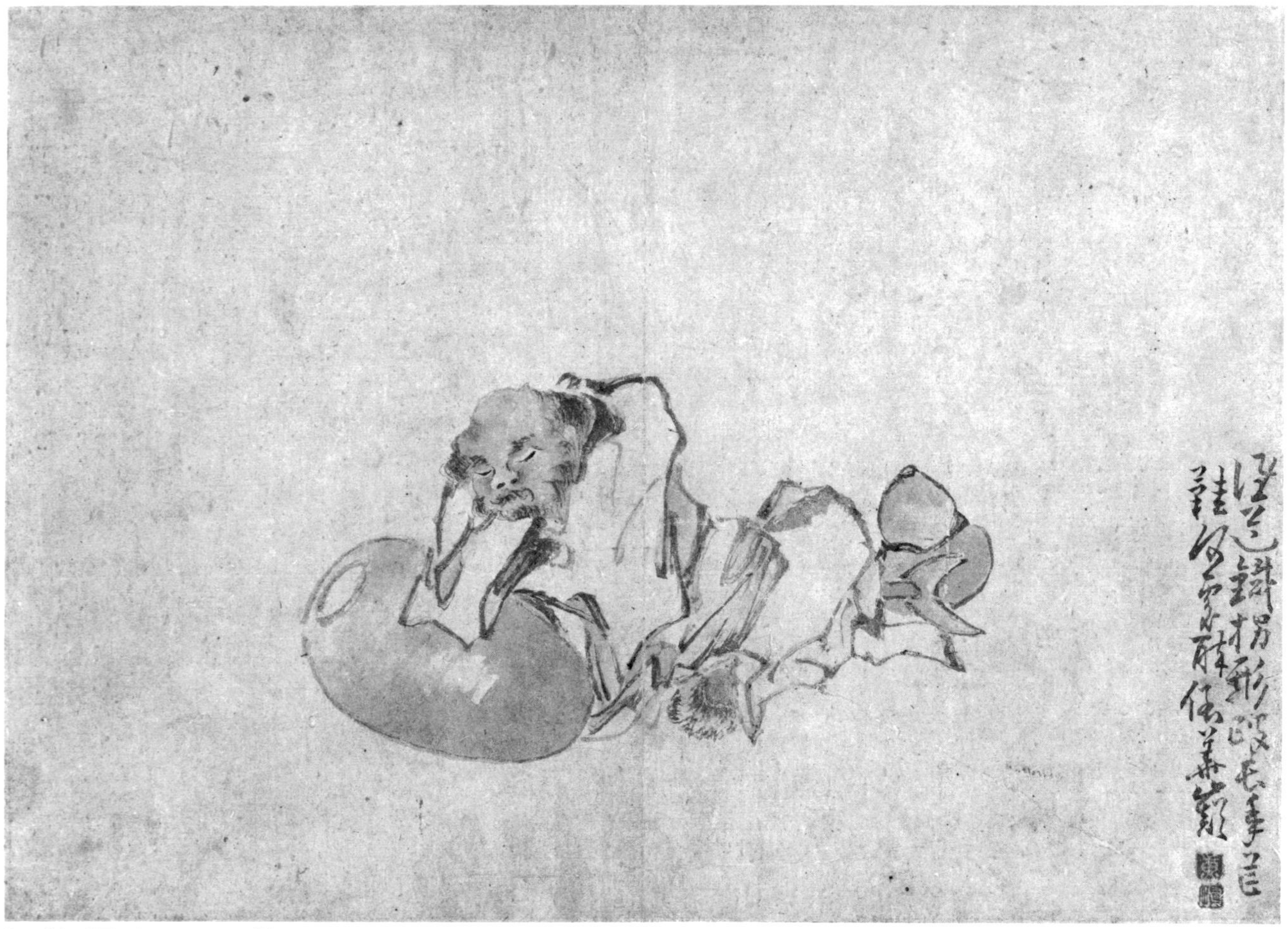

Leaf A, "Taoist Immortal"

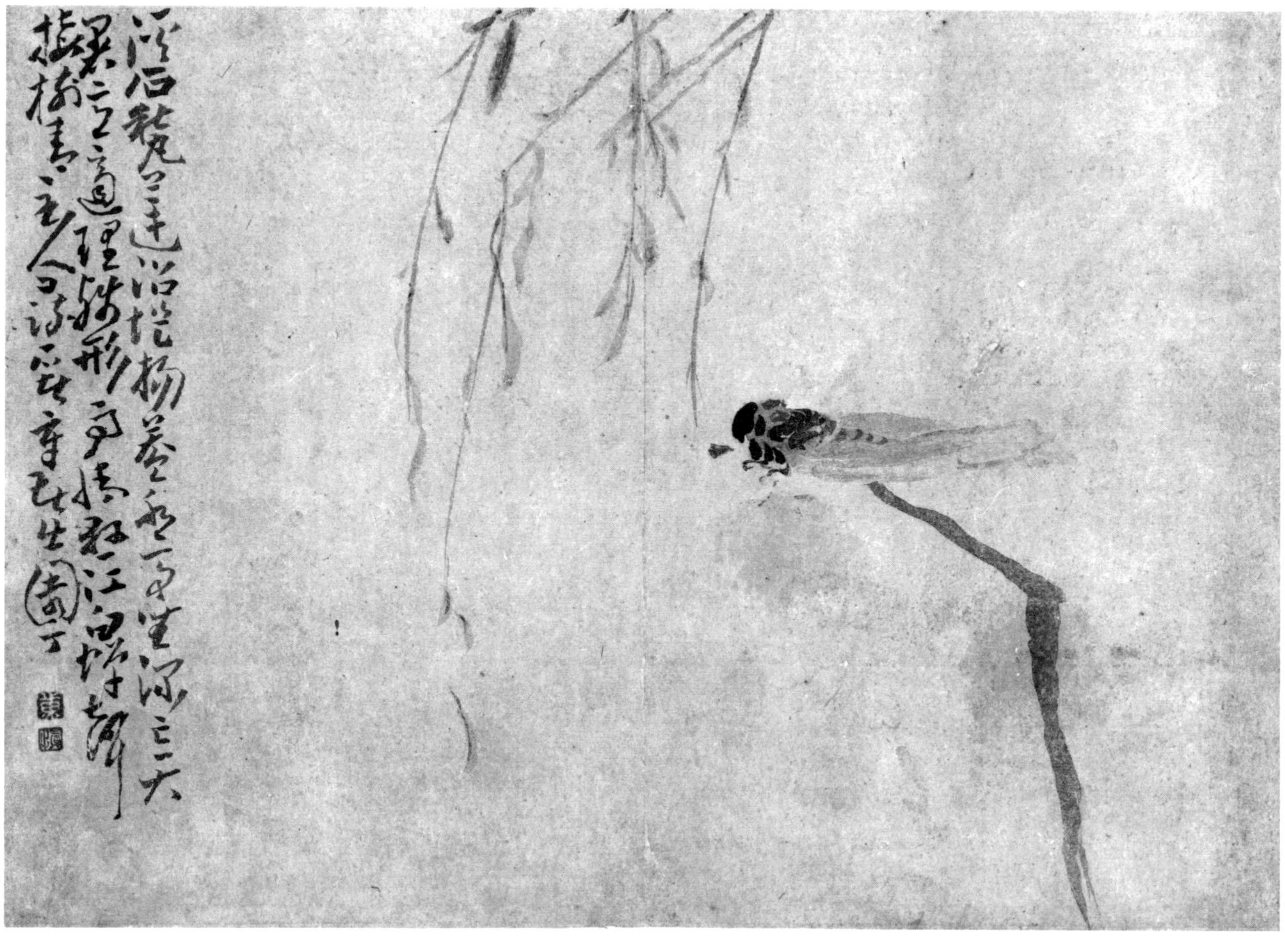

Leaf B, "Cicada"

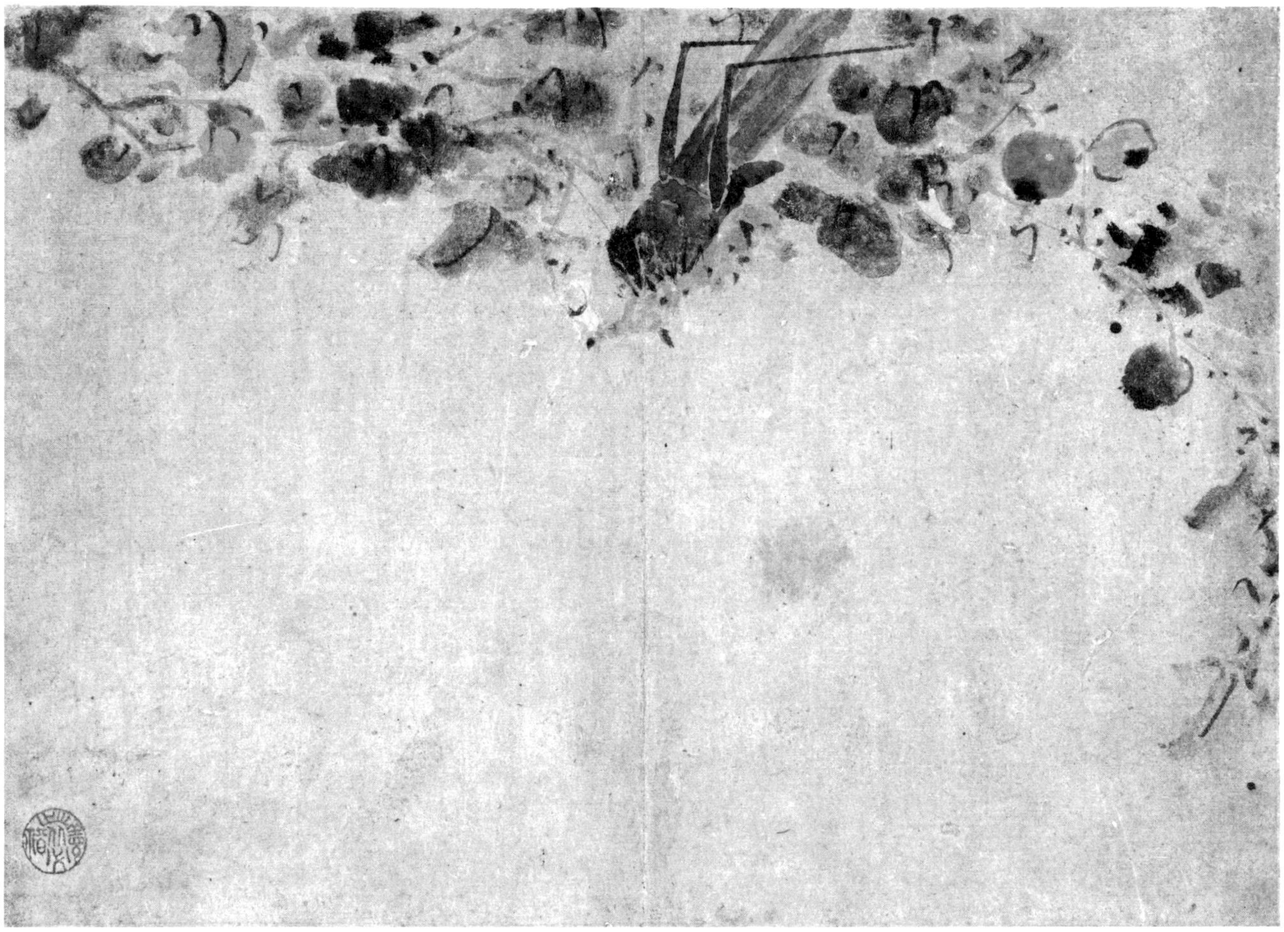

Leaf C, "Grasshopper on a Hawthorn Branch"

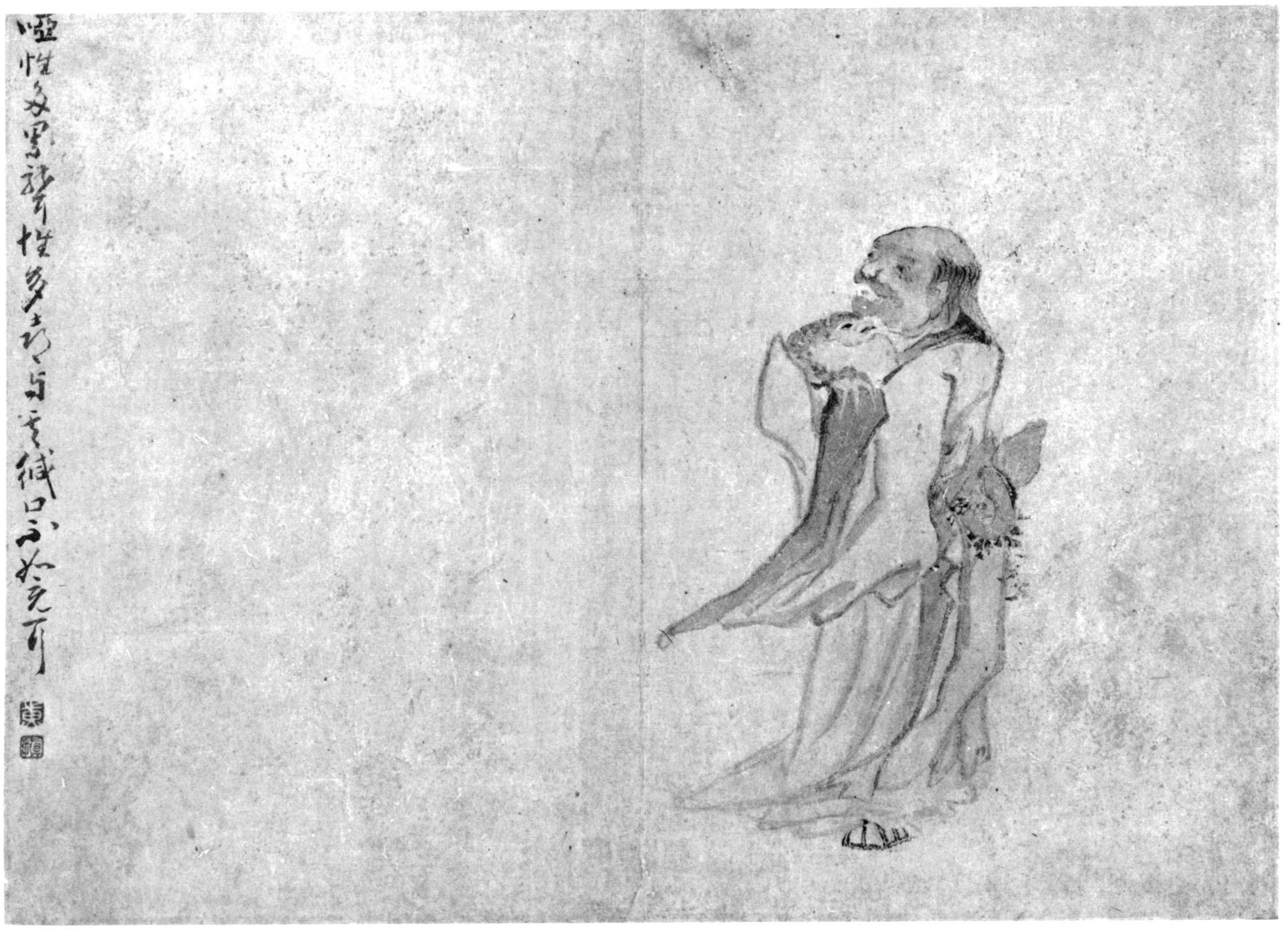

Leaf D, "Taoist Immortal Liu Hai Playing with a Toad"

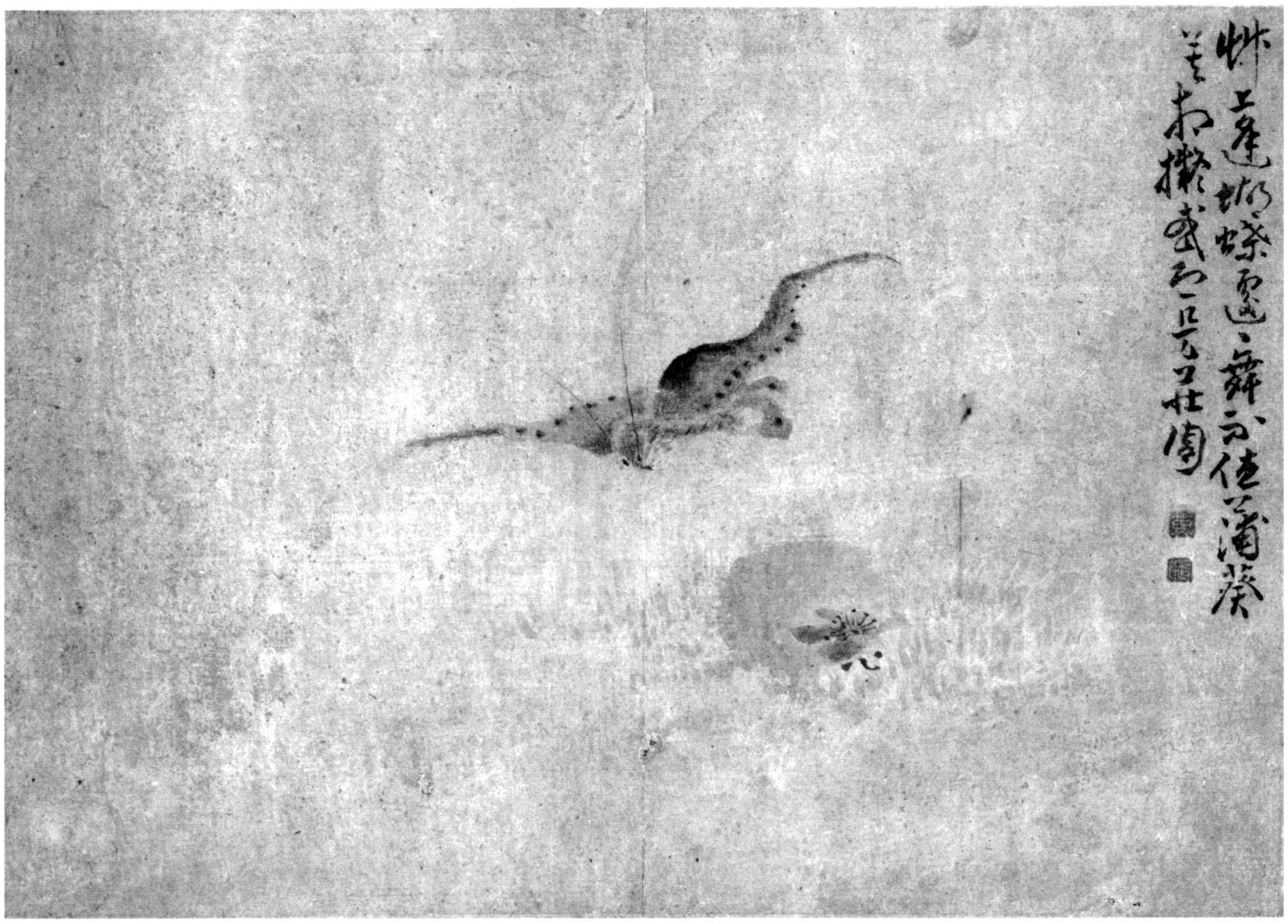

Leaf E, "Butterfly"

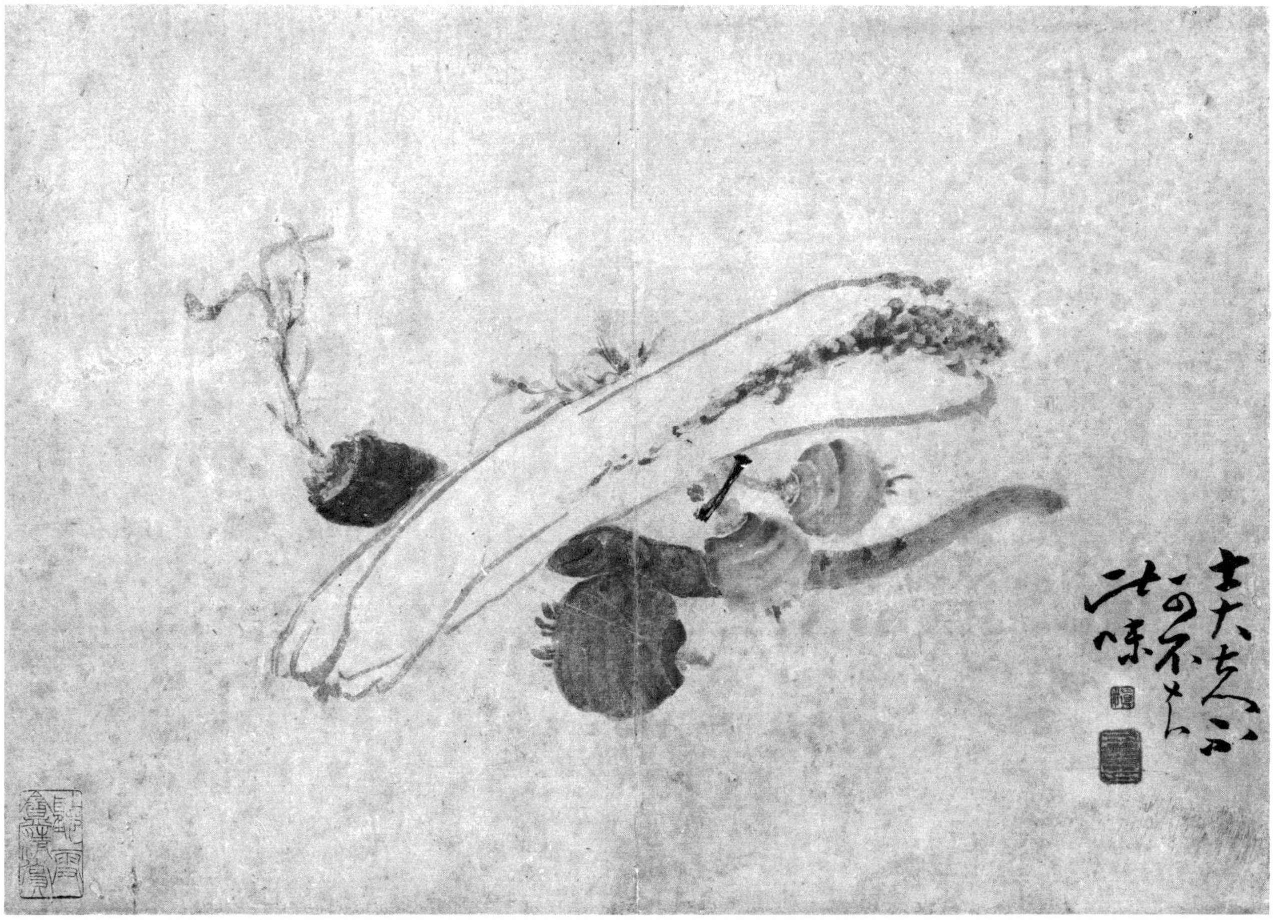

Leaf F, "Vegetables"

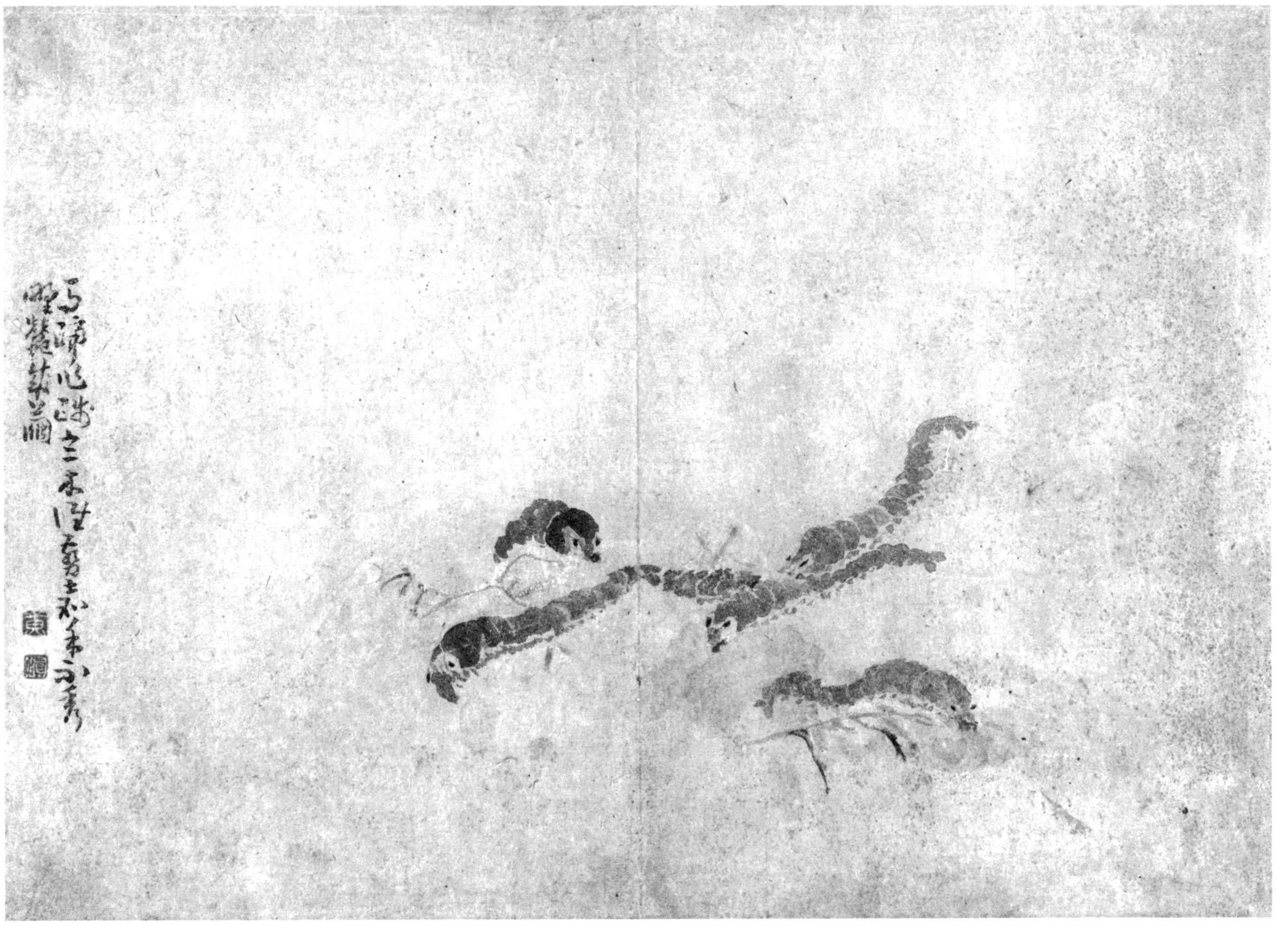

Leaf G, "Silkworms"

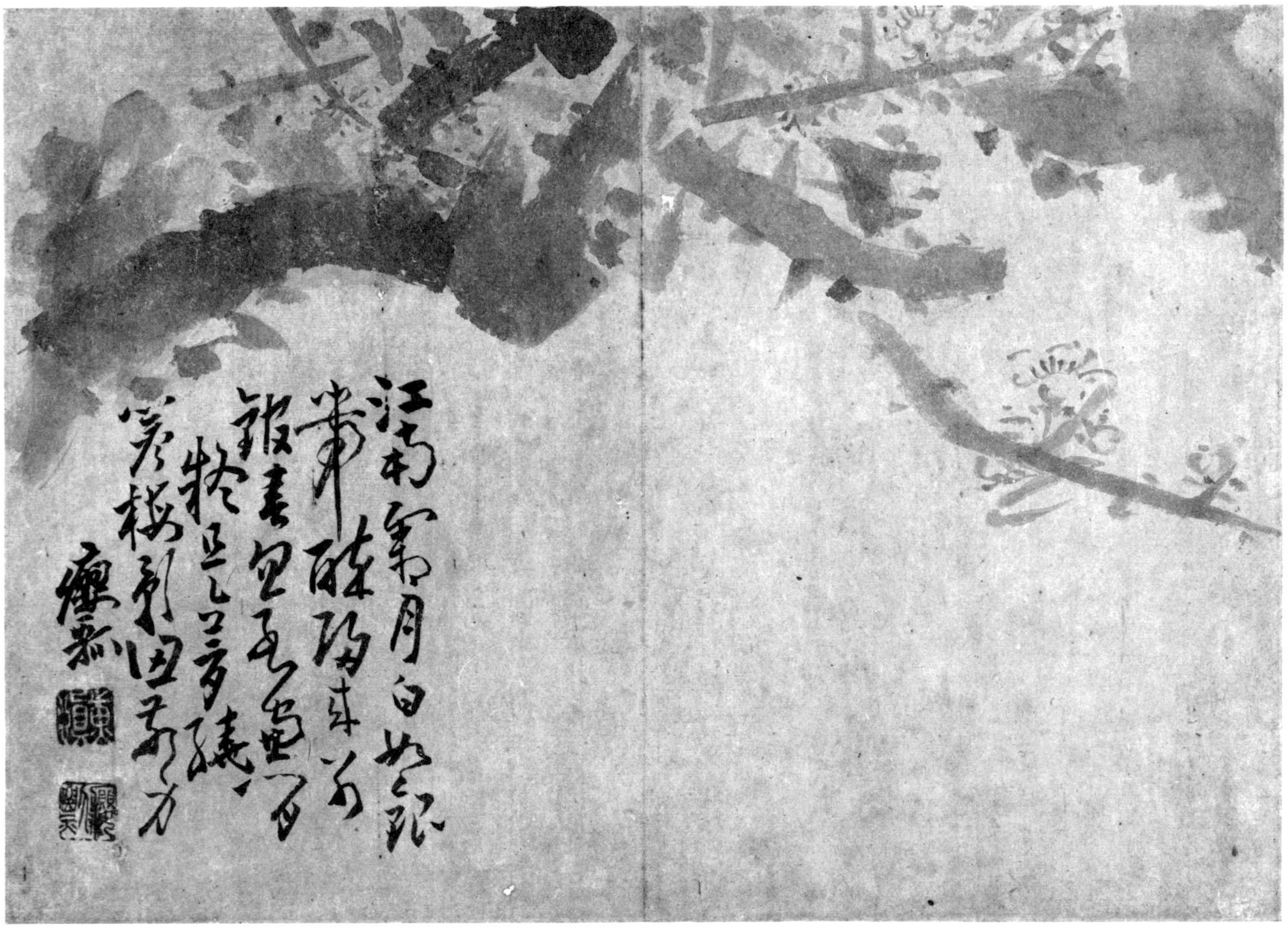

Leaf H, "Plum Blossoms"

# 55 Huang Shen (1687–ca. 1768)

## *Man Appreciating an Ink Slab (Shang-yen t'u)*

Undated
Hanging scroll, ink and color on paper
106.0 x 51.2 cm (3 ft. 5¾ in. x 20⅛ in.)

ARTIST'S INSCRIPTION (7 character regulated verse in 8 lines in 5 columns of cursive script):

A rock of Spring Mountain from the Ancient Gate of Heaven,
Everywhere rubbed smooth, down to its emerald traces,
Round like the eyes of a myna or crane, clear like pure water.
All night clever craftsmen hacked away marsh reeds to find it;
A splinter of it permeated the lake, killing snakes and dragons.
Its light radiating through the window dims sun and moon.
Light penetrates the surface of the lake without sullying its purity,
Thousands of hands groping in the transparent water retrieved this stone.

ARTIST'S SIGNATURE: Ying-p'iao-tzu, Shen.

ARTIST'S SEALS: Huang Shen (square intaglio); Ying-p'iao (square relief).

Edward L. Elliott Family Collection (L33.75)

PUBLISHED: Suzuki Kei, comp., *Chūgoku kaiga sōgō zuroku: daiikkan, Amerika–Kanada hen* (Comprehensive illustrated catalogue of Chinese paintings: volume 1, American and Canadian collections) (Tokyo: University of Tokyo Press, 1982), p. 129, pl. A17–043.

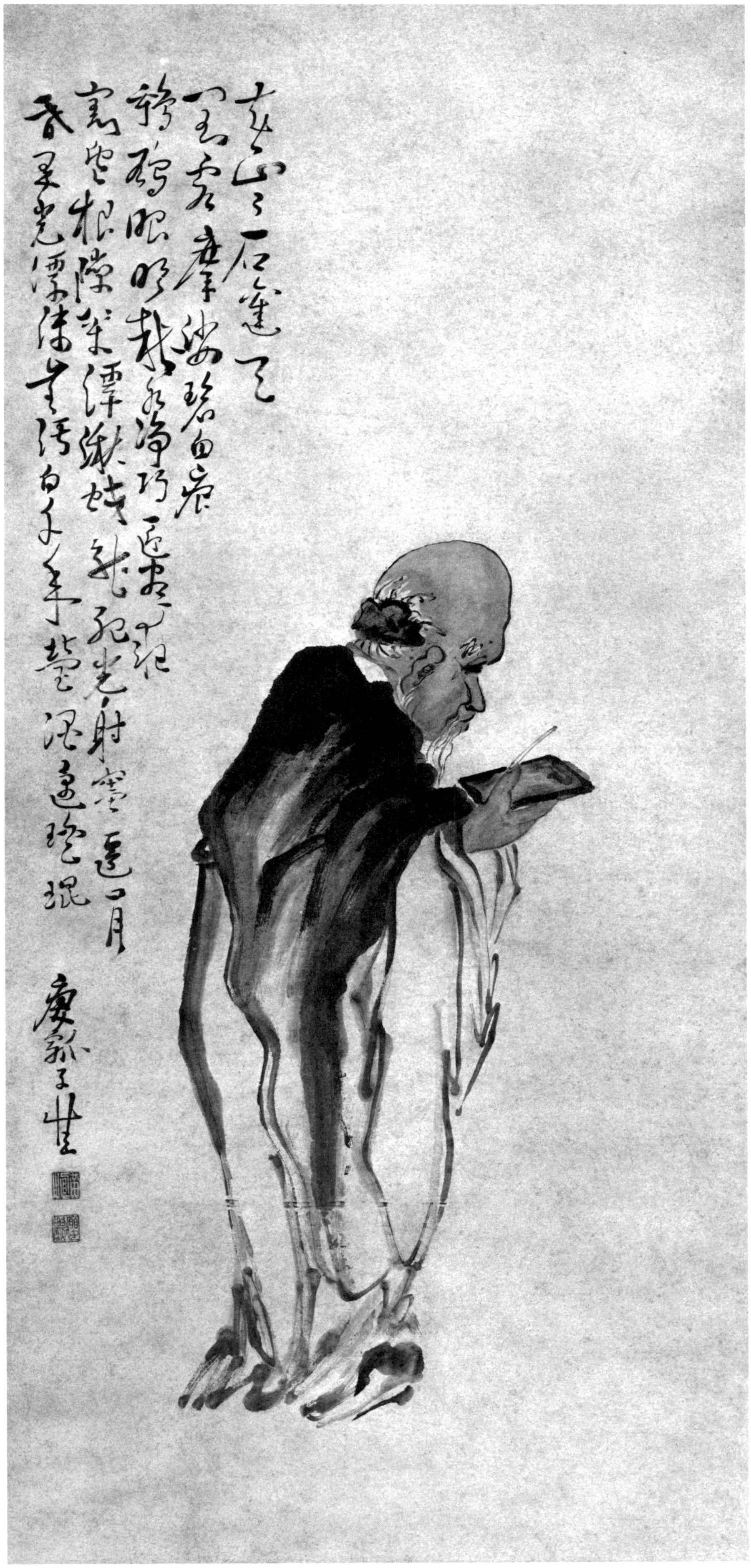

# 56 Ch'en Chuan (fl. 1710–40)

## *Plum Blossoms (Mo-mei ts'e)*

Undated

Album of six leaves of painting (A–F) followed by two leaves of colophons (G, H), ink on paper

Painting, average measurements, each leaf: 23.1 x 15.9 cm (9 1/8 x 6 1/4 in.); colophons (G): 27.5 x 37.1 cm (10 7/8 x 14 5/8 in.); (H): 23.5 x 10.8 cm (9 1/4 x 4 1/4 in.)

ARTIST'S INSCRIPTIONS:

Leaf A (5 character couplet in 2 columns of running script):

Mist obscures a rainy Lantern Festival;
Hints of spring penetrate the moss in the old forest.

Leaf B (5 character regulated verse in 8 lines in 5 columns of running script):

Seized with a fresh desire to search for plum blossoms, straightaway I entered the spring forest.
It was a fair and breezy day.
I noticed the homes on the shady lake.
How could I be merciless and break off those green wands of plum?
Still I could not help being attracted by the luxuriant blossoms.
After returning home my clothes were saturated with their fragrance,
And only then did I realize how near to the plums I had reclined.

Leaf C (5 character regulated verse in 8 lines in 3 columns of running script):

In the clearing after a snow, the wintry plum blossoms:
On a chilly morning their beauty gleams;
Their new finery is reflected in the water.
Green birds perch among the branches and sing.
Silently the mist rises among the trees.
Imperceptibly fragrance issues from the petals of their dresses.
In spring, although the pavilions and terraces are far away,
Who would not venture to gaze at the flowers before returning home?

Leaf D (5 character quatrain in 2 columns of running script):

Inspired I go to greet [the plums] moist with mist;
With sober mind I meditate upon them in the dawn.
My thoughts are not yet profound enough to understand their essence,
So it is in vain that I grow old living in this plum blossom village.

Leaf E (5 character regulated verse in 8 lines in 5 columns of running script):

At the foot of the mountain by overgrown paths, plums are everywhere in the gardens.
Heartsick and resentful because of spring's brevity,
Already I notice the heavy perfume of the season's end.
A nomad girl plays her flute;
The Lantern Festival is observed in the cities along the rivers.
Filled with adoration I face the pure fragrant flowers.
Besides expressing my affection what else can I say?

Leaf F (5 character quatrain in 2 columns of running script):

Old plum so distant and alone,
Standing on the empty mountain, touched with sadness;
How is it no one comes to console you?
They have been delayed for days by the raging blizzard.

ARTIST'S SEALS: Ch'en Chuan (tall rectangle relief; A–F); Wan-teh-t'ang (square relief; F).

COLOPHONS:

1. Leaf G by Wang Mei-ting (*chin-shih*, 1793): prose, 64 characters in 6 columns of running script. Signature: Untrammeled painter of the Thirty-six Peaks, Wo-yün-wai-shih, playfully inscribed this in a temporary studio at Ku-Wu [Kiangsu province]. Seal: Mei-ting chih yin (square, half relief, half intaglio).
2. Leaf H by Yung-ching (b. 1716):
   a) 102 characters in 4 columns of free-form regular script, quoted from the *Anthology of Tao-ku-t'ang* (*Tao-ku-t'ang chi*) by Hang Shih-chün (1696–1773).
   b) 46 characters in 2 columns of free-form regular script, quoted from the *Anthology of Fan-hsieh-shan-fang* (*Fan-hsieh-shan-fang chi*) by Li O (1692–1752).
   Seal: Su-chü-chu-jen (tall rectangle, half relief, half intaglio).

COLLECTORS' SEALS:

1. K'ung I (dates unknown): K'ung I shih (oval relief; lower left, Wang's colophon).
2. Unidentified owners: Chieh han-mo-yüan (tall rectangle intaglio; lower left, Wang's colophon); Chien-ch'ing kuo-yen (tall rectangle relief; lower left, Wang's colophon).

Edward L. Elliott Family Collection (L235.70)

PUBLISHED: Ishikawa Jun et al., eds., *Bunjinga suihen* (Selection of the finest Chinese and Japanese literati paintings), vol. 9 (Tokyo: Chūōkōron-sha, 1976), p. 182, fig. 33 (Leaf D); Suzuki Kei, comp., *Chūgoku kaiga sōgō zuroku: daiikkan, Amerika–Kanada hen* (Comprehensive illustrated catalogue of Chinese paintings: volume 1, American and Canadian collections) (Tokyo: University of Tokyo Press, 1982), p. 139, pl. A17–069.

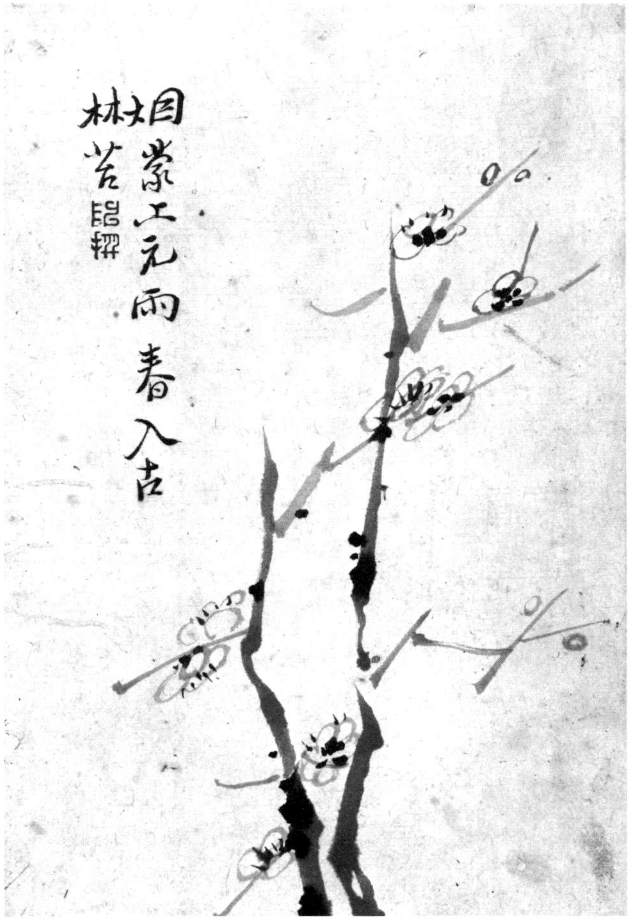

Leaf A

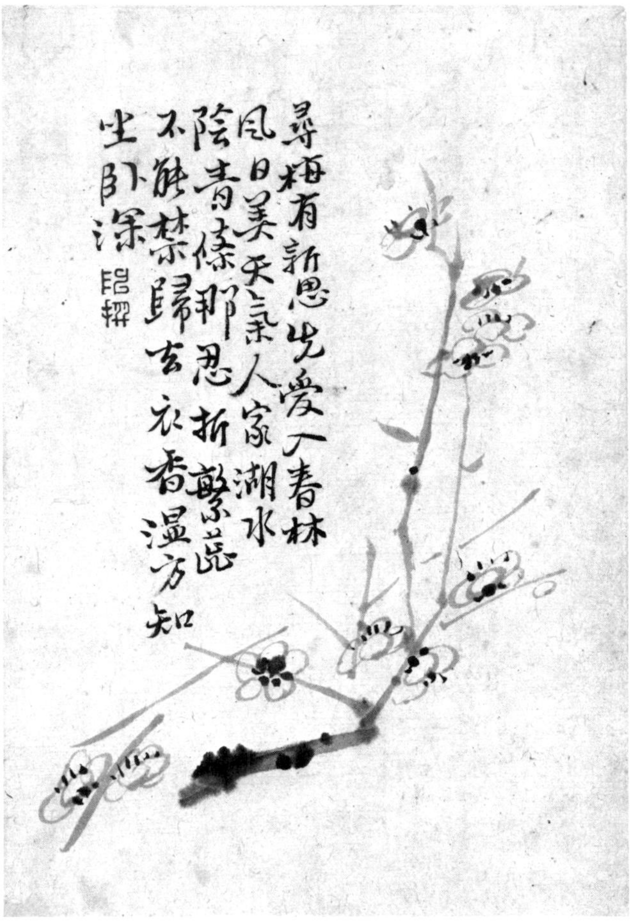

Leaf B

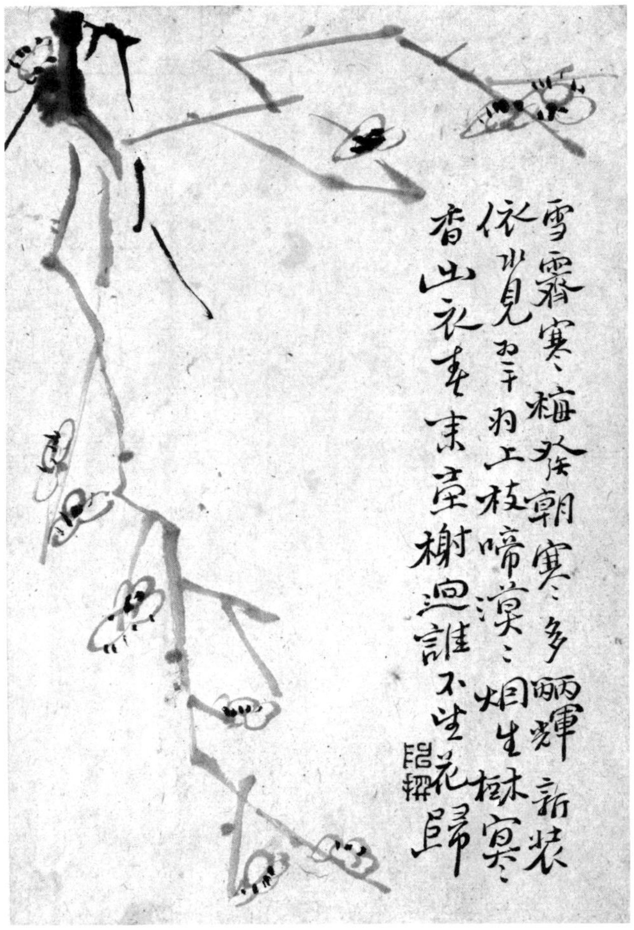

Leaf C

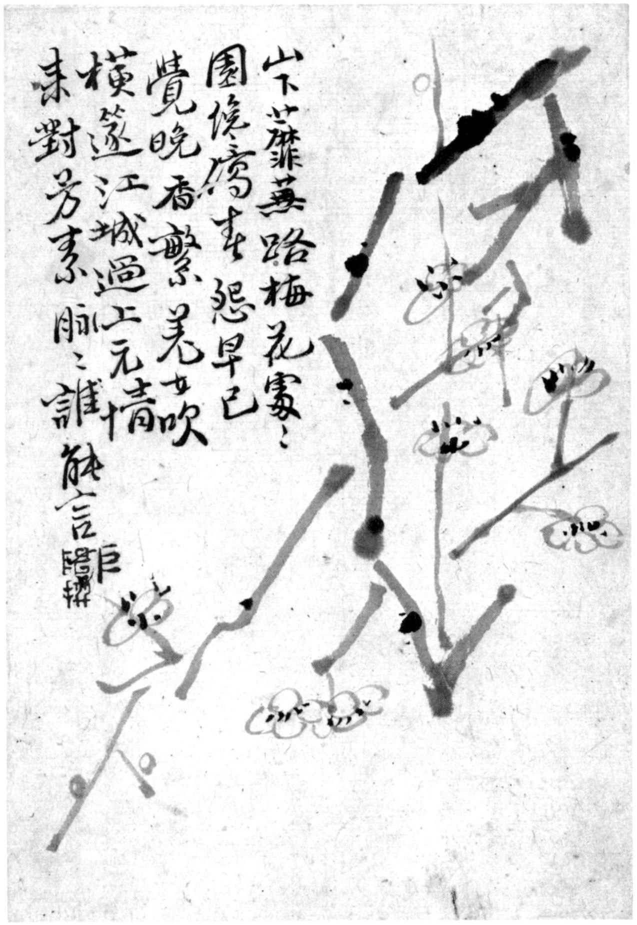

Leaf E

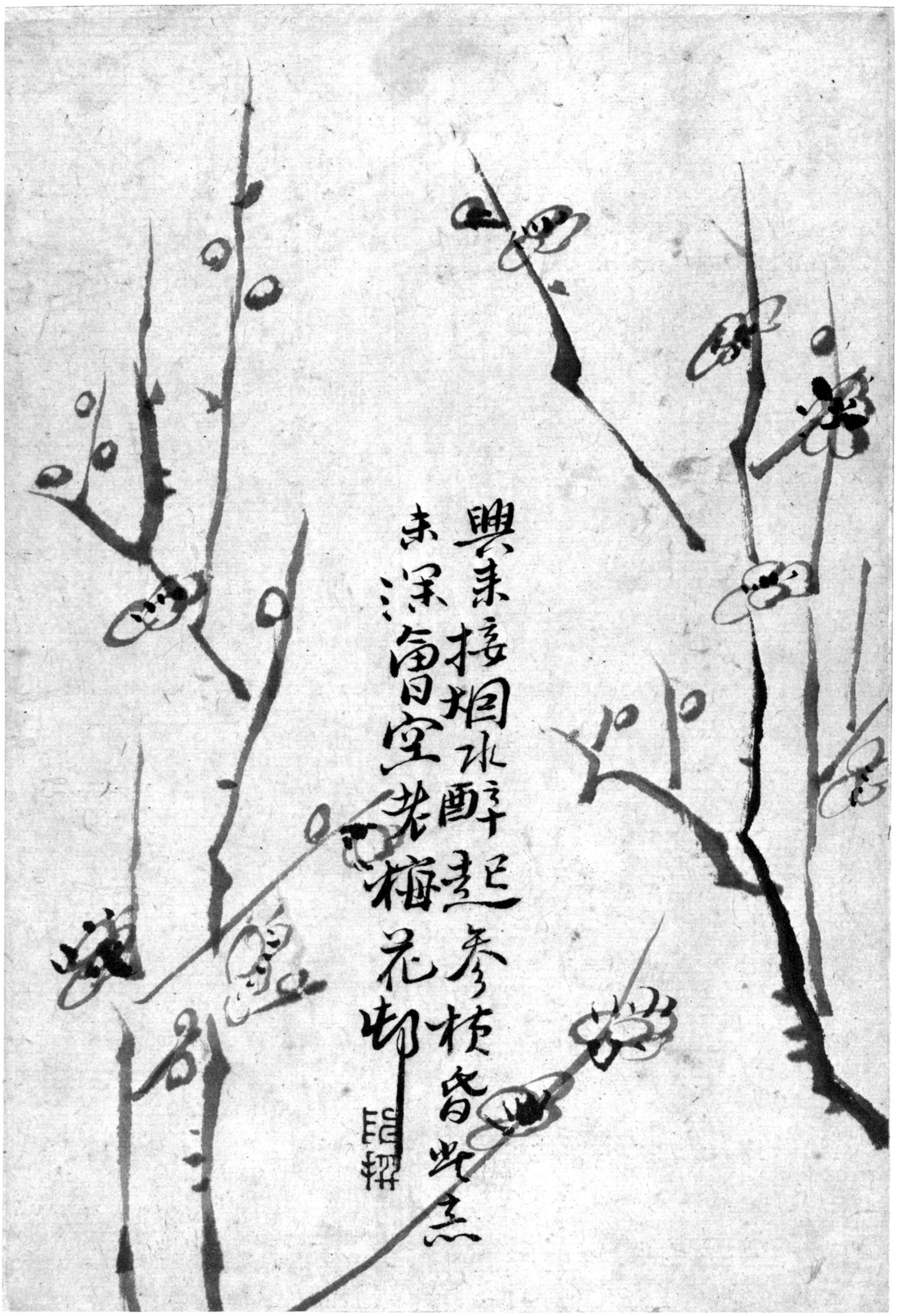

Leaf D

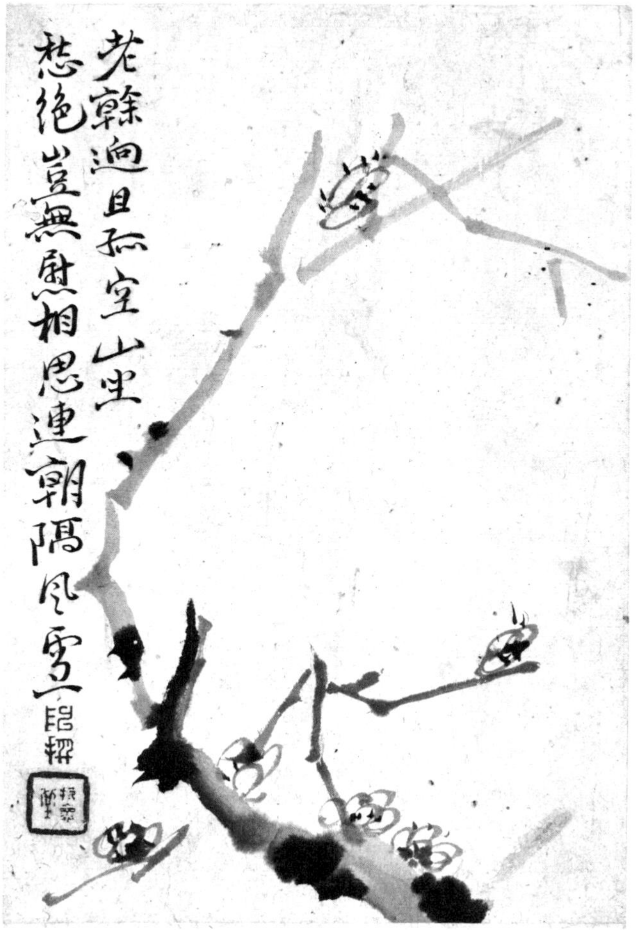

Leaf F

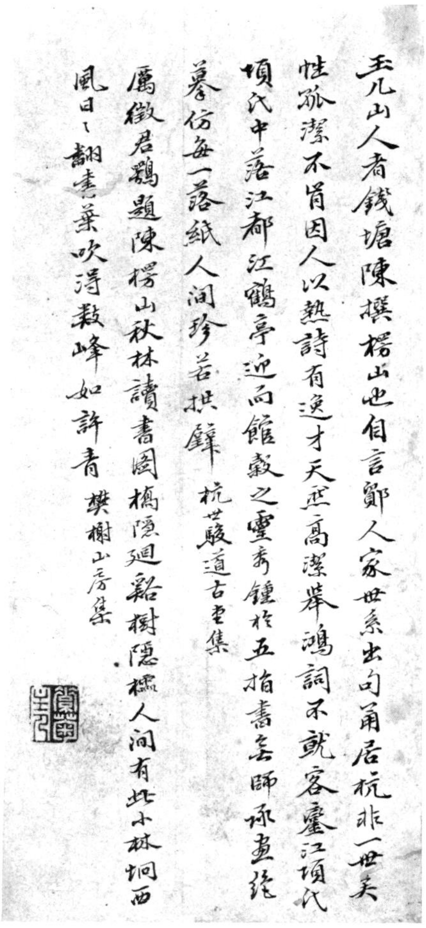

Leaf H, colophons by Yung-ching

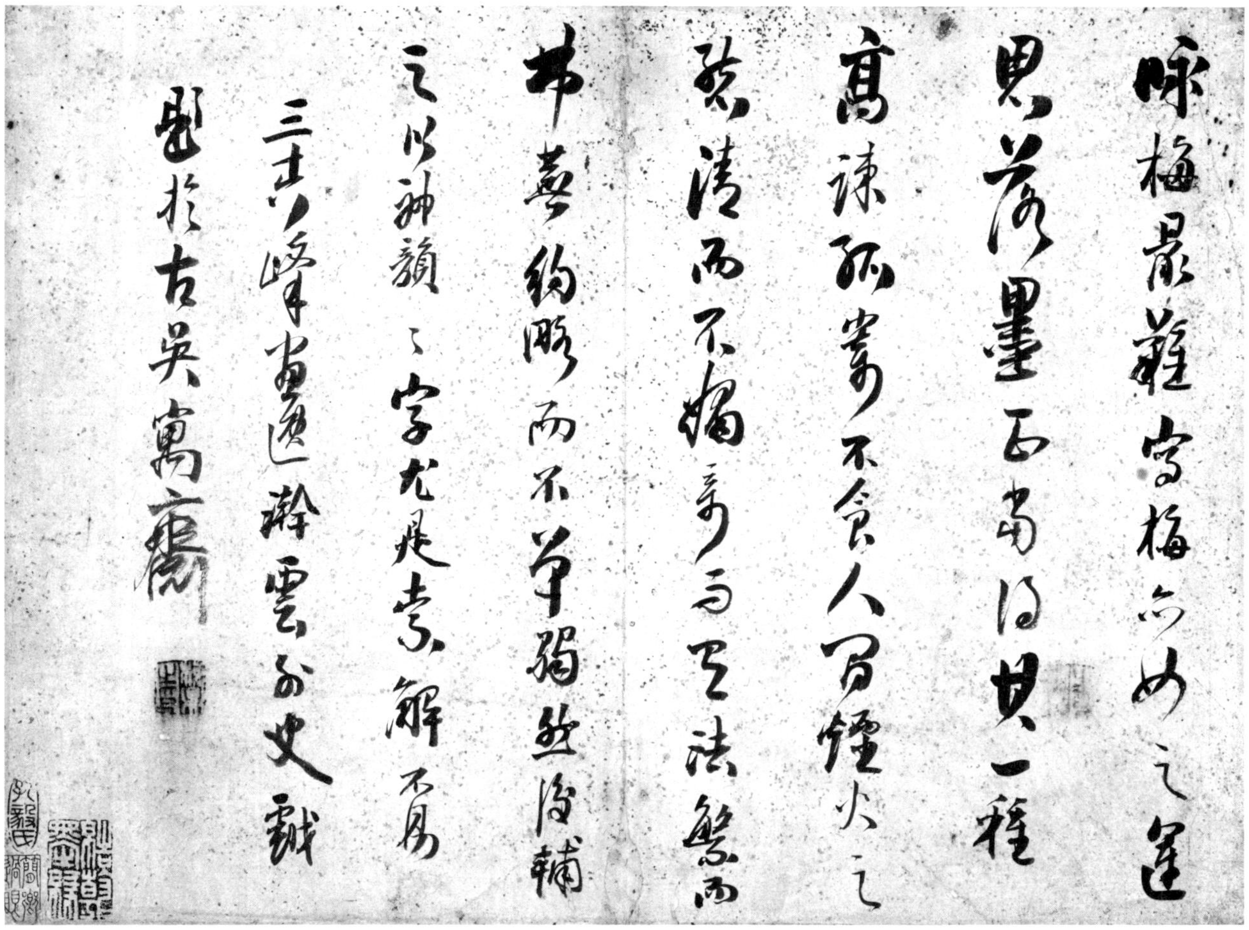

Leaf G, colophon by Wang Mei-ting

# 57 Pien Shou-min (fl. ca. early 18th century)

## *Flowers and Vegetables (Hua-hui shu-kuo ts'e)*

Dated 1747
Album of twelve leaves of painting (A–L) followed by one leaf with a colophon (M), ink on paper
Average measurements, each leaf: 24.1 x 30.7 cm ($9^1/_2$ x $12^1/_8$ in.)

ARTIST'S INSCRIPTIONS:
Leaf A, "Plum Blossoms" (5 character quatrain, followed by a 3 character note, in 10 columns of running script):

I want to be the plum blossoms' friend,
But I often worry that I cannot be their equal.
So from now on I will fast,
And drink only water and read books by the immortals.
[Quoted from Fang-weng's (Lu Yu's; 1125–1210) verse.]

Leaf B, "Lotus Pods": no inscription.

Leaf C, "Peonies" (4 characters in 1 column of running script): "Unique Flower in Spring."

Leaf D, "Pomegranates" (5 character quatrain in 8 columns of running script):

Glistening with pulp, the fruit have long been attached to their twigs.
The wind blowing off the fields cannot shake them loose.
[Use] a golden knife and jade-cool emerald juice [pours forth];
Late at night, it refreshes one's mouth, dry from wine.

Leaf E, "Clams" (rhymed prose poem, followed by a note, totaling 111 characters in 9 columns of running script):

Tightly closed within hard shells, the clams lie side by side at the bottom of the pond.
They do not know of the old maples broken by the wind.
Belonging to the family of Mollusca,
The patterns on their shells are inferior to those of the miterwort.
They spread out on the cool water bed among the fish.
With a net held by two bamboo stalks they can be lifted out of the water,
Or one may search for them with short wooden sticks, beating the dark mud into a dough.
The setting is an uncultivated field, dotted with old trees blowing in the west wind as the sun sets;
And noisy sparrows have already passed by.
The clams' shells start to open as the broth begins to boil.
Through the slight opening, one can see the yellowish white of their soft, finely textured flesh.
I do not know what makes us meet here together,
But just eat these and discard any fatty morsels [you may find].
I did not awaken until it was already past six o'clock in the morning.
In my dream I called again and again for the knife and little serving trays for clams.
I am lingering here just waiting for the clams;
That is why I do not return home in early spring.

Rhymed after the section entitled "Tranquility on the Hsiang River" ["Hsiang-chiang ching"] quoted from the *P'u-shu-t'ing* by Chu I-tsun [1629–1709].

Leaf F, "Pine" (7 character quatrain in 5 columns of running script):

Soaked by rain, scarred by frost, the pine has survived for many hundreds of years.
Holding the wind in his mouth and riding the waves, the old dragon pine looks sad.
Wildly my brush gives birth to clouds and mist, rising straight to the pine atop Lotus Peak.

Leaf G, "Lotus" (rhymed prose poem in 49 characters, followed by a 35 character note, in 7 columns of running script; rhyme scheme: *chien-tzu-mu-lan-hua*):

The young lotuses are small, and fish somersault among green water weeds.
Tiny newly opened lotus buds break through the mirror surface of the water, so picturesque;
Their green leaves are half-unfurled, but their miniature fragrant hearts remain closed.
When the buds swell the lotus plants will shade a pair of mandarin ducks.

The day after the Dragon Boat Festival of the *ting-mao* year [1747], I spontaneously wetted my dry brush and painted young lotuses. When I was ready to inscribe a poem on the finished painting, I looked over my desk and found Shih Hsiao-yu's verse, which is light and enjoyable. Therefore I transcribed it on my painting.

Leaf H, "Day Lily" (5 character quatrain in 6 columns of running script):

Everyone says living in a mountain is ideal
And regrets not being able to go there sooner.
There is absolutely no cause for worry in the mountains.
Moreover, they are filled with lilies known as "Unmindful of Worldly Cares."

Leaf I, "Eggplants": no inscription.

Leaf J, "Bamboo Shoots and Mushrooms" (rhymed prose poem, 57 characters in 15 columns of running script):

Bamboo in the southern regions is greener even than jade.
When the ground is frozen and covered with hard ice, all the plants wither,
Except the bamboo shoots, which sprout and tear through the ground.
For a hundred days there has been no meat in my humble kitchen,
Still, when my hungry stomach is filled with bamboo shoots I feel satisfied.
Do not say that the mountain dweller is undernourished;
He enjoys the delicious bamboo shoots with their jadelike texture and golden husks.
And in the snow there are still wild mushrooms.

Leaf K, "Banana Trees": no inscription.

Leaf L, "Taro Roots and Peapods" (prose, 48 characters in 10 columns of running script):

> Those who like to eat peas had better steam them, while those who favor taro roots should bake them. The best time for peas is in cool autumn; for taro roots it is the end of winter. It is best to bake taro roots at midnight, while peas should be steamed before noon. When the vegetables reach maturity, then they are succulent. People who do not grow old living in the wild cannot grasp this principle easily.

ARTIST'S SIGNATURES: Shou-min (A–C, I–K); Ch'o-ch'o-lao-jen painted and inscribed this (D); Wei-chien-chü-shih painted and inscribed this (E, G, H); Wei-chien-chü-shih, Pien Shou-min, painted and inscribed this (F); Wei-chien-chü-shih (L).

ARTIST'S SEALS: Shou-min (tall rectangle relief; A, C, I, J, L); Shou-min (tall rectangle intaglio; H, K); Shou-min (square intaglio; B, F, G); I-kung (square relief; B, H, K); I-kung (square intaglio; C, D, I, J, L); I-kung (tall rectangle intaglio; E–G); Wei-chien chü-shih (square intaglio; D); Chiu-hou ch'ang ch'eng lao-hua-shih (square intaglio; J); Hua-ch'an (tall rectangle intaglio; L).

COLOPHON by I T'u (fl. late 19th century): 81 characters in 5 columns of regular script (M). Signature: In the second lunar month of the twelfth year of the T'ung-chih era [1873], I T'u wrote this. Seals: I T'u (tall rectangle intaglio); T'ao-fang (oval relief).

COLLECTORS' SEALS:

1. Kung Shao-wen (dates unknown): Kung Shao-wen shou-ts'ang shu-hua yin (square intaglio; all except E); Tsun Shan-ku-shih-chu-jen p'ing-sheng chih ai chih wu (square relief; A).
2. Lin Hsiung-kuang (fl. ca. late 19th–early 20th century): Lang-an mi-wan (tall rectangle relief; E).
3. Unidentified owners: I hsin-hui chin hsing ch'i so-chien (square intaglio; D); Ju nan-shan chih shou (oval intaglio; F); Hsia-ching-lu (square relief; E); Sheh chia mao jan (tall rectangle relief; E).

Edward L. Elliott Family Collection (L47.70)

PUBLISHED: Suzuki Kei, comp., *Chūgoku kaiga sōgō zuroku: daiikkan, Amerika–Kanada hen* (Comprehensive illustrated catalogue of Chinese paintings: volume 1, American and Canadian collections) (Tokyo: University of Tokyo Press, 1982), pp. 140–41, pl. A17–071.

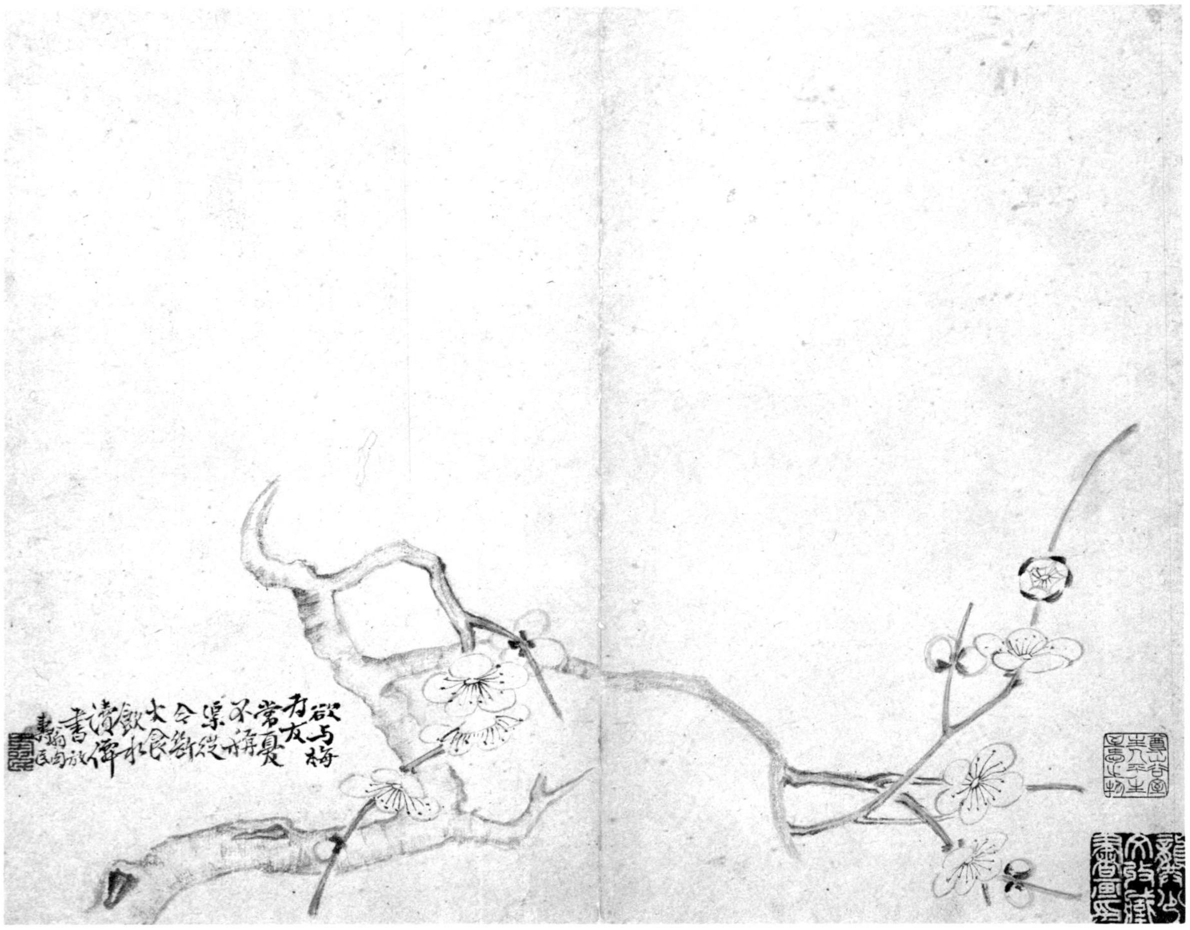

Leaf A, "Plum Blossoms"

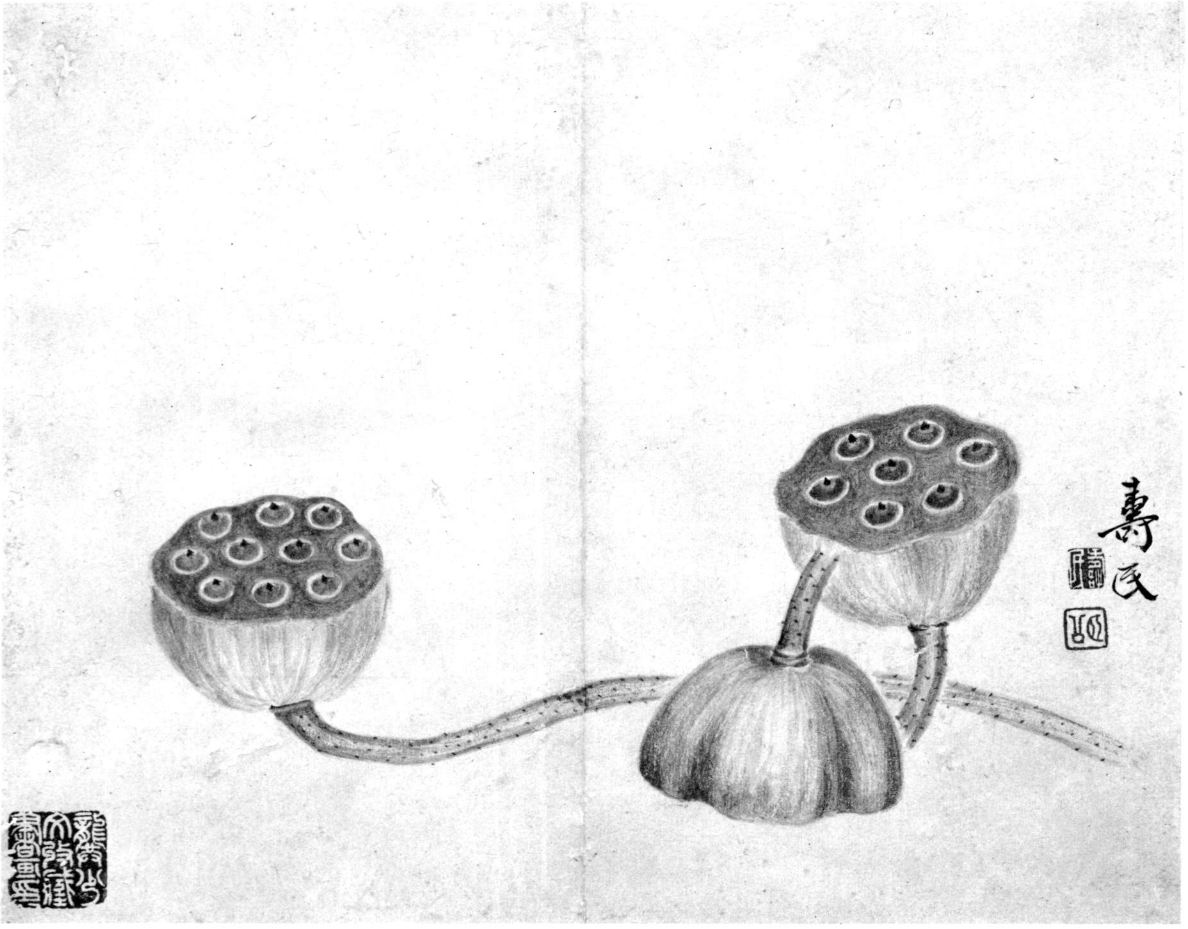

Leaf B, "Lotus Pods"

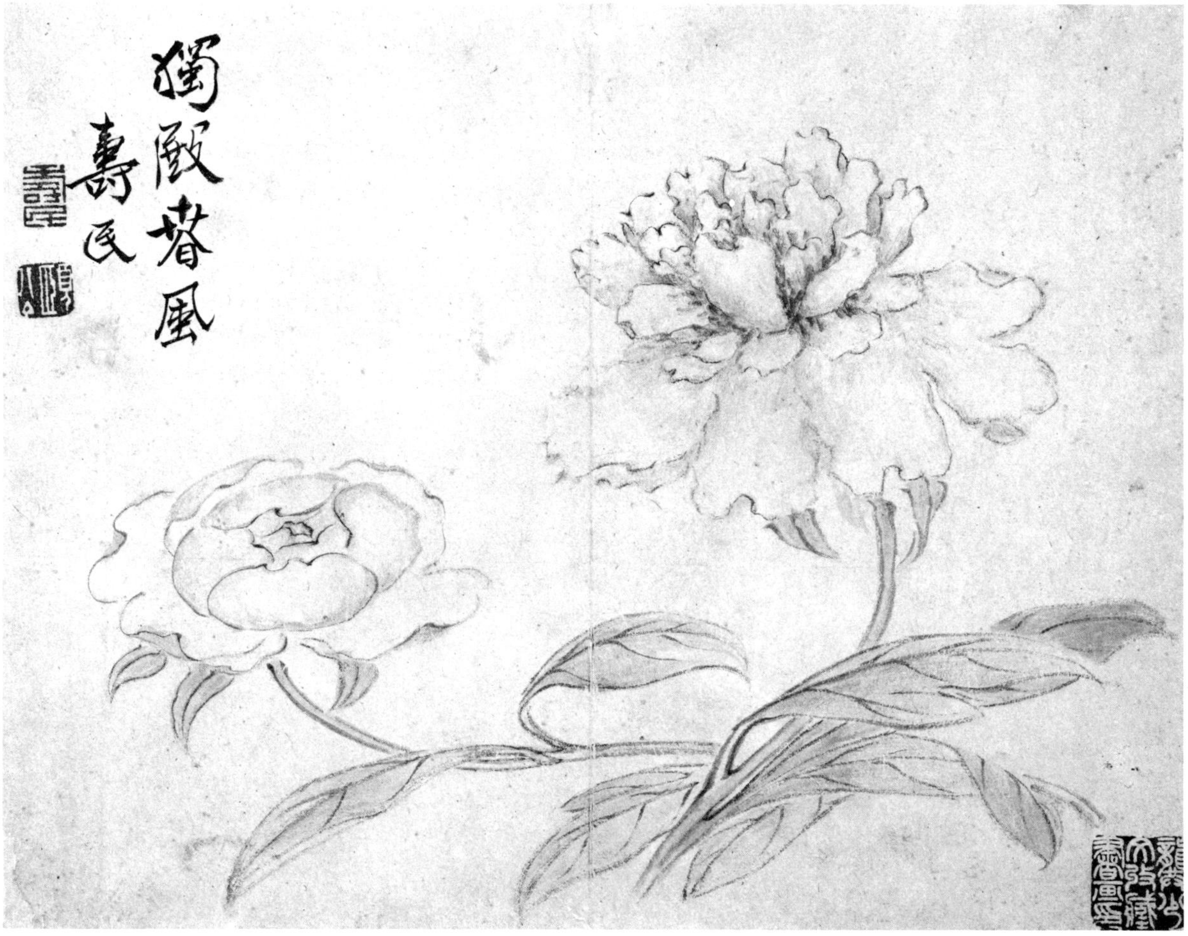

Leaf C, "Peonies"

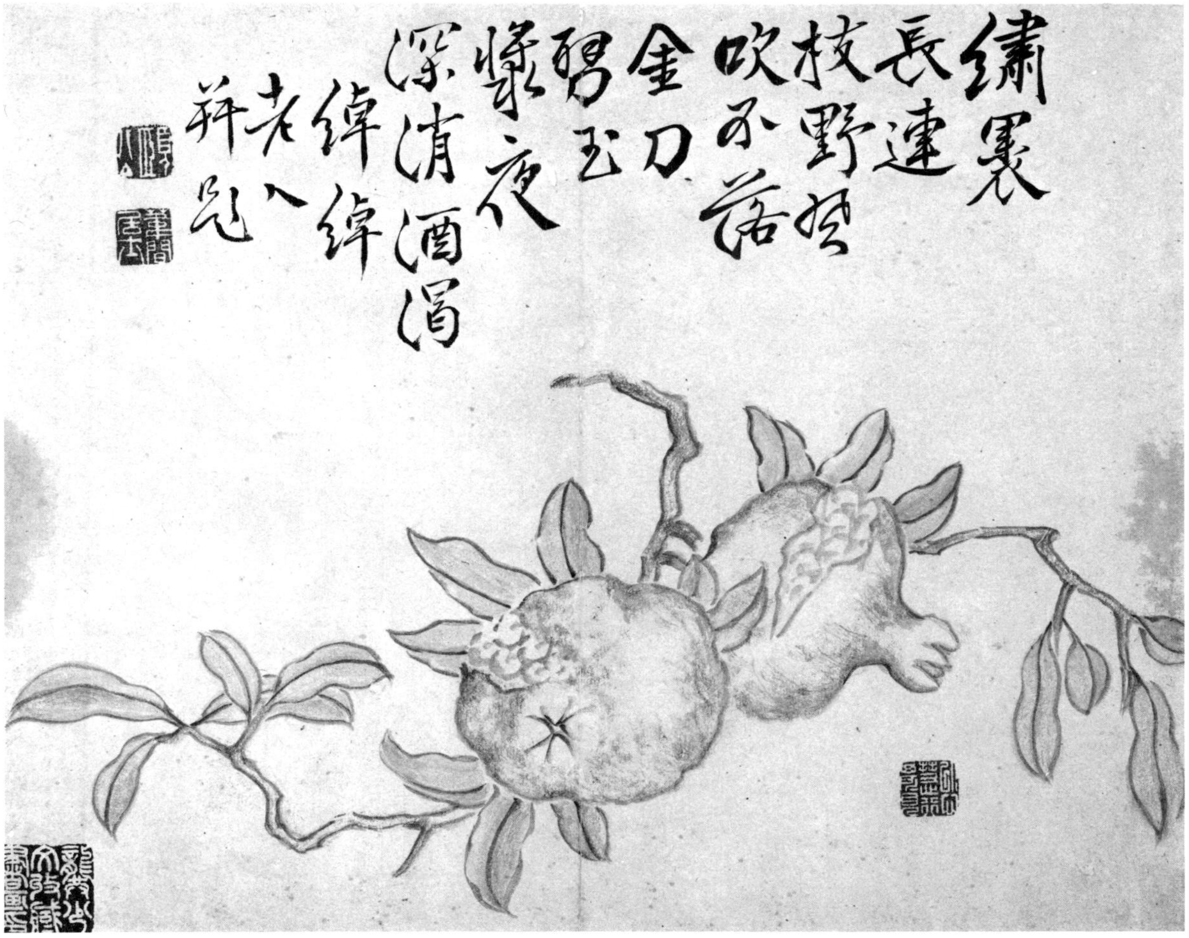
Leaf D, "Pomegranates"

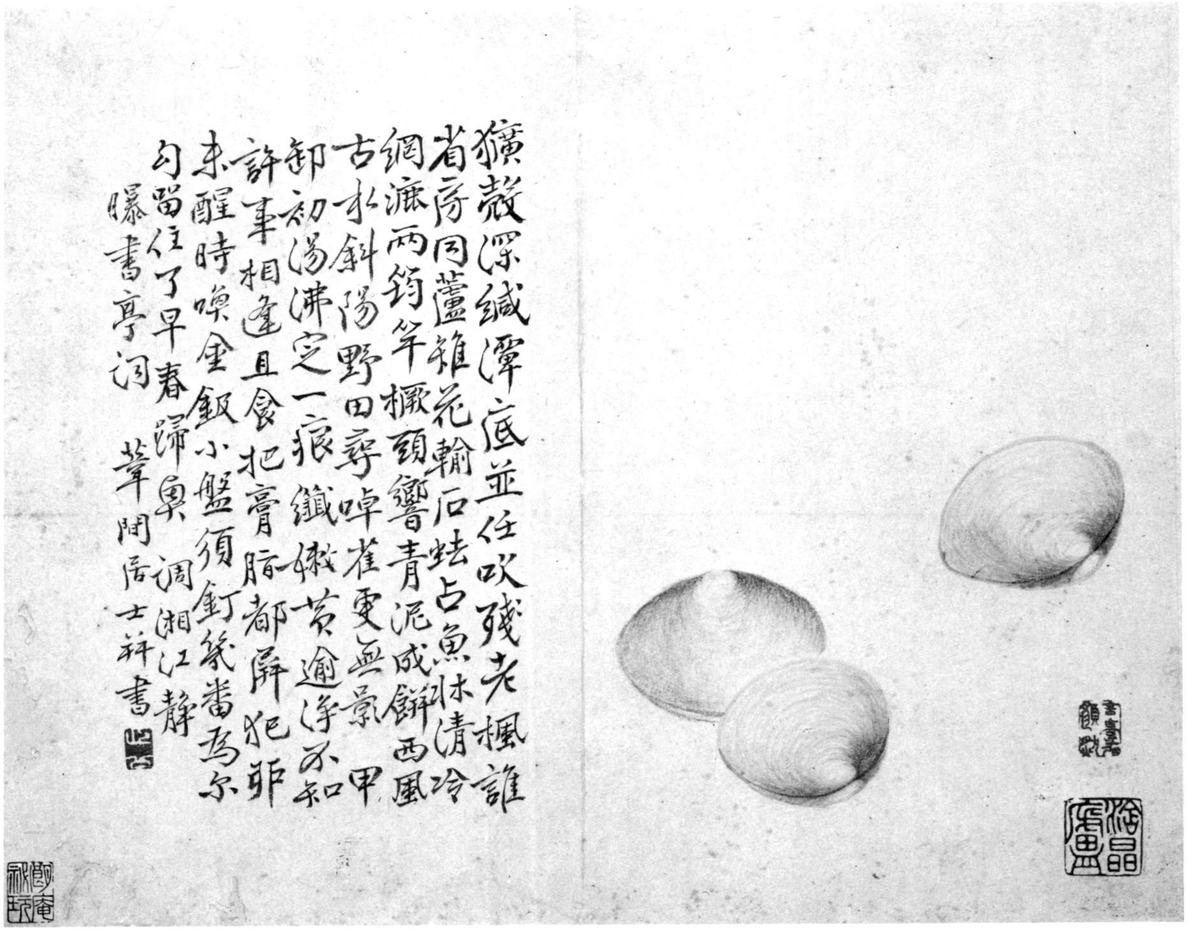

Leaf E, "Clams"

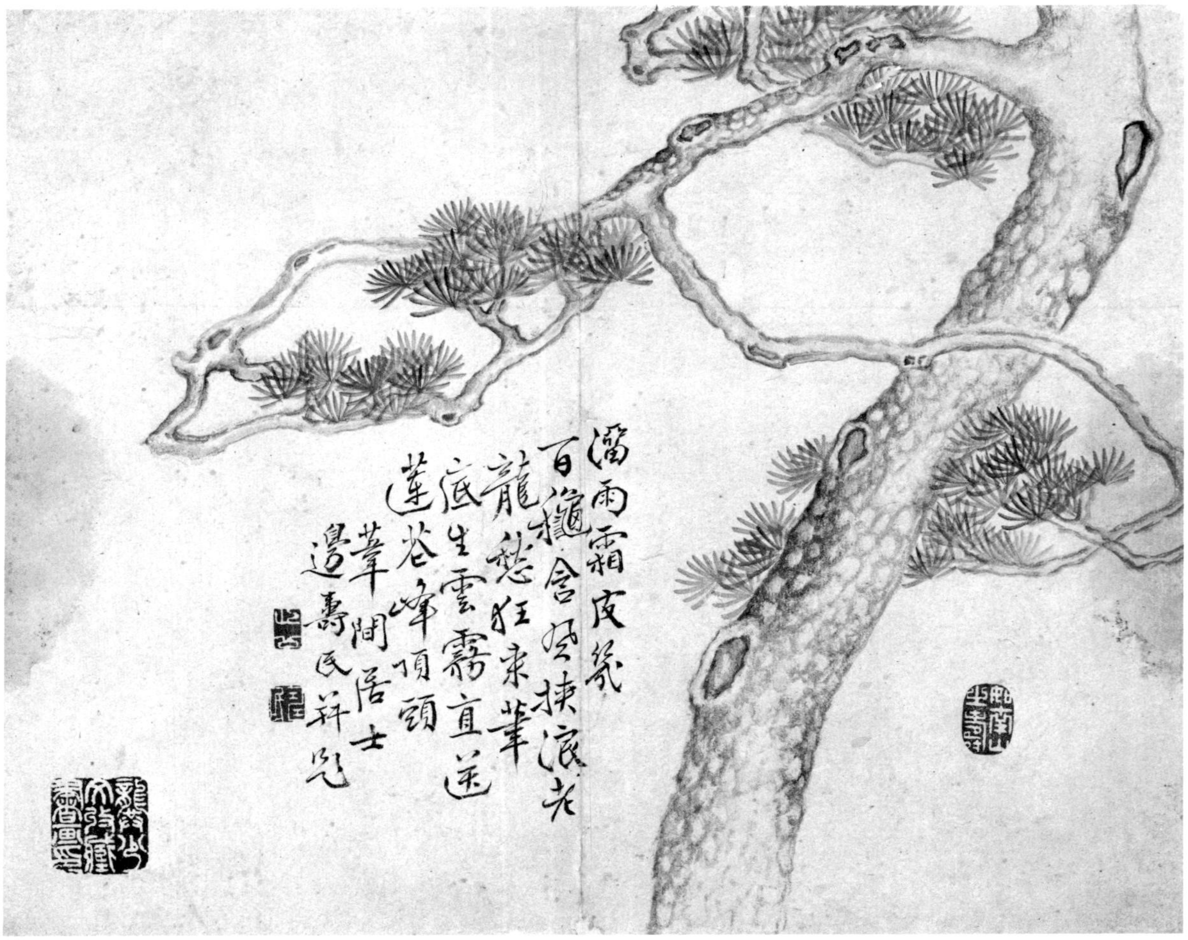

Leaf F, "Pine"

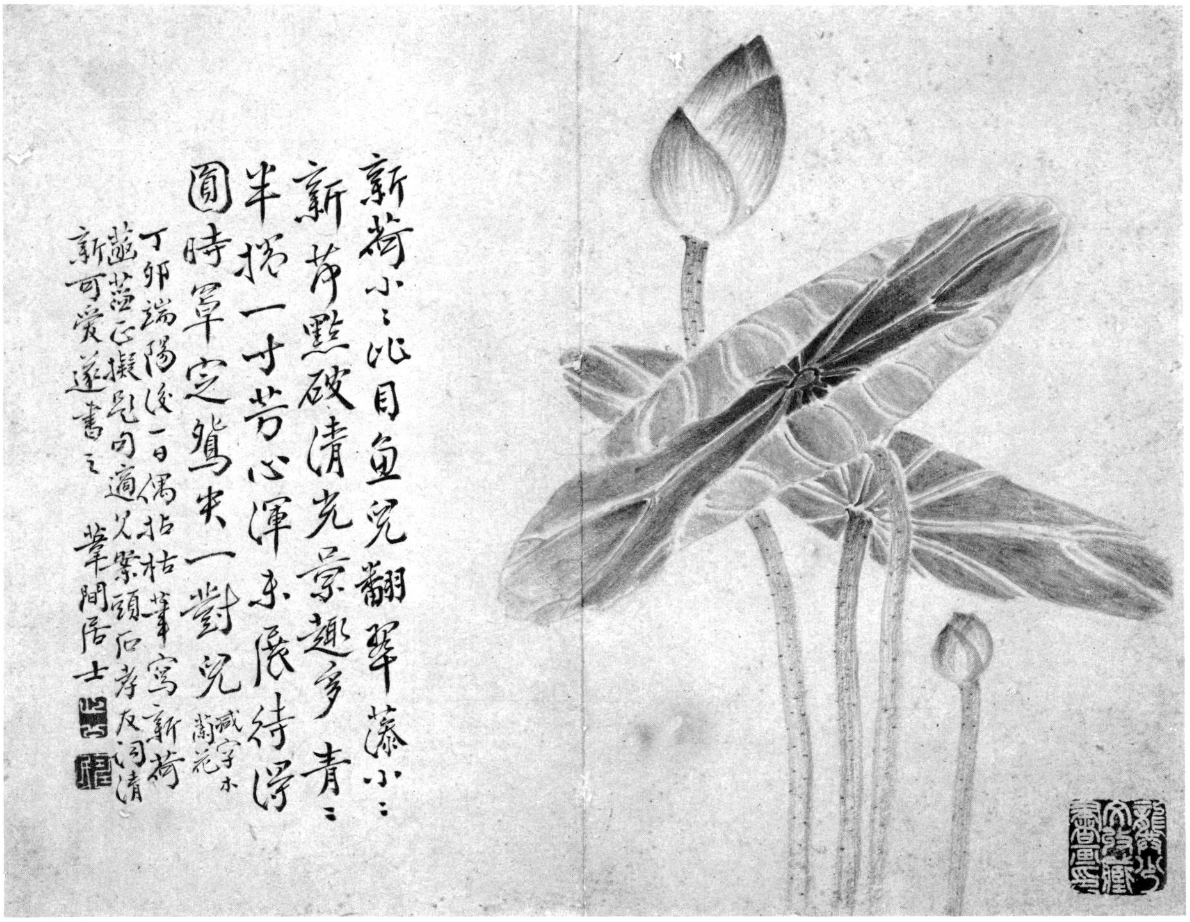

Leaf G, "Lotus"

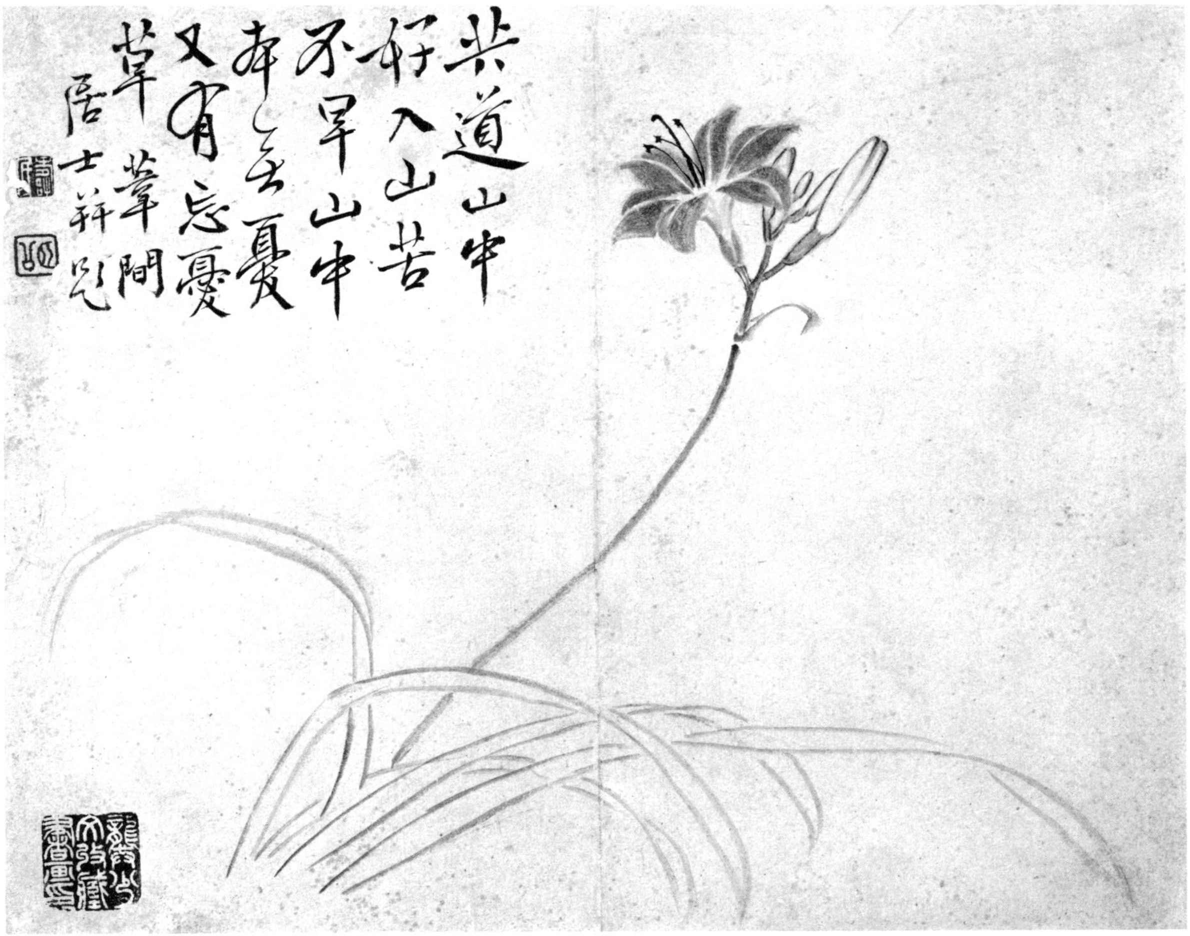

Leaf H, "Day Lily"

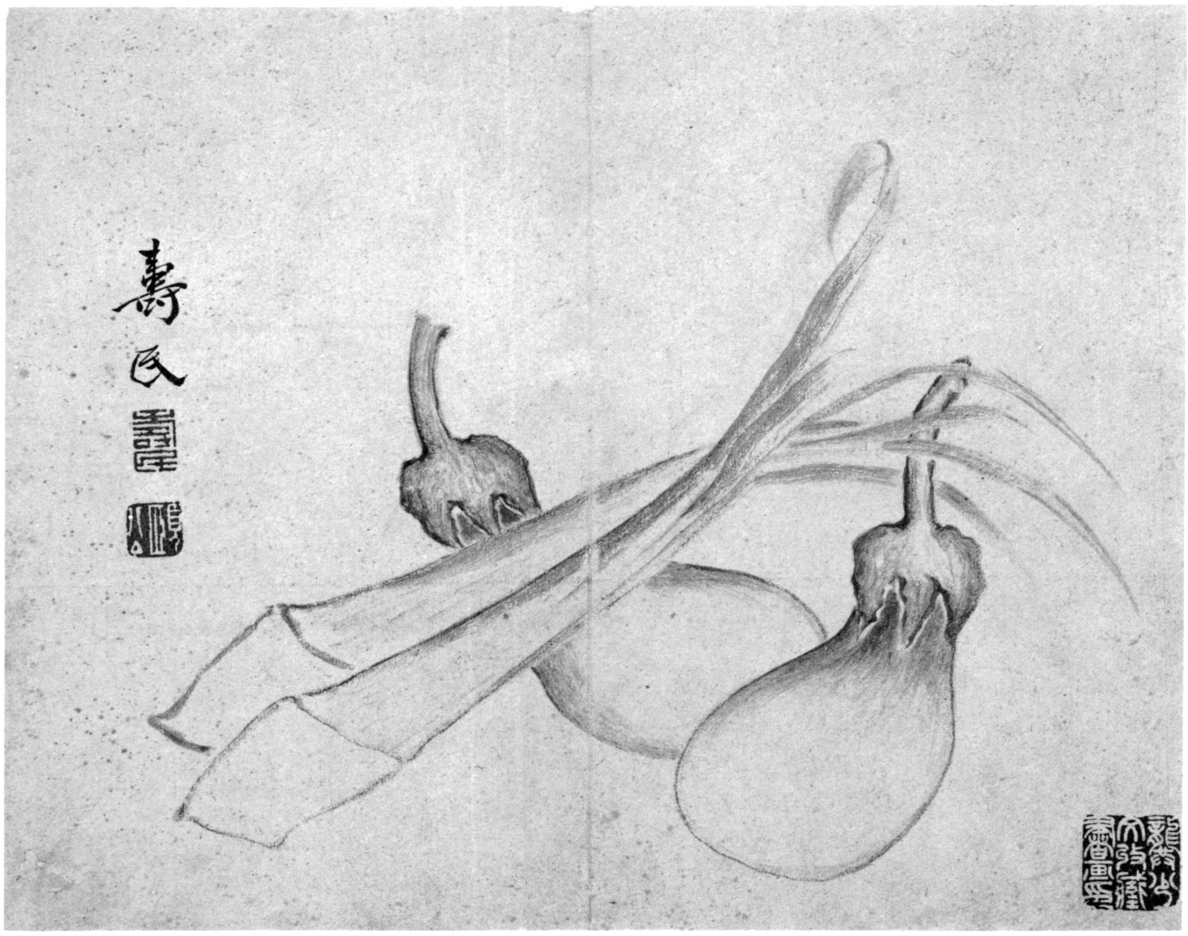


Leaf I, "Eggplants"

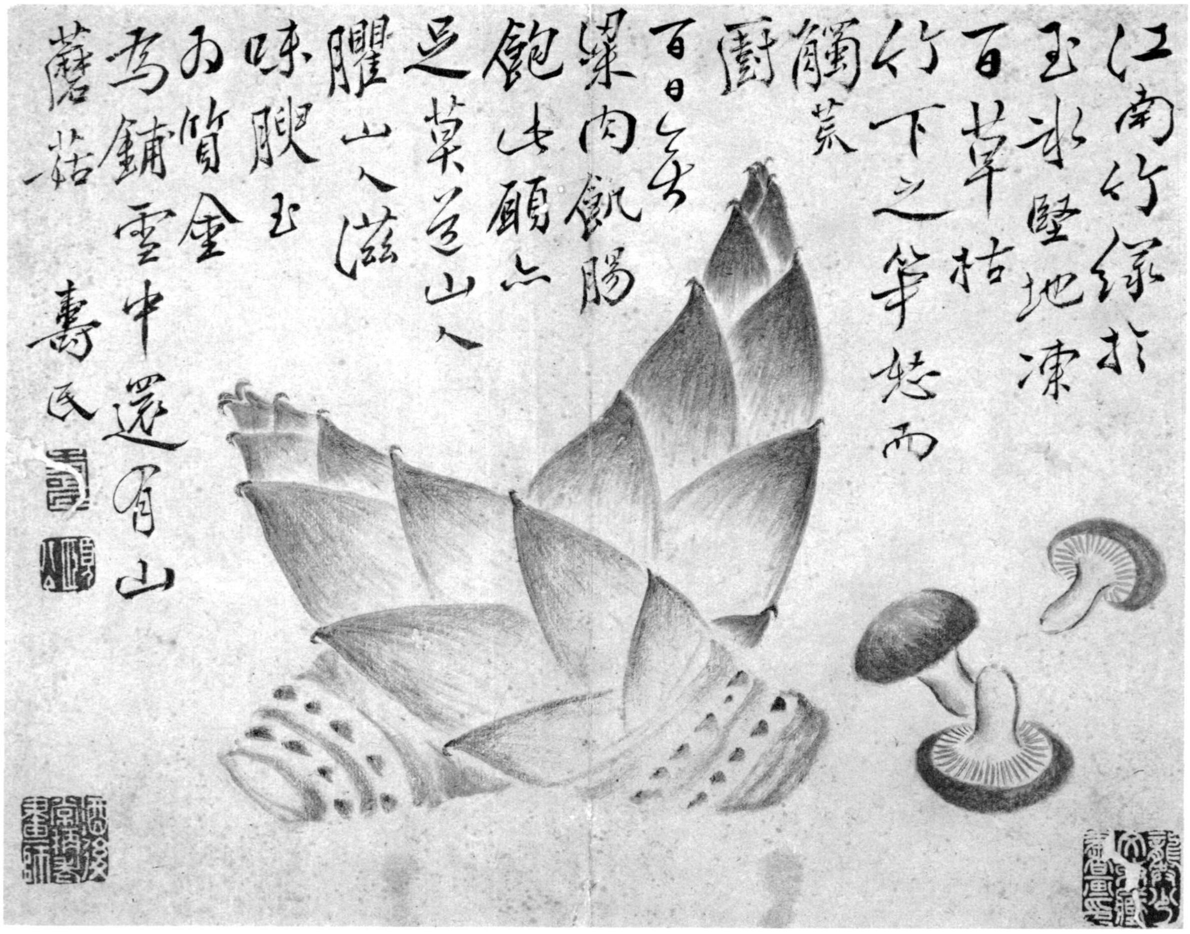


Leaf J, "Bamboo Shoots and Mushrooms"

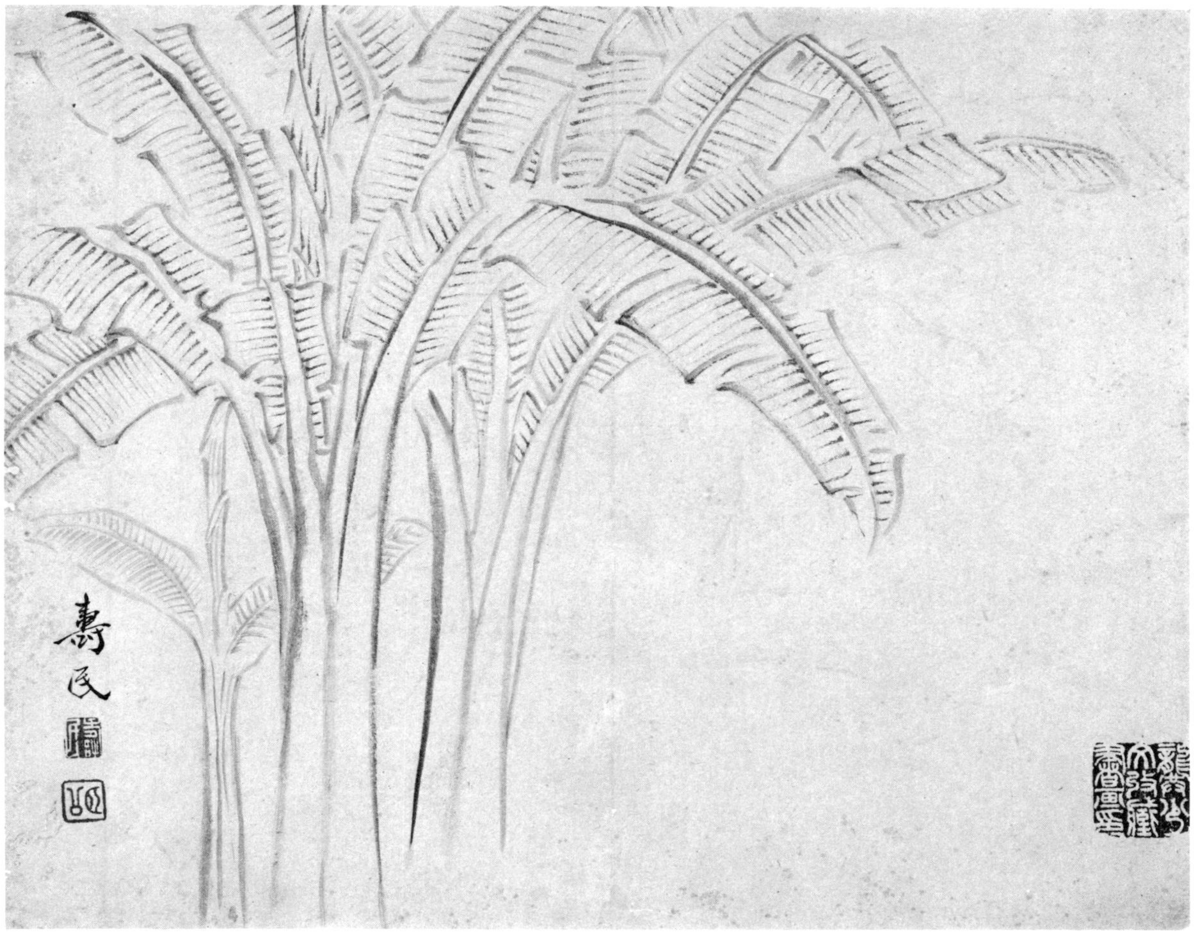


Leaf K, "Banana Trees"

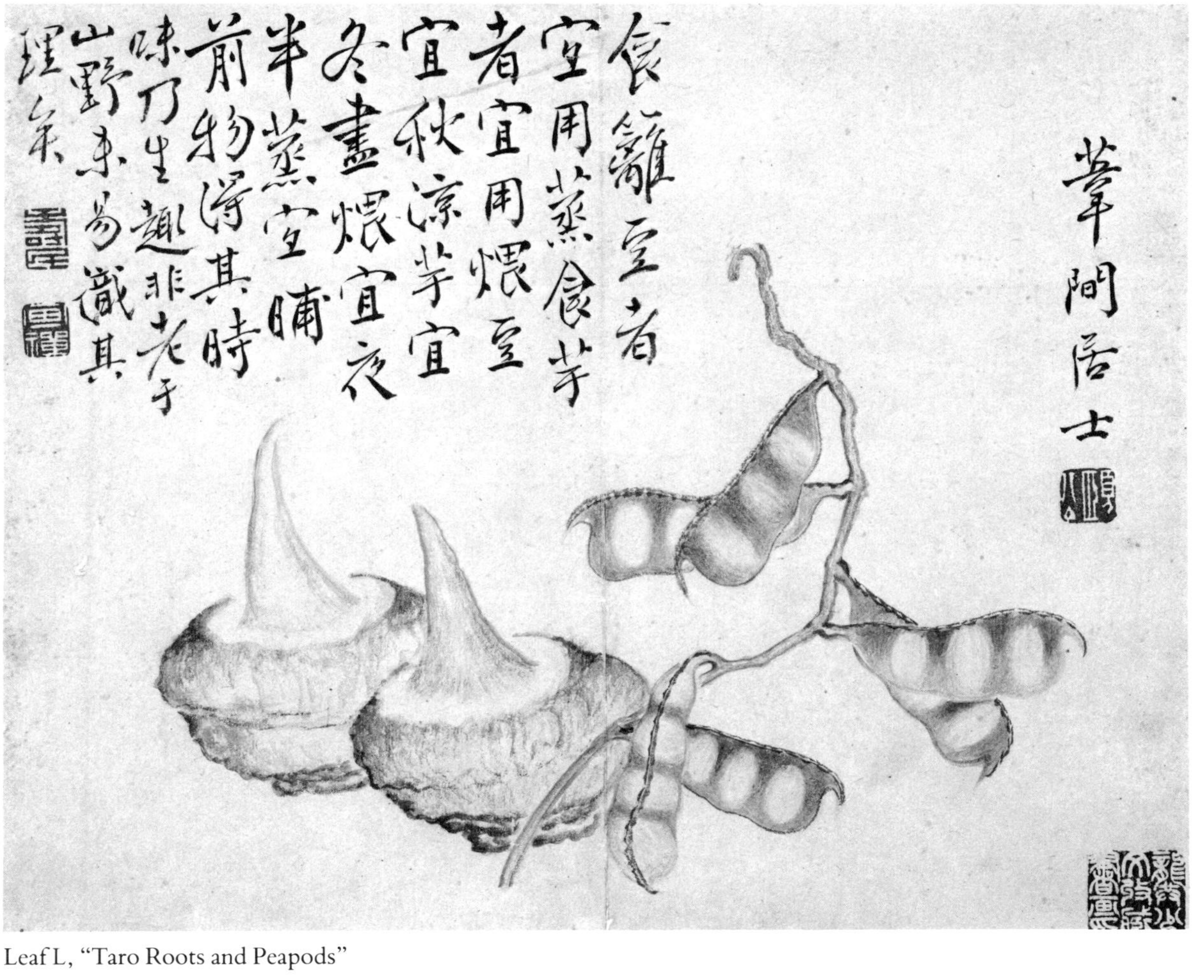


Leaf L, "Taro Roots and Peapods"

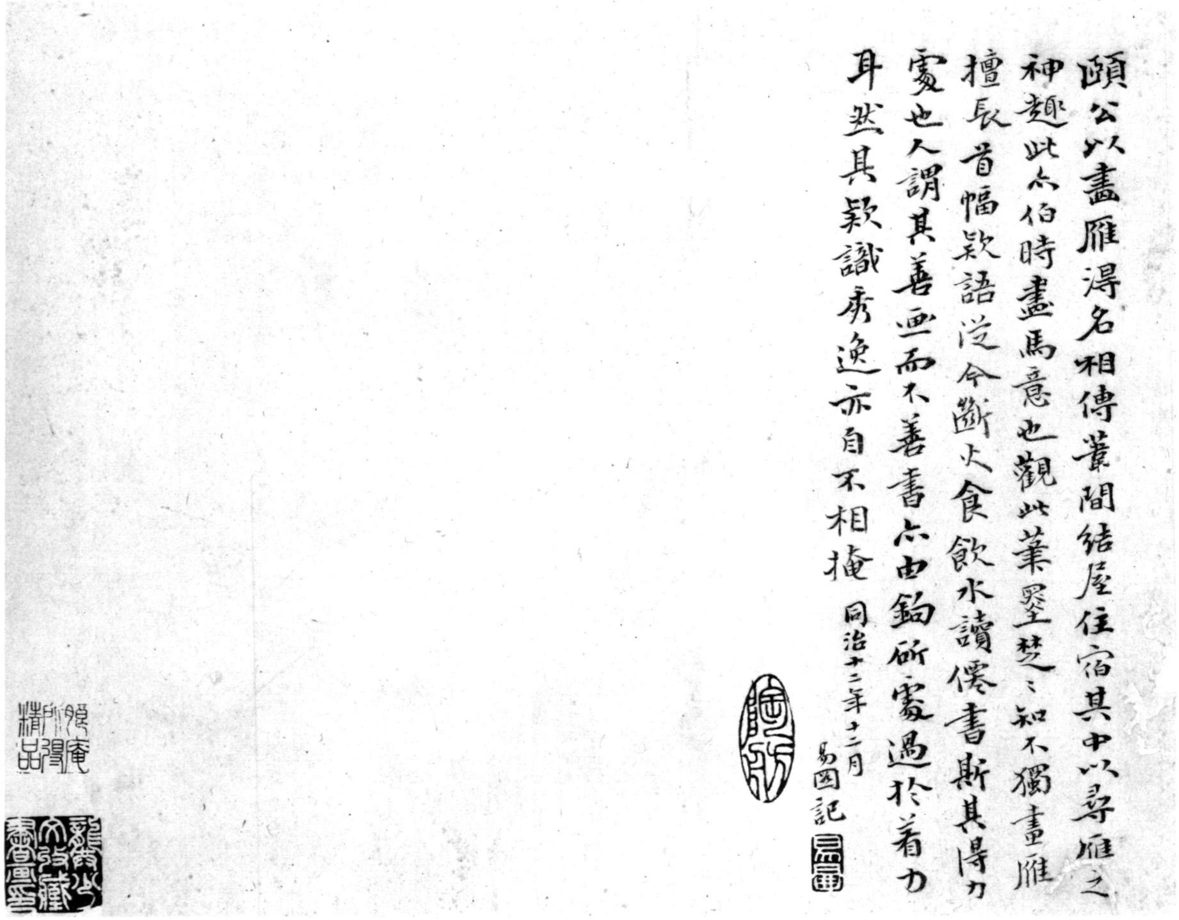
頤公以畫雁得名相傳叢間結屋住宿其中以尋雁之
神趣此亦伯時畫馬意也觀此葉翌楚楚知不獨畫雁
擅長首幅款語從今斷火食飲水讀儒書斯其得力
處也人謂其善畫而不善書亦由鉤所處過於着力
耳然其款識秀逸亦自不相掩 同治十二年十二月 易圖記

Leaf M, colophon by I T'u

# 58 Tai Li (fl. ca. early 18th century)

## *Ink Plum (Mo-mei)*

Dated 1746
Hanging scroll, ink on paper
132.2 x 47.6 cm (4 ft. 4 in. x 18¾ in.)

ARTIST'S INSCRIPTION (9 character regulated verse in 8 lines, followed by a 49 character note, in 4 columns of running script):

Last night, the west wind bent the tips of a thousand
branches.
And tossed about a small ferry and blew it into the
hollow of a sandbank.
By the deserted bridge, there are only old plums leaning
against the corner of the cold house.
Their tangled fragmentary shadows seem to rub silently
against the window screens.
Half-withered, half-alive, they look like tender mulberry
shoots.
On the verge of blooming yet still closed, numerous buds
hold onto their fragrance.
Even though a painter may have marvelous skill, at this
scene he must withdraw his hand, unable to paint it.
I love the plums' pure fragrance so much that I compose this
poem and laugh at what I've written.

In summer, on the eleventh day of the sixth lunar month in the eleventh year of the Ch'ien-lung era [1746], I copied a poem with lines, each of nine characters, on the painting. The poem was written by a monk at Mount T'ien-mu. I presented the painting to my knowledgeable elder brother, Ling-lao, on his fortieth birthday. From younger brother Tai Li, Shih-p'ing-shan-jen, done at the time I moved my painting studio to Pao-ting Hut, in the northern part of the city.

ARTIST'S SEAL: Tai Li (squat rectangle intaglio).

Edward L. Elliott Family Collection (L34.75)

PUBLISHED: Suzuki Kei, comp., *Chūgoku kaiga sōgō zuroku: daiikkan, Amerika–Kanada hen* (Comprehensive illustrated catalogue of Chinese paintings: volume 1, American and Canadian collections) (Tokyo: University of Tokyo Press, 1982), p. 151, pl. A17–093.

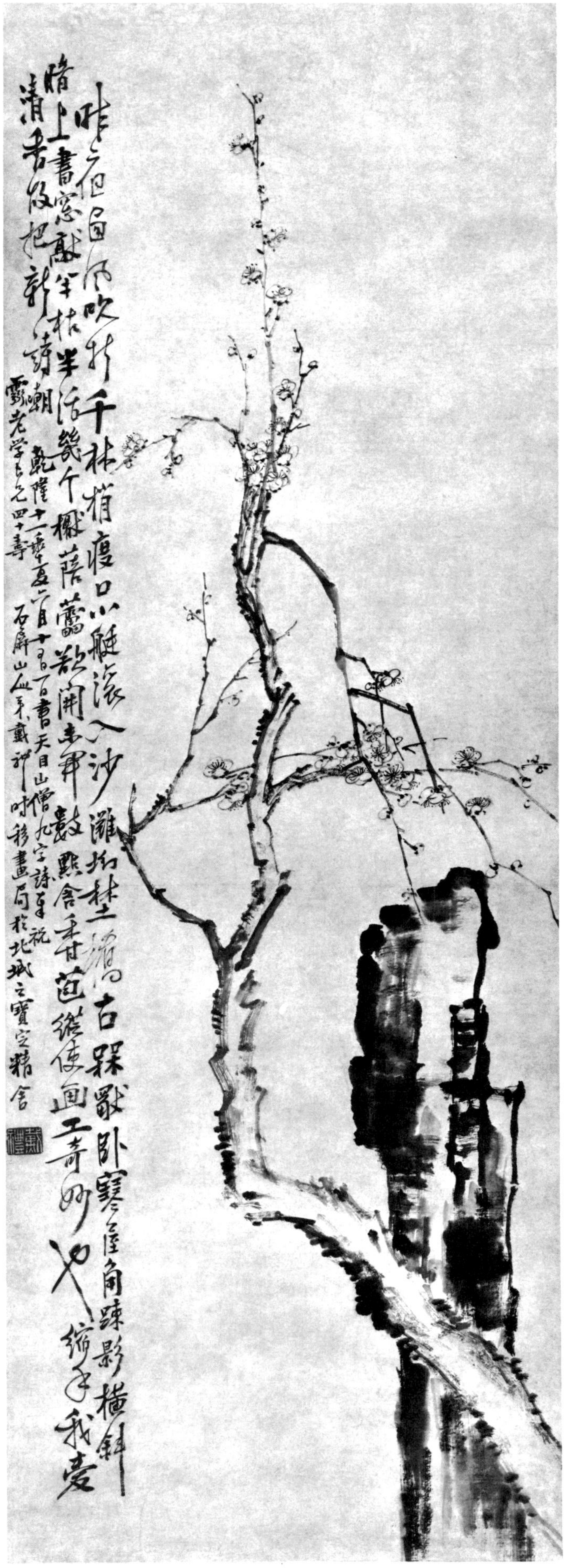

# 59 Chang Yin (1761–1829)

## *Men under Pine Trees (Sung-p'ing tso t'iao)*

Undated
Hanging scroll, ink on paper
137.2 x 39 cm (4 ft. 6 in. x 15³/₈ in.)

ARTIST'S INSCRIPTION (7 character couplet in 2 columns of free-form regular script):

> Sitting cross-legged on the soft grass under the pines,
> We feast our eyes on the mountains south of the river
> just before a rain.

ARTIST'S SIGNATURE: Chang Yin wrote this at the Ch'ing-shui Studio by the river.

ARTIST'S SEAL: Chang Yin yin (square intaglio).

Edward L. Elliott Family Collection (L205.70)

PUBLISHED: Ch'en Jen-t'ao, *Chin-kuei ts'ang-hua chi* (Chinese paintings from the King Kwei [Chin-kuei] collection) (Hong Kong: T'ung-ying, 1956), vol. 1, pl. 66; Ch'en Jen-t'ao, *Chin-kuei ts'ang-hua p'ing-shih* (Annotated catalogue of Chinese paintings from the King Kwei [Chin-kuei] collection) (Hong Kong: T'ung-ying, 1956), vol. 2, pp. 256–57; Suzuki Kei, comp., *Chūgoku kaiga sōgō zuroku: daiikkan, Amerika–Kanada hen* (Comprehensive illustrated catalogue of Chinese paintings: volume 1, American and Canadian collections) (Tokyo: University of Tokyo Press, 1982), p. 127, pl. A17–074.

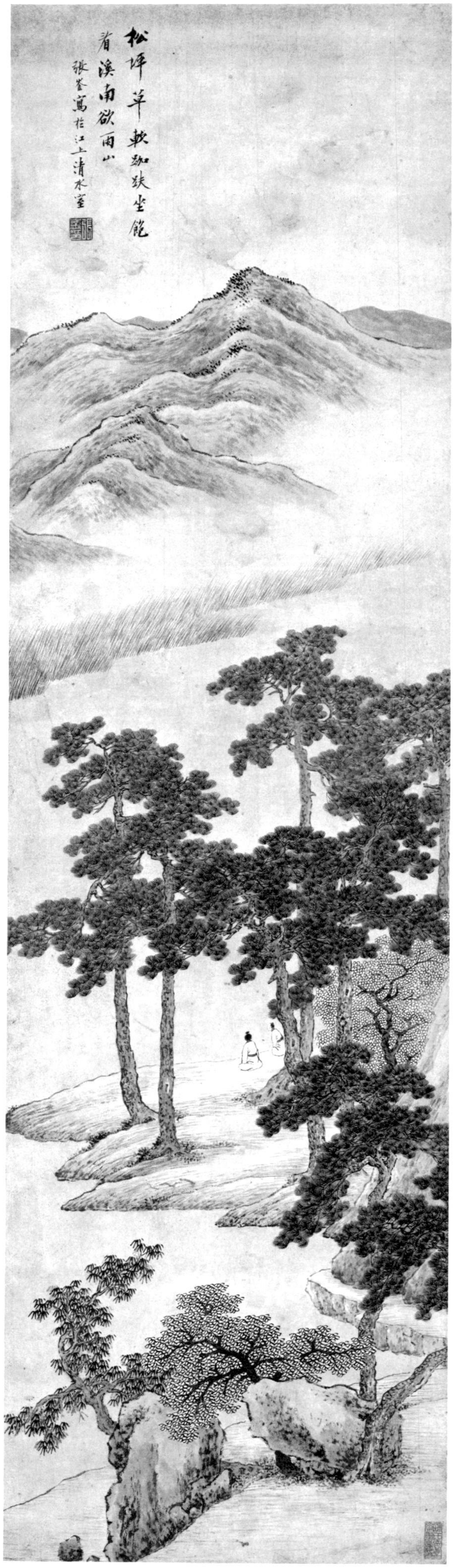

# 60 Ch'ien Tu (1763–1844)

## *Landscape in the Style of Tung Ch'i-ch'ang (Lin Tung Ch'i-ch'ang Wan-luan ts'ao-t'ang t'u)*

Dated 1803
Hanging scroll, ink on paper
106.8 x 51.0 cm (3 ft. 6 in. x 20 in.)

ARTIST'S INSCRIPTION (prose, 11 characters in 2 columns of regular script; lower left): Painted in the third lunar month of the *kuei-hai* year [1803], for my venerable senior, Shao-sung.

ARTIST'S SIGNATURE: Ch'ien Tu from Ch'ien-t'ang [in Chekiang province] made this.

ARTIST'S SEALS: Ch'ien Tu (square intaglio); Shu-mei (square relief).

ARTIST'S TRANSCRIPTIONS (3 inscriptions composed by Tung Ch'i-ch'ang; upper edge):

1. Prose, 27 characters in 4 columns of running script: "Cozy Thatched Hut" ["Wan-luan ts'ao-t'ang t'u"]. In the tenth lunar month of the *ting-yu* year [1597] I returned home from north of the Yangtze River and visited Chung-ch'un [Ch'en Chi-ju; 1558–1639] at the Tu-shu-t'ai [Studio] at K'un-shan [in Kiangsu province]. There I made this painting as a farewell present for him. Signature: Tung Ch'i-ch'ang.
2. Prose, 41 characters in 5 columns of running script: At the winter solstice of the same year, Chung-ch'un brought this painting with him when he visited me. He insisted that I color the painting. I had, by chance, obtained Li Ch'eng's [919–967] *Remote Temple in Misty Mountains* [*Yen-juan hsiao-shih*], painted in the blue and green style, and Kuo Ho-yang's [Kuo Hsi; ca. 1010–ca. 1090] handscroll *Autumn Clearing among Streams and Mountains* [*Hsi-shan ch'iu chi*]. All day long we sighed and enjoyed the paintings with admiration. Signature: Ch'i-ch'ang recorded this.
3. Prose, 24 characters in 2 columns of running script: Since I have seen the paintings by Li Ch'eng and Kuo Hsi, I no longer want to color this painting. The painting by Mi Yüan-chang [Mi Fu; 1052–1107] of the T'ang emperor Wen-huang [Hsüan-tsung; r. 712–56] was so marvelous that it discouraged other painters. The same is true now. Signature: Hsüan-tsai, again, made this record.

ARTIST'S TRANSCRIPTIONS: 20 poems attributed to Emperor Ch'ing Kao-tsung (r. 1736–95). Fourteen of the poems are on the painting, 5 are on a separate paper attached to the top, and 1 is on another sheet of paper attached to the bottom.

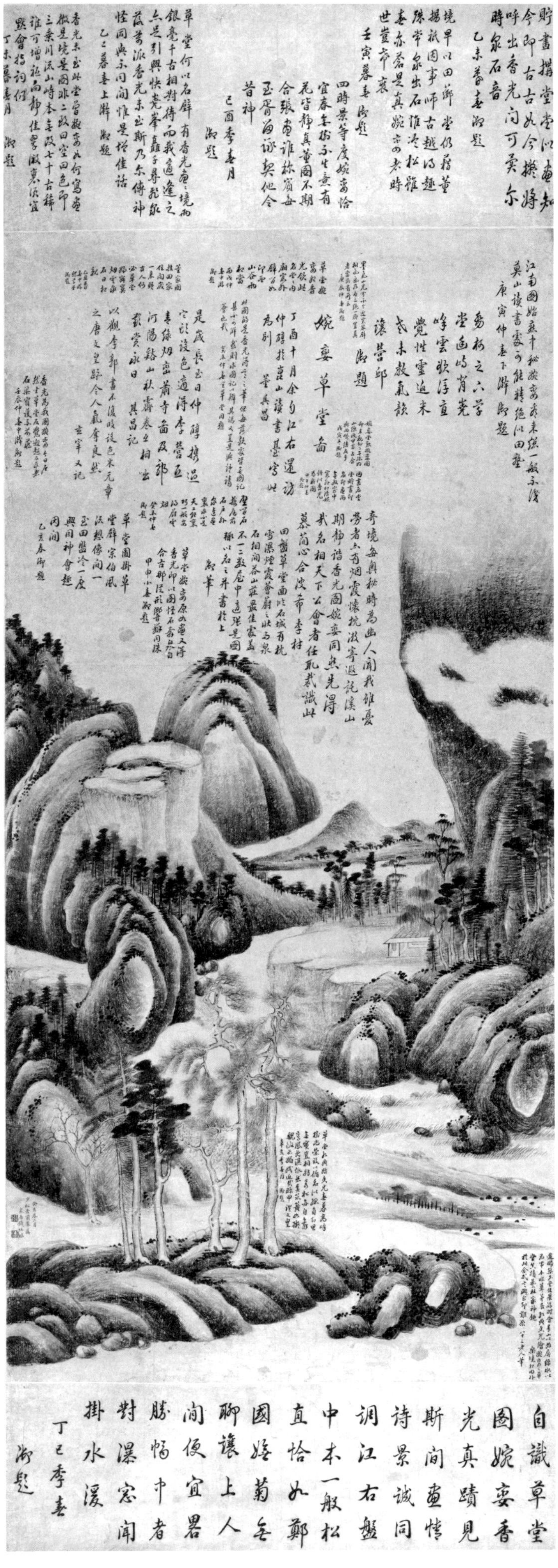

COLLECTORS' SEALS:

1. Fang Meng-yüan (1815–1889): Ts'eng tsai Fang Meng-yüan chia (square relief; lower left).
2. Shen Chung-li (dates unknown): [ ] [ ] Shen Chung-li chien-ts'ang shu-hua yin (rectangle intaglio; lower left).
3. Unidentified owner: T'ien-sheng wo-ts'ai pi yu yung (squat rectangle relief; lower left).

Edward L. Elliott Family Collection (L206.70)

PUBLISHED: Suzuki Kei, comp., *Chūgoku kaiga sōgō zuroku: daiikkan, Amerika–Kanada hen* (Comprehensive illustrated catalogue of Chinese paintings: volume 1, American and Canadian collections) (Tokyo: University of Tokyo Press, 1982), p. 127, pl. A17–017.

# 61 Ch'ien Tu (1763–1844)

## *Boat Returning Home (Ho-hu kuei-chuo)*

Dated 1815
Hanging scroll, ink and color on paper
119.8 x 29.0 cm (3 ft. 11 1/8 in. x 11 3/8 in.)

ARTIST'S INSCRIPTIONS:

1. Prose, 32 characters in 4 columns of regular script (upper right, painting): "Returning Boat on Crane Lake." Master Wu-chuang lived for a time at Wei-t'ang [in Chekiang province] and often missed his hometown. So he asked me to make this painting to illustrate his recollections.
2. 7 character verse in 16 lines, followed by a 51 character note, in 11 columns of free-form regular script (upper left, silk mounting above painting).

ARTIST'S SIGNATURES: Ch'ien Shu-mei [Ch'ien Tu] inscribed this on the fifteenth day of the eighth lunar month in the autumn of the *i-hai* year [1815] (1st inscription); Ch'ien Shu-mei blew on his hands to warm them and inscribed this (2nd inscription).

ARTIST'S SEALS: Shu-mei (square relief); Hu-kung (square intaglio); Ch'ien Shu-mei (square relief).

LABEL by Chiao-hsüeh (late 18th–early 19th century; separate strip of paper, upper right): 5 characters in 1 column of clerical script: "Returning Boat on Crane Lake." Wu-chuang asked Chiao-hsüeh to write this label. Seal: [ ] [ ] ssu-yin (square intaglio).

COLOPHONS (on silk mounting, clockwise):

1. Chang Liu (ca. late 18th–early 19th century): 7 character verse in 16 lines, followed by a 6 character note, in 10 columns of running script. Signature: Old Ginger, Chang Liu, wrote this. Seal: Lao-chiang (tall rectangle intaglio).
2. Chiang Ch'ing (ca. late 18th century–early 19th century): 7 character verse in 16 lines, followed by a 20 character note, in 5 columns of running script. Signature: Manuscript of Yü-ch'u-shan-min, Chiang Ch'ing. Seals: Chiang Ch'ing ssu yin (square intaglio); Yü-ch'u-shan-min (square intaglio).
3. Kuo Lin (1767–1831): 7 character verse in 16 lines, followed by an 8 character note, in 4 columns of running script. Signature: P'ing-chia, Kuo Lin. Seals: Ch'en Lin ssu yin (square intaglio); Ling-fen-kuan-chu (square relief).
4. Ch'en Hung-shou (1768–1822): 7 character verse in 16 lines, followed by an 11 character note, in 23 columns of running script. Signature: Man-sheng, Hung-shou, wrote this. Seals: Hung-shou (square intaglio); Man-sheng (square intaglio).
5. Chiang Ti-sen (ca. late 18th–early 19th century): 7 character verse in 16 lines, followed by a 5 character note, in 7 columns of regular script. Signature: Kuo-yin, Chiang

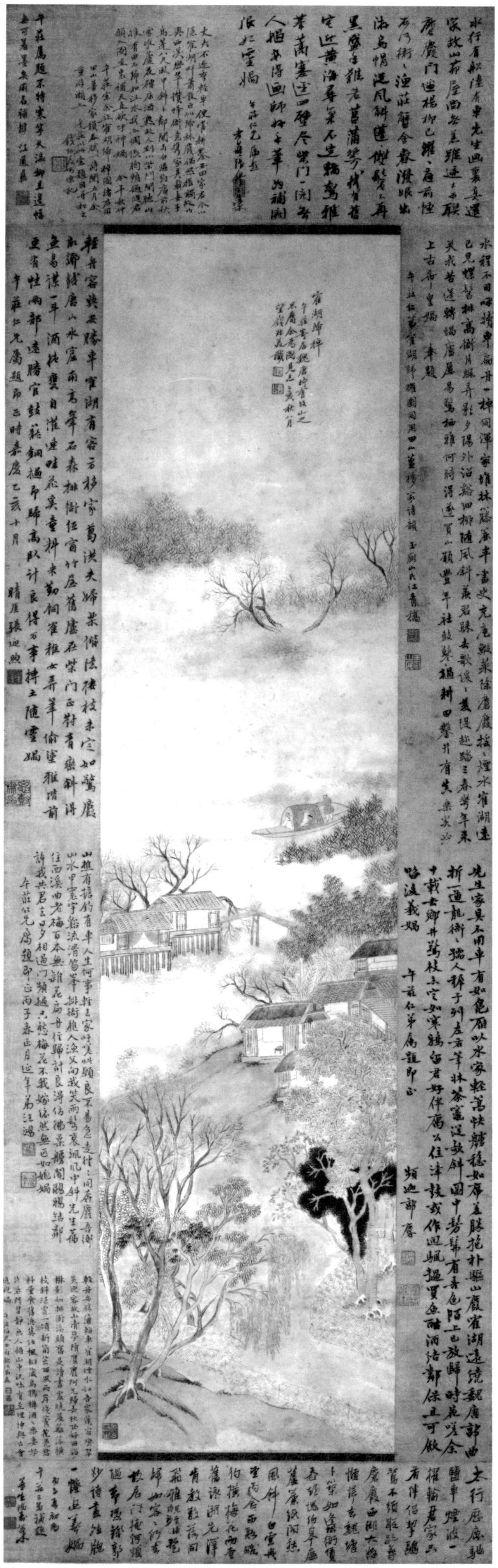

Ti-sen. Seals: Yüeh Sen (square relief); Chiang P'ei shih (square, half relief, half intaglio).

6. Wang Hung (ca. late 18th–early 19th century): 7 character verse in 16 lines, followed by an 8 character note, in 5 columns of running script. Signature: In the first lunar month, in the spring of the *ping-tzu* year [1816], Yen-nien, his junior, Wang Hung inscribed this. Seals: Hung (square intaglio); Yen-nien (square relief).
7. Chang Ying-hsü (ca. late 18th–early 19th century): 7 character verse in 16 lines, followed by a 15 character note, in 5 columns of running script. Signature: In the tenth lunar month of the *i-hai* year of the Chia-ching era [1815], Ch'ing-yai, Chang Ying-hsü, inscribed this. Seals: Ch'ing-yai (square intaglio); Ssu-shu-chai yin (square relief).
8. Chiang Feng-i (ca. late 18th–early 19th century): prose, 23 characters in 2 columns of free-form regular script. Signature: Chiang Feng-i. Seal: Chiang Feng-i (square relief).

COLLECTOR'S SEAL: Unidentified owner: Yüan-su hsien-sheng (square, half relief, half intaglio; lower left, painting).

Gift of Mrs. Edward L. Elliott (80–42)

PUBLISHED: Suzuki Kei, comp., *Chūgoku kaiga sōgō zuroku: daiikkan, Amerika–Kanada hen* (Comprehensive illustrated catalogue of Chinese paintings: volume 1, American and Canadian collections) (Tokyo: University of Tokyo Press, 1982), p. 127, pl. A17–020.

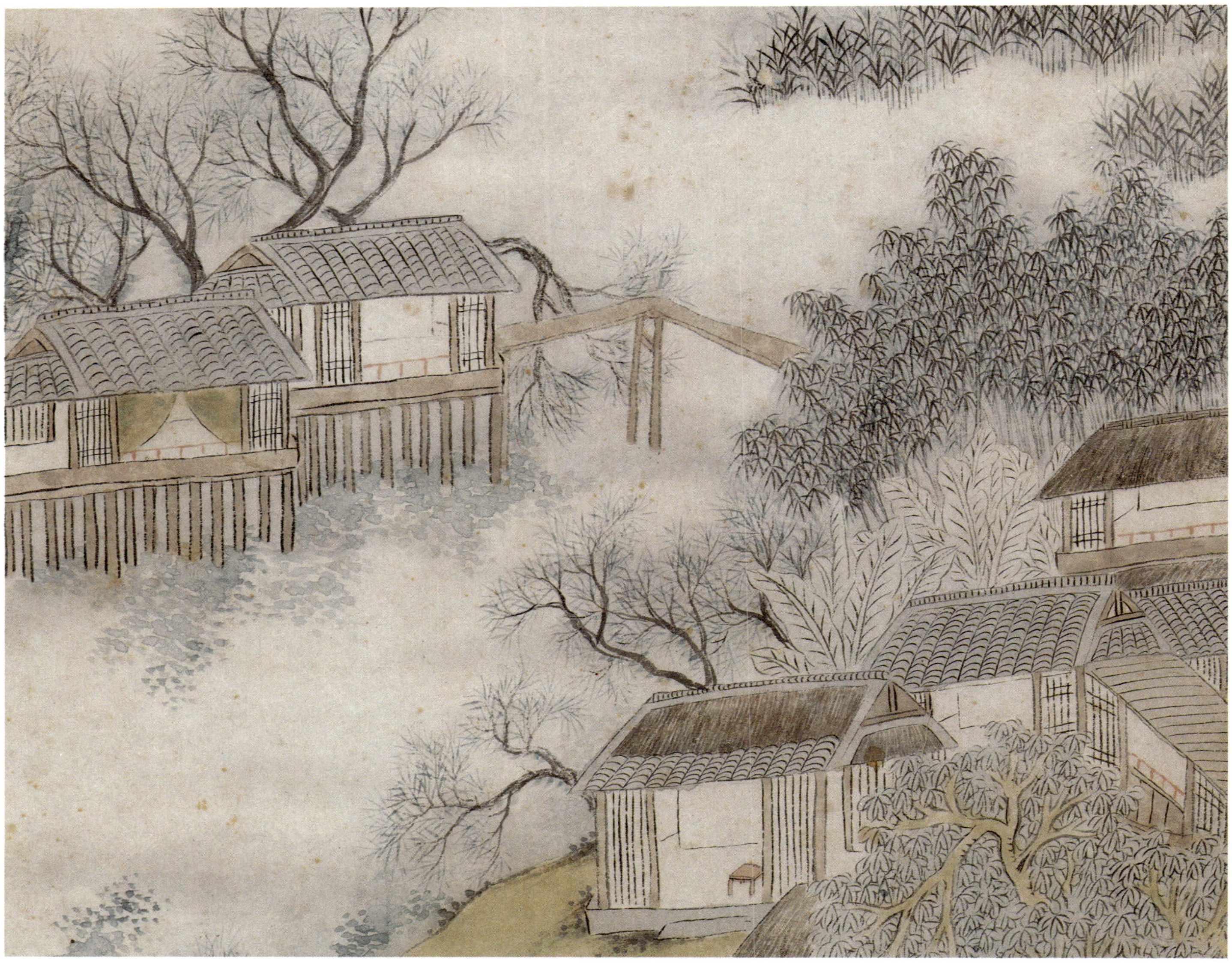

## 62 Tseng Yen-tung (ca. late 18th–early 19th century)

*Six Crabs (Liu-chia-ling-fei shang-sheng)*

Undated
Hanging scroll, ink on paper
68.0 x 28.0 cm (26³/4 x 11 in.)

ARTIST'S INSCRIPTION (prose, 6 characters in 1 column of cursive script): The *Liu-chia-ling-fei* [*Scripture*], the "Great Vehicle" [of Taoism].

ARTIST'S SIGNATURE: Ch'i-tao-shih made this in the Wen-chieh Studio.

ARTIST'S SEALS: Yen-tung (square intaglio); Tseng shih (square relief); Ts'ao-ni chih chung (tall rectangle relief); Tsun-ch'ien feng-wei (square intaglio).

Edward L. Elliott Family Collection (L209.70)

PUBLISHED: Suzuki Kei, comp., *Chūgoku kaiga sōgō zuroku: daiikkan, Amerika–Kanada hen* (Comprehensive illustrated catalogue of Chinese paintings: volume 1, American and Canadian collections) (Tokyo: University of Tokyo Press, 1982), p. 127, pl. A17–010.

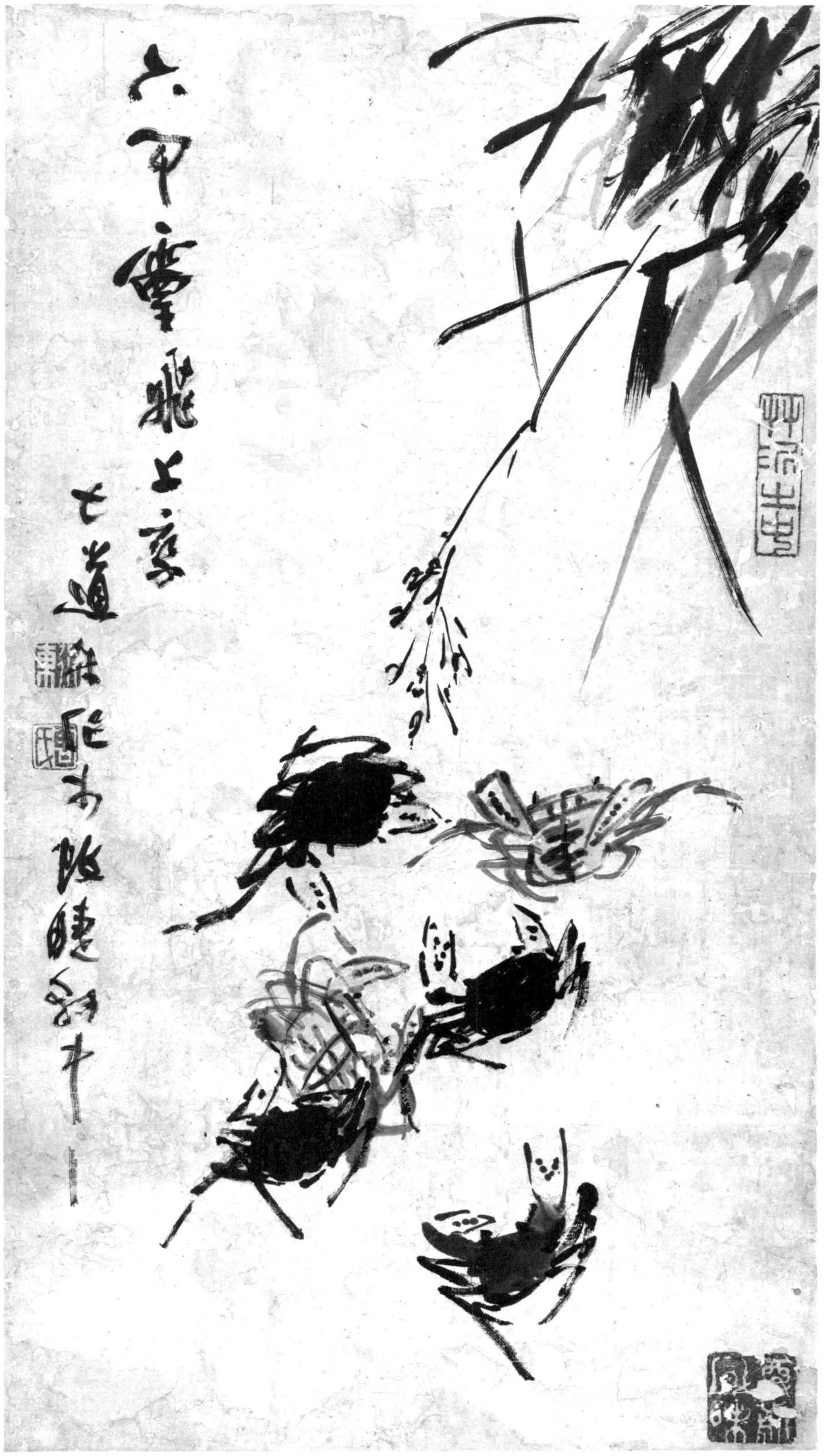

# 63 Tseng Yen-tung (ca. late 18th–early 19th century)

## *Man on a Donkey (Ch'i lü t'u)*

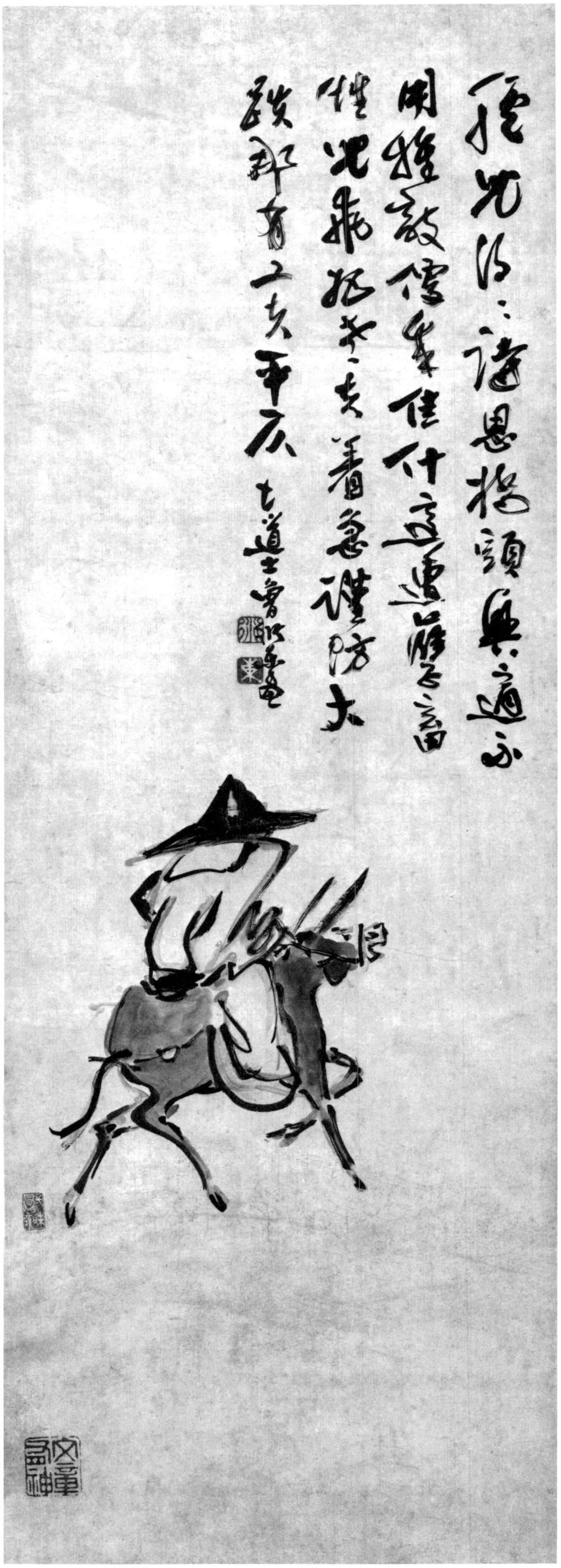

Undated
Hanging scroll, ink and color on paper
102.0 x 36.3 cm (3 ft. 4 1/8 in. x 14 1/4 in.)

ARTIST'S INSCRIPTION (40 characters in 4 columns of running script):

[Riding] a cantering donkey on a bridge evokes poetic inspiration.
If the inspiration is just right, then an excellent poem will result, almost without effort.
Nevertheless this obstinate beast with intractable character makes me anxious.
I must take care to prevent a fall,
So how can I have time to concentrate on rhyming?

ARTIST'S SIGNATURE: Ch'i-tao-shih, Tseng Yen-tung, painted this.

ARTIST'S SEALS: Yen-tung (square, half relief, half intaglio); I-wei feng-liu (tall rectangle intaglio); Wen-chang yu-shen (square relief).

Edward L. Elliott Family Collection (L113.71)

PUBLISHED: Suzuki Kei, comp., *Chūgoku kaiga sōgō zuroku: daiikkan, Amerika–Kanada hen* (Comprehensive illustrated catalogue of Chinese paintings: volume 1, American and Canadian collections) (Tokyo: University of Tokyo Press, 1982), p. 129, pl. A17–036.

# 64 Jen I (1840–1896)

## *Hens and Rocks (Chi-ch'ün hu-shih)*

Dated 1872
Hanging scroll, ink and color on paper
148.4 x 40.3 cm (4 ft. 10 1/2 in. x 15 7/8 in.)

ARTIST'S SIGNATURE: In the first lunar month of the spring of the *jen-shen* year of the T'ung-chih era [1872], Po-nien, Jen I, painted this at Huang-hsieh-p'u [Shanghai].

ARTIST'S SEALS: I yin (square intaglio); Jen Po-nien (square relief).

Edward L. Elliott Family Collection (L26.72)

Unpublished.

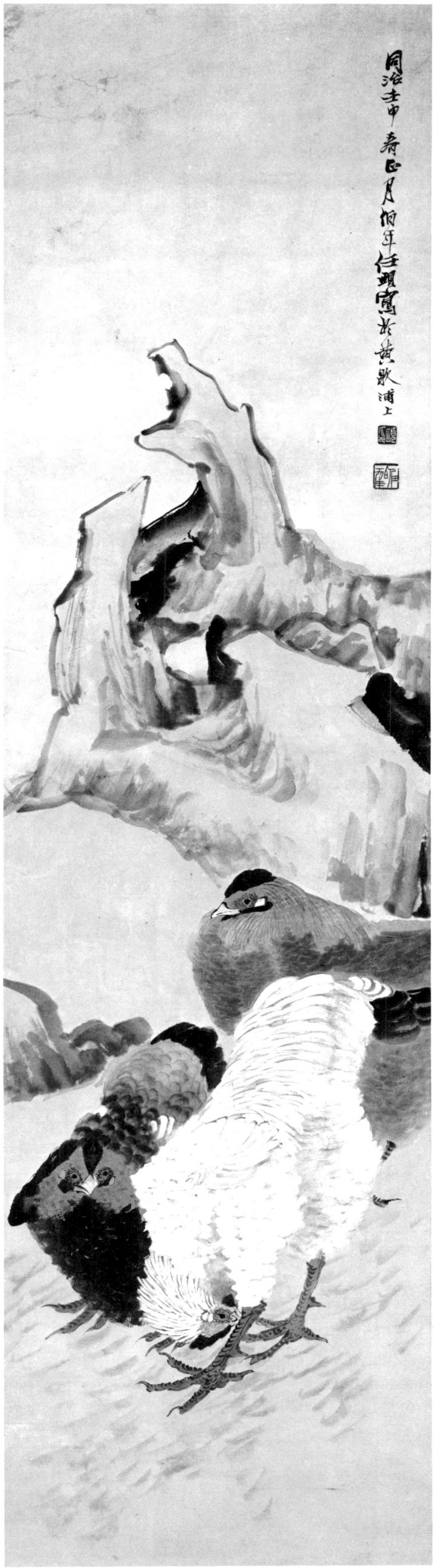

# 65 Jen I (1840–1896)

## *Immortal with a Toad (Liu Hai hsien)*

Dated 1891
Hanging scroll, ink and color on paper
145.0 x 78.5 cm (4 ft. 11 in. x 30¾ in.)

ARTIST'S SIGNATURE: Jen I wiped away his sweat and painted this in the summer of the *hsin-mao* year of the Kuang-hsü era [1891].

ARTIST'S SEAL: Jen Po-nien (square intaglio).

Edward L. Elliott Family Collection (L211.70)

Unpublished.

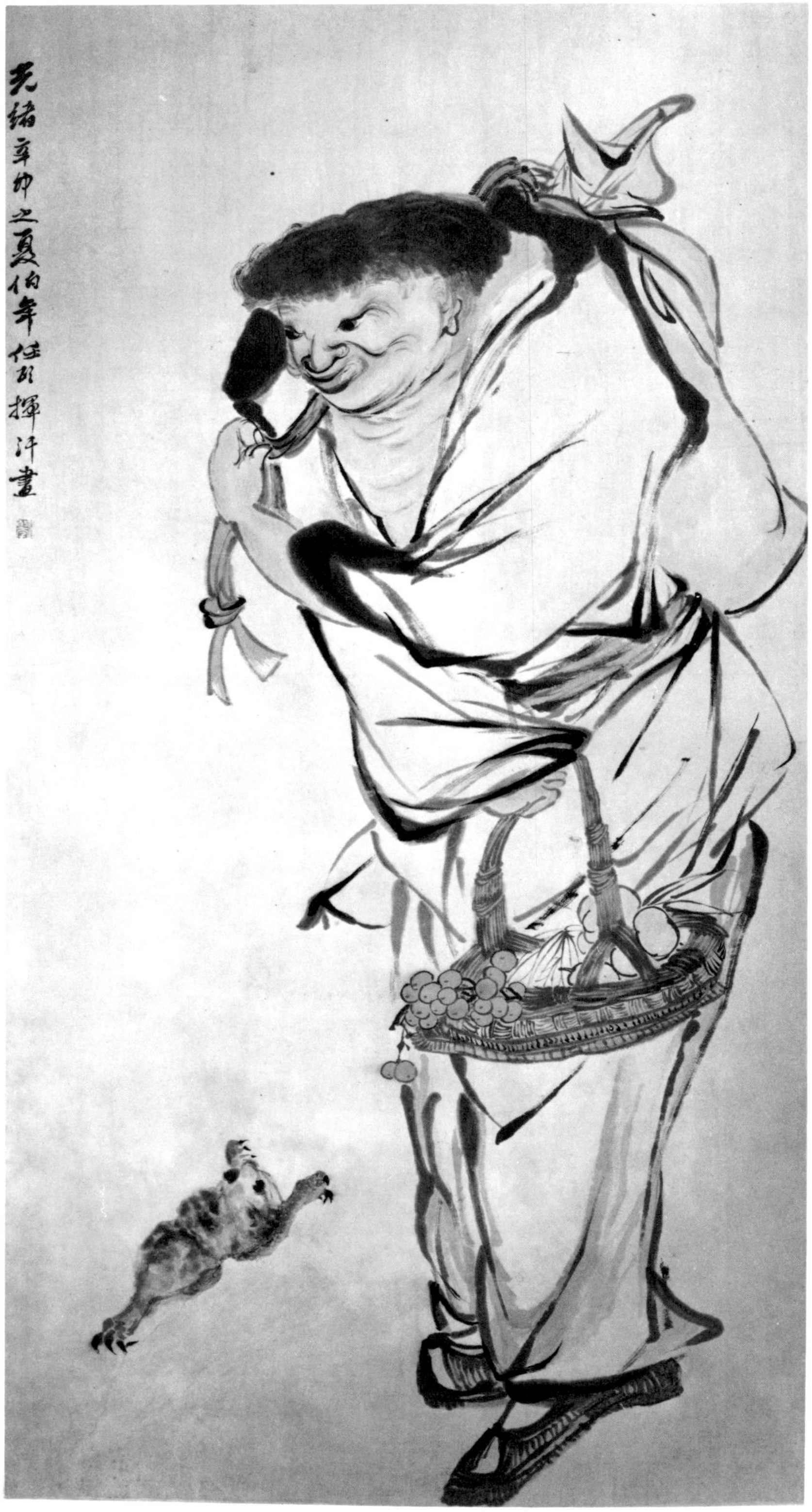

# 66 Wu Ch'ang-shih (1844–1927)

## *Vegetables (Ts'ai-ken t'u)*

Dated 1915
Hanging scroll, ink and color on paper
128.1 x 32.5 cm (4 ft. 2 1/2 in. x 12 3/4 in.)

ARTIST'S INSCRIPTIONS (from top to bottom):

1. 5 character couplet, followed by 7 character verse in 6 lines, in 6 columns of running script:

When autumn frost penetrates into the vegetables' roots
they become juicy.
If you often eat the roots you will [not succumb to]
starvation.
At home I used to grow a plot of winter vegetables;
So now as I paint them I think of my old town.
My sharp desire for the vegetables wets my brush,
so the colors penetrate into the paper.
The taste of the vegetables is so delicious that I am
driven to write this poem.
How can meat eaters ever understand?

2. 7 character quatrain in 2 columns of running script:

Cheap, fatty pork and lean, stringy meat are often
served at mealtimes.
I sigh over the bitter sour taste which does not
tempt me to eat.
Lamentably, my little Wu-yüan garden may have been hurt
by snow;
Or a plot of juicy vegetables may have been dried
out by the [merciless] wind.

ARTIST'S SIGNATURES: On a snowy day in the *i-mao* year [1915], Wu Ch'ang-shih from An-chi [in Chekiang province] painted this in his seventy-second year [*sui*] (1st inscription); Fou signed this again (2nd inscription).

ARTIST'S SEALS: Ch'ang-shih (square intaglio); Chün-ch'ing chih yin (square relief); Wu Ch'ang-shih (square relief).

Edward L. Elliott Family Collection (L115.71)

Unpublished.

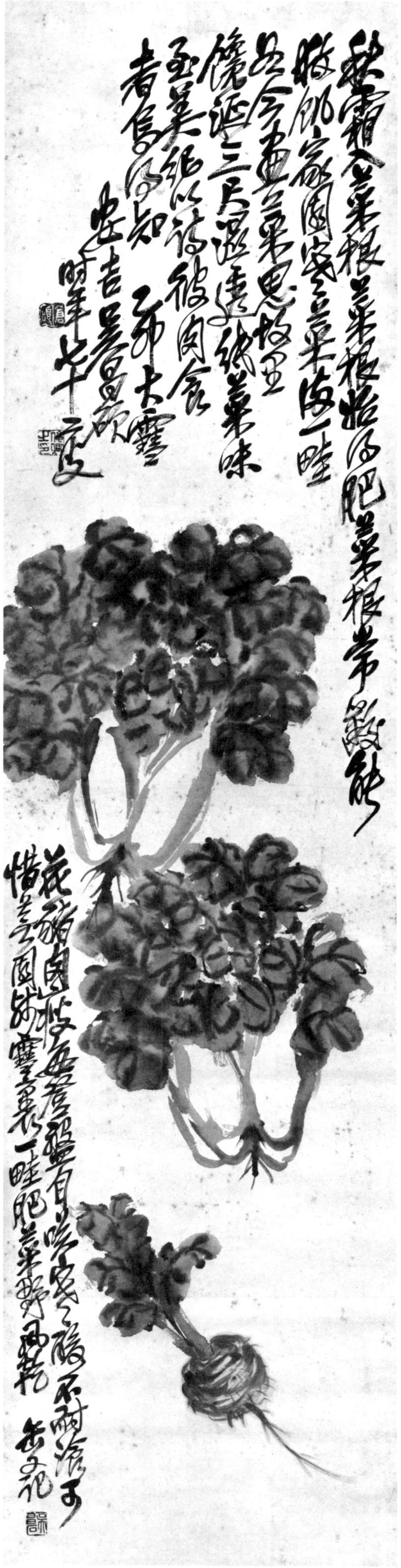

# 67 Wu Ch'ang-shih (1844–1927)

## *Landscape (Shan-shui)*

Dated 1921
Hanging scroll, ink on paper
136.5 x 37.2 cm (4 ft. 5¾ in. x 14⅝ in.)

ARTIST'S INSCRIPTION (7 character quatrain in 3 columns of running script):

> The willow tree gently swaying back and forth sweeps
> the distant sandbank.
> The east wind sends my boat to a pavilion across the river.
> Do you know where the sound of the bell comes from
> at dusk?
> There is nothing but a vast patch of green on the distant
> mountain beyond the river.

ARTIST'S SIGNATURE: In the late spring of the *hsin-yu* year [1921], Wu Ch'ang-shih, Lao-fou painted this in his seventy-eighth year [*sui*].

ARTIST'S SEALS: Ch'ang-shih (square intaglio); Pan-jih-ts'un (square relief).

Edward L. Elliott Family Collection (L116.71)

Unpublished.

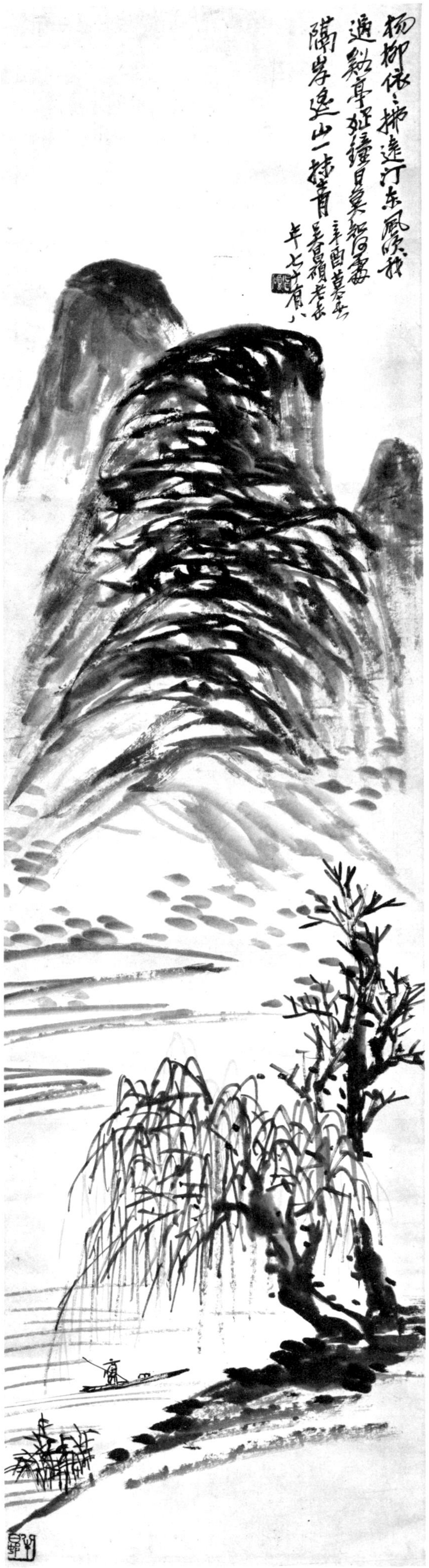

# 68 Wu Ch'ang-shih (1844–1927)

## *Plums and Daffodils (Mei-hua shui-hsien)*

Dated 1923
Hanging scroll, ink and color on paper
137.0 x 34.0 cm (4 ft. 6 in. x $13^{3}/_{8}$ in.)

ARTIST'S INSCRIPTION (5 character quatrain, followed by a 6 character note, in 1 column of running script):

> Bright beauty of Mount Lo-fu [metaphor for plum blossoms],
> Graceful Nymph of the Lo River [metaphor for daffodils]:
> Near a jeweled terrace in bright moonlight,
> They stand side by side above wind-swirled dust.
>
> In the style of Hsi-hsieh-chü-shih [Chin Nung; 1687–1764].

ARTIST'S SIGNATURE: Eighty-year-old man, Wu Ch'ang-shih.

ARTIST'S SEALS: Wu Ch'ang-shih (square relief); Wu Chün chih yin (square intaglio).

Edward L. Elliott Family Collection (L28.72)

Unpublished.

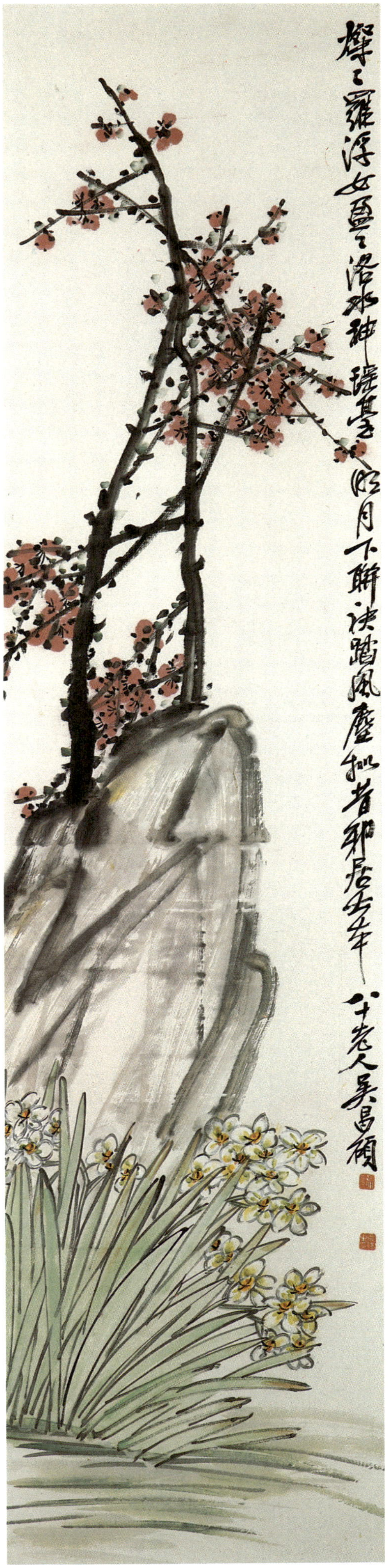

# 69 Feng Tzu-k'ai (1898–1975)

## *The Pine Tree at Your House (Chün chia lao-shu)*

Ca. 1940
Hanging scroll, ink and color on paper
Painting: 55.5 x 39.2 cm (21 7/8 x 15 3/8 in.); calligraphy: 28.2 x 39.2 cm (11 1/8 x 15 3/8 in.)

ARTIST'S INSCRIPTION (7 character couplet, followed by a 6 character note, in 2 columns of running script; upper right, painting):

> At your house it is only the old pine
> That stands when the spring wind comes as if no wind had come at all.
>
> Respectfully submitted to Master Ch'ang-wen for his appraisal.

ARTIST'S SIGNATURE: Tzu-k'ai painted this.

ARTIST'S SEALS: Feng Tzu-k'ai (square intaglio); Yüan-yüan-t'ang hua-yüan (oval relief; lower left, painting).

ARTIST'S COLOPHON (7 character quatrain in 6 columns of running script, on a separate sheet of paper above painting):

> I open the curtain to the west wind in the clearing after the rain
> And leisurely lean against the window of the small pavilion to listen to the singing of the passing nightingales.
> White clouds scud aimlessly back and forth.
> Do not scold the mountain's monks for not welcoming and bidding them farewell.

ARTIST'S SIGNATURE: Tzu-k'ai.

ARTIST'S SEAL: Shih-men Feng shih shu-hua (square intaglio).

Edward L. Elliott Family Collection (L221.70)

Unpublished.

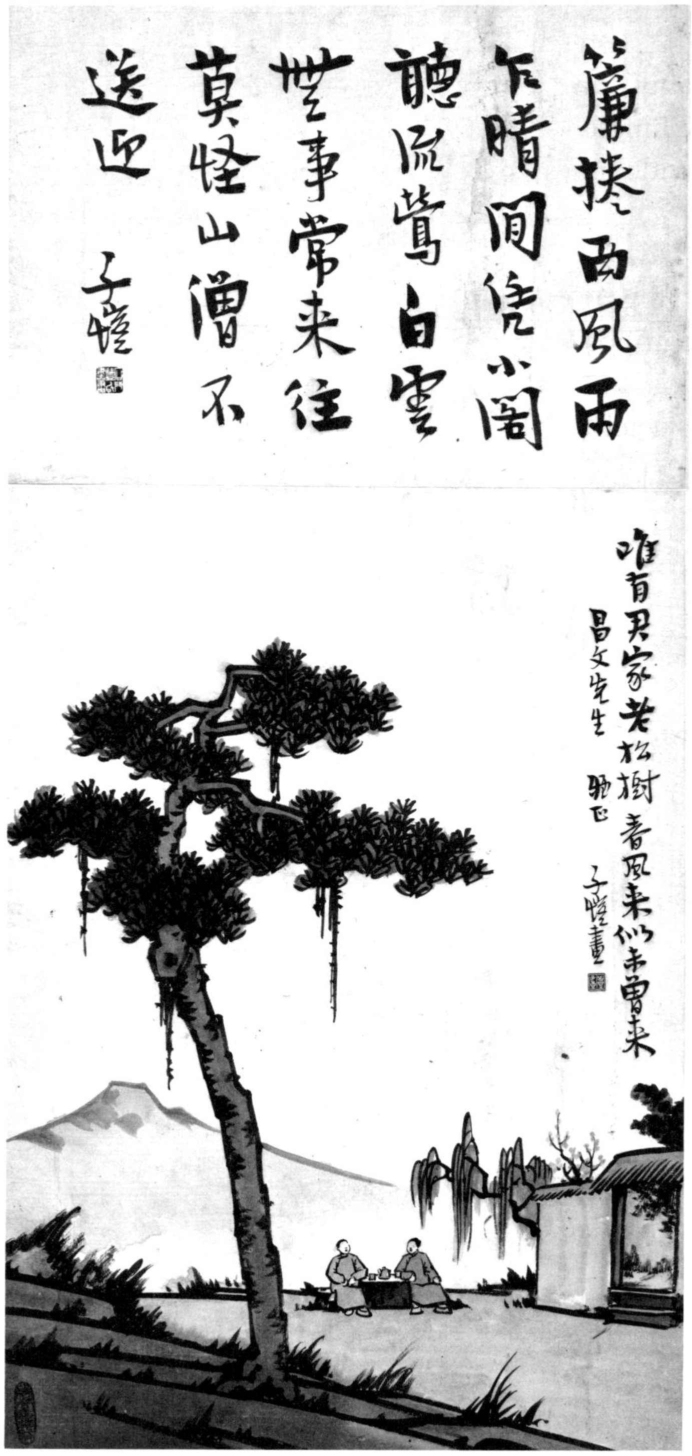

PAINTER, MUSICIAN, AND ESSAYIST, Feng Tzu-k'ai was a prolific and versatile twentieth-century artist. His family owned a dye shop in Shih-men, Chekiang province. When he was seven years old, Feng taught himself painting by tracing copies of painting manuals.[1] At seventeen he entered the First Normal School in Hang-chou and studied under Li Shu-t'ung (1880–1942), a pioneer in bringing Western-style art to China who later became a monk.[2] Under Li's influence Feng Tzu-k'ai became a pious Buddhist and devoted art teacher. He wrote on art and translated enormous compendiums of Chinese, Japanese, and Western literature, painting, and music.[3] In 1921 Feng entered the Kawabata Art School in Tokyo. There he began to draw cartoons in a style influenced by the Japanese artist Takehisa Yumeji (1844–1934). Feng's cartoons are famous for their formal clarity and satirical wit.[4]

Feng Tzu-k'ai painted five basic themes, which he listed in 1941: Modern Illustrations of Classical Verses, (Ku-shih hsin-hua); A Child's World (Erh-t'ung-hsiang); Benevolence (Hu-sheng hua-chi); Images of War (Chan-cheng hsiang); and Mirror of Society (She-hui-hsiang).[5]

Feng's early style reflects the techniques he derived from Western painting through his teacher Li Shu-t'ung and his education at the Kawabata Art School. His interest in adapting Western methods to Chinese subjects led him to concentrate on simple forms, economic brushwork, and contrasts between wide and narrow shapes and between areas of solid and void. In his "modern illustrations of classical verses" made before 1930, the scene is usually framed by lines, with the verse inscriptions as captions outside the frame—a Western treatment of a picture, rather than the traditional Chinese approach, in which the calligraphy is a part of the composition. His calligraphy of the same period is characterized by relaxed compositions and modulated brushstrokes, which reflect Feng's free and lively spirit.

In 1937, during the Sino-Japanese War, Feng Tzu-k'ai and his family left his hometown and fled to Kueichou, in southwest China. Despite the mitigating circumstances, the journey broadened his vision of Chinese landscape and inspired Feng to turn to traditional Chinese painting idioms. To express his new feelings about his native land, he chose subjects that he first encountered in the painting manuals of his childhood. In the landscape sections of his pre-1950 illustrations, Feng now built up mountains with complicated shapes filled with short, assertive texture strokes derived from the *Mustard Seed Garden Painting Manual* (*Chieh-tzu yüan*; 1679). Because of his training in Western painting he was able to suggest a sense of volume and space in his landscapes. The inscriptions on these paintings, written within the picture frame, serve as a part of the composition in the manner of the Chinese literati tradition. In his calligraphy he adopted a square composition and less modulated brushwork than he had used in his early work.

The experiences of the war and the instability of postwar China had a profound effect on Feng. His calligraphy reflected an increasing solemnity and seriousness, and the paintings of his late period exhibit simplified compositions and careful brushwork.

The style of *The Pine Tree at Your House* indicates that it was made between 1930 and 1950, when Feng had returned to Chinese-style compositions and technique, but had not yet acquired the restraint of his later years. The painting shows a conversation between two friends, seated on chairs at the far end of a courtyard. The positioning of the large slanting pine tree on the lower left, the diagonal layout of the small house on the right, and the tiny figures in front of the distant center mountain all serve to define the pictorial space as three-dimensional. The foreground pine is delicately drawn, while the figures in the distance are represented with abbreviated strokes.

"In my paintings," the artist said in an article in 1935, "I like to represent the overall impression of an image and leave out the details. For example, when representing man's features, I simply represent his mouth. It does not mean that man can only eat and speak—it is because the mouth is the most sensitive organ in one's face, the organ that conveys one's feelings."[6]

The topic being discussed by the men in the painting is the pine tree that shelters them. It symbolizes an unconquerable spirit, unmoved by outside changes. The verse inscribed on the painting, which touches upon this sentiment, reflects a placid state of mind and spirit. The mood of the inscription suggests a date for the painting in the early 1940s, after Feng Tzu-k'ai had settled in the Kueichou and Chungking areas. Another painting, also called *The Pine Tree at Your House*, has an identical verse and similar composition and brushwork, and is dated to 1940,[7] which supports an approximate date for the scroll in the early 1940s.

PAO-CHEN CH'EN

NOTES

1. Feng Tzu-k'ai, "Hsüeh hua hui-i" (Recollections of how I learned painting), in *Feng Tzu-k'ai wen-chi* (The collected writings of Feng Tzu-k'ai) (Peking: Jen-min wen-hsüeh ch'u-pan-she, 1957), pp. 95–100.
2. Feng Tzu-k'ai, "Huai Li Shu-t'ung hsien-sheng" (In memory of my teacher Li Shu-t'ung), in *Feng Tzu-k'ai wen-chi*, pp. 188–94.
3. For a bibliography of Feng's writings, see P'an Wen-yen, ed., *Feng Tzu-k'ai hsien-sheng nien-piao* (The chronological biography of Feng Tzu-k'ai) (Singapore: Yen-po-yüan, 1979); Joseph Schyns et al., *1500 Modern Chinese Novels and Plays* (Peking: Catholic University, 1948), p. 34, no. 56; pp. 178–79, nos. 264, 265.
4. See Feng Tzu-k'ai, "Man-hua te yu-lai" (The origin of cartoons), in *Man-hua te miao-fa* (How to draw cartoons) (Shanghai: K'ai-ming shu-tien, 1947), pp. 6–19.
5. Feng Tzu-k'ai, *Tzu-k'ai man-hua ch'üan-chi* (Complete cartoons of Feng Tzu-k'ai) (Shanghai: K'ai-ming shu-tien, 1947), pp. 1–3.
6. P'an Wen-yen, ed., *Feng Tzu-k'ai hsien-sheng nien-piao*, pp. 9–10.
7. Feng Tzu-k'ai, *Feng Tzu-k'ai man-hua ch'üan-chi*, pt. 1, pl. 57.

# 70 Kuo Ta-wei (b. 1919)

*Scale (Ch'eng)*

Undated
Hanging scroll, ink on paper
69.4 x 26.7 cm (27 3/8 x 10 1/2 in.)

ARTIST'S SIGNATURE (lower right): Ta-wei.

ARTIST'S SEAL: Kuo Ta-wei (square relief).

INSCRIPTION by Ch'i Pai-shih (1863–1957) (prose, 25 characters in 2 columns of running script; left):

> Hook a mouse onto the scale and title it "self-weighing"; I sometimes do things this way. My student, you do not have to write an inscription. I have done it for you, Pai-shih. Seal: Ch'i Pai-shih (square intaglio).

Edward L. Elliott Family Collection (L146.69)

Unpublished.

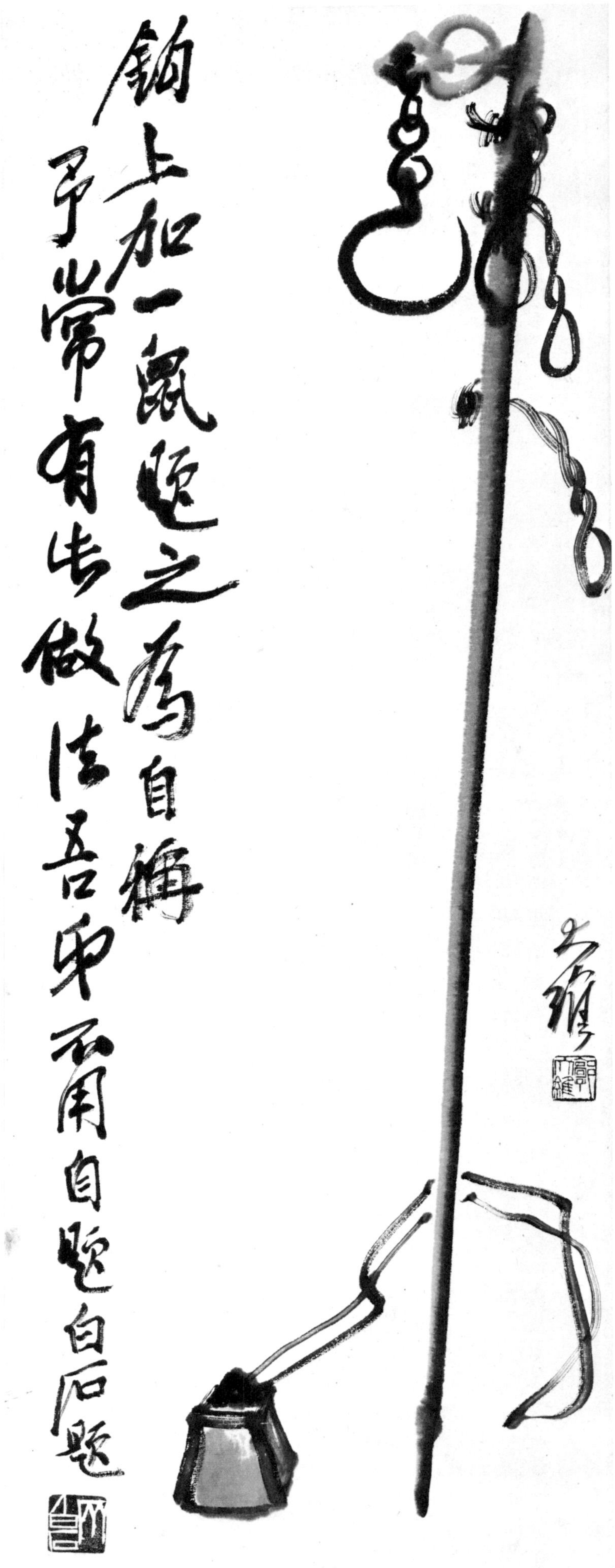

# Selected Bibliography

Full references for sources used in the preparation of this book are in the notes following each chapter or essay. This selected bibliography includes the most frequently used sources as well as publications of interest to the general reader.


Acker, William R. B. *Some T'ang and Pre-T'ang Texts on Chinese Painting*. Leiden: E. J. Brill, 1954.

Barnhardt, Richard. *Marriage of the Lord of the River: A Lost Landscape by Tung Yüan*. *Artibus Asiae* Supplementum 27 (1970).

———. *Along the Border of Heaven: Sung and Yüan Paintings from the C. C. Wang Family Collection*. New York: The Metropolitan Museum of Art, 1983.

Bary, Theodore de, ed. *Self and Society in Ming Thought*. New York: Columbia University Press, 1970.

Bush, Susan. *The Chinese Literati on Painting: Su Shih (1037–1101) to Tung Ch'i-ch'ang (1555–1636)*. Harvard-Yenching Institute Studies, no. 27. Cambridge, Mass.: Harvard University Press, 1971.

———, and Murck, Christian, eds. *Theories of the Arts in China*. Princeton: Princeton University Press, 1983.

Cahill, James. *Hills beyond a River: Chinese Painting of the Yüan Dynasty, 1279–1368*. New York and Tokyo: Weatherhill, 1976.

———. *Parting at the Shore: Chinese Painting of the Early and Middle Ming Dynasty*. New York and Tokyo: Weatherhill, 1978.

———. *An Index of Early Chinese Painters and Paintings: T'ang, Sung, and Yüan*. Berkeley: University of California Press, 1980.

———. *The Compelling Image: Nature and Style in Seventeenth-century Chinese Painting*. Cambridge, Mass.: Harvard University Press, 1982.

Chang Kuang-pin, ed. *Yüan ssu-ta-chia* [The four great masters of the Yüan]. Taipei: National Palace Museum, 1975.

Ch'en Fang-mei. *Tai Chin yen-chiu* [A study of Tai Chin]. Taipei: National Palace Museum, 1981.

Cheng Chin-fa. "Mi Fu Shu-ssu t'ieh" [Mi Fu's writing on Shu silk]. Master's thesis, National Taiwan University, 1974.

Chou, Ju-hsi. "In Quest of the Primordial Line: The Genesis and Content of Tao-chi's *Hua-yü lu*." Ph.D. dissertation, Princeton University, 1969.

Ecke, Tseng Yu-ho. *Chinese Calligraphy*. Philadelphia: Philadelphia Museum of Art; and Boston: Boston Book and Art, 1971.

Edwards, Richard, ed. *The Painting of Tao-chi, 1641–ca. 1720*. Ann Arbor: Museum of Art, University of Michigan, 1967.

———. *The Art of Wen Cheng-ming (1470–1559)*. Ann Arbor: Museum of Art, University of Michigan, 1976.

Fong, Wen C. "Toward a Structural Analysis of Chinese Landscape Painting." *Art Journal* 28 (1969): 388–97.

———. "How to Understand Chinese Painting." *Proceedings of the American Philosophical Society* 115 (1971): 282–92.

———. *Summer Mountains: The Timeless Landscape*. New York: The Metropolitan Museum of Art, 1975.

———. *Returning Home: Tao-chi's Album of Landscapes and Flowers*. New York: George Braziller, 1976.

———, and Fu, Marilyn. *Sung and Yüan Paintings*. New York: The Metropolitan Museum of Art, 1973.

Fu, Marilyn, and Fu, Shen C. Y. *Studies in Connoisseurship: Chinese Paintings from the Arthur M. Sackler Collection in New York and Princeton*. Princeton: The Art Museum, 1974.

Fu Shen. *Yüan-tai huang-shih shu-hua shou-ts'ang shih-lüeh* [A brief history of Yüan dynasty imperial collections of calligraphy and painting]. Taipei: National Palace Museum, 1981.

Fu, Shen C.Y., in collaboration with Fu, Marilyn W.; Neill, Mary G.; and Clark, Mary Jane. *Traces of the Brush: Studies in Chinese Calligraphy*. New Haven: Yale University Art Gallery, 1977.

Fung (Feng) Yu-lan. *A History of Chinese Philosophy*. Translated by Derk Bodde. 2 vols. Princeton: Princeton University Press, 1953.

Ho, Wai-kam; Lee, Sherman E.; Sickman, Laurence; Wilson, Marc F., eds., *Eight Dynasties of Chinese Painting*. Cleveland: Cleveland Museum of Art and Indiana University Press, 1980.

Hsü Fu-kuan. *Chung-kuo i-shu ching-shen* [The spirit of Chinese fine arts]. Taipei: Hsüeh-sheng shu-chü, 1974.

Huang Miao-tzu. "Tu Ni Yün-lin chüan cha-chi" [Notes on reading Ni Tsan's biography]. In *Chung-hua wen-shih lun-ts'ung*, 3rd ser. Peking: Chung-hua shu-chü, 1962.

Kōhara Hironobu, ed. *To Kisho no shoga* [Tung Ch'i-ch'ang: the man and his work]. 2 vols. Tokyo: Nigen-sha, 1981.

Kuo Shao-yü. *Chung-kuo wen-hsüeh p'i-p'ing shih* [History of Chinese literary criticism]. Shanghai: Chung-hua shu-chü, 1961.

Lawton, Thomas. *Freer Gallery of Art, Fiftieth Anniversary Exhibition, II: Chinese Figure Painting*. Washington, D.C.: The Smithsonian Institution, 1973.

Ledderhose, Lothar. *Mi Fu and the Classical Tradition of Chinese Calligraphy*. Princeton: Princeton University Press, 1979.

Lee, Sherman E., and Fong, Wen C. *Streams and Mountains without End: A Northern Sung Handscroll and Its Significance in the History of Early Chinese Painting*. *Artibus Asiae* Supplementum 14 (1956).

Lee, Sherman E., and Ho, Wai-kam. *Chinese Art under the Mongols: The Yüan Dynasty (1279–1368)*. Cleveland: Cleveland Museum of Art, 1968.

Li, Chu-tsing. "Rocks and Trees and the Art of Ts'ao Chih-po." *Artibus Asiae* 23 (1960): 153–92.

———. *The Autumn Colors on the Ch'ao and Hua Mountains: A Landscape by Chao Meng-fu*. *Artibus Asiae* Supplementum 21 (1964).

Liu, James J. Y. *The Art of Chinese Poetry*. Chicago: University of Chicago Press, 1962.

Liu Hsieh. *Wen-hsin tiao-lung* [The literary mind and the carving of dragons]. Translated by Vincent Yu-chung Shih. New York: Columbia University Press, 1959.

Loehr, Max, *The Great Painters of China*. New York: Harper and Row, 1980.

Lovell, Hsin-chung. "Wang Hui's *Dwelling in the Fu-ch'un Mountains*: A Classical Theme, Its Origins and Variations." *Ars Orientalis* 8 (1970): 217–42.

Maeda, Robert. *Two Twelfth-century Texts on Chinese Painting*. Michigan Papers in Chinese Studies, no. 8. Ann Arbor: Center for Chinese Studies, University of Michigan, 1970.

Mather, Richard B., trans. *A New Account of Tales of the World*. Minneapolis: University of Minnesota Press, 1976.

Munakata, Kiyohiko. *Ching Hao's "Pi-fa chi": A Note on the Art of Brush*. *Artibus Asiae* Supplementum 31 (1974).

Nakata Yūjirō and Fu Shen, eds. *Obei shūzō Chūgoku hōsho meisekishū* [Chinese calligraphy in American and European collections]. 5 vols. to date. Tokyo: Chūōkōron-sha, 1981– .

Nelson, Susan E. "Rocks beside a River: Ni Tsan and the Ching-Kuan Style in the Eyes of Seventeenth-century Critics." *Archives of Asian Art* 33 (1980): 65–88.

Sirén, Osvald. *Chinese Painting: Leading Masters and Principles*. 7 vols. New York: Ronald Press, 1956–58.

Soper, Alexander C. *Kuo Jo-hsü's Experiences in Painting*. Washington, D.C.: American Council of Learned Societies, 1951.

Suzuki Kei. *Mindai kaiga shi kenkyū: Seppa* [A Study of Ming dynasty painting history: the Che School]. Tokyo: University of Tokyo Press, 1968.

———, comp. *Chūgoku kaiga sōgō zuroku: daiikkan, Amerika-Kanada hen* [Comprehensive illustrated catalogue of Chinese paintings: American and Canadian collections: volume 1]. 6 vols. Tokyo: University of Tokyo Press, 1982.

*Suzuki Kei sensei kanreki-kinen: Chūgoku ega-shi ron* [Celebrating Suzuki Kei's sixtieth birthday: collected essays on Chinese painting history]. Tokyo: Yoshikawa, 1981.

Szechuan Provincial Museum, comp. *Kung Pan-chien shan-shui-hua k'o-t'u kao: Sze-ch'uan-sheng po-wu-kuan teng shou-ts'ang* [Kung Hsien's sketchbooks for instructing students: based on works in the Szechuan Provincial Museum and other collections]. Ch'eng-tu: Szechuan jen-min ch'u-pan-she, 1981.

Ts'ao P'ei-lien, ed. *Ch'ing-pi-ko ch'üan-chi* (The complete collected works of the Pure and Secluded Pavilion [of Ni Tsan]). Yüan-tai chen-pen wen-chi hui-k'an, vol. 10. Taipei: Kuo-li chung-yang t'u-shu-kuan, 1970.

Vanderstappen, Harrie. "Painters at the Early Ming Court (1368–1435) and the Problem of a Ming Painting Academy." *Monumenta Serica* 15 (1956): 258–302; and *Monumenta Serica* 16 (1957): 315–46.

Whitfield, Roderick. *In Pursuit of Antiquity: Chinese Paintings of the Ming and Ch'ing Dynasties from the Collection of Mr. and Mrs. Earl Morse*. Princeton: The Art Museum, 1969.

Wilson, Marc. "Kung Hsien: Theorist and Technician in Painting." *The Nelson Gallery and Atkins Museum Bulletin* 4 (1969).

Wright, Arthur, and Twichett, Denis, eds. *Confucian Personalities*. Stanford: Stanford University Press, 1962.

Wu, William. "Kung Hsien's Style and His Sketchbooks." *Oriental Art* 16 (1970): 72–80.

Yang Jen-k'ai. "Yeh-mao-t'ai Liao-mu ch'u-t'u ku-hua te shih-tai chi ch'i-t'a" [Ancient paintings excavated from the

Liao dynasty tomb at Yeh-mao-t'ai, their dates and other problems]. *Wen-wu* 1975: 37–39.

Yü Chien-hua, ed. *Shih-t'ao Hua-yü lu* [Shih-t'ao's (Tao-chi's) recorded sayings on painting]. Peking: Jen-min mei-shu ch'u-pan-she, 1962.

# *Index of Chinese Names*

Note: All references to figures are in *italics*; principal references to painters are in **boldface**. Alphabetization is all the way through to the first comma or parenthesis. All dates are A.D. unless otherwise indicated.

*This index was compiled by Robert J. Palmer, with Chinese glossary by Shou-chien Shih.*

# *Credits*

*The photographs of works in the collection of The Art Museum, Princeton University, are by Clem Fiori, Blawenburg, New Jersey, and the Meriden Gravure Company, Meriden, Connecticut.*

## I. IMAGES OF THE MIND

The Art Museum, Princeton University: fig. 116, Museum Purchase, John Maclean Magie and Gertrude Magie Fund; figs. 51, 59, 135, 135a, b, 141, DuBois Schanck Morris Collection; figs. 43, 148, 152, 154a, 154b, Gifts of Mr. and Mrs. Earl Morse; fig. 87, Gift of Arthur M. Sackler Foundation (Chester D. Carter Collection); fig. 134, C. O. von Kienbusch, Jr., Memorial Collection. Cleveland Museum of Art: fig. 39, Gift of Katherine Holden Thayer; fig. 121, Intended gift of Mr. and Mrs. A. Dean Perry; figs. 143a, b, Purchase, J. H. Wade Fund. Photographs courtesy of the James and Lucy Lo Photography Archive, Princeton, New Jersey: figs. 4, 6, 7, 8, 12. The Metropolitan Museum of Art, New York: figs. 131a–d, 164a, b, Gifts of Douglas Dillon; figs. 145a–d, 165, 166, Lent by Douglas Dillon; figs. 47, 64, 64a, 104, 118, 156, Gifts of the Dillon Fund; figs. 110, 120, Gifts of J. Pierpont Morgan, by exchange; fig. 58, Gift of Irene and Earl Morse. Museum of Fine Arts, Boston: figs. 41, 54, Chinese and Japanese Special Fund. Nelson Gallery–Atkins Museum, Kansas City: figs. 28, 28a, 40, 45, Nelson Fund; figs. 65, 65a, Gifts of the Kenneth A. and Helen F. Spencer Foundation Fund.

## II. THE EIGHT VIEWS OF THE HSIAO AND HSIANG RIVERS

Photographs by Alfreda Murck: figs. 1–7, 9–13.

## III. THE MIND LANDSCAPE OF HSIEH YU-YÜ

Cleveland Museum of Art: fig. 10, Purchase, John L. Severance Fund. Photograph courtesy of the James and Lucy Lo Photography Archive, Princeton, New Jersey: fig. 5.

## IV. CATALOGUE

Cleveland Museum of Art: no. 47, fig. b, Intended gift of Kelvin Smith. The Fogg Art Museum, Harvard University, Cambridge, Massachusetts: no. 22, fig. c, Paul Bernat Fund. The Metropolitan Museum of Art, New York: no. 36, fig. a, Lent by Douglas Dillon. Nelson Gallery–Atkins Museum, Kansas City: no. 23, fig. b; no. 25, fig. c, Nelson Fund. Yale University Art Gallery, New Haven, Connecticut: no. 47, fig. a, Leonard C. Hanna Fund.